D0171354

Middle East

Andrew Humphreys
Lou Callan
Paul Greenway
Anthony Ham
Pertti Hämäläinen
Paul Hellander

Ann Jousiffe
Cathy Lanigan
Gordon Robison
Jeff Williams
Pat Yale

LONELY PLANET PUBLICATIONS
Melbourne • Oakland • London • Paris

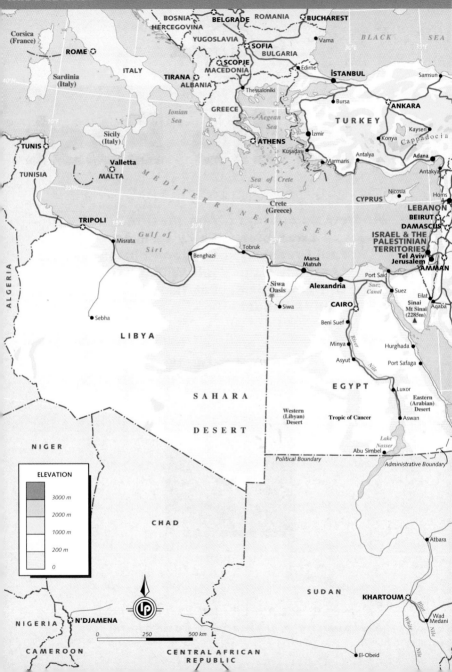

Middle East
3rd edition – January 2000
First published – April 1994

Published by
Lonely Planet Publications Pty Ltd A.C.N. 005 607 983
192 Burwood Rd, Hawthorn, Victoria 3122, Australia

Lonely Planet Offices
Australia PO Box 617, Hawthorn, Victoria 3122
USA 150 Linden St, Oakland, CA 94607
UK 10a Spring Place, London NW5 3BH
France 1 rue du Dahomey, 75011 Paris

Photographs
All of the images in this guide are available for licensing from
Lonely Planet Images.
email: lpi@lonelyplanet.com.au

Front cover photograph
Camels milling around Birqash camel market, Egypt (Greg Elms)

ISBN 0 86442 701 8

text & maps © Lonely Planet 2000
photos © photographers as indicated 2000

Printed by SNP Printing Pte Ltd, Singapore

Contents – Text

ISRAEL & THE PALESTINIAN TERRITORIES 312

JORDAN 404

KUWAIT 450

LEBANON 469

LIBYA 520

THE UNITED ARAB EMIRATES   791

YEMEN   831

LANGUAGE   873

GLOSSARY   885

ACKNOWLEDGMENTS   889

INDEX   901

Contents – Maps

The Authors

Andrew Humphreys

Andrew was the coordinating author and updated the introductory chapters and the Egypt and Syria chapters. He has been living, travelling and working in the Middle East on and off since 1988 when he first went to Cairo on holiday and took three years to leave. Originally trained in London as an architect, while in Egypt he slid over into writing through a growing fascination with Islamic buildings. Following a spell in mainstream journalism based for several years in the Baltic States, Andrew hooked up with Lonely Planet for a return to the Middle East and has since authored or co-authored guides to Central Asia, Israel & the Palestinian Territories, Jerusalem, Egypt, Cairo and Syria.

Lou Callan

Lou updated the Oman and UAE chapters. With an affinity for languages and an itchiness for travel, she fell into the job of phrasebooks editor at LP some years back. After a brief stint as a guidebook editor she packed up and followed her husband Tony to a life among the red dunes of Al-Ain in the UAE.

Paul Greenway

Paul updated the Bahrain, Iran and Qatar chapters. Gratefully plucked from the blandness and security of the Australian Public Service, he has worked on about a dozen Lonely Planet books, including *Mongolia*, *Iran*, *Madagascar* and *Bali & Lombok*. During the rare times that he's not travelling – or writing, reading and dreaming about it – Paul relaxes to (and pretends he can play) heavy rock, eats and breathes Australian Rules football, and will go to any lengths (eg staying in Mongolia and Iran) to avoid settling down.

Anthony Ham

Anthony updated the Iraq chapter. After completing a Masters in Middle Eastern politics and working as a lawyer with clients from across the Middle East, Asia, and Africa, Anthony set out to travel the world, particularly the Middle East. He now lives in Melbourne.

Pertti Hämäläinen

Pertti updated the Yemen chapter. He was born in Turku, Finland, and lives in Helsinki. Pertti has an MSC in Applied Mathematics from the University of Turku and runs a consulting company of his own, specialising in local area networks and data communications. He was introduced to travelling by his first wife Tuula, in the late 1970s. Her great interest in Islamic architecture led them to southern Arabia in 1984 and many times since. Pertti is a member of die Deutsch-Jemenitische Gesellschaft eV and the American Institute for Yemeni Studies.

Paul Hellander

Paul updated the Israel & the Palestinian Territories chapter. He has never really stopped travelling since he was born in England to a Norwegian father and English mother. He graduated with a degree in Ancient, Byzantine and Modern Greek before arriving in Australia in 1977, via Greece and 30 other countries. He subsequently taught Modern Greek and trained interpreters and translators for 13 years before throwing it all away for a life as a travel writer. Paul joined Lonely Planet in 1994 and wrote the *Greek phrasebook* before being assigned to *Greece* and *Eastern Europe*. Paul has also updated *Singapore* and covered Singapore in *Malaysia, Singapore & Brunei* and *South-East Asia*. Paul can usually be found in cyberspace at paul@planetmail.net. When not travelling, he resides in Adelaide, South Australia, where he has a predilection for cooking Thai food and growing hot chillies. He was last seen heading for Greece and Cyprus.

Ann Jousiffe

Ann updated the Libya chapter. A London-based freelance writer and photographer, Ann has travelled widely around the Mediterranean, North Africa and the Middle East pursuing her love of ancient ruins and deserts. She has a strange affinity with the letter L – lives in London and the Languedoc, writes about Lebanon and Libya (for LP) and her hobbies are loafing around museums and lager drinking. Her current 'work in progress' is a book about Libya.

Cathy Lanigan

Cathy updated the Lebanon chapter. She has travelled extensively in the Middle East, Europe, Asia, Africa and Australia over the past 16 years, and between travelling she has worked as a journalist, an organiser for environmental organisations and a local government politician. Cathy worked as an editor on Lonely Planet's Middle Eastern titles for two years before moving to Lonely Planet's London office for a year to help to set up book production there. She is now back in Melbourne working as a publishing manager for Lonely Planet and spends her weekends in the beautiful Victorian village of Metung.

Gordon Robison

Gordon updated the Kuwait and Saudi Arabia chapters. He has written for Lonely Planet for more than 10 years: he is the author of *Arab Gulf States*, and has co-authored or contributed to *USA*; *Bahrain, Kuwait & Qatar* (to be published in 2000); *UAE & Oman* (to be published in 2000), *Middle East* and *West Asia on a shoestring*. Gordon grew up in Maine and Vermont in the northeastern USA. After a year in Saudi Arabia he moved to Cairo in 1988 where he spent more than six years reporting for the American ABC Radio News, *The Irish Times*, *The Washington Times*, *The Miami Herald* and the *Sunday Times* (London), among others. Gordon now lives in Atlanta where he works for CNN International. He is married to Dona Stewart and they have two daughters, Halle and Mallory.

Jeff Williams

Jeff updated the Jordan chapter. He is a Kiwi from Greymouth on New Zealand's wild west coast and lives in subtropical Brisbane with his wife Alison and son Callum. When not travelling he likes skiing and camping and is just about to break his neck rollerblading. Jeff is variously author, co-author or contributor to Lonely Planet's *New Zealand*; *Australia*; *Western Australia*; *Tramping in New Zealand*; *Outback Australia*; *USA*; *Washington, DC & the Capital Region*; *West Africa*, *Africa*, *South Africa, Lesotho & Swaziland* and *İstanbul to Cairo*.

Pat Yale

Pat updated the Turkey chapter. She first went to Turkey in 1974 in an old van that didn't look as if it would make it past Dover. She has since been back innumerable times and is co-author of Lonely Planet's *Turkey*. She has also worked on Lonely Planet's *Ireland* and *Britain* guides and wrote the original *London* city guide. At the time of writing Pat was living in a pasha's house amid the fairy chimneys of Göreme in Cappadocia.

FROM THE AUTHORS

Andrew Humphreys Credit is due to Siona Jenkins, my co-author in Egypt, and to Colin Clement for allowing me to crib from him in Alexandria.

Lou Callan For their help during this and for putting up with all my questions and phone calls, I'd like to thank the following people: David Whitfield in Muscat; Egbert van Meggelen at Abu Dhabi National Hotels Company; Abdullah Mohammed al-Amry at the Oman embassy in Abu Dhabi; Ali bin Amer Al Kiyumi at the Ministry of Regional Municipalities & Environment in Muscat; Tariq Awad al-Jabry, Mohammed Rafi-Uz- Zaman and Mansour Ahmed Abood at Al-Ain Municipality; Alistair MacKenzie and Tim Binks at Explorer Publishing in Dubai; Peter Ochs and Christopher Beale in

Muscat. I owe very special thanks to Tony Cleaver, my tireless travel companion and darling husband.

Paul Greenway I would like to thank several people in Iran: Koulak Amanpour at the Rahe Ayandeh Internet centre in Tehrān; Farrokh Karami from the ITTO; and staff at the Khayyam Hotel, Tehrān. During this trip I also missed meeting two friends, but I hope they stay in touch: Amir Asghari Fard, in Tehrān, and Komeil Noofeli, in Shīrāz. Thanks to Brian Christie and Matthew Poulton for sharing their experiences of Iran. And *salut* to Chechete, a remarkable 70-year-old French lady whose undiminishing love of travel to places like Iran is an inspiration.

Anthony Ham Thanks to Damien Bown and the Iraqis in Australia who have helped with their wisdom about their homeland.

Pertii Hämäläinen Thanks to all the friendly people of Yemen, especially those below 15 years of age, whose enthusiastic help and advice to the visitor always makes visiting Yemen so enjoyable – you are too numerous to list here! Special thanks go to Zahra Abdrabo from Aden, Hassan Bahameed from Say'un, Kai Granholm from Riyadh and Dr J Veerman from San'a. And, finally, thanks to my wife Raija for her spirited support on the road.

Paul Hellander During a busy and invigorating stay in Israel many people offered invaluable assistance to me as I juggled and filtered a mind-numbing amount of information. Thanks to the Israel Government Tourist Office for the wealth of printed material and especially to David Beirman from the Sydney office. A big *todah* to fellow author Daniel Robinson for his selfless assistance with background data; to David Martin of the British Council in East Jerusalem for help with the West Bank; to Ohad & Einav Sharav for their invaluable contributions to language and history queries; to Amichay Ne'eman of Tel Aviv for his generous hospitality; to Deborah Lipson of the Tower of David Museum for her insight into history; to Dave Cohen of Tel Aviv for his views on the travel scene; to Danny Flax and Chaim Rockman of Jerusalem for their practical help; to Russell Kibel of Eilat for a warm welcome; to the people of Israel for their patience and understanding of my often seemingly trivial questions and for their enduring tenacity and resilience while sometimes living 'on the edge'.

Ann Jousiffe As always I came away from Libya with warm feelings of gratitude to the many people who have smoothed the path during research. I would like to particularly thank Abdulrazzag Gherwash at Winzrik for all his support, both during the research trip and afterwards supplying late information down the fax. Thanks also to Dr Abdulrahman Yedder of the

Ministry of Tourism for many fascinating insights into the history and culture of Libya. Last but not least thanks to my husband, Peter, whose moral support and practical help have, as always, been a vital ingredient in putting the whole thing together.

Cathy Lanigan Thanks to the many people in Lebanon who helped along the way. In particular I'd like to thank Aly Harakeh, Maha Al Azar and Anne Renehan of the *Daily Star*; freelance journalist Samar Kadi; Australian ambassador John Fennessy and his wife Marion; Fadi Mazraany; the Mayor of Tyre; Toufic Mishlawi of the *Middle Eastern Reporter*; Therese Nasr and Paul Khauli of Levant distributors; the staff at the Tripoli and Zahlé tourist offices; and Rania from Tania Travel. In London thanks to Yvonne and Abdallah Jarrah at the London Lebanese tourist office; Nicola Duncan from Wimbledon Flight Centre; and LP authors Andrew Humphreys, Damien Simonis, Steve Fallon & Charlotte Hindle. Thanks to Jen Loy in the US office and to Michelle Glynn, Verity Campbell and Geoff Stringer in the Melbourne office for their support. A special thanks to my partner John van der Knijff and mate Indra Kilfoyle for the support, laughs and invaluable cartographic help.

Gordon Robison Thanks to Ali Khalil and Sarah Chalabi in Kuwait for all their help and hospitality. Ashraf Fouad and Miram Amie were also, as always, very generous with their time and insights. A big thank you goes to my mother, Sylvia Robison, for her help collecting the Saudi Arabia material.

Jeff Williams Thanks to many people both in Australia and the Middle East. Particular thanks to Andrew Humphreys who comes up with so many good ideas, asks me along for the ride and shows me how to down beer in İstanbul, Damascus and Amman (and his favourite coffeehouses in Cairo). Also to Gadi Farfour, his partner, who made it up to Al-Deir, Petra, to teach me how to take photos; Hani and Yousef in Amman; Ammar in Shmeisani; Joseph Habboushe on the Internet; Trev and Özlem in Fethiye; Eric, Hakan and Özgur in Ölüdeniz; 'Uncle' Ali in Çanakkale; Anne and Andrew from NZ; Stephanie and Mehmet in Göreme; Hashmet the guide dog; Tuku Huda for 'the art of tying postcard'; Volcan in Ankara; 'the Worst Taxi Driver in Jordan'; Hans and Sylvia for the bar story; and the Bedouin people of Wadi Rum. And for the cycling notes – Etienne Le Roux, Julie Norton and Bryan Keith – you are legends.

Pat Yale Thanks to all the many Turks who went out of their way to help me. Special thanks are due to Tom Brosnahan, co-author of Lonely Planet's *Turkey*; to Paul Stockley and Yilmaz Özlük in İstanbul; and to the staff of Argeus Travel, Kirkit Voyage, Neşe Tour and Ötüken Voyage in Cappadocia. Thanks to the friends who have helped to make my stay in Göreme such a joy – there are too many of you to name but I owe you a big *teşekkür ederim*!

This Book

This book originally grew out of the Middle East section of Lonely Planet's *West Asia on a shoestring*. Many people have helped to create this 3rd edition. Among the major contributors to past editions were Andrew Humphreys, Tom Brosnahan, Geert Cole, Rosemary Hall, Ann Jousiffe, Leanne Logan, Gordon Robison, David St Vincent, Damien Simonis, Tony Wheeler, Pertti Hämäläinen, Diana Saad and Neil Tilbury.

From the Publisher

This edition of *Middle East* was coordinated in Lonely Planet's Melbourne office by Alan Murphy and then Justin Flynn after Alan left to do some researching work of his own. Bethune Carmichael, Susan Holtham, Sarah Mathers, Lyn McGaurr, Fiona Meiers, Lara Morcombe, Anne Mulvaney, Krish Naidoo, Cherry Prior, Julia Taylor and Rebecca Turner assisted with the editing and proofing. Sonya Brooke oversaw the mapping and design and was helped by Shahara Ahmed, Katie Butterworth, Heath Comrie, Hunor Csutoros, Gadi Farfour, Anna Judd, Brett Moore, Sarah Sloane, Maree Styles and Rodney Zandbergs. Special thanks to Trudi Canavan, Sarah Jolly, Kate Nolan and Mick Weldon for the illustrations, Quentin Frayne for the Language chapter, Simon Bracken for the front cover and Jeremy Smith for 'The Hanging Gardens of Babylon' boxed text.

THANKS
Many thanks to the travellers who used the last edition and wrote to us with helpful hints, advice and interesting anecdotes. Your names appear in the back of this book.

Foreword

ABOUT LONELY PLANET GUIDEBOOKS

The story begins with a classic travel adventure: Tony and Maureen Wheeler's 1972 journey across Europe and Asia to Australia. Useful information about the overland trail did not exist at that time, so Tony and Maureen published the first Lonely Planet guidebook to meet a growing need.

From a kitchen table, then from a tiny office in Melbourne (Australia), Lonely Planet has become the largest independent travel publisher in the world, an international company with offices in Melbourne, Oakland (USA), London (UK) and Paris (France).

Today Lonely Planet guidebooks cover the globe. There is an ever-growing list of books and there's information in a variety of forms and media. Some things haven't changed. The main aim is still to help make it possible for adventurous travellers to get out there – to explore and better understand the world.

At Lonely Planet we believe travellers can make a positive contribution to the countries they visit – if they respect their host communities and spend their money wisely. Since 1986 a percentage of the income from each book has been donated to aid projects and human rights campaigns.

Updates Lonely Planet thoroughly updates each guidebook as often as possible. This usually means there are around two years between editions, although for more unusual or more stable destinations the gap can be longer. Check the imprint page (following the colour map at the beginning of the book) for publication dates.

Between editions up-to-date information is available in two free newsletters – the paper *Planet Talk* and email *Comet* (to subscribe, contact any Lonely Planet office) – and on our Web site at www.lonelyplanet.com. The *Upgrades* section of the Web site covers a number of important and volatile destinations and is regularly updated by Lonely Planet authors. *Scoop* covers news and current affairs relevant to travellers. And, lastly, the *Thorn Tree* bulletin board and *Postcards* section of the site carry unverified, but fascinating, reports from travellers.

Correspondence The process of creating new editions begins with the letters, postcards and emails received from travellers. This correspondence often includes suggestions, criticisms and comments about the current editions. Interesting excerpts are immediately passed on via newsletters and the Web site, and everything goes to our authors to be verified when they're researching on the road. We're keen to get more feedback from organisations or individuals who represent communities visited by travellers.

Lonely Planet gathers information for everyone who's curious about the planet – and especially for those who explore it first-hand. Through guidebooks, phrasebooks, activity guides, maps, literature, newsletters, image library, TV series and Web site we act as an information exchange for a worldwide community of travellers.

Research Authors aim to gather sufficient practical information to enable travellers to make informed choices and to make the mechanics of a journey run smoothly. They also research historical and cultural background to help enrich the travel experience and allow travellers to understand and respond appropriately to cultural and environmental issues.

Authors don't stay in every hotel because that would mean spending a couple of months in each medium-sized city and, no, they don't eat at every restaurant because that would mean stretching belts beyond capacity. They do visit hotels and restaurants to check standards and prices, but feedback based on readers' direct experiences can be very helpful.

Many of our authors work undercover, others aren't so secretive. None of them accept freebies in exchange for positive write-ups. And none of our guidebooks contain any advertising.

Production Authors submit their raw manuscripts and maps to offices in Australia, USA, UK or France. Editors and cartographers – all experienced travellers themselves – then begin the process of assembling the pieces. When the book finally hits the shops, some things are already out of date, we start getting feedback from readers and the process begins again ...

WARNING & REQUEST

Things change – prices go up, schedules change, good places go bad and bad places go bankrupt – nothing stays the same. So, if you find things better or worse, recently opened or long since closed, please tell us and help make the next edition even more accurate and useful. We genuinely value all the feedback we receive. Julie Young coordinates a well travelled team that reads and acknowledges every letter, postcard and email and ensures that every morsel of information finds its way to the appropriate authors, editors and cartographers for verification.

Everyone who writes to us will find their name in the next edition of the appropriate guidebook. They will also receive the latest issue of *Planet Talk*, our quarterly printed newsletter, or *Comet*, our monthly email newsletter. Subscriptions to both newsletters are free. The very best contributions will be rewarded with a free guidebook.

Excerpts from your correspondence may appear in new editions of Lonely Planet guidebooks, the Lonely Planet Web site, *Planet Talk* or *Comet*, so please let us know if you *don't* want your letter published or your name acknowledged.

Send all correspondence to the Lonely Planet office closest to you:

Australia: PO Box 617, Hawthorn, Victoria 3122
USA: 150 Linden St, Oakland, CA 94607
UK: 10A Spring Place, London NW5 3BH
France: 1 rue du Dahomey, 75011 Paris

Or email us at: talk2us@lonelyplanet.com.au

For news, views and updates see our Web site: www.lonelyplanet.com

HOW TO USE A LONELY PLANET GUIDEBOOK

The best way to use a Lonely Planet guidebook is any way you choose. At Lonely Planet we believe the most memorable travel experiences are often those that are unexpected, and the finest discoveries are those you make yourself. Guidebooks are not intended to be used as if they provide a detailed set of infallible instructions!

Contents All Lonely Planet guidebooks follow roughly the same format. The Facts about the Destination chapters or sections give background information ranging from history to weather. Facts for the Visitor gives practical information on issues like visas and health. Getting There & Away gives a brief starting point for researching travel to and from the destination. Getting Around gives an overview of the transport options when you arrive.

The peculiar demands of each destination determine how subsequent chapters are broken up, but some things remain constant. We always start with background, then proceed to sights, places to stay, places to eat, entertainment, getting there and away, and getting around information – in that order.

Heading Hierarchy Lonely Planet headings are used in a strict hierarchical structure that can be visualised as a set of Russian dolls. Each heading (and its following text) is encompassed by any preceding heading that is higher on the hierarchical ladder.

Entry Points We do not assume guidebooks will be read from beginning to end, but that people will dip into them. The traditional entry points are the list of contents and the index. In addition, however, some books have a complete list of maps and an index map illustrating map coverage.

There may also be a colour map that shows highlights. These highlights are dealt with in greater detail in the Facts for the Visitor chapter, along with planning questions and suggested itineraries. Each chapter covering a geographical region usually begins with a locator map and another list of highlights. Once you find something of interest in a list of highlights, turn to the index.

Maps Maps play a crucial role in Lonely Planet guidebooks and include a huge amount of information. A legend is printed on the back page. We seek to have complete consistency between maps and text, and to have every important place in the text captured on a map. Map key numbers usually start in the top left corner.

Although inclusion in a guidebook usually implies a recommendation we cannot list every good place. Exclusion does not necessarily imply criticism. In fact there are a number of reasons why we might exclude a place – sometimes it is simply inappropriate to encourage an influx of travellers.

Introduction

Turbulent politics, some alarming leaders, a handful of terrifying extremist organisations and a correspondingly unflattering media profile have done the Middle East few favours when it comes to selling the place as a destination to potential western visitors. Even Egypt, Israel and Turkey, all long-standing staples of the European and American package-tour trade can't completely escape the blight. All three still occasionally fall victim to shrill headlines and the knee-jerk 'stay away' responses they inspire in too many. Which is all a pity, because for anybody who can see beyond those headlines the countries of the Middle East are some of the most friendly in the world.

In setting our boundaries, we've chosen a modern political definition of the Middle East, hence the inclusion of Libya, Turkey and Iran. It makes for a fascinating area, stretching from the vast sand seas of the Sahara in the south-west, up to the mountainous wooded shores of the Caspian and Black seas in the north. Africa (in the form of Sudan and Chad), Asia (in Pakistan and Afghanistan) and Europe (Greece and Bulgaria) are all neighbours. Historically, the Middle East is where the three continents have always met, traded and clashed, resulting in the region's rich accumulation of the detritus of five millennia's worth of major civilisations and cultures. Every town, valley and hillside is a living museum of humankind's history: that's the field on which Ramses triumphed over the Hittites; this is where Alexander the Great sought the Oracle's advice; here is where Cleopatra bathed; this is the route walked by Christ; that's where Richard the Lionheart set up camp; and this is where Napoleon put ashore. It's no wonder the Middle East is so turbulent when so much of its territory means so much to so many.

Although it helps, it isn't necessary to have any appreciation of history to be awed by much of what there is to see here. The Pyramids and temples of Egypt speak for themselves, as do the ghostly ruins of the Roman desert cities in Libya and Syria, the towering mud cities of Yemen and the elegant tiled mosques of Iran. And the scenery can be stunning. Captivated by the desert scenes in *Lawrence of Arabia* and *The English Patient*? Then head off to Jordan, Egypt, Libya or Oman. Sand with sea more your thing? The beaches of Sinai and along Israel's and Turkey's Mediterranean coasts are pure paradise, while the underwater landscapes of the Red Sea are equal to anything above sea level. In addition, the food is excellent, costs are low, the people are extremely hospitable, and getting around will prove to be very easy. A few bureaucratic problems aside the main difficulty most visitors find when visiting the Middle East is with such a large and diverse region, so densely packed with must-see sites, how do you decide where to go and what to leave out? As problems go, that's not a bad one to face.

Is it Safe?

Safety is a very subjective issue. Perceptions of the issue as far as the Middle East is concerned are shaped for most people by ever present news stories of conflict, kidnappings and bombings. It's a lopsided picture. Imagine somebody whose image of the USA is built solely on CNN reports of Waco-style incidents, or a person whose view of the UK has been formed purely on the evidence of the behaviour of its football fans abroad. Just as mainstream society in the USA and UK has little to do with the headline-making elements mentioned, so day-to-day life in the Middle East rarely involves guns, bombs and other elements of terror. There are trouble spots, southern Lebanon, for example, south-eastern Turkey, middle Egypt and West Bank towns such as Hebron, but these are well defined and easily avoided.

Facts about the Region

HISTORY
This section sketches out the broadest sweeps of Middle Eastern history – for further details see the more specific History sections in the individual country chapters.

Cradle of Civilisation
If Africa is the birthplace of humanity, the Middle East can make strong claims to being the birthplace of civilisation. The Fertile Crescent of Mesopotamia (ancient Iraq) and the valley of the Nile River were sites of some of the earliest known organised societies.

About 5000 BC a culture known as Al-Ubaid first appeared in Mesopotamia. Little is known about it except that its influence eventually spread down what is now the coast of the Gulf but was then a string of islands. Stone Age artefacts have also been found in Israel's Negev desert and in the West Bank town of Jericho.

Sometime around 3100 BC the kingdoms of Upper and Lower Egypt were unified under Menes; the fact that there were two kingdoms for Menes to conquer implies that a relatively organised society already existed in Egypt at that time. The earliest settlements in the Gulf also date from this period and are usually associated with the Umm an-Nar culture (centred in today's United Arab Emirates), about which relatively little is known. The Levant (present-day Lebanon, Syria and Israel) too was well settled by this time, and local powers included the Amorites and the Canaanites. In Mesopotamia it was the era of Sumer, arguably the world's first great civilisation.

In the late 24th and early 23rd centuries BC Sargon of Akkad conquered much of the Levant and Mesopotamia. At its southern edge Sargon's empire contended with a powerful kingdom called Dilmun, centred on the island of Bahrain in the Gulf. Dilmun's civilisation arose around 3200 BC and was to continue in one form or another for nearly 2000 years.

The patriarch Abraham also came from Mesopotamia, having been born, according to tradition, in Ur of the Chaldees on the Euphrates River. His migration from Ur to Canaan is usually dated around 1800 BC. Other powers in the region at that time included the Hittite and Assyrian empires and, in Greece and Asia Minor, Mycenae and Troy.

The 7th century BC saw both the conquest of Egypt by Assyria and, far to the east, the rise of the Medes, the first of many great Persian empires. In 550 BC the Medes were conquered by Cyrus the Great, usually regarded as the first Persian shāh, or king.

Over the next 60 years Cyrus and his successors Cambyses (reigned 525-522 BC) and Darius I (reigned 521-486 BC) swept west and north to conquer first Babylon and then Egypt, Asia Minor and parts of Greece. After the Greeks stemmed the Persian tide at the Battle of Marathon in 490 BC, Darius and Xerxes (reigned 486-466 BC) turned their attention to consolidating their empire, though Xerxes launched another invasion of Greece in 480 BC.

Egypt won independence from the Persians in 401 BC only to be reconquered by them 60 years later. But the second Persian occupation of Egypt was brief. Little more than a decade after they arrived, the Persians were again driven out of Egypt, this time by the Greeks.

The Hellenistic World
In 336 BC Philip of Macedon, a warlord who had conquered much of mainland Greece, was murdered. His son Alexander assumed the throne and began a series of conquests that would eventually encompass most of Asia Minor, the Middle East, Persia and north-western India.

Under Alexander, the Greeks were the first to impose any kind of order on the Middle East as a whole. Traces of their rule ring the eastern Mediterranean from Eph-

Alexander the Great (356-323 BC)

One of the greatest figures to ever shape the Middle East, Alexander rode out of Macedonia in 334 BC to embark on a decade-long campaign of conquest and exploration. His first great victory was against the Persians at Issus in what's now south-eastern Turkey. After this he swept south conquering the Phoenician seaports and passing into Egypt where he founded the Mediterranean city that still bears his name (one of no less than 17). In Egypt he made a pilgrimage across the Western Desert to the oasis of Siwa to visit the legendary oracle of Amun-Ra, who he sought to have recognise him as a son of Zeus, god of gods. He came away satisfied and returned north, heading for Babylon. Crossing the Tigris and the Euphrates he defeated the Persians again before pushing his army up into Central Asia and northern India. Eventually fatigue and disease brought the drive to a halt and the Greeks turned around and headed back home. Alexander succumbed to illness and died in Baghdad en route. His legacy was to spread the Greek language and culture all around the eastern Mediterranean and all across the known ancient world.

esus in Turkey down and around to the oasis of Siwa in Egypt's Western Desert. Far greater than the archaeological evidence are the legends and tales of the Greeks, the *Iliad* and the *Odyssey*, and the descriptions left by their historians such as Strabo, Herodotus and Pliny. Taken together, all of these writings present us with strong clues to the state of the Middle East 300 years before Christ and 900 years before the coming of Islam.

Following Alexander's death, his empire was promptly carved up by his generals, who spent the next 40 years fighting each other. From the melee emerged three main dynasties: the Antigonids in Greece and Asia Minor; the Ptolemies in Egypt; and the Seleucids, who controlled the swath of land

running from modern Israel and Lebanon through Mesopotamia to Persia.

This is not to say that peace reigned. Having finished off a host of lesser competitors, the heirs to Alexander's empire then proceeded to fight each other. The area of the eastern Mediterranean splintered into an array of different local dynasties with fluctuating borders as different parts were conquered and lost. Eventually the entire region fell before the Romans.

Romans & Christians

Rome's legionaries conquered most of Asia Minor in 188 BC, then Syria, Palestine and the North African territories of Carthage in 64 and 63 BC. When finally Egypt fell in 30 BC, the Romans controlled the whole of the

Mediterranean world. This left the area covered by this book divided largely among two empires and their client states until the coming of Islam. Asia Minor, the Levant and Egypt were dominated by Rome (known, after 395 AD, as the Eastern Roman, or Byzantine, empire), while the Sassanians, a dynasty based in what's now Iran, ruled the east. Only the nomads of the desert and the frankincense kingdoms of South Arabia remained independent of the great powers of the day.

While the mighty empire of Rome suffered no great external threats to its eastern Mediterranean empire, there was plenty of trouble fomenting within. The Jews went into open revolt in 66 AD and it took four years for the legionaries to quell the uprising. In retaliation, Jerusalem was razed to the ground and rebuilt as a Roman city and the Jews were sent into exile (an exile which could be said to have ended only with the creation of the state of Israel in 1948). One of the rebellious orators who had been stirring up anti-Roman sentiments was Jesus of Nazareth (see the boxed text 'Jesus Christ' in the Israel & the Palestinian Territories chapter) but it wasn't until almost 300 years after his death that his preaching fully manifested itself – in 331

The Seven Wonders of the Ancient World

 Off the top of your head, how many of the Seven Wonders can you name? Most people rarely get beyond two or three, and then usually with some accompanying confusion over the status of the list: are the Wonders from the Bible? Are they mythological? Did they ever exist at all?

The answer to the last of these questions is a definite yes, at least in six-sevenths of the case.

The Wonders come to us through the writings of classical historians. They belong to the Hellenistic world of the eastern Mediterranean and the seven are all, bar one, sites that could easily be reached by sea from the centres of Greece and Rome. The origins of the list are lost, but the principal text describing the wonders was compiled by Philo of Byzantium, writing in 225 BC. The list has varied through the ages and the number of Wonders has run up to 10, but since the advent of printing, in the Middle Ages, there has been a popular consensus fixing the seven as: the Statue of Zeus at Olympia; the Temple of Artemis at Ephesus; the Hanging Gardens of Babylon; the Mausoleum of Halicarnassus; the Pharos at Alexandria; the Colossus of Rhodes; and the Pyramids in Egypt.

The Pyramids may be the only surviving Wonder but work done by archaeologists has fairly conclusively proven that five of the other Wonders did also indisputably exist. A question mark is attached only to the Hanging Gardens.

By comparing their findings with ancient classical texts, the archaeologists have succeeded in completely demystifying the Wonders. We not only know that they existed, we also have a very good idea of what they looked like, how they were built and for what purpose – the Wonders were no more than monuments to the wealth and greatness of the cities that built them. They were the Statue of Liberty and Sydney Opera House of the classical world. The exception is the Pyramids; ironically the one Wonder that still exists proves the greatest mystery of all.

Anybody interested in reading more about the Wonders and the archaeological detective work that led to their rediscovery, is recommended to look out for the superb *The Seven Wonders of the World* by John & Elizabeth Romer.

AD the newly converted emperor Constantine of Rome declared Christianity the official religion of the empire.

The Coming of Islam

For several hundred years prior to the coming of Islam, the Byzantines and the Sassanians were almost constantly at war, a fact that probably explains the weakened state in which the Arab armies were to find the two empires.

Mohammed, born around 570 AD in the Arabian town of Mecca, began to preach three years after the first revelation, which he received at around the age of 40. His teachings challenged the pagan religion of the Meccans, who worshipped many gods represented to them by idols. As a result, in 622 Mohammed and his followers (known as Muslims) were forced to flee to Medina, an oasis town some 360km to the north. This *Hejira*, or migration, is taken to mark the start of the new Muslim era. The Hejira is year 0 in the Islamic calendar, as Christ's birth is in the Christian calendar.

In Medina, Mohammed rose to become a successful religious, political and military leader. He brought all the region's tribes into his fold and eventually gathered an army of 10,000 troops and conquered his home town of Mecca.

Mohammed died in 632 but under his successors, known as caliphs (from the Arabic word for 'follower'), the new religion continued its rapid spread, reaching all of Arabia by 634. Egypt, Syria and Palestine were wrested from the Byzantines by 646, while most of Iraq, Iran and Afghanistan were taken from the Persian Sassanian dynasty by 656.

The governance of this empire initially fell to the Prophet's companions. Successive leaders of the Muslim community took the title of 'caliph', an Arabic word meaning 'successor', 'lieutenant' or 'viceroy'.

Arguments over the leadership quickly arose and just 12 years after the Prophet's death a dispute over the caliphate opened a rift in Islam that grew into today's divide between Sunni and Shi'ite Muslims (see the Religion section later in this chapter). Civil war broke out, ending with the rise to power of Mu'awiyah, the Muslim military governor of Syria, who was also a distant relative of the Prophet.

Early Islam

Mu'awiyah moved the capital from Medina to Damascus and established the first great Muslim dynasty called the Umayyad (or Omayyad) dynasty.

The Umayyads were descended from a branch of the Quraysh, the Prophet's tribe, known more for expediency than piety. Mu'awiyah's father was one of the last people in Mecca to embrace Islam and had long been Mohammed's chief opponent in the city. By moving the capital to Damascus the Umayyads were symbolically declaring that they had aspirations far beyond the rather ascetic teachings of the Quran (Koran).

The Umayyads gave the Islamic world some of its greatest architectural treasures, such as the Dome of the Rock in Jerusalem and the Umayyad Mosque in Damascus. History, however, has not been kind, remembering them largely for the high living, corruption, nepotism and tyranny that eventually proved to be their undoing.

In 750 the Umayyads were toppled in a revolt fuelled by accusations of impiety. Their successors, and the strong arm behind the revolt, were a dynasty called the Abbasids.

The Abbasid caliphate created a new capital in Baghdad and the early centuries of its rule constitutes what has been remembered ever since as the golden age of Islamic culture and society. The most famous of the Abbasid caliphs was Haroun ar-Rashid (reigned 786-809) of *The Thousand and One Nights* fame – a warrior king who led one of the most successful early Muslim invasions of Byzantium, almost reaching Constantinople (Istanbul). He also presided over an extraordinary burst of creativity in the arts, medicine, literature and science. Al-Ma'mun, Haroun's son and main successor, founded the Beit al-Hikmah, or 'House of Wisdom', a Baghdad-based academy dedicated to translating Greek and Roman works of science and philosophy into Arabic. It was only through these translations that most of the classical literature we know today was saved for posterity.

After Haroun's death the empire was effectively divided between two of his sons. Predictably, civil war ensued. In 813 one son, Al-Ma'mun, emerged triumphant and reigned as caliph for the next 20 years. But Al-Ma'mun's hold on power remained insecure and he felt compelled to surround himself with Turkish mercenaries. Over time the caliph's Turkish bodyguards became the real rulers of an empire that itself was rapidly shrinking.

By the middle of the 10th century the Abbasid caliphs were the prisoners of their Turkish guards, who spawned a dynasty of their own, the Seljuks (1038-1194). The Seljuks extended their reach throughout Persia, Central Asia and Afghanistan. They also took control of Armenia, Azerbaijan and a large part of Anatolia where the Seljuk Sultanate of Rum made its capital at Konya. The resulting pressure on the Byzantine empire was intense enough to cause the emperor and the Greek Orthodox Church to swallow their pride and appeal to the Roman Catholic pope for help.

The Crusades

In response to the eastern empire's alarm, in 1095 Pope Urban II called for a Christian military expedition to liberate the holy places of Jerusalem. Rome's motives were not entirely benevolent: for his part Urban was eager to assert Rome's primacy in the east, particularly in the Holy Land.

After linking up with the Byzantine army in 1097, the Crusaders successfully besieged Antioch (modern Antakya, in Turkey) and then marched down the coast before turning inland, towards Jerusalem. A thousand Muslim troops held Jerusalem for six weeks against some 15,000 Crusaders before the city fell on 15 July 1099. The victorious Crusaders massacred the local population – Muslims, Jews and Christians alike – plundered the non-Christian religious sites and turned the Dome of the Rock into a church.

These successes were short-lived. It took less than 50 years for the tide to begin to turn against the Crusaders and only 200 before they were driven out of the region once and for all.

The Muslim leader responsible for removing the Crusaders from Jerusalem (in 1187) was Salah ad-Din al-Ayyub, better known in the west as Saladin (see the boxed text 'Saladin' in the Syria chapter). He and his successors (known as the Ayyubids) battled the Crusaders for 60 years until they were unceremoniously removed by their own army, a strange soldier-slave caste, the Mamluks.

The Mamluks ran what would today be called a military dictatorship. But the only way to join their army was to be press-ganged into it. Non-Muslim boys were captured or bought outside the empire (often in Europe or Central Asia), converted to Islam and raised in the service of a single military commander. They were expected to give this commander total loyalty, in exchange for which their fortunes would rise (or fall) with his. Sultans were chosen from among the most senior Mamluk commanders but it was a system that engendered vicious, bloody rivalries, and rare was the sultan who died of natural causes.

The Mamluks were to rule Egypt, Syria, Palestine and western Arabia for nearly 300 years (1250-1517) and it was they who succeeded in ejecting the western Crusaders from the Near East, prising them out of their last stronghold of Acre (modern-day Akko in Israel) in 1291.

The Rise of the Ottomans

In 1258, just eight years after the Mamluks first seized power in Cairo and began their bloody dynasty, a boy named Osman was born to the chief of a pagan Turkish tribe in western Anatolia. Osman, the first ruler of what would become the Ottoman empire, converted to Islam in his youth. He began his military career by hiring out his tribe's army as mercenaries in the civil wars then besetting what was left of the Byzantine empire. Payment came in the form of land.

Rather than taking on the Byzantines directly, Osman's successors patiently picked up the bits and pieces of the empire that Constantinople could no longer control. By the end of the 14th century the Ottomans had conquered Bulgaria, Serbia, Bosnia, Hungary and most of the territory that makes up present-day Turkey. They had also moved their capital across the Dardanelles to Adrianople, today the Turkish city of Edirne. In 1453 Sultan Mehmet II took Constantinople, the hitherto unachievable object of innumerable Muslim wars almost since the 7th century.

On a battlefield near Aleppo 64 years later an army under the sultan Selim the Grim routed the Mamluks and, at one stroke, the whole of the eastern Mediterranean, including Egypt, was absorbed into the Turkish empire.

The empire reached its peak, both politically and culturally, under Süleyman the Magnificent (reigned 1520-66), who led the Ottoman armies west to the gates of Vienna, east into Persia, and south through the holy cities of Mecca and Medina and into Yemen. His control also extended throughout North Africa. He cracked down on corruption, reformed the Ottoman legal system and was the patron of the great architect Sinan, who designed the Süleymaniye Mosque in İstanbul and oversaw the reconstruction of the Grand Mosque in Mecca.

After Süleyman, however, the Ottoman empire went into a long, slow period of decline. Only five years after his death Spain and Venice destroyed virtually the entire Ottoman navy at the Battle of Lepanto (in the Aegean Sea), a loss which eventually cost the Sublime Porte (as the Ottoman government was known) control of the western Mediterranean. North Africa soon fell under the sway of local dynasties. The Ottomans were driven out of Yemen in 1636, and conflict with the Safavids – Persia's rulers from the early 16th century to the early 18th century – was almost constant.

Enter Europe

Europe's colonial expansion into the Middle East began in 1498, when the Portuguese explorer Vasco de Gama visited Oman's northern coast, the Strait of Hormuz (then the seat of an independent kingdom) and the Sheikhdom of Julfar, near modern Ras al-Khaimah in the UAE. In 1507 Portugal

Süleyman the Magnificent (1494–1566)

Süleyman I, Sultan of the Ottoman empire from 1520 to 1566, was variously known as 'the Lawgiver' and 'the Magnificent'. He shattered the army of the Kingdom of Hungary and laid siege to Vienna, and his navy challenged the Portuguese in the Indian Ocean. He was also responsible for building many public works – mosques, aqueducts and bridges – particularly in İstanbul, but also elsewhere; for instance, the existing walls and some of the gates of Jerusalem were built under his patronage. Of even more relevance to today's traveller is the fact that it was also via the Constantinople of Süleyman that coffee was first introduced to Europe.

annexed the Yemeni island of Suqutra and occupied Oman. Its power eventually extended as far north as Bahrain. Although Portugal retained control of Bahrain until 1602, and was not driven out of Oman until 1650, the area was important to it only as a way-station on the route to India. Little, if any, effort was made to penetrate Arabia's interior.

In the 18th century the European powers began further nibbling away at the ailing Ottoman empire.

In 1798 Napoleon invaded Egypt in what he thought would be the first step towards building a French empire in the Middle East and India. The French occupation of Egypt lasted only three years but left a lasting mark: until very recently French was the second (sometimes the first) language of choice for the Egyptian upper classes. Even today, Egypt's legal system is based on a French model.

The British, protecting their own Indian interests, forced the French out of Egypt in 1801, and several years of unrest followed. In 1805 Mohammed Ali, an Albanian soldier in the Ottoman army, emerged as the country's strongman and became the Ottoman sultan's khedive, or viceroy. Mohammed Ali, whose descendants ruled Egypt in some form or other until 1952, set about modernising the country, particularly by sending large numbers of Egyptians to study in Europe.

In 1818 Mohammed Ali obliged the sultan by sending an army, led by his son Ibrahim, to retake Arabia, much of which had been conquered by Bedouin warriors led by the ancestors of today's Saudi royal family.

As time passed, and it became increasingly obvious that the sultan was ever more dependent on him for military backing, Mohammed Ali's ambitions grew. In the 1830s he invaded and conquered Syria, and by 1839 he had effective control of most of the Ottoman empire. İstanbul itself would probably have been his next target had not the European powers, alarmed by the idea of the Ottoman government collapsing, forced him to withdraw to Egypt. In exchange, the sultan recognised Mohammed Ali as a separate ruler owing only nominal allegiance to

the Porte (which was more an acknowledgment of reality than anything else).

In 1869 Mohammed Ali's grandson, Ismail, opened the Suez Canal. But within a few years his government was so deeply in debt that in 1882 the British, who already played a large role in Egyptian affairs, occupied the country.

At the same time, the Ottoman empire was becoming increasingly dependent on the good will of the European powers and was weakening its own position by ceding authority over its subjects to various foreign governments. In 1860 the French sent troops to Lebanon after a massacre of Christians by the local Druze. Before withdrawing, the French forced the Ottomans to set up a new administrative system for the area guaranteeing the appointment of Christian governors, over whom the French came to have great influence. In 1911, after a short struggle between Rome and the Turks, Tripoli and Cyrenaica (Libya) went to the Italians.

The Modern Middle East

With the outbreak of WWI in 1914 the Ottoman empire sided with Germany, and Sultan Mohammed V declared a *jihad*, or holy war, calling on Muslims everywhere to rise up against Britain, France and Russia. To counter the sultan, the British negotiated an alliance with Hussein bin Ali, the Grand Sherif of Mecca. In 1916 Sherif Hussein agreed to lead an Arab revolt against the Turks (his nominal overlords) in exchange for a British promise to make him King of the Arabs after the war.

The British never had any serious intention of keeping this promise. At the same time that they were negotiating with Sherif Hussein, they were holding talks with the French on how to carve up the Ottoman empire. Britain had also given the Zionist movement a promise, known as the Balfour Declaration (after the then-British foreign secretary), that it would 'view with favour the establishment in Palestine of a national home for the Jewish people' after the war. (For more on the background to Zionism and the Arab-Israeli conflict, see the boxed text 'Fifty Years & More of War' in the Israel & the Palestinian Territories chapter.)

In the closing year of the war the British occupied Palestine and Damascus. After the war a settlement modelled on the Sykes-Picot Agreement – the secret Anglo-French accord that divided the Ottoman empire into British and French spheres of influence – was implemented and given the formal rubber-stamp approval of the newly created League of Nations: France took control of Syria and Lebanon, while Britain retained Egypt and was given control of Palestine, Transjordan and Iraq. These territories were formally held under 'mandates' from the League of Nations, but in practice the system amounted to little more than direct colonial rule.

The war also meant the end of the Ottoman dynasty. Stripped of its Arab provinces, the Ottoman monarchy was overthrown and a Turkish Republic was declared under the leadership of Mustafa Kemal, a soldier who became Turkey's first president in 1923. Atatürk, as he was known, launched a drive for modernisation, which he regarded as synonymous with secularism. (For more on this see History and the boxed text 'Atatürk' in the Turkey chapter.)

Atatürk's secularism found an echo in Persia where, in 1923, Rezā Khān, the commander of a Cossack brigade who had risen to become war minister, overthrew the Ghajar dynasty. To emphasise his nationalist credentials, he changed his name from Khān to the more Persian-sounding Pahlavī, which also happened to be the name of the language spoken in pre-Islamic Persia. He initially moved to set up a secular republic on the Turkish model, but after protests from the country's religious establishment he had himself crowned shāh instead.

In 1934 he changed the country's name from Persia to Iran.

Further Independence & Pan-Arabism

The Middle East was only of marginal importance during WWII. Egypt and Libya were briefly central to the war, with decisive battles fought at Tobruk and El Alamein in the desert west of Alexandria. But the region's problems began in earnest soon after the war was over.

Since taking control of Palestine in 1918, the British had been under pressure to allow unrestricted Jewish immigration to the territory. With tension rising between Palestine's Arab and Jewish residents, they had refused to do this and, in the late 1930s, had placed strict limits on the number of new Jewish immigrants.

Several plans to partition Palestine were proposed during the 1930s and 40s, but WWII (briefly) put an end to all such discussion. When the war ended, Britain again found itself under pressure to allow large-scale Jewish immigration, particularly in the wake of the Holocaust.

In early 1947 the British announced that they were turning the entire problem over to the newly created United Nations (UN). The UN voted to partition Palestine, but the Arab side rejected the plan. Britain pulled out and the very next day the Jews declared the founding of the state of Israel and war immediately followed.

The disastrous performance of the Arab armies in the 1948 Arab-Israeli War had far-reaching consequences. Recriminations over the war, and the refugee problem it created, laid the groundwork for the 1951 assassination of King Abdullah of Jordan. Syria, which had gained independence from France in 1946, became the field for a seemingly endless series of military coups in which disputes over how to handle the Palestine problem often played a large part.

It was in Egypt that the 'Disaster of 1948', as many Arabs still call it, truly made its power felt. The Egyptian army blamed the loss on the country's corrupt and ineffective politicians. In July 1952 a group of young officers toppled the monarchy. Initially an aged and respected army general was installed as the country's president, but it soon emerged that the real power lay with one of the coup plotters: Gamal Abdel Nasser. By 1954 he was the country's acknowledged leader. After facing down the combined powers of Israel, Britain and France over the Suez Crisis of 1956, Nasser also emerged as the pre-eminent figure in the Arab world and a central player in the politics of nationalism, socialism and decolonisation that gripped much of the developing world throughout the 1950s and 60s.

But despite this prominence, Nasser was never able to realise his dream of a Pan-Arab state. In 1958 he merged Egypt and Syria to form the United Arab Republic. The marriage of the two countries was unhappy from the outset, and the union was dissolved three years later. A 1963 attempt to unite Egypt, Syria and Iraq never got off the ground.

The Arab-Israeli Wars

The one common ground shared by all Arab countries was their opposition to the Jewish state of Israel in their midst. Nasser gave rabble-rousing speeches about liberating Palestine. By early 1967 the public mood engendered throughout the Arab world by these speeches was beginning to catch up with him. Nasser fell victim to accusations that he was 'hiding' behind the UN troops who had been stationed on the Sinai peninsula since the Suez Crisis.

On 16 May 1967 Nasser demanded that the UN forces be withdrawn. Somewhat to his surprise the UN complied immediately. The Egyptian army moved into key points in the Sinai and announced a blockade of Straits of Tiran, effectively closing the southern Israeli port of Eilat. The Egyptian army was mobilised and the country put on a war footing.

Israel responded on 5 June 1967 with a pre-emptive strike that wiped out virtually

Gamal Abdel Nasser (1918-70)

Arguably the most important Arab world figure of the 20th century, the first president of the newly independent republic of Egypt was regarded as a pharaoh, with a touch of the Che Guevara. He stood defiant against the old regional rulers of Britain and France, while playing off against the other the new superpowers of the Soviet Union and the USA. Under Nasser, Egypt became a beacon for all those countries in Africa and Asia that had recently thrown off European colonial administrations. His rousing pan-Arab speeches gave the nations of the Middle East and North Africa the belief that together they might not only free themselves of western dominance, but even achieve political and economic parity. From Algeria to Iraq and Yemen, Nasser was a bona fide hero. But, all real attempts at any kind of political union failed and the brave new Egypt came crashing down on 5 June 1967 when Israel wiped out the Egyptian air force in a surprise attack. With it went the confidence and credibility of Nasser. He never recovered and died of heart failure soon after.

the entire Egyptian air force. The war lasted only six days, and when it was over Israel controlled all of the Sinai peninsula and the Gaza Strip. The West Bank, including Jerusalem's Old City, had been seized from Jordan and the Golan Heights from Syria. To the 'Disaster of 1948' was now added the 'Humiliation of 1967'.

The year 1970 saw the ascension of new leaders in both Egypt and Syria: Anwar Sadat and Hafez al-Assad respectively. The decade also began with the last remnants of colonial rule departing from the Middle East when the British, in late 1971, pulled out of the Gulf.

Preparations were also well under way for the next Middle Eastern war. The Arab states were constantly under pressure from their citizens to reclaim the land lost in 1967.

The war began on 6 October 1973, when Egyptian troops crossed the Suez Canal, taking Israel almost entirely by surprise. After advancing a short distance into the Sinai, however, the Egyptian army stopped, giving Israel the opportunity to concentrate its forces against the Syrians on the Golan Heights and then to turn back towards Egypt. When the war ended in late 1973 the Israelis actually occupied more land than they had when it began. Months of shuttle diplomacy by the US secretary of state, Henry Kissinger, followed. Pressure on the USA to broker a deal was fuelled when the Gulf States embargoed oil supplies to the west 10 days after the war began. The embargo was relatively short-lived but if the goal was to get the west's attention, it was certainly successful.

The embargo also led to a huge, and basically permanent, increase in the price of oil, which led in turn to a flood of money landing in the laps of the Gulf's sheikhs. An enormous building boom began throughout the Gulf.

All of this shifted the balance of power in the Middle East. The oil states, rich but underpopulated and militarily weak, gained at the expense of poorer, more populous countries. Huge shifts of population followed the two oil booms of the 1970s as millions of Egyptians, Syrians, Jordanians, Palestinians and Yemenis went off to seek their fortunes in the oil states (including Iraq where, in the late 1980s, over a million Egyptians alone were working).

Peace & Revolution

Anwar Sadat's dramatic visit to Jerusalem in 1977 opened the way for an Egyptian-Israeli peace process which culminated, in March 1979, with the signing of a peace treaty between the two countries. In response, Arab leaders meeting in Baghdad voted to expel Egypt from the Arab League.

Meanwhile, one of the few friends Sadat had left in the region had troubles of his own. Discontent with the Shāh of Iran's autocratic rule and his personal disregard for the country's Shi'ite Muslim religious traditions had been simmering for years. Political violence slowly increased throughout 1978. The turning point came in September of that year, when Iranian police fired on anti-shāh demonstrators in Tehrān, killing at least 300. The momentum of the protests quickly became unstoppable.

On 16 January 1979 the shāh left Iran, never to return (he died in Egypt in 1980). The interim government set up after his departure was swept aside the following month when the revolution's leader, the hitherto obscure Āyatollāh Rūhollāh Khomeinī, returned to Tehrān from his exile in France. (For more on Khomeinī and the Iranian Revolution, see the Iran chapter.)

After the Revolution

Iran's Islamic Revolution seemed to change everything in the Middle East, ushering in a period of instability that lasted until nearly the end of the 1980s.

In 1979 militants seized the Grand Mosque in Mecca – Islam's holiest site – and were only ejected several weeks later after bloody gun battles inside the mosque itself. In November of that year student militants in Tehrān overran the US embassy, taking the staff there hostage. In 1980 Turkey's government was overthrown in a military coup, capping weeks of violence between left and right-wing extremists. Further east, Iraq invaded Iran, launching what would become the longest, bloodiest and, arguably, most pointless war in modern history.

Tensions were further escalated in 1981 when President Sadat of Egypt was assassinated by Muslim militants. The following year Israel invaded Lebanon, further contributing to the cycle of chaos and destruction that had gripped that country since 1975. In 1986 clashes between the US and Libya came to a head with the American air strikes on Tripoli, while the following year saw an escalation in violence in Israel & the Palestinian Territories with the beginning of the *Intifadah*.

Over the 15 years of Lebanon's civil wars an extraordinary cast of foreign characters intervened on one side or another (in some cases switching sides as time went on): the USA, the UK, France, Iran, Iraq, Israel and Syria all got deeply involved in the Lebanese mess at one time or another. In the early and mid-1980s Lebanon became a depressing metaphor for the entire region. By the end of the decade it had become so violent and so dangerous that few foreigners dared venture there. The fighting in Lebanon only limped to a close in late 1990 when Syria moved in to put an end to it with the tacit approval of the USA.

Still, there were occasional bright spots. Turkey returned to democratic rule in 1983, albeit with a new constitution barring from public office anyone who had been involved in politics prior to the 1980 coup. In 1985 the Israelis withdrew from most of Lebanon. In 1988 Iran and Iraq grudgingly agreed to a cease-fire. The following year Egypt was readmitted to the Arab League and Jordan held its first elections in more than 20 years.

The Middle East Today

The last decade in the Middle East began with a short war and has since been dominated by the quest to bring a settled peace to the region.

In August 1990, Iraq invaded Kuwait. Within days King Fahd of Saudi Arabia had asked the USA to send troops to defend his country against a possible Iraqi attack. The result was a US-led coalition that, under the operational moniker 'Desert Storm,' engaged in a six week bombing campaign and a four day ground offensive that drove Iraq out of Kuwait. See History in the Kuwait chapter for more details.

While attempting to solicit Arab support for the anti-Iraq coalition, US president, George Bush, had promised to make a new effort to achieve Arab-Israeli peace once the Iraqis were out of Kuwait. This took the form of endless shuttling between Middle Eastern capitals culminating in a US-sponsored peace conference in Madrid in October 1991. It achieved little, and two years of further negotiations seemed similarly fruitless until in the late summer of 1993 it was revealed that Israel and the PLO had been holding secret talks in Norway for 18 months. The 'Oslo Accord' was cemented with a handshake between Yasser Arafat and Israeli prime minister Yitzhak Rabin on the White House lawn in September 1993. The following year Israel withdrew from the Gaza Strip and the West Bank town of Jericho.

After some initial hesitation, in 1994 Jordan became the second Arab country to sign a formal peace treaty with Israel.

Tragically, the peace process was pulled up short by the November 1995 assassination of Rabin and the subsequent election to power of hardline candidate Binyamin Netanyahu. The new Israeli prime minister was a firm advocate of tougher policies against the Palestinians, and for four years Netanyahu's Israel and the Arab world remained locked in an antagonistic stalemate.

As we go to press that stalemate remains, but prospects for a way forward are looking brighter than they have done at any time since 1993. Netanyahu has been voted out of office and instead the Israelis have a prime minister, Ehud Barak, who has indicated his willingness to pull his troops out of occupied South Lebanon, to talk with the Syrians on the issue of occupied Golan, and to reopen negotiations with the Palestinians. At the same time, Jordan is reaping the economic benefits from its peace with Israel, and despite a belligerent national press, Egypt's business community is leading the way in normalising relations between Cairo and Tel Aviv. With a new crowned king in Jordan, long-time frosty relations between Amman and Damascus are on the thaw, while Gaddafi's agreement to hand over the Lockerbie bombing suspects means that international sanctions against Libya have recently been lifted. Even Iran, which is the most shunned of all pariah states, enjoyed a little good humoured banter with the US state department following its national football team's victory over the Americans in the 1998 World Cup.

In a neighbourhood as traditionally rough as this, it's impossible to predict what the coming years will hold, but considering that only three of the 16 countries in this book existed as independent entities as we entered the 20th century, one has to make a few allowances for growing pains.

GEOGRAPHY

The Middle East is a somewhat vaguely defined area where the three continents of the Old World meet. The region could essentially be defined as south-west Asia but because present international borders and age-old cultural exchanges draw Turkey, Egypt and Libya into the picture, Europe and Africa are also included.

The core of the Middle East consists of the Arabian peninsula and the Levant, but the region can be said to extend north up to the natural boundaries of the Black and Caspian seas and the Caucasus Mountains.

Many people immediately visualise sand dunes on hearing the term Middle East but the reality is that sand deserts form only a tiny percentage of the whole area. They are mainly to be found in Saudi Arabia, Egypt and Libya, and even in those countries rocky plains are much more common. Mountains and high plateaus abound in many countries: in Turkey, Iran and Yemen much of the area lies above 1000m. The highest mountains in the Middle East include the 5671m-high Kūh-é Damāvand in

Iran, the 5137m-high Ağrı Dağı (Mt Ararat) in Turkey and the 3660m-high Jebel an-Nabi Shu'ayb in Yemen.

The biggest rivers in the area include the Nile, bringing African waters through Egypt, and the Euphrates and Tigris, flowing from the Anatolian highlands through Syria and Iraq to the Gulf. Otherwise, with the exception of those in Turkey and north-western Iran, rivers flowing all year round and reaching the sea are a rarity in the region, due to the arid climate.

CLIMATE

This section gives an overview of the Middle East's climate pattern and characteristics. Of course, within a region as vast as this there are considerable variations and these are discussed in the individual country chapters. More details on how the climate affects travel are given under When to Go in the Regional Facts for the Visitor chapter.

Temperatures & Humidity

Temperatures vary wildly depending on the time of year and location. The low-lying coast lands of the Red Sea, Arabian Sea and the Gulf are hot to the extreme throughout the year, with humidity continuously exceeding 70%. Expect daytime temperatures between 40° and 50°C during the summer, and way above 30°C in the winter, with nights not much cooler. Along the southern coasts of the Black and Caspian seas the mild climate resembles that of Central Europe.

On the other hand, temperatures drop consistently as altitude increases. The rule of thumb is that for every 100m of ascent the temperature drops by 0.5° to 0.7°C: many high plateaus are quite hot during the summer days but still freezing cold at night.

Mountains with snow caps are to be seen in Turkey, Iran and even as far south as Lebanon and northern Israel. Winters are regularly snowy in the nonarid highlands of Turkey and Iran, and in the coldest winters it may very occasionally snow in the highest spots of the Hajar Mountains in northern Oman and as far south as the mountains of Yemen.

Rainfall

Most of the Middle East is arid or semi-arid, including the greater part of the Arabian peninsula and Egypt, and most of Jordan, Iraq, Iran and Libya. In many regions annual rainfall hardly reaches 100mm. Most of Egypt, south-eastern Saudi Arabia and western Oman are extremely arid, with years often passing without rain. Dasht-é Kavīr, or the Great Salt Desert of Iran, is the largest area in the world with absolutely no vegetation. However, mountain ridges and two separate moist climate systems guarantee that considerable variation occurs within most of the countries.

The coastal areas of Turkey, Syria and Lebanon all get an ample amount of rain from the Mediterranean climatic system. So do north-eastern Iraq and north-western Iran, where a narrow slip of this type of climate extends from the Black Sea, along the western Agros Mountains, all the way to Khūzestān and beyond, bringing cyclonic rains in winter. Annual rainfall can reach 600mm in some areas, while in others it can even go up to 2000mm. Further south there tends to be less rain, although southernmost Arabia and, occasionally, south-eastern Iran are affected by the Indian monsoon system; in the mountains of Yemen annual rainfall can exceed 2000mm.

ECOLOGY & ENVIRONMENT

When it comes to the environment the Middle East has an ever increasing litany of woes. Perhaps the single biggest problem is the lack of water. Resources throughout the region are stretched to their capacity and beyond. In Jordan, for example, a very visible result of diminishing water resources is the virtual disappearance of the Azraq oasis in the east of the country, and all the wildlife that went with it. It is estimated that 20 species of fauna have disappeared from the country in the last 20 years, and even more are threatened with extinction. Neighbouring Saudi Arabia will also run out of ground water long before it runs out of oil.

It's a problem that has great political ramifications: Syria and Iraq have protested to Turkey over that country's building of dams at the headwaters of the Tigris and Euphrates rivers, while Egypt has threatened military action against Sudan or any other upstream country that endangers its access to the waters of the Nile. Demand far exceeds supply, and wastage on the land and in the cities exacerbates the situation. Experts often predict that the next big Middle Eastern conflict will be triggered not by rival land claims but over water rights.

Beyond the water problem, ecological and environmental issues relevant to the Middle East are similar to those elsewhere in the world: air and water pollution, deforestation, soil erosion, habitat and wildlife destruction and conservation of natural resources are all becoming increasingly pertinent.

When discussing environmental matters there is often a danger of over-simplification. It is easy to regard the issues in isolation when, in fact, they are all inter-related and linked to wider economic, social and political situations on a national, regional and global scale.

For example, in countries such as Yemen and Egypt, an ever-increasing human population puts great demands on the land and other natural resources. One of the ways of combating this is to lower the rate of population growth. To suggest that the solution simply involves contraception or a change in cultural attitudes is a narrow view. Conservationists who prefer a broad perspective point out that the rapid population growth is closely linked to poor living conditions, which in turn is linked to social issues such as lack of education and healthcare. They argue that it is not reasonable to expect people with little money or food to worry about conservation in its widest sense; the root of the problem – poverty – desperately needs to be addressed.

However, in this respect the Middle East straddles the environmental dilemma. Israel, which is by no means a poor country, was recently damned by criticism from Greenpeace for fouling the Jordan River with industrial sewage. This came on the heels of a 1997 disaster when a bridge over the polluted Yarkon River collapsed during an international sporting event and two of the fatalities were discovered to be as a result of the athletes swallowing the toxic water.

There are bright spots. In recent years Egypt has appointed a minister of the environment and begun investing money in protectorates, while in Oman and the UAE the fight against desertification has resulted in much 'greening' of the region. Recycling programs are well established in the UAE and the newspapers in both countries are constantly featuring advertorials on conservation and protection of the environment. The UAE, along with Israel and Oman, also has active breeding programs for endangered species (see the Flora & Fauna section later in this chapter).

Tourism & the Environment

As one of the Middle East's largest industries, tourism itself is a major environmental issue. Greenpeace Mediterranean (☎ 01-785 665, fax 785 667, email gp.med@cyberia .net.lb, PO Box 13-6590, Beirut) considers tourism to be one of the major causes of coastal destruction in Lebanon, and that's certainly also the case in Egypt and Turkey. It cites the dozens of yacht ports, 'land reclamation' projects and hotels that have been established illegally along the coast.

Problems also arise when destinations cannot cope with the number of tourists they attract, so that natural and social environments quickly become damaged. The prime example of this is the Red Sea coral reefs, which are under enormous threat from irresponsible tourism and opportunistic development. Also, sites such as Petra are now having to consider limiting the number of visitors to lessen the human wear and tear on the monuments and surrounding landscape.

The gradual erosion of traditional life as a result of mass tourism is also a problem. Sexual promiscuity, public drunkenness among tourists and the wearing of unsuitable clothing are all of concern: people virtually walk around Göreme, a small Anatolian village, in beachwear.

Guidelines for Responsible Tourism A British organisation called Tourism Concern (☎ 020-7753 333, Stapleton House, 177-281 Holloway Rd, London N7 8NN) has come up with some guidelines for travellers who wish to minimise any negative impact they may have on the countries they visit. These guidelines include:

- Save precious natural resources. Try not to waste water. Switch off lights and air-conditioning when you go out. Avoid establishments that clearly consume limited resources such as water and electricity at the expense of local residents.
- Support local enterprise. Use locally owned hotels and restaurants and support trade and craft workers by buying locally made souvenirs.
- Ask before taking close-up photographs of people. Don't worry if you don't speak the language. A smile and gesture will be understood and appreciated.
- Respect for local etiquette earns you respect. Politeness is a virtue in most parts of the world but remember that different people have different ideas about what's polite. In many places, tight fitting wear, revealing shorts or skimpy tops are insensitive to local feelings. Loose lightweight clothing is preferable. Similarly, public displays of affection are often culturally inappropriate.
- Learning something about the history and current affairs of a country helps you understand its people and helps prevent misunderstandings and frustrations.
- Be patient, friendly and sensitive. Remember that you are a guest.

To which we would add:

- Leave it as you found it: as long as outsiders have been stumbling over the ancient monuments of the Middle East, they have also been chipping bits off or leaving their own contributions engraved upon them. When visiting historical sites, consider the irreparable damage you inflict upon them when you climb to the top of a pyramid, or take home an unattached sample of carved masonry.
- Don't litter. Resist the local tendency of indifference to littering and bin your rubbish or, if there are no bins, carry it with you until you can dispose of it properly.
- Do as requested: strange to say, but despite warnings and posted signs to the contrary,

divers and snorkellers continue to destroy coral by touching it and treading on it, and despite instructions to the contrary, drivers in national parks still insist on heading off the beaten track, in some cases causing great damage to the fragile environment.

FLORA

Not surprisingly, Middle Eastern flora tends to be at its lushest and most varied in the north, where the climate is less arid. That said, after millennia of woodcutting much of Turkey and Syria is now largely denuded. Only the Mediterranean coast west of Antalya, the Black Sea area and north-eastern Anatolia still have forests of considerable size. Yew, lime and fir trees predominate in areas where vegetation has not been reduced to scrub. The Iranian landscape is far more pristine and large areas – especially the Alborz Mountains region – remain densely forested with broad-leaved deciduous trees.

In Lebanon, the Horsh Ehden Forest Nature Reserve is the last archetype of the ancient natural forests of Lebanon and is home to several species of rare orchids and other flowering plants. The cedars which Lebanon is famous for are now confined to a few mountain-top sites, most notably at Bcharré and near Barouk in the Chouf Mountains.

The forests of the north give way to the cultivated slopes of the Jordan Valley where cedar, olives and eucalyptus are dominant.

South towards the Dead Sea the vegetation gives way to mud and salt flats. South and west of the Dead Sea the only other spread of greenery is Egypt's Nile Delta, a fertile agricultural region.

Although much of the Arabian peninsula is desert, the varied terrain of the UAE and Oman makes for an equally wide variety of plants. In the UAE, outside of the mountain areas, much of the vegetation you are likely to see is, in fact, not indigenous but rather part of the local government's 'greenery' program. Even in the Buraimi oasis natural groves of date palms have been supplemented by acres of grass and trees planted in municipal parks.

FAUNA

Due to its position at the junction of three natural zones, the Middle East at one time was a sanctuary for an amazing variety of larger mammals, including leopard, cheetah, oryx, aardwolf, striped hyena and caracal. Crocodile used to inhabit the Nile and lions roamed the Persia of old. Unfortunately, all of these are either now extinct in the region or on the brink of extinction due to intense hunting. These days you'll be lucky to see any mammals other than domesticated camel, donkey and buffalo.

Turkey and Iran have similar animal life to that in the Balkans and much of Europe (bear, deer, jackal, lynx, wild boar and wolf), while in the hotter, southern regions of the Middle East the only largish mammals likely to be seen are ibex or other relations of this deer-like animal. Desert regions are full of small rodents such as the desert fox, sand rat, hare and jerboa but most of these are nocturnal.

Your best chance of spotting anything of interest lies in visiting a reserve, although in the Middle East these are few and far between. It is possible to see gazelle and oryx, once common features of the desert landscape, at the Shaumari Wildlife Reserve in the east of Jordan. In Lebanon there are about 30 different species of mammal at the Al-Chouf Cedar Reserve (☎/fax 05-503 230, email arzshouf@cyberia.net.lb), including mountain gazelle, striped hyena, lynx and hyrax. Israel, Lebanon and Oman also have active breeding programs for endangered species; one of the best Israeli reserves to visit for wildlife is Ein Gedi on the shores of the Dead Sea, while the Omani government's breeding centre for endangered species is at Beit al-Barakah, west of Muscat.

Birds

In contrast to the region's lack of high profile wildlife, the variety of bird life is exceptionally rich. As well as indigenous species, the Middle East serves as a pit stop on migration routes between Asia, Europe and Africa. Israel claims to be the world's second largest fly way (after South America) for migratory birds and the Society for the Protection of the Nature of Israel (SPNI) (☎ 03-638 8677, fax 688 3940, email tour ism@spni.org.il) has an excellent map and guide, *The Bird Trails of Israel*, detailing 14 birdwatching centres. Egypt's Sinai peninsula and Al-Fayoum oasis, Wadi Araba in Jordan and the tidal wetlands around Dubai (ie the Khor Wildlife Sanctuary) also receive an enormous and varied amount of ornithological traffic – both Egypt and Dubai have recorded sightings of over 400 different species (for more on bird life in Oman and the UAE see those country chapters).

Turkey's native birds include eagles, vultures and storks. Among the numerous *kuş cenneti* (bird paradises) it has set aside for migratory visitors are Meriç Delta (Graeco-Turkish border); Kuş Gölü (Bird Lake); Gediz Delta and Big Menderes Delta (all near İzmir); Göksu Delta (near Silifke); Seyhan-Ceyhan Delta (near Adana); the Turkish Lake District (around Eğirdir); Ereğli Marshes (near Konya); Sultan Marshes (near Niğde); Seyfe Gölü (near Kırşehir); and Kızılırmak Delta. *Tukiye'nin Önemli Kuş Alanlari* (Turkey's Important Places for Birds) is a book that highlights all the best birdwatching spots but is not translated into English.

Contact the following organisations for more information:

Israel International Birdwatching Centre
(☎ 07-374 276, fax 370 098)
PO Box 774, 88106 Eilat, Israel
UAE Emirates Bird Records Committee
(☎ 9714-472 277, fax 472 276)
PO Box 50394 Dubai, UAE

Marine Life
The Red Sea is teeming with an amazing spectacle of colour and form. Reef sharks, stingrays, turtles, dolphins, colourful corals, sponges, sea cucumbers and a multitude of molluscs all thrive in these waters.

Coral is what makes a reef and, although thought for many centuries to be some form of flowering plant, it is in fact an animal. Both hard and soft corals exist, their common denominator being that they are made up of polyps – tiny cylinders ringed

by waving tentacles that sting their prey and draw it into the stomach. During the day corals retract into their tube and only at night do they display their real colours.

There are about a thousand fish species in the Red Sea, many of them are endemic. Most of them closely associated with the coral reef, and live and breed in the reefs or nearby beds of seagrass. These include grouper, wrasse, parrotfish and snapper. Others, such as shark and barracuda species, live in open waters and usually only venture into the reefs to feed or breed.

When snorkelling or diving, the sharks you are most likely to encounter include white or black-tipped reef sharks. Tiger sharks, and the huge, plankton-eating whale sharks, are generally found in deeper waters only. No divers or snorkellers have ever been killed by sharks in the Red Sea and there are no sea snakes here.

The most common type of turtle in these waters is the green turtle, although the leatherback and hawksbill are occasionally sighted.

GOVERNMENT & POLITICS
Leaving aside the matter of Israel and the widely unloved Iran, the countries of the Middle East are still far from being a homogeneous bunch. Territorial disputes and rival claims on water rights, as well as ideological clashes, not to mention the wedges driven in by external influences, have all combined to ensure that the post-colonial notion of a powerful Pan-Arab union has rarely ever looked like becoming a reality.

The Pan-Arab dream has its origins in 1945 with the convening of the Arab League of Nations, which brought together in a proposed political and economic union the seven independent Arab states of the time (Egypt, Lebanon, Transjordan, Syria, Iraq, Saudi Arabia and Yemen). Although the league has since swollen to 21 members, the unified front the organisation aimed to present has constantly been undermined by internal dissension to the extent that the whole idea of a political merging in the Arab world has been completely discredited.

In 1979 Egypt, home of the Arab League, was ostracised from the organisation after signing a peace treaty with Israel at Camp David. Respectability has since, to some extent, been restored but the downgraded Egypt now vies for the mantel of regional superpower with Jordan and Syria. Relations between the three, especially Jordan and Syria, have traditionally been, at best, lukewarm, although there has been some improvement recently with the new King of Jordan, Abdullah II, receiving a warm welcome in Damascus on an early visit there.

The question of Palestine continues to affect all Middle Eastern relations to some extent; at the time of writing Turkey was out of favour with the Arab world because of an accord on military cooperation between itself and Israel.

Ranks were split by Iraq's invasion of Kuwait. During the protracted and bloody war against Iran, Iraq had enjoyed the support of most of the Middle East's Arab nations (Syria alone has good relations with the Persian mullahs), but Saddam Hussein found himself out of sympathy when he committed his act of aggression against a fellow Muslim Arab state. Only Jordan, Yemen and the Palestinians abstained from joining the US-led Desert Storm coalition.

The 1991 Desert Storm affair also served to illustrate just how large an influence the oil producing Gulf States had acquired in the politics of the region. Had the super-rich Saudi Arabia not itself felt threatened by Saddam and made an appeal for help, it is unlikely that the USA would have moved to directly intervene. And without coercion from the White House, it is also almost certain a country like Egypt would have remained inactive: many of the region's poorer nations still resent the Gulf States for their perceived failure to share around the dividends of their oil wealth.

ECONOMY

The Middle East is an area of great economic disparities. At one end are those citizens of the Gulf States – notably Kuwait and the UAE – and, to some extent, Libya,

who have per capita incomes comparable to those of citizens in the richest western countries. At the other end of the spectrum lies Yemen, by almost any measure one of the poorest countries on earth.

There are two industries that dominate the economic life of most of the countries covered by this book: oil and tourism. This is something of an over-simplification, but while there are exceptions to the rule (agriculture, for example, remains a key sector of the economy in many countries), oil and tourism, whether directly or indirectly, are the Middle East's main sources of income.

The Middle Eastern oil industry got its start in Persia (present-day Iran), where oil was found in commercial quantities in 1908. The next major strikes were in the Kurdish region of northern Iraq in 1927 and in Bahrain in 1932. By the time WWII broke out in Europe, the Middle East in general, and the Gulf in particular, was known to contain some of the richest oil fields on earth.

Today oil is the economic mainstay of Iran, Iraq, Libya and all of the Gulf States. It is also an important source of income for Egypt, Syria and Yemen. Many of the region's countries that do not possess oil remain indirectly dependent on it in the form of remittances sent home by people working in the oil states.

The only countries that have neither oil of their own in significant quantities nor large numbers of their citizens working in the oil states are Israel, Lebanon and Turkey. In the case of Israel, decades of political isolation have led the Jewish state to look beyond the Middle East for its economic strategies and the country has developed a variety of industries such as chemicals, plastics, electronic equipment, military technology and computers.

Lebanon's once thriving economy, traditionally based on free trade, banking and service industries, is slowly being rebuilt after it was thrown into turmoil by 17 years of fighting, but it's still struggling, with about 50% of the national budget being spent on debt servicing. Lebanon's major source of income is remittances from nationals abroad, which accounts for an extraordinary 25% of the GDP, with agriculture and industry other significant contributors.

Turkey has traditionally relied on agriculture (it's a net exporter of food and the biggest wool producer in Europe), however, manufacturing and services have now come to dominate the economy. In this respect Turkey has provided something of a model for other Middle Eastern states such as Egypt and Jordan, which have long been struggling to reform and modernise their ageing industrial bases. Both are at last starting to make some headway, largely by opening up former big state monopolies to privatisation. The same process is also going on in Syria, though here the shackles are coming off at a much slower rate.

Turkey also benefits more than most from the very lucrative tourism industry that annually brings billions into the region. Its government, along with those of Egypt and Israel, has worked hard to convert the country's natural beauty and vast wealth of religious and archaeological treasures into cash in the bank. And while Saudi Arabia may forbid tourism and Iran and Iraq make little effort to attract foreign visitors, most other countries in the region have caught on; tourism is a rapidly growing industry in Jordan, Syria, Yemen, Bahrain, Oman, the UAE and even Libya.

Tourism, however, is an uncertain source of income. The Gulf War destroyed the 1990-91 tourist season throughout the region, a spate of bombings in Jerusalem and Tel Aviv in 1996 resulted in the tourists staying away from Israel in droves for the rest of that year, while at the time of research Egypt's hotel occupancy rates had still to recover from the high profile terrorist attacks that occurred in late 1997.

The region's political troubles also negatively impact upon national economies in the form of military spending. In Israel and Syria severe strain is placed on the economy by defence spending, which in each case swallows up over 50% of the national budget. Iran, Iraq and Egypt also spend well beyond their means on military resources,

in the case of the latter as a result of an entrenched military elite that objects to any attempt to scale back its privileges, even as regional tensions have eased.

It's often said that the Middle East is potentially one of the richest regions of the world but in the present turbulent climate it's unlikely that wealth will ever be fully realised.

POPULATION & PEOPLE

The most populous countries in the Middle East are Turkey, Egypt and Iran, each with approximately 60 million inhabitants. The remaining countries have a combined population of 100 million; the smallest – Bahrain and Qatar – have only about half a million inhabitants each.

The people of the Middle East are descendants of those who built many ancient civilisations. While the Turks and Persians (Iranians) are distinctive groups with their own countries, customs and languages, for Arabs the picture is less clear.

Arabs

The question of who exactly are the Arabs is still widely debated; is it all the people speaking Arabic, or only the residents of the Arabian peninsula?

Fourteen centuries ago, only the nomadic tribes wandering between the Euphrates River and the central Arabian peninsula were considered Arabs, distinguished by their language. However, with the rapid expansion of Islam, the language of the Quran was spread to vast areas.

Although the Arabs were relatively few in number in most of the countries they conquered, their culture quickly became established through language and intermarriage. The term 'Arab' came to apply to two groups: in addition to the original nomadic Arabs, the settled inhabitants of these newly conquered provinces also became known as Arabs when they adopted the language.

In the 20th century rising Arab nationalism legitimised the current blanket usage of the term to apply to all the peoples of the Middle East save the Persians and Turks. That said, many Egyptians bridle at the label as it conflicts with claims to a pharaonic heritage.

Tribes The basic structure of traditional Arab society has always been formed by families, extended families and tribes. Both wandering nomads and settled farmers divide into tribes and subtribes, the latter occupying a more or less strictly defined territory.

Belonging to a unit gives a member both rights and obligations. Conflicts are resolved within the smallest unit both participants belong to, and the smaller the number of people involved, the closer the opponents are to each other within the tribal structure. If a tribesman kills a member of another tribe, everybody in his tribe is responsible for compensation. In the course of recent history, tribal conflicts have increasingly been settled with money. Tribal killings are still a reality on the Arabian peninsula but their number has been on a slow but steady decline since money from oil exports has started coming into the region.

Every tribe elects a sheikh, a respected and supposedly wise man who is to resolve the conflicts arising within the tribe according to *Shari'a*, the Islamic law.

The Bedouin The most romanticised group of Arabs is no doubt the Bedouin (also called Bedu). While not an ethnic group, they are the archetypal Arabs – the camel-herding nomads who travel all over the deserts and semi-deserts in search of food for their cattle. From among their ranks came the warriors who spread Islam to North Africa and Persia 14 centuries ago.

Today Bedouin are found mainly in Jordan, Iraq, Saudi Arabia, Yemen, Egypt's Sinai peninsula and in the Wahiba Sands in Oman. Their numbers are unknown due to their habit of wandering in regions where no census-takers venture.

While some of them have settled down to enjoy the facilities of modern life, many maintain semi-traditional lifestyles. Their customs derive from the days of early Islam, and the hospitality towards strangers that Arabs are so famous for (and proud of)

certainly takes its most genuine forms among the Bedouin.

For more information see the boxed text 'The Bedouin' in the Jordan chapter.

Persians

Persians are descendants of the Elamite and Aryan races (from southern Russia) who first settled in the central plateau of what is now Iran in the 2nd century BC. The Persians, or Fārsīs, retained their own language even though they were among the first to adopt the new religion of Islam and welcomed the Arabic script for writing Persian. Although Iran is the home of the Persian people, a significant percentage of the population south of the Gulf in Bahrain, Oman and Qatar is also of Persian descent.

Turks

The Turkish peoples originated in Central Asia where they ruled several empires before being pushed westwards by the Mongols. At first they were shamanist nomads but at one time or another these early Turks followed each of the great religions of the region including Buddhism, Nestorian Christianity and Judaism. During their western migrations they became familiar with Islam and it stuck. The Turks kept their own language even after conversion. During the 400 year Ottoman empire, when Turks ruled most of the Middle East, they became known as Shimaliyya (Northerners) throughout the Arab world.

Kurds

The Kurds are spread across a large area of the Middle East, including a good part of eastern Turkey (with a Kurdish population of maybe 12 million), Iran, north-eastern Iraq and Syria. Although they have been around longer than any other people in the region (since at least the 2nd millennium BC), the Kurds have never had a nation of their own. For more information on the Kurds see the boxed text 'The Kurds' in the Iraq chapter.

The Druze

The Druze have no homeland or language of their own and their nation, such as it is, is defined by their religion, an off-shoot of Islam. Like Muslims, the Druze believe in Allah and his prophets but they believe that Mohammed was succeeded by a further divine messenger. The Druze also hold the non-Islamic belief of reincarnation.

Most of the Druze nation lives in Lebanon and Syria and a few villages in the Galilee and the Golan regions of Israel. Having never had a state of their own the Druze tend to hold allegiance to whatever country they live in.

Jews, Armenians & Others

There are, of course, numerous other population groups in the Middle East, the most high profile of which have always been the Jews. Following their exile from Jerusalem at the hands of the Romans, the Jews spread far and wide, many settling in near-neighbouring countries. Until the middle of the 20th century and the creation of the Jewish home-state, Egypt, Syria, Iran and Iraq were all home to significant Jewish populations. For more background on the Jewish people see the Israel & the Palestinian Territories chapter.

Armenians, like Kurds, form a small group badly treated by history. They have lived in eastern Anatolia for millennia, almost always as subjects of some greater state such as the Byzantines, Persians, Seljuks or Ottomans. In the early 20th century the Orthodox Christian Armenian minority made the error of siding with the Russians against the Muslim Turk majority. The Armenians were massacred; hundreds of thousands died and they were almost wiped out in Turkey. Elsewhere in the Middle East there are significant Armenian communities in Syria, Iran and Israel.

At its southernmost fringes, the Middle East also includes African peoples, most notably the Nubians, the dark-skinned people of Nubia, the region between Aswan in the south of Egypt and Khartoum in Sudan, which was known in ancient times as Cush. Since the drowning of their homelands caused by the creation of Egypt's High Dam, many Nubians have migrated north to the cities of Cairo and Alexandria in search of a livelihood.

ARTS

The arts of the Middle East are largely the arts of Islam, typified in the minds of the non-Muslim by exotic curves and arabesques, and by intricate geometric patterning. Artistic tradition in the western sense of painting and sculpture has historically been largely absent, as Islam has always regarded the depiction of living beings as idolatrous. There have been some exceptions. The long-standing figurative art traditions in Asia Minor, Persia and further east were never completely extinguished by Islam; the Turks and Iraqis continued to produce beautiful illuminated manuscripts, while the Persians maintained their art of miniature painting – which is still practised today in places like Esfahān in present-day Iran.

Since the pervasive influence of Europe in the region, beginning in the 19th century, western-style painting and sculpture have come to take their place in the Middle Eastern artistic repertoire, but are few artists have been able to reconcile these mediums with their heritage, and all too often results rely heavily on ill-appropriated European models.

In the areas of calligraphy, metalwork, ceramics, glass, carpets and textiles, however, Islamic art has a cultural heritage of unsurpassable richness – one that, in turn, has had great influence on the west. Middle Eastern artisans and crafts people (Armenians, Christians and Jews as well as Muslims) have for more than 1200 years applied complex and sumptuous decorations to often very practical objects to create items of extraordinary beauty. Plenty of such items are on view in the region's museums such as the Topkapı Palace in İstanbul or the Islamic Museum in Cairo, but to appreciate the achievements of Islamic art it is only necessary to visit one of the older mosques in which tiling, wood carving, inlaid panelling and calligraphy are often combined in exaltation of Allah. Islamic art is, for a Muslim, foremost an expression of faith.

continued on page 44

ARABIC MUSIC OF THE MIDDLE EAST

In most countries of the Middle East music is everywhere. Egypt, Lebanon, Syria, Jordan, the Arabs of the Palestinian Territories – these are not societies that recognise the concept of personal space. You will be bombarded with tinny pop blasted out of shop doorways or from street traders' cassette decks, thumping from the interiors of passing cars, or wafting down from the balconies of apartment blocks. In taxis it's not uncommon to have to ask the driver to turn the music down.

As in the west, the diversity of music is huge and it's impossible to do it justice in such a brief space, and although we make the division here into three broad musical types there are many, many artists who fail to fit neatly under any of these headings or conversely crossover into all three.

The Classical Style

Tonality and instrumentation aside, classical Arabic music differs from that of the west in one big respect, which is that in the Middle East the orchestra is always there primarily to back the singer.

The all-time voice of classical Arabic music is Egyptian-born songstress Umm Kolthum, who was at her peak in the 1940s and 50s but whose voice remains ubiquitous on radios and cassette decks all throughout the Middle East today (see the boxed text).

The kind of orchestra that backs such a singer is a curious cross-fertilisation of east and west. Western-style instruments such as violins and many of the wind and percussion instruments predominate, next to such local species as the *oud* and *tabla* – see the illustrations. The

---

Umm Kolthum

From the 1940s through into the 70s, the voice of Umm Kolthum was the voice of the Arab world. To the uninitiated she can sound incredibly rough and raucous, but her protracted love songs and *qasa'id* (long poems) were the very expression of the Arab world's collective identity. Egypt's love affair with Umm Kolthum (where she's known as 'Kawkab ash-Sharq', or 'Nightingale of the East') was such that on the afternoon of the first Thursday of each month, streets would become deserted as the whole country sat beside its radios to listen to her regular live-broadcast performance. When she died in 1975 her death caused havoc, with millions of mourners pouring out onto the streets of Cairo. Her appeal hasn't been purely confined to the Arab world either; former Led Zeppelin vocalist Robert Plant was reported as saying that one of his lifetime ambitions was to re-form the Middle Eastern Orchestra, Umm Kolthum's group of backing musicians.

Top: The *oud* (meaning 'wood' in Arabic) can be tuned in a number of different ways. (Photo by Geert Cole)

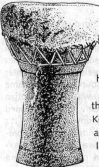

sounds that emanate from them are anything but western. There is all the mellifluous seduction of Asia in the backing melodies, the vaguely melancholic, languid tones you would expect from a sun-drenched and heat-exhausted Middle Eastern summer.

Although they never achieved the heights scaled by Umm Kolthum, the 1950s – the golden age of Arab music – gave rise to a lesser pantheon of stars that notably included Abdel Halim Hafez and Syrian-born Farid al-Atrache, two male crooners who owed much of their popularity to their omnipresence on cinema screens in countless Cairo-produced romantic movies. As with Umm Kolthum, both of these male artists remain loved and widely listened to.

Of all these golden era singers, only one is still active and that's Fairouz (see the boxed text), whose popularity even surpasses that of Umm Kolthum in her native Lebanon.

Top Left: The *tabla* is one of the most commonly played percussion instruments.

Bottom Right: The *oud* has a deep, pear shaped body and between four and six strings.

Fairouz

A Lebanese torch singer with a voice memorably described as 'silk and flame in one', Fairouz has enjoyed star status throughout the Arab world since recording her first performances in Damascus in the 1950s. Along with her writers, the Rahbani brothers, Fairouz embraced a wide range of music forms from flamenco to jazz and during the 1960s and 70s became the perfect embodiment of free-wheeling Beirut, then often referred to as the 'Paris of the Middle East'. During the civil war she became a symbol of hope for reunity and an icon for the Lebanese identity (though, in disgust, she sat out the fighting in Paris). At the end of the hostilities, in 1994, she returned to give a concert to 40,000 in downtown Beirut. Now in her late 60s, she has resettled in her homeland, living in the hills above Beirut, but she rarely performs as her voice is no longer up to it.

Pop

Characterised by a clattering, hand-clapping rhythm overlaid with synthesised twirlings and a catchy, repetitive vocal, the first pop music came out of Cairo in the 1970s. As the Arab nations experienced a population boom and the mean age decreased, a gap in popular culture had developed that the memory of the greats couldn't fill. Enter Arabic pop. The blueprint for the new youth sound (which became known as *al-jeel*, from the word for generation) was set by Egyptian Ahmed Adawiyya, the Arab world's first 'pop star'. But to unattuned ears, the Arabic pop of the 1980s is music to be driven insane to. It's cheesy and one dimensional and much of it sounds like it came preprogrammed out of a Casio keyboard – hunt down a copy of the excrutiating *Lo Laki* by Ali Hameida, which was played everywhere nonstop for several years after its release in 1988, like an uptempo electronic version of the Chinese water torture.

During the 1990s, there's been a calculated attempt to create a more upmarket sound. Tacky electronics have been replaced with moody pianos, Spanish guitars and thunderous drums. Check out Amr Diab, whose heavily produced songs have made him the best selling artist ever in the Arab world (achieved with his 1996 album *Nour al-Ain*).

Diab is Egyptian but in recent years the Egyptians have been beaten at their own game and many of the current biggest selling artists come from elsewhere. Heading the current crop of megastar singers (and the Arab music scene is totally dominated by solo vocalists, there are no groups) are Majida al-Rumi of Lebanon and Iraq-born Kazem al-Saher. Unfortunately, in the largely shrink-wrapped word of pop, regional influences are minimised and most artists have a tendency to sound the same, no matter where they come from.

UK Egypt Remix

After Indian *raga* in the late 60s, West African sounds and Zulu a cappella singing in the mid-80s (courtesy of the efforts of Peter Gabriel and Paul Simon), and the current fad for Cuban *son*, could the Arabic music of the Middle East be the next to find a mass western audience? While it's unlikely that even the biggest of Arab superstars like Amr Diab could pick up fans much north of Aleppo, there is the phenomenon of Natacha Atlas. An Anglo-Arab with roots in Egypt and Morocco, Atlas is a sort of ethnic techno artist whose work (recorded in London and Cairo) fuses traditional Egyptian musicianship with the UK dance club scene. Although she tends to warble and overplay the oriental card, she nevertheless has a following among the trend-setting London crowd. She's released three albums since 1995 (*Diaspora*, *Halim* and *Gedidia*) of which the last is possibly the best.

CHRIS MELLOR

RUSSELL MOUNTFORD

CHRIS MELLOR

Many Arabic musical instruments look and sound different to their western counterparts. One of the most odd-looking instruments is the *habban* (top left) which sounds similar to a Scottish bagpipe but is shriller in tone.

CHRIS MELLOR

CHRIS MELLOR

Arabic music is a mixture of unharmonised melodies and rhythms that are derived from the combination of percussion, string and wind instruments.

Traditional Music

Each of the Arabic countries of the Middle East has its own minority groups – ethnic, regional or religious – and most of these groups have their own music traditions. The most high profile is the Nubian music of southern Egypt. Unlike much

Arabic music with its jarring use of quarter tones, the Nubian sound is extremely accessible, mixing simple melodies and soulful vocals, and with a rhythmical quality that's almost African and a brass sound that's almost New Orleans. About the biggest name is Ali Hassan Kuban, who has toured all over Europe as well as in Japan, Canada and the US. He has several CDs out on the German Piranha label (www.piranha.de), including *From Nubia to Cairo* and *Walk Like a Nubian*. There's also a loose grouping of musicians and vocalists recording under the name Salamat who have several CDs out, also on Piranha. including the highly recommended brassy *Mambo al-Soudani*.

Not as high profile as the Nubians, the other notable Arabic folk music comes from the Bedouin (for details on these people see the aside in the Jordan chapter). Whether produced by the Bedouin of Egypt, Syria or Libya, the music is raw and totally traditional with little or no use of electronic instruments. The sound is dominated by the *mismar*, a twin-pipe clarinet, and the *rabab*, a twin-stringed prototype cello.

Much more refined than the Bedouin sound but equally dominated by traditional instrumentation is what's known as Sufi music. Sufis are religious mystics who use music and dance to attain a trance-like state of divine ecstasy. The music is bewitchingly hypnotic – a simple repeated melody usually played on the *nay* (see illustration), accompanied by recitations of Sufi poetry. There's a fascinating two-CD set called *Sufi Soul* with an accompanying booklet available on a German label NetworkMeiden GMBH.

Top Right: The *daff*, similar to the European tambourine, consists of goat or fish skin stretched from one side to the other.

Bottom Left: The *nay* is a single reed, open-ended flute-like instrument; while the *qanun* has at least 81 strings stretched across its length.

STUART KINLOCH

Left: Giant hoarding on a Cairo Highway advertising the latest releases by the stars of the moment.

A Listening Guide

Classical

In the last couple of years some of the big western record labels have begun systematically releasing the best of Arabic music on various series of well-packaged CDs. As a consequence, it's now fairly easy to find high quality recordings by classic Arab artists in the world music sections of better western CD & record stores such as HMV, Virgin or Tower. (In the Middle East you'll be able to get all the following on humble cassette.)

Umm Kolthum – well served by a collection called *La Diva* that presently runs to four CDs, although for her best single performance, *Inta Omri* (You Are My Life), you'll have to search for a CD put out by Golden Records of Beirut.

Fairouz – lots and lots available on various small labels but a good place to start is with a compilation CD called *The Legendary Fairouz* put out by EMI records in their Hemisphere series.

Abdel Halim Hafez – EMI Arabia is in the process of releasing a superb series of original soundtracks to Abdel Halim's films from the 1950s and 60s. One in particular to look out for is *Banaat al-Yom* (Girls of the Day) with music by Mohammed Abdel Wahab, one of the great classical composers.

Also highly recommended is a series put out by Virgin France called Arabian Masters including CDs devoted to Umm Kolthum, Fairouz,

The Music Scene in the Middle East

Sadly, it's very difficult to get to see live music almost anywhere in the Middle East. Artists don't generally perform gigs and there are no live music clubs as such. Other than the odd festival, like Lebanon's Baalbek festival or the Bosra festival in Syria, your best chance of catching a performance is at a wedding or party, which is the scene on which nearly all Arab singers and musicians get their start. Thursday night is the big wedding night and favoured venues are open-air restaurants or hotels.

Anyway, when it comes to Arabic pop, its true home is not on stage but on cassette. Artists have traditionally had little regard for production values and the music is slapped down in the studio and mass produced on cheap tapes in their thousands. Few people can afford quality tape decks anyway, so who cares about the quality of sound? Every town and city has numerous kiosks and shops selling tapes of whatever's the flavour of the moment, plus a selection of the classics. Shopkeepers are usually only too happy to play cassettes before you buy, although at only a dollar or two a pop you can afford to take risks.

Andrew Humphreys

A Listening Guide

Abdel Halim Hafez and Mohammed Abdel Wahab, and one double CD called *Les Plus Grands Classiques de la Musique Arabe* with a track from each of these artists plus half a dozen others including the wonderful *Batwanes Beek* by Algerian-Lebanese singer Warda.

Pop

Modern Arabic pop is far less well represented on CD as the people it appeals to most – the lower waged majority of the population – don't own CD players. However, some of the upmarket artists with an eye on the international market are beginning to venture into this format. Golden boy Amr Diab has a slickly done 'best of' package released on EMI Arabia, while Kazem al-Saher is represented by a CD in Virgin France's Arabian Masters series. *Camelspotting* (complete with spoof Trainspotting sleeve) is a compilation album put out by EMI showcasing platinum-selling singers from the Arab-speaking world – it's all sugary, soul-free stuff, although there's a great track by Yemeni singer Osama al-Attar.

Otherwise, you'll have to pick up cassettes while in the Middle East. Ask for *Kalimat* or *Tawq al-Yasmeen* by Majida al-Roumy (anthemic); *Zahma* by Ahmed Adawiyya (groundbreaking); *Shababik* or *Al-Malek* by Mohammed Mounir (jazzy); *Nazra* by Hakim (streetsound); *Awedony* or *Nour al-Ain* by Amr Diab (chic); *Ana wa Leila* by Kazem al-Saher (classy) or anything by George al-Rassy (earthy).

continued from page 37
Literature

Poetry has traditionally been the pre-eminent literary form in the Middle East and all the best known figures of classical Arabic and Persian literature are poets – men regarded as possessing knowledge forbidden to ordinary people, supposedly acquired from demons. The favourite demon seems to have been alcohol. Abu Nuwas, faithful companion to the 8th century Baghdad caliph Haroun ar-Rashid, and a rather debauched fellow, left behind countless odes to the wonders of wine, as did the Persian Omar Khayyām, famed 11th century composer of *rub'ai* (quatrains). (The current Iranian regime now prefers to celebrate Khayyām for his work as a mathematician.)

Arab literature in the form of novels and short stories is only as old as the 20th century. An increased exposure to European influences, combined with nascent Arab nationalism in the wake of the Ottoman empire's decline, led to the first stirrings, but it's been a slow growth since then. Political and religious censorship, low literacy rates and poverty meant that in much of the Middle East there existed an almost solely academic perception of publishing. Literature was narrow in its appeal and overly political. The Egyptians and Lebanese did most to expand the boundaries but much of the credit for the maturing of Arabic literature can be credited to one single author, Naguib Mahfouz, the most important writer of fiction in Arabic this century.

A life-long native of Cairo, Mahfouz began writing in the 1930s. From western-copyist origins he went on to develop a voice that was uniquely of the Arab world and that drew its inspiration from story-telling in the coffeehouses and the dialect and slang of the streets. His achievements were recognised internationally when he was awarded the Nobel Prize for Literature in 1988. Much of his work has since been made available in English-language translations – look out particularly for the haunting *Miramar*, set in Alexandria, *Arabian Nights & Days* which takes up where *The Thousand and One Nights* left off, and the folkloric *The Harafish*, which is possibly the definitive Mahfouz novel.

After Cairo, the other beacon for Arab literature is Beirut. As well as being the focus of Lebanese literary life, Beirut has been the refuge of Syrian writers escaping their repressive regime and of refugee Palestinians. Of the latter category Liana Badr, who fled to Beirut after the Israelis captured her home town of Jericho in 1967, has two books available in English (*The Eye of the Mirror* and the short story collection, *A Balcony over the Fakihani*), both of which draw heavily on her first-hand experiences of upheaval.

Of the native Lebanese writers, the best represented in translation is Hanan al-Shaykh, who writes extremely poignant but humorous novels (*Beirut Blues*, *The Story of Zahra* and *Women of Sand and Myrrh*) that resonate beyond the bounds of the Middle East.

The literary scenes of the more cloistered countries of Libya, Yemen and the Gulf States are unsurprisingly much less developed than elsewhere in the Middle East, although now and again they do throw out the odd surprise. In 1988 a book called *Cities of Salt* by Abdelrahman Munif, a relatively unknown author even in his own homelands of Saudi Arabia and Iraq, caused a stir by being picked up by a major US publishing house. The book (and its two successors) have sold extremely well and remained firmly in print.

Turkey's best-known writer is probably Yaşar Kamal, winner of the 1998 Nobel Prize for Literature. His famous and very readable *Mehmet My Hawk* deals with near-feudal life in the villages of the eastern Mediterranean. Author of the moment is Orhan Pamuk whose books are walking out of the bookshops in record numbers. *The Black Book* is the Kafkaesque tale of an abandoned husband's search for his wife in İstanbul, but it's pretty heavy going.

For Jewish-Israeli literature see the Israel & the Palestinian Territories chapter.

Film

Of all the Middle East countries only Egypt, Lebanon, Iran and Turkey have any strong film-making traditions. Of these, Egypt's film industry is reckoned to be in serious decline. In its halcyon years, Cairo's film studios would be turning out more than 100 movies annually, filling cinemas throughout the Arab world, but these days the average number of films made is around 20 a year. Most of these are genre movies relying on moronic slapstick humour and hysterics rather than acting, and usually a little belly-dancing thrown in for spice. The one director of note is Yousef Chahine, a staple of international film festivals (which is virtually the only place you'll get to see his work) and recipient of a lifetime achievement award at Cannes in 1997.

Lebanon's small film industry is showcased each year at the Beirut International Film Festival. Some of the well-known filmmakers include Maroun Baghdadi (who won an award at the Cannes Film Festival), Samir Nasri, Mohammed Sweid and Paris-based Jocelyn Saab who made the popular *Once Upon a Time Beirut*. If you get a chance, see *West Beyrouth* (1998), the story of three teenagers. The film begins on 13 April 1975, the first day of the Lebanese civil war; the cinematography is supremely slick, which is not surprising given that first-time director Ziad Doueirim, born in Lebanon, and lived his first 20 years there, was Quentin Tarratino's cameraman on *Reservoir Dogs*, *Pulp Fiction* and *Jackie Brown*.

It's a shame that the best-known film about Turkey is the American-made, racist *Midnight Express* when Turkish directors have produced so much better and more interesting portrayals of the country. Nor are these particularly uncritical. Yilmaz Günay's Palme d'Or-winning *Yol* (The Road) has only recently been shown in Turkish cinemas; its portrait of what happens to five prisoners on a week's release was too grim for the authorities to take. Günay's *The Herd* has also been shown in the west. More recently, Reis Çelik's *Hoşçkal Yarın* (Goodbye Tomorrow) told the story of the three student leaders of Turkey's revolutionary left in the 1970s.

The real success story of the region is Iranian cinema. Despite serious straitjacketing by the authorities regarding content, Iranian directors have been turning out some extremely sophisticated and beautifully made films that have won tremendous plaudits on an international level. Their accent on character and story stands in refreshing contrast to much of modern cinema, particularly that which comes out of Hollywood. A mark of how widely this work is hailed is the fact that as this book was in production London's National Film Theatre was holding a festival of Iranian cinema with screenings of over 50 different films. It's even reached the point where new Iranian films are regularly given first-run screenings in western cinemas. Names to look out for are Abbas Kiaorstami, regarded as Iran's pre-eminent film-maker and whose *The Taste of Cherry* won the Palm d'Or at Cannes in 1997, Mohsen Makhmalbaf and Jafar Panahi, whose charming *The White Balloon* is widely available in an English-subtitle video.

SOCIETY & CONDUCT

With the notable exception of Israel, the whole of the Middle Eastern region is predominantly Muslim. Religious values still greatly dictate social life. There is a strong emphasis on family and hospitality, and women tend to take a back seat to men in all matters other than the domestic.

This expression of religious values is at its most extreme in Saudi Arabia, which is one of the most insular societies on Earth. Alcohol and pork are illegal, and so are theatres and cinemas. At prayer time all shops must close. The public profession of all faiths other than Islam is banned. Non-Muslims may not enter mosques and they are barred from Mecca and may visit only the outskirts of Medina. (For details on visiting mosques see the special section 'Mosques' in the Iran chapter.) Public observance of the Ramadan fast is *mandatory* for Muslims and non-Muslims alike, with prison sentences for anyone caught smoking, drinking or eating in public.

Even Iran looks positively liberal compared with Saudi Arabia; although the dress restrictions are if anything stricter, especially as regards women (see Women Travellers in the Iran chapter for more details).

The Gulf States other than Saudi are more relaxed, and social etiquette for visitors is fairly much in line with that in countries like Egypt, Jordan, Lebanon and Syria. Alcohol and pork are available, though rarely obvious, theatres and cinemas are popular, and the only time most shops close is possibly for noon prayers and on Friday, the holy day of the Islamic week. People are generally very easy-going towards foreigners and forgiving of any social errors. Having said that, there are a few things that genuinely do cause offence, including inappropriate dress and open displays of affection – kissing and hugging in public are taboo and even holding hands is frowned upon. Vocal criticism of the government or country is also to be avoided.

Dress

Advice on how to dress is given in the Women Travellers section in the Regional Facts for the Visitor chapter, but what you wear is important for men too. Look around you: the only people wearing shorts or tatty clothes are kids, labourers or the poor. Shorts are only appropriate in the coastal resort regions of Turkey, Sinai and in Israel, where pretty much anything goes. The further away from the tourist areas and the big cities you go, the more conservative Middle Eastern society is and the more you need to be aware of what you wear.

Alcohol

Despite the popular impression of the Middle East as an abstemious region, the only countries to ban alcohol outright are Iran, Libya and Saudi Arabia. In all the other countries booze is tolerated to some degree. In most of the Gulf States alcohol is restricted to hotel restaurants and bars, but elsewhere you'll find it served in small local bars and nightclubs. That said, Middle Eastern bars are always very discrete. Other than in Israel and Turkey, drinking in public is rarely possible and most countries will impose a fine on anyone openly carrying alcohol on the streets.

RELIGION

The Middle East is the birthplace of the big three monotheistic world religions: Judaism, Christianity and Islam. The followers of these religions worship the same God, the main difference among them being their understanding of when the revelations ceased to flow unto Earth. While Judaism adheres to the Old Testament, Christianity tags on the teachings of the New Testament, and the Muslims claim that their holy book, the Quran, contains the final revelations of God, clearing up the points not made clear by earlier prophets.

Islam

Islam was founded in the early 7th century by the Prophet Mohammed who was born around 570 AD in the city of Mecca. At the age of 40 Mohammed began to receive revelations from the archangel Gabriel containing the words of God (Allah). The revelations continued for the rest of Mohammed's life and they were written down in the Quran (from the Arabic word for 'recitation') in a series of *suras* (verses).

Unlike the Torah and Bible, which are the interpretative work of many individuals, the Quran is said to be the direct word of Allah. Since its transcription by Mohammed, not one dot of the book has been altered.

By Mohammed's time religions such as Christianity and Judaism had become complicated by factions, sects and bureaucracies, to which Islam offered a simpler alternative. The new religion did away with hierarchical orders and complex rituals, and instead offered believers a direct relationship with God based only on their submission to God ('Islam' is derived from the Arabic word for submission) signified by observance of the five pillars of the faith:

Shahada Muslims must publicly declare that 'there is no God but God and Mohammed is his Prophet' (in Arabic, *ha il allah Mohammed ar rasul allah*).

Salat Pray five times a day: at sunrise, noon, mid-afternoon, sunset, and night. It's acceptable to pray at home or elsewhere, except for Friday noon prayers which are performed at a mosque

Islam & the West

Islam has been much maligned and misunderstood in the west in recent years. Any mention of it usually brings to mind one of two images: the 'barbarity' of some aspects of Islamic law such as flogging, stoning or the amputation of hands; or the so-called fanatics out to terrorise the west.

For many Muslims, however, and particularly for those in the Middle East, Islam is stability in a very unstable world. Many of them are keenly aware that Muslims are seen as a threat by the west and are divided in their own perceptions of western countries. Not without justification, they regard the west's policies, especially towards the Arab world, as aggressive and they often compare its attitudes to them with those of the medieval Crusaders. Despite this view that western culture is dangerous to Muslim values and the growing influence of anti-western religious groups, many Muslims still admire the west. It is common to hear people say they like it but that they are perplexed by its treatment of them.

If the west is offended by the anti-western rhetoric of the radical minority, the majority of Muslims see the west, especially with its support of Israel, as a direct challenge to their independence.

Although the violence and terrorism associated with the Middle East is often held up by the western media as evidence of blind, religiously inspired blood-thirstiness, the efficient oppression of the Palestinian Arabs by Israeli security forces has until fairly recently barely rated a mention. The sectarian madness of Northern Ireland is rarely portrayed as a symbol of Christian 'barbarism' in the way political violence in the Middle East is summed up as simple Muslim fanaticism. It is worth remembering that while the 'Christian' west tends to view Islam with disdain, if not contempt, Muslims accord Christians great respect as believers in the same God.

Just as the west receives a distorted view of Muslim society, so too are western values misread in Islamic societies. The glamour of the west has lured those able to compete (usually the young, rich and well educated), but for others, it represents the bastion of moral decline.

These misunderstandings have long contributed to a general feeling of unease and distrust between nations of the west and the Muslim world, and often between individuals of those countries. As long as this situation persists, Islam will continue to be seen in the west as a backward and radical force bent on violent change, rather than as simply a code of religious and political behaviour that people choose to apply to their daily lives, and which makes an often difficult life tolerable for them.

(for details on the workings of a mosques see the special section 'Mosques' in the Iran chapter). The act of praying consists of a series of predefined movements of the body and recitals of prayers and passages of the Quran, all designed to express the believer's absolute humility and God's sovereignty. Before praying, the believer washes to indicate a willingness to be purified – there are ablution fountains in mosques for this purpose.

Zakat Give alms to the poor to the value of one-fortieth of the believer's annual income. This used to be the responsibility of the individual but zakat now usually exists as a state-imposed welfare tax administered by a ministry of religious affairs.

Ramadan Fast during daylight hours during the month of Ramadan. During this month, Muslims abstain from eating, drinking, smoking and sexual intercourse from sunrise to sunset. The purpose of fasting is to bring people closer to God. (For more details on Ramadan see Public Holidays in the Regional Facts for the Visitor chapter.)

Haj Every Muslim capable of affording it should perform the haj, or pilgrimage, to the holiest of cities, Mecca, at least once in his or her life-time. The reward is considerable: the forgiving of all past sins.

Muslims also believe in the angels who brought God's messages to humans, in the prophets who received these messages, in the books in which the prophets expressed these revelations, and in the last day of judgement. The Quran mentions 28 prophets, 21 of whom are also mentioned in the Bible; Adam, Noah, Abraham, David, Jacob, Joseph, Job, Moses and Jesus are given particular honour, although the divinity of Jesus is strictly denied. The Quran also recognises the Scriptures of Abraham, the Torah of Moses, the Psalms of David and the Gospels of Jesus as God's revelation.

Shi'ite & Sunni Despite Mohammed's original intentions, Islam did not remain simple. The Prophet died with no sons, which led to a major dispute over the line of succession. Competing for power were Abu Bakr, the father of Mohammed's second wife Aisha, and Ali, Mohammed's cousin and the husband of his daughter Fatima. Initially, the power was transferred to Abu Bakr, who became the first caliph, or successor, with Ali reluctantly agreeing.

Abu Bakr's lineage came to an abrupt halt when his successor was murdered. Ali reasserted his right to power and emerged victorious in the ensuing power struggle, moving his capital to Kufa (later Najaf, in Iraq), only to be assassinated himself in 661. The Umayyad dynasty, after defeating Ali's successor, Hussein, in 680 AD at Kerbala, rose to rule the vast majority of the Muslim world, marking the start of the Sunni sect. Those who continued to support the claims of the descendents of Ali became known as Shi'ites.

Beyond this early dynastic rivalry, there is little difference between Shi'ite Islam and Sunni Islam but the division remains until today. Sunnis comprise some 90% of the world's more than 800 million Muslims, but Shi'tes are very close to being a majority of the population in Iraq and con-

stitute a clear majority in Bahrain and Iran. There are also Shi'te minorities in almost all Arab countries.

Judaism

The foundation of the Jewish religion is the Torah, or the first five books of the Old Testament. The Torah contains the revelation from God via Moses more than 3000 years ago, including, most importantly, God's commandments (of which there are 613 in all). The Torah is supplemented by the rest of the books of the Old Testament, of which the most important are the prophetic books, giving much of the substance to the religion.

These books are complemented by the Talmud, a collection of another 63 books, written in the early centuries AD and containing most of what separates Judaism from other religions. Included are plenty of rabbinical interpretations of the earlier scriptures, with a wealth of instructions and rulings for the daily life of a Jew.

The Talmud was written when the Jewish Diaspora began: after the Romans crushed the Jewish state and destroyed the Temple in Jerusalem in 70 AD, many Jews were either exiled or sold into slavery abroad. The Jewish religion was kept intact, however, within families, who passed the teachings from generation to generation.

Unlike Christians or Muslims, Jews have never actively sought converts from the followers of other religions.

Christianity

Jesus preached in what is present-day Israel but Christians form only minority groups in all Middle Eastern countries. Their numbers range from zero in Saudi Arabia (only Muslims can have Saudi nationality) to about 13% of the population of Egypt and Syria.

By far the biggest Christian sect in the region is formed by the Copts of Egypt, who make up most of that country's Christian population. Originally it was the apostle Mark who established Christianity in Egypt and by the 4th century it had become the state religion. The Coptic Church split from the Byzantine Orthodox Church in the 5th

Libya

PATRICK SYDER

Yemen

BETHUNE CARMICHAEL

Egypt

THOMAS HARTWELL

United Arab Emirates

CHRIS MELLOR

Oman

ABDULLA AHMED AL-HABSI

The hospitality of the peoples of the Middle East is legendary and language barriers are quickly broken by ready smiles and offers of tea.

ABDULLA AHMED AL-HABSI

Oman

JOHN BORTHWICK

Turkey

SARA-JANE CLELAND

Jordan

THOMAS HARTWELL

Egypt

DAMIEN SIMONIS

Syria

Despite the wealth of archaeological and architectural treasures, it's the people of the Middle East who leave the most lasting impression.

century after a dispute about the human nature of Jesus, with Dioscurus, the patriarch of Alexandria, declaring Jesus to be totally divine. Internationally, the most famous Egyptian Copt today is the former UN secretary-general, Boutros Boutros-Ghali.

The Christians of Syria belong to many churches in all main branches of the religion – Orthodox, Catholic and Protestant. This richness reflects the country's location on major routes along which the religion spread to Europe and Asia, and by which people and ideas have flowed into the area for centuries. Lebanon and Jordan have sizeable Christian populations too, and the former's one million Maronites also have followers all over the world.

And of course, while Christians form only 2.4% of the population of Israel, almost all factions of the religion are represented there, keeping watch over Christianity's holy sites.

However, the number of Christians in the Middle East is definitely in decline. The reasons are demographic. Over the centuries Christians, in Egypt and Syria in particular, have moved from the country to the city and this urbanisation has led to a fall in birth rates. Also, traditionally Christian church schools have provided a better education than Muslim state schools, which again has had the effect of lowering the birth rate. The professional qualifications resulting from the better education and subsequent wealth have also meant that Middle East Christians are far more able to emigrate. Syrian and Egyptian churches have found it impossible to staunch the flow as parishioners trickle away to Australia and the USA.

For a fascinating exploration of Christianity in the Middle East today read William Dalrymple's *From the Holy Mountain.*

Regional Facts for the Visitor

PLANNING
When to Go
When planning a trip to the Middle East, the two main things to keep in mind are the weather and the religious holidays and festivals. Despite persistent bad press, security fears should rarely be an issue – for more on this matter see the Dangers & Annoyances section later in this chapter.

Weather Most of the Middle East is best visited in autumn and spring (September to November and March to May). Though the stereotypical images are of a baking blood-red sun, in actual fact December and January can be fairly bleak and overcast everywhere in the region save for southern Egypt, Yemen and the Gulf. On the other hand, unless you really are an avid sun-worshipper or water sports freak, the summer months of June through to September should definitely be avoided. It's just too hot to do anything. This particularly applies the farther south you're heading; July and August visitors to the pharaonic sites in places like Aswan and Luxor in Egypt are obliged to get up at 5 am to beat the heat.

There are exceptions; for example, you should not venture into the east of Turkey before May or after mid-October unless you're prepared for the cold, as there will still be lots of snow around, perhaps even enough to close roads and mountain passes. Parts of Syria and northern Iran also suffer from miserable weather between November and March or April.

There are more details on weather conditions under Climate in the individual country chapters.

Religious Holidays & Festivals The main one you may want to avoid is Ramadan. Although non-Muslims are not bound by the fasting, most restaurants and cafes throughout the region (with the exception of those in hotels) will be closed. Transport is on a go-slow and office hours are erratic to say the least. In addition, going all day without food or drink doesn't improve many people's moods.

If you're visiting Turkey, you might also want to avoid Kurban Bayram which lasts a full week. Hotels are jam-packed, banks closed and transport booked up weeks ahead.

The other big Muslim feasts only last a day or two and shouldn't prove too disruptive to most travel plans. In fact, if at all possible it is well worth trying to time your visit to tie in with something like Eid al-Kebir or the Prophet's Birthday as these are wonderfully colourful occasions.

Iran also has a couple of festivals to possibly avoid during Moharram, the month of mourning, and the Persian New Year celebrations, while in Israel quite a few religious holidays such as Passover and Easter cause the country to fill up with pilgrims, prices to double and public transport to grind to a halt. There are several Jewish holidays in autumn that also make it tricky to get around.

See the Public Holidays & Special Events section later in this chapter for more details of all these events and for dates. See also the Planning sections in the individual country chapters.

Maps
A general Middle East map is not going to be of much use for anything except the broadest of planning. You really need separate country maps. There's no shortage of these on the market but we've found the best of what's available in the west to be those produced by Freytag & Berndt and GeoCenter. Once you are in the region, you will find that every country also has piles of locally produced maps available, which vary in type and quality from government survey maps to free tourist office hand-outs.

Also check out Lonely Planet's new city map series. *City Map – Jerusalem* and *City Map – İstanbul* are currently available.

The Middle East in Brief

Bahrain Bahrain is the easiest of the Gulf States to visit and a good bet for travellers on a budget. But periodic political violence is something to be aware of, and keep an eye on, when planning a trip.

Egypt Security has been beefed up since the terrorist attacks of late 1997 and tourists have begun to return in numbers. However, middle Egypt continues to be a centre of unrest and visitors should completely avoid travelling in this region – not that there is anything much to see there anyway.

Iran The Iranians are the region's most welcoming and hospitable people and their country is one of the safest in which to travel in the Middle East; the only problem for some nationalities lies in obtaining a visa.

Iraq At the time of writing Iraq is not issuing visas to travellers, only to aid workers and journalists. That said, a handful of determined souls do manage to find their way in.

Israel & the Palestinian Territories The scary headlines of bombings and rioting have been largely absent from the world's press for some time now. However, there is an ever present danger of violence errupting in the Palestinian Territories so always check the situation before heading off around the West Bank or to Gaza.

Jordan Still one of the safest and most friendly countries in the region – the odd bout of debilitating bowel problems aside.

Kuwait While not entirely recovered from Saddam's invasion, Kuwait is nevertheless open to visitors.

Lebanon Now the fighting is over and the kidnapping has long ceased, Lebanon is starting to regain the interest of the adventurous traveller. As long as you keep away from the south the country is fairly safe.

Libya Although a conservative country Libya is also one of the most hospitable in the Middle East, but due to its unpredictability it is prudent to keep a close eye on the current situation before travelling. Periodic unrest has occurred in the Jebel Akhdar area in the last few years.

Oman One of the least developed and most charming of the Gulf States, Oman probably has the greatest potential for the traveller.

Qatar While visas are not easy to arrange, Qatar is modern and safe and there's enough to see and do to justify a stopover for a few days.

Saudi Arabia Saudi Arabia actively discourages tourism and visas are hard to come by. Once in, it's easy to get around and travel is surprisingly hassle free.

Syria Despite its bad political reputation Syria is an extremely safe country to visit, free of any hotspots or violent political activity. It is, however, a police state, so watch what you say and to whom you say it.

Turkey Western Turkey is safe but east of Amasya, Kayseri and Gaziantep, exercise caution; travel on major routes to major cities and tourist sites in daylight only. Avoid completely the border areas with Iraq and north-eastern Syria.

United Arab Emirates A union of seven very different sovereign sheikhdoms that are rapidly becoming a major upmarket tourist destination. The best place in the Gulf for the independent traveller.

Yemen A lack of resources and recurrent political crises have hampered the development of the tourism industry, but this is amply compensated by the natural hospitality of the ever-optimistic Yemenis.

Latest Travel Advice

Lonely Planet's Web site (www.lonelyplanet.com) posts regular upgrades on several Middle Eastern countries which, as well as containing information on what's new etc, also include the latest safety information. See Internet Resources in this chapter for more information.

The US State Department's Bureau of Consular Affairs (Washington DC 20520, USA) offers periodically updated Consular Information Sheets which include entry requirements, medical facilities, crime information and other topics – however, it has to be said these err heavily on the side of overcaution and are often out of date. They also have recorded travel information on ☎ 202-647 5225.

If you are on the Internet, you can subscribe to a mailing list for all State Department travel advisories by sending a message containing the word 'subscribe' to travel-advisories-request@stolaf.edu (St Olaf College, Northfield MN, USA). You can check out current and past advisories at www.stolafedu/network/travel-advisories.html.

You can get British Foreign Office travel advisories from the Travel Advice Unit (☎ 020-7270 4129, fax 7270 4228), Foreign & Commonwealth Office, Room 605 Clive House, Petty France, London SW1H 9HD. Regularly updated Foreign Office travel advice is also displayed on BBC2 Ceefax, pp 564 ff.

Australians can ring the Department of Foreign Affairs and Trade in Canberra (☎ 02-6261 3305) for advisories or visit the Consular Travel Advice Web site (www.dfat.gov.au/consular/advice).

What to Bring

Clothes Temperatures are generally hot or warm, so you won't need many clothes. Bear in mind the modesty issue though (see the Society & Conduct section in the Facts about the Region chapter), and bring some light, baggy tops and trousers. Should you need to, you'll have no problem buying clothes anywhere in the Middle East – Egypt, Israel and Turkey especially.

Note that in most places, especially in cities, local people dress smartly if they can afford to, so it might be worth taking a lightweight shirt and a pair of chinos or a skirt that you can keep clean and wear when the occasion demands it. They will be useful when it comes to visa applications or crossing borders, or if you are invited to somebody's house. Also, a lot of hotel bars and nightclubs have some kind of loose dress code. Military-style clothing or baggage is definitely not a good idea.

Equipment There are few camping grounds in the Middle East, so it's not worth lugging around a tent and camping gear. A sleeping bag is useful in the cooler months, particularly if you're sleeping outside (for example on the roofs of hostels in Jerusalem) or staying at some of the more rough and ready budget accommodation options like the treehouses in Turkey or beach camps in Sinai; a lightweight one-season bag will do. Otherwise, at least bring a sheet liner.

Other useful items include a basic medical kit, mosquito repellent, sun cream and block, torch/flashlight and spare good-quality batteries, and several passport-sized photos – because every time you apply for a visa you're going to need at least two or three. A universal washbasin plug is a good idea as is a small padlock to secure the contents of your pack, a compact travel alarm, a Swiss Army-style knife, and a length of cord for drying clothes.

Women should bring preferred sanitary protection – you can't always find anything other than tampons and they're pricey.

Outside of the big cities, tourist resorts and traveller haunts like Cappadocia in

Turkey and Dahab in Sinai, any English-language reading matter can be hard to come by so make sure you bring your own paperbacks.

VISAS & DOCUMENTS
Passport
Some countries require that your passport is valid for at least three months beyond the time you plan staying in their country, so renew yours if it's near the end of its lifespan. Make sure it has plenty of blank pages too – at least two for every country you intend visiting (one for the visa, one for the entry and exit stamps).

Visas
Visas are an annoying, expensive and time-consuming piece of red tape. Effectively they are permits to enter certain countries and are stamped in your passport. You can either get them before you go or along the way. The advantage of predeparture collection is that it doesn't waste travelling time and 'difficult' embassies are sometimes less difficult when you are in your own country. There is also never any guarantee that the Iranians or Libyans, and sometimes the Syrians, are going to grant you a visa; if you apply from home first, you at least know where you stand before setting off. If you are turned down in your home country, there's usually nothing to stop you trying again while on the road.

Some visas are free but most require forms, photos and cash. Sometimes, other requirements can pop up. Some embassies request a letter from an employer or, if you're applying abroad, a letter of introduction from your embassy, while if the Israeli officials don't like the look of you they may ask to see that you have a sufficient amount of money to cover your stay. Some embassies also ask to see a 'ticket out', which means that before you can obtain a visa to get into a country you must have a ticket to prove that you intend leaving again.

For further details see the Visas & Documents section in the individual country chapters.

Travel Insurance
However you're travelling, it's worth taking out travel insurance. Work out what you need. You may not want to insure that grotty old backpack but everyone should be covered for the worst possible case: an accident, for example, that will require hospital treatment and a flight home. It's a good idea to make a copy of your policy, in case the original is lost. If you are planning to travel for a long time, the insurance may seem very expensive but if you can't afford it, you may not be able to afford to deal with a medical emergency in the Middle East. See Health Insurance under Health later in this chapter for more details.

Student Cards
An International Student Identity Card (ISIC) can come in useful in the Middle East. Egypt, Israel and Turkey have student discounts variously on flights and rail travel and reduced admissions at museums, archaeological sites and monuments of anything between 25 to 33% for card holders. A student card also gets the holder 50% off admissions to museums and cultural sites in Iran, while in Syria it slashes admissions to almost all historical sites to about a tenth of the normal foreigners' price. Bear in mind that a student card issued by your own university or college may not be recognised elsewhere: it really should be an ISIC.

Other Documents
If you plan to drive, get an International Driving Permit from your local automobile association. They are valid for one year only. If you plan to take your own car you will need a *carnet de passage* (a booklet that is stamped on arrival in and departure from a country to ensure that you export the vehicle again, after you've imported it) and third-party insurance or a Green Card (see Car & Motorcycle in the Getting Around the Region chapter for more information).

Photocopies of all your important documents, including your passport data pages, airline tickets and credit cards, will help speed up replacement if they are lost or stolen. Some airlines require photocopies of your student card before they give you your student-discounted tickets.

EMBASSIES & CONSULATES

Embassies – that is your own embassies abroad – are really not much use; they won't bail you out of trouble and will no longer hold mail; even their newspapers tend to be well out of date. Generally speaking, they won't help much in emergencies if the trouble you are in is remotely your own fault. In genuine emergencies you might get some assistance but only if all other channels have been exhausted. For example, if you have all your documents and money stolen they will help with getting a new passport but a loan for an air ticket home is out of the question.

Some embassies do post useful warning notices about local dangers or potential problems. The US embassies are particularly good for providing this information and it's worth scanning their notice boards for 'travel advisories' about security, local epidemics, dangers to lone travellers etc.

For the addresses and contact details of embassies and consulates, see the Facts for the Visitor sections in the individual country chapters.

CUSTOMS

Customs regulations vary from country to country but in most cases they aren't that different from what you'd expect in the west – a couple of hundred cigarettes and a couple of bottles of booze. The exceptions are, of course, in dry countries like Iran, Libya, Saudi Arabia and some of the Gulf States where it is strictly forbidden to take alcohol into the country.

Electronics always arouse plenty of interest too, especially in Egypt, Libya, Syria and Iran. Items like laptop computers and especially video cameras may incur heavy taxes, or they may be written into your passport to ensure that they leave the country with you and are not sold. If you are carrying this sort of thing, it's better not to be too obvious about it.

In many Middle Eastern countries, particularly those in the Gulf and Iran, video and even audio cassettes come in for scrutiny and may be taken off you for examination. In Iran, Libya and Saudi Arabia books and magazines will also be given a careful going through for any pornographic or other incendiary material. Even something as innocuous as *Newsweek* may be confiscated because, for example, a woman in an ad is deemed to be wearing a dress that's cut too low. The simple rule is don't take in any print material that you're not prepared to lose.

MONEY

Details on the currencies used in each country, places to change money and advice on specific exchange rates are given in the individual country chapters. Throughout this general section we have quoted prices in US dollars (US$) as these rates are more likely to remain stable than local currencies which may go up and down.

Costs

The Arab Gulf States, Libya and Israel aside, travel in the Middle East is cheap. Real shoestringers could conceivably get by on no more than US$10 to US$15 a day, although a more realistic budget that allows for site admissions, a varied diet and an improved chance of getting hot water at the hotel might be US$30 to US$40 a day.

When estimating your own costs take into account extra items such as visa fees (which can top US$50 depending on where you get them and what your nationality is), long-distance travel, plus the cost of organised tours or activities such as camel trekking, snorkelling or diving.

More details of costs are given under Money in the individual country chapters.

Exchanging Money

Check around when looking to exchange your cash as rates do vary. A good general rule is never change cash at borders or airports. Also be on the lookout for hidden extras like commission. Official moneychangers rather than banks often offer the best deals. Throughout the Middle East avoid accepting torn or particularly tatty notes as you will have difficulty disposing of them.

Cash & Travellers Cheques Most travellers carry a mix of cash and travellers cheques. Cash is quicker to deal with, can be exchanged almost any place and gets better rates, but it cannot be replaced. Travellers cheques are accepted everywhere in the Middle East except for Iraq and Libya; it's also difficult to find places to cash them in Iran and Yemen, though it's not impossible. If your travellers cheques are lost or stolen you get a refund. When you buy your cheques make sure you are clear about what to do when the worst happens – most companies give you a 24 hour international phone number to contact. Well-known brands of cheque such as American Express (Amex) and Thomas Cook are better to deal with as they're the most widely accepted; both companies have offices in the Middle East.

It's worth carrying a mix of high and low denomination notes and cheques so that if you're about to leave a country, you can change just enough for a few days and not have too much local currency to get rid of.

ATMs Most of the larger banks in the region – with the exception of those in Iran, Iraq, Libya, Syria and Yemen – now have Automatic Teller Machines (ATMs) linked up to one of the international networks (eg MasterCard/Cirrus or Visa/Plus or GlobalAccess systems). In countries like Bahrain, Egypt, Israel, Lebanon, Oman, Qatar, Saudi Arabia, Turkey and the UAE it's possible to travel around without cash, just getting by on your plastic. Major credit and credit/debit cards, especially Visa and MasterCard, are readily accepted and many machines will also take bank-issued cash cards (which you use at home to withdraw money directly from your bank account). Make sure you remember your PIN (personal identification number), and it is also a good idea to check out what sort of transaction fees you are likely to incur from both your own bank and the banks whose machines you will be using while you travel. See Money in the individual country chapters for more details.

Credit Cards Countries like Iran, Libya and Yemen aside, credit cards are fairly widely accepted in the Middle East, although in Syria and Jordan their use is often restricted to top end hotels. Israel, Lebanon and the Gulf States, on the other hand, are fully plastic societies in which you could probably get by without ever having to handle cash. Visa, MasterCard and American Express are the most popular. It's possible to get cash advances on credit cards in several countries in the region including Egypt and Israel – see Money in those individual country chapters for more details.

International Transfers Bank-to-bank transfers are possible but unless your home bank has links with a banking group in the country you're travelling in, it is a very complicated, time-consuming and expensive business, especially when you get outside the major capitals. Unless you are going to be in that one place for at least a couple of weeks don't attempt it. A cash advance on a credit card is much simpler. Alternatively, Western Union Money Transfer has representatives in quite a few Middle East countries including Bahrain, Egypt, Israel, Qatar and Turkey.

Black Market There is still black-market activity in some Middle Eastern countries, notably Iran, Libya and Syria. If you do play the black market don't do it on the street – a dealer with a front, a travel agent or tailor shop, for example, is safest. Big notes are worth much more than small ones – 100 US$1 bills are worth less than one US$100 bill.

Security

The safest place to carry your money is right next to your skin. A money belt, pouch or an extra pocket inside your jeans will help to keep things with their rightful owner. Remember that if you lose cash you have lost it forever, so don't go overboard on the convenience of cash versus the safety of cheques. A good idea is to put aside a separate emergency stash, say US$50, for use if everything else disappears.

Tipping

Tipping is expected in all Middle Eastern countries except Yemen where this practice simply does not exist. Called *baksheesh*, it is more than just a reward for having rendered a service. Salaries and wages are much lower than in western countries, so baksheesh is regarded as an often essential means of supplementing income. To a cleaner in a one or two-star hotel who might earn the equivalent of US$50 per month, the accumulated daily dollar tips given by guests can constitute the mainstay of his or her salary.

For western travellers who are not used to continual tipping, demands for baksheesh for doing anything from opening doors to pointing out the obvious in museums can be quite irritating. But it is the accepted way. Don't be intimidated into paying baksheesh when you don't think the service warrants it, but remember that more things warrant baksheesh here than anywhere in the west.

In hotels and restaurants, while a service charge is often included at the bottom of the bill, the money goes into the till; it's necessary therefore to leave an additional tip. Services such as opening a door or carrying your bags warrant a small tip; a guard who shows you something off the beaten track at an ancient site should receive something a little more substantial – for a guide to tipping levels see the Money section in individual country chapters.

One last tip: carry lots of small change with you but keep it separate from bigger bills, so that baksheesh demands don't increase when they see that you can afford more.

Bargaining

In Middle Eastern countries, bargaining over prices is a way of life. People from the west often have difficulty with this concept,

and are used to things having a fixed value, whereas in the Middle East commodities are often considered worth whatever their seller can get for them.

In markets selling basic items like fruit and vegetables *some* sellers will invariably put their asking price high when they see you as a wealthy foreigner. If you pay this – whether out of ignorance or guilt about how much you have compared to locals – you may be considered foolish, but you'll also be doing fellow travellers a disservice by creating the impression that all foreigners are willing to pay any price named. Having said that, many sellers will quote you the same price that locals pay, particularly away from cities or tourist areas. It is very important not to go around expecting *everybody* to charge high. It helps of course to know the price of things. After the first few days in a country (when you'll inevitably pay over the odds a few times) you'll soon get to learn the standard prices for basic items.

Bazaars & Souqs In the bazaars and souqs, where many of the items are specifically for tourists, it's a completely different story: bargaining is very much expected. The vendor's aim is to identify the highest price you're willing to pay. Your aim is to find the price below which the vendor will not sell.

People have all sorts of formulas for working out what this should be but there are no hard and fast rules. The vendor will always first quote you a price inflated anywhere between two-fold and four-fold. Decide what you want to pay or what others have told you they've paid, and your first offer should be about half this. At this stage, the vendor may laugh or feign outrage, while you plead abject poverty. The vendor's price then starts to drop from the original quote to a more realistic level. When it does, you begin making better offers until you arrive at a mutually agreeable price. Tea or coffee might be served as part of the bargaining ritual but accepting it doesn't place you under any obligation to buy.

If a seller won't come down to a price you feel is fair, it either means he really isn't making any profit, or that if you don't pay his price, he knows somebody else will. Remember the sellers are under no more obligation to sell to you, than you are to buy from them. You can go elsewhere, or (if you really want the item) accept the price.

POST & COMMUNICATIONS

Post and telephone services are quite reliable in most of the Middle East, though in rural areas the service can range from slow to nonexistent – it definitely pays to make your calls or send your mail from the main centres. For more specific details, such as rates and prices, see Post & Communications in the individual country chapters.

Sending Mail

Letters sent from a major capital take about a week to reach most parts of Europe, and anything between a week and two weeks to reach North America or Australasia. If you're in a hurry, either DHL or Federal Express has offices in almost every capital city in the Middle East.

Receiving Mail

If you need to receive mail, you can use the *poste restante* service, where letters are sent to a post office (usually in a capital city or major town) for you to collect. Letters should be addressed in this form:

> Your NAME
> Poste Restante
> General Post Office
> City
> Country

To collect your mail, go to the main post office in that town and show your passport. Letters sometimes take a few weeks to work through the system, so have them sent to a place where you're going to be for a while, or will be passing through more than once.

Some hotels and tour companies operate a mail-holding service, and Amex customers can have mail sent to Amex offices. Details are given under Post & Communications in the individual country chapters.

Telephone & Fax

Most cities and large towns have public telephone offices (either part of the post office, or privately run) where you can make international calls and send faxes and telegraphs. Card phones are starting to appear in many countries, including Egypt, Jordan, Syria, Turkey and Yemen, from which you can direct dial internationally but at present the service is limited. The exceptions are Bahrain, Israel, Oman, Qatar and the UAE, where virtually all public phones offer international direct dial.

Costs for international calls start at about US$3 per minute, and only a few countries offer reduced rates at night. The other problem is the waiting time between placing your call with the operator and actually getting through, which can be minutes or hours depending on the locality and time of day.

Email & Internet Access

The Middle East is joining the communications revolution but as yet hooking up is still difficult in most of the region's countries – with the notable exception of Israel and perhaps Turkey. Compuserve has nodes in both of these countries and, in each case, there are several other competing servers. Egypt, Jordan and Lebanon also have several ISPs.

The number of Internet cafes is also growing and you'll find them everywhere throughout the Middle East, particularly in Egypt, Lebanon and Turkey, three countries where the Netsurfing bug has really bitten – see the country chapters for details.

The only countries that outright ban the Internet and where you won't find any publicly accessible terminals are Libya, Syria and Saudi Arabia.

INTERNET RESOURCES

The Internet is a rich resource for travellers. You can research your trip, hunt down bargain air fares, book hotels, check on weather conditions or chat with locals and other travellers about the best places to visit (or avoid!).

There's no better place to start your explorations than the Lonely Planet Web site (www.lonelyplanet.com). Here you'll find succinct summaries on travelling to most places on earth, postcards from other travellers and the Thorn Tree bulletin board, where you can ask questions before you go or dispense advice when you get back. You can also find travel news and updates to many of our most popular guidebooks, and the sub-WWWay section links you to the most useful travel resources elsewhere on the Web.

Much of the Middle East has been slow to embrace the Internet – governments in the region are wary of encouraging a system that allows for an unregulated flow of information. As a result many of the best Arab-oriented Web sites emanate from Europe or America, developed largely by either expatriate or Middle Eastern students or by trade associations dealing with the Middle East. There's some good stuff out there – whether you want to find out the current prayer times or arrange yourself a marriage ... Of course, there's a lot of dross too, but the following Web sites are some of the better ones.

Egypt

ce.eng.usf.edu/pharos/
   The Egypt World Wide Web index with hundreds of links broken down into categories including Egyptology, travel, media and cooking. This is *the* place to start surfing.
pharos.bu.edu/Egypt/Cairo/home
   Billing itself as The Cairo Guide, this contains a lot of information similar to that contained in this book.
interoz.com/Egypt
   The official site of the Egyptian Ministry of Tourism. Pretty standard stuff like travel tips and travel news updates but it also has more interesting features such as the virtual dive centre with plenty of graphics and descriptions of dive sites over wrecks.
www.metimes.com
   The online edition of the weekly *Middle East Times*. Includes all the articles the censors wouldn't allow into the print edition. No fee.

Israel

www.infotour.co.il/
   The Israeli Government Tourist Office's Web page. Good for seeing what the IGTO want you to know, plus other useful links on the country.

www.birzeit.edu/
   The Web site of Birzeit University, 20km north of Jerusalem. A one-stop shop for all you could want to know about the Palestinian Territories, including a link to all the useful Palestinian Web sites.
www.visit-palestine.com/
   The official tourism Web site of the Palestinian Ministry of Tourism & Antiquities. Comprehensive data on the seven main Palestinian towns.
www.jpost.co.il/
   The Internet version of the English-language daily *The Jerusalem Post*, which includes daily news, columns, features and reviews – and there's no subscription fee.
www1.huji.ac.il/jeru/jerusalem.html
   A virtual tour through the Old City of Jerusalem with links to information on other parts of the country.
www.israelhotels.org.il/
   The home page of the Israel Hotel Association. Good for getting an overview of Israeli hotels, although only members of the IHA are listed.

Jordan

www.jordan-online.com
   Run by Baladna Community Services, this site is excellent for the latest current affairs, cultural info and links to chat sites about Jordan
www.access2arabia.com/jordantimes
   Run by the best of the English-language newspapers in Jordan, and updated daily.
www.arabia.com/Jordan
   This colourful site run by the Jordan Tourism Board is a must for all visitors.
www.arabia.com/JordanToday
   Check out this for the freebie tourist pamphlet which lists hotels, restaurants etc.

Lebanon

www.dailystar.com.lb
   This is the online edition of one of Lebanon's English-language daily papers. It also has some excellent links.
www.embofleb.org
   Maintained by the US embassy in Lebanon, this has good general information on the country, especially concerning visas, and some good links.

Libya

home.earthlink.net/~dibrahim
   This site is called 'Libya, Our Home' and has all kinds of goodies.
members.aol.com/libyapage/index.htm
   Libya Resources on the Net.

Oman

www.oman.org
By far the best, biggest and most informative site on Oman, this is specifically set up for travellers, researchers and journalists and is linked with the Oman Studies Centre which has masses of information on culture and lifestyle, as well as a comprehensive bibliography.

www.omanet.net
Information on politics, economy, foreign affairs, commerce and media and other links.

Syria

www.syriatourism.org
The official Ministry of Tourism site has some good site descriptions but precious little else.

www.teshreen.com
Home site of the Damascus-based English-language newspaper *Syria Times*. While it is updated daily there's next to nothing here beyond a few headlines. If you want to know what Assad is doing today then this is where to look.

www.syria-net.com
A link site strong on business and academic material but also with feeds to a few travellers' reports and other tourism related pages.

Turkey

www.turkishdailynews.com
The *Turkish Daily News* site has current information, weather and, in the classifieds section, ads for rental apartments, jobs as English teachers and translators etc.

www.milliyet.com/e/
Milliyet, a prominent national daily news paper, provides news in ambitious English.

www.turkey.org
The official Turkish government site has visa, passport, consular and economic information, email addresses of Turkish diplomatic missions, and useful links to other sites related to Turkey.

www.mfa.gov.tr
Lists all the embassies in Turkey and has some interesting cultural information as well.

UAE

www.emirates.org.ae
General information on travel within the UAE including things to see and do, news and media, arts and crafts.

www.uaeforever.com
Breaks up information by emirates and has comprehensive lists of travel agents in each city as well as things to see and do. It also includes lists of government departments and embassies.

www.godubai.com
A large site with lists of travel agencies, airlines, libraries and links to other sites. It also has information on the Emirates Environmental Group, as well as promotions and giveaways.

Yemen

www.al-bab.com
A well-organised site that includes a wealth of articles and links.

www.y.net.ye
TeleYemen hosts most of the Yemeni sites and this, their homepage, has a good links section.

BOOKS

Most books are published in different editions by different publishers in different countries. As a result, a book might be a hardcover rarity in one country while it's readily available in paperback in another. Fortunately, bookshops and libraries search by title or author, so your local bookshop or library is best placed to provide you with information on the availability of the following recommendations.

The books listed here contain general information about the Middle East. Other books more relevant to individual countries are listed under Books in each chapter.

Lonely Planet

Lonely Planet has several detailed guides to various countries in the Middle East, including travel guides for the following: *Arab Gulf States, Egypt, Iran, Israel & the Palestinian Territories, Jordan, Syria, Lebanon, Turkey* and *Yemen*. Due on the bookshelves soon is *İstanbul to Cairo*, the definitive overland guide for those looking to rage their way through the Middle East on a pittance. As well, there are city guides for *Cairo, Jerusalem* and *İstanbul*, travel atlases for *Egypt, Israel & the Palestinian Territories, Jordan, Syria & Lebanon* and *Turkey*, and an *Arabic* and *Turkish* phrasebook.

Lonely Planet's travel literature series, *Journeys*, includes *The Gates of Damascus* by Lieve Joris, *Kingdom of the Film Stars* and *Travels in Jordan* both by Annie Caulfield, which are described in the Syria and Jordan chapters, respectively.

Travel

The Holy Mountain, by William Dalrymple. An ambitious attempt by the most fêted travel writer of the moment to revisit the roots of Christianity in the troubled spots of eastern Turkey, Lebanon, Palestine and middle Egypt. Beautifully written and highly recommended.

Expats, by Christopher Dickey. A side of the Middle East rarely written about – expatriate life in Libya, Egypt and the Gulf. Well observed and fluidly written by a former *Newsweek* correspondent.

Baghdad Without a Map, by Tony Horwitz. Should really be subtitled, 'the trials and misadventures of a freelance journalist awash in the Middle East'. Among other places, Cairo-based Horwitz trips up in Baghdad, Beirut, Tehrān and Yemen. Sober reading for anyone who thought they might make some easy cash by flogging their travel diary on getting back home.

An Australian Odyssey: From Giza to Galipolli, by Garrie Hutchinson. The skeleton of the book is a pilgrimage to WWI ANZAC sites of the Middle East but the author's travels from Cairo to Jordan and Syria into Turkey (with a hijacked detour into Libya) make fun reading.

Arabia Through the Looking Glass, by Jonathan Raban. One of the most readable of English travel writers, in this early book Raban visits the Arab Gulf countries during the oil boom. His observations on expatriate life in the region are as valid today as they were when he visited in early 1979.

East is West; Valleys of the Assassins; Beyond the Euphrates, by Freya Stark. Probably the most famous of a number of distinguished women travellers in the Middle East, Stark wrote more than 20 books recounting her travels throughout the region.

Pillars of Hercules, by Paul Theroux. The normally acerbic and grumpy Theroux lightens up a little as his exploratory jaunt around the fringes of the Mediterranean takes in seaside Turkey, Syria, Israel and Egypt. You still wouldn't want him as your travelling companion but he's great in book form.

Sandstorms, by Peter Theroux. A memoir of Theroux's seven years stationed as a journalist in Riyadh, bookended by stays in Cairo.

History & Politics

The Arab World: Forty Years of Change, by Elizabeth Fernea & Robert Warnock. A wide-ranging and very readable overview of trends and events in the recent history of the Middle East. It makes a great primer for a trip to the region.

From Beirut to Jerusalem, by Thomas Friedman. The recent history of the Middle Eastern conflicts as witnessed by a Pulitzer prize-winning journalist. The book is an excellent read for anyone seeking a fuller understanding of the causes and effects of the constant strife that afflicts the region.

A Peace to End All Peace: Creating the Modern Middle East, 1914-1922, by David Fromkin. For some background on how the Middle East came to be the mess that it is, this book is absolutely essential. Fromkin defines the region broadly, even taking in Central Asia, as he details the western machinations during and immediately after WWI that laid the groundwork for the Middle Eastern politics we know today.

Money For Old Rope; Tribes With Flags, by Charles Glass. Two collections of articles and essays on Levantine politicking by veteran journalist Glass. Both include accounts of his kidnapping and subsequent escape from pro-Iranian guerrillas in Beirut.

Arabia Without Sultans, by Fred Halliday. A detailed and quite accurate account of the development of the Arab Gulf countries in recent decades, with some 180 pages devoted to Yemen.

A History of the Arab Peoples, by Albert Hourani. While not exactly holiday reading, this is possibly the single best book on the development and sociology of the modern-day Arab world.

The Middle East, by Bernard Lewis. A recent and very erudite overview of Middle Eastern history from the rise of Christianity to the present day.

The Arabs, by Peter Mansfield. In addition to an overview of the history of the Middle East, Mansfield comments on the individual countries in the region.

People & Society

Nine Parts of Desire, by Geraldine Brooks. An investigation into the life of women under Islam. As befits a *Wall Street Journal* correspondent, the book succeeds in maintaining a degree of objectivity, and interview sources range from village girls to Queen Noor of Jordan and the daughter of President Rafsanjānī of Iran.

The Hidden Face of Eve: Women in the Arab World, by Nawal El-Saadawi. Considers the role of women in world history, Arab history and literature, and contemporary Egypt. El-Saadawi is a psychiatrist, feminist, novelist and writer of nonfiction and all her books, many of which have been translated into several languages, are well worth reading for the insight they provide into the lives of women in the Arab world.

Price of Honour, by Jan Goodwin. The blurb on the back of this book includes the terms 'horrific', 'abused', 'oppressed' and 'restrictions', and that's all within a single sentence. Goodwin has clocked up the miles and the hours in her quest to expose the Muslim world's mistreatment of women, but you can't help but suspect she already had her script written long before she set about her research.

The New Arabians, by Peter Mansfield. An introduction to both the history and society of the Gulf, though the focus is mostly on Saudi Arabia and the general tone of the book is fairly uncontroversial.

Islam

Living Islam, by Akbar Ahmed. Highly recommended as a sensitive introduction to Islam by a Pakistani scholar who has dedicated himself to bridging the mutual ignorance and misunderstanding between the Muslim and non-Muslim worlds; based in part on a BBC TV series.

Islam, by Alfred Guillaume. Dry as dust but dense with information on history, doctrine and practice.

Art & Culture

Islamic Arts, by Jonathan Bloom & Sheila Blair. Part of Phaidon's beautifully formatted Arts & Ideas series, this is an excellent introduction to the subject; the text is lively and concise and there are some great photos.

Oriental Rugs & A Buyer's Guide, by Essie Sakhi. As well as colour photographs, the book includes useful information on the history of Persian carpets, how they are made, and even more importantly, what to look for when buying one.

Calligraphy and Islamic Culture, by Annemarie Schimmel. A good book dealing with Arabic calligraphy, a most intricate and complex art form.

Islamic Art, by David Talbot Rice. A useful general reference on both artistic and architectural forms throughout the Islamic world.

For literature by Middle Eastern writers see the Arts section in the Facts about the Region chapter.

NEWSPAPERS & MAGAZINES

There are no English-language daily or weekly newspapers that cover the whole of the Middle East or have any kind of regional distribution. Instead almost all the countries have their own English-language press. These vary greatly in quality. Many papers are state-run and contain little for anyone with interests beyond those of what the president did this week. Nongovernment papers are, in most Middle Eastern countries outside of Israel, subject to censorship but as long as they stay away from military topics, wayward interpretations of Islam and say only good things about the country's leaders, this doesn't affect the reporting too much. About the best English-language papers in the region are *The Middle East Times*, published in Egypt but featuring some regional coverage, and the *Daily Star*, published out of Beirut. Both of these papers are only available in their own local markets but they both have good Web sites – see Internet Resources earlier this chapter.

For details of other English-language papers see Newspapers & Magazines in the individual country chapters.

The Middle East (IC Publications) is an internationally-distributed monthly magazine with a mix of politics, financial and economic analysis, features on social and cultural affairs, sport, arts, health and recreation. It's published in London but you should be able to find it in better newsagencies in big cities in the USA and Australia, and throughout the Middle East itself.

PHOTOGRAPHY & VIDEO
Film & Equipment

Most types of film are available in the Middle East though they may not be easily found outside of the big cities. Colour-print processing is usually quite adequate, while B&W and slide processing is not that good.

Film prices are usually similar, if not more expensive, to prices in western countries, so you may want to bring your own supply. In some countries, film may have been stored for ages in less than ideal conditions, so always check the 'use by' date.

Cameras and lenses collect dust quickly in desert areas. Lens paper and cleaner can be difficult to find in some countries, so bring your own. A dust brush is also useful.

Technical Tips

In most Middle Eastern countries, early morning and late afternoon are the best times to take photographs. During the rest of the day, sunlight can be too bright and the sky too hazy, causing your photos to look washed out. There are a few remedies for this: a polarisation filter will cut glare and reflection off sand and water; a lens hood will cut some of the glare; Kodachrome film, with an ASA of 64 or 25, and Fujichrome 50 and 100 are good slide films to use when the sun is bright.

Many religious sites and other buildings are not lit inside and you'll need long exposures (several seconds), a powerful flash or faster film. A portable tripod can be very useful.

Video

Properly used, a video camera can give a fascinating record of your holiday. As well as videoing the obvious things – sunsets, spectacular views – remember to record some of the ordinary everyday details of life in the country. Often the most interesting things occur when you're actually intent on filming something else. Remember too that, unlike still photography, video 'flows' – so, for example, you can shoot scenes of countryside rolling past the train window, to give an overall impression that isn't possible with ordinary photos.

Video cameras these days have amazingly sensitive microphones, and you might be surprised how much sound will be picked up. This can also be a problem if there is a lot of ambient noise – filming by the side of a busy road might seem OK when you do it, but viewing it back home might simply give you a deafening cacophony of traffic noise. One good rule to follow for beginners is to try to film in long takes, and don't move the camera around too much.

Make sure you keep the batteries charged and have the necessary charger, plugs and transformer for the country you are visiting. In most countries, it is possible to obtain video cartridges easily in large towns and cities, but make sure you buy the correct

format. It is usually worth buying at least a few cartridges duty free to start off your trip.

Finally, remember to follow the same rules regarding people's sensitivities as for still photography – having a video camera shoved in their face is probably even more annoying and offensive than a still camera. Always ask permission first.

Restrictions

In most Middle Eastern countries, it is forbidden to photograph anything even vaguely military in nature (bridges, train stations, airports and other public works). The definition of what is 'strategic' differs from one country to another, and signs are not always posted, so err on the side of caution.

Photography is usually allowed inside religious and archaeological sites, unless there are signs indicating otherwise. As a rule, however, do not photograph inside mosques during a service.

Many Middle Easterners are sensitive about the negative aspects of their country, so exercise discretion when taking photos in poorer areas.

Also, be aware that certain countries, like Iran, are very suspicious of video cameras and may not allow you to take one into the country. See Photography & Video in the individual country chapters for further details.

Photographing People

As a matter of courtesy, do not photograph people without asking their permission first. Children will almost always say yes, but their parents or other adults might say no. In the more conservative Muslim countries, such as Iran, Saudi Arabia and Libya, you should not photograph women. In countries where you can photograph women, show them the camera and make it clear that you want to take a picture of them. Sometimes their male companions may object.

TIME

Egypt, Israel, Jordan, Lebanon, Libya, Syria and Turkey are two hours ahead of GMT/UTC. Bahrain, Iraq, Kuwait, Qatar, Saudi Arabia and Yemen are three hours

Time Differences

When it's noon in the following Middle Eastern capitals, the time elsewhere is:

city	Paris	London	New York	LA	Hong Kong	Sydney	Auckland	daylight saving
Amman	10 am	9 am	4 am	1 am	5 pm	7 pm	9 pm	yes
Baghdad	10 am	9 am	4 am	1 am	5 pm	7 pm	9 pm	n/a
Beirut	11 am	10 am	5 am	2 am	6 pm	8 pm	10 pm	yes
Cairo	11 am	10 am	5 am	2 am	6 pm	8 pm	10 pm	yes
Damascus	11 am	10 am	5 am	2 am	6 pm	8 pm	10 pm	yes
Doha	10 am	9 am	4 am	1 am	5 pm	7 pm	9 pm	no
Dubai	9 am	8 am	3 am	12 am	4 pm	6 pm	8 pm	no
İstanbul	11 am	10 am	5 am	2 am	6 pm	8 pm	10 pm	yes
Kuwait	10 am	9 am	4 am	1 am	5 pm	7 pm	9 pm	no
Manama	10 am	9 am	4 am	1 am	5 pm	7 pm	9 pm	no
Muscat	9 am	8 am	3 am	12 am	4 pm	6 pm	8 pm	no
Riyadh	10 am	9 am	4 am	1 am	5 pm	7 pm	9 pm	no
San'a	10 am	9 am	4 am	1 am	5 pm	7 pm	9 pm	no
Tehrān	9.30 am	8.30 am	3.30 am	12.30 am	4.30 pm	6.30 pm	8.30 pm	yes
Tel Aviv	11 am	10 am	5 am	2 am	6 pm	8 pm	10 pm	yes
Tripoli	11 am	10 am	5 am	2 am	6 pm	8 pm	10 pm	n/a

ahead; and Iran is 3½ hours ahead. See the boxed text to find out what the time is in your city when it's noon in the Middle Eastern capitals and which countries have daylight saving.

Time is something that Middle Eastern people always seem to have plenty of – something that should take five minutes will invariably take an hour. Trying to speed things up will only lead to frustration. It is better to take it philosophically than try to fight it.

ELECTRICITY

The electric current in most Middle Eastern countries is 220V AC, 50 Hz, though in some both 220V and 110V are in use in dif-ferent areas – see the boxed text 'Electrical Conversions'. Bring along an adapter and transformer if necessary because these sorts of things are hard to find locally.

WEIGHTS & MEASURES

All the countries in this book use the metric system. There is a standard conversion table at the back of this book.

In Iran, you may still come across the *sīr* (about 75g) and the *chārak* (10 *sīr*) in some remoter places. Gold and other precious metals are still measured by the *mesghāl*, equal to 4.7g.

In the souqs of Oman, silver jewellery is often sold according to weight measured in

Electrical Conversions

country	voltage	plug
Bahrain	230	3-pin UK-style
Egypt	220 & 110	round 2-pin
Iran	220	round 2-pin
Iraq	n/a	n/a
Israel	220	round 2-pin
Jordan	220	round 2-pin
Kuwait	220 & 240	2 & 3-pin UK-style
Lebanon	220 & 110	round & flat 2 pin
Oman	220 & 240	3-pin UK-style
Qatar	230	3-pin UK-style
Saudi Arabia	220 & 110*	n/a
Syria	220	round 2-pin
Turkey	220	round 2-pin**
UAE	240 & 220***	3-pin UK-style
Yemen	220	3-pin UK-style

*   Both 220 and 110 are found at various places in the kingdom, but the latter is more widespread.

**   There are two sizes in use in Turkey. Most common is the small-diameter prong; the other is the large-diameter, grounded plug used in Germany and Austria.

*** The current is 240V in Abu Dhabi and 220V in the rest of the Emirates.

tolas. Tolas are sometimes called 'thallers' after the Maria Theresia dollar, an 18th century Austrian coin which became the model for Arabia's common currency of the 19th and early 20th centuries. One tola is equal to 11.75g.

HEALTH

Travel health depends on your predeparture preparations, your daily health care while travelling and how you handle any medical problem that does develop. While the potential dangers can seem quite frightening, in reality few travellers experience anything more than an upset stomach. For more in-formation, see also Health in the individual country chapters.

Predeparture Planning

Immunisations Plan ahead for getting your vaccinations: some of them require more than one injection, while some vaccinations should not be given together. Note that some vaccinations should not be given during pregnancy or to people with allergies – discuss this with your doctor.

It is recommended you seek medical advice at least six weeks before travel. Be aware that there is often a greater risk of disease with children and during pregnancy.

Discuss your requirements with your doctor, but vaccinations you should consider for this trip include the following (for more details about the diseases themselves, see the individual disease entries later in this section). Carry proof of your vaccinations, especially yellow fever, as this is sometimes needed to enter some countries.

Diptheria & Tetanus Vaccinations for these two diseases are usually combined and are recommended for everyone. After an initial course of three injections (usually given in childhood), boosters are necessary every 10 years.

Polio Everyone should keep up to date with this vaccination, which is normally given in childhood. A booster every 10 years maintains immunity. The risk of contracting polio is low in most Middle Eastern countries, with the exception of Turkey and Yemen.

Typhoid Vaccination against typhoid may be required if you are travelling for more than a couple of weeks in most countries of the Middle East. It is now available either as an injection or as capsules to be taken orally.

Hepatitis A Hepatitis A, the most common travel-acquired illness, exists in all Middle Eastern countries, but can easily be prevented by vaccination.

Hepatitis A vaccine (eg Avaxim, Havrix 1440 or VAQTA) provides long-term immunity (possibly more than 10 years) after an initial injection and a booster at six to 12 months.

Alternatively, an injection of gamma globulin can provide short-term protection against hepatitis A – for two to six months, depending on the dose given. It is not a vaccine, but ready-made antibodies collected from blood donations. It is reasonably effective and, unlike the vaccine, it is protective immediately, but because it is a blood product, there are current concerns about its long-term safety.

Hepatitis A vaccine is also available in a combined form, Twinrix, with hepatitis B vaccine. Three injections over a six-month period are required, the first two providing substantial protection against hepatitis A.

Hepatitis B Endemic in all Middle Eastern countries, travellers who should consider vaccination against hepatitis B include those on a long trip, as well as those going to places where blood transfusions may not be adequately screened or where sexual contact or needle sharing is a possibility. Vaccination involves three injections, with a booster at 12 months. More rapid courses are available if necessary.

Meninogococcal Meningitis Vaccination is recommended for travellers to Egypt. It is also required of all haj pilgrims entering Saudi Arabia. A single injection gives good protection against the major epidemic forms of the disease for three years. Protection may be less effective in children under two years.

Rabies Vaccination should be considered by those who will spend a month or longer in a country where rabies is common, especially if they are cycling, handling animals, caving or travelling to remote areas, and for children (who may not report a bite). Pre-travel rabies vaccination involves having three injections over 21 to 28 days. If someone who has been vaccinated is bitten or scratched by an animal, they will require two booster injections of vaccine; those not vaccinated require more.

Medical Kit Check List

Following is a list of items you should consider including in your medical kit – consult your pharmacist for brands available in your country.

☐ **Aspirin** or **paracetamol** (acetaminophen in the USA) – for pain or fever
☐ **Antihistamine** – for allergies, eg hay fever; to ease the itch from insect bites or stings; and to prevent motion sickness
☐ **Antibiotics** – consider including these if you're travelling well off the beaten track; see your doctor, as they must be prescribed, and carry the prescription with you
☐ **Loperamide** or **diphenoxylate** – 'blockers' for diarrhoea; **prochlorperazine** or **metaclopramide** for nausea and vomiting
☐ **Rehydration mixture** – to prevent dehydration, eg due to severe diarrhoea; particularly important when travelling with children
☐ **Insect repellent, sunscreen, lip balm** and **eye drops**
☐ **Calamine lotion, sting relief spray** or **aloe vera** – to ease irritation from sunburn and insect bites or stings
☐ **Antifungal cream** or **powder** – for fungal skin infections and thrush
☐ **Antiseptic** (such as povidone-iodine) – for cuts and grazes
☐ **Bandages, Band-Aids (plasters)** and other wound dressings
☐ **Water purification tablets** or **iodine**
☐ **Scissors, tweezers** and a **thermometer** (note that mercury thermometers are prohibited by airlines)
☐ **Syringes** and **needles** – in case you need injections in a country with medical hygiene problems. Ask your doctor for a note explaining why you have them.
☐ **Cold** and **flu tablets, throat lozenges** and **nasal decongestant**
☐ **Multivitamins** – consider for long trips, when dietary vitamin intake may be inadequate

Malaria Medication Antimalarial drugs do not prevent you from being infected but kill the malaria parasites during a stage in their development and significantly reduce the risk of becoming very ill or dying. Expert advice on medication should be sought, as there are many factors to consider, including the area to be visited, the risk of exposure to malaria-carrying mosquitoes, the side effects of medication, your medical history and whether you are a child or an adult or pregnant. Travellers to isolated area in high risk countries may like to carry a treatment dose of medication for use if symptoms occur.

Health Insurance A travel insurance policy to cover theft, loss and medical problems is a wise idea. There is a wide variety of policies and your travel agent will have recommendations. The international student travel policies handled by STA or other student travel organisations are usually good value. Some policies offer lower and higher medical expenses options but the higher one is chiefly for countries like the USA which have extremely high medical costs. Check the small print.

Some policies specifically exclude 'dangerous activities' which can include scuba diving, motorcycling, even trekking. If such activities are on your agenda you don't want that sort of policy. You may prefer a policy that pays doctors or hospitals directly rather than requiring you to pay on the spot and claim later. If you have to claim later make sure you keep all documentation. Some policies ask you to call back (reverse charges) to a centre in your home country where an immediate assessment of your problem is made.

Check if the policy covers ambulances or an emergency flight home. If you have to stretch out you will need two seats and somebody has to pay for them!

Many policies exclude cover for travel in war zones, which may include several countries in the Middle East. (Some insurers, particularly in the USA, still consider the Gulf a war zone, for example.)

Travel Health Guides There are a number of books on travel health, including:

CDC's Complete Guide to Healthy Travel, Open Road Publishing, 1997. The US Centers for Disease Control & Prevention recommendations for international travel
Staying Healthy in Asia, Africa & Latin America, by Dirk Schroeder, Moon Publications, 1994. Probably the best all-round guide to carry, as it's compact but very detailed and well organised
Travellers' Health, Dr Richard Dawood, Oxford University Press, 1995. Comprehensive, easy to read, authoritative and also highly recommended, although it's rather large to lug around
Where There is No Doctor, by David Werner, Macmillan, 1994. A very detailed guide intended for someone, such as a Peace Corps worker, going to work in an underdeveloped country, rather than for the average traveller
Travel with Children, by Maureen Wheeler, Lonely Planet Publications, 1995. Includes advice on travel health for young children

There are also a number of excellent travel health sites on the Internet. From the Lonely Planet homepage, *www.lonelyplanet.com*, there are links at *www.lonelyplanet.com/health/health.htm/h-links.htm*, to the World Health Organization, Centers for Diseases Control & Prevention in Atlanta, Georgia, and the Stanford University Travel Medicine Service.

Other Preparations Make sure you are healthy before you start travelling. If you are going on a long trip make sure your teeth are OK. If you wear glasses take a spare pair and your prescription.

If you require a particular medication take an adequate supply, as it may not be available locally. Take part of the packaging showing the generic name rather than the brand, which will make getting replacements easier. It is a very good idea to have a legible prescription or letter from your doctor to show that you legally use the medication in order to avoid any problems at customs.

Basic Rules

Food There is an old colonial adage which says: 'If you can cook it, boil it or peel it you can eat it ... otherwise forget it'. Vegetables and fruit should be washed with purified water or peeled where possible. Beware of ice cream which is sold in the street or anywhere it might have been melted and refrozen; if there's any doubt (eg a power cut in the last day or two), steer well clear. Shellfish such as mussels, oysters and clams should be avoided as well as undercooked meat, particularly in the form of mince. Steaming does not make shellfish safe for eating.

If a place looks clean and well run and the vendor also looks clean and healthy, then the food is probably safe. In general, places that are packed with travellers or locals will be fine, while empty restaurants are questionable. The food in busy restaurants is cooked and eaten quite quickly with little standing around and is probably not reheated.

Water The number one rule is *be careful of the water* and especially ice. If you don't know for certain that the water is safe, assume the worst. Reputable brands of bottled water or soft drinks are generally fine, although in some places bottles may be refilled with tap water. Only use water from containers with a serrated seal – not tops or corks. Take care with fruit juice, particularly if water may have been added. Milk should be treated with suspicion as it is often unpasteurised, though boiled milk is fine if it is kept hygienically. Tea or coffee should also be OK, since the water should have been boiled.

Water Purification The simplest way of purifying water is to boil it thoroughly. Vigorous boiling should be satisfactory; however, at high altitude water boils at a lower temperature, so germs are less likely to be killed. In these environments, boil the water for longer.

Consider purchasing a water filter for a long trip. There are two main kinds of filter. Total filters take out all parasites, bacteria and viruses and make water safe to drink. They are often expensive, but they can be more cost effective than buying bottled water. Simple filters (which can even be a nylon mesh bag) take out dirt and larger foreign bodies from the water so that chemical solutions work much more effectively; if

Nutrition

If your diet is poor or limited in variety, if you're travelling hard and fast and therefore missing meals or if you simply lose your appetite, you can soon start to lose weight and place your health at risk.

Make sure your diet is well balanced. Cooked eggs, tofu, beans, lentils (dhal in India) and nuts are all safe ways to get protein. Fruit you can peel (bananas, oranges or mandarins for example) is usually safe (melons can harbour bacteria in their flesh and are best avoided) and a good source of vitamins. Try to eat plenty of grains (including rice) and bread. Remember that although food is generally safer if it is cooked well, overcooked food loses much of its nutritional value. If your diet isn't well balanced or if your food intake is insufficient, it's a good idea to take vitamin and iron pills.

In hot climates make sure you drink enough – don't rely on feeling thirsty to indicate when you should drink. Not needing to urinate or small amounts of very dark yellow urine is a danger sign. Always carry a water bottle with you on long trips. Excessive sweating can lead to loss of salt and therefore muscle cramping. Salt tablets are not a good idea as a preventative, but in places where salt is not used much, adding salt to food can help.

water is dirty, chemical solutions may not work at all. It's very important when buying a filter to read the specifications, so that you know exactly what it removes from the water and what it doesn't. Simple filtering will not remove all dangerous organisms, so if you cannot boil water it should be treated chemically. Chlorine tablets will kill many pathogens, but not some parasites like giardia and amoebic cysts. Iodine is more effective in purifying water and is available in tablet form. Follow the directions carefully and remember that too much iodine can be harmful.

Medical Problems & Treatment

Self-diagnosis and treatment can be risky, so wherever possible seek medical help. Although we do give treatment dosages in this section, they are for emergency use only. Medical advice should be sought before administering any drugs.

An embassy or consulate can usually recommend a good place to go for such advice. So can five-star hotels, although they often recommend doctors with five-star prices. (This is when that medical insurance really comes in useful!) In Syria, Libya and Jordan and Egypt (away from Amman and Cairo) standards of medical attention are so low that for some ailments the best advice is to get on a plane and go somewhere else.

Note that antibiotics should ideally be administered only under medical supervision. Take only the recommended dose at the prescribed intervals and use the whole course, even if the illness seems to be cured earlier. Stop immediately if there are any serious reactions and don't use the antibiotic at all if you are unsure that you have the correct one. Some people are allergic to commonly prescribed antibiotics such as penicillin; carry this information (eg on a bracelet) when travelling.

In many countries if a medicine is available at all it will generally be available over the counter and the price will be much cheaper than in the west. However, be careful of buying drugs in developing countries, particularly where the expiry date may have passed or correct storage conditions may not have been followed. Bogus drugs are common and it's possible that drugs which are no longer recommended, or have even been banned, in the west are still being dispensed in many Middle Eastern countries.

Environmental Hazards

Sunburn In the tropics, the desert or at high altitudes you can get sunburnt surprisingly quickly, even through cloud. Use a sunscreen, a hat, and a barrier cream for your nose and lips. Calamine lotion or a commercial after-sun preparation are good for mild sunburn. Protect your eyes with good quality sunglasses, particularly if you will be near water, sand or snow.

Prickly Heat Prickly heat is an itchy rash caused by excessive perspiration trapped under the skin. It usually strikes people who have just arrived in a hot climate. Keeping cool, bathing often, drying the skin and using a mild talcum or prickly heat powder or resorting to air-conditioning may help.

Heat Exhaustion Dehydration and salt deficiency can cause heat exhaustion. Take time to acclimatise to high temperatures,

---

Everyday Health

Normal body temperature is up to 37°C (98.6°F); more than 2°C (4°F) higher indicates a high fever. The normal adult pulse rate is 60 to 100 per minute (children 80 to 100, babies 100 to 140). As a general rule the pulse increases about 20 beats per minute for each 1°C (2°F) rise in fever.

Respiration (breathing) rate is also an indicator of illness. Count the number of breaths per minute: between 12 and 20 is normal for adults and older children (up to 30 for younger children, 40 for babies). People with a high fever or serious respiratory illness breathe more quickly than normal. More than 40 shallow breaths a minute may indicate pneumonia.

drink sufficient liquids and do not do anything too physically demanding.

Salt deficiency is characterised by fatigue, lethargy, headaches, giddiness and muscle cramps; salt tablets may help, but adding extra salt to your food is better.

Anhidrotic heat exhaustion is a rare form of heat exhaustion that is caused by an inability to sweat. It tends to affect people who have been in a hot climate for some time, rather than newcomers, and it can progress to heatstroke. Treatment involves removal to a cooler climate.

Heatstroke This serious, occasionally fatal, condition can occur if the body's heat-regulating mechanism breaks down and the body temperature rises to dangerous levels. Long, continuous periods of exposure to high temperatures and insufficient fluids can leave you vulnerable to heatstroke.

The symptoms are feeling unwell, not sweating very much (or at all) and a high body temperature (39° to 41°C or 102° to 106°F). Where sweating has ceased, the skin becomes flushed and red. Severe, throbbing headaches and lack of coordination will also occur, and the sufferer may be confused or aggressive. Eventually the victim will become delirious or convulse. Hospitalisation is essential, but in the interim get victims out of the sun, remove their clothing, cover them with a wet sheet or towel and then fan continually. Give fluids if they are conscious.

Fungal Infections Hot-weather fungal infections are most likely to occur on the scalp, between the toes or fingers (athlete's foot), in the groin (jock itch or crotch rot) and on the body (ringworm). You get ringworm (which is a fungal infection, not a worm) from infected animals or by walking on damp areas, like shower floors.

To prevent fungal infections wear loose, comfortable clothes, avoid artificial fibres, wash frequently and dry carefully. If you do get an infection, wash the infected area daily with a disinfectant or medicated soap and water, and rinse and dry well. Apply an antifungal powder like the widely available Tinaderm. Try to expose the infected area to air or sunlight as much as possible and wash all towels and underwear in hot water as well as changing them often.

Motion Sickness Eating lightly before and during a trip will reduce the chances of motion sickness. If you are prone to motion sickness try to find a place that minimises movement – near the wing on aircraft, close to midships on boats, near the centre on buses. Fresh air usually helps; reading and cigarette smoke don't. Commercial motion-sickness preparations, which can cause drowsiness, have to be taken before the trip commences. Ginger (available in capsule form) and peppermint (including mint-flavoured sweets) are natural preventatives.

Infectious Diseases

Diarrhoea Simple things like a change of water, food or climate can all cause a mild bout of diarrhoea, but a few rushed toilet trips with no other symptoms is not indicative of a major problem.

Dehydration is the main danger with any diarrhoea, particularly in children or the elderly as dehydration can occur quite quickly. Under all circumstances *fluid replacement* (at least equal to the volume being lost) is the most important thing to remember. Weak black tea with a little sugar, soda water, or soft drinks allowed to go flat and diluted 50% with clean water are all good. With severe diarrhoea a rehydrating solution is preferable to replace minerals and salts lost. Commercially available oral rehydration salts (ORS) are very useful; add them to boiled or bottled water. In an emergency you can make up a solution of six teaspoons of sugar and a half teaspoon of salt to a litre of boiled or bottled water. You need to drink at least the same volume of fluid that you are losing in bowel movements and vomiting. Urine is the best guide to the adequacy of replacement – if you have small amounts of concentrated urine, you need to drink more. Keep drinking small amounts often. Stick to a bland diet as you recover.

Gut-paralysing drugs such as loperamide or diphenoxylate can be used to bring relief from the symptoms, although they do not actually cure the problem. Only use these drugs if you do not have access to toilets, eg if you *must* travel. Note that these drugs are not recommended for children under 12 years.

In certain situations antibiotics may be required: diarrhoea with blood or mucus (dysentery), any diarrhoea with fever, profuse watery diarrhoea, persistent diarrhoea not improving after 48 hours and severe diarrhoea. These suggest a more serious cause of diarrhoea and in these situations gut-paralysing drugs should be avoided.

In these situations, a stool test may be necessary to diagnose what bug is causing your diarrhoea, so you should seek medical help urgently. Where this is not possible the recommended drugs for bacterial diarrhoea (the most likely cause of severe diarrhoea in travellers) are norfloxacin 400mg twice daily for three days or ciprofloxacin 500mg twice daily for five days. These are not recommended for children or pregnant women. The drug of choice for children would be co-trimoxazole with dosage dependent on weight. A five day course is given. Ampicillin or amoxycillin may be given in pregnancy, but medical care is necessary.

Two other causes of persistent diarrhoea in travellers are giardiasis and amoebic dysentery.

Giardiasis This is caused by a common parasite, *Giardia lamblia*. Symptoms include stomach cramps, nausea, a bloated stomach, watery, foul-smelling diarrhoea and frequent gas. Giardiasis can appear several weeks after you have been exposed to the parasite. The symptoms may disappear for a few days and then return; this can go on for several weeks.

Amoebic dysentery Caused by the protozoan *Entamoeba histolytica*, amoebic dysentery is characterised by a gradual onset of low-grade diarrhoea, often with blood and mucus. Cramping abdominal pain and vomiting are less likely than in

other types of diarrhoea, and fever may not be present. It will persist until treated and can recur and cause other health problems.

You should seek medical advice if you think you have giardiasis or amoebic dysentery, but where this is not possible, tinidazole or metronidazole are the recommended drugs. Treatment is a 2g single dose of tinidazole or 250mg of metronidazole three times daily for five to 10 days.

Cholera Cholera vaccination is not very effective. The bacteria responsible for this disease are waterborne, so attention to the rules of eating and drinking should protect the traveller. Outbreaks of cholera are generally widely reported, so you can avoid such problem areas. The disease is characterised by a sudden onset of acute diarrhoea with 'rice water' stools, vomiting, muscular cramps, and extreme weakness. You need medical help – but treat for dehydration, which can be extreme, and if there is an appreciable delay in getting to hospital then begin taking tetracycline. The adult dose is 250mg four times daily. It is not recommended for children aged eight years or under nor for pregnant women. An alternative drug is Ampicillin, though people with allergies to penicillin should not take it.

Typhoid Typhoid fever is a dangerous gut infection caused by contaminated water and food. Medical help must be sought.

In its early stages sufferers may feel they have a bad cold or flu on the way, as early symptoms are a headache, body aches and a fever which rises a little each day until it is around 40°C (104°F) or more. The victim's pulse is often slow relative to the degree of fever present – unlike a normal fever where the pulse increases. There may also be vomiting, abdominal pain, diarrhoea or constipation.

In the second week the high fever and slow pulse continue and a few pink spots may appear on the body; trembling, delirium, weakness, weight loss and dehydration may occur. Complications such as pneumonia, perforated bowel or meningitis may occur.

Hepatitis Hepatitis is a general term for inflammation of the liver. It is a common disease worldwide. There are several different viruses that cause hepatitis, and they differ in the way that they are transmitted. The symptoms are similar in all forms of the illness, and include fever, chills, headache, fatigue, feelings of weakness and aches and pains, followed by loss of appetite, nausea, vomiting, abdominal pain, dark urine, light-coloured faeces, jaundiced (yellow) skin and yellowing of the whites of the eyes. People who have had hepatitis should avoid alcohol for some time after the illness, as the liver needs time to recover.

Hepatitis A is transmitted by contaminated food and drinking water. You should seek medical advice, but there is not much you can do apart from resting, drinking lots of fluids, eating lightly and avoiding fatty foods.

Hepatitis E is transmitted in the same way as hepatitis A; it can be particularly serious in pregnant women.

Hepatitis B has almost 300 million chronic carriers throughout the world. It is spread through contact with infected blood, blood products or body fluids, for example through sexual contact, unsterilised needles and blood transfusions, or contact with blood via small breaks in the skin. Other risk situations include having a shave, tattoo or body piercing with contaminated equipment. The symptoms of hepatitis B may be more severe than type A and the disease can lead to long term problems such as chronic liver damage, liver cancer or a long term carrier state.

Hepatitis C and **D** are spread in the same way as hepatitis B and can also lead to long term complications.

There are vaccines against hepatitis A and B, but there are currently no vaccines against the other types of hepatitis. Following the basic rules about food and water (hepatitis A and E) and avoiding risk situations (hepatitis B, C and D) are important preventative measures.

Tetanus This potentially fatal disease is found worldwide. It is difficult to treat but is preventable with immunisation. Tetanus occurs when a wound becomes infected by a germ which lives in the soil and faeces of horses and other animals, so clean all cuts, punctures or animal bites. Tetanus is known as lockjaw, and the first symptom may be discomfort in swallowing, or stiffening of the jaw and neck; this is followed by painful convulsions of the jaw and whole body.

Rabies Rabies is a fatal viral infection found in all Middle Eastern countries and is caused by a bite or scratch by an infected animal. Dogs and cats are noted carriers. Any bite, scratch or even lick from a mammal should be cleaned immediately and thoroughly. Scrub with soap and running water, and then clean with an alcohol or iodine solution. If there is any possibility that the animal is infected, medical help should be sought immediately to prevent the onset of symptoms and death. Even if the animal is not rabid, all bites should be treated seriously as they can become infected or can result in tetanus. A rabies vaccination is now available and should be considered if you are in a high-risk category – eg, if you intend to explore caves (bat bites could be dangerous) or work with animals or travel so far off the beaten track that medical help is more than two days away.

Meningococcal Meningitis Sub-Saharan Africa is considered the 'meningitis belt' but there are recurring epidemics in other regions including Saudi Arabia and the Nile Valley.

The disease is spread by close contact with people who carry it in their throats and noses (coughs and sneezes). They may not be aware that they are carriers.

This very serious disease attacks the brain and can be fatal. A scattered, blotchy rash, fever, severe headache, sensitivity to light and neck stiffness which prevents forward bending of the head are the first symptoms. Death can occur within a few hours, so immediate treatment is important.

Treatment is large doses of penicillin given intravenously, or, if that is not possible, intramuscularly (ie, in the buttocks). Vaccination offers good protection for over a year, but you should also check for reports of current epidemics.

Tuberculosis Although this disease is widespread in many developing countries, it is not a serious risk to travellers. Young children are more susceptible than adults and vaccination is a sensible precaution for children under 12 travelling in endemic areas. TB is commonly spread by coughing or by unpasteurised dairy products from infected cows. Milk that has been boiled is safe to drink; the souring of milk to make yoghurt or cheese also kills the bacilli.

Schistosomiasis Known as bilharzia, this disease is carried in water by minute worms. The larvae infect certain varieties of freshwater snails, found in rivers, streams, lakes and particularly behind dams. The worms multiply and are eventually discharged into the water surrounding the snails. The Nile and the Nile Delta are infested with the bilharzia parasite. The disease is common in Yemen and is also found in Iraq, Saudi Arabia, Syria and the south-west of Iran.

The worm enters through the skin and attaches itself to your intestines or bladder. The first symptom may be a general feeling of being unwell, or a tingling and sometimes a light rash around the area where it entered. Weeks later a high fever may develop. Once the disease is established abdominal pain and blood in the urine are other signs. The infection often causes no symptoms until the disease is well established (several months to years after exposure) and damage to internal organs has become irreversible.

Avoiding swimming or bathing in fresh water where bilharzia is present is the main method of preventing the disease. Even deep water can be infected. If you do get wet, dry off quickly and dry your clothes as well.

A blood test is the most reliable way to diagnose the disease, but the test will not show positive until a number of weeks after exposure.

Diphtheria Diphtheria can be a skin or more dangerous throat infection. It's spread by contaminated dust contacting the skin or inhalation of infected cough or sneeze droplets. Frequent washing and keeping the skin dry will help prevent skin infection. Treatment requires close medical supervision.

Sexually Transmitted Diseases (STDs) HIV/AIDS and hepatitis B can be transmitted through sexual contact – see the relevant sections earlier for more details. Other STDs include gonorrhoea, herpes and syphilis; sores, blisters or rashes around the genitals and discharges or pain when urinating are common symptoms. In some STDs, such as wart virus or chlamydia, symptoms may be less marked, especially in women. Chlamydia infection can cause infertility in men and women before any symptoms have been noticed. Syphilis symptoms eventually disappear completely but the disease continues and can cause problems in later years. While abstinence from sexual contact is the only 100% effective prevention, using condoms is also effective. The treatment of gonorrhoea and syphilis is with antibiotics. The different sexually transmitted diseases each require specific antibiotics.

HIV/AIDS Infection with the human immunodeficiency virus (HIV) may lead to acquired immune deficiency syndrome (AIDS), which is a fatal disease. Any exposure to blood, blood products or body fluids may put the individual at risk. The disease is often transmitted through sexual contact or dirty needles – vaccinations, acupuncture, tattooing and body piercing can be potentially as dangerous as intravenous drug use. HIV/AIDS can also be spread through infected blood transfusions; some developing countries cannot afford to screen blood used for transfusions.

If you do need an injection, ask to see the syringe unwrapped in front of you, or take a needle and syringe pack with you.

Fear of HIV infection should never preclude treatment for any serious medical conditions.

Insect-Borne Diseases

Malaria This serious disease is spread by mosquito bites. It does not occur in Bahrain, Kuwait, Israel, Jordan, Lebanon or Qatar, but is endemic in certain rural areas of other Middle Eastern countries (see Health in each individual country chapter for details).

If you are travelling in endemic areas it is extremely important to avoid mosquito bites and to take tablets to prevent this disease. Symptoms range from fever, chills and sweating, headache, diarrhoea and abdominal pains to a vague feeling of ill-health. Seek medical help immediately if malaria is suspected. Without treatment malaria can rapidly become more serious and can be fatal.

If medical care is not available, malaria tablets can be used for treatment. You need to use a malaria tablet which is different from the one you were taking when you contracted malaria. The standard treatment dose of mefloquine is two 250mg tablets and a further two six hours later. For Fansidar, it's a single dose of three tablets. If you were previously taking mefloquine and cannot obtain Fansidar, then other alternatives are Malarone (atovaquone-proguanil; four tablets once daily for three days), halofantrine (three doses of two 250mg tablets every six hours) or quinine sulphate (600mg every six hours). There is a greater risk of side effects with these dosages than in normal use if used with mefloquine, so medical advice is preferable. Be aware also that halofantrine is no longer recommended by the WHO as emergency standby treatment, because of side effects, and should only be used if no other drugs are available.

Travellers are advised to prevent mosquito bites at all times. The main messages are:

- wear light-coloured clothing
- wear long trousers and long-sleeved shirts
- use mosquito repellents containing the compound DEET on exposed areas (prolonged overuse of DEET may be harmful, especially to children, but its use is considered preferable to being bitten by disease-transmitting mosquitoes)
- avoid perfumes or aftershave

- use a mosquito net impregnated with mosquito repellent (permethrin) – it may be worth taking your own
- impregnating clothes with permethrin effectively deters mosquitoes and other insects

Leishmaniasis This is a group of parasitic diseases transmitted by sandfly bites, found in many parts of the Middle East. Cutaneous leishmaniasis affects the skin tissue causing ulceration and disfigurement and visceral leishmaniasis affects the cells of internal organs. The disease rarely causes serious illness, but it is often misdiagnosed and therefore treated incorrectly. Treatment of the disease is with drugs containing antimony.

Avoiding sandfly bites is the best precaution. The bites generally occur at night, are usually painless, only slightly itchy and are yet another reason to cover up and apply repellent, especially between late afternoon and dawn.

Cuts, Bites & Stings

Cuts & Scratches Wash well and treat any cut with an antiseptic such as povidone-iodine. Where possible avoid bandages and Band-Aids, which can keep wounds wet. Coral cuts are notoriously slow to heal and if they are not adequately cleaned, small pieces of coral can become embedded in the wound.

Bites & Stings Bee and wasp stings are usually painful rather than dangerous. Calamine lotion will give relief or ice packs will reduce the pain and swelling. There are some spiders with dangerous bites but antivenenes are usually available. There are also various fish and other sea creatures which can sting or bite dangerously or which are dangerous to eat. For example, sea urchins, blowfish, fire coral, feathery lionfish, moray eels, turkeyfish, stonefish and triggerfish should all be avoided. Seek local advice before entering unfamiliar water.

Scorpions Scorpion stings are a serious cause of illness and occasionally death in the Middle East, although effective antivenenes are available. Shake shoes, clothing and towels before use. Inspect bedding and don't put hands or feet in crevices where they may be lurking. A sting usually produces redness and swelling of the skin, but there may be no visible reaction. Pain is common, and tingling or numbness may occur. At this stage, cold compresses on the bite and pain relief (eg, paracetamol) are called for. If the skin sensations start to spread from the sting site (eg, along the limb), then immediate medical attention is required.

Snakes To minimise your chances of being bitten always wear boots, socks and long trousers when walking through undergrowth where snakes may be present. Don't put your hands into holes and crevices, and be careful when collecting firewood.

Snake bites do not cause instantaneous death and antivenenes are usually available. Keep the victim calm and still, wrap the bitten limb tightly, as you would for a sprained ankle, and then attach a splint to immobilise it. Then seek medical help, if possible with the dead snake for identification. Don't attempt to catch the snake if there is even a remote possibility of being bitten again. Tourniquets and sucking out the poison are now comprehensively discredited.

Jellyfish In the Gulf and Red Sea, jellyfish are the most common problem. Local advice is the best way of avoiding contact with these sea creatures and their stinging tentacles. Stings from most jellyfish are simply irritating rather than painful. Dousing in vinegar will deactivate any stingers which have not 'fired'. Calamine lotion, antihistamines and analgesics may reduce the reaction and relieve the pain.

Bedbugs & Lice Bedbugs live in various places, but particularly in dirty mattresses and bedding. Spots of blood on bedclothes or on the wall around the bed are signs that it's time to find another hotel. Bedbugs leave itchy bites in neat rows. Calamine lotion or Stingose spray may help.

All lice cause itching and discomfort. They make themselves at home in your hair (head lice), your clothing (body lice) or in your pubic hair (crabs). You catch lice through direct contact with infected people or by sharing combs, clothing and the like. Powder or shampoo treatment will kill the lice and infected clothing should then be washed in very hot water.

Women's Health

Gynaecological Problems Antibiotic use, synthetic underwear, sweating and contraceptive pills can lead to fungal vaginal infections, especially when travelling in hot climates. Fungal infections are characterised by a rash, itch and discharge and can be treated with a vinegar or lemon-juice douche, or with yoghurt. Nystatin, miconazole or clotrimazole pessaries or vaginal cream are the usual treatment. Maintaining good personal hygiene and wearing loose-fitting clothes and cotton underwear may help prevent these infections.

Sexually transmitted diseases are a major cause of vaginal problems. Symptoms might include a smelly discharge, painful intercourse and sometimes a burning sensation when urinating. Medical attention should be sought and male sexual partners must also be treated. For more details see the section on Sexually Transmitted Diseases earlier. Besides abstinence, the best thing is to practise safe sex using condoms.

Pregnancy It is not advisable to travel to some places while pregnant as some vaccinations are not advisable during pregnancy (eg, yellow fever). In addition, some diseases are much more serious during pregnancy (eg, malaria) and may increase the risk of a stillborn child.

Most miscarriages occur during the first three months of pregnancy. Miscarriage is not uncommon and can occasionally lead to severe bleeding. The last three months should also be spent within reasonable distance of good medical care. A baby born as early as 24 weeks stands a chance of survival, but only in a good modern hospital. Pregnant women should avoid all unnecessary medication, although vaccinations and malarial prophylactics should still be taken where needed. Additional care should be taken to prevent illness and particular attention should be paid to diet and nutrition. Alcohol and nicotine, for example, should be avoided.

WOMEN TRAVELLERS

Middle Easterners are conservative, especially about matters concerning sex and women (and by that read local women, not foreign women).

An entire book could be written from the comments and stories of women travellers about their adventures and misadventures in the Middle East. Most of the incidents are nonthreatening nuisances, in the same way a fly buzzing in your ear is a nuisance: you can swat him away and keep him at a distance but he's always out there buzzing around.

Attitudes Towards Women

Some of the biggest misunderstandings between Middle Easterners and westerners occur over the issue of women. Half-truths and stereotypes exist on both sides: many westerners assume all Middle Eastern women are veiled, repressed victims, while a large number of locals see western women as sex-obsessed and immoral.

For many Middle Easterners, both men and women, the role of a woman is specifically defined: she is mother and matron of the household. The man is the provider. However, as with any society, generalisations can be misleading and the reality is far more nuanced. There are thousands of middle and upper middle class professional women in the Arab World and especially in Iran who, like their counterparts in the west, juggle work and family responsibilities. Among the working classes, where adherence to tradition is strongest, the ideal may be for women to concentrate on home and family, but economic reality means that millions of women are forced to work (but are still responsible for all domestic chores).

The issue of sex is where the differences between western and Middle Eastern women are most apparent. Premarital sex (or, indeed, any sex outside marriage) is taboo, although, as with anything forbidden, it still happens. Nevertheless, it is the exception rather than the rule – and that goes for men as well as women. However, for women the issue is potentially far more serious. With the possible exception of the upper classes, women are expected to be virgins when they get married and a family's reputation can rest upon this point. In such a context, the restrictions placed on a young girl – no matter how onerous they may seem to a westerner – are intended to protect her and her reputation from the potentially disastrous attentions of men.

The presence of foreign women presents, in the eyes of some Middle Eastern men, a chance to get around these norms with ease and without consequences. That this is even possible is heavily reinforced by distorted impressions gained from western TV, and it has to be said, by the behaviour of some foreign women in the country – as one young man in Egypt remarked when asked why he persisted in harassing every western woman he saw, 'For every ten that say no, there's one that says yes'. So, as a woman traveller you can expect some verbal harassment at the very least. Sometimes it will go as far as pinching bottoms or brushing breasts but physical harassment and rape are not significant threats.

Treatment of foreign women tends to be at its best in strictly Islamic societies such as Iran (providing of course you adhere to the prevailing social mores; see the boxed text 'Women in Iranian Society' in the Iran chapter), and at its worst in Egypt, Israel and Turkey, where sexual harassment can be a real holiday-souring nuisance.

Safety Precautions

There are a number of things that you can do to lessen the harassment but top of the list is to dress modestly. The woman wearing short pants and a tight T-shirt on the street is, in some local's eyes, confirmation of the worst views held of western women. Generally, if you're alone or with other women, the amount of harassment you get will be directly related to how you dress: the more skin that is exposed, the more harassment you'll get – although it has to be said in some places nothing you can do short of garbing yourself in full Saudi-style *chador* is ever going to completely leave you free of unwanted attention. For more on the dress issue see the following What to Wear section.

Other helpful tips include the following:

- Wear a wedding band. Generally, Middle Eastern males seem to have more respect for a married woman.
- If you are unmarried but travelling in male company say you are married rather than girlfriend/boyfriend or just friends.
- It's better not to let on if you are travelling alone or just in the company of another female friend – always say that you are with a group.
- Avoid direct eye contact with local men; dark sunglasses could help.
- Don't respond to any obnoxious comments – act as if you didn't hear them.
- Be careful in crowds and other situations where you are crammed between people, as it is not unusual for crude things to happen behind you.
- Don't sit in the front seat of taxis unless the driver is a woman.
- On public transport, sit next to a woman if possible.
- Be very careful about behaving in a flirtatious or suggestive manner, it could create more problems than you ever imagined.
- If you need help for any reason (directions etc), ask a woman first. That said, local women are less likely than men to have had an education that included learning in English – you'll find this a major drawback in getting to meet and talk with them.
- Be wary when horse or camel riding, especially at touristy places. It's not unknown for a man to ride close to you and grab your horse, among other things. Riding in front of a man on a camel is simply asking for trouble.

One other bit of advice is that if you're hassled on buses or have men show up at your hotel door, then complain to the driver or manager. You are paying for these services and have a right to be allowed to use them without hassle, and if you don't complain it adds to the belief that foreign women don't mind.

What to Wear

This differs from country to country, though on the whole a certain amount of modesty is advisable. In Egypt, Iraq, Israel, Jordan, Lebanon, Syria and Turkey attitudes towards women are more relaxed than in Iran, Libya, Yemen and the Gulf countries. In the former group of countries, women can generally wear what they like at beach resorts and in big cities – within reason. Outside of these areas, however, it is better to ensure that legs, arms, shoulders and the neckline are covered. Baggy T-shirts and loose cotton trousers or long skirts won't make you sweat as much as you think and will protect your skin from the sun as well as from unwanted comments. Wearing a bra will avoid countless unwelcome confrontations, and a hat or headscarf is also a good idea.

As with anywhere, take your cues from those around you: if you're in a rural area and all the women are in long, concealing dresses, you should be conservatively dressed.

In the very traditional societies of Iran and Saudi Arabia, although it is not necessary for foreign women to wear the *chador* (the one-piece cloak associated with Muslim countries), it is essential for them to cover all parts of the body except the hands, feet and face (from hairline to neckline), and to ensure that the outer layer of clothing gives no hint of the shape of the body. For more on this see the boxed text 'Dress Code' in the Iran chapter. See also the boxed text 'Boys, Girls & the Veil' in the Egypt chapter.

GAY & LESBIAN TRAVELLERS

With the exception of Egypt, Lebanon, Turkey and Israel, homosexuality is illegal in all Middle Eastern countries. Penalties include fines and/or imprisonment, and in Iran, Saudi Arabia and Yemen the death penalty may be invoked. Even in those countries where homosexuality is not prohibited by law, it remains fairly low key, with a few exceptions – Bodrum in Turkey and Tel Aviv in Israel both have vibrant gay scenes. However, in general, as a westerner, you are unlikely to encounter prejudice or harassment as long as you remain discreet, although this may not be the case if you become involved with a local. For more information on gay-friendly bars and hotels see the *Spartacus International Gay Guide* and Gay & Lesbian Travellers in the individual Egypt, Israel, Jordan, Lebanon and Turkey chapters.

DISABLED TRAVELLERS

Generally speaking, scant regard is paid to the needs of disabled travellers in the Middle East. Steps, high kerbs and other assorted obstacles are everywhere, streets are often badly rutted and uneven, roads are made virtually uncrossable by heavy traffic, while many doorways are low and narrow. Ramps and specially equipped lodgings and toilets are an extreme rarity. You will have to plan your trip carefully and will probably be obliged to restrict yourself to luxury-level hotels and private, hired transport. The happy exception is Israel – see the Disabled Travellers section in that chapter. There are also agencies in Oman and the UAE specialising in making arrangements for disabled travellers – see those chapters.

Otherwise, before setting off for the Middle East, disabled travellers could get in touch with their national support organisation (preferably with the travel officer, if there is one) – in the UK contact RADAR (☎ 020-7250 3222) at 250 City Rd, London EC1V 8AS or the Holiday Care Service (☎ 01293-774 535).

TRAVEL WITH CHILDREN

Taking the kids can add another dimension to a trip to the Middle East, although there are a few provisos that should be born in mind. Firstly, it's a good idea to avoid travel in the summer as the extreme heat can be quite uncomfortable and energy sapping. With infants, another problem may be cleanliness. It is impractical to carry more than about a half dozen washable nappies around with you, but disposable ones are not always that easy to come by – although in Egypt, Israel, Lebanon and Turkey there should be no problem. Powdered milk is widely available, as is bottled water. As for hotels, you are going to want something

with a private bathroom and hot water, which will normally preclude most budget accommodation. The good news is that children are made a big fuss of in the Middle East. They'll help break the ice and open doors to closer contact with local people.

For more comprehensive advice on the dos and don'ts of taking the kids in your luggage, see Lonely Planet's *Travel with Children* by Maureen Wheeler.

DANGERS & ANNOYANCES

The Middle East has a reputation for being a dangerous area because of political turmoil, the Arab-Israeli conflict and the emergence of Islamic fundamentalism in many countries. Don't let this deter you from travelling. The trouble spots are usually well defined, and as long as you keep track of political developments, you are unlikely to come to any harm.

Theft & Violence

In general theft is not much of a problem in Middle Eastern countries and robbery (mugging) even less of one, but don't let the relative safety lull you. Take the standard precautions.

Always keep valuables with you or locked in a safe – never leave them in your room or in a car or bus. Use a money belt, a pouch under your clothes, a leather wallet attached to your belt, or extra internal pockets in your clothing. Keep a record of your passport, credit card and travellers cheque numbers separately; it won't cure problems, but it will make them easier to bear.

However, beware of your fellow travellers; there are more than a few backpackers who make their money go further by helping themselves to other people's.

BUSINESS HOURS

The end-of-week holiday throughout the Middle East is Friday except in Israel, Lebanon and Turkey. In Israel it's Saturday (Shabbat), while in Lebanon and Turkey it's Sunday. In countries where Friday is the holiday, most embassies and government offices are also closed on Thursday, though private businesses and shops are open on Thursday mornings and many stores will reopen in the evening on Friday.

In many countries, shops have different hours at different times of the year, depending on the seasons (they tend to work shorter hours in summer) and during Ramadan, the month-long fasting period for Muslims, when almost everything shuts down in the afternoon in many Middle Eastern countries.

PUBLIC HOLIDAYS & SPECIAL EVENTS

All Middle Eastern countries, save Israel, observe the main Islamic holidays of Ramadan, Eid al-Fitr, which marks the end of Ramadan, Eid al-Adha, which marks the pilgrimage to Mecca, and the Prophet's Birthday. Countries with a major Shi'ite population also observe Ashura, the anniversary of the martyrdom of Hussein, the third imam of the Shi'ites. Most of the countries in this book also observe both the Gregorian and the Islamic new year holidays. Every country also has its own national days and other public holidays – for details refer to the individual country chapters.

Islamic New Year Also known as *Ras as-Sana*, literally 'the head of the year'.

The Prophet's Birthday Also known as *Moulid an-Nabi*, 'the feast of the Prophet'.

Ramadan Ramadan (Ramazan in Iran and Turkey) is the ninth month of the Muslim calendar, when Muslims fast during daylight hours. How strictly the fast is observed depends on the country but most Muslims conform to some extent. Foreigners are not expected to follow suit, but it is impolite to smoke, drink or eat in public during Ramadan – in the more strictly Islamic countries flaunting your nonobservance of the fast will get you into trouble, especially in Saudi Arabia where jail sentences are handed out to anyone seen so much as smoking during daylight hours. Business hours tend to become more erratic and usually shorter, and in out-of-the-way places you may find it hard to find a restaurant that opens before sunset. As the sun sets each day, the fast is broken with *iftar* (breaking the fast), at which enough food is usually consumed to compensate for the previous hours of abstinence.

Eid al-Fitr This feast marks the end of Ramadan fasting; the celebrations last for three days.

Eid al-Adha This feast marks the time that Muslims make the pilgrimage to Mecca.

Islamic Calendar All Islamic holidays are celebrated within the framework of the Muslim calendar, while secular activities are planned according to the Christian system, except in Saudi Arabia, where the Muslim calendar is the principal one used, and in Iran, where the Iranian solar calendar is used.

The Muslim year is based on the lunar cycle and is divided into 12 lunar months,

Islamic Holidays

Hejira Year	New Year	Prophet's Birthday	Ramadan	Eid al-Fitr	Eid al-Adha
1420	17.04.99	26.06.99	09.12.99	08.01.00	16.03.00
1421	06.04.00	14.06.00	27.11.00	27.12.00	06.03.01
1422	26.03.01	03.06.01	16.11.01	16.12.01	23.02.02
1423	15.03.02	23.05.02	05.11.02	05.12.02	12.02.03

each with 29 or 30 days. Consequently, the Muslim year is 10 or 11 days shorter than the Christian solar year, and the Muslim festivals gradually move around our year, completing the cycle in roughly 33 years.

Year zero in the Muslim calendar was when Mohammed and his followers fled from Mecca to Medina (which occurred in 622 AD in the Christian calendar). This *Hejira*, or migration, is taken to mark the start of the new Muslim era, much as Christ's birth marks year zero in the Christian calendar.

ACTIVITIES

Although the Middle East is a region not generally associated with activities, its wide variety of terrain – from deserts to beaches to snowcapped mountains – does offer quite a few opportunities to do things other than visit museums and old stones.

Archaeological Digs

With its wealth of ancient history, the Middle East offers unparalleled opportunities for visiting archaeological sites. In Israel, it is also possible to work on archaeological digs. The busy archaeological season is May to September.

Cycling

See the Bicycle section in the Getting Around chapter for details about cycling around the Middle East, including practicalities and organisations to contact.

Desert Safaris & Drives

One of the most rewarding parts of Middle Eastern desert to explore is Wadi Rum in Jordan. There are plenty of operators there who organise anything from afternoon camel treks to safaris and hikes lasting several days. Oman is the other great desert exploration country – see the Activities section in that country chapter.

In Egypt there are plenty of small Bedouin operators who lead groups into the Sinai interior on overnight or two or three day camel treks – see the Sinai section for more details. It's also possible to head off into the less visited Western desert as part

of a 4WD safari, organised out of Cairo. Israel's Negev desert is less attractive than deserts elsewhere, but there are some fun truck tours organised by the Metzoke Dragot company in the Dead Sea region.

Diving

The Red Sea is one of the world's top diving sites. Its waters are teeming with a dazzling array of colourful coral and fish life, supported by an extensive reef system. The best place to experience the Red Sea is from one of the resorts on southern Sinai or south along Egypt's Red Sea coast. Eilat in Israel and Aqaba in Jordan are not as good.

Most of the clubs in these places offer every possible kind of dive course. The average open-water certification course for beginners, either with CMAS, PADI or NAUI, takes about five days and usually includes several dives. The total cost varies between US$280 and US$400 depending on the operator and location. A day's diving (two dives), including equipment and air fills, costs US$50 to US$95. An introductory dive is around US$60. Full equipment can be hired for about US$20 per day.

For more details see the Diving & Snorkelling section under Sinai in the Egypt chapter.

Hiking & Trekking

There's a wealth of superb hiking opportunities, both leisurely and more strenuous, though you have to be careful in picking the right time of year for your visit. In Jordan, from June to August it's too hot for any walking but outside of the summer months the Wadi Rum area offers some of the most spectacular Middle Eastern desert scenery. The Upper Galilee and Golan regions of Israel have plenty of trails through semi-mountainous, wooded terrain with a good series of hostels providing accommodation. (For more on hiking in Israel see the Activities section in that country chapter.) In Iran, the Alborz Mountains are a popular destination for walking, though the region lacks any infrastructure and places to stay are hard to come by. Hiking and mountain trekking are also becoming increasingly popular in Turkey, particularly in the north-east.

Skiing

While not an obvious Middle Eastern activity, Turkey, Iran, Lebanon and even Mt Hermon in Israel all get some snow each year. The season starts around the middle of January and lasts until late March or April.

Water Sports

The Red Sea resort of Eilat in Israel is possibly the Middle East's water-sports capital, although places like Sharm el-Sheikh and Hurghada in Egypt, Aqaba in Jordan and many of Turkey's Mediterranean beach resorts all offer ample opportunities for year-round sailing, snorkelling, water-skiing and windsurfing. For the region's best windsurfing spot though, head to Moon Beach in Sinai. Water sports are also popular throughout the UAE, and the tourist industry is increasingly pushing the country as a winter 'sea & sun' destination. However, most water-sport facilities are tied either to a big hotel or a private club and are not generally accessible to nonguests and nonmembers.

For more on water sports in Israel see the Activities section in that country chapter.

Yacht Cruising

Turkey has lots of possibilities for yacht cruising, from day trips to two-week luxury charters. Kuşadası, Bodrum and Marmaris are the main centres, with more resorts developing yachting businesses all the time. You can hire crewless bareboats or flotilla boats, or take a cabin on a boat hired by an agency. Ask anywhere near the docks for information.

COURSES
Language

Various institutes and colleges in Egypt, Jordan, Lebanon and Yemen offer short intensive courses in Arabic and there are plenty of places in İstanbul at which to study Turkish. It's also possible to take up Hebrew and biblical studies in Israel. See Courses in the specific country chapters for more details.

WORK

It is quite possible to pick up work in the Middle East in order to extend your stay and eke out your savings – but you have to know where to look and what you are looking for. Forget places like Iran, Libya and Syria or the Gulf countries (although it is quite possible to work in the latter if you can secure a job in advance); realistically, your best options are Egypt, Israel and Turkey, that is the places where other foreigners gather in numbers. See Israel & the Palestinian Territories chapter for information about working on a kibbutz or a moshav.

English Tutoring

Teaching centres – both of the respectable kind and cowboy outfits – can be found throughout the Middle East. Cowboy outfits are often desperate for teachers and will take on people whose only qualification is that their mother tongue is English. Pay is minimal and you'll probably have to stay on a tourist visa, which will be up to you to renew. However many long-termers finance their stays this way, particularly in Cairo and İstanbul. In Cairo your first port of call should be the ILLI at 34 Sharia Talaat Harb, which is a privately run chain of English-language schools. It's on the 5th floor above the El-Abd bakery. Otherwise, visit the British Council for a list of schools to contact. In İstanbul try English Fast at Altiyol, Yogurtcu Sukru Sokak 29 in the Kadikoy district or, again, visit the British Council.

Your chances of getting a job are greatly improved if you have a certificate in CELTA (Certificate in English Language Teaching to Adults). This is what used to be known as TEFL and basically it's your passport to work abroad. To get the qualification you need to attend a one month intensive course, which you can do in your home country via an English language training centre. In the UK contact International House (IH) (☎ 020-7491 2598, Web site www.international-house-london.ac.uk) which runs more than a dozen courses

Cover up or else, Egypt

A sure way to grab your attention, Israel

Advertising the latest release, Jordan

Haj wall painting, Egypt

Beware the 'Ship of the Desert'

In-your-face advertising, Egypt

DIANA MAYFIELD

Fishing boats, Antalya, Turkey

JULIET COOMBE

Donkey carts, Siwa Oasis, Egypt

CHRIS MELLOR

Causeway, Manama, Bahrain

ANDREW HUMPHREYS

City tram, Alexandria, Egypt

TONY WHEELER

Abras, ferries which run across Dubai Creek, UAE

a year (in 1999 the course cost UK£967). IH has 110 affiliated schools in 30 countries worldwide, including Egypt (Cairo) and Turkey (İstanbul) and then, once you have completed the course, you can apply for any advertised positions. Alternatively, you could fly out to Cairo and do the CELTA course at the IH school there (see addresses below); with the course costing only UK£575 in Cairo, depending on the price of your flight, this is a cheaper way to do it than at IH in London. Successful trainees are sometimes taken on. Otherwise, you are already in a position to look for employment elsewhere.

The other big employer of English-language teachers is the British Council. Its overseas teaching centres don't often take on people who just turn up at the door (most recruiting is done in the UK – contact the Information Centre ☎ 0161-957 7755, fax 957 7762, Web site www.britishcouncil.org) but you may be lucky. For British Council addresses in the Middle East see the Cultural Centres heading in the capital cities throughout this book.

Working at a Backpackers

In Israel (Jerusalem, Tel Aviv and Eilat) and various places in Turkey (particularly İstanbul, Selçuk, Bodrum, Fethiye and Cappadocia), it's usually possible to pick up work in a hostel, typically cleaning rooms or looking after reception. It doesn't pay much but it does usually get you a free room, a meal or two a day plus some beer money. The only way to find this kind of work is to ask around.

Copy Editing

There are literally dozens of English-language newspapers and magazines published in the Middle East. Unless you have the proper training and experience you're unlikely to be offered any work in the way of journalism but there's often a need for people with good English-language skills who can copy edit. The amount of work available and money to be made obviously depends on whether the paper or magazine is daily,

weekly or monthly – whatever the case, you aren't going to make much but it may be enough to cover the cost of your accommodation. The only way to find such work is to pick up the newspapers and phone.

ACCOMMODATION

In all the countries covered in this book, you'll find a wide range of places to stay, from international-class Hiltons and Sheratons in the capitals and resorts, through reasonably priced, comfortable, mid-range hotels, down to the most basic lodging houses out in the sticks or in the rough end of town.

Standards vary between countries but quality generally reflects price – although in some countries, such as Libya and the Arab Gulf States, it can be difficult to find really cheap accommodation at all. Hotels at the top end of the range have clean, air-con, self-contained rooms with hot showers and toilets that work all the time. In the mid-range, rooms are self-contained, but there may not always be hot water, and there will probably be fans instead of air-con. Near the bottom end, hotel rooms are not always clean, in fact they are sometimes downright filthy, showers and toilets are usually shared and they're often in an appalling state. The very cheap hotels are just dormitories where you're crammed into a room with whoever else fronts up. Some of the very cheapest places are probably too basic for many tastes and not always suitable for women travelling alone.

In some countries hotels will want to keep your passport in the 'safe' overnight. This is generally to ensure payment – tell them you need it to change money at the bank. If you want to hang on to it, the hotel may insist on advance payment for the room.

Camping

Camping in the Middle East is possible but it's always better to stick to officially sanctioned camp sites because many areas which are military or restricted zones aren't always marked. There are official camping grounds in Egypt, Iran, Israel, Lebanon and Saudi Arabia.

Hostels

There are international youth hostels in Bahrain, Egypt, Israel, Qatar, Saudi Arabia and the UAE. It's not usually necessary to hold a HI card to stay at these places but it will get you a small discount.

For further details and other types of accommodation see the individual country chapters.

FOOD

The quality of food varies considerably from country to country – in terms of local cuisine, the best is in Lebanon and Turkey, the worst is in Egypt. For a look at what to expect see the special section 'Middle Eastern Cuisine'.

Local-style food is usually safer than western-style food because it's cooked much longer (sometimes all day) and the ingredients are invariably fresh. On the other hand, food in a smarter restaurant may have been lingering in a refrigerator.

Even travellers with sensitive stomachs can usually eat traditional Middle Eastern food if they ease themselves in gently to the change of diet. In any kind of restaurant, you might get a bit of stomach trouble if plates or cutlery aren't clean, but that can happen anywhere, and it doesn't happen often.

Where to Eat

A pleasant feature of Middle Eastern travel is the availability of street food – ideal if you're on the move, or prefer to eat little and often. Street food is nearly always cooked in front of you and rarely involves plates or knives.

The best place to eat, if you are lucky enough to be invited, is invariably somebody's house, but most days you will be heading for a restaurant. As well as local restaurants, every country in the region also has western-style restaurants, which range from burger bars to five star haute cuisine establishments. Mid-range restaurants cater mainly to well-off locals and foreigners and often serve only international dishes.

Vegetarian Food

Vegetarians should have no trouble eating in the Middle East, even though the concept of vegetarianism is rarely understood. A friend ordered vegetable casserole at a Cairo restaurant and was served up a hunk of lamb in broth. When he complained about his order the waiter replied, 'But there are vegetables in there'. Misconceptions aside, avoiding meat is easy as salads, dips, pulse-based dishes and pureéd and stuffed vegetables feature heavily on most restaurant menus, and there's always the fall-back of the ubiquitous street food staple, felafel.

Fruit

Availability depends on the season but the choice is usually good. The main fruits you'll find are oranges, pomegranates, bananas (usually small and green), pineapples, grapes, guavas and mangoes. Melons of all types are also very common, from honeydews to great green watermelons. In countries like Syria and Lebanon, a big plate of fruit is often served complimentary at the end of a meal.

continued on page 89

The Coffeehouse

The coffeehouse (in Arabic *qahwa*, the same word as for coffee; in Persian it's *chāykhānē*, or teahouses) is the great social institution of the Middle East. Or rather it is for around half the population – with very few exceptions, Arabic woman do not frequent qahwas. There's no reason, however, why a western woman shouldn't, especially in the less staunchly Muslim countries like Egypt, Jordan, Lebanon and Syria.

Typically just a collection of battered chairs and tables in a sawdust-strewn room open to the street, the qahwa is a relaxed and unfussy place to meet locals who are often curious to question any *khwajas* (foreigners) who come and sit among them. Conversation is inevitably accompanied by the incessant clacking of slammed domino and backgammon pieces and the bubbling sound of smokers drawing hard on their *narjilehs*, the cumbersome water pipe, also known as a *sheesha*.

MIDDLE EASTERN CUISINE

This section describes the kind of indigenous food that you're likely to encounter throughout much of the region, Iran and the Gulf States aside. Iran has its own very distinctive cuisine, which is briefly described in that chapter, while the Gulf States … well, they've never been known for their cuisine and almost everything on the menu in these countries is imported. Note that while many dishes described on the following pages are found in Turkey, they often go by a different name – see the Food section in the Turkey chapter.

Top: The humble glass of tea, always served sweet and hot (Photo by Diana Mayfield)

Right: The wholesale fruit and vegetable market in the early morning, Mina Qaboos, Oman

CHRIS MELLOR

MIDDLE EASTERN CUISINE

Street Food

Street food in the Middle East is good and cheap, although often limited; the two main standbys are *felafel* and *shwarma*. Felafel (called *ta'amiyya* in Egypt) is mashed chickpeas and spices balled up and deep fried. You usually buy felafel in the form of a sandwich, with several balls stuffed inside a pocket of pita-type bread along with salad and perhaps humous. Shwarma is the Middle Eastern equivalent of the Greek *gyros* sandwich or the Turkish *döner kebab*. Strips of lamb or chicken are sliced from a spit, sizzled on a hot plate with chopped tomatoes and garnish, and then stuffed in a pocket of pita-type bread.

In Egypt you'll also find plenty of *fuul* sellers – fuul is fava beans mashed into a thick, lumpy paste, usually ladled into a piece of pita-type bread. Another Egyptian favourite is *kushari*, a mix of noodles, rice, black lentils, fried onions and tomato sauce. The ingredients are served together in a bowl for sit-down meals, or spooned into a polythene bag or plastic tub for takeaway. You can recognise kushari joints by the great tureens of noodles and rice in the windows.

PAUL GREENWAY

Left: A *shwarma* seller in Jordan waits for a hungry passerby

Mezze

A traditional Middle Eastern meal starts with *mezze*, which is a selection of hot and cold starters. In a good restaurant you'll find 20 or more available. Order as many or as few as you choose. It is quite acceptable to just make a meal of mezze. If there are, say, two of you dining then a spread of maybe six mezze plus bread will usually make for a totally satisfying meal. Note that because of the imprecise nature of transliterating Arabic into English, spellings will vary; for example, what we give as kibbeh may appear variously as kibba, kibby or even gibeh.

Baba Ghanouj A lumpy paste of mashed eggplant mixed with tomato and onion and sometimes, in season, pomegranate. Done well, it has a delicious smoky taste.

Borek Triangles of light pastry stuffed with usually either salty white cheese or spinach or spicy minced meat. Also known in Lebanon and Syria as *fatayer*.

Fattoush Similar to tabbouleh but with the addition of pieces of crunchy, deep fried bread.

Humous Cooked chickpeas ground into a paste and mixed with tahina, garlic and lemon. This is available in every restaurant and is often done badly – woody tasting and watery; at it's best it should be thick and creamy.

Kibbeh Minced lamb, burgul wheat and pine seeds shaped into a patty and deep fried.

Kibbeh Nayeh Minced lamb and cracked wheat served raw like steak tartare.

Kibda Liver, often chicken liver *kibda firekh* or *kibda farouj*, and usually sauteed in lemon or garlic. Done correctly they should have an almost pâte-like consistency.

Labneh A cheesy yoghurt paste which is often heavily flavoured with garlic or sometimes, even better, with mint.

Loubieh French bean salad with tomatoes, onions and garlic.

Mashi Various vegetables, such as courgettes *kousa*, vine leaves, peppers, or white and black aubergines, stuffed with minced meat, rice, onions, parsley and herbs and then baked. Very popular in Egypt.

Muttabel Similar to babaghanouj but the blended eggplant is mixed with tahina, yoghurt and olive oil to achieve a creamier consistency.

Shinklish A salad of small pieces of crumbled tangy, eye-wateringly strong cheese mixed with chopped onion and tomato.

Tabbouleh A bulgur wheat, parsley and tomato based salad, with a sprinkling of sesame seeds, lemon and garlic.

Tahina A thin sesame seed paste.

Right: Spices of all tastes and colours abound at a spice market in Egypt

CHRIS MELLOR

Bread

Known as *khobz* or *a'aish* (which literally translates to 'life'), bread is eaten in copious quantities with every meal. It's unleavened and comes in flat disks about the size of a dinner plate. It's used in lieu of knives and forks to scoop up dips and ripped into pieces that are used to pick up the meat. You can also often get *a'aish bi zaatar*, which is bread with spices, seasoned with thyme and a mixture of other herbs.

Top: Giant loaves on sale in the back streets of Malatya, Eastern Anatolia, Turkey

Bottom: An Egyptian bread vendor displays his wares.

JULIET COOMBE

Top: Dates for sale,
Ta'izz, Yemen

Main Courses

Meat *Kofta* and *kebab* are the two most popular main dishes throughout much of the Middle East. Kofta is ground meat peppered with spices, shaped into small sausages, skewered and grilled. Kebab is skewered, flame-grilled chunks of meat, usually lamb. There are a few regional specialities, especially in Syria and Lebanon, where menus will often include *kebab halebi* (Aleppan kebab), a standard kebab but served in a heavy, chopped tomato sauce, or *kebab Iskendrun*, which is a spicy kebab.

You'll also commonly find *shish tawouq*, which is a kebab with pieces of marinated, spiced chicken instead of lamb. The meat usually comes on a bed of *badounis* (parsley) and may be served in upmarket restaurants with grilled tomatoes and onions. Otherwise you eat it with bread, salad and tahina.

Chicken is common, roasted on a spit and, in restaurants, ordered by the half. In Egypt you'll often be offered *hamam* (pigeon), which is usually served stuffed with rice and spices. It's also served as a stew cooked in a deep clay pot, known as a *tagen*, with onions, tomatoes, and rice or cracked wheat.

Stews Stews are usually meat or vegetable or both and, although not available everywhere, make a pleasant change from chicken and kebabs. *Fasoolyeh* is a green bean stew, *biseela* is made of peas, *batatas* of potato, while *bamya* is okra. Stews are usually served on *ruz* (rice) or, more rarely, *makarone* (macaroni).

Desserts

Pastries Middle Easterners love sugar and their desserts are assembled accordingly; the basic formula is lightweight pastry heavily drenched in honey, syrup and/or rose water. When buying from a pastry shop you order by weight – 250g ('roba kilo'), which is generally the smallest amount they are prepared to weigh out, is more than enough for one person. The most common pastry types are:

Asabeeh Rolled filo pastry filled with pistachio, pine and cashew nuts and honey. Otherwise known as 'lady's fingers'.

Baklawa A generic term for any kind of layered flaky pastry with nuts, drenched in honey.

Barazak Flat, circular cookies sprinkled with sesame seeds. Very crisp and light.

Isfinjiyya Coconut slice.

Kunafa Shredded wheat over a creamy sweet cheese base baked in syrup.

Mushabbak Lace-work shaped pastry drenched in syrup.

Zalabiyya Pastries dipped in rose-water.

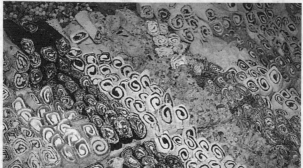

Top: A tempting array of delicious sweets at an İstanbul market

Bottom: The honey-drenched *baklawa* is a favourite dessert in the Middle East.

Top: Almond and date traditional dish

Middle: Served at its best, humous, the most ubiquitous of all mezze, is thick and creamy and if eaten with fresh bread is almost a meal in itself.

Bottom: Turkish *dolma* (stuffed vine leaves or vegetables) is prepared in a variety of delicious ways.

CHRIS MELLOR

EDDIE GERALD

GLENN BEANLAND

ANDREW HUMPHREYS

PAUL DOYLE

CHRIS MELLOR

Top Left: Street food is often literally that: food sold from street-vendors' carts. Pictured here is a *kushari* (a mix of noodles, rice, black lentils, fried onions and tomato sauce) seller in Islamic Cairo.

Top Right: Refreshing, chilled herbal and seed-based drinks, such as the aniseed-tasting *ar'zus*, are sold by traditionally costumed strolling vendors in cities like Cairo, Jerusalem, Aleppo and Damascus.

Bottom: The bread of the Middle East is invariably unleavened and comes in large flat disks which are sometimes (such as in Iran) so big that they are rolled up like a newspaper and carried under the arm.

continued from page 82

DRINKS

Nonalcoholic Drinks

Tea & Coffee In the Middle East tea *(shai)* and coffee *(qahwa)* are drunk in copious quantities and are served strong.

Tea comes in two sorts: there's the tea bag type (always called 'Lipton tea', or *shai libton*, whatever the brand) and local tea. Local tea is made with green leaves (often imported from China) and it is served in small glasses, often with *na'ana* (mint). It's incredibly sweet unless you ask for only a little sugar *(shwayya sukkar)* or medium *(wassat)*. If you want no sugar at all, ask for it *bidoon sukkar* (without sugar), but it tastes bitter and has a strong tannin aftertaste.

Coffee is usually Turkish coffee in small cups and is also sweet. If you want less sugar ask for it *mazboota*; without sugar ask for *sada* (plain). It is very thick and muddy so let it settle a bit before drinking. Don't try and drink the last mouthful (which in cups this size is only about the second mouthful) because it's like drinking silt.

The traditional Arabic or Bedouin coffee is heavily laced with cardamom and drunk in cups without handles that hold only a mouthful. Served without sugar, it is poured from a silver or brass pot and your cup will be refilled until you make the proper gesture that you have had enough – hold the cup out and cover it with your hand. It is good etiquette to have at least three cups although you are unlikely to offend if you have less. Coffee is then followed by tea ad infinitum.

Western-style instant coffee is usually called Neskaf. It comes in a small packet with a cup of hot water and a jug of milk.

Other Nonalcoholic Drinks Juice stalls selling delicious freshly squeezed fruit juices *(aseer)* are quite common. Popular juices include lemon, orange, carrot, mango, pomegranate, rockmelon and sugarcane and you can have combinations of any or all of these. Steer clear of the stalls which add milk to their drinks.

Other traditional drinks include *ayran* (yoghurt and water mixed), which is tangy, refreshing and healthy. Another favourite, served hot in the winter, cold in the summer, is *sahlab* (*sahlep* or *salep* in Turkey). It is made up of sahlab powder (like tapioca), milk, coconut, sugar, raisins, chopped nuts, rose-water and a glacé cherry garnish (most cheap places will have simpler versions).

International and local brands of soft drink are sold everywhere. A tiny shop in a remote village may have little of anything at all, but the chances are they'll have a few dusty bottles of sweet, sticky Coke for sale.

Alcohol

Many Middle Eastern countries have several locally brewed alcoholic beverages, including beer (and nonalcoholic beer), wine (red, white and rosé) and *araq*, the indigenous firewater. It is similar to Turkish *raqi* and, yes, the effect is the same. It is usually mixed with water and ice and drunk with food. The best araq comes from Lebanon.

In larger cities and tourist resorts, you can find imported spirits and beer. For attitudes towards alcohol in the Middle East see Society & Conduct in the Facts about the Region chapter.

SHOPPING

One of the highlights of the Middle East is the covered souqs and bazaars where anything can be found if you look long and hard enough. Nothing beats the excitement of the expedition up and down the back alleyways of the bazaars, past pungent barrels of basil and cloves from the spice stalls through to medieval caravanserais. Take your sense of humour and curiosity with you, and if you want to buy something, be prepared to bargain – see Bargaining earlier in this chapter.

The list of things to buy varies from country to country (see the individual country chapters), but includes: handicrafts; *kilims* (rugs) and carpets; pearls, silver and gold; cotton clothing including *kufeyya* (headscarves), *galabiyyas* (long, loose robes worn by men), caftans and embroidered dresses; Bedouin woven bags; decorative daggers and swords; copperware and brassware; olive and cedar woodcarvings; bottles of

That Special Something

For the connoisseur of kitsch the Middle East is an absolute dream. How about one of the following:

Mother-of-Pearl Telephone A real telephone but in a wooden casing with inlaid mother-of-pearl (actually plastic) patterning. Not only is it hideous but it's about the shape and size of a typewriter. Available in the Souq al-Hamadiyya, Damascus.

Pyramid Paperweight A clear resin pyramid with a golden sphinx inside. When you shake it golden 'snow' rains down. Or maybe it's acid rain. Available in Egypt just about anywhere tourists congregate.

Inflatable Arafat Just put your lips to the back of his head and blow for a life-size, pear-shaped, air-filled bust of everybody's favourite kufeyya-wearing world leader. Gathering dust on shelves in Gaza City.

Now-you-see-him-now-you-don't Khomeinī Plate A plate which you tilt one way to get a stern-looking āyatollāh, then tilt another way for a cheery prime minister Khatamī. Available, along with some splendid keyrings, pennants, wall plaques and so on, at the Shrine of Khomeinī, south of Tehrān.

Ephesus Clock A plastic version of a Roman gate with arch stones for nine o'clock through to three o'clock but any time (in the open portal) between three and nine o'clock is anybody's guess.

The Green Book At last count Gadaffi's little book of guidance had been translated into no less than 84 languages so you can even take one home for your friend in Lithuania or Bhutan. Available in all good bookshops everywhere.

King Tut Galabiyya Perfect for lounging around the house, a short-sleeved, brightly coloured robe that is usually too short and festooned with a giant iron-on reproduction of the famous funerary mask.

King Tut Hologram Lamp White plaster bust of the famous boy-king that appears to float like a hologram when plugged in. Available in Cairo's Khan al-Khalili for a mere US$50.

Priapus from Ephesus A small replica of the (in)famous, generously endowed statue on display at the museum here. If you can attach these to the wall they make great coat hangers.

Your Name in Sand Small bottles of coloured sand with your name incorporated into them. You write your name on a piece of paper in the morning and pick up the item in the afternoon. Do not pay in advance. Available around Wadi Rum and Petra in Jordan.

---

coloured sand; kohl; silk scarves; inlaid backgammon boards and jewellery boxes; water pipes and meerschaum pipes; embroidered tablecloths and cushion covers; leather and suede; frankincense and incense.

In addition there's heaps of tacky souvenirs and kitsch, from Khomeinī watches to hieroglyphic drawings – see the boxed text 'That Special Something'.

At the other extreme are the duty-free shops of the UAE airports, reputed to be among the largest and cheapest in the world, where you'll find the latest in electronic goods and hi-tech gadgets.

Getting There & Away

This chapter gives you information on getting to and from the Middle East by air, land and sea. For details of travel between the countries of the Middle East see the following Getting Around chapter.

AIR

Airports in the Middle East of most use to tourists and with frequent flights to/from other parts of the world are Cairo, İstanbul, Tel Aviv and Dubai. The first three are the region's big tourism hubs, while Dubai is a major link in intercontinental routes between Europe and South-East Asia and Australasia. Outside of these four, most of the Middle East is still seen primarily as a business destination, a fact reflected in the expense of flying there.

What this means in practice is that when booking a flight to the Middle East, you shouldn't automatically aim for the airport

nearest to where you are going. For instance, your destination might be Jordan but you may find tickets to Tel Aviv significantly cheaper, even taking into account the cost of the overland trip to Amman.

Also, look out for cheap charter flight packages from Western Europe to destinations in Turkey, Egypt and Israel. Some of the flight-plus-accommodation packages offered by travel agencies can work out to be cheaper than a standard flight, although often the dates can be very restrictive.

Bizarrely, it can also often be cheaper to take a transcontinental flight involving a change of planes or a transit stop in the Middle East than to buy a ticket just to that place. This can be true even for tickets sold through the same travel agency and with the same airline. For example, a London-Karachi ticket via Dubai may cost less than the cheapest available London-Dubai ticket. The catch is that the first ticket may not allow a stopover in Dubai, may restrict it to the return leg or may only allow it for an extra charge.

The UK

You can get to the Middle East on direct flights from almost any European city of any size but London has the greatest number of options, closely followed by Frankfurt.

Fares from London are usually cheaper than from other European cities. The real bargains used to be with the Eastern European airlines but for the last few years the best deals have been with Olympic Airways. You will probably have to change planes at Athens, which must be one of the world's most unpleasant airports, but if you are heading to İstanbul or Cairo Olympic's fares are hard to beat.

Although publications like London's weekly *Time Out* and the travel pages of the national Sunday papers are full of ads for cheap flights, when you make the call it's rare to be offered a price that's anywhere

---

Warning

The information in this chapter is particularly vulnerable to change: prices for international travel are volatile, routes are introduced and cancelled, schedules change, special deals come and go, and rules and visa requirements are amended. Airlines and governments seem to take a perverse pleasure in making price structures and regulations as complicated as possible. You should check directly with the airline or a travel agent to make sure you understand how a fare (and ticket you may buy) works.

The upshot of this is that you should get opinions, quotes and advice from as many airlines and travel agents as possible before you part with your hard-earned cash. The details given in this chapter should be regarded as pointers and are not a substitute for your own careful, up-to-date research.

Air Travel Glossary

Baggage Allowance This will be written on your ticket and usually includes one 20kg item to go in the hold, as well as one item of hand luggage.

Bucket Shops These are unbonded travel agencies specialising in discounted airline tickets.

Bumped Just because you have a confirmed seat doesn't mean you're going to get on the plane (see Overbooking).

Cancellation Penalties If you have to cancel or change a discounted ticket, there are often heavy penalties involved; insurance can sometimes be taken out against these penalties. Some airlines impose penalties on regular tickets as well, particularly against 'no-show' passengers.

Check-In Airlines ask you to check in a certain time ahead of the flight departure (usually one to two hours on international flights). If you fail to check in on time and the flight is overbooked, the airline can cancel your booking and give your seat to somebody else.

Confirmation Having a ticket written out with the flight and date you want doesn't mean you have a seat until the agent has checked with the airline that your status is 'OK' or confirmed. Meanwhile you could just be 'on request'.

Courier Fares Businesses often need to send urgent documents or freight securely and quickly. Courier companies hire people to accompany the package through customs and, in return, offer a discount ticket which is sometimes a phenomenal bargain. In effect, what the companies do is ship their freight as your luggage on regular commercial flights. This is a legitimate operation, but there are two shortcomings – the short turnaround time of the ticket (usually not longer than a month) and the limitation on your luggage allowance. You may have to surrender all your allowance and take only carry-on luggage.

Full Fares Airlines traditionally offer 1st class (coded F), business class (coded J) and economy class (coded Y) tickets. These days there are so many promotional and discounted fares available that few passengers pay full economy fare.

ITX An ITX, or 'independent inclusive tour excursion', is often available on tickets to popular holiday destinations. Officially it's a package deal combined with hotel accommodation, but many agents will sell you one of these for the flight only and give you phoney hotel vouchers in the unlikely event that you're challenged at the airport.

Lost Tickets If you lose your airline ticket an airline will usually treat it like a travellers cheque and, after inquiries, issue you with another one. Legally, however, an airline is entitled to treat it like cash and if you lose it then it's gone forever. Take good care of your tickets.

MCO An MCO, or 'miscellaneous charge order', is a voucher that looks like an airline ticket but carries no destination or date. It can be exchanged through any International Association of Travel Agents (IATA) airline for a ticket on a specific flight. It's a useful alternative to an onward ticket in those countries that demand one, and is more flexible than an ordinary ticket if you're unsure of your route.

No-Shows No-shows are passengers who fail to show up for their flight. Full-fare passengers who fail to turn up are sometimes entitled to travel on a later flight. The rest are penalised (see Cancellation Penalties).

Air Travel Glossary

On Request This is an unconfirmed booking for a flight.

Onward Tickets An entry requirement for many countries is that you have a ticket out of the country. If you're unsure of your next move, the easiest solution is to buy the cheapest onward ticket to a neighbouring country or a ticket from a reliable airline which can later be refunded if you do not use it.

Open Jaw Tickets These are return tickets where you fly out to one place but return from another. If available, this can save you backtracking to your arrival point.

Overbooking Airlines hate to fly empty seats and since every flight has some passengers who fail to show up, airlines often book more passengers than they have seats. Usually excess passengers make up for the no-shows, but occasionally somebody gets 'bumped' onto the next available flight. Guess who it is most likely to be? The passengers who check in late.

Point-to-Point Tickets These are discount tickets that can be bought on some routes in return for passengers waiving their rights to a stopover.

Promotional Fares These are officially discounted fares, available from travel agencies or direct from the airline.

Reconfirmation If you don't reconfirm your flight at least 72 hours prior to departure, the airline may delete your name from the passenger list. Ring to find out if your airline requires reconfirmation.

Restrictions Discounted tickets often have various restrictions on them – such as needing to be paid for in advance and incurring a penalty to be altered. Others are restrictions on the minimum and maximum period you must be away, such as a minimum of 14 days or a maximum of one year.

Round-the-World Tickets RTW tickets give you a limited period (usually a year) in which to circumnavigate the globe. You can go anywhere the carrying airlines go, as long as you don't backtrack. The number of stopovers or total number of separate flights is decided before you set off and they usually cost a bit more than a basic return flight.

Stand-by This is a discounted ticket where you only fly if there is a seat free at the last moment. Stand-by fares are usually available only on domestic routes.

Transferred Tickets Airline tickets cannot be transferred from one person to another. Travellers sometimes try to sell the return half of their ticket, but officials can ask you to prove that you are the person named on the ticket. This is less likely to happen on domestic flights, but on an international flight tickets are compared with passports.

Travel Agencies Travel agencies vary widely and you should choose one that suits your needs. Some simply handle tours, while full-service agencies handle everything from tours and tickets to car rental and hotel bookings. If all you want is a ticket at the lowest possible price, then go to an agency specialising in discounted fares.

Travel Periods Ticket prices vary with the time of year. There is a low (off-peak) season and a high (peak) season, and often a low-shoulder season and a high-shoulder season as well. Usually the fare depends on your outward flight – if you depart in the high season and return in the low season, you pay the high-season fare.

near as attractive as the one that's quoted. As far as Middle East flights are concerned there are no dedicated specialists and the best bet is to call Campus Travel, Trailfinders and STA Travel, and then plump for the best deal.

Campus Travel
(☎ 020-7730 8111) 52 Grosvenor Gardens, London SW1W 0AG. Also has offices in universities/colleges around the country.
STA Travel
(☎ 020-7361 6262) 74-88 Old Brompton Rd, London SW7. Also has branches in Bristol, Manchester and most big university cities.
Trailfinders
(☎ 020-7938 3366) 42-48 Earls Court Rd, London W8. Also has branches in Bristol, Manchester and other big cities.

If you're looking to fly into Egypt then it's also worth calling Suleiman Travel (☎ 020-7244 6855), a reputable Egypt specialist that often manages to undercut the competition, particularly on services to places like Sharm el-Sheikh in Sinai and Aswan in Upper Egypt.

The USA & Canada
There are more flights from the USA than from Canada, but still not that many. Royal Jordanian flies New York-Amman five times a week and Chicago-Amman twice weekly. EgyptAir flies between New York and Cairo four times a week and Los Angeles and Cairo once a week. During the high season EgyptAir offers one extra flight per week from New York and LA. Other New York-Cairo flights are offered by TWA. To/from Israel, you can choose from El Al, Tel Aviv links with New York and Los Angeles and TWA's New York-Tel Aviv flights. Saudia services operate to/from Jeddah and Riyadh, linking with both New York and Washington. Kuwait Airways flies between New York and Kuwait City three times per week.

From Montreal and Toronto, El Al flies twice a week to Tel Aviv.

As well as these direct flights there are connections with changes for other Middle Eastern airports from various cities in North America. The cheapest way to get from North America to the Middle East by air might be to fly to London and buy a ticket from a bucket shop there, but this would depend on the fare to London and the time you would have to spend in London waiting for a flight out.

Discount travel agents can be found through the *Yellow Pages* or the major daily newspapers. *New York Times*, *Los Angeles Times*, *Chicago Tribune* and *San Francisco Examiner* all produce weekly travel sections filled with travel agents' ads. Council Travel, America's largest student travel organisation, has around 60 offices in the USA; its head office (☎ 800-226 8624) is at 205 E 42 St, New York, NY 10017. Call it for the office nearest you or visit its Web site at www.ciee.org. STA Travel (☎ 800-777 0112) has offices in Boston, Chicago, Miami, New York, Philadelphia, San Francisco and other major cities. Call the tollfree 800 number for office locations or visit its Web site at www.statravel.com.

In Canada, *Toronto Star*, Toronto's *Globe & Mail*, *Montreal Gazette* and *Vancouver Sun* carry travel agents' ads and are a good place to look for cheap fares. Travel CUTS (☎ 800-667 2887) is Canada's national student travel agency and has offices in all major cities. Its Web site is found at www.travelcuts.com.

Australia & New Zealand
There are no longer tight constraints on ticket discounting in Australia, but for Australians and New Zealanders there are still few route options to the Middle East. EgyptAir has a regular service from Sydney via South-East Asia to Cairo, from where there are connections to almost all other Middle Eastern destinations. However, the aircraft and in-flight service are much better with Gulf Air and Emirates, both of which fly out of Sydney and Melbourne to Abu Dhabi and Bahrain. Gulf Air's RTW fare could be good value if you also want to visit London and stop over in Asia. Emirates has good connections with other Mid-

dle Eastern capitals like Beirut and Cairo and will pay for a hotel if the layover stretches to eight hours.

If you're heading for Tel Aviv then Qantas Airways and El Al via Asia are the best. Other options include Alitalia via Milan, Lufthansa Airlines via Frankfurt or KLM-Royal Dutch Airlines via Amsterdam.

In both Australia and New Zealand, STA Travel and Flight Centres International are big dealers in cheap air fares. Check the travel agents' ads in the *Yellow Pages* and ring around.

On From the Middle East by Air

Air Passes At the time of writing Emirates (www.ekgroup.com) has something called the Arabian Airpass that allows cut-price travel around the Middle East. To qualify you need to buy a flight to Dubai and then onward flights (a minimum of two, maximum of six) to cities such as Cairo, Amman, Damascus and Muscat, these are available from US$40.

Europe/USA/Australasia Buying cheap air tickets in the Middle East isn't easy. Usually the best deal you can get is an airline's official excursion fare and no discount on single tickets unless you qualify for a youth or student fare. Some travel agencies in the Middle East will knock the price down by up to 10% if you're persistent, but may then tie you into fixed dates or flying with a less popular airline.

The nearest thing you'll find to a discount ticket market in the Middle East is offered by some travel agencies in Israel, particularly in Tel Aviv, and in İstanbul, especially around Taksim Square and in Sultanahmet. As well as discounts on tickets to Western Europe and North America, the İstanbul agencies have cheap deals to places like Moscow (US$90), Mumbai/Delhi (from US$299), Tokyo (from US$395), Singapore/Bangkok (from US$335) and San Francisco (from US$350).

Africa The widest choice of African destinations is offered by EgyptAir but, despite the proximity, there is nothing cheap about flying from the Middle East into Africa. In fact, for most African capitals a ticket bought in London will be cheaper than one bought in the Middle East. The best bet is to buy your African ticket with a stopover in the Middle East.

As an idea of prices, Cairo to Addis Ababa (Ethiopian Airlines and EgyptAir) is US$584 one way, or US$811 return; Nairobi (Kenya Airways) is US$622 one way; and Khartoum (EgyptAir and Sudan Airways) is US$394 one way or US$480 return.

You can get the odd cheap deal in Tel Aviv. For example, at the time of writing Balkan Air was offering a one-way fare of US$410 to Johannesburg but with a 30 hour stopover in Sofia.

Yemen, of course, also has good connections with the countries on the east coast of Africa – see that chapter for details.

Central Asia & the Caucasus There are a small but rapidly growing number of flights from the Middle East to Central Asian and Caucasus destinations. There are regular flights between İstanbul and Almaty (Turkish Airlines, three times weekly, US$180 one way), Bishkek (Kyrgyzstan Airlines, twice weekly, US$280 one way), Baku (Turkish Airlines, three times weekly, US$240 one way) and Tashkent (Uzbekistan Airways, twice weekly, US$510 one way). There are also daily İstanbul-Ashghabat flights (Turkmenistan Airlines, US$250, one way).

From Iran there are flights (on Iran Air or Iran Asseman) from Tehrān once a week to Almaty (US$300 one way), Ashghabat (US$176 one way) and Tashkent (US$205 one way). From Mashhad there are flights three times a week to Ashghabat (US$90 one way), once a week to Bishkek (US$155 one way) and twice a week to Dushanbe (US$90 one way). There's also a weekly flight connecting Tabriz and Baku (US$200 one way).

From Tel Aviv, Uzbekistan Airways flies to Tashkent twice a week for US$300 one way. There are also Uzbekistan Airways flights connecting Tashkent with Bahrain, Sharjah and Jeddah.

LAND

If you are travelling independently overland to the Middle East – whether hitching, cycling, driving your own car or coming by train or bus – you can approach the region from three main directions:

- From the west (Europe), including routes through Greece by bus, train and car; through Bulgaria by bus, train and car; by direct bus to İstanbul from many Western European cities or by train to İstanbul via Bucharest or Budapest; or via the Caucasus into eastern Turkey or north-western Iran.
- From the east (Asia), including by bus or train through Turkmenistan (possibly); or by train, bus, motorbike or car through Pakistan.
- From the south (Africa), including routes through Sudan and Chad, or across North Africa via Tunisia into Libya.

Greece

The easiest and most common overland route into the Middle East is via Greece to İstanbul. (Ferries from Greece across the Aegean to Turkey and across the Mediterranean to Haifa in Israel are described later in this chapter.)

Bus A bus to İstanbul departs from Athens' Peloponnese train station at 7 pm daily, except Wednesday. The journey costs 17,000dr (US$58) and takes about 22 hours – slightly less than the train and a somewhat more pleasant prospect. Try to book your seat a day ahead. You can also pick up the bus in Thessaloniki (US$37) from the train-station forecourt at 2.30 am (except Thursday) and at Alexandroupolis (US$14) at 8.30 am (again, except Thursday).

Alternatively, you can make your own way to Alexandroupolis and take a service from the intercity bus station to the border town of Kipi (three departures a day, US$2.40). You can't walk across the border but it's easy enough to hitch – you may be lucky and get a lift all the way to İstanbul. Otherwise, take a bus to İpsala (5km east

beyond the border) or Keşan (30km east beyond the border), from where there are many buses to the capital.

Train This is a must for masochists. Greece's sole rail link with Turkey is the daily Thessaloniki-İstanbul service. The train leaves İstanbul late in the evening, arriving in Thessaloniki late the next afternoon; in the reverse direction, it leaves Thessaloniki at 10.20 pm. However, the timetable is subject to seasonal changes so don't count on these times. Although the 1400km trip is supposed to take 16 hours, delays of more than five or six hours at the border are common, especially on the eastbound leg, and the train can get uncomfortably crowded and hot. And, despite being an overnight international journey, only 2nd class seats are available (US$38).

Car & Motorcycle The two border posts between Greece and Turkey are at Kastanies and Kipi. If you're lucky you may get through in an hour or two.

Bulgaria

If you plan on leaving the Middle East via Bulgaria, nationals of the USA and the EU are admitted without a visa for stays of less than 30 days. Travellers of other nationalities (including Aussies, Kiwis and Canadians) need a transit visa, which is issued at the border for US$68.

Bus There are regular daily buses from Sofia to İstanbul (US$25). They most likely also pick up in Plovdiv and Svilengrad.

Train The *Balkan Express* runs from Hungary (Budapest) via Bulgaria (Sofia) to İstanbul (US$37, 12 hours). The train leaves Sofia at 8.40 pm. In the reverse direction, it departs İstanbul's Sirkeci station at 10.20 pm.

Car & Motorcycle Bulgaria's main road crossing point with Turkey, open 24 hours, is at Kapitan-Andreevo, on the E5 road from Svilengrad; over the fence lies the Turkish border post of Kapıkule, 18km west of Edirne. The second is at Malko Târnovo, 92km south of Burgas. Motorists in transit through Bulgaria may only be allowed to cross at Kapitan-Andreevo, depending on the current regulations.

Hitching A cheaper option is to catch a domestic train to Svilengrad and take a bus or taxi or hitch the 14km from here to Kapitan-Andreevo. You may not be allowed to walk to the border on the Bulgarian side; you may be required to hitch a lift or hire a taxi. After the formalities, you enter the Turkish town of Kapıkule by crossing the river Tunca at the Gazi Mihal Bridge and passing some fragments of Byzantine city walls. City bus No 1 runs from Kapıkule to the centre of Edirne; there are *dolmuşes* (shared taxis) on this route as well, but both are infrequent in the early morning and late at night. It's also easy to enter Bulgaria this way, although the Bulgarian taxi drivers will probably want hard currency.

The Rest of Europe

It's still fairly easy to get to İstanbul by train or bus (which is as far into the Middle East as public transport from the west penetrates). You'll probably find, though, that unless you're travelling from somewhere relatively nearby like Eastern Europe, taking the train works out no cheaper than flying. The advantages are that the train journey is much more pleasant and an experience in itself.

Bus Buses to İstanbul run from many European cities. One of the main operators from Western Europe is Eurolines, which sells tickets through various agencies. Two of the best Turkish companies – Ulusoy and Varan – operate big Mercedes buses on European routes and are also reliable. For details get in touch with the bookings office of any international bus station or any travel agency dealing in bus tickets.

During summer there are regular bus services to İstanbul from the following cities: Bucharest, Tirana, Rome and Turin; Bregenz, Graz, Innsbruck, Salzburg, Vienna and Wiener Neustadt in Austria; several German cities; Paris and Strasbourg in France; Basel and Zürich in Switzerland, Amsterdam, Brussels and London. Sample one-way fares to İstanbul are US$175 from Frankfurt, US$155 from Munich and US$110 from Vienna. Return fares are discounted by about 20%. Ask about student, youth or child discounts.

Train The *İstanbul Express* and *Skopje-İstanbul Express*, which used to connect İstanbul and Munich, no longer run. Aside from the Thessaloniki train and the *Balkan Express* (described under Bulgaria earlier), the only other service connecting the Middle East with Europe is the *Bosfor Express*. This leaves İstanbul for Bucharest, Romania, daily at 8.45 pm and arrives the next day at 1.10 pm (US$25).

With a change of trains it's possible to get to İstanbul from more European cities. Through tickets can be bought at almost any international railway booking office in Europe, but it's advisable to make inquiries some weeks ahead, especially in summer when demand is greatest.

The Caucasus

Georgia To travel to Georgia, you must first obtain a visa from the Georgian consulate in Trabzon. A bus departs from Trabzon's Russian bazaar at 7 pm daily and arrives at Batumi in the middle of the night. You may prefer to take a morning minibus to Rize or Hopa and pick up another heading for the border at Sarp (US$5 in all). On the other side of the border taxis will be waiting to run you to Batumi (US$10). Ask to be dropped near the train station.

Armenia At present it is not possible to cross between Armenia and Turkey. It is unwise to attempt crossing from Iran while the fighting continues between Armenia and Azerbaijan over disputed land near the Iranian border. Some intrepid travellers have recently succeeded but we don't recommend that anyone try to follow in their footsteps. It's even unclear where the current border crossing is between Iran and Armenia.

Azerbaijan Some of the buses from Trabzon to Tbilisi continue to Baku (US$75, plus a US$10 'tip' payable on the bus if you're going to Tbilisi, US$25 for Baku). It's a fairly gruelling journey with a three to four hour delay at Sarp on the border with Turkey and Georgia – mainly because the Georgians and Azaris buy up and take home half of Turkey. Trabzon to Tbilisi takes the best part of 19 hours.

The border at Āstārā (Iran) and Astara (Azerbaijan) is closed to foreigners, though it is open to Iranians and Āzārīs. Check the current situation with the Russian embassy in Tehrān. Boats between Bandar-é Anzalī (on Iran's Caspian coastline) and Baku still run once a fortnight, but only in summer – see the Sea & River section later in this chapter. The only real alternative is the weekly flight on Iran Air between Tabrīz and Baku.

Afghanistan

Until the Soviet invasion of Afghanistan in 1979, the most popular route with overland travellers was through the Khyber Pass from Peshawar to Jalalabad, west to Kabul and on through Herat into Mashhad in Iran. However, for the last 20 years only journalists, aid workers and a handful of the most intrepid travellers have ventured into the country. At the time of writing, hostile relations between Afghanistan's conquering Taliban and neighbouring Iran meant that borders were firmly closed and gaining entry into Afghanistan overland was a very remote possibility.

Turkmenistan

The only recognised border is at Sarakhs (Iran) and Saraghs (Turkmenistan). It's easy to reach the border by train or bus from either side, and cross the border independently. There are also direct buses between Mashhad (Iran) and Mary (Turkmenistan), but no direct trains across the border.

Pakistan

The only proper border crossing for foreigners is between Mīrjāvé (Iran) and Taftan (Pakistan). Foreigners normally pass through this border easily unless they cross

by train (because they may have to wait up to 10 hours for Iranians and Pakistanis to clear customs and immigration). It's best to catch public transport to either side of the border, cross it independently and then catch onward public transport.

Africa

Travel between Africa and the Middle East is extremely problematic at the time of writing. Although the Nile ferry which connects Aswan in Upper Egypt to Wadi Halfa in Sudan began running again in early 1998, Sudan is still unsafe for travel. Most East African overlanders now skip Sudan by flying from Egypt down to Addis Ababa in Ethiopia, although the current clashes on the Eritrean-Ethiopian border also place a big question mark over the validity of this option. See later in this chapter for details of Red Sea sailings.

SEA & RIVER

The Mediterranean routes have been popular with western travellers for many years and are fairly well publicised. However, it's not always easy to get information on many of the other services to the Middle East as the usual travel trade publications tend to ignore their existence. Your best bet is to get in touch with the carrier or its nearest agent some time in advance, and not to take too seriously what other sources tell you. This advice is particularly important if your itinerary depends on catching a particular ferry, or if you intend to ship your vehicle on one.

You're unlikely to regret taking an adequate supply of food and drink with you on any of these ships; even if it is available on board you're pretty stuck if it doesn't agree with you or your budget. Many people may find deck class on some of the longer sailings, such as the eight day Karachi-Jeddah run, a little too much to bear.

As well as the services listed below, some cruise liners call at Middle Eastern ports such as Aden, Suez, Alexandria or Muscat, but these are outside the scope of this book. A good travel agent should be able to tell you what's available this season.

Unless stated otherwise, all services run in both directions and all fares quoted below are single. A slight discount may apply on return tickets as well as student, youth or child fares on some lines. Schedules tend to change at least annually according to demand; fares, too, often fluctuate according to season, especially on the Mediterranean routes.

Although vehicles can be shipped on most of the following routes, bookings for them may have to be made some time in advance. The charge usually depends on the length or volume of the vehicle and should be checked with the carrier. As a rule motorcycles cost almost nothing to ship and bicycles are free.

Mediterranean Sea

Of all the scheduled services listed in this chapter, those in the Mediterranean offer the nearest thing to most people's idea of a cruise. Some of the ships even have discos, duty-free shops, casinos and swimming pools. However, travelling in deck class on the Piraeus-Haifa run is unlikely to damage your shoestring credentials.

Thomas Cook's *Greek Island Hopping* covers most domestic and international services in the eastern Mediterranean, not just those between the Greek islands. It includes summaries of sights and budget accommodation in most ports.

Between Greece & Israel Salamis Lines and Poseidon Lines operate weekly ferries between Piraeus, the port of Athens, and Haifa (see the Israel chapter). All stop at Rhodes and Limassol (Cyprus), some also at Iraklio. Departures from Piraeus are on Monday and Thursday, and from Haifa on Thursday and Sunday evenings; these are open to frequent seasonal change and you should check with a ticket agent in good time before making concrete travel plans.

The cheapest Piraeus-Haifa tickets are US$96 for deck class, US$106 for a pullman seat and from US$125 per person in a four-berth cabin. Students and those under 26 get a discount of about 20%. These prices are for one-way voyages in the low

season; in the high season, prices go up by between 11 and 15%.

A disembarkation fee of US$22 is charged for each stopover en route. The charge for a vehicle is US$44. Travellers with camper vans can sleep in the van on deck and avoid expensive cabin costs when travelling on Poseidon Line's *FB Sea Symphony*. The Piraeus-Haifa run takes about 58 hours, so take plenty of food and drink, or money, for the voyage.

Alternatively, it's possible to take the ferry only as far as Rhodes and change there for Marmaris in Turkey.

Contact details for the shipping companies are given later in this section.

Between Italy, Greece & Turkey Several shipping lines operate car and passenger ferries from Italy and Greece to Turkey in summer, and small ferries shuttle between the Greek islands and the Turkish mainland. A hydrofoil service operates in high summer between Rhodes and Fethiye. Timetables and fares are notoriously fickle and the few dependable services generally vary according to demand and are most frequent in summer; some stop running or only operate irregular services at other times. Various petty restrictions apply; it is much easier to get a ticket on a Turkish ship from Turkey or a Greek ship from Greece, unless you already hold a return ticket. Turkish Maritime Lines (Venice to Çeşme, İzmir and Antalya), European Seaways (Brindisi/Bari-Mykonos-Çeşme), Med Link Lines (Brindisi-Igoumenitsa-Patras-Çeşme) and Stern Ferrylines (Brindisi/Bari-Çeşme) have all been recommended. For more information see the Getting There & Away section of the Turkey chapter.

Between Cyprus & Turkey Several companies run *feribotlar* (car ferries) and *ekspresler* (hydrofoils) between Taşucu on Turkey's eastern Mediterranean coast and Kyrenia (Girne in Turkish) in northern Cyprus, selling tickets from offices in the main square. Passenger tickets cost less on the car ferry but the trip is longer. Provided your visa allows for multiple entries within its period of validity, you shouldn't have to pay for a new one when you come back into Turkey. If you do need a new visa, expect long queues, so try to be off the boat early.

The best ferry company is Fergün Express (☎ 324-741 2323, fax 741 2802, in Kyrenia 392-815 2344, fax 815 3866) which has daily express departures at 11 am and 1 and 3 pm, and a car ferry (the MF *Fatih*) leaving at midnight from Monday to Friday. The return express service from Kyrenia runs daily at 9.30 am and 1 and 2 pm, while the car ferry's return is at 11.30 am. A one-way ticket on the express service costs US$27 and a return ticket will set you back US$50. On the car ferry, the passenger fare is US$18/34 a single/return; a car costs US$38 one way.

Turkish Maritime Lines (☎ 324-741 4785) has a car ferry, the MV *Ayvalık*, departing from Taşuçu at midnight from Sunday to Thursday and returning from Kyrenia at noon Monday through Friday. Başak Denizcilik (☎ 324-741 6296, fax 741 4624) has car ferries departing from Taşucu at midnight on Wednesday, Saturday and Sunday and returning at noon the following day. Tickets cost US$17/32 one way/return, plus US$38 for a car.

Ertürk (☎ 324-741 4033, fax 741 4325, in Kyrenia ☎ 081-52308 or 081-53784), with its main office in Çeşme, west of İzmir, operates the MF *Ertürk I*, departing from Taşucu at midnight from Sunday to Thursday and arriving at Kyrenia the next day at 7.30 am. From Kyrenia the ferry leaves at noon on Monday to Friday, arriving in Taşucu at 4 pm. Tickets cost US$14 one way for passengers and US$65 per car.

Black Sea
Russia Karden Line ferries run between Trabzon and Sochi in Russia, departing from Trabzon on Monday and Thursday at 6 pm and returning from Sochi on Tuesday and Friday at 6 pm. Cabin tickets (US$60) are available in Trabzon from Navi Tour (☎ 462-326 4484), İskele Caddesi Belediye Duükkanları. At the time of writing most people had to get a visa from a Russian

consulate in their home country to use this service, but that may change.

Red Sea & Gulf of Aden
Sudan Ferries bound for Port Sudan leave from Suez; the voyage, via Jeddah in Saudi Arabia, takes about four days. Information and tickets are available from Yara Tours & Shipping (☎ 393 8861) at Sharia Mohammed Sabri Abu Alam in central Cairo. In Saudi Arabia contact Al-Aquel Travel (☎ 02-647 5337). See the Egypt and Saudi Arabia chapters for more information.

Arabian Sea & Indian Ocean
The Pan-Islamic Steamship Company sails about once a month between Karachi and Jeddah. In the *haj* season only pilgrims are carried. The sailing to Jeddah takes seven or eight days. For information and tickets contact its office in Karachi (see Shipping-Line Addresses later). There are also offices in Yemen and the other Gulf States.

Caspian Sea
Azerbaijan Infrequent passenger-cum-cargo boats between Bandar-é Anzalī (Iran) and Baku (Azerbaijan) only run in summer – and then only once a fortnight. You may be able to hitch a ride on a cargo ship at any time, however, but don't count on it. Outside the two countries, tickets and information can be obtained through IRISL (Iran's national shipping line) in London on ☎ 020-7378 7121.

Nile River
Sudan The twice-weekly steamer service linking the railheads of Wadi Halfa in Sudan and Aswan in Egypt recommenced operations in early 1998 after being suspended for four years. Ferries depart Aswan in southern Egypt every Monday afternoon at around 3 pm, arriving in Wadi Halfa, Sudan, about 8 am Tuesday morning. You can go 1st/2nd class, at a cost of E£142/88.50 (US$42/26). First class means bunks in small cabins, second means seats. The fare includes a meal and tea, and soft drinks are also available on board.

Tickets are bought at the Nile Valley Navigation Office in Aswan (☎ 097-303 348), next to the tourist office, one street in from the Corniche. The office is open from 8 am to 2.30 pm every day except Friday. Note that the office will not sell you a ticket unless you've got a Sudanese visa. You will also be asked for a yellow fever certificate on the boat.

Shipping-Line Addresses

The head office of the following shipping lines is listed first under each heading, followed by a selection of any offices or agents outside the Middle East.

Adriatica Line
(☎ 041-781611, fax 781894)
Zattere 1411, PO Box 705, Venice 30123, Italy
(☎ 081-227 002, fax 223 749)
Crete Travel Bureau, 20-22 Odos Epimenidou, PO Box 1069, Iraklio, Crete, Greece
(☎ 061-421995) Charilaos Cacouris Company Odos Othonos Amalias 8, PO Box 1012, Patras, Greece
(☎ 020-7373 6548) Serena Holidays, 40-42 Kenway Rd, London SW5 0RA, UK
Arkadia Lines
(☎ 01-612 3402, fax 612 6206)
Kifissias 215, Maroussi, Athens 15124, Greece
(☎ 01-422 2127, fax 422 3640)
Piraeus 42, Akti Poseidonos and Loudovikou, Piraeus 18531, Greece
Black Sea Steamship Company
(☎ 0482-25 35 39) Potyomkintsev ploshchad 1, 270026 Odessa, Ukraine
Fayaz Trading, Construction & Shipping Company
(☎ 02-647 4208) Al-Mina'a St, Jeddah, Saudi Arabia
Khazar Shipping Company
(☎ 020-7378 7121) ISRL, TR House, 134-8 Borough High St, London SE1 1LB, UK
Minoan Lines
(☎ 01-689 8340, fax 689 8344)
Odos Kifissias 64B, Maroussi, Athens 15125, Greece
(☎ 071-207 1068, 207 0874)
Euroferries Ancona Ltd, Stazione Marittima Porto, Ancona, Italy
(☎ 081-330301, fax 330308)
Odos 25 Avgustou 17, Iraklio, Crete, Greece.
Misr Edco Shipping Co SAE
(☎ 03-483 2397, fax 483 8898)
Sharia al-Central, Al-Mansheiyya, Alexandria, Egypt

(☎ 06-40213/4, fax 40168)
Telstar Travel & Tourism, Jebel Amman, 3rd Circle, Riyadh Centre, Al-Riyadh building, PO Box 194, Amman, Jordan
(☎ 02-682 3759, 647 5251)
Yousef bin Ahmed Kanoo, PO Box 812, Kilo 4, Mecca Rd, Jeddah, Saudi Arabia
Pan-Islamic Steamship Company
(☎ 021-241 2110, fax 241 2276)
Writers' Chambers, Mumtz Hasan Road, PO Box 4855, Karachi, Pakistan
Poseidon Line
(☎ 01-429 2046, fax 429 2041, Web site www.greekislands.gr/greece.htm) Akti Miaouli 35-39, Piraeus 18536, Greece
(☎ 04-867 4444, fax 866 1958)
Caspi Travel, 76 Ha'Atzmaut St, Haifa, Israel
(☎ 020-7431 4560, fax 7431 5456)
Viamare Travel 2 Sumatra Rd, London NW6 1PU, UK
Salamis Lines
(☎ 01-429 4325, fax 429 4557, Web site www.viamare.com/salamis/salprc.htm) Fillelinon 9, Piraeus 18536, Greece
(☎ 04-867 1743, fax 867 0530)
Allalouf & Co Shipping Ltd, 40 HaNamal St, Haifa, Israel. See also Viamare Travel under Poseidon Line earlier
Shipping Corporation of India
(☎ 022-202 6666, fax 202 2949)
Shipping House, 245 Madame Cama Rd, Mumbai, India 400021
Strand Cruise & Travel Centre
(☎ 020-7836 6363, fax 7497 0078)
Charing Cross Shopping Concourse, The Strand, London WC2N 4HZ, UK
Turkish Maritime Lines
(☎ 212-249 9222 for reservations, ☎ 244 2502 for information, fax 251 9025) TDI Denizyollari Acentesi, Rıhtım Caddesi, Karaköy, İstanbul, Turkey
(☎ 020-7499 9992, fax 7499 9995)
Sunquest Holidays Ltd, 23 Princes St, London W1R 7RG, UK
(☎ 41-520 8819, fax 520 4009)
BassaniSpA, Via XXII Marzo 2414, 30124 Venice, Italy
(☎ 392-366 5786, fax 366 7840)
Kıbrıs Türk Denizcilik Ltd Şti, Bülent Ecevit Bulvarı 3, Gazimagosa (Famagusta), Turkish Republic of Northern Cyprus

ORGANISED TOURS

Three main sorts of tours are available: package tours, overland tours and inclusive tours. Package tours are mainly to the resort areas of Turkey, Egypt and Israel.

Overland Tours

For people with time to spare, especially if lone travel does not appeal, these trips are ideal. You travel in an 'overland truck' with about 15 to 28 other people, a couple of drivers/leaders, plus tents and other equipment. Most of the hassles such as border crossings are taken care of by the leader. Disadvantages include a fairly fixed itinerary and the possibility of spending long amounts of time with a bunch of other people, not all of whom you will necessarily get along with.

Most main overland operations are in the UK:

African Trails
(☎ 020-8742 7724, fax 8742 8621)
3 Flanders Rd, Chiswick, London W4 1NQ. Egypt to Turkey in six weeks for UK£600.
Dragoman
(☎ 01728-861 133, fax 861 127)
96 Camp Green, Kent Rd, Debenham, Suffolk IP14 6LA. Overland specialists with numerous itineraries through North Africa and the Middle East (often as part of a larger African or Asian itinerary).
Economic Expeditions
(☎ 020-8995 7707, fax 8742 7707, email ecoeped@mcmail.com) 29 Cunnington St, Chiswick, London W4 5ER. Middle East overland trips from İstanbul to Cairo (five weeks) costing UK£380.
Encounter Overland
(☎ 020-7370 6845, fax 7244 9737, email ad venture@encounter.co.uk) 267 Old Brompton Rd, London SW5 9JA. Extensive overland tours taking in the ME as part of a larger Asia or Africa trip and a round-Egypt 21 day excursion or a Cairo to Tunis trip through Libya.
Hinterland Travel
(☎ 01883-743 584, 743 861, fax 743 912)
2 Ivy Mill Lane, Godstone, Surrey RH9 8NH. Small overland specialist. Options include a 21 day Syria, Jordan and Lebanon trip and an 88 day odyssey taking in Syria, Jordan, Lebanon, Egypt, Turkey, Iran, Lebanon, Saudi Arabia, UAE and Oman.
New Frontier Expeditions
(☎ 01702-307 848, fax 305 367)
96B West Road, Westcliff-on-Sea Essex SSO 9DB. İstanbul to Cairo in five weeks for UK£400 and İstanbul-Aqaba-İstanbul in seven weeks for UK£550.

Oasis Overland
(☎ 020-8759 5597, fax 8897 2713)
33 Travellers Way, Hounslow, London TW4 7QB. Overland outfit that runs a five week Turkey-Syria-Jordan-Egypt trip (UK£590).

In North America and Australia overland companies are represented by specialist travel agencies – see the following Inclusive Tours section.

Inclusive Tours

You can reach the Middle East from your home country on a tour which includes your international flight, internal transport, accommodation, food, local guide and so on. These tours range from one week Nile cruises to expeditions into little visited regions of Libya. The following is a selection of the most interesting options:

Australia
Adventure World
(☎ 1800-133 322 or 02-9956 7766, fax 9956 7707) 73 Walker St, North Sydney, NSW 2060. Also in Adelaide, Brisbane, Melbourne and Perth. Agents for the UK's Explore Worldwide and Exodus.
Insight International
(☎ 02-9512 0767, fax 9438 5209)
Suite 201, 39-41 Chandos St, St Leonards, NSW 2065. Three to 15 day packages, including a grand Jordan, Israel and Sinai tour and Nile cruises.
Passport Travel
(☎ 03-9867 3888, fax 9867 1055)
Suite 11a, 401 St Kilda Rd, Melbourne, Victoria 3004. Middle East specialist with no packages and no brochures; instead Passport assists in arranging itineraries for individuals or groups. For example, at the time of writing it was putting together a made-to-order Persian carpet tour through Iran.
Peregrine
(☎ 03-663 8611, fax 663 8618)
258 Lonsdale St, Melbourne, Victoria 3000. Also in Adelaide, Brisbane, Perth and Sydney. Agents for the UK's Dragoman and The Imaginative Traveller.
Ya'lla
(☎ 03-9510 2844, fax 9510 8425, email yal lamel@yallatours.com.au) West Tower, 608 St Kilda Rd, Melbourne, VIC 3000. Wide variety of pick 'n' mix packages and private arrange-

ment tours in Dubai, Egypt, Israel, Jordan, Lebanon, Syria, Turkey and Yemen.

UK

Arab Tours
(☎ 020-7935 3273, fax 7486 4237)
78 Marylebone Lane, London W1M 5FF. Middle East specialist with tours to Libya.

Caravanserai Tours
(☎ 020-8691 2513, fax 8469 3091, email caravanserai@musicfarm.demon.co.uk) 225A Lewisham Way, London SE4 1UY. Specialises in Iran, Libya and Syria and offers tailor-made arrangements and group travel.

Crusader Travel
(☎ 020-8744 0474, fax 8744 0574)
57 Church St, Twickenham TW1 3NR. Primarily diving packages in the Red Sea out of Eilat, Nuweiba and Taba. Also does special diving for the disabled. Apart from diving, it has a seven day jeep safari through the Bzburun peninsula in Turkey, trekking in Lycia and rafting on the Coruh.

Exodus
(☎ 020-8675 5550, fax 8673 0779)
9 Weir Rd, London SW12 0LT. Lots of themed two week itineraries ('Taurus Mountain Trek', 'Valleys of the Assassins') taking in one or more of the following: Egypt, Iran, Jordan and Syria, Turkey and Yemen.

Explore Worldwide
(☎ 01252-319 448, fax 343 170)
1 Fredrick St, Aldershot, Hampshire GU11 1LQ. Small group exploratory holidays with titles like 'Lawrence's Arabia', 'Crusader Castles & Desert Cities' taking in one or more of Egypt, Israel, Iran, Jordan, Lebanon, Oman, Syria and Yemen.

High Places
(☎ 0114-275 7500, fax 275 3870, email highpl@globalnet.co.uk) Globe Works, Penistone Rd, Sheffield S6 3AE. Mountain trekking in Yemen, hiking in Wadi Rum and camel trekking in Sinai, with tours to Oman to come.

Prospect Music & Art Tours
(☎ 020-8995 2151, fax 8742 1969)
454-458 Chiswick High Road, London W4 5TT. Cultural tours to Libya, Syria, Lebanon and Jordan.

The Imaginative Traveller
(☎ 020-8742 8612, fax 8742 3045)
14 Barley Mow Passage, Chiswick, London W4 4PH. Small group tours to a single country with a few linkages (Jordan and Syria, Syria and Lebanon). Does a Red Sea Diving for Beginners trip based in Hurghada.

Top Deck
(☎ 020-7244 8641, fax 7373 6201, email topdeck@dial.pipex.com) 131-135 Earls Court Rd, London SW5 9RH. Tours to Egypt, Israel and Jordan, either each country separately or all three combined in one 28 day package. Also has an 11 week London to Kathmandu overland trip passing through Turkey, Syria, Jordan and Iran.

Travelbag Adventures
(☎ 01420-541 007) 15 Turk St, Alton, Hants GU34 1AG. Small group 'adventure' tours with structured itineraries to Egypt, Iran, Jordan and Turkey.

USA

Adventure Center
(☎ 1800-227-8747, fax 510-654-4200, email tripinfo@adventure-center.com) 1311 63rd St, suite 200, Emeryville, CA 94608. Agents for the UK's Dragoman, Encounter Overland and Explore Worldwide.

Archaeological Institute of America
(☎ 617-353-9361, fax 353-6550)
Boston University, 656 Beacon St, Boston, MA 02215-2010. Ancient civilisation tours to the Aegean coast, Arabian Peninsula, Jordan and Syria led by prominent scholars. Itineraries include visits to archaeological sites, ongoing digs and museums. Many of the tours are cruises.

Archaeological Tours
(☎ 212-986-3054) 271 Madison Ave, suite 904AB, New York, NY 10016. Specialised tours to Anatolia, Ancient Egypt, Eastern Turkey, Syria and Jordan, Oases of the Western Desert and Yemen led by distinguished scholars.

Distant Horizons
(☎ 1800-333-1240, fax 562-983-8833, email disthoriz@aol.com) 30 Elm Ave, Long Beach, CA 90802. Small but long-established company offering group (max 15) travel to Iran, Oman and Yemen led by scholars. Tours are pricey (US$4000 to US$6000 for around two weeks) but sound fascinating.

Geographic Expeditions
(☎ 415-922-0448, fax 346-5535, email info@geoex.com) 2627 Lombard St, San Francisco, CA 94123. Offers 23 days in Iran (US$4990), 17 days in Yemen (US$3590) and a 22 day 'Sands of Araby' tour, which takes in Cairo, Upper Egypt, Petra, Damascus, Aleppo and Palmyra (US$5290).

Getting Around the Region

AIR

With no regional rail network to speak of and distances that make the bus a discomforting test of endurance, flying is certainly the most user-friendly method of transport in the Middle East. Tickets are more flexible than buses or trains, schedules more rigidly adhered to, refunds easier to get and information more readily available.

Flying isn't an option for getting to or from Iraq, nor is flying possible between Israel and most other Middle Eastern countries, except for Egypt, Jordan and Turkey. But, these exceptions aside, almost every Middle Eastern capital is linked to each of the others. See the Regional Flights table for schedules and sample fares.

Flights are usually operated by state airlines, most of which are reasonable (if often overpriced) and some of which, such as Emirates and Gulf Air, are truly excellent. If you're in a capital city, it's usually worth buying your ticket through a reputable travel agency. It can provide you with all the available choices without you having to visit several different airline offices. The price you pay will usually be the same.

Travel agency adresses are found in the Information sections of individual cities.

BUS

Bus is the universal mode of transport in the Middle East. Throughout most of the region buses will take you to almost anywhere of any size; on many routes there may be no other form of public transport. The exception is the Gulf States, where car ownership levels are so high that little demand for public bus services exists. It's not too difficult to get between the main towns in Saudi Arabia and Oman by bus, but Bahrain, Kuwait, the UAE and Qatar have few, if any, domestic services.

Most Middle Eastern countries can be reached by direct international bus from other parts of the region:

Aleppo (Syria)
 Several buses daily to İstanbul (US$20, 22 hours) via Ankara; and numerous daily buses to Beirut (US$6.50, six to seven hours).
Amman (Jordan) ·
 Two direct buses daily to Damascus (US$6.50, seven hours); daily direct buses to King Hussein Bridge for Israel (US$8.50, 45 minutes); daily direct buses to Riyadh, Dammam and Jeddah in Saudi Arabia and beyond (US$45, all up to 24 hours depending on destination); and direct buses to Baghdad, Iraq (US$17, 14 hours).
Ankara (Turkey)
 One daily bus to Tehrān (US$25, 28 hours);

How to Get Where You're Going

This chapter outlines the various ways of getting around the region. It's a directory that should be used for general planning. If you want to travel, for instance, between Turkey and Israel, this chapter will give you an overview of the options: air, land or sea; train vs bus, and so on. So you decide to go by bus from İstanbul to Damascus, from Damascus to Amman, and Amman to Jerusalem – you should then go to the Getting There & Away section of Turkey for further details on buses to Syria. If instead of a bus direct from İstanbul to Damascus you opt to travel through Turkey in stages, the Getting There & Away section in Turkey identifies the border crossing point to head for (in this case either Reyhanli or Yayladaği near Antakya). Border crossing details will then be found under Antakya.

Once in Syria, consult that chapter's Getting There & Away section for the best way to continue on to Jordan. Simple.

two daily buses to Aleppo (US$25, 10 hours); two daily buses to Damascus (US$30, 14 hours).

Baghdad (Iraq)
Two daily buses to Amman ($US20, 14 hours); Iraq's other borders still remain closed to tourists.

Beirut (Lebanon)
Direct buses daily to Damascus (US$4, four hours) and Aleppo (US$6.50, six to seven hours).

Cairo (Egypt)
Direct buses to Jerusalem/Tel Aviv Sunday, Monday, Wednesday and Thursday (S$35, 10 hours); one bus weekly to Jeddah via the Red Sea ferry from Port Suez (US$140, 52 hours); once a week to Benghazi (US$78, 20 hours) and twice weekly to Tripoli ($US130, 36 hours). There are also services direct to Libya from Alexandria.

Damascus (Syria)
Two buses daily to Amman (US$6, six or seven hours); several daily departures for İstanbul (US$32, 30 hours) via Ankara (US$26); hourly buses to Beirut (US$4, four hours); and one departure weekly to Cairo (US$43, 30 hours).

Dubai (UAE)
Twice daily buses to Muscat (US$20, five hours); and twice weekly buses to Damascus and Amman via Saudi Arabia (US$80, 36 hours).

İstanbul (Turkey)
One daily bus to Tehrān (US$40, 35 hours); two buses a day to Aleppo (US$34, 16½ hours); two buses a day to Damascus (US$37, 20 hours).

Jeddah (Saudi Arabia)
Direct buses operate several times per week from İstanbul via Ankara, Damascus and Amman. Several Turkish companies compete with Saudi Arabia's national bus company SAPTCO on the route. The Sáudi buses tend to be newer and better maintained. For northbound travel you should visit the main bus terminals in Riyadh or Jeddah to check schedules and fares, as these change frequently. You should be aware that around pilgrimage time buses to and from Jeddah are sold out well in advance.

Jerusalem (Israel)
Direct buses daily to Cairo (US$35, 12 to 14 hours); unscheduled excursion buses to Amman with Mazada Tours in Jerusalem (see Israel chapter).

Muscat (Oman)
Twice daily buses to Dubai (US$20, five hours).

Riyadh (Saudi Arabia)
See Jeddah.

Tehrān (Iran)
Several buses daily to Ankara and İstanbul (69,000/81,000/115,000 rials for buses with 32/29/22 seats); and several buses weekly to Damascus.

Tel Aviv (Israel)
Direct buses daily to Cairo (US$35, 13 hours); and unscheduled excursion buses to Amman with Mazada Tours in Tel Aviv (see Israel chapter).

Tripoli (Lebanon)
There are two buses a week to both Alexandria (US$130, 20 hours) and Cairo (US$150, 35 hours).

For further details of these services see the Getting There & Away sections of the relevant cities.

Even in those countries without any international bus services it's usually possible to get to at least one neighbouring country by using domestic services, making your own way across the border and picking up another domestic service or taxi in the next country. This method is usually cheaper and it avoids one of the big problems of international services: waiting for the vehicle to clear customs at each border. This can mean delays of several hours. However, if you are planning on using domestic buses make sure you know that there will be onward transport on the other side of the border.

It's always advisable to book bus seats in advance at the bus station; the bus station is usually the only ticket outlet and source of reliable information about current services. That said, trying to find information can be frustrating if you don't speak the language.

The cost and comfort of bus travel vary enormously throughout the region, and further details are given in the individual country chapters. One most typical nuisance, however, is the Middle Eastern bus drivers' fondness for loud videos (a fondness presumably shared by local passengers); sleep is almost always impossible. Another potential source of discomfort is that there doesn't yet seem to be such a concept as a nonsmoking bus.

TRAIN

No Middle Eastern country has an extensive railway network and there are few international services. Most railway lines in the region were built primarily for strategic or economic reasons, and many are either no longer in use or only carry freight. However, where there is a choice (such as in Iran and Egypt) the trains are usually much more comfortable than the buses and compare favourably in price. On the other hand, they are less frequent and usually slower, while many stations are some distance out of the town centres they serve. In general, tickets are only sold at the station and reservations are either compulsory or recommended.

The only functioning international passenger services within the region are:

Amman-Damascus
One weekly train connects the capitals of Jordan and Syria. It's a slow diesel train with ancient carriages that leaves Damascus at 7.30 am on Sunday, returning from Amman the next day. The journey takes anything between eight and 11 hours, and tickets cost US$6 – but see the Damascus Getting There & Away section for further details.
İstanbul-Aleppo
There is one weekly service between these two cities – at the time of research it was not actually running but it was due to restart in the near future; see the Aleppo section for further details.

TAXI

In the west taxis are usually an avoidable luxury. In the Middle East they are often neither. Many cities, especially in the Gulf States, have no other form of urban public transport, while there are also many rural routes that are only feasible in a taxi or private vehicle.

The ways in which taxis operate vary widely from country to country, and often even from place to place within a country. So does the expense of using them. Different types of taxi are painted or marked in different ways, or known by different names, but often local people talking to foreigners in English will just use the blanket term 'taxi'. If you want to save money, it's important to know which is which. Details of local peculiarities are given in the country chapters.

Regular Taxi

The regular taxi (also known as agency taxi, telephone taxi, private taxi or, in Israel, special taxi) are found in almost every Middle Eastern town, sometimes even in quite tiny settlements.

In some places there's no other public transport but in most, regular taxis exist alongside less expensive means of getting around (although these usually shut down overnight). They are primarily of use for transport within towns or on short rural trips, but in some countries hiring them for excursions of several hours is still cheap. They are also often the only way of reaching airports or seaports.

For details see the individual country chapters.

Shared Taxi

A compromise between the convenience of a regular taxi and the economy of a bus, the shared taxi picks up and drops off passengers at points along its route and runs to no particular schedule (although in most places to a fixed route). It's known by different names – collect, collective or service taxi in English, *servees* in Arabic, *sherut* in Hebrew, *dolmuş* in Turkish and just *tāksī* in Persian. Most shared taxis take up to four or five passengers, but some seat up to about 12 and are indistinguishable for most purposes from minibuses.

Shared taxis are much cheaper than private taxis and, once you get the hang of them, can be just as convenient. They are dearer than buses, but more frequent and usually faster, because they don't stop so often or for so long. They also tend to operate for longer hours than buses. They can be used for urban, intercity or rural transport, but not necessarily all three in a particular place.

Fixed-route taxis wait at the point of departure until full or nearly full. Usually they pick up or drop off passengers anywhere en route, but in some places they have fixed halts or stations. Sometimes each service is allocated a number, which may be indicated on the vehicle. Generally a flat fare applies for each route, but sometimes it's possible to pay a partial fare.

Shared taxis without routes are supreme examples of market forces at work. If the price is right you'll quickly find a taxi willing to take you almost anywhere, but if you're prepared to wait a while, or to do your journey in stages, you can get around for almost nothing. Fares depend largely on time and distance but can also vary slightly according to demand.

Beware of boarding an empty one, as the driver may assume you want to hire the vehicle for your exclusive use and charge you accordingly. It's advisable to watch what other passengers pay and to hand over your fare in front of them. Passengers are expected to know where they are getting off. 'Thank you' in the local language is the usual cue for the driver to stop. Make it clear to the driver or other passengers if you want to be told when you reach your destination.

CAR & MOTORCYCLE

The advantages of having your own vehicle are obvious. You aren't tied to schedules, you can choose your own company, set your own pace, take the scenic route, declare your vehicle a smoking or no-smoking zone and won't be at the mercy of dishonest taxi drivers or have to fight for a place on a bus. And you can avoid all the hassles that go with carrying your world on your back.

But for the vast majority of short-term visitors to the Middle East the advantages of being attached to one vehicle are far outweighed by the disadvantages. The main problem isn't the expense of obtaining a *carnet de passage* (see under Carnets later). It's not the often hair-raising driving found on Middle Eastern roads. Nor is it the variable quality of the roads themselves or the sheer distance between places of interest. Nor is it even the millstone-around-the-neck worry of serious accident, breakdown or theft.

The one overwhelming obstacle that puts all these difficulties into the shade is sim-

ply establishing a feasible route through the Middle East. This can be hard enough if you're relying on public transport, but at least there's nearly always the alternative of flying if a particular overland route proves too difficult or dangerous. This is hardly an option if you have a car with you, and air freighting even a motorcycle isn't cheap. Selling or dumping a temporarily imported vehicle in the Middle East is more or less ruled out by customs regulations. It's at least theoretically possible to have it put under customs seal in one country and to return for it later, but this is a hassle to arrange, requires backtracking and somewhat negates the point of bringing a vehicle in the first place. Car ferries can get around some of these problems but shipping a car isn't cheap, often requires an advance booking and won't help you out in every eventuality.

Overland access from Europe being restricted, it's hard to think of a route through the Middle East that would justify the expense and hassle of bringing a car and getting it out again. Even in the Gulf States, it would make more sense for short-term visitors to rent a car locally. For long-term residents it would probably be cheaper and more straightforward to buy one there and sell it before leaving.

Motorcycles are rare sights on most of the Arabian Peninsula; elsewhere in the region they are fairly popular as a means of racing around in urban areas, but little used as long-distance transport. They are particularly popular in Afghanistan, where two wheels are better than four at swerving around potholes, and few people can afford cars, anyway. Women motorcyclists are a rare breed throughout the region.

If you do decide to motorcycle through the Middle East, try to take one of the more popular Japanese models if you want to stand any chance of finding spare parts. Even then, make sure it's in very good shape before setting out. Motorcycles can be shipped or, often, loaded as luggage onto trains.

Even if you do work out a feasible route that justifies taking your own vehicle, you'll face mountains of paperwork and red tape before you leave home. The documents usually take a month or more to obtain, and just finding out the current regulations can be difficult. It's best to get in touch with your automobile association (eg the AA or RAC in the UK) at least three months in advance. Note that the following rules and conventions may not apply if you stay more than three months in any one country, or if you're going for any purpose other than tourism.

Carnets

A carnet de passage is a booklet that is stamped on arrival at and departure from a country to ensure that you export the vehicle again after you've imported it. It can be issued by a motoring organisation in the country where the vehicle is registered. The situation on carnets alters frequently, but many Middle Eastern countries require them.

The sting in the tail with a carnet is that you have to lodge a deposit to secure it. If you default on the carnet – that is, you don't have an export stamp to match the import one – then the country in question can claim your deposit, which can be up to 300% of the new value of the vehicle. You can get around this problem with bank guarantees or carnet insurance but you still have to fork out in the end if you default.

Should the worst occur and your vehicle is irretrievably damaged in an accident or catastrophic breakdown, you'll have to argue it out with customs officials. Having a vehicle stolen can be even worse, as you may be suspected of having sold it.

Other Documents

An International Driving Permit (IDP) is compulsory for foreign drivers and motorcyclists in Bahrain, Egypt, Iran, Iraq, Saudi Arabia, Syria and Yemen. Most foreign licences are acceptable in the other Gulf States, Israel, Lebanon and Turkey, and for foreign-registered vehicles in Jordan, but even in these places an IDP is recommended.

For the vehicle you'll need the registration documents. Check with your insurer whether you're covered for the countries you intend to visit and whether third party cover is included. You'll also need a green card, issued by insurers. Insurance for some countries is only obtainable at the border.

Breakdowns & Spare Parts

Mechanical failure can be a problem as spare parts – or at least official ones – are often unobtainable. Fear not: ingenuity often compensates for factory parts.

Generally Land Rovers, Volkswagens, Range Rovers, Mercedes and Chevrolets are the cars for which spare parts are most likely to be available, although in recent years Japan has been a particularly vigorous exporter of vehicles to the Middle East. In more anti-western countries, such as Iran, Syria and Iraq, spare parts for US vehicles may be very hard to find. One tip is to ask your vehicle manufacturer for a list of any authorised service centres it has in the countries you plan to visit. The length of this is likely to be a pretty good reflection of how easy it is to get spare parts on your travels.

Road Rules & Conditions

One of your enduring memories of the Middle East will undoubtedly be the driving standards. With the partial exception of Oman, the driving is appalling by western norms. Fatalism rules supreme. Many regulations are, in practice, purely cautionary. Car horns, used at the slightest provocation, take the place of caution and courtesy. At least theoretically, driving throughout the region is on the right, although many motorcyclists consider themselves exempt from this convention. You're unlikely even to know what the speed limit is on a particular road, let alone to be forced to keep to it. As a rule only non-Middle Easterners wear motorcycle helmets or car safety belts in most countries of the region.

The main roads are good or at least reasonable in most parts of the Middle East, but there are plenty of unsurfaced roads and the international roads are generally narrow and crowded.

Remember that an accident in the more remote parts of the region isn't always handled by your friendly insurance company. 'An eye for an eye' is likely to be the guiding principle of the other party and their relatives, whether you're in the wrong or not. Don't hang around to ask questions or gawp. Of course we're not saying that you shouldn't report an accident, but it may be more prudent to head for the nearest police station than to wait at the scene. Except in well-lit urban areas, try to avoid driving at night, as you may find your vehicle is the only thing on the road with lights.

A warning triangle is required for vehicles (except motorcycles) in most Middle Eastern countries; in Turkey two triangles and a first-aid kit are compulsory.

Petrol

Usually two grades are available; if in doubt get the more expensive one. Petrol stations are few and far between on many desert roads. Away from the main towns, it's advisable to fill up whenever you get the chance. Locally produced maps often indicate the locations of petrol stations. Diesel isn't readily available in every Middle Eastern country, nor is unleaded petrol.

Rental

In most large Middle Eastern cities it's fairly easy, if rarely cheap, to rent a vehicle. Some agencies can arrange vans, minibuses and buses for groups, but most deal only in cars; extremely few rent out motorcycles or bicycles. Before hiring a self-drive vehicle, ask yourself seriously how well you think you can cope with the local driving conditions and whether you know your way around well enough to make good use of one. Also compare the cost with that of hiring a taxi for the same period.

BICYCLE

While on the road researching this book we encountered maybe a half dozen touring cyclists, ranging from a bloke concentrating on exploring Sinai by bike to a young Welsh guy who was cycling through Turkey, Syria, Jordan, Saudi Arabia and Iran as part of a mammoth two year round

the world expedition. The ambitions of the rest of the cyclists fell somewhere in-between. It's clear then that although the numbers doing it are small, cycling round the Middle East is a viable proposition.

Most of the people we spoke to reckoned that the most enjoyable cycling was in Turkey and Syria (this is backed up by readers' letters). Although hilly, the scenery in Turkey is particularly fine and accommodation is fairly easy to come by even in the smallest villages. This is definitely not the case elsewhere and in Syria in particular you have to expect to spend the odd night in a tent. That said, cyclists in Syria frequently receive invitations from people along the way to come home, meet the family, eat and stay over. In Turkey if you get tired of pedalling it's also no problem to have your bike transported in the luggage hold of the big modern buses they have there. A couple writing in the guestbook at the Al-Haramein Hotel in Damascus (a good source of cycling information) reported that their tandem was accommodated without them having to remove the panniers. And there's no charge for this.

By far the major difficulty cited by all cyclists was the heat. This is at its worst from June to August and cycling in these summer months is definitely not recommended. May to mid-June and September through October are the best times for two-wheel touring of this region. Even then, most cyclists found it necessary to make an early morning start and have done with most of the pedalling by early afternoon. Although one or two of the cyclists had been a little worried beforehand at the thought of being stuck for spares on the road, there are bicycle repair shops in most major towns and the locals are excellent 'bush mechanics'.

The positive aspects are that cyclists are given fantastic welcomes – a trademark of the Middle East – showered with food and drink, and, as mentioned above, sometimes offered free accommodation. Even the police are helpful and friendly. There are a couple of exceptions – along Jordan's King's Highway persistent children block the road demanding gifts, and in Sinai kids throw stones at cyclists (maybe because of the cycling shorts, we don't know) – but these are minor blips of annoyance.

Practicalities

Carry a couple of extra chain links, a chain breaker, spokes, a spoke key, two inner tubes, tyre levers and a repair kit, a flat-head and phillips screwdriver, and Allen keys and spanners to fit all the bolts on your bike. Check the bolts daily and carry spares. Fit as many water bottles to your bike as you can – it gets hot. Make sure the bike's gearing will get you over the hills, and confine your panniers to 15kg maximum. In your panniers include a two person tent (weighing about 1.8kg) that can also accommodate the bike where security is a concern; a sleeping bag rated to 0°C and a Therm-a-Rest; small camping stove with gas canisters; cooking pot; utensils; Katadyn water filter (two microns) and Maglite. Wear cycling shorts with chamois bum and cleated cycling shoes. Don't fill the panniers with food as it is plentiful and fresh along the route.

Contacts

If you are considering cycling the Middle East but have a few pressing questions that first need answering, one place to go is the Thorn Tree on Lonely Planet's Web site (www.lonelyplanet.com). Post your query on the Activities branch and there's a strong likelihood somebody will respond with the information that you're looking for.

Alternatively, you could contact the CTC (Cyclists' Touring Club) (☎ 01483-417 217, fax 426 994, email cycling@ctc.org.uk), a UK-based organisation which, among other things, produces information sheets on cycling in different parts of the world and has a useful Web site (www.ctc.org.uk). Last time we checked there was definitely a dossier on Egypt and by now there may also be sheets on other Middle Eastern countries. The club also publishes a good glossy, bi-monthly magazine that always carries one or two travel-type cycling pieces.

HITCHING

Although many travellers hitchhike, it is not a totally safe way of getting around. There is no part of the Middle East where hitching can be recommended for unaccompanied women. Just because we explain how hitching works doesn't mean we recommend it.

Hitching as commonly understood in the west hardly exists in the Middle East (except Israel). Although in most countries you'll often see people standing by the road hoping for a lift, they will nearly always expect (and be expected) to offer to pay. Hitching in the Middle Eastern sense is not so much an alternative to the public transport system as an extension of it. The going rate is usually roughly the equivalent of the bus or shared taxi fare, but may be more if a driver takes you to an address or place off their route. You may well be offered free lifts from time to time, but you won't get very far if you set out deliberately to avoid paying for transport.

Hitching is not illegal in any Middle Eastern country and in many places it is extremely common. However, while it's quite normal for Middle Easterners, Asians and Africans, it isn't something westerners are expected to do. In many Middle Eastern countries, westerners who try to set a precedent of any kind often attract considerable attention. While this can work to your advantage, it can also lead to suspicion from the local police.

Throughout the Middle East a raised thumb is a vaguely obscene gesture. A common way of signalling that you want a lift is to extend your right hand, palm down.

BOAT

Practicality is the essence of Middle East ferry services, not luxury. Even in 1st class you shouldn't expect your voyage to be a pleasure cruise, while deck class often means just that. In summer, conditions may be a little too hot for many people. While food and drink of some sort may be available on board, many passengers prefer to take their own. Vehicles can be shipped on all the following services, but advance arrangements may have to be made.

For the latest information, get in touch with the head office or local agent of the respective company some time in advance.

Red Sea

The Amman-based Arab Bridge Maritime Company sails at least once daily between Nuweiba in Sinai and Aqaba. The journey takes three hours or so. There is also a catamaran plying the same route which does the journey in one hour. See the Egypt and Jordan chapters for more details.

The Alexandria-based Misr Edco Shipping Company and four Saudi companies sail between Jeddah and Suez. The journey takes about 36 hours direct, about 72 via Aqaba. Buy tickets and check timetables and routes directly from the shipping company or its agent rather than through a travel agency if you don't want to be given misleading information (see the Shipping Line Addresses list in the Sea & River section of the regional Getting There & Away chap-

ter). Misr Edco sails about twice weekly between Port Safaga (Egypt) and Jeddah.

Persian Gulf & Sea of Oman

If you want to visit the Gulf States but don't want to fly and can't get into Saudi Arabia, you can always sail. The shortest sailing, across the Strait of Hormuz between Bandar-é Abbās and Sharjah, takes about 12 hours. Fares start at around US$50 in 3rd (deck) class. Other less frequent services link Būshehr and Bahrain, Būshehr and Kuwait, Bandar-é Abbās and Muscat, Bandar-é Abbās and Doha and Chābahār and Muscat. These only have 1st-class (cabin) accommodation but are much cheaper than the equivalent airfare. Most are overnight journeys. All these ships are operated by Valfajre-8 Shipping Company, owned by Islamic Republic of Iran Shipping Lines (IRISL; see the Getting Around section of the Iran chapter). Outside the region tickets can be obtained through IRISL in London.

Bahrain

The only island-state in the Arab world, this tiny country (about the size of Singapore, but with a fraction of its population) is unique in several ways, not least because Arabs and foreign expatriates mix more easily here than anywhere else in the region. Bahrain is the easiest of the Gulf states to visit, and is good value for those on a budget. It's a good introduction to the Gulf, though anyone visiting an Arab country for the first time should still be prepared for a little culture shock. While Bahrain is one of the most liberal countries in the Gulf, it is still, by western standards, a very conservative place.

Facts about Bahrain

HISTORY

A general history of the Middle East can be found in the Facts about the Region chapter.

Bahrain occupies a strategic position on the great trade routes of antiquity, with good harbours and abundant fresh water, and its people have always been natural merchants. As far back as the 3rd millennium BC this island was the seat of Dilmun, one of the great trading empires of the ancient world.

From 2200 to 1600 BC Dilmun controlled a large section of the western shore of the Gulf. At times its power probably extended as far north as modern Kuwait and as far inland as the Al-Hasa oasis in eastern Saudi Arabia. Between 1600 and 1000 BC, Dilmun fell into decline and by about 600 BC it had been fully absorbed by Babylon.

From the 9th to the 11th century AD Bahrain was part of the Umayyad and, later, Abbasid empires. It was once again on the trade routes between Mesopotamia and the Indian subcontinent, and as one of the Gulf's main pearling ports clearly had economic value.

It was not until the mid-18th century that the Al-Khalifa, the family that now rules Bahrain, first arrived in the area. They ini-

The State of Bahrain

Area: 692 sq km
Population: approx 620,000
Population Growth Rate: 3.8%
Capital: Manama
Head of State: The Emir, Hamad bin Isa al-Khalifa
Official Language: Arabic
Currency: Bahraini dinar (BD)
Exchange Rate: BD0.377 = US$1

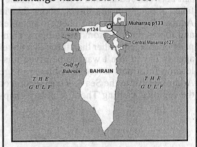

- **Best Nightlife** – the sunsets from anywhere along the King Fahd Causeway or from Al-Budayyi' are superb
- **Best Walk** – the Marina Corniche is the centre for activities such as horse riding and water sports, and is particularly pleasant during the late afternoon
- **Best View** – the tower near the Saudi Arabia border offers superb views of Bahrain and Saudi, and the sea in between
- **When in Rome ...** shopping in the souq, rather than the modern shopping centres, is always fun

tially settled in Zubara, on the north-western edge of the Qatar peninsula, and involved themselves in the region's lucrative pearling trade. They drove the Persians out of Bahrain in about 1782. Three years later, however, the Al-Khalifa were driven out by an Omani invasion and they did not return until 1820.

Bahrain was the first place on the Arabian side of the Gulf where oil was discovered (see the boxed text 'Oil & the Gulf' later in this chapter). The discovery of oil couldn't have come at a better time for Bahrain as it roughly coincided with the collapse of the world pearl market. Until that time pearling had been the mainstay of Bahrain's economy.

Bahrain's drive for modernisation began under Sheikh Hamad bin Ali and grew under his son, Sheikh Sulman, who came to power when Sheikh Hamad died in 1942. Sulman's 19 years on the throne saw an increase in the country's standard of living as oil production boomed in Saudi Arabia, Kuwait and Qatar.

Sheikh Sulman died in 1961 and was succeeded by his son, Sheikh Isa bin Sulman al-Khalifa. He reigned until his death on 6 March 1999, and was replaced by his son, Sheikh Hamad bin Isa al-Khalifa. Bahrain became independent on 14 August 1971. The emir issued a constitution in May 1973, and an elected National assembly convened that December. The Assembly, however, was dissolved only 20 months later when the emir decided that radical assembly members made it impossible for the executive branch to function.

During the 1970s and 80s, Bahrain experienced a huge degree of growth, partly from the skyrocketing price of oil, but also because in the 70s it was well ahead of most of the Gulf in terms of infrastructure. In recent years, Bahrain's status as an entrepôt has declined but its economy has become more diversified and less dependent on oil.

Bahrain Today

During the last decade Bahrain has been rocked by sporadic waves of unrest. The troubles began in 1994 when there were riots after the emir refused to accept a large petition calling for greater democracy. There was more unrest in April 1995, and again in the spring of 1996, when bombs

---

What to See

In Manama, the highlight is undoubtedly the comprehensive **Bahrain National Museum**. The **Beit al-Quran** is interesting, and a good general introduction to Islam. The **souq** is extensive and appealing, although not as memorable as souqs in other cities in the region.

Outside the capital, the burial mounds at **A'ali** are eerie and unexcavated and anyone interested in archaeology should explore the ruins at **Qala'at al-Bahrain** and the temples at **Ad-Diraz** and **Barbar**. The **Riffa Fort** and **Qala'at Arad** are nicely restored, as is the **Beit Sheikh Isa bin Ali** house, which provides a glimpse of Bahrain's elite before the advent of oil. Traditional handicrafts can be bought at workshops in the villages of **Karbabad** and **Al-Jasra**, as well as at the **Craft Centre** in Manama.

---

exploded at both the Diplomat and Meridien hotels. And in 1997, a series of arson attacks were perpetrated by unemployed local Bahrainis, angry that jobs were being taken by workers from Asia.

GEOGRAPHY

Bahrain (692 sq km) is a low-lying archipelago of about 33 islands, including the disputed Hawar Islands (also claimed by Qatar), and a few specks of sand that disappear at high tide. Bahrain Island (about 586 sq km) is the largest of the archipelago. The population is heavily concentrated in the northern third of Bahrain Island, and in the southern edge of Muharraq Island.

CLIMATE

Bahrain can get extremely hot and humid from June to September. From November to March is quite pleasant with warm days and cool nights, and temperatures that vary between a minimum of 14°C and a maximum of 24°C. The average temperature in winter (December to February) is 18°C with

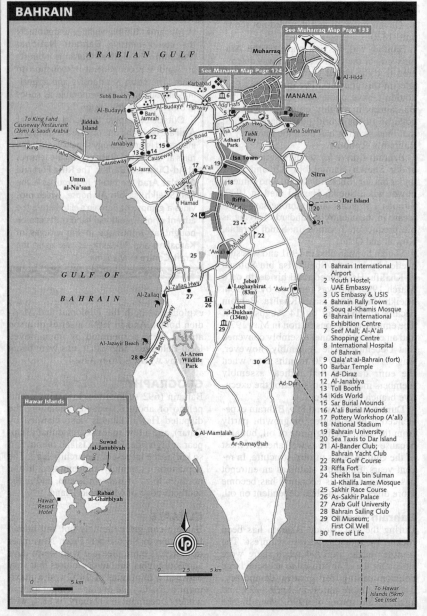

BAHRAIN

ARABIAN GULF

See Muharraq Map Page 133

Muharraq

Al-Hidd

See Manama Map Page 124

MANAMA

Karbabad
Subh Beach
Al-Budayyi
Bani
Jamrah
Al-Budayyi Highway
Jidd Hafs

Juffair

Mina Sulman

To King Fahd
Causeway Restaurant
(2km) & Saudi Arabia

Jiddah
Island

Al-
Janabiya

Sar

King Fahd Causeway

Al-Jasra

Umm
al-Na'san

Isa Sulman Hwy
Tubli
Bay
Adhari
Park

Isa Town

A'ali

Riffa

Hamad

Riffa Ave

Sitra

Dar Island

GULF OF
BAHRAIN

Al-Zallaq

Al-Zallaq Hwy

'Awali

Muaskar Hwy

Jebel
Lughaybirat
(83m)

'Askar

Al-Jazayir Beach

Zallaq Beach Highway

Al-Areen
Wildlife
Park

Jebel
ad-Dukhan
(134m)

Ad-Dur

Al-Mamtalah

Ar-Rumaythah

Hawar Islands

Suwad
al-Janubiyah

Rabad
al-Gharbiyah

Hawar
Resort
Hotel

0   5 km

0   2.5   5 km

To Hawar
Islands (5km)
See Inset

1 Bahrain International
   Airport
2 Youth Hostel;
   UAE Embassy
3 US Embassy & USIS
4 Bahrain Rally Town
5 Souq al-Khamis Mosque
6 Bahrain International
   Exhibition Centre
7 Seef Mall; Al-A'ali
   Shopping Centre
8 International Hospital
   of Bahrain
9 Qala'at al-Bahrain (fort)
10 Barbar Temple
11 Ad-Diraz
12 Al-Janabiya
13 Toll Booth
14 Kids World
15 Sar Burial Mounds
16 A'ali Burial Mounds
17 Pottery Workshop (A'ali)
18 National Stadium
19 Bahrain University
20 Sea Taxis to Dar Island
21 Al-Bander Club;
   Bahrain Yacht Club
22 Riffa Golf Course
23 Riffa Fort
24 Sheikh Isa bin Sulman
   al-Khalifa Jame Mosque
25 Sakhir Race Course
26 As-Sakhir Palace
27 Arab Gulf University
28 Bahrain Sailing Club
29 Oil Museum;
   First Oil Well
30 Tree of Life

77% humidity, and in summer (June to August) temperatures average 35°C with 59% humidity. In summer, dust storms and hot winds may often help to make life even more uncomfortable.

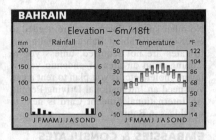

GOVERNMENT & POLITICS
Bahrain is an absolute monarchy through the emir, Sheikh Hamad bin Isa al-Khalifa. He replaced his father Sheikh Isa bin Sulman al-Khalifa, who died in early 1999. Sheikh Khalifa bin Sulman al-Khalifa is the prime minister, and Sheikh Sulman bin Hamad al-Khalifa is the crown prince. Bahrain is the only Gulf state to adopt a strict rule of primogeniture within the royal family. The royal family certainly has its opponents, but they're generally tolerated (and even liked) by the people of Bahrain.

POPULATION & PEOPLE
About 620,000 people live in Bahrain, of which about half are under 25 years old. Nearly 40% of residents (and 60% of the workforce) are non-Bahrainis or expatriates. Manama is probably the most cosmopolitan city in the Gulf, populated by more western businesspeople, Filipino shopworkers and Pakistani and Indian shop owners than Bahrainis. Bahrainis are Arabs, though many are at least partially of Persian ancestry.

RELIGION
The state religion of Islam is followed by about 85% of the population, of which about 70% are Shi'ite. The Sunni minority includes the royal family. (For an explanation of

Sunni and Shi'ite sects see the Religion section in the Facts about the Region chapter.)

LANGUAGE
Arabic is the official language but English is also widely spoken among the cosmopolitan population. See the Language chapter at the end of this book for details.

Facts for the Visitor

PLANNING
The best time to visit Bahrain is between November and February, when it's not too hot. Avoid visiting during Ramadan, when things slow down significantly, and during Muslim festivals when merrymakers (both Arab and foreign) from Saudi Arabia and Kuwait visit and hotel rooms become difficult to find.

VISAS & DOCUMENTS
Visas
Most nationalities need a visa, which can be obtained at the border with Saudi Arabia or at Bahrain's international airport. Visas are generally valid for up to two weeks but extensions are possible (see later). A two week visa on arrival costs BD5 for Australians, New Zealanders, Europeans and Canadians. UK citizens are charged nothing for a one month visa, while US citizens are charged BD10/15 for a visa for three days/one week. There is a foreign exchange office next to the immigration counter at the airport and at the border with Saudi Arabia.

US residents and Canadians can obtain a five-year multiple-entry visa at a Bahrain embassy/consulate for about US$40. Most other nationalities can get an (extendable) visa from a Bahrain embassy or consulate for about US$25/40 for three/seven days – but it's easier to get a visa on arrival. If you're transiting Bahrain, and travelling on to Saudi Arabia by land (and can prove it), the visa fee on arrival for all nationalities is BD2.

If you have an Israeli stamp in your passport or any other evidence of a visit to Israel, you will be denied entry to Bahrain.

Visa Extensions Visa extensions are available in Manama at the General Directorate of Immigration & Passports (☎ 535 111). You must firstly find a sponsor – a Bahraini friend, or your hotel will oblige. Then fill out a form, and provide the directorate with your passport and one passport-size photo. Extensions cost BD15 for one week and BD25 for more than one week and up to one month; they will take up to a week to process.

To avoid this, your hotel (if you're staying at a good one) can sponsor your extension and deal with the directorate for a fee of about BD5. Foreigners overstaying their visas are fined about BD30 per week.

Visas for Neighbouring Countries You need a visa to enter the following neighbouring countries of Bahrain:

Iran Only tourist visas are available for Iran, not transit visas. The application requires one passport-sized photo, photocopies of the information pages of your passport and, crucially, a letter of sponsorship from someone in Iran. The application is sent to Tehrān and can take two to three weeks to process. The cost is BD19.

Kuwait Only residents of Bahrain can obtain a visa in Bahrain for Kuwait.

Oman Getting an Omani visa is fairly straightforward. You will need one passport-size photo and the application form must be typed. It takes two to four days to process and costs BD7.

Qatar There is no Qatari embassy in Bahrain.

Saudi Arabia Only residents of Bahrain can obtain a visa in Bahrain for Saudi Arabia.

United Arab Emirates Only residents of Bahrain can obtain a visa in Bahrain for the United Arab Emirates (UAE), and hotels have to be pre-booked before you apply.

Yemen You will need two passport-size photos, a copy of your passport, and a letter from your place of business in Bahrain (whether travelling on business or not) or from the travel agency arranging your tickets. A one week visa will cost you BD25 and can be issued on the same day if you go to the embassy.

Other Documents

No other special documents are needed to enter or move about Bahrain. Health certificates are not required, unless you're coming from an area of endemic yellow fever, cholera etc. If you plan to rent a car, you need an International Driving Permit. An International Student Card is next to worthless in Bahrain.

EMBASSIES & CONSULATES
Bahraini Embassies & Consulates

Diplomatic representation abroad includes:

Canada
    Consulate:
    (☎ 450-931 7444, fax 931 5988)
    Rene, Levesque West Montreal, Quebec H3H
    IR4
France
    Embassy:
    (☎ 01 47 23 48 68, fax 01 47 20 55 75)
    Bis, Place Des Stats UNIS 75116 Paris
Germany
    Embassy:
    (☎ 228-957 6100 fax 957 6190)
    Plittersdorfet Str 91 53173 Bonn
UK
    Embassy:
    (☎ 020-7370 5132, fax 7370 7773)
    98 Gloucester Rd, London SW74 AU
USA
    Embassy:
    (☎ 202-342 0741, fax: 362 2192)
    3502 International Drive, NW Washington DC
    20008

Embassies & Consulates in Bahrain

The nearest embassies representing Australia, Canada and Ireland are in Riyadh, Saudi Arabia. Most of the embassies are in the 'diplomatic area' in Manama, between King Faisal Hwy and Sheikh Hamad Causeway. Opening hours are generally from around 8 or 8.30 am to somewhere between noon and 2 pm. The Saudi embassy is only open from 9 to 11 am. All embassies and consulates are closed on Thursday and Friday.

France
Embassy:
(☎ 291 734, fax 293 655)
Al-Fatih Hwy
Germany
Embassy:
(☎ 530 210, fax 536 282)
Al-Hassaa Bldg, Sheikh Hamad Causeway
Kuwait
Embassy:
(☎ 534 040, fax 533 579)
King Faisal Hwy
Netherlands (handles all Benelux countries)
Consulate:
(☎ 713 162, fax 212 295)
ABN Bldg
Oman
Embassy:
(☎ 293 663, fax 293 540)
Al-Fatih Hwy
Saudi Arabia
Embassy:
(☎ 537 722, fax 533 261)
King Faisal Hwy
UAE
Embassy:
(☎ 723 737, fax 727 343)
Juffair
UK
Embassy:
(☎ 534 404, fax 536 109)
Government Ave
USA
Embassy:
(☎ 273 300, fax 272 594)
Just off Sheikh Isa bin Sulman Hwy,
Al-Zinj

CUSTOMS

Foreigners (but only non-Muslims) can import duty free 1L of wine or spirits, or six cans of beer. All passengers are allowed to bring in 200 cigarettes or 50 cigars, and 250g of loose tobacco; and eight ounces (227ml) of perfume.

Visitors fill out a disembarkation card on arrival, which you must keep and return to the immigration authorities on departure.

MONEY
Costs

If you stay in budget hotels, walk a lot, don't drink alcohol and eat in cheap restaurants, it's possible to get by on BD10/8 per person per day travelling as a single/double, but BD12/10 is more realistic.

See the Accommodation and Getting Around sections later in this chapter for more information on costs.

Currency

The Bahraini dinar (BD) is divided into 1000 fils. Notes come in denominations of 500 fils, and BD1, 5, 10 and 20. Coins are 5, 10, 25, 50 and 100 fils. The Bahraini dinar is a convertible currency and there are no restrictions on its import or export. You may be offered some Saudi riyals as change, at the rate of BD1 = 10SR, but unless you're going to Saudi, insist on change in Bahraini currency.

Exchange Rates

The dinar is pegged to the US dollar and rarely fluctuates.

country	unit		dinar
Australia	A$1	=	BD0.241
Canada	C$1	=	BD0.253
euro	€1	=	BD0.431
France	10FF	=	BD0.670
Germany	DM1	=	BD0.221
Japan	¥100	=	BD0.333
New Zealand	NZ$1	=	BD0.208
UK	UK£1	=	BD0.627
USA	US$1	=	BD0.377

Exchanging Money

Money (travellers cheques and cash) can be changed at banks or moneychangers. There's little to choose between the two in terms of exchange rates (as little as BD0.01 per US dollar usually), and neither place usually charges commission – although it's always wise to check first. The main difference is that banking hours are restricted to Saturday to Wednesday from 7.30 am to noon and until 11 am on Thursday, whereas moneychangers keep longer hours.

Currencies for other Gulf states are easy to buy and sell at banks and moneychangers.

Credit Cards & ATMs

Credit cards are widely accepted throughout Bahrain and if you have your PIN number it's also very easy to obtain money from ATMs. Most branches of the British Bank of the Middle East have ATMs that accept Visa, Cirrus and MasterCard cards, while the Bank of Bahrain & Kuwait (BBK) has ATMs that take Visa, MasterCard, Cirrus, Maestro and American Express (Amex) cards.

Tipping

A service charge is added to some bills in Bahrain but it generally goes to the shop, not the staff. An appropriate tip for good service would be around 10%.

POST & COMMUNICATIONS
Postal Rates

Postcards cost 155/205 fils to Europe/North America and Australasia. Letters cost 205/255 fils per 10g. Parcels cost a standard minimum of BD3 for the first 500g to all western countries, and BD1/1.500 for every extra 500g.

Sending Mail

Mail to and from Europe and North America takes about one week – allow 10 days to and from Australia. The main post office (GPO) is in Manama, and there are smaller post offices in major residential areas around the country, and at the airport. Most major international express mail and package companies have offices in Manama.

Telephone

The country code for Bahrain is 973, followed by the local number. There are no area or city codes.

Bahrain's excellent telecommunications system is run by the government monopoly, Bahrain Telecommunications Company (BATELCO). Virtually every country can be dialled direct from most payphones, and some specially marked booths also accept Visa and MasterCard. International calls

from Bahrain cost BD0.510 per minute to most western countries, including Europe, Australia and North America. Rates are reduced to BD0.390 between 7 pm and 7 am every day, as well as all day Friday and on public holidays. There are several help lines with English-speaking operators including local directory assistance (☎ 181); international directory assistance (☎ 191); and the international call operator (☎ 151).

Bahrain is linked to over 100 countries through the Home Country Direct Dial service. Refer to the front of the (English-language) Bahrain telephone book for details, or ring the special inquiries number (☎ 100).

Local calls anywhere within Bahrain cost 100 fils for six minutes. Blue payphones take coins and require a minimum of 100 fils. Red payphones take phonecards, which are widely available in denominations of one, two, 3.5, 6.5 and 15 dinars.

Fax

Fax services are available at most mid-range and top end hotels, and at the BATELCO building in Manama.

Email & Internet Access

The only Internet service provider is BATELCO. There is an Internet centre in Manama (see the Manama section later in this chapter for more details).

BOOKS
Lonely Planet

Lonely Planet publishes several detailed guides to various countries in the Middle East. For information on titles, see Books in the Regional Facts for the Visitor chapter.

Guidebooks

Anyone living and working in Bahrain should pick up the detailed but dated *Bahrain: A MEED Practical Guide*; the most interesting *Bahrain Island Heritage* by Shirley Kay; or *Resident in Bahrain*, by Parween Abdul Rahman & Charles Walsham, which is particularly useful for businesspeople. More generally, *Bahrain: A Heritage Explored*, by Angela Clark, is the best all-round guide to the country's architecture, archaeology and traditions.

History & Archaeology
Possibly the best book on Bahrain is *Looking for Dilmun* by Geoffrey Bibby. The book provides a fascinating picture of life in Bahrain in the 1950s and 60s.

Archaeology and history buffs might also be interested in *Bahrain Through the Ages: The Archaeology* and *Bahrain Through the Ages: The History* by Sheikh Haya Ali al-Khalifa & Michael Rice. Both are available in Bahrain, but are bulky and expensive at about BD22.

More general Middle East titles, some of which contain coverage of Bahrain, are listed in the Books section in the Regional Facts for the Visitor chapter at the beginning of this book.

NEWSPAPERS & MAGAZINES
The *Gulf Daily News* and the less interesting broadsheet, the *Bahrain Tribune*, are both English-language dailies with good international news and sports coverage. They both cost 200 fils. The former contains a good classifieds section and a very useful 'What's On' column. The monthly *Bahrain This Month* magazine (BD1) is also an excellent information source for entertainment, sports and local events. Also worth picking up is the annual *Visitor's Complete Guide to Bahrain* (BD1.500), and the pocket-sized, and free, bi-monthly *What's On in Bahrain*.

RADIO & TV
Radio Bahrain broadcasts in English 24 hours a day on several FM and MW frequencies, the main one being 96.5 FM. FM and MW radio stations established for US forces based in the Gulf are also easy to pick up, as are Voice of America, the BBC World Service, and other European services on short wave.

Bahrain Television broadcasts Channel 55 in English (from late afternoon), and the BBC World Service is shown in English on Channel 57. Most satellite programs, such as CNN and MTV, are available in top end hotels. All radio and television programs are listed in the two English-language dailies, and in *Bahrain This Month*.

PHOTOGRAPHY & VIDEO
Plenty of shops in Manama, and elsewhere around Bahrain, sell popular brands of print and slide film, and video cassettes. A roll of 24/36 colour print film costs about BD1/1.200. Colour print film can be developed in many places, often in less than 30 minutes, for 500 fils for developing, plus 100 fils per print. Slide developing is more expensive and can take up to two days. Many photo shops around central Manama can also take passport photos for about BD2 (for four).

LAUNDRY
The best way to get your clothes cleaned is through your hotel, or at one of the numerous small laundries around central Manama. A small Indian or Pakistani-run laundry charges about 200 fils for a shirt, skirt or trousers.

HEALTH
Bahrain has a highly developed health-care system, and while treatment is not free, by western standards it is moderately priced. If you're staying in a mid-range or top end hotel, it should have a doctor on call to deal with minor ailments. A list of good hospitals is included in the Manama section later in this chapter. There are plenty of well-stocked pharmacies in all residential areas and the English-language dailies list those that are open 24 hours.

For more detailed health information, refer to the Health chapter.

DANGERS & ANNOYANCES
A series of bomb blasts and arson attacks in 1996 and 1997 led to heightened security throughout Bahrain, and a severe government crack-down on dissent. Sporadic anti-government violence remains a problem but nothing worth mentioning has happened since 1997. There is no evidence that tourists have ever been targeted and Bahrain remains safe to visit.

BUSINESS HOURS

Shops and offices are generally open Saturday to Wednesday from around 7 am to 2 pm. Many shops, particularly in the souqs, reopen from about 4 to 8 pm.

PUBLIC HOLIDAYS & SPECIAL EVENTS

In addition to the main Islamic holidays described in Public Holidays & Special Events in the Regional Facts for the Visitor chapter, Bahrain observes:

New Year's Day
  1 January
Ashura
  10th day of *Muharram* (changeable) – Ashura marks the death of Hussein, grandson of the Prophet. Processions led by men flagellating themselves take place in many of the country's predominantly Shi'ite areas.

ACCOMMODATION

Bahrain's only youth hostel is in the suburb of Juffair, south-east of central Manama (see the Manama section later for details). Good cheap hotel rooms with air-con, private bath (with hot water) and TV (not satellite) cost from BD7/10 for singles/doubles. Bahrain has a glut of four and five-star hotels, which can mean some bargains if you look out for ads in the English-language dailies, and ask at hotel reception desks.

FOOD

Refer to the special section 'Middle Eastern Cuisine' in the Facts about the Region chapter for a rundown on regional food and drinks.

There is no such thing as typical 'Bahraini cuisine'. In fact, restaurants serving any kind of Arabic food are scarce. Most cheap restaurants are owned by, and cater to, Asian workers. Many of these tiny Indian and Pakistani places have an extremely limited menu, often consisting of biryanis and samosas and little else. But the food is always cheap and filling. Chinese and Filipino food is a bit more expensive and tends to be better quality.

There are plenty of western fast food outlets in the major shopping centres and around the main streets of Manama. The service may be quick, but the food isn't cheap.

Anyone staying a while should pick up the *Bahrain Restaurant Guide* (BD1). This excellent pocket-sized booklet highlights the best of the 2000 or so restaurants throughout the country and is updated every year.

DRINKS

Nonalcoholic drinks consist of soft drinks, delicious fruit juice, and milk shakes. Alcohol is expensive – a can of beer starts from 900 fils, and spirits from BD1.200. Any place called a 'coffeeshop' in all but the top end hotels is a bar, often dark, dingy and uninviting.

SPECTATOR SPORTS

Soccer (football) is the major sport played in Bahrain. Games are held at the immense National Stadium, and at smaller grounds in the residential areas of Muharraq, Riffa and Isa Town. Also popular among locals are volleyball, badminton, basketball, cricket and handball.

The Equestrian & Horse Racing Club holds races every Friday, between October and March, at the Sakhir Race Course near 'Awali. The Bahrain Motor Club organises popular motor racing and go-kart rallies, and in the Riffa Valley, the 18 hole Riffa Golf Course has been carved out of the desert.

SHOPPING

Bahrain's specialities – pearls and gold – are good value, but shoppers should know something about quality and price before spending too much. Locally produced items include pottery from A'ali, woven baskets from Karbabad, hand-woven cloth from Bani Jamrah and textiles from Al-Jasra. For more information, refer to the relevant sections in the Around Bahrain Island section later. If you're not heading to Iran, Bahrain is also one of the best places in the Gulf to look for Persian carpets.

Getting There & Away

Refer to the Getting There & Away chapter at the beginning of this book for information about international travel to and from Bahrain and the region in general.

AIR
Airports & Airlines
Bahrain is a part-owner of Gulf Air, which regularly flies between Bahrain and London, Frankfurt, Amsterdam, Rome and Paris. Gulf Air also flies frequently to major cities on the sub-continent, and three times a week to Melbourne/Sydney in Australia. Other regional airlines, such as Saudia and Royal Jordanian, also fly to and from Bahrain, and have connections to Europe and North America. There are rarely any special deals or cheap periods for flights to Bahrain, but *from* Bahrain there are occasional special deals to Europe, and more often to places in the Middle East, eg the UAE and Oman. Check the windows of the travel agents in the souq for the latest offers.

Departure Tax
The departure tax is BD3. You can pay this at the airport, or sometimes at the travel agency or airline office if you buy your ticket in Bahrain.

LAND
The only land border is with Saudi Arabia, across the incredible King Fahd Causeway (see the Around Bahrain Island section later in this chapter for details). Bahrain is, therefore, often used as a transit point for international travel to/from eastern Saudi.

Most tourists won't have a car, or be allowed to drive between Saudi and Bahrain in a rental car, nor have a Saudi visa long enough to enjoy a leisurely drive to/from Bahrain, so this border is normally only crossed by foreigners using the Saudi-Bahrain bus service (see the following section). From Bahrain, it is possible to charter a taxi to the border, cross the border on foot, and then hitch a ride into Saudi.

Bus
Saudi Bahraini Transport Co (SABTCO) (☎ 263 244, fax 244 297) runs a bus service between Manama and Alkhobar and Dammam in Saudi Arabia. Buses leave six times a day every day, between 8 am and 8.30 pm, and cost BD4 one way. From Dammam, there are regular connections to Riyadh (Saudi) and Doha (Qatar).

From Manama, SABTCO also has daily buses as far as Amman (Jordan) for BD25; Damascus (Syria), BD25; Abu Dhabi, Dubai and Sharjah (UAE), all for about BD17; and Kuwait, BD14. All departures are from the international bus station in Manama, where the SABTCO office is located.

Private Vehicle
To get on the causeway to Saudi Arabia, all drivers (and passengers in taxis) must pay a toll of BD2, regardless of whether they're travelling to Saudi or just as far as the border. The toll booth is on the western side of the intersection between the appropriately named Causeway Approach Rd and Janabiyah Hwy.

Anyone crossing the border from Bahrain to Saudi will be given a customs form to complete, and drivers entering Bahrain from Saudi must purchase temporary Bahraini insurance and sign a personal guarantee.

SEA
There is currently no passenger ferry service between Bahrain and any other country in the region.

Getting Around

BUS
Bahrain has a good public bus system linking most of the major towns and residential areas. The fare is 50 fils per trip. Buses run about every 40 minutes between 6 am and 9 pm. Manama's main bus terminal is on

Government Ave, and there are user-friendly bus terminals in Isa Town, Muharraq and Riffa. A few private buses and minibuses are starting to ply the main routes and cost about 100 fils per trip.

LONG-DISTANCE TAXI

Taxis in Bahrain have meters, but foreigners have to be very persistent before drivers will use them. The flag fall is 800 fils, which will take you 1.5km. Thereafter the meter ticks over in 100 fils increments every 1km. Fares officially increase by 50% between 10 pm and about 6 am. Taxis will often negotiate rates for long-term hire, but using the meter will normally be cheaper. However, if you're visiting more than one tourist attraction a fair distance from town, it's probably cheaper to rent a car than charter a taxi at the metered rate.

Small trucks, and other vehicles with a yellow circle painted on the door, are unmetered taxis. Expect to pay around BD1 for most trips inside Manama, but save yourself grief by sticking to metered taxis.

CAR & MOTORCYCLE

If you're driving around Bahrain, buy a good road map (not usually provided in rental cars, but available in bookshops in Manama). Some roads farther south of the Tree of Life are off limits.

Speed limits and the wearing of seat belts are rigorously enforced in Bahrain, and drink driving laws are also strict. Driving is on the right-hand side. Speed limits are 60km/h in towns; 80km/h in outer limits of suburbs; and 100km/h on highways. Petrol costs 80 fils per litre for lower grade and 100 fils for premium. Petrol stations are well-signposted and common, especially along the highways.

Rental

Major international car rental companies, such as Hertz (☎ 321 287), Europcar (☎ 692 999), Budget (☎ 534 100) and Avis (☎ 531 144), have offices at the airport and in Manama. These companies charge from BD10/60 for one day/week for the smallest four-door

sedan. A few local companies, such as Oscar Rent-a-Car (☎ 291 591), charge a dinar or so less per day, but are not as reliable.

Rates exclude petrol but include unlimited mileage and insurance. To avoid the excess of BD200 to BD300 in the case of an accident, it's probably wise to pay the extra BD2 waiver per day. Rates are for a minimum of 24 hours. Companies normally only accept drivers over 21 years old (over 25 for more expensive models), and foreigners must have an International Driving Permit. There is nowhere to rent a motorcycle.

ORGANISED TOURS

One of the best of the few tour agencies in Bahrain is the government-run Gulf Tours (☎ 294 446, fax 291 947). It runs *dhow* (an Arab sailing vessel) cruises for BD3/6 for a half/full day; trips to Dar Island (see under Other Islands later in this chapter) for BD12; and half-day sightseeing tours around Manama for BD7. However, if you're travelling in a group of two or more it's cheaper to hire a car (see Car & Motorcycle earlier in this chapter).

Manama

Manama is the very new capital of a very old place – many of the hotels and official buildings along Government Ave sit on reclaimed land. But don't be fooled – only a few blocks inland from the shiny new hotels are sections of the city that have changed little in the last 50 years. Manama means 'Sleeping Place', and in many ways the moniker is still appropriate.

Orientation

Manama's main road is Government Ave. Bab al-Bahrain, and the small roundabout in front of it, is a hub of activity, and the gateway to the souq to the south.

Information

Tourist Offices There is a confusing array of 'tourist offices', but none that can offer independent advice in a convenient location. The Tourist Department (☎ 231 375), upstairs in the Bab al-Bahrain building, is not interested in providing general information to tourists, and neither are the Gulf Tours office and the souvenir shop downstairs. The Directorate of Tourism & Archaeology (☎ 211 199) is inconveniently located and more involved in organising travel fairs than helping tourists.

Money There are several banks along the sidestreet that runs from the GPO to the car parks in front of the Regency Inter-Continental hotel. There are also a number of banks and moneychangers on Government Ave between the GPO and the Delmon International Hotel. There are ATMs at most branches of the British Bank of the Middle East and the Bank of Bahrain & Kuwait (BBK), and an ATM for Amex cards can be found in the transit lounge of the airport. The Amex office (☎ 228 822, fax 224 040) is in the ABN building on Al-Furdah Ave. Refer to Money in the Facts for the Visitor section earlier in this chapter for information about changing money.

Post The GPO is open from 7 am to 7.30 pm every day except Friday. Poste restante facilities are available.

Telephone There are telephone booths and payphones for local and international calls all over the city. International calls can also be made at the BATELCO building in Manama. Refer to Post & Communications in the Facts for the Visitor section earlier in this chapter for details about costs.

Email & Internet Access There are very few Internet centres in Manama, and only one that's both reliable and convenient. The Idea Gallery (☎ 714 828) charges BD2 per hour. It's located in the Al-Adliya district, south of the Gulf Hotel near the Titus Arch Restaurant; its Web site is at www.ideagal .com.

Bookshops Branches of the Al-Hilal chain of bookshops can be found in many top end

hotels and upmarket shopping centres, and in the souq. Books Plus in the Seef Mall has a wide range of books, including some Lonely Planet titles.

Cultural Centres The main western cultural centres are:

Alliance Française de Bahrein
　(☎ 683 295) Isa Town, off the 16th December Hwy.
British Council
　(☎ 261 555) Ahmed Mansour al-Ali Bldg, Sheikh Isa bin Sulman Hwy.
USIS
　(☎ 273 300) at the US embassy has a library (open to all).

Medical Services Medical treatment is relatively easy to obtain in Bahrain. The American Mission Hospital (☎ 253 447) is the oldest, and smallest, but is well-equipped. Other good hospitals include the International Hospital of Bahrain (☎ 591 666) and the Sulmaniya Hospital (☎ 255 555).

Emergency The emergency number for fire, police and ambulance is ☎ 999. In the event of a traffic accident ring ☎ 688 888.

Bahrain National Museum
This museum is by far the most popular tourist attraction in Bahrain. The collection is very well labelled and signposted in English. Free films are sometimes shown in the small auditorium, exhibitions of art and sculpture in the foyer, a museum shop, and a small cafeteria. The museum is open Saturday, Sunday and Tuesday from 7 am to 2 pm; Wednesday and Thursday from 8 am to 2 pm, and 4 to 8 pm; and Friday from 3 to 8 pm. Admission is 500 fils.

Heritage Centre
The Heritage Centre was originally built in 1937 to house the Ministry of Justice & Islamic Affairs. The rooms surrounding the courtyard contain photographs of state occasions and of numerous Arab and foreign dignitaries from Bahrain throughout the

BAHRAIN

MANAMA

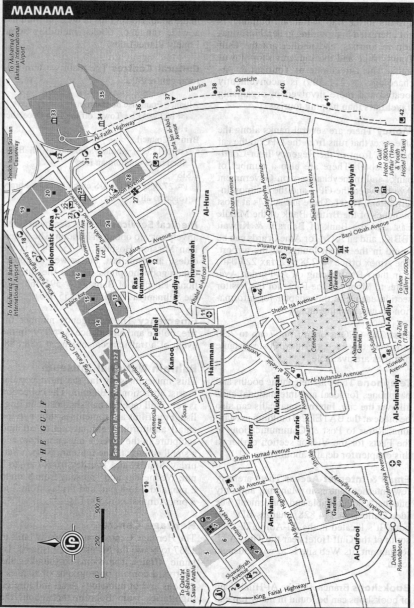

PLACES TO STAY		8	International Bus Terminal;	32	Sail Monument
9	Tylos Hotel; The Saddle		SABTCO Office	33	Bahrain National Museum
	Restaurant & Bar	10	Kid's Kingdom	34	Arts Centre
15	Sheraton Bahrain	11	American Mission Hospital	35	Marina Club
16	Bahrain Hilton	12	Wind Tower	36	Funland Centre;
19	Holiday Inn	13	UK Embassy		Jet Ski Hire
20	The Diplomat	14	Bahrain Commercial Complex	38	Gulf Tours Dock
		17	Saudi Embassy	39	Hawar Resort Hotel Booking
PLACES TO EAT		18	Kuwaiti Embassy		Office
26	Isfahani Restaurant	21	Avis Rent a Car	40	Dolphin Park
27	French Corner Cafe	22	Post Office (Diplomatic Area)	41	Horse & Camel Rides
37	Laialy Zaman	23	German Embassy	42	Al-Fatih Mosque
		24	General Directorate of	43	Al-Qudaybiyah Palace
OTHER			Immigration & Passports	44	Old Palace
1	Pearl Monument	25	Beit al-Quran	45	Bank of Bahrain & Kuwait
2	Al-Osra Supermarket	28	GOSI Shopping Complex;		(ATM)
3	Petrol Station		Delmon Cinemas; Arcadia	46	Awal Cinema
4	Police Station		(Video Arcade)	47	Craft Centre
5	Fish Market	29	Abu Bakr al-Sadiq Mosque	48	Directorate of Tourism &
6	Central Market	30	French Embassy		Archaeology
7	Lulu Shopping Centre	31	Omani Embassy	49	Sulmaniya Hospital

20th century. There are also displays about pearl diving, seafaring, musical instruments and the various uses of the date palm. The upper level houses a series of exhibits of antique weapons, games, medicine and traditional costumes. The centre was closed at the time of research, but promises to be bigger and better soon. It is open from 8 am to 2 pm Saturday to Wednesday, and from 10 am to 5 pm Thursday. Admission is free, but photography is prohibited.

Wind Towers

Bahrain's pre-electricity form of air-conditioning can be seen in the older parts of town. The towers are designed to catch even slight breezes and funnel the air down into surrounding houses. There is an interesting wind tower along Road 609. Walk south of the Hilton/Sheraton roundabout along Palace Ave for about 10 minutes and turn right at the Al-Baraka Car Centre.

Friday Mosque

Friday mosque, built in 1938, is easily identifiable by its colourful mosaic minaret, the mosque's most interesting architectural feature. The juxtaposition of the mosque with

the tall, modern Bahrain Tower nearby provides a perfect reflection (literally) of old and new Manama.

Bab al-Bahrain

The 'Gateway to Bahrain' was built by the British in 1945 and restored in 1986 to give it more of an Islamic look. The small square in front of the bab was once the terminus of the customs pier (which provides some idea of the extent of land reclamation in the area). The building now houses the Tourist Department, the Gulf Tours office and a souvenir shop.

Beit al-Quran

Beit al-Quran (House of the Quran) was opened in 1990 as a museum and research centre. The museum's centrepiece is a large and striking collection of Qurans, manuscripts and woodcarvings. Everything is well labelled in English, and the museum is a good introduction to Islam in general, and Islamic calligraphy in particular. Admission is free but a donation is requested, and visitors should dress conservatively. The main entrance is on the southern side. The museum is open Saturday to Wednesday from

9 am to noon and 4 to 6 pm, and Thursday from 9 am to noon. It has an excellent but pricey craft and bookshop in the foyer.

Al-Fatih Mosque

Al-Fatih Mosque is the largest building in the country (about 6300 sq metres), and capable of holding up to 7000 worshippers. Non-Muslims are welcome to visit Saturday to Wednesday between 8 am and 2 pm. Visitors should check in at the small library immediately to the right inside the main door. Women will be given, and are expected to wear, a hooded black cloak while inside the prayer hall. Wearing shorts is prohibited.

Places to Stay – Budget
Hostels
Youth Hostel (☎ 727 170, No 1105 Rd 4225, Juffair) is spartan but clean, with toilets and showers in a separate building, and kitchen facilities available. Beds cost BD2 per person for YHA members, BD4 for nonmembers. The hostel is in the suburbs of south-eastern Manama, but signposted in English from Al-Fatih Hwy, and easy enough to reach by taxi or bus.

Hotels All of the following hotels have aircon, TV (not satellite) and an attached bathroom with hot water.

Al-Kuwait Guest House (☎ 210 781, fax 210 764), just off Al-Khalifa Ave, has small, spartan, uncarpeted rooms – many badly in need of some renovation, so check out a few rooms. It's in an interesting part of town though, and good value at BD7/10 for singles/doubles.

Ad-Dewania Hotel (☎ 263 300, fax 259 709) is down a tiny lane off Sheikh Abdulla Ave. It's quiet, central and has friendly staff. The rooms are tiny, but clean and well furnished, and cost BD10/15.

Seef Hotel (☎ 224 557, fax 593 363), just north of Government Ave, is quiet, but the rooms are small and poorly furnished. Rooms cost a negotiable BD8/12, but get one with a view and sea breezes.

Bahrain Hotel (☎ 227 478, fax 213 509, Al-Khalifa Ave) is one of the best in this range. Quiet, pleasant rooms – although many without outside windows – cost a reasonable BD7/10.

Capital Hotel (☎ 255 955, fax 211 675, Tujjaar Ave) has singles/doubles/triples for BD10/13/19, but it's only good value if the management agrees to discount to a more reasonable BD8/10/15. The hotel is in the souq, which provides interesting views from the room's tiny balcony.

Places to Stay – Mid-Range
Bab al-Bahrain Hotel (☎ 211 622, fax 213 661), just off Government Ave, is an old favourite. It is central (and noisy), but it's just a budget-style place with a mid-range price. Unless you can negotiate down from the official rate of BD18/30/36 for singles/doubles/triples, try somewhere else.

Al-Jazira Hotel (☎ 211 810, fax 210 726, Al-Khalifa Ave) is good value, and better than most in the area. The bright, well-furnished singles/doubles cost a reasonable BD12/15, and the staff are friendly.

Sahara Hotel (☎ 225 580, fax 210 580) is one of several mid-range places around Municipality Square. It offers a balcony with good views, and is decent value for BD10/18.

Adhari Hotel (☎ 224 242, fax 214 707, Municipality Ave) is in a good, central location and has small but well-appointed rooms with a balcony for BD18/24.

Places to Stay – Top End
The rates quoted in this section are the main rack rates. Corporate discounts of up to 30% are available, and some offer weekend discount packages.

The Diplomat (☎ 531 666, fax 530 843), across from the museum, charges from BD78 to BD90 for a double. It is one of the better located hotels, and many rooms have great views.

Regency Inter-Continental (☎ 227 777, fax 229 929, email bahrain@interconti.com) costs BD72/82 for singles/doubles, and is convenient and popular.

Sheraton Bahrain (☎ 533 533, fax 534 069, Palace Ave) costs from BD72/82. It is a favourite among businesspeople.

CENTRAL MANAMA

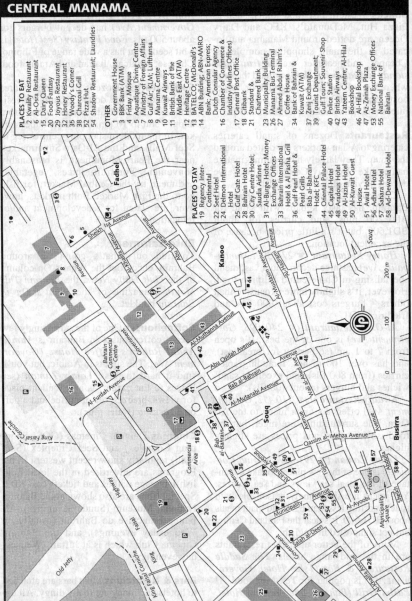

PLACES TO EAT
2 Kwality Restaurant
6 Al-Osra Restaurant
15 Dairy Queen
20 Food Fantasy
29 Joyous Restaurant
32 Honey Restaurant
35 Woody's Corner
38 Charcoal Grill
52 Pizza Hut
54 Shadow Restaurant; Laundries

OTHER
1 Government House
3 BBK Bank (ATM)
4 Friday Mosque
5 Aquatique Diving Centre
7 Ministry of Foreign Affairs
8 Gulf Air; KLM; Lufthansa
9 Manama Centre
10 Kuwait Airways
11 British Bank of the
   Middle East (ATM)
12 Heritage Centre
13 BATELCO; McDonald's
14 ABN Building; ABN-AMRO
   Bank; American Express;
   Dutch Consular Agency
16 Chamber of Commerce &
   Industry (Airlines Offices)
17 General Post Office
18 Citibank
21 Standard &
   Chartered Bank
23 Municipality Building
26 Manama Bus Terminal
27 Ahmed Abdul Rahim's
   Coffee House
34 Bank of Bahrain &
   Kuwait (ATM)
37 Zeni Exchange
39 Tourist Department;
   Gulf Tours; Souvenir Shop
40 Police Station
42 British Airways
43 Yateem Centre; Al-Hilal
   Bookshop
46 Al-Hilal Bookshop
47 Az-Zeinah Plaza
53 Money Exchange Offices
55 National Bank of
   Bahrain

PLACES TO STAY
19 Regency Inter-
   Continental
22 Seef Hotel
24 Delmon International
   Hotel
25 Gulf Gate Hotel
28 Bahrain Hotel
30 City Centre Hotel;
   Saudia Airlines
31 Al-Burge Hotel; Money
   Exchange Offices
33 Bahrain International
   Hotel & Al Pasha Grill
36 Gulf Pearl Hotel &
   Pearl Grills
41 Bab al-Bahrain
   Hotel; KFC
44 Oriental Palace Hotel
45 Capital Hotel
48 Aradous Hotel
49 Al-Jazira Hotel
50 Al-Kuwait Guest
   House
51 Awal Hotel
56 Adhari Hotel
57 Sahara Hotel
58 Ad-Dewania Hotel

Places to Eat

Snacks Western fast food joints, such as Pizza Hut, McDonald's, KFC and Dairy Queen, are dotted around Manama and located in the main shopping complexes. Cheaper, and healthier, are the *fruit juice stands* and *sandwich shops* around the souq where a small but tasty sandwich or burger costs about 500 fils, and delicious fruit juices and milk shakes cost from 200 fils.

Restaurants Dozens of small eateries catering to Asian workers are dotted around the souq. They largely have unimaginative names like 'Bombay Cafeteria', but serve decent biryanis for about 500 fils.

Charcoal Grill, next to the Bab al-Bahrain, has tasty kebabs with salad for BD1.200 plus, and curries for about BD1.600, but it's a little pricey because of the excellent location.

Honey Restaurant (☎ 274 392, *Municipality Ave*) has nice decor, and a vast menu specialising in Chinese and Filipino food. However, it's slightly more expensive than others – burgers cost about 800 fils, and fried rice BD1.

Al-Osra Restaurant (☎ 240 098, *Government Ave*) is one of the best. It's open from 7 to 1 am (so perfect for breakfast), and has over 100 dishes, including spicy curries (from 800 fils), and excellent sandwiches and burgers (about 400 fils).

Kwality Restaurant (☎ 210 413, *Government Ave*) offers a similar menu to the Al-Osra. The surroundings are nicer, but the food isn't as good and prices are slightly higher.

Laialy Zaman (☎ 293 097, *Marina Corniche*) is one of the few places to take advantage of the local sea views and sea breezes. Yet prices are surprisingly reasonable with snacks costing less than BD1 and main meals about BD1.500. It's near the Funland Centre, but not signposted in English.

Many of the better upmarket restaurants are in the mid-range hotels. *The Saddle Restaurant & Bar* (*Tylos Hotel, Government Ave*) is popular for Tex-Mex food. *Al Pasha Grill* (*Bahrain International Hotel, Government Ave*) is good value, with meals from BD1. *Pearl Grills* (*Gulf Pearl Hotel, Government Ave*) has decent burgers for about 500 fils. *Food Fantasy* (*Seef Hotel*) is a bit seedy, but has a wide range of Filipino, Chinese, Mexican, Italian and Arabic food.

Self-Catering Dozens of grocery stores ('cold stores') are dotted around the residential areas, and are usually open from about 7 am to 10 pm. There are supermarkets in the modern shopping centres (eg in Seef Mall), and the Al-Osra Supermarket, near the Pearl Monument, is reasonably convenient. For fruit, spices, vegetables and meat, try the Central Market; for fish, go to the Fish Market. Both markets, however, are slated for redevelopment and/or relocation.

Entertainment

To find out what's going on around Bahrain, check out the What's On column of the *Gulf Daily News*, the *Bahrain This Month* magazine or the *What's On in Bahrain* booklet.

Coffeehouses One of the surprisingly few decent coffeehouses in Bahrain is *Ahmed Abdul Rahim's Coffee House* (*Government Ave*). The sign is in Arabic, but you'll find it hard to miss. *Laialy Zaman* (see Places to Eat earlier) is an excellent place for views, breezes, tea or coffee and a puff on a *sheesha* (water pipe).

Cinemas Delmon Cinemas (GOSI Shopping Complex) and Seef Cineplex (Seef Mall) regularly show recent western films. Programs are advertised in the local English-language dailies and tickets cost BD2. Special films are also shown at the Bahrain National Museum (Sunday evenings), Alliance Française de Bahrein (usually on Wednesday evenings), and the Bahrain Cinema Club which is at Juffair (Wednesday evenings).

Bars & Nightclubs Most bars are attached to hotels and many are really dingy. All top end hotels have decent bars, and many feature 'happy hours', but prices are still high.

Conventional hotel bars range from the generic **Clipper Room** *(Regency Inter-Continental)*, bizarrely thematic **Sherlock Holmes** *(Gulf Hotel)*, and the charming **Hunter's Lodge Bar** *(Adhari Hotel)*. Currently trendy nightspots include **Barnaby Joes**, **The Saddle** *(Tylos Hotel)* for country music, and **U2opia** *(Delmon International Hotel)*.

Serious nightclubbers should pick up the detailed *Bahrain Restaurant Guide* (see Food in the Facts for the Visitor section earlier in this chapter), which lists recommended bars and nightclubs. Live shows are listed in the 'Showtime' section of *Bahrain This Month*, and in the English-language dailies.

Concerts & Theatre The Bahrain International Exhibition Centre often has recitals of Bahraini music. The Beit al-Quran features occasional Quran recitals, and Qala'at Arad often features traditional music on Thursday and Friday afternoons.

Shopping

Most shops in the souq are open from about 8 am to 12.30 pm and 3.30 to about 8 pm, and on Friday morning. Some locals prefer to shop at the modern, western-style shopping centres, which are wonderfully air-conditioned and open all day. In Manama, the Yateem Centre and GOSI Shopping Complex are new. In the suburbs, the Seef Mall is the biggest and best.

The **Craft Centre** is the best place to watch handicrafts being made, and to do some souvenir shopping. The centre is relaxed and friendly, and open Saturday to Wednesday from 8.30 am to 1.30 pm, and from 9 am to noon on Thursday.

Getting There & Away

Refer to the Getting There & Away chapter earlier in the book for information about international travel to Manama.

Air Bahrain International Airport is one of the busiest in the Gulf. General flight information is available by phoning ☎ 325 555.

Most airline offices are situated around the Bab al-Bahrain in the Chamber of Commerce & Industry building, or inside the Manama Centre. You'll find Gulf Air in the latter (☎ 335 777), or at the airport (☎ 338 844).

Getting Around

To/From the Airport The airport is on Muharraq Island, about 6km from central Manama. Bus No 1 runs between the airport and the Manama bus station on Government Ave about every 40 minutes between 6 am and 8.45 pm. A metered taxi from central Manama to the airport should cost about BD2. For trips *from* the airport there is a BD1 surcharge, and drivers are very reluctant to use the meter.

Taxi Taxis are easy to find, and there are taxi stands outside the Bab al-Bahrain and many upmarket hotels. Refer to the Getting Around section earlier in this chapter for details about hiring taxis.

Around Bahrain Island

KARBABAD

This village is famous for its basket weaving. Village folk sit outside their homes making baskets, place mats and chicken coops from the plentiful date palms that surround the village.

Karbabad is a short walk from Qala'at al-Bahrain (see the following section), and accessible from Manama along Sheikh Khalifa bin Sulman Hwy (the western extension of King Faisal Hwy). It's best to charter a taxi as there are no public buses to Karbabad.

QALA'AT AL-BAHRAIN

Also known as Bahrain Fort, the site has been undergoing extensive renovation (and will be for many years to come). Despite the renovations, and the on-going archaeological dig near the main fort, the site remains open every day during daylight. However, the site is a rather unimpressive collection of dirt and rocks, and may be of limited interest to anyone not interested in archaeology. Admission is free.

The site appears to have been occupied from about 2800 BC. The oldest excavated part of the site is the portion of a defensive wall from the City II period (circa 2000 BC), which indicates that this spot on the north coast of Bahrain Island was important.

The excavated remains of Cities III and IV, referred to as the Kassite and Assyrian buildings, date from 1500 to 500 BC, and include the ruins of a house with a 3m-high entrance.

The site is about 5km west of Manama and easy to reach by car. Drive along King Faisal Hwy, and its extension, Sheikh Khalifa bin Sulman Hwy, and follow the signs. Then drive along a dirt track over a low hill to the site. It is not accessible by public bus.

BARBAR TEMPLE

Barbar is a complex of three 2nd and 3rd millennium BC temples, probably dedicated to Enki, the God of Wisdom and the Sweet Waters Under the Earth.

The excavated complex can be seen from a series of walkways, which provide a great overview, but it's hard to understand without a detailed map (eg in *Bahrain: A Heritage Explored* by Angela Clark, or whatever guidebook or map is available at the site). There is officially no admission fee but a guide pressures visitors to sign a guest book and make a donation (BD1 is enough). It's open every day during daylight hours.

Take the Al-Budayyi' Hwy west from Manama and turn right at the sign for Barbar. If you follow this road the temple is on the right. The closest bus stop is near Ad-Diraz Temple (see the following section), about 30 minutes walk away.

AD-DIRAZ TEMPLE

The Ad-Diraz Temple dates from the 2nd millennium BC, and is several centuries younger than the Barbar Temple, from

which it differs significantly. The site is small, and only worth visiting if you're keen on exploring even more ruins. Ad-Diraz is open every day during daylight hours, and admission is free. The turn-off for the temple is clearly signposted along Al-Budayyi' Hwy from Manama (but not if you're driving in the other direction). Bus No 5 from Manama stops near the temple.

AL-BUDAYYI'

This small village marks the western edge of Bahrain Island. The beach has stunning views at sunset, and of the incredible King Fahd Causeway. The mammoth building overlooking the sea is **Sheikh Hamad's Fort House**, a private residence sadly not open to the public. Al-Budayyi' is at the end of Al-Budayyi' Hwy and is accessible by bus No 5 from Manama.

SOUQ AL-KHAMIS MOSQUE

The original mosque is believed to have been built in the early 8th century but an inscription dates the construction of most of the remains as the second half of the 11th century. Nevertheless, it is the first mosque built in Bahrain, and one of the oldest in the region.

The complex is open to visitors from 7 am to 2 pm Saturday to Wednesday, and from 8 am to noon Thursday and Friday. Admission is free. It's about 2.5km southwest of Manama. Take the Sheikh Sulman Hwy to Al-Khamis village, the mosque is on the right side of the road. It is also accessible from Manama on bus Nos 2 and 7.

ADHARI PARK

Adhari Park is a garden and amusement area, featuring a natural spring running into a pool containing fish and tortoises. It is a welcome respite from the noise and pollution of the city. Admission is free, but each ride costs about 400 fils. Adhari Park is open daily from 8 am to noon and 3.30 to 9 pm, but is empty most weekdays (Saturday to Wednesday). It is poorly signposted, and only accessible heading south-west from Manama along Sheikh Isa bin Sulman Hwy.

A'ALI

There are over 100,000 burial mounds in Bahrain. The most impressive are the ones often referred to as the **Royal Tombs**, near the village of A'ali. These are the largest burial mounds in Bahrain reaching up to 15m in height and 45m in diameter. The area is not signposted and has no designated entrance and there are no explanations, but it's a great place to wander around.

A'ali village is the site of Bahrain's best-known **pottery workshop**. Pottery and ceramics are on sale at several stalls around the sleepy village, and in the souvenir shop in the Bab al-Bahrain in Manama. The village also boasts a 'traditional' Arabic bakery, and the Muharraqi Gallery, which features modern Bahraini art.

From Manama, take the Sheikh Sulman Hwy south past Isa Town, then turn west along A'ali Hwy and follow the signs to the village, pottery workshop or mounds. Buses are problematic: take Bus No 2 or 7 from Manama to Isa Town, and then bus No 9 or 15 to A'ali village.

SAR

Sar was the site of another settlement from the Dilmun period. Hundreds of **burial mounds** are being successfully excavated, and archaeologists are excited about their finds. When excavations are finished, there are plans to turn the site into a major tourist attraction, including a museum. Like the mounds at A'ali, the area has no designated entrance or explanations.

Although the site seems close, there is no access from the Causeway Approach Rd. Instead, go to Sar village following the signposted road heading south from Al-Budayyi' Hwy, or from Janabiyah Hwy, and then follow the signs to the burial mounds. Bus No 12 goes to Sar village, from where it's about 1.5km to the burial mounds.

KING FAHD CAUSEWAY

The causeway connecting Saudi Arabia and Bahrain is an impressive piece of engineering. Near the bridge and border, and on an island there are two tall, thin towers, one on the Bahrain side of the border, the other on the Saudi side of the border. *King Fahd Causeway Restaurant* (open from 9 am to 11 pm daily) in the tower on the Bahraini side offers very mediocre food, but the views from the tower are superb. All drivers (and passengers in taxis) must pay a BD2 toll per vehicle at a booth along the Causeway Approach Rd, whether going to Saudi or not. No local public bus travels along the causeway.

AL-JASRA

Al-Jasra House is one of several historic homes around Bahrain that have been restored to their original condition. This one is famous as the birthplace of the former emir, Sheikh Isa bin Sulman al-Khalifa. The house is open Sunday to Tuesday from 8 am to 2 pm, Wednesday and Thursday from 9 am to 6 pm, and Friday from 3 to 6 pm. Admission is 200 fils.

In the residential area, a few hundred metres before Al-Jasra House, is the government-run **Al-Jasra Handicraft Centre**. This modern, well laid out collection of workshops specialises in textiles, basketweaving and mirrors. It's open from about 9 am to 4 pm daily and is adjacent to a stop for Bus No 12.

From the Causeway Approach Rd, look for the exit to Al-Jasra (before the toll booth), and then go past two roundabouts and the Handicraft Centre, to reach Al-Jasra House (the house is not particularly well signposted).

RIFFA FORT

The Riffa Fort stands majestically overlooking the Riffa Valley. It was originally built in the 17th century and restored completely in 1983. The limited captions and explanations are in Arabic, and the rooms are mostly empty, but it's interesting enough and the views over the valley are appealing.

The fort is open from Sunday to Tuesday from 8 am to 2 pm, Wednesday and Thursday from 9 am to 6 pm, and Friday from 3 to 6 pm. Admission is 200 fils. The fort is easy to spot from several main roads but is surprisingly hard to reach and poorly signposted. Access to the fort is only possible along Sheikh Hamood bin Sebah Ave, which is off Riffa Ave. Bus Nos 7 and 11 go past the turn-off along Riffa Ave.

AL-AREEN WILDLIFE PARK

This interesting little (10 sq km) preserve is a conservation area for species indigenous to the Middle East and North Africa. After a short introductory film (in Arabic only), a small bus leaves roughly every hour for a jaunt (providing commentary in Arabic and English) past some of the 240 species of birds and mammals, consisting mostly of onyx and gazelle.

The park has peculiar opening times – from 8 to 11 am daily, reopening between 3 and 5 pm from February to July, and 2 and 4 pm from September to January. It's closed during Ramadan and August. It's best to call the park office (☎ 836 116), or take a look at the 'What's On' column in the *Gulf Daily News* before heading out. Admission to the wildlife park will set you back BD1.

From Manama, follow the signs to Riffa and then 'Awali along Sheikh Sulman Hwy, and then continue towards to Al-Zallaq. The turn-off to the park is along the Zallaq Beach Hwy.

TREE OF LIFE

The Tree of Life is a lone tree, famous because it somehow survives in the barren desert, presumably fed by an underground spring. Although it's touted as a major tourist attraction, there is nothing else to see or do here, and it's quite a distance from Manama.

The best time to visit is around dusk – but leave before it's too dark, and don't park any vehicle in a sandy area. The site is not easy to find: follow the Sheikh Sulman Hwy to Riffa, then head towards 'Awali (or vice-versa), and follow the signs along the Muaskar Hwy. It's best to go with a knowledgeable local, or on an organised tour.

Muharraq

Just over the bridge from Bahrain Island is Muharraq Island. The attractions on the island are easy to reach on foot from the Muharraq bus station – bus Nos 2 and 7 travel between the bus stations in Muharraq and Manama at least every hour. Alternatively, charter a taxi to one place, and walk to one or more of the other attractions.

BEIT SHEIKH ISA BIN ALI & BEIT SEYADI

These two traditional houses offer a fascinating look at pre-oil life in Bahrain. Beit Sheikh Isa bin Ali (being renovated at the time of research) was built around 1800. While the rooms are bare, the different sections of the house are well captioned in English.

Beit Seyadi is a smaller house of similar age but the restoration work is not quite as advanced. It's still worth a look, however. An old mosque is attached to the house.

Beit Sheikh Isa bin Ali is open Saturday to Wednesday from 9 am to 2 pm, and Thursday from 9.30 am to 5 pm. Beit Seyadi is open Saturday to Thursday from 2 to 6 pm. Admission to both is free.

From Manama take the Sheikh Hamad Causeway and look for the signs at the roundabout on the corner of Sheikh Sulman and Sheikh Abdulla avenues. To avoid getting a little lost, ask for directions if walking from one house to the other.

QALA'AT ABU MAHIR

Qala'at Abu Mahir dates back to the 16th century, though it has been rebuilt several times since. It consists of a single watchtower with a narrow building attached to its landward side, but the building is not particularly impressive. The fort is in the grounds of the Muharraq coastguard station, so access is usually limited but if you present yourself at the gate on a weekday (Saturday to Wednesday) morning and ask nicely they may let you in. From Manama, take the Sheikh Hamad Causeway, and turn right along Khalifa al-Kebir Ave.

MUHARRAQ

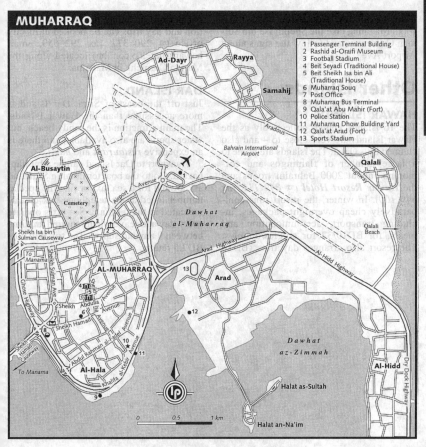

1 Passenger Terminal Building
2 Rashid al-Oraifi Museum
3 Football Stadium
4 Beit Seyadi (Traditional House)
5 Beit Sheikh Isa bin Ali
  (Traditional House)
6 Muharraq Souq
7 Post Office
8 Muharraq Bus Terminal
9 Qala'at Abu Mahir (Fort)
10 Police Station
11 Muharraq Dhow Building Yard
12 Qala'at Arad (Fort)
13 Sports Stadium

QALA'AT ARAD

Qala'at Arad (Arad Fort) was built in the early 15th century by the Portuguese. Although parts have been beautifully restored, there is little to see inside except an old well. Still, the location overlooking the bay is superb. The fort is open Sunday to Tuesday from 8 am to 2 pm, Wednesday and Thursday from 9 am to 6 pm, and Friday from 3 to 6 pm. Admission is free. During late afternoon on Thursday and Friday the fort hosts a craft market with children's

rides and traditional bands. Check *Bahrain This Month* for details.

From Manama, take the Sheikh Hamad Causeway, and follow the signs along Khalifa al-Kebir Ave and Arad Hwy.

RASHID AL-ORAIFI MUSEUM

This private art gallery is dedicated to the work of its artist/owner, most of which is based on Dilmun-related themes. The museum is open Saturday to Thursday from 8 am to noon and 4 to 8 pm, and Friday from

8 am to midday. Admission costs BD1. From Manama, take the Sheikh Isa bin Sulman Causeway, and follow the signs along Airport Ave.

Other Islands

HAWAR ISLANDS

The 16 islands known collectively as the Hawar Islands are very close to – and also claimed by – Qatar. The islands are home to a large number of flamingos and cormorants, about 2000 Bahraini troops and the *Hawar Resort Hotel* (☎ *849 111, fax 849 100*). In winter, the resort runs comparatively cheap overnight packages, including transport, accommodation and meals, for BD19/32 for singles/doubles. The resort also arranges day trips (BD10 per person) including lunch. Accommodation and day trips can be booked at its city office (☎ 290 377, fax 292 659, email hawar@batelco.com.bh) located along the Marina Corniche in Manama.

DAR ISLAND

Just off the coast of Sitra, Dar Island is more accessible than the Hawar Islands. The main attraction is the sandy beach, but water sports are also available, and there is an expensive *restaurant* and *bar*.

Transport to Dar Island can be a bit haphazard. Go to the boat terminal in Sitra and ask around for a sea taxi or ring the special number listed at the telephone box clearly indicated in the terminal. Sea taxis operate every day and leave when required anytime between 9 am and sunset. The trip will cost BD2.5 return.

Egypt

Birthplace of one of the greatest civilisations the world has known, modern Egypt still retains the glory of the pharaohs in the extraordinary monuments they left behind, dotting the entire country. The centuries following the long era of pharaonic rule brought Greeks, Romans, Arabs, Turks and Europeans – to mention only the main players – to the seat of power, and they have all left their mark.

Modern Cairo, the over-bloated capital and the continent's largest city is a chaotic collision of the Arab world, Africa and the remnants of 19th century colonialism.

Through it all flows the Nile, without which Egypt could not exist. On either side of the Nile lie harsh deserts, occasionally softened by pockets of life in the oases. Southeast of the famous Suez Canal stretches Sinai, a region of awesome beauty and a place of refuge and conflict for thousands of years. An unparalleled paradise off the Red Sea coast combines with the natural and architectural marvels on land to make this a fascinating destination.

Facts about Egypt

HISTORY

After enduring 2200 years of rule by foreigners, begun by Alexander the Great and maintained by the Romans, Arabs, Turks, French and the British, the rule of Egypt was finally put in the hands of the Egyptians following the Revolution of 1952. (For the events prior to this see the general history of the Middle East described in the Facts about the Region chapter.) Colonel Gamal Abdel Nasser, leader of the revolutionary Free Officers, ascended to power and was confirmed as president in elections held in 1956. That same year, the colonial legacy was finally and dramatically shaken off in full world view when Nasser successfully faced down Britain, France and Israel over the

The Arab Republic of Egypt

Area: 997,738 sq km
Population: 61.5 million
Population Growth Rate: 2.1%
Capital: Cairo
Head of State: President Hosni Mubarak
Official Language: Arabic
Currency: Egyptian pound (E£)
Exchange Rate: US$1 = E£3.41

- **Best Dining** – grilled fish at an open-air restaurant in the Anfushi district of Alexandria
- **Best Nightlife** – smoking a sheesha in some Cairo coffeehouse at 2 am or starlit desert nights out in the oases
- **Best Walk** – getting lost in the narrow, twisting backstreets of Islamic Cairo
- **Best View** – sunrise as seen from the peak of Mt Sinai
- **Best Activity** – diving or snorkelling off the south Sinai coast
- **When in Rome ...** find yourself a good coffeehouse with a TV and drop in on Friday afternoon to watch the locals watching football

Suez Canal. Egypt became a beacon for all those countries in Africa, Asia and the Arab world that had recently thrown off European colonial administrations.

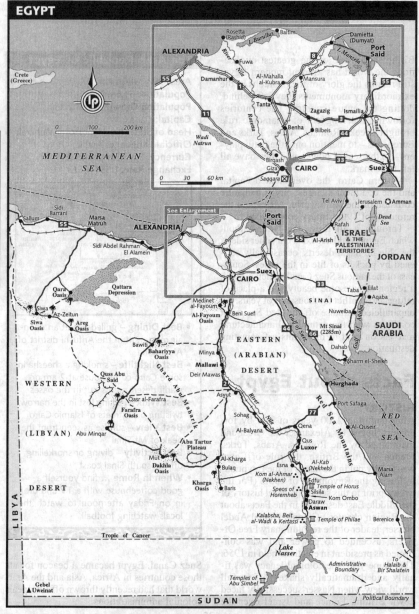

Pharaonic Egypt

About 5000 years ago an Egyptian king named Menes unified Upper and Lower Egypt for the first time. For centuries beforehand, communities had been developing along the Nile. The small kingdoms eventually developed into two important states, one covering the valley as far as the Delta, the other consisting of the Delta itself. The unification of these two states, by Menes in about 3000 BC, set the scene for the greatest era of ancient Egyptian civilisation. More than 30 dynasties, 50 rulers and 2700 years of indigenous – and occasionally foreign – rule passed before Alexander the Great ushered in a long, unbroken period of foreign domination.

Little is known of the immediate successors of Menes except that, attributed with divine ancestry, they promoted the development of a highly stratified society, patronised the arts and built many temples and public works.

In the 27th century BC, Egypt's pyramids began to appear. King Zoser and his chief architect, Imhotep, built what may have been the first, the Step Pyramid at Saqqara. Zoser ruled from the nearby capital of Memphis.

For the next three dynasties and 500 years – a period called the Old Kingdom – the power of Egypt's pharaohs and the size and scale of their pyramids and temples greatly increased. The size of such buildings symbolised the pharaoh's importance and power over his people. The pyramid also gave the pharaoh steps to the heavens, and the ceremonial wooden barques buried with him provided him with symbolic vehicles to the next life. The last three pharaohs of the 4th dynasty, Cheops, Chephren and Mycerinus, built the three Great Pyramids of Giza.

By the beginning of the 5th dynasty (about 2490-2330 BC) it is clear the pharaohs had ceded some of their power to a rising class of nobles. In the following centuries Egypt broke down into several squabbling principalities. The rise of Thebes (Luxor) saw an end to the turmoil and Egypt was reunited under Mentuhotep II, marking the beginning of the Middle Kingdom. For 250 years all went well, but more internal fighting and 100 years of occupation by the Hyksos, invaders from the north-east, cast a shadow over the country.

The New Kingdom, its capital at Thebes and later Memphis, represented a blossoming of culture and empire in pharaonic Egypt. For almost 400 years, from the 18th to the 20th dynasties (1550-1150 BC), Egypt was a great power in north-east Africa and the eastern Mediterranean. Renowned kings and queens ruled an expanding empire from Memphis, and built monuments that even today are unique in their immensity and beauty. The most startling of them is perhaps the Temple of Amun at Karnak, just north of Luxor. But by the time Ramses III came to power (1198 BC) as the second king of the 20th dynasty, disunity had again set in. The empire continued to shrink and Egypt was attacked by outsiders. This was the state of affairs when Alexander the Great arrived in the 4th century BC.

EGYPT

Sadat, Egypt's second president, initiated a complete about face. Where Nasser looked to the USSR for his inspiration, Sadat looked to the USA. Then, in the wake of the 1973 war with Israel, the Egyptian president travelled to Jerusalem in search of peace. The quest ended in 1979 with the co-signing of the Camp David Agreement. This was a complete abandonment of Nasser's pan-Arabist principles and Sadat's peace was viewed by the Arab world as no less than a betrayal. It cost Sadat his life at the hands of an assassin.

Sadat's murderer was a member of the Muslim Brotherhood, an uncompromising political organisation that aimed to establish an Islamic state in Egypt. Mass round-ups of Islamists were immediately carried out on the orders of Sadat's successor Hosni Mubarak, a former air force general and vice president.

Mubarak was able to rehabilitate Egypt in the eyes of the Arab world, without abandoning the treaty with Israel. And for almost a decade he managed to keep the lid on the Islamist extremists.

But in the early 1990s the lid blew off. During the 1980s discontent had been brewing among the poorer sections of society. Government promises had failed to keep up with the population explosion and a generation of youths were finding themselves without jobs and living in squalid, overcrowded housing with little or no hope for the future. With a repressive political system that allowed little chance to legitimately voice opposition, the only hope lay with the Islamic parties and extreme action.

There were frequent attempts on the life of the president and his ministers and frequent clashes with the security forces. Several groups of foreign tourists were shot at or bombed in the last months of 1992 and into 1993, resulting in a handful of deaths. The government responded with a heavy-handed lightning crackdown, arresting thousands. By the mid-1990s, the violence had receded from the capital, retreating to the religious heartland of middle Egypt.

Egypt Today

Over the last 10 years the country's public debt has fallen. Foreign currency reserves have climbed. The pound is stable. Inflation is under control. Population growth has been checked. The Egyptian president is a respected guarantor of peace and a vital ally of the west in the Middle East. On the home front, the government looks stable. But as anyone who wasn't on Mars in late 1997 knows terrorist violence is far from being completely a thing of the past. The sickening one-two of the fire bomb attack on a tour bus outside the Egyptian Museum in Cairo, followed a few weeks later by the

What to See

Cairo is overwhelming but allow at least two or three days to see the **Pyramids**, the **Egyptian Museum** and to spend time wandering around the neighbourhoods of **Islamic Cairo**. Next priority should be the tombs and temples of **Luxor** followed perhaps by a couple of days kicking back in **Aswan**, using the lazy Nileside town as a base for a visit to the grand temple at **Abu Simbel**.

Egypt's pharaonic splendours are at least equalled by the underwater scenery off the Red Sea coast, particularly off **southern Sinai**; hours spent snorkelling or diving in the warm waters here can be complemented by camel treks or a trip to nearby **Mt Sinai** and **St Katherine's Monastery**. Alternatively, many travellers rave over the far western desert oasis of **Siwa**, which is an idyllic place to drop out of the rat race for a couple of days.

massacre of 58 holidaymakers at the Temple of Hatshepsut in Luxor, stunned the world. The world responded by staying away and tourism figures plummeted. Since that time Egypt has been frantically wooing back the holidaymakers with high profile events like opera at the Pyramids and shopping festivals and millions spent on tourist office advertising. It's a strategy that seems to have paid off and at the time of writing Egypt's international profile is all pharaohs and frolicking at the Red Sea.

It's an attractive combination but one that's very much at odds with the Egypt experienced by the majority of the 60-plus million who actually live there. Until more is done to bridge this disparity the sunny outlook of the tourist posters is bound to remain tinged with the threat of dark clouds.

GEOGRAPHY

For most Egyptians the fertile Nile Valley is Egypt. To the east of the valley is the

Eastern (Arabian) Desert – a barren plateau bounded on its eastern edge by a high ridge of mountains. To the west is the Western (Libyan) Desert – a plateau punctuated by huge clumps of bizarre geological formations and luxuriant oases.

Terrain in Sinai slopes from the high mountain ridges, which include Gebel Musa (Mt Sinai) and Gebel Katherina (Mt St Katherine; the highest in Egypt at 2642m), in the south to desert coastal plains and lagoons in the north.

CLIMATE

Egypt's climate is easy to summarise. Most of the year, except for the winter months of December, January and February, it is hot and dry. Temperatures increase as you travel south from Alexandria. Alexandria receives the most rain – approximately 190mm a year – while far south in Aswan any rain at all is rare.

Summer temperatures range from 31°C (87°F) on the Mediterranean coast to a scorching 50°C (122°F) in Aswan. At night in winter the temperatures sometimes plummet to as low as 8°C, even in the south.

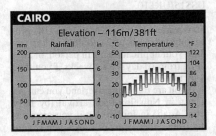

GOVERNMENT & POLITICS

The bulk of power is concentrated in the hands of the president (present incumbent, Mohammed Hosni Mubarak), who is nominated by the People's Assembly and elected by popular referendum for six years. This term can be renewed at least once, although, at the time of writing, Mubarak was close to completing a third term and had in-

Boys, Girls & the Veil

The most visible sign of the return to 'traditional values' that has swept not just Egypt but much of the region in recent years (see the boxed text 'Dress Code' in the Iran chapter) has been the huge number of women adopting more conservative dress and wearing the *hejab*, or headscarf. But, again, as with the whole issue of women in the Middle East, it's all far more complex than first meets the eye.

For every woman who adopts the hejab for religious reasons, there are others who wear it because it allows them to walk around more freely – not many men would dare hassle a *muhaggaba* (girl/woman who keeps her hair covered with a scarf)! By wearing the hejab perhaps some women feel they don't have to worry about fashion, or because it *is* the fashion. Check out the different styles of wearing a headscarf.

dicated he was going for a fourth. There is no question of him failing to secure further time in office. Mubarak himself admits democracy in Egypt is 'limited' and there are no serious opposition parties to the ruling National Democratic Party (NDP). In the last elections most seats were contested by rivals from within the NDP.

The president appoints vice presidents and ministers, as well as 10 members of the 454-member People's Assembly and 70 of the 210-member *Majlis ash-Shura* (Advisory Council).

POPULATION & PEOPLE

Egypt is the most populous country in the Arab world and has the second highest population in Africa after Nigeria. The population was counted at 61.5 million in 1997. It is predicted by some to reach 65 million by the year 2000.

Anthropologists divide Egyptian people very roughly into three racial groups, of which the biggest is descended from the

Hamito-Semitic race that has peopled the Nile (as well as many other parts of north Africa and neighbouring Arabia) for millennia. Included in this race are the Berbers, a minority group who settled around Siwa in the country's Western Desert. The second group, the truly Arab element, is made up of the Bedouin Arab nomads who migrated from Arabia and who also live in desert areas, particularly Sinai. The third group are the Nubians, in the Aswan area.

RELIGION
About 90% of Egypt's population are Muslims; most of the rest are Coptics. Generally speaking the two communities enjoy a more or less easy coexistence. Though western newspapers from time to time run stories claiming that Copts are a persecuted minority, virtually all prominent Christians in Egypt insist they are neither persecuted nor a minority. Intermarrying between Christians and Muslims is forbidden.

LANGUAGE
Arabic is the official language of Egypt. The dialect here varies markedly from that spoken in Jordan, Syria, Lebanon, Palestine and elsewhere (see the Language chapter at the back of this book) but because of Cairo's traditional status as the cultural capital of the Arab world and its correspondingly voluminous output of film, TV and song, most Arabic speakers understand Egyptian Arabic.

English is widely spoken in towns, cities and tourist centres, while Egypt's hawkers and touts are renowned for their knowledge of languages.

Facts for the Visitor

PLANNING
The best time to go to Egypt depends on where you want to go. June to August is unbearable in Upper Egypt with daytime temperatures soaring to 40°C. Summer in Cairo is almost as hot, and the combination of heat, dust, pollution, noise and crush makes

walking the city streets a real test of endurance. But then a scorching sun might be exactly what's wanted for a week or two of slow roasting on the beaches of southern Sinai.

For visiting Upper Egypt, winter is easily the most comfortable time – though hotel rates are at a premium. However, in Cairo from December to February skies are often overcast and evenings can be chilly, while up on the Mediterranean coast, Alexandria is subject to frequent downpours resulting in flooded and muddy streets.

The happiest compromise for an all-Egypt trip is to visit in spring (March to May) or autumn (October and November).

VISAS & DOCUMENTS
Visas
All foreigners entering Egypt, except nationals of Malta, South Africa, Zimbabwe and Arab countries, must obtain visas from Egyptian embassies or consulates overseas or at the airport or port upon arrival. As a general rule, it is cheaper to get a visa at Cairo airport, where the entire process takes only a few minutes and costs US$15/UK£10.

Elsewhere, processing of visa applications varies. In the USA and the UK, processing takes about 24 to 48 hours if you drop your application off in person, or anything from 10 days to six weeks if you send it by mail.

If you are travelling overland you can get a visa in Nuweiba upon arrival (by ferry from Aqaba in Jordan) but if you are coming from either Israel or Libya, you *cannot* get a visa at the border. Instead, you have to get the visa beforehand at either the embassies in Tel Aviv or Tripoli, or the consulate in Eilat (see the Israel & the Palestinian Territories and Libya chapters for details).

A single-entry visa is valid for three months and entitles the holder to stay in Egypt for one month. Multiple-entry visas (for three visits) are also available but although good for presentation for six months, they still only entitle the bearer to a total of one month in the country.

Sinai Permits It is not necessary to get a full visa if your visit is confined to the area of Sinai between Sharm el-Sheikh and Taba (on the Israeli border), including St Katherine's Monastery. Instead you are issued with an entry stamp, free of charge, allowing you a 14 day stay. Points of entry where such visa-free stamps are issued are Taba, Nuweiba (port) and Sharm el-Sheikh (airport or port).

Visa Extensions & Re-Entry Visas Extensions of your visa beyond the first month can easily be obtained for anything up to 12 months and cost E£8.20. If you do not have a multiple-entry visa, it is also possible to get a re-entry visa, valid to the expiry date of your visa and any extensions, at most passport offices. A single/multiple re-entry visa costs E£10/14.

Visas for Neighbouring Countries You need a visa to enter the following neighbouring countries of Egypt:

Eritrea Visas valid for one month are issued within 24 hours. You need a letter of recommendation from your embassy and two photos. You may be asked to show a return or onward air ticket. Visas cost E£135.

Ethiopia You need a letter of recommendation from your embassy and two photos, and you must be able to show a return air ticket. If you fulfil these requirements the visa is issued the next day and costs US$63.

Jordan Visas cost from nothing for Australians to E£63 for UK citizens, E£77 for US citizens and E£91 for Canadians. Apply in the morning and collect the visa at 2 pm. You need one photo.

Kenya Visas valid for three months and good for travel for one month cost E£26 for

most western nationalities. You need one photo.

Libya Don't count on getting a Libyan visa in Cairo. The embassy must contact Tripoli and there is little likelihood of permission being given.

Saudi Arabia Go to a consular building in Garden City near the Canadian embassy, which will issue transit visas for those who are passengers on a boat from Suez to Eritrea via Jeddah. Phone the embassy for the address. The consulate in Suez also supposedly issues transit visas.

Sudan Obtaining a visa for Sudan in Cairo would seem to be governed by cloud formations, coffee grinds, or the Nikkei index. The consul himself said it would take at least a month to commune with Khartoum on the question of a visa, but a German girl and her US friend got their visas in less than a week. To make the application, you need four passport-sized photos and a letter of recommendation from your embassy. They do not take your passport while processing your application. If successful you pay US$64 cash (they will not accept other currencies) on receipt of the visa, which is valid for use within a month and good for a month's stay.

Syria Visas are issued the same or next day depending on how early in the morning you get your application in. You need two photos. For Australians it's free, US citizens pay E£116, UK citizens pay E£210 and most other nationalities pay E£185.

Other Documents

It is well worth having a student card as it entitles you to a 50% discount on admission to almost all of the antiquities and museums, as well as significant reductions on train travel. Travellers have reported using a wide range of other cards to get student discounts for museum entry and transport, from HI cards to Eurail cards.

An International Driving Permit is required if you want to drive a car in Egypt.

EMBASSIES & CONSULATES
Egyptian Embassies & Consulates

Following are the Egyptian embassies and consulates in major cities around the world:

Australia
  Embassy:
  (☎ 06-273 4437/8)
  1 Darwin Ave, Yarralumla, Canberra 2600
  Consulate:
  (☎ 03-9654 8869/8634)
  9th floor, 124 Exhibition St, Melbourne 3000
  Consulate:
  (☎ 02-9362 3483)
  335 New South Head Rd, Double Bay, Sydney 2028
Canada
  Embassy:
  (☎ 613-234 4931/35/58)
  454 Laurier Ave East, Ottawa, Ontario K1N 6R3
  Consulate:
  (☎ 514-866 8455)
  1 Place Sainte Marie, 2617 Montreal, Quebec H3B 4S3
France
  Embassy:
  (☎ 01 47 23 06 43, 01 53 67 88 30)
  56 Ave d'Iena, 75116 Paris
  Consulate:
  (☎ 01 45 00 49 52, 01 45 00 77 10)
  58 Ave Foch, 75116 Paris
  Consulate:
  (☎ 91 25 04 04)
  166 Ave d'Hambourg, 13008 Marseilles
Germany
  Embassy:
  (☎ 228-956 8311/2/3)
  Kronprinzenstrasse 2, Bad Godesberg, 53173 Bonn
  Embassy branch:
  (☎ 30-477 1048)
  Waldstrasse 15, 13156 Berlin
  Consulate:
  (☎ 69-590557/8)
  Eysseneckstrasse 34, 60322 Frankfurt-am-Main
Ireland
  Embassy:
  (☎ 1-660 6566)
  12 Clyde Rd, Dublin 4
Netherlands
  Embassy:
  (☎ 70-354 2000)
  Badhuisweg 92, 2587 CL, The Hague

Sudan
  Embassy:
  (☎ 11-778741, fax 778741)
  Sharia al-Gama'a, al-Mogran, Khartoum
  Consulate:
  (☎ 11-772191)
  Sharia al-Gomhurriya, Khartoum
UK
  Embassy:
  (☎ 020-7499 2401)
  26 South St, Mayfair, London W1
  Consulate:
  (☎ 020-7235 9777/9719)
  2 Lowndes St, London SW1
USA
  Embassy:
  (☎ 202-895 5400)
  3521 International Court NW, Washington DC 20008
  Consulate:
  (☎ 212-759 7120/1/2)
  1110 2nd Ave, New York, NY 10022
  Consulate:
  (☎ 415-346 9700/2)
  3001 Pacific Ave, San Francisco, CA 94115
  Consulate:
  (☎ 713-961 4915/6)
  Suite 2180, 1990 Post Oak Blvd, Houston, TX 77056
  Consulate:
  (☎ 312-828 9162/64/67)
  Suite 1900, 500 N Michigan Ave, Chicago, IL 60611

Embassies & Consulates in Egypt

Most embassies and consulates are open from around 8 am to 3 pm Sunday to Thursday.

Australia
  Embassy:
  (☎ 575 0444, fax 578 1638)
  World Trade Centre, 11th floor, 1191 Corniche el-Nil, Cairo
Canada
  Embassy:
  (☎ 354 3110, fax 356 3548)
  5 Al-Saraya al-Kubra, Garden City, Cairo
Denmark
  Embassy:
  (☎ 340 2503, fax 341 1780)
  12 Hassan Sabry, Zamalek, Cairo
Eritrea
  Embassy:
  (☎ 303 0517)
  13 Mohammed Shafik, Mohandiseen, Cairo

Ethiopia
Embassy:
(☎ 335 3696, fax 335 3699)
6 Abdel Rahman Hussein, Doqqi, Cairo
France
Embassy:
(☎ 570 3916, fax 571 0276)
29 Sharia al-Giza, Giza
Consulate:
(☎ 393 4645)
5 Sharia Fadl (off Talaat Harb), Cairo
Consulate:
(☎ 482 7950)
2 Midan Orabi, Mansheya, Alexandria
Germany
Embassy:
(☎ 341 0015, fax 341 0530)
8 Hassan Sabry, Zamalek, Cairo
Consulate:
(☎ 545 7025)
5 Sharia Mena, Rushdy, Alexandria
Ireland
Embassy:
(☎ 340 8264, fax 341 2863)
7th floor, 3 Abu al-Feda, Zamalek, Cairo
Consulate:
(☎ 546 4686)
36 Sharia Kafr Abdu, Rushdy, Alexandria
Israel
Embassy:
(☎ 361 0528, fax 361 0414)
18th floor, 6 Ibn al-Malek, Giza
Consulate:
(☎ 586 0492)
207 Sharia Abdel Salem Aref, Alexandria
Jordan
Embassy:
(☎ 348 5566, fax 360 1027)
6 Al-Shaheed Basem al-Khatib, Doqqi, Cairo
Kenya
Embassy:
(☎ 345 3907, fax 344 3400)
7 Sharia al-Mohandis Galal, Doqqi, Cairo
Lebanon
Embassy:
(☎ 361 0623, fax 361 0463)
5 Ahmed Nessim, Giza, Cairo
Libya
Embassy:
(☎ 340 1864, fax 340 0072)
7 Sharia Salah ad-Din, Zamalek, Cairo
Netherlands
Embassy:
(☎ 340 1936, fax 341 5249)
18 Hassan Sabry, Zamalek, Cairo
Consulate:
(☎ 482 9044)
3rd floor, 18 Tariq al-Horeyya, Alexandria

New Zealand
New Zealand's affairs are handled by the UK
embassy.
Saudi Arabia
Embassy:
(☎ 349 0757, fax 349 3495)
2 Ahmed Nessim, Giza
Consulate:
(☎ 482 9911)
Port Tawfiq
Consulate:
(☎ 222 461)
9 Sharia Batalsa, Alexandria
Sudan
Embassy:
(☎ 354 5043, fax 354 2693)
4 Sharia al-Ibrahimy, Garden City, Cairo
Consulate:
(☎ 354 9661)
1 Mohammed Fahmy as-Said, Garden City
Syria
Embassy:
(☎ 377 7020, fax 335 8232)
18 Abdel Rahim Sabry, Doqqi, Cairo
UK
Embassy:
(☎ 354 0850, fax 354 0959)
7 Ahmed Ragheb, Garden City, Cairo
Consulate:
(☎ 546 7001)
3 Sharia Mena, Rushdy, Alexandria
USA
Embassy:
(☎ 355 7371, fax 357 3200)
5 Sharia Latin America, Garden City, Cairo
Consulate:
(☎ 472 1009)
3 Sharia al-Faraana, Alexandria

CUSTOMS

The duty-free limit on arrival is 1L of alcohol, 1L of perfume, 200 cigarettes and 25 cigars. On top of that, you can buy another 3L of alcohol (4L in Alexandria) plus a wide range of other duty-free articles within the next 30 days at branches of the Egypt Free Shops company which can be found scattered around the country.

MONEY
Costs

By international standards Egypt is still fairly cheap. It is possible to get by on US$15 a day or maybe less if you are willing to stick to the cheapest hotels (you can get a bed for as little as E£7 – US$2), eat the staple snacks of *fuul* (fava bean paste) or *ta'amiyya* (felafel), and limit yourself to one historic site per day. The major expense is going to be the admission fees to tourist sites. A complete visit to the Pyramids will cost E£80 (US$27) in admission charges, and if you want to see the mummies at the Egyptian Museum, the combined fee is E£60 (US$20).

Currency
The official currency is the Egyptian pound (E£) – in Arabic, a *guinay*. One pound consists of 100 piastres (pt). There are notes in denominations of 10, 25 and 50pt and one, five, 10, 20, 50, 100 and E£200 (the last is new and is rarely seen). Coins in circulation are for denominations of 10, 20 and 25pt.

Prices can be written with or without a decimal point. For example, E£3.35 can also be written as 335pt.

Exchange Rates
Exchange rates for a range of foreign currencies were as follows when this book went to print:

country	unit		Egyptian pounds
Australia	A$1	=	E£2.22
Canada	C$1	=	E£2.27
euro	€1	=	E£3.65
France	10FF	=	E£5.50
Germany	DM1	=	E£1.87
Israel	1NIS	=	E£0.82
Japan	¥100	=	E£2.96
Jordan	JD1	=	E£4.82
New Zealand	NZ$1	=	E£1.80
UK	UK£1	=	E£5.49
USA	US$1	=	E£3.41

Exchanging Money
Money can be officially changed at commercial banks, foreign exchange (forex) bureaus and some hotels. Rates don't tend to vary much especially on the US dollar but if you're extra keen to squeeze out the very last piastre then the forex bureaus generally offer marginally better rates than the banks and they usually don't charge a commission fee.

Look at the money you're given when exchanging and don't accept any badly defaced, shabby or torn notes as you'll have great difficulty off-loading them.

While there is no problem cashing well known brands of travellers cheques at major banks, like Banque Masr or National Bank of Egypt, many forex bureaus don't take them.

Credit Cards & ATMs
American Express (Amex), Visa and MasterCard are becoming ever more useful in Egypt and are now accepted quite widely in shops and restaurants – though away from tourist establishments they are far less common, and in remote areas they remain useless. Visa and MasterCard can be used for cash advances at Banque Masr and the National Bank of Egypt.

ATMs have spread rapidly throughout the country; as well as in Cairo you'll find them in Alexandria, Luxor and Aswan, Hurghada and Sharm el-Sheikh. There are two sorts: those belonging to Banque Masr (MasterCard/Cirrus or Visa/Plus) and those belonging to the Egyptian British Bank (EBB) (MasterCard/Cirrus or Visa/Plus or GlobalAccess).

International Transfers
Western Union, the international money transfer specialist, operates jointly in Egypt with Masr America International Bank and IBA business centres.

POST & COMMUNICATIONS
Post
Postcards and letters up to 15g cost 80pt to most countries and take four or five days to get to Europe and a week to 10 days to the USA and Australia. Stamps are available at post offices, and some souvenir kiosks, shops, newsstands and the reception desks of major hotels. Sending mail from the post boxes at major hotels instead of from post offices seems to be quicker.

Receiving Mail
Letters usually take a week to arrive from Europe, and a week to 10 days from the USA or Australia. Poste restante in Egypt func-

tions remarkably well and is generally free (though in Alexandria there's a small fee to collect letters).

Telephone

The country code for Egypt is ☎ 20. Area codes for some cities and towns within Egypt are:

Al-Arish	☎ 068
Alexandria	☎ 03
Al-Fayoum	☎ 084
Al-Quseir	☎ 088
Aswan	☎ 097
Bahariyya	☎ 018
Beni Suef	☎ 082
Cairo	☎ 02
Dahab	☎ 062
Dakhla	☎ 092
El Alamein	☎ 03
Farafra	☎ 1405
Hurghada	☎ 065
Ismailia	☎ 064
Kharga	☎ 092
Kom Ombo	☎ 097
Luxor	☎ 095
Marsa Matruh	☎ 03
Minya	☎ 086
Na'ama Bay	☎ 062
Nuweiba	☎ 062
Port Said	☎ 066
Qena	☎ 096
Sharm el-Sheikh	☎ 062
Siwa	☎ 046
Sohag	☎ 093
Suez	☎ 062
Taba	☎ 062

To make a national or international call use one of the bright orange card phones in the *centrales* (telephone offices). Phonecards for these are bought from the desk, and cost E£15 or E£30. Alternatively, you can book a call at the desk which must be paid for in advance (there is a three minute minimum). The operator directs you to a booth when a connection is made. There are different rates for day (8 am to 8 pm) and night (8 pm to 8 am) calls.

There's now also the option of making international calls from the new, privately

operated card phones, though these work out slightly more expensive than calls made at the centrale.

Fax

Fax machines are available for sending and receiving documents at the main centrales in the big cities, at most three to five-star hotels and at some of the smaller hotels as well. From a telephone office, a one page fax to the UK or USA costs about E£14, and E£20 to Australia. Hotel rates are quite a bit more.

Email & Internet Access

Egypt has taken up the Internet in a big way and there are cybercafes throughout the country including in Cairo, Alexandria, Sharm el-Sheikh, Dahab, Hurghada, and Luxor and Aswan – for addresses see the relevant city sections. Unfortunately Internet connection can be infuriatingly slow, a result of too much demand on insufficient international bandwidth. There are also problems with plugging your laptop into the wall in hotel rooms – there is a variety of phone sockets and in many cases the phone cable is wired straight into the wall.

BOOKS

Recommended travel literature includes *In An Antique Land* by Amitav Ghosh, which is a wonderfully observed account of the author's stay in a Delta village. There's also *Beyond the Pyramids* by Douglas Kennedy – some parts are noticeably weaker than others and it is very dated but this is one of the few travelogues written about Egypt in recent years. From past years look out for the entertaining *Flaubert in Egypt*, which reprints extracts from diaries Flaubert kept when he visited the country for a few months in 1849. *A Thousand Miles Up the Nile* by Amelia Edwards gives a good idea of travel in Egypt before air-con buses and air travel turned it into a five day jaunt from Europe.

Of the forests and forests of historical volumes, *The Complete Pyramids* by Mark Lehner and the companion volume, *The Complete Valley of the Kings*, by Nicholas Reeves & Richard H Wilkinson, are two superb compendiums of pharaonic information accompanied by good photos and specially drawn illustrations. *Alexandria Rediscovered* by Jean-Yves Empreur is an excellent and beautifully illustrated exploration of Graeco-Roman Alexandria including sections on the Pharos lighthouse and the search for Alexander's tomb. The authoritative book on the modern capital is *Cairo: The City Victorious* by Max Rodenbeck, an entertaining and prodigiously researched anecdotal meander through 5000 years of history.

NEWSPAPERS & MAGAZINES

Egyptian Gazette is Egypt's awful daily English-language newspaper. *Al-Ahram Weekly* and *Middle East Times* both appear every Thursday and do a much better job of keeping English-readers informed of what's going on. *Cairo Times* is a fortnightly glossy with great writing. It contains mainly hard news and analysis but there are good cultural features and a lively 'around town' section. *Egypt Today* is an ad-saturated general-interest glossy with excellent listings.

An extremely broad range of western newspapers and magazines are sold at hotel bookshops and street side newsstands. Papers are just a day old and monthly magazines usually make it within a week of their home publication dates, but expect to pay up to twice the cover price.

RADIO & TV

Nile TV, which is based in Cairo, broadcasts news and current affairs exclusively in English and French from 7 am each day until past midnight. There's a nightly English-language news bulletin on Channel Two at 8 pm.

Many hotels have satellite TV – even some of the budget places.

Radio-wise, FM95 broadcasts news in English on 557 kHz at 7.30 am and 2.30 and 8 pm daily. This is the European-language station and, in addition to English-language programs, it has programs in French, German, Italian, and Greek. BBC and Voice of America (VOA) broadcasts can be picked up on medium wave at various times of the

morning and evening. The BBC can be heard on both 639 kHz and 1320 kHz, and VOA on 1290 kHz.

PHOTOGRAPHY & VIDEO

Film generally costs as much as, if not more than, it does in the west; for example, Kodacolor 100/200 (36 exposures) costs about E£22, while for Kodachrome 100 slide film, you'll pay E£24 (36 exposures). Colour print processing costs from E£2 to E£5 depending on whether it's a one hour or overnight service, plus from 50 to 135pt per print depending on print size.

LAUNDRY

There are a few self-service laundries around Cairo but virtually none elsewhere. Another option is to take your clothes to one of Egypt's many 'hole-in-the-wall' laundries where they wash and iron your clothes by hand. The process is fascinating to watch. The *mukwagee* (ironing man) takes an ancient iron that opens at the top, places hot coals inside and then fills his mouth with water from a bottle on the table. The water is sprayed from his mouth over the clothes as he vigorously irons. Most hotels can organise to have your washing done.

TOILETS

Public toilets, when they can be found, are bad news: fly-infested, dirty and smelly. Some toilets are still of the 'squat over a hole in a little room' variety. Only in midrange and top end hotels will toilet paper be provided; most toilets come equipped with a water squirter for washing yourself when you're finished.

In cities it's a good idea to make a mental note of all western-style fast food joints, like McDonald's and KFC, and of the five-star hotels, as these are the places where you'll find the most sanitary facilities.

GAY & LESBIAN TRAVELLERS

There are no national support groups or gay information lines but there are a few places that are recognised gay hang-outs. Chief of these is Casanova's disco at the Burg Hotel on Gezira (closed at the time of writing but it may reopen again). The Taverne du Champs de Mars and Jackie's Disco, both in the Nile Hilton Hotel, are also popular with gay people.

PUBLIC HOLIDAYS & SPECIAL EVENTS

In addition to the main Islamic holidays described in the Regional Facts for the Visitor chapter, Egypt celebrates the following holidays:

New Year's Day
    1 January – official national holiday but many businesses stay open.
Christmas
    7 January – Coptic Christmas is a fairly low key affair and only Coptic businesses are closed for the day.
Easter
    March/April – the most important date on the Coptic calendar.
Sham an-Nessim
    1st Monday after Coptic Easter – Coptic holiday with pharaonic origins, it literally means 'the smell of the breeze'. It is celebrated by all Egyptians with family picnics and outings.
Sinai Liberation Day
    25 April – official national holiday. Celebrates Israel's return of Sinai in 1982.
May Day
    1 May – official national holiday.
Revolution Day
    23 July – official national holiday commemorating the 1952 coup when the Free Officers seized power from the puppet monarchy.
National Day
    6 October – celebrates Egyptian successes during the 1973 War with Israel. The day is marked by military parades and air displays and a long speech by the president.

COURSES

Several institutions in Cairo offer Arabic courses. The full-blown option is to sign up at the Arabic Language Institute (☎ 354 2964, fax 355 7665, email alu@auc.acs.eun.eg), a department of the American University in Cairo (AUC; PO Box 2511, Cairo 11511). It offers intensive instruction in Arabic language at elementary, intermediate and advanced levels with courses lasting one year. The institute also offers summer programs.

The Arabic Department (☎ 303 1514, fax 344 3076) at the British Council (192 Sharia el-Nil, Agouza, Cairo, Web site www.britcoun.org) also offers colloquial and classical courses spread over six or 12 weeks.

The third and cheapest option is to study at one of the two International Language Institutes (ILI) – in Mohandiseen (☎ 346 3087, fax 303 5624, email ili@starnet.com.eg) at 3 Sharia Mahmoud Azmy, Sahafayeen; or in Heliopolis (☎ 291 9295, fax 418 7273) at 2 Sharia Mohammed Bayoumi.

ACCOMMODATION

Officially, camping is allowed at only a few places around Egypt and facilities are rudimentary. There are a few private hotels around the country also allow campers to set up in their backyard.

Egypt has 15 hostels recognised by Hostelling International (HI). Having an HI card is not absolutely necessary as nonmembers are admitted but a card will save you between E£2 and E£4, depending on the hostel.

Budget accommodation is comprised of two, one and no-star hotels. Often the ratings mean nothing at all, as a hotel without a star can be as good as a two star hotel, only cheaper. You can spend as little as E£10 a night for a clean single room with hot water or E£40 or more for a dirty double room without a shower. Generally the prices quoted include any charges and quite often breakfast – but don't harbour any great expectations about breakfast as it is usually a couple of pieces of bread, a chunk of frozen butter, a dollop of jam, and tea or coffee. Most hotels will tell you they have hot water when they don't. They may not even have warm water. Before paying, turn the tap on and check for yourself or keep an eye out for an electric water heater when viewing the bathroom.

FOOD

While there are many wonderful things about Egypt, food isn't one of them. The cuisine is crude: salads are boring, vinegary and often far from fresh; vegetables have the flavour boiled out of them; typical main dishes of potato, rice and meat are heavy and oily. In fact, Egypt introduced the world to one of the most revolting dishes of all time – *molokhiyya*. Made by stewing the molokhiyya leaf in chicken stock, the resulting soup looks like green algae and has the consistency of mucus.

It is possible to eat well (and cheaply) in Egypt, if you can accept the lack of variety and pack your taste buds off on holiday.

Street food isn't bad. Its most ubiquitous elements are fuul and ta'amiyya. Fuul is mashed fava beans, usually ladled into a piece of *shammy* bread (like pitta), which sells for 35 to 50pt. Ta'amiyya is a slightly larger, flatter version of the mashed chickpea balls that are known elsewhere in the Middle East as felafel. A ta'amiyya sandwich costs about 50pt and two make a substantial snack.

Running a close second in national affections after fuul and ta'amiyya is *kushari*, a mix of noodles, rice, black lentils, fried onions and tomato sauce. The ingredients are served up together in a bowl for sit-down meals, or spooned into a polythene bag for takeaway. It's very good. You can recognise kushari joints by the great tureens of noodles and rice in their windows. You'll also see plenty of shwarma (see the Middle Eastern Cuisine special section in the Regional Facts for the Visitor chapter), but it's rarely good in Egypt.

The Levantine practice of dining on mezze doesn't carry through to Egypt, where main meals tend to be grilled meat with accompanying rice and bread. Expect lots of kebabs, kofta, lamb, chicken and pigeon – the last is something of a national delicacy, usually served up stuffed with rice.

DRINKS
As in the rest of the Middle East, *shai* and *ahwa* – tea and coffee – are both served strong and sugary. On practically every street in every town throughout Egypt, there is a juice stand where you can get a drink squeezed out of just about any fruit or vegetable in season.

For beer in Egypt say 'Stella'. It's a yeasty lager, the taste of which varies enormously by batch.

SPECTATOR SPORT
Football is king in Egypt. Of the Arab nations, Egypt is the one country with players of international capacity (Hazem Emam, formerly of Cairo club Zamalek, now currently plays for Udinese of Italy). In conversation with any Egyptian male, premier teams Zamalek and Al-Ahly arouse greater passions than almost any other subject. Demand for tickets makes them hard to get, especially for derbies. The season begins in September and continues until May. The big matches are held in the Cairo Stadium in Medinat Nasr.

SHOPPING
Egypt is both a budget souvenir and a kitsch-shopper's paradise. Tourists with shelf space to fill back home can indulge in an orgy of alabaster pyramids, onyx pharaonic cats, sawdust stuffed camels, and the ubiquitous painted papyrus. Hieroglyphic drawings of pharaohs, gods and goddesses embellish and blemish everything from leather wallets to engraved brass tables. Every town and village in Egypt has a small souq but there's no doubt that the best is Cairo's great Khan al-Khalili bazaar – although you will have to be prepared to bargain hard.

Getting There & Away

AIR
Airports
Egypt has a handful of airports but only six are international ports of entry: Cairo, Alexandria and, increasingly gaining status, the 'international' airports at Luxor, Aswan, Hurghada and Sharm el-Sheikh. Most air travellers enter Egypt through Cairo. The other airports (Alexandria excepted) tend to be used by charter and package-deal flights.

Warning On arrival at the airport, if you're not with a group, you may be approached by a man or woman with an official-looking badge that says 'Egyptian Chamber of Tourism' or something similar. These people are not government tourism officials, they are hotel touts. These touts will tell you that the hotel you're heading for is closed/horrible/very expensive and suggest a 'better' place, for which they earn a commission. Many taxi drivers will also try it on too. Do not be swayed by anyone who tries to dissuade you from going to the hotel of your choice. Hotels do not open and close with any great frequency in Cairo and if it's listed in this book then it is very unlikely to have gone out of business in the meantime. Some taxi drivers will stall by telling you that they don't know where your hotel is – in that case tell them to let you out at Midan Tahrir (or the Nile Hilton) and it's a short walk to almost all the budget hotels from there.

Airlines & Routes

Egypt's international and national carrier is EgyptAir. It's not a particularly good airline and fares are not cheap. You can usually get a seat on a much better carrier for the same price if not less. All the major European airlines fly direct into Cairo and more often than not, one of them will have some kind of discounted deal on offer at the time you are looking around. Try a couple of the travel agents mentioned in the Regional Getting There & Away chapter and find out what they come up with. For shorter trips, it's worth looking into packages or combined air fare and hotel deals offered by many of the high street travel agents.

Buying Tickets in Egypt

Air tickets bought in Egypt are subject to some hefty government taxes, which make them extremely expensive. Always fly in on a return or onward ticket. If you do have to buy a ticket in Cairo, see Travel Agencies in the Cairo city section later in this chapter for addresses.

LAND

Egypt has land borders with Israel & the Palestinian Territories, Libya and Sudan, but in the case of the last there is no open crossing point. The only way to travel between Egypt and Sudan is to fly or take the Wadi Halfa ferry – see under Sea later in this section.

Israel & the Palestinian Territories

There are two ways to do this: if you want to go directly to Tel Aviv or Jerusalem you go via Rafah; but if you want to spend time in Sinai enroute then you can also go via Taba.

Most nationalities do not need a visa to enter Israel but if you are returning to Egypt then you must have a re-entry or multiple-entry visa – see Visas & Documents earlier in this chapter.

Rafah There is a bus at 5.30 am every Sunday, Monday, Wednesday and Thursday from central Cairo to Tel Aviv and Jerusalem operated by Travco (☎ 340 4493) of 13 Mahmoud Azmy, Zamalek. Tickets are E£136 one way and the journey takes 10 hours. Tickets can be bought from Travco directly or from the Masr Travel offices at 7 Talaat Harb and on the 1st floor of the Cairo Sheraton hotel. The many travel agencies around Midan Tahrir can also sell tickets, but we really don't recommend that you deal with these companies. There's a E£17 departure tax to be paid at the border.

Taba Another possible route is to catch a bus to Taba in Sinai. Once at Taba you can walk across the border (which is open 24 hours) into Israel and take a taxi to Eilat (4km from the border) from where there are frequent buses onward to Jerusalem and Tel Aviv (but not on Friday evenings or before sundown Saturday, the Jewish holy day of Shabbat).

Libya

There are direct buses running between Cairo, Benghazi and Tripoli (Tarabulus). There are buses to the same destinations from Alexandria. For more details see Getting There & Away in the Cairo and Alexandria sections. A more laborious, but cheaper, alternative would be to get local transport to Sallum in the far north-west of Egypt (there are buses from Alexandria) and a service taxi to the border. From there you can get Libyan transport heading west.

SEA
Europe
There are no passenger boats operating between Egyptian ports and any ports in Europe at present.

Sudan
Via Wadi Halfa A boat leaves Aswan every Monday at around 3 pm, arriving in Wadi Halfa, Sudan, about 8 am Tuesday morning. You should be at the port at the High Dam by noon.

You can travel 1st or 2nd class, at a cost of E£142/88.50 and tickets are bought at Nile Valley Navigation Company based in Aswan (☎ 303 348), next to the tourist office, one street in from the Corniche. Note that the office will not sell you a ticket unless you've got a Sudanese visa stamp in your passport.

If you want to take a vehicle into Sudan, the Nile Valley Navigation Company also has a cargo ferry that will carry up to five or six cars. However, there are no fixed departures and you have to pay for the entire boat, a whopping E£8000.

Via the Red Sea At present there are no scheduled ships heading from Egypt to Port Sudan. You can get a boat from Jeddah but your transit visa will only be issued if you ensure that it leaves the same day that you arrive from Suez. For more information call the MenaTours office in Suez (☎ 228 821). You can also try to find a private yacht heading south, but there are very few and they may not be willing to take on passengers. Mohammed Moseilhy at Damanhur Shipping Agency in Suez can sometimes help find willing yacht owners; you can call him on ☎ 330 418.

Jordan
There's a sea link between Egypt and Jordan via Nuweiba in Sinai. A ferry and a catamaran both shuttle over from Aqaba and back, making one round trip a day. The ferry leaves Nuweiba at 3 pm and takes three hours. Tickets cost US$32 one way, or US$20 for children between five and 12 years of age. You must be at the port at least three hours before departure. The catamaran also leaves at 3 pm but it only takes one hour to reach Aqaba. A ticket costs US$42 one way (US$26 for children aged three to 10 years, US$16 for those under three). You must be at the harbour two hours before departure.

Tickets must be paid for in dollars and you must have a Jordanian visa before boarding.

Saudi Arabia & Kuwait
There are regular ferries between Jeddah and Suez (about 36 hours). Several lines compete on the route and fares can vary from one agent to another but, generally, tickets range from around E£145 for deck class to E£300 for 1st class. Most of the ferries on the route also carry cars, at a significant cost. Getting a berth during the *haj* is virtually impossible. You can get information at Masr Travel agencies, or buy a ticket directly from its office in Port Tawfiq, Suez.

There are also regular services between Hurghada on the Red Sea coast, and Dubai in Saudi Arabia. Tickets can be booked with MenaTours in Cairo (☎ 348 2230).

You can purchase tickets through to many destinations in the Gulf, either at Cairo's Sinai terminal or Turgoman garage in Cairo or in Alexandria. From Cairo to Riyadh (daily departures at 1 pm) the fare is E£250 to E£275, and to Kuwait E£380.

Getting Around

AIR
EgyptAir is the main domestic carrier. Air Sinai, which to all intents and purposes is EgyptAir by another name, is virtually the only other operator. Fares are expensive

and probably out of the range of most budget travellers. In general, it is only worth flying if your time is very limited.

During the high season (October to April), many flights are full so it's wise to book as far in advance as you can.

Sample fares one way/return are:

from	to	one way (E£)	return (E£)
Aswan	Abu Simbel		290
Cairo	Abu Simbel	818	1631
	Alexandria	248	490
	Aswan	576	1146
	Hurghada	453	900
	Luxor	419	832
	Sharm el-Sheikh	477	948
Luxor	Aswan	190	380
	Hurghada	190	380

BUS

Buses service just about every city, town and village in Egypt. Deluxe buses travel between some of the main towns such as Cairo and Alexandria and around Sinai. These services are good with comfortable seats and air-con. The bulk of buses running south of Cairo along the Nile tend to be more basic.

Often the prices of tickets for buses on the same route will vary according to whether or not they have air-con and video, how old the bus is and how long it takes to make the journey – the more you pay, the more comfort you travel in and the quicker you get there.

Tickets can be bought at the bus stations or often on the bus. Hang on to your ticket until you get off, as inspectors almost always board the bus to check fares. There are no student discounts on bus fares.

TRAIN

Although trains travel along more than 5000km of track to almost every major city and town in Egypt, the system is badly in need of modernisation and most services are grimy and battered and a poor second option to the deluxe bus. The exceptions are some of the trains to Alexandria and the tourist trains down to Luxor and Aswan – on these routes the train is the preferred option rather than the bus.

If you have an International Student Identification Card (ISIC) discounts of about 33% are granted on all fares except the wagon-lit services to Aswan and Luxor.

SERVICE TAXI

Travelling by 'ser-vees' is one of the fastest ways to go from city to city. Service taxis are generally big Peugeot 504 cars that run intercity routes. Drivers congregate near bus and train stations and tout for passengers by shouting their destination. When the car's full, it's off. A driver won't leave before his car is full unless you and/or the other passengers want to pay more money. Service taxi fares are usually cheaper than either bus or train fares and there are no set departure times – you just turn up and find a car.

CAR & MOTORCYCLE

Driving in Cairo is a crazy affair, but in other parts of the country, at least in daylight, it isn't so bad. Driving is on the right-hand side in Egypt. For more information on road rules, suggested routes and other advice, it might be worth picking up a copy of *On the Road in Egypt – A Motorist's Guide* by Mary Dungan Megalli.

Petrol is readily available. Normal, or *tamaneen*, costs 90pt a litre but is tough on the engine. Better is the higher-octane super, or *tisa'een*, at E£1 a litre. Lead-free was introduced in 1995, but with only a handful of pumps in Cairo (mainly in Mohandiseen, Zamalek and Ma'adi) and Alexandria, there might be a queue. When travelling out of Cairo, remember that petrol stations are not always that plentiful; when you see one, fill up.

Rental

Several car-rental agencies have offices in Egypt including Avis, Hertz and Budget. Their rates match international charges and finding a cheap deal with local dealers is virtually impossible. No matter who you go with, make sure you read the fine print.

EGYPT

An International Driving Permit is required and you can be liable for a heavy fine if you're caught renting a car without one. Drivers should mostly be over the age of 25.

As an indication of prices, for a small car like a Suzuki Swift you'll be looking at about US$33 to US$40 per day, plus up to US$0.20 for each extra kilometre. A Toyota Corolla is about US$56 to US$60 per day, plus around US0.25 per kilometre. These prices generally include insurance and the first 100km but check this before signing. For unlimited kilometres, you'll be looking at about US$47/70 per day respectively for the previously mentioned cars.

Some companies, such as Europcar, offer the option of one-way rentals from, for example, Cairo to Sharm el-Sheikh.

Cairo

Few other countries can be so dominated by their capital: Cairo is Egypt. Both of them are known by the same name, Masr, and for Egyptians, to speak of one is to speak of the other at the same time. The city's stature spreads beyond borders – to millions of Arabic speakers, Cairo is the semi-mythical capital of the Arab world. The so-called 'Mother of the World', Cairo nurtures around 16 million Egyptians, Arabs, Africans and sundry international hangers-on. She's overburdened with one of the world's highest densities of people per square kilometre, which makes for a seething compress of people, buildings and traffic and all the attendant cacophony and jostling for space that that brings. It's a city travellers either love or hate, but few come away indifferent.

HISTORY
Cairo is not a pharaonic city, though the presence of the Pyramids leads many to believe otherwise. At the time the Pyramids were built the capital of ancient Egypt was Memphis, 22km south of the Giza plateau.

The core foundations of the city of Cairo were laid in 969 AD by the early Islamic Fatimid dynasty. There had been earlier set-tlements, notably the Roman fortress of Babylon and the early Islamic city of Fustat, established by Amr ibn al-As, the general who conquered Egypt for Islam in 642 AD. Much of the city the Fatimids built remains today: the great Fatimid mosque and university of Al-Azhar is still Egypt's main centre of Islamic study, while the three great gates of Bab an-Nasr, Bab al-Futuh and Bab Zuweila still straddle two of Islamic Cairo's main thoroughfares.

Under the rule of subsequent dynasties Cairo swelled and burst its walls but at heart it remained a medieval city for 900 years. It wasn't until the mid-19th century that Cairo started to change in any significant way.

Before the 1860s Cairo extended west only as far as what is today Midan Opera.

Cairo Highlights

- **The Pyramids at Dawn** – with hawkers and camel owners in your face it's hard to be duly awed by the world's greatest ancient wonders, but at dawn, it's a different story: you have them to yourself
- **Fishawi's at 2 am** – any time of the day is fine at Cairo's oldest coffeehouse but after midnight the visitors are gone and the place returns to the locals
- **Sunset Felucca Rides** – drift on the Nile and watch the sun sink behind the Cairo skyline
- **Tutankhamun at the Egyptian Museum** – badly displayed but still some of the most magnificent objects held by any museum anywhere in the world
- **Up the Minarets at Bab Zuweila** – lots of Cairo's minarets are climbable but for peering into the heart of the medieval city the best view is from either of the two towers atop Bab Zuweila
- **Early Morning at the Hanging Church** – this is one of the most serene and understatedly attractive sites in Cairo, best visited early, before the coach parties arrive

The future site of modern central Cairo was then a swampy plain subject to the annual flooding of the Nile. In 1863, when the French-educated Ismail came to power, he was determined to upgrade the image of his capital, which he believed could only be done by dismissing what had gone before and starting afresh. For 10 years the former marsh became one vast building site as Ismail invited architects from Belgium, France and Italy to design and build a new European-style Cairo beside the old Islamic city.

Since the Revolution, Cairo has grown spectacularly in population and urban planners have struggled to keep pace.

ORIENTATION

Finding your way about the vast sprawl of Cairo is not as difficult as it may first seem. Midan Tahrir is the centre. Northeast of Tahrir is Downtown. Centred on Sharia Talaat Harb, Downtown is a noisy, busy commercial district and it's where you'll find most of the cheap eating places and budget accommodation. Midan Ramses, location of the city's main train station, marks the northernmost extent of Downtown.

Heading east, Downtown ends at Midan Ataba and Islamic Cairo takes over. This is the old medieval heart of the city, still very much alive today. At its centre is the great bazaar of Khan al-Khalili.

The West Bank of the Nile is less historical and much more residential than areas along the east bank. The primary districts, north to south are Mohandiseen, Agouza, Doqqi and Giza, all of which are heavy on concrete and light on charm. Giza covers by far the largest area of the four, stretching some 20km west either side of one long, straight road that ends at the foot of the Pyramids.

INFORMATION
Visas

All visa business is carried out at the Mogamma (open from 8 am to 2 pm Saturday to Thursday), the 14 storey monolithic white building on Midan Tahrir. Foreigners go up to the 1st floor, pass through the door on the right then circle around to the left and straight down the corridor ahead. Go to window No 42 to collect a form and you'll be told where to go next.

Tourist Offices

Cairo's main tourist office (☎ 391 3454) is at 5 Sharia Adly, close to Midan Opera. It's open daily from 8.30 am to 8 pm (9 am to 5 pm during Ramadan).

Money

There are banks and forex bureaus all over town but it's worth knowing that the Banque Masr branches at the Nile Hilton and Helnan Shepheard's hotels are open 24 hours. Otherwise the city's foreign exchange bureaus tend to close at 8 pm. There are ATMs in the foyers of the Cairo Marriott (in Zamalek), Nile Hilton and Semiramis InterContinental hotels; at the main entrance to the Al-Bustan shopping centre on Sharia al-Bustan, Downtown; at the British Council in Agouza; and at the EBB on Abu al-Feda in Zamalek.

The main Amex office (☎ 574 7991, fax 578 4003) is at 15 Qasr el-Nil, Downtown, while the most central branch of Thomas Cook (☎ 574 3955, fax 576 2750) is at 17 Mahmoud Bassiouni, Downtown.

Post & Telephone

Cairo's GPO, on Midan Ataba, is open from 7 am to 7 pm Saturday to Thursday, and from 7 am to noon on Friday and public holidays. The poste restante is down the sidestreet to the right of the main entrance, through the last door (opposite the EMS fast mail office). It's open from 8 am to 6 pm, except Friday and holidays when it's open from 10 am to noon.

There are several telephone centrales around Cairo, and most have a few card phones. In central Cairo there are offices on the northern side of Midan Tahrir, near the tourist information office in Sharia Adly, and on Sharia Mohammed Mahmoud in Bab al-Luq.

EGYPT

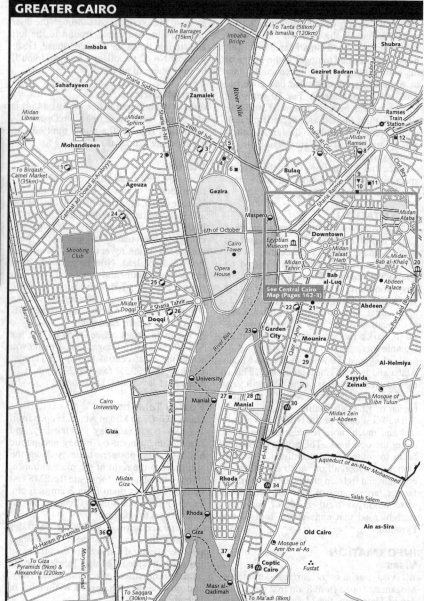

See Central Cairo
Map (Pages 162-3)

GREATER CAIRO

EGYPT

To
Nile Barrages
(15km)

To Tanta (58km)
& Ismailia (120km)

Imbaba
Bridge

Imbaba

Shubra

Sahafayeen

Geziret Badran

Sharia Sudan

Zamalek

River Nile

Ramses
Train
Station

Midan
Libnan

Midan
Sphinx

26th of July

Sharia el-Nil

Sharia al-Gisr

Midan
Ramses

12

Mohandiseen

To Birqash
Camel Market
(35km)

Agouza

Gezira

Bulaq

Shooting
Club

24

6th of October

Maspero

Egyptian
Museum

Downtown

Midan
Ataba

Cairo
Tower

Opera
House

Midan
Talaat
Harb

Midan
Bab al-Khalq

20

25

Midan
Doqqi

Sharia Tahrir

26

Doqqi

Midan
Tahrir

Bab
al-Luq

Abdeen
Palace

Abdeen

22 21

River Bus

23 Garden
City

Mounira

Al-Helmiya

29

Sayyida
Zeinab

Mosque of
ibn Tulun

University

27 28

Manial

Manial

30

Midan Zein
al-Abdeen

Cairo
University

Giza

Aqueduct of an-Nasr Mohammed

Midan
Giza

Rhoda

Salah Salem

Ain as-Sira

35

Rhoda

36

Al-Haram (Pyramids Rd)

Giza

Old Cairo

To Giza
Pyramids (9km) &
Alexandria (220km)

37

Mosque of
Amr ibn al-As

Fustat

38 Coptic
Cairo

To Saqqara
(30km)

Masr al-
Qadimah

To Ma'adi (8km)

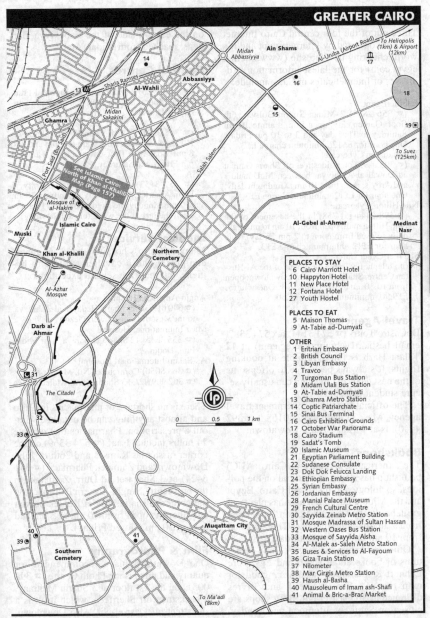

EGYPT

GREATER CAIRO

PLACES TO STAY
6 Cairo Marriott Hotel
10 Happyton Hotel
11 New Place Hotel
12 Fontana Hotel
27 Youth Hostel

PLACES TO EAT
5 Maison Thomas
9 At-Tabie ad-Dumyati

OTHER
1 Eritrian Embassy
2 British Council
3 Libyan Embassy
4 Travco
7 Turgoman Bus Station
8 Midam Ulali Bus Station
9 At-Tabie ad-Dumyati
13 Ghamra Metro Station
14 Coptic Patriarchate
15 Sinai Bus Terminal
16 Cairo Exhibition Grounds
17 October War Panorama
18 Cairo Stadium
19 Sadat's Tomb
20 Islamic Museum
21 Egyptian Parliament Building
22 Sudanese Consulate
23 Dok Dok Felucca Landing
24 Ethiopian Embassy
25 Syrian Embassy
26 Jordanian Embassy
28 Manial Palace Museum
29 French Cultural Centre
30 Sayyida Zeinab Metro Station
31 Mosque Madrassa of Sultan Hassan
32 Western Oases Bus Station
33 Mosque of Sayyida Aisha
34 Al-Malek as-Saleh Metro Station
35 Buses & Services to Al-Fayoum
36 Giza Train Station
37 Nilometer
38 Mar Girgis Metro Station
39 Haush al-Basha
40 Mausoleum of Imam ash-Shafi
41 Animal & Bric-a-Brac Market

Email & Internet Access

Three out of the four central Cairo Internet cafes are operated by InternetEgypt and it's worth checking its Web site (www.internet egypt.com) for the latest information. Addresses of Internet cafes in Cairo include:

InternetEgypt
(☎ 356 2882) 2 Midan Simon Bolivar, 6th floor, Garden City; open from 9 am to 10 pm Saturday to Thursday and 3 to 10 pm Friday. One hour for E£12, minimum charge E£3.
Mohandiseen Cybercafe
(☎ 305 0493) on a sidestreet off Sharia Gamiat ad-Dowal al-Arabiyya, between McDonald's and Arby's; open from 10 am to midnight daily. One hour for E£12, minimum charge E£3.
Nile Hilton Cybercafe
(☎ 578 0444 ext 758) in the basement of the Nile Hilton mall; open from 10 am to midnight daily (closed from noon to 2 pm Friday). One hour for E£12, minimum charge E£3.
St@rnet Cyber Café
(no telephone) in the basement of the Al-Bustan Centre, Sharia al-Bustan, Downtown; open from 10.30 am to 10.30 pm daily. One hour for E£9.90, minimum charge E£5.50.

Travel Agencies

DeCastro Tours (☎ 574 3144, fax 574 3382, email hesham1@brainy1.ie-eg.com) at 12 Talaat Harb is fairly reliable at booking flights. It's always been able to offer some of the best deals in town and can usually secure student discounts.

The official Egyptian government travel agency, Masr Travel (☎ 393 0168, fax 392 4440), is at 7 Talaat Harb, Downtown.

Bookshops

The American University in Cairo (AUC) bookshop has stacks of material on the politics, sociology and history of Cairo, Egypt and the Middle East but it also has plenty of guidebooks and some fiction. It's open from 9 am to 4 pm Sunday to Thursday and from 10 am to 3 pm on Saturday.

Other bookshops with very good selections of books about Cairo and Egypt are Lehnert & Landrock (also very good for maps) at 44 Sharia Sherif and Livres d'France at 36 Qasr el-Nil. Both shops are closed on Saturday afternoon and Sunday.

There's a large secondhand book market on the eastern side of the Ezbekiyya Gardens, reached from Midan Ataba.

Cultural Centres

France
(☎ 355 3725) 1 Madrassat al-Huquq al-Fransiyya, Mounira; open from 9 am to 9 pm Sunday to Thursday
UK
(☎ 345 3281) British Council, 192 Sharia el-Nil, Agouza; open from 9 am to 2 pm and 3 to 8 pm Monday to Thursday and from 9 am to 3 pm Friday and Saturday
USA
(☎ 357 3133) American Studies Library, 5 Latin America, Garden City; open from 10 am to 7 pm Monday and Wednesday and 10 am to 4 pm the rest of the week (closed Saturday)

Medical Services

Many of Cairo's hospitals have antiquated equipment and a cavalier attitude to hygiene, but there are several exceptions:

Anglo-American Hospital
(☎ 340 612/3/4/5) Sharia Hadayek al-Zuhreyya, to the west of Cairo Tower, Gezira
Masr International Hospital
(☎ 335 3345) 12 Sharia al-Saraya, near Midan Fini, Doqqi
As-Salam International Hospital
(☎ 363 8050) Corniche el-Nil, Ma'adi
(☎ 302 9091/2/3) 3 Sharia Syria, Mohandiseen

There is no shortage of pharmacies in Cairo and almost anything can be obtained without a prescription. Pharmacies that operate 24 hours include Isaaf (☎ 574 3369) on the corner of sharias Ramses and 26th of July, Downtown, and Zamalek Pharmacy (☎ 341 6424) at 3 Shagaret ad-Durr, Zamalek. In the city centre, Anglo-Eastern Pharmacy on the corner of sharias Abdel Khalek Sarwat and Sherif is open from 10 am to 3 pm and 6.30 to 10 pm (closed Friday).

Film & Photography

One Downtown place recommended for quality and price is the Photo Centre (☎ 392 0031) on the 1st floor at 3 Sharia Mahrany, a backstreet off Sherifeen, which itself is a sidestreet off Qasr el-Nil. Also Downtown, there's a Kodak shop on Sharia Adly between sharias Sherif and Mohammed Farid.

ISLAMIC CAIRO

The term Islamic Cairo is a bit of a misnomer, as the area is no more or less Islamic than most other parts of the city but maybe the profusion of minarets on the skyline gives the impression of piety.

The best place to start exploring is the area around the great bazaar, **Khan al-Khalili**. It's very easy to find from central Cairo – from Midan Ataba head straight along Sharia al-Azhar or Muski; alternatively, it's a short taxi ride; ask for 'Al-Hussein' – the name of both the midan and the mosque at the mouth of the bazaar. The fare should be no more than E£3 from Downtown. Before diving into the bazaar, it is worth taking time out to visit one of Cairo's most historic institutions, **Al-Azhar**, not only one of Cairo's earliest mosques but also the world's oldest surviving university. It's open daily, and admission is E£12.

One of the best walks in Cairo is north from Khan al-Khalili up towards the old **northern wall** and **gates**. The square-towered Bab an-Nasr (Gate of Victory) and the rounded Bab al-Futuh (Gate of Conquests) were built in 1087 as the two main northern entrances to the new walled Fatimid city of Al-Qahira. You can walk along the top of the walls and explore inside the gates via the roof of the Mosque of al-Hakim. Admission to the gates is E£6.

South of Khan al-Khalili a busy market street runs down to the twin-minareted gate of **Bab Zuweila**, the sole surviving gate from the old city's southern wall. The view from the minarets is about the best in Cairo – access is through the **Mosque of al-Mu'ayyad**, and admission is E£12.

Continuing south from Bab Zuweila, you pass through the **street of the tentmakers**, a covered bazaar filled by craftsmen specialising in appliqué work, and 500m farther you emerge in a large square dominated by the twin **Mosque-Madrassa of Sultan Hassan** and **Mosque of ar-Rifai**. The former dates from the 14th century, the latter from 1912;

admission to both is E£12 (the interior of Sultan Hassan is by far the more impressive).

The Citadel

Overlooking the two grand mosques is Cairo's **Citadel**, begun by Saladin (Salah ad-Din) back in the 12th century. Its walls encircle an assortment of three very different mosques, several palaces housing some fairly indifferent museums, and a couple of terraces with fine views over the city. Admission is E£20.

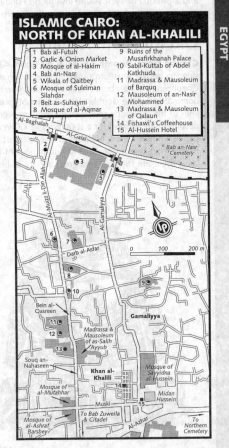

ISLAMIC CAIRO: NORTH OF KHAN AL-KHALILI

1 Bab al-Futuh
2 Garlic & Onion Market
3 Mosque of al-Hakim
4 Bab an-Nasr
5 Wikala of Qaitbey
6 Mosque of Suleiman Silahdar
7 Beit as-Suhaymi
8 Mosque of al-Aqmar
9 Ruins of the Musafirkhanah Palace
10 Sabil-Kuttab of Abdel Katkhuda
11 Madrassa & Mauseoleum of Barquq
12 Mausoleum of an-Nasir Mohammed
13 Madrassa & Mausoleum of Qalaun
14 Fishawi's Coffeehouse
15 Al-Hussein Hotel

EGYPTIAN MUSEUM

More than 100,000 relics and antiquities from almost every period of ancient Egyptian history are housed in the Egyptian Museum. To put that in perspective, if you spent only one minute at each exhibit it would take more than nine months to see everything.

With so much to see, trying to get around everything in one go is liable to induce chronic pharaonic phatigue. The best strategy is to spread the exploration over at least two visits, maybe tackling one floor at a time.

Admission to the museum is E£20 (E£10 for students). Access to the Royal Mummy Room costs an additional E£40 (E£20 for students); tickets for this are bought at the 1st floor entrance to the room. The museum is open from 9 am to 4.45 pm daily, but closes between noon and 2 pm on Friday. If you're visiting on Friday morning, you can't get back in with the same ticket in the afternoon.

Old Kingdom Rooms

Ground Floor, Rooms 32, 37 & 42 Room 42 holds what some consider to be the museum's masterpiece, a larger-than-lifesize statue of Chephren (Khafre), builder of the second pyramid at Giza. Room 32 is dominated by the double statue of Rahotep and Nofret – the simple lines of the limestone sculpture make them seem almost contemporary, despite being around for a staggering 4000 years. Also in here are the panels known as the Meidum Geese, part of a frieze that originates from a mud-brick mastaba at Meidum, near Al-Fayoum (to this day, the lakes there are still host to a great variety of bird life).

Top: The mask of Tutankhamun (Photo by Chris Mellor)

Bottom Left: An elaborate pectoral made of gold, silver, semi-precious stones and glass that was found in the wrappings of Tutankhamun's mumm

Bottom Right: Sandsto bust of Akhenaten fou in Karnak at the temple of Aten. Displayed in Room 3 on the ground floor.

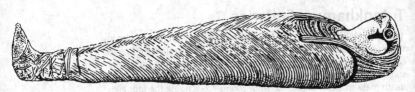

Akhenaten Room

Ground Floor, Room 3 This room is devoted to the 'heretic king' who set up ancient Egypt's first and last monotheistic faith. Compare the bulbous bellies, hips and thighs, the elongated heads and thick, Mick Jagger-like lips of these statues with the sleek, hard-edged norm of typical pharaonic sculpture. Also very striking is the delicate but unfinished head of Nefertiti, wife of Akhenaten.

Royal Tombs of Tanis

1st Floor, Room 2 One of two new galleries opened in 1998, this is a glittering collection of gold and silver encrusted amulets, gold funerary masks, daggers, bracelets, collars, gold sandals and finger and toe coverings from five intact New Kingdom tombs found in the Delta site of Tanis.

Top: Mummified falcon, found in room 53 on the 1st floor among many animal mummies.

EGYPTIAN MUSEUM

Ground Floor

NW Stairs   NEW KINGDOM   NE Stairs

MIDDLE KINGDOM

OLD KINGDOM

LATE PERIOD

SW Stairs   SE Stairs

1, 6, 7, 3, 8, 5, 9, 10
11, 12, 13, 14, 15
16, 17, 18, 19, 20
21, 22, 23, 24, 25
26, 27, 28 Atrium 33, 29, 30
31, 32, 34, 35
36, 37, 38, 39, 40
41, 42, 43, 44, 45
51, 46, 47, 48, 49, 50, 51

Library   Bookshop   Entrance   Gift Shop & Cafeteria   Tourist Police

First Floor

NW Stairs   NE Stairs

1, 2, 3, 4, 5
6, 8, 9, 10
11, 12, 13, 14, 15
16, 17, 19, 20
21, 22, 24, 25
26, 27, 29, 30
31, 32, 34, 35
36, 39, 40
41, 42, 43, 44, 45
48
51, 46, 47, 49, 50, 51
53, 54, 55, 56

Royal Mummy Room Tickets

SW Stairs   SE Stairs

Tutankhamun Galleries

Tutankhamun Galleries

1st Floor Without doubt, the exhibit that outshines everything else in the museum is the treasure of this young and comparatively insignificant pharaoh who ruled for only nine years. About 1700 items are spread throughout a series of rooms. Room 3 contains the astonishing death mask made of solid gold, while rooms 7 & 8 house the four gilded shrines that fitted inside each other and held the gold sarcophagus of Tutankhamun at their centre.

Graeco-Roman Mummies

1st Floor, Room 14 This room contains a small sample of the stunning portraits painted onto wooden panels then placed over the embalmed faces of Graeco-Roman period mummies. Most of these portraits were discovered in the Al-Fayoum oasis, just south-west of Cairo.

Royal Mummy Room

1st Floor, Room 56 This room houses the bodies of 11 of Egypt's most illustrious kings and queens, who ruled Egypt between 1552 and 1069 BC, including Ramses II.

Bottom: Tutankhamun's legendary and exquisite mask of beaten gold inlaid with lapis lazuli and other gems

EDDIE GERALD

Mosque of ibn Tulun

Also not to be missed is the **Mosque of ibn Tulun**, 800m south-west of the Citadel. It's quite unlike any other mosque in Cairo mainly because the inspiration is almost entirely Iraqi – the closest thing to it are the ancient mosques of Samarra. Admission is E£6. Right next door to Ibn Tulun is the **Gayer-Anderson Museum**, two 16th century houses restored and furnished by a British major between 1935 and 1942. The attraction of the museum is not the exhibits themselves but the houses, their puzzle of rooms and the lavish decor. Well worth a visit, the place is open from 8 am to 4 pm daily and admission is E£16.

OLD CAIRO

Once known as Babylon, this part of Cairo pre-dates the coming of Islam and remains to this day the seat of the Coptic Christian community. There is a Coptic **museum** with mosaics, manuscripts, tapestries and Christian artwork. Al-Muallaqa, or **Hanging Church**, is the centre of Coptic worship. Among the other churches and monasteries here, **St Sergius** is supposed to mark one of the resting places of the Holy Family on its flight from King Herod. The easiest way to get here from Midan Tahrir is by metro (50pt). Get out at the Mar Girgis station.

FELUCCA RIDES

You can hire a felucca for about E£15 an hour from the Corniche by the Semiramis Hotel but the best place is about 800m to the south, to the Dok Dok landing stage, just short of the bridge over to Le Meridien hotel.

PLACES TO STAY – BUDGET
Camping

The only camping in all of Cairo is at *Motel Salma* (☎ 384 9152, fax 385 1010) next to the Wissa Wassef Art Centre at Harraniyya, south of Giza. Although inconvenient in that it's miles and miles from anywhere, it does have views of the Pyramids from the back of the site. Overland tour companies occasionally stop here. Camping costs E£7 per person with your own tent or camper van.

Hostels

HI Manial Youth Hostel (☎ 364 0729, fax 398 4107, 135 Abdel Aziz el-Saud, Manial) is in reasonable nick with clean toilets, although the beds are nothing great. For HI members it costs E£12 in three-bed dorms or E£8 in six-bed dorms; nonmembers pay E£4 more. There are no rooms for couples or families.

Hotels & Pensions

The inexpensive hotels and pensions are concentrated Downtown, mainly on and around Sharia Talaat Harb.

At last visit there were no less than three hotels called *Sultan* (☎ 577 2258, 4 Souq at-Tawfiqiyya), plus *Safary Hotel* (☎ 575 0752) and *Hotel Venice*, all occupying one building off the top end of Talaat Harb, constituting a backpackers' ghetto on a colourful market street. Give or take a pound, there's little between them. They offer grubby, cramped dorms (from E£5 to E£9 for a bed), one or two of the places have doubles (E£16 to E£20), and in all cases over-burdened, unsanitary bathroom facilities are shared.

Dahab Hotel (☎ 579 4400, 26 Mahmoud Bassiouni, Downtown) is supposed to re-create the feel of a Sinai beach camp with a collection of whitewashed huts on a rooftop, with cushioned communal spaces open to the sky, bamboo screens and Bob Marley on the cassette deck. The downside is the number of street hustlers the management allows to hang around – female travellers be warned. Beds in dorms are E£12 (shared showers), while a sparse double with private shower is E£35.

Hotel Minerva (☎ 392 0600/1/2, 39 Talaat Harb, Downtown) has a ground floor reception hidden down the alley opposite the Al'Américaine cafe, while the hotel itself occupies the 6th and 7th floors. The not-so-obvious location means this old place is often overlooked, but the rooms are kept clean, as are the communal showers and toilets, and it's good value with singles/doubles at E£16/28, or doubles with shower at E£32.

CENTRAL CAIRO

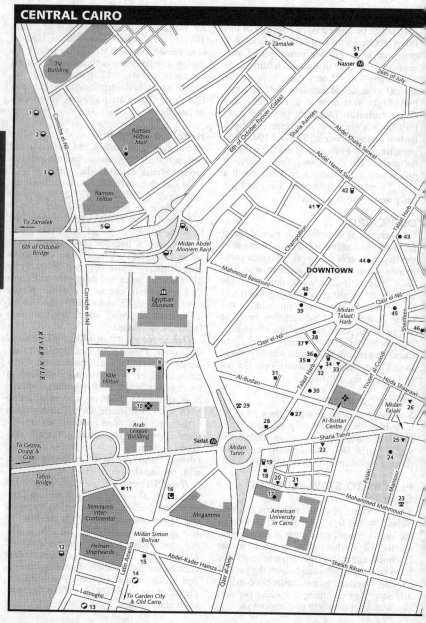

EGYPT

TV Building

Ramses Hilton Mall

Ramses Hilton

To Zamalek

6th of October Bridge

Coniche el-Nil

Coniche el-Nil

RIVER NILE

Egyptian Museum

Nile Hilton

Arab League Building

To Gezira, Doqqi & Giza

Tahrir Bridge

Semiramis Inter-Continental

Helnan Shepheards

Mogamma

Midan Simon Bolivar

Abdel-Kader Hamza

Latin America

Lazoughli

To Garden City & Old Cairo

To Zamalek

Nasser Ⓜ

26th of July

6th of October flyover (Galaa)

Sharia Ramses

Abdel Khalek Sarwat

Abdel Hamid Said

Talaat Harb

Champollion

DOWNTOWN

Mahmoud Bassiouni

Midan Abdel Moniem Raid

Qasr el-Nil

Midan Talaat Harb

Qasr el-Nil

Sheriffeen

Talaat Harb

Yousef al-Guindi

Hoda Shaarawi

Midan Falaki

Al-Bustan

Al-Bustan Centre

Sharia Tahrir

Midan Tahrir

Sadat Ⓜ

Mansour

Falaki

Mohammed Mahmoud

American University in Cairo

Sheikh Rihan

Qasr al-Ainy

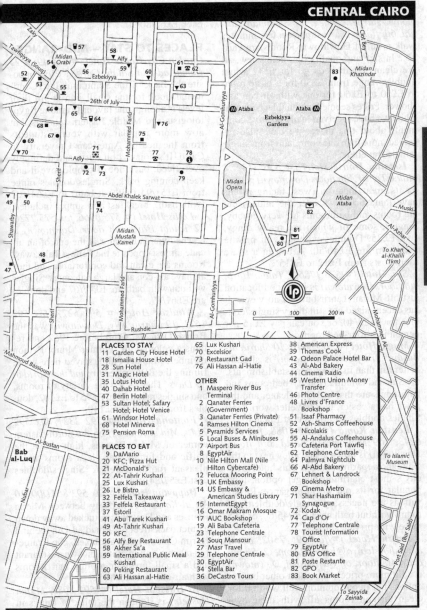

CENTRAL CAIRO

EGYPT

0   100   200 m

PLACES TO STAY
11 Garden City House Hotel
18 Ismailia House Hotel
28 Sun Hotel
31 Magic Hotel
35 Lotus Hotel
40 Dahab Hotel
47 Berlin Hotel
53 Sultan Hotel; Safary Hotel; Hotel Venice
61 Windsor Hotel
68 Hotel Minerva
75 Pension Roma

PLACES TO EAT
9 DaMario
20 KFC; Pizza Hut
21 McDonald's
22 At-Tahrir Kushari
25 Lux Kushari
32 Le Bistro
32 Felfela Takeaway
33 Felfela Restaurant
37 Estoril
41 Abu Tarek Kushari
49 At-Tahrir Kushari
50 KFC
56 Alfy Bey Restaurant
58 Akher Sa'a
59 International Public Meal Kushari
60 Peking Restaurant
63 Ali Hassan al-Hatie

65 Lux Kushari
70 Excelsior
73 Restaurant Gad
76 Ali Hassan al-Hatie

OTHER
1 Maspero River Bus Terminal
2 Qanater Ferries (Government)
3 Qanater Ferries (Private)
4 Ramses Hilton Cinema
5 Pyramids Services
6 Local Buses & Minibuses
7 Airport Bus
8 EgyptAir
10 Nile Hilton Mall (Nile Hilton Cybercafe)
12 Felucca Mooring Point
13 UK Embassy
14 US Embassy & American Studies Library
15 InternetEgypt
16 Omar Makram Mosque
17 AUC Bookshop
19 Ali Baba Cafeteria
23 Telephone Centrale
24 Souq Mansour
27 Masr Travel
29 Telephone Centrale
30 EgyptAir
34 Stella Bar
36 DeCastro Tours

38 American Express
39 Thomas Cook
42 Odeon Palace Hotel Bar
43 Al-Abd Bakery
44 Cinema Radio
45 Western Union Money Transfer
46 Photo Centre
48 Livres d'France
51 Isaaf Pharmacy
52 Ash-Shams Coffeehouse
54 Nicolakis
55 Al-Andalus Coffeehouse
57 Cafeteria Port Tawfiq
62 Telephone Centrale
64 Palmyra Nightclub
66 Al-Abd Bakery
67 Lehnert & Landrock Bookshop
69 Cinema Metro
71 Shar Hashamaim Synagogue
72 Kodak
74 Cap d'Or
77 Telephone Centrale
78 Tourist Information Office
79 EgyptAir
80 EMS Office
81 Poste Restante
82 GPO
83 Book Market

New Palace Hotel (☎ 575 1283, email *mony@starnet.com.eg, 17 Suleiman Halabi, 6th floor*) is a vast place a few minutes walk north of Downtown. Rooms are variable in size and quality but, being new, all are clean. Dorm beds go for E£12 while doubles range from E£30 for a basic room to E£50 to E£60 for one with air-con and shower. Prices seemed negotiable. Note that while we have received many positive comments about this place, we have also received more than one complaint from single female travellers.

Ismailia House Hotel (☎ 356 3122, *1 Midan Tahrir, 8th floor, Downtown*) gets by on its great location (west facing rooms have fantastic views over the midan) but the rooms and bathrooms are very grubby. Singles, some of which are really dingy, cost E£25. Doubles without/with private bathroom are E£40/50. A bed in a share room costs from E£12 to E£15.

Sun Hotel (☎ 578 1786, *2 Talaat Harb, 9th floor, Downtown*) is in a good location just off Midan Tahrir but has no views. It has decent-sized but still dingy singles/doubles for E£25/40, or you can pay E£15 per person in a four-bed room.

Magic Hotel (☎ 579 5918, *10 Sharia al-Bustan, 3rd floor, Downtown*) is slightly better run than its two sister establishments, the Sun and Ismailia House – bedrooms and bathrooms are that little bit cleaner and the place has a cosier, less traveller-worn feel. Singles/doubles with fans cost E£25/40.

Pension Roma (☎ 391 1088, fax 579 6243, *169 Mohammed Farid, 6th floor, Downtown*) is down a side alley next to the Gattegno department store. This hotel is the city's most charming budget option, long popular for its old world elegance. Reservations are necessary. Single/double/triple rooms without bath are E£25/45/60, or E£5 more with private shower.

Berlin Hotel (☎/fax 395 7502, email *berlinhotelcairo@hotmail.com, 2 Shawarby, 4th floor, off Qasr el-Nil, Downtown*) is a bit more pricey than most other budget options but in our opinion well worth it for clean air-con rooms all with their own shower. Singles/doubles/triples will set you back E£60/80/90.

PLACES TO STAY – MID-RANGE

Garden City House Hotel (☎ 354 4969, *23 Kamal ad-Din Salah, Garden City*) opposite the back of the Semiramis InterContinental (look for the small sign at 3rd floor level) is a long-time favourite among Egyptologists and Middle Eastern scholars, but now more popular with young students from the nearby American University in Cairo. It's noisy, a bit dusty and definitely overpriced, but a lot of people love it and keep coming back. Singles/doubles range from E£51/94 (without bath) to E£64/102 (with bath), breakfast and supper included.

Lotus Hotel (☎ 575 0966, fax 575 4720, *12 Talaat Harb, 7th floor, Downtown*) is reached via an elevator at the end of an arcade almost opposite the Felfela Takeaway. Rooms are clean and comfortable and they all have air-con and large balconies. Singles without/with bath are E£47/67 and doubles are E£67/87.

Windsor Hotel (☎ 591 5277, fax 592 1621, *19 Sharia Alfy, Downtown*) was the British Officers' Club before 1952 and retains a colonial air. Former Monty Python member, Michael Palin, stayed here while filming the BBC series *Around the World in 80 Days*. There's a wide variety of rooms, and singles range from E£75 to E£102, doubles from E£102 to E£140.

Fontana Hotel (☎ 592 2321, fax 592 2145, *Midan Ramses*) on the north-eastern corner of Midan Ramses, high above the traffic and fumes, has clean rooms and a pleasant rooftop cafe/bar. Singles/doubles cost E£57/84.

Happyton Hotel (☎/fax 592 8671/00, *10 Ali al-Kassar*) is halfway between Midan Ramses and Downtown, tucked away down a quiet backstreet off Emad ad-Din (behind Karim Cinema). It's a relaxed, good value-for-money option with its own restaurant and a small, open-air rooftop bar. Rooms with air-con cost E£40/52.

Al-Hussein Hotel (☎ 591 8089, *Midan Hussein*) is right in the thick of things in the Khan al-Khalili bazaar. The rooms are clean and the restaurant on the roof has fantastic views over the rooftops – pity that the food is so lousy. Air-con singles/doubles with bath and views cost E£60/70; smaller rooms without bath or views cost E£35/45.

PLACES TO EAT
Street Food

There are fuul and ta'amiyya places on nearly every street in Cairo but *At-Tabie ad-Dumyati* at 31 Orabi, north of Midan Orabi, is a personal favourite. It does fuul with tomatoes and onions, egg and *pasturma* (clarified butter). You can take away or eat in the restaurant section.

Felfela Takeaway on Talaat Harb beats all other competition Downtown. Place your order, pay at the tills, then present your ticket at the busy counter, way at the back, to get your food.

The other good Egyptian street food is kushari, and all the best kushari joints are Downtown and include: *At-Tahrir* at 19 Abdel Khalek Sarwat, east off Talaat Harb, with another shop on Sharia Tahrir, in Bab al-Luq; *Abu Tarek* at 40 Champollion, reckoned to be *the* best; the *Lux* on Sharia 26th of July and also on the southern side of Midan Falaki; and *International Public Meal Kushari*, distinguishable by its red-painted window frames, on the corner of Emad ad-Din and Alfy.

Budget Dining

Akher Sa'a at 8 Sharia Alfy (the sign is in Arabic only but look for the Christian bookshop next door) is a hugely popular fuul and ta'amiyya takeaway joint with a no-frills restaurant next door. The menu is limited but you can get things like omelettes (with pasturma is good) and tahina and bread. The bill is never more than E£3 to E£4. It's open 24 hours a day.

Excelsior, on the corner of Talaat Harb and Adly, serves terrible, overpriced food, but the macaroni and cannelloni (both around the E£5 mark) are digestible. Most people just order a beer and grab a seat at the window to watch the goings-on outside.

Restaurant Gad on Sharia Adly, opposite the synagogue, is popular for lunch with Downtown office workers. Though gloomy and grim inside it has an extensive menu of Egyptian dishes and you can eat for less than E£10 if you forgo the meat. The 'special Gad rice' (E£11), which is done with nuts, sultanas, vegetables and chicken, is good, if a bit oily.

Felfela Restaurant (☎ 392 2751, 15 Sharia Hoda Shaarawi) is perpetually packed with tourists, coach parties and locals, but it does deserve its popularity. Give the meat dishes a miss, as they are all over-priced and done better elsewhere; instead order a selection of fuul, ta'amiyya, salads and other side dishes like tahina and *baba ghanoug* (puree of grilled aubergines with tahina and olive oil). A bill for two can come in at less than E£20. You can also get beer here.

Maison Thomas (☎ 340 7057, 157 26th of July, Zamalek) is Cairo's only continental-style deli. It does by far the best pizza in Cairo, with prices ranging from E£15 to E£20 for a 'regular', which is easily enough for two. It also has excellent though pricey sandwiches and salads. Eat in or takeaway; it's open 24 hours a day.

Restaurants

Alfy Bey Restaurant (☎ 577 4999) on Sharia Alfy has been in business since 1938 and the food, while basic, is very good and represents excellent value with most mains in the E£8 to E£12 range. Choose from dishes like lamb chops, kebab, grilled chicken or stuffed pigeon; but there's no beer. It's open from 11 to 1 am.

Ali Hassan al-Hatie (☎ 591 6055, 391 8829) has two branches – ignore the one just south of the Windsor Hotel and head for the branch tucked away down an alley off Sharia 26th of July – the interior is utilitarian but the traditional Egyptian food is good and filling. Try the *moza* (roast lamb on rice, E£15).

Da Mario at the Nile Hilton is one of the better value hotel restaurants. It serves a variety of very well presented pastas in gigantic portions for E£18 to E£25. The courtyard garden setting is also pleasant and wine and beer are available. It's open from noon to 2 am.

Estoril (☎ 574 3102) at 12 Talaat Harb (down the alley next to the Amex office) is an old-style eatery with traditional Egyptian grills and salads plus Lebanese mezze. Quality is variable but if you stick with a selection of starters accompanied by beer then you'll come away happy.

Le Bistro at 8 Hoda Shaarawi, 200m beyond the Felfela, has cooking that is sufficiently Gaelic to ensure that the place is heavily patronised by Cairo's French-speaking community. The menu features some good salads (all less than E£10) and plenty of beef and chicken-in-sauce dishes for around the E£20 mark.

Peking Restaurant (☎ 591 2381, 14 Sharia Ezbekiyya) just north of 26th of July is a very passable Cantonese restaurant. Expect to spend between E£20 to E£30 per person, without drinks.

ENTERTAINMENT

On Wednesday and Saturday nights from 9 pm (9.30 pm in winter) you can see a display of Sufi dancing in the Mausoleum of al-Ghouri in Islamic Cairo. Admission is free and it's advisable to come early, especially in winter, as the small auditorium can get quite crowded.

The best belly-dancers perform at Cairo's five-star hotels with tickets at E£175 a pop, but the *Palmyra*, just off 26th of July, is a cavernous place with the full Arab music contingent and belly-dancers (from about 1 to 4 am), with an admission of just E£3 (a Stella costs E£12). Similar establishments are the *New Arizona* and the *Shererazad*, both on Sharia Alfy.

There are also several local bars on and around Sharia Alfy including *Cafeteria Port Tawfiq* at the western end on Midan Orabi. *Cap d'Or* on Abdel Khalek Sarwat is a little more salubrious and is possibly the best of central Cairo's local bars. The staff and regulars here are quite used to seeing foreigners. The same applies to the cramped *Stella Bar* on the corner of Hoda Shaarawi and Talaat Harb, near Felfela Restaurant.

For real nightowls, one of Cairo's oldest and most famous coffeehouses is *Fishawi's*, open 24 hours a day. It's a few steps off Midan Hussein in Khan al-Khalili.

GETTING THERE & AWAY
Air
EgyptAir has a number of offices around towns including its main sales office on Sharia Adly (☎ 392 7649), another office on the corner of Talaat Harb and Sharia al-Bustan (☎ 393 2836) and one in the garden courtyard of the Nile Hilton (☎ 576 5200).

Bus
The main bus station is the Turgoman garage, on Sharia al-Gisr, 1km north-west of the intersection of sharias Galaa and 26th of July. It's in an awkward location in that it's too far to walk to from central Cairo and the only way to get there is by taxi (E£2 from Downtown). From here West Delta Bus Co and Superjet buses go every 30 minutes to Alexandria (E£16 to E£25, 2½ hours). West Delta also has four services a day to Marsa Matruh (E£25 to E£35, five hours). Superjet has three Hurghada services a day (E£45 to E£47, six hours), while Upper Egypt Travel has at least nine. There's a daily bus to Al-Quseir (E£55) at 10 pm and one to Marsa Alam (E£65) at 6.30 pm.

Upper Egypt Travel has luxury buses from Turgoman to Luxor (E£50, 10 to 11 hours) departing daily at 8.30 pm and to Aswan (E£55, 12 hours), departing at 5.15 pm.

Delta and Suez buses go from a station at Midan Ulali, just south of Midan Ramses, and include one every 30 minutes to Ismailia (E£6, 2½ hours) and another every 15 minutes to Suez (E£6, 1½ to two hours).

Sinai Buses Sinai buses mostly go from the Sinai bus station in Abbassiyya. This is some distance north of the city centre and to get here you need to take bus No 983 or 948 or minibus No 32 from the station at Midan Abdel Moniem Riad. Alternatively, a taxi to/from Downtown should cost E£6. From here there are frequent services to Sharm el-Sheikh (E£35 to E£65, seven hours), a few of which go on to Dahab (E£55 to E£70, nine hours), Nuweiba (E£50, nine hours) and Taba (E£50 to E£70, 10 hours).

Western Oases Buses All Western oases buses go from a small station tucked tight against the western wall of the Citadel, just south of Midan Salah ad-Din. Note that there are no direct buses from here to Siwa – to get there take a bus to Alexandria or Marsa Matruh, and then another onwards. There are four buses a day to Bahariyya (Bawiti) (E£12.25, six hours), two of which go via Farafra (E£25 or E£30, 10 to 11 hours). To Dakhla (Mut) there are three daily buses via Asyut and Al-Kharga.

Israel & the Palestinian Territories For details on buses to Tel Aviv and Jerusalem, see the Getting There & Away section earlier in this chapter.

Libya Superjet has a daily 7 am Libya service departing from the Turgoman garage. The fare to Benghazi is E£100, while to Tripoli it's E£205. The East Delta Bus Co runs a bus to Tripoli (E£180) at 10 am every Monday and Thursday.

Train
Ramses station (Mahattat Ramses), on Midan Ramses, is Cairo's main train station. The daily wagon-lit sleeper for Upper Egypt departs Cairo at 7.45 pm each evening, arriving in Luxor at 5.10 am the next morning and Aswan at 9.30 am. An evening meal and early breakfast are included in the fare of E£314.50 one way or E£579 return. The wagon-lit booking office (☎ 574 9474, fax 574 9074) is in a building just south of the main station building, across the car park – follow the blue on yellow signs that read 'Res. Office'.

Aside from the wagon-lit train, foreigners can only travel on the No 980, departing Cairo daily at 7.30 am, and the No 996, leaving at 10 pm. First/2nd class fares on the night train are E£51/31 to Luxor, while to Aswan they're E£63/37. Students pay two-thirds of the full fare. Tickets can be bought from the ticket office beside platform 11, which is on the other side of the tracks from the main hall. You must buy your tickets at least a couple of days in advance.

The best trains running between Cairo and Alexandria are the Turbini (also known as the Spanish trains). They make only one stop, at Sidi Gaber station in Alexandria, and they take 2½ hours. They depart Cairo at 9 am and 3 and 6 pm and tickets for 1st/2nd class air-con cost E£22/17. The next best trains are the Faransawi, the 'French-line' services, which take 2¾ hours and cost E£20/12 in 1st/2nd class.

Service Taxi
Most service taxis depart from lots around Ramses train station and Midan Ulali. They depart for Alexandria (E£10), Ismailia (E£5), Port Said (E£8), Al-Arish (E£12, five hours) and Rafah (E£15, six hours).

GETTING AROUND
To/From the Airport
Bus No 356 airport service runs at 20 minute intervals from 5.45 am to 11 pm between Midan Abdel Moniem Riad (behind the Egyptian Museum) in central Cairo and bus stations II and I at the airport; to find the buses at either bus station, head out into the car park and you'll spot the stand, if not a waiting bus.

If you decide to grab a taxi, then the going rate to central Cairo is around E£25 to E£30. Avoid the large 'official' airport taxis as they have a fixed rate of E£46.

Bus & Minibus
Cairo's main local bus and minibus stations are at Midan Abdel Moniem Riad. From here, services leave for just about everywhere in the city.

Microbus
Destinations are not marked in any language, so microbuses are hard to use unless

you are familiar with their routes. Position yourself beside the road that leads where you want to go and when a microbus passes, yell out your destination – if it's going where you want to go and there are seats free it'll stop.

Metro

The Metro system is startlingly efficient, and the stations are cleaner than any other public places in Cairo. It's also extremely inexpensive and, outside rush hours, not too crowded. You are most likely to use the Metro if you're going down to Old Cairo (served by a station called Mar Girgis). A short-hop ticket (up to nine stations) costs 30pt.

Taxi

If it's too far to walk, then the easiest way of getting around Cairo is to flag down a taxi. They're cheap enough to make the hassle of the buses redundant. Use the following as a rough guide to what you should be paying for taxi rides around Cairo:

Downtown to the Airport	E£25
Downtown to Heliopolis	E£10
Downtown to Khan al-Khalili	E£3
Downtown to Zamalek	E£3
Midan Tahrir to the Citadel	E£4
Midan Tahrir to Midan Ramses	E£2
Midan Tahrir to the Pyramids	E£15

River Bus

The river bus terminal is at Maspero, on the Corniche in front of the big round TV building. From here, boats depart every 15 minutes for Masr al-Qadima (Old Cairo). The trip takes 50 minutes and the fare is 50pt.

Around Cairo

MEMPHIS & SAQQARA

There is not much left of the former pharaonic capital of Memphis, 24km south of Cairo, but the museum (admission E£14) contains a fairly impressive statue of Ram-

ses II. A few kilometres away is Saqqara, a vast site strewn with pyramids, temples and tombs. The star attraction here is the **Step Pyramid** of Zoser, the first decent attempt at a pyramid. Entrance for the entire North Saqqara area is E£20. It's open from 7.30 am to 4 pm (5 pm in summer).

It's possible to hire a horse or camel at the Pyramids of Giza to head down to Saqqara but you'll spend much of the day in the saddle. You really need a full day to get even a superficial view of the area, and transport to get around the Saqqara site is essential.

Getting There & Away

A taxi from central Cairo will cost about E£80 shared among a maximum of seven

The Pyramids of Memphis

'It is through deeds such as these that men go up to the gods or that gods come down to men.' That was the comment of the Greek historian Philo on the Pyramids. He wrote that during an era that we tag 'ancient' – the world of 'ancient Greece'. Yet when Philo penned his comment the Pyramids were already almost 3000 years old. We are closer in time to Philo than he to the Pyramids.

And considering the Seven Ancient Wonders, one has to wonder: had the Pharos of Alexandria survived, would it still be regarded as such a marvel compared with towers like the Empire State Building or Kuala Lumpur's Petronas Towers? And would the Colossus of Rhodes measure up against the Statue of Liberty, or the Temple of Artemis against St Peter's or St Paul's? Unfair comparisons perhaps, but to this day the Pyramids remain the oldest, largest and most accurate stone structures ever made. In 5000 years nothing built has ever equalled them. It's unlikely anything ever will.

THE PYRAMIDS

Even more than their age, the wonder of the Pyramids lies in their twin mysteries: What were they built for? And how were they built? The traditionally accepted notion that they are tombs built on the order of the pharaohs by vast teams of workers tens of thousands strong is constantly being challenged, and new theories ranging from the highly unlikely through to the wild and wacky are constantly being propounded.

There's an admission fee of E£20 for the plateau and then the same again to enter each of the Pyramids. The Pyramid chambers are open from 8.30 am to 4 pm, but the site itself is open from about 7 am to 7.30 pm. Note that the Pyramids are closed on a rotating basis, and only two are open for the public to clamber inside at any one time. This is to allow for necessary periodic restoration work.

Pyramid of Cheops (Khufu)

The oldest at Giza and the largest in Egypt, the Great Pyramid of Cheops stood 146.5m high when it was completed around 2600 BC. Although there is not much to see inside the pyramid, the experience of climbing through such an ancient structure is unforgettable though completely impossible if you suffer from even the tiniest degree of claustrophobia.

Along the eastern and southern sides of the Pyramid of Cheops are five long pits which once contained the pharaoh's boats. One of these ancient wooden vessels, possibly the oldest boat in existence, was unearthed in 1954. It was restored and a glass **museum** was built over it to protect it from damage from the elements. Entry costs E£20.

Pyramid of Chephren (Khafre)

Top: The Turks used the Sphinx for target practice and shot off its nose and beard. Part of the fallen beard is now in the British Museum, London. (photo by Patrick Horton)

Bottom: Various theories have them built by angels, the devil or spacemen – it's easy to laugh but gaze on the Pyramids and you'll see why so many believe they could only come of unearthly origins.

South-west of the Great Pyramid, and with almost the same dimensions, is the Pyramid of Chephren. At first it seems larger than that of

JOHN BORTHWICK

Cheop's, his father, because it stands on higher ground and its peak still has part of the original limestone casing which once covered the entire structure. Among the most interesting features of this pyramid are the substantial remains of Chephren's mortuary temple outside to the east.

Pyramid of Mycerinus (Menkaure)

At a height of 62m (originally 66.5m), this is the smallest of the three pyramids. Extensive damage was done to the exterior by a 16th century caliph who wanted to demolish all the pyramids.

The Sphinx

Known in Arabic as Abu al-Hol (Father of Terror), the Sphinx is carved almost entirely from one huge piece of limestone left over from the carving of the stones for Cheops' Pyramid. It is not known when it was carved but one theory is that it was Chephren who thought of shaping the rock into a lion's body with a god's face, wearing the royal headdress of Egypt. Another theory is that it is the likeness of Chephren himself that has been staring out over the desert sands for so many centuries.

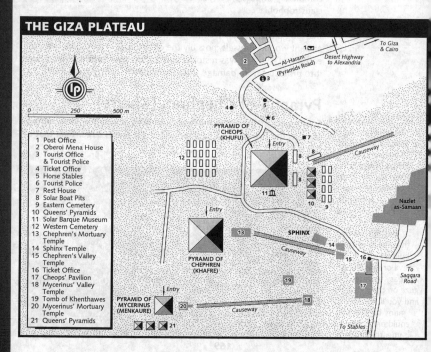

THE GIZA PLATEAU

0   250   500 m

1 Post Office
2 Oberoi Mena House
3 Tourist Office
  & Tourist Police
4 Ticket Office
5 Horse Stables
6 Tourist Police
7 Rest House
8 Solar Boat Pits
9 Eastern Cemetery
10 Queens' Pyramids
11 Solar Barque Museum
12 Western Cemetery
13 Chephren's Mortuary
   Temple
14 Sphinx Temple
15 Chephren's Valley
   Temple
16 Ticket Office
17 Cheops' Pavilion
18 Mycerinus' Valley
   Temple
19 Tomb of Khenthawes
20 Mycerinus' Mortuary
   Temple
21 Queens' Pyramids

To Giza & Cairo
Al-Haram (Pyramids Road)
Desert Highway to Alexandria

PYRAMID OF CHEOPS (KHUFU)
Entry
Causeway

Nazlet as-Samaan

PYRAMID OF CHEPHREN (KHAFRE)
Entry
SPHINX
Causeway

To Saqqara Road

PYRAMID OF MYCERINUS (MENKAURE)
Entry
Causeway

To Stables

people. This is the best way for those on a tight budget to get to and around Saqqara. Stipulate the sights you want to see and how long you want to be out, and bargain hard.

Alternatively, you could join one of the inexpensive tours run by Salah Mohammed Abdel Hafez (☎ 298 0650, mobile 012-313 8446, email samo@intouch.com). You'll need to arrange the tour at least one day in advance (leave a message on the answering machine if he's not there).

BIRQASH CAMEL MARKET

Until 1995 Egypt's largest souq al-gamaal (camel market) was among run-down tenements in Imbaba, one of Cairo's western suburbs. The city's growing population forced its relocation to Birqash, 35km northwest of Cairo, on the edge of the Western Desert.

The market is an easy half-day trip from Cairo, but like all of Egypt's animal markets, it's not for animal lovers or the faint-hearted. Hundreds of camels are sold here every day, most having been brought up the 40 Days Road from western Sudan. The market is most lively on Friday and Monday mornings from about 6 to 9 am; admission is E£3, plus E£2 for a camera and E£15 for a video.

Getting There & Away

The cheapest way to get to the market is to take a taxi (E£4) to the site of the old camel market at Imbaba, from where microbuses (E£1) shuttle back and forth to Birqash.

Alternatively, on Friday only, the Sun Hotel (see Places to Stay in the Cairo section earlier in this chapter) organises a minibus tour to the souq, leaving from the hotel at 7 am and returning at about noon. The charge is E£20 per person (minimum five people); you must book a day or two in advance.

The final option is to hire a taxi to take you all the way there and back. Depending on your bargaining skills, you'll be looking at around E£70; make sure to negotiate waiting time.

Nile Valley

AL-FAYOUM OASIS

About 100km south-west of Cairo, Al-Fayoum is a large irrigated oasis about 70km wide and 60km long.

There's not an awful lot to see in the main town, Medinet al-Fayoum, but you can explore such features of the oasis as the salty lake of **Birket Qarun** and the Ptolemaic temple known as **Qasr Qarun**, the springs of **Ain as-Siliyiin**, the Hawara, Lahun and Meidum **pyramids**, or the **Museum of Kom Aushim** at Karanis on the road to Cairo.

It is possible to camp in the grounds of the Museum of Kom Aushim for E£4, or at the lake; get a permit from the tourist police. Otherwise, there's the *Youth Hostel* (☎ 343 682) 1km east of the centre of town, which costs E£3 for members and E£5 for nonmembers; *Palace Hotel* (☎ 351 222) on the canal in the town centre has good, clean singles/doubles (including breakfast) without bath for E£20/35, or with bath for E£30/45.

Getting There & Away

There are regular buses between Medinet al-Fayoum, east of the town centre, and Cairo's Ahmed Helmy station (E£4, three hours), behind Midan Ramses. Service taxis also run to both these destinations.

MINYA

Because so many of the 'troubles' have been based in the countryside around here, Minya has become something of an armed fortress, with nervous policemen patrolling in tanks and personnel carriers. Even with this, it remains a pleasant town with a long Corniche along the Nile and some great, if shabby, early 20th-century buildings testifying to its former prosperity as a centre of the cotton industry. Keep in mind that while you can usually (but not always) wander around the town relatively freely, the police will want to accompany you to monuments in the countryside.

EGYPT

Information

There's a tourist office (☎ 320 150) in the governorate building and another in the train station (☎ 342 044) – the train station tourist office is open until 8 pm. Banque Masr's branch on Midan as-Sa'a does Visa card cash advances but it does take some time. There are a couple of other banks for cash advances and travellers cheque transactions, including National Bank which is on the corner of Al-Gomhuriyya and the Corniche.

The post office is open from 8 am to 2 pm daily except Friday. The telephone centrale is in the train station and sells phonecards.

Things to See

About 7km south-east of the town, near the ferry landing on the east bank, is a large Muslim and Christian cemetery called **Za-wiyyet al-Mayyiteen** (Place of the Dead). The cemetery consists of several hundred mud-brick mausolea stretching for 4km

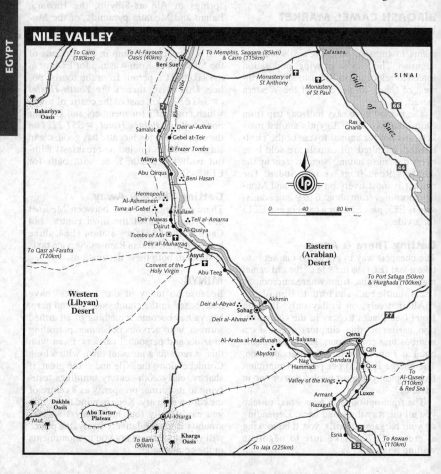

NILE VALLEY

To Cairo (180km)
To Al-Fayoum Oasis (40km)
Beni Suef
To Memphis, Saqqara (85km) & Cairo (115km)
Zafarana
Monastery of St Anthony
Monastery of St Paul
SINAI
Gulf of Suez
66
Bahariyya Oasis
River Nile
Samalut
Deir al-Adhra
Gebel at-Teir
Frazer Tombs
Ras Gharib
44
Minya
Abu Qirqus
Beni Hasan
LP
0   40   80 km
Hermopolis
Al-Ashmunein
Tuna al-Gebel
Mallawi
Deir Mawas
Tell al-Amarna
Dairut
Al-Qusiya
Tombs of Mir
Deir al-Muharraq
To Qasr al-Farafra (120km)
Asyut
Convent of the Holy Virgin
Abu Teeg
Eastern (Arabian) Desert
To Port Safaga (50km) & Hurghada (100km)
Akhmin
Western (Libyan) Desert
Deir al-Abyad
Sohag
77
Deir al-Ahmar
Al-Araba al-Madfunah
Al-Balyana
Qena
Qift
Abydos
Nag Hammadi
Dendara
Qus
To Al-Quseir (110km) & Red Sea
Valley of the Kings
Luxor
Dakhla Oasis
Mut
Abu Tartur Plateau
Al-Kharga
Armant
Razagat
Esna
2
To Aswan (110km)
To Baris (90km)
Kharga Oasis
To Jaja (225km)
53

EGYPT

Troubles in the Nile Valley

In 1992, the current round of Islamist-instigated violence broke out in Cairo and Upper Egypt. Although massive police action crushed the movement's radical wings in Cairo, it has proved far more difficult to do the same in the Nile Valley area between Minya and Qena. Easy escape routes to the desert and the hiding places afforded by crops such as sugar cane make it difficult for the police to fully control the area.

For now independent travel is definitely *not* recommended anywhere between Minya and Qena, and it is quite likely that anyone who attempts to visit ancient sites such as Tuna al-Gebel, Tell al-Amarna, the monasteries near Sohag, or Abydos will be escorted out of the area by the local police, whether they like it or not. Make sure that you check the safety of the area with your embassy before attempting to travel here.

from the road to the hills and is said to be one of the largest cemeteries in the world.

About 20km south of Minya, on the east bank, **Beni Hasan** is a necropolis with more than 30 distinctive Middle Kingdom tombs carved into a limestone cliff, though only four are on view; it's open from 7 am to 5 pm. Admission is E£12. Look for the wall paintings of wrestlers doing a little more than wrestling in the Tomb of Baqet. To get there from Minya, take a microbus to Abu Qirqus (40pt) and then a pick-up to the river. The boat across costs E£2 each if there are six people or more. Otherwise it's E£4.50 a person.

Places to Stay & Eat

Majestic Hotel (☎ 364 212) on Al-Gomhuriyya is the cheapest place in town (and maybe the dustiest too) – a three-bed room costs E£13.50.

Palace Hotel (☎ 324 071) on Midan Tahrir is worth a look-in for the decor even if you don't intend staying – a huge painted

Nefertiti greets you at the bottom of the stairs, while the rooms have very high ceilings and the central lobby is big and airy, if a little shabby. Singles/doubles are E£12/16 without bath or E£21/28 with.

Hotel Seety (☎ 363 930, 71 Saad Zaghloul) is half a block south of the train station and despite its run-down appearance, has clean and comfortable rooms that are cheap at E£8/10 without bath or E£10/14 with.

Savoy Hotel (☎ 363 270) directly opposite the train station on Midan al-Mahatta exudes decrepit grandeur with a big hall and high, painted ceilings. Singles/doubles/triples cost E£20/30/36 with bathroom, or E£15/25/30 without.

Akhenaten Hotel (☎ 365 917/8) on the Corniche has 42 clean rooms with air-con, some of which have great views of the Nile. Get one of these rooms and in terms of value for money, this is the best place to stay. Singles/doubles cost E£33.10/42.50 without breakfast, or a few pounds extra with air-con.

Nefertiti & Aton (☎ 331 515, fax 326 467) is on the Corniche about 1km north of the town centre. It's a four star hotel that has rooms facing the Nile for US$51/61, not including taxes. It also has three restaurants and two bars.

There are a lot of the usual cheap fuul and ta'amiyya stands scattered around Midan al-Mahatta, Midan Tahrir and along the market street stretching south off the latter. Otherwise, *Cafeteria Ali Baba*, on the Corniche just north of Sharia Port Said, serves a satisfying meal of the usual favourites – kebabs or another meat dish, salad, tahina and a soft drink for about E£10. *Al-Sadhi*, to the right of Savoy Hotel, has good meals for around E£12. Other than that, most of the restaurants are at the hotels.

Getting There & Away

At present, the police insist that foreigners travel only by train, not bus. The trip from Cairo (four hours) costs E£23 in 1st class or E£14/6.50 in 2nd class with/without air-con. Trains heading south depart frequently, with the fastest trains leaving Minya between about 11 pm and 1 am. Fares from Minya will set you back (1st class/2nd class with air-con/2nd class without): Asyut E£13/8/3.40; Sohag E£21/13/5.80; Qena E£31/19/9; Luxor E£31/24/10; and Aswan E£49/30/13.20.

QENA & DENDARA

Qena has little going for it other than its proximity to the **Temple of Hathor**, Dendara. The temple is dedicated to the goddess Hathor, and, although built by the Ptolemies, retains the Egyptian style and serves their beliefs. Hathor, the goddess of pleasure and love, is figured on the 24 columns of the Outer Hypostyle Hall, and on the walls are scenes of Roman emperors as pharaohs. The views from the roof are magnificent. It's open from 7 am to 6 pm, and admission is E£12.

Places to Stay & Eat

If you must stay in Qena, there's *Happyland Camp* 100m from the temple, basically a hotel with overpriced beds. There's a possibility of camping in its messy garden. Other not-great choices in town include *New Palace Hotel* (☎ *322 509*), just behind the Mobil petrol station and a few cheap dives along Sharia al-Gomhuriyya.

Cafe Nasr has good, cheap food such as spinach, tahina, salad and tea for E£2.50, while *Restaurant Hamdi* serves full meals of chicken and vegetables for around E£7. There are several kushari, kofta and ta'amiyya places along the main street.

Getting There & Away

The bus station is in front of the train station. However, buses not originating or terminating here pass along the main road and drop (and might pick up) passengers at the bridge over the canal. There are two Superjet buses to Cairo (E£25) at 7 am and 8 pm. There are 11 buses to Aswan (E£7) from 6.30 am to 7.45 pm, and most stop in Luxor (E£2). A few other buses only go as far as Edfu or Luxor. There are nine buses to Hurghada and six of them go on to Suez (E£22 to

E£38; nine to 10 hours). Superjet also has services to Hurghada (E£15) and Suez (E£40). There are also buses for coastal destinations such as Al-Quseir (E£7).

LUXOR

The sheer grandeur of Luxor's monumental architecture and its excellent state of preservation, have made this village-city one of Egypt's greatest tourist attractions. Built on and around the 4000-year-old site of ancient Thebes, Luxor is one of the world's greatest open-air museums, a time capsule of a glorious long-gone era.

History

Following the collapse of centralised power at the end of the Old Kingdom period, the small village of Thebes, under the 11th and 12th dynasty pharaohs, emerged as the main power in Upper Egypt. Rising against the northern capital of Heracleopolis, Thebes reunited the country under its political, religious and administrative control and ushered in the Middle Kingdom period. The strength of its government also enabled it to re-establish control after a sec-

---

Where First?

If you don't have the luxury of several days in Luxor, choosing what to miss can be difficult. Our highlights would be as follows:

- **The Hypostyle Hall, Karnak** – lose yourself in a stone papyrus forest
- **Valley of the Kings** – see how Egypt's ancient rulers tried to confound both thieves and mortality
- **Temple of Hatshepsut** – walk through the temple carved out of the Theban hills for one of the few women to rule ancient Egypt
- **Tomb of Nefertari** – get an idea of how Theban tombs looked before time and the breath of thousands of tourists dulled them

ond period of decline; liberate the country from foreign rule; and bring in the New Kingdom dynasties.

At the height of its glory and opulence, from 1570 to 1090 BC, all the New Kingdom pharaohs (with the exception of Akhenaten, who moved to Tell al-Amarna) made Thebes their permanent residence; the city had a population of nearly one million and the architectural activity was astounding.

Orientation

What most visitors today know as Luxor is actually three separate areas: the city of Luxor itself, the village of Karnak, 2km to the north-east, and the monuments and necropolis of ancient Thebes on the West Bank of the Nile.

In the town there are only three main thoroughfares: Sharia al-Mahatta, Sharia al-Karnak and Al-Corniche. Another road you may want to know if you're looking for cheap accommodation is Sharia Television, where there are many cheap hotels.

Information

Visa Extensions The passport office (☎ 380 885) is almost opposite Isis Hotel, south of the town centre. It's open from 8 am to 2 pm from Saturday to Thursday.

Tourist Offices The tourist police and tourist office (☎ 372 215, 373 294) are in the Tourist Bazaar on Al-Corniche, next to New Winter Palace Hotel. The office is open from 8 am to 8 pm, except on Friday when it closes at 1 pm. Travellers can leave messages on a notice board next to the main information counter. There is another tourist office at the train station that is supposedly open the same hours, although it hardly ever seems to be staffed, and a third at the airport that is open from 8 am to 8 pm daily.

Money The Bank of Alexandria has a branch on the Corniche, a little way up from the Hotel Mercure. Banque Masr is on Sharia Nefertiti, around the corner from the Mercure, and the National Bank of Egypt is

down on the Corniche near the Old Winter Palace. In addition, there is an exchange booth open quite long hours on the Corniche in front of the Tourist Bazaar.

Amex and Thomas Cook are at Old Winter Palace Hotel.

Post & Telephone The GPO is on Sharia al-Mahatta and there's a branch office in the Tourist Bazaar. The central telephone centrale is on Sharia al-Karnak and is open 24 hours; there's another branch below the resplendent Old Winter Palace Hotel (open from 8 am to 10 pm) entrance and a third at the train station (open from 8 am to 8 pm).

Email & Internet Services Rainbow Internet Cafe, at Nadi az-Zubaat (the Officers' Club) on Al-Corniche just north of Sharia as-Sayyed Yasouf is open from 9 am to 2 pm and 6 pm to midnight. Because there is no local server you have to pay for the line to Cairo and they charge E£45 for an hour's use. On the West Bank, Osman International Phone Line (☎ 310 110), just up from the ferry landing, charges E£22.50 for 30 minutes and is open between 7 pm and midnight.

Museums

On Al-Corniche, about halfway between the Luxor and Karnak temples, **Luxor Museum** has a small but well-chosen collection of relics from the Theban temples and necropolis. The displays include pottery, jewellery, furniture, statues and stelae. The museum is open daily from 9 am to 1 pm and 4 to 9 pm in winter and 9 am to 1 pm and 5 to 10 pm in summer. Admission costs E£30.

Down the steps just opposite Mina Palace Hotel on Al-Corniche is the recently opened **Mummification Museum**, which, though small, contains well presented displays telling you everything you ever wanted to know about mummies and mummification. The well-preserved mummy of a 21st dynasty official, Maserharti, as well as a host of mummified animals (including a ram, crocodile, cat and baboon) are all on display.

EGYPT

EGYPT

LUXOR (EAST BANK)

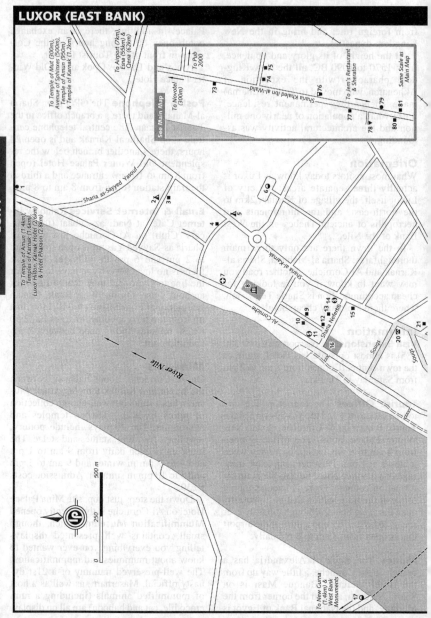

LUXOR (EAST BANK)

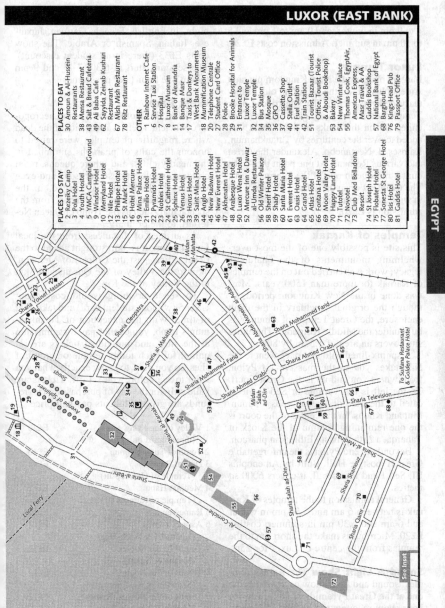

PLACES TO STAY
2 Rezeiky Camp
3 Pola Hotel
4 Youth Hostel
5 YMCA Camping Ground
9 Windsor Hotel
10 Merryland Hotel
12 Nile Hotel
13 Philippe Hotel
15 St Mark Hotel
16 Hotel Mercure
19 Mina Palace Hotel
21 Emilio Hotel
22 Pyramids Hotel
23 Nobles Hotel
25 St Catherine Hotel
26 Sphinx Hotel
26 Venus Hotel
33 Horus Hotel
39 Saint Mina Hotel
44 Anglo Hotel
45 New Radwan Hotel
46 New Everest Hotel
47 Akhenaten Hotel
48 Arabesque Hotel
50 Luxor Wena Hotel
52 Mercure Inn & Dawar
  al-Umda Restaurant
56 Old Winter Palace
58 Sherif Hotel
59 Shady Hotel
60 Santa Maria Hotel
61 Everest Hotel
63 Oasis Hotel
64 Grand Hotel
65 Atlas Hotel
69 Fontana Hotel
70 Moon Valley Hotel
71 Happy Land Hotel
71 Novotel
73 Club Med Belladona
  Resort
74 St Joseph Hotel
75 Flobater Hotel
77 Sonesta St George Hotel
80 Isis Hotel
81 Gaddis Hotel

PLACES TO EAT
30 Amoun & Al-Hussein
  Restaurants
38 Mensa Restaurant
43 Salt & Bread Cafeteria
49 Ali Baba Cafe
62 Sayyida Zeinab Kushari
  Restaurant
67 Mish Mish Restaurant
78 Ritz Restaurant

OTHER
1 Rainbow Internet Cafe
6 Service Taxi Station
7 Hospital
8 Luxor Museum
11 Bank of Alexandria
14 Banque Masr
17 Taxis & Donkeys to
  West Bank Monuments
18 Mummification Museum
20 Telephone Centrale
27 Student Card Office
28 Police
29 Brooke Hospital for Animals
31 Entrance to
  Luxor Temple
32 Luxor Temple
34 Bus Station
35 Mosque
36 GPO
37 Cassette Shop
40 Stella Outlet
41 Fuel Station
42 Train Station
51 Tourist Bazaar (Tourist
  Office, Tourist Police
  & Aboudi Bookshop)
53 Bakery
54 New Winter Palace
55 Thomas Cook, EgyptAir,
  American Express,
  Masr Travel & AA
  Gaddis Bookshop
57 National Bank of Egypt
68 Barghouti
76 Kings Head Pub
79 Passport Office

EGYPT

The museum is open from 9 am to 1 pm and 4 to 9 pm in winter, and 9 am to 1 pm and 5 to 10 pm in summer. Admission costs E£20.

Luxor Temple

Largely built by the New Kingdom pharaoh Amenophis III, on the site of an older sanctuary dedicated to the Theban triad, Luxor Temple is a strikingly graceful piece of architecture on the banks of the Nile. It was added to over the centuries by Tutankhamun, Ramses II, Nectanebo, Alexander the Great and various Romans. At one point the Arabs built a mosque in one of the interior courts. The temple is open daily from 6 am to 9 pm in winter and 6 am to 10 pm in summer, and admission is E£20.

Temples of Karnak

This site is possibly one of the most overwhelming monuments of the pharaonic legacy; work was carried out on the temples of Karnak for more than 1500 years. Most was done in the New Kingdom period, although the original sanctuary of the main enclosure, the Great Temple of Amun, was built under the Middle Kingdom. The entire site covers an area of 1.5km by 800m.

A sphinx-lined path that once went to the Nile takes you to the massive 1st Pylon, from where you end up in the Great Court. To the left is the Temple of Seti II, dedicated to the triad of Theban gods – Amun, Mut and Khons. In the centre of the court is the one remaining column of the Kiosk of Taharqa, a 25th dynasty Ethiopian pharaoh.

Beyond the 2nd Pylon is the unforgettable Great Hypostyle Hall. Built by Amenophis III, Seti I and Ramses II, it covers 6000 sq metres.

General admission to the temples of Karnak is between 6 am and 5.30 pm in winter and 6 am and 6.30 pm in summer; costing E£20. Microbuses make the short run to the temples from the centre of Luxor for 25pt.

Sound & Light Show The Karnak temples' sound and light show easily rivals the one at the Great Pyramids of Giza. The 1½ hour show recounts the history of Thebes.

There are three or four performances a night, in English, French, German, Japanese, Italian, Spanish or Arabic. The show costs E£33 (there is no student discount). The sessions start at 6.30, 7.45 and 9 pm (about one hour later in summer).

West Bank

The West Bank of Luxor was the necropolis of ancient Thebes, a vast city of the dead where magnificent temples were raised to honour the cults of pharaohs entombed in the nearby cliffs, and where queens, royal children, nobles, priests, artisans and even workers built tombs that ranged, in the quality of their design and decor, from the spectacular, such as the Tomb of Queen Nefertari, to the ordinary.

As an idea of distances, from the local ferry landing it is 3km straight ahead to the ticket office, past the Colossi of Memnon, 4km to the Valley of the Queens and 8km to the Valley of the Kings.

To see everything would cost about US$65 (without student card) and take a lot of time. With the exception of Tutankhamun's tomb, you cannot pay for admission at the sites, and individual tickets are required for each tomb, temple or group of sites, so you need to know exactly what you want to see before you set off. Tickets are valid only for the day of purchase and no refunds are given. Students pay half price.

1 Valley of the Kings (three tombs only)	E£20
2 Tomb of Tutankhamun	E£40
3 Deir al-Bahri (Temple of Hatshepsut)	E£12
4 Medinat Habu (Temple of Ramses III)	E£12
5 Ramesseum	E£12
6 Assasif Tombs (Kheru-Ef & Anch-Hor)	E£12
7 Tombs of the Nobles (Menna & Nakht)	E£12
8 Tombs of the Nobles (Sennofer & Rekhmire)	E£12
9 Tombs of the Nobles (Ramose, Userhet & Khaemhet)	E£12

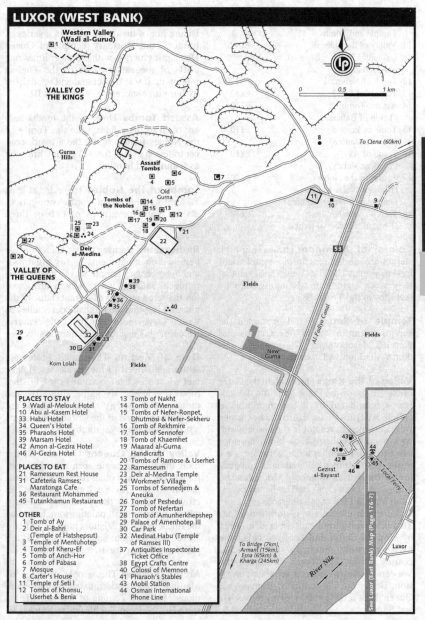

LUXOR (WEST BANK)

0   0.5   1 km

EGYPT

Western Valley
(Wadi al-Gurud)

VALLEY OF
THE KINGS

Gurna
Hills

To Qena (60km)

Assasif
Tombs

Old
Gurna

Tombs of
the Nobles

Deir
al-Medina

VALLEY OF
THE QUEENS

Fields

Al-Fadiya Canal

Fields

New
Gurna

Kom Lolah   Fields

To Bridge (7km),
Armant (15km),
Esna (65km) &
Kharga (245km)

River Nile

Luxor

Gezirat
al-Bayarat

Local Ferry

See Luxor (East Bank) Map (Page 176-7)

PLACES TO STAY
9   Wadi al-Melouk Hotel
10 Abu al-Kasem Hotel
33 Habu Hotel
34 Queen's Hotel
35 Pharaohs Hotel
39 Marsam Hotel
42 Amon al-Gezira Hotel
46 Al-Gezira Hotel

PLACES TO EAT
21 Ramesseum Rest House
31 Cafeteria Ramses;
    Maratonga Cafe
36 Restaurant Mohammed
45 Tutankhamun Restaurant

OTHER
1   Tomb of Ay
2   Deir al-Bahri
    (Temple of Hatshepsut)
3   Temple of Mentuhotep
4   Tomb of Kheru-Ef
5   Tomb of Anch-Hor
6   Tomb of Pabasa
7   Mosque
8   Carter's House
11 Temple of Seti I
12 Tombs of Khonsu,
    Userhet & Benia

13 Tomb of Nakht
14 Tomb of Menna
15 Tombs of Nefer-Ronpet,
    Dhutmosi & Nefer-Sekheru
16 Tomb of Rekhmire
17 Tomb of Sennofer
18 Tomb of Khaemhet
19 Maarad al-Gurna
    Handicrafts
20 Tombs of Ramose & Userhet
22 Ramesseum
23 Deir al-Medina Temple
24 Workmen's Village
25 Tombs of Sennedjem &
    Aneuka
26 Tomb of Peshedu
27 Tomb of Nefertari
28 Tomb of Amunherkhepshep
29 Palace of Amenhotep III
30 Car Park
32 Medinat Habu (Temple of
    Ramses III)
37 Antiquities Inspectorate
    Ticket Office
38 Egypt Crafts Centre
40 Colossi of Memnon
41 Pharaoh's Stables
43 Mobil Station
44 Osman International
    Phone Line

Colossi of Memnon These 18m-high statues are all that remain of a temple built by Amenophis III. The Greeks believed that they were statues of Memnon, slain by Achilles in the Trojan War.

Temple of Seti I Seti I expanded the Egyptian empire to include Cyprus and parts of Mesopotamia. The temple is seldom visited but well worth a look.

Valley of the Kings Once called the Gates of the Kings, or the Place of Truth, the valley is dominated by a barren mountain called Al-Qurn (The Horn). The tombs were designed to resemble the underworld, with a long, inclined rock-hewn corridor descending into either an antechamber or a series of sometimes pillared halls and ending in the burial chamber. More than 60 tombs have been excavated in the valley, although not all belong to pharaohs.

Some are closed for restoration work. Tutankhamun's tomb, discovered in 1922 by Howard Carter and far from being the most interesting, requires a separate ticket costing E£40. The Tomb of Ay in the Western Valley also has a separate admission. Better are the tombs of Ramses VI, Queen Tawsert/Sethnakt, Tuthmosis III and Saptah.

Deir al-Bahri (Temple of Hatshepsut) Rising out of the desert plain in a series of terraces, the Mortuary Temple of Queen Hatshepsut merges with the sheer limestone cliffs of the eastern face of the Theban mountain. It was desecrated and vandalised by her bitter successor, Tuthmosis III.

Assasif Tombs Three of the tombs here are open to the public. Like the Tombs of the Nobles farther south, the artwork concentrates on events from everyday life such as fishing and hunting.

Tombs of the Nobles There are at least 12 tombs in this group worth visiting; tickets are sold for groups of two or three tombs.

Ramesseum Ramses II was keen to leave behind him monuments to his greatness, and his mortuary temple was to be the masterpiece. Sadly, it lies mostly in ruins, and the shattered remains of a giant statue of the pharaoh inspired the English poet Shelley to write 'Ozymandias' in the 19th century, ridiculing his aspiration to immortality.

Deir al-Medina This small Ptolemaic temple dedicated to the goddesses Hathor and Maat was later occupied by Christian monks – hence its name, literally 'the monastery of the city'. Near the temple are the tombs of some of the workers and artists who created the royal tombs.

Valley of the Queens Only five of the more than 70 tombs are open here. They belong to queens and other royal family members from the 19th and 20th dynasties. The crowning glory is the Tomb of Nefertari, whose stunning wall paintings are hailed as the finest in Egypt. Visitors must pay a hefty E£100 admission to enter the tomb and are permitted to stay for 10 minutes only.

Medinat Habu The temple complex of Medinat Habu is dominated by the enormous Mortuary Temple of Ramses III, inspired by the temple of his father, Ramses II.

Places to Stay

Perhaps more than at any tourist destination in Egypt, the cost of accommodation in Luxor fluctuates seasonally. Some hotels drop their charges by 50% in the low season, although others don't bother altering them at all.

Try to avoid the squawking hotel touts who pounce on travellers as they get off the train/bus – they get a 25 to 40% commission for bringing you in, which ends up being factored into your bill.

Camping *YMCA* (☎ 372 425) camping ground on Sharia al-Karnak costs E£4 per night, including the use of its 20 showers.

Rezeiky Camp (☎ 381 334, fax 381 400) charges E£10 per person to pitch a tent and E£10 for a vehicle, for which you get access to the swimming pool and showers. The camp is in the midst of transforming itself into a hotel by the addition of air-con motel-style rooms for E£30/50 a single/double, but you're paying for the privilege of having the pool on your doorstep.

Hostels *Youth Hostel* (☎ 372 139) is in a street just off Sharia al-Karnak. The slightly dingy rooms have at least three beds and the showers tend to get swampy. The cost is E£8.10 with a membership card, or E£10.10 without. Breakfast is E£2.50 extra.

Hotels – South of Sharia al-Mahatta

Anglo Hotel (☎ 381 679) is the closest place to the train station. It costs E£10/20 for a single/double room with breakfast and shared bathroom. It's fairly clean and the management is friendly, but the proximity of the train station means it can be noisy.

Warning

Female travellers should exercise extreme caution when looking for a place to stay in Luxor. Several have reported being sexually assaulted after being given spiked drinks by hotel staff.

Oasis Hotel (☎ 381 699) on Sharia Mohammed Farid has spacious double rooms and more poky singles. Quite a few travellers stay here, and their reports have invariably been good. Singles/doubles with air-con cost E£6/13.

Grand Hotel (☎ 382 905) off Sharia Mohammed Farid is clean and welcoming, has a small rooftop terrace with great views and decent shared bathrooms with hot water. Singles/doubles with fan go for E£6/10.

Atlas Hotel (☎ 373 514) off Sharia Orabi costs E£8 per person (plus E£2 for breakfast) for a room with bath, some also with air-con. It's not a bad place and with 40 rooms it's rarely full.

Fontana Hotel (☎ 380 663) is one of the better deals in Luxor. The owner asks for E£6 per person for a room with fan and E£8/15 for singles/doubles with air-con and private bathroom. The rooms are spotlessly clean and there's a kitchen (of sorts), rooftop terrace and washing machine for guests to use.

The homey *Sherif Hotel* (☎ 370 757) on a small street off the very beginning of Sharia Television has 15 rooms, six with their own bathroom and four with air-con. Singles/doubles with shared bathrooms and fans go for E£7/14; those with air-con are E£12/19. It's a good deal and convenient.

Happy Land Hotel (☎ 371 828), on Sharia Qamr, is run by Mr Ibrahim. Here is where you see the fierce competition among budget hotels in Luxor at work. The rooms are spotless and toilet paper, soap and mosquito coils are provided, as well as free laundry. The cheapest rooms are E£6 per person in a dormitory with fan, including breakfast, while a good single with private bath costs E£10. It's about a 10 minute walk from the train station. Alternatively, take a minibus from the station to one stop south of the Novotel on Al-Corniche. The hotel is signposted.

A good option just south of Sharia Al-Mahatta is the newly opened *New Everest Hotel* (☎ 370 017), on a small sidestreet. It has 12 clean rooms, four of which have air-con. Singles/doubles with shared facilities cost E£5/10 without breakfast; air-con doubles

EGYPT

with their own bath go for E£20, including breakfast.

On Sharia Television, are several mid-range places offering comfortable rooms with all the necessary mod cons. **Shady Hotel** (☎/fax 374 859) charges E£50/70 for clean rooms on the street side but you will pay E£10 extra for the supposedly quieter pool side.

Further down Sharia Television is the blue and yellow **Golden Palace Hotel** (☎ 382 972, fax 382 974). At only E£40/70 for clean, air-con singles/doubles with TV, fridge and telephone, it is an excellent deal. There is also a reasonable sized pool and plans for a roof garden.

Mina Palace Hotel (☎ 372 074) is on Al-Corniche just opposite the entrance to the Mummification Museum. Although it is getting slightly run-down, the Nile views are great. It has singles/doubles with air-con and private bathrooms for E£76/86, although at the time of writing the management was willing to drop the price to almost half this. Ask for a corner room with two balconies – one looking towards Luxor Temple and the other over the Nile.

Hotels – North of Sharia al-Mahatta

The friendly **Saint Mina Hotel** (☎ 375 409) is an excellent deal if you've got a little extra money. The hotel's 20 rooms, half of which have private bathrooms, are very clean with air-con or fans. Singles/doubles with bath are E£30/50, and without bath E£25/45. It's as good as some of the mid-range places that charge double the price.

Sphinx Hotel (☎ 372 830) has singles/doubles for E£12/16, which may or may not include breakfast, depending on how well you can haggle. The rooms are musty and run-down, although the staff are friendly.

Venus Hotel (☎ 382 625) has 30 reasonable rooms with bath. Popular with backpackers, singles/doubles with their own bathroom cost E£15/20 and the hotel has a restaurant with blaring satellite TV and bar. There's also a 6th floor terrace where you can down a cold Stella for E£6.

The high-rise **Pola Hotel** (☎ 380 551, fax 380 552) just off Sharia al-Karnak opposite Rezeiky Camp has wonderful views from the roof, plus a pool, bar and restaurant. The shoddily-built rooms go for US$28/35, but the management is desperate to fill the hotel and at the time of writing was offering discounts of up to 50%.

About 3km north of the town centre, opposite the Luxor Hilton, is the five storey **Karnak Hotel** (☎ 374 155). If you want to be out of the bustle of Luxor, but stay on the East Bank, this is a great place to be. It has a garden plus a clean pool and has received rave reviews from some travellers. Prices in winter are US$40/50, including breakfast, but they go down by 20% in the summer.

Hotels – West Bank

The best place to stay on the West Bank in the budget price range is **Marsam Hotel** (☎ 382 403), also known as Ali Abd al-Rasul Hotel or Sheikh Ali Hotel. A local institution, its very simple but clean singles/doubles with shared bathrooms cost E£25/35 including breakfast.

Abu al-Kasem Hotel (☎ 310 319) is near the Temple of Seti I on Sharia Wadi al-Melouk. It has 20 dusty singles/doubles with fans and bathrooms for E£35/50. Although it's basically clean, it's looking a bit scruffy these days. The best rooms overlook the mountains and there's a great view from the roof.

Pharaohs Hotel (☎/fax 310 702) is the oldest mid-range place to stay on the West Bank. It has 14 old rooms and 15 new ones, all with air-con and bathrooms. Although it's not beautiful, the location can't be beaten. Singles/doubles in the new building cost E£55/110.

Far better, but farther from the monuments, are two new hotels that have recently opened in the area known as the Gezira, just up from the ferry landing. **Amon al-Gezira Hotel** (☎ 310 912) is a small, spotlessly clean family-run hotel in which five of the nine rooms have their own bathrooms and there is a terrace on each floor as well as a great roof terrace and garden. Doubles go for E£60 to E£70 with air-con. The other new addition is *Al-Gezira Hotel* (☎/fax 310 034), with 11 rooms, some with great Nile views, and all with their own bathrooms and either air-con or ceiling fan. Singles/doubles cost E£40/60. There is also a very pleasant roof restaurant overlooking the Nile where you can eat a filling Egyptian meal for E£20. Stella is available for E£7. To get to the hotel take the small track that goes beside the bicycle hire and video rental shop just up from the local ferry landing.

Places to Eat

Budget Dining Sharia al-Mahatta has a number of good sandwich stands and other cheap eats possibilities, as well as a few juice stands at its Luxor Temple end. The other cheap eats area is Sharia Television, which is where you'll find *Sayyida Zeinab*, one of Luxor's best kushari joints.

Salt & Bread Cafeteria on Midan al-Mahatta across from the train station serves cheap meals for about E£5. It offers a wide range of entrees, including kebab, pigeon and chicken.

Mensa Restaurant on Sharia al-Mahatta has basic food that's slightly overpriced. Dishes include sandwiches, chicken and pigeon stuffed with rice. You can have almost a full meal for about E£8.50.

Al-Hussein on Sharia al-Karnak does a good fish in a tomato and basil sauce and the pizzas are acceptable, if smallish, for E£7. The soups are sometimes good, sometimes watery. Most main dishes cost E£7 to E£10 before service is added on.

Amoun Restaurant also on Sharia Karnak serves oriental kebab, chicken, fish and various rice and vegetable dishes for similar prices to those at the neighbouring Al-Hussein. These are two of the town's most popular eating houses for tourists.

Ali Baba Cafe on the corner of Sharia Mohammed Farid and Sharia al-Karnak is popular with locals and tourists. Although part of Luxor Wena Hotel, it has its own street entrance and has reasonably priced mezze and meals such as shish kebab and *shish tawouk* (chicken on skewers).

Mish Mish Restaurant on Sharia Television serves good basic meals for less than E£10. Try the Mish Mish salad, a mixed platter with homous and cold meats, enough to constitute a light meal, for E£6.

Sultana Restaurant on Sharia Television is a tiny place, popular with travellers, where a reasonable *bram* (vegetable stew) served steaming in a clay pot, costs only E£7.50 and pizzas go for between E£9 and E£11.

Restaurants *Kings Head Pub* (☎ 371 249), on Sharia Khaled ibn al-Walid, near the passport office, continues to be one of Luxor's most popular bar/eateries. It's a laid-back place to spend an afternoon catching up on foreign newspapers or tucking into toasted sandwiches and chips.

Ritz Restaurant (no phone) in a small alley off Sharia Khaled ibn al-Walid between the Sonesta St George and Isis hotels is a new place that offers a variety of mains starting from E£15 and has soups starting at E£3.50.

Jem's (☎ 383 604), also on Khaled ibn al-Walid (which has become Luxor's restaurant strip), serves very good Egyptian and European meals, including a vegetarian set menu for E£30. Filling appetisers and salads are cheaper at about E£8.

Some of the best and most atmospheric meals in Luxor can be found on the West Bank. *Tutankhamun Restaurant* (☎ 310 118), down by the local ferry dock, is run by a former cook at one of the French archaeological missions in Luxor who serves up excellent stews and other dishes. A meal usually costs about E£10 to E£15.

Al-Gezira Hotel also serves Egyptian specialities; the surroundings are pleasant and its roof restaurant looks out over the Nile. Meals here cost E£20 and beer is available for E£7.

Restaurant Mohammed (☎ 311 014) is basically a large room in owner Mohammed Abdel Lahi's mud-brick house, which is just along from Pharaohs Hotel. It's very popular with French archaeologists and other foreign residents in the area. You can get good, basic Egyptian food, as well as

EGYPT

EGYPT

standard chicken and French-fry platters. A full kofta meal costs E£8 and duck goes for E£15. Portions are generous and Stella is available for E£7.

Getting There & Away

Air The EgyptAir (☎ 380 580) office is on Al-Corniche, next to Amex. EgyptAir flies daily between Cairo, Luxor and Aswan. A one-way ticket to Luxor from Cairo costs E£419 and there are frequent daily departures. There are also daily flights from Luxor to Aswan (E£190 one way) and three flights per week to Sharm el-Sheikh (E£415 one way). In the high season, there are several flights a day to Abu Simbel (E£832 return) via Aswan and one flight a week to Hurghada (E£190 one way).

Bus The bus station is behind Luxor Temple on Sharia al-Karnak (the garage on Sharia Television is not an official pick-up point).

From Luxor, there is only one daily departure to Cairo and it leaves at 7 pm (E£50, 10 to 11 hours). Seven buses leave for Aswan (E£6.50 to E£8, four to five hours) between 6.30 am and 2.30 pm but only the last one has air-con.

To Hurghada (E£12.25, five hours) there are four buses a day, all of which go on to Suez (E£30.25 to E£40.25).

There are 10 buses to Qena but you may not be allowed to take them because of the jittery police.

Three buses go to Kharga each week: Saturday, Monday and Wednesday at 8.30 am. Tickets cost E£22, but the buses do not use the new Armant-Kharga road and instead go via Asyut.

From time to time there is a 'direct' bus to Dahab for E£80. However, some travellers have reported that 'direct' means going via Cairo on a nightmarish 24 hour odyssey. When tourism is up, some tourist companies offer direct air-con coaches that are more expensive but far more reliable. The tourist office will know if either has started again.

Train The only sleeper to Cairo is the wagon-lit train that departs daily at 8.30 pm.

The fare is E£314.35 one way. Otherwise the only two other Cairo trains that foreigners are allowed to take depart at 8.15 am (with 1st and 2nd class fares of E£51/28) and 11.30 pm (E£51/31). Student discounts are available on both these services.

First and 2nd class tickets to Aswan (four hours) cost E£20/12 on the 6 am train and E£22/14 on the 5.15 pm service.

Service Taxi The service taxi station is on a street off Sharia al-Karnak, a couple of blocks inland from the Luxor Museum.

From Caravans to Kebabs

For hundreds of years camels from Sudan have been brought to Egypt in large caravans along the Darb al-Arba'een (the 40 Days Road), the treacherous desert route thought to have been named after the number of days it took to journey from Sudan's Darfur province to southern Egypt.

In the centuries following their introduction into the region – thought to have been by the Persians in the 6th century BC – the camels brought slaves, ostrich feathers, precious stones, animal skins and other goods to Egypt, where they were used by the country's pharaonic overlords or, in later times, distributed to the great empires in Greece, Persia, Rome and Europe. But by the 18th and 19th centuries the gradual introduction of steamers and trains in Egypt and Sudan meant that camels were no longer the most efficient way to get goods from south to north. The establishment of air links between the two countries this century seemed to seal the fate of the caravans as relics of a bygone age.

But the camels have continued to come. Now, however, they themselves are the cargo. Some are used for agricultural work, others are exported to other Middle Eastern countries, but many – if not most – are destined for the dinner tables of poor Egyptians (yes, that cheap kebab does taste a bit strange ...).

Regular destinations include Aswan (E£8, 3½ hours), Esna (E£2, 45 minutes), Edfu (E£4, two hours), Kom Ombo (E£8, 2½ hours) and Qena (E£2).

Getting Around
To/From the Airport Luxor airport is 7km east of town and the official price for a taxi is E£10, although they'll usually ask for more. There are no buses to and from the airport into town.

Motorcycle A few hotels have started renting out motorcycles for about E£40 to E£60 per day. If you are interested, hunt around a bit and check the condition of the bikes carefully.

Bicycle Luxor is bursting with bicycle rental shops and almost all hotels have bikes too. Prices range from E£4 to E£10 per day.

Hantour For about E£6 per hour you can get around town by *hantour* (horse and carriage). Rates are, of course, subject to haggling, squabbling and, occasionally, screaming.

ESNA
The hypostyle hall, with its 24 columns still supporting a roof, is all that remains of the **Temple of Khnum** constructed by Egypt's Ptolemaic rulers. The temple is open from 6 am to 5.30 pm (6.30 pm in summer), and admission costs E£8 (E£4 for students).

Getting There & Away
Buses from Luxor cost E£2 but service taxis are often more convenient and cost the same.

EDFU
The attraction in this town 53km south of Esna is the Greek-built **Temple of Horus**, the falcon-headed son of Osiris. It took about 200 years to complete and has helped with knowledge about the pharaonic architecture it imitates. It is open from 7 am to 4 pm in winter and 6 am to 6 pm in summer. Admission is E£20 (E£10 for students).

There are two cheap hotels in Edfu, near the temple, and a couple of small places to eat off the square.

Getting There & Away
There are frequent connections to Edfu from Luxor and Aswan. Service taxis are the best bet. They cost E£5 from Luxor and E£3.50 from Aswan. The buses are E£4 and E£2.50 respectively. There is a morning bus to Marsa Alam (E£7) on the Red Sea coast.

KOM OMBO
The dual **Temple of Sobek & Haroeris** (the local crocodile-god and the falcon-headed sky-god, respectively) stands on a promontory at a bend in the Nile near the village of Kom Ombo, where in ancient times sacred crocodiles basked in the sun on the river bank. The temple is open from 8 am to 4 pm, and admission is E£10 (E£5 for students).

Getting There & Away
Kom Ombo is an easy day trip from Aswan. Service taxis cost E£1.50 and can drop you at the turn-off from where it's a 2km walk or hitch to the temple. Otherwise, from the Cleopatra Hotel in Kom Ombo, take a covered pick-up (25pt) to the boat-landing on the Nile about 800m north of the temple, then walk the remainder.

ASWAN
Over the centuries Aswan, Egypt's southernmost city, has been a garrison town, the gateway to Africa and the now inundated land of Nubia, a prosperous marketplace at the crossroads of the ancient caravan routes and, more recently, a popular winter resort.

It is the most attractive of the Nile towns – a drink on the terrace of the Old Cataract Hotel overlooking the river, Elephantine Island and the flocks of felucca sails on the Nile will convince the most sceptical.

Orientation
There are only three main avenues and most of the city is along the Nile or parallel to it. The train station is at the northern end of

ASWAN

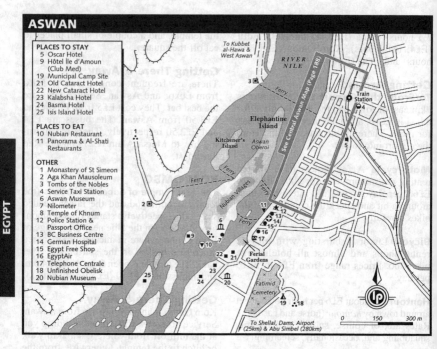

PLACES TO STAY
5   Oscar Hotel
9   Hôtel Ile d'Amoun
    (Club Med)
19 Municipal Camp Site
21 Old Cataract Hotel
22 New Cataract Hotel
23 Kalabsha Hotel
24 Basma Hotel
25 Isis Island Hotel

PLACES TO EAT
10 Nubian Restaurant
11 Panorama & Al-Shati
    Restaurants

OTHER
1   Monastery of St Simeon
2   Aga Khan Mausoleum
3   Tombs of the Nobles
4   Service Taxi Station
6   Aswan Museum
7   Nilometer
8   Temple of Khnum
12 Police Station &
    Passport Office
13 BC Business Centre
14 German Hospital
15 Egypt Free Shop
16 EgyptAir
17 Telephone Centrale
18 Unfinished Obelisk
20 Nubian Museum

To Kubbet al-Hawa & West Aswan

RIVER NILE

Ferry

Train Station

Elephantine Island

Kitchener's Island

Aswan Oberoi

Ferry

Nubian Villages

Ferry

Ferial Gardens

Fatimid Cemetery

To Shellal, Dams, Airport (25km) & Abu Simbel (280km)

See Central Aswan Map (Page 188)

0   150   300 m

town, three blocks east of the river and its
boulevard, the Corniche el-Nil, along which
you'll find most of the public utilities and
better hotels and restaurants.

Information

Tourist Office There are two tourist offices; one (☎ 312 811) is next to the train
station and the other (☎ 323 297) is on a
sidestreet, one block in from the Corniche.
Both offices are open from 8.30 am to 2 pm
and 6 to 8 pm Saturday to Thursday; on Friday they are open from 10 am to 2 pm and
6 to 8 pm.

Money The main banks have branches on
the Corniche. Banque Masr and the Banque
du Caire will issue cash advances on Visa and
MasterCard. There is also an ATM beside the
Banque du Caire (although it doesn't always
work). The Bank of Alexandria accepts Eu-

rocheques. Banque Masr also has a foreign-
exchange booth (open from 8 am to 3 pm and
5 to 8 pm daily) next to its main building.

Post & Telephone The GPO is also on the
Corniche, next to the municipal swimming
pool. However, poste restante must be collected from the smaller post office on the
corner of sharias Abtal at-Tahrir and Salah
ad-Din (go around the back, opposite the
Victoria Hotel). Both are open from 8 am to
2 pm daily except Friday.

International telephone calls can be made
from the telephone centrale, which is on the
Corniche towards the southern end of town,
just past the EgyptAir office. There are card
phones here (and usually stocks of cards). The
office is open from 8 am to 10 pm daily.

Email & Internet Access The governorate has five computers that it currently

lets you use for free between 9 am and 1.30 pm. The computers can be found at the governorate's Information & Decision Support Center; it's hard to miss – just look for the big sign saying 'Internet' beside the cinema. Also, Rosewan Hotel has recently started its own cybercafe. As in Luxor, the connection is through Cairo so you're paying for a long-distance call. There is a flat rate of E£1.50 per minute.

East Bank

Nubian Museum Showcasing the history, art and culture of Nubia from prehistoric times down to the present, the collection is housed in a well-designed modern building, loosely based on traditional Nubian architecture. The museum entrance is opposite Basma Hotel, about a 10 minute walk from the EgyptAir office. It is open from 9 am to 1 pm and then from 5 to 9 pm. Admission is E£20.

Unfinished Obelisk This huge discarded obelisk lies on the edge of the northern granite quarries that supplied the ancient Egyptians with most of the hard stone used in pyramids and temples. Three sides of the shaft, which is nearly 42m long, were completed except for the inscriptions and it would have been the largest single piece of stone ever handled if a flaw had not appeared in the granite. Admission to the site is E£20. Private taxis will charge about E£2 to take you to the site.

The River Nile

Feluccas & Ferries The river is at its most picturesque in Aswan and no visit would be complete without at least an hour spent sailing around the islands in a felucca. The official government price for hiring a felucca capable of seating one to eight people is E£15 per hour, but with a bit of bargaining you should be able to hire a boat for three or four hours for about E£35 to E£45.

Elephantine Island Once the core of what is now Aswan, the island is characterised by its huge grey boulders. Excava-

tions have revealed a small town, temples, fortifications and a Nilometer at the southern end of the island. There is a small museum (admission E£10).

Kitchener's Island Lord Kitchener turned this island into a flourishing garden, which it remains. Admission is E£5 and you have to hire a boat to get there.

West Bank

Mausoleum of Aga Khan The elaborate resting place of the Aga Khan is modelled on Fatimid tombs in Cairo. Unfortunately, it's currently closed to the public.

Monastery of St Simeon This well-preserved 6th century Coptic Christian monastery is a half-hour hike or short camel ride from the felucca dock near the Mausoleum of Aga Khan. The monastery is open from 9 am to 5 pm; admission is E£12.

Tombs of the Nobles A few of these Old and Middle Kingdom tombs of local dignitaries are worth exploring. Admission to the tombs is E£12. Hours are from 8 am to 4 pm in winter and 8 am to 5 pm in summer.

Places to Stay

Camping There's an official *camping ground* next to the unfinished obelisk, which is a 20 to 25 minute walk from the area around EgyptAir. Facilities are basic (filthy toilets and cold showers only) but there are grassy spaces for setting up tents and a few trees to provide shade. It costs E£3 per person plus E£5/2 for a car/motorcycle.

Hostels *Youth Hostel* (☎ 322 235) is on Sharia Abtal at-Tahrir, near the train station at the side entrance of the governorate-run hostel, which, just to confuse you, also calls itself a youth hostel. The 'real' youth hostel charges members E£7.60 for a bed in a dorm, while nonmembers pay E£8.60.

Hotels – North of the Train Station *Rosewan Hotel* (☎ 304 497) has been popular with budget travellers for quite a few years but the rooms are now a bit over-priced. It has fairly clean, simple, rather small singles/doubles/triples with shower/toilet combinations for E£12/22/33.

Mena Hotel (☎ *304 388*) has carpeted rooms with air-con, TV, phone, shower, toilet and small balcony for E£25/35. (There are also a few cheaper rooms with poor air-con or just fans.) There's a colourful roof garden with cushioned chairs that is ideal for an evening beer (E£5).

New Abu Simbel Hotel (☎ *306 096*) is several blocks north of the train station and although it's out of the centre, the management is friendly and there's a pleasant garden where you can relax and cool off with a cold Sbeer. At E£25/35, the screened rooms with private bathroom and air-con, are good value.

Hotels – South of the Train Station

Marwa Hotel is entered from an alley off Sharia Abtal at-Tahrir, directly across the street from the Youth Hostel. The rooms are simple and a little cramped, but at E£5 a person in a share room of three or four beds, it is fairly popular. A few rooms have air-con, for which you pay E£2 more.

Abu Simbel Hotel (☎ *302 888*) not far from the tourist office on the Corniche has singles/doubles with showers for E£29.50/38.50. The view of the Nile from the tiny balcony of each room is fantastic, and for some people makes up for the tiny bathrooms and shabby state.

Abu Shelib Hotel (☎ *303 051*) at the southern end of Sharia as-Souq is next to a mosque. Rooms are clean and simple, with fans and/or air-con, and toilet/shower combinations (big bathrooms in some). Singles/doubles are E£20/30, but you may be able to negotiate.

Hotel Orabi (☎/*fax 317 578*) on a quiet sidestreet just off the souq is relatively new and its central location is an advantage for exploring the souq and the Corniche. The staff are friendly, the rooms are modern and comfortable, and the communal bathrooms are clean. The cost is E£10/15 for singles/doubles with air-con but shared bath-

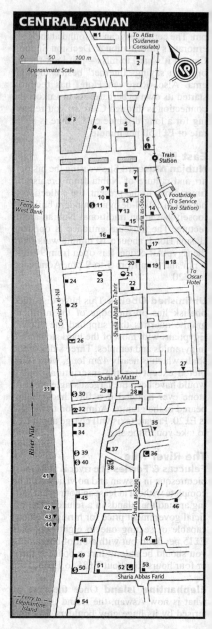

CENTRAL ASWAN

CENTRAL ASWAN

PLACES TO STAY
1 New Abu Simbel Hotel
2 Mena Hotel
5 Rosewan &
   As-Saffa Hotels
8 Marwa Hotel
10 Youth Hostel
14 Noorhan Hotel
15 Al-Amin Hotel
16 Ramses Hotel
18 Bob Marley Hotel
19 New Brethren Hotel
20 Cleopatra Hotel
22 Nubian Oasis Hotel
24 Abu Simbel Hotel
28 Aswan Palace Hotel
29 Happi Hotel
31 Isis Hotel
33 Al-Salam Hotel
34 Hathor Hotel
37 Victoria Hotel

45 Horus Hotel
46 Keylany Hotel
47 Hotel Orabi
48 Memnon Hotel
49 Philae Hotel
51 Al-Amir Hotel
53 Abu Shelib Hotel

PLACES TO EAT
7 Restaurant Derwash
9 Al-Dar Restaurant
12 An-Nasry
13 Esraa (Kofta Place)
17 Medina Restaurant
27 Al-Masry Restaurant
35 Al-Sayyida Nefissa
   Restaurant
41 Saladin Restaurant
42 Aswan Moon Restaurant
43 Emy Restaurant
44 Monalisa Restaurant

OTHER
3 Governorate Building
4 Governorate Internet
   Centre
6 Tourist Office
11 Tourist Office & Nile Valley
   Navigation Office
21 Bus Station
23 Share Taxi Stand
25 Cultural Centre
26 GPO
30 Banque Masr
32 Card Phones
36 Mosque
38 Post Office
   (Poste Restante)
39 Banque du Caire
40 Bank of Alexandria
50 Banque du Caire
52 Mosque
54 Thomas Cook

EGYPT

room. A bed in a triple with a fan is E£6 per person.

Keylany Hotel (☎ 317 332) has brand new rooms with ceiling fans and pine furniture and their own spotless bathrooms. Singles go for E£7 and doubles cost E£14. This is definitely one of the better options in the budget range.

Ramses Hotel (☎ 324 000, fax 315 701) on Sharia Abtal at-Tahrir is a good deal and, according to some, the best value hotel in Aswan. Singles/doubles with shower, toilet, air-con, colour TV, mini-fridge and Nile views cost about E£35/55.

Oscar Hotel (☎/fax 306 066) has become a travellers' favourite. Rooms cost E£40/70, but can be bargained down. Some have balconies and bedside reading lights. There's also a rooftop terrace where beers (E£6) are available.

Al-Salaam Hotel (☎ 302 651, 303 649) on the Corniche can be considered a fair deal for the price. Singles/doubles cost E£25/40 with fans, E£35/50 with air-con. Most of the freshly painted rooms have private bathrooms and some have great views of the Nile.

Horus Hotel (☎/fax 313 313) on the Corniche has large and comfortable singles/doubles with air-con and bath for E£40/50. Some rooms have great Nile views. Ask for a room that has been renovated. There is a rooftop bar and restaurant.

Places to Eat
Restaurant Derwash on the southern side of the midan in front of the train station has been recommended by some travellers. *Medina Restaurant* on Sharia as-Souq, across from Cleopatra Hotel, is recommended for its kofta and kebab deals, and is often patronised by travellers. It also serves a vegetarian meal for E£4.50. *Al-Sayyida Nefissa* tucked away in a side alley in the heart of the souq is a good-value place serving kofta for E£6, soup for E£1, and a meal of rice, salad, vegetables and bread for E£2.50.

Al-Masry Restaurant (☎ 302 576) on Sharia al-Matar serves kebabs and kofta only, but it's clean with attractive Arabesque tiled walls, and the meat is excellent and comes with bread, salad and tahina. Expect to pay around E£16.

The tiny *Restaurant el-Nil* is on the Corniche a few doors along from Thomas Cook. A full meal with fish (carp from Lake Nasser), chicken or meat with vegetables, rice, salad, tahina and bread should cost about E£9.

Getting There & Away

Air EgyptAir has daily flights from Cairo to Aswan (E£576 one way, 1¼ hours). The one-way hop to Luxor is E£190; to Hurghada via Luxor it's E£374. The return flight from Aswan to Abu Simbel costs E£290 and includes bus transfers between the airport and the temple site.

Bus The bus station is in the middle of town on Sharia Abtal at-Tahrir. In their zeal to 'protect' foreigners, some policemen have been forbidding foreigners even from taking buses out of Aswan. There seem to be no hard and fast rules, although at the time of writing Abu Simbel buses were definitely off limits.

There are two buses a day for Cairo (E£40 and E£55, 12 hours), and hourly buses to Luxor (E£6.50/15, four to five hours) via Kom Ombo, Edfu and Esna. There are also five buses going through to Hurghada (E£25, seven hours) and a daily bus for Marsa Alam (E£12, five hours).

Train The wagon-lit train (No 85) costs E£300 one way to Cairo and departs at 3 pm. Express train Nos 981 and 997 to Cairo leave at 5 am and 8.45 pm. The 1st/2nd class fare is E£63/37; student discounts are available. Tickets for the train to Luxor (four hours) cost E£22/12 in 1st/2nd class on the afternoon service, and a few pounds more on the morning train. Both trains also stop at Kom Ombo and Edfu.

Service Taxi At the time of writing the police in Aswan were forbidding foreigners from taking service taxis, often turning them back at the checkpoint just north of town. As with all such directives, people do get around the rules but in general it's better to take the bus or train, or else get a group of people together and hire a private taxi.

Felucca Aswan is the best place to arrange overnight felucca trips. At the time of writing trips north of Edfu were forbidden for security reasons so, unless things change, you are limited to trips to Kom Ombo (one night, two days) or, the most popular option, Edfu (three days, two nights).

Officially, feluccas can carry a minimum of six passengers and a maximum of eight, for the following prices: E£25 per person to Kom Ombo, E£45 to Edfu. On top of this you must add E£5 for police registration, plus there's the cost of food supplies.

Boat to Sudan See the Getting There & Away section earlier in this chapter.

Getting Around

To/From the Airport The airport is 25km south-west of town and the taxi fare is about E£20.

Taxi A taxi tour that includes the Philae Temple, High Dam and unfinished obelisk near the Fatimid Cemetery costs around E£30 for five to six people.

Bicycle There are a few places at the train station end of Sharia as-Souq where you can hire bicycles for about E£5 a day – try around the Marwa and Ramses hotels.

AROUND ASWAN
Temple of Philae

South of Aswan and relocated to another island to save it from being flooded in the 1960s (see the following High Dam section), the Temple of Philae was dedicated to Isis, who found the heart of her slain brother, Osiris, on Philae Island (now submerged). Most of the temple was built by the Ptolemies and Romans, and early Christians turned the hypostyle hall into a chapel. It is possible to organise taxi trips to the boat landing at Shellal south of the Old Dam, or you can walk if you can get a lift to the dam.

The temple complex is open from 8 am to 4 pm in winter and 7 am to 5 pm in summer; admission is E£20. Tickets are purchased from the small office before the boat landing at Shellal. The boat costs about E£14 (maximum eight people) for the return trip.

A sound & light show (E£33) is held here – there are usually three performances a night.

High Dam

The controversial Sadd al-Ali, the High Dam, 17km south of Aswan, is 3.6km across, 980m wide at its base and 111m high at its highest point. About 35,000 people helped build this enormous structure and 451 of them died during its construction. When it was completed in 1971 the water that collected behind it became Lake Nasser, the world's largest artificial lake. In creating the lake, a number of pharaonic monuments had to be rescued in a US$40 million UNESCO effort – taken to pieces and rebuilt at new sites above the risen water line.

Most people get to the High Dam as part of an organised trip to sites around Aswan but many are disappointed by the visit, expecting more spectacular views.

ABU SIMBEL

Carved out of a mountainside and the single most photogenic of all Egypt's monuments, Ramses II's **Great Temple of Abu Simbel** was one of the monuments moved out of the way of the rising waters of Lake Nasser in the 1960s. The temple was dedicated to the gods Ra-Harakhty, Amun, Ptah and the deified pharaoh himself. Guarding the entrance, the four famous colossal statues of Ramses II sit majestically, each more than 20m tall, with smaller statues of the king's mother, Queen Tuya, his wife Nefertari and some of their children.

The other temple at the Abu Simbel complex is the rock cut **Temple of Hathor**.

The admission fee for both temples is E£36 (E£18 for students).

Places to Stay

There are two hotels at Abu Simbel. The four star *Nefertari Hotel* (☎ 400 508/9) is about 400m from the temples, overlooking Lake Nasser. It has singles/doubles costing US$72/90 including breakfast but not taxes.

You can also camp for about E£20 – you get to use the showers and pool.

The three star *Nobaleh Ramses Hotel* (☎/fax 400 380) is about 1.5km from the temple site and charges US$50/82.50 half-board, including tax, although deals are possible.

Getting There & Away

Although there is a perfectly good road between Aswan and Abu Simbel, at the time of writing the police had deemed it off limits to all foreigners. As a result, EgyptAir had halved its fare and most visitors were seeing the temple in the company of a plane-load of package tourists (see the Aswan Getting There & Away section).

Western Oases

The five main oases of the Western Desert are attracting a growing number of travellers, but still remain off the main tourist trail. The government has dubbed the string of oases the New Valley Frontier District and hopes to develop the area, and so create new possibilities for an exploding population. Asphalt roads link all the oases now, four of them in a long loop from Asyut around to Cairo. Siwa, out near the Libyan frontier, is now linked by road to Bahariyya, but no public transport uses this route as yet. There is limited accommodation in all of the oases, and infrequent buses link all but Siwa.

KHARGA OASIS

About 235km south of Asyut is the largest of the oases, Kharga. The town, Al-Kharga, is the administrative centre of the New Valley governorate, which also includes Dakhla and Farafra oases. The town is of little interest, but to the north you'll find the **Temple of Hibis**, built to the god Amun by the Persian Emperor Darius I. To the east are the crumbling remains of the **Temple of An-Nadura**, built by the Romans. Just north of the Temple of Hibis is the Coptic **Necropolis of Al-Bagawat**, dating as far back as the 4th century.

Places to Stay & Eat

You can *camp* in the grounds of the Kharga Oasis Hotel for E£7 per person and use the toilet and shower inside.

Newly built *Dar al-Bayda Hotel (☎ 921 717)* has clean, pleasant singles/doubles, most with fans, for E£14/20. Breakfast is E£4 extra.

Waha Hotel (☎ 920 393) is a reasonable cheapie but the singles are cramped and windowless and the shared bathrooms can be filthy. Singles/doubles cost E£7/14 without bath or E£15/20 with bath.

Hamad Allah Hotel (☎ 920 638, fax 925 017) is popular with overland tour groups. Singles/doubles with bath, fridge, TV and breakfast cost E£31/53, or E£45/75.25 with air-con.

Kharga Oasis Hotel (☎ 921 500) is another modern homage to concrete, but has a nice palm-filled garden and terrace. Singles/doubles cost E£55/77 without air-con, or E£61/83 with. Prices include breakfast and taxes.

Restaurants are few and far between in Kharga and the best places to eat are the hotels. At *Hamad Allah Hotel* set lunch (E£17) and dinner (E£19) are available and there's a bar. *Kharga Oasis Hotel* restaurant has lunches for E£21 and dinners for E£24. Otherwise, try *Al-Ahram* at the front of the Waha Hotel, which sells chicken, and vegetable dishes.

Getting There & Away

EgyptAir flies from Cairo to Al-Kharga and back again on Sunday and Wednesday; the fare is E£450 each way.

Four buses leave Al-Kharga daily for Cairo (E£23.25, seven to eight hours) and there are several buses from Al-Kharga to Asyut (E£6 to E£7, three to four hours).

Buses to Dakhla (E£5 to E£7, three hours) leave at 7 am, noon and 2.30 pm and there's a bus to Luxor each Friday, Sunday and Tuesday at 7.30 am.

A service taxi to Dakhla takes three hours and costs E£7.

There's also a train from Al-Kharga to Luxor every Friday at 7 am. The trip takes about seven hours and tickets (3rd class only) cost E£9.80 (students E£4.90).

DAKHLA OASIS

Located 190km west of Kharga, Dakhla was created from more than 600 natural springs and ponds. It contains two small towns, Mut and Al-Qasr. Mut is the bigger and has most of the hotels and public utilities. There are government-run **hot springs** 3km to its north. Another 30km brings you to the remarkable medieval mud-brick town of **Al-Qasr**. Watch out for the 12th century minaret.

Places to Stay

It's possible to *camp* near the dunes west of Mut or in Al-Qasr, on a desert plateau just north of town, but you should check with the tourist office first.

Other than a fairly unpleasant *Government Rest House* (in the same building as the tourist office) that charges just E£4.35 per person, the only option in Al-Qasr is the friendly *Al-Qasr Hotel (☎ 876 013)* on the main road near the entry to the old town. It has four big screened rooms with narrow balconies for E£5 per person; breakfast is E£2 extra. Shared bathrooms are clean and, contrary to the norm, have hot water only.

A reasonable deal in Mut itself is *Gardens Hotel (☎ 821 577)* where singles/doubles without bath or fan cost E£12/16; with bath they cost E£15/20 (triples E£24).

Another cheap alternative is *Nasser's Hotel*, on the edge of Sheikh Waley, a village about 5km east of Mut on the road to Kharga oasis (or 20 minutes by bicycle from Mut). It has five rooms for E£10 per person, including breakfast.

Bedouin Camp (☎ 830 604/5) is 7km north of Mut, on a desert hilltop near the small desert village of Al-Dohous. It has eight reed huts and three mud-brick rooms that are simple but very clean and quiet and have great views. Rooms are E£15 per person, including breakfast.

Mebarez Hotel (☎/fax 821 524) on the road to Al-Qasr is popular with groups. Singles/doubles with bath and air-con cost

E£44/58. Without bath the rooms cost E£28/42.

Places to Eat

There aren't too many restaurants or cafes in Mut but *Ahmed Hamdy's Restaurant* is popular with travellers and serves chicken, kebab, vegetables and a few other small dishes plus excellent, freshly squeezed lime juices and beer. Confusingly, there are two restaurants with almost the same name, a result of a dispute between two brothers. Ahmed Hamdy's is the original – it's the one closest to Mebarez Hotel.

The nearby *Abu Mohammed Restaurant* is the place to go for an E£8 to E£10 meal that will fill you to bursting point. Seemingly unending serves of soups, vegetables, rice, kebab, salads, sweets and nonalcoholic Stella emerge from a pristine kitchen.

Getting There & Away

EgyptAir flies from Mut to Cairo every Sunday and Wednesday at 8 am. A one-way ticket will cost you E£500.

Bus services to Cairo (E£42, eight to 10 hours) via Kharga oasis (E£8) and Asyut (E£15) leave every day at 7 pm and 8 pm. You can also go to Cairo via Farafra and Bahariyya oases at 6 am and 6 pm for E£35.

Service taxis leave from the bus station, and cost E£7 to Al-Kharga and E£15 to either Farafra oasis or Asyut. There are also microbuses to Farafra oasis for E£12 to E£15.

FARAFRA OASIS

About 300km north-west of Dakhla, Farafra is the smallest and most untouched of the oases. There is really nothing much to see here, except for the palms and fruit trees bearing everything from dates to apricots. About 45km north of town is the stunning **White Desert**, to which you can organise excursions from the town.

Places to Stay & Eat

There are only two places to stay in town. The government-run *Al-Farafra Tourist Rest House* is next to the new hospital, about 1km out along the road to Bahariyya.

It costs E£10 per person in rooms (that aren't great) with fan and three beds.

Far better is the tastefully designed mud-brick *Al-Badawiyya Safari & Hotel* (☎ 345 8524 in Cairo), which is one of the best hotels in the oases. The rooms come in different styles and start with large quads with shared bathrooms for E£10 per person. Double rooms with shared bath are E£15 per person, while you're looking at E£50 to E£70 for large double and triple rooms, with their own bathroom, sitting area and TV.

The choice of where to eat is similarly limited. *Hussein's* is the larger of the two restaurants in town but even here most of the pots are empty by 7 pm, so come early. Check the prices beforehand – he's been known to charge E£2 for a cup of tea.

There is also the tiny *Nice Time* restaurant, which is off the main road and has become something of a travellers' hang-out, and the *Al-Badawiyya*, hotel where the food is more expensive but fresh and good. They can also scrounge up a beer.

Getting There & Away

There is a bus from Farafra to Cairo (E£25, 10 to 11 hours) via Bahariyya (E£10, 2½ hours) every day between 10 and 11 am. Another leaves Farafra at about 11 pm and arrives in Cairo at 6 am. Every Saturday, Monday and Thursday there is a third bus at 9 am. There are two buses a day from Farafra to Dakhla (E£12, four to five hours) – the first leaves between 1 and 2 pm and the other between 1 and 2 am.

Microbuses to Dakhla leave from in front of the Mabrouk Cafeteria whenever they have a full load and a seat costs about E£15.

BAHARIYYA OASIS

About 185km north-east of Farafra and 330km south-east of Cairo is the oasis of Bahariyya. Buses will bring you to **Bawiti**, the main village. The attractions are limited here to various **springs**. One of the best, Bir al-Ghaba, is accessible only by 4WD. Ask at the Alpenblick Hotel in Bawati, which has a camp site there. You can also walk to **Black Mountain**.

Places to Stay & Eat

Government Rest House is 7km from town near Bir al-Mattar. For E£5 per night (including transport) you can stay here, but it is very basic and in need of renovation.

Government-run **Paradise Hotel** (☎ 802 600) in the centre of town has recently been renovated, although it remains quite basic. There are six rooms with three beds and it costs E£3.50 per person. Breakfast on the small vine-covered terrace is an extra E£1.50.

Ahmed's Safari Camp (☎ 802 090) about 4km west of the centre has become a bit of a favourite among travellers and trans-Africa groups. It has a range of options (prices are per person): cool, pleasant, domed double rooms with private bathroom for E£12.50 including breakfast; rooms with shared facilities for E£5 per person; basic reed huts at E£3; or a roof where you can sleep under the stars for E£2.

Alpenblick Hotel (☎ 802 184), which is more expensive, is a relatively attractive two storey place with a variety of clean rooms. Large doubles without/with private bath (and hot water) cost E£35/46 including breakfast. Budget rooms cost E£17 (breakfast is E£5 extra).

The Alpenblick also has 15 huts with mattresses out at Bir al-Ghaba. The enclosure is watched by a warden, who will also help out with tea and firewood. It costs E£10 a night and is very peaceful, but you must bring your own food.

Unless you make your own meals, your food will be limited to the hotels or the town's one restaurant, **Popular Restaurant** (also known as Bayoumi's), which serves a selection of dishes like chicken, soup, rice and vegetables for around E£12. It's also open for breakfast.

Getting There & Away

There are daily buses to Cairo (E£12) at 7 am and 3 pm and another sometime between midnight and 1 am. Also, each Saturday, Monday and Thursday at about 11.30 am, you can catch a bus originating in Farafra on its way to Cairo for the same price.

Heading to Farafra (E£18.25) you can pick up one of the buses from Cairo, which are supposed to leave Bahariyya at 8 am, noon and 3 and 6.30 pm.

Supposedly, there's always a service taxi going to Sayyida Zeinab in Cairo between 3 and 4 pm, but this could be earlier or later and not every day. Ask at Popular Restaurant. A service taxi to Farafra (and they're not very frequent) will also cost E£15. Microbuses to either place cost about the same but are more frequent. They can be caught opposite the police intelligence office or, again, ask at Popular Restaurant.

If you want to get a taxi to Siwa, expect to pay at least E£550.

SIWA OASIS

The lush and productive Western Desert oasis of Siwa, famous throughout the country for its dates and olives, is 300km south-west of Marsa Matruh and 550km west of Cairo, near the Libyan border. There are no banks here so bring all the money you'll need.

Things to See & Do

Apart from date palms, there are a couple of **springs** where you can swim, the remains of a **temple** to Amun, some Graeco-Roman **tombs** and a small **museum** of local traditions. The town centre is marked by the remnants of a medieval mud brick **fortress** and **minaret** – the only one in the country where the muezzin still climbs to the top and doesn't use a loudspeaker. Several shops around town sell local crafts such as basketware and jewellery.

Places to Stay

Palm Trees Hotel (☎ 460 2204) just off the main square is a popular place to stay. It has clean rooms with fans, screened windows and small balconies and charges E£5/6 per person in a double room without/with private bath.

In close competition with the Palm Trees Hotel, is **Yousef Hotel** (☎ 460 162) in the town centre. Some of the rooms here are tiny, but everything is clean, the beds are comfortable, and the showers steaming with hot water. It's E£5 per night, without breakfast.

Next door is the oasis' long-time hotel *Al-Medina*. It's E£5 a night here too, but considerably more grotty. Both places are close to mosques.

If you head directly south of the main square you'll soon arrive at *Cleopatra Hotel* (☎ 460 2148). Rooms in its original building cost E£10/14 for singles without/with bathrooms, and E£13/18 for doubles. Far better are the more expensive chalets where rooms with ceiling fan and simple wooden furniture go for E£25/34. None of the prices include breakfast.

Next up is the cheapest and scummiest place in Siwa, *New Siwa Hotel*. It's E£2.50 a bed. A walk down the main road and off to the right is *Badawi Hotel*, run by a young gent of the same name. For E£5 you get a comfortable bed and maybe a fan; however, mixed couples wanting to stay here must be able to show their marriage certificate.

Just in from the telephone centrale is the brand new *Alexander Hotel* (☎ 460 2081). With nine rooms and eight more planned, it has an inside staircase down to Alexander the Great restaurant below. The spotless singles/doubles are E£12/25 with bath, not including breakfast.

Opposite the tourist office is the 20 room *Arous al-Waha Hotel* (☎ 460 2100). Although it resembles a modern government building rather than a hotel the management is friendly and helpful. Rooms have bathrooms with constant hot water and fans. Singles/doubles with breakfast cost E£54/72.

Places to Eat

The ever popular *Abdu Restaurant* across the road from Yousef Hotel serves a wide range of traditional dishes, vegetable stews, couscous and roasted chickens. It also serves a very tasty pizza for E£5, though you might be waiting an hour or so for it.

Just as popular these days is *Alexander Restaurant* opposite Al-Medina hotel.

Yousef, the original chef at Alexander Restaurant, recently opened his own place around the corner. His *Alexander the Great Restaurant* offers much the same fare as the others, including the curries that appeared on all the town's menus after three Pakistanis spent a month in the oasis a couple of years back. It also has plenty of vegetarian dishes.

There are several places dotted around the square where you can have a sheesha or a cup of coffee and play some backgammon. *Bakri's Cafe* (also known as Sohag Rest House) next to Abdu Restaurant is one of the most popular.

Getting There & Away

There is a daily bus at 7 am to Alexandria (E£15, eight hours), stopping at Marsa Matruh (E£8, four hours) on the way. There's a second bus to Alexandria, once again via Marsa Matruh, departing at 10 am, which has air-con and costs E£25 (E£10 to Matruh). You should book ahead for these services. There is an additional daily service to Marsa Matruh at 2 pm that costs E£9; no bookings are taken.

Although there is a road linking the oases of Siwa and Bahariyya, there is no public transport. Also, although asphalted, it is in bad shape and few people take it. Some entrepreneurial types in town will take you if you can manage the E£550 they're charging.

Alexandria & the Mediterranean Coast

ALEXANDRIA

Alexandria (Iskendariyya) is often said to be the greatest historical city with the least to show: it was founded by Alexander the Great, yet it bears no trace of him; it was the site of one of the wonders of the ancient world, but there's not a single notable monument in the city today; it was ruled by Cleopatra and was a rival of Rome, yet it's now a provincial city overcrowded with people and short on prestige.

The reality of modern-day Alexandria is a grubby compress of apartment blocks jostling at the seafront. First time visitors

Cleopatra (65-30 BC)

Cleopatra, of Elizabeth Taylor and four hour bore-athon film fame, belonged to the Ptolemaic dynasty, established in Egypt by a former general of Alexander the Great. She and her younger brother Ptolemy XIII together ruled Egypt, until Cleopatra got cosy with Julius Caesar and had her sibling rival tossed into the Nile. Following the assassination of Caesar, Cleopatra found herself a new protector – and husband – in Marc Antony, a strong contender for the vacated role of Emperor of Rome. But the union of the Egyptian queen and the Roman general was not popular in Rome, especially with Caesar's nephew Octavian, whose sister was already married to Antony. In the ensuing power struggle, the Egyptian fleet was defeated at Actium in 31 BC by the superior forces of Octavian (who later became Emperor Augustus). As the victorious Roman fleet sailed towards Egypt, Cleopatra, rather than face capture, reputedly put an asp to her breast and so ended the Ptolemaic dynasty.

can't help but be disappointed. But to judge Alexandria on first appearances is to sell the city short. It's a city of nuances and shades, with plenty to be discovered if you're prepared to invest the time.

History

Established in 332 BC by Alexander the Great, the city became a major trade centre and focal point of learning for the entire Mediterranean world. Its ancient library held 500,000 volumes and the Pharos lighthouse was one of the Seven Wonders of the World (see boxed text 'The Pharos of Alexandria'). Alexandria continued as the capital of Egypt under the Romans and their eastern offshoot, the Byzantine empire. From the 4th century onwards the city declined into insignificance. Napoleon's arrival and Alexandria's subsequent redevelopment as a major port attracted people from all over the world, but the 1952 Revolution put an end to much of the city's pluralistic charm.

Orientation

Alexandria is a true waterfront city, nearly 20km long from east to west and only about 3km wide. The focal point of the city is Midan Ramla, also known as Mahattat Ramla (Ramla station) because this is the central terminus for all the city's tram lines. Immediately adjacent is Midan Saad Zaghloul, a large square running back from the seafront and joining Midan Ramla at the corner. Around these two midans, and in the streets to the south and west, are the central shopping area, the tourist office, airline offices, restaurants and most of the cheaper hotels.

Information

Visa Extensions The passport office is at 28 Talaat Harb. You'll need one photo and a photocopy of the relevant pages of your passport (available from the machines out front) and the passport itself. The office is open from 8 am to 1.30 pm daily except Friday.

Tourist Office The tourist office (☎ 807 9885) open from 8 am to 6 pm is on the south-west corner of Midan Saad Zaghloul.

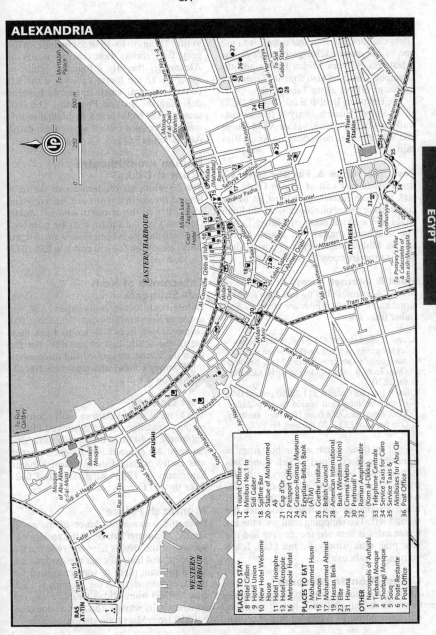

ALEXANDRIA

To Montazah Palace

To Fort Qaitbey

RAS AT-TIN

WESTERN HARBOUR

EASTERN HARBOUR

ANFUSH

ATTAREEN

To Pompey's Pillar & Catacombs of Kom ash-Shuqqafa

To Sidi Gaber Station

Masr Train Station

EGYPT

PLACES TO STAY
8 Hotel Crillon
9 Hotel Union
10 New Hotel Welcome House
11 Hotel Triomphe
13 Hotel Acropole
16 Metropole Hotel

PLACES TO EAT
15 Mohammed Hosni
17 Trianon
19 Mohammed Ahmed
23 Hassan Bleik
31 Elite
32 Havana

OTHER
1 Necropolis of Anfushi
3 Terbana Mosque
4 Shorbagi Mosque
5 Souq
6 Poste Restante
7 Post Office
12 Tourist Office
14 Minibus No.1 to Sidi Gaber
18 Spitfire Bar
20 Statue of Mohammed Ali
21 Cap d'Or
22 Passport Office
24 Graeco-Roman Museum
25 Egyptian-British Bank (ATM)
26 Goethe Institut
27 British Council
28 American International Bank (Western Union)
29 Cinema Metro
30 Pastroudi's
32 Roman Amphitheatre (Kom al-Dikka)
33 Telephone Centrale
34 Service Taxis for Cairo
35 Service Taxis & Minibuses for Abu Qir
36 Post Office

Money For changing cash or cashing travellers cheques, the simplest option is to use one of the many exchange bureaus on the sidestreets between Midan Ramla and the Corniche. There are also dozens of currency exchange offices along Talaat Harb.

The Egyptian-British Bank (☎ 483 2839) at 47 Sultan Hussein, only a five minute walk east of the centre, has an ATM where you can get cash advances on your Visa card.

Post, Telephone & Fax The GPO is a small office just east of Midan Orabi. To pick up poste restante you must go to the mail sorting centre one block west of Midan Orabi and a block north of Midan Tahrir. The telephone centrales at Midan Ramla and on Midan Gomhuriyya opposite Masr train station are open 24 hours a day.

Email & Internet Access At the time of writing Alexandria has no less than four Internet cafes, two of which are close by Sidi Gaber train station.

Access Cybercafe (☎ 425 5766, Web site www .cyberaccess.com.eg) 1st floor of the shopping mall beside the new Zahran Mall, Smouha. Open from 9 am to midnight daily. One hour for E£10.

Click-It Internet Cafe (☎ 311 7520) ground floor of the shopping mall beside the new Zahran Mall, Smouha. Open from 10.30 to 1 am daily. One hour for E£12, 30 minutes for E£7.

To get to them, catch a minibus from in front of the Cecil Hotel to Sidi Gaber bus station, then head south, away from the train station, until you hit the main road, where you take a right. After 200m you'll reach a roundabout at which you take the second left. The shopping mall with the Internet cafes is between the mosque and the new pink multi-storey Zahran Mall. It's a 10 minute walk in all.

Graeco-Roman Museum

Ancient Alexandria is almost as intangible to us as Atlantis but the 40,000 artefacts collected in the 24 rooms of this excellent museum go some way towards bringing it to life. Things to look out for include, in the very first room, three carved heads of Alexander, the city's founder, while in room No 18 the fourth cabinet on the left contains several small terracotta lanterns depicting the ancient Pharaohs. The museum (☎ 483 6434) is at 5 Al-Mathaf ar-Romani and is open from 9 am to 4 pm daily. Admission is E£16.

Roman Amphitheatre (Kom al-Dikka)

The 13 white marble terraces of the only Roman theatre in Egypt were discovered in 1964. It's at the northern end of Midan Gomhuriyya (the square with the train station) and the site is open from 9 am to 4 pm daily; admission fee will cost you E£6 (E£3 for students).

Catacombs of Kom ash-Shuqqafa

Dating back to the 2nd century AD, the tombs of Kom ash-Shuqqafa held about 300 corpses. Open from 8.30 am to 4 pm, they are in the south-west of the city, not far from the famed, misnamed and disappointing **Pompey's Pillar** and tram line No 16. Admission is E£12.

Fort Qaitbey

The Mamluk sultan Qaitbey built a fortress on the foundations of the destroyed Pharos lighthouse in 1480. In the 19th century Mohammed Ali expanded its defences, but it was badly damaged during British bombardments in 1882. Admission is E£12. Take the No 15 tram.

Montazah Palace

Once the summer residence of the royal family, Montazah Palace, at the eastern extremity of the city, is now reserved for the president and his VIPs but the gardens are still a pleasant place to wander around for the day. Admission to the grounds is E£2. Bus No 260 from Midan Orabi passes the gardens on its way to Abu Qir, as does bus No 250 from Masr train station.

EGYPT

The Pharos of Alexandria

According to classical accounts, the Egyptian coast was notoriously treacherous with hidden rocks and sand banks and a flat featureless shoreline offering little in the way of navigation aids. So it was that Ptolemy I ordered a great tower to be built, one that took a dozen years to complete and was finally inaugurated in 283 BC. The finished structure was of such massive proportions and of such a unique nature that ancient scholars regarded it as one of the Seven Wonders of the World.

The tower became a lighthouse in the 1st century AD, when the Romans added a beacon, probably in the form of an oil-fed flame that was reflected by sheets of polished bronze.

In all, the Pharos withstood winds, floods and the occasional tidal wave for a total of 17 centuries. However, in 1303 a violent earthquake rattled the entire eastern Mediterranean from Egypt to Greece and the Pharos was totally destroyed. A century later the sultan Qaitbey quarried the ruins for the fortress that he built on the same site.

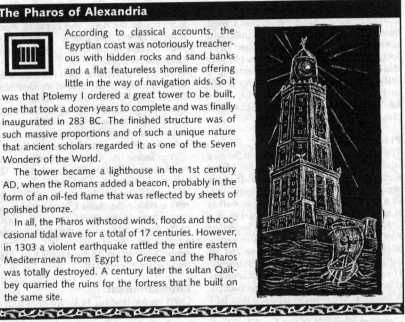

Places to Stay

New Hotel Welcome House (☎ 480 6402, *8 Sharia Gamal ad-Din Yassin*) on the street behind the Cecil is easily the best of three otherwise grotty hostels occupying the top two floors of this building. Rooms vary in quality but an attempt has been made to look after them. Try to get one of the three doubles that overlook the harbour; these have their own shower and toilet units and are a bit of a bargain at E£16.

Hotel Acropole (☎ 480 5980, *1 Gamal ad-Din Yassin, 4th floor*) has rooms with great views over Midan Saad Zaghloul but none overlooking the harbour. Some of the rooms are also very shabby but the place has a pleasant rambling, chaotic appeal. Rates are between E£15 and E£20 for a single, and E£25 to E£35 for a double, depending on the room.

Hotel Triomphe (☎ 480 7585, *2 Gamal ad-Din Yassin, 5th floor*) has no rooms with sea views either. It's a similar sort of place

to the Acropole but considerably more scruffy. Room rates are roughly the same.

Hotel Union (☎ 480 7312, fax 480 7350, *164 Sharia 26th of July, 5th floor*) one block back from the Cecil offers great value with three star accommodation at more or less budget rates. The rooms are some of the cleanest in Alexandria with sparkling tiled bathrooms. Most also have balconies and fantastic harbour views. Singles/doubles without bath cost E£30/38, or E£45/60 with bath. Breakfast is E£8 extra. Reservations are recommended.

Hotel Crillon (☎ 480 0330, *5 Sharia Adib Ishaq, 4th floor*) two blocks back from the Cecil runs a close second to the Union in the cleanliness stakes – although a few of the rooms are notably not as good as the rest. Most rooms have balconies with that great harbour view. Doubles with shower are E£53, while those with a bathroom are E£67. Reservations are a must.

Metropole Hotel (☎ 482 1465, fax 482 2040, 52 Sharia Saad Zaghloul) has a good, central location just off Midan Ramla, with most rooms overlooking Midan Saad Zaghloul and the harbour. It's a classy old joint that has been recently renovated, earning itself a four star rating. Singles go for E£160 to E£180, while doubles are E£180 to E£190. Breakfast is obligatory (E£14), plus there's 19% in taxes to be added.

Places to Eat

The place for cheap eating is around the area where Sharia Safiyya Zaghloul meets Midan Ramla, and along Sharia Shakor Pasha, one street over to the west. There are plenty of little fuul and ta'amiyya places here as well as sandwich shops and the odd *kushari* joint.

Mohammed Ahmed (317 Sharia Shakor Pasha) specialises in fuul, but also serves ta'amiyya, omelettes, fried cheese and all the usual salad and dip accompaniments. The food's a bit greasy but Alexandrians swear by it and the place is always packed. A full meal will come to no more than E£4 to E£6 per person.

Hassan Bleik (18 Sharia Saad Zaghloul) next to Sofianopoulo Coffee Store is a venerable Lebanese restaurant nestled behind a patisserie. Never mind the grubby tablecloths, it has an excellent menu of traditional Levantine dishes like *kibbeh* (meat-filled cracked wheat croquettes in yoghurt sauce), fatta with chickpeas and lamb, and chicken livers. Prices for dishes are from E£6 to E£14. It's open from noon to 6 pm only.

Havana (☎ 483 0661) at the junction of Sharia Ahmed Orabi and Sidi al-Metwali in Attareen is primarily a bar (see the following Entertainment section) but it also serves great food. The fried calamari is superb, and heaped up with fries and salad it's a bargain at E£10. The pizzas are also highly recommended (E£9 to E£18), while other dishes include omelettes (E£5 to E£8), chicken livers (E£9.50) and – the owner is Coptic Christian – roast pork (E£13.50).

Elite (☎ 482 3592, 43 Sharia Safiyya Zaghloul) near Cinema Metro faintly resembles an old US diner and seems sealed in a 1950s bubble. The menu is displayed outside, beside the door, and contains meals from spaghetti bolognaise at E£4.50 to grilled meats in the E£25 to E£30 range. Beer is served (E£5.25).

Some of Alexandria's best restaurants for straightforward good-value streetside dining can be found in the Anfushi, south of Fort Qaitbey, particularly along Sharia Safar Pasha, where there are at least half a dozen restaurants specialising in grilled meats and fish – we recommend *Mohammed Hosni*.

Alexandria has a great cafe scene. The best known is *Pastroudi's*, founded in 1923 by Greeks and immortalised in Durrell's *Alexandria Quartet*. It's at 39 Tariq al-Horreyya, beside the Amir Cinema. *Trianon*, which faces Midan Ramla, was a favourite of the Alexandrian-Greek poet Cavafy, who worked in offices above. It's still immensely popular and a good place for a continental-style breakfast.

Entertainment

Our vote for best bar in Egypt goes to the *Havana*. It's run by Nagy whose father bought the place from a departing Greek in the 1950s. Since that time some of the details may have changed but a cosmopolitan, *laissez-faire* air still prevails at its six tables.

Almost as good as the Havana is *Cap d'Or* at 4 Sharia Adib, just south of Sharia Saad Zaghloul, which has the feel of an Andalusian tapas bar. Plenty of people come here to eat calamari, shrimp or fish, all of which are excellent, but it's an equally fine place just to pull up a stool and settle in for a Stella. The nearby *Spitfire Bar* just north of Sharia Saad Zaghloul has a totally different atmosphere and feels almost like a Bangkok bar – but without the women of course.

Getting There & Away

Air There are direct international flights from Alexandria to Athens (Olympic Airways) and Frankfurt (Lufthansa), and to Saudi Arabia and Dubai (EgyptAir).

Air travel to Alexandria from within Egypt is expensive; the one-way fare for the 40 minute flight from Cairo is E£248.

Bus Long-distance buses all go from one garage behind Sidi Gaber train station; the No 1 minibus from outside the Cecil Hotel connects it with the city centre.

From here Superjet has buses to Cairo (E£20 to E£31, 2½ hours) every 30 minutes from 5.30 am to 10 pm.

West Delta has 12 buses a day to Marsa Matruh (E£15 to E£23, depending on the bus), of which the 6 pm service goes on to Sallum (E£20, nine hours), while the 11 am service goes via Marsa Matruh to Siwa (E£25, nine hours).

For Sinai there's just one service a day at 6.30 to 9 to Sharm el-Sheikh (E£77, seven hours). There's also one Superjet bus daily to Port Said (E£22, four hours) and one to Hurghada (E£75, nine hours) at 8 pm. West Delta has four services a day to Port Said (E£17 to E£20), two to Ismailia (E£17) at 7 am and 2.30 pm, and two to Suez (E£20) at 6.30 am and 2.30 pm. The Upper Egypt Bus Company also has a Hurghada (E£55) bus departing at 6.30 pm daily.

Train Alexandria's main train terminal is Masr station (Mahattat Masr), although Sidi Gaber, which serves the populous eastern suburbs, is almost as busy. Cairo-bound trains leave from here at least hourly, from about 5 am to 10 pm (there's also one at 3.25 am), stopping five minutes later at Sidi Gaber station. The best trains, the Turbini (also known as the Spanish trains), depart Mahattat Masr at 8 am and 2 and 7 pm and tickets for 1st/2nd class air-con cost E£22/17.

Service Taxi The service taxi depot is across the midan from the Masr train station. The fares are between E£8 and E£10 to Cairo or Marsa Matruh, depending on whom you talk to.

Getting Around

To/From the Airport The airport (☎ 420 1036) is south-west of the city centre. To get there, you can take bus No 203 from Midan Ramla or No 703 from Midan Orabi. A taxi should cost no more than E£10.

Bus & Minibus As a visitor to Alexandria, you won't use the buses at all – the trams are a much better way of getting around.

Tram Tram is still the best way to travel in Alexandria. Midan Ramla is the main tram station and from here lime-yellow-coloured trams go west and blue ones go east.

Taxi A short trip, say from Midan Ramla to Masr train station, will cost E£2, while between E£3 and E£4 is reasonable for a trip to the eastern beaches.

EL ALAMEIN

The beginning of General Montgomery's offensive on 23 October 1942 ruined Field Marshall Rommel's hopes of pushing his Afrika Korps through to the Suez Canal forever. Within two weeks he was on the run, and El Alamein, 105km west of Alexandria, went down as the first great turning point of WWII. Today, a **war museum** and the Commonwealth, German and Italian **war cemeteries** mark the scene of one of the biggest tank battles in history.

Should you want to stay overnight, *Al-Amana Hotel*, almost opposite the museum, has simple double rooms that are nothing special – but a damn sight better than rooms in the rest house down the road. A room costs E£20/30 without/with bath. It also has a small cafeteria where you can get chicken and rice meals, omelettes and fuul as well as drinks and biscuits.

Getting There & Away

Catch any of the Marsa Matruh buses from Sidi Gaber in Alexandria. Alternatively service taxis leave from the lot in front of Alexandria's train station and cost about E£6.

MARSA MATRUH

The large waterfront town of Marsa Matruh, built around a charming bay of clear Mediterranean waters and clean white sandy beaches, is a popular summer destination with Egyptians. Away from the sand, the town itself, with a population of about

EGYPT

80,000, is dull and very unattractive. Outside of the summer season, it's also completely dead, with most of the hotels and restaurants closing down over winter.

There are really only two streets in Marsa Matruh that you need to know: the Corniche, which runs all the way around the waterfront, and Sharia Iskendariyya, which runs perpendicular to the Corniche, towards the hill behind the town. The tourist office (☎ 493 1841) is on the ground floor of the governorate building one block west of Sharia Iskendariyya on the corner of the Corniche. It's open daily from 8.30 am to 6 pm (until 9 pm in summer).

You can change cash and travellers cheques at the National Bank of Egypt, a few blocks west of Sharia Iskendariyya and south of the Corniche or there are several exchange bureaus on Sharia al-Galaa.

The GPO is on Sharia ash-Shaata, one block south of the Corniche and two blocks east of Sharia Iskendariyya. It's open from 8.30 am to 3 pm (closed Friday and Saturday). The 24 hour telephone centrale is across the street from the GPO.

Things to See & Do

Set in the caves Rommel used as his headquarters during part of the El Alamein campaign is the rather poor **Rommel Museum**, which contains a few photos, a bust of the Desert Fox, some ageing German, Italian and British military maps and what is purported to be his greatcoat. The museum is about 3km east of the town centre, out by the beach of the same name.

Cleopatra's Beach or **Shaata al-Gharam** (Lovers' Beach), which are about 14km and 17km respectively west of town, are better, but best of all is **Agiba Beach**, about 24km west of Marsa Matruh. It is a small but spectacular beach, accessible only by a path leading down from the clifftop.

Places to Stay

The more expensive hotels are along the Corniche. Others are dotted around the town, most of them not too far from Sharia Iskendariyya.

Although there are no official camp sites, it may be possible to pitch a tent along the beach or at Rommel's Beach – check with the tourist office.

Youth Hostel (☎ 493 2331) a couple of blocks south of Awam Mosque is just about OK. Members pay E£8 for a comfortable enough bunk bed in a cramped room of six or eight. There seems to be no problem if nonmembers stay.

Ghazala Hotel (☎ 493 3519) just off Sharia Iskendariyya is the most popular backpackers' stop; the entry is sandwiched between some shops and is easily overlooked. The charge is E£10 per person for a basic but clean bed. Most rooms have balconies (but no view to speak of) and the shared toilet/shower combinations are clean, if lacking in hot water.

Hotel Hamada (☎ 493 3300) has a great central location just off Sharia Iskendariyya and, while basic, is at least clean. It charges E£15/20 for singles/doubles with shared bathrooms and toilets.

Hotel Dareen (☎ 493 5607) has OK rooms that are not very well kept but at least the sheets are clean and there's hot water in the ensuite bathrooms. Singles/doubles are E£30/45 (E£10 more in summer) with breakfast, or E£5 cheaper if you want to skip the stale bread and jam.

Rommel House Hotel (☎ 493 5466, fax 347 1496) on Sharia al-Galaa, east of Sharia Iskendariyya, has rooms with bath, TV, fridge and breakfast for E£83/111 in summer or E£43/63 in winter.

There is a string of places on the waterfront heading west of Sharia Iskendariyya with little to choose between them; they all have good sea views but little else in the way of nearby amenities. The first of them, the 10 storey *Royal Palace Hotel*, used to have very reasonably priced rooms (less than E£50 in summer) that came with bath, balcony and breakfast, but it was under going renovation when we last visited, which may mean a jump in prices when it reopens.

Hotel Beau Site (☎ 493 8555, fax 493 3319) is easily Matruh's most attractive option – if you have the money. The 'luxury' rooms on the beach cost E£390/577 in summer, or about half that in winter. The rooms come with breakfast and all mod cons. There are some tiny rooms available above the disco with great balconies for substantially cheaper rates.

Places to Eat
The dining situation in Matruh is less than impressive. When we last visited, which admittedly was in winter, we had a hard time getting anything to eat at all. The two main options were *Camona Tourist Restaurant* on the corner of sharias Al-Galaa and Iskendariyya, and another corner *kebab restaurant* about 200m west of that. Both the places had kebab, kofta and chicken, and the latter also served *fiteer*, the Egyptian pancake/pizza. There's also a good takeaway in *Abu Rabie* at the train station end of Sharia Iskendariyya; it does fuul, ta'amiyya, salads and good *gamboury* (shrimp) or calamari sandwiches for about E£1.25 each.

Beau Site Restaurant in the hotel of the same name is fairly good, but beware of the prices.

Getting There & Away
Air EgyptAir flies between Cairo and Marsa Matruh for E£344 one way.

Bus Marsa Matruh has two bus stations: the main station is up near the railway line and there's a second, small station consisting of just a kiosk near the tourist office. From this latter station Superjet has two services a day, one to Alexandria (E£24, four hours) at 2.30 pm and one to Cairo (E£37, five hours) at 3 pm. West Delta has at least seven buses a day to Alexandria (E£11 to E£15) going from the main bus station, plus another three from the tourist office station – these latter three are luxury buses and cost E£20 or E£23. It has four services to Cairo daily, one from the main bus station at 7.30 am (E£25 but no air-con) and three later air-con services from the tourist office station all at E£35. Buses

to Sallum (E£6.25 to E£10, four hours) all depart from the main bus station and there are nine services a day, starting at 7 am. Rough buses without air-con run to Siwa at 7.30 am and 1.30 and 4 pm. The fare is E£7 on the first two buses and E£10 on the third.

Train Don't do it. Even the station master at Marsa Matruh says that the trains are 'horrible'.

Service Taxi The service taxi lot in Marsa Matruh is across from the bus station. Service taxis to Siwa cost E£10, if there are enough people going. Other fares include Sallum for E£10 and Alexandria for E£8.

SALLUM
About 214km west of Marsa Matruh, Sallum (pronounced saLOOM) is in the proverbial middle of nowhere. The water is crystal clear but is spoiled by the rubbish on the beach. Head east for a while and you can pick yourself out some secluded stretch of sand. At the eastern entrance to the town is a WWII Commonwealth war cemetery, a somewhat more modest version of the El Alamein cemetery.

The accommodation in town is dire and you should plan to avoid having to stay overnight here.

Getting There & Away
Buses for Marsa Matruh (E£8, four hours) depart three times a day and at least one of these goes straight on through to Alexandria (E£20, eight hours). A service taxi to Marsa Matruh will cost about E£10.

Libya The border crossing point of Amsaad, just north of the Halfaya Pass, is 12km west of Sallum. Service taxis run up the mountain between the town and the Egyptian side of the crossing for E£2 to E£3. Once through passport control and customs on both sides (you walk through), you can get a Libyan service taxi on to Al-Burdi for about LD1. From there you can get buses on to Tobruk and Benghazi.

Suez Canal

The Suez Canal, one of the greatest feats of modern engineering, links the Mediterranean with the northern end of the Red Sea. Opened in 1869 the canal severed Asia from Africa, and is now an important source of revenue for Egypt in the form of fees charged for its use by the world's tankers.

The three principal cities along the canal are not top of the list of tourist attractions, but Port Said and, to a lesser extent Ismailia, are full of some of the best examples of late 19th and early 20th century colonial-style architecture.

PORT SAID

A city of 400,000 people Port Said was founded in 1859 and is a duty-free zone. It is effectively built on an island, connected to the mainland by a bridge to the south and a causeway to the west.

The tourist office (☎ 235 289) at 43 Sharia Palestine has maps and information about the Suez Canal and the port. It's open from 9 am to 1.30 pm and 3 to 8 pm from Saturday to Thursday, closed Friday.

There are a number of banks on Sharia al-Gomhuriyya and the GPO is opposite Ferial Gardens, one block north.

There are two telephone centrales: one is on Sharia Palestine two blocks north-west of the tourist office; the other is behind the governorate building. Both are open 24 hours a day.

Things to See & Do

If you've ever seen a picture of Port Said, it was probably of the striking green domes of **Suez Canal House**. One of the best views of the canal used to be from this white-columned building south-west of the ferry terminal and tourist office, which was built in time for the inauguration of the canal in 1869 but it's now off-limits to visitors.

At the top end of Sharia Palestine, the **National Museum** houses a varied collection representative of prehistoric and the pharaonic periods, plus Islamic and Coptic

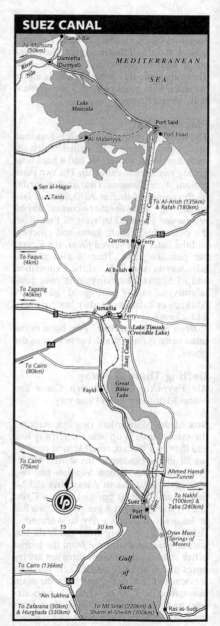

SUEZ CANAL

exhibits. It's open from 9 am to 4 pm daily and admission is E£6.

The small **Military Museum** on Sharia 23rd of July has some interesting relics from the 1956 Anglo-French War and the 1967 and 1973 wars with Israel, as well as a small display of ancient pharaonic and Islamic conflicts. It's open from 9 am to 2 pm Saturday to Thursday and 10 am to 1.30 pm on Friday.

Places to Stay

Youth Hostel (☎ 228 702) on Sharia 23rd of July, near the stadium, is the cheapest place to stay in Port Said. It costs E£3.25/4.25 with/without membership card. It has basic bunk beds, with 20 beds per room. It's OK, but in a highly inconvenient location.

Greek-owned *Akri Palace Hotel* (☎ 221 013, 24 Sharia al-Gomhuriyya) has reasonably clean singles/doubles for about E£13/25 or doubles with bath for E£37.

Two blocks north-west from the Akri is *Mereland Hotel* (☎ 227 020) in a lane between Sharia Saad Zaghloul and Sharia an-Nahda. It offers big clean rooms for E£15/20 with decent communal bathrooms or E£24/35 with private bath; breakfast is extra.

Hotel de la Poste (☎ 224 048, 42 Sharia al-Gomhuriyya) has a fading elegance which the management has attempted to salvage through careful renovation. Singles/doubles on the street side with bath and balcony cost E£35/44 without breakfast. Other rooms cost E£28/38.

Places to Eat

Not surprisingly, there are plenty of seafood restaurants in Port Said. One of the cheapest is *Galal* on the corner of sharias al-Gomhuriyya and Gaberti. A plate of calamari will set you back E£12; fish dishes start at around E£14.

At the front of *Hotel de la Poste* there's a bar, cafe and restaurant. The restaurant has cheap hamburgers, sandwiches, salads and what is called pizza.

Getting There & Away

Bus Superjet buses to Cairo (E£15, three hours) leave 11 times a day from in front of the train station. It also has a bus to Alexandria (E£22, four hours) at 4.30 pm.

East Delta Bus Co leaves from a bus station near Ferial Gardens (also known as the 'Lux terminal'); buses to Cairo depart hourly between 6 am and 6 pm, with fares from E£13 to E£15. There are four buses to Alexandria (E£17 to E£22), and buses south to Ismailia (E£5) depart hourly between 6 am and 6 pm. Buses to Suez (E£7.50, 2¼ hours) depart at 6 and 10 am and 1 and 4 pm.

Train There are four trains a day to Cairo but this is an extremely slow and uncomfortable way to travel.

Service Taxi Service taxis leave from a mucky lot on Sharia an-Nasr, north-west of the train station, but there doesn't appear to be a lot happening in the afternoon. Fares include: Cairo (E£8), Qantara (E£2.50), Ismailia (E£3.50) and Suez (E£6).

ISMAILIA

Ismailia was founded by and named after Ismail Pasha, the ruler of Egypt during the construction of the Suez Canal in the 1860s. Ferdinand de Lesseps, the director of the Suez Canal Company, lived here until the canal was completed.

If Ismailia can claim to have a main street, it's probably Sharia Sultan Hussein, which runs between the railway line and the Sweetwater Canal. The tourist office is useless here. Banks, telephone and post office can all be found near the train station.

The small **Ismailia Museum** has an interesting collection of ancient artefacts. The house where Ferdinand de Lesseps lived is not open to the public but it's one of many buildings built here by Europeans that are worth a look. You might want to spend time on some of the **beaches** of Lake Timsah.

Places to Stay & Eat

The high-rise *Youth Hostel* (☎ 322 850) on a beach around Lake Timsah has rooms with two/four/six beds for E£18/15/8 including breakfast. The rooms are clean and comfortable with lockers and views over the

EGYPT

lake. They don't seem too concerned about whether or not you have a membership card.

Nefertari Hotel (☎ 322 822, 41 Sharia Sultan Hussein) has clean, comfortable singles/doubles with bath and air-con for E£36/54, including breakfast. They also have a small bar with dim red lights.

George's and ***Nefertiti*** (☎ 220 494), both on Sharia Sultan Hussein, serve fish and meat dishes. The fish at the Greek-run George's is an institution; the place has an intimate atmosphere and a lovely old bar that has been enticing drinkers for more than 40 years. Nefertiti is cheaper, with meals ranging from E£12 to E£25, but the decor is bland. Both are open until 10 pm.

King Edward (☎ 325 451, 171 Sharia at-Tahrir) is more expensive. It serves meat and fish dishes for around E£15 to E£30, as well as pizza from E£6.50. The chicken curry is quite good and makes a nice change from the usual fare.

Getting There & Away

Bus There are two bus stations in Ismailia. On Midan Orabi, West Delta Bus Co has frequent departures to Cairo (E£6, 2½ hours) at 7 am and 2.30 pm buses to Alexandria (E£17). The East Delta Bus Co station is on Sharia al-Gomhuriyya, on the other side of the railway line. It also has frequent buses to Cairo for E£6. East Delta buses to Port Said leave every 30 to 45 minutes and cost E£4, and to Suez every 15 to 20 minutes for E£3.50. Buses to Sinai also leave from here. There are buses every hour or so to Al-Arish (three hours) from 8 am to 5 pm. They usually cost E£7, but prices may fluctuate for through buses from Cairo. There are buses to Sharm el-Sheikh (E£25) at 6.30 am, noon and 2.30, 3.30, 9, 10 and 11 pm and midnight.

Train There are about 10 trains a day to both Cairo and Port Said but the service is slow and uncomfortable and no cheaper than the bus.

Service Taxi Service taxis depart from the lot across the road from East Delta Bus Co

station. Destinations include Suez (E£3), Port Said (E£3.50), Cairo (E£5) and Al-Arish (E£7).

SUEZ

Suez, which sprawls around from the entrance of the canal at Port Tawfiq down along the western side of the gulf, suffered badly in the 1967 and 1973 wars, and is above all a transit point for tankers, pilgrims to Mecca and people travelling between Sinai and the rest of the country. It's a good place to watch the passing tankers.

The tourist office is in Port Tawfiq, the GPO is on Sharia Hoda Shaarawi and the telephone centrale can be found on Sharia Saad Zaghloul. Most banks have branches around town.

Places to Stay & Eat

Youth Hostel (☎ 221 945) is on the main road heading west out of Suez. It's cheap (E£5 with membership card, E£6 without), grungy and a long way from anything.

In the centre of Suez, there's a handful of cheapies clustered around Sharia at-Tahrir (known locally as Sharia an-Nimsa) and Sharia Talaat Harb. About the best of a pretty bad bunch is ***Hotel d'Orient*** on Sharia Hoda Shaarawi, which has basic rooms for E£10/12.

If you have a hankering to stay in Port Tawfiq, the cheapest place there seems to be ***Arafat Hotel*** (☎ 338 355) in the street of the same name. Singles/doubles/triples cost E£15/22/33 without bath or E£24/30/37 with. The hotel has recently been renovated and is well run and spotlessly clean. There are even snacks and toiletries on sale in the lobby.

For views of the canal try ***Green House Hotel*** (☎ 331 553, fax 331 554) on the road out of Suez to Port Tawfiq, on the corner of sharias Port Said and Al-Geish. The hotel has a 24 hour restaurant, pool (E£3 for nonguests) and bar. Comfortable rooms with bath, air-con, TV, fridge and balcony with a view of the canal cost US$38/48, not including breakfast and tax.

Red Sea Hotel (☎ 334 302, fax 334 301, 13 Sharia Riad) in Port Tawfiq is Suez's premier establishment. Its 81 rooms have TV, bath, phone and air-con and are comfortable and clean. Rooms cost US$43/50, not including breakfast and tax. It has a 6th floor *restaurant* with a great panoramic view of the canal; meals cost between E£12 and E£33.

For the cheap old favourites like ta'amiyya and shwarma, a wander around the streets bounded by Sharia Talaat Harb, Sharia Abdel as-Sarawat, Sharia Banque Masr and Sharia Khedr will soon reveal what you're after.

Fish Restaurant just up from White House Hotel on Sharia as-Salaam is exactly what it calls itself. The day's catch is sold by weight and grilled, but sometimes it's overcooked. A big meal will cost around E£25; it's open to 2 am.

Getting There & Away

Bus Buses to Cairo, Alexandria and the other canal cities leave from East Delta Bus Co's Arba'een bus station on Sharia al-Faarz, not far from the centre of town. Buses to Cairo (E£6/7, 1½ hours) leave every 30 minutes from 6 am to 8 pm. Buses to Ismailia (E£3) depart every 15 to 20 minutes. There are three buses directly to Port Said (E£7.50) at 7 and 9 am and 3.30 pm, and two to Alexandria (E£20) at 7 am and 2.30 pm.

Buses to the Sinai peninsula also leave from the East Delta Bus Co station. Five buses go nonstop to Sharm el-Sheikh (E£20, 5½ hours) along the direct route down the Gulf of Suez. They go on to Dahab (E£23, 6½ hours) and Nuweiba (E£25). A bus leaves for St Katherine's Monastery (E£17, five hours) via Wadi Feran at 11 am.

Minibuses sometimes run to destinations in Sinai too – you'll be looking at about E£15 per person to St Katherine's Monastery, E£20 to Sharm el-Sheikh or Nuweiba and E£35 to Dahab. Ask around at the bus station for more details.

For buses to the Red Sea coast, Luxor and Aswan, you must go to Upper Egypt Bus Co's station about 3km north of town, just before the train station. There are buses heading to Hurghada (E£25 to E£35) almost every hour. Most of these go on to Qena (E£26/30, nine to 10 hours).

There are six buses a day to Luxor (E£35 to E£37, 10 hours), three of which continue to Aswan (E£40 to E£45, 14 hours).

Train Only a masochist would want to travel to or from Suez by train. The train station is 2km west of the Arba'een bus station; a microbus shuttles between them for 25pt. Six Cairo-bound trains depart daily (E£2.60/1.05 for 2nd/3rd class, 2¼ hours) and only make it as far as Ain Shams, 10km north-east of central Cairo. There are also nine very slow trains to Ismailia (E£2.40/1.10 for 2nd/3rd class, 2½ hours).

Service Taxi Service taxis depart from near the bus station to many areas serviced by buses and trains. Destinations include Cairo (E£5), Ismailia (E£3), Port Said (E£6) and Hurghada (E£20, 3½ to four hours). The only place in Sinai served by service taxi is El-Tor (E£10).

Red Sea Coast

Egypt's Red Sea coast stretches for more than 800km from Suez in the north to the village of Bir Shalatein near the disputed border with Sudan in the south. Famed for its brilliant turquoise waters, splendid coral and exotic creatures of the deep, the Red Sea attracts more than 200,000 tourists annually. It's Egypt's most rapidly developing area, with more hotels and resorts constructed here in the last few years than anywhere else in the country. Unfortunately, much of the development during the freewheeling boom of the last decade has gone unchecked, resulting in massive environmental damage.

HURGHADA (AL-GHARDAKA)

Little more than a decade and a half ago Hurghada had two hotels separated by nothing more than virgin beach. A one-time isolated and modest fishing village, it's now

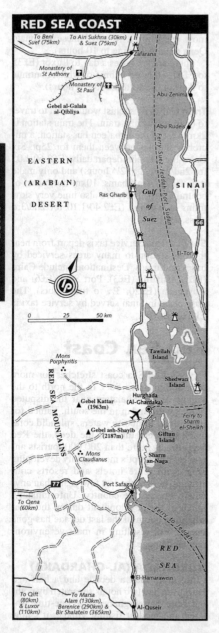

RED SEA COAST

To Beni Suef (75km)
To Ain Sukhna (30km) & Suez (75km)
Zafarana
Monastery of St Anthony
Monastery of St Paul
Gebel al-Galala al-Qibliya
Abu Zenima
Abu Rudeis
EASTERN (ARABIAN) DESERT
Ras Gharib
SINAI
Gulf of Suez
66
El-Tor
44
Tawilah Island
Mons Porphyritis
Shedwan Island
RED SEA MOUNTAINS
Gebel Kattar (1963m)
Hurghada (Al-Ghardaka)
Ferry to Sharm el-Sheikh
Gebel ash-Shayib (2187m)
Giftun Island
Mons Claudianus
Sharm an-Naga
Port Safaga
77
To Qena (60km)
Ferry to Jeddah
RED SEA
El-Hamarawein
To Qift (80km) & Luxor (110km)
To Marsa Alam (130km), Berenice (290km) & Bir Shalatein (365km)
Al-Quseir

0   25   50 km

home to more than 35,000 people and packed with more than 100 resorts and hotels catering to sun-seekers and diving enthusiasts on package tours from all over the world. But while the crystal-clear waters and fascinating reefs have made Hurghada Egypt's most popular resort town, if you're not into beaches, diving or snorkelling (or chunks of concrete, iron rods and empty oil drums – the results of the ongoing construction boom) then this ever-developing resort town has little to offer.

Orientation

The main town area, called **Ad-Dahar**, where virtually all the budget accommodation is located and most of the locals live, is at the northern end of the stretch of resorts that makes up the whole area. The main road through Ad-Dahar is Sharia an-Nasr, which is the highway linking Hurghada to Port Safaga and Suez. A few kilometres down the coast is **Sigala**, where new hotels, restaurants and resorts are springing up like mushrooms. This is also where you'll find the port for boats to Sharm el-Sheikh. South of Sigala, a road winds down along the coast through the **'resort strip'**.

Information

Hurghada's tourist office (☎ 446 513) is a large marble building south of Sigala on the main road leading to the resort strip. It's open from 8.30 am to 3 pm daily except Friday.

In Ad-Dahar, branches of Banque Masr, the National Bank of Egypt (with an ATM machine) and the Bank of Alexandria are dotted along Sharia an-Nasr. The GPO is on Sharia an-Nasr, towards the southern end of Ad-Dahar. The 24 hour telephone centrale is farther north-west along the same road. Opposite the telephone centrale is a fax booth (fax 544 581) open daily (except Friday) from 8 am to 2 pm and 8 to 10 pm.

Aboudi Bookshop in Ad-Dahar on Sharia al-Mustashfa has Hurghada's first Internet cafe, and it is currently charging E£20 for an hour's use between 10 am and 5 pm, or E£25 between 5 pm and midnight.

Beaches

There are two public beaches, one in Ad-Dahar and a much smaller version in Sigala near the port. Though relatively clean, the sand resembles fine dirt and the rubbish bobbing around in the water is very off-putting. Also, the beach at Sigala is next to a mosque, which makes stripping down to anything more daring than long trousers and a T-shirt inappropriate. Women may also feel uncomfortable sunbathing or swimming in Ad-Dahar as men often congregate along the beach wall to sit and stare. Admission to either costs E£1.

Your only other option close to town is to pay to use one of the beaches at the resorts, or head to the small beach at Al-Sakia restaurant in Sigala, where there's a minimum charge of E£15 (including a drink). Unfortunately, being so close to the port, the water here is still pretty dirty.

Snorkelling

Hurghada is crawling with dive clubs and agents for snorkelling trips. One of the popular snorkelling day trips is to Giftun Island, which costs between E£25 to E£40. Some of the reputable dive clubs take snorkellers out to better sites, and by going with one of them, you're almost assured of reef protection practices being put into action.

Diving trips of one day or more are possible. Subex (☎ 547 593) in Ad-Dahar is highly recommended for shorter trips, and Rudi Kneip (☎ 442 960) in Sigala has years of experience taking diving safaris.

Places to Stay

Ad-Dahar *Happy House (☎ 549 611)* on the main square by the mosque in the centre of Ad-Dahar is a humble pension charging E£15 for a single room, or E£10 per person in a double, including breakfast. A room with its own bathroom goes for E£25.

St George's Hotel (☎ 548 246) just by Aladdin's Lamp Restaurant in the centre of Ad-Dahar is a pleasant family-run place with newly renovated rooms without bath or breakfast for E£20/30. With bath they cost E£25/35.

There are a couple of places in the upper end of the budget bracket nearby on Sharia al-Sheikh Sebek. *Gobal Hotel (☎ 546 623)* has singles/doubles with breakfast and sometimes with private bath for E£15/25. All rooms have fans but the bathrooms are not great. *Happy Land Hotel (☎ 547 373)* has clean rooms without/with bath for E£25/30 a double, breakfast not included. All rooms have phones.

Ramses Ghardaka (☎ 548 941) also on Sharia an-Nasr is more expensive than most other options but far better. It has very clean singles/doubles with air-con, telephone and fridge for E£45/55, including breakfast. Without air-con, rooms go for E£40/50.

Ritz Hotel (☎ 547 031) is a laid-back place, next to a tiny tourist police office, with air-con singles/doubles for E£30/60. There's a restaurant and bar, and you get access to the beach at Sand Beach Hotel for E£5.

California Hotel (☎ 549 101) is a bargain for this area. It sports exotic murals and has rooms with private bath and balcony on the new 2nd floor. The older rooms with shared bathrooms cost E£10/15 including breakfast and the new rooms are a bit more.

Four Seasons (☎ 549 260) has 14 rooms with private bathrooms, six of which have air-con. Those without air-con (but with fan, balcony and breakfast) are good value at E£15/25. Air-con rooms cost a little more. For E£5 you can also use the beach at Geisum Village hotel.

Alaska Hotel (☎ 548 413) on the slope up behind Aboudi Bookshop, charges E£8.50 per person plus E£2 for breakfast and is a good, comfortable place to stay.

Geisum Village (☎ 548 048, fax 547 995) is the cheapest of the three places on the beach. It charges E£80/140 for half-board singles/doubles.

Sigala Should you want to be close to the port, try *Abu Nawas Hotel (☎ 442 830)* behind the post and telephone office. It has big, clean rooms with fan and communal bathrooms for E£15/25, but it's a tad overpriced and usually empty. There's a pleasant

HURGHADA, AD-DAHAR

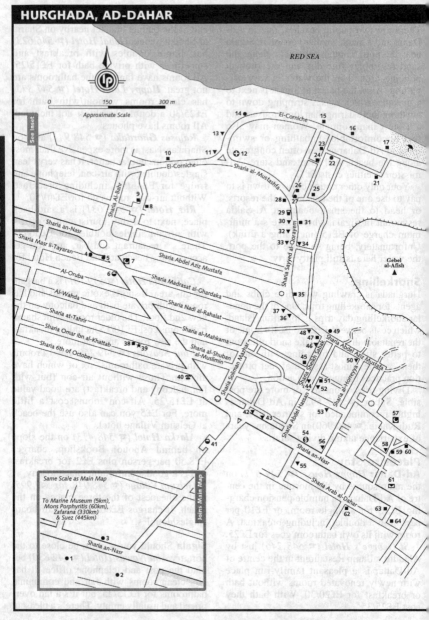

RED SEA

0   150   300 m

Approximate Scale

See inset

El-Corniche

El-Corniche

Sharia al-Mustashfa

Sharia Al-Bahr

Sharia an-Nasr

Sharia Masr li-Tayaran

Sharia Abdel Aziz Mustafa

Al-Oruba

Sharia Madrasat al-Ghardaka

Al-Wahda

Sharia Nadi al-Rahalat

Sharia at-Tahrir

Sharia Omar ibn al-Khattab

Sharia al-Mahkama

Sharia 6th of October

Sharia al-Shuban al-Muslimin

Sharia Soliman Mazhar

Sharia Sayyed al-Qoraiym

Gebel al-Afish

Sharia Abdel Aziz Mustafa

Sharia Sheikh Sabek

Sharia al-Horreyya

Sharia Abdel Hasan

Sharia an-Nasr

Sharia Arab al-Dahar

Same Scale as Main Map

To Marine Museum (5km),
Mons Porphyritis (60km),
Zafarana (330km)
& Suez (445km)

Sharia an-Nasr

Joins Main Map

EGYPT

HURGHADA, AD-DAHAR

PLACES TO EAT
11 Bar BQ Inn
13 Cafe Cheers
30 Belgian Restaurant
32 Portofino
33 Norhan
34 Red Sea Restaurant II
36 Bell Riviera
37 Egyptian Corner
42 Omar Khayyam Restaurant
43 Happy Land Restaurant
44 La Torta
46 Young Kang
48 Pizza Tarboush
50 Scruples Biliardeni
52 Aladdin's Lamp
53 Pharaoh's Restaurant
55 Scruples Restaurant & Bar
56 Red Sea I Restaurant
58 Zeko

PLACES TO STAY
8 Al-Gezira & Horus Hotels
9 Sea Horse Hotel & La Bamba Disco
10 Shedwan Golden Beach Hotel
15 Three Corners Village
16 Sand Beach Hotel
17 Geisum Village
19 Sindbad Sea View
20 Casablanca Hotel
21 Al-Arousa Hotel
23 California Hotel
24 Pharaohs Hotel
25 Alaska Hotel
26 Four Seasons
28 Three Corners Empire Hotel
31 Sindbad Inn
35 Shakespear Hotel
38 Ritz Hotel
45 Happy Land Hotel
47 Gobal Hotel
51 St George's Hotel
59 Happy House
60 Africa Hotel
62 Ramses Hotel
63 Sunshine House
64 Hotel Sosna

OTHER
1 Passports & Immigration Office
2 Governorate Building
3 Cultural Centre
4 Masr Travel
5 EgyptAir
6 Superjet Bus Station
7 Main Mosque
14 Public Hospital
18 Aquarium
22 National Parks Office
22 Subex Diving Centre
27 Aboudi Bookshop
29 Peanuts Bar & Market Place Shopping Centre
39 Tourist Police
40 Telephone Centrale
41 Service Taxi Station
49 Al-Shaymaa Sea Trips & Boho Bike Shop
54 Banque Masr & National Bank of Egypt (ATM)
57 Mosque
61 GPO
65 Upper Egypt Bus Co Bus Station
66 Bank of Alexandria
67 Safa Hospital

Public Beach

To Sigala (6km)

To Sigala (3.5km), Airport (12.5km), New Hurghada (14km) & Port Safaga (53km)

EGYPT

streetfront terrace where you can get a beer. Otherwise, there's a bewildering array of mid-range places on and around Sharia Sheraton and more seem to be opening every month.

Places to Eat

The following are in Ad-Dahar, which has the greatest concentration of places to eat.

Bell Riviera on Sharia Abdel Aziz Mustafa (not to be confused with its more expensive sister restaurant with the similar name across the road) has excellent lentil soup for E£3, spaghetti for E£3.50, pizzas for between E£7 and E£10 and calamari for E£9. You can also get breakfast for E£4. Avoid the toilets.

Next door *Egyptian Corner* is a tiny little place popular with travellers. It has a very limited menu that includes a E£5 breakfast, spaghetti bolognaise for E£4 and simple meals like chicken for E£8.

Scruples Restaurant & Bar on Sharia an-Nasr across from the National Bank is a 'pub and steak house' that has a couple of other outlets around Ad-Dahar. A reasonable fillet of beef with rice and vegetables will set you back about E£25. The same management also runs a pool hall, *Scruples Biliardeni*, at the end of Sharia Abdel Aziz Mustafa, where you can get the same menu as at the original Scruples, and beer for E£7.

Red Sea I Restaurant (☎ 547 704) on a street off Sharia an-Nasr is popular with package tourists wanting a night away from their resorts. The rooftop terrace gets quite crowded in the evenings. With a wide selection of seafood, plus Egyptian dishes and pizza, you can tailor the menu to fit most budgets. Main courses go for between E£15 and E£40.

Down by Sharia Sayyed al-Qorayem, the road running from Shakespear Hotel around to Shedwan Golden Beach Hotel (on the Corniche), is lined with shops and restaurants. *Norhan* is an unpretentious little diner with a few terrace tables and a limited menu. Mains such as shepherds pie or chicken range from E£5 to E£9 and come with a complimentary soft drink (no beer is served). Pizza starts at E£6 and is cheap enough though a bit doughy.

Cafe Cheers is a small roadside restaurant on Sharia el-Corniche that purports to be open 24 hours a day and has beer in frosty mugs for E£7.50, as well as burgers, pizzas and a few kebab meals for reasonable prices.

Portofino (☎ 546 250) is across the road from Red Sea II Restaurant on Sharia Sayyed al-Qorayem and is a friendly Italian place with good, medium priced Italian (and some Egyptian) food. Its pasta dishes are about the best in town and prices start around E£15. Most evenings the gregarious owner wanders around happily talking to customers.

Getting There & Away

Air There are daily flights between Hurghada and Cairo (E£453 one way), plus three flights per week to Sharm el-Sheikh (E£330) and one each week to Luxor.

Bus Two bus companies operate services from Hurghada. Superjet has its bus station near the main mosque in Ad-Dahar from where there are three buses a day to Cairo (E£47, six hours) and a daily bus to Alexandria (E£75, nine hours). Upper Egypt Bus Co operates from the main bus station at the southern end of Ad-Dahar from where it runs buses every couple of hours to Cairo (E£35 to E£45, six hours). A couple of these set down in Suez as well. About 10 Upper Egypt Bus Co buses go daily to Qena (E£8, three hours), and there are four daily services to Luxor (E£20 to E£22, five hours), all of which go on to Aswan (E£35 to E£40). There are buses to Marsa Alam and Bir Shalatein via Al-Quseir (E£12) at 5 am, 3 pm and midnight.

Service Taxi The service taxi station is near the telephone centrale in Ad-Dahar. Taxis go to Cairo for E£30 per person (six hours). Others go to Al-Quseir (E£7), Qena (E£10), Marsa Alam (E£15) and Suez (E£20, 3½ to four hours). They don't usually go to Luxor or Aswan, although you

could always talk one into going. If you bargain hard it'll cost about E£200 for a car that seats seven people.

Boat At the time of writing, two vessels were plying the waters from Hurghada to Sharm el-Sheikh, departing daily (except Wednesday and Friday) from Hurghada. The old ferry takes five to seven hours to cover the 144km and the cost is E£100 one way. The boat departs from the old port in Sigala sometime between 9 and 10 am; you should be there at least 30 minutes beforehand. The second boat is a luxury high-speed ferry operated by Travco that departs Hurghada every Monday (5 am and 3.30 pm), Tuesday (6 am and 8 pm) and Saturday (6 am). It also leaves from the old port in Sigala and costs US$33 per person and US$75 per car. The boat is air-con and makes the trip to Sharm el-Sheikh in 1½ hours.

There is also a 'flying boat' from Hurghada to Dubai (Saudi Arabia). At the time of writing there were departures four days a week and tickets cost E£160 per person and E£340 per car; the trip takes three hours. Call MenaTours in Cairo (☎ 348 2230) for more information.

AL-QUSEIR

Until the 10th century Al-Quseir was one of the most important exit points for pilgrims travelling to Mecca. There's not much to do in this medieval port town of 4000 people but some of the **beaches** out of town are worth exploring on a hire bicycle.

Places to Stay & Eat

The only choice for travellers on a tight budget is *Sea Princess Hotel* (☎ 431 880) just south of the bus stop. Small cabin-like singles/doubles with fan cost E£15/20 plus tax.

About 1.5km south of the Sea Princess is the four star *Fanader Hotel* (☎ 430 861, fax 431 415). Named after a rocky islet just to the south, it has 55 adjoining domed bungalows plus two large villas for US$35/60 a single/double for half-board.

Foodwise, the options are very limited. The people at *Sea Princess Hotel* can cook you up something. Otherwise, there are a few ta'amiyya and fish joints around it and the bus station. At **Fanader Hotel**, the buffet dinner costs E£60 and is open to nonguests.

Getting There & Away

Bus There are four buses that go all the way through to Cairo (E£55, 11 hours) via Hurghada (E£10 and E£15). There are two buses south to Marsa Alam (E£5) at 11.30 am and 1 pm and four buses daily to Qena (E£5 to E£10, four hours).

Service Taxi The service taxi station is at the southern end of town. The officially prescribed fares are: Cairo E£35, Suez E£25, Qena E£8 and Hurghada E£7. As in Hurghada you have to hire the entire taxi for the trip to Luxor. Drivers ask for about E£250 but if you're lucky you may be able to bargain them down.

Getting Around

There is a no-name bike shop virtually opposite the service taxi station. The owner wants E£15 for a day's bike rental, but this can probably be bargained down.

MARSA ALAM

Marsa Alam is a fishing village 132km south of Al-Quseir. A road also connects the village with Edfu, 230km across the desert to the west. There are some quiet beaches around and, if you have the equipment, some reasonable diving.

You can ask for a room at Pharaoh's Gold Mining company's **rest house** (istiraha) on the northern edge of town. The only alternative apart from simply pitching a tent somewhere on the beach is **Coral Cove Beach Safari Camp** (☎ 364 7970) which is 7km north of town. It has large tents for E£55 per person per night including breakfast.

Getting There & Away

The bus to Aswan (E£10.50) via Edfu (E£9) leaves from the cafes at the junction at about 7 am. There are three buses a day to Al-Quseir (E£5, 1½ hours).

Sinai

It was in Sinai, on Mt Sinai, that Moses received the Ten Commandments, but over the centuries the sixth has been broken here with monotonous regularity. Armies have crossed backwards and forwards, most recently from Israel, which occupied the peninsula from 1967 until 1982, when, under the Camp David Agreement, it agreed to pull out.

The area is populated mainly by Bedouin, although Egyptians are settling here, mostly to take full advantage of the tourist trade.

The splendours of the underwater kingdom of the Red Sea and the grandeur of the desert mountains are Sinai's attractions not to be missed.

RAS MOHAMMED NATIONAL PARK

Declared a national marine park in 1988, the headland of Ras Mohammed is about 30km west of Sharm el-Sheikh. Camping permits cost E£5 per person per night and are available from the visitors' centre inside the park but camping is allowed only in designated areas. Vehicles are permitted to enter (US$5 per person), but access is restricted to certain regions and, for conservation reasons, it's totally forbidden to drive off the official tracks. Take your passport with you, and remember that it is not possible to go to Ras Mohammed National Park if you only have a Sinai permit in your passport.

SHARM EL-SHEIKH & NA'AMA BAY

The south coast of the Gulf of Aqaba, between Tiran Island in the strait and Ras Mohammed, features some of the world's most amazing underwater scenery.

Na'ama Bay is a resort that has grown from virtually nothing since the early 1980s, while Sharm el-Sheikh, initially developed by the Israelis, is a long-standing settlement. They are 6km apart.

Information

The passport office in Sharm el-Sheikh is open from 9.30 am to 2 pm daily except Friday but visa extensions are available only at the office in El-Tor. There is no tourist office but the tourist police office is up on the hill in Sharm el-Sheikh. They also have a booth next to Marina Sharm Hotel in Na'ama Bay.

Banque Masr, the Bank of Alexandria and the National Bank of Egypt have branches in Sharm el-Sheikh (on the hill) and in Na'ama Bay. At the time of writing there were three ATMs in Na'ama Bay: in the lobby of Mövenpick Hotel, at the entrance to Sanafir Hotel and outside Banque Masr (under Best Tours) in the shopping bazaar. A machine at the Sharm el-Sheikh branch of Banque Masr (beside the telephone centrale) should also be working by the time this book is published.

The post office is in Sharm el-Sheikh on the hill. It is open from 8 am to 3 pm daily except Friday. The nearby telephone centrale is open 24 hours.

There is a cybercafe/bar just off the boardwalk at the Hilton Fayrouz in Na'ama Bay charging E£15 per hour.

Diving & Snorkelling

Na'ama Bay itself has no reefs, but the stunning Near and Middle gardens and the even more incredible Far Garden can be reached on foot from the bay. Some of the most spectacular diving is off Ras Mohammed and in the Straits of Tiran. There is also good snorkelling at most of the popular coastal dive sites, including Ras um Sid near the lighthouse at Sharm. The deep drop-offs and strong cross currents at Ras Mohammed are not ideal for snorkelling. There are several wrecks, including the prized *Thistlegorm*. Any of the dive clubs and schools can give you a full rundown of the possibilities. Among the better and more established are Aquamarine Diving Centre (☎ 600 276); Aquanaute (☎ 600 187); Camel Dive Club (☎ 600 700); Red Sea Diving Club (☎ 600 342); and Red Sea

Footprints in the Sand Only, Please

Although much of Sinai is hot dry desert, it is not devoid of life. A very delicate ecosystem is in place; however, it's under direct threat from the onslaught of tourism.

Sinai is a unique land of craggy mountains sliced by dry, gravel wadis in which the odd acacia tree or clump of gnarled tamarisk manages to survive. On the edge of all this are the coastal dunes where a variety of plants tenuously hold onto life in loose, sandy soil. Once every few decades, when storm clouds gather over the mountains and dump colossal amounts of water on this parched landscape, the entire scene is transformed into a sea of greenery. Seeds that have lain dormant in the soil for years suddenly burst into life. For Sinai's wildlife, such as the gazelle and rock hyrax (as well as for the goats herded by local Bedouins), these rare occasions are times of plenty.

Up until relatively recently, the only people to wander through this region were Bedouin on camel; nowadays, groups of tourists looking for outback adventure and pristine spots are ploughing their way through in 4WD vehicles and quads (four wheeled motorcycles) that churn up the soil, uproot plants and create erosion. Aware of the danger this poses to Sinai's ecosystem, authorities have banned vehicles from going off-road in certain areas, such as Ras Mohammed National Park but banning something and actually enforcing it in areas as vast as these are two different things. Rangers do patrol protectorates but it's largely up to tourists themselves to follow the rules. If you really want to explore the region in depth, do it in the age old fashion – go by foot or hire a camel.

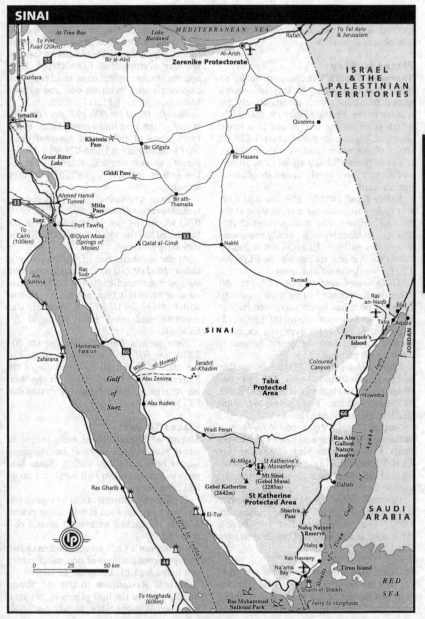

SINAI

MEDITERRANEAN SEA

At-Tina Bay

*To Port
Fuad (20km)*

Lake
Bardawil

Rafah

*To Tel Aviv
& Jerusalem*

Al-Arish

Zerenike Protectorate

Suez Canal

Bir al-Abd

55

Qantara

ISRAEL
& THE
PALESTINIAN
TERRITORIES

Ismailia

3

Quseima

**Khatmia
Pass**

Bir Gifgafa

Bir Hasana

Great Bitter
Lake

Giddi Pass

3

**Ahmed Hamdi
Tunnel**

33

Bir ath-
Thamada

**Mitla
Pass**

Suez

Port Tawfiq

*To
Cairo
(100km)*

Oyun Musa
(Springs of
Moses)

Qalat al-Gindi

Nakhl

33

Ras
Sudr

Tamad

Ain
Sukhna

Ras
an-Naqb

Eilat

Taba

Aqaba

SINAI

**Pharaoh's
Island**

JORDAN

Hammam
Fara'un

Zafarana

66

Wadi al-Homur

Abu Zenima

Serabit
al-Khadim

**Taba
Protected
Area**

Coloured
Canyon

Gulf
of
Suez

Nuweiba

Abu Rudeis

66

Wadi Feran

**Ras Abu
Gallum
Nature
Reserve**

Ras Gharib

Al-Milga

**St Katherine's
Monastery**

Mt Sinai
(Gebel Musa)
(2285m)

Gebel Katherine
(2642m)

**St Katherine
Protected
Area**

Dahab

SAUDI
ARABIA

El-Tor

Ferry to Jeddah

**Sharira
Pass**

**Nabq Nature
Reserve**

Nabq

Ras Nasrany

Tiran Island

RED
SEA

Na'ama
Bay

Sharm el-Sheikh

Straits of Tiran

Gulf of Aqaba

*To Hurghada
(60km)*

Ras Mohammed
National Park

Ferry to Hurghada

0   25   50 km

EGYPT

Diving College (☎ 600 313). There's a modern decompression chamber just outside Sharm el-Sheikh.

Places to Stay

Sharm el-Sheikh The cheapest, but by no means the best, place to stay in an area geared to tourists with comparatively fat wallets is the *Youth Hostel* (☎ 660 317), which is up on the hill. A bed in a fairly standard eight-bed dorm costs E£18.60 (E£19.60 for nonmembers) with breakfast. It's open from 6.30 to 9 am and 2 to 10 pm, and doesn't seem overly fussed about membership cards.

Safety Land (☎ 660 359, fax 660 458) was undergoing extensive renovation at the time of writing. The management claims that singles/doubles in its newly renovated bungalows will cost E£37/54 not including breakfast. Air-con rooms will be E£70/90/120 for singles/doubles/triples.

Al-Kheima Camp (☎ 660 167, fax 660 166), the first place you pass on your way from the port, has bamboo-covered huts at E£36/45 and air-con rooms for E£92/115. Breakfast is E£8. However, it's inconveniently located and the desert behind is strewn with garbage.

Clifftop Hotel (☎ 660 251) has reasonable singles/doubles/triples with TV, air-con, fridge, phone and bathroom for US$50/65/78 including breakfast. You also get to use the beach at Marina Sharm Hotel.

Sunset Hotel (☎/fax 661 673/4) is a brand new three star and one of the better deals in town with singles/doubles for E£100/120 including breakfast. As with most of the other hotels along here, you can use the beach at Ras Um Sid.

Palermo Resort (☎ 661 561) is another three star hotel with singles/doubles for US$31/40 including breakfast. They have a large pool and a section of beach at nearby Ras Um Sid.

Na'ama Bay *Pigeon House* (☎ 600 996, fax 600 965) on the northern edge of town is only a budget option because everything else around here is so expensive. It has three

types of rooms. Bottom rung are the basic huts with fans that go for E£38/56/76 a single/double/triple. Then there are the small rooms, which though clean and comfortable are way overpriced at E£65/85/105. Both options involve shared communal facilities. Superior rooms with air-con and private bathrooms go for E£120/170/205.

Sanafir Hotel (☎ 600 197, fax 600 196) is one of the best mid-range places. It has two classes of rooms and seasonal rates. You'll be looking at US$64/78/99 for a 'superior' air-con single/double/triple in the low season, and US$82/98/126 in the high season.

Not as nice to look at but slightly cheaper is *Kahramana Hotel* (☎ 601 071, fax 601 076) which sits one block away from the beach and has singles/doubles for US$50/60 including breakfast.

At the northern end of Na'ama Bay is *Oasis Hotel* (☎ 602 624). It has rooms with air-con but shared baths for US$32/39 including breakfast (but not taxes). Rooms with baths go for US$37/44. There are also concrete and reed huts available for E£40/60.

Near here is *Paradise Village* (☎ 601 280/8, fax 601 289) at the northern end of the main road. Guests have the use of the Sonesta's beach facilities and singles/doubles/triples go for a relatively reasonable E£130/200/270.

Places to Eat

Sharm el-Sheikh There are a couple of small restaurants/cafes in the shopping bazaar behind the bus station. *Sinai Star* serves some excellent fish meals for about E£12 per person.

Brilliant Restaurant offers a range of traditional Egyptian food at reasonable prices. A plate of chicken with salad should cost about E£15.

Fisherman's Cafe serves chicken or fish with generous portions of rice, salad, tahina and bread for E£1. Beers are E£10.

Safsafa Restaurant in the old Sharm 'mall' is one of the best places in this area. It's a small, eight-table, family-run affair and locals say the fish here is the freshest in Sharm. A plate of calamari and rice, with tahina and babaghanoug, will cost you E£18.

Al-Fanar at Ras Um Sid beach at the base of the lighthouse is an open-air Bedouin-style restaurant with sunken alcoves and not-so-cheap prices (a substantial lunch will cost upwards of E£30), but the view of the sea is marvellous, the food is good and you can get a cold Stella (E£10).

Na'ama Bay *Tam Tam Oriental Cafe* is one of the cheapest restaurants in Na'ama Bay and is deservedly popular. Jutting out onto the beach, it's a laid-back place where you can delve into a range of Egyptian fare including mezzes for E£3.75 a bowl, kushari for E£7.50, and roast pigeon for E£17. Wash it all down with a Stella (E£7.50). There are sheeshas too for E£3.50.

Chef Jurgen's Restaurant over at the Pigeon House is deservedly popular. Pasta dishes here start at E£10.50 and there's a good selection of vegetarian food, plus fruit and pancakes for dessert. Beers are E£9.50.

Another popular choice is *Danadeer Restaurant* (☎ 600 321) just along from the Sanafir on a corner opposite the Falcon al-Diar hotel. There is a selection of seafood and Egyptian dishes on offer and you can get a fish meal for about E£35.

The usual fastfood outlets are also represented here: *McDonald's*, *KFC* and *Pizza Hut* are all on or close to the street that runs in front of the Sanafir. There is even a newly opened *Hard Rock Cafe* (☎ 602 665), which is very popular with the young middle class Cairenes who flock here on weekends and national holidays.

Getting There & Away

Air EgyptAir flies daily to Cairo (E£477) and three times a week to Hurghada (E£330). On Saturday and Thursday there are also flights to Luxor (E£415).

Air Sinai currently flies from Cairo to Sharm el-Sheikh every Monday in winter only. The one-way fare is E£477 and these flights proceed to Tel Aviv.

Bus The bus station is behind the Mobil Station halfway between Na'ama Bay and Sharm el-Sheikh. East Delta Bus Co's direct services to Cairo (seven hours) run between 7.30 am and 4.30 pm and cost between E£40 and E£50; there are also four buses between 10 pm and midnight and a seat on one of those costs E£65. Superjet has a bus to Cairo (E£55) leaving at 11 pm from its bus station next to East Delta Bus Co.

It is cheaper, but more time-consuming, to get a bus to Suez and then another bus or service taxi from there to Cairo. Buses to Suez (E£25 or E£30, 5½ hours) depart almost every hour throughout the day.

Seven buses go to Dahab (E£10, 1½ hours) – the 9 am and 5 pm buses go on to Nuweiba (E£25) and the 9 am bus then continues all the way to Taba (E£35). The 7.30 am bus goes on to St Katherine's Monastery (E£25).

Boat There is a ferry between Sharm el-Sheikh and Hurghada on Monday, Wednesday and Friday, leaving the harbour at 9 or 10 am. Tickets can be booked through most hotels or at Thomas Cook in Na'ama Bay. For details see the Hurghada Getting There & Away section in the Red Sea Coast section earlier in this chapter.

Travco (☎ 661 111) operates a high-speed air-con ferry that travels between Sharm and Hurghada in 1½ hours (although some travellers have said that it can take much longer). The boat departs on Monday at 7.30 am and 6 pm, Tuesday at 8.30 am and 10.30 pm, and Saturday at 6 pm. A ticket costs US$33 (vehicles US$75). For more information contact the Travco office at Riu Palace Hotel.

DAHAB

The village beach resort of Dahab (literally, 'gold') is 85km north of Sharm el-Sheikh on the Gulf of Aqaba. There are two parts to Dahab: in the new part, referred to by locals as Dahab City, are the more expensive hotels and bus station. The other part of Dahab, named Assalah, was a Bedouin village, about 2.5km north of town. It now has more budget travellers and Egyptian entrepreneurs than Bedouin in residence.

Information

There is a branch of the National Bank of Egypt at Novotel Holiday Village (open from 9.30 am to 12.30 pm and 6.30 to 8.30 pm) and another near the bus station. A rather dubious looking Banque 'de' Caire is just along from the Snapper Photo Shop in Assalah. It's open daily from 9 am to 2 pm (9 to 11 am on Friday) and 6 to 9 pm.

The post and telephone offices are opposite the bus station in Dahab City. The latter is open 24 hours a day and has a card phone. There are also two card phones in Assalah – one at the Oxford supermarket and the other at the papyrus shop in the heart of the bazaar, both of which sell phonecards.

At the Snapper Photo Shop on the bay, you can send emails for 50pt per minute, with a minimum charge of E£3. Emails can also be sent at White Hawk Souvenir Shop (☎ 640 377) opposite the entrance to Auski camp. It charges E£25 per hour or E£7.50 for 15 minutes.

Activities

After loafing around, diving is the most popular activity in Dahab. The town's various dive clubs all offer a full range of diving possibilities; however, you should choose your club carefully as some places have lousy reputations when it comes to safety standards – among the better are Inmo, Nesima and Fantasea.

Snorkellers tend to head for Eel Garden, just north of town. You can hire snorkelling gear from places along the waterfront.

In the morning, camel drivers and their charges congregate along the waterfront to organise camel trips to the interior of Sinai. Prices for a day trip including food start at E£50.

Places to Stay

Most, if not all, budget travellers head straight for Assalah. There's a plethora of so-called camps, which are basically compounds with simple stone and cement huts of two or three mattresses, generally costing E£5 to E£10 per person. Many of the camps are introducing proper rooms with private bathrooms, but these are considerably more expensive than the huts. Prices are always negotiable. *Auski*, *Bishbishi* and *Mirage Village* are all good camps.

Heading south from Assalah *Starcosa Hotel* (☎ 640 388) is a comfortable place to stay offering single/double rooms with fans, private bathroom and hot water for E£37/60.

Lagona Dahab Village (☎ 640 352, fax 640 351) is in the middle of nowhere on the beach between Dahab City and Assalah. The dome-shaped rooms cost E£50/80 for a single/double with fans, including breakfast and taxes. Rooms with air-con are about E£20 per person more. It is a comfortable enough place but it has the air of a structured resort. There's a restaurant where alcohol is not served.

Close to Dahab City are a few upmarket hotels.

Places to Eat

There is a string of places to eat along the waterfront in Assalah. They serve breakfast, lunch and dinner, and most seem to have identical menus hanging up out the front – a meal will generally cost you between E£6 to E£15. *Jays Restaurant* on the strip in Masbat is a favourite of locals and serves the usual mixture of Egyptian and western fare. Few people seem to stay at *Dolphin Camp* but the food here is good, the servings generous and it's one of the few camps where you can enjoy a beer with your meal. *Tota*, a ship-shape place in the heart of Assalah, has the best Italian cuisine on the strip. *Italy Pizzeria* next door does arguably better pizzas.

Getting There & Away

Bus The bus station is in Dahab City. The most regular connection is to Sharm el-Sheikh (E£10, 1½ hours) with buses at 8.30 and 10 am and 1, 2.30, 9 and 10 pm. Buses to Nuweiba (E£8) leave at 10.30 am and

6.30 pm. The 10.30 am service goes on to Taba (E£20). The 9.30 am bus to St Katherine's Monastery (E£15) takes two to three hours. Buses to Cairo (nine hours) leave at 8.30 am and 1 and 2.30 pm (all E£55) and at 10 pm (E£70). Buses for Suez (E£28, 6½ hours) depart at 8.15 and 10 am and 9 pm.

Service Taxi As a rule, service taxis are much more expensive than buses – they know you're only using them because the bus doesn't suit.

NUWEIBA

The beach and port town of Nuweiba, hardly Sinai's most attractive spot, is 87km north of Dahab. It is divided into three parts. To the south is the port with a major bus station, banks and fairly awful hotels. A few kilometres farther north is Nuweiba city, where the tourist resort hotels and one of the area's two dive centres are located, as well as a couple of good places to eat. Tarabin is a farther 2km out, draped along the northern end of Nuweiba's calm bay. Once a tranquil beachside oasis, it's rapidly turning into a party and pick-up place, especially during Israeli holidays.

Information

The post and phone offices are near the hospital on the exit road from Nuweiba city. There's another post office as well as two banks on the road leading into the port. The National Egyptian Bank has a branch inside Helnan Nuweiba Hotel at Nuweiba city.

Activities

Once again, underwater delights are the feature attraction and scuba diving and snorkelling the prime activities. Diving Camp Nuweiba (☎ 500 402) is in Helnan Nuweiba Hotel camping area.

Holiday Village organises fairly expensive jeep and camel treks to sights such as Coloured Canyon, Khudra oasis, 'Ain Mahmed and 'Ain Furtaga. Try your luck with the Bedouin people of Tarabin.

At the Bedouin village of Mizela, 1km south of Nuweiba port, you can swim in a bay that has been frequented, for the past few years at any rate, by a dolphin. The village elders charge visitors E£10 to swim and E£10 for a mask and snorkel.

Places to Stay

Nuweiba Port There are three fairly unimpressive hotels you can stay in by the port. *Motel Marina* is the best of the trio. Tiny doubles without/with shower and aircon are E£30/75. The only other option in the vicinity is *Nuweiba Hilton Coral Resort* (☎ 520 320, fax 520 327) on the beachfront just north of the port. Singles/doubles start at US$115/149 including taxes and breakfast.

Nuweiba City With your own tent, you can camp at *Morgana Restaurant* for E£3, but there's precious little shade. *Helnan Nuweiba Hotel* (E£10) and *City Beach Village* (E£5) also take campers.

There are a couple of simple camps with a few huts along the beach south of Al-Waha Tourism Village including *Habiba* and the relaxing *Duna*.

Helnan Nuweiba Hotel (☎ 500 401, fax 500 407) caters mainly to package tourists or middle class Cairenes. It has singles/doubles with breakfast from US$45/60 plus taxes. Next door in its *Holiday Camp* there are cheaper cabins at E£46/62 for singles/doubles including breakfast.

Further down the road is *Al-Waha Tourism Village* (☎/fax 500 420/1) which has 16 large tents at E£12.50 per person. Stuffy, pastel-toned wooden huts cost E£55 a double. It also has slightly better air-con rooms with bathrooms at E£80/100.

City Beach Village halfway between Nuweiba city and Tarabin is not a bad option if you just want to sit all day on a tranquil beach. You can pitch a tent for E£5, camp out in one of its reed huts for E£10 per person or go for a clean, comfortable single/double room for E£45/55, in which case breakfast is included.

Tarabin As Tarabin develops along Dahab lines, the choice of accommodation is becoming wider. You can get a mattress in a bamboo or concrete hut at one of the camps for E£5, and there are a couple of hotels.

Places to Eat

Apart from the hotels and camps, there's not much to speak of at the port or in Tarabin. In Nuweiba city *Dr Shishkebab* and *Sendbad* are both excellent budget diners.

Getting There & Away

Bus Buses going to or from Taba stop at Helnan Nuweiba Hotel and Dr Shishkebab in Nuweiba city. They usually also call in at the port but do not stop at Tarabin.

Buses generally meet incoming ferries. The bus from Taba to Cairo (E£50) via St Katherine's Monastery (E£10) stops at Helnan Nuweiba Hotel around 10 to 10.30 am. There's another bus to Cairo (E£55) at 3 pm. Buses to Sharm el-Sheikh (E£20) via Dahab (E£10) leave at 6.30 am and 4 pm; to Taba at 6 am (E£10) and noon (E£19); and to Suez at 6 am (E£25; six hours via Nakhl).

Service Taxi There is a big service taxi station by the port. The fare to Suez is E£40 and it's E£50 to Cairo.

Boat For information about ferries and speedboats to Aqaba in Jordan, refer to Sea in the Getting There and Away section earlier in this chapter.

TABA

This busy crossing point into Israel is open 24 hours.

There is a small post and telephone office in the 'town', along with a hospital, bakery and an EgyptAir office (often closed). You can change money at booths of Banque du Caire (unreliable opening hours) and Banque Masr (open 24 hours) both 100m before the border, or at Taba Hilton Hotel.

Getting There & Away

Air EgyptAir has flights between Cairo and Ras an-Naqb airport (which is 38km from Taba) each Monday for E£497.

Bus East Delta Bus Co runs several buses from Taba. The 10 am bus goes to Nuweiba (E£10), St Katherine's Monastery (E£25) and on to Cairo (E£60). Another bus to Cairo (E£65) leaves at 2 pm and goes via Nakhl. Other buses leave at 9 am and 3 pm for Sharm el-Sheikh (E£35), stopping at Nuweiba (E£10) and Dahab (E£15). To Nuweiba only there's another bus at 2 pm. To Suez (E£40, five hours via Nakhl) there's one at 7 am.

Service Taxi A taxi (up to seven people) to Nuweiba costs E£210 and E£300 to Sharm el-Sheikh. You may also find a minibus or two that will take you to Dahab for about E£15 per person. Your bargaining power increases if the bus is not too far off.

ST KATHERINE'S MONASTERY

There are 22 Greek Orthodox monks living in this ancient monastery at the foot of Mt Sinai. The monastic order was founded in the 4th century AD by the Byzantine empress Helena, who had a small chapel built beside what was believed to be the burning bush from which God spoke to Moses. The chapel is dedicated to St Katherine, the legendary martyr of Alexandria, who was tortured on a spiked wheel and then beheaded for her Christianity.

In the 6th century Emperor Justinian ordered the building of a fortress with a basilica and a monastery as well as the original chapel. It served as a secure home for the monks of St Katherine's and as a refuge for the Christians of southern Sinai. St Katherine's is open to visitors from 9 am to noon daily except Friday, Sunday and holidays.

Information

In the village of Al-Milga, about 3.5km from the monastery, there's a post office, phone exchange, bank and variety of shops and cafes. Banque Masr here will change cash or travellers cheques and may accept Visa and MasterCard for a cash advance. It's open from 9 am to 2 pm and 6 to 9 pm.

Mt Sinai

At a height of 2285m Mt Sinai (Gebel Musa is the local name) towers over St Katherine's Monastery. It is revered as the place Moses received the Ten Commandments from God. It is easy to climb – you can take the gentle camel trail or the 3000 Steps of Repentance, carved out by a monk. It takes two to three hours, and most people either stay overnight or climb up in time for sunrise – bring a torch (flashlight). It gets freezing cold in winter.

Places to Stay & Eat

St Katherine's Monastery runs a *hostel* that offers a bed in a single-sex dormitory (seven beds) for E£35, and rooms with three beds and private bathroom for E£40 per person. The facilities are basic.

Beside the roundabout 2km west of the monastery is the expensive *St Katherine's Tourist Village* (☎ 470 333, fax 470 323) where singles/doubles/triples cost US$130/156/197 including breakfast and dinner.

Off to your right about 400m before you reach the mosque in Al-Milga is a cluster of three hotels. *Daniela Village* (☎ 470 225) has 52 stone bungalows with comfortable enough rooms for US$49/65/79 including breakfast.

In Al-Milga there's a *bakery* opposite the mosque and a couple of well stocked *supermarkets* in the shopping arcade. Just behind the bakery are a few small restaurants, the most reasonable of which is *Kafeteria Ikhlas*; try its chicken meal with soup for E£12. Just by the bus stop *Katrien Rest House* (no accommodation) is open for lunch only and also serves a filling chicken, rice and vegetable meal. Across the square, near the bank, is the popular *Restaurant for Friends* where meals go for about E£8.

Getting There & Away

Bus Buses leave from the square in Al-Milga to Cairo (E£40, seven hours) at 10 am; Suez (E£20, five hours) at 6 am; Sharm el-Sheikh (E£20) via Dahab (E£15) between noon and 1 pm; and Taba (E£20) via Nuweiba (E£15) at 3.30 pm.

Service Taxi Service taxis travel in and out of the village irregularly and infrequently. At the monastery taxis often wait for people coming down from Mt Sinai in the early afternoon. Count on between E£10 and E£20 per person to Dahab or Nuweiba.

AL-ARISH

Al-Arish is the capital of the north Sinai governorate and has a population of about 40,000. The palm-fringed beaches and comparatively unspoiled nature make it a pleasant place for a swim.

Every Thursday, a **souq** is held in the oldest part of town and Bedouin come in from the desert to trade silver, beadwork and embroidered dresses. There's also the **Sinai Heritage Museum** on the outskirts of town along the coastal road to Rafah. Otherwise, the main attraction is the **beach**. The parade of palms, fine white sand and clean water makes this one of the nicer Mediterranean spots in Egypt.

Places to Stay

Golden Beach Hotel (☎ 342 270) has concrete bungalows with up to three beds at E£15 per bungalow. Just up the road and slightly better is *Moon Light Hotel* (☎ 341 362) with singles/doubles at E£15/30. Both places are on the beach but facilities are very basic.

Behind the New Golden Beach is *Mecca Hotel* (☎/fax 344 909), a friendly, good, clean place that has singles/doubles with fan and hot water for E£30/40.

One of the better deals is *Green Land Beach Hotel* (☎ 340 601) virtually right on the beach. Clean and comfortable double/triple rooms with bathroom cost E£25/30. Breakfast is extra and most of the rooms have terraces.

Farther west are Al-Arish's two luxury establishments, the *Semiramis* and *Egoth Oberoi*.

Places to Eat

There's not a huge range of places to eat in Al-Arish. About as good as you'll find in the budget range is *Aziz Restaurant* on Sharia Tahrir. It has good meals of fuul and ta'amiyya as well as grilled chicken, kofta, rice and spaghetti. It's also open for breakfast.

Sabry opposite Aziz in the back corner of a little square makes the best felafel. At *Sammar Restaurant* (signposted in Arabic) on Sharia Tahrir you can get kebab and kofta.

At the junction of sharias Fuad Zikry and 23rd of July is *Fairuz Restaurant* (☎ 343 307). It serves kofta, kebab, fish and chicken in reasonably generous portions, although it's closed in winter.

On the beach, among the palms, is the classier *Maxim*, which specialises in fish dishes costing about E£25 to E£40. It serves good food, but is open in summer only.

Getting There & Away

Air EgyptAir has two flights a week between Cairo and Al-Arish for E£328 one way.

Bus Buses for Cairo (five hours) leave Al-Arish at 7 am (E£25) and 4 pm (E£35). There is a bus via Qantara (E£5) to Ismailia (E£7, three hours) every hour until 3 pm. For Suez, you have to go to Ismailia and take another bus from there. At 7.15 and 10.30 am there's a bus to Rafah (E£1.50). The bus bypasses Rafah town and takes you directly to the Egyptian border post.

Service Taxi A cheaper alternative to the expensive Sinai buses to Cairo is a service taxi, which costs about E£12 per person.

Iran

Over the centuries, Persia has attracted some of the region's more gruesome invaders, and later, some of the world's more eccentric explorers. Only in the past few years has Iran recovered from the excesses of the Islamic Revolution, and the aftermath of the Iran-Iraq War, and the Iranian government is again (tentatively) starting to promote tourism. Iran boasts excellent transport, a good range of accommodation and plenty of ancient ruins, glorious mosques and labyrinthine bazaars to explore, as well as decent skiing and trekking. From some, the major attraction is that Iran is cheap, and often very good value.

Forget the media images of fervent anti-western marches and secret police: Iran is a remarkably safe and hospitable country. Women should hold no fears: if you dress and act according to (admittedly strict) local rules, you will be treated well, and suffer little, if any, of the hassles women often endure in Pakistan and Turkey. Post-revolutionary Iran is now one of the most fascinating, welcoming and inexpensive countries in the Middle East.

Facts about Iran

HISTORY

A general history of the Middle East is given in the Facts about the Region chapter at the beginning of this book.

In the 6th century BC Cyrus the Great emerged as the first notable Persian ruler. The Achaemenid empire he founded lasted from 558 to 330 BC and his successors, Darius I and Xerxes, expanded their rule all the way to India in the east and the Aegean Sea in the west. Even Egypt came under Persian rule and the magnificent complex of Persepolis became the hub of the empire.

Xerxes' defeat by the Greeks at Marathon marked the end of the great Achaemenid period of Persian history. It was Europe's turn

The Islamic Republic of Iran

Area: 1,648,195 sq km
Population: approx 70 million
Population Growth Rate: approx 3.5%
Capital: Tehrān
Head of State: Āyatollāh Alī Khameneī is the 'supreme leader'; the elected president is Hojjat-ol-Eslām Seyed Mohammed Khatamī
Official Language: Persian (Fārsī)
Currency: Iranian rial
Official Exchange Rate: US$1 = 1756 rials

- **Best Dining** – slurp on a bowl of *ābgūsht* (stew) at a cafe by a stream along the walking trail starting from Darband, north of Tehrān
- **Best Walk** – stroll along the banks of Rūd-é Zāyandé in Esfahān, and visit the teahouses in the old bridges
- **Best View** – the views of picturesque valleys and of the mighty Kūh-é Damāvand mountain from Reine are superb
- **Best Activity** – wander around the bazaars in Kermān, Esfahān and Shīrāz
- **When in Rome ...** watch the prayers on Friday mornings, or religious holidays, at Tehrān University or Meidūn-é Emām Khomeinī in Esfahān

IRAN

to conquer and, in the 4th century BC, Alexander invaded Persia and 'accidentally' burned down Persepolis. After his death the Greek influence rapidly waned, starting with the breakaway region of north-east Persia, which was ruled by the Parthians.

The Sassanians controlled Persia from 224 to 638 but through these years of Persian history there was continuing conflict with the Roman and, later, the Byzantine empires. Weakened by this scrapping, the Zoroastrian Persians fell easy prey to the spread of Islam and the Arabs. Between 637 and 642 nearly all of Persia was taken by the Arabs and the Zoroastrian religion was superseded by Islam. Arabs maintained control over Persia for nearly 600 years but towards the end of that period they were gradually supplanted by the Turkish Seljuk dynasty. The Seljuks heralded a new era of Persian art, literature and science, marked by such people as the mathematician-poet Omar Khayyām. Then in 1194 the Seljuk era abruptly collapsed when the Mongol Genghis Khan swept in and commenced a cold-blooded devastation that was to last for two centuries.

Another invasion by Tamerlane in 1380 didn't help matters, but in 1502 the Safavid era commenced and heralded a Persian renaissance. Under Shāh Abbās I (1587-1629) foreign influences were again purged from the country, and the architectural miracles he later performed in Esfahān have left a permanent reminder of this period.

The decline of the Safavids following Shāh Abbās I's death was hastened by an invasion from Afghanistan, but in 1736, Nāder Shāh, a tribal leader from the northeast, overthrew the impotent Safavids and proceeded to chuck out Afghans, Russians and Turks in all directions. It was a relief to all, both within Persia and without, when he was assassinated in 1747.

The following Zand and Ghajar periods were not notable except for a brief reign of glory under Karīm Khān-é Zand at Shīrāz. In 1926 Rezā Khān Pahlavī, a Cossack officer in the imperial army, founded the Pahlavī dynasty. Foreign influence – and

What to See

Of the main cities, **Shīrāz** has plenty of attractions, **Esfahān** is the most architecturally stunning and **Yazd** boasts a fascinating old, inhabited city; **Tehrān** has little to offer, but does boast several great museums. Iran has excellent ruins: **Persepolis** is one of Iran's highlights, as is the ancient city of **Bam** and the remote **Throne of Soleimān**. Naturally, mosques are plentiful, and they are particularly stunning in Esfahān and Yazd; non-Muslims can visit the very sacred **Holy Shrine of Emām Rezā** in Mashhad. There are also charming gardens and mausoleums in, and/or near, Shīrāz, Kāshān and Esfahān.

Every town has a bazaar; the ones in Kermān, Esfahān and Shīrāz are particularly long and colourful. More adventurous travellers can go hiking, and skiing is almost world-class and cheap. The countryside is picturesque in the far western and eastern sections of the Caspian provinces, and the **Alī Sadr Caves** are ideal for anyone tired of bazaars, mosques and ancient ruins.

oil – soon became an important element in Iran's story. In WWII, Iran was officially neutral, but Rezā Khān was exiled to South Africa because he was thought to be too friendly with the Axis powers. His 22-year-old son, Mohammed Rezā, succeeded him. After the war, the invading Russian forces were persuaded to depart, the shāh assumed near-absolute power and Iran firmly aligned itself with the west.

The government of Mohammed Rezā was repressive, but Iran was rapidly modernised. Illiteracy was reduced, women emancipated, land holdings redistributed, health services improved and a major industrialisation program embarked upon. The 1974 oil price revolution became the shāh's undoing: he allowed US arms merchants to persuade him to squander Iran's vast new wealth on huge arsenals of useless weapons. The flood of petrodollars lined the pockets of a select few, while galloping inflation made the majority worse off than before.

Since the early days of the Pahlavī era there had been a smouldering resistance that occasionally flared into violence. Students wanted faster reform, devout Muslims wanted reforms rolled back, and everybody attacked the Pahlavīs' conspicuous consumption. As the economy went from bad to worse, the growing opposition made its

presence felt with sabotage and massive street demonstrations. The shāh introduced martial law, and hundreds of demonstrators were killed in street battles in Tehrān. The shāh finally fled the country in January 1979, and died a year later.

Āyatollāh Khomeinī returned to Iran on 1 February 1979 to be greeted by adoring millions. His fiery brew of nationalism and Muslim fundamentalism had been at the forefront of the revolt, but few realised how much deep-rooted support he had and how

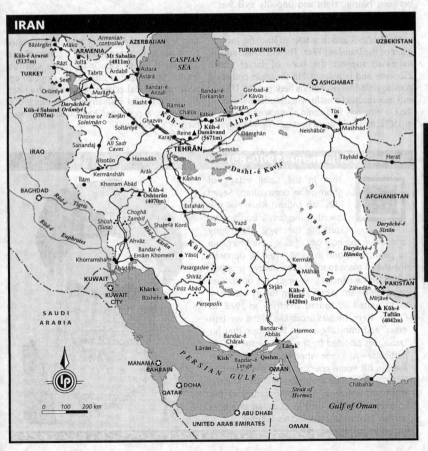

strongly he reflected the beliefs and ideals of millions of his people.

Khomeinī's intention was to set up a clergy-dominated Islamic republic – the first true Islamic state in modern times. He went about achieving this with brutal efficiency: opposition disappeared; executions took place after meaningless trials; minor officials took the law into their own hands; and policies were implemented that were confrontationist and unashamedly designed to promote similar Islamic revolutions elsewhere.

The main opponent in this primordial battle between Islamic right and ungodly evil was (and continues to be) the USA. The reasoning behind this is that the USA provided support to the Pahlavīs and then later to Iraq, the instigator of the Iran-Iraq War. The USA also continues to support the state of Israel and Zionism, and is responsible for trade embargoes against Iran. Relations between the USA and Iran reached a nadir when students seized the US embassy in Tehrān along with 52 staff in 1979, and held them hostage for 444 days.

In 1980, Saddam Hussein made an opportunistic land grab in south-west Iran, taking advantage of Iran's domestic chaos, on the pretext that the oil-rich province of Khūzestān was historically part of Iraq. Although Iraq was better equipped, Iran drew on a larger population and a fanaticism fanned by the rhetoric of the *mullahs* (Muslim teachers). For the first time since WWI the world witnessed the hideous spectre of trench warfare and poison gas. A cease-fire was finally negotiated in mid-1988, with neither side achieving its objectives.

Iran Today

Khomeinī died in 1989, leaving an uncertain legacy to the country he had dominated for a decade. Āyatollāh Alī Khameneī was appointed his successor as Iran's spiritual leader, but inherited little of his popular appeal or political power. Two months later, Hojjat-ol-Eslām Rafsanjānī was elected as president, a post that has previously been largely ceremonial.

IRAN

Āyatollāh Khomeinī (1900-89)

Born in the small village of Khomein in central Iran, Seyed Rūhollāh Mūsavī Khomeinī followed in the family tradition by studying theology, philosophy and law in the holy city of Qom. He first came to public attention in 1962 when he opposed the shāh's plans to reduce the clergy's property rights and emancipate women. His outspoken opposition earned him exile in Turkey before he was shunted off to Iraq and then, in 1978, to France. Here, he was accessible to the western press, and ironically, it was in Europe that his cause was boosted by the media – the BBC in particular – at a time when he was little known even in his home country. After the shāh fled in 1979, Āyatollāh Khomeinī returned to a tumultuous welcome, and took control of the country. When he died in 1989 an unprecedented 10 million attended his funeral.

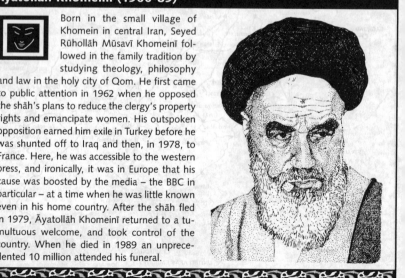

In 1997, the moderate, and potentially more visionary, Hojjat-ol-Eslām Seyed Mohammed Khatamī easily beat another candidate (who was backed by the Iranian parliament) to become president. Khatamī attracted a large vote from women and youth, both of which groups hope that Khatamī will change many of the more stern impositions of the Islamic Republic.

However, there has been virtually no liberalism since Khatamī came to power, because hardline factions, dedicated to the Islamic Revolution, control the corridors of power within the government. In 1998, several liberal Iranian writers were murdered by persons linked to the Iranian Ministry of Interior (ie security forces). The murderers were eventually caught, and their actions made public, thereby indicating that Khatamī remains in control, however precariously. Meanwhile, Iran's economic outlook appears bleak because the price of oil and carpets – its two major exports – is plummeting. Iran can no longer afford to carry the heavy burden of subsidies it provides its populace, but the reduction or abolition of these subsidies could cause political and social unrest.

Throughout 1999 Iran held numerous boisterous celebrations to commemorate the 20th anniversary of the Islamic Revolution, and the 10th anniversary of the Āyatollāh Khomeinī's death, which re-enforced the ideals of the Islamic Revolution.

GEOGRAPHY
Iran covers 1,648,195 sq km, which makes it more than three times larger than France. The two great deserts, Dasht-é Kavīr and Dasht-é Lūt, occupy most of the north-east and east of the central plain. There are three dominant mountain ranges: the volcanic Sabalān and Tālesh ranges in the north-west; the vast, old and virtually insurmountable Zāgros range; and the Alborz range, between Tehrān and the Caspian Sea, home to Iran's highest peak, Kūh-é Damāvand (5671m).

The settled areas are almost entirely confined to the foothills of these mountains, although oasis towns, such as Kermān, are growing in size and importance. Iran is par-

ticularly susceptible to earthquakes: there have been almost 1000 registered quakes in the past 20 years.

Most rivers drain into the Persian Gulf, the Caspian Sea, or one of a number of salty and swampy lakes, such as Daryāche-yé Orūmīyé, Iran's largest lake.

CLIMATE
With a few exceptions, Iran is hot and dry in summer and cold and dry in winter. North of the Alborz Mountains, especially along the Caspian coast, rainfall is heavy, but the rest of Iran experiences little precipitation. The summer can get pretty hot down south: in the desert and along the Persian Gulf coast, debilitating humidity and summer temperatures over 40°C are common. Away from the coast most of the main cities are at a fairly high altitude, which tends to moderate the heat; on the other hand it makes the winters colder. In midwinter, Tehrān and Mashhad are usually cold, and snow is common in the higher regions of the west and south-east.

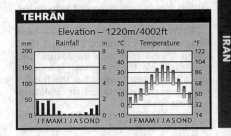

TEHRĀN
Elevation – 1220m/4002ft

GOVERNMENT & POLITICS
After the Islamic Revolution in 1979, 98% of the population apparently voted to implement a unique form of Islamic government, with three levels of political power. Firstly, there's a parliament called the *Majlis*, which comprises Islamic experts and revered Islamic leaders from around the country, and includes a representative from the Jewish and Zoroastrian communities, and two from the Armenian Christians. The

Majlis approves (but does not instigate, in theory) laws and economic decisions, but under the constitution it can 'investigate and examine all affairs of the country'.

The Majlis is dominated by the *velayat-é faqih*, or supreme leader. The first supreme leader was the revered Āyatollāh Khomeinī – refer to the boxed text 'Āyatollāh Khomeinī' earlier in this section. The current supreme leader, Āyatollāh Alī Khameneī, has enormous power: he can select (and sack) the commander of the armed forces; declare war or peace; and veto the election of (and dismiss) the president. The Majlis is elected by the Iranian people every four years, but the candidates are carefully vetted before the elections. The Speaker of the Majlis is Hojjat-ol-Eslām Alī Akbar Nateq Nouri.

The second level of power, the Council of the Guardians, 'safeguards the Islamic Ordinances and Constitution', and comprises 12 Islamic jurists and religious experts, all selected by the Supreme Leader. The Council's main purposes are to uphold Islamic values, ensure that the parliament remains free of corruption and approve the handful of presidential candidates.

Thirdly, the president manages (and elects himself) a cabinet, although final control always rests with the Majlis. The president is elected every four years (and only allowed two terms), but the Iranian people normally only have four candidates to choose from.

As promised by President Khatamī, Iran held its first municipal elections in February 1999. A high percentage of Iranians, particularly the youth and women, again voted for candidates who support the liberalisation espoused by Khatamī. The vote was mostly free of incident and violence, and some candidates from banned, but tolerated, opposition parties were allowed to participate.

POPULATION & PEOPLE

Iran's population is around 70 million – and rising very fast. More than 65% of inhabitants can be classified as Persians, descendants of the Aryans who first settled in the central plateau of Iran in about 2000 BC. About 25% of the population are Āzārīs, who live in the north-westernmost region of Iran. Turkmen (2% of the population) are a fierce nomadic race of horse people and warriors who inhabit Iran's far north-east.

Other inhabitants include the Lors (2%) – thought to be part Persian, part Arab – a semi-nomadic people who live in the western mountains south of Kermānshāh, and speak Lorī, a Persian dialect. Kurds (5%) mostly inhabit the western mountains between Orūmīyé and Kermānshāh. (Iran's treatment of the Kurds compares favourably with that of most neighbouring countries.) Arabs (4%) mostly live on the south coast and Persian Gulf islands, and in Khūzestān.

More than 300,000 nomads still roam the plains and mountains. The Baluchīs are semi-nomadic and inhabit Balūchestān, a formerly semi-autonomous territory now divided between Iran and Pakistan. Ghashghā'īs of south-west Iran are traditionally wandering herdspeople.

RELIGION

Most Iranians belong to the *Shi'ite* branch of Islam. Less than 8% of the population (Kurds, Baluchīs, Turkmen and about half the Arabs) are *Sunni*. The official figures for minorities – Christians (0.7%), Jews (0.3%) and Zoroastrians (0.1%) – are probably underestimated as many followers of other faiths call themselves Muslims in official documents.

Most Iranian Christians are Armenians, predominantly members of the Gregorian Church; the rest are mainly Assyrians. There are also a few Protestants, including Adventists, Anglicans and Lutherans, as well as Latin-rite Catholics. Jews first settled in Iran following the Babylonian captivity of 597 BC at the invitation of Xerxes I, whose wife, Esther, was Jewish. Some 30 synagogues operate in Iran today. Iran is a centre of Zoroastrianism, and followers are found mainly in Yazd, Tehrān and Kermān.

Baha'i, a religion founded in Iran which regards itself as 'pure Islam', is followed by about 300,000 Iranians. The religion is not recognised by the Iranian authorities, however, and many followers have been persecuted or forced to keep a very low profile or have emigrated.

LANGUAGE

Although the vast majority of Iranians speak the national language Persian (Fārsī), it's the mother tongue of only about 60% of the population. The most important minority languages are Āzarī, Kurdish, Arabic, Baluchī and Lorī.

English is understood by many educated middle-class men and women in the major cities, most employees of mid-range and top end hotels and restaurants, and most staff in travel agencies and tourist offices. A surprising number of Iranians have studied, worked or lived in Germany and speak passable German.

Most towns, squares, streets and tourist attractions are signposted in English. However, if you're travelling independently and using budget accommodation and restaurants, you cannot rely entirely on English. The Language chapter at the back of this book lists some important Fārsī words and phrases.

Facts for the Visitor

PLANNING

The climate in most areas is mild and pleasant from mid April to early June, and late September to early November. Winter is the most agreeable time to visit the southern

---

Dress Code

From the moment you enter Iran, you are legally obliged to observe its rigid dress code. You will be reprimanded for any lapses, though foreigners are unlikely to get into serious trouble providing they quickly make amends. The dress code is strictly enforced during Ramazān, when Iranians avoid wearing red and other loud colours. Colours are also subdued in the mourning month of Moharram.

Women Females older than seven must wear the *hejāb* (modest dress) whenever in the actual or potential sight of any man who isn't a close relative. All parts of the body, except hands, feet and the face above the neckline and below the hairline, must be covered, and the shape of the body must be disguised. The outfit commonly associated with Iranian women is the *chādor*, a tent-like cloak (normally black), draped loosely over the head, legs and arms. However, it's not necessary to go this far: the standard dress for many Iranian women is a full-length skirt, or trousers (jeans will do), worn beneath a loose-fitting, below-the-knees black or dark blue coat, known as a *roupush*. Hair is hidden beneath a large, plain headscarf (although it's acceptable to allow a very modest fringe to show).

Foreign woman visiting Iran can wear a baggy shirt, or loose-fitting jacket, which comes down to at least their mid-thighs, over a long, loose, ankle-length skirt – plus socks and a headscarf. In Iran, foreign women can easily buy a roupush, which allows the freedom of wearing just a light vest or bra only underneath – a lot cooler in summer.

Apart from plain rings, jewellery and make-up should be discreet to the point of invisibility.

Men Men must wear full trousers; shorts are only acceptable when swimming and playing sport. Short sleeve shirts are normally acceptable, except when visiting particularly holy places. During Ramazān, it's recommended that you stick to long sleeves.

coast and Persian Gulf islands, while the west and the north-east are at their best from late spring to early summer, and late summer to early autumn. Some prefer not to visit during Ramazān (Ramadan), although it won't affect your travels too much. For about 10 days before and after the Iranian New Year (which starts on about 21 March), transport and accommodation is very scarce, so it's best to avoid travelling around Iran at this time.

Maps

The maps of the cities in this book should satisfy most travellers, although a more detailed map of Iran is a good idea. Gita Shenasi (☎ 21-679 335, fax 675 782), 15 Kheyābūn-é Ostad Shahrīvar, Tehrān, PO Box 14155/3441, publishes an impressive array of maps of Iran and all major cities. Some maps are sold at bookshops throughout Iran, but the better maps are only available at Gita Shenasi's office. Its *General Map of Iran* (1:1,000,000) published in English, is the best; and the new *A Tourist Guide to Tehrān* is the best map of that mammoth metropolis. The best dual-language (ie Fārsī and English) is the *Tourist Map of the Islamic Republic of Iran* (1:2,500,000) published by the Ministry of Culture & Islamic Guidance, although it's not widely available in Iran. The best English-language map probably available in your country is *Iran* (1:2,000,000) published by GeoCenter.

VISAS & DOCUMENTS
Visas

Visitors from Slovenia, Macedonia (ie the Former Yugoslav Republic of ...) and Turkey can get a three-month tourist visa on arrival. Japanese travellers can get a three-month tourist visa at any Iranian consulate/embassy without a problem. However, everyone else needs a visa prior to arrival, and getting one is a hassle. Don't let this put you off – just allow plenty of time.

The best general advice is to apply for a two-week or one-month tourist (or business) visa (extendable) in your home country if you're flying into Iran, or a five to 10 day transit visa (extendable) along the way

if you're travelling overland to Iran. Multiple entry visas are only issued to foreign workers and diplomats.

If you can't get a tourist visa in your home country, don't give up. Either telephone the Iranian embassy/consulate in a neighbouring country, or drop in at every Iranian mission on your way to Iran. If you can only get a short transit visa, don't worry – getting an extension inside Iran is far easier than obtaining any sort of visa in the first place.

When applying for a visa, you must complete two or three application forms (in English); provide up to four passport-sized photos – complete with the hejāb (head covering) for women; and pay a fee (which varies according to nationality). You may also be asked to provide photocopies of your airline tickets in and out of Iran, and provide a 'letter of introduction' from your embassy. Visa costs are difficult to understand but the cost for most travellers seems to be the equivalent of $US50.

If you have access to the Internet, check out these informative Web sites:

- www.salamiran.org – managed by the Iranian embassy in Ottawa, Canada
- www.iran-embassy.org.uk – Iranian consulate in London, UK
- www.daftar.org – Iranian embassy in Washington, USA

Two final points: every part of every day counts towards the length of your visa; and passport stamps issued on entry, and for visa extensions, often use the Islamic calendar, so make sure you know the expiry date in the Gregorian (western) calendar.

If you have an Israeli stamp in your passport or any other evidence of a visit to Israel, you will be refused a visa and denied entry into the country.

Transit Visa A transit visa is valid for five or 10 days and is extendable; sponsors are not normally required. This visa is normally requested by, and given to, foreigners who are travelling overland into and out of Iran. Transit visas are normally valid for three months, ie you must enter Iran within three months of the date of visa issue. (Before obtaining an Iranian visa in Turkey, you will probably need a Pakistani visa.)

Tourist & Business Visa Tourist (and business) visas are mainly for people flying in and out of Iran for business, to visit family or on an organised tour. These visas are for two weeks or one month, and can also be extended. If you ask for a one-month tourist visa, you may also need to provide a brief itinerary of your trip. Tourist visas are also normally valid for three months.

Regulations about whether you need a sponsor in Iran for a tourist visa differ from one embassy/consulate to another. If you're arranging your tourist (or business) visa through a relative, travel agency or business contact in Iran, they will need your full personal and passport details, and brief itinerary. A week or so later, your sponsor will send you an authorisation number from the Ministry of Foreign Affairs in Tehrān, which you then use to collect your visa from the relevant embassy. Or so the theory goes.

If you don't have a sponsor in Iran contact a travel agency in Iran (see Organised Tours in the Getting Around section later), or a visa service agency in your home country. These agencies may charge up to US$50 for their services (on top of the visa fee), but you're usually under no obligation to take any of their tours, and using an agency avoids the hassle of getting the visa yourself.

Visa Extensions You can get one or two (and sometimes three) extensions of up to two weeks each without too much hassle, but don't expect extensions totalling more than one month.

You can normally only apply for an extension two or three days before the visa is due to expire. The best places to get extensions are Tehrān; Tabrīz (as much as 30 days is possible); Esfahān (only 10 days); Shīrāz (seven to 10 days regularly given, but 15 or more is possible if you ask nicely); Kermān; and Mashhad (30 days is possible). The locations of the visa offices are provided in the relevant sections.

To get an extension obtain and fill out (English is usually OK) the visa extension form from the visa office, and take the form to a large Bank Melli branch for the relevant stamp (10,000 rials). The visa office will also want one or two photocopies of your passport and original Iranian visa, and two passport-sized photos. (Remember, women must be photographed in hejāb.) Once accepted, you can normally collect your passport (and, hopefully, visa extension) the next day.

Visas for Neighbouring Countries Iran is a bad place to get visas for most neighbouring countries, because many staff don't speak English; bureaucracy reigns supreme and waiting is seemingly endless; most missions are in Tehrān, which is a nightmare to get around, and not a great place to wait around for visas; and letters of introduction from your embassy are commonly required.

Armenia A three week visa costs about US$50, takes about two weeks to issue and requires two photos.

Azerbaijan The embassy was unwilling to provide information, because the situation about visas and foreigners crossing from Iran to Azerbaijan was unknown even to them. Staff strongly suggested that foreigners get visas elsewhere.

Pakistan Visas for up to one month cost about 30,000 rials, require two photographs and they can be picked up the following day.

Syria Visas cost about US$35 and they can be obtained on the same day providing you apply between 9 and 11 am, but a letter of introduction is required.

Turkey Most nationalities can obtain a visa at the border with Turkey, but you can check this with the Turkish embassy in Tehrān or the consulates at Orūmīyé and Tabrīz.

IRAN

Turkmenistan Transit visas of about five days are issued in a few days, cost about US$20, require three photos and may need a letter of introduction from your embassy.

United Arab Emirates Visitors normally need a sponsor, but a one month visa can be obtained without a sponsor if you're willing to wait for 10 to 15 days. Three photos are required, and it costs 30,000 rials.

Driving Licence & Permits
To drive around Iran you must have an International Driving Permit. If bringing in a vehicle, get a *carnet de passage* and a *diptyque* or a *triptyque* from the relevant international automobile organisation in your country. No other permit is required to travel around Iran.

Student & Youth Cards
With a current International Student Card, you can often get a 50% discount on the high entrance fees at some tourist sites but you'll have to be insistent with the ticket sellers.

EMBASSIES & CONSULATES
Iranian Embassies & Consulates
For addresses of Iranian embassies in neighbouring Middle Eastern countries see the relevant country chapter.

Australia
    Embassy:
    (☎ 02-6290 2421, fax 6290 2431)
    25 Culgoa Crt, O'Malley, ACT 2606
Canada
    Embassy:
    (☎ 613-2354 726, fax 2325 712, Web site www.salamiran.org)
    245 Metcalfe St, Ottawa, Ontario, K2P 2K2
France
    Embassy:
    (☎ 01 47 20 30 95, fax 01 40 70 01 57)
    4 Ave d'Iena, 75016, Paris
Germany
    Embassy:
    (☎ 228-816 110, fax 376 154)
    Godesberger Allee 133-137, 5300, Bonn
    Consulate:
    (☎ 69-560 0070, fax 560 0071)
    Guiollettstrasse 56, 6000 Frankfurt

Consulate:
    (☎ 40-5144 060, fax 5113 511)
    Bebelalle 18, 2000 Hamburg
    Consulate:
    (☎ 89-9279 060, fax 9810 105)
    Mauerkircherstrasse 59, 8000 Munich
Ireland
    Embassy:
    (☎ 1-885 881, fax 834 246)
    72 Mount Merrion Ave, Blackrock, Dublin
Netherlands
    Embassy:
    (☎ 70-3469 353, fax 3924 921)
    Duinweg 24, 2585 JX s'Gravenhage
New Zealand
    Embassy:
    (☎ 04-3862 983, fax 3863 065)
    The Terrace, Wellington
UK
    Embassy:
    (☎ 020-7584 8101, fax 7589 4440)
    27 Princes Gate, London SW7 IPX
    Consulate (for visas):
    (☎ 020-7937 5225, visa info line ☎ 0906-802 0222, fax 7938 1615, Web site www.iran-embassy.org.uk)
    50 Kensington Court
USA
    Embassy:
    (☎ 202-9654 990, Web site www.daftar.org)
    Iranian Interests Section at the Embassy of Pakistan, 2209 Wisconsin Ave NW, Washington, 20007

Embassies & Consulates in Iran
Most countries are represented in Iran. The missions listed below are in Tehrān unless stated otherwise. Most are open from around 8 or 9 am to 2 or 3 pm Sunday to Thursday.

Armenia
    Embassy:
    (☎ 6704 833, fax 6700 657)
    1 Kheyābūn-é Ostad Shahriar
Australia
    Embassy:
    (☎ 8724 456, fax 8720 484)
    13 Kheyābūn-é 23, Kheyābūn-é Khalid Islambuli
Azerbaijan
    Embassy:
    (☎ 2294 458, fax 2284 929)
    50 Kheyābūn-é Aghdasiyeh
Canada
    Embassy:
    (☎ 8732 623, fax 8733 202)
    57 Kheyābūn-é Shahid Sarafraz

France
 Embassy:
 (☎ 6706 005, fax 6706 544)
 85 Kheyābūn-é Nōfl-Lōshātō
Germany
 Embassy:
 (☎ 3114 111, fax 398 474)
 324 Kheyābūn-é Ferdōsī
Ireland
 Embassy:
 (☎/fax 2222 731)
 10 Razan Shomali, Kheyābūn-é Mir Damad
Netherlands
 Embassy:
 (☎ 8906 011, fax 8892 087)
 36 Kūché-yé Jahansouz, Kheyābūn-é
 Sarbedaran
New Zealand
 Embassy:
 (☎ 8757 052, fax 8757 056)
 57 Kheyābūn-é Javad Sarafraz
Oman
 Embassy:
 (☎ 2056 831, fax 2044 672)
 12 Kūché-yé Tandis, Kheyābūn-é Africa
Pakistan
 Embassy:
 (☎ 934 332, fax 935 154)
 Kheyābūn-é Ahmad Eitemad Zadeo, Jamshid
 Abad Shomali. Closed Thursday.
 Consulate:
 (☎/fax 051-29 845)
 Kheyābūn-é Emām Khomeinī, Mashhad
 Consulate:
 (☎ 0541-23 389, fax 23 666)
 Kheyābūn-é Pahlavanī, Zāhedān
Syria
 Embassy:
 (☎ 2059 031, fax 2059 409)
 22 Kheyābūn-é Arash
Turkey
 Embassy:
 (☎ 3115 299, fax 3117 928)
 314 Kheyābūn-é Ferdōsī
 Consulate:
 (☎ 0441-228 970, fax 231 800)
 Kheyābūn-é Beheshtī, Orūmīyé
 Consulate:
 (☎ 041-407 590)
 516 Kheyābūn-é Sharī'atī, Tabrīz
Turkmenistan
 Embassy:
 (☎ 2542 178, fax 2580 432)
 39 5th Kheyābūn-é Golestān,
 Consulate:
 (☎ 051-47 066, fax 99 940)
 24 Kūché-yé Konsūlgarī, Mashhad. Closed
 Friday and Sunday.

United Arab Emirates
 Embassy:
 (☎ 8781 333, fax 8789 084)
 355 Kheyābūn-é Vahid Dastjerdi
 Consulate:
 (☎ 0761-38 262)
 Kheyābūn-é Naseer, opposite Sharī'atī
 Hospital, Bandar-é Abbās
UK
 Embassy:
 (☎ 6705 011, fax 6708 021)
 143 Kheyābūn-é Ferdōsī
USA
 Embassy:
 (☎ 8782 964, fax 8773 265)
 US Interests Section in the Swiss embassy,
 59 Kheyābūn-é West Farzan. Open 8 to 11
 am from Saturday to Wednesday only.

CUSTOMS

You may bring into Iran duty-free 200 cigarettes, 200 cigars or 200g of tobacco, and a 'reasonable quantity' of perfume. But no alcohol. It's best to avoid bringing in any foreign magazines because there is bound to be a picture in one of them that, according to customs regulations, will 'promote moral and ideological perversion'; if so, it will be confiscated.

At international airports, cabin luggage – but rarely hand luggage – may be inspected thoroughly. At the Iranian borders, foreigners are often given special treatment and breeze through customs and immigration very quickly.

You may officially take out Iranian handicrafts up to the value of 150,000 rials (so keep a receipt handy); two Persian carpets or rugs; and 150g of gold and 3kg of silver (but neither with gemstones). If you exceed the stated values, or quantities, you officially need an export permit from the local customs office, but foreigners are normally given some leeway and allowed to take home a reasonable amount of souvenirs. Visitors must not take out more than 200,000 rials in cash.

On arrival, you have to fill out a Disembarkation Card, and, possibly, a Customs Declaration, which you must keep and then return to customs and immigration when you leave.

IRAN

MONEY

Costs

If you change money at the 'street rate', Iran is extremely cheap. Cheap hotels cost from about 10,000/15,000 rials for singles/doubles; meals start at 2000 rials for hamburgers and about 3500 rials for *chelō kabāb* (see Food, later in this chapter); transport is about 1000 rials for each hour of travel in a bus. Therefore a bare minimum, for budget hotels, Iranian food and overland, public transport, is about 40,000/30,000 rials per person per day, travelling as a single/double. Unless you thrive on discomfort, however, allow about 70,000/50,000 rials. Add to this, extra money for internal flights, long-distance chartered taxis and souvenirs.

Dual Pricing There are three circumstances where foreigners are charged more than locals. Firstly, all tickets on international flights and ferries bought in Iran must be paid for in US dollars (cash or credit cards). Secondly, foreigners are often charged 10,000 to 15,000 rials to enter a tourist attraction, while Iranians pay as little as 500 rials. Thirdly, most mid-range hotels and all top end hotels are allowed to charge foreigners in US dollars. However, most mid-range places will accept rials, and negotiate; top end hotels rarely do either.

Currency

The official unit of currency is the rial. In conversation, Iranians usually refer to the *tōmān*, a unit of 10 rials, although in writing, prices are mostly expressed in rials. Since the unit of currency is often omitted, you have to make absolutely sure whether you're talking about rials or tōmāns before settling on a price. There are coins for 250, 100 and 50 rials, and notes for 10,000, 5000, 1000, 500, 200 and 100 rials. The 100 and 200 rials notes are rare, and the 5000 and 10,000 rials notes come in two different versions.

Exchange Rates

At the time of research, the *official* exchange rates, set by the Central Bank of Iran, were:

country	unit		rials
Australia	A$1	=	1121 rials
Canada	C$1	=	1178 rials
euro	€1	=	1863 rials
France	10FF	=	2840 rials
Germany	DM1	=	952 rials
Japan	¥100	=	1605 rials
New Zealand	NZ$1	=	904 rials
UK	UK£1	=	2826 rials
USA	US$1	=	1756 rials

These rates are virtually meaningless, however, but make sure the banks in Iran don't use these rates when changing travellers cheques, or giving cash advances. There are three ways to change money (preferably US dollars): at the official, and unfavourable, exchange rate at a bank; at the favourable 'street rate' at a legal, though uncommon, money exchange office; and on the illegal black market, anywhere.

Exchanging Money

Ironically, the major currency for tourism and trade is the US dollar. Bring only US dollars in *cash*, although UK pounds and German Deutschmarks (both in cash) are accepted at most banks and money exchange offices.

Don't bring any types of travellers cheques of any denomination or currency unless you absolutely, positively must. The only banks where you can reliably change travellers cheques are: the Bank Melli branches at the international airport and on Kheyābūn-é Ferdōsī, both in Tehrān; and in Shīrāz. And when you change travellers cheques you may have to wait an hour for the paperwork, while the exchange rate will be far less than the 'street rate' and you may be charged up to 10% commission. American Express (Amex) travellers cheques are not accepted anywhere because of the US trade embargo.

The major branches of most banks will change US dollars in cash (and often Deutschmarks and UK pounds) at the rate of about US$1 to 5750 rials. Money exchange offices happily offer a 'street rate' of about US$1 to 7500 rials, and, usually, Deutschmarks at about DM1 to 4400 rials and UK pounds at about UK£1 to 12,000 rials. Black market traders on the street want only US dollars, and offer about US$1 to 7800 rials, but it's not worth the risk of getting caught by police, or indeed the risk of getting ripped off. (The rate will increase if there are any real or possible future economic or social problems.) Change as much money as you can at the money exchange offices mentioned in the relevant sections later in this chapter.

Top end hotels will change money at the bank rate (ie about US$1 to 5750 rials), while some mid-range hotels, and a few budget places, will change money at the 'street rate' (ie about US$1 to 7500 rials) if you ask discreetly.

Other Currencies In Bandar-é Abbās, there is a black market in United Arab Emirates (UAE) *dirhams*, and in the north there is a small trade in Russian *roubles*. Turkish *lira* is treated with scorn everywhere, except near the Turkish border, and Pakistani *rupees* are bought and sold at Zāhedān. You can often buy currencies of neighbouring countries with rials at major towns near the relevant border, but the black market traders at either side of the borders are the easiest way of initially changing money.

Credit Cards & ATMs
Some mid-range hotels, all top end hotels, major souvenir shops, larger travel agencies and all airline offices accept Visa and/or MasterCard – but not Amex. However, if your Visa or MasterCard has been issued in the USA, it may not be accepted because of the USA trade embargo. Before you use a credit card, find out which exchange rate the bank(s) will use.

You can also use Visa or MasterCard for cash advances (in rials) at the central branches of Bank Melli at most major cities. However, banks usually charge up to 5% commission, you may have to wait an hour or two for authorisation and the exchange rate will be unfavourable compared to the 'street rate'.

Tipping & Bargaining
In most cases, tipping is no more and no less than it should be – an optional reward for good service.

Fares in private taxis are always negotiable, but not in any other form of transport – including a shared taxi – because these prices are set by the government. Rates in all hotels are open to negotiation, except most top end places. Prices in restaurants are set; food in bazaars (but not in shops) is sometimes negotiable, but probably not worth the effort. Everything else is definitely negotiable, particularly handicrafts.

POST & COMMUNICATIONS
Postal Rates
Postcards by air mail to Europe, North America and Australasia cost 400 rials. The cost for a normal-sized letter by air mail to these regions is about 1000 rials. The cost for packages per 500g/1kg is 17,500/39,225 rials for Australasia; 15,750/27,450 rials for Europe; and 17,500/30,950 rials for North America.

Sending Mail
The Iranian international postal service is generally reliable and reasonably swift; the domestic service is reliable, but slow. Some of the Iranian stamps are very colourful – leave enough space on your envelope or postcard for the stamps.

Sending parcels out of Iran is a major exercise in form shuffling. Take your unwrapped package to the *daftar-é amānāt-é postī* (parcel post counter) at the *postkhūné-yé markazī* (head post office) in any provincial capital. The package will be checked, packaged and signed for in triplicate. Major post offices offer an EMS express mail and parcel service.

Receiving Mail
You can receive mail, including parcels, at the head post office in any major city; the most reliable poste restante services are at the post office at Meidūn-é Emām Khomeinī (Tehrān) and at the head post offices in Shīrāz and Esfahān. Poste restante mail is normally

IRAN

held indefinitely, despite requests for it to be forwarded. There is a nominal collection fee and you need to take your passport.

Telephone

The country code for Iran is ☎ 98, followed by the area code (minus the zero), then the subscriber number. Area codes for major cities and regions are:

Bam	☎ 03447
Bandar-é Abbās	☎ 0761
Būshehr	☎ 0771
Chālūs	☎ 0191
Esfahān	☎ 031
Ghazvīn	☎ 0281
Hamadān	☎ 0261
Kermān	☎ 0341
Kermānshāh	☎ 0431
Kīsh Island	☎ 07653
Mākū	☎ 04634
Mashhad	☎ 051
Nōshahr	☎ 0191
Orūmīyé	☎ 0441
Rāmsar	☎ 01942
Rasht	☎ 0131
Shīrāz	☎ 071
Tabrīz	☎ 041
Tehrān	☎ 021
Yazd	☎ 0351
Zāhedān	☎ 0541

Making telephone calls within Iran, and overseas, is fairly easy. In Tehrān, you can buy a *kard telefon*, but very few telephones accept these telephone cards. Most public telephone boxes are only good for local calls. They only accept 5 or 10 rial coins, but because these coins are almost impossible to find, locals usually use private telephones in shops (50 rials per three minutes). Local calls are so cheap that your hotel will probably let you make a few local calls for nothing. Airports and major bus stations usually have at least one free public telephone.

International calls can be made at a *markazī-é telefon* or *edāre-yé koll-yém okhābarāt* (telephone office), or from a smaller, private telephone office, in any town – but it's far easier from major cities.

Long-distance calls can also be made from most hotels for an additional fee. International calls are charged a minimum period of three minutes, plus each subsequent minute (or part thereof). The cost per minute is 8200 rials to Europe; 10,500 rials to Australasia; and 15,400 rials to North America.

Fax & Telegram

Faxes can often be sent from the main post and/or telephone office in any provincial capital, and from most mid-range and top end hotels. Sending a fax from Iran isn't cheap (about 12,000 rials per page to Europe), so if you only want to send a few words, a telegram may be cheaper (less than 200 rials per word to Europe) but not, of course, as quick. Telegrams (in English) can be sent overseas from most main telephone offices.

Email & Internet Access

There are a couple of Internet service providers in Iran, one of the largest of which is Neda Net (www.neda.net.ir). The Net is not widely available to the general public, however; it's derided by the authorities and prohibitively expensive for most locals. Internet centres (cafes) are located in Tehrān and Yazd – refer to those sections for details.

BOOKS

One of the classics is *The Road to Oxiana*, by Robert Byron, widely acknowledged as one of the great travel books of its era. Although Byron has a scholarly preoccupation with Islamic architecture, the book is lively and worth bringing.

Many books have been written about personal experiences before, during or after the Islamic Revolution (1979). *Out of Iran*, by Sousan Azadi, is a revealing, though one-sided, autobiography of the western Iranian elite who stayed in Iran after the Revolution. *Lifting the Veil* (first published as *Behind Iranian Lines*) by John Simpson & Tira Shubart is one of the best accounts of life after the Revolution.

One of the few authentic travel narratives is *Danziger's Travel: Beyond Forbidden*

Frontiers, by Nick Danziger, who travelled throughout the region with no regard for tiresome formalities like visas. The book is loaded with enough hair-raising adventures to make all travellers feel inadequate. *A Short Walk in the Hindu Kush*, by Eric Newby, is a glorious and eccentric account of a haphazard jaunt to the Hindu Kush, via Iran. The fearless Freya Stark wrote several accounts of her travels around Iran in the 1930s, including *Valleys of the Assassins*.

Some novels in English, French and German are available from a couple of bookshops in Tehrān, but you would be well advised to bring your own reading material. Most bookshops in Iran also carry a number of excellent souvenir books (mostly English, but often in French and German) about Iranian poetry, handicrafts, culture and attractions like Esfahān, Persepolis and Bam.

More general Middle East titles, some of which also contain coverage of Iran, are listed in the Books section in the Regional Facts for the Visitor chapter at the beginning of this book.

NEWSPAPERS & MAGAZINES

If you ignore the extreme bias against the USA and Israel, the English-language daily newspapers printed in Tehrān are not too bad. *Iran Daily* is easy to read; *Iran News* toes the official line, but has a good world news section and some handy classifieds; and *Tehran Times* has the best cartoons and classifieds. *Kayhan International*, however, is a translation of the uninteresting government mouthpiece printed in Fārsī.

In a few major cities, the latest issues of *Time*, *Newsweek* and *National Geographic* are sometimes available but prices are high.

RADIO & TV

All Iranian radio and television stations are heavily controlled by the state. Most of the numerous radio stations are based in Tehrān, and relayed to each province. As well as programs in minority languages such as Kurdish, Lorī and Āzārī, there are programs in English, Spanish, French and Arabic – but don't rely on them for impartial news coverage. The BBC World Service, most European international radio services and Voice of America can be picked up clearly in most parts of Iran.

Iranian television is so boring that most Iranians don't bother watching it. International satellite stations, such as MTV and CNN, are only available at top end hotels and in upper class homes (with special permission). From cities along the coast of the Persian Gulf, and islands within the Gulf, English-language television stations, including the BBC, can be picked up from Bahrain and Kuwait.

PHOTOGRAPHY & VIDEO

Most towns have at least one photographic shop for film and/or development, though the range of available film and camera equipment is limited (except in Tehrān and Mashhad). A roll of 24 print film costs about 11,500 rials; slide film, including processing, is 29,000 rials. All over Iran there are small backroom photographers; many of them do passport photos very cheaply (about 9000 rials for four).

Bring your own video cassettes, but remember that customs officials are eager to confiscate blank or used video cassettes on arrival if they believe there's any likelihood of something 'immoral' on the tape. One way around this is to keep video tapes in their original wrappings until you have passed through customs.

LAUNDRY

There are reliable laundry services in most cities but no do-it-yourself laundrettes. Many hotels also have a laundry service for guests. Invariably, your clothes will be scrubbed thoroughly, lovingly ironed, and wrapped in a newspaper. Prices are cheap. You should wash your 'smalls' in a hotel sink; hot water is plentiful and washing detergent and soaps are widely available.

TOILETS

Toilets are either the European sit-down type, or the Middle Eastern squat kind, but a US$40 hotel room may still have a hole in

IRAN

the ground, so always be prepared for this. Public toilets are uncommon and generally unpleasant. Toilet paper is only reliably provided in top end hotels, but is available in most grocery shops in major cities.

HEALTH

No compulsory vaccinations are needed before visiting Iran. Malaria is very uncommon, but there have been rare cases of cholera.

If you're mildly sick, seek advice from someone at your hotel, or an Iranian friend. They should be able to find a reputable doctor who speaks English and will hopefully come to your hotel. If your situation is more serious, your embassy should be able to recommend a reputable doctor and/or hospital and possibly arrange everything.

The standard of medical facilities varies greatly. The best place to get ill or injured is Tehrān, which has a disproportionate number of doctors and medical establishments. Doctors' surgeries and pharmacies (drug stores) are often clustered around major hospitals; surgeries often have signs outside their building with the doctor's name and specialty in English. Pharmacies are usually well-stocked (but always check expiry dates) and staff often speak English.

For more general health information see the Health section in the Regional Facts for the Visitor chapter.

WOMEN TRAVELLERS

The big hassle is having to cover up – see the boxed text 'Dress Code' earlier in this chapter. The good news is that any woman who has travelled – make that struggled – through Pakistan and/or Turkey will feel far more comfortable and at ease in Iran. The sexual harassment and constant come-ons from the local males that are common in these other countries (and indeed throughout much of the Middle East) are largely absent in Iran. By comparison, women enjoy considerably more independence in Iran than elsewhere in the region (see the boxed text 'Women in Iranian Society'). One welcome consequence of this is that female visitors will find it quite easy to meet and chat with Iranian women.

DANGERS & ANNOYANCES

Open hostility towards western visitors (including Americans) is extremely rare. The Iranian police have a far better reputation for probity and efficiency than their counterparts in other countries in the region. There are a number of police forces (the exact name of the forces, and their uniforms, even confuse locals), but as long as you behave yourself, and dress appropriately, you will normally receive nothing but a smile, and a helping hand if you need it. If you're arrested, or taken away for questioning, demand identification, insist on telephoning your consulate/embassy, and find an interpreter if you don't speak Fārsī.

A few travellers have been stopped in the street by bogus plain-clothes policemen. *Never* show or give any important documents or money to any policeman in the street; always insist on going to the police station, or claim that your valuables are at your hotel. If the 'policeman' won't accompany you to the police station, or your hotel, loudly enlist support from locals.

Baggage inspections, and occasional body frisks, are routine for everyone on entry to some public buildings, train stations and ports, at all airports, and at some public gatherings. There are frequent roadblocks/checkpoints around the countryside, especially near the borders of Afghanistan and Pakistan, but these are normally painless.

Iran is no stranger to political crises, and huge, often frightening, government-organised marches are sometimes held in major cities. Always stay well clear of all political marches and gatherings.

In February 1999, a German working in Iran was taken hostage and killed near Qom. A few months later, three Italian workers were kidnapped near Bam, and then released unharmed a week later. These incidents were not politically motivated, but undertaken by Iranian drug traffickers seeking money or the release of colleagues from prison. There is no evidence that foreigners are being targeted (almost all drug-related crime is against locals), but it pays to be aware of the situation and spend as little

Women in Iranian Society

Most visitors to Iran understandably equate the strict dress regulations imposed on Iranian (and foreign) women with oppression of Iranian women in general. Iranian women are often paradoxically better off than women in many other Islamic countries and societies, where the laws and traditions about divorce (and child custody), polygamy (for men), female infanticide, rape, female circumcision and the minimum age of marriage (for women), as well as education, dress and suffrage, are often very strict.

In Iran, women are able to receive the same level of education as males, and women are as (under)represented in positions of power in Iran as in many western countries: in Iran, many women are doctors, and some are family court judges and members of parliament. President Khatamī was elected in 1997 with a very strong female vote, and he subsequently appointed a female vice-president and two female cabinet ministers.

In more secular countries such as Jordan, Lebanon and Turkey, and more liberal countries with a significant foreign population such as Bahrain and the United Arab Emirates, there are little or no legal restrictions for women, but strict traditions about dress, behaviour and marriage prevail in many families.

In Saudi Arabia, Iraq, Afghanistan and Iran, however, women are legally required to wear the hejāb (ie cloak and head covering), and men and women are commonly segregated in restaurants and public transport. Saudi Arabia goes further: men and women often use separate entrances to public buildings, and local women cannot drive cars or travel on any transport without an accompanying male. The regulations imposed on women by the ruling (but internationally unrecognised) Taliban forces in Afghanistan are so severe they offend almost every Muslim: women must cover all parts of the body and are rarely allowed outside their homes, and cannot get education or work.

---

time as possible between Bam and the Pakistan border, and avoid anywhere near the Afghanistan border.

BUSINESS HOURS

Few places have uniform opening and closing times, but most close on Friday. Most government offices open from 8 am to 2 pm Saturday to Wednesday, and close at noon on Thursday. Many shops and businesses close during the afternoon for a 'siesta' (from about 1 pm to 3 or 4 pm), and open again in the evenings. Along the blistering Persian Gulf, the 'siesta' sensibly stretches until about 5 pm. The only thing that does not stop during the 'siesta' is public transport.

PUBLIC HOLIDAYS & SPECIAL EVENTS

In addition to the main Islamic holidays described in the Public Holidays & Special Events section in the Regional Facts for the Visitor chapter at the beginning of this book, Iran observes:

Ghadir-é Khom
    18 Zu-l-Hejjé (changeable) – the day that the Prophet Mohammed appointed Emām Alī as his successor
Ashura
    9 & 10 Moharram (changeable) – anniversary of the martyrdom of Hussein, the third emām of the Shi'ites; celebrated with religious dramas and sombre parades
International Qods Day
    Last Friday of Ramazān (Ramadan) (changeable) – when many Iranians take to the streets to protest against the Israeli 'occupation' of Palestine
Arbaeen
    20 & 21 Safar (changeable) – the 40th day after 9 & 10 Moharram (mentioned above)
Anniversary of Khomeini's rise to power
    11 February (22 Bahman)
Oil Nationalisation Day
    20 March (29 Esfand)

Nō Rūz
    around 21 to 24 March (1 to 4 Farvardīn) –
    Iranian New Year (see below)
Islamic Republic Day
    1 April (12 Farvardīn) – anniversary of the establishment of the Islamic Republic of Iran in 1979.
Sīzdah Bedar
    2 April (13 Farvardīn) – 13th day after the Iranian New Year, when most Iranians leave their houses for the day.
Death of Emām Khomeinī
    4 June (14 Khordād) – particularly chaotic in Tehrān and Qom.
Arrest of Emām Khomeinī
    5 June (15 Khordād)
Anniversary of a bomb blast in 1980
    28 June (7 Tīr) – happened at a meeting of the Islamic Republic Party.
Day of the Martyrs of the Revolution
    8 September (17 Shahrīvar)

Nō Rūz

The Iranian New Year, or Nō Rūz, is a huge family celebration. Starting on about the spring equinox (around 21 March), Iranians traditionally return to their home villages and towns to celebrate with friends and relatives. It's exceptionally difficult to find hotel accommodation about 10 days before and after the New Year, and all forms of public transport are very heavily booked. Most businesses (but not hotels), including many restaurants, will close for about five days after the start of the New Year. This is *not* a good time to travel around Iran.

ACCOMMODATION

In Iran our term 'budget' hotels encompasses *mosāferkhūnés* (basic guesthouses), a few backpacker lodges and one and two-star hotels, all of which offer reasonable prices for foreigners. 'Mid-range' is two and three-star hotels and 'top end' is four and five-star hotels. There are also 'homestays' (a room in someone's home) and 'suites' (fully equipped apartments) in the Caspian provinces.

All but the cheapest places have rooms with private bathrooms (and hot water), and a fan and/or heater. Don't bother paying more for a room with a telephone (which you probably won't use), fridge (which may not work) or TV (only the top end places have satellite TV). The price difference between a double room in a good mid-range hotel (price negotiated and payable in rials) and a top end hotel (not negotiable, and payable in US dollars) can be as much as US$70 per day, but the main difference is that the top end place has satellite TV and maybe a tennis court and/or swimming pool.

Most mid-range hotels, and all top end places, can – and will – charge foreigners much more than Iranians, and in US dollars. Most mid-range hotels are open to negotiation, however, and will accept rials at a negotiable rate – top end hotels will rarely do either. All guests (Iranian and foreign) must fill out a registration form, which can be tiresome if there is no common language. Hotel management usually want to keep your passport during your stay, because a police/security officer may come at any time and ask to see it. Check-out is usually at 2 pm.

Some mosāferkhūnés will not accept foreigners due to local police regulations – this tends to happen in Būshehr, Bandar-é Abbās, Hamadān, Tabrīz, Kermānshāh, Esfahān, Mashhad, Kāshān and Rasht. You can avoid this discrimination by obtaining a special permit from the local police station allowing you to stay at any mosāferkhūné in that town/city. The permit is often not worth the hassle because there's always a mosāferkhūné somewhere that *will* accept foreigners.

Camping is not really a viable option. There are no camp sites, and authorities don't like anyone – least of all foreigners – pitching tents in the countryside except nomads.

FOOD

Iranian food varies considerably from the Middle Eastern norm. The diet is heavily based on rice, bread, fresh vegetables, herbs and fruit. Rice in general is called *berenj*. *Chelō* is boiled and steamed rice and is often the base for meals such as *chelō morgh* (chicken and rice). Rice cooked with other ingredients, such as nuts and spices, is called *polō*. Saffron is frequently used to flavour and colour the rice.

Iranian bread, known generally as *nūn*, is always fresh and delicious. *Lavāsh* is a flat and very thin type of bread that is folded twice into a square; *sangak* is thicker, oval-shaped and pulpy, and baked on a bed of stones to give it its characteristic dimpled look; *taftūn* is crisp, thick and oval-shaped, with a characteristic ribbed surface; and *barbarī* is crisp and salty, with a glazed and finely latticed crust.

Māst is similar to Greek or Turkish yoghurt. It's commonly used as a cooking ingredient, often mixed with rice, and comes with diced cucumber or other vegetables, fresh herbs and spices.

Sūp (Iranian soup) is thick and filling. Even thicker is *āsh*, more of a pottage or broth; thicker still is *ābgūsht*, which is commonly served as a main dish. *Khōresht* is a blanket term for any kind of thick meaty stew with vegetables and chopped nuts. It's usually delicious and a tasty alternative to boring, ubiquitous kabābs. One popular delicacy is *fesenjān* – a stew of duck, goose or chicken in a rich sauce of pomegranate juice and chopped walnuts.

The main dish in restaurants is the *kabāb*, a long thin strip of meat or mince served as chelō kabāb (with a mound of rice), or with bread and grilled tomatoes. There are different varieties: *fillé kabāb* is made from lamb, and invariably delicious; *kabāb-é makhsūs* is a larger strip of decent meat; *kabāb-é barg* is thinner and varies in quality; *kabāb-é kūbīdé* is made of minced meat with heaven knows what else; and *jūjé kabāb* is made of chicken, and is more expensive.

The main vegetarian alternative is soup and salad, often part of a meal in any decent restaurant anyway. Vegetarians can easily buy their own food at the market: nuts, fruits and vegetables, such as cucumbers, tomatoes and pickles, are excellent, commonly available and cheap. There is also plenty of fresh bread, as well as cheese and eggs for nonvegans.

DRINKS

The national drink is undoubtedly *chāy* (tea). It's always served scalding-hot, black and strong, and traditionally in a small glass cup, but western-style tea bags are a depressingly common alternative these days. Only upmarket hotel restaurants will offer milk with tea (or coffee).

Ghahvé (Iranian coffee) is the same as Turkish coffee. Remember to let the brew settle and then only drink three-quarters of it. Iranian coffee is served strong, black and sweet. 'Nescafe' is the generic term for western-style powdered coffee, often served from sachets with powdered milk and sugar. If you prefer the real stuff, bring it from home or Turkey, and ask for hot water.

All sorts of delicious fresh fruit juices and milkshakes are available. Outside Tehrān, the tap water varies widely in quality, but it's generally safe to drink everywhere. Bottles of mineral water are not widely available, so one excellent way to replenish the internal liquid supply is to slurp on a cold water fountain at an airline office, bank or museum.

Dūgh is made of churned sour milk or yoghurt, mixed with either sparkling or still water and often flavoured with mint and other ground herbs – definitely an acquired taste. All sorts of soft drinks (sodas) are available, including the USA icons Pepsi and Coke. *Mā'-osh-sha'īr* ('Iranian beer'), often labelled as 'nonalcoholic malt beverage', tastes like, well, nonalcoholic beer.

SPECTATOR SPORTS

Football (soccer) is the major sport. The national competition lasts from about October to June, and games are played throughout the country on Thursday and Friday. Iran has a fine international side that qualified for the 1998 World Cup, and several Iranians play in major European football leagues.

Second in popularity is wrestling, which you can sometimes witness (if you ask around) at a *zurkané*. Cricket is played at Chābahār and Tehrān but if the 'gentlemen's

IRAN

game' is a little too sedate for you, go to the auto drag races at Āzādī Stadium in Tehrān. (Most visitors will appreciate the extreme irony of paying money to witness hundreds of Iranian cars scream around in a frenzied circle.)

In Sīstān va Balūchestān province, there is traditional camel racing.

SHOPPING

Iran is a buyers' market for souvenirs, and you'll find it hard not to pick up a thing or two (or more). Thanks largely to the shortage of tourists, mass production is not common, prices are low and the quality is generally high. Naturally, the bazaar is the best place to start looking, but in Esfahān, Shīrāz and any place where foreign tourists are more common, it's harder to get a good price. Some great souvenirs include ceramics, hand-beaten bronzeware and copperware, inlaid boxes, tea-sets, hubble-bubble pipes, jewellery, spices, silk products, glassware, miniatures and, of course, carpets and rugs – refer to the boxed text 'Persian Carpets' later in this chapter.

If you don't like bargaining, and don't have time to look around, the government-run Iran Handicrafts Organisation has stores in most provincial capitals. Often knowing the best place to buy a souvenir is as important as getting a good price – refer to Shopping in the Esfahān, Kermān, Mashhad, Shīrāz, Tehrān and Yazd sections for more ideas of what to buy.

General Export Restrictions

Officially, you need permission to export anything 'antique' (ie more than 50 years old), including handicrafts, gemstones, coins and manuscripts. There is also some sort of prohibition on the export of large quantities of saffron. To send home by mail a few books (whether old or new; Islamic or not), get permission from the Ministry of Culture & Islamic Guidance in Tehrān. Travellers have also reported troubles in sending carpets (but not kilims) home by mail – refer to the boxed text 'Persian Carpets' later in this chapter for details.

If you're worried about whether an expensive item will be confiscated, contact the *edāré-yé gomrok* (local customs office) before buying anything, or place it carefully in your hand luggage, which is rarely searched on departure.

Getting There & Away

AIR

Airports & Airlines

Iran's main international airport is in the western suburbs of Tehrān. For details of getting to/from the airport see the Getting Around section of Tehrān.

The national carrier is Iran Air, though a few smaller Iranian airlines, such as Iran Asseman, also offer a handful of international flights. Iran Air is not a bad airline but it doesn't serve alcohol and female passengers have to wear the hejāb. It has a vast network of flights between Tehrān and Europe and Asia, and between Tehrān, Ahvāz, Bandar-é Abbās, Būshehr, Esfahān, Shīrāz and Tabrīz and the Middle East and Central Asian republics. Iran is also reasonably well covered by other regional airlines like Gulf Air, Emirates and Kuwait Airways. There are no flights on any airline directly between Iran and North America or Australia.

Flights to Iran are not particularly cheap, but flying into regional centres such as Shīrāz, Tabrīz and Bandar-é Abbās is cheaper than flying to (and nicer places to start/finish your trip than Tehrān). The number of flights and fares generally increase during the Iranian summer, and flights are heavily booked about 10 days before and after the Iranian New Year (which starts on about 21 March).

Buying International Tickets in Iran

Foreigners must pay for tickets on international flights out of Iran with US dollars (cash or major credit cards). There are no particularly cheap flights from Iran, and flights are no cheaper at travel agencies than airline offices. One-way fares are expensive. For example, on Iran Air, a flight from Tehrān to London (also good for connections to the USA) costs US$690; to Frankfurt (for connections elsewhere in Europe), US$645; and to Kuala Lumpur (for connections to Australia), US$644.

Departure Tax

The tax for all international flights is a hefty 70,000 rials, but if you buy your international ticket within Iran the departure tax is often included, especially on Iran Air and Gulf Air. Check with the airline when you book your ticket or confirm your reservation.

LAND
Border Crossings

Afghanistan No border is open with Afghanistan.

Armenia & Azebaijan Between Iran and Azerbaijan, the border crossing at Āstārā/Astara is currently closed to foreigners; and between Iran and Armenia the situation is unclear and the crossings themselves unsafe – check with the relevant embassies/consulates first.

Iraq The situation concerning Iran-Iraq border crossings is unclear and the crossings themselves unsafe – check with the relevant embassies/consulates first.

Pakistan The only border crossing between Iran and Pakistan is at Mīrjāvé/Taftan – see the Getting There & Away chapter at the beginning of this book for details.

Turkey There are two crossings. Serō (Iran) and Yüksekova (Turkey) is rarely used by foreigners because it involves travelling through parts of east and south-east Turkey, which is unsafe because of conflict between Turkish authorities and Kurdish separatists. It is far safer, easier and often more convenient to cross at Bāzārgān and Gürbülak.

There are direct Iran-Turkey (or vice versa) buses across the border but it is far quicker to catch a bus, minibus or shared taxi to either border, cross the border independently, and then catch onward transport rather than wait for the rest of the bus to clear customs and immigration. Foreigners are usually whisked across the border very quickly.

Turkmenistan The only border crossing between Iran and Turkmenistan is at Sarakhs/Saraghs – see the Getting There & Away chapter at the beginning of this book for details.

SEA
Azerbaijan

The only ferry to/from Iran across the Caspian Sea is the service between Baku (Azerbaijan) and Bandar-é Anzalī, but this only operates in summer. For more details see the Getting There & Away chapter at the beginning of this book.

Kuwait & the UAE

Passenger ferries reliably sail across the Persian Gulf between Būshehr, Bandar-é Abbās and Bandar-é Lengé, and Kuwait and the UAE. The ferries are operated by the Valfajre-8 Shipping Company, whose head office (☎ 889 2933, fax 892 409) is on Kūché-é Abyar, corner of Shahīd Azadī and Karīm Khān-é Zand streets in Tehrān.

from	to	cost US$ (one way/ return)	day(s)
Khorram-shahr	Kuwait	120/232	Sat, Mon, Wed
Būshehr	Qatar	105/210	temporarily suspended at time of research
Bandar-é Abbās	Dubai	55/110	Tues
Bandar-é Abbās	Sharjah	38/76	once a week; days changeable

IRAN

Getting Around

AIR

Iran is one of the cheapest countries in the world for domestic flights, especially if you've changed money at the 'street rate'. Try to book tickets as soon as possible, although you can usually get on the flight you want (except during the Iranian New Year). If the airline office or travel agency claim the flight is 'full', you will still probably have luck with a standby ticket at the airport. If you pre-book domestic flights overseas, tickets must be paid for in foreign currency, and cost a lot more.

The main domestic airline, Iran Air, has regular services to just about anywhere you want to go. The airline is reliable, safe, efficient and fully computerised. Ask for the very useful pocket-sized timetable from an Iran Air office. Other smaller airlines, such as Iran Asseman, Caspian Airlines and Kish Airlines, have limited and erratic schedules, and are not as reliable. Contact details for Iran Air offices are mentioned in the individual Getting There & Away sections later in this chapter. For other airlines, book at an authorised travel agent.

All of the following Iran Air services are at least daily:

from	to	one way (rials)	hours
Bandar-é Abbās	Esfahān	122,000	1½ hrs
	Shīrāz	79,500	70 mins
	Tehrān	161,500	2 hours
Esfahān	Mashhad	128,000	1½ hrs
	Shīrāz	70,000	70 mins
	Tehrān	70,000	1 hour
Kermān	Tehrān	122,500	70 mins
Kermānshāh	Tehrān	74,000	1 hour
Mashhad	Shīrāz	144,500	1¾ hrs
	Tehrān	116,000	1¾ hrs
Orūmīyé	Tehrān	94,500	80 mins
Rasht	Tehrān	70,000	1 hour
Shīrāz	Tehrān	106,500	1½ hrs
Tabrīz	Tehrān	87,000	70 mins
Tehrān	Yazd	85,500	80 mins
Tehrān	Zāhedān	160,000	2 hours

BUS & MINIBUS

Iran is extremely well covered by bus and minibus. Fares are very cheap and services are regular. Most buses are comfortable, with individual cushioned seats; and standing is not normally allowed. The best companies, with the most extensive networks, are TBT and Cooperative Bus Company No 1, while Sayro Safar has the most modern fleet. It's normally OK to go on whatever bus is heading your way, but you may want to look around for a decent bus for long or overnight trips.

There are usually two classes of long-distance bus: 'lux', which is cheaper, and 'super', which is more expensive and more comfortable. However, for short distances, the difference is marginal. Don't count on averaging more than 60km/h on most routes. Although many journeys run overnight, it's difficult to sleep well on buses, though some prefer travelling at night in summer, when the daytime heat can be unbearable.

In a few remote places, you may need to hail a passing bus (or minibus or shared taxi); roadblocks, roundabouts and junctions are the best places to hail something. In most towns, you can buy tickets up to one week in advance at the terminal, or at a bus company office (if there is one) in town. From one major city to another, eg Shīrāz to Esfahān, a bus from one company or another leaves every 15 minutes or so, but departures are less frequent in more remote places, and between smaller towns.

Minibuses are often used for shorter distances and between less populated places. Minibuses are often faster than buses, and carry fewer passengers, so they spend less time dropping off and picking up passengers. However, minibuses are not as comfortable; you can't pre-book a ticket; they usually only leave when full; and as many passengers as possible are squeezed in.

TRAIN

There are services from Tehrān to Tabrīz, Ahvāz, Esfahān, Bandar-é Abbās, Kermān and Mashhad, but Iran is not nearly as well covered by train as it is by bus and plane. Trains can be comfortable (in 1st class), efficient, reasonably fast, cheap and good for overnight travel, but they're far less frequent than buses, minibuses and shared taxis; schedules are infrequent to popular places like Esfahān and Kermān, and nonexistent to places like Shīrāz; buying a ticket can be difficult; departure and arrival times for most places along a route are often lousy; and waiting for a train is just a waste of time.

All trains have two classes; some have three. It's always worth paying a little more for 1st class compartments, but if you buy a ticket from any town along a route (ie not at the starting or finishing point), you may only be able to buy a 2nd class ticket (but you can probably upgrade to 1st class along the way). On trains that travel overnight, 1st class has sleepers – four or six bunks in a small carriage, like in India, Pakistan and Turkey. In Tehrān, Esfahān, Tabrīz and Mashhad, tickets are available up to 15 days in advance for a 20% surcharge, but it's often not possible to book a return ticket. Food and drink is normally available on longer trips.

LONG DISTANCE TAXI

Shared taxis – often referred to as a *savarī* – are normally available between any major town less than four hours away by car. Speed is the main advantage, because shared taxis are generally more uncomfortable than the bus (but better than the minibus). Shared taxis cost about three times more than the 'lux' ticket on a bus, but are still cheap, and worth using for a quick trip, especially through dull countryside. If you wish to speed up a departure, or crave a little extra comfort, pay for an empty seat, or charter the entire vehicle. Shared taxis normally leave from inside, or just outside, the relevant bus terminal, though some towns have special terminals.

CAR & MOTORCYCLE

Driving your own vehicle obviously gives you more flexibility, but distances across Iran are great, the countryside is often boring, and the traffic is truly horrendous – nearly 14,000 people die on Iranian roads each year. Road surfaces throughout Iran are generally excellent, but the roads are poor or unpaved in remote desert and mountainous regions. Just about every road sign you'll ever need is in English. Never drive off the main road near the Pakistani, Iraqi or Afghani borders.

In theory, the rule of the road is to drive on the right. Leaded petrol currently costs 200 rials per litre (but is due to rise to 350 rials soon). Unleaded petrol is rarely available (or leaded fuel is sold as 'unleaded'). Petrol stations are open every day in, or just outside of, every major town. The outskirts of every city, town and village has filthy shops where you can arrange repairs.

The main automobile organisation is the Touring & Automobile Club of the Islamic Republic of Iran (☎ 8740 411, fax 8740 410), 12 Kheyābūn-é Nobakht, Kheyābūn-é Khorramshahr, Tehrān, PO Box 15875/5617. If you are driving, carry a good map, preferably in Fārsī and English (see Maps under Planning earlier in this chapter).

Rental

A couple of car rental agencies in Tehrān advertise in the *Tehrān Times* and *Iran News*. For example, '24 Hours Rent Cars' (☎ 021-824 490) has a vast number of tariffs, starting from about 130,000 rials per day. But remember: you can hire a taxi *and* a driver for about 90,000 rials per day, and the driver can cope with the appalling traffic.

ORGANISED TOURS

Few travel agencies in Iran organise trips for foreigners around Iran; but the agencies listed on the next page (all are based in Tehrān) can arrange some expensive tours.

The Getting Around the Region chapter at the beginning of this book also has a list of foreign agencies that organise trips to and around Iran.

Azadi International Tourism Organisation (☎ 8732 191, fax 8732 195, email aito@ www.dci.co.ir) Kheyābūn-é 8th, Kheyābūn-é Ahmād Gassir; PO Box 15875/1765

Caravan Sahra Co
(☎ 7502 229, fax 767 184, email caravan@neda.net) 125/4 Kheyābūn-é Sharī'atī; also has an office in the Laleh International Hotel

Iran Tours Corporation
(☎ 2255 440, fax 2254 330, email itcorp@sama.dpi.net.ir) 242 Kheyābūn-é East Vahid Dastgerdi

Iran Touring & Tourism Organisation
(☎ 656 715, fax 656 800) 154 Bolvār-é Keshāvarz

Tehrān

Iran is not blessed with one of the world's loveliest capitals. It suffers from pollution, chronic overcrowding and a lack of any responsible planning, so if you're expecting an exotic crossroads steeped in oriental splendour, you'll be sadly disappointed. However, the hotels and restaurants are good, its facilities are better than those in most places in the provinces, and there are some great museums. Most travellers end up in Tehrān for a couple of days anyway.

ORIENTATION

Tehrān is so vast that getting hopelessly lost at least once is a near certainty, but thankfully about 90% of the streets that you're likely to use are marked in English. If you need landmarks: the Alborz Mountains are to the north, and the huge telephone office at Meidūn-é Emām Khomeinī dominates inner southern Tehrān. Many north-south roads slope down as they head south, such as Kheyābūn-é Valī-yé Asr, which runs for more than 20km from Tajrīsh to the train station.

If you're using public transport, get to know the names and locations of the main squares as soon you can, and if you're staying a while, pick up the excellent *A Tourist Guide to Tehrān* map – see Maps under Planning earlier in this chapter.

INFORMATION
Visa Extensions

Tehrān used to be the worst place for visa extensions but you can now obtain an extension within 24 hours from friendly, English-speaking staff. Go to Department of Foreign Affairs (☎ 936 555) in the building occupied by the Disciplinary Force of the Islamic Republic of Iran, on Kheyābūn-é Khalantarī, just off Kheyābūn-é Nejātollāhī. It's open from 8 am to 1.30 pm daily except Friday.

Tourist Offices

There is *still* no tourist office in Tehrān. The tourist information booths at the train station and both airport terminals have English-speaking staff but are no good for any general information.

Money

If you arrive by air, change some money at a bank in the airport to pay for a taxi, at least. Most of the banks located along Kheyābūn-é Ferdōsī, and around Meidūn-é Ferdōsī, change money. The best is Bank Melli on Kheyābūn-é Ferdōsī, which also changes travellers cheques and gives cash advances on Visa and MasterCard. There are some black marketeers around Meidūn-é Ferdōsī, but the best place to change money is one of the money exchange offices along northern Kheyābūn-é Ferdōsī.

Post & Communications

The most convenient post office (which has a poste restante) and telephone office are around Meidūn-é Emām Khomeinī. Other post offices and telephone offices are located around major squares in the city.

Email & Internet Access Tehrān boasts a few Internet centres. The best is Rahe Ayandeh (☎ 8865 423, email cybercafe@neda.net) on Bolvār-é Keshāvarz, which charges 10,000 rials per 30 minutes. Staff are cluey and friendly but access is often very slow.

Bookshops

There are several bookshops around the city. The best are: Bookshop Sirus, Gulestan Bookshop and Argentin Bookshop, and there are good (but expensive)

GREATER TEHRĀN

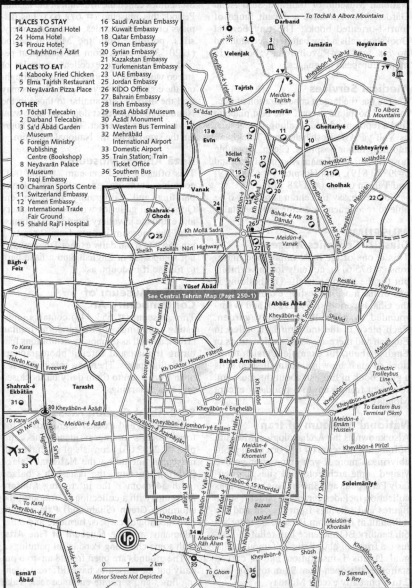

PLACES TO STAY
14 Azadi Grand Hotel
24 Homa Hotel
34 Pirouz Hotel;
   Chāykhūn-é Āzārī

PLACES TO EAT
4 Kabooky Fried Chicken
5 Elma Tajrīsh Restaurant
7 Neyāvarān Pizza Place

OTHER
1 Tōchāl Telecabin
2 Darband Telecabin
3 Sa'd Ābād Garden
   Museum
6 Foreign Ministry
   Publishing
   Centre (Bookshop)
8 Neyāvarān Palace
   Museum
9 Iraqi Embassy
10 Chamran Sports Centre
11 Switzerland Embassy
12 Yemen Embassy
13 International Trade
   Fair Ground
15 Shahīd Rajī'ī Hospital

16 Saudi Arabian Embassy
17 Kuwait Embassy
18 Qatar Embassy
19 Oman Embassy
20 Syrian Embassy
21 Kazakstan Embassy
22 Turkmenistan Embassy
23 UAE Embassy
25 Jordan Embassy
26 KIDO Office
27 Bahrain Embassy
28 Irish Embassy
29 Rezā Abbāsī Museum
30 Āzādī Monument
31 Western Bus Terminal
32 Mehrābād
   International Airport
33 Domestic Airport
35 Train Station; Train
   Ticket Office
36 Southern Bus
   Terminal

IRAN

bookshops inside most top end hotels. The National Museum of Iran and Sa'd Ābād Garden Museum have a decent range of tourist-oriented books. The tiny Ferdōsī Bookshop sells a few battered, secondhand novels, and pre-Revolutionary books, in major European languages.

Medical Services

Tehrān has the largest concentration of doctors and hospitals in Iran. The best place to find a reputable doctor is along streets such as Valī-yé Asr, Keshāvarz and Tāleghānī, and near major hospitals. Clean, reputable hospitals include Emām Khomeinī Hospital (☎ 9380 819), Pārs Hospital (☎ 6500 519) and Tehrān Clinic (☎ 8728 113).

Your embassy in Tehrān should also be able to recommend a doctor and hospital.

MUSEUMS
Glass & Ceramics Museum

This is one of the most impressive museums (☎ 675 614), not only for the exhibits but for the building itself. The building is one of the most interesting examples from the Ghajar period (1779-1921), and is surrounded by a small but lovely **garden**. Each piece in the museum is labelled in English and there are some explanations in English about, for example, Persian traditions of glass blowing. A small shop sells a guidebook in English about the museum. It's open from 9 am to 5 pm daily except Monday.

National Museum of Iran

Also known as the Archaeological Museum of Iran, this museum (☎ 672 061) will probably mean more if you come after you've visited some archaeological sites, particularly Persepolis and Shūsh. This marvellous collection includes ceramics, pottery, stone figures and carvings from the 5th and 4th millennium BC. From Persepolis, there's a 6th century BC audience hall relief of Darius I, a frieze of glazed tiles, a famous trilingual Darius I inscription and a carved staircase. It's open from 9 am to 1 pm and 2 to 5 pm daily except Monday.

Islamic Arts Museum

Sometimes called the Museum of the Islamic Period, this museum (☎ 672 655) has displays of carpets, textiles, ceramics, pottery, silks, portraits from the Mongol period (1220-1380), coins from the Sassanian period (224-637), and excellent examples of stucco work from various mosques throughout the country. However, some visitors may find the displays are similar to those in the National Museum next door, and may want to visit one or the other. The opening hours are the same as for the National Museum.

Rezā Abbāsī Museum

This often-ignored museum (☎ 863 001) contains stunning examples of Islamic painting and calligraphy from ancient Qurans, and galleries with delicate pottery and exquisite jewellery from several dynasties. The museum is open from 9 am to 1 pm and 2 to 6 pm daily except Tuesday. It's not signposted in English, and a little hard to find so if in doubt, ask.

Tehrān Museum of Contemporary Art

This museum (☎ 653 445) contains interesting paintings from modern Iranian artists, as well as temporary exhibitions featuring Iranian and foreign photographers and calligraphers. There is a cafe inside. It's open from 9 am to 6 pm daily but is closed on Friday morning.

Sa'd Ābād Garden Museum

In the pretty and extensive grounds of the former shāh's summer residence, this complex (☎ 2282 031) consists of several small museums, including the **National Palace (White) Museum**, the last shāh's palace (with 54 rooms); the interesting **Military Museum**, with a collection of armoury; the enormous **Green (Shahvand) Palace**, with its collection of carpets, furniture and other oddments; and the **Museum of Fine Arts**, with some charming Persian oil paintings.

The grounds are open from 8 am to 6 pm daily but the museums have different opening times and separate entrance fees. Take a shared (or private) taxi from Meidūn-é Tajrīsh, or walk about 1.5km from Tajrīsh, along Kheyābūn-é Shahīd Ja'afarī.

Carpet Museum

The Carpet Museum (☎ 653 200) contains more than 100 pieces from all over Iran, from the 18th century to the present. Although the exhibition is not vast, it more than makes up for it in quality. It's open from 9 am to 6 pm daily except Monday. There's a decent cafe inside.

Golestān Palace & Gardens

This complex includes an **Ethnographical Museum** (☎ 311 0653), with a colourful exhibition of wax dummies wearing ethnic costumes and holding traditional cooking and musical implements; and the magnificent **Golestān Palace**, with displays of diamonds and photography. The complex is open from 8 am to 3 pm Saturday to Wednesday.

National Jewels Museum

There are so many jewels on display here that it's overwhelming, even vulgar. This museum (☎ 3110 101) is only open for a few hours each week (currently from 2 to 4 pm from Sunday, Monday and Tuesday), so ring ahead if you're coming a long way. It's in a vault in the basement of Bank Melli. Look for the huge black gates, and a couple of machine-gun-toting guards.

Neyāvarān Palace Museum

There is nothing particularly stunning inside this museum (☎ 2282 012) but the **gardens** are lovely. Take a shared taxi east of Meidūn-é Tajrīsh, and ask to be dropped off at the end of Kheyābūn-é Shahīd Bāhonar, about 100m from the entrance.

MOSQUES

There are surprisingly few mosques and mausoleums worth visiting in Tehrān. The 18th century **Emām Khomeinī Mosque** is a working mosque, one of the largest and busiest in Tehrān. The **Sepahsālār Mosque & Madrassa** is Tehrān's largest and most important Islamic building. It was built between 1878 and 1890, after the golden age of Persian architecture had passed, so it's ungainly and gaudy, but the eight minarets are impressive, and the poetry, inscribed in several ancient scripts in the tiling, is famous.

US DEN OF ESPIONAGE

The only indication that this vast complex used to be the US embassy is a single faded symbol of the bald eagle on one of the entrances. Now called the US Den of Espionage, and used to train the Revolutionary Guards, the building is closed to visitors, but there are fascinating **murals** on the southern walls, and a **bookshop** (with erratic opening hours) on the corner. Be very discreet about taking any photos in the area.

PLACES TO STAY – BUDGET

Most cheap places are within a 1km radius of Meidūn-é Emām Khomeinī, though this area is noisy and grubby and only a few decent restaurants. There are also some cheapies in the bazaar district, but many won't accept foreigners, and most are unsavoury.

Arya Hotel (☎ 3113 011, Kheyābūn-é Amīr Kabīr) is located behind a mosque so it's probably noisy. Rooms are tiny, but reasonably clean, for 16,500 rials a double. *Chehel Sotoun Hotel* (☎ 312 248) is in the same lane as the Arya. Clean but basic doubles cost 17,000 rials; and a grubby dorm bed costs only 6000 rials.

Hotel Khazar Sea (☎ 3113 760, Kheyābūn-é Amīr Kabīr) is often recommended for its friendliness, but the rooms, for about 13,500 rials, are fairly basic. There are plenty of other ordinary but cheap places along southern Kheyābūn-é Mellat, and southern Kheyābūn-é Sa'dī, south of the intersection with Amīr Kabīr.

Hotel Khayyam (☎ 3113 757, fax 301 497, Kheyābūn-é Amīr Kabīr) is off the main road, quiet and worth paying more for. The rooms are small, but nicely furnished, and cost a negotiable 65,000/80,000 rials a double without/with bathroom. It also has a decent *restaurant*.

IRAN

IRAN

CENTRAL TEHRĀN

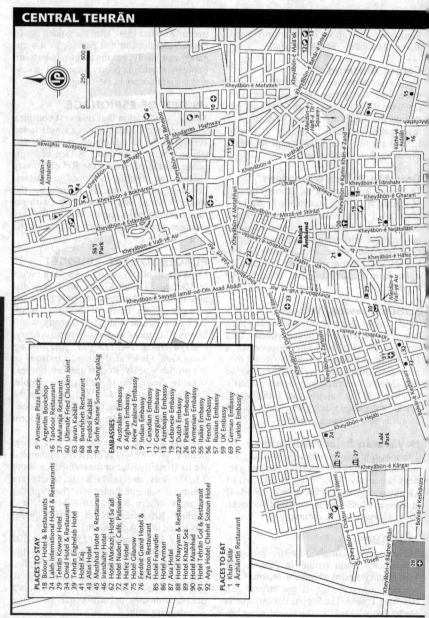

PLACES TO STAY
18 Bolour Hotel & Restaurants
24 Laleh International Hotel & Restaurants
29 Tehrān Kowsar Hotel
34 Omid Hotel & Restaurant
39 Tehrān Enghelab Hotel
41 Hotel Kaj
43 Atlas Hotel
45 Mashhad Hotel & Restaurant
46 Iranshahr Hotel
62 Hotel Markazi; Hotel Sa'adi
72 Hotel Naderi; Café; Patisserie
74 Hafez Hotel
75 Hotel Gilanow
76 Ferdosi Grand Hotel &
    Zeitoon Restaurant
85 Hotel Farvardin
86 Hotel Arman
87 Asia Hotel
88 Hotel Khayyam & Restaurant
89 Hotel Khazar Sea
90 Hotel Mashhad
91 Hotel Tehrān Gol & Restaurant
92 Arya Hotel; Chehel Sotoun Hotel

PLACES TO EAT
1 Khān Sālār
4 Ārzhāntin Restaurant
5 Armenian Pizza Place;
  Argentin Bookshop
16 Tandoor Restaurant
37 Maharaja Restaurant
60 Ultimate Fried Chicken Joint
63 Javan Kabābi
68 Banafsheh Restaurant
84 Ferdösi Kabābi
94 Sofre Khane Sonnati Sangalag

EMBASSIES
2 Australian Embassy
6 Afghan Embassy
7 New Zealand Embassy
9 Indian Embassy
11 Canadian Embassy
12 Georgian Embassy
13 Azerbaijan Embassy
19 Lebanese Embassy
22 Dutch Embassy
26 Pakistan Embassy
53 Armenian Embassy
56 Italian Embassy
57 French Embassy
59 UK Embassy
69 German Embassy
70 Turkish Embassy

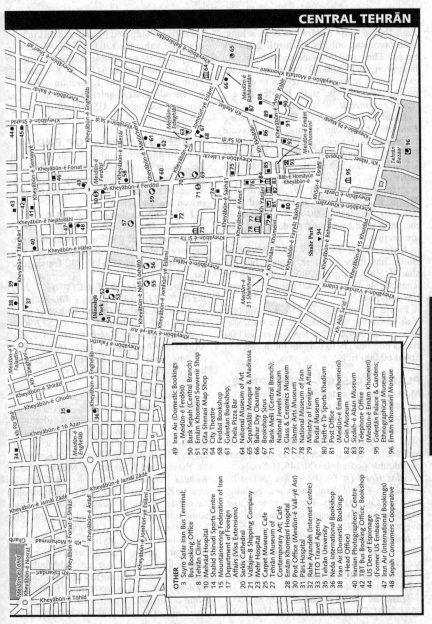

CENTRAL TEHRĀN

OTHER
3 Sayro Safar Iran Bus Terminal; Bus Booking Office
8 Tehran Clinic
10 Mehrād Hospital
14 Shahid Shirudi Sports Centre
15 Mountaineering Federation of Iran
17 Department of Foreign Affairs (Visa Extensions)
20 Sarkis Cathedral
21 Valfajre-8 Shipping Company
23 Mehr Hospital
25 Carpet Museum; Cafe
27 Tehrān Museum of Contemporary Art; Café
28 Emām Khomeini Hospital
30 Post Office (Meidūn-e Vali-yé Asr)
31 Pārs Hospital
32 Rahe Ayandéh (Internet Centre)
33 ITTO Travel Agency
35 Tehran University
36 Neda International Bookshop
38 Iran Air (Domestic Bookings – Head Office)
40 Iranian Photographers' Centre
42 TBT Bus Booking Office; Bookshop
44 US Den of Espionage (Former US Embassy)
47 Iran Air (International Bookings)
48 Sepah Consumers Cooperative

49 Iran Air (Domestic Bookings) – Meidūn-e Ferdōsī)
50 Bank Sepah (Central Branch)
51 Emām Khomeini Souvenir Shop
52 Gita Shenasi Map Shop
54 City Theatre
58 Ferdōsi Bookshop
61 Gulestan Bookshop; Chela Pizza Bar
64 National Museum of Art
65 Sepahsālār Mosque & Madrassa
66 Bahar Dry Cleaning
67 Bookshop Sirus
71 Bank Melli (Central Branch); Glass & Ceramics Museum
73 Islamic Arts Museum
77 National Jewels Museum
78 National Museum of Iran
79 Ministry of Foreign Affairs; Postal Museum
80 Haft-e Tir Sports Khadium
81 Post Office (Meidūn-e Emām Khomeini)
82 Coin Museum
83 Sizdah-é Aban Museum
93 Telephone Office (Meidūn-e Emām Khomeini)
95 Golestán Palace & Gardens; Ethnographical Museum
96 Emām Khomeini Mosque

Hotel Tehrān Gol (☎ *3113 477, Kheyābūn-é Amīr Kabīr*) has been a long-time favourite, but it's often full and very noisy. The singles/doubles, with private bathroom, cost 25,000/40,000 rials – but the exact cost for foreigners seems to depend on the mood of the staff. It does have a handy *restaurant*.

Hotel Arman (☎ *3112 323, Kheyābūn-é Ekbātān*) has clean rooms, with private bathroom and air-con, for a reasonable US$10/12 – and staff will probably want US dollars. It's just off the main road, and fairly quiet.

Asia Hotel (☎ *3118 551, Kheyābūn-é Mellat*) is central, clean and new, and good value for 50,000/90,000 rials. It has been recommended by several readers, and staff are friendly.

Hafez Hotel (☎ *6709 063, Kūché-yé Bank*) has large, modern rooms, but the shared toilets are grimy. It's good value for a negotiable 40,000/60,000 rials, and is central and quiet.

Pirouz Hotel (☎ *5376 958, Kheyābūn-é Valī-yé Asr*) is convenient to the train station, but overpriced for foreigners: 90,000 rials a double. Try to bargain them down to about 60,000 rials.

PLACES TO STAY – MID-RANGE

Most of the mid-range places are overpriced because foreigners are charged more than Iranians, so try to negotiate a decent price.

Ferdōsī Grand Hotel (☎ *6459 991, fax 6451 449, 24 Kheyābūn-é Mesrī*) is stylish and central, and the service is good. Singles/doubles cost 160,000/246,100 rials.

Atlas Hotel (☎ *8900 286, fax 8800 407, Kheyābūn-é Tāleghānī*) costs a negotiable 150,000/250,000 rials. The rooms are quiet and have huge baths, and some have views over a courtyard.

Bolour Hotel (☎ *8829 881, 191 Kheyābūn-é Gharanī*) has cosy rooms, the staff are friendly and it has two good *restaurants* – no wonder it's often full. Rooms cost US$30/40 including breakfast.

Mashhad Hotel (☎ *8825 145, fax 882 2681, 190 Kheyābūn-é Shahīd Mofatteh*)

has large, beautifully furnished rooms, and is central. Compared to others in this range, it's good value for 120,000/150,000 rials – and prices are negotiable at quieter times.

Omid Hotel (☎/fax *6414 564, Kheyābūn-é East Nosrat*) just off Kheyābūn-é Kārgar has friendly staff, a quiet location and large modern rooms for US$35/40 including breakfast.

PLACES TO STAY – TOP END

Most of the four and five-star hotels in Tehrān are hopelessly inconvenient to the rest of the city, and ludicrously overpriced. Some of the more central and reasonably priced are listed here.

Laleh International Hotel (☎ *656 021, fax 655 517, Kheyābūn-é Dr Hosein Fātemī*) is one of the few top end places in the city centre. It has all the amenities you would hope for at US$117/132 for singles/doubles.

Tehrān Enghelab Hotel (☎ *6467 251, fax 6419 311, 50 Kheyābūn-é Tāleghānī*) is also central, and willing to deduct at least 15% from the standard rate of US$72/96.

Tehrān Kowsar Hotel (☎ *8908 371, fax 8891 615, Kheyābūn-é Shahīd Malaee*) just off Meidūn-é Valī-yé Asr is quiet, central but overpriced at US$50/66.

PLACES TO EAT
Street Food

There are dozens of almost identical *kabābīs* in and around Meidūn-é Emām Khomeinī, along Kheyābūn-é Ferdōsī, and around the corner of Kheyābūn-é Jomhūrī-yé Eslāmī and Kheyābūn-é Mellat. *Javan Kabābī* (*Kheyābūn-é Jomhūrī-yé Eslāmī*), next to Kūché-ye' Alipour Karam, is an old favourite. *Ferdōsī Kabābī* is also good: some staff speak English, and a full chicken kabāb meal costs about 10,000 rials.

The best western-style fast food restaurants are along the upper reaches of Kheyābūn-é Valī-yé Asr, around Meidūn-é Tajrīsh and near the corner of Kheyābūn-é Valī-yé Asr and Kheyābūn-é Enghelāb. *Elma Tajrīsh Restaurant* (*Meidūn-é Tajrīsh*) serves scrumptious pizzas, plus salad and drink, for about 9000 rials. *Armenian Pizza Place (Meidūn-é Ārzhāntīn)* is also worth a visit. *Banafsheh Restaurant (Kheyābūn-é Sa'dī)* is obvious by the bright red furniture and pictures of hamburgers on the window. It has a friendly manager and good fast food.

Restaurants
Tandoor Restaurant (☎ 8825 705, Kūché-yé Ardalān) in Hotel Tehrān Sara is popular with expats. *Maharaja Restaurant (☎ 6462 765, Kheyābūn-é Valī-yé Asr)* in Jahan Hotel also has tasty curries from about 12,000 rials. *Ārzhāntīn Restaurant (Meidūn-é Ārzhāntīn)* is a green place opposite the main square offering western-style hamburgers, tasty Chinese food and other meals such as steak for about 10,000 rials.

The best, and most convenient, restaurants are often in the hotels. *Zeitoon Restaurant* under the Ferdossi Grand Hotel has a menu in English and huge western meals, such as trout and chicken schnitzel for 14,000 rials. *Bolour Hotel* has a restaurant on the 6th floor serving Iranian and western food, and a classy *Chinese-Korean restaurant* on the 1st floor. *Omid Hotel* is very good, with dishes from 10,000 rials, and excellent service. *Mashhad Hotel* is classy, but overpriced, and the superb views are blocked by an annoying row of shrubs. The several restaurants at the *Laleh International Hotel* are quite affordable for budget-minded travellers who order wisely.

ENTERTAINMENT
Tehrān has plenty of cinemas, but they only show (often violent) Iranian films – go to witness a slice of Iranian life, not for the quality of the film. One of the few inner city theatres that features cultural events and traditional performances that foreigners are welcome to attend is the City Theatre. The English-language newspapers normally advertise upcoming events.

Teahouses
Sofre Khane Sonnati Sangalag, in southern Shahr Park, is a marvellous place to un-wind, enjoy traditional hospitality and admire locally made carpets and gold products around the room. *Khān Sālār (Kūché-yé Alvānd)* also has some traditionally inspired surroundings, though the food is not exceptional. *Chāykhūn-é Āzārī (☎ 537 3665, Kheyābūn-é Valī-yé Asr)* is another popular, large, traditional-style teahouse, complete with tiling and fountains.

The teahouses in Tehrān are disappointing, however – they're far better in Esfahān, Kermān and Shīrāz.

SHOPPING
The Tehrān Bazaar is a huge marketplace. Among the carpets and various tacky souvenirs, you can also pick up intricate glassware, and just about anything else. Sadly, the bazaar is gradually declining in size, importance and quality of merchandise, but it's still worth a wander around, though the bazaars are better in Kermān, Esfahān and Shīrāz. The main entrances are along Kheyābūn-é 15 Khordād.

The branches of the Iranian Handicrafts Organisation have a good selection of souvenirs, and there are many interesting souvenir shops along northern Kheyābūn-é Valī-yé Asr (anywhere north of Enghelab Ave) and Kheyābūn-é Ferdōsī.

GETTING THERE & AWAY
The individual Getting There & Away sections later in this chapter have more details about air, bus, train and shared taxi services to/from Tehrān. The Getting There & Away section at the beginning of this chapter has details about flights to/from Tehrān and the Getting There & Away chapter at the beginning of this book has details about international air and bus services to/from Tehrān.

Air
Iran Air flies every day between Tehrān and most cities and larger towns in Iran. Services are less frequent on the other smaller airlines, such as Iran Asseman and Kīsh Airlines.

Most international airline offices (and many travel agencies) are along, or very near, Kheyābūn-é Nejātollāhī but it's often easier to purchase a ticket on a domestic flight at a reputable travel agency. Iran Air has three offices: the office on Meidūn-é Ferdōsī (☎ 8826 532) handles domestic flights only; main office for domestic flights (☎ 91 111, 9112 650 for reservations) can be found along Kheyābūn-é Tāleghānī; and the office for international flights (☎ 9112 591, 6001 191 for reservations) is along Kheyābūn-é Nejātollāhī.

Bus

There are four bus terminals, but you can pre-book tickets at the TBT office on Kheyābūn-é Gharanī, or at the 'The Union of Countrys Travelling Companies' at the Sayro Safar Iran bus terminal.

The Western Bus Terminal caters for all places west of Tehrān, and anywhere along the Caspian Sea west of, and including, Chālūs. To get to the terminal, take a shared taxi to Meidūn-é Āzādī, and walk the rest of the way.

The Southern Bus Terminal has buses to the south and south-east of Tehrān. Take a shared taxi heading south from the south-western corner of Meidūn-é Emām Khomeinī.

The small Eastern Bus Terminal has buses to anywhere east, and anywhere along the Caspian Sea east of Chālūs. Take a shared taxi to Meidūn-é Emām Hussein, and another shared taxi – or try the electric trolleybus.

The private terminal run by Sayro Safar Iran at Meidūn-é Ārzhāntīn has buses to Esfahān, Kermān, Mashhad, Rasht, Shīrāz and Yazd.

Train

All train services around the country start and finish at the impressive train station in southern Tehrān. Destinations, and times of arrivals and departures, are helpfully listed in English on a huge board at the entrance, and the knowledgeable staff at the information booth (☎ 556 114) speak English.

There are daily services between Tehrān and Ahvāz, Gorgān, Tabrīz and Mashhad (up to nine a day); and less frequently to Bandar-é Abbās (Sunday, Tuesday and Thursday),

Esfahān (Saturday, Monday and Wednesday), and Kermān (Monday, Wednesday and Friday). Refer to the individual Getting There & Away sections later in this chapter for details about the length and cost of the various train journeys.

You may be able to buy a ticket at an office upstairs in the main building at the station if you ask at the information booth. If not, go to the chaotic ticket office (not signposted in English), 200m east of the train station. The train station and ticket office are easy to reach by any shared taxi heading south from the south-western corner of Meidūn-é Emām Khomeinī.

Shared Taxi

Most towns within about four hours by car from Tehrān are linked by shared taxi. Shared taxis leave from specially designated sections inside, or just outside, the appropriate bus terminals, depending on the destination (refer to the Bus section earlier). For instance, shared taxis to Rasht leave from Meidūn-é Āzādī, near the Western Bus Terminal.

GETTING AROUND
To/From the Airport

If you're arriving in Tehrān for the first time, it's wise to pay for a private taxi to your hotel. Avoid the taxi drivers who huddle immediately outside the domestic and international terminals, and walk for about two minutes towards the main gate and catch a chartered taxi (about 12,000 rials), or shared taxi, to Tehrān. At either airport, the driver will avoid paying the car park entrance fee and drop passengers off about 200m from the international terminal, or about 50m from the domestic terminal. If travelling by public transport, catch bus No 511 or 518 from Meidūn-é Enghelāb to the domestic (not international) terminal, or take a shared taxi to Meidūn-é Āzādī and another to either terminal.

Bus

Extensive bus services cover virtually all of Tehrān. They're often crowded, but cheap – 100 rials across most of central Tehrān.

Some useful routes include: No 126 between Meidūn-é Tajrīsh and Meidūn-é Ārzhāntīn; No 127 between Meidūn-é Tajrīsh and Meidūn-é Valī-yé Asr; and Nos 128 and 144 between Meidūn-é Valī-yé Asr and Meidūn-é Emām Khomeinī.

Taxi

Shared taxis travel every nano-second along the main roads, linking the main squares: Emām Khomeinī, Vanak, Valī-yé Asr, Tajrīsh, Ārzhāntīn, Āzādī, Ferdōsī, Enghelāb, Haft-é Tīr, Rāh Āhan and Emām Hussein. Any shared taxi can be hired for a private trip; anything from a private taxi agency will cost more.

Underground

All the chaos around the main squares is a result of the *long* overdue construction of an underground/subway system. When this will be finished is anyone's guess.

Around Tehrān

NORTH OF TEHRĀN

If Tehrān is getting you down, head for the hills to the north. **Tajrīsh** is a charming area in northern Tehrān, populated by upper-class Tehrānīs.

Tehrān boasts two **telecabins** (chair lifts). The Tōchāl telecabin is long, and has a tea-house at both chairlift stations and a restaurant at the top. The telecabin from Darband has prettier scenery, more drink stalls and cafes along the way, and is cheaper; and if you want to walk some of the way, the trail up from Darband is far easier. Both telecabins are only open a few days a week, however, but always on Thursday and Friday. To both, take a shared taxi from Meidūn-é Tajrīsh.

REY

Rey is now sadly swallowed up by the urban sprawl of Tehrān, but it does boast the lovely **Mausoleum of Shah-é Abdal-Azim**, which contains a shrine to the brother of Emām Rezā (of Mashhad fame); **Tabarak**

Fortress, on a nearby hill; the 12th century **Toghoral Tomb Tower** in the town centre; and the **Cheshmeh Alī** mineral springs. To find these places, hire a local taxi in Rey. From Tehrān, minibuses and shared taxis leave from the Southern Bus Terminal.

KŪH-É DAMĀVAND

This magnificent conical volcano (5671m) is the highest in the country. If you intend to go mountain climbing, contact the Mountaineering Federation of Iran (☎ 021-836 641, fax 834 333), 15 Kheyābūn-é Varzandeh; or the *Mountaineering Hostel* in Reine (where you can stay for 10,000 rials per double). Even if you're not a mountain climber, there are plenty of gentle hiking trails in the area, and the village of **Reine** is pretty. Take a shared taxi or minibus from Tehrān's Eastern Bus Terminal towards Āmol, get off at the junction to Reine, and take another shared taxi up the hill. It's worth chartering a taxi from Tehrān.

THE HOLY SHRINE OF EMĀM KHOMEINĪ

When completed, the Resting Place of His Holiness Emām Khomeinī will be one of the greatest Islamic complexes in the world, though it's currently surprisingly unimpressive. (Apparently, the Āyatollāh asked that his shrine become a public place where people can enjoy themselves, rather than a mosque.) There are several decent restaurants in the complex, as well as some shops. It's open every day but avoid mourning days. The shrine is on the road between Tehrān and Qom – take a bus, minibus or shared taxi from the Southern Bus Terminal in Tehrān.

BEHESHT-É ZAHRĀ

The main military cemetery for those who died in the Iran-Iraq War is an extraordinary, but eerie, place. Foreigners and non-Muslims are welcome to walk around but avoid mourning days. It can be combined with a trip to the Holy Shrine of Emām Khomeinī. The cemetery is about 500m east from the back of the Shrine, past a huge civilian cemetery and over the main road.

Central Iran

The dry and dusty plain of central Iran is relatively sparsely populated, especially in the east of the region where the two great deserts of Iran are located. The main drawcard is Esfahān, but the towns of Yazd and Kāshān also have many worthwhile attractions.

QOM

The main attraction of this holy city is **Hazrat-é Masumeh**, the tomb of Fātemé (sister of Emām Rezā), who died and was buried here in the 9th century. This extensive complex was built under Shāh Abbās I, and the other Safavid kings, all anxious to establish their Shi'ite credentials. You can walk around the perimeter of the complex, but non-Muslims are not allowed inside.

There is a huddle of guesthouses directly opposite the (dry) river from the shrine complex. *Safa Hotel* (☎ *0251-58 457*) costs a reasonable 13,500/17,000 rials for singles/doubles. Nearby, *Mohammed Hotel* costs 20,000 rials per room.

Minibuses and shared taxis regularly travel to Tehrān, Kāshān and Esfahān. Qom is also on the Tehrān-Esfahān train line, but departures from Qom are usually late at night.

ESFAHĀN

The cool blue tiles of Esfahān's Islamic buildings, and the city's majestic bridges, contrast perfectly with the hot, dry Iranian countryside around it. The architecture is superb, the climate is pleasant, and there's a relaxed atmosphere compared with other Iranian towns. It's a city in which to walk, get lost in the bazaar, doze in beautiful gardens, and meet people.

Esfahān had long been an important trading centre, but it reached its peak when Shāh Abbās, who united Persia and then purged it of foreign invaders, came to power in 1587. He set out to make Esfahān a great city, and the famous half-rhyme *Esfahān nesf-é jahān* ('Esfahān is half the world') was coined at this time to express its grandeur.

Orientation

The main road, Kheyābūn-é Chahār Bāgh, was built in 1597, and was once lined with many palaces. Most travellers base themselves along the middle section of the road, ie Chahār Bāgh Abbāsī, between Sī-o-Sé Bridge and Meidūn-é Takhtī.

Information

Visa Extensions Ten-day extensions can be obtained in less then 24 hours from the 2nd floor of the Foreign Affairs Branch (☎ 688 644) opposite Esfahān University. Take a shared taxi from the southern end of Sī-o-Sé Bridge, and keep your eye out for a sign in English.

Tourist Office The tourist office (☎ 228 491) is on the ground floor of the Alī Ghāpū Palace, on Meidūn-é Emām Khomeinī. The office is not as useful as it used to be, but it does offer a useful (free) map.

Money The central branches of Bank Melli and Bank Mellat have foreign exchange facilities, but it's better to change money at the 'street rate' in the official money exchange office on Kheyābūn-é Sepāh. A few souvenir shops along Chahār Bāgh Abbāsī, and around Meidūn-é Emām Khomeinī, may also change money, but be discreet.

Post & Communications The main post office is along Kheyābūn-é Neshāt, but there's a far more convenient office on Meidūn-é Emām Khomeinī. The central telephone office is easy to find on Kheyābūn-é Beheshtī.

Jāme' Mosque

This mosque is more a museum of Islamic architecture: it displays styles from the simplicity of the Seljuk period (1038-1194), through the Mongol period (1220-1380) and on to the more baroque, Safavid period (1502-1722). A history of the mosque is written in English (well, sort of) on a notice board at the entrance of the mosque but it's rather hard to understand.

ESFAHĀN

PLACES TO STAY
2 22 Bahman Hotel
3 Azadi Hotel & Restaurant
5 Persia Hotel
7 Amir Kabir Hotel; Pizza/Hamburger Joint
8 Naghsh-é Jahan Hotel; Piroozy Hotel & Restaurant; Nobahar Restaurant
21 Shad Hotel
23 Abbāsī Hotel, Chehelsotoun & Nagh-é Jahan Restaurant
25 Aria Hotel
27 Pars Hotel
28 Hotel Alī Ghapū & Restaurant
31 Sa'adī Hotel
32 Tourist Hotel
33 Tous Hotel
34 Sahel Hotel & Bame Sahel Teahouse
39 Pol & Park Hotel
40 Kowsar International Hotel
43 Julfa Hotel

PLACES TO EAT
6 Restorān-é Sa'dī
30 Restaurant Shahrzad
35 Maharaja Restaurant
37 Sahelteria Restaurant

OTHER
1 Jāme' Mosque
4 Stadium
9 Bank Mellat (Central Branch)
10 Money Exchange Office
11 Bank Melli (Central Branch)
12 Main Post Office
13 Police Headquarters
14 Decorative Arts Museum of Iran
15 Natural History Museum
16 Chehel Sotūn Palace; Teahouse
17 Local Bus Station
18 Esfahān Hospital
19 Main Telephone Office
20 Hasht Behesht Palace
22 Chahār Bāgh Madrassa
24 Kish Airlines Office
26 Iran Handicrafts Organisation; Iran Air Office; Bookshops
29 Iran Air Office
36 Train Ticket Office
38 Paddleboat Hire
41 Bethlehem Church
42 Vank Cathedral & Museum

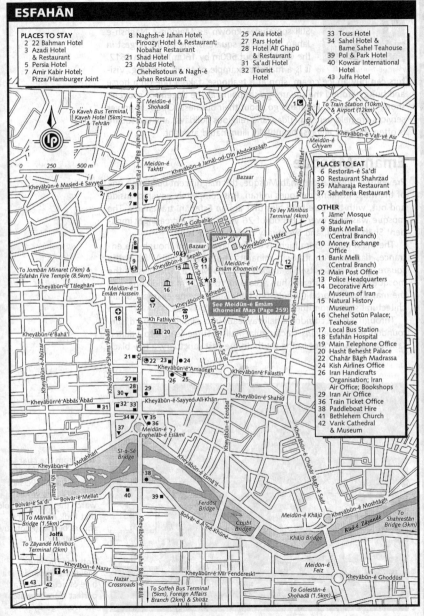

IRAN

MEIDŪN-É EMĀM KHOMEINĪ

Still sometimes known as Meidūn-é Naghsh-é Jahān, this huge square is one of the largest in the world (about 500m by 160m). Built in 1612, it is a majestic example of town planning. Visitors can buy an ice cream, stop at a teahouse, take a ride on a horse and buggy around the square, go shopping at the dozens of souvenir shops or just watch Esfahānīs go about their business. Open-air prayer services are held here on Friday, and religious holidays, and the square is often (but not always) beautifully illuminated at night.

Emām Mosque

Previously known as the Shāh Mosque, this magnificent building is one of the most stunning mosques in Iran. It is completely covered, inside and out, with the pale blue tiles that are an Esfahānī trademark. The mosque was built over a period of 26 years by an increasingly impatient Shāh Abbās I, and eventually completed in 1638.

The main dome (54m high) is double-layered, and though the entrance, flanked with its twin minarets (both 42m high), faces the square, the mosque itself is angled towards Mecca. The tiles of the mosque take on a different hue according to the light conditions, and the magnificent portal (about 30m tall), is a supreme example of architectural styles from the Safavid period (1502-1722).

Through a short corridor, a hallway leads into a inner courtyard, surrounded by four *eivāns* (rectangular halls). Three lead into vaulted sanctuaries; the largest to the south. In the east sanctuary, a few black

Top: From the *talar* (verandah) of the Alī Ghāpū Palace, Persia's Safavid rulers would watch the games of polo that took place in the square below. (Photo by Chris Mellor)

Bottom: The huge Meidūn-é Khomeinī is a hive of activity and a perfect place to watch the world go by.

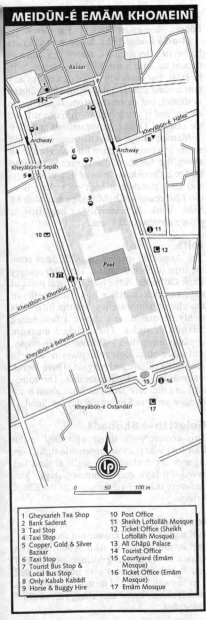

MEIDŪN-É EMĀM KHOMEINĪ

1 Gheysarieh Tea Shop
2 Bank Saderat
3 Taxi Stop
4 Taxi Stop
5 Copper, Gold & Silver Bazaar
6 Taxi Stop
7 Tourist Bus Stop & Local Bus Stop
8 Only Kabab Kabādī
9 Horse & Buggy Hire
10 Post Office
11 Sheikh Loftollāh Mosque
12 Ticket Office (Sheikh Loftollāh Mosque)
13 Alī Ghāpū Palace
14 Tourist Office
15 Courtyard (Emām Mosque)
16 Ticket Office (Emām Mosque)
17 Emām Mosque

paving stones under the dome create seven clear echoes when stamped upon. To the east and the west of the mosque, there are two *madrasés* (theological schools).

The best time for photographs is around 11 am. The mosque is open to visitors from 7 am to 7 pm daily except Friday morning.

Alī Ghāpū Palace

This six storey palace was built in the 18th century as a functioning seat of government. Many of the murals and mosaics which once decorated the many small rooms, corridors and stairways have been destroyed, but the fretwork stalactites on the top floor, chiselled out in the shapes of musical instruments, are beautiful. The palace is almost completely devoid of any furniture, but the views of the square from the top floor are superb.

The palace is open from about 7 am to noon and 3 to 7 pm daily.

Sheikh Lotfollāh Mosque

This small mosque was also built during the time of Shāh Abbās I, and dedicated to his father-in-law, Sheikh Lotfollāh, a holy preacher. This beautifully proportioned and decorated 17th century mosque, which boasts some of the best mosaics from the era, took nearly 20 years to complete. The mosque is unusual because there is no minaret or courtyard.

The pale tiles of the dome change colour, from cream to pink, depending on the light conditions. The figure painted in the middle of the floor under the dome is a peacock; at certain times of the day the sunlight enhances the peacock's tail. The mosque was once called the 'Women's Mosque', because there is apparently a tunnel between this mosque and the Alī Ghāpū Palace, which allowed women from the old dynasties to attend prayers without being seen in public.

The mosque is open from about 7 am to noon and 3 to 7 pm daily.

Chahār Bāgh Madrassa

No doubt you'll pass this theological college many times while walking along Chahār Bāgh Abbāsī. Built in the early 18th century, the courtyard is extraordinarily beautiful and restful. It's currently undergoing extensive restoration, but should be open to visitors soon.

Chehel Sotūn Palace

This marvellous building was constructed as a reception hall by Shāh Abbās I in the 17th century. The small museum inside contains a collection of ceramics, old coins, pottery, and several Qurans. Six friezes were painted on the inside walls, depicting such scenes as the gory battle between Shāh Abbās and the Uzbeks. Although many exhibits are not labelled in English, it's still worth visiting.

If you bring your own food and drink, you can enjoy a picnic in the extensive gardens or by the large pool. The best time for photos is early morning, and it's usually lit up (but rarely open) at night. The grounds and museum are open from about 8 am to noon and 2.30 to 7 pm daily.

Hasht Behesht Palace

This small garden palace was built in the 11th century. It has some charming and impressive mosaics and stalactite mouldings, but has been *very* slowly undergoing renovation for at least 20 years. There is nothing much inside, and you can easily admire the palace from the surrounding Shahīd Raja'ī park without paying the entrance fee.

Other Museums

The Natural History Museum was built during the Timurid period (1380-1502). Inside the building, which is quite interesting in itself, there's a haphazard display of molluscs, stones and stuffed animals – but few explanations are in English. Nearby, the new Decorative Arts Museum of Iran has interesting displays of modern art and miniatures.

Bridges

One of your lasting impressions of Esfahān will be the old bridges that cross the Rūd-é Zāyandé river. Several have charming tea-houses – see under Places to Eat following.

Sī-o-Sé Bridge links the upper and lower halves of Kheyābūn-é Chahār Bāgh, and was named because it has 33 arches. It was built in 1602 and is attractive, though not of any outstanding architectural merit. Khājū Bridge is shorter, but more attractive. It doubles as a dam, and if you look hard you can still see the original 17th century paintings and tiles.

Mārnān Bridge is not that interesting, but serves as a finishing point for a pleasant stroll along the banks of the river. Shahrestān Bridge is the oldest – most of its present stone and brick structure is believed to date from the 12th century. Chubī Bridge was built by Shāh Abbās II, primarily to help irrigate palace gardens in the area.

Jolfā

The Armenian quarter of Jolfā dates from the time of Shāh Abbās I. The 17th century Vank Cathedral is the historic focal point of the Armenian church in Iran. The exterior of the church is unexciting but the interior is richly decorated, and shows a fascinating mixture of styles. The attached museum contains more than 700 handwritten books, and other ethnological displays relating to Armenian culture and religion. There's even a small drawing by Rembrandt. The cathedral and museum are open from about 8 am to noon and 2 to 5 pm every day but Sunday.

Golestān-é Shohadā

This cemetery for those who died in the Iran-Iraq War is an unforgettable sight. Foreigners are welcome to walk around but avoid Fridays and mourning days. The cemetery is about 1.5km south of the Khājū Bridge.

Jombān Minaret

In Kaladyn, about 7km west of the city centre, is the tomb of Abu Abdollah. It's known as the Shaking Minarets because if you lean hard against one minaret it will start to sway back and forth – and so will its twin. Take a shared taxi along Kheyābūn-é Tāleghānī.

Esfahān Fire Temple

This disused fire temple, perched on top of a small hill, is 1.5km farther west along the same road from the Jombān Minaret. Dating from Sassanian times (224-637), these ancient mud-brick ruins provide good views of the city and Rūd-é Zāyandé.

Places to Stay – Budget

It's best to find somewhere within walking distance of Chahār Bāgh Abbāsī, though most places situated on or near the main road will be very noisy. Some cheap guesthouses will not accept foreigners.

Amir Kabir Hotel (☎/fax 296 154, *Kheyābūn-é Chahār Bāgh-é Pā'īn*) is deservedly popular. The rooms could be cleaner, but it's friendly and central. Singles/doubles/triples with communal bathroom costs 15,000/20,000/30,000 rials, and dorm beds are 10,000 rials per person.

Shad Hotel (☎ 236 883, *Kheyābūn-é Chahār Bāgh-é Abbāsī*) is very friendly and a good, central option. Small, clean twin rooms cost 20,000 rials with a shared bathroom, but it's often full. *Sa'adī Hotel* (☎ 236 363, *Kheyābūn-é Abbās Ābād*) has large, comfortable rooms, and is very good value if you can negotiate down to 40,000/50,000 rials for singles/doubles.

Sahel Hotel (☎ 234 585, *Meidūn-é Enghelāb-é Eslāmī*) is in a noisy, but very handy, part of town. The rooms are clean, and good value for 20,000/40,000 rials.

Naghsh-é Jahan Hotel (☎/fax 282 148, *Kheyābūn-é Chahār Bāgh-é Pā'īn*) is quite good value and central and charges 45,000/60,000/72,000 rials for its singles/doubles/triples, with a shared bathroom, but further discounts are often possible.

Pars Hotel (☎ 261 018, *Kheyābūn-é Chahār Bāgh Abbāsī*) is friendly, and staff speak some English. Rooms with fridge and TV, but a shared bathroom, cost 20,000/45,000 rials for a double/triple.

Places to Stay – Mid-Range & Top End

Aria Hotel (☎ 227 224, *Kheyābūn-é Amadegh*) is in a good, quiet location and the manager speaks English. Singles/doubles with a private bathroom and sometimes a balcony are good value for 75,000/100,000 rials, including breakfast.

Kaveh Hotel (☎ 420 531) at the northern Kaveh bus terminal is ideal for late night or early morning departures, and is still close to town. Large doubles, with TV and bathroom, cost about 60,000 rials.

Abbāsī Hotel (☎ 226 009, fax 226 008, *Kheyābūn-é Amadegh*) luxuriously created in the shell of an old caravanserai is undoubtedly the most romantic place to stay in Esfahān; some rooms are surprisingly ordinary, but the setting is superb. Foreigners are currently (over)charged US$78/112, but it costs nothing to enter the hotel to see the decorations, and magnificent courtyard.

Kowsar International Hotel (☎ 240 230, fax 249 975, *Bolvār-é Mellat*) is the other major top end hotel. It charges foreigners a ridiculous US$74/115.

Places to Eat

Nobahar Restaurant (☎ 257 587, *Kheyābūn-é Chahār Bāgh-é Pā'īn*), signposted in English and right next to the Naghsh-é Jahan Hotel, is one of the best Iranian restaurants along the main road. There's a menu in English, the service is good and the food is tasty. Try the mixed kabābs (7500 rials).

Restorān-é Sa'dī (*Kheyābūn-é Chahār Bāgh-é Pā'īn*) is not marked in English, but is downstairs and immediately opposite the Amir Kabir Hotel. It has a menu in English, with helpful explanations of the dishes. Main dishes start from about 6000 rials.

Sahelteria Restaurant (*Meidūn-é Enghelāb-é Eslāmī*) next to the cinema is a popular place for locals. The food is cheap, but unexciting, and the service is reasonably quick.

Pizza/Hamburger Joint is the moniker we've given the place a few doors south of the Amir Kabir Hotel. It offers tasty chips (French fries), hot dogs, pizza (8000 rials) and scrumptious western-style hamburgers (2500 rials).

Restaurant Shahrzad (*Kheyābūn-é Abbās Ābād*) is well worth a splurge. Western-style meals, such as a schnitzel with the trimmings, cost about 12,000 rials; kabāb-type meals are about 10,000 rials. The service is excellent, and the decor is charming.

Chehelsotoun Restaurant in the glorious Abbāsī Hotel is worth visiting for the sheer elegance. The prices are not outrageous considering the decor and service – about 20,000 rials a dish.

Teahouses

One thing you must do in Esfahān is enjoy a pot of tea (or two) at one of the *teahouses* under one of the bridges – the best are arguably under the Chubī and Khājū bridges. The *teahouse* in the gardens of the Chehel Sotūn Palace is also charming and *Bame Sahel Teahouse*, on the top floor the Sahel Hotel, has great views. *Gheysarieh Tea Shop* at the far northern end of Meidūn-é Emām Khomeinī has wonderful views of the mammoth square.

Shopping

The bazaar, linking Meidūn-é Emām Khomeinī with Jāme' Mosque, about 2km away, is a highlight of Esfahān. The bazaar was mostly built during the early 16th century, though most of it dates back almost 1300 years. Esfahān is one of the best places to buy miniatures, picture-frames, carvings and inlaid boxes. Avoid the shops lined along the main square; prices will be lower farther into the bazaar.

Getting There & Away

Air Iran Air has two offices: one (☎ 228 999) on Kheyābūn-é Chahār Bāgh Abbāsī and the other (☎ 228 200) in a nearby shopping complex along Kheyābūn-é Amadegh. Iran Air flies daily to Mashhad (128,000 rials), Shīrāz (70,000 rials) and Tehrān (70,000 rials); and less regularly to Bandar-é Abbās, Kermān and Zāhedān.

Bus Although there are two major bus terminals, every bus you'll need leaves from the more convenient Kaveh bus terminal, about 5km north of Meidūn-é Shohadā. Among other places, buses regularly go to

Hamadān (9000 rials, seven hours); Kāshān (3500 rials, four hours); Kermān (9500 rials, 12 hours); Kermānshāh (9000 rials, nine hours); Shīrāz (7800 rials, eight hours); Tehrān (15,000 rials by 'express', seven hours); and Yazd (4500 rials, five hours).

Train Overnight express trains leave Esfahān for Tehrān (10 hours) on Tuesday, Friday and Sunday (6650/15,650 rials, 2nd/1st class), via Kāshān and Qom. From Esfahān, *all* trains go north towards Tehrān; there is no train to Yazd or beyond.

The unsignposted train ticket office (☎ 224 425) is on Meidūn-é Enghelāb-é Eslāmī. The train station is on the way to the airport. Passengers with pre-booked train tickets can catch a special bus from outside the Kowsar International Hotel – tee this up with the ticket office.

Getting Around

The airport is about 12km from the city centre. To the airport, catch a shared taxi from Meidūn-é Takhtī and another from Ghods or Lalé squares; *from* the airport, plenty of shared taxis head to the city. Many shared taxis ply the streets, but beware: Esfahānī taxi drivers have a deservedly bad reputation for overcharging all visitors, foreign or Iranian.

KĀSHĀN

Kāshān is an attractive oasis town with a surprising number of things to see. The centre of town is the stretch of Kheyābūn-é Mohtasham between Meidūn-é Emām Khomeinī and Meidūn-é Kamāl-ol-Molk, about 700m to the south.

Things to See

The revered Shāh Abbās I would be disappointed with his unimpressive mausoleum, **Zeyārat-é Habīb ibn-é Mūsā**, about 100m north of Meidūn-é Emām Khomeinī. The large **Soltaniye Mosque** is lost in the midst of the labyrinthine bazaar, north of Meidūn-é Kamāl-ol-Molk. **Agha Bozorg Madrassa**, a mosque and theological school famous for its lovely portal and minarets, is 100m south of

Kamāl-ol-Molk. **Borujerd Museum** contains charming wall paintings and a lovely courtyard. It's just off Kheyābūn-é Alavī, about 500m south of Kamāl-ol-Molk. Nearby is the recently renovated **Home of Tabatabai.**

Places to Stay & Eat

Hotel Sayyah (☎ *0361-445 35)* about 100m west of Meidūn-é Emām Khomeinī costs a negotiable US$15/20 for small, pleasant singles/doubles. It has the best *restaurant* in town. The pink, unsignposted *guesthouse*, a few metres west of the Sayyah, is far better value for 15,000/20,000 rials. *Amīr Kabīr Hotel* (☎ *0361-300 091)* about 2km before the gardens at Fīn (see Around Kāshān following) has decent, but overpriced, rooms for US$25/40, and a good *restaurant*.

Getting There & Away

Kāshān is well connected by bus, minibus and shared taxi with Esfahān, Qom and Tehrān; many services leave from Meidūn-é 15 Khordād, about 600m west of Meidūn-é Emām Khomeinī. Every week, three express trains go to Tehrān, via Qom, and to Kermān, via Yazd.

AROUND KĀSHĀN
Abyaneh

Most of the remains of this village date back to the Safavid period (1502-1722). Although recognised for its antiquity and uniqueness by UNESCO, Abyaneh is less interesting than the magnificent old city of Yazd, and not as accessible. However, some visitors love Abyaneh. Take any bus south from Kāshān, get off at the signposted turn-off to Abyaneh and then wait for another lift (or walk the final 12km). Alternatively, charter a taxi from Kāshān.

Tārīkhī-yé Fīn Gardens

About 8km south-west of Kāshān, these beautiful gardens have buildings from the Safavid (1502-1722) and Ghajar (1779-1921) periods, as well as **pools**, orchards and a charming *teahouse*. On the way, you can visit the delightful **Shrine of Ibrahim**, with its exquisite tilework and pretty court-yard. To get to the gardens, charter a taxi, or catch a minibus from Meidūn-é 15 Khordād in Kāshān.

Ārān

Only a few kilometres north of Kāshān, Ārān boasts the **Holy Shrine of Hel-ibn-Ali**, one of the most impressive in the region. Charter a taxi, or catch a minibus from Meidūn-é 15 Khordād in Kāshān.

YAZD

Yazd is a relaxed, tree-lined town with enough sights to justify a couple of days – the town is also surprisingly good value. Wedged between the northern Dasht-é Kavīr desert, and the southern Dasht-é Lūt, Yazd boasts the best old – and inhabited – city in Iran. Yazd was an important centre for the pre-Islamic religion, Zoroastrianism, and the city has always been renowned for its weaving.

Information

The large, unsignposted building opposite the bus terminal is responsible for visa extensions. The tourist office (☎ 47 111) is in the middle of the old city – head up Kheyābūn-é Sayyed Gol-é Sorkh, turn east (right) down a road that starts opposite a telephone booth, and keep walking and asking for directions. You can change money at the central branch of Bank Melli, or at the favourable 'street rate' at Amin Money Exchange. Ask at the Aria Hotel (see Places to Stay later in this section) about how to find the informal Internet Centre, located in the suburbs.

Old City

According to UNESCO, Yazd is one of the oldest towns in the world. Every visitor should spend a few hours getting completely lost in this living museum. Look for the tall *bādgīrs* (wind-towers) on rooftops, designed to catch even the lightest breeze and direct it to underground living rooms. Ask the tourist office for directions to the interesting old Mahmoudi and Rasoulian **houses**. The twin minarets of the Jāme' Mosque (see Mosques & Shrines following) serve as a vital landmark when you get lost.

IRAN

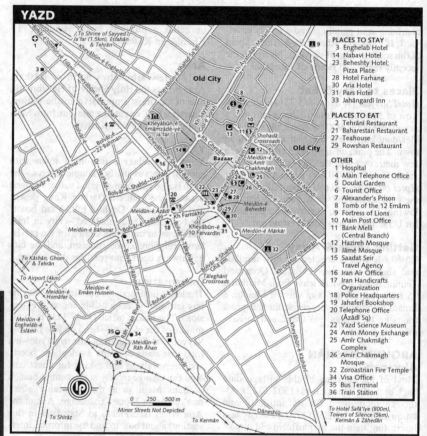

YAZD

PLACES TO STAY
3 Enghelab Hotel
14 Nabavi Hotel
23 Beheshty Hotel;
    Pizza Place
28 Hotel Farhang
30 Aria Hotel
31 Pars Hotel
33 Jahāngardī Inn

PLACES TO EAT
2 Tehrānī Restaurant
21 Baharestan Restaurant
27 Teahouse
29 Rowshan Restaurant

OTHER
1 Hospital
4 Main Telephone Office
5 Doulat Garden
6 Tourist Office
7 Alexander's Prison
8 Tomb of the 12 Emāms
9 Fortress of Lions
10 Main Post Office
11 Bank Melli
    (Central Branch)
12 Hazireh Mosque
13 Jāmé Mosque
15 Saadat Seir
    Travel Agency
16 Iran Air Office
17 Iran Handicrafts
    Organization
18 Police Headquarters
19 Jahaferī Bookshop
20 Telephone Office
    (Āzādī Sq)
22 Yazd Science Museum
24 Amin Money Exchange
25 Amīr Chakmāgh
    Complex
26 Amir Chākmagh
    Mosque
32 Zoroastrian Fire Temple
34 Visa Office
35 Bus Terminal
36 Train Station

To Shrine of Sayyed/Ja'far (1.5km), Esfahān & Tehrān

Old City

Old City

Kheyābūn-é Emāmzādé-yé Ja'far

Bazaar

Shohadā Crossroads

Meidūn-é Amīr Chakhmāgh

Meidūn-é Beheshtī

Meidūn-é Azadī

Meidūn-é Bāhonar

Meidūn-é Markār

Kheyābūn-é 10 Farvardin

Meidūn-é Emām Hussein

Meidūn-é Homáfer

Meidūn-é Enghelāb-é Eslāmī

Tāleghāni Crossroads

Meidūn-é Rāh Ahan

To Kāshān, Ghom & Tehrān
To Airport (4km)
To Shirāz
To Kermān
Dāneshjū

To Hotel Safā'īye (800m),
Towers of Silence (5km),
Kermān & Zāhedān

0 250 500 m
Minor Streets Not Depicted

Zoroastrian Sites

The **Towers of Silence** include several disused Zoroastrian buildings, such as a well, kitchen, lavatory and two small bādgīrs. It's also a great area for **hiking**. The towers are about 7km south of Meidūn-é Markār; the best way to get there is to charter a taxi.

The *āteshkadé*, or **Zoroastrian fire temple**, attracts followers from around the world. The sacred flame has apparently been burning since about 470 AD, and was transferred from its original site in 1940. Find someone

to explain things to you, or it will all be a bit incomprehensible. The building is open every day from 7 am to noon and 4 to 7 pm.

About 50km from Yazd, **Chak Chak** is another important shrine. It's best to get permission from the authorities at the āteshkadé in Yazd before going there. The only way to Chak Chak is to charter a taxi.

Mosques & Shrines

Yazd has dozens of mosques. The magnificent 14th century **Jāme' Mosque** dominates the old city. It has a remarkably high, tiled entrance portal, flanked with two magnificent minarets and adorned with an inscription from the 15th century. The beautiful mosaics on the dome, and on the mehrāb (niche pointing towards Mecca), are also superb. The 11th century **Tomb of the 12 Emāms** has fine inscriptions, and though seemingly neglected, it's well preserved.

The impressive twin-minareted entrance to the **Amīr Chakmāgh Complex** is not actually a mosque, but leads to a **bazaar** and the **Takyeh Mosque**. The **Shrine of Sayyed Ja'far** is decorated inside with tens of thousands of mirror tiles, and has exquisite mosaics and lovely **gardens**. To get there, take a shared taxi north-west along Bolvār-é Jomhūrī-yé Eslāmī.

Places to Stay

A few dives near Meidūn-é Mārkār cost about 8000/10,000 rials for singles/doubles. *Pars Hotel* (☎ 627 24) is one of the best for 15,000/18,500 rials, but it's very noisy and not signposted in English.

Aria Hotel (☎ 304 11, *Kheyābūn-é 10 Farvadīn*) has simple rooms (many in desperate need of renovation) with private shower but a shared toilet for 20,000/40,000 rials. Despite the drawbacks, it's the best of an ordinary lot.

Beheshty Hotel (☎ 247 17, *Kheyābūn-é Emām Khomeinī*) gets mixed reviews so check out a few rooms. Decent rooms cost a negotiable 25,000/35,000 rials. It's not signposted in English and it's a little back from the road and easy to miss.

Hotel Farhang (☎ 665 012, *Kheyābūn-é Emām Khomeinī*) is way overpriced at 90,000/100,000 rials, though the reasonable rooms, with a private bathroom, do include three beds. *Nabavi Hotel* (☎ 661 289, *Kheyābūn-é Sayyed Gol-é Sorkh*) has huge rooms – with three beds, fridge and sitting room – but it's overpriced for a negotiable 110,000 rials per room.

Enghelab Hotel (☎ 656 111) just off Bolvār-é Jomhūrī-yé Eslāmī is arguably the better of the top end hotels, and it costs US$35/45.

Places to Eat

Meidūn-é Beheshtī has dozens of places for Iranian-style hamburgers and kabābs. *Baharestan Restaurant* is one of the best. *Rowshan Restaurant* (☎ 36 470, *Kheyābūn-é 10 Farvadīn*) can dish up some reasonable kabābs for about 8000 rials.

Pizza Place is the rather obvious name we've given to a tiny, popular place just up from the Beheshty Hotel. It's unsignposted in English, so look for the black and yellow neon sign. For a tasty breakfast, tea and the hubble-bubble, try the great *teahouse* near Hotel Farhang – look for the picture of Donald Duck at the entrance!

Tehrānī Restaurant (*Bolvār-é Jomhūrī-yé Eslāmī*) is a little pricey, and not particularly convenient, but the food is tasty and the service is good. Dishes cost from 10,000 rials. *Hotel Safā'iye* in southern Yazd has the best restaurant of the upmarket hotels, and has excellent service and a charming setting.

Shopping

All sorts of beautiful stuff from a silk called *tirma* is made in Yazd province, and can be bought in the **bazaar**. Yazd is also famous for intricate glassware and leather bags.

Getting There & Away

Air Iran Air (☎ 28 030) flies daily to Tehrān (85,500 rials); and less often to Bandar-é Abbās, Mashhad, Shīrāz and Zāhedān.

Bus & Minibus Many bus companies have offices along Kheyābūn-é Emām Khomeinī. Buses leave from the bus terminal, accessible by shared taxi from Meidūn-é Beheshtī and Meidūn-é Āzādī. Yazd is well-connected to all major cities, including Esfahān (4500 rials, five hours), Kermān (5200 rials, six hours) and Shīrāz (6900 rials, seven hours).

Train Yazd is on the railway line between Tehrān (9600/21,850 rials, 2nd/1st class) and Kermān, but departures are infrequent. Current details are available from the train station, or from Saadat Seir Travel Agency (☎ 660 693, fax 666 599), where train tickets can be bought one month in advance.

IRAN

SEMNĀN

This ancient town, which probably dates back to the Sassanian period (224-637), is fairly appealing. The east-west road, Kheyābūn-é Emām, is an extension of the thoroughfare from Tehrān; and north-south Kheyābūn-é Ghods is the road from Mashhad.

The 15th century **Jāmé Mosque**, with its impressive entrance portal, interesting stucco and 21m minaret, dominates the town. About 200m east, **Emām Khomeinī Mosque** has a very attractive entrance portal.

Hotel Kormesh next to the park on Meidūn-é Emām is the best hotel: it has decent rooms without/with bathroom for a bargain 12,000/17,500 rials. *Mohel Restaurant* near the Emām Khomeinī Mosque is the best place to eat.

The bus terminal is about 3km west of the bazaar. To anywhere east of Semnān, hail down any bus heading along the main road outside the bus terminal. The minibus terminal, about 1.5km north of the bazaar, has services to nearby towns. Semnān is also on the railway line between Tehrān and Mashhad.

SHĀHRŪD

Shāhrūd is a pleasant place to break up the long overland journey between Tehrān and Mashhad. The main road is Kheyābūn-é 22 Bahman, which stretches from the bus terminal in the south to the turn-off to Bastām and Mashhad in the north. Only 7km from Shāhrūd, the pretty village of **Bastām** has a beautiful mosque, possibly dating from the 11th century.

New Islami Hotel set back a little from Meidūn-é Jomhūrī-yé Eslāmī has decent, but basic, rooms for 13,500 rials. *Hotel Reza* at the northern end of 22 Bahman has good rooms, with a large bathroom, for a negotiable 40,000 rials a double. *Hotel Reza* has a decent restaurant and there are other good *restaurants* along northern 22 Bahman.

The bus/minibus terminal is about 5km south of Jomhūrī-yé Eslāmī, but to anywhere to the west, and Gorgān, hail something at the roundabout, about 500m north of Hotel Reza. The Tehrān-Mashhad train also stops at Shāhrūd.

Eastern Iran

The east and south-east are different from central Iran, less developed certainly but also steeped in archaeological and historical interest. The perennial civil war in Afghanistan, and the smuggling of drugs and other illegal goods through Iran from Afghanistan and Pakistan, creates a certain amount of tension in many places in eastern Iran. You should be extremely careful when travelling overland anywhere near the Afghan border.

MASHHAD

Mashhad (The Place of Martyrdom) is extremely sacred to Shi'ites as the place where the eighth grandson of the Prophet Mohammed, Emām Rezā, died in 817. The story spread that Emām Rezā had been poisoned, so his tomb became a major Shi'ite pilgrimage site. At the time of Iranian New Year (about 21 March), and the height of the pilgrimage season (mid-June to late July), Mashhad almost bursts: more than 12 million pilgrims visit Mashhad each year. There are also a few attractions near Mashhad, and the city is a natural staging post if you're travelling to/from Turkmenistan.

Information

It's relatively easy to get a 30 day visa extension within 24 hours from the visa/passport office at Meidūn-é Rāhnamā'ī in the north-west of the city (charter a taxi there). The tourist office (☎ 717 057) is more concerned with visiting pilgrims than foreign tourists, so it isn't worth trying to find; the tourist information booth at the train station is more helpful. The central branches of Bank Melli, Bank Mellat and Bank Sepah will change money, and there's a foreign exchange counter in the departure lounge at the airport. Black marketeers hang around Bank Melli, but it's best to change money at the Sepehri Exchange Office.

Āstān-é Ghods-é Razavī

The Holy Shrine of Emām Rezā, and the surrounding buildings, are known collectively

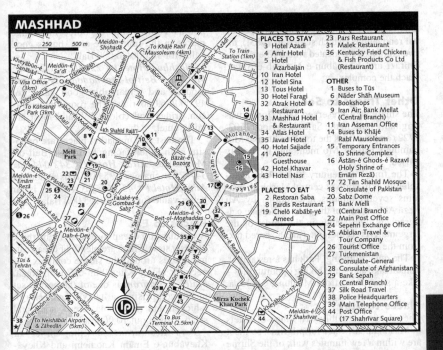

MASHHAD

PLACES TO STAY
3 Hotel Azadi
4 Amir Hotel
5 Hotel Āzarbaijan
10 Iran Hotel
12 Hotel Sina
13 Tous Hotel
30 Hotel Faragi
32 Atrak Hotel & Restaurant
33 Mashhad Hotel & Restaurant
34 Atlas Hotel
35 Javad Hotel
40 Hotel Sajjade
41 Alborz Guesthouse
42 Hotel Khavar
43 Hotel Nasr

PLACES TO EAT
2 Restoran Saba
8 Pardis Restaurant
19 Chelō Kabābī-ye Ameed
23 Pars Restaurant
31 Malek Restaurant
36 Kentucky Fried Chicken & Fish Products Co Ltd (Restaurant)

OTHER
1 Buses to Tūs
6 Nāder Shāh Museum
7 Bookshops
9 Iran Air; Bank Mellat (Central Branch)
11 Iran Asseman Office
14 Buses to Khājé Rabī Mausoleum
15 Temporary Entrances to Shrine Complex
16 Āstān-é Ghods-é Razavī (Holy Shrine of Emām Rezā)
17 72 Tan Shahīd Mosque
18 Consulate of Pakistan
20 Sabz Dome
21 Bank Melli (Central Branch)
22 Main Post Office
24 Sepehri Exchange Office
25 Abidian Travel & Tour Company
26 Tourist Office
27 Turkmenistan Consulate-General
28 Consulate of Afghanistan
29 Bank Sepah (Central Branch)
37 Silk Road Travel
38 Police Headquarters
39 Main Telephone Office
44 Post Office (17 Shahrīvar Square)

as the Āstān-é Ghods-é Razavī, and comprise one of the marvels of the Islamic world. The original tomb chamber of Emām Rezā was built in the early 9th century, but later destroyed, restored and destroyed again. The present structure in the centre of the complex was built under the orders of Shāh Abbās I at the beginning of the 17th century.

As well as the shrine, the complex contains two mosques, four museums, 12 lofty eivāns or halls (two of them coated entirely with gold), six theological colleges, several libraries, a post office and a bookshop. The remarkable **Azīm-é Gōhar Shād Mosque** has a 50m blue dome and cavernous golden portal. The **Moghaddas Museum** houses a 16th century gold bas-relief door, and a vast collection of gifts given to Emām Khomeinī by various world leaders. Next door, the less interesting **Markazī Museum** has many Islamic ornaments and writing implements, a

huge 800-year-old wooden door and a one tonne stone drinking vessel made in the 12th century. Downstairs from the Markazī Museum is the fascinating **Stamp and Coin Museum**. The **Ghods-é Razavī Museum** has a display of carpets, calligraphy and hand-inscribed Qurans – probably the largest public display in Iran.

The Holy Shrine itself is strictly closed to non-Muslims, but it's generally fine to visit the rest of the complex. Please dress extremely conservatively and behave impeccably, and avoid large religious gatherings and the main pilgrimage season. Non-Muslims may feel more comfortable with a Muslim guide or friend, but it's not mandatory – ask around outside the shrine or at your hotel. If you go alone, report to the unmarked Foreigner's Registration Office in the Administration Office, in the far west of the complex.

The complex is open daily from about 7 am to late in the evening. During the perpetual renovations (which started in 1983!), the two entrances are located where Kheyābūn-é Shīrāzī and Kheyābūn-é Novvāb-é Safavī reach the complex.

Other Things to See
The small, well-preserved **Sabz Dome**, was originally built in the Safavid period (1502-1722) and contains the tomb of Sheikh Mohammed Hakīm Mo'men, but is usually closed.

The fine 16th century **Khājé Rabī Mausoleum**, 4km north of central Mashhad, contains several famous inscriptions by Alī Rezā Abbāsī, one of the greatest Persian calligraphers, and stands in the midst of the large **martyrs' cemetery**. Take a shared taxi from the train station.

The quiet **Kūhsangī Park** has a restaurant, a small lake and some hiking opportunities – take a shared taxi from Meidūn-é Shohadā.

Places to Stay
There is an incredibly vast range of hotels in Mashhad. All cater for pilgrims, so most are within a few minutes walk of the Shrine Complex, and some will not accept foreigners at any time. In the off-season, the prices of mid-range hotels are negotiable.

There are a few decent places near the corner of Kheyābūn-é Emām Rezā and Kheyābūn-é Dānesh. *Hotel Nasr* (☎ 97 943) charges 20,000/40,000 rials for singles/doubles, and is cleaner and quieter than most. *Alborz Guesthouse* (☎ 825 097) is another good cheapie for 10,000/15,000 rials, although it's noisy. *Hotel Sajjade* (☎ 45 238) is central and good value for 17,500/22,000 rials.

Tous Hotel (☎ 22 922) at the point where Kheyābūn-é Shīrāzī reaches the shrine complex is central but quiet, and worth paying a little extra: 25,000 rials per room.

Just up from the corner of Kheyābūn-é Shīrāzī and Kheyābūn-é Āzādī are several good options. *Hotel Azarbaijan* (☎ 54 001) is probably the best value: decent, basic but noisy rooms cost 22,000/30,000 rials.

Javad Hotel (☎ 24 135, fax 650 080) is not as comfortable as other mid-range places in the immediate area, but is good value for 30,000/60,000 rials.

Mashhad Hotel (☎ 22 701, fax 26 767, *Meidūn-é Beit-ol-Moghaddas*) is central, modern and remarkably good value for 49,000/76,000 rials. The rooms have air-con, fridge and colour TV, and most are fairly quiet.

The best two upmarket places are opposite each other facing Meidūn-é Beit-ol-Moghaddas. *Atrak Hotel* (☎ 342 044, fax 347 772) charges 135,000 rials a double. *Atlas Hotel* (☎ 45 061, fax 47 800) is far better value for 60,000/105,000 rials.

Places to Eat
A popular and cheap local dish is the thick *ābgūsht* stew. There are plenty of cheap eating houses around the shrine complex, especially along Kheyābūn-é Emām Rezā. *Malek Restaurant* is one of the best: a set menu comprising a tasty *chelō morgh* (chicken and rice), cola, bread, soup and salad costs about 10,000 rials.

Pars Restaurant, on the corner of Kheyābūn-é Emām Khomeinī and Kheyābūn-é Pāsdārān, serves tasty Iranian food (about 8000 rials a plate) in a friendly atmosphere. *Restoran Saba* is handy to the chain of hotels around the corner of Kheyābūn-é Shīrāzī and Kheyābūn-é Āzādī, and has the usual range of kababs.

There isn't much in the way of fast food. *Kentucky Fried Chicken & Fish Products Co Ltd* (well, that's the name outside), opposite Javad Hotel, is popular with the younger crowd.

The best restaurants are in the mid-range hotels. *Atrak Hotel* is elegant, but most items are overpriced: from 13,000 rials, plus 15% tax. *Mashhad Hotel* has Iranian meals for about 11,000 rials, and excellent, self-serve breakfasts (7500 rials) for the public and guests.

Shopping
Mashhad has several bazaars, including the 700m long **Bāzār-é Rezā**. Among the range

of tacky souvenirs, the bazaars sell gorgeous fabrics, rugs, turquoise (but beware of fakes) and saffron.

Getting There & Away

Refer to the Getting There & Away chapter at the beginning of this book for details about international air, train and bus services to/from Mashhad.

Air Iran Air (☎ 51 492) flies many times a day to Tehrān (116,000 rials); daily to Esfahān (128,000 rials) and Shīrāz (144,500 rials); and less often to Ahvāz, Bandar-é Abbās, Rasht, Tabrīz, Yazd and Zāhedān. Some other domestic airlines, such as Iran Asseman (☎ 58 200), also link Mashhad with Tehrān and Esfahān.

Bus From the bus terminal (easy to reach by shared taxi along Kheyābūn-é Emām Rezā), a plethora of buses go to every major city, and regional town, but most trips to/from Mashhad are *very* long and often *very* boring. Some of the more popular routes are to: Gorgān (8000 rials, nine hours); Shāhrūd (11,500 rials, 10 hours); Tehrān (12,000 rials, 14 hours); and Zāhedān (12,500 rials, 15 hours).

Train Up to nine trains travel between Tehrān and Mashhad every day for 12,000/24,000 rials (2nd/1st class). Some are 'express', and take 13 hours.

Getting Around

The Mashhad Taxi Agency has a counter outside the airport, but you must still negotiate a reasonable fare. A public bus travels regularly between the airport and the corner of Kheyābūn-é Emām Rezā and Kheyābūn-é Fedā'īyān-é Eslām.

AROUND MASHHAD
Tūs (Ferdowsi)

Tūs (also known as Ferdowsi) is a former regional capital, but is now better known for the **Mausoleum of Ferdōsī**, dedicated to a famous poet. A cafe inside the gardens serves drinks and simple meals during the day. The 14th century **Hordokieh Mausoleum**, about 1km south of Ferdōsī's mausoleum, is the only remaining structure of the original city of Tūs. Minibuses and shared taxis leave about every 30 minutes from Meidūn-é Shohadā in Mashhad.

Neishābūr

Neishābūr is the home town of the famous poet Omar Khayyām. The **Mausoleum of Omar Khayyām** is unimpressive but the gardens surrounding it are attractive. The grounds also contain the fine 16th century **Mausoleum of Mohammed Mahrūgh**. In the town centre, a partially restored **caravanserai** contains some uninspiring **souvenir shops**, and a small **museum**.

Tourist Hotel (☎ *0551-33 445*) in the centre of town charges 90,000/120,000 rials for singles/doubles, and has an excellent *restaurant*. Several minibuses leave every morning from the Mashhad bus terminal; or hop on any bus heading towards Semnān. It's easy to combine Neishābūr with a trip to the charming 17th century **Ghadamgāh Mausoleum**, just off the main Mashhad-Neishābūr road.

Sarakhs

Sarakhs is on the border with Turkmenistan – refer to the Getting There & Away chapter at the beginning of this book for details about crossing the border to Turkmenistan. If you're going to Sarakhs, allow time to visit the vast **Sheikh Loghmān Bābā Tower** on the outskirts of town.

Six buses travel every day from the bus terminal in Mashhad to Sarakhs (three hours). There's a train (also three hours) that leaves Mashhad every day at 3.30 pm (but arrives when the border is closed), and leaves Sarakhs at 6.30 am (before the border is open).

ZĀHEDĀN

Zāhedān is dusty and featureless, but it's the nearest major town to the border with Pakistan, so most overland travellers end up here for a day or two, much to their frustration.

Information

The 'Police Dept of Alien Affairs' handles visa extensions. The central branch of Bank Melli changes money, including Pakistani rupees. There is a small black market for Pakistani and Afghan currency (and foreign passports) in the bazaar – but be *very* discreet. It's easier to change money with a black marketeer at the border.

Places to Stay

There are a few places in the grubby bus terminal area. *Abuzar Hotel* (☎ 228 692) is convenient and good value at 9000/12,500 rials for singles/doubles with shared bathroom, but it's noisy and often full.

Hotel Momtazhirmand (☎ 222 827) is the best cheapie and a good place to meet other travellers. Basic but acceptable rooms with shared bathroom cost 12,000/16,000 rials. It's along the first laneway on the left heading north from the intersection of Kheyābūn-é Emām Khomeinī and Kheyābūn-é Doktor Sharī'atī.

Sāleh Hotel (☎ 231 797, fax 226 330) just south-west of Meidūn-é Āzādī is the best in

the mid-range bracket. It charges 60,000/90,000 rials for a double without/with bathroom, but you'll have to negotiate to get this price.

Esteghlal Grand Hotel (☎ 238 052, fax 222 239, Meidūn-é Āzādī) is large, new and expensive at 163,000/240,000 rials.

Places to Eat

Several *restaurants* around the bus terminal area; the one in *Abuzar Hotel* is the most popular and hygienic. *Hotel Momtazhirmand* has a decent restaurant, and is the best in the budget range. *Saleh Hotel* also has a good restaurant. There are a couple of decent *kabābīs* near Saleh Hotel.

Getting There & Away

Refer to the Getting There & Away chapter at the beginning of this book for details about travelling to/from Pakistan by train and bus.

Air Iran Air (☎ 220 812) flies every day to Tehrān (160,000 rials); and less often to Esfahān, Kermān, Mashhad and Yazd. Iran

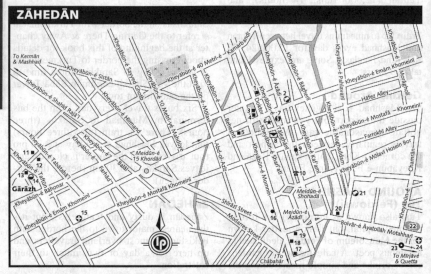

ZĀHEDĀN

Asseman also has regular flights to Tehrān; its representative is Khaterat Zāhedān Travel & Tours (☎ 225 001).

Bus The bus terminal is a grotty, sprawling mess in the west of the city. The bus companies have offices all over the terminal area, so you'll have to ask around. Buses leave many times a day to Bam (5500 rials, five hours); Bandar-é Abbās (10,500 rials, 17 hours); Esfahān (13,800 rials, 21 hours); Kermān (5500 rials, six hours); Mashhad (12,500 rials, 15 hours); Shīrāz (13,500 rials, 17 hours); Tehrān (16,000 rials, 22 hours); and Yazd (8500 rials, 14 hours).

MĪRJĀVÉ

Mīrjāvé is the closest village to the border with Pakistan – refer to the Getting There & Away chapter at the beginning of this book for information about crossing the border.

Mirjaveh Inn (☎ 05448-4386) is a more pleasant alternative than most hotels in Zāhedān, and costs a negotiable 40,000 rials per double. Shared taxis, and occasional minibuses, to Mīrjāvé, and the border,

15km farther east, regularly leave from the bus terminal in Zāhedān.

KERMĀN

Kermān is a pleasant desert city with enough attractions to justify a stopover for a day or more. For many centuries, the livelihood of Kermān depended on its place along the Asian trade routes, but from about the beginning of the Safavid period (1502-1722) the city has relied more on the production of carpets – still one of the major, local industries.

Information

Visa extensions can be obtained at the 'Aliens' Bureau' (☎ 222 240); it's currently in the Police Headquarters – but the bureau does often move to other buildings in the streets immediately surrounding the post and telephone offices. The tourist office (☎ 228 030) is friendly but of little help. The central branch of Bank Melli will change money but you'll get a better rate if you ask the manager at your hotel.

Mosques & Mausoleums

Built in 1349, the well-preserved **Jāme'** **Mosque**, in the bazaar district, has four lofty eivāns, shimmering blue tiles and a unique clock tower. The **Emām Mosque** was constructed in the 11th century, and includes remains of the original mehrāb and minaret, though much of the building has been rebuilt since. The 14th century **Pā Manār Mosque** has fine original tilework in its portal, and the twin-domed **Mausoleum of Mushtaq Alīshāh** is also worth a quick look around.

Museums

The **Ganj Alī Khan Bath Museum** is a fascinating, though slightly tacky, museum with a small collection of wax dummies indicating the purpose of a bathhouse. On the other side of the pleasant **Ganj Alī Courtyard** is the small **Coin Museum**. The **Kermān Contemporary Arts Museum** contains a large collection of watercolours, mostly by local artists, and has a delightful garden.

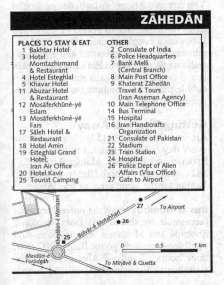

ZĀHEDĀN

PLACES TO STAY & EAT	OTHER
1 Bakhtar Hotel	2 Consulate of India
3 Hotel Momtazhirmand & Restaurant	6 Police Headquarters
	7 Bank Melli (Central Branch)
4 Hotel Esteghlal	8 Main Post Office
5 Khavar Hotel	9 Khaterat Zāhedān Travel & Tours (Iran Asseman Agency)
11 Abuzar Hotel & Restaurant	
12 Mosáferkhūne-yé Eslam	10 Main Telephone Office
	14 Bus Terminal
13 Mosáferkhūne-yé Fars	15 Hospital
	16 Iran Handicrafts Organization
17 Sāleh Hotel & Restaurant	21 Consulate of Pakistan
18 Hotel Amin	22 Stadium
19 Esteghlal Grand Hotel; Iran Air Office	23 Train Station
	24 Hospital
	26 Police Dept of Alien Affairs (Visa Office)
20 Hotel Kavir	
25 Tourist Camping	27 Gate to Airport

27 To Airport
26
Kheyābān-é Montazeri
Bolvār-é Motahhari
25
0   0.5   1 km
Meidān-é Forūdgāh
To Mīrjāvé & Quetta

IRAN

Other Things to See

Just beyond the eastern edge of Kermān, Ja-baliyé Dome is small, octagonal and of unknown age or purpose. The area around it is excellent for hiking. Take a shared taxi from Meidūn-é Shohadā. The strange Moayedī Ice House has been renovated with *khesht* (a common form of locally made brick, dried in the sun), and is now used as a library and children's park. The gardens around the Kermān National Library are lovely.

Places to Stay

Bahar Guest House (☎ 222 590) just south of Meidūn-é Tohid is central and very cheap – 6500 rials per person – but is extremely reluctant to take foreigners.

Guest House Saady (☎ 43 802) is just off Kheyābūn-é Āyatollāh Sadūghī – look for the painted sign in English on the corner. It has a number of good, cheap and quiet singles/doubles for 14,000/24,000 rials. *Omid Guest House* (☎ 220 581, Mei-dūn-é Ghareny) is a little noisy, but decent enough, for 13,000/20,000 rials – look for the sign in English 'Omid Inn Special Parking'.

Kermān Hotel (☎ 225 065, fax 232 385) is near the bus terminal, but not much else. The rooms are a bit grubby, and cost a negotiable 53,000 rials a double.

Akhavan Hotel (☎ 41 411, fax 49 113, Kheyābūn-é Āyatollāh Sadūghī) is the best mid-range place. It has large, well-furnished rooms, and the managers speak good English. Staff may start mumbling about 150,000/210,000 rials, but will quickly negotiate down to a reasonable 60,000/90,000 rials.

Hotel Milad (☎ 45 862) has decent rooms, with private bathroom, for 25,000/50,000 rials. It's next to the Akhavan Hotel, but not signposted in English. *Naz Hotel* opposite the Akhavan is reasonable for 53,000 rials for doubles and worth trying if the manager at the Akhavan won't negotiate sensibly.

Kermān Grand Hotel (☎ 45 203, fax 44087, Bolvār-é Jomhūrī-yé Eslāmī) is the upmarket hotel, and overpriced at US$53.

Places to Eat

Hot Chips (well, that's the name on the wall) just south of Meidūn-é Āzādī is a pleasant place for western-style fast food, and one of plenty of modern, trendy places along the roads spreading out in all directions from Āzādī.

The hotel restaurants are best. *Akhavan Hotel* has a set menu of fish/meat/ chicken, soup, bread, salad, rice and a drink, for about 13,000 rials. *Kermān Hotel* has a decent 'restourant', as does *Amin Hotel* (Kheyā-būn-é Doktor Chamrān). *Khan-é Sayyah Kermān Restaurant* in the grounds of the Kermān Contemporary Arts Museum has delightful and traditional decor and furniture, and tasty food from about 12,000 rials a dish.

Vakīl Teahouse (☎ 225 989) inside the bazaar is a glorious, subterranean old bathhouse, with elegant brickwork. It offers lunch, tea and the hubble-bubble. *Khayyam Teahouse* between Naz Hotel and Meidūn-é Āzādī is large and has a huge range of hub-ble-bubbles. It's not signposted in English, so look for the lurid purple and silver entrance.

Shopping

You can spend hours just wandering around the 1.5km-long Bāzār-é Vakīl, most of which dates from the Safavid period (1502-1722). It houses a couple of museums (see Museums earlier), a few mosques and a glorious teahouse (see Places to Eat earlier). Kermān is a good place to buy tea-sets and hubble-bubble pipes, and anything made from copper and bronze.

Getting There & Away

Air Iran Air (☎ 235 153) flies to Tehrān every day (122,500 rials); and less often to Esfahān and Zāhedan. Mahan Air (☎ 251 542) also has several flights a week to Tehrān for the same price as Iran Air.

Bus & Minibus From the orderly terminal (accessible by shared taxi from Meidūn-é Shohadā and Meidūn-é Āzādī), buses and minibuses regularly go to: Bam (5200 rials, three hours); Bandar-é Abbās (7600 rials, eight hours); Esfahān (9500 rials, 12 hours);

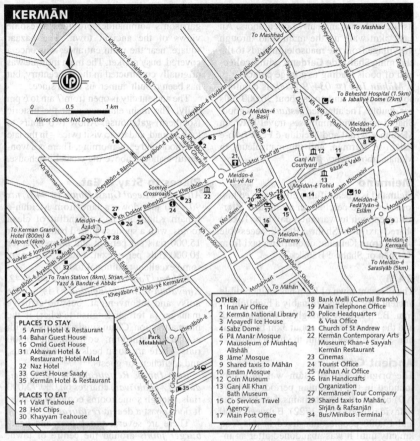

KERMĀN

0   0.5   1 km

Minor Streets Not Depicted

To Mashhad

To Mashhad

To Beheshtī Hospital (1.5km)
& Jabaliyé Dome (7km)

To Kerman Grand
Hotel (800m) &
Airport (4km)

To Train Station (8km), Sīrjān,
Yazd & Bandar-é Abbās

To Māhān

To Meidūn-é
Sarasīyāb (5km)

Ganj Alī
Courtyard

Bāzār-é Vakīl

Meidūn-é
Basij

Meidūn-é
Shohadā

Meidūn-é
Vali-yé Asr

Somiyé
Crossroads

Meidūn-é
Āzādī

Meidūn-é
Ghareny

Meidūn-é
Tohid

Meidūn-é
Feda'īyān-é
Eslām

Meidūn-é
Kermānī

Park
Motahhari

PLACES TO STAY
5   Amin Hotel & Restaurant
14 Bahar Guest House
16 Omid Guest House
31 Akhavan Hotel &
    Restaurant; Hotel Milad
32 Naz Hotel
33 Guest House Saady
35 Kermān Hotel & Restaurant

PLACES TO EAT
11 Vakil Teahouse
28 Hot Chips
30 Khayyam Teahouse

OTHER
1   Iran Air Office
2   Kermān National Library
3   Moayedī Ice House
4   Sabz Dome
6   Pā Manār Mosque
7   Mausoleum of Mushtaq
    Alishāh
8   Jāme' Mosque
9   Shared taxis to Māhān
10 Emām Mosque
12 Coin Museum
13 Ganj Alī Khan
    Bath Museum
15 Co Services Travel
    Agency
17 Main Post Office
18 Bank Melli (Central Branch)
19 Main Telephone Office
20 Police Headquarters
    & Visa Office
21 Church of St Andrew
22 Kermān Contemporary Arts
    Museum; Khan-é Sayyah
    Kermān Restaurant
23 Cinemas
24 Tourist Office
25 Mahan Air Office
26 Iran Handicrafts
    Organization
27 Kermānseir Tour Company
29 Shared taxis to Māhān,
    Sīrjān & Rafsanjān
34 Bus/Minibus Terminal

IRAN

Shīrāz (10,800 rials, eight hours); Tehrān (10,500 rials, 18 hours); Yazd (5200 rials, six hours); and Zāhedān (5500 rials, six hours).

Train To Tehrān (15 hours) via Yazd, Kāshān and Qom, trains leave Kermān on Tuesday, Thursday and Saturday afternoons. Tickets (14,000/30,000 rials for 2nd/1st class) are on sale between 6 am and 1.30 pm on the day of departure. The train station is about 8km south-west of town – take a shared taxi from Meidūn-é Āzādī.

Shared Taxi From Meidūn-é Āzādī, shared taxis travel to Rafsanjān, Māhān and Sīrjān; for Māhān, also leaving from Meidūn-é Fedā'īyān-é Eslām. To Bam, and sometimes Zāhedān, taxis leave from Meidūn-é Sara-sīyāb, about 5km east of Meidūn-é Kermānī.

AROUND KERMĀN
Māhān

In Māhān, there's the **Mausoleum of Shāh Ne'matollāh Valī**, dedicated to a well-known local poet and mystic. It dates from the early 15th century, and is renowned for its tilework and ancient wooden doors. An easy 5km walk up the main road through the village from the mausoleum leads to the charming **Shāhzāde Gardens**, with a collection of pools leading to a large **palace**.

Māhān Inn (☎ 03479-2700) is comfortable and clean, and costs about 90,000 rials per double. The attached *restaurant* is good. Shared taxis and minibuses travel between Meidūn-é Āzādī and Meidūn-é Fedā'īyān-é Eslām in Kermān, and the mausoleum in Māhān, about every hour.

Meimand

Meimand is a beautiful, well-preserved historical village perched on a hill, and interesting enough to warrant a day trip. Take a shared taxi from Shahr-é Bābak, accessible by bus from Kermān; or charter a taxi from Kermān or Shahr-é Bābak.

BAM

The pleasant town of Bam has an incredible ancient city – unquestionably a highlight of Iran. Bam is easy enough to walk around, and the ancient city is about 3km from Meidūn-é Emām Khomeinī, the town centre.

Ancient City

The original city of Bam was probably founded in the Sassanian period (224-637 AD) but most of the remains date from the Safavid period (1502-1722). Between 9000 and 13,000 people once lived in this 6 sq km city until it was abandoned after an invasion by the Afghans in 1722.

All of the steep, narrow stairways lead to the pinnacles of the outer wall for a definitive outlook over the old and new towns. The inner citadel contains a fortified 17th century residence known as the Chahār Fasl. In the garrison, shout something and listen to the extraordinary echo – archaeologists believe this is an ancient loudspeaker system. Nearby are the 14th century stables, which once housed 200 to 300 horses.

On the way up to the governor's residence, there are some very dark and scary dungeons – obviously built for those who

displeased the governor. The residence of the garrison's commander provides awesome views of the ancient town. The bazaar square, near the main entrance, was once a covered, busy market. The main mosque was originally constructed in the 9th century, but has been rebuilt numerous times since.

The ancient city is open from 7 am to 6 pm daily. The main entrance is at the historic (southern) **gatehouse**. Allow two hours to look around, and try to visit twice – in the late afternoon and early morning. There is a wonderful teahouse above the citadel gatehouse.

Places to Stay & Eat

Alī Amirī's Legal Guest House (☎ 4481, fax 90 085) just down a lane from Meidūn-é Emām Khomeinī has a handful of clean rooms, with a spotless shared bathroom, for 15,000 rials per person; and dorm beds for 10,000 rials per person. Guests can enjoy some excellent traditional food.

Akhbar Tourist Guest House (☎ 5842, Kheyābūn-é Saled Jamaladin) is a little noisy and inconvenient, but the effusive manager (a former English teacher) is the main attraction. Clean singles/doubles, with a shared bathroom, cost 20,000/40,000 rials. There are dorm beds for 15,000 rials, and a kitchen for guests.

Bam Inn & Restaurant (☎ 3323, Meidūn-é 17 Shahrīvar) charges 60,000/72,000 rials, though some rooms could be cleaner. It does boast a decent *restaurant*.

There are several **snack bars** and **hamburger joints** around the centre of town, and a **teahouse** in the old city. *Bamargh Restaurant* opposite the entrance to the old city has a charming setting.

Getting There & Away

Iran Asseman flies between Bam and Tehrān on Thursday and Sunday for 152,000 rials. At the time of research, the location of the Iran Asseman office in Bam was uncertain. Try to buy your ticket out of Bam before you come, or ask your hotel in Bam about the office.

If you started very early, you could do a day trip to Bam from Kermān. Buses leave

Bam from offices along the main street to: Bandar-é Abbās (7500 rials, eight hours); Kermān (5200 rials, three hours); Tehrān (16,500 rials, 21 hours); Yazd (8500 rials, nine hours); and Zāhedān (6500 rials, five hours). Alternatively, catch onward transport in either direction at the large roundabout along the Kermān-Zāhedān road.

Southern Iran

Most travellers to southern Iran understandably concentrate on Shīrāz and its nearby attractions, such as Persepolis, but there are several other worthwhile places to visit for a glimpse of Arab life along the Persian Gulf. Iran has several islands in the Gulf, but only the duty-free islands of Kīsh and Qeshm are equipped for tourism.

BANDAR-É ABBĀS
Bandar-é Abbās is the busiest port in Iran, and the major city along the Persian Gulf. In summer, it gets sizzling hot and very humid, but it's a very pleasant place to visit in winter. There's not much to see or do, but the city – known simply as Bandar by the locals – is a stepping-off point for the nearby islands (see Persian Gulf Islands later). Bandar's population is a fascinating mix of Arabs and black Africans, with a large Sunni minority.

Orientation & Information
The main east-west thoroughfare changes its name from Bolvār-é Beheshtī (in the east), to Kheyābūn-é Emām Khomeinī (through the centre of town), and then Bolvār-é Pāsdārān (in the west). The city centre is Meidūn-é 17 Shahrīvar, where the police headquarters (for visa extensions) and Bank Melli are located. The money exchange offices on Kheyābūn-é Emām Khomeinī are better places to change money.

Places to Stay
Many budget places won't accept foreigners. **Bandar Guest House** (that's the name we've given it) is above the bazaar, along the esplanade, but not signposted in English. It's noisy but clean, and certainly cheap: 6000 rials for a dorm bed and 8000/10,000 rials for singles/doubles. **Maharaja Guest House** (not signposted in English) near the corner of the esplanade and Kheyābūn-é Abūzar is basic and convenient, but the area is dodgy at night. Foreigners are charged a negotiable 30,000 rials for a room with three beds.

Safa Hotel (☎ 22 651, Kheyābūn-é Asad Ābādī), about 500m north-west of Meidūn-é 17 Shahrīvar, has reasonable doubles, some with air-con, from 15,000/25,000 rials. **Hotel Ghods** (☎ 22 344, Kheyābūn-é Emām Khomeinī) about 200m east of 17 Shahrīvar is the recognised 'tourist hotel'. It has large, well-furnished rooms, and good service, for a negotiable 60,000 rials per person.

Hotel Hamzeh (☎ 23 771, Kheyābūn-é Abūzar) is the best in the mid-range, but overpriced for a negotiable 70,000/100,000 rials. **Homa Hotel** (☎ 553 080, fax 517 32, Kheyābūn-é Meraj) is luxurious, but inconveniently located about 2.5km west of the city centre. Rooms cost US$71/95.

Places to Eat
Safa Kabābī directly under Safa Hotel is one of the best places for kabābs. Kheyābūn-é Sayyādān, between Meidūn-é Shohādā (in western Bandar) and the sea, has several trendy places for hamburgers and pizzas. **Nofl Loshato** is popular, and one of the best.

Most of Bandar's hotels serve decent fare. **Hotel Ghods** serves good food, at good prices. **Persian Restaurant** (Kheyābūn-é Emām Khomeinī) about 50m west of Meidūn-é 17 Shahrīvar is the best place for chelō khōresht (stew and rice), and other traditional food, for about 11,000 rials, with soup and a drink. **Customs Restaurant & Club** is an unusual looking place, about 500m east of 17 Shahrīvar.

Getting There & Away
Refer to the Getting There & Away chapter at the beginning of this book for details about international ferry services to/from Bandar-é Abbās.

IRAN

Air Iran Air (☎ 39 595), about 600m west of Meidūn-é 17 Shahrīvar, flies every day to Tehrān (161,500 rials) and Shīrāz (79,500 rials); and less regularly to Esfahān, Mashhad and Rasht. Iran Asseman (☎ 29 096), along the esplanade, also flies to Tehrān and Shīrāz for the same price as Iran Air.

Bus The bus terminal is in the far east of the city – you may need to take two shared taxis, or charter one directly. Buses regularly go to all major places including: Bam (7500 rials, eight hours); Bandar-é Lengé (4000 rials, three hours); Būshehr (13,500 rials, 14 hours); Esfahān (12,500 rials, eight hours); Kermān (7600 rials, eight hours); Shīrāz (9500 rials, 10 hours); and Yazd (11,800 rials, 10 hours).

Train The train to Tehrān (21 hours) leaves every Monday, Wednesday and Friday, and tickets cost 35,500 rials in 1st class (no 2nd class). The station is in the far north of the city – charter a taxi. There is a handy ticket office (unsignposted in English), one door east of the Bala Parvaz Travel Agency, and almost opposite Hotel Ghods.

Boat Boats to Hormoz and Qeshm islands leave every few minutes from the main jetty, opposite the bazaar. Ferries to Qeshm (and across the Persian Gulf) leave several times a day from the Shahīd Bāhonar docks, about 6km west of the city centre. Tickets for international ferries are available at travel agencies around the town, or from Valfajre-8 (☎ 559 075), between the city centre and docks.

MĪNĀB

The pleasant town of Mīnāb is an easy day trip from Bandar-é Abbās. The region is famous for ceramics and mosaic tiles; both are for sale at the markets.

Mīnāb Inn (☎ 07623-2263) is nicely located inside a park, 3km past the main bridge as you come from Bandar. Very pleasant singles/doubles cost a reasonable 35,000/45,000 rials. The charming *restaurant* is open to guests and the public. *Sadaf Hotel* (☎ 07623-

8999), not far from the bus terminal, has clean rooms for 25,000/35,000 rials.

About every hour, minibuses and shared taxis leave from a designated spot about 100m north of Meidūn-é 17 Shahrīvar in Bandar-é Abbās.

BANDAR-É LENGÉ

Lengé is an infectiously lethargic place, and a pleasant overnight stop before or after visiting Kīsh Island, or as a day trip from Bandar-é Abbās. There is nothing to do, but the **beach**, about 1km east of the docks, is reasonable.

Hotel Amid (☎ 07622-2311, Kheyābūn-é Enghelāb), about 150m north of the docks, charges 25,000 rials for a three-bed room with a shared bathroom. The *restaurant* downstairs is the best place to eat. *Hotel Babu*, the unmistakable four-storey place in the bazaar, charges 21,000 rials for a double with a shared bathroom.

Iran Air (☎ 07622-2799) flies every day to Tehrān, via Shīrāz. From the bus terminal, about 2km east of the docks, buses go to Bandar-é Abbās (4000 rials, three hours) about every hour, and daily to Būshehr and Shīrāz.

PERSIAN GULF ISLANDS

Iran has 16 islands in the Persian Gulf, of which three are still claimed by the UAE. Eleven of the 16 are inhabited, but foreigners are only welcome to Kīsh, Qeshm and Hormoz islands.

Kīsh Island

The main attraction of Kīsh for Iranians is duty-free electrical goods, but it also promotes itself as a 'resort', so it's very expensive. There is no real centre on the island, but most facilities are in the north-east, where the banks and Kīsh Tourism Organisation are located; Saffein village is in the north-west.

Things to See & Do Among the unrestrained development are the limited ruins of the **ancient cities** near Saffein. Kīsh has several sandy **beaches**, but females must use Ladies Beach No 1 or Ladies Beach No 2; and men, the Men's Beach. Iran's only **div-**

ing centre (☎ 2771) is at Shayan Hotel. The island also has theme parks, such as **Family Park** and **Deers Park**, and an **aquarium**.

Places to Stay & Eat *Sahra Guest House* (☎ 2110) near the port and *Sahar Guest House* (☎ 2067) south of the airport charge from 65,000 rials for a double, but are almost permanently full. Ask around the port for other cheap guesthouses or apartments. *Didar Hotel* (☎ 2706) in Saffein charges a negotiable 100,000 rials for a huge room. Plenty of other expensive, top end places are dotted around the island.

Venus Burger is a western-style hamburger joint in the shopping district. *Kando Restaurant* and the nearby *Sahel Restaurant* are reasonably priced. There are a handful of cheap *cafes* and *restaurants* in Saffein.

Getting There & Away Iran Air (☎ 2274) has regular flights from Tehrān, and Kīsh Airlines (☎ 2259) flies from Tehrān, Shīrāz, Esfahān and Mashhad.

Ferries operated by Valfajre-8 sail from three ports: irregularly from Būshehr and Bandar-é Abbās, and every night from Bandar-é Lengé. Far better is the speedboat from Bandar-é Chārak – an easy ride from Lengé by shared taxi.

Hormoz Island

The 42 sq km Hormoz Island is worth a visit, and easily accessible from Bandar-é Abbās. The only village is also called Hormoz, and the rest of the island is virtually uninhabited. About 750m to the north of Hormoz village are the ruins of a 16th century **Portuguese castle**. It's the most impressive colonial fortress in Iran, but badly neglected.

Speedboats travel between the jetty (opposite the bazaar) in Bandar-é Abbās and Hormoz village (30 minutes) about every hour.

Qeshm Island

Qeshm is the largest island (1335 sq km) in the Persian Gulf. The island is mountainous, dotted with villages and gradually being developed as a rival duty-free resort to Kīsh. The main town is Qeshm.

Things to See & Do Conical **water reservoirs** are scattered all over the island, with the highest concentration around Qeshm town. A few Arab-style **mosques** are also dotted around the island. The remains of the **Portuguese fortress** in Qeshm town are not nearly as impressive as the ruins on Hormoz. **Lāft** is a pretty village, with windtowers, wells and an empty **beach**.

Places to Stay & Eat In Qeshm town *Gheshm Inn* (☎ 7629-2001) is pleasant, and has very good doubles for 45,000 rials. They have an excellent *restaurant*. Like Kīsh, there are plenty of other top end places around the island, such as *International Gheshm* (☎ 07629-5305).

Getting There & Away Refer to Getting There & Away in the Bandar-é Abbās section earlier for information about boat transport to Qeshm.

Qeshm Air (☎ 0761-570 361), next to the Iran Air office in Bandar-é Abbās, has daily flights from Tehrān (160,000 rials), and from most major mainland cities. The Qeshm Air office is also a source of useful information about the island.

SHĪRĀZ

Shīrāz was one of the most important cities in the medieval Islamic world, and was the Iranian capital during the Zand period (1747-79), when many of its most beautiful buildings were built or restored. Through its many artists and scholars, Shīrāz has been synonymous with learning, poetry, roses and, at one time, wine.

Shīrāz is probably the most pleasant of the large Iranian cities after Esfahān. It is relaxed and cultivated, and has generous inhabitants, wide tree-lined avenues, and enough monuments, gardens and mosques to keep most visitors happy for several days.

Orientation

Most of the things to see, and many of the tourist facilities, are along, or near, the wide, tree-lined Bolvār-é Karīm Khān-é Zand – often simply called 'Zand'. The city

IRAN

SHĪRĀZ

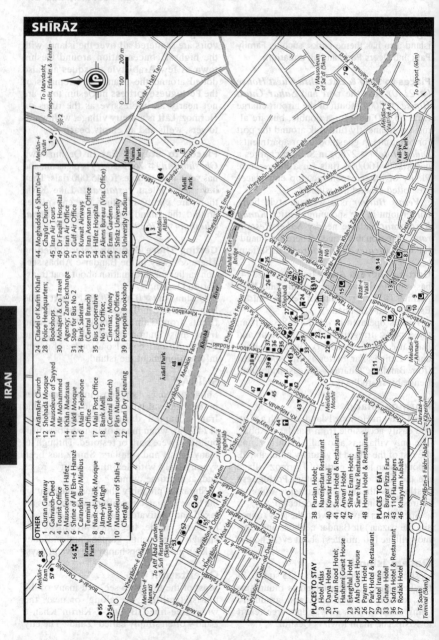

To Marvdasht,
Persepolis, Esfahān & Tehrān

To Mausoleum
of Sa'di (5km)

To Airport (6km)

To Affī Ābād Garden
(5km) & Sufi Restaurant

To South
Terminal (5km)

To Ghadamgah
(5km)

To Kāzerūn

OTHER
1   Quran Gateway
2   Gahvārch-Deed
4   Tourist Office
5   Mausoleum of Hāfez
6   Shrine of Alī Ebn-e Hamzé
7   Carandish Bus/Minibus
     Terminal
8   Nasir-ol-Molk Mosque
9   Jāmé-yé Atigh
     Mosque
10 Mausoleum of Shāh-e
     Cherāgh
11 Arāmāné Church
12 Shohadā Mosque
13 Mausoleum of Sayyed
     Mir Mohammed
14 Khān Madrassa
15 Vakil Mosque
16 Main Telephone
     Office
17 Main Post Office
18 Bank Melli
     (Central Branch)
19 Pārs Museum
22 Ozari Dry Cleaning
24 Citadel of Karīm Khāni
28 Police Headquarters;
     Bookshops
30 Mohājeri & Co Travel
     Agency; Zand Exchange
31 Stop for Bus No 2
     (Central Branch)
34 Bank Saderat
     (Central Branch)
35 Bus Cooperative
     No 15 Office;
     Cinemas; Money
     Exchange Offices
39 Persepolis Bookshop
44 Moghaddas-é Sham'ūn-é
     Ghayūr Church
45 Iran Air Tours
49 Dr Faqihi Hospital
50 Iran Air Office
51 Gulf Air Office
52 Kuwait Airways
53 Iran Asseman Office
54 Hāfez Hospital
55 Aliens Bureau (Visa Office)
56 Eram Gardens
57 Shīrāz University
58 University Stadium

PLACES TO STAY
3   Hotel Atlas
20 Darya Hotel
21 Arvan Rood Hotel;
     Hashemi Guest House
23 Esteghlal Hotel
25 Mah Guest House
26 Payam Hotel
27 Park Hotel & Restaurant
29 Hotel Irano
33 Ghane Hotel
35 Sadra Hotel & Restaurant
37 Rodaki Hotel
38 Parsian Hotel;
     Narenjestan Restaurant
40 Kowsar Hotel
41 Sasan Hotel & Restaurant
42 Anvari Hotel
47 Shīrāz Eram Hotel;
     Sarve Naz Restaurant
48 Homa Hotel & Restaurant

PLACES TO EAT
32 Burger Pizza Fars
43 110 Hamburgers
46 Khayyām Kabābi

centre is Meidūn-é Shohadā, still widely known as Meidūn-é Shahrdārī.

Information

Visa Extensions Shīrāz is a great place to extend your visa. Extensions of seven to 10 days are given without hassle, and an extension of 15 days or more is possible if you ask nicely. The 'Aliens Bureau' is a little hard to find behind the Hāfez Hospital – ask for directions.

Tourist Offices The tourist office (☎ 220 791) hands out some brochures (in German and English) and a good (free) map, but the office itself is not particularly useful. It's opposite Melli Park and is not well-signposted.

Money The central branches of the major banks will change money. The best is Bank Melli, which also gives cash advances on MasterCard and Visa, and accepts travellers cheques. The Bank Melli branch at the airport will also change money. To obtain the favourable 'street rate', go to one of the money exchange offices along Zand. The black marketeers hang around Bank Melli and the Citadel of Karīm Khān.

Post & Communications The telephone office is along Kheyābūn-é 22 Bahman, and the well-organised post office is easy to find along a laneway off 22 Bahman.

Citadel of Karīm Khān

Dominating the city centre is a well-preserved citadel with four circular towers. During the Zand period, it was part of a royal courtyard that Karīm Khān planned to rival that of Esfahān. Currently, there is little to see inside, but restoration is continuing. It's open from 8 am to 6 pm daily.

Pārs Museum

Opposite the citadel, this small museum contains an exhibition relating to the life of Karīm Khān, along with other historic artefacts. Opening hours are erratic but it's worth a peek.

Vakīl Mosque

The 'Regent's Mosque' has two vast eivāns to the north and south, and a magnificent inner courtyard surrounded by beautifully tiled alcoves and porches. Although the structure of the mosque dates from 1773, most of the tiling, with its predominantly floral motifs, was added in the early Ghajar era (about 1820). The best time for a look is during noon prayers (from about noon to 1.30 pm).

Shohadā Mosque

The 'Martyrs' Mosque' is one of the largest and oldest mosques in Iran. Founded at the start of the 13th century, it has been partially rebuilt many times, and now has very little in the way of tiling or other decorations. It does boast some impressive barrel vaulting, however, and a huge courtyard (over 11,000 sq metres). The only time you'll be able to look around is on Friday.

Mausoleum Shāh-é Cherāgh

The tomb of the 'King of the Lamp' houses the remains of Sayyed Mīr Ahmad (another brother of Emām Rezā of Mashhad fame) who died, or was killed, in Shīrāz in 835. A mausoleum was originally erected over the grave in the mid-14th century, and it's now an important Shi'ite place of pilgrimage. Past the shrine, a small, unmarked **museum** contains a display of fine china and glassware. The mausoleum and museum are open daily from about 7 am to 10 pm.

Khān Madrassa

This theological college was built in 1615, but has since been extensively damaged by earthquakes, so only a small part remains. The mullahs' training college (still in use today) has a fine stone-walled inner courtyard set around a small garden. This place is also often closed, but if you find the caretaker he'll happily open it up.

Mausoleum of Hāfez

The tomb of the celebrated poet Hāfez is surrounded by a charming garden and flanked by two pools. The marble tombstone,

IRAN

engraved with a long verse from the poet's works, was placed here, inside a small shrine, by Karīm Khān in 1773. In 1935, the octagonal pavilion was erected above it.

A wonderfully atmospheric *teahouse* is in a private, walled garden inside the grounds, and there's a library and bookshop nearby. The mausoleum is open from about 8 am to 9 pm daily. Take a shared taxi from Meidūn-ē Shohadā.

Mausoleum of Sa'dī

The tomb of another local poet, Sa'dī, is tranquil, but not as impressive as Hāfez's. The unattractive marble tomb, which dates from the 1860s, is in an octagonal stone colonnade, inscribed with various verses from Sa'dī. The grounds are open every day during daylight hours.

A small, underground *teahouse* is located around a fish pond inside the complex, and there are plenty of shops and *kabābīs* near the entrance. Take a shared taxi from Meidūn-é Shohadā, and another from Meidūn-é Atlasī or Meidūn-é Valī-yé Asr; or charter something directly there.

Eram Gardens

Famous for its cypress trees, the 'Garden of Paradise' is better arranged than the other gardens in Shīrāz. Alongside a pretty pool is the charming 19th century **Eram Palace**, though it's not normally open to visitors. The gardens are open every day during daylight hours. Take any shared taxi along Zand heading towards the university.

Afīf Ābād Garden

These picturesque gardens contain the **Afīf Ābād Palace**, once owned by the shāh. Built in 1863, and influenced by the Ghajar style of architecture, the lower floor of the palace is now an interesting **military museum**. The gardens are only open from 4.30 to 7.30 pm every day, and they're a fair way from the city centre, so it's best to charter a taxi.

Quran Gateway

Mir Alī, grandson of Emām Musā Kazem, is buried at this impressive site. There are great views and hikes in the area, and a charming *teahouse*. It's particularly pleasant in the evening. Stop here if you've chartered a vehicle to Persepolis or beyond; or charter a taxi or walk from the Mausoleum of Hāfez.

Places to Stay – Budget

One place to check around and find something at the standard and price you want is Kheyābūn-é Pīrūzī, where there are about a dozen places for about 15,000/20,000 rials for singles/doubles. *Darya Hotel* (☎ 220 858) has a good range of rooms, and a manager who speaks English.

Esteghlal Hotel (☎ 227 728, Kheyābūn-é Dehnadī) is central, but now a little overpriced. Small, clean singles/doubles/triples, with private bathroom, cost 24,000/30,000/35,000 rials. It's just off the main road, and quieter than most places.

Payam Hotel (☎ 227 994, Kheyābūn-é 22 Bahman) is a friendly place on a quiet street. Rooms with a shared bathroom costs 15,000/30,000 rials. The upper floors have views, while the lower floors overlook an uninspiring courtyard.

Ghane Hotel (☎ 225 374, Kheyābūn-é Tōhid) is set back from the main road, and quieter than other places. The rooms are small, but decent enough, and cost a reasonable 18,000/20,000 rials with shared bathroom.

Anvarī Hotel (☎ 337 591, Kheyābūn-é Anvarī), also called Madaen Hotel, is the best of three cheapies in a row. Staff are friendly, and the rooms, with private bathroom, are clean and comfortable. Doubles cost 30,000 rials; singles are negotiable and cost about 18,000 rials. *Sasan Hotel* (☎ 337 830) next to the Anvarī is also comfy, but a little overpriced for a negotiable 40,000/50,000 rials.

Places to Stay – Mid-Range & Top End

Sadra Hotel (☎ 224 740, Kheyābūn-é Rūdakī) is one of three good mid-range places along a quiet street. It has clean, large singles/doubles with fridge and lovely bathroom for a negotiable 75,000/90,000 rials.

Kowsar Hotel (☎ *335 724, fax 333 117, Bolvār-é Karīm Khān-é Zand*) has large rooms, with a fridge and TV, for 70,000/120,000 rials. The staff speak English, but some travellers have complained about shonky bills and accounting procedures with credit cards.

Shīrāz Eram Hotel (☎ *337 201, fax 335 292, Bolvār-é Karīm Khān-é Zand*) has large, well-furnished rooms with a fridge, sunny bathroom and enormous beds, for a negotiable 100,000/150,000 rials, including breakfast.

Park Hotel (☎ *221 426, fax 221 429, Meidūn-é Shohadā*) has large rooms, with balconies. It's pretty good value because foreigners can pay in rials: 139,000/210,000 rials, including breakfast. The pool is permanently empty.

Homa Hotel (☎ *228 000, fax 48 021, Kheyābūn-é Meshkin Fām*) is the top end place, with all the luxuries you'd expect, such as tennis courts and a swimming pool (with water), for US$71/103.

Places to Eat

Zand is lined with plenty of cheap *kabābīs* and *hamburger joints*, but Shīrāz is one place where you may want to spend a few more rials and enjoy some decent meals.

110 Hamburgers (*Kheyābūn-é Anvarī*) is the best place for fast food, and is a short distance from most hotels. A large western-style burger, Iranian-style chips (French fries) and cola costs about 5000 rials. *Burger Pizza Fars* on the corner of Bolvār-é Karīm Khān-é Zand and Kheyābūn-é Sa'dī also serves burgers, but the scrumptious pizzas are its speciality.

Sufi Restaurant near the Afīf Ābād Garden is a long way from the city centre and hopeless for public transport, but worth visiting for good food and atmosphere. Expect to pay for about 14,000 rial per person, including soup and the mandatory visit to the salad bar.

Sadra Hotel has one of the best hotel restaurants. *Park Hotel* has a decent restaurant, with meals from 12,500 rials, and is also good for set-priced breakfast (about 8600 rials). *Sarve Naz Restaurant* on the 1st floor of the Shīrāz Eram Hotel is elegant, and has a menu in English. A huge roast chicken, among other western-style dishes, costs 11,500 rials.

Teahouses

The teahouses in Shīrāz are not as charming as those in Esfahān, but there are some pleasant places for a cuppa at the Hāfez and Sa'dī mausoleums, and at the Quran Gateway and Bāzār-é Vakīl.

Shopping

The **Bāzār-é Vakīl** (Vakil Bazaar) was constructed by Karīm Khān as part of a plan to make Shīrāz into a great trading centre. The vaulted brick ceilings ensure that the interior is cool in the summer and warm in the winter. It's one the finest bazaars in Iran, and houses its own **bathhouse** and a few *teahouses*. The **Bāzār-é Nō** (New Bazaar) is also worth a stroll around. Shīrāz is a good place to buy printed fabrics, tea-sets and hubble-bubble pipes made from copper and bronze.

Getting There & Away

Air Iran Air (☎ 330 041) flies many times a day to Tehrān (106,500 rials) and Esfahān (70,000 rials); daily to Bandar-é Abbās (79,500 rials), Bandar-é Lengé (72,500 rials) and Mashhad (144,500 rials); and less regularly to Ahvāz and Būshehr. Iran Asseman (☎ 308 841) has a similar schedule with identical prices. Gulf Air (☎ 301 962) has an office along Zand.

Bus & Minibus The main bus/minibus terminal is the Carandish bus terminal, also known as the Termīnāl-é Bozorg. Bus tickets can also be bought in advance at one of the bus company offices along Zand. Buses and minibuses leave regularly for Bandar-é Abbās (9500 rials, 10 hours); Bandar-é Lengé (10,200 rials, 11 hours); Būshehr (5500 rials, five hours); Esfahān (7800 rials, eight hours); Kermān (10,800 rials, eight hours); Tehrān (13,500 rials, 16 hours); and Yazd (6900 rials, seven hours).

Shared Taxi From the Carandish bus terminal, shared taxis leave for regional towns, including Marvdasht (for Persepolis), and occasionally travel all the way to Esfahān.

Getting Around
To/From the Airport Bus No 10 travels between the airport and a stop behind the Citadel of Karīm Khān. Shared taxis for the airport leave irregularly from Meidūn-é Valī-yé Asr; from the airport, there are plenty of shared taxis.

Bus The handy bus No 2 starts from the corner of Zand and Kheyābūn-é Sa'dī, and passes the tourist office, the Hāfez mausoleum and Meidūn-é Golestān (for the Carandish Bus Terminal).

AROUND SHĪRĀZ
Naghsh-é Rostam
Hewn out of a cliff, the four tombs of Naghsh-é Rostam are believed to be those of Darius I, Artaxerxes, Xerxes I and Darius II (from left to right as you look at the cliff). There are also eight **reliefs** from later in the Sassanian period (224-637 AD) depicting scenes of imperial conquests and royal investitures, and what is probably a **fire temple** from the Achaemenian period (559-330 BC). The best time for photos is before mid-afternoon.

The only restaurant in the area is *Takhte Tawoos* on the road between Persepolis and Naghsh-é Rostam.

If you want to avoid paying the (high) entrance fee, you can see most of the tombs from outside the fence. Naghsh-é Rostam is 6km along the road north from Persepolis. If you haven't chartered a taxi, you can walk there, or share or charter a taxi from Persepolis.

Pasargadae
Begun under Cyrus (Kouroush) the Great in about 546 BC, the city of Pasargadae was superseded soon after Cyrus' death by Persepolis. It's nowhere near as visually stimulating as Persepolis, and what remains is widely scattered, so you'll need your own transport.

The first structure you'll see is the six tiered **Tomb of Cyrus**, one of the best preserved of the remains. Within walking distance of the tomb (but you'll need to ask exact directions) are the insubstantial remains of three **Achaemenian Palaces**; and the ruins of a tower on a plinth, known as the **Prison of Solomon**. Other remains are farther afield.

Pasargadae is 130km north of Shīrāz. If you haven't chartered a taxi directly there, get a minibus to Marvdasht from Shīrāz, another minibus or shared taxi to Sā'adatshahr, and another shared taxi to Pasargadae. Alternatively, catch a bus between Shīrāz and Esfahān, and hitch a ride to Pasargadae from the turn-off.

Fīrūz Ābād
The remains of the old cities of Fīrūz and Gūr, dating back to the Sassanian period (224-637 AD), are often ignored. About 6km before Fīrūz, on the road from Shīrāz, an abandoned chairlift leads to the ruins of the three storey **Doktar Palace**. About 2km farther towards Fīrūz, an unsignposted rocky trail leads to the **Ardeshir Fire Temple**.

There's at least one bus and several minibuses every day between Shīrāz and Fīrūz. To see as much as possible, charter a taxi from Shīrāz or Fīrūz.

BŪSHEHR
Būshehr is the most pleasant town along the Persian Gulf. It lacks the frantic bustle of Bandar-é Abbās, and is mostly free of the complete and utter lethargy of Bandar-é Lengé. The highlight is the **old city**, one of the largest living museums of traditional Bandarī architecture in Iran, and thankfully spared from the destructive effects of development. The centre of town is Meidūn-é Shohadā, in the bazaar district.

Places to Stay & Eat
There is a dire shortage of budget accommodation, and most cheap places, such as *Hafez Hotel* in the bazaar district, will only accept foreigners with special permission from the local police station. Ask around

the bazaar for something cheap and available to foreigners.

Rezā Hotel (☎ *27 171, Meidūn-é Ghods)* is the recognised 'tourist hotel'. It's comfortable, but not cheap: 90,000 rials for a double with bathroom, fridge, air-con and telephone.

Azadi Restaurant *(Kheyābūn-é Shohadā)* is the best place to eat. ***Lian Restaurant***, on Kheyābūn-é Leyān (the pedestrian mall heading south-west of the main square) is also good.

Getting There & Away

Iran Air (☎ 22 041) flies to Tehrān every day (73,500 rials), and less often to Esfahān and Shīrāz. Buses go to all major destinations, including Bandar-é Abbās (13,500 rials, 14 hours), Bandar-é Lengé (9200 rials, nine hours) and Shīrāz (5500 rials, five hours). Valfare-8 ferry company (☎ 24 234), in the port area, operates ferries to Kīsh Island.

AHVĀZ

Much of Ahvāz was devastated by unremitting Iraqi bombardments throughout the Iran-Iraq War, and has since been ruined by uncontrolled redevelopment. There is no need to spend too long here: Andīmeshk is a better base for visiting Shūsh or Choghā Zambīl.

Hotel Star (☎ *061-218 125)* has good singles/doubles, with fan and shared bathroom, for only 15,000/20,000 rials. It's a white, three storey building on the corner of an unmarked lane and Kheyābūn-é Emām Khomeinī. ***Hotel Iran*** (☎ *061-218 200, Kheyābūn-é Sharī'atī)* has comfortable rooms with bathroom and fan for 30,000/42,500 rials. ***Restaurant Khayyām*** on Meidūn-é Shohadā has great views and meals.

Iran Air (☎ 22 096) flies every day to Tehrān and Esfahān, and less often to Mashhad and Shīrāz. Iran Air has two offices: one (☎ 45 398) is on the road to the airport; the other (☎ 42 094) is in the northern Kiyan Pars district.

Buses and minibuses leave from different places in the western suburbs. You can charter a taxi to the terminal you need. Express trains (16 hours) travel overnight to Tehrān every day.

ANDĪMESHK

Andīmeshk is the best place to base yourself while exploring the south-west region, and visiting Shūsh and/or Choghā Zambīl (though there is now a hotel in Shūsh).

The best hotels in Andīmeshk are along the main road heading north from the highway. They all charge about 50,000 rials for a reasonable double room. ***Hotel Apadana*** is a bit dated; ***Hotel Rostam*** opposite is slightly better; and ***Hotel Eghbal*** on the square in the middle of town is the best.

Some bus companies in Andīmeshk have direct services to Tehrān. To avoid going to the large, and very dreary, town of Dezfūl nearby for other bus services, hail down a bus from the roundabout along the main highway in Andīmeshk. Several trains leave for both Ahvāz and Tehrān from the station daily, about 150m west of Hotel Eghbal.

SHŪSH (SUSA)

Shūsh was one of the great ancient cities of Iran, and one of the earliest to be explored by archaeologists. It was an important regional centre from at least the 4th millennium BC, and reached its peak in the 13th century BC and again in the 6th century BC. It must have been as grand as Persepolis, but there's now very little to see.

Ancient City

The city was built on four small mounds. The largest mound contains the remains of the **Royal Town**, once the quarter of the court officials. North-west of this was the **Apadana**, where Darius I built his residence and two other palaces. Two well-preserved foundation tablets found beneath the site of **Darius' Palace** record the noble ancestry of its founder. The mound labelled as the **Artisans' Town** dates from the Seleucid (331-190 BC) and Parthian (190 BC-224 AD) periods. The **Acropolis** was built by the French Archaeological Service at the end of the 19th century as a necessary defence against the unpacified Arab tribes of the region, but is

PERSEPOLIS

In about 512 BC, Darius I (the Great) began constructing this massive and magnificent complex as a summer capital. It was completed by a host of subsequent kings over the next 150 years. The original name was Pārsā but the Greeks, who invaded and destroyed the city in 331 BC, bestowed upon it the name Persepolis.

The Site

At the top of the grand entrance stair is **Xerxes Gateway**, with three separate doors and a hallway. It once covered an area of more than 600 sq metres. The remaining doors are still covered with inscriptions and carvings in the ancient Elamite language. To the east, near the **Unfinished Gate**, are some double-headed eagles.

The southern door of Xerxes Gateway leads to the immense **Apadana Palace**, where the kings received visitors. Inside, the **Court of Apadana** was built from stone somehow excavated from nearby mountains. The roof of the **Central Hall of Apadana Palace** was supported by 36 stone columns, each 20m high. The stairways are decorated with superb reliefs, each representing ancient nationalities.

Behind the Central Hall, and connected by another stairway, is the **Palace of Darius I**. Once the private residence of Darius I, it was filled with statues covered with jewels, but only the carvings along the staircase remain.

The **Palace of 100 Columns** was probably one of the largest buildings constructed during the Achaemenid period (559-330 BC), and contained 100 columns about 14m high, each with reliefs showing Darius struggling with evil spirits. **Darius' Treasury** was a large collection of rooms housing the wealth of the city. Overlooking all of this are the **Tomb of Artaxerxes II**, and the larger **Tomb of Artaxerxes III**, which are both carved into the rockface of the mountains that overshadow the site.

The small **Persepolis Museum** contains some ceramics, carvings, cloth and coins, with captions in English.

Top: The great winged bulls of Xerxes Gateway (Both photos by Bradley Mayhew)

Left: The most striking aspect of Persepolis is the abundance of beautifully styled bas reliefs.

Persepolis is open every day during daylight hours. An impressive sound and light show runs every evening (at 6 pm) for one month from the start of the Iranian New Year (approximately 21 March), and continues on Thursday and Friday evenings until late September.

Getting There & Away

By public transport, catch a minibus from the back of the Carandish Bus Terminal in Shīrāz to Marvdasht, and then take a shared taxi to Persepolis (14km). Alternatively, catch a Shīrāz-Esfahān bus and ask to be let off at the Persepolis (Takht-é Jamshīd) junction; from here it's a 4km walk or look for a shared taxi, from the obvious turn-off along the main road. Chartering a taxi from Shīrāz will allow visitors to also see Naghsh-é Rostam and Pasargadae (see the Around Shīrāz section earlier in this chapter).

Top: Several columns of the 100 that once supported Darius' palace (Photo by Bradley Mayhew)

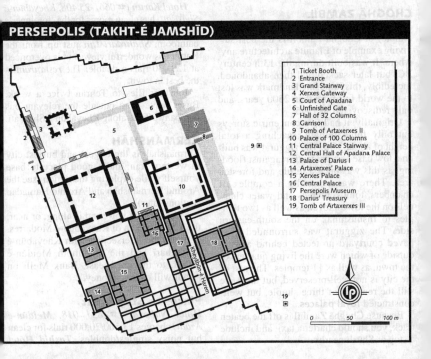

PERSEPOLIS (TAKHT-É JAMSHĪD)

1 Ticket Booth
2 Entrance
3 Grand Stairway
4 Xerxes Gateway
5 Court of Apadana
6 Unfinished Gate
7 Hall of 32 Columns
8 Garrison
9 Tomb of Artaxerxes II
10 Palace of 100 Columns
11 Central Palace Stairway
12 Central Hall of Apadana Palace
13 Palace of Darius I
14 Artaxerxes' Palace
15 Xerxes Palace
16 Central Palace
17 Persepolis Museum
18 Darius' Treasury
19 Tomb of Artaxerxes III

Kheyābān-é Haram

0 50 100 m

not currently open to the public. The complex is open daily from 8 am to 6 pm.

Tomb of Dānyāl

Dominating Shūsh, Daniel's Tomb is interesting, mainly because it's dedicated to a Jewish prophet.

Places to Stay & Eat

A new (and yet to be named) *hotel* is open close to the ancient city. Decent rooms cost 15,000 rials and it has a great *restaurant*.

Getting There & Away

Minibuses regularly leave Andīmeshk for Shūsh town, and the ancient city (which is in the middle of town). From Ahvāz, there are regular minibuses, or just get off a bus along the road heading north. A chartered taxi is a good option, because you can combine it with a side trip to Choghā Zambīl.

CHOGHĀ ZAMBĪL

The well-preserved *ziggurat* (pyramidal temple) of Choghā Zambīl is the best surviving example of Elamite architecture anywhere. It was built during the 13th century BC, but later sacked and then abandoned. Incredibly, this imposing landmark was lost to the world for more than 2500 years, and only rediscovered in 1935.

Originally, it had five concentric storeys but only three remain, reaching a total height of about 25m. The ziggurat was built on a low base as a precaution against flooding, as this was once a fertile and forested area. There was originally a complex of chambers, tombs, tunnels and water channels on the lowest level, as well as two temples to Inshushinak on the south-eastern side. The ziggurat was surrounded by a paved courtyard protected behind a wall, outside of which were the living quarters of the town, as well as 11 temples. The rest of the city is not well-preserved, but there are still the remains of three simple, but well-constructed **royal palaces**.

Because Choghā Zambīl is off the beaten track, you should charter a taxi, and include a stop at Shūsh nearby.

Western Iran

There is evidence of settlement in western Iran as early as the 6th millennium BC, and many of the earliest empires and kingdoms of Persia had their capitals here. Standing at the frontiers with Mesopotamia and Turkey, much of the region has been vulnerable to incursions from the west throughout its long history. During the Iran-Iraq War, the region was thrown into turmoil; towns were bombed and, in some cases, occupied by Iraqi forces. This area is often ignored by travellers, but there's enough to see to justify a detour.

KHORRAM ĀBĀD

Khorram Ābād is a pleasant town, and a decent stopover. It's famous for the impressive and dominating **Falak-ol-Aflak** fortress, which is undergoing renovation, but worth a look for the **views**.

Hotel Karun (☎ 0661-25 408, Kheyābūn-é Sharī'atī) has clean rooms for the 'foreigner's price' of 50,000/60,000 rials without/with bathroom. *Shahrdari Inn* just up from the Karun has wonderful views but is overpriced at 129,030 rials a double. The *restaurant* is the best in town.

Iran Air flies to Tehrān twice a week. Buses leave from outside the relevant bus company offices along Kheyābūn-é Sharī'atī.

KERMĀNSHĀH

Kermānshāh is the largest and busiest city in western Iran, and a good place to base yourself while exploring the region (see the Around Kermānshāh and Around Hamadān sections later).

Most of what you need is along, or near, the 1.5km stretch of Kheyābūn-é Modarres, between the intersection with Kheyābūn-é Motahharī and the mammoth Meidūn-é Āzādī, to the north-east. Bank Melli on Āzādī will change money.

Places to Stay & Eat

Hotel Nabovat (☎ 831 018, Meidūn-é Āzādī) charges 13,500/20,000 rials for clean but noisy singles/doubles. *Toshid Hotel*

(Meidūn-é Āzādī) is also noisy and basic, but cheap for 7500/10,000 rials.

Soroush Hotel (☎ 27 001, *Kheyābūn-é Motahharī*) is a little inconvenient, but it's the best option. The rooms with private bathrooms are small but cosy, and the management will accept 65,000 rials per double, including breakfast.

There are plenty of *kabābīs* and *cake shops* around Āzādī. The best places for lunch and a pot of tea are the restaurants at Tāgh-é Bostān (see Around Kermānshāh following).

Getting There & Away
Iran Air (☎ 53 814), about 2km north of Meidūn-é Āzādī, flies every day to Tehrān (74,000 rials), and less regularly to Mashhad.

The bus and shared taxi terminal is about 8km north of Āzādī. Buses regularly go to Esfahān (9000 rials, nine hours); Hamadān (5400 rials, three hours); Orūmīyé (11,500 rials, 11 hours); Tabrīz (13,800 rials, 11 hours); and Tehrān (7500 rials, nine hours).

AROUND KERMĀNSHĀH
Bīsotūn
Overlooking the main road to Hamadān are two eroded **Parthian bas-reliefs**. The one on the left shows King Mithradites standing before four supplicants. The one on the right depicts several scenes relating to Gotarzes II. About 50m to the north, the unimpressive mid-2nd century BC **sculpture of Hercules** lies under a tacky tin shelter.

About 100m south of Hercules, the **tablet of Darius I** represents Darius' hard-fought victory over several rebel princes. In the cliffs, another 200m towards Kermānshāh, the vast unfinished **stone panel** was probably started in about the 7th century BC, but its intended purpose remains a mystery.

The bas-reliefs are about 2km west of Bīsotūn village. Take any bus between Kermānshāh and Hamadān, or a minibus from Kermānshāh.

Tāgh-é Bostān
These fascinating **bas-reliefs** and carved alcoves date back to the Sassanian period (224-637 AD), and overlook a large pool and pleasant **garden**. The figures in the large grotto are believed to represent Khosrō II, a contemporary of the Prophet Mohammed, and a famous hunter. Next to it, a small arched recess carved in the 4th century shows Shāpūr II and his grandson, Shāpūr III. Farther along, carvings depict the investiture of Ardeshīr II. Take a shared taxi (or walk about 4km) from the huge square next to the bus terminal in Kermānshāh.

HAMADĀN
Hamadān has always been a major stop on the ancient royal road to Baghdad, and it remains an important trading and transit centre. Hamadān is a popular retreat for Iranians and there's a few things to see in the city, and nearby (see the Around Hamadān section later in this chapter and the Around Kermānshāh section earlier).

Orientation & Information
The centre of town is the huge Meidūn-é Emām Khomeinī. Bank Melli dominates the northern side of the square, and is the only place to change money. There is a great bookshop at the Bouali Hotel. The main post office, about 700m south of the main square, also handles local, interstate (between provinces in Iran) and international telephone calls.

Things to See
About 200m north of the main square, **Jāme' Mosque** has 55 columns, and was built during the Ghajar period (1779-1921). Also, worth a look is the **Shrine of Abdollah**, about 600m north-west of the main square. Another 200m farther east, the well-preserved 12th century **Dome of Alavīyān** has outstanding stucco ornamentation.

The **Mausoleum of Ester va Mōrdekhāy** is the most important Jewish pilgrimage site in Iran. Jews believe that it contains the body of Esther, the Jewish wife of Xerxes I, who is credited with organising the first Jewish emigration to Persia in the 5th century. If you ring the bell at the entrance, someone should open it up.

Obviously modelled on the Dome of Kāvūs near Gorgān, the **Avicenna Memorial**, built in memory of the local famous poet, Bū Alī Sīnā, has a library and museum. The **Museum of Natural History** has a wide collection of stuffed animals and other exhibits, all labelled in English. It's at the end of Bolvār-é Azadegan, about 5km from the city centre – charter a taxi.

Some ruins of the ancient city can be seen around **Hekmatāné Hill**, but most items of interest are in the National Museum of Iran in Tehrān.

Places to Stay
The best three cheapies are only a few metres from Meidūn-é Emām Khomeinī. *Ekhbatan Hotel* (☎ 224 024, *Kheyābūn-é Shohadā*) has very small and basic, but cleanish, rooms for 12,500 rials. *Hamadān Guest House* (☎ 227 577, *Kheyābūn-é Ekbātān*) is the best place. It has a large number of clean rooms, all with a shared bathroom, for 25,000 rials. *Yass Hotel* (☎ 223 464, *Kheyābūn-é Shohadā*) is decent value providing you can negotiate a room for the rial equivalent of US$10/15 for singles/doubles.

Bouali Hotel (☎ 52 822, fax 52 824, *Kheyābūn-é Bū Alī Sīnā*) 1.2km south of the main square has excellent rooms, but is way overpriced for foreigners: US$58 a double.

Places to Eat
All the best *kabābīs* are based around Meidūn-é Emām Khomeinī. *Shilan Restaurant* (*Kheyābūn-é Bū Alī Sīnā*) about 400m south of the main square offers a decent selection of Iranian meals for about 7000 rials a dish. *Hamadān Guest House* has a simple restaurant. *Bouali Hotel* has an elegant restaurant with excellent western food for about 13,000 rials; this place is worth a splurge.

Getting There & Away
A few bus companies have offices along Kheyābūn-é Shohadā. The bus terminal is along Kheyābūn-é Ekbātān, about 1.2km north of the main square. Buses regularly go to Esfahān (9000 rials, seven hours);

Ghazvīn (4300 rials, four hours); Kermānshāh (5400 rials, three hours); Shīrāz (10,500 rials, 15 hours); and Tehrān (5500 rials, five hours). The minibus terminal is about 200m north-east of the bus terminal.

AROUND HAMADĀN
Ganjnāmé is a charming piece of greenery, 8km south-west from Hamadān. There are a pair of famous **Achaemenian rock carvings** of Darius I, and his son Xerxes I – a translation of the writing is in English nearby. More enticing is the attractive **waterfall**, and there are plenty of **hiking trails** in the area. The best way there is to charter a taxi.

The remarkable **Alī Sadr Caves**, approximately 100km north of Hamadān, are about 40m high, and contain several huge lakes with clear water up to 8m deep. The entrance fee includes an interesting tour in a paddle-boat. *Alī Sadr Hotel* (☎ 08262-2099) charges US$15/20 for comfortable singles/doubles. There are *kabābīs* in the vicinity, and even a *café* inside the cave. Minibuses travel to Alī Sadr village from the minibus terminal in Hamadān. Alternatively, charter a taxi.

GHAZVĪN
Ghazvīn is a pleasant stopover, and the best place from which to visit the Mausoleum of Soltānīyé and the Castles of the Assassins (see those sections later for details). Most of the life support systems are within a few hundred metres of the town centre, Meidūn-é Sabze.

Things to See
The ancient **Jāme' Mosque**, 700m south of Meidūn-é Sabze, has some features dating back to the Arab period (637-1050), including an exquisitely decorated prayer hall. About 300m farther south, the 16th century **Shrine of Hussein** is particularly beautiful, and revered by all Iranians. **Al Nabī Mosque** in the middle of the bazaar district, about 300m west of Sabze, was built mainly during the Safavid period (1502-1722). **Ghazvīn Museum**, on Meidūn-é Sabze, is also worth a visit.

Places to Stay & Eat

Hotel Iran (Meidūn-é Sabze) is the best place. It's central and has clean singles/doubles with private shower (but shared toilet) for 13,000/17,500 rials. *Khaksar Hotel* (☎ 24 239, *Bolvār-é Āyatollāh Tāleghānī*) about 300m east of Sabze has decent, no-frills rooms for 20,000 rials. *Albors Hotel* (☎/fax 26 631), almost opposite the Khaksar, has luxurious rooms for 110,400/168,000 rials, but try to negotiate for an 'Iranian price'. It has a small *coffeehouse*.

Eghbali Restaurant (☎ 23 347, *Bolvār-é Āyatollāh Tāleghānī*) about 200m east of Sabze is the best place in town – try the tasty khōresht.

Getting There & Away

Buses and shared taxis to Zanjān, Tehrān, Hamadān, Rasht and Tabrīz leave from the bus terminal near Meidūn-é Darvāzeh in the south-eastern suburbs; or from various roundabouts in different places around town – ask your hotel or taxi driver for details. Ghazvīn is on the train line between Tabrīz and Tehrān, but arrival and departure times are antisocial. The train station is about 2km south of Meidūn-é Sabze.

MAUSOLEUM OF SOLTĀNĪYÉ

The famous mausoleum of the Mongol Soltān Oljeitū Khodābandé was originally built as the final resting place of Alī, the son-in-law of the Prophet Mohammed, but this never eventuated. It has one of the largest domes in the world – 48m high, and nearly 25m in diameter – and the views from the top are superb.

The mausoleum is not far from the main road between Zanjān and Ghazvīn. Take any bus, minibus or shared taxi between the two towns, get off at the junction and catch another shared taxi to Soltānīyé village. To walk (5km) there from the main road, get off at the point where the mausoleum looks closest to the road.

CASTLES OF THE ASSASSINS

In the southern foothills of the Alborz Mountains are the historic fortresses known as the Castles of the Assassins. The castles were the heavily fortified lairs of the adherents of a bizarre religious cult, based loosely on the precepts of the Ismaili sect. (The word 'assassin' originates from the name of this sect.) Sadly, little more than rubble remains, but the **views** and the stunning **landscape** are the main attractions.

All but one of the castles are *only* accessible to experienced and well-equipped trekkers. A complete tour would take a very tough six days; guides and donkeys can be hired in villages along the way. The only accessible castle is **Alamūt**, reached by a paved road heading north-east from Ghazvīn. Charter a taxi, or organise something with the Hotel Iran in Ghazvīn.

ORŪMĪYÉ

Orūmīyé lies to the west of the lake of the same name. Despite its relatively remote position, the town lies on an increasingly important trade route with Turkey, so the city is more Turkish and Āzārī than Persian.

Orientation & Information

There are many facilities on Kheyābun-é Emām Khomeinī, between Meidūn-é Faghīyé and Meidūn-é Enghelāb. The tourist office (☎ 45 018), just south of Bolvār-é Modarres, about 800m north-west of Meidūn-é Enghelāb, is helpful. Turkish lira can be bought and sold with rials or US dollars (at the bank rate) at Bank Melli on Enghelāb. Black marketeers also hang around the Bank Melli building.

Things to See

The large **Jāme' Mosque**, near Meidūn-é Faghīyé, has some fine plaster mouldings, and a large dome. The 12th century **Sé Dome** is notable for its stucco and stalactite decorations – take the second lane on your left along Kheyābun-é Jāmbāzān, north of the intersection with Kheyābun-é Dastgheib (about 800m south-east of Rezā Hotel).

The **Orūmīyé Museum** has a mildly interesting display – it's along Kheyābun-é Beheshtī, about 1.2km south-east of Meidūn-é Enghelāb. The Assyrian, Armenian,

Nestorian and Roman Catholic communities have interesting **churches**, several of which are around Enghelāb and the nearby Meidūn-é Ghods – ask locals for directions.

Places to Stay & Eat

Rezā Hotel (☎ 26 580) next to the underpass on the corner of Kheyābūn-é Emām Khomeinī and Kheyābūn-é Be'sat is a bargain because foreigners can easily obtain the 'Iranian price'. Large, comfortable rooms cost 20,000 rials per person, and it has the best *restaurant* in town.

Khorram Hotel (☎ 25 444, *Kheyābūn-é Emām Khomeini*) about 200m south-west of the underpass has friendly management, and good doubles for about 25,000 rials. *Hotel Iran Setareh* (☎ 54 454, *Kheyābūn-e' Be'sat*) about 700m south-east of the Rezā has clean and comfortable singles/doubles for 17,5000/20,000 rials.

Hotel Be'sat (☎ 36 128) about 200m down from the Rezā is a last resort for 25,000 rials a double.

Getting There & Away

Iran Air (☎ 40 530) flies twice a day to Tehrān (94,500 rials), and less regularly to Mashhad. Iran Air's office is virtually opposite the museum.

Some bus companies have booking offices along Kheyābūn-é Emām Khomeinī. The terminal for buses, minibuses and shared taxis is north-east of the town centre – catch a shared taxi along Kheyābūn-é Emām Khomeinī. Buses regularly go to Kermānshāh (11,500 rials, 11 hours), Mākū (3900 rials, four hours) and Tabrīz (5500 rials, five hours). For other destinations, get connections in Tabrīz or Kermānshāh.

SERŌ

This nondescript village is on the border with Turkey. There is nowhere to stay. Buses and shared taxis regularly travel between Serō and Meidūn-é Tōhīd in northern Orūmīyé.

THRONE OF SOLEIMĀN

This large and remote fortified settlement is built around a small lake on a hilltop and dates from the Achaemenid (559-330 BC), Parthian (190 BC-224 AD), Sassanian (224-637 AD) and Arab (637-1050) periods. The oldest remaining structures are the ruins of a **Sassanian palace** and the substantial **fire temples**. The complex is open daily from 7 am to 7 pm.

The top of the conical **Prison of Soleimān** mountain, about 2.5km west of the ruins, offers superb **views** of the countryside, village and ancient city. The general area is great for **hiking**.

Hotel Randji (☎ 04837-3179) in nearby Takāb village has large, comfortable rooms for 50,000 rials.

To reach these impressive ruins, go to Takāb on a series of minibuses from Tabrīz, via Meyāndo'āb and Shāhīn Dezh; or from Zanjān, by direct bus. From Takāb, take a minibus to Nosratabad village, and then walk to the ruins. Alternatively, charter a taxi from Takāb.

GHARA KELĪSĀ

The Church of St Thaddaeus is probably the most remarkable Christian monument in Iran. (It's often called Ghara Kelīsā, but the church is more accurately known as Kelīsā-yé Tādī – the Church of St Thaddaeus.)

The period of construction is unknown, and very little remains of the original church. It was largely rebuilt after extensive earthquake damage in the 13th century, but there are some older parts, perhaps from the 10th century. The church has one service a year, on the feast day of St Thaddaeus (around 19 June), when Armenian pilgrims from all over Iran attend the ceremonies. The church is open every day during daylight hours.

From Mākū, catch any bus or shared taxi towards Bāzārgān, get off at a junction with the sign to 'Kandi Kelisa', and take another shared taxi (or charter it). The easiest way is to charter a taxi from Mākū or Bāzārgān.

MĀKŪ

Many travellers stop in Mākū just before, or after, crossing the border with Turkey. Everything is along one very long road, part of the main thoroughfare between Tabrīz and the Turkish border. You can change US dollars, Turkish lira and Iranian rials with dealers along the main road.

Places to Stay & Eat

Hotel Alvand (☎ *23 491*) on the town's main square has nice singles/doubles with shared bathroom for 15,000/20,000 rials. *Hotel Lalah* (☎ *3441*) opposite has larger and some quieter rooms with shared bathroom for the same price.

Mākū Inn (☎ *23 212*) about 300m up from the Lalah is off the main road and is quiet. It's good value for 70,350/105,570 rials, and also boasts the only proper *restaurant* in town.

Getting There & Away

Buses to Tabrīz and Orūmīyé leave about every hour or so in the morning from the terminal, 3km from the town centre and on the road to Tabrīz. Shared taxis to Bāzārgān leave from outside Hotel Alvand; and to Tabrīz and Orūmīyé, from outside the bus terminal.

BĀZĀRGĀN

Bāzārgān is on the Iran-Turkey border – refer to the Getting There & Away section earlier in this chapter for details about crossing the border.

The main road from Mākū goes through Bāzārgān and stops at the border. The road is lined with a dozen cheap hotels such as *Hotel Jafapour* which is right next to the border and costs about 10,000 rials per person. From the border, shared taxis regularly go to Mākū and to Tabrīz when there are enough passengers.

TABRĪZ

Tabrīz had a spell as the Persian capital during the Safavid period (1502-1722), but these days it's just another unexciting Iranian city. For most travellers, Tabrīz is a stopover on the way to/from Turkey.

Information

Tabrīz is, however, one of the best places to arrange visa extensions, which are available at the police headquarters. The tourist office (☎ 68 491) is helpful – look for the sign next to Golshan Hotel – but the office at the airport is better (if it's open). Bank Melli is not a great place to change money. If you want to change money at the 'street rate', make discreet inquiries in the bazaar, or at your hotel.

Things to See

Although badly damaged by earthquakes, the 15th century **Kabūd Mosque** is still notable for the extremely intricate tilework. It's normally closed, but the key is available from the nearby **Āzarbāyjān Museum**, which has some mildly interesting exhibits.

The huge, crumbling **Citadel of Tabrīz** was built in the early 14th century, but is permanently fenced off while restoration continues. One of the more interesting local churches is the old, but substantially rebuilt, **Maryam-é Moghaddas Church**. **Elgolī** is a large, pleasant park – take a shared taxi from Meidūn-é Shahrdārī.

Places to Stay

Golshan Hotel (☎ *69 273*) on the corner of Kheyābūn-é Emām Khomeinī and Kheyābūn-é Anvarī is the cheapest option. Basic dorm-style beds cost 9000 rials, while the other rooms are better for 15,000/25,000 rials without/with bathroom.

Park Hotel (☎ *551 852, Kheyābūn-é Emām Khomeinī*) has good value singles/doubles for 20,000/30,000 rials with shower (shared toilet) and fridge, though some rooms are musty. *Morvarid Hotel* (☎ *60 520, Meidūn-é Fajr*) is friendly, and charges 21,000/27,500 rials. Rooms have private bathroom, fridge and B&W TV, but many are noisy.

Hotel Iran (☎ *459 515, Kheyābūn-é 22 Bahman*) is near the train station, but is inconvenient to the rest of the city. It's friendly and good value for a negotiable 20,000/40,000 rials.

Ark Hotel (☎ *551 277*) at the back of the citadel is also recommended for 25,000 rials for doubles. *Azarbaijan Hotel* (☎ *559 051, Kheyābūn-é Sharī'atī*) recognisable by the red and white columns on the outside is worth a splurge for 50,000/70,000 rials.

IRAN

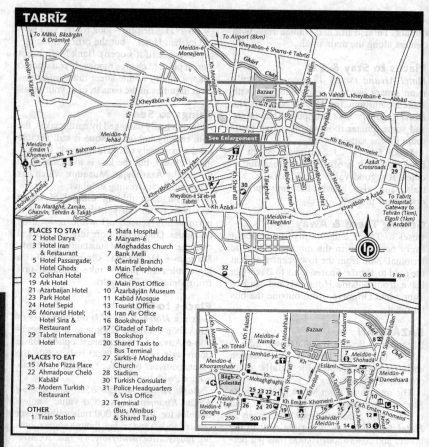

TABRĪZ

PLACES TO STAY
2 Hotel Darya
3 Hotel Iran & Restaurant
5 Hotel Passargade; Hotel Ghods
12 Golshan Hotel
19 Ark Hotel
21 Azarbaijan Hotel
23 Park Hotel
24 Hotel Sepid
26 Morvarid Hotel; Hotel Sina & Restaurant
29 Tabrīz International Hotel

PLACES TO EAT
15 Afsahe Pizza Place
22 Ahmadpour Chelō Kabābī
25 Modern Turkish Restaurant

OTHER
1 Train Station

4 Shafa Hospital
6 Maryam-é Moghaddas Church
7 Bank Melli (Central Branch)
8 Main Telephone Office
9 Main Post Office
10 Āzarbāyjān Museum
11 Kabūd Mosque
13 Tourist Office
14 Iran Air Office
16 Bookshops
17 Citadel of Tabrīz
18 Bookshop
20 Shared Taxis to Bus Terminal
27 Sarkīs-é Moghaddas Church
28 Stadium
30 Turkish Consulate
31 Police Headquarters & Visa Office
32 Terminal (Bus, Minibus & Shared Taxi)

Places to Eat

There are plenty of *kabābīs*, *hamburger joints* and *teahouses* along Kheyābūn-é Emām Khomeinī. *Modern Turkish Restaurant*, downstairs and signposted in English, is one of the better places. *Ahmadpour Chelō Kabābī* is not signposted in English, so look for the words 'Chelo Kabab' and 'Chicken Kebab' on the window. *Afsahe Pizza Place* (*Kheyābūn-é Emām Khomeinī*) has decent pizzas for about 9000 rials. The restaurant in *Hotel Iran* is worth a visit.

Shopping

The labyrinthine bazaar was built more than 1000 years ago but most of it dates to the 15th century. Tabrīz is renowned for carpets, silverware, jewellery, silk and spices, such as henna.

Getting There & Away

Refer to the Getting There & Away chapter at the beginning of this book for full details about international flights to/from Tabrīz.

Air Iran Air (☎ 552 000) flies several times a day to Tehrān (87,000 rials) and less regularly to Rasht and Mashhad.

Bus, Minibus & Shared Taxi The bus/minibus terminal is in the south of the city – take a taxi from the corner of Kheyābūn-é Emām Khomeinī and Kheyābūn-é Sharī'atī. Buses regularly go to Jolfā (4500 rials, three hours); Kermānshāh (13,800 rials, 11 hours); Mākū (4300 rials, four hours); Orūmīyé (5500 rials, five hours); Rasht (8500 rials, eight hours); and Tehrān (9300 rials, nine hours). From the bus terminal, shared taxis go to Orūmīyé, Mākū and Bāzārgān.

Train Trains leave every day at about 5 pm for Tehrān (12 hours). Tickets, which cost 14,500/20,500 rials (2nd/1st class), should be booked at least one day in advance at the station, accessible by shared taxi along Kheyābūn-é Emām Khomeinī and Kheyābūn-é 22 Bahman.

AROUND TABRĪZ
Marāghé
The former capital of the Mongol dynasty (1220-1380) is famous for its four ancient brick **tomb towers**, and its ceramics and mosaic tiles. The tombs are difficult to find so charter a taxi. *Aria Hotel* (☎ 0422-2294), halfway between the train station and the large Meidūn-é Mosallā, has decent, cheap rooms. Buses regularly go to Tabrīz and Orūmīyé from the terminal, 1.5km west of Meidūn-é Mosallā.

Kandovan
The region around this remarkable village has **rock formations** similar to Cappadocia in central Turkey, though unlike in its Turkish cousin, in Kandovan many homes are still inhabited. Kandovan is about 50km south-west of Tabrīz. Catch a minibus from Tabrīz to Oshu, then a shared taxi to Kandovan; or, better, a chartered taxi from Tabrīz.

JOLFĀ
Jolfā is near the border between Iran and Azerbaijan and Armenia – refer to the Get-

ting There & Away chapter at the beginning of this book for details about crossing the two borders.

Jolfa Hotel, along the western end of the main road, is grubby but acceptable. Jolfā is regularly linked by bus with Tabrīz, and with minibuses from the nearby junction town of Marand.

ARDABĪL
Near the border with Azerbaijan, Ardabīl boasts the impressive **Mausoleum of Sheikh Safī-od-Dīn**; a great **bazaar**; and the hot mineral springs at **Sareyin** nearby.

Noisy but cheap *Ojahan Inn* (☎ 0451-22 481, Meidūn-é Emām Khomeinī) is 12,500 rials a room. *Hotel Sheikh Safī* (☎ 0451-24 111, Kheyābūn-é Sharī'atī) charges 25,000/35,000 rials for singles/doubles and is the best option.

Iran Air (☎ 0451-249 83) flies between Ardabīl and Tehrān every day. There are also regular buses to Tabrīz, Rasht and Zanjān.

Caspian Provinces

The Caspian region, known as the Shomāl (North), has a varied terrain, with thick forests, mountains and a coastal plain up to 100km wide, and is particularly wet and densely populated. There are few beaches or other seaside attractions however, and tourism, though important, is very much a do-it-yourself affair.

RASHT
Rasht is a popular weekend retreat, and holiday destination, for Tehrānīs. The city has little to offer travellers, but it's a good place to unwind while exploring the region (see the Around Rasht section following). Rasht is one of the wettest places in Iran, and can be uncomfortably humid in summer.

Orientation & Information
The city centre is the chaotic Meidūn-é Shohadā. On this square are the post office and police headquarters (where visa extensions are usually possible). About 200m

IRAN

Persian Carpets

Persian carpets (or rugs) are more than just a floor-covering to an Iranian: they are a display of wealth, an investment, an integral part of religious and cultural festivals, and used in everyday life (eg as a prayer mat).

Types of Carpet Persian carpets often come in three sizes: the *mian farsh* is up to 3m long and up to 2.5m wide; the *kellegi* is about 3.5m long and nearly 2m wide; and the *kenareh* is up to 3m long and 1m wide.

A *kilim* is a double-sided flat-woven mat, without knots, which is thinner and softer than knotted carpets. They are popular as prayer mats and wall-hangings.

Making Carpets/Rugs Most handmade carpets are made from wool. The wool is spun, usually by hand, and then rinsed, washed and dried. It's then dyed, usually by chemicals. Nomadic carpet weavers often use high-grade wool, and create unique designs, but they use unsophisticated horizontal looms so the carpets are often less refined. In villages, small workshops use upright looms, which create carpets with more variety and extras, such as fringes, but the designs are often uninspiring. City factories usually mass-produce carpets of monotonous design and variable quality.

Carpets are made with Persian knots, which loop around one horizontal thread, and under the next; or Turkish knots, looped around two horizontal threads, with the yarn lifted between them. But the difference is not obvious to the layman (or tourist).

---

south-west is Meidūn-é Sabze. The major banks will change money, but the best place is Mehra Pooya Currency Exchange, near Hotel Golestān (see Places to Stay).

Places to Stay

Sedaghat Guest House (☎ 46 088, *Kheyābūn-é Sharī'atī*) is 100m east of Meidūn-é Shohadā and up four flights of stairs. It has clean double rooms, with shared bathroom, for 15,000 rials.

Hotel Golestān (☎ 25 257, *Bolvār-é Emām Khomeinī*), about 100m south-east of Shohadā, has quiet doubles for 20,000 rials but many are without outside windows. *Fārs Hotel* (☎ 25 257) opposite has clean, quiet rooms for about the same price.

Carvan Hotel (☎ 22 613, *Bolvār-é Emām Khomeinī*) is the best budget place: it's friendly and has singles/doubles, with a shared bathroom, for 15,000/20,000 rials.

Ordibehesht Hotel (☎ 22 210, *Meidūn-é Shohadā*) is convenient, and has well-furnished doubles for a negotiable 144,000 rials.

Places to Eat

There are several decent *hamburger joints* around Sabze and Shohadā squares. *Grand Father Pitza Restaurant* (*Kheyābūn-é A'lam-ol-Hodā*) between Meidūn-é Shohadā and Meidūn-é Sabze has tasty pizzas for about 9000 rials. *Ordibehesht Hotel* has a good choice of delicious Iranian and western food for about 12,000 rials a dish. *Carvan Hotel* has a cheap restaurant with a limited menu.

Getting There & Away

Iran Air (☎ 24 444) flies every day to Tehrān (70,000 rials), and less regularly to Bandar-é Abbās, Mashhad and Tabrīz. To the Iran Air office, take a shared taxi from Meidūn-é Shohadā towards the suburb of Golsar.

Buses head in all directions from the bus terminal, accessible by shared taxi heading south-east along Bolvār-é Emām Khomeinī. Tickets are also available at bus company offices around Shohadā. Minibuses leave from a special terminal in the far eastern

Persian Carpets

The higher number of knots per sq cm, the better the quality – and, of course, the higher the price. A normal carpet has up to 30 knots per sq cm; a medium-grade piece 30 to 50 knots; and a fine one, 50 knots or more. A nomadic weaver can tie around 8000 knots each day; a weaver in a factory about 12,000 knots.

Buying Carpets/Rugs If you don't know much about Persian carpets take a trustworthy, and knowledgeable Iranian friend with you when shopping. You might be able to pick up a bargain in Iran but dealers in western countries often sell Persian carpets for little more than you'd pay in Iran (plus postage), and you're less likely to be ripped off by your local warehouse dealer than a savvy Iranian bazaar merchant. Unless you're an expert, never buy a carpet as an investment.

Before buying anything, lie the carpet on the floor and check for any bumps or imperfections. Small bumps will usually flatten out with wear, but large bumps will remain. To check that a carpet is handmade, turn it over: the pattern will be distinct on the underside, the more distinct the better the quality.

Taking Them Home Posting a carpet/rug home adds about one-third more to the cost. Currently, each foreigner can take out of Iran (by air, land or sea) one Persian carpet or two small Persian rugs totalling 12 sq metres. However, one traveller recently needed special permission from the post office in Tehrān to post a carpet home, so check the regulations (with the post office and not the carpet salesman!) before forking out any money.

---

suburbs – charter a taxi. Shared taxis to Ghazvīn, Tehrān, Rāmsar and Bandar-é Anzalī leave from around Shohadā.

AROUND RASHT
Māsūlé

Māsūlé is one of the most beautiful villages in the region, and a great area for **hiking**.

Monfared Masooleh Hotel (☎ 01864-3250) has good singles/doubles for 35,000/50,000 rials, and has a stupendous rooftop *restaurant*. You may also be able to get a *room* in a local home for about 35,000 rials a double.

From Meidūn-é Sabze in Rasht, take a shared taxi to Fūman, then another past stunning scenery to Māsūlé. Chartering a taxi allows a leisurely drive, and stops for photos.

Bandar-é Anzalī

Anzalī is a popular resort for Iranians. The town centre is Meidūn-é Emām Khomeinī, just past the second bridge from Rasht. From the **promenade**, you can organise boat trips into the 450 sq km **Anzalī Lagoon**, home to several species of water birds. In summer ferries leave from here to sail up the Caspian to Baku in Azerbaijan – see the Getting There & Away chapter at the beginning of this book for details.

Tehrān Hotel (Meidūn-é Emām Khomeinī) is charming and cheap – 12,000 rials for a double – but often full. *Hotel Ancient Golsang* (☎ 0181-22155) next door has pleasant singles/doubles for 50,000/85,000 rials. *Hotel Iran* about 200m east of Emām Khomeinī has a good *restaurant* and charming *coffeehouse*.

Shared taxis leave for Rasht from around Emām Khomeinī. Regular minibuses and shared taxis to Āstārā depart from a junction just south of the town centre.

ĀSTĀRĀ

This town is on the border with Azerbaijan – refer to the Getting There & Away chapter at the beginning of this book for information about crossing the border.

IRAN

Hotel Aras is the best of the cheapies around Meidūn-é Shahrdārī. *Astara Guest House* (☎ 01854-6063) only metres from the border is charming but overpriced at US$40 a double. Plenty of shared taxis and minibuses head towards Rasht, Bandar-é Anzalī and Ardabīl – from where there are onward connections elsewhere.

SĀRĪ

Sārī is smaller and less developed than Rasht, but makes a reasonable stopover. The centre of town is Meidūn-é Sā'at (Clock Square). Things to see include the 15th century **Shrine of Yahyā** at the end of a laneway opposite Hotel Nader; the nearby **Soltān Zein-ol-Ābedīn Tower**; and the **Shrine of Abbās**, about 2.5km east of Clock Square.

Places to Stay & Eat

Hotel Nader (☎ 02431-2357, *Kheyābūn-é Jomhūrī-yé Eslāmī*) 200m south-west of Meidūn-é Sā'at charges 13,500/17,500 rials for noisy but cleanish singles/doubles. *Hotel Asram* near the bus terminal is large and modern, and has a good *restaurant*, but the rooms are expensive at US$30/42.

Getting There & Away

Sārī is a stopover on the regular Iran Air flights between Tehrān and Mashhad. The Iran Air office (☎ 20 921) is about 1.2km south-west of Meidūn-é Sā'at. The bus terminal is about 3km north-east of Meidūn-é Sā'at, but for Gorgān, buses leave from a special terminal, 2km east of Meidūn-é Sā'at. Trains to Tehrān leave three days a week, and to Gorgān every day. The train station is about 1km south of Meidūn-é Sā'at.

RĀMSAR

Rāmsar is one of the more attractive seaside resorts, but the **beaches** are disappointing. The last shāh built a **palace** in the wooded hills overlooking Rāmsar, and it houses a **museum** that seems to be permanently closed. The main road is Kheyābūn-é Motahharī, and the centre is Meidūn-é Enghelāb, where Bank Melli is located.

Places to Stay & Eat

You can usually stay in a local *home* for about 15,000/25,000 rials for singles/doubles. Ask at the snack bars and restaurants along the main road, or just look lost for a few minutes – someone will offer you something soon enough.

Nazia Suites (☎ 6600, 4588) just up from Meidūn-é Enghelāb is a collection of furnished apartments for 35,000 to 60,000 rials. *Rāmsar Grand Hotel* (☎ 3592, fax 5174) dominates the town centre and is set on a splendid hillside. Comfortable rooms start from a non-negotiable US$42/65.

Several reasonable *kabābīs* and *hamburger joints* are dotted along the main road; *Golesorkh Restaurant* is about the best. *Shaghayegh Restaurant* in the Rāmsar Grand has expensive food in luxurious surroundings; you can also enjoy tea in a very sumptuous lounge.

Getting There & Away

Although there are no regular flights to/from Rāmsar, there's an Iran Air office (☎ 2788) along the main road. From the terminal in western Rāmsar, frequent minibuses and shared taxis go to Rasht and Chālūs. To Chālūs, Sārī and Gorgān, you can also catch any bus along a road one block north of Kheyābūn-é Motahharī. Direct buses to Tehrān leave from a terminal about 500m north of the Rāmsar Grand Hotel.

NŌSHAHR & CHĀLŪS

Nōshahr is far nicer than Chālūs, a sprawling industrial town and junction only 5km west of Nōshahr. But the only reason to stay in either place is to explore the nearby attractions (see Around Nōshahr & Chālūs following).

Places to Stay & Eat

Shalizar Restaurant & Hotel (☎ 34 264) has charming, well-furnished rooms for US$25/30 for single/doubles, but the management is willing to discount to a more reasonable 60,000/70,000 rials. It's easy to find in central Nōshahr.

Two comfortable, mid-range places are opposite each other at the official western entrance to Nōshahr – check out both and negotiate. *Hotel Malek* (☎ *24 107*) charges 100,000 rials. *Hotel Kourosh* (☎ *2396*) charges 50,000/60,000 rials.

A few decent *pizzerias* and *hamburger joints* are spread along the main road. The *restaurants* in the Malek, Shalizar and Kouroush hotels are good.

Getting There & Away

The terminal for all public transport in any direction is in western Chālūs, a few hundred metres from the road heading south to Tehrān. To some places to the west of Chālūs, however, you often need a connection in Tonekābon, west of Chālūs.

AROUND NŌSHAHR & CHĀLŪS

There are some half-decent **beaches** along the road between Nōshahr and Nūr. **Nūr**, about 50km east of Nōshahr, retains some semblance of quaintness, and has the nice *Nūr Hotel*. **Namak Abrūd**, about 10km west along the main road from Chālūs, has a **telecabin** to the top of Kūh-é Medovin mountain (1050m). The small **Sīsangān National Park**, 31km east of Nōshahr, is a lovely pocket of rare forest.

GORGĀN

Gorgān is a nice place to break up a journey to/from Mashhad. Kheyābūn-é Emām Khomeinī stretches north from Meidūn-é Emām Khomeinī to Meidūn-é Shahrdārī.

Things to See

In the bazaar, **Jāme' Mosque** has a traditional sloping tiled roof and an unusual minaret. About 200m west, the **Shrine of Nūr** is a small polygonal tomb tower, with outer walls decorated with simple brickwork designs. **Gorgān Museum**, about 1km west of Meidūn-é Shahrdārī, has some mildly interesting displays.

Places to Stay & Eat

Tourist Home next to the terminal for minibuses to Gonbad-é Kāvūs (see Getting

There & Away following) has basic but acceptable singles/doubles for 9000/12,500 rials. *Taslimi Hotel* (☎ *4814*) 200m south of Meidūn-é Shahrdārī charges a negotiable 60,000 rials for decent rooms. *Tahmasebi Jadid Hotel* (☎ *2780*) 500m down from Meidūn-é Emām Khomeinī also charges 60,000 rials, but won't negotiate. There are plenty of unmemorable *kabābīs* around the main squares.

Getting There & Away

From the bus terminal, 2km north-west of Meidūn-é Shahrdārī, buses regularly go in all directions. Minibuses for Sārī leave from a special terminal about 3km south-west of Meidūn-é Emām Khomeinī.

From Gorgān, the daily train to Sārī leaves at the ungodly hour of 4.30 am, and the Gorgān-Tehrān train (6000/14,300 rials for 2nd/1st class) departs every day. The train station is about 300m west of the bus terminal.

AROUND GORGĀN

Nahar Khorān

Nahar Khorān, about 6km south of Gorgān, is a picturesque pocket of forest with plenty of **hiking trails**. *Hotel Shahrdārī Gorgān* (☎ *0271-8077*) is a grand, old place, which charges 65,000 rials for doubles. *Nahar Khorān Inn* (☎ *0271-21 278*) has rooms and cabins for US$15. Take a shared taxi, or a bus, from Meidūn-é Khakh, which is about 1km east of Meidūn-é Shahrdārī, in Gorgān. The walk back to Gorgān from Nahar Khorān is pleasant and very easy to follow.

Gonbad-é Kāvūs

In this unexciting town is a spectacular **tomb tower** built by Ghābus ibn-é Vashmgīr. This earliest of skyscrapers is about 55m tall, and has a circular structure with 10 buttresses rising from the base to an 18m-high pointed dome. From Gorgān, minibuses leave about every hour from a terminal 5km north of Meidūn-é Shahrdārī.

IRAN

Iraq

The Republic of Iraq

Area: 434,924 sq km
Population: 21.7 million (1998 estimate)
Population Growth Rate: 3.2%
Capital: Baghdad
Head of State: President Saddam Hussein
Official Language: Arabic
Currency: Iraqi dinar
Exchange Rate: US$1 = ID1200

Long ago in the fertile valleys between the Tigris and Euphrates rivers, a great civilisation was born. It was to leave an indelible mark on the future of the world. This land was known as Mesopotamia, from the Greek meaning 'between two rivers', and is now part of modern Iraq. It was here that human beings first began to cultivate their land and where writing was invented.

Recent history has dealt less kindly with Iraq; few countries in the region have experienced such political turbulence and, in the early years of independence, so many changes of regime.

In the mid-1970s the country began to reap considerable benefits from its huge oil reserves and planned to plough some of this money into tourism. Iraq's industrial infrastructure, educational system, and nationwide literacy campaigns were the envy of many countries in the region.

However by the end of the 1980-88 Iran-Iraq War, Iraq's economy was in tatters. Before the country had a chance to rebuild, it was plunged once again into crisis with its invasion of Kuwait, the subsequent Gulf War, and the imposition of debilitating UN economic sanctions against it.

Facts about Iraq

HISTORY

For a general history of the Middle East, see the Facts about the Region chapter.

Iraq became independent in 1932 after a period of Ottoman and then British rule. On 14 July 1958, the monarchy was overthrown in a military coup and Iraq became a republic, ushering in a period of instability characterised by a series of coups and counter-coups that continued throughout the 1960s.

The Arab-Israeli conflict of 1967 caused Iraq to turn to the Soviet Union for support, accusing the USA and UK of supporting Israel. On 17 July 1968, a bloodless coup by the Ba'ath Party, a secular socialist party founded in Syria in 1942, put General Ahmad Hassan al-Bakr in power.

IRAQ

Despite some minor border skirmishes with Iran over the question of sovereignty over the Shatt al-Arab waterway in 1969, the 1970s represented a period of relative stability for Iraq. In 1975, Iraq and Iran decided to settle their differences, and a boundary line was drawn down the middle of the Shatt al-Arab (Iraq had been granted exclusive control of the waterway in 1937). Iran also stated that it would stop giving aid to Iraqi Kurds. By the end of 1977, Kurdish had become an official language and greater autonomy had been granted, offering hope for a lasting peace between the Kurds and Iraqi authorities, conflict between whom had been simmering since 1961. These factors resulted in Iraq becoming a more stable country, and the growing oil revenues brought about an unprecedented improvement in the economy.

In 1979 Saddam Hussein replaced Al-Bakr as president, the revolution in Iran took place and relations between the two countries quickly sank to an all-time low.

IRAQ

Iraq declared that it was dissatisfied with the 1975 boundary agreement of the Shatt al-Arab and wanted a return to the exclusive control of the waterway. The Iraqi government had always been dominated by Arab *Sunni*, even though *Shi'ites* form a majority of the Iraqi population, and Hussein became increasingly concerned about the threat of a Shi'ite revolution in his own country. Indeed, attempts were made by Iran to incite rebellion among Iraq's Shi'ites.

Clashes took place along the border during 1980 and full-scale war broke out on 22 September, with Iraqi forces entering Iran along a 500km front. The eight years of war that followed were characterised by human-wave infantry advances and the deliberate targeting of urban residential areas by enemy artillery, all for little territorial gain. The waters of the Persian Gulf also became a battleground as oil and other supply ships were destroyed, causing major disruptions to shipping in the area.

In March 1988 Kurdish guerrillas occupied government-controlled territory in Iraqi Kurdistan, and the Iraqi government in response killed many more thousands of civilians, forcing many more to escape to Iran and Turkey. It is alleged that chemical weapons were used – an allegation that Iraq continues to deny.

In August 1988 the UN brokered a cease-fire between Iran and Iraq. In the eight years of war, millions of lives had been lost on both sides, and the economic cost to Iraq is estimated at more than US$100 billion.

As Iraq started to emerge from the ravages of the war, relations with neighbouring Kuwait began to sour. In July 1990, Hussein accused the Kuwaitis (with some justification) of waging 'economic warfare' against Iraq by attempting to artificially hold down the price of oil, and of stealing oil from the Iraqi portion of an oilfield straddling the border.

Arab attempts to mediate a peaceful end to the dispute failed and on 2 August 1990 Iraq sent its troops and tanks into Kuwait. The UN quickly passed a series of resolutions calling on Iraq to withdraw. Instead,

on 8 August, Iraq annexed the emirate as its 19th province.

Western countries, led by the USA, began to enforce a UN embargo on trade with Iraq by stopping and searching ships bound for Iraq and Jordan. In the months that followed, more than half a million troops from 27 countries flooded into Saudi Arabia as the diplomatic stand-off over Kuwait deepened. At the end of November, the USA and the UK secured a UN resolution authorising the use of force to drive Iraq out of Kuwait if Baghdad did not voluntarily pull out before 15 January 1991.

Despite frantic last-minute attempts by international leaders to broker a deal, the deadline passed, the Iraqis did not budge, and within hours a barrage of Tomahawk cruise missiles was launched against strategic targets in Baghdad and elsewhere. Allied (mostly US) aircraft began a five week bombing campaign over Iraq and Kuwait. In contrast, the subsequent ground offensive lasted only 100 hours. While there were relatively few casualties on the Allied side, controversy has persisted over the number of civilian and military deaths in Iraq and Kuwait: estimates range from 10,000 to more than 100,000.

A cease-fire was announced by the USA on 28 February and Iraq agreed to comply fully with all UN Security Council resolutions. The Security Council demanded full disclosure, inspection and destruction of the country's biological, chemical, ballistic and nuclear weapons stockpiles and development programs before UN sanctions would be lifted.

The elite remnants of the Iraqi army turned their guns on Kurdish and Shi'ite uprisings in the north and south, causing a further mass exodus into neighbouring countries, particularly Iran and Turkey. This led the Allied forces to impose two 'no-fly' zones, in the north and south, to protect the civilian population from Iraqi air raids.

As malnutrition increased and medical care became inadequate throughout Iraq, the food for oil plan was introduced in 1996.

Under this program, Iraq was permitted to export US$2 billion of oil over a six month period in order to buy food and medicine, although limited hard currency reserves and extensively damaged infrastructure prevented full implementation of the plan.

Iraq Today

Tensions between Iraq and the UN (principally the USA) have risen and fallen cyclically since mid-1996. In August of that year, the Iraqi army moved into an area forbidden to it by international rules, resulting in the US destruction of air defences in southern Iraq. In November 1997 and then again in January and February of the following year, Iraqi-US stand-offs threatened to spill over into open military confrontation – avoided on the latter occasion only through the last minute intervention of UN Secretary-General Kofi Annan.

In early August 1998, Iraqi hopes for an imminent lifting of the crippling economic sanctions were dashed as its relationship with the UN again deteriorated. Weapons inspectors were denied access to sites and the Iraqi government announced the suspension of all cooperation until the sanctions were removed. The USA, with British backing, responded with four days of air strikes in December, drawing protests from Russian, Chinese and Arab representatives at the UN.

At the time of writing, UN inspection activities in Iraq are still suspended. The two sides remain frozen in hostility and the sanctions that have devastated the Iraqi economy remain in force.

GEOGRAPHY

Iraq has a total land area of 434,924 sq km, consisting of four distinct regions. The first, the upper plain, stretches north-west from Hit and Samarra to the Turkish border between the Euphrates and Tigris rivers and is the most fertile region, although high soil salinity reduces the cultivable potential to 12% of arable land. The second, the lower plain, stretches from Hit and Samarra southeast to the Gulf and contains the marshes –

an area of swamps, lakes and narrow waterways, flanked by high reeds. The third, the mountainous region, is in the north-east. The fourth, the desert region, lies to the west of the Euphrates, stretching to the borders of Syria, Jordan and Saudi Arabia.

The Tigris and Euphrates rivers converge near Baghdad, then diverge again, before meeting at Qurna to form the wide Shatt al-Arab River which flows through Basra into the Gulf. Above Baghdad the rivers have strong retaining banks, but further south they often flood in spring.

CLIMATE

Iraq is hot in summer (May to September); the average summer temperature in Baghdad is 34°C and in Basra 37°C; the north is slightly cooler. In the south there is high humidity and in the central plains there are dust storms. Contact-lens wearers beware – these storms can be agonising.

Winter can be cold and the mountains become covered with snow. The average winter temperature in Baghdad is 11°C and in Basra 14°C. Rain falls between October and March and is pretty scanty, except in the north-east.

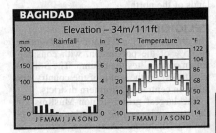

BAGHDAD — Elevation – 34m/111ft

GOVERNMENT & POLITICS

Power in the Republic of Iraq is concentrated in the hands of President Saddam Hussein. After holding a number of senior Ba'ath Party positions in the 1960s, Hussein was effectively elevated to second in command in 1968, a position he held until he seized power in 1979. As president, Hussein is also

IRAQ

commander of the armed forces, has executive power, and appoints the Council of Ministers. Nominal legislative and executive powers are exercised by the Revolutionary Command Council (RCC), operating under the strict control of the Ba'ath Party and Hussein. There is also a 250 member National Assembly, elected from a list of government-approved candidates every four years under a system of proportional representation.

An ally of the western powers throughout the Iran-Iraq war, Hussein has become an international pariah since the invasion of Kuwait. His reputation in western policy circles and continued hold on power are key reasons for Iraq's ongoing isolation.

POPULATION & PEOPLE

The population of Iraq was estimated to be 21.7 million in July 1998. Baghdad has a population of over five million, Basra nearly two million and Mosul 1.5 million.

Arabs make up 80% of the population and Kurds (concentrated primarily in the north) approximately 15%. Other minority groups are the Marsh Arabs, Yezidis, Turkomans, Assyrians, Chaldeans, the nomadic tribes who live in the western desert, and the Jezira Bedouin who live in the highlands of the north.

RELIGION

The official religion is Islam. Muslims make up 95% of the population, with considerably more Shi'ites than Sunni. The Shi'ites tend to live in the south of the country, the Sunni in central and northern districts.

The largest group of non-Muslims are Christians who belong to various sects, including Chaldeans, Assyrians, Syrian and Roman Catholics, Orthodox Armenians and Jacobites. Other religious minorities are the Yezidis, often erroneously called devil worshippers, and the Sabaeans, or Mandeans, who are followers of John the Baptist.

Serious religious conflicts in Iraq have been rare, and tensions between the various communities have occurred primarily because of political manipulation rather than fundamental doctrinal differences.

LANGUAGE

Arabic, the official language, is spoken by 80% of the population. The Kurds speak Kurdish, an Indo-European language. The Turkomans, who live in villages along the Baghdad to Mosul highway, speak a Turkish dialect. Persian is spoken by minorities near the Iranian border, while similar numbers speak Assyrian and Chaldean. English is quite widely spoken in urban centres.

Facts for the Visitor

VISAS & DOCUMENTS

At the time of writing, Iraqi embassies overseas were still not issuing visas to visitors. Some adventurous travellers have applied for visas at the Iraqi embassy in Jordan and were not refused outright. Some were even given cause to believe that their applications might be successful. However, we are not aware of anyone being granted a visa, other than journalists and aid workers; those who applied reported waits of up to three months before a refusal was issued.

EMBASSIES & CONSULATES

Some of Iraq's embassies overseas include:

Australia
    Embassy:
    (☎ 02-6286 1333)
    48 Culgoa Circuit, O'Malley 2606
France
    Embassy:
    (☎ 01 45 01 51 00)
    53 rue de la Faisanderie, Paris 75016
Jordan
    Embassy:
    (☎ 21 375)
    1st Circle, Jebel Amman, Amman
UK
    Embassy:
    (☎ 020-7584 7141, 7584 7146)
    22 Queen's Gate, London SW7
USA
    Embassy:
    (☎ 202-483 7500)
    Iraqi Interests Section, c/o Embassy of Algeria, 1801 Peter St NW, Washington, DC 20036

MONEY

There are 1000 fils to the Iraqi dinar.

BOOKS

If you are interested in archaeology, there are many books available about Iraq's ancient sites. *Nineveh & its Remains* by Austen Henry Layard is particularly interesting; Layard was the pioneer as far as excavations in the Middle East are concerned. This book also gives an insight into the lives of ordinary people in Iraq in the 19th century.

Essential reading for anyone hoping to catch a glimpse of the marshes is the excellent *The Marsh Arabs* by Wilfred Thesiger, who felt a great affinity with the Marsh Arabs and lived with them for five years in the 1950s.

Gavin Young also visited the marshes in the 1950s at the instigation of Thesiger. He returned again in the 70s to see how much the Marsh Arabs had changed. *Return to the Marshes* is an account of this visit. Large colour photographs by Nik Wheeler accompany the text. Another collaboration by these two is *Iraq, Land of Two Rivers,* which has interesting descriptions and photographs of the landscape and people.

The Longest War by Dilip Hiro is a detailed account of the Iran-Iraq War. Hiro also published a painstaking account of the events surrounding the 1991 Gulf War. In a conflict characterised by partial media reporting on both sides, Hiro's detailed narrative, *Desert Shield to Desert Storm*, is about as objective as it gets. For general information on Iraq, see the Books section in the Regional Facts for the Visitor chapter.

FOOD & DRINKS

Food in Iraq is similar to that of other Middle Eastern countries (see the special section 'Middle Eastern Cuisine').

Tea, drunk sweet without milk, is the most popular hot drink, followed by thick, black coffee. Other drinks include fruit juices, soft drinks and alcohol, including locally made arak.

SHOPPING

Iraq is known for Bedouin and Kurdish rugs, copperware and jewellery.

Getting There & Away

AIR

Although there are international airports at Baghdad and Basra, Iraqi Airways, Iraq's flag carrier, has been grounded since the Gulf War, and no other international carriers fly to the country.

LAND & SEA

At the time of writing, there were overland routes to Iraq from Jordan, Syria and Iran, although none were open to foreigners.

The train from Istanbul to Baghdad has been suspended since the Iran-Iraq War, and there have been no passenger ships operating to or from Iraq since the start of the war.

Getting Around

With the grounding of Iraqi Airways, internal flights between Baghdad, Basra and Mosul have been suspended.

Iraq has a good road network and there are buses between towns and cities, plus a rail line connects Baghdad to Mosul and Basra. Shared taxis are used between towns and cities in the north of Iraq.

Baghdad

For many people, the name of this ancient city conjures up vivid images: starry skies, golden domes and minarets; women shrouded in black gliding through narrow streets with old houses leaning precariously towards one another; or shafts of sunlight filtering through gloomy bazaars, their open shop fronts overflowing with exotic merchandise. Compared with these images, one's first impression of Baghdad can be disappointing, for it is not a city that makes an immediate impact. The old Baghdad has almost disappeared and the Iran-Iraq and Gulf wars destroyed much of the modern city.

Baghdad was founded by Al-Mansur, the second caliph of the Abbasid dynasty, in 762 AD. The city he built was on the western bank of the Tigris, enclosed within a circular wall and called Medinat as-Salaam, which meant City of Peace; it became known as the Round City. The caliph's palace and the grand mosque were in the centre with four roads radiating from them. The city expanded beyond the wall and was eventually joined by a bridge of boats to the eastern bank, where a district called Rusafah grew up. By 946 this district had grown sufficiently large to rival the Round City.

Baghdad reached the height of its prosperity and intellectual life in the 8th and 9th centuries under the caliphs Mahdi and Haroun ar-Rashid. It was the richest city in the world, the crossroads of important trade routes to the east and west, and supplanted Damascus as the seat of power in the Islamic world. Arabic numbers, the decimal system and algebra all came into being at this time. Advances were also made in medicine, and magnificent buildings were constructed with beautiful gardens.

From the mid-9th century onwards, the Abbasid caliphate became weakened by internal conflict, and civil war between Ar-Rashid's two sons resulted in the partial destruction of the Round City. Total destruction came about when the Mongols sacked Baghdad, killed the caliph and many of the residents, and destroyed the irrigation system. In 1534 it became part of the Ottoman empire and centuries of neglect followed.

Efforts were made to improve the city in the early years of the 20th century. The administration was reformed, hospitals and schools were built and a postal service developed, but these improvements were belated and inadequate. Baghdad's greatest developments took place when large oil revenues started to flow in after 1973. However, all developments were curtailed by the wars of the 1980s and 90s.

Orientation

The city extends along both sides of the Tigris. The eastern side is known as Rusafah and the western as Karkh. The core of the city is a 3.5km by 2km area in Rusafah, extending from Midan Muadham in the north to Midan Tahrir in the south. Sharia Rashid is the main street of this area and contains the city's financial district, and the copper, textile and gold bazaars.

Running parallel to Sharia Rashid is Sharia al-Jamouri, which has some historical mosques and government offices. South of Sharia Rashid is Sharia Sadoun, a newer commercial area. Parallel to here along the river bank is Sharia Abu Newas with many outdoor cafes.

Sharia Damascus in Karkh stretches from the Iraqi Museum to the international airport road. The Central train station, Alawi al-Hilla bus/taxi station, Al-Muthana airport and Zawra Park are along here. Sharia Haifa, parallel to the river, is another major street in Karkh.

Since the 1950s the city has expanded enormously, and planned middle-class neighbourhoods have sprung up between the city centre and the Army Canal. On the western bank are a number of residential areas including affluent Mansour, which is surrounded by a race track and has trendy boutiques and fastfood restaurants. A number of embassies are in Mansour.

Museums

Baghdad has numerous excellent museums and interesting mosques. Many museums are free, others have only a nominal fee, and most are closed on Friday. In Karkh, near the Alawi al-Hilla bus/taxi station, is the large, well-organised **Iraqi Museum** that has a collection carefully labelled in English and Arabic that is from prehistoric, Sumerian, Babylonian, Assyrian and Abbasid times. Near Midan Rusafah, the **Baghdad Museum** houses an interesting collection of life-sized models in tableaux depicting traditional Baghdadi life.

The **Museum of Pioneer Arts** on Sharia Rashid is worth a visit just for the wonderful old Baghdadi house in which the art collection is hung. The rooms are built around a central courtyard with a fountain in the middle. It's a peaceful retreat where you can sit and relax after the hustle and bustle of Sharia Rashid. Some of the rooms are traditionally furnished, and the guest rooms upstairs are the nicest of all.

Housed also in a large traditional Baghdad house, the **Museum of Popular Heritage**, on the western side of Sharia Haifa, has some fine examples of traditional Iraqi crafts, including woodwork, metalwork, basketwork and carpets, all tastefully displayed.

The **Saddam Art Centre**, on the western side of Sharia Haifa, is a beautiful building with high ceilings, white walls and chandeliers. It was opened only in 1986 and the works in the permanent collection are mainly from the 1970s and 80s. The **Museum of Modern Art** on Midan Nafura near the Tahrir bus station is a bit of a letdown after the Saddam Art Centre, but it has some interesting temporary exhibitions.

Mosques

Never go into a mosque in Iraq unless you are invited. If you want to go inside one, stand at the entrance and someone will soon appear and indicate whether or not you are welcome inside. You must of course be dressed modestly and women must cover their heads.

The **Kadhimain Mosque** is the most important in Iraq after those at Kerbala and Najaf. Inside are the shrines of the two *imams* (religious teachers) Musa al-Kadhim and Mohammed al-Jawad. The very large and elaborate mosque has gold-coated domes and minarets and was built in 1515.

The **Caliph's Mosque** is on the eastern side of Sharia al-Jamouri, between Wathba and Amin squares. It's a new mosque with an ancient minaret that dates from 1289. Built 40 years ago, the **14th Ramadan Mosque** on Midan Fardous, Sharia Sadoun, has lovely arabesques and glazed wall tiles. Another attractive mosque is the **Ibn Bunnieh Mosque** in front of Alawi al-Hilla bus station. Yet another is the **Umm Attubol Mosque** on the road to the international airport. It has an unusual architectural style, very ornate and delicate, and gives the impression of being modelled in icing sugar.

The **Marjan Mosque**, on the eastern side of Sharia Rashid, was built in 1357, and in its early days served as the Murjaniyya School. Early this century, most of it was pulled down and rebuilt as a mosque. A little way down the opposite side of the road is the Murjin Khan, where the scholars used to live. It has been converted into a restaurant.

Mustansiriyya School

Opposite the Baghdad Museum, turn left at the mosque to get to the school entrance. The school was built in the reign of the 36th Abbasid caliph, Mustansir Billah, and was the most highly esteemed university of that time. It was completed in 1232 and is an outstanding example of Abbasid architecture.

Abbasid Palace

From Sharia Rashid, turn left at Midan Maidan and take the road to the right of the mosque. The palace is at the bottom of the road on the right, overlooking the Tigris. Because of its resemblance in style and structure to the Mustansiriyya School, some scholars believe it is the Sharabiyya School mentioned by old Arab historians.

Zawra Park

This vast park on Sharia Damascus, opposite Al-Muthana airport, is a little parched-looking compared with European parks, but parts of it, like the Islamic garden where fountains play, are attractive. There's a good view of the city from the 54m-high Baghdad Tower in the park.

There is also a zoo, a swimming pool and a planetarium in the park.

Other Attractions

When it's not too hot, Baghdad is a fascinating city to explore on foot. If and when it gets onto the tourist map, the bazaars of Sharia Rashid will be where visitors go to see the 'real' Baghdad.

A far more interesting area, and one that gives a greater insight into the city, is that behind the Saddam Art Centre on Sharia Haifa. Here, you will see men in *galabeyyas* (long loose shirts), sitting in coffeehouses smoking water pipes or sitting cross-legged on the pavement selling their wares; little shops selling fresh herbs, spices or fruit and vegetables; men covered in oil mending old cars; narrow streets of old crumbling houses with overhanging balconies; and barefoot children playing in the streets. Fascinating though this area is, it is also a sad testimony to Iraq's enormous social and economic problems.

Around Baghdad

BABYLON, KERBALA & NAJAF

Ancient Babylon and the important Muslim shrines of Kerbala and Najaf all lie south of Baghdad, and it's quite possible to visit them all in a day trip from the capital.

Babylon

Babylon lies 90km south of Baghdad and 10km north of Hillah, and is perhaps the most famous of Iraq's ancient sites. The ancient city reached its height during the reign of Nebuchadnezzar II (605-563 BC). With its high walls and magnificent palaces and temples it was regarded as one of the most beautiful cities in the world. It was most renowned for its Hanging Gardens, one of the Seven Wonders of the World.

All that remains of the ruins of Babylon is a huge and magnificent lion, eroded by time and the weather.

Kerbala

Kerbala is 108km south-west of Baghdad and is of great religious significance to Muslims because of the battle of Kerbala in 680

The Hanging Gardens of Babylon

The Hanging Gardens of Babylon were located a long way from the heartland of the Classical world. Perhaps that is why they have always been one of the most mysterious and perplexing of the Seven Wonders – some people suggest they may not have existed at all. But many rulers in the ancient Middle East decorated their palaces with luxurious gardens to provide relief and shelter from the surrounding desert climate.

The Hanging Gardens were built by the Babylonian King Nebuchadnezzar II around 590 BC, perhaps as a gift for his Median bride Amitiya to remind her of her lush, mountainous homeland. The construction of the gardens was probably based on the traditional Mesopotamian Step Pyramid or ziggurat design. The wide steps or terraces, rising in ever diminishing layers, would have contained deep garden beds and boxes for plantations. The terraces would have been planted with palms, cypresses and fruit trees. Other shrubs must have been planted along the terrace edges with their foliage spilling over the brickwork to give the 'hanging garden' effect that amazed visitors to Babylon more than 2000 years ago.

Jeremy Smith

AD. The battle between those who believed the rulers of the Islamic community must be the direct descendants of Mohammed, and those who argued that virtue alone bestowed legitimacy upon leaders, led to the schism between the Sunni and Shi'ite sects. Hussein ibn Ali, who has become revered as leader of the Shi'ites, and his brother Abbas, grandsons of the Prophet Mohammed, were killed in the battle, and their shrines are contained in the two mosques here, thus making Kerbala one of the greatest pilgrimage centres in the Islamic world. Non-Muslims are not allowed to enter the shrines but, with the permission of an attendant, may be able to walk around the surrounding courtyards.

Najaf

Najaf is 160km south of Baghdad, just west of the Euphrates. It was founded by Haroun ar-Rashid in 791 AD. In the city centre is a mosque containing the tomb of Ali ibn Abi Talib (600-661), cousin and son-in-law of Mohammed and founder of the Shi'ites, thus making this mosque one of the sect's greatest shrines.

It is a great honour for Muslims to be buried in graveyards in either Kerbala or Najaf. The latter especially seems to have graveyards all over the place and it's fascinating, if a little macabre, to wander around them. Many of the graves are small shrines.

THE ARCH OF CTESIPHON

Little is left of the city of Ctesiphon, apart from the arch. It is 30km south-east of Baghdad, east of the Tigris. The city was built in the 2nd century BC by the Parthian Persians. The arch was part of a great banqueting hall and, apparently, is the widest single-span vault in the world. It survived the disastrous flooding of the Tigris in 1887, which destroyed much of the rest of the building.

Basra

Basra was founded by the caliph Omar in 637 AD. It was originally a military base but rapidly grew into a major Islamic city. It be-

came the focal point of Arab sea trade during the 16th century, when ships left its port for distant lands in the east. Its strategic position has made it the scene of many battles, sometimes between the Marsh Arabs and the Turks and sometimes between invading Persians and Turks.

In 1624 Ali Pasha repulsed a Persian attack and, in the period of peace that followed, Basra became a mecca for poets, scientists and artists. The peace was shortlived; Ali Pasha's son imposed a buffalo tax upon the Marsh Arabs and the fighting and instability resumed.

Basra is Iraq's main sea port and second largest city, 550km south-east of Baghdad and 130km from the Gulf. There are extensive palm groves on the outskirts of the city and most of Iraq's dates are grown in and around Basra.

Orientation & Information

The city comprises three main areas – Ashar, Margil and Basra proper. Ashar is the old commercial area and includes the Corniche, which runs alongside the Shatt al-Arab River; Sharia al-Kuwait; and Sharia ath-Thawra, where banks and the old Iraqi Airlines office are found. Basra's bazaars are also here and behind them is the Ashar bus garage. The central post office is on the road to the west of the bus garage.

The Basra train station is in Margil, which also includes the port and a modern residential area to the north-west of Ashar.

Basra proper is the old residential area to the west of Ashar. Here you can see the lovely 19th century houses called *shenashils* by the canal that flows into the Shatt al-Arab. One of these is the Basra Museum. Further along this road is the Baghdad bus station from where intercity buses leave.

Basra Museum

The contents of the museum are nothing special – just a few objects from Sumerian, Babylonian and Islamic times – but it's worth coming here to see the beautiful shenashil houses with high pointed windows and ornate, wooden overhanging balconies.

IRAQ

Not far from the museum is the derelict **St Thomas Chaldean Church**.

Floating Navy Museum

This museum is in Ashar at the northern corner of the Corniche. Its exhibits include guns from both sides in the Iran-Iraq War, models of ships and parts from wrecked Iranian aircraft and ships.

Museum for The Martyrs of the Persian Aggression

This white building has some war-wrecked vehicles in the grounds, while inside are heart-rending displays of the sufferings of the ordinary people of Basra during the war with Iran. The museum is on the north-eastern corner of Sharia Istiklal.

Basra Bazaar

Basra's bazaar in Ashar is one of the most atmospheric in Iraq, and was once home to a particularly good gold bazaar with some very fine pieces of jewellery. In parts you can see old houses with wooden facades and balconies tilting at such precarious angles that it's amazing they manage to stand at all.

Sinbad Island

Sinbad is supposed to have started his voyages from here. The island used to be attractive, with outdoor restaurants and gardens, but it suffered extensive bombing and now is a little dreary.

Nasiriyya

Nasiriyya is 375km south-east of Baghdad, on the northern bank of the Euphrates. Most people stay here only to visit Ur of the Chaldees, but it's a pleasant, relaxed place to spend a day or two. The centre of Nasiriyya is Midan Haboby.

Nasiriyya Museum

The museum has an interesting collection from Sumerian, Assyrian, Babylonian and Abbasid times. It's on the southern side of the river, a pleasant 20 minute walk along the river bank. Walk south along Sharia Neel and turn right into the road that runs by the river; walk along here and cross over the bridge; take the first turning right and the museum is on the right.

AROUND NASIRIYYA
Ur of the Chaldees

Ur is one of the most impressive ancient sites in Iraq. It was mentioned in the Bible as being the birthplace of Abraham, and its earliest buildings date from 4000 BC. For three successive dynasties it was the capital of Sumeria, although it reached its height during the third and last dynasty (2113-2095 BC). The ziggurat is impressive and the royal tombs well preserved.

The Marshes

The marshes originally covered an area of approximately 10,000 sq km between the Tigris and the Euphrates, stretching from Basra in the south, Nasiriyya in the west and Kut in the north. Some parts were permanent, and others were temporary marshland, changing with the seasons.

The marshes were a world of vast expanses of water and shallow lagoons. Here it is sometimes possible to see the Marsh Arab dwellings known as *sarifas*, with their ornate latticework entrances. The people row long slender canoes known as *mashufs* through the high reeds. There is archaeological evidence that life has continued here, almost unchanged, for 6000 years and the marshes are also home to many species of water birds. Sadly, much of the marshes were drained in the late 1980s and most Marsh Arabs have moved to refugee camps, mainly in Iran.

Mosul

Mosul, 396km north of Baghdad, is Iraq's third largest city. It's also the most ethnically mixed, with Arabs, Kurds, Assyrians and Turkomans.

In Abbasid times, Mosul achieved commercial importance because of its position on the caravan route from India and Persia to the Mediterranean. Its most important export was cotton. The word 'muslin' is derived from Mosul, and cotton is still produced here today. Mosul was devastated by the Mongols in the 13th century but began to revive under the Ottomans.

The main street and commercial area is Sharia Nineveh, along which are several old houses that are fine examples of 19th century Mosul architecture. The old part of the city is a maze of narrow streets off both sides of Sharia Nineveh, west of the bazaar.

The city centre is Midan Babatub, a huge open area with a fountain in the middle. The bazaar is between here and Sharia Nineveh. Sharia Duwasa runs south from Midan Babatub. Behind the eastern side of the square is the Babatub bus station. The central post office is on the eastern side of the station.

Mosul Museum

This museum has a large collection of finds from the successive civilisations of Iraq, from prehistoric to Islamic times, with an emphasis on finds from Nineveh to Nimrud. It's on the western side of the river.

Mosul House

This beautiful old house, built around a central courtyard, has a facade of Mosul marble. It houses life-sized models depicting traditional Mosul life. Admission is free but the museum is difficult to find and doesn't have a sign in English. Walking west along Sharia Nineveh, turn left at the crossroads before the Clock & Latin Church, take the second turning left along here, go under the arches and the house is on the right. It has a large wooden entrance.

Mosques

Believed to be the burial place of Jonah, the **Mosque of Nebi Yunus**, on the eastern side of the Tigris, is built on a mound beneath which are buried some ruins of Nineveh, but because of the sanctity of the site, excavation is impossible. A little community of mud-brick houses and narrow winding streets has grown up around the mosque. Take a bus from the Babatub garage towards the Ash-Shamal bus station and look out for the mosque on the right, about 3km from the Horeyya Bridge.

The **Great Nur ad-Din Mosque** was built in 1172 by Nur ad-Din Zanqi and is famed for its remarkably bent minaret, which stands 52m high and has elaborate brickwork. To get there, walk west along Sharia Nineveh and turn right at the crossroads before the Clock & Latin Church; the mosque is on the right.

Churches

Mosul has a higher proportion of Christians than any other Iraqi city. The **Clock & Latin Church** is a good place to start because it's easy to find and also sells a booklet called *The Churches of Mosul*. This booklet contains a numbered list in Arabic and English of the major churches in Mosul, and a map of sorts that will help you find them, or at least enable you to get assistance from someone. The church is on the southern side of Sharia Nineveh. Inside is lots of blue Mosul marble, lovely brickwork in blue, brown and cream, and stained-glass windows of abstract patterns.

Many of the churches are near this one, but hidden away in the labyrinth of old Mosul's fascinating backstreets.

Other Attractions

The imposing ruins of **Bash Tapia Castle**, rising high above the Tigris on its western bank, are now the only part of Mosul's city wall still in existence. Just a few minutes away, a little further south on the river bank, are the remnants of the 13th century palace of the sultan Badr ad-Din called **The Black Palace** (Qara Serai).

Between the two ruins is the **Chaldean Catholic Church of Al-Tahira**, or the Church of the Upper Monastery. The oldest part was built in 300 AD as a monastery, and in 1600 was added to and became a church. In the street running parallel to this is the Syrian Orthodox Al-Tahira Church, which dates from 1210.

IRAQ

AROUND MOSUL
Nineveh
The ancient city of Nineveh was the third capital of Assyria. Up until King Hammurabi's death it was a province of Babylonia, but after this time it developed as an independent kingdom. By 1400 BC it had become one of the most powerful countries in the Middle East, but by 500 BC it had been destroyed by the Medes of Northern Persia. For 200 years prior to this, however, Nineveh was the centre of the civilised world.

Nineveh is on the outskirts of Mosul, on the eastern bank of the Tigris. Its walls measured 12km in circumference and there were 15 gates, each named after an Assyrian god. Several have been reconstructed. The Shamash gate is just beyond the Ash-Shamal bus garage. The Nergal gate is about 2km from the university and it has a small museum with some Assyrian reliefs and a model of the city of Khorsabad, which was the fourth capital of Assyria. To get there you must walk south from the university and then turn left just before the reconstructed walls on both sides of the road. You will see the gate just along here on the right.

Nimrud
Nimrud, the second capital of Assyria, is 37km south-east of Mosul and one of the best preserved of Iraq's ancient sites. The city wall has an 8km circumference containing several buildings, the most impressive being King Assurnasirpal II's palace. On either side of the entrance are two huge sculptures of human-headed lions with hawk wings. Inside are some beautiful bas-relief slabs.

Hatra
Hatra is 110km to the south-west of Mosul. Once an important city, it dates from the 1st century AD. In architecture, sculpture, metalwork and military expertise, Hatra was no less advanced than Rome. The ruins contain many fine pieces of sculpture.

North-East Mountains

Scenically this area contrasts starkly with the rest of the country, consisting of high mountains and fertile valleys. Much of it is in the Kurdish Autonomous Region. The Kurds are descendants of the Medes and have inhabited 'Kurdistan' since Parthian times (see History in the Facts about the Region chapter).

ARBIL
Arbil, 84km from Mosul, is one of the oldest continuously inhabited cities in the world, and headquarters of the Kurdish Autonomous Region. Its beginnings are buried in the mists of antiquity, but there is archaeological evidence that Neolithic peoples roamed the area 10,000 years ago.

Fortress
The modern town occupies the top of a mound formed by successive building over a long period of time. It is dominated by a fortress, behind which are three large 19th century Kurdish houses which, along with the fortress, have been turned into museums. The houses have ceilings decorated with floral patterns and coloured-glass windows. One has a room with an interesting collection of everyday Kurdish objects and handicrafts, another an art gallery showing works by contemporary Iraqi artists. Nearby is a large bathhouse, also part of the house.

Arbil Museum
The museum was opened in 1989 and has a comprehensive collection from Sumerian to Abbasid times. From Midan Nishteman, walk away from the fortress, along the main road, cross Midan Media, and the museum is on the left.

SHAQLAWA & GULLY ALI BEG
The road from Arbil winds steeply upwards to Salahuddin at 1090m above sea level, and then on to Shaqlawa, 50km from Arbil. This is an idyllic town surrounded by mountains

The Kurds

Iraq is home to over four million Kurds, the overwhelming majority of whom are Sunni Muslims and live in the northern provinces of the country. These provinces form part of the ancient Kurdish homeland of Kurdistan, which extended across the modern borders with Iran, Turkey and Syria. The 1961 Kurdish campaign to secure independence from Iraq laid the foundations for an uneasy relationship between the Kurds and the Iraqi state. Cycles of conflict and détente have consistently characterised this relationship ever since, as greater official recognition and freedom have been alternately offered and denied, culminating frequently in brutal repression. This process was tragically re-enacted after the 1991 Gulf War when over two million Kurds were forced to flee across the mountains to the relative safety of Turkey and Iran, countries with their own restive Kurdish populations. Under UN protection, the Kurdish Autonomous Region was set up in northern Iraq. However, ongoing Iraqi and external interference, and the often bitter rivalry between the Patriotic Union of Kurdistan (PUK) and the Kurdistan Democratic Party (KDP), ensure that these tentative moves towards autonomy remain precarious. Like many Kurds in neighbouring countries, Iraqi Kurds continue to face an uncertain future.

and orchards where pears, apples, grapes, pomegranates, almonds and walnuts grow in profusion.

From Shaqlawa the mountain ranges begin to close in and the scenery becomes more rugged and dramatic. Gully Ali Beg, 60km from Shaqlawa, is a narrow 10km-long pass with a lovely 80m-high waterfall tumbling into it.

DOHUK

Dohuk is a small Kurdish town 73km north of Mosul. It's a pleasant place, with an interesting market, but serves mainly as a base from which to explore the surrounding mountains.

AMADIYA

Amadiya is 90km from Dohuk. The road passes through scenery that, as the road unfolds, becomes more and more spectacular. It winds through several villages – firstly Zawila, then Suara Tuga, which has a wonderful view of the plain of Sarsang, then through Anshki to Sulaf, a village with waterfalls and lots of cafes where you can sit and enjoy the views. The road finally ends at Amadiya, an extremely picturesque village on a plateau 1985m above sea level, surrounded by magnificent mountains and endless green valleys.

ZAKHO

Zakho, near the Turkish border, is Iraq's most northerly town and is famous for its old stone bridge, well preserved and still in constant use. Its age is unknown but it's reputed to have been built by a local Abbasid ruler and is at the far side of town. The approach to Zakho is spectacular, crossing many high mountain ridges.

SINJAR

The town of Sinjar is 160km west of Mosul on the slopes of the Jebel Sinjar range in the desert, near the Syrian border. It is most renowned for being the town of the Yezidis, the so-called devil worshippers who are of Kurdish stock.

What they actually believe is that the devil is a fallen angel, bringing evil to the world, and must be appeased so he will once again take up his rightful place among the angels. The Yezidis will never say his name, Shaitan, or any similar-sounding word. Their religion contains elements of nature worship, Islam and Christianity. In October a festival is held at the shrine of Sheikh Adi, the sect's founder. Like the Kurds, the Yezidis are friendly and hospitable.

IRAQ

Israel & the Palestinian Territories

One of the golden rules for successful travelling is to avoid discussing religion and politics. In Israel, however, they collide inseparably, both with each other and with virtually everything else. This is the Holy Land; this is Palestine.

A land of incredible contrasts, Israel offers a wealth of changing landscapes, different climates, culture, history and, of course, religion. Its tiny size makes this all the more remarkable. Slightly smaller than New Jersey or Belgium and about half the size of Tasmania, Israel contains almost every type of geographical terrain: mountains, sub-tropical valleys, fertile farms and deserts.

Jewish, Muslim and Christian pilgrims are drawn here by the conviction that 'this is where it happened'. Such beliefs, combined with Israel's strategic location, have made this probably the most hotly disputed area in the world.

Facts about Israel & the Palestinian Territories

HISTORY

A general history of the Middle East is given in the Facts about the Region chapter at the beginning of this book. In the 1930s Hitler's rise to power in Germany sent hundreds of thousands of Jews fleeing from Europe to swell the numbers in the 'Promised Land'. The indigenous Arabs of Palestine saw no reason why they should suffer for the misfortunes of war-torn Europe and responded with riots against the unwelcome and ever-increasing number of newcomers. In 1948 Britain washed its hands of the whole mess and cleared out. Immediately the Jews declared the land as their own in-

The State of Israel

Area: 28,000 sq km (including the Gaza Strip and the West Bank)
Population: 6.03 million (including the Gaza Strip and the West Bank)
Population Growth Rate: 2.2%
Capital: Jerusalem – also claimed as capital by the Palestinians
Head of State: Prime Minister Ehud Barak with a president, Ezer Weizmann, having a largely symbolic role
Official Languages: Hebrew & Arabic
Currency: new Israeli shekel (NIS)
Exchange Rate: US$1 = 4.07NIS

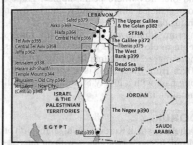

- **Best Dining** – Tel Aviv's countless restaurants and snack bars
- **Best Nightlife** – a camp site meal at night in the Judean Desert
- **Best Walk** – along the walls of Jerusalem's Old City
- **Best view** – from the rim of the Maktesh Ramon crater in the Negev Desert
- **Best activity** – diving the Red Sea at Eilat
- **When in Rome ...** getting invited to a *sukka* celebration during Sukkot
- **And avoid** – rip-off taxi drivers of Jerusalem and Tel Aviv

dependent state, called Israel, and began to fight it out with the Arabs.

Israel emerged victorious from that first Arab-Israeli bout, as it did again during the 1956 Suez Conflict. An even more decisive victory over the combined forces of Egypt, Jordan and Syria achieved in just six days in 1967 established Israel as the Middle East's pre-eminent military superpower. However, early defeats in the following 1973 war left Israel considerably less sure of its security. Negotiations began which resulted in the signing of the Israel-Egypt Peace Treaty of 1979 (the Camp David Accord), a peace which although a little frosty has so far been maintained.

Peace with Egypt failed to address the issue of the Palestinian Arabs, great numbers of whom had been made refugees in 1948 and 1967, while those remaining in Gaza and the West Bank lived under Israeli occupation. During the 1970s and 1980s, under the spearhead of Yasser Arafat's PLO, a campaign of international terrorism was waged to bring the Palestinian plight to international attention. The world's response was repulsion. This began to change in 1987 with the *intifada*, a spontaneous popular uprising to which the Israelis were seen to respond with a brutal heavy-handedness. Worldwide TV screenings of Israeli soldiers firing on unarmed Arab youths did much to rehabilitate the Palestinians and demonise the Jewish state.

In 1991 Israeli officials sat down to talk with a Palestinian delegation for the first time. This ultimately led to the White House lawn where Arafat and Israeli prime minister Rabin signalled their intentions of peace and made their Nobel Peace Prize-winning handshake.

Since then the Gaza Strip and several towns in the West Bank have been handed over to Palestinian autonomous rule and elections have confirmed Arafat as undisputed leader of his people. However, a comprehensive settlement with the Palestinians is still some distance in the future with the really sticky issues such as the status of Jerusalem and the future of the two million

What to See

Allow as much time as you can for **Jerusalem**, a place that needs to be absorbed not 'done'; two days here is the absolute minimum but give it a week if you've got it. Jerusalem is also the best base for visiting the **Dead Sea** and **Masada**, two sites which come high on most itineraries.

From the Holy City, head up to **Tiberias** on the shores of Galilee and aim to spend a full day there, perhaps cycling around the lake. Next morning head for **Safed** and plan to spend the night in the Crusader city of **Akko**.

Some time should be allotted for **Tel Aviv** – a great Mediterranean city with a laid-back, hip lifestyle. The **Negev Desert** should be high on your list. Try trekking in the **Maktesh Ramon** – an enormous natural crater then head down to **Eilat** for a spot of diving and swimming in the **Red Sea**.

Palestinian refugees in Egypt, Jordan and Lebanon still to be discussed. Add to that Syria's demands for the return of the Israeli annexed Golan Heights and the continued confrontation with Hezbollah in southern Lebanon and Israel is still some way off sleeping easy at night.

In October 1998 at Wye River in the USA President Bill Clinton, morally encouraged by the ailing King Hussein of Jordan, rekindled the peace process by getting Yasser Arafat and Binyamin Netanyahu and the Israelis together once more. The ensuing Wye River Accord, which called for the Israelis to hand over a further 13% of the West Bank to the Palestinians, demanded that the Palestinians abrogate the clauses in the Palestinian National Charter calling for the destruction of the State of Israel and redouble their efforts against terrorism. A foiled attack on a school bus at the Israeli settlement of Gush Katif in the Gaza Strip and failed suicide bomber attack in Jerusalem's Mahane Yehuda market

ISRAEL & THE PALESTINIAN TERRITORIES

Fifty Years & More of War

There are Israelis who claim that God gave the land to the Jews and, therefore, it would be blasphemous to surrender 1mm of it. There are Arabs who equate Israel with the Crusader states of the Middle Ages and view its destruction as a religious duty, saying it represents an infidel incursion into the sacred lands of Islam.

These are, of course, extreme examples, but they serve to illustrate the depth of the feelings and enmities born of nearly a century of conflict between Arabs and Jews over the sliver of land traditionally known as Palestine.

Zionism has its roots in 19th century Europe (thus the Arab claim that Israel is little more than a relic of the colonial era). Though the idea of a Jewish state did not originate with him it was first put forward in a systematic way by an Austrian journalist, Theodor Herzl, who believed that Jews could never gain true acceptance in European society. Herzl's 1896 book *Der Judenstaat* (The Jewish State), called for the establishment of a Jewish homeland, and the following year he organised the first International Zionist Congress in Basel, Switzerland. The Congress' final resolution stated that 'the goal of Zionism is the establishment for the Jewish people of a home in Palestine guaranteed by public law'.

In November 1917 the British Cabinet, in a statement known as the Balfour Declaration, gave the cause its formal backing. When Britain took control of Palestine near the end of WWI Zionists hoped the declaration would serve as a licence for unrestricted Jewish immigration. The arrival of Jewish settlers, however, led to tension with Palestine's Arab population and, eventually, to violence. In the late 1930s Britain clamped strict limits on Jewish immigration, a policy which was continued throughout WWII.

In February 1947 the British, despairing of ever reconciling Arabs and Jews and far more concerned with post-WWII reconstruction at home, announced that they would withdraw from Palestine the following year and turned the problem over to the United Nations.

In November 1947 the UN voted to partition Palestine into Arab and Jewish states and to turn Jerusalem into an international city. Predictably, neither side was satisfied with the plan. The Jews, however reluctantly, accepted it while the Arabs rejected it outright. War broke out when Britain withdrew in May 1948, and the formal partition lines quickly came to mean nothing. Jewish forces sought to gain control of as much of Palestine as possible while the combined armies of Egypt, Jordan and Lebanon (along with smaller contingents from Syria, Iraq and Saudi Arabia) endeavoured to wipe out the new Jewish state.

The 1949 armistice agreements which ended the previous year's Arab-Israeli War effectively defined the Jewish state's borders for the next 18 years. The only portions of historical Palestine left under Arab control were the Gaza Strip, which was occupied by the Egyptian army, and the area now known as the West Bank, which was occupied, and later annexed, by the Jordanians.

By the time of the Suez Crisis in 1956 the basic elements which defined the Arab-Israeli conflict for the next 35 years were in place: Israel, its population swelled by successive waves of Jewish immigration, possessed most (after 1967, all) of historical Palestine. The Palestinians lived as refugees either in other Arab countries or under Israeli occupation. Arab governments refused to talk to Israel under any circumstances and Israel loudly proclaimed its desire for peace while working furiously to create what former Israeli defence minister Moshe Dayan called 'facts on the ground' – essentially geographic and demographic alterations to secure the territory under their control. These changes tended both to reinforce Israel's long-term strategic position and to convince Arabs that Israel had no

Fifty Years and More of War

intention of either giving up land or of allowing the Palestinian refugees to finally return to what had once been their homes.

In such an explosive situation no event or gesture, however seemingly innocuous, managed to remain devoid of political content. The combination of time, physical separation and an unbroken stream of propaganda on both sides led many Arabs and Israelis to develop somewhat cartoon-like images of each other.

The 1991 Gulf War changed the strategic equation in the region by leaving both sides of the Arab-Israeli conflict politically weakened and anxious to score points with the international community. Even so, it took months of US coaxing to get both sides to agree to attend a peace conference in Madrid in October of the same year. Among the major sticking points was Israel's insistence that it would not deal directly with the Palestine Liberation Organization (PLO), which it considered a terrorist group. After the ceremonial opening session in Madrid, nearly two years of inconclusive bilateral talks with Syria, Lebanon, Jordan and a group of non-PLO Palestinians followed.

Then, in August 1993, the news broke that Israel and the PLO had been holding secret talks for some 18 months in Norway. The following month Israel and the PLO formally recognised each other. Then, on 13 September, PLO chairman Yasser Arafat and Israeli Prime Minister Yitzhak Rabin shook hands in Washington on the White House lawn after watching their deputies sign a joint Declaration of Principles. The Declaration laid out a timetable for future talks on the details of an Israeli withdrawal from the Gaza Strip and the West Bank town of Jericho, the redeployment of Israeli forces away from the West Bank's other population centres, the granting of limited autonomy to Palestinians throughout the West Bank and Gaza Strip and elections for a Palestinian Authority to run the self-rule areas.

At the Washington ceremony almost every speaker, whether Israeli, Palestinian, American or Russian, stressed the length of the road that still had to be travelled before a true and lasting peace could be achieved. Their point was driven home by the charges of betrayal with which rejectionists on both sides greeted the accords.

Between the need of both Arafat and Rabin to cover their flanks politically, a series of provocations by extremists on both sides and the simple fact that neither Israel nor the PLO really had much trust in the other, the talks on a detailed agreement dragged on for months beyond the original timetable. An accord was finally signed, in Cairo, in May 1994 and Israeli troops withdrew from Gaza and Jericho. Further talks led to Palestinian elections and the withdrawal of most Israeli troops from the West Bank's main population centres at the end of 1995, a process that went forward despite the assassination of Prime Minister Rabin by a Jewish extremist opposed to the peace process on 4 November 1995.

Working with Arafat, Rabin's successor, Shimon Peres, sought to push the peace process forward. The job was complicated by an increasingly strong backlash from Hamas, a Palestinian Muslim fundamentalist group originally supported by the Israelis themselves as an alternative to the PLO, and by the doubts about the peace process that Hamas' terror bombings sowed in the Israeli public. In May 1996 these doubts brought down Peres, who narrowly lost the prime ministership to Benjamin Netanyahu in a general election. The 1996 election was also Israel's first in which the prime minister was directly elected in a separate vote from the one for seats in parliament. This gave Netanyahu much greater power within the Israeli government.

The new prime minister appointed one of the most right-wing governments in the country's history, and promised to be much tougher on security issues than his predecessor. While saying he wanted only to put the peace process on a sounder footing, he subjected Arafat to what the Palestinians, and most other Arabs, saw as a series of deliberate slights and public humiliations. Tension once again rose throughout the region. In September 1996 there were widespread clashes between Israelis and Palestinians, including the Palestinian police, that left dozens dead. Peace talks with Syria and Lebanon, slow-moving under Peres, ground to a halt with the installation of the new government. But, the election of Labour's Ehud Barak in May 1999 brought renewed hope in the peace process and within months of his landslide victory, a timetable for a permanent settlement was agreed upon.

Though Israel and Jordan have drawn increasingly close to one another on the governmental level since they signed a peace treaty in October 1994, contact between the two peoples remains more limited. As has been the case with Egypt, there are many Israeli tourists who visit Jordan, but few Jordanians have ever shown any interest in taking their holidays in Israel.

Egypt has been at peace with Israel since 1979, yet many Egyptians and Israelis continue to express bitter attitudes toward one another. That reality, and the chilly official relationship between Egypt and Israel for most of the years since 1979, underscores the fact that peace per se is neither friendship nor reconciliation. In time enemies may become friends and allies (think of Germany and France), but this is a slow process and the change in attitudes that it requires cannot be brought about overnight by a piece of paper.

in November of 1998, combined with increasing opposition from within Netanyahu's coalition government, all but completely stalled the peace process.

Israel & the Palestinian Territories Today

On the back of a landslide election victory in May 1999 Prime Minister Ehud Barak immediately set about to resuscitate the faltering peace process which had stalled somewhat during the three years Binyamin Netanyahu's Likud-led government was in power.

In September, Barak and Arafat signed the Sharm el-Sheikh Memorandum, also known as Wye-II, outling a timetable for a permanent settlement by 13 September 2000 – the seventh anniversary of the Oslo Accords.

The final status talks have now begun and the most controversial issues – the status of Jerusalem and the Palestinian refugees among others – are finally on the negotiating table.

While those extremists opposed to the settlement threaten to derail it by launching terrorist attacks, most Israelis and Palestinians continue to support the peace process.

GEOGRAPHY

Israel (including the Gaza Strip and the West Bank) has a total land area of 28,000 sq km.

The country's geography is dominated by the Rift Valley, part of the great Syrian-African Rift and the longest valley in the world, stretching from East Africa to southern Turkey. This trough runs the length of the eastern side of Israel, starting in the south as the arid Arava Valley, then filling with the Dead Sea before becoming the Jordan Valley, to contain the Sea of Galilee and furrowing between the mountains of the Golan Heights and the Galilee as the Hula Valley.

Between the mountain-fringed 'Valley' and the Mediterranean is the narrow sandy coastal plain which forms the heartland of Israel. The population centres are denser towards the more mountainous and better-watered north, while to the south is the Negev, an arid desert plain.

CLIMATE

Climatic conditions vary considerably from region to region. In general, Israel's climate is temperate with two seasons: winter when it's cold and rainy, and summer, which is hot and dry. Rainfall is concentrated between November and March and can vary from more than 1000mm a year on Mt Hermon in the Golan to less than 100mm in Eilat on the Red Sea.

Temperature-wise, Israeli winters can be surprisingly severe, often catching travellers with inadequate clothing. Even in summer a warm sweater is needed in many places, as evening temperatures drop considerably from the daytime high.

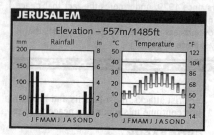

FLORA & FAUNA
Society for the Protection of Nature in Israel (SPNI)

The aims of the SPNI are the conservation and protection of antiquities, plant and animal life and the environment. For the traveller, the SPNI provides an excellent source of information on all of these areas. The main offices are in Tel Aviv and Jerusalem, both with large and extremely well stocked shops with the best range of books and pamphlets on nature and wildlife that you're going to find in Israel.

The SPNI also operates around 20 to 30 field schools throughout the country. Staffed by enthusiastic specialists these are great places to visit for information on local hikes, places of beauty and indigenous wildlife. Some of the schools also offer accommodation. Contact one of the two main offices for a complete list of addresses:

Jerusalem (office and bookshop)
(☎ 02-624 4605, fax 625 4953, email tourism@spni.org.il) 13 Heleni HaMalka St, PO Box 930, Jerusalem 96101
Tel Aviv
(☎ 03-638 8674, fax 688 3940, email tourism@spni.org.il) 19 HaSharon St, Tel Aviv 66183, near the central bus station

GOVERNMENT & POLITICS

Israel is a secular, parliamentary and democratic republic, figureheaded by a largely symbolic president – a post held presently by Ezer Weizmann. The Knesset is Israel's parliament, a single-chambered house of 120 members (MKs). It is located in Jerusalem. The current prime minister is Erhud Barak who leads the left wing AVODA Labor Party. This marks a swing back to the traditionally labour dominated political scene. At the time of writing it was too early to see what effect the new government will have on Israeli domestic and international politics.

Former military man Ariel Sharon plays a larger-than-life role in the political scene and his appointment as defence minister has caused considerable angst to both Palestinians and Israeli 'doves' who view his often provocative politics as destabilising.

Yasser Arafat decided in May 1999 to withdraw from his proclaimed aim of declaring an independent Palestine, preferring instead to see if the new government would be any more accommodating to Palestinian claims. Israel's future political direction will depend largely on the outcome of the 1999 general elections.

POPULATION & PEOPLE

Israel, including the Gaza Strip and the West Bank, has a population of 6.03 million. Of this number 4.78 million (79.3%) are Jews, 901,000 (14.9%) are Muslims, 129,000 (2.1%) are Christians and 99,000 are Druze (1.6%).

Jews

'Two Jews equals three opinions' is more than just an amusing aphorism – despite the international image of the Jews of Israel as a homogenous people the truth is that they are a deeply divided nation, driven by a bewildering array of schisms. Divisions exist along the lines of secular vs nonsecular, hawks vs doves, oriental vs European, those who use coffee creamer vs those who don't – everything is an issue here to be debated and argued in cafes and newspaper columns, on TV talk shows and at the dining room table.

The most basic ethnic divide is into the Ashkenazi Jews from Eastern Europe, and the Sephardic Jews, originally from Spain but more recently from the Arab and Muslim countries (also called oriental Jews).

Palestinian Arabs

The Arab population is concentrated mainly in Gaza and the West Bank. More than 80% are Sunni Muslims, the remainder are Christians.

Considerable controversy exists over the origins of the Palestinians and this subject is at the very heart of the Palestine 'problem'. The Israelis commonly contend that they are descended from the Arabs who invaded Palestine in the 7th century or even that most of them are descendants of immigrants from neighbouring countries who came to Palestine at the turn of the 19th century. Palestinians, on the other hand, claim that their ancestry goes beyond that and that their ancestors appeared along the south-east Mediterranean coast more than five millennia ago and settled down to a life of fishing, farming and herding. Nearly 10% of the Arabs are Bedouin, mainly concentrated in the Negev where they continue to live in tents and breed sheep, goats and camels.

Druze

Nearly 10% of the non-Jewish population belong to this mysterious religious sect. The Druze have no homeland or language of their own and their nation, such as it is, is defined by their religion, an offshoot of Islam. Like Muslims, the Druze believe in Allah and his prophets but they believe that Mohammed was succeeded by a further divine messenger. The Druze also hold the non-Islamic belief of reincarnation.

Most of the Druze nation lives in Lebanon and Syria; in Israel they inhabit a few villages in Galilee, on Mt Carmel, and also in the Golan.

ARTS
Music

Israel has long been associated with excellence in classical music. This really started in the 1930s when Jewish musicians, including some of the best of Europe's composers, performers and teachers, fled to Palestine to escape Nazism. The Israel Philharmonic Orchestra remains world-renowned and the country still produces top class musicians, most notably violinist Yitzhak Perlman.

Klezmer More elementally Jewish in nature, klezmer is traditional Yiddish dance music born in the communities of Eastern and Central Europe – think *Fiddler on the Roof*. Centred on violins, the sound can range from weeping melancholy through to wild thigh-slapping, high-kicking exuberance. In the last 20 years it's a musical form that has experienced something of a revival and Perlman recently dug around in his Jewish roots to record a klezmer album which was extremely well received.

Literature

Israeli The Israeli author SY Agnon was honoured with the Nobel Peace Prize for Literature in the 1960s but these days the most well represented Israeli writer in translation is Amos Oz, whose books appear in no less than 22 languages. Although much of the charm and colour in his novels is drawn from the Jewish characters and settings, the themes are universal and rise above national self-absorbency. Almost rivalling Oz in his collection of international accolades is David Grossman, about whom comparisons with Gunter Grass and Garcia Marquez have been drawn; his most recent novel to be translated into English is *The Zigzag Kid*, but it's for *See Under Love* that he's most widely known. Belonging to a generation older than Oz and Grossman,

Who are the Israelis?

It is easy for an outsider to assume that Israel is made up of a homogeneous Jewish society, given this nation's recent history. Israel is indeed made up primarily of Jews, but there is as much cultural diversity among the Jews as there is among other nations with mixed ethnic and religious groupings. Israel is also home to significant numbers of Muslims and smaller groups of Christians and other religious, racial and linguistic minorities.

According to 1998 statistics provided by the Israeli Bureau of Statistics the population of Arabs in the West Bank, Gaza including areas under both Israeli and Palestinian authority control is about 2.9 million.

The Jewish Israelis constitute a varied group with four main cultural groupings. The **Ashkenazi** in classical Hebrew means 'Germany'. These Jews originated from Central and Eastern Europe, particularly Germany. They are also descendants of Ashkenazim who emigrated to North and South America, South Africa and Australia. Some of them still use Yiddish as their common language, a combination of Hebrew and medieval German, written in Hebrew characters.

The **Sephardi** (Sephard is the Hebrew for 'Spain') Jews are descendants of those expelled from Spain and Portugal in the 15th century. The majority of the Jews in Palestine until the 19th century were Sephardim. The Spanish Jews spoke Ladino, a mixture of Hebrew and Spanish, written in Hebrew characters. It's still spoken today by some older Sephardim. Less educated and generally speaking less wealthy than the Ashkenazim, the Sephardim claim that they have been treated as 2nd class citizens. The prevalence of Ashkenazim in politics and other positions of power is often cited as proof of this.

The **Oriental Jews**, also referred to as Sephardi, originate from various Muslim and Arabic-speaking countries. The most high profile are the Yemenite Jews. They arrived in Israel soon after its independence, when a massive airlift called 'Operation Magic Carpet' brought virtually the entire community to Israel. The Iraqi Jews arrived at around the same time. There are also Afghan, Bukharan (from Central Asia), Cochin (from Cochin in India) and Iranian Jewish communities in Israel.

AB Yehoshua, a native of Haifa, is still producing highly regarded work. His most recent work in English translation is *Mr Mani*, a sweeping six generational epic of a wandering Jewish family.

SOCIETY & CONDUCT
Israeli Society

Israeli society is unique in that it is the only Jewish country in the Middle East with a religion that stands alone among a sea of Islam. Nonetheless, Israel does have sizeable communities of non-Jews including Muslims and Christians. Israeli society itself is fragmented into groups ranging from secular (nonreligious) Jews to ultra-orthodox conservative Jews at the other end of the spectrum.

The Palestinians themselves are split across two main groups: the Israeli Arabs – some of whom are Christians – and the Muslim Palestinians living in the Palestinian Territories yet still subject to some or little control from Israel itself.

RELIGION

Israel's religious scene is not surprisingly dominated by Judaism, which constitutes approximately 80% of believers in Israel & the Palestinian Territories. Muslims make up 15% of that total and Christians and other sects make up 5% of the total. While all three major religious groups share many common features throughout their dogmas, relations are at best politely cordial and at

Who are the Israelis?

Finally there are the **Ethiopians** who were airlifted to Israel from their famine-struck country in two massive operations in 1985 and 1991. Many Jews, especially Ashkenazim, have found it hard to accept that these black people really share their faith.

The Muslims in Israel are mainly represented by the **Palestinian Arabs**, 80% of whom are Sunni Muslims. They live mainly in the West Bank and in the Gaza strip. About 10% of Arabs in Israel are **Bedouins**. These are tribes of traditionally nomadic people and are still mainly concentrated in the Negev, continuing to live in tents while breeding sheep, goats and camels.

Christians in Israel are mainly represented by **Christian Arabs**, most of whom are living in Nazareth, Bethlehem and Northern Israel. The remainder consist mainly of Armenians, foreign clergymen, monks, nuns and those working for Christian organisations.

Israel is also home to a number of minority groups of whom the **Druze** are the most prominent; having neither a homeland nor a language of their own their religion is an offshoot of Islam. In Israel they inhabit a few villages in the Galilee, on Mt Carmel, and also in the Golan. Most of the Druze are Israeli citizens and, like any other citizen perform military service.

The **Samaritans** are one of the world's smallest minorities, numbering only 584 people. The Samaritans claim to be both Palestinians and Israelites – they speak Arabic but pray in ancient Hebrew. According to their history they are descendants of the tribes of Joseph and until the 17th century they possessed a high ,priesthood descending directly from Aaron through Eleazar and Phinehas. The Circassians are an independent group in the Muslim community, numbering some 4000 people.

The **Circassians** originated in the Caucasian Mountains of Russia, immigrating to Palestine in the 1890s. Mostly loyal to the State of Israel, the community is concentrated in two villages in the Galilee.

Finally, the **Hebrew Israelite Community** have attracted controversy ever since the first arrivals in 1969. They claim to be the most authentic descendants of the Jews exiled from Israel 4000 years ago, but this is treated with deep scepticism by the authorities and they have been refused Israeli citizenship. They live mainly in Dimona in the Negev Desert.

worst hostile. Many Christian Arabs have left Muslim-dominated communities for other parts of Israel or abroad, dramatically shifting the demographic balance in some cases.

LANGUAGE

Israel's national language is Hebrew, followed by Arabic. English is widely spoken; there will nearly always be someone nearby who understands it. Most of the important road signs are in all three languages. With Jews arriving in Israel from around the world, many other languages are commonly understood. French, German and Yiddish are the main ones, but also Spanish and Russian. Most Arabs are fluent in Hebrew and English as well as Arabic. Many also speak other European languages very well, especially in the tourist centres.

The Palestinian Arabs' common language is a Syrian dialect of Arabic.

Facts for the Visitor

PLANNING

If you can, avoid visiting Israel during the Jewish holidays of Pesah (Passover), which coincides with the Christian Easter, and Rosh HaShanah, Yom Kippur and Sukkot, which fall around October (the dates vary each year). At these times shops and all businesses including cafes and restaurants close, public transport is nonexistent and accommodation prices double.

Lonely Planet has a highly detailed, slimline 1:250,000 *Israel & the Palestinian Territories travel atlas*, designed specifically to complement the *Israel & the Palestinian Territories* guide. Otherwise, the best of the internationally available sheet maps is Hallwag's 1:500,000 *Israel Road Map*, which clearly marks the hierarchy of roads, denotes the territory of the West Bank (many maps don't), includes within its bounds Beirut, Damascus and Amman, and also has inset street plans of the major Israeli cities. Hildebrand's 1:360,000 *Travel Map of Israel* isn't bad either, although despite the larger scale it's not as clear as Hallwag.

For a wider choice or something more specialised, wait until you reach Israel where you'll be able to pick up high quality locally produced city maps, street atlases, topographical surveys – in fact more or less anything you could imaginably want.

VISAS & DOCUMENTS
Visas
With all but a few exceptions, a tourist visa is not required to visit Israel, just a passport, valid for at least six months from your date of entry. Exceptions include holders of passports from most African and Central American countries, India, Singapore and some of the ex-Soviet republics.

Tourists are normally allowed a three month visit, although visitors entering through land borders with Egypt and Jordan are initially only granted a month's stay.

If you look 'undesirable' or are suspected of looking for illegal employment, on arrival immigration officials may question the purpose of your visit and ask to see evidence of a return flight/ferry ticket and financial support. Travellers singled out and then found to have insufficient money to cover their proposed stay have, in the past, been prevented from entering the country and put on the next flight home. More commonly, if unimpressed, immigration may only allow you a shorter stay, say one month.

Visa Extensions If after your initial three month stay you want more time, you need to apply for a visa. You do this at offices of the Ministry of the Interior, which are located in most major towns and cities. You have to be able to convince the civil servants that you can support yourself without needing to work illegally. The process costs 90NIS and one passport-sized photo is required.

Visas for Neighbouring Countries The only neighbouring countries you are going to be able to visit from Israel directly are Jordan and Egypt. Both countries maintain diplomatic mission in Tel Aviv and Eilat, the latter handy for travellers heading for Petra in Jordan or the Sinai in Egypt. It is not possible to obtain visas for other neighbouring countries such as Lebanon or Syria: an indication in your passport that you have been to Israel will in any case preclude you from visiting these countries.

The Israeli Stamp Stigma

Israel is, of course, the venue for that popular Middle Eastern game, the Passport Shuffle which involves getting in and out of the country but avoiding being stamped with any incriminating evidence to tell that you were ever there. This game was devised because those countries which refuse to recognise Israel (Iran and all Arab countries other than Egypt and Jordan) refuse to allow anyone across their borders whose passport is marred by evidence of a visit to the Jewish State. Israeli immigration officials will, if asked, stamp only your entry permit and not your passport. This is fine if you are flying both into and out of Israel but if crossing by land into either Egypt or Jordan, the Arab immigration officers are generally not so obliging and their entry stamps will be a dead giveaway – although some wily travellers have reported getting away with stamps on a separate piece of paper, especially at the Allenby Bridge border crossing into Jordan.

Other Documents

The only officially required document for travellers in Israel is a valid passport but, if you have them, bring along your Hostelling International (HI) card and International Student Identity Card (ISIC), which entitles the holder to a 10% discount on Egged bus fares over 10NIS, 20% off fares on Israel State Railways and substantial discounts at most museums and archaeological sites. Student cards issued by your individual university or college are often not recognised.

The Green Card is a pass to all the archaeological sites in Israel and is worth obtaining if you plan to visit many of the sites. International drivers licences are not mandatory, but always useful to have in case of unexpected problems like a vehicle accident.

EMBASSIES & CONSULATES
Israeli Embassies & Consulates

Australia
  Embassy:
  (☎ 02-6273 1309)
  6 Turrana Ave, Yarralumla, Canberra, ACT 2600
  Consulate:
  (☎ 02-9264 7933)
  37 York St, Sydney, NSW 2000
Canada
  Embassy:
  (☎ 613-567 6450)
  50 O'Conner St, Suite 1005, Ottawa, Ontario KIP 6L2
  Consulate:
  (☎ 514-393 9372)
  1155 Blvd Rene Levesque Ouest, Suite 2620, Montreal, Quebec H3B 4S5
France
  Embassy:
  (☎ 01 40 76 55 00)
  3 rue Rabelais, F-75008 Paris
  Consulate:
  (☎ 9177 3990)
  146 rue Paradis, Marseille F-13006
Germany
  Embassy:
  (☎ 228-934 6500)
  Simrockallee 2, Bonn D-53173
  Consulate:
  (☎ 030-893 2203)
  Schinkelstrasse 10, Berlin D-14193

Ireland
  Embassy:
  (☎ 01-668 0303)
  Berkeley Court Hotel, Suite 630, Landsdowne Rd, Ballsbridge, Dublin 4
Netherlands
  Embassy:
  (☎ 070-376 0500)
  47 Buitenhoff, The Hague 2513 AH
New Zealand
  Embassy:
  (☎ 04-472 2362)
  DB Tower, 111 The Terrace, PO Box 2171, Wellington
UK
  Embassy:
  (☎ 020-7957 9500)
  2 Palace Green, London W8 4QB
USA
  Embassy:
  (☎ 202-364 5500)
  3514 International Drive NW, Washington DC 20008
  Consulate:
  (☎ 212-499 5400)
  800 Second Ave, New York NY10017
  There are nine Israeli consulates in the USA; phone one of the above two for contact details.

Embassies & Consulates in Israel

Although Israelis lay claim to Jerusalem as the capital of the Jewish State this is not recognised by most of the international community. Instead, most foreign embassies are in Tel Aviv. Some countries also maintain consulates in Jerusalem and a few in Haifa.

Check with the embassy or consulate concerned regarding opening hours, since they are subject to frequent change.

Australia
  Embassy:
  (☎ 03-695 0451)
  37 HaMelekh Shaul Ave, Tel Aviv
Canada
  Embassy:
  (☎ 03-636 3300)
  3 Nirim St, Tel Aviv
Egypt
  Embassy:
  (☎ 03-524 5371)
  54 Basel St, off Ibn Gvirol St, Tel Aviv
  Consulate:
  (☎ 07-636 7882)
  68 Ha'Efroni St, Eilat

France
  Embassy:
  (☎ 03-524 5371)
  112 Herbert Samuel Esplanade, Tel Aviv
  Consulate:
  (☎ 02-625 9481)
  6 Emile Botta St, West Jerusalem
  Consulate:
  (☎ 02-628 2387)
  Sheikh Jarrah, East Jerusalem
  Consulate:
  (☎ 07-360 111)
  8 Kikar Nemerim, Eilat
  Consulate:
  (☎ 04-851 3111)
  37 HaGefen St, Haifa
Germany
  Embassy:
  (☎ 03-693 1313)
  3 Daniel Frisch St, Tel Aviv
Ireland
  Embassy:
  (☎ 03-696 4166)
  3 Daniel Frisch St, Tel Aviv
Jordan
  Embassy:
  (☎ 03-751 7722)
  14 Abba Hillel Silver St, Ramat Gan, Tel
  Aviv
Netherlands
  Embassy:
  (☎ 03-695 7377)
  Asia House, 4 Weizmann St, Tel Aviv
  Consulate:
  (☎ 04-824 3298)
  24A Vitkin, Haifa
UK
  Embassy:
  (☎ 03-524 9171)
  192 HaYarkon St, Tel Aviv
  Consulate:
  (☎ 02-582 8281)
  19 Nashashibi St, Sheikh Jarrah, East
  Jerusalem
  Consulate:
  (☎ 07-637 2344)
  14 Tsofit Villas, Eilat
USA
  Embassy:
  (☎ 03-519 7575, fax 516 0315, email acs
  .amcit-telaviv@dos.us-state.gov)
  71 HaYarkon St, Tel Aviv
  Consulate:
  (☎ 02-625 3288)
  18 Agron St, West Jerusalem
  Consulate:
  (☎ 02-625 3288, fax 272 2233)
  27 Nablus Rd, East Jerusalem
  Consulate:
  (☎ 04-853 1470)
  12 Yerushalayim St, Haifa

MONEY
Costs

There are no two ways about it: compared to other countries in the region like Egypt, Jordan or Turkey, Israel is expensive. Compare prices with Australia, New Zealand, the UK or USA, however, and there's little to complain about.

Accommodation can be quite cheap – many private hostels offer clean sheets, hot showers and possibly air-con for somewhere between 20 to 30NIS per night (US$5 to US$7.50). Dining could well be the area that busts your budget apart. While it is possible to survive on three felafel sandwiches a day at a cost of around 6NIS, a more realistic figure would be 30 to 50NIS (US$7.50 to US$12.50) per day, which allows for a little indulgence bolstered with a lot of street food.

Museum and gallery admissions are pricey, often in the region of 20NIS (US$5) but this is offset by the relatively cheap cost of transport; the hour long bus ride between Tel Aviv and Jerusalem, for instance, is less than 14NIS (approximately US$3.50).

On an individual budget of 100 to 150NIS per day (about US$25 to US$37.50), it should be possible to get decent accommodation, eat well and travel around.

Currency

The national currency is the new Israeli shekel (NIS). The Hebraically correct plural is *shekelim* but even Israelis when speaking English tend to Anglicise and use 'shekels'. The new shekel is divided into 100 agorot. There are coins of 10 and 50 agorot, one and five NIS and notes of five, 10, 20, 50, 100 and 200NIS.

Most Israelis talk in terms of US dollars, not shekels, and top end hotels, HI hostels, most car hire companies and many airlines all accept payment in US dollars – this is worth doing as it saves you the 17% Value Added Tax (VAT).

Exchange Rates

country	unit		New Israeli shekel
Australia	A$1	=	2.6NIS
Canada	C$1	=	2.7NIS

Egypt	E£1	=	1.2NIS
euro	€1	=	4.7NIS
France	10FF	=	7.0NIS
Germany	DM1	=	2.4NIS
Japan	¥100	=	3.5NIS
Jordan	JD1	=	5.8NIS
New Zealand	NZ$1	=	2.2NIS
UK	UK£1	=	6.7NIS
USA	US$1	=	4.1NIS

Exchanging Money

Generally speaking there is little variation in the rates of exchange on offer but you ought to check on the commission, sometimes voracious, charged by the banks. The best deals are offered by the Arab moneychangers in Jerusalem and the specialist exchange bureaus in Jerusalem and Tel Aviv, none of which take any commission at all.

After the dollar one foreign currency is as good as any other and moneychangers and banks will take whatever you've got, though exchange rates on the Egyptian pound are very poor.

Although banking hours vary, generally they are from 8.30 am to 12.30 pm and 4 to 5.30 pm from Sunday to Tuesday and Thursday, and from 8.30 am to noon on Wednesday, Friday and eves of holy days.

Some bank branches also have currency exchange ATMs which accept several of the major international currencies and offer the convenience of 24 hour accessibility, seven days a week; the drawback is a whopping transaction charge.

Holders of travellers cheques will have no trouble getting them cashed – Eurocheques can even be exchanged at post offices. Beware though, commission charges can be as high as 20NIS *per cheque* regardless of the amount, so shop around. The best bet is to go to one of the no-commission currency exchange bureaus or to one of the American Express (Amex) or Thomas Cook offices or agents – see the individual city sections for addresses.

Credit Cards & ATMs

Credit cards are accepted almost everywhere and many bank foyers are equipped with cash dispensing ATMs which accept, among others, Amex, Diners Club, Euro-Card and Visa.

Money Transfers

For anyone unfortunate enough to run out of money, the Israeli Post Office operates a Western Union international money transfer service.

Tipping & Bargaining

Not so long ago, apparently, no one tipped in Israel. Now your bill arrives appended with a large handwritten 'Service is not included' and delivered by a waiter or waitress with a steely smile that reads, '15%. No less'. Tipping usually only applies to restaurants.

Note that taxi drivers in Israel do not expect to be tipped; they're usually content just to overcharge.

Taxes & Refunds

Israel slaps Value Added Tax (VAT) on a wide range of goods but tourists are entitled to a refund on most items purchased with foreign currency in shops that are registered with the Ministry of Tourism (there'll be a sign in the window or at the till). The purchases need to be wrapped in a sealed plastic bag, of which at least one side must be transparent with the original invoice displayed inside the bag so that it can be read without opening the bag. The bag needs to remain sealed for the duration of your time in Israel. Claim your refund from the Bank Leumi counter in the departure lounge at Ben-Gurion airport in Tel Aviv.

POST & COMMUNICATIONS
Post

Letters posted in Israel take seven to 10 days to reach North America and Australia, and a little less to Europe. Incoming mail is fairly quick, taking about three or four days from Europe and around a week from places farther afield. At the time of writing, a normal air mail letter to Europe cost 1.80NIS, to the USA 2.20NIS and to Australia 2.70NIS.

Poste restante seems to work quite well; for post restante addresses see the individual city sections in this chapter. Remember that Amex offices (in Jerusalem and Tel Aviv) will receive mail for card holders.

Telephone

To call Israel from abroad the international dialling code is ☎ 972. Regional telephone codes are as follows:

Jerusalem and the West Bank	☎ 02
Tel Aviv and Surrounds	☎ 03
Haifa and the North Coast	☎ 04
The North including the Galilee, the Upper Galilee and the Golan	☎ 06
The Negev, down to Eilat, the Gaza Strip and the Dead Sea Region	☎ 07
The Coastal Plain (south of Tel Aviv)	☎ 08
Sharon District (north of Tel Aviv)	☎ 09

Israel has a state-of-the-art card-operated public telephone system. International calls can be made from any street call box with telecards bought from lottery kiosks, news stands or bookshops.

For the purposes of charging, standard rate operates between 8 am and 10 pm; calls are 25% cheaper from 10 pm to 1 am and all day Saturday and Sunday, while all week between 1 and 8 am calls are 50% cheaper.

You can also make discount international calls from the offices of Solan Telecom, located in most towns and cities throughout Israel and open 24 hours, although in practice the savings are nothing substantial.

There's a wide range of local and international phonecards available. Lonely Planet's eKno Communication Card (see the insert at the back of this book) is aimed specifically at travellers and provides cheap international calls, a range of messaging services and free email – for local calls, you're usually better off with a local card. You can join online at www.ekno.lonely planet.com, or by phone from Israel by dialling ☎ 1-800-945-9176. Once you have joined, dial ☎ 1-800-945-9177 to use eKno from Israel.

Fax

To send a fax or telex, go to a post office. Faxes are charged at 17NIS for the first sheet and 9NIS for subsequent sheets. Faxes can also be sent from Solan Telecom offices at a cost of 12NIS per sheet, irrespective of the destination and they'll receive faxes for you for a small fee.

Email & Internet Access

There are Internet cafes in most major cities. See under each individual city entry for address details. Longer term visitors with their own laptop PCs may consider taking out a local email service. There are a number of service providers, but we used Netvision (☎ 04-856 0660, fax 04-855 0345, email admin@netvision.net.il) with considerable success and lack of fuss. Visit their Web site (www.netvision.net.il/ser vices) for all the details.

Israel's phone plugs are similar to the wide modular UK plugs but they use a different polarity in the wiring. You will need to either bring an Israel-specific adapter with you, or buy one locally. Connecting your PC from your hotel room is no problem as long as you have the correct adapter. Phone networks are now all-digital.

BOOKS

The Israeli propensity for navel-gazing means that most of the titles mentioned here are also available in bookshops in Tel Aviv and Jerusalem too. Try the shops belonging to the Steimatzky chain.

Winner Takes All by Stephen Brook, despite being a little dated (it was written in 1990), is nevertheless still the best available primer for a visit to Israel. Far more illuminating and entertaining is *Jerusalem: City of Mirrors* by Amos Elon, an internationally respected Israeli writer who has spent most of his life in the city of which he writes. Mark Twain's *The Innocents Abroad*, written in 1871, is still one of the best books dealing with the tourist experience in the Holy Land.

For the uninitiated a good place to start with history is with Amos Oz who, although primarily a novelist, has had three collections of essays (In the Land of Israel, The Slopes of Lebanon and Israel, Palestine and Peace) published on the state of Israel and the prospects of peace. The BBC's The Fifty Year War: Israel & the Arabs was published in 1998 to accompany the television series of the same name. It is a concise, seemingly unbiased account of the conflict co-written by both a Jew (Ahron Bregman) and an Arab (Jihan El-Tahri) and contains some hitherto unpublished secret interviews with key players on both sides.

Published also in 1998 is Israel: A History by Martin Gilbert, an authoritative, somewhat dry, but very readable account of the history of Israel during the last 100 years. Soldier of Peace by Dan Kurzman and published in the same year is a detailed and gripping account of the life of former prime minister Yitzhak Rabin who was assassinated in Tel Aviv in 1995.

Of the authors writing from a Palestinian perspective, the most eloquent is Edward Said whose views are expounded in The Palestinian Question. Far more emotive and gritty is Gaza: Legacy of Occupation by Dick Doughty and Mohammed El-Aydi, which focuses on the tragedies of Palestinian life in the Strip.

NEWSPAPERS & MAGAZINES

Unless you read Hebrew or Arabic, your appreciation of Israel's extensive press will be limited. Jerusalem Post is the country's only English-language daily (but no Saturday edition). Though indispensable for its coverage of Israeli life, its pronounced right-wing leanings are a turn-off to many. Buy it on Friday, however, for the extensive 'what's on' supplement. In East Jerusalem only, you can pick up the weekly pro-Palestinian Jerusalem Times.

Western newspapers and magazines are easily found and they're usually only a day old – the best selection is carried by the Steimatzky bookshops.

RADIO & TV

National Radio 1 (576 AM in Tel Aviv and the central region, 1458 AM in Jerusalem and Eilat) has English-language news bulletins at 7 am and 1 and 8 pm, as well as a current affairs program at 5 pm daily. The BBC World Service can be picked up on 639 and 1323 kHz and 227 MW, while Voice of America is on 1260 kHz.

Israel has two state TV stations, both of which carry masses of English-language programming (English news on Channel 1 is at 6.15 pm during the week, 4.30 pm Friday and 5 pm Saturday). These are supplemented by Arabic language Jordan TV and Middle East TV, a Christian station administered by North Americans. The majority of the Israeli population also has cable which gives access to an additional 32 channels including CNN, Sky, BBC World, Discovery and MTV.

For TV and radio listings pick up the Jerusalem Post.

PHOTOGRAPHY & VIDEO

Whatever you run out of or whatever needs replacing, you'll be able to find it in Israel but there's little doubt that it would have been way cheaper back home.

One-hour film processing and all types of film are available in most places. Choices are more limited in the West Bank towns.

LAUNDRY

Many of the better hostels have laundry facilities, otherwise coin operated laundrettes are common. One machine load costs about 8NIS and dryers are about 4NIS for a 10 minute cycle.

WOMEN TRAVELLERS

Unfortunately a lot of what we say in the Regional Facts for the Visitor chapter also applies in Israel. Although Israeli men are not known for their gentlemanly conduct towards women, most of the problems will occur in Arab areas, particularly those that are most heavily visited by tourists. We recommend women take special care in the Old City of Jerusalem and on the Mount of Olives where attacks have frequently occurred, and in the towns of Nazareth and Akko. Women might also be harassed by

Israeli beach Romeos in Tel Aviv. The best advice is to ignore them totally.

GAY & LESBIAN TRAVELLERS

The most popular gay spot is *Cafe Nordau* at 145 Ben Yehuda St in freewheeling Tel Aviv where homosexuality is one of the causes they champion along with animal rights and ecology. In Jerusalem, as far as we could discern the choices were *Orion* or *Yellow Submarine* clubs. *Tmol Shilshom* cafe/bookshop in the central Nahalat Shiv'a quarter is gay-run but other than a shelf of second-hand gay fiction that doesn't amount to much.

There must be more and we suggest that you call the gay switchboard (☎ 03-629 2797) between the hours of 7.30 and 11.30 pm on Sunday, Tuesday and Thursday. The Society for the Protection of Personal Rights (SPPR) (☎ 03-620 4327, fax 525 2341, email sppr@netvision.net.il) at PO Box 37604, Tel Aviv 61375 also operates a gay hotline (☎ 03-629 3681) and publishes *Israel Update,* an English-language newsletter – send a self-addressed envelope.

DISABLED TRAVELLERS

Many hotels and most public institutions in Israel provide ramps, specially equipped toilets and other conveniences for the disabled. In particular, several of the HI affiliated hostels, including the one in Tel Aviv and the Beit Shmuel in Jerusalem, have rooms specially adapted for wheelchair access. Anyone with any particular concerns might try contacting Milbat – The Advisory Centre for the Disabled (☎ 03-530 3739) – at the Sheba Medical Centre in Tel Aviv for information and advice.

Yad Sarah Organisation (☎ 02-624 4242) at 43 HaNevi'im St in Jerusalem also loans wheelchairs, crutches and other aids free of charge (a deposit is required). It's open to visitors from 9 am to 7 pm Sunday to Thursday and from 9 am to noon on Friday.

SENIOR TRAVELLERS

Most senior travellers visiting Israel will be on some kind of organised tour with most conveniences laid on – coach tours, hotels and even restaurants. Still, even the most cosseted of tours cannot take away the occasional struggle with narrow stairways, cobbled streets, hills and other natural impediments that are part of visiting Israel – particularly its archaeological sites. The heat can be a particular problem for older travellers, especially in July and August when Tel Aviv can become very uncomfortable.

DANGERS & ANNOYANCES

While security and safety in a large sense are not matters which should concern the average visitor, theft is just as much of a problem in Israel as it is anywhere else. The standard precautionary measures should be taken. Always keep valuables with you or locked in a safe – never leave them in your room or in a car or bus (unhappily there are more than a few fellow travellers who make their money go further by helping themselves to other people's). Use a money belt, a pouch under your clothes, a leather wallet attached to your belt, or extra internal pockets in your clothing. Keep a record of your passport, credit card and travellers cheque numbers.

Travelling on intercity buses, you generally stow large bags in the luggage hold. This is a virtually trouble-free system, but keep valuables with you just in case. Crowded tourist spots and markets are an obvious haunt for pickpockets, so take extra care.

BUSINESS HOURS

The most important thing to know is that on Shabbat, the Jewish Sabbath, most Israeli shops, offices and places of entertainment close down. Shabbat starts at sundown Friday and ends at sundown on Saturday. During this time you'll find it tough to get anything to eat, you can't easily change money and your movements are restricted because most buses aren't running. You need to plan for Shabbat in advance and work out where you'll be and what you can do to avoid being overtaken by the countrywide inactivity. The country kicks back into action on Saturday evening when the cafes, bars and restaurants always experience a great post-Shabbat rush.

Predominantly Muslim areas like East Jerusalem, the Gaza Strip and the West Bank towns remain open on Saturday but are closed all day Friday. Christian-owned businesses (concentrated in Jerusalem's Old City and in Nazareth) close on Sunday.

Israeli shopping hours are 8 am to 1 pm and 4 to 7 pm (or later) Monday to Thursday, and 8 am to 2 pm Friday, with some places opening after sundown on Saturday.

PUBLIC HOLIDAYS & SPECIAL EVENTS

In addition to the main Islamic holidays described in Public Holidays & Special Events in the Regional Facts for the Visitor chapter Israel observes the following holidays.

Orthodox Christmas
  5-6 January
Armenian Christmas
  19 January
Tu BiShvat
  22 January – New Year for Trees
Black Hebrew Day of Appreciation & Love
  February
Purim
  21 March – Feast of Lots
Good Friday
  March/April
Easter Sunday
  March/April
Pesah
  20-26 April – Feast of Passover
Armenian Holocaust Memorial Day
  24 April
Mimouna
  27 April – North African Jewish festival
Orthodox and Armenian Good Friday
  28 April
Orthodox and Armenian Easter Sunday
  30 April
Yom HaSho'ah
  4 May – Holocaust Memorial Day
Yom Ha'Atzmaut
  10 May – Independence Day
Lag b'Omer
  23 May – A festival celebrating a break in the plague that killed Rabbi Akiva's students
Liberation of Jerusalem Day
  4 June
Shavuot
  9 June – Pentecost
Tisha B'Av
  10 August

Rosh HaShanah
  30 September – Jewish New Year
Yom Kippur
  9 October – Day of Atonement
Sukkot
  14-20 October – Festival Commemorating 40 years in the Wilderness
Hanukkah
  22-28 December – Festival of Lights
Western Christmas
  25 December

Jewish

Rosh HaShanah The 'head of the year', or Rosh HaShanah, is Jewish new year. As with all Jewish holidays, prayer services begin on the eve of the holiday.

Yom Kippur Known as the Day of Atonement, Yom Kippur ends the 10 days of penitence which begin on New Year's Day. For the observant, Yom Kippur means 25 hours of complete abstinence from food, drink, sex, cosmetics (including soap and toothpaste) and animal products. The time is spent in prayer and contemplation and all sins are confessed.

Sukkot & Simhat Torah On the Festival of Sukkot most Jews, religious or not, erect home-made *sukkot* (shelters) in commemoration of the 40 years which the ancient Israelites spent in the wilderness after the exodus. The sukkot, hammered together from plyboard but with a roof only of loose branches through which the sky can be seen, sit out on the balconies of apartments, in gardens and even in hotels and restaurants.

Hanukkah Also known as the Festival of Lights, Hanukkah celebrates the triumphant Maccabaean revolt. Its symbol is the *menorah* (a seven-branched candelabrum), and one of its candles is lit each night for a week. A special Hanukkah lamp should also be displayed by each house, usually hung in the window – in Mea She'arim these are often hung outside the building.

Purim Feast of Lots, is remembrance of the hatred born of the Jews' refusal to assimilate

ISRAEL

and their unwillingness to compromise religious principle by bowing before the secular authority. Despite such a serious, if highly relevant, theme, the holiday has a carnival atmosphere and fancy dress is the order of the day: the streets are filled with proud parents and their Batmen, Madonnas and Power Rangers. In the evening it's then the turn of the dames, fairies and gangsters.

For a nation of nondrinkers, Purim is an opportunity for Israelis to atone: according to tradition they are supposed to get so drunk that they can't distinguish between the words 'bless Mordechai' and 'curse Haman'.

Pesah Pesah, the Feast of Passover, celebrates the exodus of the Jews, led by Moses, from Egypt. The festival lasts a full week during which time most Jewish shops (including food shops and markets) are closed (or open for limited hours). The production of everyday bread is substituted for *matza*, a flat tasteless variety which is made in discs of up to 1m in diameter. There's no public transport on either the first or last day of the festival.

Holocaust Day (Yom HaSho'ah) Periodically throughout the day sirens wail to signal two minutes of silence in remembrance of the six million victims of the Holocaust – it's an incredibly moving and eerie experience as everyone and everything stops.

Independence Day (Yom Ha'Atzmaut) On 14 May 1948 Israel became an independent state and since this day has been celebrated by Jews worldwide (note, the date changes with the lunar calendar).

Christian

Christmas Day Apart from 25 December, Christmas is celebrated on 7 January by the Orthodox and on 19 January by the Armenians. The event to attend is the midnight mass on Christmas Eve (24 December), held at Bethlehem's Church of the Nativity. During the day a procession departs from Jerusalem for the church but, due to the popularity of the service, not everyone gets in. Pew space inside the church is reserved

for ticket-holding observant Catholics only (the tickets, which are free, must be applied for in advance at the Terra Sancta office in the Christian Information Centre at Jaffa Gate in Jerusalem's Old City).

Easter Celebrated first by the Roman Catholics and the Protestants and then about two weeks later by the Orthodox Church, Easter means absolute chaos in Jerusalem's Old City. The Via Dolorosa and the narrow streets around the Church of the Holy Sepulchre become clogged with pilgrims staking out their spots for the various services and processions. Note that at this time pilgrims fill many of the cheap hostels in Jerusalem's Old City and completely block-book everything in Bethlehem.

Celebration of the Baptism of Jesus Christ The traditional site where John the Baptist baptised Jesus Christ is on the west bank of the Jordan River, a few kilometres from Jericho. The area has long been off-limits for security reasons and a baptism site farther up the river was provided near the Sea of Galilee at Kibbutz Degania. However, the Roman Catholics have recently been able to organise a special celebration at the revered site in October. Contact the Christian Information Centre in Jerusalem for details, including transport arrangements.

Special Events
Jerusalem Musical Encounters
    February
International Festival of Poets (Jerusalem)
    March
International Judaica Fair (Jerusalem)
    March
Ein Gev Music Festival (Ein Gev, The Galilee)
    April
Israel Festival (Jerusalem)
    May-June
Blues Festival (Haifa)
    June
Hebrew Song Festival (Arad)
    June
Israel Folkdance Festival (Karmiel)
    June
International Film Festival (Jerusalem)
    June

Klezmer Festival (Safed)
    August
Red Sea Jazz Festival (Eilat)
    August
Fringe Theatre Festival (Akko)
    October
Film Festival (Haifa)
    October
Jerusalem Marathon (Jerusalem)
    October
International Christmas Choir Assembly (Nazareth)
    December

ACTIVITIES
Hiking
With its changing landscapes, Israel offers a wealth of superb hiking opportunities, both leisurely and more strenuous. In particular look at exploring the Maktesh Ramon (see Mitzpe Ramon in The Negev section), the world's largest crater, and Ein Avdat (also in The Negev section) which involves some canyon climbing to reach an ice-cold spring. Other excellent hikes include the route through Wadi Qelt (see Around Jericho in The Gaza Strip & the West Bank section) and various trails in the Golan region – see Information in The Upper Galilee & the Golan section.

We really can't stress enough that anyone interested in hiking should visit the SPNI in Jerusalem and Tel Aviv (see Flora & Fauna earlier in this chapter).

Cycling
Tours can be arranged with the Israel Cyclists' Touring Club, an affiliate of the International Bicycle Touring Society. Each tour is accompanied by a certified guide and an escort to handle any technical problems. You might also contact the Jerusalem Cycle Club (☎ 02-561 9416).

Water Sports
While Eilat is overrated, the beaches at Bat Yam, a suburb of Tel Aviv, Tel Aviv itself, Netanya and Dor are all excellent. As you travel towards Haifa the water becomes polluted and jellyfish are a problem. With the Red and Mediterranean seas and the Sea of Galilee, there are ample opportunities to

swim, windsurf and sail. Eilat is the water sports capital offering everything from parascending to waterskiing. It's also a major scuba diving centre – although the sites along the Sinai coast are far superior. An interesting option is to dive at Caesarea where you can explore the underwater ruins of Herod's city. Contact the Diving Club at Caesarea (☎ 06-636 1787).

WORK
Many people automatically associate a visit to Israel with a spell as a kibbutz or moshav volunteer and every year thousands of young people from all over the world descend on the Holy Land for the experience. Many volunteers are actually extremely disappointed with what they encounter. The hostels of Tel Aviv are full of former kibbutzers who couldn't wait to get out. Before committing yourself to a volunteer program you should study carefully what it actually involves.

Kibbutz Volunteers
There are basically three ways to go about becoming a volunteer. The first two involve contacting a kibbutz representative office in your own country and either joining a group of about 15 people or travelling as an individual. The kibbutz representatives charge a basic registration fee (about US$50) and arrange your flight – which generally costs more than you'd pay if you shopped around yourself. If you choose to join a group you have no option but to fly with them, but as an individual you can register and then make your own travel arrangements. To find out more, contact your nearest kibbutz representative's office:

Australia
    (☎ 02-9360 6300) Kibbutz Program Centre, 104 Darlinghurst Rd, Darlinghurst, NSW 2010
    (☎ 03-9272 5331, fax 9272 5640) Kibbutz Program Desk, 584 St Kilda Rd, Melbourne, Victoria 3004
Canada
    Kibbutz Aliyah Desk, 1000 Finch Ave West, Downsview, Ontario M3J 2E7
    Kibbutz Aliyah Desk, 5800 Cavendish Blvd, Cote St Luc, Quebec PQ H4W 2TS

New Zealand
(☎ 4-844 229) Kibbutz Program Desk, Jewish Community Centre Bldg, Kensington St, PO Box 27-156, Wellington

UK
(☎ 020-8458 9235) Kibbutz Representatives, 1A Accommodation Rd, London NW11
(☎ 020-7831 7626, fax 7404 5588) Project 67, 10 Hatton Garden, EC1

USA
(☎ 212-318 6130, fax 318 6134)
Kibbutz Aliyah Desk, 110 East 59th St, New York, NY 10022
Kibbutz Aliyah Desk, 870 Market St (1083), San Francisco, California 94102
Israel Aliyah Centre (Kibbutz), 4200 Biscayne Blvd, Miami, Florida 33137
Kibbutz Aliyah Desk, 2320 W Peterson, Suite 503, Chicago, Illinois 60659

Alternatively, would-be volunteers can make their own way to the kibbutz offices in Tel Aviv to apply there in person for a place. Your success at being accepted is dependent not only on there being a suitable vacancy, but on your being able to convince the kibbutz officials that you are not a drug-crazed, beer-guzzling, youngster-perverting layabout.

There are three main offices in Tel Aviv to apply to:

Kibbutz Volunteer Centre
(☎ 03-527 8874) 18 Frishman St, corner of Ben Yehuda. Open from 8 am to 2 pm Sunday to Thursday.

Meira's
(☎ 03-523 7369, fax 524 3811)
73 Ben Yehuda St, entrance behind the restaurant. Open from 9.30 am to 3 pm Sunday to Thursday.

Project 67
(☎ 03-523 0140, fax 524 7474)
94 Ben Yehuda St. Open from 9 am to 5 pm Monday to Thursday and from 9 am to noon Friday.

Moshav Volunteers

The differences between being a volunteer on a moshav as opposed to a kibbutz are that the work is generally much harder, though often more varied and occasionally more interesting, and the money is slightly better.

Although there are moshav representatives in some countries, prospective volunteers can save themselves around US$100 by making their own way to Tel Aviv. The official moshav main office (☎ 03-258 473) is downstairs at 19 Leonardo de Vinci St. From Tel Aviv central bus station take bus No 70. It's open from 9 am to noon Sunday to Thursday. You can also try Project 67 or Meira's (see the previous Kibbutz Volunteers section for addresses).

Each volunteer has to take out a health insurance policy which includes coverage for hospitalisation. Volunteers are often in short supply, so as long as you present yourself as hard-working, punctual and well-behaved, you should have no problems and will probably find work in a day or two.

COURSES

Some of the Israeli universities operate overseas student programs in various subjects, including Hebrew, Arabic and Middle East studies. It is not always necessary to speak Hebrew to enrol, although you will often need to study the language as part of the curriculum. Contact the nearest Israeli government tourist information office in your home country for information.

Language

After a few weeks in Israel, it's not uncommon for travellers to find that they want to learn Hebrew or Arabic. Unfortunately, finding a place to learn Hebrew in Israel is neither cheap nor easy, and to learn Arabic can be even harder.

The *ulpanim* (language schools) network caters for new Jewish immigrants and is generally not welcoming of non-Jews. However, you might try contacting the Ulpan Office, Division of Adult Education (☎ 02-625 4156), 11 Beit Ha'am, Bezalel St, Jerusalem 94591.

The Ulpan Akiva Netanya (☎ 09-835 2312/3, fax 865 2919), PO Box 6086, Netanya 42160, is an international school for Jews and non-Jews and has various programs for learning Hebrew and Arabic. Fees for the 24 day program are US$1875, including tuition, cultural activities, accommodation and meals. Courses of eight, 12 and 16 to 20 weeks are also available for varying fees.

Kibbutz Ulpan is a 4½ or six month program for those who want to learn Hebrew and experience kibbutz life. Students spend half the day at work and the other half studying, six days a week. For more information contact your nearest kibbutz office or the Kibbutz Aliyah Desk (☎ 212-318 6130, fax 318 6134) at 110 East 59th St, 4th floor, New York, NY 10022, USA.

Birzeit University north of Jerusalem on the West Bank offers courses in Arabic language and literature to beginners and more experienced students. For full details check out the Birzeit University Web site (www.birzeit.edu/index.html).

ACCOMMODATION
Camping

While there are numerous countrywide camping areas, usually equipped with all necessary amenities, they aren't always the expected cheap alternative and it's often better value to check into a hostel. Pitching your tent for free seems to be tolerated on most public beaches, though notable exceptions include the Dead Sea shore, the Mediterranean coast north of Nahariya and in the Gaza Strip. Be careful, theft is very common on beaches, especially in Eilat, Tel Aviv and Haifa.

Hostels

Israel had, at last count, 32 HI-affiliated hostels. In the Dead Sea region and Mitzpe Ramon they are the sole budget accommodation choice but elsewhere privately owned hostels usually offer better value and service. For a list of HI hostels and further information contact the Israel Youth Hostels Association (☎ 02-655 8400, fax 655 8432, email iyha@netvision.net.il), Binyanei Ha'Umah Conference Centre (6th floor), PO Box 6001, Jerusalem 91060. The Binyanei Ha'Umah Conference Centre is west of the city centre, about 500m south of the new bus station and the office is open Sunday to Thursday from 8.30 am to 3 pm and Friday from 9 am to

noon. Visit their Web site for further details: www.youth-hostels.org.il.

Kibbutz Guesthouses

The kibbutzim have had to search for alternatives to agriculture for income, and in recent years they have been developing the guesthouse concept. They mainly fit into the mid-range price and have good facilities such as swimming pools or beaches, renowned restaurants and special activities for guests. The Kibbutz Hotels Reservations Office (☎ 03-524 6161, fax 527 8088), 90 Ben Yehuda St, PO Box 3194, Tel Aviv 61031, publishes a booklet listing all their hotels, restaurants and camp sites with prices, amenities and a map (also available at government tourist offices).

B&Bs

In many popular tourist areas you will find accommodation in private homes. In some places they form the bulk of moderately priced rooms. They can be found by inquiring at the local tourist office, looking for signs posted in the street or in some places by simply hanging out at the bus station with your bags.

Jerusalem is well-served by B&Bs. The Home Accommodation Association of Jerusalem (HAAJ) maintains a growing list of more than 30 establishments. These range from self-contained apartment studios to simple rooms with private facilities. In many cases breakfast is offered as part of the deal. Prices range from US$25 to US$70 and in at least 13 cases, bookings can be made effortlessly via email.

Check the HAAJ's Web site (www.bnb.co.il) for further details.

Hotels

In comparison to the number of lower and mid-range priced beds available, Israel has a disproportionately high percentage of luxury accommodation. Prices at these hotels compare favourably with those in other parts of the world and attuned as they are to a predominantly North American clientele, the facilities and level of service are top class.

FOOD

Despite constant claims that Israel has an incredible variety of international cuisine due to its worldwide immigration, you'll find much of the food expensive and disappointing.

Budget travellers can shop in the street markets, grocery shops and supermarkets, choose from the good range of quality vegetables and fruit and cook for themselves in their hostel's communal kitchen.

Much of what's on offer is similar to standard Middle Eastern fare with the exception of the traditional Eastern European dishes such as schnitzel, goulash and gefilte fish.

Italian pasta restaurants abound and there are always the fast food chains like Mc Donald's and KFC that spring up like mushrooms almost overnight.

DRINKS

Although alcohol is absolutely permissible Israelis do not drink very much. Usually, wine is only drunk on holy days such as Shabbat and during Passover. Spirits are hardly touched at all. Israel also has a national brewery and its product, bottled under the labels Maccabee and Gold Star, isn't bad.

SHOPPING

Israel is full of shops stocked with tacky souvenirs more expensive than in neighbouring countries. To find bargains and quality items you will need time to shop around and patience to haggle. It is hard to think of much in Israel that will appeal to budget travellers that cannot be found for less elsewhere in the Middle East. Exceptions are items of religious interest and Armenian ceramics.

Getting There & Away

AIR

El Al is Israel's national carrier and operates a wide range of services to and from Israel. Security is tight on El Al services and it is recommended that you check in earlier than usual. In some cities in Israel you can check in downtown, thus avoiding delays at the airport.

Fares into Israel are not particularly cheap and getting a stopover in Israel on a round the world ticket can be a challenge. Sample return fares from the USA range from US$760 to US$970. From Australia the cheapest tickets are just under A$2000.

From the UK a typical return fare will cost about UK£180. Web surfers might like to try their luck on www.TRAVEL.com where you can check your own itinerary, get a price quote and book your ticket online.

The main international airport is Ben-Gurion airport in Tel Aviv, though a number of international charter flights fly to Eilat or to Ovda airport 70km from Eilat.

Buying Tickets in Israel

Despite the long queues, the Israel Student Travel Association (ISSTA) offices do not always offer very competitive fares. See the Travel Agencies listings under Information in the Jerusalem and Tel Aviv sections. It's worth checking around the hostels and travellers' bars as many of these advertise cut-price flights. In Tel Aviv, for example, ask at the No 1 or Gordon hostels and look at the noticeboard in Buzz Stop bar; in Jerusalem ask at the Palm or Tabasco hostels; and in Eilat ask at any of the hostels mentioned in the Eilat section. The average cheapest single ticket prices that LP dug up were US$113 to Athens, US$130 to London and US$350 to New York.

Departure tax is included in all quoted ticket prices.

LAND

Egypt and Jordan have open land borders with Israel; Lebanon and Syria do not. If you are planning to visit Lebanon or Syria then do so before going to Israel, as evidence of a visit to the Jewish state will without exception bar you from entry (see the boxed text 'The Israeli Stamp Stigma' earlier in this chapter).

Private cars may cross the borders but not taxis or hire cars. Drivers and riders of motorcycles will need the vehicle's registration papers and liability insurance, although for Israel an international drivers' permit is not necessary – a domestic licence will do.

Egypt

There are two border crossing points, Rafah and Taba; which one you use depends on where you are in Israel and whether it's Sinai or Cairo you're heading for.

Note, if your visit to Egypt is confined to just Sinai (crossing at Taba only) then no Egyptian visa is necessary – you'll be issued a 14 day pass at the border.

Rafah This is the nearest border crossing to Tel Aviv and Jerusalem and can be crossed individually or by scheduled bus. Cars and motorcycles may also cross here. The crossing point is technically within the Gaza Strip but access to the border crossing is via a protected road from Israel proper running alongside the actual border.

Taba This is the most convenient place to cross if you are planning a visit to Sinai. The border is open 24 hours but this is subject to occasional change and you will want to time your crossing to be able to find transport on the other side. Unlike Rafah, where you can be held up for three or four hours, it's normally possible to stroll through the formalities at Taba in around 30 minutes.

Jordan

Travellers may cross into Jordan at three designated border crossings.

Allenby/King Hussein Bridge This crossing is only 30km from Jerusalem on one side and 40km from Amman on the other. Crossing can take anything up to three hours depending on the traffic – try to avoid being there between 11 am and 3 pm which is the busiest time. This crossing can be the most daunting of the crossings, but is the fastest way into Jordan from Tel Aviv or Jerusalem.

Jordan River The least used of the three border crossings is 6km east of Beit She'an up in the Galilee region and not particularly convenient for anywhere. However, if you don't already have your Jordanian visa they are issued here and it is considerably closer to northern Israeli cities like Tiberias or Haifa.

Arava Opened in August 1994 this crossing (known as Wadi Araba to the Jordanians) is just 2km north-east of central Eilat. The huge volume of coach traffic at this crossing often means delays of up to three hours. This crossing is handy for access to southern Jordan and for visitors wanting to make day trips to Petra from Eilat.

SEA

Israel is connected via Haifa to mainland Europe with a regular ferry service from Piraeus, near Athens in Greece. The Piraeus-Haifa run usually involves a stopover in Rhodes, or sometimes Crete, with all ferries stopping additionally at Lemesos (Limassol) in Cyprus. Departures at the time of writing were every Thursday and Sunday.

Getting Around

AIR

Arkia, Israel's domestic airline (which has extended its operations to include charters to and from abroad), operates scheduled flights connecting Jerusalem, Tel Aviv, Haifa, Rosh Pina, Kiryat Shmona and Eilat. Fares are Tel Aviv to Eilat US$80, Tel Aviv to the Galilee US$46 and Haifa to Eilat US$94.

You can book at these Arkia offices:

Ashdod
   (☎ 08-852 1212, fax 856 8838)
   Kanyon Ashdod, Nordau St
Bat Yam
   (☎ 03-507 3366, fax 507 6657)
   35 Rothschild Blvd
Beersheba
   (☎ 07-628 7444, fax 628 7450)
   183 Keren Kayemet St
Eilat
   (☎ 07-638 4888, fax 637 3370)
   Red Canyon Centre

Haifa
(☎ 04-861 1606, fax 867 1661)
80 Ha'Atzmaut St
Jerusalem
(☎ 02-625 5888, fax 623 5758)
Klal Centre, 97 Jaffa Rd
Kiryat Shmona
(☎ 06-695 9901, fax 695 9904) Pal Bldg
Netanya
(☎ 09-884 3143, fax 882 5904)
110 Shtamper St
Rosh Pina
(☎ 06-693 5302) airport
Tel Aviv
(☎ 03-524 0220, fax 524 0229) 11 Frishman St

Arkia also has its own Web site (www
.arkia.co.il) where you can view the latest
timetables and prices.

BUS

Israel's small size and excellent road system
have combined to make bus travel the
choice of public transport. Israel's bus network is dominated by Egged, the second
largest bus company in the world after Grey-
hound. For information on schedules and
prices call ☎ 1770-225 555 (no area code).

In Nazareth, East Jerusalem and the West
Bank around 30 small Arab companies provide buses. While the Jewish buses tend to
be modern, air-con, cleaner and faster, Arab
services are antiquated and slow.

Fares are generally very cheap and ISIC
holders are entitled to a discount of about
10% on inter-urban fares.

Jewish bus schedules are affected by public holidays and usually don't run on Shabbat.
Arab buses operate every day as normal.

TRAIN

The small passenger network of the Israel
State Railways (ISR) is even cheaper than
the buses but, due to the location of most of
the stations away from city and town centres,
it is less convenient. ISIC holders get a 20%
discount. The main line is from Tel Aviv
Central (North) to Haifa, with some trains
continuing to Nahariya. The train is probably
a better option for travellers heading straight
for Akko from Tel Aviv. The quality and service of the trains is now very good.

TAXI
Sherut/Service Taxi

Like its neighbours, Israel is the land of the
shared taxi. Most commonly called the
sherut, the Arabs call it *servees*, or taxi service. On Shabbat, sheruts provide the only
transport on certain major intercity routes.
In the West Bank, where Egged is limited to
Jewish settlements, the service taxis save
hours of travelling time compared to the
local Arab buses.

Special Taxis

Drivers of 'special' (ie nonshared) taxis
have a lousy reputation for overcharging,
unhelpfulness and being impolite. Be sure
that the meter is used; tourist offices can advise how much to pay. Taxi drivers are not
normally tipped.

CAR & MOTORCYCLE

Driving in Israel presents no particular problems other than frenetic driving by Israelis
and main highways with frequent traffic
lights. Good roads, beautiful scenery and
short distances make Israel a great place to
drive in. Also, in places like the Golan and
the Negev, the buses do not cover so much
ground and having your own vehicle can
help you to really see the area. With overland entry to Israel so limited, bringing your
own vehicle makes little sense.

Rental

If you are on a budget, sharing a car can still
be the most economical way to see specific
areas, if not the entire country. Eldan and Reliable are inexpensive local firms.

BICYCLE

If planning a bicycle tour, bear in mind the
hot climate, frequent rainfall in certain areas,
innumerable steep hills, and the fact that
most drivers fail to recognise your status as
a road user. Despite these factors, there are a
few cyclists to be seen pedalling around.

HITCHING

This was once a common way for locals and
travellers to get around Israel. Hitching is

still possible but not as easy as it used to be. Women should not hitch without male company. Israelis are actively encouraged to give lifts to male soldiers, so bear in mind that if you are hitching you will be last in line for a lift if there are any soldiers to be seen. Female soldiers are now forbidden to hitch because of potential dangers.

Sticking out your thumb is not the locally accepted way to advertise to drivers that you are hitching. The local signal is to point to the road with your index finger.

Jerusalem

Jerusalem, highly disputed capital of Israel, is perhaps the most fascinating city in the world, as well as one of the most beautiful. It is, surely, the holiest city of all.

History

Originally a small Jebusite settlement on the slopes of Mt Moriah, Jerusalem was captured in 997 BC by the Israelite King David, who made it his capital. Mt Moriah was the plateau on which Abraham, patriarch of the Jews, is said to have offered his son as a sacrifice to God, and so on this site David's son and successor, Solomon, built the great First Temple which though long gone still remains central to the Jewish faith. The temple was destroyed during the conquest of Nebuchadnezzar, King of Babylon, in 586 BC and the Jews suffered their first period of exile.

The Babylonians gave way to the Persians under whose benevolent rule the Jews were allowed to return and reconstruct the temple (the 'Second Temple'). The Persians went, swept aside by Alexander the Great who died shortly after to be succeeded by the Seleucid dynasty which in turn collapsed before the Romans around 63 BC. Herod the Great was installed to rule what the Romans called the Kingdom of Judea. Later, the city was administered through a series of procurators; Pontius Pilate, who ordered the crucifixion of Jesus, was the fifth.

Jesus had very little impact on the course of history while he was alive and it wasn't until some 300 or more years after his death, with the conversion of Constantine, that the ministry of the Nazarene began to make any historical impact. The swell of discontent flooded into open revolt in 66 AD (the First Revolt) resulting in the Romans destruction of the Second Temple. A Second Revolt occurring in 132 AD took the Romans four years to put down and in its aftermath they banished the Jews from Jerusalem and all Palestine. The Jews were scattered north to Babylon and Europe and west across northern Africa to Spain creating a Diaspora which, in popular myth, remained in exile until the creation of the State of Israel in 1948. The Romans also razed Jewish Jerusalem and rebuilt the city as Aelia Capitolina, the basis of today's Old City.

The conversion of the Eastern Roman Emperor Constantine to Christianity in 331 AD and the religion's subsequent legalisation triggered a wave of biblically inspired building in the 'Holy City', with churches and monasteries being erected over many of the sites associated with the life of Jesus.

After weathering a short-lived invasion by the Persians, the Byzantines buckled under the sudden onslaught of Islam. Jerusalem fell in 638 AD and was designated a Holy City of Islam because of the Muslim belief that their Prophet Mohammed had ascended to heaven from within its walls. For a time Christians, Muslims and Jews were all permitted access to the city but persecution of non-Muslims in the 10th century led to the Crusades. The Christian knights held the city from 1099 but lost it to Salah ad-Din (known to the west as Saladin) in 1187 who did, however, once again open the city to all faiths.

In 1517 the Ottoman Turks absorbed Jerusalem into their expanding empire and the city remained under rule from Istanbul for 400 years. However, Turkish interest in the region was minimal and a vacuum existed in which petty landlords fought for authority. It was into this vacuum that large

JERUSALEM

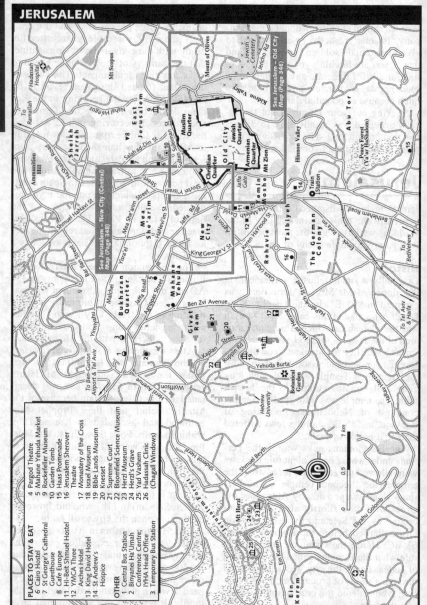

To Ramallah
To Ben Gurion Airport & Tel Aviv
To Tel Aviv & Haifa
To Bethlehem

Hadassah Hospital
Mt Scopus
Mount of Olives
Jewish Cemetery
Jericho Rd
Abu Tor
Peace Forest (Ya'ar HaShalom)

Sheikh Jarrah
Ammunition Hill
HaShlom Road
Nablus Road
Shmuel HaNavi St
Bar Ilan Street

East Jerusalem
Salah ad-Din St
Nahal HaEgoz
Sultan Suleiman St
Shivtei Yisrael St

Muslim Quarter
Jewish Quarter
Christian Quarter
Armenian Quarter
Old City
Jaffa Gate
Mt Zion
Yemin Moshe

See Jerusalem – Old City Map (Page 346)
Kidron Valley
Hinnom Valley
Train Station

Mea She'arim
Mea She'arim St
HaNevi'im St
Jaffa Rd
Jaffa Road
Street
Malchei Yisrael St
Shivtei Yisrael
Ethiopia St

New City
Agron St
HaMelekh David St
Jaffa Rd
King George V St

Bukharian Quarter
Malchei
Yirmeyahu
Herzl Avenue
Agrippas Street
Mahane Yehuda

See Jerusalem – New City (Central) Map (Page 348)

Ben Zvi Avenue
Givat Ram
Kaplan Street
Ruppin Rd
Yehuda Burla
Botanical Garden
Hebrew University

Kerem HaYesod
Gaza (Aza) Rd
Rehavia
Talbiyeh
The German Colony
Emek Refa'im St
Bethlehem Road
HaPalmach St
Derech Hebron
HaRav Herzog
Ramban
Wolfson

Sderot Herzl
Shmuel Beyth
Jerusalem Forest
Mt Herzl
Ein Kerem
Elyaohu Golomb
HaMevasser

1 km
0.5

numbers of Jewish immigrants began arriving from the mid-19th century on.

Jerusalem became a hotbed of Arab-Jewish nationalistic struggles which intensified during the 1930s. A proposal put forward by the British, successors in Jerusalem to the Ottomans, to make the city an international enclave were rejected. The city was fought over in 1948 with the end result that the Arabs got the Old City and East Jerusalem while the Jews held the western, newer parts of the city.

The Six Day War in 1967 resulted in Jerusalem being re-unified under Israeli rule. The city continues to play a key role in the Palestine problem. According to opponents of Israel, the Jewish state has no right to declare Jerusalem its capital.

Orientation

Jerusalem can be divided into three parts: the walled Old City; predominantly Arab East Jerusalem; and the rapidly expanding Jewish New City (also referred to as West Jerusalem).

Information

Tourist Offices The main city tourist information office (☎ 625 8844) is in the City Hall Complex on Safra Square at the eastern end of Jaffa Rd. It goes by the grand name of the Jerusalem Information & Tourism Centre and is open from 8.30 am to 4.30 pm Sunday to Thursday, and from 8.30 am to noon on Friday but is closed on Saturday. There's also a second, now privately run tourist information office at Jaffa Gate in the Old City, open the same hours as the main tourist office.

Christian Information Centre (☎ 627 2692, fax 628 6417) on Omar ibn al-Khattab Square, opposite the entrance to the Citadel, is very good on everything pertaining to the city's Christian sites. Practising Catholics apply here for tickets for the Christmas Eve Midnight Mass in Bethlehem. The centre is open from 8.30 am to 1 pm Monday to Saturday and is closed on Sunday. The Jewish Student Information Centre (☎ 628 2643, fax 628 8338, email jseidel@jer1.co.il) is at 5 Beit El St in the Jewish Quarter of the Old City (adjacent to the Hurva Synagogue).

Money If you want the best deal when changing money, go to the legal money-changers in the Old City and East Jerusalem. The two just inside Damascus Gate seem to give a better price than anywhere else. The moneychanger just inside Petra Hostel near Jaffa Gate seems to be open when the others are closed. In the New City go to Change Point at 33 Jaffa Rd or 2 Ben Yehuda St, neither of which charge commission. Both close early on Friday and are closed all day Saturday.

Amex (☎ 624 0830, fax 624 0950) is at 19 Hillel St in the New City; the local agent for Thomas Cook is Aweidah Tours (☎ 628 2365, fax 628 2366) at 23 Salah ad-Din St in East Jerusalem.

Post & Communications The main post office (☎ 624 4745) and poste restante is at 23 Jaffa Rd. The main section is open from 7 am to 7 pm Sunday to Thursday, and 7 am to noon Friday; closed Saturday.

For discount international telephone calls go to Solan Telecom which is at 2 Luntz, a small pedestrianised street running between Jaffa Rd and Ben Yehuda St. It's open 24 hours a day, seven days a week.

Email & Internet Access Travellers can send and receive email at the Strudel Internet cafe/wine bar (☎ 623 2101, fax 622 1445, email strudel@inter.net.il) at 11 Mounbaz St near the Russian Compound in the New City. It has four computer stations linked to the Web through Netscape and computer time is charged at 6NIS for 15 minutes.

Nearby is Netcafe (☎ 624 6327, email info@netcafe.co.il) at 9 Helene HaMalka St where you can surf and email for 14NIS for 30 minutes or 25NIS for one hour. It's open from about 10 am to late on weekdays, 10 am to 3 pm on Fridays and 9 pm to late on Saturdays.

Travel Agencies The student travel agency ISSTA (☎ 625 7257) is at 31 HaNevi'im St,

The Significance of Jerusalem

Perhaps no other city in the world carries the same religious significance for the world's three major monotheistic religions as Jerusalem. Its historical and religious importance has been repeatedly testified to by a never-ending series of skirmishes, crusades and wars ever since the Holy City was founded by David 1000 years before the birth of Jesus Christ. Doomsday watchers have often mused that Jerusalem may well be the site of the world's last battle; Messianics believe that the Messiah will come to Jerusalem to deliver the world at the end of the 20th century while Jews, Arabs, Christians and pilgrims from all over the world are drawn inexorably to the City as if by magnetism.

For Christians Jerusalem is the site of the trial and execution of Jesus Christ, though it took 300 years for the effect of Christianity to permeate the walls of the city and take hold. It is the city to which throngs of pilgrims converge yearly to visit the Church of the Holy Sepulchre where Christ was buried, to walk the Via Dolorosa through the City's narrow streets where Jesus was taken on his last walk to the Cross at Calvary, a small quarry, now the site of the Church of the Holy Sepulchre. It is home to permanent Christian communities of Greek Orthodox, Catholic, Armenian Orthodox, Protestant and other Christian denominations and although numerically small, they wield considerable power over the control of the Old City.

To Muslims, Jerusalem is the city from where Mohammed made his ascent to heaven on his Night Journey. The rock from which Mohammed is believed to have ascended to heaven is the centrepiece of the fabulous Dome of the Rock mosque that now sits in the centre of the raised hillock called the Haram ash-Sharif or Temple Mount as it is known in English. For Muslims the rock within the dome is considered to be the foundation stone of the world. To

---

open Sunday to Tuesday and Thursday from 9 am to 6 pm, and Wednesday and Friday from 9 am to 1 pm; closed Saturday. Egged Tours (☎ 625 3454) is at 44A and 224 Jaffa Rd, while Mazada Tours (☎ 623 5777), which operates a bus service to Cairo, is at 9 Koresh St, a couple of blocks south of Jaffa Rd.

Bookshops Steimatzky has three branches all within a few hundred metres of each other in Jerusalem's New City; they're at 39 Jaffa Rd, just east of Zion Square, at 7 Ben Yehuda St and at 9 King George V St. Probably Jerusalem's best bookshop, however, is Sefer VeSefel, a creaky little place with floor to ceiling new and second-hand titles, fiction and nonfiction. It's upstairs at 2 Ya'Avetz St which is a little alley linking Jaffa Rd with Mordechai Ben Hillel St. It's open from 8 am to 8 pm Sunday to Thursday, 8 am to 2.30 pm Friday and from the end of Shabbat to 11.30 pm Saturday.

Laundry With only two machines but plenty of charm, coffee and good home-cooking while you wait, Tzipor Hanefesh (☎ 624 9890) is a friendly three storey cafe/laundrette. One machine load costs 10NIS and a 45 minute drying cycle costs the same. It's at 10 Rivlin St, in the trendy central area of Nahalat Shiv'a.

Medical Services In case of medical emergencies call ☎ 101 or contact the Magen David Adom (☎ 523 133). In the Old City the Orthodox Society (☎ 627 1958) on Greek Orthodox Patriarchate Rd in the Christian Quarter operates a low-cost clinic that, we're told, welcomes travellers. It also does dental surgery. The clinic is open from 8 am to 3 pm Monday to Saturday, closed Sunday.

Emergency The central police station (in emergencies dial ☎ 100) is near the Russian Compound in the New City. The city's

The Significance of Jerusalem

Palestinians, Jerusalem is the notional capital of their nascent state and carries as much political significance for them as it does religious.

Jews have long considered Jerusalem as their ancestral and spiritual home. Israelis today regard Jerusalem as their capital. Exiled on a number of occasions from Jerusalem, Jews still look back to the days when the first and second temples still existed and most hanker after rebuilding the temple: a dream confounded by the fact that the Dome of the Rock is now sitting more or less where the Second Temple was located before its destruction by the Romans in 70 AD. Jerusalem to Jews is quintessentially Jewish and it is no accident that it is here that the greatest number of religious orthodox Jews have made their home.

Jerusalem can also have a strange psychological effect on some people. Many visitors to the city do not willingly leave and instead succumb to what is known as the 'Jerusalem Syndrome'. Seemingly normal, balanced people upon arrival in Jerusalem begin to feel that they are there by Divine command or that they are a reincarnated biblical figure. Bearded and biblically-garbed individuals wandering the streets of Jerusalem are not unusual. As with everything else in Israel, opinions vary on what causes the syndrome. It's been suggested that these are people who have arrived in Israel hoping to find peace and calm, possibly looking for an escape from some kind of turmoil back home, and when instead they encounter the conflict and tension that underlies life in Jerusalem, their minds snap. Although the ages and backgrounds vary, a significant proportion of those afflicted with the syndrome are unmarried 20 to 30 year old Christians or Jews from North America and Western Europe who grew up in religious homes.

lost and found office can also be found here. The rape crisis centre can be contacted by phoning ☎ 514 4550.

The Old City

Tightly bound by stone walls, the Old City is divided into four quarters (Armenian, Christian, Jewish and Muslim) and focused on three centres of gravity: the Haram ash-Sharif (Temple Mount) site of the Dome of the Rock; the Jewish Western Wall; and the Church of the Holy Sepulchre, built over the site of the Crucifixion.

Walls, Gates & the Citadel The Old City walls are the legacy of Süleyman the Magnificent and were built between 1537 and 1542, but have since been extensively renovated. One of the best ways to see the Old City and its surroundings is to stroll around the ramparts. It isn't possible to make a complete circuit of the wall because the Haram ash-Sharif stretch is sealed off

for security reasons. Instead the walk is in two sections: Jaffa Gate north to St Stephen's Gate (via New, Damascus and Herod's Gates) and Jaffa Gate south to Dung Gate (via Zion Gate). While you can descend at any of the gates, getting up onto the walls is only possible at Jaffa and Damascus gates. Women should not do this walk alone because of the danger of assault or sexual harassment.

There are seven open gates. The recently restored **Jaffa Gate**, so named because it was the start of the old road to Jaffa, is now the main way of entry to the Old City from the New City. It's dominated by the minaret and towers of the **Citadel (Tower of David)** – one of the country's most impressive restoration projects, and a major museum complex which is definitely worth a visit.

Moving clockwise, **New Gate**, which also gives access to the New City, is the most recent gate and dates from 1887. Down the hill,

HARAM ASH-SHARIF & DOME OF THE ROCK

For many visitors to Israel this spectacular site in the centre of Jerusalem's Old City is the reason for visiting this holy but controversial city. The gleam of the golden cupola of the Dome of the Rock Mosque is indelibly identified with the visual image of Jerusalem on travel posters seen all over the world. Seen from any angle of Jerusalem, but particularly in the crisp early morning light from the Mount of Olives, the site is a photographer's delight, yet a religious and political headache for the two major religions in Jerusalem contesting its ownership – Judaism and Islam.

The Haram ash-Sharif (Temple Mount to the Jews) is the biblical Mt Moriah on which Abraham was instructed by God to sacrifice his son in a test of his faith. Today it's a tranquil flat, paved area the size of a couple of adjacent football fields, fringed with some attractive Mamluk buildings and with the Dome of the Rock positioned roughly in the centre and the Al-Aqsa Mosque to the south.

Entrance to the Haram itself is free, but to visit the two mosques (highly recommended) and the uninspiring museum, a ticket must be purchased for 30NIS (students 22NIS). Get the ticket from the ticket kiosk just inside the Bab al-Maghariba.

Visiting hours are slightly confusing as they are based around Muslim prayer schedules, but basically the Haram is open from 8 am to 3 pm Saturday to Thursday (closed Friday). During prayers (approximately from 11.30 am to 12.30 pm in winter and 12.30 to 1.30 pm in summer) the museum shuts and entry to the mosques is for Muslims only. Note also that during the month of Ramadan the Haram is only open from 7.30 to 10 am and it's completely closed on Muslim holidays. Visitors must be suitably dressed.

ERIC WHEATER

ANDREW HUMPHREYS

Top: Inside and out, the Dome is covered with a bright confection of mosaics and scrolled verses from the Quran. (Photo by Russell Mountford)

Bottom Left: Side doorway of the workaday Al-Aqsa Mosque

Bottom Right: Fine Mamluk architecture fringes the Haram ash-Sharif.

SH-SHARIF &

Dome of the Rock

Enclosing the sacred rock upon which Abraham prepared to sacrifice his son and from which, according to Islamic tradition, the Prophet Mohammed launched himself to the heavens to take his place alongside Allah, the Dome of the Rock was constructed between 688 and 691 AD under the patronage of the Umayyad caliph Abd al-Malik. His motives were shrewd as well as pious – the caliph was concerned that the imposing Christian Church of the Holy Sepulchre was seducing Arab minds.

During the reign of Süleyman the Magnificent what remained of the original interior mosaics were removed and replaced, while the external mosaics were renewed in 1963. Essentially, however, what you see today is the building as conceived by Abd al-Malik – except the gold that originally covered the dome disappeared long ago, melted down to pay off some caliph's debts. The present convincing anodised aluminium dome has been financed by Gulf State Arab countries.

Al-Aqsa Mosque

Believed by some to be a conversion of a 6th century Byzantine church, Muslims maintain that Al-Aqsa was built from scratch in the early 8th century by the son of Abd al-Malik, patron of the Dome. The original structure was twice destroyed by earthquakes in its first 60 years and the present-day mosque is a compendium of restorations and rebuildings. The intricately carved *mihrab* (prayer niche indicating the direction of Mecca), however, does date from the time of Salah ad-Din.

Right: Dome of the Rock: the centrepiece of the Haram ash-Sharif

ANTHONY PIDGEON

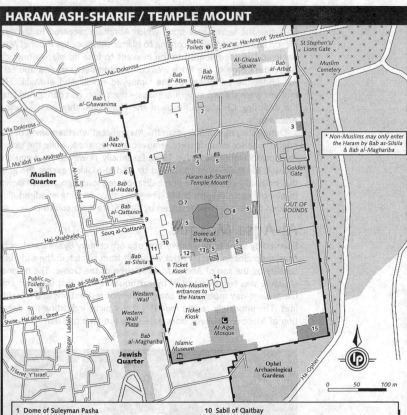

HARAM ASH-SHARIF / TEMPLE MOUNT

* Non-Muslims may only enter the Haram by Bab as-Silsila & Bab al-Maghariba

1 Dome of Suleyman Pasha

2 Sabil – Public Fountain

3 Solomon's Throne

4 Sabil of Sheikh Budir

5 The Stairs of Scales of Souls
Muslims believe that scales will be hung from the column-supported arches at the top of these stairs on Judgment Day to weigh the souls of the dead.

6 Small Wall
A little visited northern extension of the Western Wall.

7 Dome of the Ascension
According to Muslim tradition Mohammed prayed here before his ascent.

8 Dome of the Chain
This is the smaller version of the Dome of the Rock, in the exact centre of the Haram. Mystery surrounds the reason for its construction. A popular theory is that it was a trial-run for the real thing; another is that it was the Haram's treasury. Its name comes from the legend that Solomon hung a chain from the dome and those who swore falsely whilst holding it were struck by lightning.

9 Gate of the Cotton Merchants
This is the most imposing of the Haram's gates. Make a point of departing through here into the Mamluk-era arcaded market of the Cotton Merchants (Souq al-Qattanin).

10 Sabil of Qaitbay
Though overshadowed by its more illustrious neighbours, this is one of Jerusalem's most beautiful structures. It was built by Egyptians in 1482 as a charitable act to please Allah, and it features the only carved stone dome outside Cairo.

11 Mamluk Arcade

12 Dome of Learning
Along with parts of the facade of the Al-Aqsa Mosque, this is one of the very few remaining Ayyubid (1187-1250) structures in Jerusalem. Note the very unusual entwined columns flanking the door.

13 Summer Pulpit
Built by the Mamluks in the 14th century and renovated by the Ottomans, this was used to deliver outdoor sermons.

14 Al-Kas Fountain
One of many ablutions fountains on the Haram for the ritual washing before prayers.

15 Solomon's Stables
A cavernous vaulted hall under the Haram, constructed by the Crusaders to accommodate their horses. Unfortunately it's closed except by arrangement. This area is out of bounds.

the **Damascus Gate** gives access to/from East Jerusalem and is the most attractive and crowded of all the city gates. **Herod's Gate** also faces Arab East Jerusalem; it was close to here that the Crusaders first breached Jerusalem's walls in 1099.

St Stephen's Gate, facing the Mount of Olives, is named for the first Christian martyr, who was stoned nearby. The curious name of **Dung Gate** may be due to its location nearby what was the local rubbish dump. Its official name is Gate of the Moors because North African immigrants lived nearby in the 16th century. **Zion Gate** became known as the Gate of the Jewish Quarter in late medieval times and the many bullet marks are signs of the fierce fighting that took place here during the 1948 War.

Western Wall The Western Wall is part of the retaining wall built by Herod in 20 BC to support the temple's esplanade. As such it is the only remaining physical evidence of what was the Jew's most holy ancient shrine. The area immediately in front of the wall now operates as a great open-air synagogue.

The wall is accessible 24 hours a day and is free. We very much recommend that you make several visits here at different times of the day especially at sundown on Friday.

Jewish Quarter Flattened during the fighting in 1948, the Jewish Quarter has been almost entirely reconstructed since its recapture by the Israelis in 1967. There are few historic monuments above ground level but the digging that went on during reconstruction unearthed a number of interesting archaeological finds, the most significant of which is **The Cardo,** the main (north-south) street of Roman and Byzantine Jerusalem. A part of it has been restored to something like its original appearance while the rest has been reconstructed as an arcade of expensive gift stores and galleries of Judaica.

West of the Cardo is the **Old Yishuv Court Museum** at 6 Or HaChaim St, set up as a house with each room showing an aspect of Jewish life in the Quarter before the destruction in 1948; east of the Cardo is Hurva Square, identifiable by its graceful landmark of a lone single-brick arch, almost all that remains of the **Hurva Synagogue**. Down a narrow alleyway off the east side of the square is **Wohl Archaeological Museum**, perhaps the Jewish Quarter's most impressive complex, featuring renovated examples of the houses of wealthy Jews in Herod's Upper City.

Muslim Quarter This is the most bustling and densely populated area of the Old City and depending on your tastes it's either claustrophobic and a hassle or completely exhilarating. Clustered around the Haram ash-Sharif in narrow medieval alleys are some fine examples of **Mamluk architecture** while down by St Stephen's Gate is **St Anne's Church**, the finest example of Crusader architecture in Jerusalem. The road leading from St Stephen's Gate down into the heart of the Old City is the **Via Dolorosa**, the route traditionally believed to have been the one followed by Jesus as he carried his cross to Calvary. Though the biblical connection is of dubious authenticity, the Franciscan Fathers lead a procession along the Via Dolorosa every Friday at 3 pm.

Christian Quarter The Christian Quarter is centred around the **Church of the Holy Sepulchre** which occupies the site generally agreed to be where Jesus was crucified, buried and resurrected. The church is a messy collision of styles, originally Byzantine, extensively rebuilt by the Crusaders and interfered with and tarted up on numerous occasions since – the interior has best been described as looking like 'a cross between a building site and a used furniture depot'. The church is open daily to anyone suitably dressed. It's worth visiting the neighbouring **Lutheran Church of the Redeemer** for the excellent views over the Old City from the tower.

Armenian Quarter & Mt Zion This small and secluded quarter is not much visited but the Armenian **St James' (Jacques') Cathedral** has a sensuous aura of ritual and

ISRAEL

JERUSALEM – OLD CITY

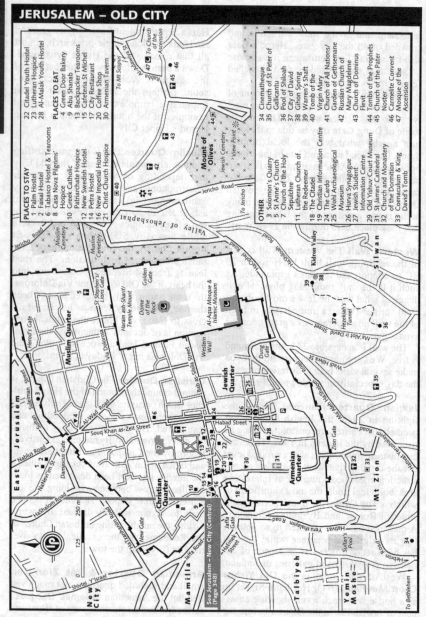

PLACES TO STAY
1 Palm Hostel
2 Faisal Hostel
6 Tabasco Hostel & Tearooms
8 Casa Nova Pilgrims'
   Hospice
10 Greek Catholic
   Patriarchate Hospice
12 New Swedish Hostel
14 Petra Hostel
16 New Imperial Hotel
21 Christ Church Hospice
22 Citadel Youth Hostel
23 Lutheran Hospice
28 Al-Malak Youth Hostel

PLACES TO EAT
4 Green Door Bakery
9 Abu Shanab
13 Backpacker Tearooms
15 Cafeteria St Michel
17 City Restaurant
20 Coffee Shop
30 Armenian Tavern

OTHER
3 Solomon's Quarry
5 St Anne's Church
7 Church of the Holy
   Sepulchre
11 Lutheran Church of
   the Redeemer
18 The Citadel
19 Christian Information Centre
24 The Cardo
25 Wohl Archaeological
   Museum
26 Hurva Synagogue
27 Jewish Student
   Information Centre
29 Old Vishuv Court Museum
31 St James' Cathedral
32 Church and Monastery
   of the Dormition
33 Coenaculum & King
   David's Tomb
34 Cinematheque
35 Church of St Peter of
   Gallicantu
36 Pool of Shiloah
37 City of David
38 Gihon Spring
39 Warren's Shaft
40 Tomb of the
   Virgin Mary
41 Church of All Nations/
   Garden of Gethsemane
42 Mary Magdalene
   Russian Church of
43 Church of Dominus
   Flevit
44 Tombs of the Prophets
45 Church of the Pater
   Noster
46 Carmelite Convent
47 Mosque of the
   Ascension

mystery lacking from every other Christian site in this most holy of cities. Unfortunately the church is only open for services, held Monday to Friday from 6.30 to 7.15 am and 2.45 to 3.30 pm, and Saturday and Sunday from 2.30 to 3 pm.

The Armenian Quarter's Zion Gate leads out to Mt Zion, site of the **Coenaculum** (also known as the Cenacle), traditionally held to be where the Last Supper took place. On the other side of the same building is **King David's Tomb**, claimed resting place of the legendary Jewish king, while around the corner is the **Church & Monastery of the Dormition** where the Virgin Mary fell into 'eternal sleep'.

Mount of Olives East of the Old City, reached through St Stephen's Gate, the Mount of Olives is where Jesus was arrested and later ascended to heaven. There are several interesting churches here as well as the biblical **Garden of Gethsemane** and the attractive **Tomb of the Virgin Mary**. However, the biggest draw is the **panorama** of the Old City from the top of the mountain – visit early in the morning for the best light. Sadly, Lonely Planet has received a number of letters from women readers who suffered unpleasant experiences while walking around here and so we have to advise females not to visit alone.

East Jerusalem

The modern, blaring, fume-hazed Palestinian part of Jerusalem, this is a district of small businesses, shops and aged hotels. On Sultan Suleiman St, just outside the Old City walls, the **Rockefeller Museum** has some impressive archaeological and architectural exhibits although the presentation is off-puttingly dour and musty compared to other more modern Israeli museums. Opposite the Sultan Suleiman St bus station **Solomon's Quarry** is a vast cave beneath the north wall of the Old City – while there's little to see it does offer cool refuge on a hot day. On Nablus Rd the **Garden Tomb** is a pretty spot, believed by some to be the site of Jesus' death and resurrection.

New City

The New City is roughly centred on the triangle of Jaffa Rd, King George V St and pedestrianised Ben Yehuda St but the most colourful and bustling district is **Mahane Yehuda**, the Jewish food market. Possibly one of the world's most reluctant tourist attractions, the Ultraorthodox Jewish district of **Mea She'arim** is the only remaining example of a *shtetl* (ghetto) as existed in pre-Holocaust Eastern Europe. Dress conservatively and photograph with discretion. The Holocaust itself is remembered at **Yad Vashem**, a moving memorial and museum complex on the outskirts of town at the edge of the Jerusalem Forest.

The country's major museum complex is the **Israel Museum**, just west of the New City. An assemblage of several major collections, it has an excellent art section and includes the Shrine of the Book, which houses some of the Dead Sea Scrolls.

Organised Tours

Bus A good introduction to the city is Egged Tours' **Route 99**, Circular Line. This service takes you on a comfortable coach to 36 of the major sites, with basic commentary in English (sort of) provided by the driver. The bus leaves from Ha'Emek St by Jaffa Gate but you can board at any of the stops and it's a continuous circular route (taking 1½ hours) ending up where it started.

Zion Walking Tours The three hour 'Four Quarters' tour of the Old City, departing Sunday to Friday at 9 and 11 am and 2 pm, is particularly good value at US$10 (students US$9) per person. Other tours include the Pre-Temple Period route, the Underground City of Jerusalem and Mea She'arim. Zion (☎ 628 7866, fax 629 0774) has its office on Omar ibn al-Khattab Square, opposite the entrance to the Citadel.

Free Walking Tours The municipal tourist office does a free Saturday morning walking tour around a different part of the city each week. Meet at 10 am by the entrance to the Russian Compound at 32 Jaffa Rd.

ISRAEL

JERUSALEM – NEW CITY (CENTRAL)

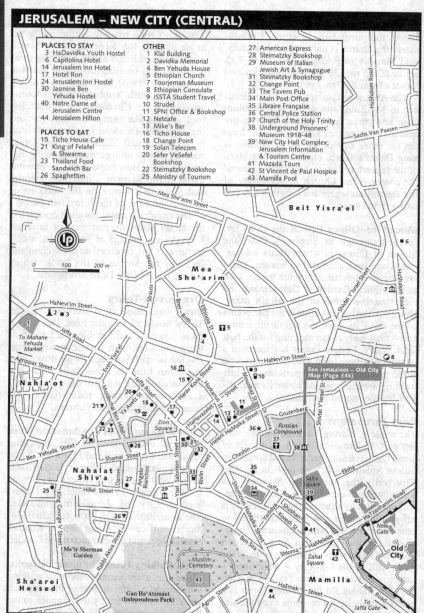

PLACES TO STAY
- 3 HaDavidka Youth Hostel
- 6 Capitolina Hotel
- 14 Jerusalem Inn Hotel
- 17 Hotel Ron
- 24 Jerusalem Inn Hostel
- 30 Jasmine Ben
  Yehuda Hostel
- 40 Notre Dame of
  Jerusalem Centre
- 44 Jerusalem Hilton

PLACES TO EAT
- 15 Ticho House Cafe
- 21 King of Felafel
  & Shwarma
- 23 Thailand Food
  Sandwich Bar
- 26 Spaghettim

OTHER
- 1 Klal Building
- 2 Davidka Memorial
- 4 Ben Yehuda House
- 5 Ethiopian Church
- 7 Tourjeman Museum
- 8 Ethiopian Consulate
- 9 ISSTA Student Travel
- 10 Strudel
- 11 SPNI Office & Bookshop
- 12 Netcafe
- 13 Mike's Bar
- 16 Ticho House
- 18 Change Point
- 19 Solan Telecom
- 20 Sefer VeSefel
  Bookshop
- 22 Steimatzky Bookshop
- 25 Ministry of Tourism

- 27 American Express
- 28 Steimatzky Bookshop
- 29 Museum of Italian
  Jewish Art & Synagogue
- 31 Steimatzky Bookshop
- 32 Change Point
- 33 The Tavern Pub
- 34 Main Post Office
- 35 Librairie Française
- 36 Central Police Station
- 37 Church of the Holy Trinity
- 38 Underground Prisoners'
  Museum 1918-48
- 39 New City Hall Complex;
  Jerusalem Information
  & Tourism Centre
- 41 Mazada Tours
- 42 St Vincent de Paul Hospice
- 43 Mamilla Pool

The Jewish Student Information Centre (see Information earlier in this section), which is committed to giving young Jews a fresh awareness of being Jewish, organises free walking tours of Jewish sites in the Old City's Jewish and Muslim quarters.

Places to Stay – Budget

The best location to stay really depends on your requirements. The Old City and East Jerusalem tend to have the cheapest places, the best atmosphere and, of course, they're the most convenient for the major sites nearby. However, some hostels and hospices have strict curfews, and being at least a good 20 minute walk from the New City centre nightlife, they aren't so great for those who want to stay out late (the Old City and East Jerusalem almost completely close down at dusk). On the other hand, with only one or two unappealing exceptions, accommodation in the New City tends to be considerably more expensive.

Old City The main contender in the popularity stakes is *Tabasco Hostel* (*☎/fax 628 3461*) on Aqabat at-Takiya St (you can see the sign from Souq Khan as-Zeit St). This place is clean and very lively though sometimes crowded. It has a busy notice board and no curfew, though you will have to identify yourself to get in after 1 am. Downstairs is the Old City's most popular partying venue (see Entertainment). It's cheap – dorm beds are 18NIS, a mattress on the roof is 15NIS, while a small private room is a hefty 75NIS.

Near Jaffa Gate is *Petra Hostel* (*☎ 628 6618*) which has a superb location on Omar ibn al-Khattab Square, so see if you can get into a dorm with a balcony overlooking the action. It's an airy, breezy place, with lots of room to move. Located in what was once a grand hotel in the old Jerusalem it is now a popular backpackers' home. Dorm beds are 23NIS and a spot on the roof with a great view of the Dome of the Rock is 15NIS.

New Swedish Hostel (*☎ 626 4124, fax 628 7884, 29 David St*) is about 100m far-

ther down into the bazaar. While it's clean and quite OK overall and draws a regular backpacker crowd, many of whom come from Sweden, it is somewhat cramped and pokey. Dorm beds cost 15NIS and tiny private rooms are between 50 and 75NIS. There is a 3 am curfew.

For a couple of better hostels, head into the bazaar along David St from Omar ibn al-Khattab Square, take the first right and then turn left immediately onto St Mark's Rd. *Citadel Youth Hostel* (*☎ 627 4375, email citadelhostel@netscape.net*) is 50m down here on the right. The reception and the small double rooms (60 to 100NIS) on the ground floor look like they've been burrowed into stone. A tight, narrow stairway leads up to some clean and comfortable dorms (beds are 20NIS), a small lounge, a kitchen, and access to the roof with views over the Old City.

Finally, tucked away on quiet Al-Malak St is the only private accommodation option in the Jewish Quarter. *Al-Malak Youth Hostel* (*☎ 628 5362*) is a cool, cosy oasis in the basement of an old house not far from the Western Wall. Dorm beds go for 20NIS and small private rooms, some of which are in a separate part of the house, go for between and 75 and 100NIS.

East Jerusalem 'Hostel Row' is the stretch of HaNevi'im St across from Damascus Gate, beside the service taxi rank. There are four possibilities here but we only recommend two. *Faisal Hostel* (*☎ 627 2492*) is the closest to the city walls and it has a nice terrace and a kitchen with free tea and coffee. Dorm beds (a bit cramped) are 20NIS and there are a few doubles at 50NIS. There's a flexible 1 am curfew. *Palm Hostel* (*☎ 627 3189*) next door to the Faisal has a great common room with plants and a glass roof. There's also a kitchen with a fridge stocked with cold beers, and videos are shown most nights. There's no curfew. Beds in large spacious dorms are 20NIS and there are a few private rooms at 80 and 100NIS.

One street east and just north of the bus park is *Cairo Hostel* (*☎ 627 7216*) at 21

Nablus St. It's a bit soulless and not particularly friendly but there's a large lounge with satellite TV and free coffee and tea in the kitchen. Dorm beds are 15NIS and private rooms that take three, maybe four people cost 60NIS.

New City *HaDavidka Youth Hostel* (☎ 538 4555, fax 538 8790, 67 HaNevi'im St) is at the junction of HaNevi'im St and Jaffa Rd. It's just a few minutes walk from the city centre and a bus ride (Nos 23 and 27 stop outside on the way to Damascus Gate) from the Old City. It has good facilities and is well maintained. Dorm beds are between US$13 and US$19 and there are usually private singles for around US$42 including breakfast.

Jerusalem Inn Hostel (☎ 625 1294, 6 HaHistradrut St) just off pedestrianised Ben Yehuda St is kept immaculately clean and there's a no smoking policy. There's no kitchen but at the reception/bar area you can get breakfast, snacks, tea, coffee and beer. The place has a midnight curfew but a deposit will get you a front door key. Dorm beds are 42NIS, singles are 96NIS while doubles are from 120NIS.

Another option is *Jasmine Ben Yehuda Hostel* (☎ 624 8021, fax 625 3032, 1 Solomon St) more or less above the Underground disco. This place is reasonably clean and well run but the management is a bit diffident and timeworn as is the feel of the hostel generally. There is a small kitchen area and tea, coffee and breakfast if you want it. Dorm beds are 30NIS.

There are several HI-affiliated hostels in the New City, the best of which is *HI-Beit Shmuel Hostel* (☎ 620 3491, fax 620 3467, 6 Shama St) next to the Hebrew Union College near the junction of HaMelekh David and Agron streets. Highly recommended, this place is more like a hotel than a hostel and it's only a few minutes walk from both the Old City and the central area of the New City. Dorm beds are around US$15 and there are usually private singles/doubles for around US$42 with breakfast included.

Places to Stay – Mid-Range

Old City *Christ Church Hospice* (☎ 627 7727, fax 627 7730, email christch@netvision.net.il) at Omar ibn al-Khattab Square opposite the Citadel entrance has pleasant staff and is very clean, quiet and comfortable, with a pretty courtyard and nice public rooms. Singles cost from US$41 to US$50, and doubles from US$72 to US$90. As well as its cheap dorm beds, the very popular *Lutheran Hospice* has an attached guesthouse in which singles/doubles go for US$40/60, with breakfast provided.

Casa Nova Pilgrims' Hospice (☎ 628 2791, fax 626 4370, 10 Casa Nova St), run by the Franciscans, has singles/doubles at US$35/60. From Jaffa Gate take the second left, Greek Catholic Patriarchate Rd, and follow it until it eventually becomes Casa Nova St. *Greek Catholic Patriarchate Hospice* (☎ 628 2023, fax 628 6652) is a bit unfriendly but the basic singles/doubles (US$32/48) are comfortable and breakfast is included. It's on St Dimitri's Rd, also an extension of Greek Catholic Patriarchate Rd.

Although owned by the Greek Orthodox Church *New Imperial Hotel* (☎ 628 2261) on your left as you enter Jaffa Gate has few religious trappings. It was built in the late 19th century and retains an air of dusty, faded grandeur although the rooms have been cleaned up and are very comfortable. Singles/doubles are a bit of a bargain starting at US$30/33.

East Jerusalem One of the best accommodation deals in the city is *St George's Cathedral Guesthouse* (☎ 628 3302, fax 628 2253, email sghotel@netvision.net.il, 20 Nablus Rd) part of the St George's Cathedral compound just 10 minutes walk from the Old City. It's a delightful building with an attractive garden. The atmosphere is very relaxed and friendly with no curfew. Comfortable rooms, most with private bathroom, cost US$50/78 for singles/doubles, with breakfast.

On the same street but a little closer to Damascus Gate is *Capitolina Hotel* (☎ 628 6888, fax 627 6301, 29 Nablus Rd), next door to the US consulate. The decor is dowdy but there are good facilities, including squash and tennis courts, and a swimming pool; singles/doubles are US$55/75.

New City Facing New Gate (and just 10 minutes walk from the city centre) the guesthouse at *Notre Dame of Jerusalem Centre* (☎ 627 9111, fax 627 1995) is one of the city's most attractive mid-range options. The rooms have three-star facilities while the majestic surroundings and views are excellent. Singles cost US$79 and doubles will set you back US$98 with breakfast included.

Equally as enchanting is *YMCA Three Arches Hotel* (☎ 569 2692, fax 623 5192, email y3arches@netvision.net.il) situated at 26 HaMelekh David St probably the best-looking YMCA in the world. Guests also have free use of the pool, gym and the squash and tennis courts. Singles/doubles will set you back US$104/127.

In the New City *Jerusalem Inn Hotel* (☎ 625 2757, fax 625 1297, 7 Horkanos St) has an almost Scandinavian looking interior with masses of open space and a large lounge and bar/restaurant. Prices range from US$52 to US$72 and US$58 to US$78 for singles/doubles. *Hotel Ron* (☎ 622 3122, fax 625 0707, email ronhotel@inter.net.il, 44 Jaffa Rd) has large and reasonably pleasant rooms although those facing the front may be a little noisy; singles/doubles are US$89/94.

Places to Stay – Top End
Jerusalem is top-heavy with luxury hotels. Most are in the New City, with just one or two in East Jerusalem and none in the Old City. In 1997 the Hilton chain opened what is now the city's brashest and most glitzy hotel, the *Jerusalem Hilton* (☎ 621 1111, fax 621 1000, email jrshiew@netvision.net.il, 7 King David St) in Mamilla, a champagne cork's arc away from the Old City walls. Singles run from US$236 to US$333, while doubles rev up at US$282 to US$380.

The country's top hotel is probably still the *King David* (☎ 620 8888, fax 620 8882, email danhtls@danhotels.co.il, 23 HaMelekh David St), given the seal of approval by a stream of visiting kings and queens, presidents and prime ministers. Singles cost from US$283 to US$506, while doubles go from US$306 to US$529.

Places to Eat
Street Food There are surprisingly few felafel places in the Old City and none of them are particularly good. The most convenient is a stall at the bottom of the slope as you enter from Damascus Gate, in the narrow frontage between the two forking roads. As you face the felafel stall look to your left and you'll see Aqabat ash-Sheikh Rihan St which contains *Green Door Bakery*. It rustles up cheese, egg and tomato pizzas (4NIS) while you wait.

Most New City felafel is sold on King George V St between Jaffa Rd and Ben Yehuda St – just follow the trail of tahina, salad and squashed felafel balls on the pavement. One of the most popular with locals is *King of Felafel & Shwarma* on the corner of King George V and Agrippas streets. If you want to sit while eating go to the curiously named *Thailand Food Sandwich Bar* (6 Ben Hillel St) where you'll pay 7NIS for felafel and 12NIS for shwarma.

Snacks *Ticho House Cafe* is a fine place to sip coffee and browse the newspapers or read a book – the ground floor of a museum and gallery, it's off the top end of Harav Kook St.

For breakfast *Cafeteria St Michel* (Omar ibn al-Khattab Square) at Jaffa Gate does a decent omelette, bread and jam, and tea or coffee. Two doors away *City Restaurant* also serves breakfast and has various Middle Eastern snacks such as grilled cheese and felafel or homous platters.

Across the square, next to the Christian Information Centre, *Coffee Shop* is a lovely place – clean, and decorated with Christian-theme Jerusalem tiles on the tables and walls. It features a modestly priced all-you-can-eat salad bar with soup and bread.

Cafe Europe (9 As-Zahra St) east of Salah ad-Din offers some of the best value quality eating in the city. The platters are particularly recommended and the ice cream cocktails are excellent if not a little pricey.

Restaurants In the Jaffa Gate area is *Armenian Tavern* (☎ *627 3854, 79 Armenian Patriarchate Rd*) with a beautiful tiled interior and a fountain gently splashing in one corner. The strongly flavoured meat dishes (30 to 40NIS) are excellent and the *khaghoghi derev*, a spiced mince meat mixture bundled in vine leaves, is highly recommended. It's open daily and is a good place to eat on Friday evenings when other places are closed.

Abu Shanab (35 Latin Patriarchate Rd) – the first left as you enter Jaffa Gate – specialises in pizza which comes in three sizes: filling (10NIS), very filling (20NIS) and 'do you want half of this?' (35NIS). Abu Shanab also does hot sandwiches, salads, lasagne and spaghetti, all about 15NIS. It's open daily from 10 am to after midnight.

There are several good pasta places in the central area, the best of which we consider to be *Spaghettim* (☎ *623 5547, 8 Rabbi Akiva St)* off Hillel St. The menu is spaghetti-only but served in more than 50 different ways from the predictable bolognaise through to ostrich in hunter sauce. Prices are 20 to 40NIS and it's open from noon to 1 am.

Self-Catering *Mahane Yehuda Market* is Jerusalem's cheapest source of food; cheaper even than the Old City. To save even more, go along just as the market closes (about 7.30 to 8.30 pm Sunday to Thursday, and 3 to 4 pm Friday) when prices are at their lowest. It's closed on Saturday.

Entertainment

East Jerusalem and the Old City close up completely at sundown with just *Abu Shanab's*, *Tabasco Tearooms* and *Backpacker Tearooms* providing any alternative to beer and a book back at the hostel. The New City, on the other hand, is buzzing, especially the Nahalat Shiv'a quarter and the area immediately west of the Russian Compound. Yoel Salomon and Rivlin, the two

parallel main streets in Nahalat Shiv'a, are lined with enough late night bars and cafes to defeat even the most ardent of pub-crawlers.

Down at the bottom of Rivlin St, *The Tavern Pub* was the original Jerusalem pub and it attracts a mainly expat, bar propping, beer drinking crowd. It's nothing special, but it's at the centre of action and the tables outside make a good vantage point for people watching. For live music – rock, folk and blues – squeeze in at *Mike's Bar*, a tiny place on Horkanus St. For jazz, try *Pargod Theatre* (☎ *623 1765, 94 Bezalel St)*. Friday afternoons used to be 1.30 to 5.30 pm jam sessions – maybe it still is, call to find out.

Jerusalem Sherover Theatre (☎ *561 7167, 20 David Marcus St)* in Talbiyeh has simultaneous English-language translation headsets available for certain performances. The Sherover is also home to the Jerusalem Symphony Orchestra while *Binyanei Ha'Umah Conference Centre* (☎ *622 2481)* is the national residence of the Israel Philharmonic Orchestra. Free classical performances are sometimes held at a number of venues including *YMCA Auditorium (HaMelekh David St)*, *Music Centre of Mishkenot Sha'ananim* (alternate Fridays) and *Beit Shmuel*, part of Hebrew Union College on King George V St (Saturday morning). Immigrant musicians also give performances at *Ticho House* every Friday morning.

Al-Masrah Centre for Palestine Culture & Art and *Al-Kasaba Theatre* (☎ *628 0957)* on Abu Obeida St off Salah ah-Din St in East Jerusalem perform plays, musicals, operettas and folk dancing in Arabic, often with an English synopsis.

Pick up the Friday edition of *Jerusalem Post* for an up-to-date and comprehensive list of events and also stop by the tourist offices for their current 'Events in Jerusalem' brochure.

Getting There & Away
Air Arkia (☎ 02-625 5888, fax 623 5758), Klal Centre, 97 Jaffa Rd, flights depart from the airport at Atarot, north of the city. These connect directly with Eilat and Rosh Pina,

with further connections to Haifa and Tel Aviv. There are no flights on Saturday.

Bus The Egged central bus station on Jaffa Rd is where most people first arrive. Buses connect to all the major areas in the country. Although the inter-urban buses usually fill up, you only need to make advance reservations for the Eilat bus. Buses for the Dead Sea are always busy and depart erratically so try to make as early a start as possible.

Tel Aviv costs 17NIS, takes 50 minutes and buses depart every 15 minutes; Eilat is 57NIS, takes 4½ hours and four buses depart each day. Buses for the 40 minute trip to Ben-Gurion airport near Tel Aviv leave at least every hour for 17NIS.

For travel in the West Bank and to Gaza use the service taxis.

Buses to Egypt (Cairo) are run by Mazada Tours (☎ 623 5777, fax 625 5454) at 9 Koresh St. Buses depart daily at 7 am. There are also overnight services on Sunday, Tuesday and Thursday, departing at 6.30 pm. The journey takes roughly 12 to 14 hours and a ticket costs US$35 one way or US$50 return. The night bus is US$40/60 for a single/return ticket.

Service Taxis Service taxis make an affordable alternative to buses and on Shabbat they are the only way of getting around. Service taxis for Tel Aviv depart from the corner of Harav Kook St and Jaffa Rd and cost 20NIS per person (30NIS on Friday and Saturday).

In East Jerusalem the service taxi rank is across from Damascus Gate. All West Bank destinations as well as Gaza depart from here. Service taxis are much faster than buses, depart more frequently and cost only a few shekels more.

Getting Around
To/From the Airport United Tours bus No 111 departs hourly from the central bus station for Ben-Gurion airport (20NIS, 45 minutes). Alternatively, take a Nesher service taxi from 21 King George V St, on the corner of Ben Yehuda St, for 30NIS. For no extra charge Nesher (☎ 623 1231, 625 7227)

will also pick up from your hostel/hotel, seven days a week, 24 hours a day, but make a reservation one day ahead.

Bus Currently, these are some of the major bus routes:

Bus No 1 Departs from platform D of the central bus station to Mea She'arim, Jaffa Gate, Mt Zion and then heads to the Old City's Jewish Quarter.

Bus No 7 Departs from the central bus station down Keren HaYesod, through Talpiot and out to Ramat Rachel.

Bus No 9 Departs from Jaffa Rd to the Israel Museum and the Givat Ram campus of the Hebrew University and then into Rehavia via Ramban St and down Keren HaYesod.

Bus No 13 Departs from Kiryat HaYovel via Jaffa Rd to Jaffa Gate.

Bus No 17 Departs to Ein Kerem.

Bus No 18 Runs the length of Jaffa Rd connecting the New City centre with the bus station.

Bus No 20 Departs from Yad Vashem via Jaffa Rd to Jaffa Gate.

Bus No 23 Departs from Yad Vashem via Jaffa Rd to Damascus Gate.

Bus No 27 Departs from Hadassah Clinic to Mt Herzl and Yad Vashem museum, along Jaffa Rd past the central bus station, left along HaNevi'im and via Strauss and Yezehekel streets to the Nablus Rd bus station near Damascus Gate.

Bus No 28 Departs from Jaffa Rd central bus station to Mt Scopus and French Hill.

Mediterranean Coast

TEL AVIV

Tel Aviv is a greatly underrated Mediterranean city, barely a century old, that thumbs its nose at the 3000 year history of Jerusalem. Forsaking synagogues for stock exchanges and tradition for fadism, the concerns of secular Tel Aviv are finance, business and fun. The city possesses an absorbing array of distinctive neighbourhoods, a result of the diverse backgrounds of its inhabitants, all of whom have arrived with the last few generations with piles of cultural baggage intact. A short walk can encompass the spicy orientalism of the Yemenite Quarter, the seedy vodka cafes of Russified lower Allenby St and the Miami chic of pastel pink and blue glass beachfront condominiums.

Orientation

Tel Aviv is a large conglomeration of suburbs sprawling across a coastal plain. Most of your time will be spent in the city's well-defined central district which occupies about 6km of seafront estate and is focused on four main streets running north-south, more or less parallel to the beachline. Closest to the sand is Herbert Samuel Esplanade while a block inland is hotel-lined HaYarkon St. Farther back is backpacker-central Ben Yehuda St, while the trendy shopping zone, Dizengoff St, more or less marks the easternmost limit of Tel Aviv for the visitor. These four streets all run virtually the entire length of the central city area, from the northern tip bordered by the Yarkon River, down as far as Allenby St and the Yemenite Quarter, the original 1930s centre of town.

Allenby St, almost a continuation of Ben Yehuda, is a fifth major street which runs south from the city centre towards the vicinity of the central bus station.

Information

Tourist Office The city tourist information office (☎ 639 5660, fax 639 5659) is on the 6th floor of the central bus station, opposite stand No 630. It's open from 9 am to 6 pm Sunday to Thursday, and from 9 am to 1.30 pm Friday; closed Saturday.

Money The best currency exchange deals are at the private bureaus around town, places that also don't charge commission. Try Sinai Exchange at 68 Ben Yehuda St, Change at 37 Ben Yehuda St, Change Spot at 140 Dizengoff St and Change Point at 94 HaYarkon St. These offices are generally open from 9 am to 8 or 9 pm Sunday to Thursday, and from 9 am to 2 pm Friday; closed Saturday. Sinai Exchange re-opens after sundown on Shabbat from 7 to 11 pm.

Tel Aviv's Amex office (☎ 524 2211, fax 523 1030) is at 120 Ben Yehuda St. It's open from 9 am to 5 pm Sunday to Thursday, closed Friday and Saturday. Thomas Cook is represented by Unitours (☎ 520 9999) at 90a HaYarkon St, open from 9 am to 5 pm Sunday to Thursday, and 8 am to 1 pm Friday.

Post & Communications The main post office is at 132 Allenby St, on the corner of Yehuda HaLevi St. It's open from 7 am to 6 pm Sunday to Thursday and from 7 am to noon Friday, closed Saturday. The poste restante is two blocks east at 7 Mikve Y'Israel St – cross Allenby St to Yehuda HaLevi St and then bear right at the fork. This is also the international telephone office, open from 8 am to 6 pm Sunday to Thursday, and from 8 am to 2 pm Friday (closed Saturday).

For discount international phone calls, faxes and telegrams go to Solan Telecom (☎ 522 9424, fax 522 9449) at 13 Frishman St, between HaYarkon and Ben Yehuda streets. It's open 24 hours a day, seven days a week.

The Internet may be accessed at the In Bar (☎ 528 2228, fax 528 2225, email barak@isralink.co.il) at Shlomo Hamelech St, at the junction with HaMelekh George St. Since this place has the virtual monopoly on private Internet access charges are an exorbitant 40NIS an hour or 30NIS for 30 minutes.

Travel Agencies ISSTA (☎ 517 0111) is at 109 Ben Yehuda St on the corner of Ben-Gurion Ave and is open from 8.30 am to 1 pm and 3 to 6 pm Sunday to Thursday, and from 8.30 am to 1 pm Friday, closed Saturday. Possibly the best place to get discounted one-way tickets out of Israel is at Mona Tours (☎ 621 1433, fax 528 3125, email miridave@netvision.net.il) at 25 Bograshov St. A one-way ticket to London at the time of research was selling for US$120. Ask for Dave Cohen.

Bookshops Steimatzky has branches at 71 and 103 Allenby St, in the central bus station, in the Dizengoff and Opera Tower shopping centres, on the corner of Dizengoff

TEL AVIV

PLACES TO STAY
3   HI-Tel Aviv Youth Hostel
15 Home Hostel
20 Dan Panorama

PLACES TO EAT
2   Humous Ashkara
6   Cafe Nordau
14 Bezalel (Felafel) Market

21 Tel Aviv Brewhouse
23 Spaghettim
25 Cafe Noir

OTHER
1   MASH
4   Branch Post Office
5   Police
7   Mazada Tours (Egypt Buses)

8   Egyptian Embassy
9   Central Train Station
10 Australian Embassy
11 Tel Aviv Museum of Art
12 HaShalom Train Station
13 Cinematheque
16 Carmel Market
17 Steimatzky Bookshop
18 Logos Live Music Bar

19 Hassan Beq Mosque
22 Great Synagogue
24 Steimatzky Bookshop
26 Main Post Office
27 Police; Lost & Found
28 International Telephone Office;
    Poste Restante
29 SPNI
30 Central Bus Station

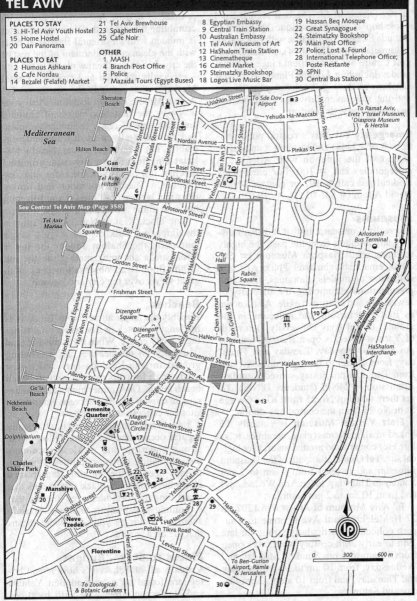

and Frishman Sts and just a few doors along at 109 Dizengoff St. The best second-hand bookshop is Book Boutique at 170 Ben Yehuda St, near the junction with Arlosoroff.

Lametayel (☎ 528 6894), in the Dizengoff Centre has an excellent range of travel guides including Lonely Planet. Here you can browse through books at your leisure and the store even provides cushions and bean bags for your comfort.

Emergency Tel Aviv's central police station (☎ 564 4444) and lost and found office is east of the junction with Allenby; in emergencies call ☎ 100. For emergency medical aid call ☎ 101 or contact Magen David Adom (☎ 546 0111).

Museums

Not really a museum, in that it doesn't display any artefacts from the past, the highly recommended **Diaspora Museum** (☎ 646 2020, email bhwebmaster@bh.org.il) is a collection of models, dioramas, films and presentations chronicling the diversity of Jewish life and culture in exile. Also known as Beit Hatefutsoth, the museum, in the grounds of Tel Aviv University 1km north of Yarkon River, is open from 10 am to 4 pm Sunday, Monday, Tuesday and Thursday, from 10 am to 6 pm Wednesday, and from 9 am to 1 pm Friday, closed Saturday. Admission is 24NIS (students 18NIS). To get there take bus No 25 from King George St or No 27 from the central bus station.

Eretz Y'Israel Museum is actually 11 linked small museums (glass, ceramics, folklore etc) constructed around an archaeological site, Tel Qasile. It's south of the Diaspora Museum and is open from 9 am to 2 pm Sunday to Thursday, to 6 pm on Wednesday) and from 10 am to 2 pm Saturday.

Tel Aviv Museum of Art (☎ 696 1297) at 27 HaMelekh Shaul Ave is home to a superb collection, particularly strong on late 19th to early 20th century works. It's open from 10 am to 6 pm Sunday, Monday and Wednesday, from 10 am to 10 pm Tuesday and Thursday, and from 10 am to 2 pm Friday and Saturday.

Yemenite Quarter

A maze of narrow dusty streets lined with crumbling buildings, the Yemenite Quarter is imbued with an oriental flavour at odds with the clean cut modernism of the rest of the city. It's one of the few places in the city – especially the loud and crowded **Camel Market** – that reminds the visitor of Tel Aviv's Middle Eastern location. Push your way past the first few metres of clothing and footwear to reach the more aromatic and enticing stalls of fresh fruits and vegetables, hot breads and spices. Nearby **Nahalat Binyamin St** is a busy pedestrianised precinct full of fashionable cafes and arty shops. On Tuesday afternoon and Friday the street hosts a craft market and fills with buskers, mime artists and dancers.

One block west of Nahalat Binyamin is the imposing bulk of Tel Aviv's major landmark, the **Shalom Tower**; the lower floors are a shopping mall while the top (30th) floor is an observation deck with great views over the city and beyond.

Beaches

Possibly the major attraction in Tel Aviv is the lengthy stretch of fine white sand fringing the city centre. When the sun is out (and it usually is) the beaches are a strutting ground for the local poseurs and a vast sandy court for pairs playing *matkot*, Israeli beach tennis. On summer nights the beaches remain crowded as they serve as impromptu sites for concerts and discos.

Bear in mind that drowning is a tragically regular occurrence – a combination of the strong undertow and reckless swimmers overestimating their capabilities. It's wise to take heed of the warning flags posted along the beaches: a black flag means that swimming is forbidden; red means that swimming is dangerous and you certainly shouldn't swim by yourself; white means that the area is safe.

Places to Stay – Budget

Virtually all of Tel Aviv's hostels and hotels are found on or around Ben Yehuda and HaYarkon streets, all with locations just minutes from the beaches, popular eating and shopping places and nightspots. The flip side is that a lot of these places, especially in the lower price bracket, tend to be quite noisy, especially if you are in a room facing the street. If serenity is your bag then consider staying in neighbouring Jaffa to the south.

The charge per night for a dorm bed in a Tel Aviv hostel is generally around the 25 to 40NIS mark – exceptions noted below. For slightly less, many places will also let you sleep on the roof. There's no curfew unless noted.

One of the better hostels is *Dizengoff Square Hostel* (☎ 522 5184, fax 522 5181, email info@dizengoffhostel.co.il, 11 Dizengoff Square) offering a great location close to plenty of cheap eating places. Favoured by long-termers, the place has a very friendly atmosphere. Dorms have six or 11 beds with showers and toilets shared between two or three rooms. The hostel also has private rooms at 90NIS per night.

Another popular hostel is the excellent *No 1 Hostel* (☎ 523 7807, email sleeping@inter.net.il, 84 Ben Yehuda St) on the 4th floor and just south of the intersection with Gordon St. Well-organised, the No 1 has an international telephone line and reception can cash travellers cheques and help with cheap flights. There's a kitchen and a lovely conservatory-like common room overlooking the city rooftops. The single-sex dorms have their own bathrooms and there are reductions for longer stays. Reception is open 24 hours.

Gordon Hostel (☎ 522 9870, 2 Gordon St) is on the seafront. There's a kitchen, TV area, rooftop bar and 24 hour cafe-bar on the ground floor. Dorm beds are 32NIS and the hostel is closed between 11 am and 2 pm. While both places are under the same 'Sleep in Israel' management, facilities here are not as flash as the No 1 Hostel and because it is slightly cheaper, it attracts a younger crowd.

New to the scene is *Hayarkon 48 Hostel* (☎ 516 8989, fax 510 3113, 48 HaYarkon St). This converted former school opened in January 1999 and offers pleasant dormitory accommodation and fully self-contained private rooms for 189NIS. Guests rave about the good showers and you also get a free breakfast and a TV and pool room thrown in for good measure.

In the Yemenite Quarter is the rustic *Home Hostel* (☎ 517 6736, 20 Alsheich St) which has reasonable dorms and if there are two of you, a small private room for 70NIS. There are cooking facilities, small courtyard, cheep beer and a free dinner on Friday evenings and a free breakfast on Saturday mornings.

Places to Stay – Mid-Range

Centrally located and offering a bit more luxury than hostels are *Kikar Dizengoff Apartments* (☎ 620 0107, fax 620 0108, email neemanam@netvision.net.il, 4 Dizengoff St). These apartments are ideal for both long and short-term stays and can't be beaten for price and quality. All rooms offer digital phones, cable TV, cooking facilities and are close to restaurants and shops. Check www.inisrael.com/kda for full details and current rates.

Gordon Inn Guest House (☎ 523 8239, fax 523 7419, email sleeping@inter.net.il, 17 Gordon St) is a hybrid hostel/hotel, beautifully kept and good value with singles from US$37 to US$41 and doubles from US$47 to US$52.

A couple of other good but more expensive mid-range options are *Astor Hotel* (☎ 522 3141, 105 HaYarkon St) with singles/doubles from US$73/$88, and the newly renovated *Hotel Metropolitan* (☎ 519 2727, fax 517 2626, email reserve@metrotlv.co.il, 11-15 Trumpeldor St) which has a terrace pool. Singles are US$102 to US$128 and doubles cost US$122 to US$164.

Places to Stay – Top End

Almost all of these places are on HaYarkon St with the beach just a quick shuffle away. Prices range from over US$100 to more than US$350 for a single room and there is quite a wide price difference depending on seasons.

ISRAEL

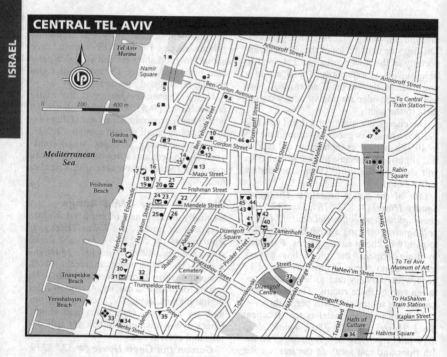

CENTRAL TEL AVIV

Tel Aviv Hilton (☎ 520 2222, fax 522 4111, Independence Park) is also in the North Central area but it compensates by having the best beach access of any hotel and also benefits from its parkland setting. Then again, it is one of Tel Aviv's most expensive.

The density of hotels starts to increase around Namir Square, which is unfortunate as this concrete complex is the most unpleasant public zone in all of Tel Aviv.

To the north of the square is *Carlton Hotel (☎ 520 1818, fax 527 1043, email request@ carlton.co.il, 10 Eliezer Peri St)* and south of the square on HaYarkon St are three virtually indistinguishable establishments: there's *Radisson-Moriah Plaza (☎ 521 6666, fax 527 1065, email radisson-moriah-il@ibm.net, 155 HaYarkon St)*; *Crowne Plaza (☎ 520 1111, fax 520 1122, 145 HaYarkon St)*; and *Ramada Continental (☎ 521 5555, fax 521 5588, email reservation@ramada.co.il, 121*

HaYarkon St). All three are right on the beach and relatively convenient for the central Tel Aviv shopping areas.

One more top end establishment is *Dan Panorama (☎ 519 0190, fax 517 1777, email danhtls@danhotels.co.il, 10 Kaufmann St)* opposite Charles Chlore Park. It is a decent enough hotel but its location on the coastal road to Jaffa makes it awkward to get to by bus (No 10) and just a bit too far from central Tel Aviv to walk on a regular basis.

Places to Eat

Street Food Felafel in Tel Aviv isn't always the best but one guaranteed good place is *Bezalel Market*, near Allenby St and the Yemenite Quarter. The 'felafel market', as it's also known, is no more than two stalls side by side but each has a fantastic array of salads and for 12NIS you are free to stuff your own pitta bread with as much felafel

CENTRAL TEL AVIV

PLACES TO STAY
1   Carlton Hotel
5   Radisson-Moriah Plaza
6   Crowne Plaza
7   Ramada Continental
9   Gordon Hostel
10 Gordon Inn Guest House
13 No 1 Hostel
19 Astor Hotel
32 Hotel Metropolitan
34 Hayarkon 48 Hostel
39 Kikar Dizengoff Apartments;
    24 Hour Laundromat
41 Dizengoff Square Hostel;
    Subway

PLACES TO EAT
18 International Bar
26 Taste of Life
28 Buzz Stop
30 The Chicago
35 Brazilian Sandwich Bar &
    Bakery

42 Derby Bar Restaurant
45 Basta La Pasta

OTHER
2   Ben-Gurion's House
3   Book Boutique
4   ISSTA Student Travel
8   British Council
11 Project 2
12 Kibbutz Hotels
    Reservation Office
14 Supersol Supermarket
15 Meira's Kibbutz &
    Moshav Office
16 Unitours
    (Thomas Cook Agent)
17 French Embassy
20 Arkia Booking Office
    (Domestic Flights)
21 Solan Telecom
22 Uni Wash
    Laundromat
23 Egged Tours

24 Branch Post Office
25 American Express
27 Mona Tours
29 US Embassy
31 Branch Post Office
33 Opera Tower
    Shopping Centre
36 Habima Theatre
37 Lametayel
    Adventure Store &
    Bookshop
38 In Bar Internet Cafe
40 Branch Post Office
43 Steimatzky Bookshop
44 Cameri Theatre;
    Steimatzky Bookshop
46 Change Spot
    (Currency Exchange,
    Phones & Fax)
47 Gan Ha'Ir
    Shopping Centre
48 City Hall
49 Rabin Memorial

and greenery as you can fit in. Otherwise the heaviest concentration of Middle Eastern fast food staples are on the southern stretches of Ben Yehuda and Dizengoff streets.

Snacks Tel Aviv's many cafes exist as centres of gossip and to provide ringside seating for the ongoing pavement carnival. Good or cheap food is not always a priority and the locals tend to fuel themselves on black coffee, croissants and cheesecake.

Cafe Noir (43 Ahad Ha'am) was the hot cafe at the time of research. It attracts a youngish clientele and its interior decor of wood and tile is very conducive to romantic evenings. It is located four blocks south of Sheinken St. *Brazilian Sandwich Bar & Bakery* at the lower end of Ben Yehuda St is a no-nonsense simple sandwich joint that does reasonable quick snacks and sandwiches for around 15NIS.

Close to Dizengoff Square is *Basta la Pasta,* no more than a hole in the wall where your pasta is cooked in front of you. Delicious pasta dishes go for no more than 12NIS. Look for the sign 'Best Italian Pasta to Go'.

For vegetarians the unique vegan tofu-cuisine at *Taste of Life (60 Ben Yehuda St)* is well worth a try. Dishes include vegetable shwarma, vegetarian hot dogs, *tamali, tofulafel,* barbecue twist burgers, cheeses, yoghurts, ice cream and shakes.

Restaurants Israelis in north Tel Aviv head for *Humous Ashkara (☎ 546 4547, 45 Yirmiyahu St)* for what they consider the best humous and fuul in town. The sign is in Hebrew only, so look out for the Coca Cola sign and the tables on the street.

Besides felafel, easily the cheapest eating in Tel Aviv can be found at the few remaining travellers bars of which *Buzz Stop, International Bar* or *MASH* (see Entertainment, later) have constantly changing menus, typically featuring English breakfasts, stir-fries and fish, chips and peas.

Just off Dizengoff Square, *Derby Bar Restaurant (☎ 523 6128, 94 Dizengoff St)* is a popular oriental place with a variety of meat and vegetable dishes and some delicious flavoured rice. A hearty meal here with beer should not set you back more than 40NIS.

Looking a bit like a refugee from South Beach Miami, the puce-painted *The Chicago* (☎ 517 7505, 63 HaYarkon St) near the corner of Trumpeldor St has regular deep pan pizzas for around 55NIS, large pizzas for 70NIS as well as chilli (25NIS) and lasagne (32NIS). There's draught beer and American sports on TV.

Pasta fans should head for *Spaghettim* (☎ 566 4467, 18 Yavne St) one block east of Allenby St. It's spaghetti only but there's a choice of more than 50 sauces – LP researchers have tried about eight and they were all good. It's open from noon to 1 am.

Tel Aviv's poshest bar/restaurant is *Tel Aviv Brewhouse* (☎ 516 8555, 11 Rothschild Ave) just south of Shalom Tower. Here, well-heeled yuppies sip four kinds of designer ales – try the Masters, a strong, dark ale with 6% alcohol – in a cosy copper and wood setting. Their food is predictable beer fare with sausages and sauerkraut being the most popular dish. Beers cost between nine and 23NIS depending on what you order.

Self-Catering For fresh fruit head for Carmel Market. For one-stop shopping there's a convenient *Supersol supermarket* at 79 Ben Yehuda St between Gordon and Mapu streets. It's open Sunday to Thursday from 7 am to midnight, Wednesday and Thursday for 24 hours, and Friday from 7 am to 3 pm; closed Saturday.

Entertainment

There's a collection of travellers bars scattered around the city but their existence is often almost ephemeral and keeping track of what's hot and what's not (or no more) is a tricky job. Possibly Tel Aviv's best travellers bar is *Buzz Stop*, a 24-hour, seven-day-a-week joint popular with dawn watchers. It's next to Planet Hollywood on the esplanade, in the lower half of the Yamit Park Plaza complex and is in the middle of all the activity.

Tel Aviv's oldest travellers bar is *MASH*, which stands for More Alcohol Served Here, up at 275 Dizengoff St in the North Central area. It's a haunt of the city's long-stay community.

On HaYarkon St, just north of the junction with Frishman St, *International Bar* is another really popular bar with a terrace out the back overlooking the seafront, a couple of pool tables and satellite TV for football fans. The barbed wire ringed view over the tatty carpark is a bit off-putting, but the sea is no more than 150m beyond that.

For live music visit *Logos*, which has local blues, R&B and rock bands playing every night at about 10 pm. It's at 8 HaShomer, a sidestreet running off Nahalat Binyamin St to HaCarmel St.

Anyone seriously interested in good cinema should go to *Cinematheque* (☎ 691 7181) part of a membership chain which shows a variety of classics, avant-garde, new wave, and off-beat movies – it's at 1 Ha'Arba'a St; follow Dizengoff St south to the junction with Ibn Gvirol St. Continue south on Ibn Gvirol, forking left onto Carlibach St and the Cinematheque will be visible to your left across a triangular piazza. During summer check to see if free films are being screened at night on the beach, near Allenby St.

Performances at *Cameri Theatre* at 101 Dizengoff St (entrance on Frishman St) are simultaneously translated into English on Tuesday. At *Habima Theatre* (on Habima Square), home of Israel's national theatre group, performances on Thursday have simultaneous English-language translation.

Getting There & Away

Air Arkia flights depart from the Sde Dov airport, north of Yarkon River. These connect directly with Eilat (several flights daily; US$80 one way) and Rosh Pina in Upper Galilee, with further connections to Haifa and Jerusalem. There are no flights on Saturday. Arkia's city offices (☎ 699 2222) are at 11 Frishman St.

Bus Doubling as a multistorey shopping centre, Tel Aviv's central bus station is a mammoth complex in which, if unlucky, you could easily spend the first few days of your visit trying to find the way out. Outgoing intercity buses depart from the 6th floor, where there's also an efficient if sullenly staffed information point. Suburban and city buses depart from the 4th floor but these are not so well signposted and you'll need to ask to find the correct bay.

There are buses to Jerusalem (17NIS, one hour) departing every 10 minutes; to Haifa (22NIS; 1½ hours) every 15 to 20 minutes; and to Eilat (37NIS, five hours) hourly between 6.30 am and 5 pm, plus an overnight service departing at 12.30 am.

Tour operators provide coach services from Tel Aviv. They travel nonstop to Cairo via the border at Rafah (where there is a change of bus) in the Gaza Strip. The journey takes roughly 10 hours and a ticket from Tel Aviv is about 90NIS (US$30) one way or 135NIS (US$45) return. To that has to be added an Israeli departure tax of 90NIS (US$30), payable usually to the bus company, and an Egyptian entry tax of E£7 (US$2.50). You can change money at the border.

There is one operator in Tel Aviv; Mazada Tours (☎ 03-544 4454), 141 Ibn Gvirol St, has daily buses departing at 9 am, arriving in Cairo at 7 pm. Also Tuesday, Thursday and Sunday overnight buses departing 8.30 pm arriving 7 am next morning.

There is also a second bus station in Tel Aviv, the Arlosoroff terminal, up by the central train station in the north-east part of town. One or two services from Jerusalem and Haifa finish up here rather than the central bus station. To get into town walk over to the bus stands on the main road and catch bus No 61 which runs down Arlosoroff St and then south along Dizengoff and King George Sts to Allenby St.

Train Tel Aviv now has one main (central) train station and one suburban stop, HaShalom on the southern line to Rehovot. The main train station (☎ 693 7515 for information) serves Haifa (19.50NIS, one to 1¼ hours) and Nahariya (30NIS, 1½ to two hours) up near the Lebanese border, both

via Netanya, with trains leaving virtually every hour between 6 am and 8 pm. The main train station is at the junction of Haifa Rd, Arlosoroff St and Petah Tikva Rd – take bus Nos 61 or 62 north up Dizengoff St. Take bus No 51 (stand 51) from the Central bus station and alight just before the Dizengoff interchange from where it's a five minute signposted walk to the train station.

Service Taxis Service taxis operate from outside the central bus station (where bus Nos 4 and 5 alight) to the suburbs, Jerusalem (25NIS) and Haifa (20NIS). On Saturday they leave from HaHashmal St, east of the bottom of Allenby St and cost about an extra 20%.

Getting Around
The Airport Bus No 222 runs up Ha-Yarkon St to the airport, with departures at 45 minute intervals between 4 am and midnight (last bus Friday 6.45 pm; first bus Saturday at noon). There are timetables posted at the stops. The city-airport fare is 15NIS and the journey takes about 45 minutes to one hour.

Bus Bus No 4 goes from the central bus station via Allenby, Ben Yehuda and north Dizengoff streets to the Reading terminal, north of Yarkon River, passing most of the city centre hostels along the way; bus No 5 goes from the central bus station, along Allenby St, up Rothschild Ave, along Dizengoff St, Nordau Ave, Ibn Gvirol St, Pinkas St, Weizmann St and Yehuda HaMaccabi St and then back – useful for the HI hostel, the Egyptian embassy, Habima Square and the Dizengoff St hostels.

JAFFA
Founded, according to the Old Testament, by Japheth, in the wake of the famed flood that shot his father Noah to fame, Jaffa came to prominence as a port during the time of Solomon. Now swallowed up by Tel Aviv, the Jaffa (Yafo in Hebrew) of today exists largely as a quaint harbourside setting for an expensive seafood meal.

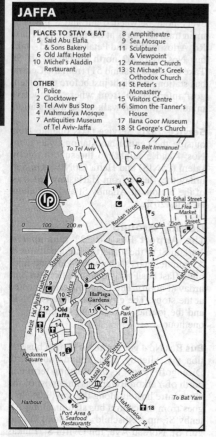

JAFFA

PLACES TO STAY & EAT
5 Said Abu Elafia
& Sons Bakery
6 Old Jaffa Hostel
10 Michel's Aladdin
Restaurant

OTHER
1 Police
2 Clocktower
3 Tel Aviv Bus Stop
4 Mahmudiya Mosque
7 Antiquities Museum
of Tel Aviv-Jaffa
8 Amphitheatre
9 Sea Mosque
11 Sculpture
& Viewpoint
12 Armenian Church
13 St Michael's Greek
Orthodox Church
14 St Peter's
Monastery
15 Visitors Centre
16 Simon the Tanner's
House
17 Ilana Goor Museum
18 St George's Church

To Tel Aviv
To Beit Immanuel
Beit Eshal Street
Flea
Market
Rodan Street
Olei Zion Street
Mifraz Shlomo Street
Retzif Ha' Aliyah Hashniya Street
Yefet Street
Rabbi Pinas St
HaPisga Gardens
Old Jaffa
Car Park
Kedumim Square
Mazal Dagim Street
Pasteur Street
Harbour
HaMigdalor St
To Bat Yam
Port Area &
Seafood
Restaurants

Every Wednesday, a free three hour guided walking tour of Old Jaffa departs from the clocktower at 9 am.

Things to See & Do

The central attraction is **Old Jaffa**, an area of narrow twisting alleys, home to galleries, art studios and a variety of unnecessary shops. The **Antiquities Museum of Tel-Aviv-Jaffa** at 10 Mifraz Shlomo St was originally a Turkish administrative and detention centre but is now home to a display of local ar-

chaeological discoveries. It's open Sunday to Thursday from 9 am to 2 pm (to 6 pm on Wednesday), and Saturday from 10 am to 2 pm; closed Friday. The grassy knoll behind the museum, known as **HaPisga Gardens**, has a small amphitheatre with a panorama of the Tel Aviv seafront as its backdrop.

A footbridge connects the gardens to **Kedumim Square** (Kikar Kedumim), Old Jaffa's reconstructed centre, ringed by restaurants, clubs and galleries but dominated by the bulk of orange-painted **St Peter's Monastery**. In a chamber underneath the square is the well-designed **Visitors Centre** where you can view partially excavated remains from the Hellenistic and Roman era and watch a six minute film on Jaffa. You can also pick up an informative free map down here. It's open daily from 9 am to 10 pm (2 pm on Friday).

Close to the Ottoman **clocktower**, east of Yefet St, is the flea market, which has a decent reputation for antiques and interesting oriental bits and pieces.

Places to Stay

A pleasant Israeli couple have converted a beautiful old Turkish house into the lovely *Old Jaffa Hostel (☎ 682 2370, fax 682 2316, email ojhostel@shani.net)*. There's a large bar/common room and airy dorms complete with armchairs and tables. A dorm bed is 35NIS while private doubles are 100NIS. There's also the option of taking a mattress on the roof for 25NIS. The hostel is in the flea market area at 8 Olei Zion St although the entrance is a little difficult to find because it's actually from Ami'ad St.

Places to Eat

Almost reason alone to visit Jaffa is *Said Abu Elafia & Sons*, a bakery at 7 Yefet St. It has become near legendary in Israel. The main attraction is their version of pizza, prepared in the traditional Arab manner of cracking a couple of eggs on top of pitta bread, stirring in tomato, cheese and olives and baking it in the oven.

For Israelis, the main culinary attraction in Jaffa is fish and both Mifraz Shlomo St and the port area have numerous outdoor restaurants, some of which also serve meat grilled on the fire. Try **Michel's Aladdin** *(5 Mifraz Shlomo St)* if only for the views from its terrace. The restaurant is in an 800 year old building that was originally a *hammam* (bathhouse). Most of the dishes are priced in the 40 to 70NIS range but there are things like blintzes at 34NIS.

Getting There & Away

From the centre of Tel Aviv it's a pleasant 2.5km stroll along the seafront to Old Jaffa. If you don't fancy walking then catch bus No 10 from Ben Yehuda St, bus No 18 from Dizengoff St, or bus Nos 18 or 25 from Allenby St. In reverse, bus No 10 for Ben Yehuda St departs from the clocktower.

NETANYA

As a sun and sand resort we would recommend francophile Netanya over more popular Eilat. It has 11km of **free beaches**, which are some of the best in the country (beware of the undertow) and a lively pedestrianised main street lined with patisseries. The local tourist information office (☎ 882 7286, fax 884 1348) is housed in a small kiosk-like building on the south-western corner of Ha'Atzmaut Square, open from 8.30 am to 4 pm Sunday to Thursday, and from 9 am to noon Friday, closed Saturday.

Places to Stay

Unfortunately budget accommodation is severely limited to the **Atzmaut Hostel** *(☎ 862 1315, fax 882 2562)*, occupying a prime position right on the south side of seafront Ha'Atzmaut Square. The rooms are air-con, clean and comfortable but a little on the expensive side at US$10 per person. The similarly pricey alternative is **Hotel Orit** *(☎ 861 6818, 21 Chen St)*, a guesthouse run by friendly Swedish Christians. Singles are 133NIS and doubles are 200NIS per person, breakfast included. It's often full with parties of Scandinavians so book ahead.

Getting There & Away

There are buses about every 15 minutes to and from Tel Aviv (10NIS, 30 minutes) and

services to Haifa (17NIS, one hour) and Jerusalem about every 30 minutes. To reach Caesarea, Megiddo, Nazareth or Tiberias, take a bus from Netanya to Hadera and change there.

HAIFA

While Jerusalem is swathed in historical mystique and Tel Aviv buzzes with unbounded credit card hedonism, Haifa, Israel's third largest city, contents itself with being the solid cornerstone of the country's technological industry. However, clinging to the wooded slopes of Mt Carmel, Haifa is not an unattractive place and the upper sections of the city include some pleasant residential areas and promenades with superb panoramic views north along the coastline. There are quite a few destinations nearby that are worth a brief visit and as the regional transport hub, Haifa makes a convenient base for some good day trips.

The Haifa Tourism Development Association organises a free guided walking tour every Saturday at 10 am. Meet at the signposted observation point on the corner of Sha'ar HaLevenon and Ye'fe Nof streets up in Carmel Central.

Orientation

Haifa is divided into three tiers ascending the slope of Mt Carmel. Whether you arrive by bus, train or boat, the first place you will see is the port area, also known as Downtown. Uphill is Hadar; most shops, businesses, eating places and hotels are here. The Carmel district occupies the higher slopes of the city, where exclusive residences benefit from cool breezes and magnificent views. Carmel Central, focused on HaNassi Ave, is a small commercial district with a cluster of bars and eating places all charging fittingly high-altitude prices.

Information

Tourist Offices Haifa's main government-run tourist information office (☎ 853 5606, fax 853 5610, email haifa5@netvision.net.il) is at 48 Ben-Gurion Ave below the Baha'i Gardens near the German Colony. It's open

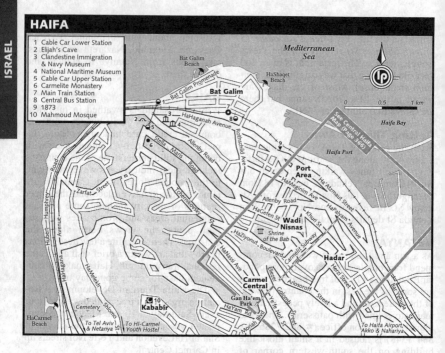

HAIFA

1 Cable Car Lower Station
2 Elijah's Cave
3 Clandestine Immigration
   & Navy Museum
4 National Maritime Museum
5 Cable Car Upper Station
6 Carmelite Monastery
7 Main Train Station
8 Central Bus Station
9 1873
10 Mahmoud Mosque

from 8 am to 6 pm Sunday to Thursday, from 9 am to 1 pm Friday and closed on Saturday. There's also a second government-run tourist information office at the port (☎ 864 5692), usually open when ferries and cruise ships arrive.

In addition, Haifa has two municipality-run tourist information offices: one at the central bus station (☎ 851 2208), open from 9.30 am to 5 pm Sunday to Thursday, from 9.30 am to 2 pm Friday, closed Saturday; another in the City Hall (☎ 835 6200) at 14 Hassan Shukri St, open from 8 am to 1 pm Sunday to Friday, closed Saturday. There is also a pre-recorded, English 'What's On' line (☎ 837 4253).

Money Banks are easily found on Ha'Atzmaut St in the port area and in Hadar on and around HaNevi'im St. All banks are closed on Saturday and Monday, and on Wednes-

day and Friday afternoons. If you're caught short of shekels out of banking hours then Haifa's port area is a popular haunt for black marketeers. While they offer a better rate than the banks they take cash only and there's a definite risk of being ripped off.

Post & Communications The main post office, poste restante and international telephones are at 19 HaPalyam Ave in the port area. It's open from 8 am to 8 pm Sunday to Thursday, from 8 am to 2 pm Friday and is closed on Saturday.

Things to See & Do
Among the beautifully manicured and dizzily sloped Persian Gardens, Haifa's most impressive attraction is the golden-domed **Shrine of the Bab**. This is one of the two main spiritual centres of the Baha'i faith. Completed in 1953, the shrine com-

bines the style and proportions of European architecture with designs inspired by the orient. To get to the shrine take bus No 22 from the central bus station; Nos 23, 25 and 26 from HaNevi'im or Herzl streets (in Hadar) also stop outside. The shrine is open from 9 am to noon daily. Admission is free. Remove your shoes before entering and don't wear shorts or bare your shoulders. The gardens remain open until 5 pm.

Higher up the hill, 200m beyond the shrine, is **Sculpture Garden** (Gan HaPesalim), a small park containing bronze sculptures.

Haifa Museum at 26 Shabtai Levi St is ostensibly three museums in one – ancient art, modern art, and music and ethnology – however the combined displays would hardly fill a telephone kiosk and there's more bare wall here than in China. It's open from 10 am to 4 pm Sunday, Monday, Wednesday and Thursday, from 4 to 7 pm Tuesday, from 10 am to 1 pm on Friday and holidays and from 10 am to 2 pm Saturday. Admission is 20NIS (15NIS students). The same ticket admits you to the **National Maritime Museum** at 198 Allenby Rd, west of the bus station, which presents a rather dry history of shipping in the Mediterranean area. It's open from 10 am to 4 pm Sunday to Thursday, and from 10 am to 1 pm Saturday.

Much more interesting is the neighbouring **Clandestine Immigration & Navy Museum** (☎ 853 6249) which deals with the successes and failures of the Zionists' illegal attempts to infiltrate into British blockaded Palestine in the 1930s and 40s. Opening hours are from 9 am to 4 pm Sunday to Thursday, and from 9 am to 1 pm Friday. Admission is 5NIS.

The **Carmelite monastery and church** was originally established in the late 12th century by the Crusaders but the present buildings date from 1836. It's worth visiting the church to view the beautiful painted ceiling. From the monastery a **cable car** descends to the Bat Galim Promenade below, beside the maritime museum and a small grotto known as **Elijah's Cave**. This is where the prophet Elijah is believed to have hidden from King Ahab and Queen Jezebel after he slew the 450 priests of Ba'al (I Kings:17-19). Holy to all three of the major monotheistic faiths, the cave is usually crammed full of praying Jews while outside the garden is a favourite picnic spot for local Christian Arabs.

Places to Stay – Budget

Hostels There's not much to choose from and most travellers end up at the pleasant and friendly **Bethel Hostel** (☎ 852 1110, 40 HaGefen St). There are no private rooms (separate male and female dorms; US$12 per night) nor a kitchen, but there is a lounge with tea and coffee-making facilities, a snack bar open for breakfast and a free evening meal on Friday.

An alternative is the peaceful **St Charles Hospice** (☎ 855 3705, fax 851 4919) in the port area, which is owned by the Latin Patriarchate and run by the Rosary Sisters. Singles/doubles cost US$30/50 with breakfast. A third option is **HI-Carmel Youth Hostel** (☎ 853 1944, fax 853 2516) but it's very inconveniently located on the southwestern approach to the city. Bus No 43 goes there from the central bus station about every hour.

Places to Stay – Mid-Range

Up in Carmel Central **Beit Shalom Guesthouse** (☎ 837 7481, fax 837 2443, 110 HaNassi Ave) is a comfortable German Protestant-run 'evangelical guesthouse', open to all (although, in summer at least, there's a minimum three night stay policy). It provides good hotel-style facilities with singles/doubles at US$50/70. You need to book ahead as it's often full.

Places to Eat

Street Food Haifa's street food is cheap, delicious and easily available. In particular, head for the HaNevi'im St end of HeHalutz St where some of the country's best felafel and shwarma is sold, alongside bakeries producing sweet pastries, ring doughnuts, sticky buns and other delights.

The other good felafel area, convenient to Bethel Hostel, is Allenby Rd, east of

ISRAEL

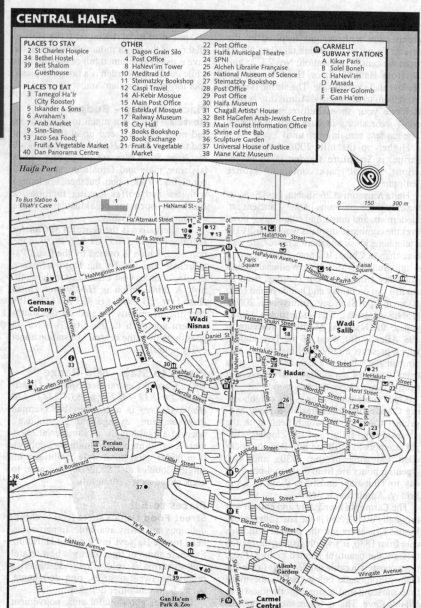

CENTRAL HAIFA

PLACES TO STAY
2 St Charles Hospice
34 Bethel Hostel
39 Beit Shalom
     Guesthouse

PLACES TO EAT
3 Tarnegol Ha'Ir
    (City Rooster)
5 Iskander & Sons
6 Avraham's
7 Arab Market
9 Sinn-Sinn
13 Jaco Sea Food;
     Fruit & Vegetable Market
40 Dan Panorama Centre

OTHER
1 Dagon Grain Silo
4 Post Office
8 HaNevi'im Tower
10 Meditrad Ltd
11 Steimatzky Bookshop
12 Caspi Travel
14 Al-Kebir Mosque
15 Main Post Office
16 Esteklayl Mosque
17 Railway Museum
18 City Hall
19 Books Bookshop
20 Book Exchange
21 Fruit & Vegetable
     Market

22 Post Office
23 Haifa Municipal Theatre
24 SPNI
25 Alcheh Librairie Française
26 National Museum of Science
27 Steimatzky Bookshop
28 Post Office
29 Post Office
30 Haifa Museum
31 Chagall Artists' House
32 Beit HaGefen Arab-Jewish Centre
33 Main Tourist Information Office
35 Shrine of the Bab
36 Sculpture Garden
37 Universal House of Justice
38 Mane Katz Museum

**Ⓜ CARMELIT
SUBWAY STATIONS**
A Kikar Paris
B Solel Boneh
C HaNevi'im
D Masada
E Eliezer Golomb
F Gan Ha'em

Haifa Port

To Bus Station &
Elijah's Cave

0   150   300 m

HaNamal St
Ha'Atzmaut Street
Jaffa Street
Sha'ar Palmer St
Elyahu St
HaNamal St
Natanson Street
Paris
Square
HaPalyam Avenue
Faisal
Square
Hammam al-Pasha St

**German
Colony**

HaMeginim Avenue
Ben-Gurion Avenue
Allenby Road
Khuri Street
HaZiyonut Boulevard
Wadi
Nisnas
Daniel St
Hassan Shukri Street
HeHalutz Street
Shmaryahu Levin St
HaNevi'im Street
**Wadi
Salib**
Shapira Street
Yehiel Street
Faisal Street

Shabtai Levi Street
Herzlia Street
Hadar
Sirkin Street
HeHalutz Street
Nordau Street
Herzl Street
Yerushalayim Street
Pevsner Street
Hillel Street
Hayam St
Balfour Street

Abbas Street
**Persian
Gardens**

HaGefen Street
HaZiyonut Boulevard
Hillel Street
Masada Street
Arlosoroff Street
Hess Street

Eliezer Golomb Street

Ye'fe Nof Street
HaNassi Avenue
Sha'ar HaLevanon St
Allenby
Gardens
Ye'fe Nof Street
Wingate Avenue

Gan Ha'em
Park & Zoo
**Carmel
Central**

Ben-Gurion Ave. For the connoisseurs *Avraham's* (☎ 852 5029, 36 Allenby Rd) proclaims itself to be the 'King of Felafel'.

Snacks There are several pleasant *konditereis* (pastry shops and cafes combined) around Hadar, many of them on Nordau St. The best coffee in town is served at a little cafe/bar on HaNevi'im St, across from the post office.

A self-service cafeteria on the 1st floor of the *Dan Panorama Centre*, adjacent to the hotel of the same name, provides some of the cheapest eating in Carmel with an odd selection ranging from burgers (from 10NIS) to Chinese stir-fry (20 to 25NIS). Carmel Central has no shortage of fashionable cafes but to avoid choking finish your food before requesting the bill.

Restaurants The Egged self-service *restaurant* at the central bus station provides the best value for money and there are several fast-food outlets around the precinct too. Around Paris Square, near the market, there are a couple of cheap places that do soups, humous, grilled meats and offal. In the Wadi Nisnas area *Iskander & Sons* (170 HaZiyonut St) has more of the same with dishes around the 20 to 25NIS mark and it's open on Saturday.

Tarnegol Ha'Ir (☎ 851 7413, 17 Ben-Gurion Ave) is an excellent chicken restaurant. The sign is in Hebrew only but just look for a frontage adorned with big red chickens. Prices for entrees are in the 25 to 30NIS range. The place is open from 11.30 am to midnight.

Sinn-Sinn (☎ 867 6161, 28 Jaffa Rd) is a reasonable Chinese restaurant which does a special set meal of appetiser, soup, main dish and rice for 31NIS. It's open daily from noon to 10 pm.

Jaco Sea Food (☎ 862 6639, 12 HaDekalim St) is a famous seafood restaurant and a bit of a Haifa institution. The seedy neighbourhood belies the establishment's culinary excellence. It's open from noon to 11 pm from Sunday to Thursday and closes earlier on Friday and Saturday.

1873 (☎ 853 2211, 102 Jaffa St) is Haifa's best restaurant with a warm and welcoming atmosphere. Housed in an old building dating back to 1873 (hence the name) the fare is classic European. It's open from noon to 3 pm and 7.30 pm to 11 pm from Sunday to Thursday with the usual restricted hours on the Shabbat. A decent feed for two will set you back about 350NIS.

Self-Catering For fruit and vegetables, shop at the great little market occupying a couple of alleys between Ha'Atzmaut St and Jaffa Rd down in the port area. For some of the country's best felafel and shwarma (and bakeries) head for the HaNevi'im end of HeHalutz St in Hadar.

Entertainment

Haifa is not renowned for entertainment but pick up a copy of the free leaflet *Events in the Haifa & Northern Region* from the tourist office or dial ☎ 837 4253 and you might find something going on.

Getting There & Away

Air Arkia, the Israeli domestic airline, flies in and out of the airport in the industrial zone east of Haifa. Flights connect directly with Eilat (US$94) with further connections to Tel Aviv and Jerusalem. Arkia's city office (☎ 864 3371) is at 80 Ha'Atzmaut St in the port area.

Bus The central bus station, on HaHaganah Ave in the Bat Galim neighbourhood of the port area, has intercity buses arriving and departing on the north side, and local buses operating from the south side.

Buses depart every 20 minutes for Tel Aviv (22NIS, 1½ hours) while there's an hourly service to Jerusalem (34NIS, two hours), with extra buses at peak times. Heading north, bus Nos 271 and 272 (express) go to Nahariya (13.50NIS, 45 to 70 minutes) via Akko, and bus Nos 251 and 252 (express) go to Akko only (10NIS, 30 to 50 minutes).

Train Haifa has three train stations but the one to use is the main station at Bat Galim, adjacent to the central bus station and reached through an underground passage next to bus platform 34. Timetables are given in English for the hourly trains south, via Netanya, to Tel Aviv (19.50NIS) and north, via Akko, to Nahariya (11NIS).

Ferry For trips to Athens, Crete and Cyprus, check out Caspi Travel (☎ 867 4444, fax 866 1958) at 76 Ha'Atzmaut St, or A Rosenfeld Shipping Ltd (☎ 861 3670, fax 853 3264) at 104 Ha'Atzmaut St. See the Sea & River section in the Getting There & Away chapter at the beginning of this book for full details.

Getting Around

Haifa has Israel's only subway system, the Carmelit, which runs from Paris Square in the port area through Hadar and up to Carmel Central – it saves a lot of legwork. A single ticket costs 4.30NIS.

DRUZE VILLAGES

The dusty Druze villages of **Isfiya** and **Daliyat al-Karmel**, on the slopes of Mt Carmel, are a popular attraction for both foreign visitors and Israelis who come to shop at the high-street bazaar (the mix of imported Indian clothing and trinkets on offer is unlikely to hold much appeal for the well-travelled). While there isn't much to see here, a visit does provide an opportunity to observe and possibly meet the Druze, a people that have a reputation for being extremely friendly and hospitable.

The Druze villages are a half-day trip from Haifa. Bus No 192 runs from Haifa's central bus station, via Herzl St, Sunday to Friday, but there are only two or three departures a day – and all are in the afternoon. It's much better to take a service taxi; they leave continually all day until about 5 pm from Eliyahu St, between Paris Square and Ha'Atzmaut St in the port area. They take about half the time of the bus and at 10NIS are no more expensive.

CAESAREA

One of the country's premier archaeological sites, Caesarea is also a fast developing coastal resort with commercialisation continuing apace with the excavations. It was originally a port founded by Herod the Great and the impressive remains are spread along a 3km stretch of the Mediterranean coast. The central attraction is a walled **Crusader city** with citadel and harbour. North, beyond the walls, littered across the beach are the skeletons of the **Roman aqueducts**, while to the south is a **Roman amphitheatre**, reconstructed as a modern-day venue for concerts.

There is a free beach south of the amphitheatre but take heed of any 'No Bathing' signs – they indicate waters dangerously polluted by the factory of the nearby kibbutz.

Places to Stay

Most people visit Caesarea as a day trip from either Tel Aviv or Haifa as accommodation here is expensive – the neighbouring *Kibbutz Sdot Yam (☎ 06-636 2211)* charges US$56/82 for air-con singles/doubles. Free camping on the beach is possible but beware, theft is common.

Getting There & Away

From Haifa or Tel Aviv and Netanya take any bus going along the coastal road to Hadera. You then have two choices: you can get off at Hadera bus station and hope for a reasonable connection with the No 76 bus which goes to Caesarea; alternatively, you can jump off the bus at the Caesarea intersection and make the 3.5km hike to the excavations.

BEIT SHE'ARIM

About 19km south-east of Haifa, the archaeological site of Beit She'arim features a network of burial caves and a few ruins from the 2nd century. Get there on bus No 338 from Haifa to Kiryat Tivon.

AKKO

Surpassing even Jerusalem, there is no city in Israel more timeless than Akko, a stone fortress city by the sea. The town has had an exceptionally long and varied history under Alexander the Great, the Egyptians and the

Romans but it came to prominence as the Crusader city of Acre. It was a hotbed of Arab hostility towards Jewish immigration in the 1930s but in the end the Jews more or less left Old Akko to the Arabs, preferring to develop their own new town outside the city walls. A fortuitous result as Akko has been passed over for development and investment and while every other place in Israel is busy packaging up its heritage for the tourist buck, Akko soldiers on oblivious, with families not artists in its houses,

household goods not souvenirs in the souq and the fish on the quay in nets and buckets not white wine sauce.

Orientation & Information

From the bus station it's a short walk south to Old Akko; turn left as you leave the station, walk one block to the traffic lights and turn right onto Ben Ami St. After walking through the pedestrianised shopping precinct, turn left onto Weizmann St and you'll see the city walls ahead.

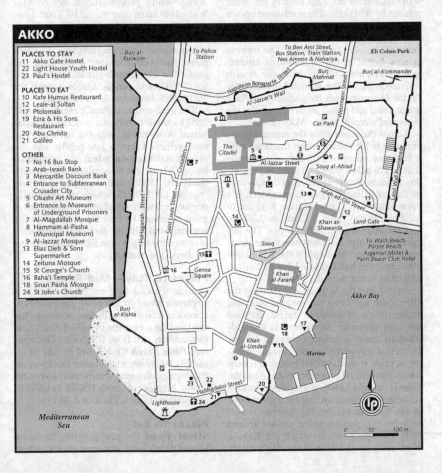

AKKO

PLACES TO STAY
11 Akko Gate Hostel
22 Light House Youth Hostel
23 Paul's Hostel

PLACES TO EAT
10 Kafe Humus Restaurant
12 Leale-al Sultan
19 Ezra & His Sons Restaurant
20 Abu Christo
21 Galileo

OTHER
1 No 16 Bus Stop
2 Arab-Israeli Bank
3 Mercantile Discount Bank
4 Entrance to Subterranean Crusader City
5 Okashi Art Museum
6 Entrance to Museum of Underground Prisoners
7 Al-Magdallah Mosque
8 Hammam al-Pasha (Municipal Museum)
9 Al-Jazzar Mosque
13 Elias Dieb & Sons Supermarket
14 Zeituna Mosque
15 St George's Church
16 Baha'i Temple
18 Sinan Pasha Mosque
24 St John's Church

The ticket office at the subterranean Crusader city (☎ 991 1764) acts as an information bureau, open from 9 am to 6 pm Sunday to Thursday, from 8.30 am to 2.30 pm Friday, and from 9 am to 6 pm Saturday.

Old Akko

Enter through walls built by Ahmed Pasha al-Jazzar in 1799 – today serving as a very physical division between the predominantly Arab Old Akko and the sprawl of the modern Jewish town to the north. The sea walls date from the 12th century but were refaced by Al-Jazzar. The north-west corner of Old Akko is secured by a fortress built, also by the ubiquitous Al-Jazzar, on 13th century Crusader foundations. The fortress is now home to the **Museum of Underground Prisoners,** dedicated to the Jewish resistance during the British Mandate. **Al-Jazzar Mosque,** with its distinctly Turkish green dome and pencil minaret, provides the dominant element on the Akko skyline.

Across the street from the mosque is the entrance to the **subterranean Crusader city,** a haunting series of echoing vaulted halls that lie 8m below the street level of present-day Akko and were at one time the quarters of the crusading Knights Hospitallers. It's open Sunday to Thursday from 8.30 am to 6.30 pm, Friday from 8.30 am to 2.30 pm and Saturday from 9 am to 6 pm. The admission cost also includes entry to the **Hammam al-Pasha** (also called the Municipal Museum), the bathhouse Al-Jazzar built in 1780 and in use until the 1940s.

As you exit the bathhouse, following the alley south will bring you into the **souq** and another slice of authentic orient. Beyond the souq, down by the harbour is **Khan al-Umdan,** once a grand caravanserai (or khan) that served the camel caravans bringing in grain from the hinterland, and is now Akko's unofficial soccer stadium. Atop the khan is an ugly Ottoman **clocktower** which you can sometimes ascend for a great view of the **harbour** below. The harbour is still very much in service and if you are around early enough you can watch the fishing boats chug in and offload the day's catch.

Throughout the day and until well after sundown, the *Akko Princess* departs regularly from the end of the breakwater and makes a 20 minute cruise around the walls.

Places to Stay – Budget

Akko has only three accommodation options in the old town. *Akko Gate Hostel* (☎ 991 0410, fax 981 5530) is a reasonable kind of place and offers more creature comforts than Paul's Hostel. The hostel is next to the Land Gate on Salah ad-Din St. Dorm beds are 30NIS while private rooms are 90NIS. Walied has taken over the old HI Youth Hostel and has renamed it **Light House Youth Hostel** (☎ 981 5530, fax 991 1982). This former mansion on the sea front near the lighthouse has been extensively renovated and now offers dorms beds (six to 10 per room) for 25NIS and single/double rooms for 70/100NIS. Breakfast is not included.

The third option is *Paul's Hostel* (☎ 991 2857) a small family-run concern in a converted Arab house near the harbour. The management keeps a low profile and the place has the laid-back feel of a communal house. There are two mixed dormitories (beds are 25NIS) and a couple of private 'rooms' for 120NIS, which are essentially dormitories with a double bed thrown in for good measure. To find the place go to the souvenir stall with the dark blue Kodak-emblazoned awning by the lighthouse and ask for Jerry, the manager.

Places to Stay – Mid-Range

Outside the Old City on Purple Beach is *Argaman Motel* (☎ 991 6691, fax 991 6690) a modern complex with free access to the sand and the great view of walled Akko. Singles/doubles cost from US$50/70. The adjacent *Palm Beach Club Hotel* (☎ 981 5815, fax 991 0434) has much better facilities, including a pool, sauna, tennis court and water sports. Singles cost from US$91 to US$116 and doubles from US$120 to US$155.

Places to Eat

Street Food For cheap eating there are several felafel and shwarma places around the junction of Salah ad-Din and Al-Jazzar streets.

Snacks For an after dinner smoke and a coffee, seek out *Leale-al Sultan* coffee shop inside Khan as-Shawarda. Here, mainly local youths sip cardamom coffee and suck on *narghiles* in this rather trendy new establishment.

Restaurants The romance of a waterfront moonlit meal means that the restaurants around the lighthouse and the harbour are easily the most popular venues for sit-down dining. Most of these places are open daily from 11 am to about midnight. Fish is the obvious thing to order but despite the quantities hauled in every morning it's still extremely expensive, clocking in at a minimum 35NIS on most menus.

The best dishes are served at *Abu Christo* (☎ 991 0065) but this is also one of the most pricey places; expect to pay around 45NIS per person whatever you order. An alternative is *Galileo* (☎ 991 4620, 176/11 HaMigdalor St) built into the sea wall almost opposite the Light House Youth Hostel.

Ezra & His Sons Restaurant and the adjacent *Ptolomais* (☎ 991 6112) on the harbour both have a more laid-back and cosy ambience, but 'plastic fantastic' furniture rules and the food, while reasonably priced (30 to 40NIS for meat dishes, more for fish) and filling, is generally unspectacular.

Self-Catering If you've got the use of a kitchen then supplies can be bought at *Elias Dieb & Sons* (no English sign) a great little cave-like supermarket on Salah ad-Din St opposite Souq al-Abiad.

Getting There & Away
Departing frequently, bus Nos 252 and 272 connect Akko with Haifa (8NIS, 30 to 50 minutes) as do bus Nos 251 and 271, but these are slower services. Bus Nos 270, 271 and 272 (express) run north to Nahariya (7NIS, 15 to 25 minutes). There are also buses about every 30 minutes to and from Safed. You can also catch one of 10 trains

daily heading north to Nahariya or south to Haifa and Tel Aviv.

NAHARIYA
One of Israel's quietest seaside resorts, Nahariya, the definitive one-street town, seems to exist in a perpetual state of Shabbat. The town's appeal – if it can be said to have any – lies solely in its beaches, although there is also an uninteresting Canaanite temple and a dull museum. The local tourist office is on the ground floor of the municipality building, just west of the bus station on HaGa'aton Blvd – maybe they can whip up some enthusiasm for the place.

Bus Nos 270, 271 and 272 (express) run to Akko (7NIS, 15 to 25 minutes), with the 271 and 272 services continuing to Haifa (10.50NIS, 45 to 70 minutes). Departures are every 20 minutes until 10.30 pm.

AROUND NAHARIYA
Rosh HaNikra
On the sensitive Israel-Lebanon border (photography could be risky), carved by the sea into the base of tall white cliffs, this series of caves was enlarged by the British for a railway and by the Israelis to improve access for visitors. The road up from Nahariya (10km to the south) halts at an observation point/tourist centre (☎ 04-985 7109) from where the only practical way to reach the caves is by cable car. The cars operate from 8.30 am to 6 pm Sunday to Thursday, and from 8.30 am to 4 pm Friday. The 30NIS fare (26NIS) is an admitted rip-off, but there is no other way down to the caves.

Bus Nos 20 and 22 from Nahariya go direct to Rosh HaNikra (7NIS, 15 minutes) but there are only three services a day. Other more frequent services pass the Rosh HaNikra junction but from there it's a 3km walk to the site.

The Galilee

With its combination of beautiful scenery and religious heritage Galilee is probably the most popular area of the country, both

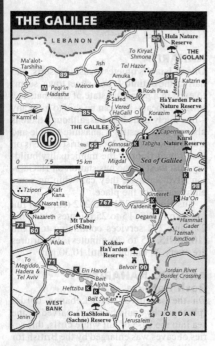

THE GALILEE

Orientation & Information

The main places of interest are concentrated in the centre of the old Arab town on and around Paul VI St. The other important street is the short Casa Nova St which intersects Paul VI St and continues up to the market – the tourist information office (☎ 657 3003, fax 657 5279) is here, just downhill from the Basilica; it's open from 8.30 am to 5 pm Monday to Friday, and from 8.30 am to 2 pm Saturday but it's closed on Sunday.

The Holy Sites

One of the Christian world's most holy shrines, the **Basilica of the Annunciation** is held by believers to stand on the site where the Angel Gabriel appeared to Mary to inform her that she was pregnant with the son of God. It's commemorated by a ponderous modern (1969) structure which is at least partially redeemed by an inventive interior.

Just up Casa Nova St from the Basilica is **St Joseph's Church**, built in 1914 and occupying the traditional site of Joseph's carpentry shop. This belief probably originated in the 17th century and today's church was built over the remains of an existing medieval church. Down in the crypt you can see an underground cave used for grain storage in pre-Byzantine times. Up the sidestreet across from the Basilica (the one with the Casa Nova Hospice on the corner), the **Sisters of Nazareth Convent** boasts one of the best examples of an ancient tomb sealed by a rolling stone; it lies under the present courtyard and can only be viewed by appointment.

At the top of Casa Nova St is the **Arab market,** occupying a maze of steep, narrow, winding streets in the midst of which is the **Greek Catholic Church** located on the site of the synagogue traditionally believed to be where Jesus regularly prayed and later taught. There's also a very attractive Greek Orthodox church, **St Gabriel's**, about a 10 minute walk north of the Basilica, two blocks west of where Paul VI St ends. Close by St Gabriel's is **Mary's Well**, also known as the Virgin's Fountain, massively renovated in 1998 and claimed by some as an alternative site where the Angel Gabriel appeared before Mary.

with Israelis and foreign visitors alike. This is Israel's lushest region, with green valleys, verdant forests, lots of fertile farmland and, of course, the Sea of Galilee itself. Serious Bible territory, Galilee is where Jesus did most of his preaching as well as a spot of water walking and some fish multiplying.

NAZARETH

Generally believed to be the home of Mary and Joseph and the infant Jesus, Nazareth usually fails to match the high expectations of pilgrims and tourists. The several important churches are unfortunately overshadowed by the unattractive and rapidly expanding modern town. Beyond the holy sites there's little here, and with few places to eat and limited accommodation options most visitors will be content to make just a half day visit to Nazareth.

Jesus Christ (0-33 AD)

Little can be reconstructed of the life of Jesus from historical sources – the oldest accounts that we have (the Christian gospels) all date from some time after his death. But we do know that he was born into turbulent times. The provinces of Judea and Samaria that were formerly the heart of a Jewish kingdom had recently been swallowed by the Roman empire. The Jews were restive under occupation and political dissent was rife. Self-styled Jewish prophets and agitators delivered impromptu marketplace speeches railing against the materialism and decadence of wealthy Jerusalemites and were contemptuous of Rome's authority. It's likely that Jesus was such a figure, a popular orator. Although we know very little about his early life, we do know that from about the age of 30 it seems that in just a couple of years he gathered a group of followers and travelled around Judea preaching. He received the attention of the people (as the gospels have it, for the miracles he performed) but he also incurred the wrath of the authorities. Jesus was crucified on the orders of the Roman governor for his preachings and beliefs. Just over 30 years later the native populace rebelled completely in an uprising it took the Romans four years to completely quell – Jerusalem was destroyed and the Jews were sent into exile.

Places to Stay & Eat

Sisters of Nazareth Convent (☎ 655 4304, fax 646 0741) provides by far the best accommodation in town. Dorm beds cost 28NIS and there are also singles/doubles for US$19/38. At Easter, especially, and through the summer, the place is busy with pilgrim groups from Europe so you'd be well advised to make a reservation if possible. To get there, go up Casa Nova St, turn left opposite the Basilica and it's up the street on the right. Look for the small sign in French 'RELIGIEUSES DE NAZARETH'. *Casa Nova Hospice (☎ 645 6660, fax 657 9630)* across from the basilica on Casa Nova St is also very popular and usually filled by Italian pilgrim groups. The rooms are pleasant and the food is good. Singles/doubles are US$39/54 and breakfast is included.

The best places to eat in Nazareth are undoubtedly in the Christian hospices. Failing that, the next best thing is to cook for yourself. The market is the place to buy fresh vegetables and fruit, and there are grocery shops and bakeries along Paul VI St in both directions from Casa Nova St. Between the Basilica and the bus station are several good felafel stalls, while a decent place for humous (14NIS), shwarma (17NIS) and a bottle of beer is *Astoria Restaurant*, on the corner of Casa Nova and Paul VI streets.

Getting There & Away

Bus From outside Hamishbir department store on Paul VI St, bus No 431 departs hourly for Tiberias (15NIS, 45 minutes); for Haifa (15NIS, 45 minutes) stand on the other side of the street. There are also several buses a day direct to Akko (take bus No 343 from the stop opposite the Egged information office; 13.40NIS) and Tel Aviv (30NIS; bus No 823 or 824).

Service Taxis Service taxis to Tiberias leave from in front of Hamishbir department store. For Haifa and Tel Aviv go to the street by the side of the Paz petrol station.

MEGIDDO

Otherwise known as Armageddon (from the Hebrew *Har Megiddo*, meaning Mt of Megiddo), the site synonymous with the last great battle on earth is today an uninspirational mound of baked earth maintained by the National Parks Authority. Excavations have unearthed the remains of 20 distinct historical periods from 4000 to 400 BC, but it takes some stretch of the imagination to see any traces of former grandeur in the modern-day site. Help, however, is given in the form of some excellent models in the visitors centre museum and by informative signs planted around the site. It's open from 8 am to 5 pm Saturday to Thursday, and from 8 am to 4 pm Friday.

The archaeological site is 2km north of Megiddo Junction, a well-signposted intersection of the main Haifa road with the Afula-Hadera highway. There are several Haifa-Afula buses passing by daily as well as half-hourly Tiberias to Tel Aviv services – ask the driver to let you off at Megiddo Junction and then walk or hitch a lift up the slight hill.

BEIT SHE'AN

The attraction here is one of the country's most extensive archaeological sites, including its best-preserved Roman amphitheatre. Excavations and restoration work are ongoing but among the other structures so far revealed are a temple, basilica, nymphaeum, a wide colonnaded Roman street leading down to the great theatre, and extensive Byzantine baths covering more than half a hectare.

The site is open to visitors from 8 am to 5 pm Saturday to Thursday and from 8 am to 4 pm Friday (closing one hour earlier in the winter). Beit She'an is a stop-off point for the Tiberias-Jerusalem bus and there are also regular services between here and Afula, making it accessible from Nazareth.

TIBERIAS

As the only town on the shores of the Sea of Galilee, Tiberias is the obvious base from which to enjoy the surrounding lakeside beauty spots. With its mix of natural spas and tombs of venerated sages, the town is a popular holiday centre where observant Jews can combine treatment of the body with purification of the soul, while the not so observant flock here too for lakeside wining, dining and the lively nightlife.

Although there isn't much to be seen of the town's rich history, there is a free two hour guided tour that goes a little way to pointing out the evidence; it departs from outside the tourist information office (in Archaeological Park beside Jordan River Hotel) at 6 pm on Sunday, Monday and Thursday, and at 9 am Wednesday.

The Old Town

As out of place as a pin-stripe suited gent at a teenage rave, the dignified little **Al-Omri Mosque** is one of the few structures of any age (mid-18th century) in Tiberias' not-so-

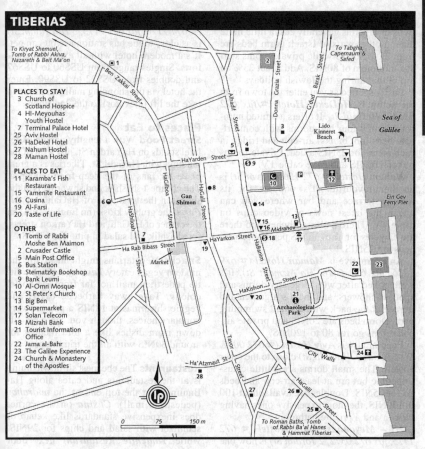

TIBERIAS

To Kiryat Shemuel,
Tomb of Rabbi Akiva,
Nazareth & Beit Ma'on

To Tabgha,
Capernaum &
Safed

Sea of
Galilee

Lido
Kinneret
Beach

Ein Gev
Ferry Pier

PLACES TO STAY
3 Church of
 Scotland Hospice
4 HI-Meyouhas
 Youth Hostel
7 Terminal Palace Hotel
25 Aviv Hostel
26 HaDekel Hotel
27 Nahum Hostel
28 Maman Hostel

PLACES TO EAT
11 Karamba's Fish
 Restaurant
15 Yamenite Restaurant
16 Cusina
19 Al-Farsi
20 Taste of Life

OTHER
1 Tomb of Rabbi
 Moshe Ben Maimon
2 Crusader Castle
5 Main Post Office
6 Bus Station
8 Steimatzky Bookshop
9 Bank Leumi
10 Al-Omri Mosque
12 St Peter's Church
13 Big Ben
14 Supermarket
17 Solan Telecom
18 Mizrahi Bank
21 Tourist Information
 Office
22 Jama al-Bahr
23 The Galilee Experience
24 Church & Monastery
 of the Apostles

Ben Zakkai Street

Alhadif Street

Donna Grazia Street

G'dud Barak Street

HaYarden Street

HaGiboa Street

HaCalil Street

Gan
Shimon

HaShiloah Street

Ha Rab Bibass Street

Market

HaYarkon Street

Midrahov

HaBanim Street

HaKishon Street

Street

Archaeological
Park

Tavor Street

City Walls

Ha'Atzmaut St

HaCalil Street

To Roman Baths, Tomb
of Rabbi Ba'al Hanes
& Hammat Tiberias

0   75   150 m

old Old Town. A second mosque, the waterfront Jama al-Bahr (1880), now stands forlorn and abandoned with plans to turn it into an Antiquities Museum apparently shelved.

Part of a modern waterfront development across from Jama al-Bahr mosque, **The Galilee Experience** is a 37 minute summation of the history, geography and spiritual significance of the region presented in the form of a state-of-the-art slide show.

St Peter's Church, on the restaurant-lined waterfront promenade, was originally built

in the 12th century by the Crusaders but the present structure dates from 1870. The boat-shaped nave is a nod to St Peter's profession as a fisherman.

A few minutes walk along Ben Zakkai St from the centre of town, the **Tomb of Rabbi Moshe Ben Maimon** is worth visiting to observe some of the rituals of Jewish sacred life. Maimonides, as Ben Maimon is better known, was one of the 12th century's most highly regarded sages and personal physician to Saladin. Modest dress is essential.

ISRAEL

Places to Stay – Budget

Beds in Tiberias generally cost a little more than in other parts of Israel; dorm beds are from 25 to 30NIS while private rooms start at a minimum of 80NIS. Add about 25% on top of that during the Jewish holidays.

Easily spotted as you enter the town from the south is *HaDekel Hotel (☎/fax 672 5318, 1 HaGalil St)*. It offers a limited number of small four bed dorms with comfortable beds (not bunks) air-con and fridge in each room for 25NIS a bed. Private rooms go for 120NIS and have cable TV.

Nahum Hostel (☎ 672 1505, Tavor St) is another favourite. It's popular for its rooftop terrace and bar where you can watch the latest news or video clips on cable TV. There's also a kitchen and there are bicycles for hire (30NIS per day). Dorm beds are 25NIS.

An alternative is *Maman Hostel (☎ 679 2986, fax 672 6616, Ha'Atzmaut St)*. It's well looked after with large airy dorms and spotless showers, and there's a garden and terrace at the back with a small swimming pool. Dorm beds are 20NIS and private air-con rooms go for 80 to 120NIS.

Popular also is *Aviv Hostel (☎ 672 0007, fax 672 3510, HaGalil St)* close to the other hostels. The small dorms are a little claustrophobic but are at least air-con and beds go for 25NIS. Doubles are available at 100 to 150NIS, the more expensive ones having air-con and a private bathroom.

HI – Meyouhas Youth Hostel (☎ 672 1775, fax 672 0372, 2 Jordan St) is now one of the country's nicest HI hostels. Accommodation is in two to four-bed dorms at 42NIS per night for nonmembers with breakfast included. There are also single/double rooms at 90/126NIS.

Places to Stay – Mid-Range

Just past Meyouhas hostel, towards the lake is the comfortable *Church of Scotland Hospice (☎ 672 3769, fax 679 0145, email scot tie@rannet.com)* with excellent facilities including a garden and private beach. B&B is US$40 to US$45 per person in larger than average singles/doubles.

Opened in 1997, *Terminal Palace Hotel (☎ 671 7176, fax 671 7175, 3 HaPrahim St)* is as close to the bus station as you can get. It's a modern hotel with all expected comforts. Singles range from US$60 to US$67 and doubles from US$72 to US$90. Enter the hotel via the shopping mall entrance and take the lift (elevator) to the 2nd floor.

Places to Eat

Street Food With a lengthy parade of felafel stands on HaYarden St, just west of the junction with HaGalil St, Tiberias is a great place for fans of the deep-fried chickpea. The cheapest shashlik and shwarma is at the shops on the west side of HaGalil; try *Al-Farsi,* the grubby kiosk (no English sign) on the corner of HaGalil and HaYarkon streets, for shashlik and salad in pitta for 13NIS.

Snacks Vegetarians might head for the modern vegan eatery *Taste of Life* on a little pedestrian mall not far from the hostel colony. Take away barbecue twists and veggie shwarmas at 18NIS a pop are very popular choices, though you can have sit-down main dishes like a tofu medley for around 39NIS with all the trimmings.

Restaurants The cheapest sit-down dining is at the restaurants and cafes along HaBanim St, at the top end of the *midrahov* (pedestrian mall). *Cusina* on the corner does inexpensive standards like kebab or schnitzel with salad and chips for 29NIS, while *Yamenite Restaurant* next door serves up *malawach*, large flaky-pastry pancakes, filled with either meat, mushrooms, egg or honey, for 16 to 18NIS each.

The waterfront restaurants are easily the most attractive places to eat – grab a table at the water's edge and you can watch the fish, some up to almost 1m in length, flit and glide through the shallows and wonder with such an abundance why the hell you have to pay 35 to 45NIS for the one on your plate. One of the better restaurants offering fish is *Karamba's Fish Restaurant (☎ 672 4505)* at the north end of the promenade and it's open daily from about noon until the early hours.

Self Catering For picnicking supplies there's a small *market* with some fruit and vegetable stalls, just south of Gan Shimon (Shimon Park), off HaYarkon St. It's open Sunday to Friday. There's also a very convenient *supermarket* behind the Al-Omri Mosque, open from 7 am to 6.45 pm Sunday to Thursday, from 7 am to 3.30 pm Friday, and from 8 am to 10 pm Saturday.

Entertainment

The cafes and bars on and around the midrahov are where the crowds form in the evening, bunching at *Le Pirat* and *Big Ben*, both of which are loud and raucous until well after midnight. There are a couple of other popular places at the northern end of the promenade. All these bars, however, are geared to the Israeli tourist which means 12NIS or more for a beer and awful music to boot. Budget travellers might prefer the rooftop bar at *Nahum Hostel* which serves bottled beer at 10NIS and has cable TV for friends of the 'box'.

Throughout the summer there are discos on the Lido Kinneret Beach and, for the suitably inebriated, departing from the same place each evening at 8 pm there are many loud disco cruise ships (20NIS per person).

Also, check the tourist information office for special events. For example, every Passover there's the Ein Gev Music Festival and there's also an annual summer Sea of Galilee Festival which attracts a lot of attention.

Getting There & Away

Bus There's a direct bus to Tel Aviv (32.50NIS, 2½ hours) departing at least every hour and services to Jerusalem (39NIS, 2½ hours) are even more frequent. There are also regular services to Haifa (22NIS, 1¼ hours), Nazareth (16.70NIS, 45 minutes), Safed (16NIS, one hour) and to Beit She'an (19NIS, 45 minutes).

Service Taxis Outside the bus station and across the grass is where a few service taxis leave in the morning for Nazareth and occasionally Haifa.

SEA OF GALILEE

Not just a natural beauty spot, the Sea of Galilee is also Israel's major water supply. A freshwater lake fed by the Jordan River, the 21km long Sea of Galilee lies 212m below sea level and, in a good summer, the lake can be as warm as 33°C.

The best way to explore the Sea of Galilee is to use Tiberias as a base and spend a day or two on a bicycle. It's 55km all the way around the Sea of Galilee and if you're in shape it's perfectly possible to cycle the entire way around in a day, taking time out at one or two of the sites. But perhaps a better way of tackling it is to take the lake in two halves, each day finishing up at Kibbutz Ein Gev, opposite Tiberias, from where there's a regular ferry crossing back.

About 6km north of Tiberias the lakeside road passes ancient **Migdal**, birthplace of Mary Magdalene; a tiny, white-domed shrine marks the site.

Within the grounds of Kibbutz Ginossar is **Yigol Allon Centre** (☎ 06-672 1495) a museum devoted to the theme 'man in the Galilee'. Its most celebrated exhibit is what shrewd tour operators have dubbed **'the Jesus boat'**, the skeletal remains of a fishing vessel, discovered only in 1986, that scientists have dated to the time of Christ's ministry.

Generally considered to be the most beautiful and serene of the Christian holy places, **Tabgha** is associated with three of the New Testament's most significant episodes: the Sermon on the Mount, the Multiplication of the Loaves and Fishes, and Jesus' post-Resurrection appearance where he conferred the leadership of the church on Peter. Each one of these events is celebrated with a church, all located within a short distance of each other.

Capernaum also has various New Testament connections – it was the home base of Jesus when he started his ministry. The ruins of a 4th century church built on the supposed site of Jesus' lodgings are now one of the major attractions of a well-labelled **archaeological museum**.

Although its marketing department would have you believe otherwise there is little of interest at **Kibbutz Ein Gev** – except the landing stage for the ferry over to Tiberias. Kibbutz Ha'On has an **ostrich farm** but that's easily topped at **Hammat Gader** where an alligator farm is just one of many attractions – others include some impressive Roman ruins and hot springs. Hammat Gader (☎ 06-675 1039, fax 675 2745) is open from 7 am to 9.30 pm Monday to Thursday, from 7 am to 11.30 pm Friday, and from 7 am to 6.30 pm Saturday and Sunday. Admission is 40NIS (students 35NIS), which gives access to all the amenities, although some health and beauty facilities are extra. The site is 8km south-east of the Sea of Galilee (21km from Tiberias). From Tiberias bus No 24 departs Sunday to Thursday at 8.45 and 10.30 am, and Friday at 8.30 and 9.30 am. Departures from Hammat Gader to Tiberias are Sunday to Thursday at noon and 3 pm, and Friday at noon and 1 pm. No buses run on Saturday.

Places to Stay

Camping If you thought camping was an alternative to paying high prices, think again. Camp sites on the shores of the Sea of Galilee, mostly run by kibbutzim, are quite expensive. However, if you have your own tent then there are 20 or so spots around the lake where you can pitch for free. The SPNI Field School and the tourist information centre at Tzemah, at the southern tip of the lake, can give you details.

Hostels An attractive alternative to Tiberias for many visitors is to stay outside the town for at least some of their time in the region. In Tabgha the modern and extremely elegant *HI – Karei Deshe-Yoram Youth Hostel* (☎ 672 0601, fax 672 4818) is set in attractive grounds with eucalyptus trees, a rocky beach and a few peacocks. Dorm beds are US$16 for members and nonmembers pay US$17.50.

Hotels The four-star-styled *Nof Ginnosar Guesthouse* (☎ 679 2161, fax 679 2170, email ginosar@netvision.net.il) run by Kibbutz Ginnosar provides comfortable accommodation beside the lake. It offers gardens, a private beach and water-sports facilities in a very quiet and unhurried atmosphere. Singles cost from around US$95 to US$126 and doubles from US$121 to US$156. Just south of Tabgha, the kibbutz is off the main road from Tiberias, and is clearly signposted.

Getting Around

Bicycle The most popular way of getting around the lake is by bicycle. The lake shore road is relatively flat and with so many sites so close together then as long as you can deal with the heat, a bike is the ideal means of transport. You can rent bicycles from several of the hostels in Tiberias, including the Aviv (☎ 06-672 0007) and Nahum (☎ 06-672 1505). It isn't necessary to be a guest at these places. Expect to pay 30 or 40NIS for the day.

Ferry Three times a day a ferry belonging to the kibbutz departs Ein Gev for Tiberias and then shuttles back. In summer 1998 the sailing times from Tiberias were 11.30 am, 1.30 and 4 pm. A one-way crossing takes 45 minutes and costs 20NIS (30NIS return). Bicycles are carried for free.

SAFED

Alternatively spelt Zefad, Tzfat or Tsfat, this is an attractive hilltop town with a rich heritage of Jewish mysticism, a heavy quota of new immigrants and an industrious artists' colony. The town is also blessed with a beautiful high-altitude setting and a temperate climate. The shortage of good budget accommodation and lack of evening entertainment weigh against an overnight stay but it's definitely worth a day visit (best made from Tiberias). Avoid Safed on the Shabbat when even the birds stay grounded.

Orientation & Information

Safed is spread over one perfectly rounded hill, with the bus station on the east side and the old town centre directly opposite on the west side – Jerusalem (Yerushalayim) St makes a complete loop connecting the two.

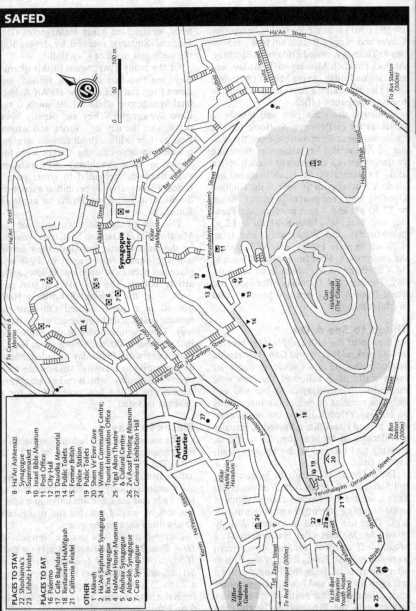

SAFED

0	50	100 m

PLACES TO STAY
22 Shoshana's
23 Lifshitz Hostel

PLACES TO EAT
16 Palermo
17 Cafe Baghdad
18 Restaurant HaMifgash
21 California Felafel

OTHER
1 Mikveh
2 Ha'Ari Sephardic Synagogue
3 Ba'na Synagogue
4 HaMeiri House Museum
5 Abuhav Synagogue
6 Alsheikh Synagogue
7 Caro Synagogue
8 Ha'Ari Ashkenazi
   Synagogue
9 Supermarket
10 Israel Bible Museum
11 Post Office
12 City Hall
13 Davidka Memorial
14 Public Toilets
15 Former British
   Police Station
19 Public Toilets
20 Shem Ve'Ever Cave
24 Wolfson Community Centre;
   Tourist Information Office
25 Yigal Allon Theatre
   & Cultural Centre
26 Zvi Assaf Printing Museum
27 General Exhibition Hall

Synagogue
Quarter

Artists'
Quarter

Gan
HaMtzuda
(The Citadel)

Ha'Ari Street
Jawitz Street
Yerushalayim (Jerusalem) Street
To Bus Station
(300m)
Hativat Yiftah Road
Kikar
HaMagnim
Yerushalayim (Jerusalem) Street
Bar Yohai Street
Ha'Ari Street
Alkabetz Street
Beit Yosef Street
Ma'alot Olei HaGardom Street
HaPalmach Street
To Bus
Station
(300m)
Aborodi
Street
Kikar
HaMa'alot
Haradum
Aliyah Bet
Keren HaYesod Street
Tet Zayin Street
Yerushalayim (Jerusalem) Street
HaPalmach Street
To Red Mosque (300m)
To Hi-Beit
Binyamin
Youth Hostel
(500m)
Zilfer
Sculpture
Garden
To Cemeteries &
Meiron

Safed's local tourist information office (☎ 692 0961) is in the Wolfson Community Centre and is open from 8 am to 4 pm Sunday to Thursday, closed Friday and Saturday. At 9.45 am each Monday to Thursday, and at 10 am on Friday, Aviva Minoff (☎ 06-692 0901) leads a walking tour of Safed from the tourist information office.

Although the main post and telephone office is on HaPalmach St (look for the radar dish next door, visible from the corner of Aliyah Bet St) some way from the centre, there is a convenient branch office at 37 Yerushalayim St. Bank branches are all on Yerushalayim St west of the Citadel. Opening hours are generally from 8.30 am to 12.30 pm and 4 to 6 pm Sunday, Tuesday and Thursday, from 8.30 am to 12.30 pm Monday and Wednesday, and from 8.30 am to noon Friday, closed Saturday. An exception is First International Bank at 34 Yerushalayim St, which is closed Sunday, Tuesday and Thursday afternoons but open from 4 to 7 pm on Monday and Wednesday.

Things to See & Do

At the top of the hill, the pleasant breeze-cooled park and viewpoint **Gan HaMetsuda** was once the site of a Crusader citadel. Its outer walls once followed the line now marked by Yerushalayim St but you can only see remains of one of the inner walls on Hativat Yiftah Rd, near the inappropriately named **Israel Bible Museum**, actually a collection of biblical themed sculpture, painting and lithography by an American-Jewish artist.

The old quarters that are the heart of central Safed tumble down from Yerushalayim St in a snakes and ladders compendium of ankle-straining stairways and slithering alleys. They are divided uncompromisingly in two by **Ma'alot Olei HaGardom St**, a broad, stiff stairway running down from Yerushalayim St. It was built by the British after the riots of 1929 to divide the town and keep the Arab and Jewish communities apart. The area to the north of the stairway is known as the **Synagogue Quarter**, the

town's old traditional Jewish neighbourhood, centred on **Kikar HaMaginim** (Defenders' Square), reached by descending the steps just north of City Hall.

Of the many synagogues in this quarter there are two that should be visited; just down from the Kikar is the **Ha'Ari Ashkenazi Synagogue** while a little south is the **Caro Synagogue**. They are usually open throughout the day to visitors, and admission is free although donations are requested. Suitable clothing must be worn (no shorts, no bare shoulders) and cardboard yarmulkes are provided to cover men's heads. Photography is permitted except on the Shabbat (sundown Friday to sundown Saturday).

The part of the old town south of the Ma'alot Olei HaGardom St stairway used to be the Arab quarter but since their defeat and subsequent withdrawal in 1948 the place has been developed by the Jews as an **artists' colony**. The best place to start any walk is at the **General Exhibition Hall**, housed in a white-domed Ottoman-era mosque just a little to the south of the stairway. The opening hours of the exhibition hall vary but it's usually open for at least a part of every day, Saturday included. Many of the individual artists' studios are also open on Saturday, which makes art appreciation one of the few possibilities for a Shabbat in Safed.

Places to Stay

On the same alley, just before Shoshanna's apartments are *Lifshitz Hostel* (☎ 052-472 360). The Lifshitz family offers accommodation from 35NIS per night. The rooms, off a central courtyard, have from two to four beds and are quite attractive in a spartan sort of way. Look for the makeshift handwritten sign on the gate.

Easily mistaken for a modern high school *HI – Beit Binyamin Youth Hostel* (☎ 692 1086, fax 697 3514, 1 Lohamei HaGeta'ot St) in South Safed suffers badly from being a 20 to 25 minute walk up a steep gradient from the town centre. You can take bus No 6 or 7 from the central bus station. It also has a very off-putting institutional air about it. A dorm bed is US$16 and there are also single (US$35) and double (US$45) rooms available.

Places to Eat

Safed is not the place to plan on breaking your diet of felafel and shwarma – away from street food our experiences of dining here were invariably disappointing. Most cafes and restaurants are on the pedestrianised part of Yerushalayim St.

Street Food There are several good felafel places on the stretch between the bus station and HaPalmach St, one of the best of which is *California Felafel*, beside the bridge.

Snacks A good snacking place is *Palermo*, which serves up reasonably priced pizza by the slice; it's on Yerushalayim St by the top of Ma'alot Olei HaGardom St.

Restaurants *Cafe Baghdad* (☎ 697 4065, 61 Yerushalayim St) is a dairy and vegetarian restaurant which, apart from reasonable dinners, does breakfasts, blintzes and sandwiches. The view from the streetside terrace is great too.

Farther west along the same street is *Restaurant HaMifgash* (☎ 692 0510, 75 Yerushalayim St) which although nothing flash, does purport to produce the best burgers in town.

Self-Catering There is a fruit and vegetable *market* on Wednesday morning next to the bus station and a *supermarket* at the eastern end of Yerushalayim St near the Javits St steps.

Getting There & Away

There are services to Haifa (25NIS, two hours) every 30 minutes until 9 pm (5.45 pm on Friday) and hourly to Tiberias (16NIS, one hour) until 7 pm (4 pm on Friday). Three buses a day go to Tel Aviv (44NIS, otherwise change at Haifa) and one a day to Jerusalem (40NIS, otherwise change at Rosh Pina).

The Upper Galilee & the Golan

The Upper Galilee is an area of lush greenery watered by the run-off from the surrounding mountains. These streams come together in the Hula Valley to form the Jordan River, provider of most of Israel's fresh water. The chain of high peaks known as the Golan (or the Golan Heights) rises to form a barrier between the fertile Jordan Valley and the arid Syrian lands to the east. The Golan also acts as a political wedge between the two neighbouring countries, with Syria asserting that there will never be peace while the Israelis occupy the Heights.

A relative lack of frequent public transport makes the Upper Galilee and Golan considerably more difficult to explore than most other parts of Israel. Those who have limited time and money might decide to take one of the tours mentioned in the following Organised Tours section and visit the area for a day with a guide to point out the major places of interest. If you're following your own schedule then we recommend planning for a couple of days in the area, staying for one or possibly two nights. The only budget accommodation to be found is in the far north at Tel Hai, near Kiryat Shmona, or in the south at Katzrin.

Information

There's a local tourism authority information station (☎ 06-693 5016, email saram@ netvision.net.il) at the Mahanayim Junction, 3km north of Rosh Pina. They're open daily from 10 am to 4.30 pm. They also have a privately maintained and potentially useful Web site (www.zimmer.co.il) with listings of accommodation options – especially for B&Bs.

Golan Tourist Association (☎ 06-696 2885, fax 696 3630, email tour@golan.org.il) is based in Katzrin and exists to promote eco-friendly tourism for groups and individuals around the region. You can also write to them at PO Box 175, 12900 Katzrin.

ISRAEL

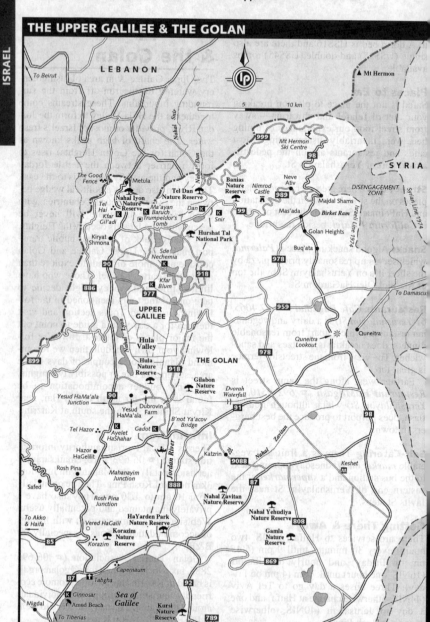

THE UPPER GALILEE & THE GOLAN

LEBANON

To Beirut

SYRIA

Mt Hermon

0   5   10 km

Mt Hermon Ski Centre

DISENGAGEMENT ZONE

The Good Fence

Metula

Neve Ativ

Nimrod Castle

Majdal Shams

Tel Hai

Kfar Gil'adi

Nahal Iyon Nature Reserve

Tel Dan Nature Reserve

Banias Nature Reserve

Mas'ada

Birket Ram

Ma'ayan Baruch

Trumpeldor's Tomb

Dan

Snir

Golan Heights

Kiryat Shmona

Hurshat Tal National Park

Buq'ata

Sde Nechemia

To Damascus

Kfar Blum

UPPER GALILEE

Quneitra

Hula Valley

Quneitra Lookout

THE GOLAN

Hula Nature Reserve

Gilabon Nature Reserve

Dvorah Waterfall

Yesud HaMa'ala Junction

Yesud HaMa'ala

Dubrovin Farm

B'not Ya'acov Bridge

Tel Hazor

Ayelet HaShahar

Gadot

Katzrin

Keshet

Hazor HaGelilit

Rosh Pina

Mahanayim Junction

Nahal Zavitan Nature Reserve

To Akko & Haifa

Rosh Pina Junction

Safed

Vered HaGalil

HaYarden Park Nature Reserve

Nahal Yehudiya Nature Reserve

Korazim Nature Reserve

Korazim

Gamla Nature Reserve

Ginnosar

Tabgha

Capernaum

Migdal

Amud Beach

Sea of Galilee

Kursi Nature Reserve

To Tiberias

For updated hiking and day trip information, the best bet is to call in at one of the two SPNI field schools in the region:

Golan
(☎ 06-696 1352, fax 696 1947) in Katzrin
Hermon
(☎ 06-694 1091, fax 695 1480) south off road No 99, near Kibbutz Snir, midway between the Tel Dan and Banias nature reserves

Organised Tours

From Akko, Walied's Gate Hostel (☎ 04-991 0410, 991 4700) runs a bus trip two or three times a week depending on demand. Departing at 8.30 am, the tour takes in Safed, the Good Fence, Banias Nature Reserve and Majdal Shams, returning to Akko about 6 pm. The cost is 150NIS per person. From Tiberias, Aviv Hostel (☎ 06-672 0007, 672 3510) organises something similar for 130NIS per person.

Egged Tours (☎ 06-672 9220) also operates from Tiberias every Tuesday, and Saturday (all year). It takes an air-con bus on a circuit of Tabgha, Capernaum, Jordan Park, Mitzpe Gadot, Metula (from where you can visit the Good Fence), Banias Nature Reserve and Bikat Ram. Some of the stops, however, are way too brief and the blatantly Zionist commentary grates rather than enlightens. The cost per person is US$38.

ROSH PINA

The busy junction at Rosh Pina is the main point of entry to the region. If you choose to travel by bus you will often have to change buses here. Proceeding north from Rosh Pina the road heads up to Metula on the Israel-Lebanon border, via Kiryat Shmona.

Rosh Pina Pioneer Settlement Site (☎ 06-693 6603) up the hill, just to the west of the junction, was the first settlement in Galilee, established in 1882. The original old houses have been renovated and it is a great spot for a meal or a drink at the local pub.

HULA VALLEY & NATURE RESERVE

This beautiful valley between the Lebanese border and the Golan mountains is a unique wetlands and wildlife sanctuary, Hula Nature Reserve (☎ 06-693 7069). There's a visitors centre which exhibits and explains much of the flora and fauna to be seen in the reserve, and rents binoculars so you can go in search of the real thing in the wild.

The reserve is open to visitors from 8 am to 5 pm Saturday to Thursday, and from 8 am to 4 pm Friday, and there are free guided tours between 9.30 am and 1.30 pm on Saturday, Sunday, Tuesday and Thursday.

Buses running between Rosh Pina and Kiryat Shmona will drop you off at a signposted junction about 2.5km from the entrance to the reserve –walk from there.

Places to Stay

Kibbutz Ayelet HaShahar (☎ 693 2611, fax 693 4777, email atlashot@netvision.net.il) has a four-storey guesthouse with horse riding and jeep trips available. Singles cost from US$83 to US$95 and doubles from US$102 to US$120. It's near Hazor Museum. North of Hula Nature Reserve and 3km along a side road to the east of main road No 90, *Kibbutz Kfar Blum* (☎ 694 3666, fax 694 8555) has a three-star guesthouse with singles costing from US$75 to US$95 and doubles from US$96 to US$136.

KIRYAT SHMONA & AROUND

The name Kiryat Shmona is Hebrew for 'Town of the Eight', after the eight Jewish settlers killed at nearby Tel Hai in 1920. Since then there have been more casualties: the town's proximity to the Lebanese border has made it the recipient of Palestinian, and more recently Hezbollah, rocket and bomb attacks. Despite its frontier-post position, Kiryat Shmona is to all appearances a standard, unexceptional new Israeli town.

North of Kiryat Shmona, on the road to Metula, is Tel Hai, where the death of the Jewish settlers occurred. The original settlement's watchtower and stockade have been converted into a museum. There's another museum, at Kibbutz Kfar Gil'adi just before Tel Hai, documenting the history of the early Zionist settlers' regiments in the British Army during WWI.

Of greater interest is the frontier town of Metula, on the border with Lebanon. The border crossing point is a place to the west of town called **The Good Fence** (HaGader Ha-Tova) from where, on a clear day, you can see across the border to several Lebanese Christian villages and Beaufort Castle to the north-west.

East of the Kiryat Shmona-Metula road is **Nahal Iyon Nature Reserve**, which encompasses the valley of the Iyon River and its several waterfalls, the most impressive of which is the 18m high **Tanur Fall**.

Places to Stay & Eat

In Kiryat Shmona *Hotel North* (☎ 694 4703, fax 694 1390, Tel Hai Blvd) is across the street from the bus station; singles/doubles are US$50/65. *HI – Tel Hai Youth Hostel* (☎ 694 1743, fax 694 0043) is a cheaper alternative offering dorm beds for US$16.50. Breakfast is included and other meals are available. At *Kfar Gil'adi Kibbutz Guesthouse* (☎ 690 0000, fax 690 0069, email kfar_giladi@kibbutz.co.il) singles cost from US$75 to US$98 and doubles from US$96 to US$136.

Getting There & Away

Kiryat Shmona is the major junction of the Upper Golan with connecting services to Tel Hai, Metula and the Israel-Lebanon border to the north, and Tel Dan, Banias, Nimrod Castle, Mt Hermon and Katzrin to the east. It's connected to the rest of Israel via bus Nos 541, 841 and 963, which run down to Tiberias (18NIS) via the Hula Valley and Rosh Pina.

THE GOLAN

Main road No 99 heads east from Kiryat Shmona, across the Iyon River and then the Snir River, one of the principal sources of the Jordan River, to reach **Hurshat Tal National Park**. A popular and often crowded picnic spot, this forested area is famous for its ancient oaks. Bus Nos 25, 26 and 36 from Kiryat Shmona will drop you off here.

Farther along road No 99 is Kibbutz Dan and **Beit Ussishkin Museum** featuring audiovisuals, dioramas and other exhibits covering the flora and fauna, geology, topography and history of the region. There is also a birdwatching centre here.

Banias Nature Reserve is probably the most spectacularly beautiful and popular spot in the entire Upper Galilee/Golan region. The heart of the reserve is a cave sanctuary while about 1km away is the **Banias waterfall**, the largest in the region. Less than 2km east of Banias, **Nimrod Castle** is the most impressive and best preserved of Israel's Crusader castles. Bus No 55 from Kiryat Shmona passes by Banias twice a day; alternatively, walk the 5km west to Kibbutz Dan where bus Nos 25, 26 and 36 run a bit more often.

Up in the north-east corner of the Golan region is the **Mt Hermon Ski Centre**. At 2224m Mt Hermon is Israel's highest peak (though only 7% of Hermon is actually in Israeli territory). There are surprisingly decent, albeit limited, skiing facilities here, based around the settlement of **Neve Ativ** where there's a ski information centre (☎ 06-698 1337). The snow season is usually from late December to early April. Prices are as bad as you probably expect them to be.

Majdal Shams and **Mas'ada** are the two largest of four Druze villages in the area. Unlike the communities on Mt Carmel, these Druze are fiercely anti-Israeli and they have protested against the occupation and subsequent annexation of this area from Syria. About 15km south from Mas'ada, the road reaches a high mound with an observation point. From here you can look across the UN-patrolled border to the Syrian ghost town of **Quneitra**, abandoned as a result of the fighting in 1967. Damascus is a mere 30km north-east of here.

Places to Stay

There's a *camping ground* (☎ 06-694 2360) at Hurshat Tal National Park where tent space costs 25NIS per person, and three-bed bungalows are 170NIS. *SPNI Hermon Field Study Centre* (☎ 06-694 1091, fax 695 1480) has guest cottages set among oak tree-shaded lawns. The price per night is approximately US$40 per person but call in advance because this place is often booked up. The Field Study Centre is near Kibbutz Snir.

KATZRIN & AROUND

The new 'capital' of the Golan, **Katzrin** is not an attractive town but it's as near to an ideal base from which to explore the area as you can get, especially for those on a tight budget. Around town there's **Golan Archaeological Museum** and **Ancient Katzrin Park**, with the remains of a 3rd century synagogue and two reconstructed houses. There is also an excellent SPNI Field Study Centre on Daliyat St on the southern edge of Katzrin.

There are some terrific hiking opportunities in the area – ask at the Field Study Centre for details about the attractive **Dvorah Waterfall** and other waterfalls, water pools and hiking in the **Gilabon Nature Reserve**.

Located south of Katzrin within the Gamla Nature Reserve is **Gamla**, a spectacular site overlooking the Sea of Galilee, believed to be the ruins of an ancient Jewish stronghold where, as at Masada on the Dead Sea, a Roman siege ended with mass suicide.

Places to Stay

SPNI's *Golan Field Study Centre* (☎ 696 1352, fax 696 1947, Daliyat St) has a modern, clean and comfortable guesthouse in which beds in air-con dorms are US$40 per person. It's often full, so phone ahead to make a reservation. To the south it has a camping ground with tent sites costing 24NIS.

Getting There & Away

Bus Nos 55, 56 and 57 connect Katzrin with Rosh Pina (11NIS, 30 minutes), just 2km east of Safed, and bus Nos 15, 16 and 19 go to Tiberias (15NIS, 45 minutes).

Bus No 55 goes twice a day from Katzrin to Kiryat Shmona via Mas'ada.

The Dead Sea

No visit to Israel would be complete without a visit and a swim in one of its best-known highlights. With a shoreline of some 90km

there is no one bathing spot but you are advised to take your dip somewhere with shower facilities – the Dead Sea has a slightly slimy quality. After the obligatory float, the next popular thing to do is to visit Masada, a place which readers' letters consistently rate as Israel's number one attraction. Not as well known or as well frequented by travellers, the Ein Gedi Nature Reserve also deserves some exploration.

Organised Tours

By far the cheapest way of sampling the Dead Sea region is to sign up for the 12 hour tour you'll see advertised in almost all the hostels in Jerusalem. It departs the Old City at 3 am each morning, getting you down to Masada in time to watch the sunrise over the desert. There's a visit to the Ein Gedi reserves and a float in the Dead Sea before photostops at Qumran and Jericho's Mount of Temptation. Despite the stopwatch-timed schedule most travellers find that they get to see all they want. SPNI Tours operates a similar program but it's about three times more expensive.

Metzoke Dragot (02-994 4222, fax 994 4333, email metzoke@netvision.net.il) in the town of the same name offers various tours and activities in the Judean Desert, with or without accommodation. They are highly recommended by those who have used them.

Getting There & Away

The entire west coast of the Dead Sea, about 90km in length, is served by a single main road (No 90) which comes off the Jerusalem-Jericho highway in the north and follows the shoreline southwards to Sodom, continuing to Eilat. The most comprehensive bus service is from Jerusalem's central bus station. Buses from there to Eilat and Beersheba go by Qumran (18NIS, one hour), Ein Gedi (25NIS, 1½ hours) and Masada, and there should be something departing at least every hour or so.

QUMRAN

Described as 'the most important discovery in the history of the Jewish people', the **Dead**

THE DEAD SEA

Caught in the Syrian African rift valley and lying some 340m below sea level, the Dead Sea is an inland lake fed by the waters of the Jordan River. The visibly falling water level of the Dead Sea is caused by over-use of the waters of the Jordan River by both Israeli and Jordanian farmers. The Sea is bordered by Jordan on the east shore and a large chunk of the western shore is within the West Bank Palestinian territory.

A visit to the Dead Seas is obligatory almost as much for its references in the Bible as it is for its uniqueness. Where else can you swim – or rather float – in a body of water at the lowest point of the earth's surface. For this reason alone a swim in the Dead Sea is undoubtedly one of the Middle East's major highlights. However, a look at what you are letting yourself into may be worth some investigation.

Top: Buy it in a pharmacy and Dead Sea mu is expensive stuff. (Pho by Lee Foster)

Mineral Waters

Compared to regular sea water, the water of the Dead Sea contains 20 times as much bromine, 15 times as much magnesium and 10 times as much iodine – it is, in effect, 33% solid substance. Bromine, a component of many sedatives, relaxes the nerves; magnesium counteracts skin allergies and clears the bronchial passages; iodine has a beneficial effect on certain glandular functions – or so it's claimed, especially by local health spa owners and the various Dead Sea cosmetic companies.

Healthy or not, soaking in the water of the Dead Sea can also be extremely painful. Wade in with any exposed cuts or grazes and you will gain instant enlightenment as to the meaning behind the phrase to 'rub salt in ones' wounds'. We guarantee that you are going to discover scratches and sores that you never knew you had. The magnesium chloride in the water gives it a revolting bitter taste and swallowing any can induce retching. Don't get the water in your eyes either as it will sting and inflame – if this happens then rinse them immediately with fresh water.

Where to go Floating

This is no Mediterranean beach break: swimming in the Dead Sea presents a challenge

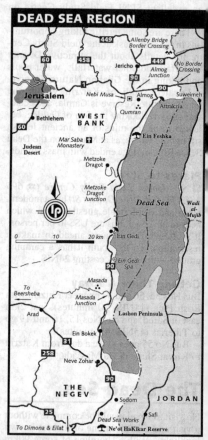

DEAD SEA REGION

- 449
- Allenby Bridge Border Crossing
- 60
- 458
- Jericho
- 449
- No Border Crossing
- Almog Junction
- 1
- 90
- **Jerusalem**
- Nebi Musa
- Almog
- Suweimeh
- Qumran
- Attrakzia
- Bethlehem
- 60
- **WEST BANK**
- Mar Saba Monastery
- Ein Feshka
- Judean Desert
- Metzoke Dragot
- Metzoke Dragot Junction
- **Dead Sea**
- Wadi al-Mujib
- 0   10   20 km
- Ein Gedi
- Ein Gedi Spa
- 90
- Masada
- To Beersheba
- Masada Junction
- Arad
- Lashon Peninsula
- Ein Bokek
- 31
- Neve Zohar
- 258
- 90
- **THE NEGEV**
- Sodom
- **JORDAN**
- 25
- Dead Sea Works
- Safi
- To Dimona & Eilat
- Ne'ot HaKikar Reserve

and requires a little preparation. With a shoreline of some 90km there is no one bathing spot but you are advised to take your dip somewhere with shower facilities – the Dead Sea has an unpleasantly slimy quality. The nicest places are the well-kept sandy beach at Ein Bokek by the main hotel area, and at Hamme Zohar, a little farther south. However, if you are short of time you may be better off using the beach at Ein Gedi which is closer to Jerusalem. There are shower facilities and shade here.

The best place to visit the Dead Sea on the Jordanian side is at the 'resort' at Suweimeh; see the Jordan chapter for more details.

ght: Palms are the only life that survives in or around the Dead Sea.

Bottom: Swimming is near impossible; all you can do is float.

ISRAEL

Sea Scrolls, now on display in Jerusalem, were found here in 1947. The site includes the settlement and caves of the Essenes, a Jewish sect who wrote the scrolls between 150 BC and 68 AD when the Romans dispersed them. The bus stops on the main road; follow the turn-off up the hill. There is a self-service *cafeteria* at the site. It's a hot climb up to the caves, so bring drinking water.

EIN GEDI

One of the country's most attractive oases, Ein Gedi is a lush area of freshwater springs, waterfalls, pools and tropical vegetation nestled in the arid desert landscape of the lowest place on earth. It's a haven for desert wildlife, which hangs in there despite the terrifyingly raucous coach loads of kids that rampage through the reserves on an almost daily basis. The beach is, undeservedly, one of the most popular on the Dead Sea.

Ein Gedi sprawls over 4km – the nature reserves, field school and youth hostel are to the north, on the west side of the road. The field school has a small museum of local flora and fauna.

About 1km farther south are the bathing beach, restaurant and camp site. Another 2.5km to the south is the turn-off for Kibbutz Ein Gedi, with the Ein Gedi Spa (Hamme Mazor) sulphur baths 2.5km beyond. Avoid weekends and holidays when Ein Gedi is noisy and crowded.

Places to Stay & Eat

You can sleep for free by the beach, but watch your gear as theft is not uncommon.

HI – Beit Sara Hostel (☎ 658 4165, fax 658 4445) charges US$16.50 for a bed in an air-con eight bed dorm. A double room is US$40 (nonmembers pay a couple of dollars more). Breakfast is included and dinner is available. Check-in is from 3 to 7 pm and check-out is 9 am. The hostel is about 250m north-west of the Ein Gedi Reserve bus stop.

SPNI Field Study Centre (☎ 658 4288, fax 658 4257) has six-bed dorm rooms for visitors at US$40 per person (US$50 in high season).

Surrounded by tree-filled gardens beside the Dead Sea, with a swimming pool and hot spa included in the price, the guesthouse at *Kibbutz Ein Gedi* (☎ 659 4222, fax 658 4328, email eb@kibbutz.co.il) is one of the most popular in the country. Terms are half-board only; singles cost from US$122 to US$143 and doubles from US$174 to US$204. Booking is recommended.

MASADA

A free-standing, sheer-sided plateau high above the Dead Sea, Masada was fortified by Herod the Great. In 66 AD the Jews rose up against the Romans in what's known as the First Revolt, and a group of them called the Zealots captured the lightly guarded Masada. After suppressing the uprising in the rest of the country the Romans turned their attention finally to the mountain-top stronghold. When defeat was inevitable the 967 men, women and children atop Masada committed mass suicide leaving only a couple of survivors left to tell the tale. The event figures large in the Israeli national psyche and the melodramatic utterance 'Masada shall not fall again' is a favoured pearl of political rhetoric.

The site and views are superb, and you can reach the top by cable car or on foot.

Places to Stay & Eat

HI – Isaac H Taylor Hostel (☎ 07-658 4349, fax 658 4650) by the Masada bus stop provides air-con dorms at $16.50 per person with breakfast included. Dinner costs around US$8 but must be ordered before 6 pm, otherwise bring plenty to eat and drink or be prepared to rely on the nearby restaurants and snack bar. Check-in is from 3 to 7 pm and check-out is by 9 am.

Sleeping out on top of Masada is no longer permitted, but the hostel does have some tent-pitching space.

Getting There & Away

There are about eight buses a day to Jerusalem (31.50NIS, 1¾ hours), four a day to Eilat (45NIS) and several to Beersheba (30NIS).

The Negev

Stretching south-west from the Dead Sea, the Negev Desert accounts for almost half of Israel's land area. Most of the Negev remains largely uninhabited and there are only a handful of towns together with kibbutzim, moshavim and an estimated 75,000 Bedouin who live a nomadic lifestyle. Many visitors only see the Negev through a bus window en route to Eilat but there are places worth a visit, not far from the main roads.

There are some excellent hikes in the Negev region taking in a surprising variety of landscapes. Particularly recommended are those around Sde Boker, Ein Avdat and Mitzpe Ramon (see individual entries in this section). SPNI has field schools at Sde Boker, Mitzpe Ramon and Eilat, and at Hatzeva, 50km south of the Dead Sea on road No 90 – these are the places to visit for detailed maps and information and recommendations on routes and desert sights.

BEERSHEBA

Unattractive, with little to see and little to do, Beersheba is unlikely to impress many visitors. It's the kind of town that gives most satisfaction when seen from the rear window of your departing bus. For the visitor, probably the greatest point of interest is the weekly Bedouin market held every Thursday morning. The museum is also pleasant but it won't take much time and as accommodation is so pricey there's little reason to stay overnight.

The local tourist office (☎ 07-623 6001/2) is on Nordau St across from the entrance to the central bus station. It's open from 8 am to 4 pm Sunday to Thursday and it's closed on Friday and Saturday.

The main post office is just north of the central bus station on the corner of HaNessi'im and Nordau streets while there are plenty of banks in the modern Kanion shopping centre beside the bus station.

The much vaunted Thursday **Bedouin market** is rather disappointing; the only traces of authenticity are found very early in the morning. The exhibits at **Negev Museum**, which occupies an old Turkish mosque in a park on Ha'Atzmaut St in the Old Town, include a history of the town itself as well as a series of archaeological artefacts from the entire Negev region. There is also a section on Bedouin culture, a collection of medieval maps of the Holy Land, and a 6th century mosaic floor depicting animals in its geometric design. The museum was closed for structural renovations at the time of our last visit but it's hoped that it will re-open by the time this book hits the shelves. The elegant building across from the museum is what used to be the governor's residence and for a while was the city hall before becoming a small contemporary **art gallery**.

Places to Stay & Eat

HI – Beit Yatziv Youth Hostel (☎ 627 7444, 627 5735, 79 Ha'Atzmaut St) isn't quite the cheapest place in town but overpriced as it is, still offers the best value for money. It's a clean, modern complex with a swimming pool, pleasant gardens and no curfew. Comfortable dorm beds in a room for six with toilet and shower are US$21. An adjoining guesthouse has singles/doubles for US$40/59. All prices include breakfast. Lunch and dinner at 45NIS are available.

The best place to eat is *Kanion shopping mall*, which has the whole lower ground floor given over to felafel, shwarma and various fast-food franchises. The other place for inexpensive food is on and around Keren Kayemet Le-Y'Israel St, which is lined with *cafes* that serve the standard versions of grilled meats and salads, along with ice cream parlours and fast food outlets. If you fancy sitting down to dine try *Yitzhak's Bulgarian Restaurant* (112 Keren Kayemet Le-Y'Israel St) which does kebabs, schnitzels, liver etc for around 30NIS.

Getting There & Away

Bus Nos 370 and 380 run every 20 minutes to Tel Aviv (17.50NIS, 80 minutes) headed for the central bus station and Arlosoroff terminal respectively. Bus Nos 470 and 446

ISRAEL

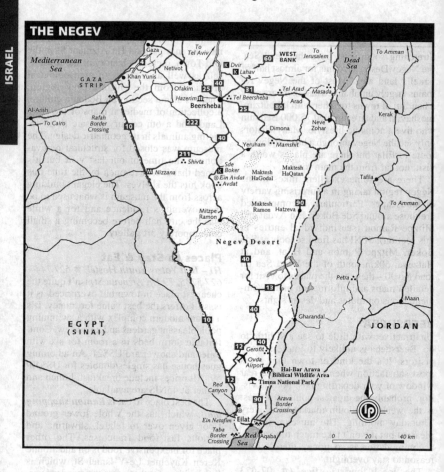

THE NEGEV

head for Jerusalem (23.50NIS, 1½ hours), with one or the other departing every 30 minutes or so between. For Eilat (35NIS, three hours), there's the hourly No 394 via Mitzpe Ramon (17.50NIS, 80 minutes) and a slow stopping service, No 397, which departs twice a day.

AROUND BEERSHEBA

Kibbutz Lahav has the Joe Alon Centre with its **Museum of Bedouin Culture**, the world's largest museum of its kind. It's off a side road that intersects with the Beersheba-Kiryat Gat road. From Beersheba bus No 369 to Tel Aviv passes the intersection quite often – from here it's an 8km hitch or walk; bus No 42 runs directly to the kibbutz but once a day only at 11.50 am, returning to Beersheba at 1.20 pm.

Anyone interested in aircraft or military history should make a trip to the **Israeli Air Force Museum** at the Hazerim IAF base near Beersheba. Hazerim (sometimes spelt Khatserim) is just 6km west of Beersheba.

From the central bus station take bus No 31 and the air base and museum is the last stop.

DIMONA

Dimona is another bleak, modern desert town, and unless you're involved in espionage (it's the site of Israel's no-longer-secret nuclear reactor) the sole attraction is the controversial Hebrew Israelite Community settlement. They live a virtually self-contained lifestyle with their own school and they make their own clothes (natural fibres only), jewellery and food (their religion prohibits meat, dairy products, fish, eggs, white sugar and white flour). They welcome visitors and their settlement is only 10 minutes walk from Dimona's bus station. However, the community prefers that you give advance notice of any visit; telephone ☎ 07-655 5400 or simply ask any of the staff in the Eternity Restaurant in Tel Aviv.

There is a small *guesthouse* which charges 80NIS per person with breakfast and dinner included. Alternatively, you can stay at *Drachim Youth Hostel (☎ 655 6811, HaNassi St)*, which the bus passes as it comes into town, where dorm beds are 44NIS.

With frequent buses from Beersheba (40 minutes) Dimona is not difficult to reach. There are also occasional buses from Arad and Mitzpe Ramon.

MITZPE RAMON

Mitzpe is Hebrew for lookout and this small, struggling desert town is so named for its location overlooking the massive **Maktesh Ramon**, or Ramon Crater, one of Israel's geological highlights. While difficult to describe without going overboard, the crater is said to remind visitors a little of the Grand Canyon and a lot of the moon. Its vital statistics are: 300m deep, 8km wide and 40km long. A few nature trails have been marked out which lead through some of the most attractive and interesting sections.

Perched on the edge of the Maktesh Ramon is an attractive aspirin-shaped **Visitors' Centre** which aims to explain everything you might want to know about the massive and intriguing crater. The roof of the building serves as an excellent viewing platform. The neighbouring **Bio-Ramon** complex is home to a collection of desert creatures.

SPNI has a field school (☎ 07-658 8615/6, fax 658 8615) on the edge of the crater which is possibly worth visiting for anybody planning any serious hiking. It's open from 8 am to 5 pm Sunday to Thursday, and from 8 am to 1 pm Friday but it's closed on Saturday. The school is about a 2km walk from the southern end of Ben-Gurion Blvd.

One of the new wave of desert tour centres springing up in the Negev, **Desert Shade** (☎ 07-658 6229, fax 658 6208) offers desert tours on camels (30NIS per hour) or in a 4WD (80NIS per person for two hours), rents mountain bikes (45NIS for a full day) and organises activities like rappelling. Desert Shade is located a few hundred metres north of the petrol station, back towards Beersheba, east of the main road at the end of a dirt road.

Places to Stay & Eat

Beautifully located near the edge of the Maktesh Ramon, the modern *HI – Mitzpe Ramon Youth Hostel (☎ 658 8443, fax 658 8074)* is also just a short walk from the Visitors' Centre. Dorm beds cost US$18 and singles/doubles are US$35/49, all with breakfast.

Chez Alexis (☎ 658 8258, 7 Ein Saharonim St) is an excellent choice for budget travellers. It's a villa that has been converted into a guesthouse and is on the western side of town. Beds are around US$12 per person and double rooms are US$30.

Next to the petrol station, *Hannah's Restaurant* serves surprisingly decent food and snacks. All Eilat-Beersheba buses take a 15 minute halt here and the custom they bring in seems to be the only thing that keeps the place going.

The restaurant next to the Visitors' Centre, the self-service *HaTsukit* (meaning The Cliff – for obvious reasons) commands a wonderful view over the crater and the food isn't bad value either – around 28 to 32NIS a dish. It's open daily from 8 am to 5 pm.

Getting There & Away

Bus No 932 stops here en route between Beersheba and Eilat (27NIS), via Dimona, but there are only about four buses a day, three of them before noon – check at the youth hostel or Visitors' Centre for the current timetables. Catch bus No 932 in both directions, at the petrol station.

Bus No 60 shuttles between Beersheba (21NIS) and Mitzpe Ramon, via Sde Boker and Ein Avdat, with departures about every hour between 6 am and 9.30 pm. Catch it from Ben-Gurion Blvd near the commercial concourse. Again check the youth hostel and Visitors' Centre for timetables.

EILAT

Distanced from the Israel of international headlines by a 200km sea of empty desert, Eilat exists almost as an 'offshore', sybaritic, mini city-state in which the major concerns are a good spot on the beach and an even tan. It's a 'wannabe' beachfront Las Vegas with glitzy ziggurat-like hotels surrounding a turquoise-blue artificial lagoon from which Walt Disney-styled glass-bottomed boats set out on cruises around the bay. However, the town's sun, sand and sea image isn't all it's cracked up to be: while there's plenty of sun, decent beaches are limited to a cluttered strip in the hotel area and views across the bay tend to be blotted by great tankers docking at the port. Eilat remains a popular stopover only by dint of its proximity to border crossing points with Egypt and Jordan.

Orientation & Information

Eilat has three parts: the town centre, the hotel area and a trailing 5km coastal strip running down to the border with Egypt at Taba. Eilat's excellent new tourist information centre is just south of the town centre on Ha'Arava Rd above Burger King; it's open from 8 am to 9 pm Sunday to Thursday, from 8 am to 2 pm Friday, and from 10 am to 2 pm Saturday. The best place to change money is at one of the no-commission exchange bureaus in the old Commercial Centre off HaTemarim Blvd in the town centre. Alternatively, the post office in the Red Canyon Centre also changes money and there are a couple of banks in the vicinity of the central bus station.

The police station (☎ 332 444, or in an emergency call ☎ 100) is on Avdat St, at the eastern end of Hativat HaNegev Ave. They're very used to travellers turning up here to report stolen bags and packs.

For medical aid call the Magen David Adom (☎ 372 333) or in emergencies dial ☎ 101.

Things to See & Do

At **Dolphin Reef** visitors can observe training demonstrations, help out at feeding time or even swim or dive with the dolphins; it's south of the port on the road down to Taba. Farther south is the **Underwater Observatory Marine Park**, which boasts, among other marine attractions, a glass-walled viewing chamber sunk 4.25m below the water's surface. In case the fish outside fail to put in an appearance there are plenty of captive specimens in the accompanying **aquarium**. For a deeper look at the underwater world, visitors can dive down to 60m in the observatory's **Yellow Submarine**, a viewing craft that takes passengers on a 50 minute cruise along the sea bed and the sheer-sided coral cliff wall. None of the above is cheap.

The Red Sea marine life can also be observed on a **glass-bottomed boat cruise**; the Stingray-like *Jules Verne Explorer* sets off from the North Beach marina four times a day for a two hour cruise around in the tight little area hemmed in by the Egyptian and Jordanian borders. Cost per person is 55NIS (children 40NIS).

Originally built as a movie set, **Texas Ranch** is an unimpressive mock Wild West town inspired by the resemblance of the local terrain to that of American cowboy country. The complex also offers horse riding and half-day camel treks.

Other than the glass-bottom boats, all the above attractions are off Mizrayim Rd, south of the HI – Eilat Youth Hostel; take bus No 15 from HaTemarim Blvd.

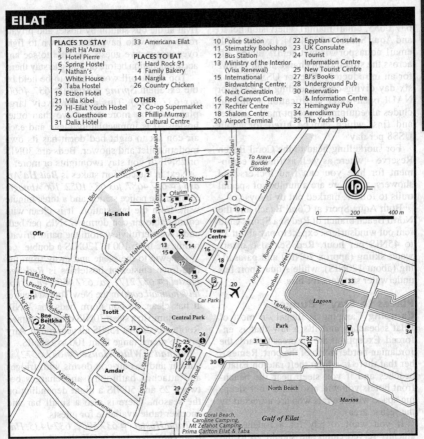

EILAT

PLACES TO STAY
3 Beit Ha'Arava
5 Hotel Pierre
6 Spring Hostel
7 Nathan's
   White House
9 Taba Hostel
19 Etzion Hotel
21 Villa Kibel
29 HI-Eilat Youth Hostel
   & Guesthouse
31 Dalia Hotel

33 Americana Eilat

PLACES TO EAT
1 Hard Rock 91
4 Family Bakery
14 Nargila
26 Country Chicken

OTHER
2 Co-op Supermarket
8 Phillip Murray
   Cultural Centre

10 Police Station
11 Steimatzky Bookshop
12 Bus Station
13 Ministry of the Interior
   (Visa Renewal)
15 International
   Birdwatching Centre;
   Next Generation
16 Red Canyon Centre
17 Rechter Centre
18 Shalom Centre
20 Airport Terminal

22 Egyptian Consulate
23 UK Consulate
24 Tourist
   Information Centre
25 New Tourist Centre
27 BJ's Books
28 Underground Pub
30 Reservation
   & Information Centre
32 Hemingway Pub
34 Aerodium
35 The Yacht Pub

Beaches

Eilat's beaches are less than impressive. The most convenient is the North Beach strip fringing the hotel area but the sands are incredibly crowded and cluttered – the best chance of avoiding the rush-hour commuter feeling is to head east towards the Jordanian border. Of the 5km of coastline stretching down to the Egyptian border, much of it resembles a building site of stones and gravel and muddy furrows, while one stretch is cordoned off and posted with unexploded mine notices. The only decent options seem to be the crowded, admission-charging Coral Beach Nature Reserve, south of the port, or the free HaDekel Beach, just north of the port.

Activities

Despite the enthusiastic PR, Eilat's waters do not offer world-class diving – serious divers should head to nearby Sinai. The best place, however, to check out the local options is around Coral Beach where you'll find Red Sea Sports Club (☎ 637 6569, fax 637 0655, email manta1@netvision.net.il) and Aqua Sport (☎ 633 4404, fax 633 3771, email aquaspor@isdnet.net.il) facing off across the street. Both charge about US$42 for an introductory dive, or US$275 for a six day diving course leading to PADI or NAUI open-water certification – this includes all equipment except mask, snorkel and fins, which can be hired for about US$8 per day.

For snorkelling head to the Coral Beach Reserve – where as well as finding equipment for hire you can find lockers and showers, and there are a number of special trails to follow, marked out by buoys.

Both Aqua Sport at Coral Beach and the North Beach branch of Red Sea Sports Club rent out windsurfers; expect to pay about 35 to 45NIS per hour. Red Sea also offers water skiing (approx 70NIS) and parasailing (about 120NIS), while Aqua Sport has underwater scooters for hire.

Places to Stay – Budget

Camping Camping is illegal on most of Eilat's beaches and it's a law that is enforced. Exceptions are the areas towards the Jordanian border north of the port. Remember that there is a high theft rate on Eilat's beaches and if you sleep near the beachfront hotels you will also share your sleeping space with the rats who are attracted by the refuse areas.

If you want to pay for a rodent-free, amenity-served camp site should go to the Coral Beach area. *SPNI Field School (☎ 637 1127, fax 637 1771, email info@eilat.spni .org.il)* has a shaded camp site that is open all year round. Cost is 20NIS per person. *Caroline Camping (☎ 637 5063)* does not cater to campers as such but offers two-person bungalows for 100NIS. It has clean bathrooms and showers and a basic cafeteria. Just a couple of hundred metres south *Mt Zefahot Camping (☎ 637 4411, fax 637 5206)*, next to the SPNI Field School, charges 20NIS for a tent site, which allows you access to hot showers, toilets and an electricity supply if wanted.

Hostels Travellers are often greeted on arrival at the bus station by hostel and private room touts who have been known to fight over prospective guests. Be sure to see any accommodation before deciding to stay there.

Top of the bill would have to be held by the excellent *Spring Hostel (☎ 637 4660, fax 637 1543)*. This comparatively large place is a bit more expensive than other hostels. It is immaculately clean and each air-con six to eight bed dorm has its own modern toilet and shower. Beds are 30NIS or 25NIS if you stay two nights or more.

Next in the comfort stakes is *Beit Ha'Arava (☎ 637 4687, fax 637 1052, 106 Almogin St)* near the police station and a three minute walk from the bus station. It is clean with comfortable air-con dorms (25NIS per bed) and a wonderful view from the patio. Private rooms are from 100 to 120NIS a double.

A newie to the scene and away from the mid-town cluster of hostelries is *Red Sea Hostel (☎ 637 2171, fax 637 4605, email hostel@hotmail.com)* in the New Tourist Centre. It has clean, air-con dorm beds for 25NIS which jump to a steep 70NIS during summer. Rooftop beds cost 15NIS all year round. Airy private rooms range from 100 to 180NIS.

Nathan's White House (☎ 637 6572) is similar and has air-con dorms with fridges and attached bathrooms and charges between 25 and 50NIS a night depending on the season. There is also a small bar and snooker table available for guests.

Taba Hostel (☎ 637 5982, 637 1435, Hativat HaNegev Ave) is OK though some of the dorms (20 to 25NIS a bed) take up to 22 people. Women's dorms are generally around the cramped nine bed mark. There is an ample sitting and patio area and breakfast costs 10NIS.

In its own category is *HI – Eilat Youth Hostel & Guesthouse (☎ 637 0088, fax 637 5835, Mizrayim Rd)*. The hostel is immaculate and there are good views towards the gulf from some of the balconies. Dorm beds are US$16.50 to US$18.50 per night and singles cost from US$36 to US$40.50 and doubles from US$52 to US$59 depending on the season.

Places to Stay – Mid-Range

Pickings here are fairly slim since most of Eilat's hotels are resorts with budget bursting tariffs. Still the following choices fill the mid-range quite adequately. New to the scene is the snazzy-looking *Hotel Pierre* (☎ 632 6601, fax 632 6602, 123 Ofarim Alley). It's smallish but comfortable rooms are equipped with fridge, phone, TV and are all air-con. Singles range in price from US$40 to US$50 and doubles from US$50 to US$60.

Next to the Rechter Centre at the bottom of HaTemarim Blvd is *Etzion Hotel* (☎ 637 0003, fax 637 0002). It has a sauna, pool and nightclub, with singles from US$60 to US$80 and doubles from US$80 to US$100.

In the expensive hotel area by the lagoon there are some more moderately priced beds available. Near to Galei Eilat Hotel, *Dalia Hotel* (☎ 633 4004, fax 633 4072) has singles from US$53 to US$79, and doubles from US$68 to US$112. *Americana Eilat* (☎ 633 3777, fax 633 4174) has a pool, nightclub and tennis, with singles from US$55 to US$75, and doubles from US$65 to US$99.

Out on Coral Beach is *Prima Carlton Eilat* (☎ 633 3555, fax 633 4088, email sales@prima.co.il) part of the Prima Hotel chain. Its decent singles run from US$84 to US$120 and doubles from US$108 to US$155.

Travellers who prefer independent apartment accommodation should look no further than *Villa Kibel* (☎ 634 5366, fax 637 6911, email russell@eilat.ardom.co.il, 18 Peres St). Owner Russell Kibel has a range of apartments large and small to cater to all tastes and numbers of guests and their prices range from US$40 to US$150. Bookings are recommended and Russell will pick you up if given notice.

Places to Eat

Street Food Most of the felafel and shwarma places are on HaTemarim Blvd near the bus station – there's a particularly good one next to the International Bird-watching Centre.

Eilat's bakers win the prize for baking Israel's smallest pitta, and getting both felafel and salad into the same piece of bread is an acquired art. Also on HaTemarim Blvd, mainly between Hativat HaNegev Ave and Almogin St, are a couple of good bakeries; the *Family Bakery* where Ofarim meets HaTemarim, is worth noting as it stays open 24 hours and has a patio with seating, and a jukebox. The sign is in Russian and Hebrew only.

Snacks None of the shopping malls has a truly recommendable eating place and you may find yourself having to resort to any of the fast food chains who have made a presence in Eilat. However *Country Chicken* (☎ 637 1312) in the New Tourist Centre gets favourable comments in the local press where it is recommended for its chicken soup and reasonable prices.

Restaurants For something more substantial, but what are basically uninspiring permutations of chips, eggs, bacon, sausage and beans, *Underground Pub* (☎ 637 0239) in the New Tourist Centre serves up these staple traveller fillers for around 13NIS, or 20NIS for a chicken schnitzel with chips.

Nothing to do with its near-namesake, *Hard Rock 91* (☎ 637 2883, 179 Elot Ave) is a dim little cellar bar but it does serve the best burgers and fries in town, and a few other dishes besides. Prices are around 15 to 20NIS. It's just west of HaTemarim Blvd.

The local branch of *Nargila* (☎ 637 6101) provides passable Yemenite food; try the malawach, a savoury or sweet pastry pancake. You'll find the Nargila next to the bus station.

Self-Catering The one saving grace of dining in Eilat is that the thermometer-busting heat means appetites tend to be smaller. If you can be satisfied with just a sandwich then there's a *Co-op supermarket* on Elot Ave, on the corner of HaTemarim Blvd, and another in the Shalom Centre.

Entertainment

The nightlife in Eilat is firmly bar-based, however, pick up the free *English in Eilat* leaflet from the tourist office to find out what else is happening.

The most popular place with travellers at the time of research was the **Underground Pub** in the New Tourist Centre, where cheap beer and food fuel a loud and lively crowd. **Hemingway Pub** is no more than a semi-circular room in a basement under a supermarket, but it pulls in a good crowd nightly.

Next Generation is run by the same management as Hemingways, but is only open three nights a week. This hot spot features '70s & 80s nights' with free drinks for appropriately-dressed patrons. It's on Market Square behind Leumi Bank, opposite the main entrance of the bus station.

Back at the marina you will find **The Yacht Pub**, part of the King Solomon's Palace Hotel complex, which features live music of varying quality.

Getting There & Away

Air Arkia flights depart several times daily from the central airport for Jerusalem (US$80) and Tel Aviv (US$80) and less frequently for Haifa (US$94). The Arkia booking office (☎ 637 6102) is in the Red Canyon centre above the post office.

For information on flights with other airlines call Eilat airport (☎ 637 3553) or Ovda airport (☎ 635 9442) which is 70km from Eilat.

Bus Bus No 394 departs for Tel Aviv (46NIS, five hours) every 1½ hours between 8 am and 5 pm with an additional overnight service leaving at 1 am. Last bus on Friday is at 3 pm; the first bus on Shabbat is at 1 pm. Bus No 444 departs for Jerusalem (57NIS, 4½ hours) at 7 and 10 am and 2 and 5 pm daily. On Friday there is no 5 pm bus, while on Shabbat there is only one bus, departing at 4 pm. There is also a Haifa service (65NIS, 6½ hours), bus No 991, departing Sunday to Thursday at 8.30 am and 11 pm and Saturday at 11 pm only. For all of these services it's advisable to book at least a day beforehand. If there are no Jerusalem or Tel Aviv buses available, go to Beersheba and change there.

Egypt If you are heading to or from Sinai, local bus No 15 runs between Eilat's central bus station and Taba (5.20NIS). The service runs every 15 to 20 minutes between 7 am and 9.30 pm (last bus on Friday is at 5 pm; first bus on Shabbat at 9 am). You can also catch the less frequent No 16 which goes Arava-central bus station-Taba but check which direction it's heading first.

Jordan Bus No 16 runs from Eilat's central bus station to the border at Arava every 20 minutes, Monday to Thursday from 7 am to 4 pm.

Getting Around

Bus Local bus No 15 is the most used service, running every day between the bus station and Taba via the hotel area and Coral Beach. Distances within the town are not so great and most people walk everywhere.

Bicycles & Scooters The heat may prove to be too much of a deterrent, but you can hire a bicycle for 60NIS a day from Doobie Scooter (☎ 633 6557, 650 3917) based in Dalia Hotel. Alternatively beat the heat and let the wind whip your hair by slapping down 70NIS for four hours or 115NIS for 24 hours for a scooter from the same company.

AROUND EILAT

Places that should be seen if you have a car or decide to take a tour include **Ein Netafim**, a small spring at the foot of a 30m waterfall, which attracts many animals who come to drink; the **Red Canyon**, one of the area's most beautiful sights, 600m long, 1m to 3m wide at its narrowest and some 10m at it deepest; and **Moon Valley**, which is Egyptian territory but can be seen from the Red Canyon.

About 25km north of Eilat and accessible by public bus, **Timna National Park** is the site of some stunning desert landscapes, enlivened with multicoloured rock formations. Any bus heading to or from Eilat passes the turn-off for the park but from the main road it is a 2.5km walk to the park's entrance.

Hai-Bar Arava Biblical Wildlife Reserve was created to establish breeding groups of wild animals threatened by extinction. Within the reserve is also the **Yotvata Visitors' Centre** (☎ 637 6018) which features an audiovisual presentation that describes the region's natural attractions, and an exhibition of maps, diagrams and photographs on the zoology, botany, geology, archaeology and history of settlement in the area. The reserve is 40km north of Eilat and all buses to and from town pass by.

The Gaza Strip & the West Bank

Formerly known as the Occupied Territories, the Gaza Strip and the West Bank are predominantly Palestinian territories captured by Israel during the Six Day War. They have remained in political limbo ever since, neither annexed outright by Israel (as were East Jerusalem and the Golan Heights), nor granted outright autonomy – although this may eventually be the result of the ongoing peace process.

Although the extents of the Gaza Strip are well defined by razor wire and watchtowers, the pre-1967 border between Israel and the West Bank (known as the 'green line') is not marked by any signs, let alone border posts, and most Israelis would be hard pressed to point out exactly where one region ends and the other begins. At the present time this has yet to become an issue as the handing back of all West Bank territories to the Palestinians is still some way down the line.

Since 1994 the Palestinians have existed under limited self-rule in the Gaza Strip and Jericho. In late 1995, the Israeli Defence Force (IDF) also withdrew from several West Bank towns, including Jenin, Nablus, Bethlehem and Ramallah, releasing them to the direct control of the Palestinian National Authority.

GAZA

Gaza was at one time one of the most strategically important towns in the Levant, a staging post on several well-trafficked trade routes linking Central Asia and Persia with Arabia, Egypt and Africa. It is said that Gaza has been taken and destroyed in war more than any town in the world.

Since the establishment of limited self-rule in 1994, Gaza is experiencing a post-*intifada* pick-up, although normal service is still some way off being resumed.

Orientation & Information

There is one long street, Omar al-Mukhtar St, which runs about 4km from Al-Shajaria Square to the seafront. Most of the city's shops, businesses and other facilities are either on Omar al-Mukhtar St or just off it. The centre of activity is Palestine Square (Midan Filisteen) which is 500m west of Al-Shajaria Square on Omar al-Mukhtar St. All Gaza's hotels and most of the restaurants are on the seafront at the extreme west end of Omar al-Mukhtar St. This coastal district is known as Rimal ('Sand') and it's the posh area, full of cool villas and Mediterranean apartment blocks, home to wealthy ex-émigré Palestinians, expat aid workers and Yasser Arafat and family.

Money is best changed at the official moneychangers around Palestine Square, which is also where most of the town's banks are located. There's an international telephone office El-Baz (☎ 282 1910, fax 286 4120) just east of Gaza's only traffic lights on Omar al-Mukhtar St. The police station is on the north side of Al-Shajaria Square, while around the corner is the post office – open from 8 am to 6 pm Saturday to Thursday but it's closed on Friday.

The Old Town

The area surrounding Palestine Square is the oldest part of town and contains most of the city's historical interest sites. Although mostly obscured by the surrounding buildings, the **Jamaa al-Akbar (Great Mosque)**, a conversion of a Crusader-era church, is the town's most distinguished structure. Non-Muslims are usually allowed to enter the mosque in between the daily prayers. Along the southern side of the mosque runs the short, vaulted **Goldsmiths' Alley**, all that remains of what, during the Mamluk-era, was a much larger covered market, similar to that in Jerusalem's Old City.

During his Egyptian campaign, Napoleon Bonaparte camped in Gaza in 1799 and commandeered an attractive Mamluk-era building as his headquarters. Known as **Napoleon's Citadel** it's now a girls school. It stands on Al-Wahida St, north of the Great Mosque. Head west (towards the sea) from the citadel and take the second right for the **Mosque of Said Hashim**, erected on the grave of the Prophet Mohammed's great-grandfather.

Places to Stay

The cheapest place in town is *Al-Amal Hotel* (☎ 286 1832, fax 284 1317, Omar al-Mukhtar St) 300m east of the seafront. Though the plumbing is a little old, it's a well-run place, immaculately clean and not badly priced at US$40/50 for a single/double. For those with a fatter wallet, the other good option is *Marna House* (☎ 282 2624, fax 282 3322) a comfortable private villa in a quiet residential street. Singles/doubles are US$60/70 with breakfast. Marna House is two blocks north of Omar al-Mukhtar St, just west of An-Nasser St.

Places to Eat

Felafel is easily found in the Palestine Square area and some of the best shwarma is here at a shop on the short street that connects the east end of the square to Wahida St; a huge piece of lafah bread stuffed with meat and salad is only 10NIS.

Fish is a local speciality and restaurants on the seafront compete for the attention of the bigger spenders. *Al Salam*, *Loveboat*, *Mirage* and *La Andalus* restaurants, set above the beach between the hotels, are all fairly modern and well-run places and you can expect to pay 60 to 80NIS per person for a meal.

Getting There & Away

The only entry/exit point at the time of writing was Erez, in the north of the Strip, though passengers to/from Egypt via the Rafah crossing will get to the crossing via a separate road corridor from Israeli territory. To get there from Jerusalem, essentially the only way nowadays is to take a special taxi from East Jerusalem with Al Zahra Taxi (☎ 628 2444) to the Erez crossing. It will cost you 180NIS.

The only entry/exit point at the time of writing is Erez, in the north of Gaza Strip. The most convenient way to get there is to take a service taxi from opposite Damascus Gate in Jerusalem. They depart every day but you may have to wait a considerable time for the car to fill up (on our last trip we waited almost three hours for the required seven people). The cost is 30NIS per person and the ride takes about an hour. Alternatively, if it's time you're short of not money, you can opt for a 'special' and pay for the entire taxi yourself, in which case the cost is 210NIS.

The other way to get to Erez is via the Israeli coastal town of Ashkelon, which is served by regular buses from Tel Aviv. From Ashkelon take a southbound bus and ask to be let off at the Yad Mordechai junction. This is only about 5km from Erez and there are usually taxis at Yad Mordechai that will ferry you to the border.

Once at Erez, for non-Israeli or non-Arab passport holders crossing into the Strip is painless and takes minutes. The only headache is the swarm of taxi drivers beyond the Palestinian checkpoint who literally fight over the right to drive you into Gaza City, some 10km away. The fare should be no more than 10NIS service or 40NIS 'special'.

Avoid crossing between 4.30 and 6 am when the border is clogged by thousands of Palestinians heading out into Israel for a day's work and likewise from 3 to 4 pm when they are returning.

Getting Around

With Gaza having a 4km long main street, the unofficial local taxi setup is great. Instead of walking, stand by the roadside and, by pointing your index finger, hail a taxi. It seems like half of the cars in town act as pirate taxis and everyone uses them. Up and

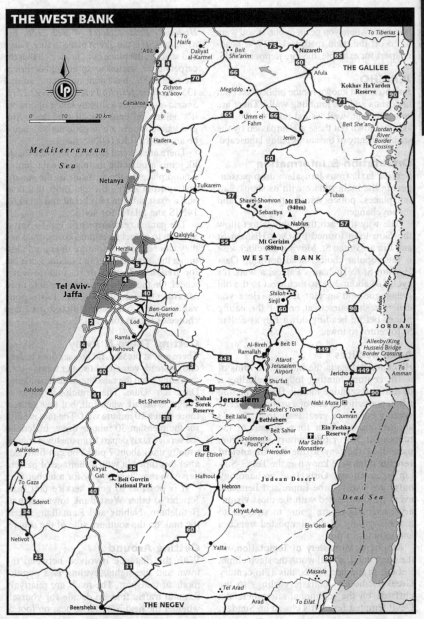

THE WEST BANK

down Omar al-Mukhtar St the fare is 1NIS, no matter where you get in or out. If you want to go off the main road, to UNRWA headquarters for example, the fare jumps to 5NIS.

JERICHO
Jericho is best known for the biblical account of Joshua and the tumbling walls. There are some ancient, well-visited ruins on the outskirts of town but these are surpassed by the shabby beauty of the surrounding landscape.

Orientation & Information
Service taxis from Jerusalem drop passengers in the main square with its shops, eating places, police station, taxi ranks and moneychanger.

The way to reach the sights is to follow the 6km loop formed by Qasr Hisham St and Ein as-Sultan St. Moving anticlockwise is the popular choice: head north up Qasr Hisham St to Hisham's Palace, a walk (or cycle) of about 2.5km, then west to the old synagogue and ancient Jericho. Here you can refresh yourself at one of the eating places before heading down Ein as-Sultan St to return to town.

Ancient Sites
Hisham's Palace is the impressive ruins of a 7th century hunting lodge, including a beautiful Byzantine mosaic floor depicting a lion pouncing on one of a group of gazelle grazing beneath a great leafy tree. There's another mosaic floor forming part of the ruins of a 5th or 6th century synagogue, passed on the way to the site of ancient Jericho, otherwise known as the Tel as-Sultan excavations. Only true archaeology buffs are likely to be impressed here and even visitors blessed with the most visionary imaginations are going to struggle to make anything of the signposted trenches and mounds of dirt.

Mount & Monastery of Temptation, on the other hand, is well worth the steep climb. Rebuilt in the late 1800s, this 12th century Greek Orthodox monastery clings to the cliffside on the traditional site where the Devil tempted Jesus. It's closed on Sunday.

Places to Stay & Eat
Hisham's Palace Hotel (☎ 992 2156, Ein as-Sultan St) is the oldest place to stay. Large and shabby, the place is so neglected that the carpets have started to sprout grass. Prices are negotiable, but count on paying around 135NIS. *New Jericho Pension* (☎ 992 2215, Sharia al-Quds) is a slightly better option but it's neither brilliant nor all that flash. Single/double rooms are negotiable but should be around the 130/160NIS mark.

There are several *cafes* and felafel/shashlik joints around the main square, including a good place on the east side of the square, just up from Zaki's bicycle shop, that does half a roast chicken plus bread and salad for 14NIS and felafel for 4NIS.

The garden *restaurants* on Ein as-Sultan St seem to attract an enthusiastic crowd and they can be worth a splurge to enjoy Palestinian meat specialities and salads. Look out for *Bedouin Tent* with its bizarre water wheel. On the same street but closer to town *Maxim* (☎ 992 2410) offers fairly good value with a barbecued mixed grill and choice of salads for 32NIS.

Getting There & Away
There are, at present, no bus services to Jericho; instead, you could use the service taxis operating from the rank opposite Jerusalem's Damascus Gate. The stretch-Mercedes or Peugeots depart when full, but that's rarely more than a 10 minute wait. The fare is 5NIS for the pleasant 30 minute drive. In Jericho the service taxis depart from the town square, usually until about 7 pm. You can find taxis after this time but with a shortage of passengers you may have to pay for a higher fare.

It is possible to get a service taxi from Jericho to other West Bank towns such as Bethlehem, Nablus and Ramallah; ask at the rank on the southern side of the square.

Getting Around
With the distance involved between the town and the sights, cycling is a popular mode of transport. The roads are relatively flat and traffic free, so decide for yourself whether the heat is easier to bear on foot or

on the saddle of a rented boneshaker. Zaki's bicycle shop is on the town square and it charges 5NIS per hour. There's a second bicycle hire place around the corner on Jerusalem St. A passport or a similar document may be asked for security.

AROUND JERICHO

About 8km before Jericho a road leads right to **Nebi Musa**, a small monastic complex revered by Muslims as the tomb of Moses, with a backdrop of the Judean Desert.

Wadi Qelt is a nature reserve with a natural spring where you can swim in a pool under a waterfall and hike along an aqueduct to **St George's Monastery**, built into the cliff face of a canyon. The hike takes about four hours. The starting point is the Wadi Qelt turn-off on the Jerusalem-Jericho road (get the bus driver to drop you off here) and the finishing point is Jericho, from where you can continue sightseeing in the town or easily find transport back to Jerusalem.

BETHLEHEM

Modern-day Bethlehem may be a cynic's delight, with Manger Square, Manger St, Star St, Shepherds' St, two Shepherds' Fields and an unheavenly host of 'Christmases' but for most travellers with even the remotest Christian background, a trip to the Holy Land without visiting the site of the Nativity is unthinkable, even if only to please a pious relative back home. Besides the pilgrimage sites, there are also some excellent excursions to places just outside the town, such as the Mar Saba Monastery and the Herodion.

Orientation & Information

With the Church of the Nativity located on its southern side, Manger Square is the centre of town. At the time of research renovations to the square, a joint Palestinian-Swedish project, were not complete but should be long-ready by the time this book gets to print. Around the square are the tourist information office, police station, post office and various shops, hotels and eating places. Milk Grotto St heads off to the south-east, past the Milk Grotto Chapel, while Paul VI St, which heads

uphill to the north-west, has the museum, outdoor market and more shops and hotels.

Manger St, which comes off the east side of the square, is the main winding route through the new town. It eventually intersects with the Jerusalem-Hebron highway opposite the Jewish shrine of Rachel's Tomb.

Things to See

Church of the Nativity, one of the world's oldest working churches, is built like a citadel over the cave where it is believed that Jesus was born. Happily, it's a suitably august and venerable building, which unlike Jerusalem's Holy Sepulchre or Nazareth's Basilica manages to avoid the 'holy site as sideshow' feel. Down Milk Grotto St is **Milk Grotto Chapel**, a kitsch little shrine that owes its existence to the Virgin Mary's lactations (at least that's how the legend goes). North of the square on Paul VI St **Bethlehem Museum** has exhibits of traditional Palestinian crafts and costumes; it's open Monday to Saturday from 10 am to noon and 2.30 to 5.30 pm; closed Sunday.

One of Judaism's most sacred shrines, and also revered by Muslims and Christians, **Rachel's Tomb** is housed in a small white domed building on the edge of town at the intersection of Hebron Rd and Manger St.

Places to Stay & Eat

Accommodation in Bethlehem is limited, especially at Christmas and Easter (some things never change) and it makes more sense to stay in nearby Jerusalem.

The best option is the recently renovated Franciscan *Casa Nova Hospice* (☎ 274 3981, fax 274 3540) next to the Church of the Holy Nativity. It has great facilities and good food, and costs US$20 for B&B, US$25 for half-board, US$30 for full board.

Alexander Hotel (☎ 277 0780, fax 277 0782) is a great hotel with an enthusiastic owner called Joseph. Its tastefully furnished rooms have a view over the valley at the back and singles cost between US$40 and US$55 and doubles between US$50 and US$85.

There are no outstanding restaurants but there are plenty of felafel and mixed grill merchants competing around Manger Square. *Reem Restaurant* down the sidestreet past the bakery on Paul VI St is inexpensive with homous and other salads for about 14NIS.

Getting There & Away

Arab bus No 22 runs frequently from East Jerusalem and stops outside Jaffa Gate en route. It's about a 40 minute ride. Service taxis (costing 3NIS) from outside Damascus Gate are more convenient; they tend to depart more frequently and make the journey in half the time of the bus.

Walking from Jerusalem to Bethlehem is a popular option. At Christmas there's an official procession, but the two to 2½ hour, up and downhill-all-the-way hike will be shared with heavy traffic.

AROUND BETHLEHEM

Past Rachel's Tomb, in the direction of Hebron, a road heads west to the pleasant Christian Arab village of **Beit Jalla** and continues to the summit of **Har Gillo** with great views. A side road leads to the attractive Salesian monastery of **Cremisan**, renowned for its wine and olive oil. Arab bus No 21 runs from Jerusalem to Beit Jalla.

Various biblical events are associated with the **Field of Ruth** and the two **Shepherds' Fields** at the village of Beit Sahur, 1km east of Bethlehem. There are the ruins of a Byzantine monastery, destroyed by the Persians in 614 AD, and a 5th century church built over a cave with a mosaic floor. Arab bus No 47 goes to Beit Sahur from Manger St and the fields are a 20 minute walk farther east, 3km or 4km from Bethlehem.

Splendid architecture and a superb location combine to make the Greek Orthodox Monastery of **Mar Saba** one of the most impressive buildings in the Holy Land. Unfortunately, it's strictly closed to women but it is worth a visit if only to view the exterior. The monastery is on the steep bank of the Kidron River in the proverbial middle of nowhere and unless you have your own car, you will have to walk the 6km from where the bus stops in the village of Abu Diye (reached by Arab bus No 60 from Bethlehem).

There are more superb views and a major archaeological site at the **Herodion**, the palace complex built by Herod between 24 and 15 BC. The Herodion is 8km south of Beit Sahur. Various buses run infrequently from Bethlehem, despite what the tourist office says; otherwise use taxis, walk or hitch. **Solomon's Pools**, with a large reservoir and a Turkish fort, are 8km south of Beit Jalla. Take Arab minibus No 1 to Dashit, the nearby Arab village, or Arab bus No 23.

HEBRON

At the time of writing, Hebron continues to be the place of greatest unrest in the West Bank. The dispute focuses on the Ibrahimi Mosque/Cave of Machpelah, a site holy to both Jews and Muslims. In order to be near the shrine, in the early 1970s a group of Jewish extremists established their presence on the fringes of entirely Arab Hebron. Since then, they have advanced into the town itself, taking possession of a central street and its buildings. Now 500 strong, the Jewish settler community is guarded by 2500 Israeli soldiers from the 12,000 Palestinians among whom they live. It's an extremely volatile situation that in autumn 1995 erupted in a series of particularly unpleasant confrontations, resulting in a number of deaths. Frequent clashes since then make visiting Hebron a potentially risky venture. Check on the current state of affairs before visiting.

Orientation & Information

The bus or service taxi will drop you off on King David St on the northern edge of the market. Heading down through the market, directly south, brings you to the Ibrahimi Mosque. It is important that when wandering through the old town you look as touristy (ie non-Jewish) as possible.

The Old Town

Supposed burial place of Abraham, to Jews the site of the **Cave of Machpelah**, over which the **Ibrahimi Mosque** was built in the 12th century, is second in sanctity only to Jerusalem's Western Wall, while to Muslims, of all the Holy Land shrines, only the

Dome of the Rock is more venerated. As such the site has always inflamed passions and been a cause of bloody tragedy, as happened in February 1994 when a Jewish settler stepped into the mosque and opened fire on a congregation of Muslims at prayer. The mosque is now segregated into separate Muslim and Jewish sections each with their own entrance. Security is tight and visitors will be brusquely frisked and questioned.

Hebron's **souq** is a compendium of Crusader and Mamluk facades, vaulted ceilings, tiny shops and narrow alleyways. Despite the tensions in the city, it's still fairly lively first thing in the morning.

Getting There & Away
Arab bus No 23 operates between Jerusalem and Hebron (3NIS) via Rachel's Tomb at Bethlehem but service taxis (5NIS), caught outside Jerusalem's Damascus Gate, depart far more frequently and are much faster.

NABLUS
Beautifully situated between the scenic mountains of Gerizim and Ebal, Nablus is the largest of the West Bank towns. It's a typical bustling Arab town, quite attractive with its breeze-block houses tumbling down the mountainsides and an enchanting old quarter. Only an hour from Jerusalem by service taxi it's well worth a day visit.

Orientation & Information
The centre of Nablus is Palestine/Al-Hussein Square, home to a small market and the terminal for many buses and service taxis. Just south of the square is the Old Town, which stretches to the east along Nasir St. Beyond the Old Town rise the slopes of Mt Gerizim, holy to the Samaritans, while Mt Ebal stands to the north.

The Old Town
From Al-Hussein Square head directly south, homing in on the minaret of **An-Nasir Mosque** on Nasir St – one of 30 minarets punctuating the Nablus skyline. Close by is an old Turkish mansion known as **Touqan Castle**. It's now privately owned, but usu-

ally visitors are welcome to look at the architecture and garden. From Nasir St walk south through Al-Beik Gate and the entrance is up the slope on your left.

East of the An-Nasir Mosque on An-Nasir St is Al-Shifa (☎ 09-838 1176), the oldest working **Turkish bath** in the country. Built around 1480 at the start of the Ottoman period, Al-Shifa has been lovingly restored and as well as the hot rooms there's a central hall with cushion strewn platforms to recline on while you sip black coffee or mint tea and puff on a nargileh. The bath is open daily for men only from about 8 am to 10 pm; Wednesday between 8 am and 5 pm is women only. It costs 10NIS to use the baths and a massage is 10NIS extra.

Places to Stay & Eat
There are only a couple of hotels in Nablus. At the bottom of the scale is *Al-Istiqlal Pension* (☎ 238 3618, 11 Sharia Hitteen) which offers men-only dorm accommodation. *Al Qasr Hotel* (☎ 238 5444, 238 5944, email alqasr@netvision.net.il, Sharia Omar Ibn al-Khatib) has singles/doubles costing US$70/95 irrespective of the season.

Along with soap, the Nablus speciality is sweets. These include all the various pastries, halvah and Turkish delight, but in particular *kanafe* (cheese topped with orange wheat flakes and soaked in honey). The best bakery to try this rich delicacy is *Al-Aqsa*, next to An-Nasir Mosque and across from the soap factory on Nasir St in the Old City.

Getting There & Away
Arab buses run to Nablus from East Jerusalem (Nablus Rd station) via Ramallah. It takes two to 2½ hours, making the service taxis (11NIS, 1¼ hours) very appealing.

AROUND NABLUS
Sebastiya
This quiet little Arab village stands about 15km north-west of Nablus up on the scenic slopes of the Samarian hills. Just above it on the summit of the peak lie the impressive ruins of Samaria, the capital of the ancient Israelite kingdom.

Jordan

Jordan is a delightful place to visit, made more so by its truly friendly people, who continually call out to you 'Welcome in Jordan!' – and they really mean it. It is usually an easy place to get around although border crossings to some of its neighbours – Israel, Iraq and Saudi Arabia – can be difficult, depending on current regional politics. Yet in the midst of all the Middle Eastern turmoil Jordan seems to retain a calmer air, a peacefulness and sanity not prevalent in surrounding countries.

In comparison with other Middle Eastern countries, travelling in Jordan can be expensive, although budget travellers seem to get by without too much difficulty. One thing that overwhelms is the sense of history. Amman, the ancient Rabbath Ammon of the Old Testament and over 5500 years old, was taken by the biblical David's army and, later, was one of the cities of the ancient Decapolis.

To the south of Amman at Madaba is the famous mosaic depicting Palestine and lower Egypt, often seen in advertisements for Israel! A few kilometres away is Mt Nebo, one of the supposed burial places of Moses. At the southern end of the Dead Sea were Sodom and Gomorrah, perhaps ... Before Christ was born Nabataean stonemasons carved out their beautiful city of Petra from towering rock walls. Nearby, Moses, at the end of the Exodus, struck the ground at Wadi Musa and 'water gushed forth'. And Aaron (the Islamic Prophet Harun), the elder brother of Moses, was buried atop Mt Hor, overlooking Petra.

Jordan is compact and has enough attractions to keep you interested for a couple of weeks, so on no account miss it.

Facts about Jordan

HISTORY

Jordan was one of many countries that escaped from a long period of Turkish rule

Hashemite Kingdom of Jordan

Area: 89,206 sq km
Population: approx 5.2 million
Population Growth Rate: 3.4%
Capital: Amman
Head of State: King Abdullah II
Official Language: Arabic
Currency: Jordanian dinar (JD)
Exchange Rate: US$1 = JD0.71

- **Best Dining** – a Bedouin meal of *mensaf* (lamb on a bed of rice and pine nuts topped with the head of the lamb), served in a dish and eaten on the floor
- **Best Nightlife** – watching nature's planetarium from your open-air desert bed in Wadi Rum
- **Best Walk** – through the labyrinthine *Siq* to the spectacular *Khazneh* (Treasury), then past the other facades of the ancient Nabataean city of Petra, to Mt Haroun and Aaron's Tomb
- **Best Views** – from the ramparts of the Dead Sea Hills down to Wadi Araba and the Dead Sea
- **Best Activity** – watching *Indiana Jones & The Last Crusade* after your first day in Petra; nearly everyone says 'I saw that today' when the Khazneh comes up in the last scenes
- **When in Rome ...** You'll continually hear 'Welcome in Jordan' – it doesn't hurt to say 'Shukran' (Thank you)

when the Ottoman empire collapsed after WWI (see the History section of the Facts about the Region chapter). The newly formed League of Nations gave Britain a Mandate over Palestine, and shortly afterwards the new state of Transjordan was made a separate entity under King Abdullah. What remained of Palestine corresponded more or less to present-day Israel and the Palestinian Territories. Britain's attempts to accommodate the international Jewish communities' desire for a homeland in Palestine and keep the Arab populace happy were ultimately unsuccessful. Immediately after WWII the British gave up and referred the mess to the United Nations (UN), which voted in favour of the partition of Palestine into separate Arab and Jewish states. Agreement could not be reached and the Arab-Israeli War broke out in 1948, ending with a comprehensive victory for Israel and Jewish occupation of the zones allocated to them under the UN partition plan as well as virtually all those assigned to the Palestinian Arabs. Transjordan took advantage of the situation and occupied the West Bank and a part of Jerusalem. This done, King Abdullah shortened his fledgling country's name to Jordan.

Abdullah was assassinated in 1951. He was succeeded the following year by his grandson Hussein, who took the throne at the immature age of 17 and managed to hold it for 48 years through insurrection attempts and major disruptions, two wars with the Israelis and a virtual civil war with the Palestinians, until his death early in 1999.

In the 1960s things were pretty rosy in Jordan with aid pouring in from the USA and a boom in tourism, mainly in Jerusalem's Old City. The situation was radically altered by the Six Day War of 1967, in which Jordan lost the West Bank and its half of Jerusalem to occupying Israeli forces. In a single blow Jordan had lost its two most important income sources: agriculture and tourism. It also experienced another huge influx of Palestinian refugees.

As the Palestinians, particularly the Palestine Liberation Organization (PLO),

What to See

North of Amman are the ancient cities of the Roman Decapolis including **Umm Qais**, **Pella** and **Jerash**; the latter is one of the most well-preserved Roman provincial cities in the Middle East. To the north-east of Amman there is a collection of **desert castles** built or taken over by 7th and 8th century Umayyad rulers. **Amman** itself is an extremely friendly, cosmopolitan city and a great place to stop for a while.

To the south of Amman are the real treasures. Along the King's Highway you encounter the mosaics of **Madaba**, the spectacular **Wadi al-Mujib**, the crusader castle of **Kerak** and then **Petra** – the remarkable Nabataean city with facades hewn into the multicoloured rock cliffs.

In the far south is magnificent **Wadi Rum** with its stone and granite rock landscapes, a one-time haunt of Lawrence of Arabia. Lastly, is the town and gulf of **Aqaba**, with many aquatic pastimes.

JORDAN

became more militant against the Israeli occupation in the early 1970s, they also posed a danger to King Hussein, given that most of them operated from Jordanian territory and virtually came to contest power in his kingdom. After bloody fighting, the bulk of the radicals were forced to move to Lebanon, where they would later become an integral part of that country's woes.

Hussein's diplomatic skills were stretched to the fullest when, during the 1991 Gulf War, the king refused to side against Iraq, largely out of fear of unrest among Jordan's pro-Saddam Palestinian populace. It was a precarious stance but the country avoided total isolation by playing a peace-broker role and complying, officially at least, with the UN embargo on trade with Iraq.

Jordan recovered remarkably well from that conflict, and despite fears of the threat of Islamic extremism, Hussein went ahead and signed a full peace treaty with Israel in 1994.

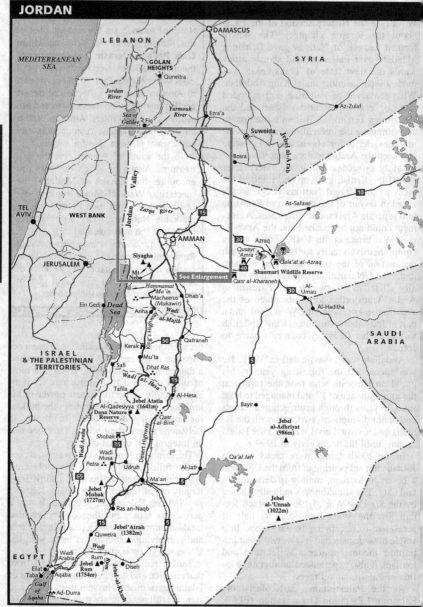

JORDAN

JORDAN

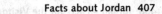

To Baghdad

IRAQ

Ar-Ruwayshid

SAUDI
ARABIA

0   25   50 km

Al-Hemma
*Umm
Qais*   0   20 km
Jisr   Der'a
Sheikh   Irbid Ramtha
Hussein   Jabir   Naşib
Pella   Jabir
Al-Mashari'a   Mafraq
Qala'at Ajlun Jerash
ar-Rabad   Umm
Deir Alla Jerash   al-Jimal
Jordan *Zarqa River*
River   Qasr
Suweileh   Zarqa   al-Hallabat
Salt   15
Al-Karama   Hammam
Wadi   as-Sarah
as-Seer AMMAN
South Shuneh
Jisr   Al-Muwaqqar
al-Malek Mt
Hussein Nebo
Suweimeh *Siyagha* Qasr al-Mushatta
Ma'in Madaba   Queen Alia
International
Airport

Jordan Today

The dividends of peace with Israel have been a huge upsurge in tourism in Jordan, not least from tens of thousands of Israelis bussing across the border to visit Petra and Wadi Rum. When King Hussein finally succumbed to the cancer that had been ailing him for so long in February 1999, it was a comparatively stable and prosperous country that was passed on to his son and nominated heir King Abdullah II. But how much that stability relied on the presence of the widely respected Hussein, and whether the new king can prove as diplomatically adept in one of the most turbulent neighbourhoods in the world, remains to be seen.

GEOGRAPHY

Jordan can easily be divided into three major regions: the Jordan Valley, the East Bank plateau and the desert. The fertile valley of the Jordan River is the country's dominant physical feature, running from the Syrian border in the north, down the border with Israel to the Gulf of Aqaba. The majority of the population live in a narrow 70km-wide strip running the length of the country on the East Bank plateau. The remaining 80% of the country is a desert, stretching to Syria, Iraq and Saudi Arabia, with climatic extremes and minimal rainfall.

Distances are short – it's only about 420km from Ramtha in the north to Aqaba in the south. From Amman to the furthest point of interest in the east, Azraq, is just 103km.

CLIMATE

Average daytime maximum temperatures in Amman range from 12°C in January to 32°C in August. The weather in the Jordan Valley is oppressive in summer: daily temperatures are well in excess of 36°C and have been recorded as high as 49°C. At the other extreme, snow in Amman is not unheard of and even Petra gets the occasional snowfall. The desert areas, with less than 50mm of rain annually, have extremely hot summers, with temperatures that can reach into the high 40s.

JORDAN

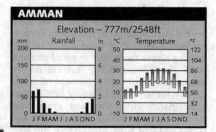

AMMAN
Elevation – 777m/2548ft

GOVERNMENT & POLITICS

Jordan is a constitutional monarchy with a democratically elected government. King Abdullah II came to power in February 1999 following the death of his much admired father, King Hussein. Hussein was highly respected both in his country and throughout the region and was a believer in some form of parliamentary democracy taking root in Jordan. It's thought that Abdullah II, born of a British mother and educated in England and the USA, shares his father's outlook.

The National Assembly (*Majlis al-Umma*) is bicameral, the Senate having half as many members as the House of Representatives. The king is vested with wide-ranging powers, although his power of veto can be overridden by a two-thirds majority of both the houses of the National Assembly. The 80 member lower house is elected by all citizens over the age of 18 years, but the prime minister is appointed by the king, as are the 40 members and president of the Senate.

Although elections are supposed to take place every four years, the first elections since Jordan lost the West Bank in the 1967 Six Day War were held in November 1989. This was the first time women were allowed to vote.

POPULATION & PEOPLE

The population of Jordan stood at about 5.2 million in 1998. Some 900,000 of whom were registered as refugees (from the wars of 1948 and 1967) with the United Nations Relief & Works Agency (UNRWA) on the East Bank. The population is growing at a relatively moderate 3.4%.

Approximately 1.7 million people live in the capital, Amman, and a further 630,000 people live in neighbouring Zarqa and suburbs. The majority of Jordanians are Arab; 60% of people are Palestinian Arabs. There are also 25,000 resident Circassians (descendants of 19th century migrants from the Caucasus in Russia) and much smaller groups of Chechens and Armenians.

The Bedouin were once originally desert dwellers and form the majority of the indigenous population, but today not more than 40,000 Bedouin can be considered to be truly nomadic.

RELIGION

More than 92% of the population are Sunni Muslims. A further 6% are Christians who live mainly in Amman, Madaba, Kerak and Salt. There are tiny Shi'ite and Druze populations, and a few hundred Bahais. All religions seem to get on harmoniously in Jordan.

The majority of Christians belong to the Greek Orthodox Church, but there are Greek Catholics, a small Roman (Latin) Catholic community, Syrian Orthodox, Coptic Orthodox and, among the non-Arabs, Catholics and Armenian Orthodox Christians.

LANGUAGE

Arabic is the official language of Jordan. English is widely spoken however, and is sufficient to get by. For details on the Arabic language, see the Language chapter at the back of this book.

Facts for the Visitor

PLANNING

Spring is the best time to visit as temperatures are mild and the winter rains have cleared the haze that obscures views for much of the year. Visiting in autumn is the next best choice.

If you go in summer, don't be caught without a hat and water bottle, especially in Wadi Rum in the south, the Desert Castle loop east of Amman and along the Jordan Valley. Winter can be bitterly cold, especially in Amman and the East Bank plateau. Aqaba is the only real exception – while scorching in summer, it can be very pleasant in winter.

VISAS & DOCUMENTS
Visas

Visas are required by all foreigners entering Jordan. These are issued at the border or airport on arrival or can be obtained from Jordanian consulates outside the country. Tourist visas are valid for stays of up to two weeks from the date of entry, but can be easily extended for up to three months. If you intend to stay beyond the two weeks your initial visa allows, you need to obtain an extension from the police (see under Information in the Amman section later in this chapter).

The cost ranges from JD16 for Australian passport holders to US$60 for US passport holders, although it averages around JD12 for most nationalities. In general, visas are cheaper to get at Jordanian consulates in neighbouring Damascus or Cairo than at the border (this is true for UK passport holders but not for US or Canadian passport holders). Multiple-entry visas are also easy to get here and are not issued at Jordan's border crossings.

Visas for Neighbouring Countries You need a visa to enter the following neighbouring countries of Jordan:

Egypt The embassy in Amman is next to the Dove Hotel, and is open for visa applications from 9 am to noon Sunday to Thursday. Passports can be picked up the following day before 3 pm. You need a passport photo and the JD17 (US$24) fee. The consulate in Aqaba on Istiqlal St is quieter, visas are cheaper at JD12 (US$17), and the staff are easier to deal with. If you are going to Egypt via the ferry, it is also possible to get your visa on arrival at Nuweiba but it's a hassle – better to get it beforehand.

Iraq Give up! You have absolutely no chance of getting a visa here. See the Iraq chapter for more details.

Israel Israeli visas are available at the land border crossings; see Getting There & Away later in this chapter for details.

Lebanon Lebanon has followed Syria's example and has virtually stopped issuing visas to those who aren't Jordanian residents. If you wish to try, the Lebanese embassy is open for applications from 8.30 to 11 am Sunday to Thursday; take a photocopy of your passport details, a passport photo and JD14 (US$20). The visa (if you get it) is valid for a month. If you are going overland you will need a Syrian visa – and this has to be obtained *before* you get to Jordan.

Saudi Arabia For details of the hoops you have to jump through to acquire a full Saudi visa see the Saudi Arabia chapter. The embassy in Amman will otherwise only issue 24 and 48 hour transit visas.

Syria Since 1996 it has been virtually impossible for those who aren't Jordanian residents to get a Syrian visa in Amman. Travellers should get one before arriving in Jordan (in Cairo, for instance). If you wish to chance it, the processing of applications seems to take about 20 days and there is no guarantee of getting a visa. You need a letter of recommendation from your embassy (for which you pay big time), a passport photo and the fee, which varies wildly between free for Australians and up to US$55 for the British. Australians and the Irish are of the few nationalities that can cross into Syria from Jordan without a visa – it is issued at the border, as long as there is no evidence that the traveller skipped into Israel. This doesn't always work though and Australian and Irish travellers should still get a visa for Syria before heading to Jordan.

Other Documents

Keep your passport handy, especially along the border area with Israel where you'll encounter numerous military checkpoints. Keep the card you receive on entry and/or that was handed to you with your visa extension as you need to present them on departure.

International Driving Permits are not needed. Student cards are not honoured at monuments or museums (everyone pays full price at Petra).

EMBASSIES & CONSULATES
Jordanian Embassies & Consulates

There is no diplomatic representation in Ireland or New Zealand for Jordan. Citizens of these countries can obtain visas on arrival (as everyone can). For addresses of Jordanian embassies in neighbouring Middle Eastern countries refer to the relevant country chapter.

Australia
Embassy:
(☎ 06-295 9951)
20 Roebuck St, Redhill, Canberra, ACT 2603

Canada
Embassy:
(☎ 613-238 8090)
100 Bronson Ave, Suite 701, Ottawa, Ontario OT K1N 6R4

France
Embassy:
(☎ 01 46 24 23 78)
80 Blvd Maurice Barres, 92200 Neuilly-Seine, Paris

Germany
Embassy:
(☎ 228-35 70 46)
Beethovenallee 21, 5300 Bonn 2 (there are also consulates in Berlin, Düsseldorf, Hanover, Munich and Stuttgart)

UK
Embassy:
(☎ 020-7937 3685)
6 Upper Phillimore Gardens, London, W8 7HB

USA
Embassy:
(☎ 202-966 2664)
3504 International Drive NW, Washington DC 2000
Consulate:
(☎ 212-752 0135)
866 UN Plaza, New York, NY

Embassies & Consulates in Jordan

Foreign embassies and consulates are in Amman (Egypt also has a consulate in Aqaba). In general the offices are open from 9 to 11 am Monday to Thursday and Saturday for submission of visa applications; most will return your passport with your visa between 1 and 3 pm the same afternoon. The conditions are constantly changing, so you'd be wise to phone ahead and check.

Australia
Embassy:
(☎ 593 0246, fax 593 1260)
Between 4th and 5th Circles, Zahran St, Jebel Amman

Canada
Embassy:
(☎ 566 6124, fax 568 9227)
Pearl of Shmeisani Bldg, Shmeisani

Egypt
Embassy:
(☎ 560 5175, fax 560 4082)
Between 4th and 5th Circles, Qurtubah St

France
Embassy:
(☎ 464 1273, fax 465 9606)
Mutanabi St, Jebel Amman

Germany
Embassy:
(☎ 593 0351, fax 568 5887)
Between 4th and 5th Circles, 31 Benghazi St, Jebel Amman

Iraq
Embassy:
(☎ 462 1375, fax 461 9172)
Near 1st Circle, Zahran St, Jebel Amman

Israel
Consulate:
(☎ 569 6511)
Le Meridien Hotel, Shmeisani

Lebanon
Embassy:
(☎ 592 9111, fax 592 9112)
2nd Circle, Jebel Amman

Netherlands
Embassy:
(☎ 661 9693, fax 661 9515)
Intercontinental Hotel, Amman

New Zealand
Embassy:
(☎ 463 6720, fax 463 4349)
4th floor, Khalas Bldg, 99 Al-Malek al-Hussein St, Downtown

Saudi Arabia
Embassy:
(☎ 592 4154, fax 592 1154)
1st Circle, Jebel Amman

Syria
Embassy:
(☎ 464 1935, fax 465 1945)
Between 3rd and 4th Circles, Afghani St, Jebel Amman

UK
Embassy:
(☎ 592 3100, fax 591 3759)
Wadi Abdoun, Abdoun
USA
Embassy:
(☎ 592 0101, fax 582 0123)
Deir Ghbar, Abdoun

CUSTOMS

You can import 200 cigarettes and up to 1L of wine or spirits into Jordan duty free. There are no restrictions on the import and export of Jordanian or foreign currencies.

MONEY

Costs

One of the biggest sightseeing expenses in Jordan is the entrance fee to Petra (JD25 for two days), but this actually represents reasonable value. At other sites, such as Jerash, foreigners pay a highly inflated entrance fee compared to locals. This duel pricing policy is widespread and only in the most basic of places do locals and foreigners pay the same.

If you are living in the most basic hotels, eating felafel and shwarma, drinking tea and using shared transport (service taxis and buses), and factoring in visa costs and entrance fees, you could survive on US$15 to US$20 per day in Jordan. For another US$15 you could live quite comfortably and eat well.

Currency

The currency in Jordan is the dinar (JD) – known as the *gee-dee* among hip young locals – which is made up of 1000 fils. You will also often hear *piastre* or *qirsh* used, which are both 10 fils, so 10 qirsh equals 100 fils. Often when a price is quoted to you the ending will be omitted, so if you're told that something is 25, it's a matter of working out whether it's 25 fils, 25 qirsh or 25 dinar! To complicate things a little further, 50 fils is commonly referred to as a *shilling*, 100 fils (officially a *dirham*) as a *barisa* and a dinar as a *lira*. In fact, Jordanians rarely use the word fils at all, except for the benefit of foreigners.

Exchange Rates

country	unit		dinar
Australia	A$1	=	JD0.46
Canada	C$1	=	JD0.47
Egypt	E£1	=	JD0.21
euro	€1	=	JD0.76
France	10FF	=	JD1.10
Germany	DM1	=	JD0.39
Japan	¥100	=	JD0.62
New Zealand	NZ$1	=	JD0.37
Syria	S£10	=	JD0.10
UK	UK£1	=	JD1.15
USA	US$1	=	JD0.71

Exchanging Money

It's not difficult to change money in Jordan, with most hard currencies being accepted. American Express (Amex) travellers cheques seem to be the most widely accepted.

Outside banking hours, there are plenty of foreign exchange bureaus in Amman, Aqaba and Irbid. Many only deal in cash but some take travellers cheques. Check their exchange rates with those in the banks before changing – often they are quite OK.

In Amman you can get Syrian pounds for about the same as the black market rate in Damascus. Conversely it isn't hard to sell Syrian pounds. The same goes for Lebanese currency in Amman. The Israeli shekel can also be traded here without problem as there are a great number of Palestinians coming and going between Jordan and the West Bank. There is no problem with Egyptian currency either – many traders move to and fro between Jordan and Cairo.

It is easy to off-load the shekel in Petra as there are now great numbers of Israeli tourists day-tripping here since the relaxation of border crossings, post the end of the intifada.

You'll have absolutely no problems with Egyptian currency in Aqaba – there are daily ferries and a need for both currencies at the border.

Credit Cards & ATMs

It is possible to survive in Jordan almost entirely by cash advance. Visa is accepted for cash advances, but only at selected branches of the following banks in Amman: Housing Bank, Bank of Jordan, ANZ Grindlays,

Cairo-Amman Bank, Arab Banking Corporation, Jordan Arab Investment Bank, and Jordan Investment & Finance Bank. In Aqaba cash advances can be made at Housing Bank and Bank of Jordan. In Irbid try Bank of Jordan.

MasterCard is also accepted for cash advances, but only at selected branches of British Bank of the Middle East, Jordan National Bank and Bank of Jordan.

ATMs are found all over Jordan and accept foreign cards (including Visa and MasterCard). If an ATM swallows your card, call ☎ 06-566 9123 (Amman).

International Transfers

Western Union operates in Jordan through the Cairo-Amman Bank. See this section in the Regional Facts for the Visitor chapter.

Tipping & Bargaining

Tips of 10% are generally expected in the better restaurants. Bargaining, especially when souvenir hunting, is essential but shop owners are unlikely to shift a long way from their original asking prices.

POST & COMMUNICATIONS

Post

Letters to the USA and Australia cost 400 fils, postcards 300 fils. To Europe, letters are 300 fils and postcards 200 fils, and to Arab countries 200 fils and 150 fils respectively. Parcel post is ridiculously expensive but admittedly very efficient. If you want to send something by air to Australia, for instance, the first kilogram will cost you JD12.7 and each subsequent kilogram JD7.500. To the UK the first kilogram is JD9.500 and each kilogram after JD3.400.

For express mail facilities, Federal Express (☎ 461 8730) is very reliable and can be found at 2nd Circle, Jebel Amman. There are several home-grown operations that carry out the same functions as FedEx; they are easy to find in Amman.

Telephone

The country code for Jordan is ☎ 962, followed by the area code (minus the zero),

then the subscriber number. Most numbers in Amman have seven digits, but some suburbs have six digits and are prefixed by 07 rather than 06. Numbers in all towns outside of Amman have only six digits (with the exception of Petra and Aqaba). Area codes for the major cities and regions are:

Amman	☎ 06
Amman suburbs	☎ 07
(Sweifieh, Abdoun etc)	
Irbid	☎ 02
Jerash, Mafraq	☎ 04
Ma'an, Petra,	☎ 03
Kerak & Aqaba	
Madaba	☎ 08
Salt	☎ 05
Zarqa	☎ 09

The local telephone system isn't too bad but numbers are changing constantly in Amman as the service is upgraded; for the latest information call directory ☎ 121. Calls cost 100 fils and most shops and hotels will let you use their phone, which is better than trying to use the few noisy public telephones.

Overseas calls can be made easily from offices in Amman and Aqaba but cost the earth, with prices up to JD2.750 per minute for a three minute minimum call. It may take up to 30 minutes or so to get the connection. In Amman a bunch of private phone/fax offices have sprung up in direct competition. They sometimes provide cheaper rates and do not impose a three minute minimum. It is not possible to make collect (reverse charge) calls from Jordan. It is best to call overseas from a private telephone bureau and leave an accessible number (such as your hotel) with the person called – get them to ring you back. To Australia, expect to pay JD2 for this service; to the USA and Europe it's JD1.500.

There are now two local companies, Alo (☎ 06-465 4545 ext 248) and JPP, which have pre-paid phonecards (from JD1 to JD15) that allow you to make local, national and international calls from their public card phones (the cards get eaten up rapidly, especially on a call to Australia).

Email & Internet Access

There are several Internet cafes in Amman, as well as the odd publicly accessible terminal in Aqaba, Irbid, Madaba and Wadi Musa – see those sections later in this chapter for further details.

BOOKS

Annie Caulfield's *Kingdom of the Film Stars: Journey into Jordan* unravels some of the tightly woven western myths about the Arab world, and does so in the intimate framework of a love story. With honesty and humour, the author tells of her relationship with a Bedouin man and offers a vividly personal account of Jordanian culture and society (see the boxed text 'Amman' below).

The Seven Pillars of Wisdom by TE Lawrence describes Lawrence's adventures in Jordan before, during and after WWI (he wrote a substantial portion of the book in Amman). Unfortunately you cannot buy it in Jordan because it is banned.

For useful guides on rock climbing, walking, and 4WD and camel treks see Tony Howard's *Treks & Climbs in the Mountains of Rum & Petra* and *Walks & Scrambles in Rum*.

More general Middle East titles, some of which cover Jordan, are listed in the Books section in the Regional Facts for the Visitor chapter.

NEWSPAPERS & MAGAZINES

The press in Jordan is given a surprisingly free reign by the government, and by the region's standards, the controls are loose. The *Jordan Times*, the daily English-language newspaper, has a reasonably impartial outlook and gives good coverage of events in Jordan, elsewhere in the Middle East and worldwide. *Arab Daily* is also a local English language daily newspaper.

RADIO & TV

Radio Jordan transmits in Arabic and English. The English-language station is on 855

JORDAN

Amman

Westerners who could afford taxis stayed up in the hills in big hotels; only locals and bus-riding backpackers lurked in the heaving lower depths of the city. The hills had trees, new houses, plate glass, air-conditioning and a clean tranquillity the better-off could retreat to and survey their city as it unravelled towards Downtown, the scruffy valley where a very different life was lived.

Downtown. Where you could eat for pennies and buy cigarettes for a quarter of the European price from Iraqi refugees squatting on the pavement, their wares set out on cardboard boxes or their own threadbare coats. Safeway, McDonald's and Pizza Hut were up in the hills, full of rich foreign-educated young Arabs who wore Versace, smoked Marlboro and liked to pepper their conversation with American-accented English. Downtown, small dusty Palestinian boys ran about with wooden trays on their heads, piled high with bread and cakes, and old men sold Bedouin coffee from elaborate silver pots as they huddled in doorways with their makeshift wheeled stoves. Cafes curled with the smoke from narjileh pipes, fat cracked from pans of felafel cooked at the roadside. Second-hand western clothes were haggled over by men wearing a hundred variations on traditional Arab dress, while veiled women struggled to cross terrifyingly busy roads with armfuls of babies. Downtown never ceased to be a racket of shouts, traffic, music ... and didn't pretend to be anything other than itself.

from *Kingdom of the Film Stars: Journey into Jordan* by Annie Caulfield
(Part of Lonely Planet's Journeys series of travel literature)

kHz AM and 96.3 kHz FM in Amman, and 98.7 kHz FM in Aqaba. It's mostly a music station.

Jordan TV broadcasts on three channels: two in Arabic, and Channel 2 is solely French and English.

PHOTOGRAPHY & VIDEO

Reputable brands of film (including slide film) are widely available at tourist sites in Jordan and in Amman itself, but don't expect to pay less than you would at home (anything up to JD8 for a 36-slide roll). Check the use-by dates before buying. In Amman there are places on Al-Malek al-Hussein, Hashemi, Al-Malek Talal and Quraysh Sts where you can get passport photos taken immediately.

Always ask permission before photographing anyone, particularly women, and be careful when taking pictures in and around Aqaba as Israel is just 'over there' and the Saudi border is only 20km away. Photographing military areas is forbidden.

LAUNDRY

There are several laundries in Downtown Amman and some good dry-cleaners. Out of Amman (and even in Amman) you can ask at your hotel to have your laundry done; be prepared to pay JD3 for a 5kg load – it comes back smelling better and folded more neatly than you could ever have hoped.

If you prefer to use a laundrette in Amman, several sidestreets off Cinema al-Hussein St have laundries.

TOILETS

Only in the major hotels will you find western style toilets. Most are 'squats' with either a hose or water bucket provided for flushing. There is also a receptacle for toilet paper – use it or you will return to find an overflow on the floor. Some of the toilets you will encounter along the Desert and King's highways are literally 'stinkers' and seldom is toilet paper provided – bring your own roll.

HEALTH

There have been several recent scares with the water supply in Amman, thought to have been contaminated by the piping in of stagnant water from Lake Tiberias. The locals have been advised to boil water for two minutes before using it. The crisis has also led to a shortage of bottled mineral water. Some unscrupulous shopkeepers and restaurateurs have been caught filling mineral water bottles with the contaminated water.

Medical services in Jordan are well developed in the larger towns and cities and many of the doctors have been trained overseas and speak English. Your embassy will usually be able to recommend a reliable doctor or hospital if the need arises.

Many drugs normally sold only on prescription in the west are available over the counter in Jordan, but as the price of antibiotics in Jordan can be outrageous, you may want to bring a supply with you. If you do, make sure you also bring a prescription or a letter from your doctor.

For more general health information see the Health section in the Regional Facts for the Visitor chapter.

GAY & LESBIAN TRAVELLERS

Although the gay and lesbian scene is very much underground, there are a couple of places in Amman that are gay friendly, such as the Internet cafe/wine bar Books@Cafe. Thursday nights at the Irish Pub (under the Dove Hotel) pulls in a young mixed gay and straight dance crowd (see under Places to Eat and Entertainment in the Amman section later in this chapter).

DANGERS & ANNOYANCES

Jordan is a safe and friendly country to travel in. The military keep a low profile and you are unlikely to experience anything but friendliness, honesty and hospitality. It is generally safe to walk around anywhere day or night in Amman and other towns. Having said this, cyclists on the King's Hwy have reported harassment by groups of children taunting, and throwing stones and other missiles. Theft is usually no problem for people who take reasonable care with their gear.

BUSINESS HOURS

Government offices are open from 8 am to 2 pm daily except Friday. Banks are open from 8.30 am to 12.30 pm and 4 to 6 pm in summer (3.30 to 5.30 pm in winter) daily except Friday. Businesses keep similar hours but are more flexible. Museums are generally closed on Tuesday.

Small shops are open for long hours, from about 9 am to 8 or 9 pm. Some close for a couple of hours mid-afternoon. Friday is pretty dead, although a few shops are open.

The souqs and street stalls are open daily, and in fact Friday is often their busiest day.

From 30 June 1999 Jordan advanced its clocks by one hour. The adjustment will be permanent (ie clocks will not be adjusted back at the end of the summer period). Jordan will therefore be in the same time zone as Iraq, Kuwait and Saudi Arabia.

PUBLIC HOLIDAYS & SPECIAL EVENTS

In addition to the main Islamic holidays described in Public Holidays & Special Events in the Regional Facts for the Visitor chapter, Jordan observes the following holidays:

Tree Day (Arbor Day)
    15 January – school children are encouraged to get out and plant trees
Arab League Day
    22 March – a low-key affair
Labour Day
    1 May – also a low-key affair
Independence Day
    25 May – speeches and flag waving
Army Day & Anniversary of the Great Arab Revolt
    10 June – military parades and remembrance services
King Hussein's Birthday
    14 November – usually turns into an exciting three day weekend, with pictures of the king and Jordanian flags everywhere, car horns honking and a gathering at the Amman stadium

COURSES

The University of Jordan (☎ 534 3555) on University St, Shmeisani, in Amman, offers summer courses in Modern Standard Arabic as well as more leisurely courses throughout the rest of the year. Inquiries should be addressed to the director of the Language Centre in the Arts Faculty. Some of the foreign cultural centres also have Arabic courses (see Cultural Centres & Libraries in the Amman section).

ARCHAEOLOGICAL DIGS

You may be able to get work on archaeological projects but it is usually unpaid. Make your inquiry six months in advance so that you can obtain the necessary permits. When applying spell out your skills (eg photography, cartography etc) as locals are usually employed to do the basic spade work.

Those interested in archaeological projects in Jordan can contact the following for more information:

American Center for Oriental Research
    (☎ 06-534 6117) ACOR, PO Box 2470, Jebel Amman, Amman, 11181, Jordan
British Institute at Amman for Archaeology & History
    (☎ 06-534 1317) PO Box 519, Al-Jubeiha, Amman, 11941, Jordan
Deutsches Evangelisches Institut für Alterturnswissenschaft des Heiligen Landes, Zweigstelle Amman
    PO Box 183, Amman 1118, Jordan
Institut Français d'Archéologie du Proche Orient
    PO Box 5348, Amman, Jordan
Near Eastern Archaeology Foundation
    Volunteer Coordinator, Near Eastern Archaeology Foundation, SACAH, A14, University of Sydney, Sydney, 2006, Australia

WORK

Work is probably not an option for most foreigners passing through Jordan. The Alternative Information Centre has a 'yellow book' with details of volunteer work in the West Bank; there may be the chance to work with Palestinian refugees.

Foreigners teach English at the American Language Center and the British Council in Amman; however, teachers are usually recruited in the USA and UK (see Cultural Centres & Libraries in the Amman section for contact details).

ACCOMMODATION

There are no youth hostels in Jordan. A bed in a shared room in a cheap hotel will cost

JORDAN

around JD3 to JD5 without a shower. It's sometimes possible to sleep on the hotel roof, which in summer is a good place to be, and will cost from JD1.500.

There is a reasonable choice of mid-range hotels in Amman, Aqaba and Petra, where a single will cost from JD10 to JD25. Insist upon the posted price, as they sometimes try and charge tourists more.

FOOD & DRINKS

Arabic food is the most prevalent. The Bedouin speciality is *mensaf*, which tastes great if you don't see it as it's served. It is spit-roasted lamb that is continually basted with spices until it takes on a yellow appearance. It is served on a bed of rice and pine nuts with the head of the lamb plonked in the centre. Oh, and the cooking fat is poured into and mixed with the rice – but not all of it. You'll definitely eat it if you go to Wadi Rum on a tour. Honoured guests get the eyes, less honoured guests the tongue. The dish is served with a sauce of cooked yoghurt that has been mixed with leftover cooking fat; it actually tastes great!

Dessert here, as in many parts of the Middle East, may be baklava or *mahalabiyya wa festaq* (milk pudding with pistachio nuts).

The universal Bedouin drink is tea (followed a close second by coffee) – as soon as you enter a compound you are sat down on the floor and offered tea, then tea, then tea. Nothing unusual, as alcohol doesn't rate highly in the region, but the quantity here is bladder-busting. Some options are *yensoon*, an aniseed based hot drink, and *zata'* (thyme flavoured tea).

Bottled mineral water is widely available, as are locally made soft drinks, Amstel beer and wine. Imported liquors are sold in Amman and Aqaba but are very expensive. A person who tested the water in the Jordan Valley said that the water supply in Amman is suspect and that tap water is often added to bottled mineral water to overcome shortages.

SPECTATOR SPORTS

Watching football in the bars or coffee-houses is free and can be lots of fun.

Amman's two main teams are Wahadat (supported by Palestinians) and Faisaly (supported by Jordanians). It would be worth going to the Sports City complex in north-west Amman to see these teams play each other (JD1.500 to JD2). Other teams that have performed well in the national competition are Irbid teams Al-Hussein Irbid and Ramth'a, and Al-Ahli.

There are often endurance horse races – a popular desert course is from Wadi Rum to Aqaba.

SHOPPING

Jordan doesn't have a lot to offer the souvenir hunter. Most things are overpriced and many come from Syria anyway, such as the inlaid backgammon boards and boxes. Bedouin rugs and tapestries made by Palestinian women are popular, though you need to check carefully to make sure they are actually handmade.

Brass and copper coffee pots are among the better buys but they're difficult to transport and usually come from Syria, where you can pick them up for less. Small bottles of coloured sand from Petra, skilfully poured into the bottle to form intricate patterns, are sold for anything from JD1 upwards.

Getting There & Away

AIR
Airports

There are two international airports – the Queen Alia international airport 35km south of Amman, which handles most international flights, and the smaller Aqaba airport from which the odd Royal Jordanian flight goes to Cairo.

Airlines & Routes

Royal Jordanian (☎ 567 8321, Web site www.rja.com.jo) is the national carrier, but from the main European capitals you can generally get cheaper deals with other airlines. Air fares vary extensively by season.

In general, it is cheaper to get a return air fare to Amman than a one-way fare. Return fares start at around US$613/793 from east coast/west coast USA, UK£280 from the UK, US$290 from Athens and İstanbul (but there are much cheaper student fares available), E£680 from Cairo, and A$1100 to A$1200 from Australia and New Zealand (usually via Cairo).

Departure Tax

There are three levels of departure tax from Jordan depending on how you leave: JD4 across all land borders, JD6 from Aqaba by sea, and JD10 by air. If you are in the country for less than 72 hours you are exempt from departure tax.

LAND
Border Crossings

Jordan, apart from a minuscule southern portion on the Gulf of Aqaba, is surrounded on all sides by other countries. There are two crossing points with Syria, three with Israel and one with Saudi Arabia. There is also one with Iraq, although foreign travellers make little use of it.

For details on international travel to the Middle East see the regional Getting There & Away chapter.

Iraq

There are two daily JETT buses between Amman and Baghdad at 8.30 am and 2 pm.

Service taxis are faster than the buses, but over a long distance the bus is probably more comfortable. You'll find taxis for Baghdad around Abdali bus station and at offices north-west of Downtown in Amman. It is not possible to get a visa for Iraq in Jordan; see the Iraq chapter for visa details.

Israel & the Palestinian Territories

Peace with Israel and the setting up of the partially autonomous Palestine National Authority has changed the border crossing situation between Jordan and Israel. There are now three border crossings. As of April 1996 private cars can be taken across the northern and southern crossings. Israeli vehicles are required to change number plates when they enter Jordan, but no such restriction applies to Jordanian vehicles going the other way. Vehicles with plates from other countries should have no problem.

Middle Eastern politics being what it is, all border crossing information should be considered highly perishable. Things can alter at short notice, and although the Jordanian-Israeli peace deal appears solid, be prepared for changes.

King Hussein (Jisr al-Malek Hussein)/ Allenby Bridge This border crossing point offers travellers the most direct route between Amman and Jerusalem/Tel Aviv. It's open daily from 8 am to midnight, but transport doesn't run during the Jewish Shabbat between sunset Friday and sunset Saturday, so this may not be a good time to cross.

From Amman's Abdali bus station you can catch a 6.30 am JETT bus or a minibus (JD1) or service taxi (JD1.500). The odd service taxi also leaves from Irbid for this crossing.

The ride to the Israeli side, although it's extremely short, can seem to last an eternity with repeated stops for passport and bag checks. The bridge itself is rather disappointing, an unimpressive 30m-long structure over what seems little more than a dribble of the Jordan River. At the time of research it was not possible to walk, hitch or take a private car across.

If you wish to return to Jordan while your present Jordanian visa is still valid, you need only keep the stamped exit slip and present it on returning by the same crossing (it won't work at the other crossings). At the Israeli border post plead with officials to stamp the Jordanian exit slip rather than your passport, especially if you intend going on to Syria – if you are, there must be no evidence of a trip to Israel in your passport. Syrian authorities just love turning travellers with Israeli passport stamps away from their border.

There are moneychanging facilities on your way to the exit.

There are two ways to Jerusalem from here. The easy way is to take a direct shared taxi (sherut) for 30NIS per person to Damascus Gate. Then there is the cheaper but more complicated way: catch a bus to Jericho (Areeha) for 6NIS, then take a service taxi from the southern side of the town's main square on to Damascus Gate (5NIS, 30 minutes).

Wadi Araba This handy crossing (Arava to the Israelis) in the south of the country links Aqaba to Eilat. The border is open from 6.30 am to 10 pm Sunday to Thursday and from 8 am to 8 pm Friday and Saturday. To get there from Aqaba you need to take a taxi (JD3) 10km to the border. Once you've crossed into Israel central Eilat is only 2km away, you can simply walk into town or catch bus No 16 (5NIS). This bus runs between Wadi Araba crossing and the Taba crossing into Egypt, via Eilat's central bus station.

There are facilities for changing money, as well as phones and cafes on both sides of the border. Both the Israelis and the Jordanians will issue visas on the spot.

Jisr Sheikh Hussein The northernmost Jordan River crossing into Israel, and perhaps the least convenient for travellers, Jisr Sheikh Hussein (Jordan River to Israelis) links northern Jordan with Beit She'an in Galilee. The crossing is open from 8 am, closing at 8 pm Sunday to Thursday, and 5 pm Friday and Saturday.

Saudi Arabia
There are regular JETT and Saptco buses departing from Amman to Jeddah at 10 am, Dammam at 11 am, and Riyadh at 11.30 am. (Hijazi bus company also has buses to Saudi Arabia for similar prices.) Transport can also be arranged to destinations beyond, such as Kuwait and Abu Dhabi in the United Arab Emirates (UAE).

Syria
Bus There are border crossings between Jordan and Syria is between Ramtha and Jabir in Jordan and Der'a in Syria. Air-con JETT and Karnak buses (respectively the Jordanian and Syrian government bus companies) run to the border and back each day from their respective capital cities. This is one of the easiest ways to make the crossing. From Amman you need to book a seat 48 hours in advance as demand often exceeds supply (see Getting There & Away in the Amman section for more details).

Train The famous Hejaz railway line built early in the 20th century to transport pilgrims to Medina from Damascus has been resurrected between Amman and Damascus. This slow diesel train with ancient carriages leaves Amman on Monday at 8 am and returns the following Sunday (JD4, 8 hours).

Service Taxi The *servees* are slightly faster than the buses and run at all hours (although it gets harder to find one in the evening). However, they usually get a far more thorough search at the border, so you often save no time at all. They leave from around Abdali bus station in Amman and travel to the Baramke terminal in Damascus.

SEA
Egypt
Ferry & Fast Boat There is at least one car ferry a day between Aqaba and Nuweiba on Egypt's Sinai peninsula. The trip takes three hours under ideal conditions; ferries depart at 3 pm (noon and 6.30 pm on Sunday). One-way tickets cost US$19. Return tickets are valid for a year and cost US$32.

There is also a fast passenger-only turbocatamaran leaving daily at noon that will whisk you to the other side in one hour. One-way tickets cost US$27 (JD21.200). Return tickets are valid for a year and cost US$42.

Beware of buying 1st class ferry tickets in Amman – there are no 1st class berths!

Getting Around

AIR
The modern Queen Alia international airport (☎ 445 1256) is about 35km south of Amman. There is also a smaller airfield in the outlying Amman suburb of Marka, from

where Royal Wings (a subsidiary of Royal Jordanian) operates flights to Aqaba (US$20, 45 minutes), the only domestic route, departing daily at 7 am, with a second flight Thursday and Friday at 8.30 am. Buses run to the airport from Abdali bus station in Jebel Amman – look for the new sign at the uphill end of the bus station.

BUS

The blue and white JETT buses run from Amman to Aqaba, King Hussein Bridge border crossing, Petra and Hammamat Ma'in. See Getting There & Away in the Petra section and Getting Around in the Amman section for details of destinations and fares.

Large (usually) air-con private buses run north from Amman to Irbid (850 fils) and south to Aqaba (JD3).

All smaller towns are connected by 20-seat minibuses. These leave when full and on some routes operate infrequently. The correct fare is nearly always posted in Arabic somewhere inside the front of the bus – just pay the driver the local rate.

SERVICE TAXI

By far the most popular mode of transport in Jordan is the service taxi. For more details see Getting Around and Getting There & Away in the Amman section. For general information see the regional Getting There & Away chapter.

TAXI

Regular taxis are quite cheap but point to the meter and make sure it is turned on (flagfall is 150 fils) or agree on a price if travelling late at night.

Don't believe taxi drivers when they say your hotel is closed or that they can't find it, as they earn a commission for every tourist they bring into certain hotels; don't let them accompany you to your hotel, as that commission will be added to your bill.

CAR & MOTORCYCLE

Vehicles drive on the right side of the road in Jordan. The speed limit is 50km/h in built up areas, 90km/h on the open road and 110km/h on the Desert Hwy. Indicators are seldom used, rules are seldom obeyed, the horn is omnipresent and pedestrians have absolutely no rights at all.

Petrol is available along the Desert and King's highways and in most sizeable towns. Expect to pay about 290 fils for a litre of regular, 360 fils for a litre of super, and best of luck if you are looking for unleaded. Diesel is about 150 fils a litre.

Motorcyclists should be aware that there are precious few mechanics in Jordan able to deal with the average modern motorcycle and its problems.

Rental

If there are four or more of you to split the cost of a rental car, it can be a good way of seeing a bit of the country – especially the Desert Castles, some of which are not accessible by public transport.

You'll be lucky to find a small rental car deal with unlimited mileage for under JD25 a day, with a three day minimum hire period (the excess is from JD200 to JD300 in the case of an accident). Limited kilometre deals work out to be much more expensive if you're going to be doing more than 100km per day. They cost from about JD20 per day plus 60 to 80 fils for every extra kilometre.

There are rental agencies in Amman and Aqaba which are much cheaper than Hertz, Avis and Budget. In Amman, try Star Rent-a-Car (☎ 06-515 4904) out by Sports City junction, and Natour (☎ 06-462 7455) at 9 Sha'ban St, Jebel Amman. In Aqaba, Rum Rent-a-Car (☎ 03-201 3581) and Moon Rent-a-Car (☎ 03-201 3316) are reasonable.

BICYCLE

Cycling is an option in Jordan but not necessarily a fun one. The desert in summer is not a good place to indulge in strenuous activity, and cyclists on the King's Highway have been stoned by groups of kids. Cycling north or south (most roads run north-south) can be hard work as there is a strong prevailing western wind that can wear you down. Bring plenty of spare parts (see Bicycle in the Getting Around the Region chapter).

JORDAN

ORGANISED TOURS

The only organised tours are those operated by JETT bus company (☎ 566 4146) from Amman to Petra and Hammamat Ma'in but these are not good value. Jordan is a finite enough commodity for you to plan your own tour. You can usually bargain with a service taxi driver in Amman to take you to just about anywhere (eg Petra or the Desert Castles) for about JD40 for a full day.

For trips to Wadi Rum, which is difficult to see completely under your own steam unless you have lots of time, try Wadi Rum Desert Service (☎ 03-201 4679), Petra Moon Tourism Services (☎ 03-215 6665) or Desert Guides (☎ 03-201 4131), all in Aqaba.

Amman

Amman at first glimpse seems like an anomaly in the desert – a larger concrete version of famed desert cities like Mali's Timbuktu or Niger's Agadez. The Downtown area is a busy, chaotic jumble of traffic – human and motorised – and just crossing the street through this is an achievement. An upwards glance to the numerous jebels reveals a rabble of houses and flats clinging to the hillsides, all pictures of boxed uniformity. As Amman is on Jordan's main highway, it's highly likely that you will pass through, and it's really quite an agreeable place with plenty of nightlife and extremely friendly people.

The area has been inhabited since at least 3000 BC. Built originally on seven hills (like Rome), Amman ('Philadelphia' in Roman times) now spreads across 19 hills. At its heart lies a well-restored 6000 seat theatre, a forum and a street of columns. To the north, across from the theatre on a hill, is the citadel, an old Roman garrison from which you can enjoy some of the best views of the city centre.

Amman is also one of the friendliest cities you're likely to visit. Most residents, whether born Jordanians or among the flood of Palestinian refugees from the wars of 1948 and 1967, are well educated, friendly,

speak a fair amount of English and are eager to chat with foreigners.

Orientation

The Downtown area of Amman, where you'll find plenty of cheap hotels and restaurants, as well as banks, post offices and the bulk of what little there is to see in the city, is at the bottom of four of the many hills that characterise the city. The main hill is Jebel Amman, where you'll find most of the embassies and some of the flash hotels. On Jebel al-Hussein are the Abdali and JETT bus stations. Eight 'circles' are found west and north-west of Downtown (some are just traffic junctions); these are used as points of reference in just about every conversation with taxi drivers.

Note that street addresses are not often used in Amman, or indeed in Jordan. It is not unusual for a street to have several names, there are very few street signs and there is a conspicuous absence of street numbers. When talking with taxi drivers it is more common to pick a landmark nearby (such as King Hussein Mosque) and the general area (eg Abdoun, Shmeisani or Jebel Amman) and ask the taxi driver to locate that first.

Information

Visa Extensions If you plan to stay in Jordan for more than 14 days, you must register with the police. In Amman you need to go to the Muhajireen police station. Take service taxi No 35 from the stand in the south of Downtown and ask for 'Markaz Amn Muhajireen'. The relevant office at the station is open daily (except Friday) from 10 am to 1 pm and the process takes about 15 minutes. Extensions of two to three months are issued free of charge and with a minimum of fuss. Failure to do so results in a JD1 fine for each day overstayed, charged on departure.

Tourist Office The Downtown Visitors' Centre (☎ 464 6264) is just south of the Roman (Philadelphia) amphitheatre; the staff speak English and give out free brochures. The Ministry of Tourism & Antiquities (☎ 464 2311) near 3rd Circle also has a few brochures. The major hotels have copies of the free *Your Guide to Amman*

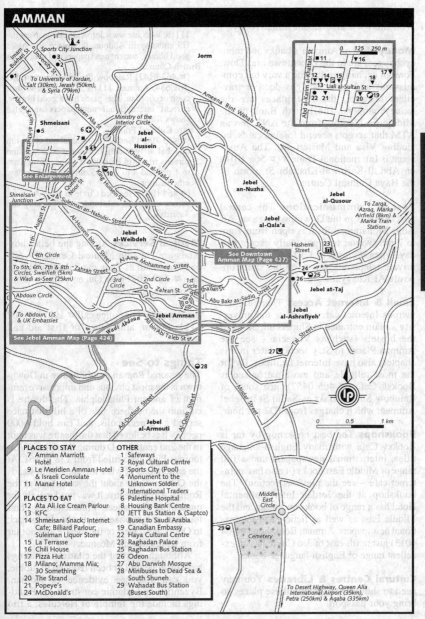

AMMAN

Jorm

Sports City Junction

To University of Jordan,
Salt (30km), Jerash (50km),
& Syria (79km)

Imam Bukhari St
University St

Shmeisani

Abd al-Karim al-Khattabi St

See Enlargement

Shmeisani
Junction

Ministry of the
Interior Circle

Queen Alia St

Jebel
al-Hussein

Khalid Ibn al-Walid St

King Hussein St

Noor St

Ameena Bint Wahab Street

Jebel
an-Nuzha

Jebel
al-Qala'a

Jebel
al-Qusour

To Zarqa,
Azraq, Marka
Airfield (8km) &
Marka Train
Station

Suleiman an-Nabulsi Street

Al-Hussein bin Ali Street

11th August St

4th Circle

To 5th, 6th, 7th & 8th
Circles, Sweifieh (5km)
& Wadi as-Seer (25km)

Abdoun Circle

To Abdoun,
US & UK Embassies

Al-Amir Mohammed Street

Zahran Street

3rd
Circle

2nd Circle

Zahran St

1st
Circle

9th

Sha'ban St

Abu Bakr as-Sadiq Street

Jebel Amman

Jebel
al-Weibdeh

Wadi Abdoun

Ali bin Abi Taleb St

See Jebel Amman Map (Page 424)

Jebel
al-Qala'a

Hashemi
Street

See Downtown
Amman Map (Page 427)

Jebel at-Taj

Jebel
al-Ashrafiyeh'

Jebel
al-Armouti

Ad-Dustour Street

Al-Quds Street

Taj Street

Misdar Street

Middle
East
Circle

Middle
East
Circle

Cemetery

To Desert Highway, Queen Alia
International Airport (35km),
Petra (250km) & Aqaba (335km)

0   125   250 m

Abd al-Khattabi St

Liali al-Sultan St

PLACES TO STAY
7   Amman Marriott
     Hotel
9   Le Meridien Amman Hotel
     & Israeli Consulate
11 Manar Hotel

PLACES TO EAT
12 Ata Ali Ice Cream Parlour
13 KFC
14 Shmeisani Snack; Internet
     Cafe; Billiard Parlour;
     Suleiman Liquor Store
15 La Terrasse
16 Chili House
17 Pizza Hut
18 Milano; Mamma Mia;
     30 Something
20 The Strand
21 Popeye's
24 McDonald's

OTHER
1   Safeways
2   Royal Cultural Centre
3   Sports City (Pool)
4   Monument to the
     Unknown Soldier
5   International Traders
6   Palestine Hospital
8   Housing Bank Centre
10 JETT Bus Station & (Saptco)
     Buses to Saudi Arabia
19 Canadian Embassy
22 Haya Cultural Centre
23 Raghadan Palace
25 Raghadan Bus Station
26 Odeon
27 Abu Darwish Mosque
28 Minibuses to Dead Sea &
     South Shuneh
29 Wahadat Bus Station
     (Buses South)

JORDAN

and *Jordan Today*. Also try *Jordan Today*'s Web site www.arabia.com/JordanToday.

Money Most of Amman's banks and moneychangers are in the Downtown area Dow. Foreign exchange rates don't vary but commissions and other charges do. For travellers cheques, the best places are the moneychangers. The British Bank of the Middle East, across from the ANZ, has an ATM that accepts several foreign cards, including Visa and MasterCard. The Amex agent is International Traders (☎ 566 1014) on Abd al-Karim al-Khattabi St, north of the Haya Cultural Centre.

Post & Communications The central post office is in the Downtown area on Al-Amir Mohammed St. It is open from 7 am to 7 pm (winter to 5 pm) daily except Friday, when it closes at 1.30 pm. You'll find private telephone offices on the street opposite Al-Khayyam Cinema.

Email & Internet Access There are numerous Internet cafes opposite the university's main entrance in Shmeisani. Some of the hostels (such as Venecia – see the Amman Places to Stay section later in this chapter) also have Internet facilities. By far the most reliable and most patronised is Books@Cafe (☎ 465 0457), just south of Rainbow St/Abu Bakr as-Sadiq St in Jebel Amman, which charges from JD2 per hour.

Bookshops The best bookshop by far is Books@Cafe with many English-language titles, international newspapers and a full range of Middle East books (it also has an Internet cafe – see the previous section). The bookshop at the Jordan InterContinental Hotel has a range of books on Jordan and the Middle East as well as fiction and international newspapers. Amman Bookshop (☎ 464 4013) just north-east of 3rd Circle has an excellent range of English-language books.

Cultural Centres & Libraries You may need to show ID to get into these places so bring your passport.

American Center
(☎ 585 9102) ALC, PO Box 676, Amman, 11118, Web site www.info&alc.edu.jo. Near the US embassy in Abdoun, this place also has a good library, current newspapers and magazines
British Council
(☎ 463 6147) Rainbow St, Jebel Amman, PO Box 634, Amman, 11118, Web site www.brit coun.org/jordan. This place has a good library, current international newspapers and also shows films.
Centre Culturel Français
(☎ 463 7009) Beside the roundabout at the top of Jebel al-Weibdeh, it also has a library and screens films (in French). It's open from 9 am to 1 pm and 4 to 7 pm Saturday to Thursday.
Goethe Institut
(☎ 464 1993) Near 3rd Circle in Jebel Amman, shows films and exhibitions on Tuesday and Saturday.

Medical Services Among the better hospitals are Hussein Medical Centre (☎ 585 6856) in Wadi as-Seer and Palestine Hospital (☎ 560 7071) on Queen Alia St (University St), Shmeisani.

Emergency For police call ☎ 192 or ☎ 462 1111. For an ambulance or first aid call ☎ 193.

Things to See
The restored **Roman amphitheatre** in Downtown is the most obvious and impressive remnant of ancient Philadelphia. The theatre is cut into the northern side of a hill that once served as a necropolis, and can hold 6000 people. It is believed that the theatre was built in the 2nd century AD during the reign of Antoninus Pius, who ruled from 138 to 161. At the eastern end of what was the forum stands the **Odeon**. Built about the same time as the Roman Amphitheatre, it was used mainly for musical performances. Philadelphia's chief fountain, or **nymphaeum**, stands with its back to Quraysh St, west of the theatre and not far from King Hussein Mosque.

Although many of the **citadel's** buildings have disappeared or been reduced to rubble, you can still see evidence of Roman, Byzantine and Islamic construction. Buildings include the **Temple of Hercules**, a trio of whose columns have been re-erected. Artefacts dating to the Bronze Age show that the hill served as a fortress or agora for thousands of years. The nearby **National Archaeological Museum** (☎ 463 8795) is worth a visit. It's open from 9 am to 5 pm Saturday to Thursday, and from 10 am to 4 pm on Friday and holidays (closed Tuesday). Admission is JD2.

The **Folklore Museum** is one of two small museums housed in the wings of the Roman theatre. The other is the **Traditional Jewels & Costumes Museum**, which has well-presented displays of traditional costumes, jewellery and utensils. Opening times are the same as at the National Archaeological Museum and entry to each is JD1.

The simple and solemn **Monument to the Unknown Soldier** is out by the Sports City complex and houses a small museum on Jordan's military history. It is open from 9 am to 4 pm daily except Saturday.

Amman has a number of imposing **mosques** with the busiest but not necessarily most impressive being the **King Hussein Mosque** (also known as the Al-Husseini Mosque) in Downtown. Here the attraction is the whole precinct rather than the building – as usual prayer times are busy but at other times the front of the mosque and the surrounding streets exude an altogether Arab flavour – it is a bustling central meeting place. The original mosque was built on this site in 640 AD by 'Umar, the second caliph of Islam; the latest version was built by King Abdullah, the present King's grandfather, in 1924 and it was restored in 1987.

The **King Abdullah Mosque** in Jebel al-Hussein was completed in 1990. It is worth a look; women should wear an *abeyya* (women's garment) with their hair well and truly covered. Admission will be about JD1.

The **Jordan National Gallery** (☎ 463 0128) at 6 Hosni Fareez St in Jebel al-Weibdeh exhibits the paintings, ceramics and sculpture of contemporary Jordanian artists; it's open from 10 am to 6 pm daily except Tuesday (and closed for lunch from 1.30 to 3.30 pm).

Amman has a disorganised but bustling **market**, with most of the Downtown seemingly embroiled in the frenetic commerce. To savour the smells and noise of the various souqs just wander up and down and between Al-Malek Talal and Quraysh Sts, and around King Hussein Mosque.

Places to Stay – Budget

Downtown Amman is thick with cheap hotels, and often cheap equals filthy.

Arab League on Hashemi St, across from King Hussein Mosque, was recommended by a couple of intrepid cyclists we met but it's nothing special – clean sheets and a sink, yes, but the rooms are small, there's a midnight curfew and absolutely no alcohol is allowed in the rooms. It costs JD5 for a double.

Cliff Hotel (☎ 462 4273), up a side alley off Al-Malek Faisal St, used to be a travellers' favourite, but now you only need to look at the stairwell to realise how much it has dropped its standards. You can sleep on the roof for JD2 or in a dorm for JD3.500. A (sometimes) hot shower costs 500 fils extra. A bed in a double (with bugs) costs JD5 or it's JD8 for the whole room.

Venecia (☎ 463 8895, email venecia@ hotmail.com) is one lane up from Cliff Hotel towards the post office. Beds in a tatty dorm cost JD3, a bed in a double costs JD5 or it's JD6 for the whole room. It has Internet access here for guests.

Park Hotel (☎ 464 8145, Al-Malek al-Hussein St) is edging a little further up the scale. It is not bad at JD10.500/14.500 for singles/doubles with phone, TV, balcony and bathroom, and the staff seem happy to bargain.

Farah Hotel (☎ 465 1443, Cinema al-Hussein St), behind the Arab Bank, is the best of the budget places. It is spotlessly clean, has friendly staff, a nice reception area (once the noisy video games are tossed out) and an outdoor tent where you can enjoy a coffee. The basic rooms are very clean and have B&W TV and phone. Most rooms have shared bathrooms that are also kept spotlessly clean. Dorms/singles/doubles are JD4/9/10 and a rooftop mattress is JD2.500.

Select Hotel (☎ 463 7101, Baoniya St, Jebel al-Weibdeh) is another nice deal. The

JORDAN

JORDAN

JEBEL AMMAN

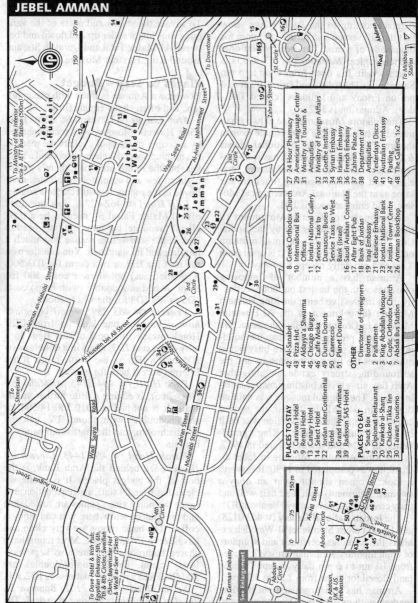

PLACES TO STAY
5   Caravan Hotel
9   Remal Hotel
13 Canary Hotel
14 Select Hotel
22 Jordan InterContinental Hotel
28 Grand Hyatt Amman
39 Radisson SAS Hotel

PLACES TO EAT
4   Snack Box
15 Diplomat Restaurant
20 Kawkab al-Sharq
25 Chicken Tikka Inn
30 Taiwan Tourismo
42 Al-Sanabel
43 Pizza Hut
44 Aldayya'a Shwarma
45 Chicago Burger
46 Caffe Moka
49 Dunkin Donuts
50 Casereccio
51 Planet Donuts

OTHER
1   Directorate of Foreigners
    Borders
2   Parliament
3   King Abdullah Mosque
6   Coptic Orthodox Church
7   Abdali Bus Station
8   Greek Orthodox Church
10 International Bus
    Offices
11 Jordan National Gallery
12 Caffe Moka
    Service Taxis to
    Damascus; Buses &
    Service Taxis to West
    Bank (Israel)
16 Saudi Arabian Consulate
17 After Eight Pub
18 Bank of Jordan
19 Iraqi Embassy
21 Lebanese Embassy
23 Jordan National Bank
24 Jordan Tower Centre
26 Amman Bookshop
27 24 Hour Pharmacy
29 American Language Center
31 Ministry of Tourism &
    Antiquities
32 Ministry of Foreign Affairs
33 Goethe Institut
34 Syrian Embassy
35 Iranian Embassy
36 French Embassy
37 Zahran Palace
38 Department of
    Antiquities
40 Yesterdays Disco
41 Australian Embassy
47 Parking
48 The Galleria 1x2

rooms cost JD11/20 and are about the same quality as those of Park Hotel, but many have balconies in the shade.

Palace Hotel (☎ 462 4326, Al-Malek Faisal St) has been described by a reader as 'not overly crappy even though it is modest'. A bed in a shared room with ensuite will cost you JD7.

Places to Stay – Mid-Range
Remal Hotel (☎ 463 0670) is tucked away on a sidestreet opposite the police department south of the Abdali bus station. It has comfortable singles/doubles that will set you back JD14/18 plus tax.

Canary Hotel (☎ 463 8353/61/62) gets its name from the resident canaries in the forecourt. It's 10 minutes walk from Downtown in Jebel al-Weibdeh, opposite the Terra Sancta college (No 4 service taxi passes by). Canary has good singles/doubles/triples for JD18/24/27 including breakfast, plus 10% tax.

Caravan Hotel (☎ 566 1195/7, email caravan@go.com.jo, Police College St) is near Jordan's biggest mosque, King Abdullah. Clean and comfortable, and with a delightful patio, it has the same rates as Canary.

Dove Hotel (☎ 569 7601, fax 567 4676, Qurtubah St, Jebel Amman) next to the Egyptian embassy (which all taxi drivers know), between 4th and 5th circles, is the best of the mid-range places. Nice rooms with all the necessities are JD20/26 plus tax. Jordan's best bar, the Irish Pub, is also here and is a good place to meet all manner of people – local and foreign. The pub shares the hotel's capable restaurant.

Manar Hotel (☎ 566 2186, fax 568 4329, Abd al-Karim al-Khattabi St) in Shmeisani has a swimming pool and the rooms are good value at JD30/40 plus taxes.

Shepherd Hotel (☎/fax 464 2401, Zeid Ben Haritha St), near 2nd Circle, is a three star place an easy walk from Downtown that has been recommended by readers.

Places to Stay – Top End
Jordan InterContinental Hotel (☎ 464 1361, fax 464 5217), between 2nd and 3rd circles, is the closest of the big hotels to Downtown and has luxuries such as swimming pool, fitness centre and car rental facilities. Singles/doubles are nevertheless expensive at JD125/135 plus 10% tax.

Radisson SAS (☎ 560 7100, fax 566 5160, Web site www.radisson.com/ammanjo) about 1km north-west of the 3rd Circle in Jebel Amman has a 24 hour business centre, car rental facilities, swimming pool and restaurants. Rooms cost from JD80/100 plus 10% tax.

Amman Marriott Hotel (☎ 560 7607, fax 567 0100, email ammanmarriott@go.com.jo, Isam al-Ajlouni St) has rooms from JD75/95 and *Le Meridien Amman (☎ 569 6511, fax 567 4261, Queen Noor St)* has rooms from JD85/126. Both are in Shmeisani and have similar facilities to Radisson SAS.

Grand Hyatt Amman (☎ 465 1234, fax 465 1634, email hyatt@go.com.jo), just north of 3rd Circle, opened at the end of 1998 – it's only for diplomats, pop stars and people on expense accounts.

Places to Eat
There are plenty of cheap eats in Downtown. The farther you get from here the higher the prices tend to be, suggesting that this is where the locals dine. We have included places to eat in some other areas for those who want a change. For more information on local cuisine see Food & Drinks in the Facts for the Visitor section earlier in this chapter.

Places to Eat – Budget
Hashem on the Alley, on Al-Amir Mohammed St, across from Venecia Hotel, is a cheap restaurant for felafel, humous and *fuul* (fava bean paste). A filling meal with bread and tea is only about 500 fils, and the place is open 24 hours.

You'll find several *shwarma stalls* dotted around the Downtown area. The price of a *shwarma* (a sandwich of meat sliced off a spit) is around 250 fils, but you'll need a couple to make a halfway decent lunch.

There are excellent *juice stalls* at the intersection of Al-Malek Faisal and Hashemi Sts (400 fils for a huge juice). For desserts you can't beat *Jabri Cafe & Patisserie* on Al-Malek al-Hussein St.

Abu Khamis & Abu Saleh Restaurant, on a lane off Al-Malek Faisal St, has a good range, including chicken, stuffed green peppers, potato chips, and a variety of meat and vegetable stews. A filling meal will cost between JD1 and JD2.

Cairo Restaurant two blocks south of King Hussein Mosque has a similar range to that of Abu Khamis but is cheaper. Sit down and enjoy a huge chicken feast (JD1.500) with the locals, although it is likely that you will not appreciate some of the side dishes.

Al-Quds Restaurant, on Al-Malek al-Hussein St, serves traditional mensaf (a communal dish of lamb on a bed of rice and pine nuts) with a delicious cooked yoghurt sauce for around JD2.500 and meat dishes from JD1.500.

Orient Restaurant, upstairs and just off Basman St, is a local favourite with a plethora of meat dishes, some vegetarian entrees and the slowest service in central Amman. Food and drinks for three cost JD10.

Bifa Billa Cafe on Cinema al-Hussein St is a fastfood place with good hamburgers (500 fils), pizzas and chips. It must do one of the region's top milk shakes.

Wimpy on Al-Amir Mohammed St has a good range of burgers for those craving such and, next door, adding to the US flavour, is a branch of *Southern Fried Chicken*.

McDonald's on Abdullah Ghousheh St, near the Roman Amphitheatre, is one of only two of this famous chain in the country. Not surprisingly it is immensely popular. No prizes for guessing the menu though.

Batata on Rainbow St, downhill from 1st Circle, serves genuine French fries (600 fils small, JD1.500 family, 100 fils for special sauces).

For cheap eats in Jebel Amman try *Snack Box* on Suleiman an-Nabulsi St, opposite King Abdullah Mosque. It's a superb example of a Middle Eastern place attempting western and Asian-style meals. The fine meat-and-pasta dishes and stir-fries (take away) cost JD2 or less, and are a tasty alternative to standard Arabic fare.

Shmeisani has heaps of western-style takeaways, including *Pizza Hut* (☎ 568 1640), *KFC* (☎ 567 1608), *Popeye's* (☎ 560 1721), *Shmeisani*, *Chili House* (☎ 568 1707), with hearty serves of good chilli for about JD3, and *TARWEA Restaurant* (☎ 566 5195) in the Haya Cultural Centre, which has good meals from JD2.

Fastfood places around Abdoun Circle (better known for its expensive restaurants) include *Pizza Hut*, *Planet Donuts*, *Chicago Burger*, *Dunkin Donuts* and *Aldayya'a Shwarma* (small 350 fils, big 500 fils).

Places to Eat – Mid-Range

Diplomat Restaurant on 1st Circle, has a good range of dishes for JD1 to JD3, including reasonable pizzas. It's open until quite late and has tables on the pavement where you can sip on an Amstel beer for JD1.800.

Books@Cafe (☎ 465 0457), downhill from 1st Circle, is expensive but extremely popular with travellers. The menu changes monthly; salads cost JD2.500, while huge 'designer' sandwiches cost JD4; add a hefty 10% tax and 10% service charge.

Kawkab al-Sharq on 2nd Circle, has a good range of local dishes as well as pizza – look for the picture of Umm Kolthum on the sign.

Chicken Tikka Inn on Al-Amir Mohammed St, north-east of 3rd Circle and not far from the Jordan Tower Centre, has great curries for around JD2.500. It is open daily from noon to 4 pm and 6.30 pm to midnight.

Taiwan Tourismo (☎ 464 1093), down a sidestreet two blocks south of 3rd Circle, behind the nearby Akilah Hospital, offers a good, filling Chinese meal for around JD5. It is open daily for lunch from noon to 3.30 pm and from 6.30 to 11.30 pm.

Shmeisani has several places where you won't come away with much change from JD10. Popular and somewhat more stylish places include *La Terrasse* (☎ 566 2831), which often has Arab musicians in the evening, *Ata Ali* for very ordinary meals but a good selection of ice cream (300 fils); and the ever popular and very upmarket *The Strand*. The easiest way to get there is

DOWNTOWN AMMAN

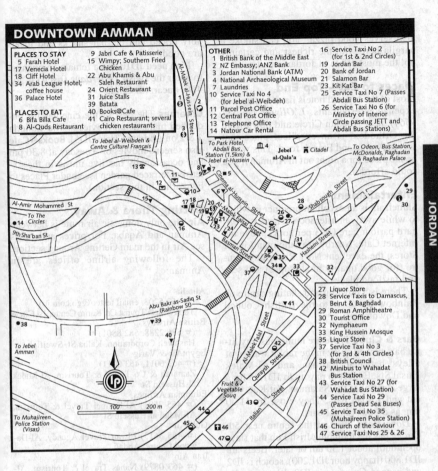

PLACES TO STAY
5 Farah Hotel
17 Venecia Hotel
18 Cliff Hotel
34 Arab League Hotel; coffee house
36 Palace Hotel

PLACES TO EAT
6 Bifa Billa Cafe
8 Al-Quds Restaurant

9 Jabri Cafe & Patisserie
15 Wimpy; Southern Fried Chicken
22 Abu Khamis & Abu Saleh Restaurant
24 Orient Restaurant
31 Juice Stalls
39 Batata
40 Books@Cafe
41 Cairo Restaurant; several chicken restaurants

OTHER
1 British Bank of the Middle East
2 NZ Embassy; ANZ Bank
3 Jordan National Bank (ATM)
4 National Archaeological Museum
7 Laundries
10 Service Taxi No 4 (for Jebel al-Weibdeh)
11 Parcel Post Office
12 Central Post Office
13 Telephone Office
14 Natour Car Rental

16 Service Taxi No 2 (for 1st & 2nd Circles)
19 Jordan Bar
20 Bank of Jordan
21 Salamon Bar
23 Kit Kat Bar
25 Service Taxi No 7 (Passes Abdali Bus Station)
26 Service Taxi No 6 (for Ministry of Interior Circle passing JETT and Abdali Bus Stations)

27 Liquor Store
28 Service Taxis to Damascus, Beirut & Baghdad
29 Roman Amphitheatre
30 Tourist Office
32 Nymphaeum
33 King Hussein Mosque
35 Liquor Store
37 Service Taxi No 3 (for 3rd & 4th Circles)
38 British Council
42 Minibus to Wahadat Bus Station
43 Service Taxi No 27 (for Wahadat Bus Station)
44 Service Taxi No 29 (Passes Dead Sea Buses)
45 Service Taxi No 35 (Muhajireen Police Station)
46 Church of the Saviour
47 Service Taxi Nos 25 & 26

JORDAN

to jump into a taxi and ask for the Haya Cultural Centre in Shmeisani.

Still in Shmeisani, three swish places are found together near a prominent cedar tree on Liali al-Sultan St. *Mama Mia* (☎ 568 2122) has delectable pizzas from JD2 to JD7 and chicken parmesan for JD3; *Milano* (☎ 568 0670) is another Italian place next door; and on the other side of Mama Mia is *30 Something* (☎ 560 4620), a Mexican restaurant that features live music by local musician Saif Shaheen.

Abdoun Circle is the most upmarket of the restaurant enclaves, popular with well-heeled Jordanians. If you are tired of Middle Eastern food, a taxi trip (JD1 from Downtown) to Abdoun Circle might be called for.

Casereccio has tasty, large wood-fired pizzas for a reasonable JD3 and tempting Nutella pizzas for dessert (JD1.500). No alcohol is served. *Caffe Moka* (☎ 592 6285) is a patisserie and cafe, and the place to be seen, but unless you get there early you won't get a seat. *Al-Sanabel* (☎ *592 5112*) also serves good pizza. You can smoke a nargila here with the richest and certainly not the most effete of Jordanian citizens.

Places to Eat – Top End

Most of the top end hotels have a couple of expensive restaurants. *L'Olivier* (☎ *581 9564*), near Abdoun Circle and down from the Orthodox, is an excellent place that serves Arabic and French food. This would be *the* place for a night out in Amman if you could afford it.

Entertainment

Shmeisani is an excellent precinct in which to while away an afternoon. There is a billiard parlour here (JD3 per hour) above the Internet Cafe. Nearby are Suleiman Liquor Stores, the excellent No 1 Recording Centre (for good quality pirate tapes) and several fastfood places.

There is a bowling and skating centre on Rainbow St, close to the British Council and Downtown.

Bars & Clubs There are numerous tiny little bars tucked away in the rabbit warren of alleys between Basman and Al-Malek Faisal Sts. Expect to pay up to JD1.75 for a large Amstel at the Salamon, Kit Kat, Orient and Jordan bars. They close by 11.30 pm, as do most hotel bars.

Dove Hotel, west of the centre near 5th Circle, has the thumping Irish Pub that stays open until about 1.30 am or later. Beers are JD1.800 (happy hour JD1.200), scotch is JD2 and canned Guinness is JD2. It's a popular meeting place for expats and embassy staff.

Bayerischer Hof (☎ *581 9730*) on Al-Hamra St in Sweifieh is a German place with a great bar serving costly wheat beer. It also has a casual dining area/beer garden on a mezzanine and a fine dining area on the lower level.

Champions (☎ *560 7607*) at Amman Marriott Hotel on Isam al-Ajlouni St is a sports bar and popular after-work venue.

After Eight next to the Granada Hotel, south of 1st Circle, is a good place to relax.

The seating is in booths, the beer is reasonably priced and the bar snacks and meals are good.

Men need JD10 and a female companion to enter the swish *Yesterdays Disco* (☎ *565 4201*) near 4th Circle.

Cinemas The best of the cinemas for un-dubbed mainstream movies is **The Galleria 1 & 2** on Abdoun Circle (JD5). **Books@Cafe** also screens movies on Tuesday at 8.30 pm and occasionally has live music in the extensive terraced garden (see under Places to Eat earlier in this section).

Getting There & Away

Air The only domestic air route is between Amman and Aqaba. For prices and times see Air in the main Getting Around section.

The following airline offices are in Amman:

Alitalia
  (☎ 462 5203, email testco@go.com.jo)
  Terra Sancta Tourist Co, Karim Centre, 1st Circle
British Airways
  (☎ 586 2288, 582 8801)
  Hashweh Corporation, Kalha St, Sweifieh
EgyptAir & Varig
  (☎ 463 6011, 463 0011)
  Zaatarah & Co Travel & Tourism, Al-Malek al-Hussein St
Ethiopian Airlines
  (☎ 465 3691) Al-Karmel Travel & Tourism, Al-Malel al-Hussein St
Gulf Air
  (☎ 465 3613) Elwan Travel Agency, Al-Dawood Centre, Abdali
Iran Air
  (☎ 463 0879) Nahas Travel & Tourism, Al-Malek al-Hussein St
KLM
  (☎ 465 5267) Al-Malek al-Hussein St
Royal Jordanian
  (☎ 566 3525) Offices in the Royal Jordanian Airlines Bldg, Abdali
  (☎ 534 6868) Jordan University
  (☎ 585 6835) Queen Alia terminal
Syria Airways
  (☎ 462 2147) Al-Amir Mohammed St

Bus & Minibus The JETT bus station is on King Hussein St, a few minutes walk north of Abdali bus station. Tickets for

JETT buses should be booked at least a day in advance. There are daily departures to Aqaba (JD4, five hours), King Hussein Bridge border crossing for the West Bank and Jerusalem (JD6.500), Petra/Wadi Musa (JD5.500), Damascus in Syria (JD4.500), and Baghdad in Iraq (JD12).

The main bus stations in Amman are Abdali (for transport north and west), and Wahadat (for transport south). From Abdali bus station, minibuses run to Suweileh (85 fils, 20 minutes), Salt (175 fils, 45 minutes), Jerash (350 fils, one hour), Deir Alla in the Jordan Valley (400 fils, one hour), Ajlun (450 fils, 1½ hours) and Irbid (530 fils, 1½ hours), and also leave from the southern end of the station for King Hussein Bridge border crossing (JD1, 45 minutes).

From Wahadat bus station minibuses depart for Madaba (these are more convenient from Raghadan bus station) (220 fils, one hour), Kerak (750 fils, two hours), Ma'an (JD1.050, 2½ hours), Hammamat Ma'in (JD1.500), and Petra/Wadi Musa (JD2, three hours). Minibuses and buses for Aqaba (JD3, five hours) leave from here.

Train The Hejaz train to Damascus leaves from a station in Marka on Monday at 8 am and costs JD4.

Service Taxi Service taxis leave from the bus stations, are faster and more convenient than buses but are more expensive. From Abdali bus station they run to Salt (350 fils, 45 minutes), Jerash (650 fils, one hour), King Hussein (JD1.500, 45 minutes), Irbid (JD1, 1½ hours), and even occasionally to the Ramtha border crossing with Syria (JD1, one hour). Taxis also run to Damascus in Syria (JD5, five hours).

Getting Around

To/From the Airports Queen Alia international airport is about 35km south of the city. Buses run every 30 minutes between 6 am and 10 pm from Abdali bus station (750 fils, 50 minutes). You can also get airport taxis for the trip into town. They cost about JD10 (JD12 between about 10 pm to 8 am).

If you need to get to the small airfield at Marka, take a Marka service taxi from the Raghadan bus station.

Service Taxi There's a standard charge of 70 to 80 fils for most service taxis, depending on the route, and you pay the full amount regardless of where you get off. Some of the more useful routes are: No 3 from Basman St for the 3rd and 4th circles; No 6 from Cinema al-Hussein St for the Ministry of the Interior Circle, going past the Abdali and JETT bus stations; and No 27 from near the fruit and vegetable souq to the Middle East Circle for Wahadat bus station.

Taxi The flag fall in a standard taxi is 150 fils, and cross-town journeys should never cost more than JD2.

Around Amman

WADI AS-SEER & IRAQ AL-AMIR
The narrow, fertile valley of Wadi as-Seer is a real contrast to the bare, treeless plateau of Amman to the east. The caves, known as 'Iraq (or 'Araq) al-Amir (Cave of the Prince) and the ruins of **Qasr Iraq al-Amir** (Castle of the Slave) are another 10km down the valley from the largely Circassian village of Wadi as-Seer.

The caves are up to the right of the road and are in two tiers; the upper one forms a long gallery along the cliff face. The castle is about 500m down the valley and can be seen from the caves. There is still some mystery about when and why it was constructed but it is believed that it was built in the 2nd century BC by Hyrcanus of the powerful Jewish Tobiad family.

Getting There & Away
There is a minibus from Ali bin Abi Taleb St in Jebel Amman (100 fils, 30 minutes). There are also minibuses from Suweileh and local town buses. Once in Wadi as-Seer you can catch a minibus right to the end of the road at 'Araq al-Amir (100 fils).

North & West of Amman

JERASH

This beautifully preserved Roman city, 51km north of Amman, is deservedly one of Jordan's major attractions, second only to Petra. The main ruins of Jerash were rediscovered in 1806 but excavations did not begin until the 1920s. They continue today and it is estimated that 90% of the city is still untouched. The site is open from 7.30 am until dark daily, and admission is JD5 for foreigners.

There's a visitors' centre with a souvenir shop and post office, and a variety of eateries. Get a copy of the Jordan Tourism Board's free *Jerash* – it has a good explanatory map. In July and August Jesarh is the scene of the Jerash Cultural Festival, featuring local and overseas artists and displays of traditional handicrafts.

History

Although discoveries indicate that the site was inhabited in Neolithic times, it was from the time of Alexander the Great (332 BC) that the city really started its rise to prominence.

In 63 BC the Roman general Pompey conquered the region and Jerash became part of the Roman province of Syria and, soon after, one of the cities of the Decapolis (the commercial league of 10 cities formed by Pompey after his conquest of Syria and Palestine in 64 BC). Jerash reached its peak at the beginning of the 3rd century AD, when it was made a colony, and then went into a slow decline.

By the middle of the 5th century Christianity had become the major religion of the region and the construction of churches proceeded at a startling rate. With the Persian invasion of 614 and the Muslim conquest of 636, followed by a series of earthquakes in 747, Jerash really hit the skids and its population shrank to about 25% of the size it had been in its heyday.

Things to See

Approaching the ruins from Amman, the **triumphal arch** is first to come into view. Behind the arch is the **hippodrome**, the old sports field that used to be surrounded by seating for up to 15,000 spectators. The **South Gate**, originally one of four in the 3500m long city wall, little of which remains, is the main entrance to the site today.

Once inside the gate, the **Temple of Zeus** is the ruined building on the left. It was built in the latter part of the 2nd century on a sacred site. The nearby **forum** is unusual because of its oval shape; some attribute this to the builders' desire to gracefully link the main north-south axis with the existing Hellenistic sacred site of the Temple of Zeus.

The **South Theatre**, behind the Temple of Zeus, was built in the 1st century and could once hold 5000 spectators. On the far side of the forum the Cardo, or **colonnaded street**, stretches for more than 600m to the North Gate. The street is still paved with the original stones, and the ruts worn by thousands of chariots over the years can clearly be seen.

Halfway along the Cardo is the **nymphaeum**, the main ornamental fountain of the city and a temple to the Nymphs. This is followed by the most imposing building on the site, the **Temple of Artemis**, dedicated to the patron goddess of the city.

In the tiny **museum** just to the east of the forum, there's a good selection of artefacts from the site. It's open daily from 7.30 am until dark, and admission is JD2.

Places to Stay & Eat

Surprisingly, there is still no hotel in Jerash, but it's an easy day trip from Amman.

Olive Branch Resort (☎ 07-923 546, fax 06-826 034) is about 5km out of town on the Ajlun road. Singles/doubles with colour TV, central heating and fan are JD26/38. A swim in its pool is JD2 for nonguests. You can camp here in your/its tent for JD4/5 per person.

Government Rest House by the entrance has an expensive restaurant; near the bus station there's the usual collection of cafes selling the usual felafel and shwarma. About

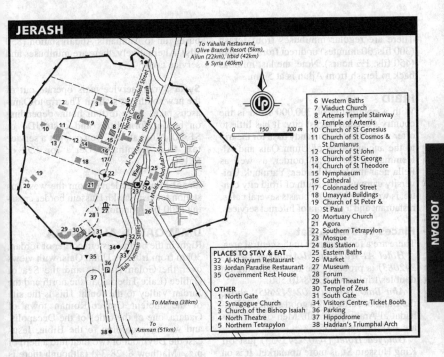

JERASH

To Yahalla Restaurant,
Olive Branch Resort (5km),
Ajlun (22km), Irbid (42km)
& Syria (40km)

0   150   300 m

6 Western Baths
7 Viaduct Church
8 Artemis Temple Stairway
9 Temple of Artemis
10 Church of St Genesius
11 Church of St Cosmos &
St Damianus
12 Church of St John
13 Church of St George
14 Church of St Theodore
15 Nymphaeum
16 Cathedral
17 Colonnaded Street
18 Umayyad Buildings
19 Church of St Peter &
St Paul
20 Mortuary Church
21 Agora
22 Southern Tetrapylon
23 Mosque
24 Bus Station
25 Eastern Baths
26 Market
27 Museum
28 Forum
29 South Theatre
30 Temple of Zeus
31 South Gate
34 Visitors Centre; Ticket Booth
36 Parking
37 Hippodrome
38 Hadrian's Triumphal Arch

PLACES TO STAY & EAT
32 Al-Khayyam Restaurant
33 Jordan Paradise Restaurant
35 Government Rest House

OTHER
1 North Gate
2 Synagogue Church
3 Church of the Bishop Isaiah
4 North Theatre
5 Northern Tetrapylon

To Mafraq (38km)

To
Amman (51km)

JORDAN

20m from the site entrance are the pleasant *Al-Khayyam* and *Jordan Paradise* restaurants. At the northern end of the ruins is *Yahalla Restaurant*, a large place with a garden and water feature. Some would say the decor was a bit garish but the food is fine.

Getting There & Away
From Amman, take a service taxi or minibus from Abdali bus station. From Jerash, there are minibuses to Ajlun, Irbid and Mafraq. All transport stops after 6 pm (and a taxi back to Amman will cost about JD7).

AJLUN
The trip to Ajlun, 22km west of Jerash, goes through beautiful small pine forests and olive groves. The attraction of the town is nearby **Qala'at ar-Rabad**, built by the Arabs as protection against the Crusaders. The castle is a fine example of Islamic mil-

itary architecture. It stands on a hill 2km west of the town and from the top you get fantastic views of the Jordan Valley to the west. It is open daily from 8 am to 7 pm (9 am to 5 pm in winter), and admission is JD1. It's a tough uphill walk but there are minibuses (in this case called service taxis) to the top (50 fils) or you can take a taxi (500 fils one way).

Places to Stay & Eat
Ajlun is definitely worth considering as an overnight stop as watching the sun set from the castle is a memorable experience. There are two expensive hotels between the town and the castle, both *Al-Rabad* and *Ajlun* have singles/doubles for JD24/32. If you have a tent it is possible to camp in the small patch of forest just to the west of the castle.

You can get felafel and shwarma near the bus station.

Getting There & Away

There are regular minibuses from Jerash (300 fils, 30 minutes) or direct from Amman (450 fils, 1½ hours). Note, the last minibus back to Jerash from Ajlun is at 5 pm.

IRBID

With a population of 300,000 Irbid is the country's second largest city. It has little to offer visitors but it is a handy base for the trip to the ancient ruins of Umm Qais and Al-Hemma, on the Syrian border, as well as Pella near the Israel border. Yarmouk University campus, 1km south of Irbid city centre, is worth visiting – it boasts several cafes, restaurant and a plethora of Internet services.

Places to Stay & Eat

There are a few cheapies in the central area.
Hotel Al-Wahadat al-Arabiyya (☎ 02-242083) is probably the best with singles/doubles/triples for JD5/8/10.500.

Abu Bakr Hotel (☎ 02-242695), above the Bank of Jordan, is a good choice if Wahadat al-Arabiyya is full. Men-only dorms are JD2, doubles JD5.

Omayed Hotel (☎ 02-245955) just off King Hussein St, is more upmarket. It is on the 2nd floor above Jordan Arab Investment Bank, and has good, clean rooms with en suite bath, TV and fan for JD14/18.

Al-Khayyam Restaurant, not far from the King Hussein St roundabout, is more of a bar than anything else, but you can get a decent meal; a generous plate of kebabs costs JD1.500, while beer is JD1.500. There are several other restaurants nearby on the roundabout, including *Meshwar* for filled sandwiches and *Automatic* for kebabs, chicken and hamburgers.

Andalusia and *Al Alali* restaurants, off King Hussein St near the roundabout, are two good choices. You reach them from a lift in the arcade: Andalusia is on the 6th floor and Al Alali is on the 8th floor. They serve standard fare but cost extra because of the height.

Getting There & Away

From the north bus station minibuses go to Umm Qais and Al-Hemma.

From the south bus station air-con Hijazi buses run to Amman's Abdali station (850 fils). Alternatively, there are minibuses and service taxis.

Syria Syrian service taxis operate out of the new south bus station. The trip to Damascus takes three to four hours depending on border formalities and costs JD4 or S£300. Alternatively, you can get a service taxi from Ramtha to Der'a for JD2 or S£150.

Israel Minibuses leave from the west bus station for Jisr Sheikh Hussein border crossing (300 fils, one hour).

UMM QAIS & AL-HEMMA

Right in the north-western corner of Jordan, 30km from Irbid, is Umm Qais, with views over the Golan Heights and the Sea of Galilee (Lake Tiberias) to the north and the Jordan Valley to the south. This is the site of the ancient Graeco-Roman town of Gadara, one of the cities of the Decapolis, and where, according to the Bible, Jesus cast the Devil out of two men into a herd of pigs (Matthew 8: 28-34) (although there is an alternative site for this episode on the eastern shore of the Sea of Galilee in Israel).

Things to See

The small **museum** is open from 8 am to 5 pm daily except Tuesday, and admission is free. It contains artefacts and mosaics from the area, including a 4th century mosaic found in one of the town's mausoleums. It is overshadowed perhaps by the headless white marble statue of a goddess found sitting in the front row of the **Western Theatre**, which is now in a very sorry state of repair. The site is open from 8 am to 7 pm daily (9 am to 5 pm in winter), and admission is JD1.

The baths of **Al-Hemma** are a farther 10km from Umm Qais, down the hill towards Yarmouk River. These baths were famous in Roman times for their health-giving properties and are still used today (although the water is sometimes very smelly).

Places to Stay & Eat

Umm Qais Hotel (☎ 02-217081) is a very comfortable place; prices vary, but JD6 per person seems the approximate figure. It also has a small restaurant.

In Al-Hemma, there is an unnamed *hotel* (☎ 02-249829 ext 5) by the baths with rooms for JD8 and *Sah al-Noum* in the village has the same rates.

Getting There & Away

There are regular minibuses to Umm Qais from Irbid (220 fils, 45 minutes) and on to Al-Hemma. You need your passport for the trip down as there's a military control point on the edge of Umm Qais and at least one other closer to Al-Hemma.

UMM AL-JIMAL

Comparatively little is known about this strange black-basalt city in the south of the Hauran (also called Jebel Druze), only about 10km from the Syrian border and about 20km east of Mafraq.

Umm al-Jimal is thought to have been founded in about the 2nd century AD and to have formed part of the defensive line of Rome's Arab possessions. It continued to flourish into Umayyad times but was destroyed by an earthquake in 747 AD and never recovered. Much of what remains is simple urban architecture – ordinary people's houses and shops – but other buildings have been identified such as a **barracks** and **church** combined, and the building known as the **Western Church**.

Getting There & Away

It is possible to see Umm al-Jimal in a day trip from Amman. Take a local bus or minibus to Zarqa (150 fils, 20 minutes), a minibus from there to Mafraq (350 fils, 45 minutes) and then another minibus on to the ruins (200 fils, 20 minutes).

JORDAN VALLEY

Forming part of the Great Rift Valley of Africa, the fertile valley of the Jordan River was of great significance in biblical times and is now the food bowl of Jordan. The river rises in the mountains of Lebanon and flows southward, draining into the Dead Sea (the lowest point on Earth at 394m below sea level). The Jordan River marks the boundary between Israel and Jordan from the Sea of Galilee to the Dead Sea.

Ambitious irrigation projects such as the East Ghor (now King Abdullah) Canal have brought substantial areas of the valley under irrigation. A new dam is being built at Al-Karama west of Amman. The hot, dry summers and short, mild winters of the Jordan Valley make for ideal growing conditions and two or even three crops a year are grown.

Apart from the Dead Sea and Pella, there is little to attract visitors to the valley today.

Have your passport with you when travelling in the area, as there are frequent military checkpoints.

Pella

Near the village of Al-Mashari'a are the ruins of the ancient city of Pella (Tabaqat Fahl), 2km east of the road.

Pella followed the fate of many other cities in the region, coming successively under the rule of the Ptolemies, the Seleucids and the Jews, who largely destroyed Pella in 83 BC because its inhabitants were not inclined to adopt the customs of their conquerors.

Pella was one of the cities of the Decapolis. It was to Pella that Christians fled persecution from the Roman army in Jerusalem in the 2nd century AD. Excavations are still in progress by an Australian team.

The points of interest include the area known as the **main mound** (with a maze of houses, shops and store houses), the **Civic Complex Church**, a 1st century odeon or **theatre**, the remains of a Roman **nymphaeum** or fountain and a Byzantine fort.

It is a steep walk up to the site, and the heat is punishing in summer, so get some water in Al-Mashari'a before heading up.

Places to Stay & Eat There is an unnamed place near the ruins that has passable doubles for JD15. The expensive *Government Rest House* at the site is the only close place to eat; wait until you get back to Al-Mashari'a.

JORDAN

Getting There & Away From Irbid you can catch an Al-Mashari'a minibus from the west bus station. From Amman, take a minibus for Suwalha (don't confuse this with Suweileh) and change for Al-Mashari'a. You can also catch a series of minibuses up the Jordan Valley from South Shuneh or down from North Shuneh.

The Dead Sea
The bathing facilities on the Jordan side of the Dead Sea are nowhere near as good as those in Israel. If you are contemplating a float at the lowest point of Earth perhaps do it from the Israeli side. For details on the qualities of the Dead Sea see Israel & the Palestinian Territories chapter. If you do decide to swim on the Jordan side make sure you are close to a shower (see the information about the Dead Sea Rest House in the following Places to Stay & Eat section) so that you can immediately wash off the encrusted salt.

At the sea's southern end the Jordanians are exploiting the high potash content of the mineral-rich water.

Places to Stay & Eat The 'resort' at Suweimeh is where most people go for a float on the eastern shore of the Dead Sea. The government-owned *Dead Sea Rest House* (☎ 08-572901) here provides day-trippers with showers, changing rooms and an air-con restaurant (buffet lunch JD6). Admission to the beach area is JD2.500, a towel is JD1.500 and lockers are 500 fils. Horribly overpriced rooms are also available here.

A farther 5.5km south, *Dead Sea Spa Hotel* (☎ 08-546101) is another expensive option.

Getting There & Away There are frequent buses from Al-Quds St in Amman to South Shuneh (400 fils, 35 minutes), from where another minibus leaves about every half an hour for the Dead Sea Rest House at Suweimeh (200 fils, 25 minutes). Friday and Sunday are the best days for hitching as families head down to the sea on their day off.

East of Amman

THE DESERT CASTLE LOOP
A string of what have become known as 'castles' lies in the desert east of Amman. Most of them were built or taken over and adapted by the Damascus-based Umayyad rulers in the late 7th and early 8th centuries. Two of the castles, Azraq and Qasr al-Hallabat, date back to Roman times and there is even evidence of Nabataean occupation.

Many of the castles can be visited in a loop from Amman via Azraq. With the exception of Qasr al-Mushatta, it is quite feasible to see all the main castles along this loop in one day using a combination of public transport and hitching. Most are never more than a couple of kilometres off the road. A private car would simplify matters, or you could arrange a taxi for the day from Amman (approximately JD35). Get a copy of the Jordan Tourism Board's free *Desert Castles*.

There are, however, a number of castles so far off the beaten track that only 4WDs and experienced guides will do, especially the little visited Qsar at-Tuba (4WD definitely needed).

Qasr al-Hallabat & Hammam as-Sarah
Qasr al-Hallabat was originally a Roman fort built as a defence against raiding desert tribes. During the 7th century it was a monastery and then the Umayyads fortified it and converted it into a country estate. It's now crumbling walls and fallen stone.

Some 2km down the road heading east is the Hammam as-Sarah bathhouse and hunting lodge built by the Umayyads. It has been almost completely reconstructed and you can see the channels that were used for the hot water and steam.

Getting There & Away From Amman's Raghadan bus station take a minibus to Zarqa (150 fils), from where you can get another to Hallabat (230 fils). The bus drives right by the two sites. From the Hammam as-Sarah it's probably easiest to hitch to the Azraq Hwy and on to Azraq. A bus from Zarqa to Azraq is 500 fils.

Azraq

The oasis town of Azraq, 103km east of Amman, is the junction of the roads heading north-east to As-Safawi and on to Iraq and south-east into Saudi Arabia.

Azraq has the only water in the whole of the Eastern Desert, and used to be one of the most important oases in the Middle East for birds migrating between Africa and Europe. It was also home to water buffalo and other wildlife. Until a few years ago, the oases had almost run dry because of the large-scale pumping from wells to supply Amman with drinking water. This process has now been reversed, but most of the wildlife has been lost and few birds stop here now.

Qala'at al-Azraq This large castle is built out of black basalt, and in its present form dates to the beginning of the 13th century. It was originally three storeys high, but much of it crumbled in an earthquake in 1927. Greek and Latin inscriptions date earlier constructions on the site to around 300 AD – about the time of the reign of Diocletian. The Umayyads followed and maintained it as a military base, as did the 14th century Ayyubids. In the 16th century the Ottoman Turks stationed a garrison here.

After the 16th century the only other recorded use of the castle was during WWI when Sheriff Hussein (father of the recently deceased King Hussein) and TE Lawrence made it their desert headquarters in the winter of 1917, during the Arab Revolt against the Turks. Lawrence's room was directly above the southern entrance.

Shaumari Wildlife Reserve This is the Royal Society for the Conservation of Nature's (RSCN) attempt to reintroduce long-absent wildlife into the region. There are over 200 wild oryx, several hundred gazelle, and ostrich and other less visible birdlife here. Unfortunately, you may not see much wildlife apart from the ostrich as the oryx and gazelle largely roam free (apparently the ostrich are now being farmed for meat and feathers). The only way to get to this small reserve, about 10km south of the old junction in Azraq, is by car or hitching.

Places to Stay & Eat *Az-Zoubi Hotel*, 1km south of the intersection and just off the road to Saudi Arabia, is the best value of the hotels. As everywhere else here, prices are negotiable, but you may be able to get a room with up to four beds for JD12. There are no singles.

The penniless may choose *Funduq al-Waha* (no sign in English), 300m north of Az-Zoubi Hotel on the same highway, where a bed costs JD3 in a shared double. The two hotels north of the intersection are well overpriced.

A bunch of small restaurants lines the 1km stretch south of the main road junction. These places are all keen for your money, so it is advisable to find out what you'll be paying before eating.

Getting There & Away A minibus leaves from near Azraq post office (north of the castle) to Zarqa (450 fils, two hours). A lift to Amman in a private car (with stops at desert castles along the way) will cost about JD8 to JD10.

Qusayr 'Amra

Heading back towards Amman on Hwy 40, *Qusayr* (Little Castle) 'Amra is the best preserved of the desert castles. The walls of the three halls are covered with frescoes, including several rather risqué nudes. The castle's plain exterior belies the beauty within. It is now a world heritage site.

Qasr al-Kharaneh

This well-preserved castle is a farther 16km along the road to Amman, stuck in the middle of a treeless plain to the left of the highway. It seems it was the only one of the castles built solely for defensive purposes, although no one really knows what its purpose was. Another popular explanation was that it was one of the first Islamic *khans*, or caravanserais (inns for travelling traders).

Qasr al-Mushatta

Qasr al-Mushatta is 35km south of Amman near the airport. It was the biggest and most lavish of all the Umayyad castles but for some unknown reason was never finished.

Getting There & Away Qasr al-Mushatta is only about 2km from Queen Ali international airport but cannot be reached on foot. The only option is to drive the 10km around the airport perimeter (you will need to leave your passport at a military checkpoint).

South of Amman

There are three possible routes south of Amman to Aqaba: the Desert Hwy, the Wadi Araba road via the Dead Sea and the King's Hwy. The last is by far the more interesting of the three, as it twists and winds its way south, connecting the historic centres of Madaba, Kerak, Tafila, Shobak and Petra.

Public transport along the highway is reliable but infrequent. Hitching is possible and, from Tafila at least, is the quickest way to go. In 1999 there was extensive reconstruction of the King's Hwy between Madaba and Kerak. Those driving their own vehicles should check with the police in either town to find out if this section of the highway is open.

MADABA

This easy-going little town 30km south of Amman is best known for its remarkable, mostly Byzantine-era mosaics, including the famous 6th century map of Palestine. Madaba makes an easy day trip from Amman or a good first stop en route between Amman and Petra.

The most interesting **mosaic** is in the Greek Orthodox St George's Church. It is a clear map of Palestine and Lower Egypt, and although it is now far from complete, many features can still be made out, including the Nile River, the Dead Sea and the map of Jerusalem showing the Church of the Holy Sepulchre. It was made around 560 AD, originally measuring a staggering 25m by 5m and consisting of more than two million pieces. The church is open from 8.30 am to 6 pm Monday to Thursday and from 10.30 am to 6 pm Friday, Saturday and Sunday; admission is JD1.

Careful excavation and restoration from 1991 to 1995 has led to the creation of an **archaeological park**. Its core takes in the sites of the 7th century churches of the Virgin and the Prophet Elias, along with parts of an earlier structure now known as Hippolytus Hall. Between the two churches are the well-preserved remains of a Roman road, which ran east to west between the then Roman city's gates. Several mosaics have been uncovered and ramps have been built to allow visitors to examine them.

By far the most impressive mosaic is in Hippolytus Hall, depicting scenes from the classical Oedipal tragedy of Phaedre and Hippolytus. The main mosaic in the Church of the Virgin, a masterpiece of geometrical design, appears to have been executed in Umayyad times, but by Christians, not Muslims.

Yet another extraordinary mosaic, dedicated to the 12 Apostles, is on view in a tastefully designed building that replaces what little was left of the Church of the Apostles, down by the King's Hwy 1km from St George's Church.

Places to Stay & Eat

Lulu's Pension (☎ 08-543678) is a 10 minute walk from St George's Church. Head out along the road for Mt Nebo, but at the second roundabout go straight. Very clean and comfortable rooms cost JD10, including breakfast.

Black Iris Hotel (☎ 08-541959, Al-Mouhafada Circle) comes recommended. It has scrupulously clean singles/doubles/triples, all with ensuites, for JD18/25/35 including breakfast.

Haret Jdoundna, a new place just 100m from the mosaic, has a wood-fired pizzeria and a restaurant serving Jordanian food. It is the prime place for package tourists in Madaba, with about 20 craft shops arrayed around it, so it's a little pricey.

Let's Go Internet Cafe, near Lulu's Pension, has chosen the wrong name we think (as far as guidebooks go) but is useful for those spending the night in Madaba. Internet access is JD2 per hour, and food and drinks are also available.

Getting There & Away

Minibuses regularly run between Madaba and Amman's Raghadan and Wahadat bus stations (220 fils, one hour).

AROUND MADABA
Mt Nebo

From this area, 10km north-west of Madaba on the edge of the Eastern plateau, it is possible to see the Dead Sea and the spires of the churches in Jerusalem on a clear day.

The Franciscan Fathers bought the site at Mt Nebo in the 1930s and have excavated the ruins of a 6th century church and monastery. Although little remains of the buildings that housed them, the mosaics from this period can be seen today, protected by a modern structure erected by the Franciscans. The main mosaic is about 3m by 9m and depicts, among other things, wine-making and hunting. The site is open daily from 7 am to 7 pm (closing 5 pm in winter), and admission is 500 fils.

Getting There & Away From Madaba take a minibus from the traffic roundabout (near the tourist office) or by Jordan Bank heading for Fasilliyeh on the Mt Nebo road (100 fils, 10 minutes). From there it's about a 5km walk (you may be able to hitch). The road from Mt Nebo down to the Dead Sea has been sealed but it is still treacherous – if driving, be extra careful.

Hammamat Ma'in

The hot springs and resort of Hammamat Ma'in lie 25km south-west of Madaba. The serpentine road crosses some of the most spectacular territory around the Dead Sea and drops fairly steeply to the springs after the first 30km. The therapeutic value of the spring waters was made famous by such figures as Herod the Great.

Before you even get into this place, you are hit for money. It's a minimum JD2 just to get into the area. Or you can pay JD4 to use the pool as well (alternatively you can pay for the pool separately once you're inside and at no extra cost). Treat these springs as a day trip only.

For a free sauna and spa, walk along the road passing under part of the hotel and after a few hundred metres you'll reach a mosque. Continue past this another 50m and you'll come to a natural sulphur spa bath. The cave to the right is as good a sauna as you'll ever have. This is, unfortunately, generally a male-dominated activity – the usual warnings to women apply.

Places to Stay & Eat The cheapest accommodation is *Safari Caravans park* just behind Drop & Shop 'supermarket' on your left shortly after entering the site. These claustrophobic little sweat boxes are JD15/20 a night for singles/doubles – plus 10% tax! This place was closed for renovations at the time of research.

Ashtar Hotel (☎ 08-545500) in the heart of the resort has rooms for US$70/90.

Getting There & Away From Amman you can catch the JETT bus from Abdali bus station for JD4 one way, or pay JD10 for the round trip, which includes admission and lunch. From Wahadat bus station there are up to four minibuses in the morning for JD1.

From Madaba catch a minibus to Ma'in (150 fils, one hour) and hitch. If you're lucky the minibus will go the whole way (500 fils).

MACHAERUS (MUKAWIR)

Perched on a 700m-high hill about 45km south-west of Madaba are the ruins of Herod the Great's fortress Machaerus. His successor, Herod Antipas, had John the Baptist beheaded here. Herod Antipas feared John the Baptist's popularity and did not take kindly to criticism of his second marriage to Herodias. When Salome, Herodias' daughter, danced for him he honoured his promise to give Salome anything she wanted – it ended up being John's head on a plate.

The fort, known to the locals as **Qala'at al-Meshneq**, is approached up a set of stairs. There's not an awful lot to see, but vestiges of Herod Antipas' palace, baths and parts of the fortress wall and defensive towers can be made out.

Getting There & Away

From Madaba take a Mukawir minibus (250 fils, 1½ hours) and tell the driver your destination; he'll let you out at an appropriate place. You can see the hill and fort to the west. Minibuses back to Madaba are infrequent and finish at 5 pm, so keep a look out.

WADI AL-MUJIB

Wadi al-Mujib cuts a massive swathe across the King's Hwy (and is also thought to be Arnon, the border between the biblical Ammonite and Moabite kingdoms). The canyon, over 1km deep, is one of the most spectacular sights in Jordan.

The road winds precariously down one side and up the other and at the bottom there is only a bridge over the wadi. Where the Wadi al-Mujib enters the Dead Sea on the new Wadi Araba road there is a spectacular view up the narrow ravine at its mouth.

In 1999 there was extensive construction on this section of the King's Hwy, check with the police in Madaba or Kerak as to whether the road is open.

KERAK

The fort town of Kerak lies about 50km south of Wadi al-Mujib on the route of the ancient caravans that used to travel from Egypt to Syria in the time of the biblical kings, and were also used by the Greeks and Romans.

The greater part of Kerak lies within the walls of the old Crusader town and is dominated by its fort – one in a long line built by the Crusaders, which stretched from Aqaba in the south right up into Turkey in the north.

The **Krak de Moabites** (fort) itself has been partially restored, and is a jumble of rooms and vaulted passages. It is still possible to see the cisterns where water was once stored, but not much else. There is

also a small **museum**. The castle is open daily (except Tuesday) during daylight hours, and admission is JD1.

Places to Stay & Eat

Towers Castle Hotel (☎ 03-354293) has clean rooms, some with private shower and toilet. Prices are flexible but it appears JD7.500/11 are the basic rates for singles/ doubles.

Rum Cottage Hotel (☎ 03-354359) is just as good and is in the centre of town. It is clean and has some large rooms; doubles with/ without private bathroom go for JD10/7.

Next to the castle and with excellent views is *Karak Rest House* (☎ 03-351148). Comfortable rooms cost JD30/40, including tax and breakfast.

The new *Al-Mujib Hotel* (☎ 03-386090) about 10 minutes from downtown and the castle is just as good as the Karak Rest House and is recommended by readers. All rooms have large bathrooms, air-con and phones; doubles are JD26 including breakfast. There is also a restaurant and an airy lobby.

There are a few cheap eateries around Kerak. *Peace Restaurant*, near Castle Hotel, serves up a filling mixed grill of meat with several dips and salad for about JD3.500, including a drink. *Al-Fed'a Restaurant*, a block farther on, serves beer (but note that we have received complaints about overcharging here).

There are also several inexpensive chicken and kebab places, and bakeries, in the centre of town.

Getting There & Away

From the bus station there are minibuses and service taxis for Amman along the Desert Hwy. Public transport also runs north along the King's Hwy as far as Ariha and south to Tafila (500 fils, 1½ hours). There are no direct buses to Petra; you have to go via the Desert Hwy and Ma'an or risk the long hitch south.

TAFILA

Wadi al-Hesa, the second great river gorge to cut through the King's Hwy, lies approximately halfway between Kerak and

Tafila. Tafila, now a busy market centre, was once a Crusader base but there's little to see from that era. Its Crusader castle is still closed to the public. You may well stop here to change minibus (for Ma'an) on the trip between Petra and Kerak.

DANA NATURE RESERVE

Stretching west from the King's Hwy town of Al-Qadesiyya, the RSCN's Dana Nature Reserve is something of a novel experiment in Jordan – an attempt to promote eco-tourism, protect wildlife and improve the lives of local villagers all at once. It is one of the most beautiful spots in Jordan. The terrain ranges from the lofty cliffs creating Wadi Dana (at 1500m above sea level) to the desert plains of Wadi Araba (at 50m below sea level) and the archaeologically significant Wadi Faynan. Visit at all costs.

Three main walking trails (Cave Trail, 4km; Ar-Rummana, 2.5km; and Campsite, 2km) have been marked out. For more difficult trails you need to hire guides (JD30 per day, maximum 10 people per guide).

Admission to the park is JD5, tent hire (maximum four people) is JD5, camping fees are JD12 per person and, thankfully, the shuttle bus is free.

You can camp at either of two camp sites: Ar-Rummana is open from 1 March to 31 October, while Feinan is open all year. *Dana Guest House* (☎ 03-368497), in the village of Dana at the eastern end of the reserve, is pricey. Singles/doubles with balcony are JD25/35, those without are JD20/25, and breakfast is included (add a 10% 'conservation' surcharge).

SHOBAK

This is yet another Crusader castle/fort in the chain and, like Kerak, it has a commanding position over some incredibly desolate land. Today the place looks more impressive from the outside, as it is built on a small knoll right on the edge of the Eastern plateau. The inside is in a decrepit state, although restoration work is underway. Shobak is at the peak of a road that loops north between Ma'an and Wadi Musa.

PETRA & WADI MUSA

If you are only going to see one place in Jordan make it majestic Petra, the ruined capital of the Nabataeans, Arabs who dominated the Transjordan area in pre-Roman times. Like Jerash, this lost city was forgotten by the outside world for 1000 years. It was rediscovered in 1812, excavations commenced in 1929 and the central city was not uncovered until after 1958.

Orientation

Wadi Musa is the small tourist town sprawled along the sides of a 4km-long valley that leads down to the entrance to Petra. The centre of Wadi Musa is defined by Shaheed roundabout and all of the main services are found near here; this is also the place to catch buses to Aqaba and Wadi Rum. From the circle it's 3km downhill (along aptly named Tourist St) to the star-studded hotels which guard the entrance to Petra. (Realise that prices increase as the altitude drops.)

Information

There's a post office in the visitors' centre at the entrance to the site. The only useful credit card in town is Visa – you can use this at the Housing Bank ATM near the circle, the Cairo-Amman Bank in the Mövenpick and the Arab Bank in the visitors' centre. You can do laundry at the Twaissi (JD6 for a 10.5kg load) and there is an Internet cafe near the central mosque.

'Ain Musa/Moses' Spring

Just before you descend to Wadi Musa, coming in on the road from Amman, you pass a small, three-domed building on the right. It's not a mosque but is supposedly the place where Moses struck the rock with his staff and water gushed forth – hence the name.

Al'Barid/Little Petra

For those who cannot afford the admission price to Petra – and yes some people come here and cannot pay – the ancient Neolithic village of Al-Beidha and the ruins at Al-Barid (also known as Little Petra) are alternatives for the impecunious. These are 8km

PETRA

This spectacular rose-stone city was built in the 3rd century BC by the Nabataeans who carved palaces, temples, tombs, storerooms and stables from the rocky cliffs. From here they commanded the trade route from Damascus to Arabia, and through here the great spice, silk and slave caravans passed. In a short time the Nabataeans made great advances – they mastered hydraulic engineering, iron production, copper refining, sculpture, stone carving – all probably because of their great success in commerce. Archaeologists believe that several earthquakes, including a massive one in 555 AD, forced the inhabitants to abandon the city.

The Site

Petra is approached through an incredibly narrow 1.2km-long defile known as the **Siq**. This is not a canyon (a gorge carved out by water) but rather one block that has been rent apart by tectonic forces. Just as you start to think there's no end to the Siq, you catch tantalising glimpses ahead of the most impressive of sights, the **Khazneh** (Treasury). Carved out of solid iron-laden sandstone to serve as a tomb, the Treasury gets its name from the story that pirates hid their treasure here. The interior is just an unadorned square hall with a smaller, similarly empty room at the back.

The other monument that shouldn't be missed is the **Ad-Deir** (Monastery), reached by a long, rock-cut staircase on the far side of the site. On the way up look out for the **Lion Tomb** – although the eroded lions astride the entrance are difficult to see at first. The Monastery has a similar facade to the Khazneh, but is far bigger and

TM FLOWER

Top: The urn of the Khazneh is pocked by rifle shots, the result of vain efforts to break it open by locals who believed it contained pirate treasure. (Photo by TM Flower)

Left: The Khazneh is the finest of all Petra's monuments, with a facade instantly familiar to viewers of *Indiana Jones & the Last Crusade*.

the views from the cliff-tops nearby are stunning (especially out to Mt Haroun).

Other interesting sites include an 8000 seat **amphitheatre**, the **Qasr al-Bint** (one of the very few free-standing buildings), the **colonnaded street**, the **Temple of the Winged Lions**, the ruins of a **Byzantine church** with possibly the world's oldest Byzantine mosaic, and the facade known as the **Royal Tombs**. Walk to the Royal Tombs – the Urn, Corinthian, Silk and Palace – to examine the eroded facades and colourful interiors.

The price of entry to Petra is JD20/25/30 for a one/two/three day pass (must be used on consecutive days). If you buy a three day pass you get a fourth day for free. Tickets are bought from the visitors' centre near the entrance gate, which also provides some information and has periodic displays. At the nearby Jeff's Bookshop you can purchase the excellent *Map of Petra* (JD5), which depicts the site in relief. The first visitors are admitted to Petra at 6 am, and it's wise to get there as early as possible to avoid the daily stampede and the heat.

High Places

The **Crusader Fort** is the easiest climb (a few minutes), while the **High Place of Sacrifice** near the Siq is a 30 minute climb. Continue on to the **Lion Fountain**, the **Garden Tomb**, the **Tomb of the Roman Soldier** and the **Triclinium**, then down to the **Pharoan Column**.

For those with time the five-hour return trip to **Mt Haroun** and **Aaron's Tomb** is not to be missed. The views from the top are superb. On the way back look for **Snake Monument** which dominates a collection of tombs – to your right as you head down into Wadi ath-Thughra.

The hike to the top of **Umm al-Biyara**, once thought to be the Biblical Sela, is tough going and takes two to three hours.

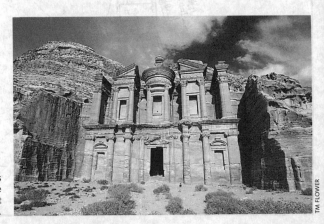

Right: It takes 30 minutes or more to walk up to the Monastery but the effort is well rewarded.

TM FLOWER

PETRA

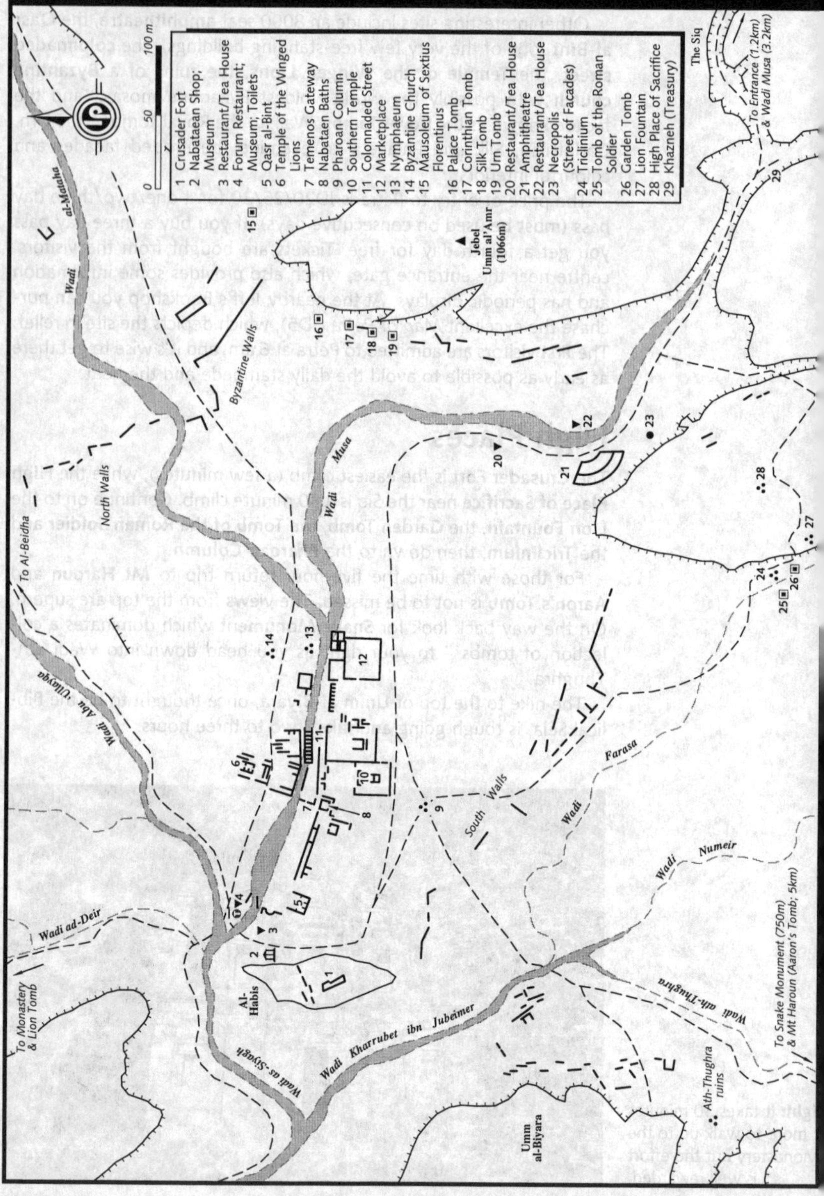

1 Crusader Fort
2 Nabataean Shop;
  Museum
3 Restaurant/Tea House
4 Forum Restaurant;
  Museum; Toilets
5 Qasr al-Bint
6 Temple of the Winged
  Lions
7 Temenos Gateway
8 Nabataean Baths
9 Pharaon Column
10 Southern Temple
11 Colonnaded Street
12 Marketplace
13 Nymphaeum
14 Byzantine Church
15 Mausoleum of Sextius
  Florentinus
16 Palace Tomb
17 Corinthian Tomb
18 Silk Tomb
19 Urn Tomb
20 Restaurant/Tea House
21 Amphitheatre
22 Restaurant/Tea House
23 Necropolis
  (Street of Facades)
24 Triclinium
25 Tomb of the Roman
  Soldier
26 Garden Tomb
27 Lion Fountain
28 High Place of Sacrifice
29 Khazneh (Treasury)

0   50   100 m

Wadi al-Matha

Byzantine Walls

Wadi Musa

Jebel
Umm al'Amr
(1066m)

To Al-Beidha

North Walls

Wadi ad-Deir

To Monastery
& Lion Tomb

Al-
Habis

Wadi Abu 'Ulleiqa

Wadi Kharrubet ibn Jubeimer

Wadi es-Siyagh

South Walls

Farasa

Wadi Numeir

Wadi ath-Thughra

To Snake Monument (750m)
& Mt Haroun (Aaron's Tomb; 5km)

Ath-Thughra
ruins

Umm
al-Biyara

The Siq

To Entrance (1.2km)
& Wadi Musa (3.2km)

29

29

north of Petra Forum Hotel. A taxi for four people with a one hour stop at the ruins will cost JD10. Make sure the driver points out the 'little' Siq al-Barid.

Places to Stay
Petra and the neighbouring village of Wadi Musa are crawling with hotels (over 70 of them) and there seems no end to the construction underway.

Places to Stay – Budget
Mussa Spring Hotel (☎ 03-215 6310) is one of the first hotels you come across after 'Ain Musa. A bed on the (enclosed) roof costs JD2, one in a room of three people or more costs JD4, and doubles are JD10/JD16 without/with own bath. The hotel can organise a lift to and from the site.

Just down the hill is the similar *Al-Anbat* (☎ 03-215 6275) (the name is Arabic for 'Nabataeans') including a well situated restaurant with splendid views over Wadi Musa. The rooms have recently been renovated and are good value at JD10 for a double; the buffet meals are also good value at US$4.50. A camp site costs from JD3 to JD5 depending on the size of the group.

Places to Stay – Mid-Range
Peace Way Hotel (☎ 03-215 6963, Housing Bank St) is a comfortable place with a good reputation – so good it can often be booked out for months in advance. Singles/doubles with heating, private bathroom (clean towels daily) and phone cost JD22/26.

Not far from the Circle are three good hotels. *Rose City Hotel* (☎ 03-215 6440, fax 215 6448) has tidy singles/doubles/triples from JD18/23/30 with breakfast included. They have an á la carte menu in the restaurant and also prepare excellent buffet meals for groups. *Elgee Hotel* (☎ 03-215 7002, fax 215 6701) has comfortable rooms with TV (free movies), phone and showers for JD15/24 including breakfast. It is popular with locals and the bar is a good place to meet Bedouin. Similar to the previous two is *Moon Valley Hotel* (☎ 03-215 6824, fax 215 7131, Tourist St).

Petra Hotel & Rest House (☎ 03-215 6014, fax 215 6868), closer to the entrance, behind the visitors' centre, has good rooms that are reasonably priced at JD31/58 in the older part and JD41/70 in the new wing. Part of it includes an old Nabataean tomb.

Places to Stay – Top End
Petra Forum Hotel (☎ 03-215 6266, fax 215 6977) is an expensive option close to Petra's entrance. You get great views over the Siq from its poolside bar. Singles/doubles are from JD80/90 including 20% tax.

King's Way Inn (☎ 03-215 6799, fax 215 6796, www.kingsway-petra.com) out on the road from Amman is a big, friendly four star place with 80 air-con rooms with satellite TV starting at JD90 plus tax. There's also a restaurant and swimming pool.

Closer to Petra, *Mövenpick Hotel* (☎ 03-215 7111, fax 215 7112) is the new five star darling of the pre-booked European set and has every creature comfort they would expect from a top end hotel in their own countries. It also has two excellent restaurants (see the following Places to Eat section) and the best bar in Wadi Musa.

Places to Eat
For the cheapest eats, investigate the little restaurants clustered around the Circle – which is also where you can buy your own foodstuffs in shops frequented mainly by locals.

Wadi Petra Restaurant, right on the Circle, is a curious little place where you can eat a few dishes beyond the usual fare. The chicken and mixed vegetable stew is good value at JD1.800.

Cleopetra (☎ 03-215 7099) serves chicken and Middle Eastern dishes. *Treasury* is another chicken place with meals for about JD2.500. *Abbysalama Flowers*, serving kebabs and chicken, gets the thumbs up from locals.

On Tourist St near Mövenpick Hotel there is another collection of eateries. The best value is *El Tafily*, which specialises in Jordanian dishes. As you head downhill you pass *Pizza Hut*, which is the same as its US

JORDAN

counterparts, *Papazzi*, which does a poor imitation of Pizza Hut (a small pizza is JD4), and the classy but expensive *Red Cave Restaurant*.

If you want an ice cream then the shop at *Mövenpick* is the place (900 fils for a scoop and JD2.500 for a big vase of fruit cocktail).

Most hotels have restaurants attached; those at *Petra Rest House*, *Petra Forum Hotel* and Mövenpick are expensive. *Al-Saraya* and *Al-Iwan*, both at Mövenpick, are excellent.

Entertainment

Bar hopping is not really possible in Wadi Musa. Beer is expensive wherever you buy it in town (a big bottle of Amstel is JD3.500). *Elgee Hotel* has a liquor store and the upstairs *Bedwin Bar* with a distinctive puffer fish light; foreigners will be gawked at here for a little while. About the only other place to buy takeaway beer is at Mövenpick, and surprisingly it is cheaper here than at the Elgee. Mövenpick also has a superb bar in the style of a lavishly decorated grand dining room but the drinks are very pricey. *Petra Palace* has a cosy sports bar that is popular with locals.

Getting There & Away

There are three JETT buses daily from Amman, which you can catch one way for a hefty JD5.500 (three hours), or take the day tour for JD32, which includes lunch. It leaves for Amman at about 3 pm.

There are a few minibuses departing from Shaheed roundabout for Amman between 5.30 am and noon, a couple for Aqaba (two hours) between 6.30 am and 3.30 pm, and one to the Government Rest House at Wadi Rum at 6 am (1½ hours); all are JD3. Minibuses depart for Ma'an (500 fils, one hour) about once an hour. From Ma'an you can get another minibus or service taxi to Amman or Aqaba, or just get off on the highway and hitch.

WADI RUM

Wadi Rum has some of the most spectacular desert scenery anywhere in the world, and is

well worth leaving the Desert Hwy for. T[...] Lawrence spent quite a bit of time here dur[...]ing the Arab Revolt and many scenes from David Lean's movie *Lawrence of Arabi*[...] were shot here. The huge sheer jebels ris[...] from the sandy valley floor overshadowing the small but growing settlement of Rum which includes the Desert Patrol Corps fort All up, villagers and Bedouin throughout the Wadi Rum area number some 4000.

Wadi Rum deserves a visit of at leas[...] three days and two nights. The silent night[...] with a stunning blanket of stars are unforgettable – have fun watching meteors and other fireworks as Orion chases Scorpi[...] across the sky. Equally memorable are the sunrises and sunsets, best observed from one of the jebels – the colour changes are dramatic and rapid.

The camel-mounted **Desert Patrol** was originally established to patrol borders and keep dissident tribes in order. Nowadays, they use blue 4WDs bristling with machine-guns. The camels, khaki robes, bandoleers, shouldered rifles and daggers at their waists are now only sported on ceremonial occasions. Yet they still revel in their photogenic nature and will pose for those who sit with them, discuss the inconsequential and share tea.

Information

There is no information office – the Government Rest House acts as a quasi tourist centre. It has a mounted copy of the hard-to-get 1:50,000 map of Wadi Rum and surrounds.

The JD1 you pay to enter Wadi Rum entitles you to a cup of tea or coffee at the entry point. If you come in a 4WD you pay an extra JD4 or JD5, depending on whether it's a rented or private vehicle.

To hire a 4WD will cost you anything from JD15 just to get down to Lawrence's Well and back, to around JD38/42 for a full day. You can also hire camels by the hour or the day – one great trip is from Wadi Rum to Aqaba.

As well as trekking around in the desert, Wadi Rum also provides some great rock-climbing possibilities. However, you have

The Bedouin

These desert dwellers, the *bedu* (the name means nomadic), number several hundred thousand, but few can still be regarded as truly nomadic. Some have opted for city life, but most have, voluntarily or otherwise, settled down to cultivate crops rather than drive their animals across the desert in search of fodder.

A few retain the old ways. They camp for a few months at a time in one spot and graze their herds of goats, sheep or camels. When the sparse fodder runs out, it is time to move on again. All over the east and south of the country you'll see the black goat-hair tents (*beit ash-sha'ar* – literally 'house of hair') set up; sometimes just one, often three or four together. Such houses are generally divided into a *haram* (forbidden area) for the women and another section for the men. The men's section is also the public part of the home. Here guests are treated to coffee and sit to discuss the day's events. Most of the family's belongings and stores are kept in the haram (strangers are not permitted inside).

The Bedouin family is a close-knit unit. The women do most of the domestic work including fetching water, baking bread and weaving clothes. The men are traditionally providers and warriors. There is precious little warring to do these days, and the traditional intertribal raids that for centuries were the staple of everyday Bedouin life are now a memory. With the kids often sent out to tend the flocks, the average Bedouin fellow can actually find himself distinctly under-employed.

Most of those still living in the desert continue to wear traditional dress, and this includes, for men, a dagger – a symbol of a man's dignity but rarely used in anger now. The women tend to dress in more colourful garb, but rarely do they veil their tattooed faces.

Although camels, once the Bedouin's best friend, are still in evidence, they are now often replaced by the Land Rover or Toyota pick-up truck – Wilfred Thesiger would definitely not approve. Other concessions to modernity are radios (sometimes even TVs), plastic water containers and occasionally a kerosene stove.

The Jordanian government provides services such as education and offers housing to the 40,000 or so Bedouin estimated to be truly nomadic, but both are often passed up in favour of the lifestyle that has served them so well over the centuries.

The Bedouin are renowned for their hospitality and it is part of their creed that no traveller is turned away. This is part of a desert code of survival. Once taken in, a guest will be offered the best of the available food and plenty of tea and coffee. The thinking is simple: today you are passing through and they have something to offer; tomorrow they may be passing your camp and you may have food and drink – which you would offer them before having yourself. Such a code of conduct made it possible for travellers to cross the desert with some sense that the odds against survival in such a hostile natural environment were not stacked so high as to be impossible.

One has to wonder, if tourists continue to pass through in ever growing numbers (and 99 times out of 100 in no danger of expiring on a sand dune), how long outsiders can expect to be regaled with such hospitality. After all, the original sense of it has largely been lost. Perhaps the moral for travellers is to be open to such things, but not to deliberately search out the Arab 'hospitality experience', reducing it to a kind of prefab high to be ticked off from the list of tourist excitements automatically claimed as a virtual right. There is a world of difference between the harsh desert existence that engendered this most attractive trait in Arab culture and the rather artificial context in which most of us experience this part of the world today.

JORDAN

to bring all your own gear. For more information see Tony Howard's *Treks & Climbs in the Mountains of Wadi Rum & Petra*.

Things to See

The enormous **Jebel Rum** (1754m) is impossible to miss, as it rises sheer-sided from the 2km-wide valley floor.

There are a few places of interest close to the village of Rum (about 30 Bedouin families). **Lawrence's Well** is 2km south-west of Rum but these days is little more than a stagnant pool.

Between the face of Jebel Rum and the resthouse you'll find the ruins of a 1st-century **Nabataean temple**, once a square courtyard with rooms on three sides.

Bedouin rock carvings can be found on the northern side of Jebel Khazali where there is a narrow siq. In fact the whole area is dotted with Thamudic and Kufic inscriptions and rock art.

It is, however, the natural grandeur that makes this place – and the serenity at night.

Places to Stay & Eat

Government Rest House has quite reasonable two-person tents out the back for JD4 a head. Camping in your own tent costs JD1. Or you can sleep on the roof (mattresses and blankets are provided) for JD2.500. Meals are around JD5 (breakfast is JD3) and beer is JD2.500. Take note that even in summer it gets pretty cool in the evenings. The resthouse has showers and luggage storage. If this doesn't appeal, head out into the desert and sleep under the stars. You may be asked by Bedouin to sleep under their tents instead – but don't turn up uninvited.

Organised Tours

There are many tour operators in Aqaba and Amman that arrange good trips to Bedouin-style camps in Wadi Rum. With a group of six or more you could expect to pay about JD25 per person per day including meals, bedding, toilets, showers, 4WD transport and entertainment. These tours give you a chance to get out into the desert well away from the resthouse.

Wadi Rum Desert Service (☎ 03-20 4679) was particularly good. Other operator are Petra Moon Tourism Services (☎ 03-21 6665) and Desert Guides (☎ 03-201 4131 both in Aqaba.

Getting There & Away

From Aqaba take a Quweira minibus (50 fils, 30 minutes) or a Ma'an minibus (JD1 one hour) to the turn-off. The turn-off fo Wadi Rum is 5km south of Quweira and th 26km of road east from there to Diseh an Tuweiseh is surfaced.

There is at least one minibus daily t Petra (JD3) leaving at 8.30 am (it leave Petra for Wadi Rum about 6.30 am). Ther is also at least one minibus daily to Aqab (JD1.500) leaving at 6.30 am. These time are subject to the usual vagaries of this kin of transport – if they fill up earlier, the leave earlier. If you miss them, you'll hav to stick out your thumb.

AQABA

Since pre-Roman times Aqaba has occa sionally been a maritime trading centre; i was a small fishing village that became major trading port, and is Jordan's only coastal town. Today it's also important as tourist centre. While the rest of the countr shivers in winter, the mercury hover steadily around 25°C in Aqaba. In summer however, temperatures and humidity ar uncomfortably high.

Information

There's an unhelpful tourist office in the visitors' centre near the old fort by the wa terfront (but it gives out free maps o Aqaba). The Egyptian consulate north o the centre issues tourist visas on the spot fo JD12 with a minimum of fuss – a great con trast to the shambles at the embassy in Amman. It is open from 9 am to noon daily except Friday.

If you are stuck without cash on a Friday or holiday, try the Cairo-Amman Bank a the Arab Bridge Maritime Company, which is open daily. Visa card holders can ge quick cash advances at Cairo-Amman Bank

AQABA

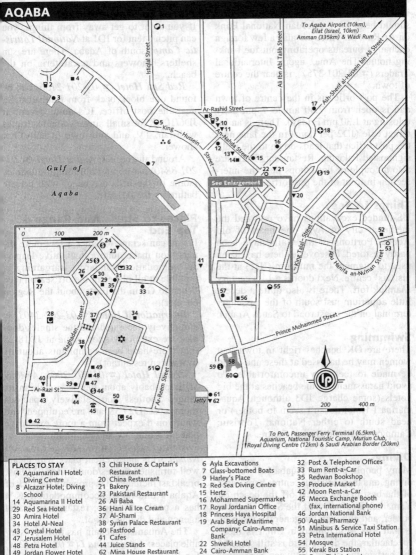

JORDAN

in the centre of town. MasterCard holders should head for the Jordan National Bank on Ar-Razi St. There are also a few foreign exchange bureaus operating outside banking hours. The Amex agent, International Traders (☎ 03-201 3757), is near the centre of town.

The post office is in the centre of town and is open from 7.30 am to 7 pm daily (closing at 1.30 pm Friday). There is an Internet cafe (JD2 per hour) in the lane near the post office that leads down to the well-signposted Pakistani Restaurant. There are also a couple of bookshops near the intersection in front of the post office.

Things to See
US-funded excavations have revealed the medieval city of Ayla, the heart of old Aqaba. Portions of the walls have been partly restored. Discoveries here have been used to augment the museum (JD1) at the visitors' centre. Next door is a 14th century Mamluk fort. There is also quite a decent little aquarium just south of the passenger terminal on the coast road to Saudi Arabia.

Swimming
There are OK beaches right in town, but women may be harassed at these and could be made to feel very uncomfortable. To avoid harassment try the beaches at the big hotels (some charge JD3 although Aquamarina I Hotel doesn't seem to bother) or head south to either National Touristic Camp or the Royal Diving Centre.

Diving
Many people come to Aqaba just for the diving, and there are four centres here. Most of the best diving is just off the beach on Yamanieh Reef north of the Saudi Arabian border, and although the general consensus is that Ras Mohammed in Sinai is more spectacular, the diving here is still some of the best in the world. Between the power station and the Saudi border well over 20 diving sites have been documented (see Activities in the Regional Facts for the Visitor chapter for more information on diving).

Places to Stay – Budget
If you want to get away from things, you can pitch a tent for JD1 at **National Touristic Camp**, south of Aqaba. There are sun shelters, showers and a cafeteria on the beach.

Red Sea Hotel (☎ 03-201 2156) can be found one block back from Raghadan St, near the post office. It's quite decent at JD6/10/18 for small singles/doubles/triples with fan, TV, and your own (usually) hot shower.

Around the corner, **Amira Hotel** (☎ 03-201 8840) has comfortable singles/doubles (some of the beds are huge) with private bathroom for JD14/18.

Places to Stay – Mid-Range & Top End
If you can scrape together a few more dinars, you make quite a qualitative leap in accommodation standards. Bargaining is possible at all places in the off season (see When to Go in the Facts about the Region chapter).

International Hotel (☎ 03-201 3403) is attractively decorated and the singles/doubles are extremely good value at JD18/28 (but there have been complaints about its overpriced restaurant).

Crystal Hotel (☎ 03-201 2001, Ar-Razi St) is probably about the best value in its range. Spotless and relatively spacious rooms cost JD25/38, and are equipped with what you'd expect from a more expensive place (ensuite, TV and mini-bar).

Alcazar Hotel (☎ 03-201 4131, An-Nahda St) is an excellent place with clean, well-furnished singles/doubles for JD39/54, breakfast included. It is probably the pick of Aqaba's mid-range accommodation as it has a pool, good pub, restaurants, travel agency and diving school.

The Aquamarina chain has three reasonable places: **Aquamarina I** (☎ 03-201 4271, fax 201 4271, King Hussein St) right on the beach, **Aqaumarina II** (☎ 03-201 5165, An-Nahda St) closer to the centre and **Aquamarina III** (☎ 03-201 6255, fax 201 3569, Abu Hanifa-an-Nu'man St) on the Circle east of the city. At all three expect to pay around JD50/65, including tax.

Radisson SAS Resort (☎ 03-201 2426, fax 201 3426, King Hussein St), on the beach and close to Aquamarina I, is expensive but in a great location. Rooms start at JD95/120 plus 20% tax (including use of its beach).

Places to Eat

Aqaba has quite a few choices when it comes to food. *Ali Baba (☎ 03-201 3901)* is the most upmarket restaurant in town. It serves a wide range of meals, including reasonable Indian biryanis for JD5, and a selection of fish dishes for about JD7.

Al-Shami (☎ 03-201 4788), off Raghadan St, is cheaper. In this air-con place you can get an excellent meal for two for JD6 with free tea and coffee. It also has great views out across the Gulf. The nearby *Syrian Palace Restaurant* is also recommended for good meals at moderate prices.

China Restaurant serves pretty good meat and rice dishes (and soups for around 500 fils) and *Pakistani Restaurant* is about as close to sub-continental fare as you will get in these parts.

Mina House Restaurant is in a small boat down by the fishing harbour; it has a great fish menu including the Arabic dish *sayadiyeh* (about JD7 per person).

There are a few places by the Aquamarina II Hotel, such as *Captain's Restaurant*, *Pizza Hut* and the fastfood *Chili House (☎ 03-201 2435)*, the last of which does a good version of this US favourite for about JD3. If it's fast chicken you want, try *Tikka Chicken (☎ 03-201 3633)* across the road.

The shops along the road out of Aqaba (Ash-Sherif al-Husseinbin Ali St) are well stocked with all sorts of food (including a bakery near Shweiki Hotel), so if you are heading for Wadi Rum stock up on goodies like dates, cheese and bread. The souq also has plenty of fresh fruit and vegetables.

There is a liquor store diagonally across from the post office.

Entertainment

Entertainment is centred around the hotels. *Radisson SAS* has two-for-the-price-of-one beers (JD3.600) during its happy hour and, later, entertainment around the pool. *Aquamarina II* also has a happy hour. There is also *Dolphin Pub* at Alcazar Hotel (with a happy hour from 7 to 9 pm) with pool table, lounge bar and two restaurants. *Harley's Place* in An-Nahda St hots up after 9 pm, sometimes with live music. Guests can visit *Murjan Club* on the reef for free.

Getting There & Away

Air For details of Jordan's only domestic route between Aqaba and Amman see the main Getting Around section earlier in this chapter.

Bus & Service Taxi JETT buses run four times daily to Amman (JD4, five hours), the last at 4 pm. A few service taxis head for Amman in the morning. You can also take a bus to Ma'an and try again from there.

If you miss the early morning Wadi Rum minibus take either a Ma'an or Quweira (300 fils) minibus. Tell the driver where you are going and he'll let you off at the turn-off, about 5km before Quweira.

One or two minibuses leave in the morning for Petra/Wadi Musa (JD3). These are less likely to run on Friday and holidays.

Sea The ferry terminal is south of the port, 7km from the city centre. A taxi between the terminal and the city centre costs JD1.500. You can buy tickets at the Arab Bridge Maritime Company in central Aqaba. For more details see the main Getting There & Away section earlier in this chapter.

Israel You may get lucky and find a service taxi running to the Wadi Araba border crossing with Israel for JD4 (JD1 per person if you can fill it), otherwise the price for a standard taxi is JD3. For more details of the crossing; see the main Getting There & Away section earlier in this chapter.

Kuwait

If you find an old map of Kuwait, worry not. After the 1991 Gulf War the government restored the ruins of Kuwait City to their exact pre-war state – right down to the pink marble steps at the entrance to Kuwait City's leading five star hotel, the Safir International.

The war is now nearly a decade past. But while the city may look the same, much has changed. Today's Kuwait is more interesting, more vibrant – and easier to visit – than the Kuwait of a decade ago.

Facts about Kuwait

HISTORY
A general history of the Middle East can be found in the Facts about the Region chapter.

The headland now occupied by Kuwait City was settled only 300 years ago. In the early 18th century Kuwait was nothing more than a few tents clustered around a storehouse-cum-fort.

Eventually the families living around the fort divided among themselves the responsibilities attached to the new settlement. The Al-Sabah family, whose descendants now rule Kuwait, were appointed to handle local law and order. The small settlement grew quickly. By 1760, when the town's first wall was built, Kuwait's dhow fleet was said to number 800 and camel caravans based there travelled often to Baghdad and Damascus.

By the early 19th century Kuwait was a thriving trading port. But trouble was always, quite literally, just over the horizon. It was often unclear whether Kuwait was part of the Ottoman empire. Though the 19th century Kuwaitis generally got on well with the Ottomans, official Kuwaiti history is adamant that the sheikhdom always remained independent. As the Turks strengthened their control of Eastern Arabia (then known as Al-Hasa) the Kuwaitis skilfully managed to avoid being absorbed by the empire. The Al-Sabah did, however, agree

The State of Kuwait

Area: 17,818 sq km
Population: 2.2 million (of whom approximately 750,000 are Kuwaitis)
Population Growth Rate: 5.25%
Capital: Kuwait City
Head of State: The Emir, Shaikh Jaber al-Ahmed al-Sabah
Official Language: Arabic
Currency: Kuwaiti dinar (KD)
Exchange Rate: US$1 = KD0.303

- **Best Nightlife** – along Arabian Gulf St between the Kuwait Towers and the Sultan Centre shopping mall.
- **Best View** – get a window seat for after-hours take-offs and landings. The stream of lights that emerges from the headland marked by the Kuwait Towers is a sight to behold.
- **Best Activity** – find an expat with a boat, hire one from the docks near the Sultan Centre or hop the ferry to Failaka Island.
- **When in Rome ...** if anyone invites you to a *diwaniya* ... go. These informal gatherings, usually at someone's home, are the place where Kuwaitis (well, Kuwaiti men) chat about everything from soccer scores to the day's debates in parliament. A uniquely Kuwaiti institution, and one worth joining.

o take the role of provincial governors of Al-Hasa on the Ottoman's behalf.

That decision led to the rise of the pivotal figure in the history of modern Kuwait: Sheikh Mubarak al-Sabah al-Sabah, commonly known as Mubarak the Great (reigned 1896-1915). Mubarak was deeply suspicious of Turkey and convinced that Constantinople planned to annex Kuwait. He overthrew and murdered his brother the emir, did away with another brother and installed himself as ruler.

In 1899 Mubarak signed an agreement with Britain. In exchange for the British navy's protection he promised not to give away territory to, take support from or negotiate with any other foreign power without British consent. The Ottomans continued to claim sovereignty over Kuwait but they were now in no position to enforce it. Britain's motive for signing the treaty was a desire to keep Germany, then the main ally and financial backer of Turkey, out of the Gulf.

Kuwait spent the early 1920s fighting off the army commanded by Abdul Aziz bin Abdul Rahman al-Saud (Ibn Saud), the founder of modern Saudi Arabia. In 1923 the fighting ended with a British-brokered treaty under which Abdul Aziz recognised Kuwait's independence, but at the price of most of the emirate's territory.

An oil concession was granted in 1934 to a USA-British joint-venture known as the Kuwait Oil Company (KOC). The first wells were sunk in 1936 and by 1938 it was obvious that Kuwait was virtually floating on oil. The outbreak of WWII forced the KOC to suspend its operations, but when oil exports took off after the war so did Kuwait's economy.

Sheikh Abdullah al-Salem al-Sabah (reigned 1950-65) became the first 'oil sheikh'. His reign was not, however, marked by the kind of profligacy with which that term later came to be associated. As the country became wealthy, health care, education and the general standard of living improved dramatically. In 1949 Kuwait had only four doctors; by 1967 it had 400.

On 19 June 1961 Kuwait became an independent state. Elections for Kuwait's first

What to See

The **National Museum** and its small gallery of works by Kuwaiti artists is essential viewing during any visit to Kuwait. The **National Assembly** building is one of the city's architectural landmarks. If you're interested in politics try to take in an Assembly session (English translation available). In the suburbs the **Tariq Rajab Museum** has a small but excellent collection of Islamic art and artefacts.

Outside Kuwait City, the archaeological site on **Failaka Island**, and the **Exhibition of Kuwaiti Sailing Ships** are both worth a few hours of your time.

National Assembly were held the following year. Although representatives of the country's leading merchant families won the bulk of the seats, radicals had a toehold in the parliament from its inception. Leftists in the National Assembly almost immediately began pressing for faster social change and the country had three Cabinets between 1963 and 1965.

In August 1976 the Cabinet resigned, claiming that the assembly had made day-to-day governance impossible. The emir suspended the constitution, dissolved the assembly and asked the crown prince (who, by tradition, also serves as prime minister) to form a new Cabinet. New elections were not held until 1981, and then only after the electoral laws had been revised virtually to guarantee that the radicals won no seats in the new parliament. This succeeded after a fashion, but the assembly's new conservative majority proved just as troublesome as the radicals had been. Parliament was dissolved again in 1986.

In December 1989 and January 1990 an extraordinary series of demonstrations took place calling for the restoration of the 1962 constitution and the reconvening of parliament. The demonstrators were met by riot police, tear gas and water cannons. In June of that year elections were held for

KUWAIT

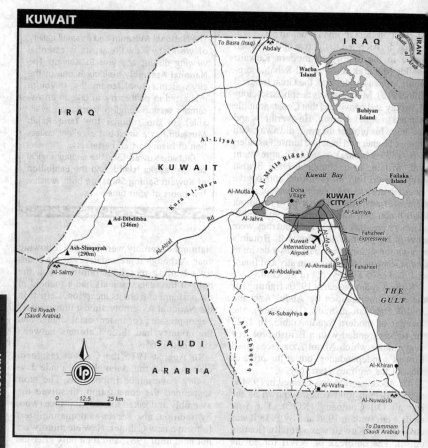

KUWAIT

To Basra (Iraq)
Abdaly
IRAQ
Warba Island
IRAQ
Bubiyan Island
Al-Liyah
KUWAIT
Al-Mutla Ridge
Kuwait Bay
Failaka Island
Al-Mutla
Doha Village
KUWAIT CITY
Ferry
Al-Salmiya
Al-Jahra
Fahaheel Expressway
Ad-Dibdibba (246m)
Kura al-Maru
Rd
Al-Atraf
Kuwait International Airport
Al-Maqwa Rd
Al-Ahmadi
Fahaheel
Ash-Shaqayah (290m)
Al-Salmy
Al-Abdaliyah
THE GULF
To Riyadh (Saudi Arabia)
As-Subayhiya
SAUDI
Ash-Shaqeeq
Al-Khiran
ARABIA
Al-Wafra
0   12.5   25 km
Al-Nuwaisib
To Dammam (Saudi Arabia)

a consultative council that was supposed to spend four years advising the government on possible constitutional changes prior to the election of a new assembly. Pro-democracy activists demanded the restoration of the old assembly and denounced the new council as unconstitutional.

Despite these political and economic tensions, by mid-1990 the country's (and the Gulf's) economic prospects looked bright, particularly with an end to the eight year Iran-Iraq War. In light of this, the following events were even more shocking to most people in the region.

On 16 July 1990 Iraq sent a letter to the secretary-general of the Arab League accusing Kuwait of exceeding its OPEC quota and of stealing oil from the Iraqi portion of an oil field straddling the border. The following day Iraqi president Saddam Hussein repeated these charges in a speech and vaguely threatened military action.

Over the next two weeks a series of envoys bent over backwards to offer Iraq a graceful way out of this manufactured dispute. Each time Iraq replied by launching another verbal salvo in the direction of Kuwait. When the tanks came crashing over the border at 2 am on 2 August, the Kuwaitis never had a chance. The Iraqis were in Kuwait City before dawn and by noon they had reached the Saudi frontier. The emir and his Cabinet fled to Saudi Arabia.

The United Nations quickly passed a series of resolutions calling on Iraq to withdraw from Kuwait. The Iraqis responded with the patently absurd claim that they had been invited in by a group of Kuwaiti rebels who had overthrown the emir. On 8 August Iraq annexed the emirate. Western countries, led by the USA, began to enforce a UN embargo on trade with Iraq, and in the months that followed more than half a million foreign troops flooded into Saudi Arabia.

At the end of November the USA and the UK secured a UN resolution authorising the use of force to drive Iraq out of Kuwait if Baghdad did not pull out voluntarily before 15 January 1991. The deadline passed, the Iraqis did not budge and within hours waves of Allied (mostly USA) aircraft began a five week bombing campaign over Iraq and Kuwait.

The ground offensive, when it finally came, lasted only 100 hours and was something of an anticlimax. Iraq's army, which had been touted in the west as one of the most fearsome military machines on earth, simply disintegrated. Allied forces arrived in Kuwait City on 26 February 1991 to be greeted by jubilant crowds and clouds of acrid black smoke which came from the hundreds of oil wells the Iraqis had torched as they retreated.

The government set about not simply rebuilding Kuwait but rebuilding it exactly as it had been before the invasion.

By the 2nd anniversary of the invasion Kuwait's government had largely succeeded in erasing the physical scars of war and occupation. But over the years tensions with Iraq have remained high. Several times in the years since liberation Iraqi troop movements have prompted the Kuwaitis,

the USA or both to mobilise troops. In 1994 Kuwait convicted several Iraqis on charges of attempting to assassinate former USA president George Bush when he visited the emirate in 1993. The plot, according to the Kuwaitis, was uncovered and foiled at the last minute.

In keeping with a promise the opposition had extracted from the emir during the occupation, elections for a new National Assembly took place in October 1992. The opposition shocked the government by winning more than 30 of the new parliament's 50 seats. Opposition MPs secured six of the 16 seats in the Cabinet, though the Al-Sabah family retained control of the key defence, foreign affairs and interior ministries. Elections in 1996 produced a parliament more to the government's liking, though the country's MPs zealously exercise their right to question ministers about anything and everything. Possibly a bit too zealously – in May 1999 the emir dissolved the assembly and ordered a snap election after MPs threatened a censure motion against the Minister for Islamic Affairs.

Kuwait Today

As the 1999 parliamentary campaign got underway the emir unexpectedly announced, and the Cabinet approved, extending the vote to Kuwaiti women. The move did not apply to the 1999 vote – but coming after the National Assembly's dissolution it did not require parliamentary approval (though it may be subject to a vote by the new assembly).

Votes for women immediately became one of the election's main issues and seemed certain to dominate debate in the new assembly. The emir's move – and the loud public debate it provoked – said more about how Kuwait has changed in the last decade than the flashy new shopping malls, swish restaurants and growing number of internet cafes ever could. Kuwait may lack the freewheeling atmosphere of, say, Dubai, but in many ways it is a more open society; an easier place for the visitor to get to know and appreciate on its own terms.

GEOGRAPHY

Kuwait's 17,818 sq km of land is mostly flat and arid with little or no ground water. The desert is generally gravelly. The country is about 185km from north to south and 208km from east to west. The only significant geographic feature is the infamous Al-Mutla ridge.

CLIMATE

In summer (April to September) Kuwait is hellishly hot. Its saving grace is that it is nowhere near as humid as Dhahran, Bahrain or Abu Dhabi. The winter months are often pleasant but can get fairly cold, with daytime temperatures hovering around 18°C and nights being genuinely chilly. Sandstorms occur throughout the year but are particularly common in spring.

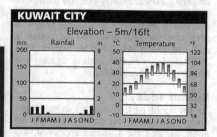

KUWAIT CITY
Elevation – 5m/16ft

GOVERNMENT & POLITICS

Under Kuwait's 1962 constitution the emir is the head of state. By tradition the crown prince serves as prime minister. The prime minister appoints the Cabinet, usually reserving key portfolios (such as interior, and foreign affairs and defence) for other members of the ruling family.

The powers of the emir, crown prince and Cabinet are tempered by the 50 member National Assembly, which must approve the national budget and also has the power to question Cabinet members. The emir has the power to dissolve the assembly whenever he pleases, but is required by the constitution to hold new elections within 90 days of any such dissolution (a requirement that, historically, has not always been honoured).

Post-War Politics

Those who remember the Kuwait of the late 1980s know that the emirate today is a vastly different place. After years marked by terrorism and the constant rumble of the Iran-Iraq War just over the horizon Kuwait (circa 1988) was a tense place.

In the wake of the Iraqi occupation a very different country rose from the ashes. Today's Kuwait boasts some of the more liberal newspapers in the region and a parliament that is unique on the Arab side of the Gulf. Kuwaitis are very open and willing to discuss the politics of the day (that itself is a change from many other Gulf countries), and if you are in the country for any length of time it is easy to keep up on local politics through Kuwait's two English-language newspapers.

Some issues to watch for: In the wake of the Emir's move to give women the vote beginning with the next parliamentary election (currently scheduled for mid-2003), you can expect voting rights issues to dominate public debate for the next few years. As you might expect in a country where foreigners outnumber citizens, immigration issues are often a hot topic in parliament. Relations with both Iran and the USA are other perennial hot topics.

POPULATION & PEOPLE

While no exact figures are available, Kuwait's population is thought to be around 2.2 million. Of these about 750,000 (around 34%) are Kuwaitis and the remaining 66% are expatriates from the Indian subcontinent, Asia, other Arab countries and, to a lesser extent, Europe, the USA and Canada.

SOCIETY & CONDUCT
Dos & Don'ts

Kuwait is a lot more relaxed about matters of public conduct than other Gulf countries. Aside from things obviously immodest by Muslim standards (skirts above the knee, halter tops etc), women can dress as they

KUWAIT

want and there is never any need for a woman to wear an *abeyya* (a long, cloak-like black garment), veil or headscarf.

Non-Muslims may enter mosques, even during prayer time, as long as proper dress is observed.

RELIGION

Kuwait's brand of Islam is not as strict as that practised in Saudi Arabia, but the country is not as liberal as Bahrain. Most Kuwaitis are Sunni Muslims, though there is a substantial Shi'ite minority.

Facts for the Visitor

PLANNING

The *Oxford Map of Kuwait* is the best of the locally available maps. A better map, easy to recognise because of its yellow cover, is published by the Ministry of Information and distributed free at Kuwaiti embassies abroad. We've never seen it on sale in Kuwait.

VISAS & DOCUMENTS
Visas

Everyone except nationals of the other Gulf States needs a visa to enter Kuwait. Kuwait does not issue tourist visas per se, but most hotels can sponsor visas for travellers holding a western passport (in the past only top end hotels provided this service, but things have loosened up a bit in recent years).

To obtain a visa this way send a fax to the hotel with your passport data, arrival and departure dates, flight numbers and reason for visit (generally 'business' though 'tourism' is increasingly OK too). Most people will receive a single-entry visa valid for one month and for a one-month stay. Travellers from western countries that played a large role in the anti-Iraq coalition (mainly the USA, UK, France and Canada) *might* receive multiple-entry visas valid for anywhere from one to 10 years. These allow the holder to come and go at will, though you can only stay in the country for one month at a time.

The hotel will charge you a fee for sponsoring the visa. This is usually KD5, but could go as high as KD12. Be sure to ask about the costs when you are making your visa arrangements. Hotels also usually require that you stay with them for three nights and some may charge you for whatever the agreed minimum number of nights was if you check out early. It usually takes three to four working days for a hotel to process a visa though at the cheapest places it may take a bit longer.

Visas are usually picked up at a Kuwaiti embassy (though in some countries it is possible to mail your passport in). While visas, once approved, can be picked up at any Kuwaiti diplomatic mission, the pickup point has to be specified at the time the papers are filed. In a few cases large hotels may leave the visa at the airport for pick-up. If they do this, be sure that the hotel provides you with a fax that includes the visa number, otherwise the airline may not let you fly.

The embassies themselves are of little use to the casual traveller as they only issue visas against instructions from Kuwait. In other words, you cannot simply walk in and apply for a visa.

If your passport contains an Israeli stamp you will be refused entry to Kuwait.

Visa Extensions It is difficult to stay in Kuwait for more than one month on a business visa. If you need to hang around for more than a month you will probably have to fly out, get a new visa and return.

Driving Licence & Permits

Driving licences from most western and Arab (and all GCC) countries are valid in Kuwait, though visitors will need to obtain 'insurance' for their licence before renting a car. See the Kuwait City Getting Around section for details.

EMBASSIES
Kuwaiti Embassies Abroad

There are Kuwaiti embassies in the following countries:

Kuwait Info. Center
0207 235 1787

Bahrain
Embassy:
(☎ 534 040)
King Faisal Hwy, Manama, opposite Holiday Inn

Canada
Embassy:
(☎ 613-780 9999)
80 Elgin St, Ottawa ON, K1P IC6

Oman
Embassy:
(☎ 699626, 699627)
Jameat A'Duwal al-Arabiya St, Medinat Qaboos Diplomatic Area, Muscat

Qatar
Embassy:
(☎ 832 111)
Diplomatic Area, beyond Doha Sheraton Hotel, Doha

Saudi Arabia
Embassy:
(☎ 01-488 3500)
Diplomatic Quarter, Riyadh

UAE
Embassy:
(☎ 02-446 888)
Diplomatic Area, Airport Rd, Abu Dhabi, behind the Pepsi Cola plant, about 10km south of the centre
Consulate-General:
(☎ 04-284 111)
Beniyas Rd, Deira, Dubai, opposite the Sheraton Hotel

UK
Embassy:
(☎ 020-7590 3400)
2 Albert Gate, Knightsbridge, London SW1X 7JU

USA
Embassy:
(☎ 202-966 0702)
2940 Tilden St NW, Washington DC 20008

Embassies in Kuwait
Some of the countries with embassies in Kuwait include:

Bahrain
Embassy:
(☎ 531 8530)
Surra district, St 1, Block 1, Bldg 24

Canada
Embassy:
(☎ 256 3025)
Da'iya district, El-Mutawakil St, Area 4, House 24, adjacent to the Third Ring Rd

France
Embassy:
(☎ 257 1061)
Mansouria district, St 13, block 1, Villa 24

Germany
Embassy:
(☎ 252 0857)
Bahiya district, St 14, block 1, Villa 13

Netherlands
Embassy:
(☎ 531 2650)
Jabriah district, St 1, block 9, House 76

Oman
Embassy:
(☎ 256 1962)
Udailia district, St 3, Block 3, House 25, by the Fourth Ring Rd

Qatar
Embassy:
(☎ 251 3606)
Istiglal St, Diplomatic Area, south of the centre off Arabian Gulf St

Saudi Arabia
Embassy:
(☎ 240 0250)
Sharq district, Arabian Gulf St

UAE
Embassy:
(☎ 252 7693)
Istiglal St, Diplomatic Area, south of the centre off Arabian Gulf St

UK
Embassy:
(☎ 240 3334)
Arabian Gulf St, near Kuwait Towers and Dasman Palace

USA
Embassy:
(☎ 539 5307)
Al-Masjid Al-Aqsa St, Plot 14, Block 14, Bayan about 17km south of the centre

MONEY
Costs
Kuwait is expensive. A rock-bottom budget would be KD17.500 (US$62) per day but you are likely to find yourself spending more than that. If you are on a tight budget it is quite easy to eat for KD1 or less but sleeping cheap is another matter. Kuwait's cheapest hotels start at around KD10 per night for a single, twice that for a double.

Visa and American Express (Amex) are widely accepted in Kuwait. Gulf Bank is your best bet if you want to get money out of an ATM. Their machines are linked into the Cirrus, Plus and Maestro networks.

Currency

Kuwait's currency is the Kuwaiti dinar (KD). The KD is divided into 1000 fils. Coins are worth five, 10, 20, 50 or 100 fils. Notes come in denominations of KD 0.25, 0.5, one, five, 10 and 20. The Kuwaiti dinar is a hard currency and there are no restrictions on taking it into or out of the country.

Exchange Rates

country	unit		dinar
Australia	A$1	=	KD0.196
Canada	C$1	=	KD0.204
euro	€1	=	KD0.332
France	10FF	=	KD0.490
Germany	DM1	=	KD0.164
Japan	¥100	=	KD0.277
New Zealand	NZ$1	=	KD0.157
UK	UK£1	=	KD0.488
USA	US$1	=	KD0.304

Exchanging Money

For a country with a highly sophisticated financial system, Kuwait can be a remarkably frustrating place to change money. Banks charge excessive commissions and money-changers often refuse to change travellers cheques. The only bright spot in this picture is that even Kuwait's cheap (if you can call them that) hotels take credit cards.

Some, but far from all, of the country's ATMs are linked into the big global networks. Gulf Bank's ATMs are on the Cirrus, Plus and Maestro systems. The Commercial Bank of Kuwait's machines are on Plus.

Tipping & Bargaining

A tip is only expected in fancier restaurants. Note, however, that the service charge added to your bill in such places goes into the till, not to wait staff.

Bargaining is not as common as you might think. If you ask for a discount at a hotel or a shop selling, say, electronics, it is likely to be offered. It is equally likely that this new price represents the bottom line. Do not expect lengthy haggling sessions.

POST & COMMUNICATIONS

Post

Post boxes are a rare sight around Kuwait City, so you will probably have to brave the lines at post offices if you need to send anything and do not already have stamps.

The postal rate for aerogrammes and for letters or postcards weighing up to 20g is 150 fils to any destination outside the Arab world. Postage for cards or letters weighing 20 to 50g is 280 fils. Ask at the post office for parcel rates as these vary significantly from country to country.

There is no poste restante service in Kuwait. Large hotels will often hold mail for their guests but otherwise you are out of luck.

Telephone

Kuwait has an excellent telephone system and calling pretty much anywhere in the world is quick and easy. Payphones take 50 and 100 fil coins, though they are increasingly giving way to card phones.

When calling Kuwait from the outside world, the country code is ☎ 965, followed by the local seven digit number. There are no area or city codes.

The USA Direct access code from Kuwait is ☎ 800 288. For MCI Worldphone dial ☎ 800 624.

Fax

Fax services are available from the government communications centres, though there are usually long queues.

Email & Internet Access

Kuwait has one very good Internet cafe in the centre of town called Cafe Olé, which has fast access via a dedicated line on new computers with Pentium II chips. See Places to Eat in the Kuwait City section for more information.

BOOKS

There are not a lot of good books on Kuwait. Geoffrey Bibby's *Looking for Dilmun* includes several chapters on the archaeological excavations on Failaka Island and also paints an interesting picture of life in Kuwait in the 1950s and 60s.

The New Arabians by Peter Mansfield has a good summary chapter on Kuwait's history through the mid-1980s. *The Modern History of Kuwait 1750-1965* by Ahmad Mustafa Abu-Hakima is a detailed account written by a Kuwaiti scholar based in Canada. It is widely available in Kuwait and is worth a look, especially for the old photographs documenting life in Kuwait in the early years of the 20th century.

The Ministry of Information publishes a number of books on the Iraqi invasion and the Gulf War. These include a rather gruesome collection of photographs of Iraqi atrocities in occupied Kuwait called *The Mother of Crimes against Kuwait in Pictures*. Michael McKinnon and Peter Vine's book *Tides of War: Eco-Disaster in the Gulf* looks at the ecological consequences of the oil slicks and oil fires left intentionally by the retreating Iraqis. See also the Books section in the Regional Facts for the Visitor chapter for more book information.

NEWSPAPERS & MAGAZINES

Arab Times and *Kuwait Times* are Kuwait's two English-language newspapers. Both provide adequate foreign coverage, largely reprinted from British newspapers and international wire services.

RADIO & TV

Radio Kuwait – also known as the Super Station – broadcasts on 99.7 FM; it plays mostly rock and roll with a bit of local news and features mixed in. The US military's Armed Forces Radio & Television Service (AFRTS) can be heard on 107.9 FM; it broadcasts a mixture of music, news and chat shows. A similar programming mix can be found on the Voice of America at 95.7 FM.

Kuwait TV's Channel 2 broadcasts programs in English each evening from around 5 pm to midnight. Many hotels, even the smaller ones, have satellite TV.

PHOTOGRAPHY & VIDEO

In theory, a photography permit is necessary to take pictures of anything in Kuwait. In practice, this is not something you need to worry about provided you exercise a modicum of common sense. Photographing obvious 'tourist' sites, such as the Kuwait Towers or the Red Fort in Al-Jahra, is never a problem. If you are discreet and do not photograph anything sensitive you should be OK. Film can be developed quickly (often in an hour or two) and cheaply so long as it is colour print film. B&W or slide film takes a lot longer and often yields mixed results. Small photo studios throughout the centre of Kuwait City can do passport photos for about KD2.

HEALTH

Health care in Kuwait is equivalent to what is available in most western countries.

The drinking water in much of the country is not good and you would be well advised to stick to bottled water. See Health in the Regional Facts for the Visitor chapter for more detailed health information.

WOMEN TRAVELLERS

Harassment of women has been a serious problem in Kuwait since liberation. The best advice is to dress conservatively, not to respond to approaches on the street and avoid eye contact with men. If you are followed go to a public place, such as the lobby of a hotel.

DANGERS & ANNOYANCES

Kuwait City and the residential sections of other urban centres like Al-Jahra and Al-Ahmadi are clear of mines. The desert is another story. Desert mine clearance is, at best, an inexact science. Sand dunes can shift, covering mines for months, or even years, only to shift again, leaving unexploded mines exposed in what are, theoretically, safe areas. This means that wadi bashing is still a very dangerous sport in Kuwait and you ought to think long and hard before indulging yourself. Desert camping in organised camping areas is a better bet. The wisest course is to camp with someone who knows the area and has been there before.

Whenever you are in the desert, or on Failaka Island: *don't pick up any unfamiliar object*. Kuwait is no longer the frighteningly unsafe place it once was – but people who keep track of these things emphasise that stuff still blows up every month. When in doubt, play it safe.

If you are going north the Iraqi border is now pretty hard to miss. A trench, fence, earth wall and various other border fortifications have replaced the open desert across which the Iraqis rolled in August 1990. That said, the unsettled situation between Iraq and Kuwait means that you really should *not* be anywhere north of the Kuwaiti army checkpoint on the Al-Mutla ridge without a very good reason. If you do run into trouble with the Iraqis (who have been known to cross into Kuwaiti territory and snatch the odd foreigner) you should know that the UN troops who patrol the border zone have no authority to help you.

BUSINESS HOURS

Shops are open from 8 or 9 am to about 1 pm and from about 4 to 6 or 7 pm from Saturday to Wednesday. Large shopping centres usually stay open to 9 pm. On Thursday most businesses will only be open in the morning. Friday is the weekly holiday and almost nothing is open during the day, though some shops may open in the late afternoon and early evening.

PUBLIC HOLIDAYS & SPECIAL EVENTS

Secular holidays are New Year's Day (1 January) and National Day (25 February). Liberation Day (26 February) is not an official holiday but everyone seems to treat it as one. In deference to the families of those still missing after the war and occupation, ceremonies marking both National Day and Liberation Day tend to be pretty muted affairs.

For religious holidays see the Regional Facts for the Visitor chapter.

ACCOMMODATION

Getting a bed for the night in Kuwait was never cheap. There are few hotel rooms in the country for less than US$50 per night. At the bottom end expect to pay at least KD15 for a single and KD20 for a double.

FOOD & DRINK

Most of Kuwait's cheapest restaurants are either Indian places that serve biryanis and little else, or small stalls that serve those Middle Eastern staples, *fuul* (fava bean paste) and *ta'amiyya* (felafel). Eating at any of these places should cost you KD1 or less. Western fastfood: burgers, pizza etc are also widely available, though they tend to cost a bit more.

Cafes, mostly in either hotels or shopping centres, offer western style snacks and sandwiches at reasonable prices, and the city is well stocked with good, upmarket eateries.

All drinks are nonalcoholic. The usual selection includes soft drinks (sodas), mineral water, fruit juice, coffee and tea.

SHOPPING

Kuwait is not exactly a shopper's paradise. You can buy traditional Bedouin weavings at Sadu House, a cultural foundation dedicated to preserving Bedouin art, but there is little else in the way of locally produced souvenirs on the market. As is the case elsewhere in the Gulf, most of the Arabian-looking things you will see for sale around the country are produced elsewhere.

Getting There & Away

AIR

Kuwait is not a particularly cheap place to fly into or from. The airlines and travel agents tightly control prices and few discounted fares are available.

Fares to the USA start at around US$1200 (flying *to* Kuwait from the USA is cheaper – in midwinter you might be able to do it for about US$800 from the east coast). Australia, relatively speaking, can be a bargain with return fares as low as KD300 (about A$1500) sometimes available. There are 10 day minimum/three month maximum stay return tickets to London starting at KD324 (A$1600) and one-way tickets at KD278 (A$1375).

Airfares to the Indian subcontinent are among the better deals that are available from Kuwait. The cheapest regular fare to New Delhi is KD129 (US$426) for a return ticket allowing a four month stay (seven day minimum).

The cheapest return fares to some other Gulf destinations include Abu Dhabi or Dubai KD76 (US$251), Bahrain KD43 (US$142), Muscat KD106 (US$350) and Riyadh KD59 (US$195).

Wherever you are going, there is an airport departure tax of KD2. Tickets sold outside Kuwait often don't include this tax, meaning that you'll have to pay it in cash at the airport. Look for 'KWD 2.000' or something similar in the 'tax' box just below the part of the ticket that shows the cities between which you are travelling.

LAND

Buses operate between Kuwait and Cairo via Aqaba in Jordan and Nuweiba in Egypt. Agents specialising in these tickets (the trip takes about two days) are in the area around the main bus station.

Getting Around

Kuwait has a very cheap and extensive system of both local and intercity buses. You can also use local taxis to get around, though these have no meters. See the Kuwait City Getting There & Away and Getting Around sections for details.

Kuwait is the most expensive place in the Gulf to rent a car. Al-Mulla is the cheapest of the larger local agencies with cars from KD7.5 per day. This rate usually includes unlimited kilometres but full insurance will cost an extra KD2 per day. Al-Mulla has offices in Kuwait Plaza (☎ 245 8600) and Safir International (☎ 250 3869) hotels.

If you hold a driving licence and residence permit from another Gulf country you can drive in Kuwait without any further paperwork. Otherwise you can drive on an International Driving Permit or a local licence from any western country, but you'll also be required to purchase 'insurance' for your licence at KD10.

Kuwait City

In the years since liberation Kuwait City has developed into a remarkably easy-going place, at least compared to what it was like in the late 1980s.

Orientation

Kuwait City's commercial centre is the area from the bay inland to Al-Soor St between the Al-Jahra Gate and Mubarak al-Kabir St. The main shopping and commercial street is Fahad al-Salem St, which becomes Ahmed al-Jaber St north of Al-Safat Square. The souq is the area between the municipal park and Mubarak al-Kabir St. Upmarket shopping places are clustered along the lower end of Fahad al-Salem St (near Kuwait Sheraton Hotel) and, increasingly, along Arabian Gulf St.

From the centre the city spreads inland becoming ever broader as it goes. The main arteries are a series of numbered ring roads and Arabian Gulf St, which continues along the coast to Al-Salmiya and beyond.

Information

Money You will find banks evenly distributed throughout the city. Moneychangers can offer slightly better rates than banks (and usually lower commissions) but finding one in the city centre that will change travellers cheques can be a problem. Try Al-Jawhara Exchange Centre in the Souq al-Watya shopping centre, next to Kuwait Sheraton Hotel. It changes travellers cheques at decent rates with no commission.

Amex (☎ 241 3000) is represented in Kuwait by Al-Ghanim Travel from its office on the 2nd mezzannine level of the Salhiya Commercial Centre. It is open from 8 am to 1 pm and 4 to 7 pm from Saturday to Thursday and is closed on Friday. Amex card holders can cash personal cheques but the office will not hold mail for Amex clients.

Post The GPO is along Fahad al-Salem St near the intersection with Al-Wattiya St. It is open from 7.30 am to 7.30 pm Saturday to

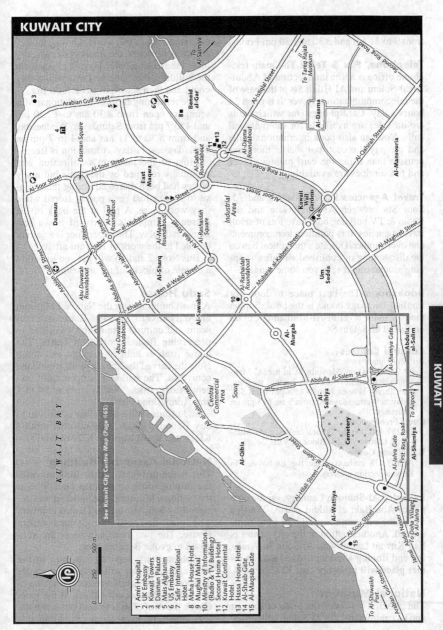

KUWAIT CITY

1 Amir Hospital
2 UK Embassy
3 Kuwait Towers
4 Dasman Palace
5 Mais Alghanim
6 US Embassy
7 Safir International Hotel
8 Maha House Hotel
9 Mughal Mahal
10 Ministry of Information (Radio & TV Building)
11 Second Home Hotel
12 Kuwait Continental Hotel
13 Hassa House Hotel
14 Al-Shaab Gate
15 Al-Maqsab Gate

Wednesday, to 3.30 pm on Thursday and from 9 to 11 am and 3.30 to 7.30 pm Friday.

Telephone, Fax & Telex The main telephone office is at the intersection of Abdullah al-Salem and Al-Hilali Sts at the base of the telecommunications tower. It is open 24 hours a day. Card phones (for which cards are on sale) are available for international calls. You can also book international calls and pre-pay the cost, but this is more expensive than using the card phones. Telex and fax services are available.

Travel Agencies Fahad al-Salem and Al-Soor Sts between Al-Jahra Gate and the Radio & TV building both have lots of small travel agencies. It is pointless to recommend one over another. Despite a theoretical ban on the discounting of published air fares, shopping around might save you some money.

Bookshops The best place to look for English-language books is the bookshop on the basement level of Al-Muthanna Centre on Fahad al-Salem St.

Cultural Centres
British Council
(☎ 253 3204) on Al-Arabi St in the Al-Mansouria district, next to Nadi al-Arabi stadium. The library is open from 4 to 8 pm from Saturday to Wednesday and from 9 am to 1 pm on Thursday.
Circle Francophone
(☎ 257 4803) at the French embassy, Al-Mansouria District, St 13, Block 1, Villa 24.
US Cultural Centre
At the US embassy (see the Embassies in Kuwait section earlier).

Laundry Al-Shurouq Laundry, on the corner of Abu Bakr al-Siddiq and Al-Wattiya Sts in the city centre, offers 24 hour turnaround. Another option in the city centre is Fajr Kuwait Laundry on Al-Soor St. Washing and ironing a medium-sized load at either place will probably cost KD2 to KD4.

National Museum
The museum was once the pride of Kuwait and its centrepiece, the Al-Sabah collection, was one of the most important collections of Islamic art in the world. During the occupation, however, the Iraqis systematically looted the exhibit halls. Having cleaned out the building, they smashed everything they could and then set what was left on fire.

The remaining ruins of the National Museum are open from 8.30 am to 12.30 pm and 4 to 7 pm from Saturday to Wednesday and from 8.30 to 11 am and 4 to 7 pm on Thursday and Friday. Admission is free.

Most of the museum's collection was eventually returned by the Iraqis but many pieces had been damaged during their transit to Iraq or had been poorly stored while they were there. A hall at the back of the museum complex's courtyard has a few items on display. The upper floor is a gallery devoted to the work of Kuwaiti artists.

Bus Nos 12 and 16 will get you to within a couple of blocks of the museum.

Sadu House
A small building near the National Museum on Arabian Gulf St, Sadu House is a museum and cultural foundation dedicated to preserving Bedouin arts and crafts. The house itself is built of gypsum and coral. Note the carved decorative work around the courtyard. The building is open daily, except Friday, from 8 am to 1 pm and 4 to 8 pm. Admission is free.

Sadu House is the best place in Kuwait to buy Bedouin goods. Pillows cost around KD15 and small bags are KD7 to KD15.

National Assembly Building
This is the distinctive white building with the sloping roofs on Arabian Gulf St near the National Museum. The building was designed by Jorn Utzon, the Danish architect who also designed the Sydney Opera House. The two sweeping roofs are supposed to evoke Bedouin tents.

Parliamentary sessions are open to the public, though you will have to have your passport or (for foreign residents) iqama to get through the security check at the gate. Check the *Arab Times* to find out when the legislature is in session. Simultaneous translation of parliamentary debates into English is available. Ask for a set of earphones as you enter the chamber.

Bus Nos 12, 21 and 29 stop a few hundred meters from the National Assembly building at the intersection of Fahad Al-Salem and Al-Hilali Sts.

Sief Palace

At the intersection of Mubarak al-Kabir and Arabian Gulf Sts north-east of the National Museum, Sief Palace is the official seat of the emir's court. The oldest parts of the building date to the turn of the century. The palace is not open to the public.

The closest you can get to the palace by bus is the intersection of Mubarak Al-Kabir and Ahmed Al-Jaber Sts. Bus Nos 11, 12, 14, 15, 16, 18, 20 and 22 all stop there.

Grand Mosque

This huge, modern mosque opposite Sief Palace was opened in 1986. It cost KD13 million to build and the government says that it can accommodate more than 5500 worshippers. The central dome is 26m in diameter and 43m high.

Kuwait Stock Exchange

The stock exchange, the Gulf's largest, is the big brown building on Mubarak al-Kabir St, a block or so inland from the Grand Mosque. Trading takes place Saturday to Wednesday from 9.30 am to noon. The exchange is an electronic market, so the 'trading floor', which occupies most of the ground level of the building, looks rather like the waiting area of an airport. You'll see lots of people sitting around tracking their investments on the tally boards hanging from the roof, but none of the running about and shouting usually associated with western financial markets.

Former Political Agent's House (Beit Dixon)

About 750m north-east of Sief Palace you will find a modest white house with blue trim. From 1904 until the late 1930s this was the Political Agency, the British headquarters in Kuwait. Freya Stark spent most

of March 1937 here. The widow of the last British political agent continued to live in the house for many years, spending her winters here well into the 1980s.

At the time of writing the building (which has not been open to the public in the past) was being restored.

There is no bus service to the house.

Kuwait Towers

Designed by a Swedish architectural firm and opened in 1979, the towers have become Kuwait's main landmark.

The largest of the three towers rises to a height of 187m. Its upper globe houses a two level observation deck. The lower globe (at 82m) has a restaurant, coffeehouse and private banquet room. The lower globe on the largest tower and the single globe on the middle tower are used to store water. The small tower with no globes is used to light up the other two.

The observation deck is open daily from 9 am to 11 pm. Admission to the observation deck costs 500 fils but entry to the restaurants is free. Because the towers overlook a palace, cameras with zoom lenses are not permitted and you will have to leave these at the ticket booth.

Tareq Rajab Museum

This museum, which is housed in the basement of a large villa, is a private collection of Islamic art assembled by Kuwait's first minister of antiquities. The collection is all the more important granted the fate that befell the National Museum's treasures.

The museum is at House 16, St 5, Block 12, in the Jabriya district, on a corner two blocks north and one block west of the New English School, near the intersection of the Fifth Ring Motorway and the Fahaheel Expressway. It is open from 9 am to noon and 4 to 7 pm from Saturday to Thursday and from 4 to 7 pm on Friday. Admission is free. There is no sign on the building but it is easily identified by its entrance – a carved wooden doorway flanked by two smaller doors on each side. All four of the door panels are worked in gilt metal.

KUWAIT

Bus Nos 25 and 32 serve Jabriya, though neither stops within easy walking distance of the museum.

Science & Natural History Museum

Though the collection seems to consist largely of stuffed animals, there is some variety. The ground floor also contains animal skeletons, including a few dinosaurs. The 1st floor has a display on space exploration. On Abdullah al-Mubarak St, the museum is open from 8.30 am to noon from Saturday to Thursday and is closed on Fridays and holidays. Admission is free.

The museum is a short distance from the main bus station on Abdullah al-Mubarak St near the intersection with Al-Hilali St.

Old City Gates

Four of Kuwait City's five gates lie along Al-Soor St, the street that follows the line of the old city wall (soor is the Arabic word for 'wall'): Al-Shaab, Al-Shamiya, Al-Jahra and Al-Maqsab. The fifth gate (Dasman Gate) once stood near Dasman Palace by the Kuwait Towers. Despite their ancient appearance the wall and gates were only constructed around 1920. The wall was torn down in 1957.

Communications Tower

The Communications tower at the intersection of Al-Hilali and Abdullah al-Salem Sts is Kuwait's tallest building. There is an observation deck about two-thirds of the way up the tower, though at the time of writing it was not open to the public.

Exhibition of Kuwaiti Sailing Ships

This small, largely unknown, tourist sight consists of about six different dhows and other traditional sailing vessels ranging in size from small fishing boats to a large ocean-going dhow. All of the boats have been carefully restored and ramps provide access for curious visitors. It's a long drive out from the city but absolutely worth the trip.

The exhibition is open every day from 8 am to 8 pm. Admission is free. To reach the site take the Al-Jahra Rd west out of Kuwait City. Follow the signs for Entertainment City and turn onto the Doha spur road.

Organised Tours

Kuwait has no formal tour industry, and no companies offering tours to the public on a regular basis.

Places to Stay – Budget & Mid-Range

Now that smaller hotels can arrange visas there is no longer any need to go upmarket just to get into the country.

All of Kuwait's hotels have air-con and private baths. TVs are also standard, as are mini-fridges (at budget level, though there probably won't be anything in them). Many hotels do not have heating in the rooms and you will certainly notice this in December and January. Most of the country's hotels also hit you for a 15% service charge – though you may be able to negotiate this away as a 'discount'.

Maha House Hotel (☎ 252 3211, fax 257 1220) on an unmarked street in the Beneid al-Gar district behind Safir International Hotel is Kuwait's cheapest hotel ('cheap', in this case, being a very relative term). It charges KD10/20 for singles/doubles. It's not as bad as it once was, but that is not saying much. You should also be aware that both the heating and the air-con are dodgy at best. From the city centre the hotel can be reached by bus No 15. Get off at the roundabout where you see the Kuwait Continental Hotel and walk towards the sea.

Second Home Hotel (☎ 253 2100, fax 253 2381) is just behind the much larger Kuwait Continental Hotel. All things considered it's probably Kuwait's best value hotel. Singles/doubles are KD15/20, for which you get small but tidy rooms. There's also a decent little coffeehouse in the lobby. *Kuwait Continental Hotel* (☎ 252 7300, fax 252 9373, Al-Dasma Roundabout) charges KD25/30.

Phoenicia Hotel (☎ 242 1051, fax 242 4402) on the corner of Fahad al-Salem and

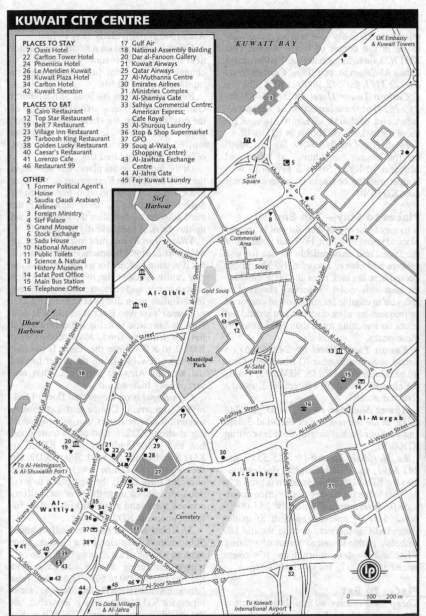

KUWAIT CITY CENTRE

PLACES TO STAY
7 Oasis Hotel
22 Carlton Tower Hotel
24 Phoenicia Hotel
26 Le Meridien Kuwait
28 Kuwait Plaza Hotel
34 Carlton Hotel
42 Kuwait Sheraton

PLACES TO EAT
8 Cairo Restaurant
12 Top Star Restaurant
19 Beit 7 Restaurant
23 Village Inn Restaurant
29 Tarboosh King Restaurant
38 Golden Lucky Restaurant
40 Caesar's Restaurant
41 Lorenzo Cafe
46 Restaurant 99

OTHER
1 Former Political Agent's
   House
2 Saudia (Saudi Arabian)
   Airlines
3 Foreign Ministry
4 Sief Palace
5 Grand Mosque
6 Stock Exchange
9 Sadu House
10 National Museum
11 Public Toilets
13 Science & Natural
    History Museum
14 Safat Post Office
15 Main Bus Station
16 Telephone Office

17 Gulf Air
18 National Assembly Building
20 Dar al-Fanoon Gallery
21 Kuwait Airways
25 Qatar Airways
27 Al-Muthanna Centre
30 Emirates Airlines
31 Ministries Complex
32 Al-Shamiya Gate
33 Salhiya Commercial Centre;
    American Express;
    Cafe Royal
35 Al-Shurouq Laundry
36 Stop & Shop Supermarket
37 GPO
39 Souq al-Watya
    (Shopping Centre)
43 Al-Jawhara Exchange
    Centre
44 Al-Jahra Gate
45 Fajr Kuwait Laundry

KUWAIT BAY

UK Embassy & Kuwait Towers

Sief Harbour

Sief Square

Central Commercial Area

Souq

Dhow Harbour

AL-Qibla

Gold Souq

Municipal Park

Al-Safat Square

Al-Murgab

Al-Salhiya

Cemetery

Al-Wattiya

To Al-Helmigaoon & Al-Shuwaikh Port

To Doha Village & Al-Jahra

To Kuwait International Airport

0   100   200 m

KUWAIT

Al-Hilali Sts is slightly musty, but generally reliable and is easily your best bet if you want to be in the centre of town. Rooms cost KD17/23 including breakfast. Farther down Fahad Al-Salam St, you'll find *Carlton Hotel* (☎ 242 3171, fax 242 5848) at KD15/20.

Carlton Tower Hotel (☎ 245 2740, fax 240 1624) at the intersection of Ahmad al-Jaber and Mubarak al-Kabir Sts is a bit more upmarket with rooms at KD30/40.

Oasis Hotel (☎ 246 5489, fax 246 5490) on the corner of Ahmad al-Jaber and Mubarak al-Kabir Sts is a favourite with budget-minded business travellers. Rooms cost KD30/40.

Places to Stay – Top End

If money is no object then Kuwait is an easy place to spend a lot of it. Five-star hotels offer the fastest and most reliable service for visa seekers and charge accordingly. The prices quoted here are rack rates and do not include the near-universal 15% service charge. Unless you're eligible for some sort of corporate or frequent-traveller discount you should not count on knocking more than KD5 or so off these prices.

Kuwait Plaza Hotel (☎ 243 6686) on Fahad al-Salam St near Al-Muthanna Centre has singles/doubles for KD48/57. This is the cheapest and most central of Kuwait's five-star hotels.

Kuwait Sheraton (☎ 242 2055, fax 244 8032) at the intersection of Fahad al-Salam and Al-Soor Sts has singles/doubles costing KD60/70.

Le Meridien Kuwait (☎ 245 5550, fax 243 8391) on Al-Hilali St has singles/doubles for KD67/78. The Meridien is probably the best value for money in this price range.

Safir International Hotel (☎ 253 0000, fax 256 3797) on Arabian Gulf St in the Beneid al-Gar district opposite the old US embassy is the favoured haunt of visiting VIPs and western journalists. It's overpriced at KD68/75 for singles/doubles.

Places to Eat

Cheap food is easy to find throughout the city centre and, contrary to popular belief, does not consist solely of biryanis. Cheap Arab food is particularly easy to find.

Cairo Restaurant on a small steet corner near the Grand Mosque and Stock Exchange has excellent fuul and ta'amiyya sandwiches for 100 fils.

Restaurant 99 on Al-Soor St near Jahra Gate is a relatively new arrival and is one of the city's best bets for cheap eats. Humous, shwarma and a wide variety of things stuffed into Lebanese-style bread are on offer for a few hundred fils.

Of the Indian biryani places that abound in the centre *Top Star Restaurant* in the souq is a good bet. Enter the souq from Al-Safat Square by the big 'Citizen' sign, take the third alley on the left after the sign and head up the stairs. A meal usually costs KD1.

Village Inn Restaurant just off Fahad al-Salem St behind Phoenicia Hotel is a good bet if you are looking for a cheap meal in the city centre. Stick to the Indian food, which is both better, and cheaper, than the Chinese food. Indian main dishes cost KD1 to KD2.

Caesar's on Abu Bakr Al-Saddiq St near Kuwait Sheraton Hotel is the centre's best bet for Chinese food. Main dishes cost KD1.2 to KD3. Note that there is another Caesars a few blocks up the street toward the Kuwait Airways building. That one serves only Indian food.

Cafe Royal is on the ground floor of Salhiya Commercial Centre and has mostly western food (omelettes, burgers etc) starting at about KD2. It also offers quite good hot and cold sandwiches for KD1.5 to KD1.8 and salads for KD1.500 to KD2. On the second mezzanine level of the same complex *Cafe Olé* is the best place to go if you need to hook up to the Internet. It offers a snack menu and good Turkish coffee. Internet access is KD2 per hour.

Al-Helmiyaon on Arabian Gulf St about 5km south of Safir Hotel is a cleaner, more modern version of a traditional Egyptian coffeehouse offering kebabs and ta'amiyya sandwiches for 250 to 500 fils, *shish tawouk* (chicken kebab) for KD1 and *sheesha* (water pipes) for 500 fils. The sign is in Arabic, but the seaside complex is large. There is no bus service down this part of Arabian Gulf St. A taxi from the centre costs KD1.5 to KD1.75.

One top end restaurant bears mention in any rundown of Kuwait's eateries. If your budget will bear it, you must visit *Mais Al-ghanim*. This Lebanese restaurant, on Arabian Gulf St, between the Kuwait Towers and the intersection with Al-Soor St, was founded in 1953 and has long been something of a local institution. Meals cost about KD3 to KD4. It is worth going out of your way for; expect queues for the garden tables in winter and the indoor (air-con) ones in summer.

Entertainment

Kuwait's newest, fanciest *cinema* is the three screen complex at Sharq Market on Arabian Gulf St. Check the *Arab Times* for show times. Admission is KD2.500, but on weekends the cinema can be very crowded and tickets should be purchased early in the day.

Getting There & Away

Air Kuwait international airport is 16km south of the city centre. Check-in time is officially two hours before your flight is due to depart, but some carriers insist on your being there three hours in advance; call the airline to double check. Note that Kuwait is pretty serious about enforcing the 'only one carry-on bag' rule. For general information, including flight arrivals and departures, call ☎ 433 5599 or 433 4499.

Bus Kuwait has only a handful of intercity bus routes. All long-haul trips cost 250 fils. Route 101 runs from the main bus station in the city centre to Al-Ahmadi and Fahaheel. Route 103 goes to Al-Jahra.

International bus services to Cairo and Dammam (Saudi Arabia) can be booked through any of the small travel agencies around the intersection of Abdullah al-Mubarak and Al-Hilali Sts.

There is no formal service-taxi system operating in Kuwait.

Getting Around

To/from the Airport Taxis charge a flat KD4 between the airport and the city. Bus

No 501 runs between the main bus station and the airport every 30 minutes from 5.30 am to 9 pm. The fare is 250 fils.

Bus The main bus station is near the Al-Hilali and Abdullah al-Mubarak Sts intersection. On printed timetables the station is referred to as 'Mircab bus station'.

Buses start running at around 5 am and continue to around 10 pm. Fares are 100, 150 or 200 fils depending on how far you travel. An office on the ground floor of the Kuwait Public Transport Company building at the main station sells a route map for 150 fils.

Taxi Kuwait's taxis have no meters. Bargaining the fare in advance may save you some grief at the end of the trip but it will also cost you money. Around town, taxis are orange coloured. In general, any trip within the city centre is about KD1. Longer trips just outside the city centre (eg from Kuwait Sheraton Hotel to Safir Hotel) cost about KD1.5.

Around Kuwait

FAILAKA ISLAND

The home of Kuwait's main archaeological site, Failaka is definitely worth a visit, though it requires a bit of extra caution. The Iraqis turned Failaka into a heavily fortified base, and after liberation it was found to be filled with mines. While the site is now open, Failaka is one of those parts of Kuwait where you should restrict yourself to well-trodden paths.

Failaka's history goes back to the Bronze Age Dilmun civilisation that was centred in Bahrain. The Greeks arrived in the 4th century BC in the form of a garrison sent by Nearchus, one of Alexander the Great's admirals. A small settlement existed on the island prior to this, but it was as the Greek town of Ikaros that the settlement became a real city or at least a large town.

As you enter the site, the road swings around to the left and ends in front of a group of prefabricated buildings. These used to house the archaeological museum and the on-site administrative offices, though at the time of writing they remained closed. From here it is a short walk to the **temple**, Failaka's centrepiece.

Ferries to Failaka depart from Ras Salmiya (also known as Ras al-Ard) on Arabian Gulf St south of the city centre. The terminal can be reached via bus Nos 14, 15, 24, 34 and 200. At the time of writing there was still only one ferry per day, departing sometime between 8 and 10 am (the schedule varies from day to day and is published a couple of weeks in advance). The trip to the island takes 1½ hours. The ferry then stays at the island for three hours before making the return trip. This is enough time for a quick look at the archaeological site and nearby parts of the town but not much else. If you miss the ferry back you will be stuck on the island until the following day. Since there are no hotels and camping is inadvisable because of the danger of land mines, don't miss the ferry! The fare is KD2.5 return. Call the ferry company on ☎ 574 2664 for information on sailing times.

To reach the site from the ferry terminal on Failaka, turn right as you exit the terminal building. Almost immediately you will see the mud house, which contains the ethnographic display, on a low hill to the right beyond a wall. The entrance is a gate in this wall with seals on either side marked 'Kuwait National Museum'.

Failaka is one of the last places in Kuwait where you can see some serious war damage. The ruins of Failaka's Post and Telecoms building are about a 15 minute walk beyond the gate to the archaeological site along the same street. What's left of the traffic department's local headquarters is across the street. If you turn left out of the ferry terminal and follow the road on foot for about 15 minutes you will come to what used to be the Failaka branch of the Science and Natural History Museum (it's on the left and there is a sign in English). This stands open to the public. The trashed exhibition hall is a sad spectacle.

AL-AHMADI

Built to house Kuwait's oil industry in the 1940s and 50s, Al-Ahmadi was named for the then emir, Shaikh Ahmed. It remains, to a great extent, the private preserve of the Kuwait Oil Company (KOC).

The **oil display centre** (☎ 398 2747) on Mid 5th St is a small, well-organised and self-congratulatory introduction to KOC and the oil business. The centre is open from 7 am to 3 pm Saturday to Wednesday. Admission is free. Al-Ahmadi also has a small, pleasant **public garden** that is worth a visit.

To reach the town take the Al-Safr Motorway south out of Kuwait City until you reach the Al-Ahmadi exit. First follow the blue signs for North Al-Ahmadi, and then the smaller white signs for the display centre and the public garden. Bus No 101 runs from the main bus station in Kuwait City to Al-Ahmadi (passing by the oil display centre as it enters town).

AL-JAHRA

Al-Jahra, 32km west of Kuwait City, is the site where invading troops from Saudi Arabia were defeated (with British help) in 1920. It was also the site of the Gulf War's infamous 'turkey shoot' – the Allied destruction of a stalled Iraqi convoy as it attempted to retreat from Kuwait.

The town's only sight is the **Red Fort** (also known as the Red Palace), a low rectangular mud structure near the highway. The fort played a key role in the 1920 battle. Coming from Kuwait City, take the second of the three Al-Jahra exits from the expressway. The Red Fort is on the right, about 200m south of (inland from) the highway, though you can't see it until you are right in front of it. In winter it is open daily from 7.30 am to 1.30 pm and 3.30 to 6.30 pm. During summer the hours are from 7 am to 1 pm and 4 to 7 pm. Throughout the year the fort is closed on Saturday afternoons. Admission is free. Still photography is permitted but videos are not. Call ☎ 477 2559 for more information.

Al-Jahra can be reached via bus No 103, which passes directly in front of the Red Fort.

Lebanon

Lebanon offers a unique blend of the ancient and ultra-modern, the traditions of the Middle East and the sophistication of Europe. You can see ruins dating back to 5000 BC during the day and rage at some of the best nightclubs you'll come across in the Middle East in the evening.

Most of the world's great civilisations have been in Lebanon at one point or another, from the Phoenicians to the Egyptians, Greeks, Romans, Byzantines, Arabs, Ottoman Turks and Crusaders, and there are still remnants of them all.

In more recent times Lebanon has been in the world headlines for the 16 year civil war that engulfed it until 1991. The country suffered physically, culturally, financially and psychologically during this period and, while there are still graphic reminders of the war, the energy and enthusiasm with which the nation is being rebuilt is inspirational. Beirut is abuzz with reconstruction and there's an air of optimism that's been missing for decades. Despite the images of war-torn Beirut that still pervade western public consciousness, it is possible to travel independently and safely throughout the country, except in the extreme south which is still under United Nations and Israeli control.

Geographically, Lebanon is as diverse as it's possible to imagine in a country so small. The Lebanese are fond of saying that it's one of the only countries in the world where you can ski in the morning and swim in the afternoon; there is a coastal plain with ancient historical cities strung along its length, a soaring mountain range with popular ski resorts and an agricultural plain bounded by a second mountain range.

Independent travellers are still a bit of a rarity in Lebanon and are made to feel very welcome; the regular offers of help and invitations are almost always genuine manifestations of hospitality and friendliness. The nation also offers some of the region's

The Republic of Lebanon

Area: 10,452 sq km
Population: approx four million
Population Growth Rate: approx 1.6%
Capital: Beirut
Head of State: President Emile Lahoud
Official Language: Arabic
Currency: Lebanese lira (LL)
Exchange Rate: US$1 = LL1508

- **Best Dining** – splurge at the delectable pâtisseries in Tripoli or Sidon
- **Best Nightlife** – go to Amor Y Libertad in Jounieh for amazing music and belly-dancing
- **Best Walk** – wander through the medieval souqs of Tripoli
- **Best View** – walk out to Kadisha Grotto for stunning views across the valley
- **Best Activity** – explore the ancient ruins of Baalbek or the caves of Jeitta Grotto
- **When in Rome ...** have a flutter on the horses at the Hippodrome in Beirut or stroll along the Corniche on a sunny weekend afternoon

most superb food as well as award-winning wineries which you can visit.

It's possible to visit Lebanon on a budget, but in general prices are more in keeping with Mediterranean Europe than the Middle East. Lebanon is well and truly prepared for receiving travellers, so now is a good time to visit before the visitor numbers return to their prewar high.

Facts about Lebanon

HISTORY

Lebanon was another country which emerged from the break-up of the Ottoman empire after WWI – events covered in the general history of the Middle East in the Facts about the Region chapter at the beginning of the book. Between the wars it was under a French mandate and then became fully independent during WWII. Its strategic Middle Eastern location and relatively stable, west-leaning government made it a major trade and banking centre, with many western multinationals basing their Middle Eastern head offices in Beirut.

But Lebanon had a fatal flaw in its national make-up: power and control rested with the right-wing Christian part of the population while the Muslims (almost half the population) felt they were excluded from real government. Add large numbers of displaced and restive Palestinians and you had a recipe for conflict. The USA helped to put down a Muslim rebellion in 1958, but in 1975 civil war broke out between a predominantly Muslim leftist coalition (allied with Palestinian groups) and Christian right-wing militias. In April 1976 Syrian forces intervened at the request of the Lebanese president, Suleiman Franjieh, to halt the defeat of the Christian forces.

Subsequently, an uneasy peace was forced upon the two sides by the Syrians. Then in 1978 the Israelis marched into southern Lebanon and set up a surrogate militia, the South Lebanon Army (SLA), led by a renegade Christian Lebanese army general, to protect northern Israel from cross-border attacks by the Palestine Liberation Organisation (PLO). Following United Nations (UN)

What to See

Beirut has a fantastic nightlife, good museums and is one of the Middle East's most cosmopolitan cities. Nowhere in Lebanon is more than a couple of hours by road from Beirut. If you only have a couple of days, also visit **Baalbek**, Lebanon's number one archaeological attraction. If you have a week, travel north and see spectacular world-class caves at **Jeitta Grotto**, the ancient city of **Byblos** with its ruins and picturesque port, and **Tripoli** for its dramatic Crusader castle, great souqs and outstanding Islamic monuments.

With two weeks you'd have time for a side-trip from Tripoli to **Bcharré** and the **Kadisha Valley**, among the most beautiful sights in Lebanon, as well as the famous **Cedars** nearby. South of Beirut are the coastal towns of **Sidon** and **Tyre**, both with ancient ruins that are worth visiting, as is the **Palace of Beiteddine**, a lavish Ottoman-style building set in a beautiful landscape.

pressure, the Israelis withdrew three months later and were replaced by UN peacekeeping forces (UNIFIL). Meanwhile in Beirut, both the Christian and Muslim militias continued building up their arsenals. In the absence of a political solution acceptable to all parties, fighting erupted frequently, only to be stopped by Syrian intervention. At the same time, the Christians started demanding that Syria withdraw its troops from Lebanon.

In June 1982 Israeli troops marched again into Lebanon, this time with the stated aim of eradicating the PLO. They laid siege to Beirut and for seven weeks relentlessly bombarded the Muslim half of the capital by air, sea and land. In August the USA arranged for the evacuation of PLO fighters to other Arab countries, and a Multinational Force (MNF) of US and Western European troops was deployed in Beirut to protect

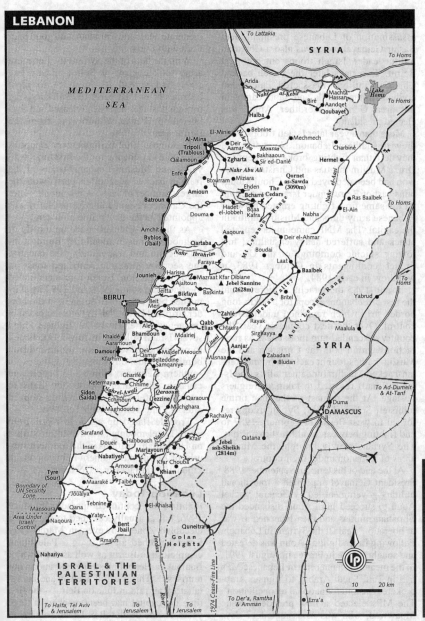

LEBANON

MEDITERRANEAN
SEA

SYRIA

To Lattakia

To Homs

Arida

Nahr al-Kebir

Machtà
Hassan
Biré
Aandqet
Qoubayet

Lake
Homs

To Homs

Halba

Bebnine

Mechmech

Charbiné

El-Minie

Al-Mina
Tripoli
(Trablous)
Qalamoun

Deir
Aamar
Zgharta

Nahr Abu

Moussa

Bakhaaoun
Sir ed-Danié

Hermel

Nahr Abu Ali

Enfe

Btourram

Miziara
Ehden

Qornet
as-Sawda
(3090m)

Nahr el-Aasi

Ras Baalbek

To Homs

Amioun

The
Bcharré Cedars

Batroun

Hadet
el-Jobbeh

Bqaa
Kafra

Deir el-Ahmar

El-Ain

Douma

Nabha

Amchit
Byblos
(Jbail)

Aaqoura

Qartaba

Boudai

Deir el-Ahmar

Nahr Ibrahim

Faraya

Laat

Baalbek

Jounieh
Harissa

Mazraat Kfar Dibiane

Ajaltoun

Jebel Sannine
(2628m)

Bikfaya
Jeitta
Baskinta

To
Homs

Yabrud

BEIRUT
Beit
Meri
Broummana

Zahlé

Britel

Baabda
Aley
Bhamdoun
Mdairiej

Qabb
Elias

Chtaura

Rayak

Sirghayya

Maalula

Khaldé
Aaramoun

Deir
al-Qamar

Majdel Meouch

Aanjar

SYRIA

Damour
Kfarhim

Beiteddine
Bamqaniye

Masnaa

Zabadani
Bludan

Gharifé
Chhime

Nahr

Ketermaya

Lake
Qaraoun
Jezzine

To Ad-Dumeir
& At-Tanf

Sidon
(Saida)
Echmoun

Qaraoun

Nahr el-Awali

Maghdouche

Machghara

Rachaiya

Duma

DAMASCUS

Sarafand

Insar

Douier

Habbouch

Nahr el Litani

Kfair

Qatana

Nabatiyeh
Marjayoun

Jebel
ash-Sheikh
(2814m)

Tyre
(Sour)

Arnoun

Kfar Chouba

Maaraké

Taibé

Khiam

Kfar Kila

Boundary of
UN Security
Zone

Jdaidya

Area Under
Israeli
Control

Mansoura

Qana

Tebnine

Yater

El-Khalsa

Naqoura

Rmaich

Bent
Jbail

Quneitra

Golan
Heights

Nahariya

ISRAEL & THE
PALESTINIAN
TERRITORIES

Jordan River

1974 Cease-Fire Line

To Haifa, Tel Aviv
& Jerusalem

To
Jerusalem

To
Jerusalem

To Der'a, Ramtha
& Amman

Ezra'a

0   10   20 km

LEBANON

Palestinian and Muslim civilians. After the assassination of Lebanese president-elect Bashir Gemayel, who was also a Christian militia leader, Israeli troops entered west Beirut. Two days later the Israeli-backed Christian militias massacred Palestinian civilians in the Chatila and Sabra camps in this area. Gemayel's brother, Amin, was elected president.

More than a year later Israeli troops withdrew to southern Lebanon. No sooner had they left than fighting broke out between Druze Muslim militias and Christian forces who had been deployed in the Chouf Mountains east of Beirut under Israeli protection. At the same time fighting erupted between Lebanese army units and Muslim militia in the capital. The MNF came under repeated attack and suffered heavy casualties; following suicide bombings of the US and French contingents in October 1983, it withdrew in early 1984.

In mid-1985 the Israelis withdrew from the rest of Lebanon, except for a 60km-long border strip which remained under Israeli control. Over the next couple of years the country descended into more chaos as rival factions within both the Christian and the Muslim camps fought each other, and Iranian-backed Muslim fundamentalists (the Islamic Jihad) resorted to taking foreigners hostage. At the request of the then prime minister, Selim al-Hoss, Syrian troops returned to west Beirut in February 1987 to end fighting between rival Muslim militias. The Syrians slowly brought the Muslim areas of Lebanon under their control.

At the end of his term, in September 1988, President Gemayel appointed a transitional military government led by General Michel Aoun to succeed him. Aoun disbanded the Christian militias and then launched a 'war of liberation' against the Syrians in Lebanon. Following fierce fighting Aoun was defeated and sought refuge in France in August 1991. In the meantime a majority of Lebanese MPs met in Taif, Saudi Arabia, to sign an Arab-brokered 'accord for national reconciliation'. The MPs elected a new president, René Moawwad, who was assassinated 17 days later. He was replaced by Elias Hrawi, a moderate Maronite Christian with good relations with Syria.

With the help of the Syrians the Lebanese army took control of Beirut and by late 1991 had spread its presence to most Lebanese areas. By early 1992 all surviving foreign hostages had been released and Syrian troops began withdrawing from the Beirut area.

In August 1992 parliamentary elections were held in Lebanon for the first time in 20 years, and Muslim fundamentalists of the Iranian-backed Hezbollah party won the largest number of seats. A few months later the Cabinet resigned and Rafik Hariri was appointed as the new prime minister.

As the new Cabinet, made up mostly of technocrats, began rebuilding Beirut's infrastructure and rehabilitating the country, the security situation remained tense in southern Lebanon. Israeli forces continued to attack the south 1991 and 1992 as skirmishes between Israeli soldiers in the border strip and Hezbollah fighters increased in frequency. After Hezbollah fighters killed seven Israeli soldiers in July 1993, Israeli forces launched week-long air, sea and land bombardments on some 80 villages in southern Lebanon, killing 113 people and causing more than 300,000 civilians to leave for safer areas. The shelling stopped after US intervention with Tel Aviv.

Trouble flared up again in April 1996 when Israel mounted a wave of air strikes on Hezbollah positions in the southern suburbs of Beirut and southern Lebanon which killed 106 refugees in a UN camp.

Lebanon Today

Fighting has continued sporadically since 1996, but is usually confined to the Israeli Occupied Zone. However, in March 1999 Israel launched air raids on a Palestinian camp close to Beirut as well as the town of Baalbek, a Hezbollah stronghold and major tourist site. This was followed by another retaliatory air raid in June on Beirut – the first time the capital had been attacked in three years. As the death toll of Israeli soldiers in its 'security zone' steadily climbs the Israeli government faces increasing pressure from its population to withdraw from Lebanon. New Israeli prime minister Ehud Barak took office in July and promised to withdraw from Lebanon within one year.

GEOGRAPHY

There are four main geographical areas, running more or less parallel to each other from north to south. They are (from west to east): the coastal plain, the Mt Lebanon range, the Bekaa Valley and the Anti-Lebanon range.

The coastal plain is quite narrow, except in the north, and is broken at several points by cliffs and buttresses of the Mt Lebanon range which run into the sea. Lebanon's main cities and towns, including Beirut and Tripoli (Trablous), are along this plain.

The Mt Lebanon range rises from the coastal plain in limestone terraces. It is cut by deep gorges and numerous rivers and streams and includes Lebanon's highest summit of Qornet as-Sawda (3090m) and the famous Cedars of Lebanon.

The eastern slopes of the Mt Lebanon range are rocky and arid and fall steeply into the Bekaa Valley, Lebanon's main agricultural region. At 800m above sea level, the fertile Bekaa, with two rivers flowing from it, is cultivated year-round.

The Anti-Lebanon range is an arid massif rising from the eastern side of the Bekaa Valley and marks the border between Lebanon and Syria. Its highest summit is Jebel ash-Sheikh (Mt Hermon) at 2814m.

CLIMATE

Lebanon has a Mediterranean climate – hot and dry in the summer, cool and rainy in the winter. About 300 days of the year are sunny.

In summer the humidity is very high along the coast and daytime temperatures average 30°C, with night temperatures not much lower. Winter is mild, with daytime temperatures averaging 15°C. In the mountains, however, summer days are moderately hot (26°C on average) and the nights pleasantly cool. Winters are cold, with snowfalls above 1300m.

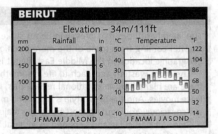

BEIRUT
Elevation – 34m/111ft

GOVERNMENT & POLITICS

Lebanon is a republic with a president, a cabinet and a unicameral National Assembly of 128 members. The parliament has legislative powers and elects the president for a six year non renewable term. The president appoints a prime minister and cabinet; both have executive powers. Under a National Covenant agreed to in 1943, the president is a Maronite Christian, the prime minister a Sunni Muslim, the deputy prime minister a Greek Orthodox, the speaker of parliament a Shi'ite Muslim and the armed forces chief of staff a Druze. Emile Lahoud was elected president in November 1998 and appointed Salim al-Hoss as prime minister. They are both keen to clean up government corruption and nepotism, and have a reputation for being honest and fair. Serving his fifth term as prime minister, Al-Hoss, an economist, is expected to reign in government spending and oversee a program of financial and social reform. Both enjoy wide support in Lebanon from Christians and Muslims, and have good relationships with other Arab countries. Former prime minister Rafiq Hariri remains a vocal and often critical presence in the parliament, as does Druze leader Walid Jumblatt.

POPULATION & PEOPLE

Lebanon has an estimated population of about four million people, 85% of whom live in urban areas – more than one million of them in Beirut. It is one of the most densely populated countries in the Middle East, with an average density of about 380 people per sq km. In addition, there are an

The Difference with Lebanese

The liberal attitudes that prevail in Beirut strike many western travellers as a breath of fresh air after coming from some of the more traditional Middle Eastern countries. Despite its firm geographic location in the Middle East, Beirut is a distinctly west-leaning city.

The more western approach to life is something you immediately notice when you arrive: there are nightclubs, international restaurants, Internet cafes and cinemas with the latest release movies. And the dress style is smart and modern; Beirutis are extremely image and fashion conscious. You could almost be in any major city in Europe.

Beirut in particular and Lebanon in general have somehow always been different to the rest of the Middle East. Why? There's no simple answer but it helps to consider some of the complex geographic, historic, religious, economic, political and cultural reasons.

Geographically and historically, Beirut has long been at a crossroads on major trade routes, giving it not only a strategic and financial importance but also access and exposure to the numerous cultures that passed through. Lebanon is also unlike most Arab countries in that it is not dominated by one sole religion. At last count there were 17 officially recognised sects in Lebanon: the tolerance and openness that this demands of a people is huge.

The system of government is unusual for the region. Many Arab countries have leaders who have been in power for long periods, whereas Lebanon's law restricts parliamentary terms and also aims to create an equitable share of power between the major religions, again requiring a level of openness and optimism.

Lebanon is also a nation with few natural resources – there's no oil, heavy industry or manufacturing. It had tourism as a thriving industry, but the civil war killed that off and visitors are only slowly coming back (there were all of 632,000 tourists in 1998). But the Lebanese in general and Beirutis in particular have long relied on their own resources and turned their astute business sense to financial and commercial enterprises. As one Lebanese journalist put it, 'The Lebanese have always been merchants and traders, they are born traders'. Many of them apply their skills at home, some live in Saudi Arabia and make a fortune for their family before returning to their home country, others go overseas and run businesses; many have ended up as heads of multinational corporations.

Relative to the rest of the Middle East, Beirutis are well educated and widely travelled. There are many more Lebanese living abroad than in Lebanon and many of them end up returning to their home country, bringing something of the west with them. Its worldliness, political and cultural history, connection to Europe and entrepreneurial drive continue to set Lebanon apart from other parts of the Middle East.

---

estimated 400,000 Palestinian refugees and more than 300,000 other Arabs, Kurds and Armenians. Although the Lebanese are of mixed ancestry, about 92% of the population are of Arab descent.

RELIGION

There are no official figures available but it's estimated that about 70% of the population is Muslim and about 30% of the population is Christian. The majority of Lebanon's Muslims are Shi'ite, although there are also significant numbers of Sunni. The largest Christian group is the Maronite sect, followed by the Greek Orthodox, the Greek Catholic, the Armenian Orthodox, the Armenian Catholic, the Syrian Catholic, the Chaldean, the Protestant and the Syrian Orthodox churches. There's also a handful of Roman Catholics, Baha'is and Jews.

The vivid memory of the devastating civil war means that there is a truce between Christians and Muslims as well as the factions within each religious group. In his five terms as prime minister Salim al-Hoss, a Sunni Muslim, has promoted a philosophy of peaceful co-existence, personified by his marriage to a Christian.

LANGUAGE

Arabic is the official language of Lebanon, but French and, to a lesser degree, English are widely spoken around the country. Most Beirutis, and people in the tourist service industry in other main towns, speak English. For a list of useful Arabic and French words and phrases see the Language guide at the back of this book.

Facts for the Visitor

PLANNING

Spring and autumn, when the climate is warm but not uncomfortable, are the best times to travel. If you want to ski November to March is the time to go. Make the tourist office in Beirut one of your first stops for a good GEO projects map of the city and brochures for all the sites and cities you plan to visit, as they contain some good maps and information and are not usually available at the sites and towns themselves. The tourist office should also have a quarterly magazine, *All Seasons*, which has useful information about attractions. A hat and sunglasses are essential in summer, while some warm clothes and a waterproof jacket are needed in winter. A torch is useful for walking around Beirut at night. Most things you'll need can be bought in Lebanon.

VISAS & DOCUMENTS
Visas

All nationalities require a visa for Lebanon. Nationals of Australia, Austria, Belgium, Canada, Denmark, Finland, France, Germany, Greece, Ireland, Italy, Japan, Luxembourg, Netherlands, Norway, Portugal, South Korea, Spain, Sweden, Switzerland,

the UK and the USA can get a tourist or business visa upon arrival at Beirut airport. Forty-eight hour transit visas are issued free of charge or for a visa good for two to 15 days it's US$17, while one for 16 to 30 days is US$34.

Visas can be obtained more cheaply in advance at any Lebanese embassy or consulate; you'll need two passport-size photographs and usually a letter of recommendation from your employer to say that you are returning to your job. They are valid for three months and cost about US$20 for a single entry visa and US$40 for a multiple entry visa (useful if you're planning to visit Syria from Lebanon and return to Beirut). They are usually issued the next day but can sometimes take longer.

If you have an Israeli stamp in your passport or any other evidence of a visit to Israel, you will be refused a visa and denied entry into the country.

Visa Extensions Visas can be extended for a further three months at no charge at the *amn al-aam*, or General Security office, on the corner of a block to the west of the Cola roundabout in Beirut. The office, open daily except Sunday from 8 am to 1 pm, is on the 2nd floor and the staff speak English. A second extension of three months is possible.

Visas for Neighbouring Countries You need a visa to enter the following neighbouring countries of Lebanon:

Egypt It's much easier to get your Egyptian visa in either Syria or Jordan but if you must do it in Lebanon then you need two photographs, a photocopy of the first three pages of your passport and preferably a letter of introduction as well. The visa takes five days to issue and costs LL50,000 for a single entry for all nationalities, or LL75,000 for multiple entry. The Egyptian embassy is open from 10 am to noon daily.

Jordan One passport photo is required and visas take one hour to be issued. Fees vary wildly according to nationality. Costs for nationals of the following countries are: Australia free, Canada LL112,000, France LL31,500, Germany LL28,000, Japan free, Netherlands LL35,000, UK LL84,000, USA LL70,000.

Syria There is no Syrian diplomatic representation in Lebanon so you cannot get a Syrian visa here.

Other Documents

Keep your passport with you at all times when travelling around Lebanon. There are Lebanese and Syrian army checkpoints all around the country, and even though identification checks are rare, being caught without your passport may cause you unnecessary delays and hassles.

Student cards are next to useless in Lebanon and do not get you any kind of discounts or cheap fares.

If you intend to drive in Lebanon an International Driving Permit (IDP) is required. Third-party insurance is not mandatory but recommended. See Car & Motorcycle in the Getting Around the Region chapter for more information about IDPs.

EMBASSIES & CONSULATES
Lebanese Embassies & Consulates

Irish and New Zealand nationals should apply to the UK consulate for visas. There is no Lebanese embassy in either Israel or Syria.

Australia
  Embassy:
  (☎ 02-6295 7378)
  27 Endeavour St, Red Hill, Canberra, ACT 2603
  Consulate:
  (☎ 03-9529 4588)
  117 Wellington St, Windsor, Victoria 3181. Issues visas to Victorian residents only.
  Consulate:
  (☎ 02-9361 5449)
  70 William St, Kings Cross, Sydney, NSW 2010. Issues visas to NSW residents only.
Canada
  Embassy:
  (☎ 613-236-5825)
  640 Lyon St, K1S 3Z5 Ottawa, Ontario

  Consulate:
  (☎ 514-276-2638)
  40 Chemin Côte Ste Catherine, H2V-2A2-PQ Montreal 153
France
  Embassy:
  (☎ 01 40 67 75 75)
  3, Rue Copernic, 75016 Paris
Germany
  Embassy:
  (☎ 0228-95 68 00)
  Rheinallee 27, D-53173 Bonn
Netherlands
  Embassy:
  (☎ 070-365 8906)
  Frederick Straat 2, 2514 LK The Hague
  Consulate:
  (☎ 020-625 8080)
  2nd floor, Zekering Straat 36, 1014 BC Amsterdam
UK
  Embassy:
  (☎ 020-7229 7265/6)
  21 Kensington Palace Gardens, London W8 4QM
  Consulate:
  (☎ 020-7727 6696)
  15 Palace Gardens Mews, London W8 4RA
USA
  Embassy:
  (☎ 202-939-6300)
  2560 28th St, Washington, DC 20008
  Consulate:
  (☎ 213-467-1253)
  Suite 510, 7060 Hollywood Blvd, Hollywood, CA 90028
  Consulate:
  (☎ 212-744-7905)
  9 East 76th St, New York, NY 10021

Embassies & Consulates in Lebanon

Nationals of Ireland and New Zealand should contact the UK embassy. The following offices are in Beirut or on the highway to Jounieh, and opening hours are generally from 8 or 9 am to 1 pm Monday to Friday.

Australia
  Embassy:
  (☎ 01-347 701)
  Farra building, Rue Bliss, Ras Beirut
Canada
  Embassy:
  (☎ 04-521 163/4, fax 521 167)
  1st floor, Coolrite Bldg, Autostrade, Jal ad-Dib

Egypt
  Embassy:
  (☎ 01-867 917, fax 863 751)
  Rue Thomas Edison, Ramlet al-Beida
France
  Consulate:
  (☎ 01-616 578, fax 616 580)
  Rue de Damas, Ras an-Naba
  Embassy:
  (☎ 05-429 629)
  Rue Mar Takla, Hazmieh
Germany
  Embassy:
  (☎ 04-914 444, fax 914 450)
  Mataileb, Rabieh
Jordan
  Embassy:
  (☎ 05-922 500, fax 922 502)
  Rue Helias Helou, Baabda
Netherlands
  Embassy:
  (☎ 01-204 663, fax 04-339 393)
  9th floor, ABM Amro Bldg, Achrafieh
Turkey
  Embassy:
  (☎ 04-406 776)
  Rabieh
UK
  Embassy:
  (☎ 04-402 025/35, fax 402 033)
  Coolrite Bldg, Autostrade, Jal ad-Dib
USA
  Embassy:
  (☎ 04-402 200/403 300, fax 402 168)
  Autostrade, Awkar

CUSTOMS

Visitors are allowed to bring in 400 cigarettes and one bottle of spirits or 200 cigarettes and two bottles of spirits. There are no restrictions on the importing and exporting of local or foreign currencies.

MONEY
Costs

Compared to most of the Middle East, Lebanon is not cheap. The main expenses are accommodation and nightlife, but if you're on a tight budget it is possible to get by on about US$15 per day. That would mean basing yourself in Beirut and Tripoli at budget hotels where a dorm bed costs about US$4, living on felafel, Lebanese pizzas and *shwarma* (sandwich of meat sliced

off a spit) for about US$6 per day and spending the remaining few dollars getting around on buses.

A more comfortable budget of US$40 a day would get you a basic single room for about US$20, simple meals at restaurants for US$5 to US$10, buses, the odd service taxi and the occasional drink at a nightclub. A double room in a mid-range hotel costs about US$35 and top end prices start at about US$70. There is an extensive bus network which is cheap: most journeys within Lebanon are US$1 or less. Most nightclubs don't have a cover charge but many will sting you LL10,000 per drink.

Currency

The currency in Lebanon is the Lebanese lira (LL), also known locally as the *pound*. There are coins of LL50, 100, 250 and 500 and notes of LL1000, 10,000 and 50,000. US dollars act as a second currency and are accepted almost everywhere. It's not unusual to pay in lira and get some of the change in US dollars, or vice versa.

Exchange Rates

country	unit		lira
Australia	A$1	=	LL987
Canada	C$1	=	LL1007
euro	€1	=	LL1619
France	10FF	=	LL2460
Germany	DM1	=	LL828
Japan	¥100	=	LL1313
New Zealand	NZ$1	=	LL800
Syria	S£10	=	LL361
UK	UK£1	=	LL2431
USA	US$1	=	LL1514

Currency from other Middle Eastern countries can be changed at banks, exchange bureaus and with moneychangers. The rates are usually at the daily posted rate but can vary slightly, so shop around.

Exchanging Money

Most banks will only change US dollars and UK pounds in cash and travellers cheques, while moneychangers, found throughout

Lebanon, will deal in almost any convertible currency. They also usually offer better rates than the banks.

Before using moneychangers find out what the current exchange rates are. Either ask at a bank or check the previous day's closing exchange rates in the English-language newspaper *The Daily Star*.

For travellers cheques, there's a commission ranging from US$1 to US$4 per cheque at most places. Again, it pays to shop around.

Credit Cards & ATMs

Travellers cheques and most international credit cards (American Express, Visa, Diner's Club, MasterCard) are accepted in the larger establishments and most restaurants and shops.

Automatic Teller Machines accept credit cards or co-branded home banking cards for Cirrus, Diner's Club, Maestro, MasterCard, Visa and Visa-Electron.

Money Transfers

Western Union operates in Lebanon in conjunction with Credit Libanais and BBAC banks.

Tipping & Bargaining

Most restaurants and nightspots include a 16% service charge in the bill but it is customary to leave an extra tip of 5 to 10% of the total.

Most things can be bargained down in Lebanon, from taxi fares to hotel charges. If you feel you're being overcharged while shopping then offer a price less than what you're really willing to pay to leave room for negotiation.

Many hotels will give you a discount if there are a few of you or if you're staying for more than three days. Or they may offer to throw in a free breakfast.

Service taxis have set prices for their routes, but regular taxis may try to overcharge you. A good way to know how much to pay for a regular taxis is to multiply the service-taxi fare to your destination by five (the number of passengers in a full car).

POST & COMMUNICATIONS

Post offices are generally open from 8 am to 1 pm Monday to Saturday, however the closing time can vary between noon and 2 pm.

Sending Mail

It's the same price to send a postcard or letter. To Europe it costs LL1250 and to Australia and the USA it's LL1500. Parcels to Europe and USA cost LL30,000 for 1kg and LL65,000 for 5kg and to Australia are LL35,000 for 1kg and LL100,000 for 5kg. You can only send letters and parcels from a post office.

Letters usually take between five to 21 days to reach Europe, the USA or Australia, and occasionally mail never arrives at its destination.

Courier service DHL has an office on Rue Banque du Liban and its counterpart Federal Express (☎ 345 385) is on Rue Emile Edde.

Receiving Mail

Receiving mail from around the world generally takes several weeks and there are no poste restante facilities. Amex provides a mail holding service for people using its travellers cheques; letters can be sent to Amex, Gefinor Centre, Beirut. If you know the hotel in which you'll be staying, its staff will keep your incoming mail for you if you let them know that you are expecting letters.

Telephone

The country code for Lebanon is ☎ 961. The area code when dialling a mobile phone is ☎ 03. Local telephone area codes are:

Greater Beirut	☎ 01
Byblos (Jbail) and Jounieh	☎ 09
Lebanon North (including Tripoli)	☎ 06
Lebanon South (including Sidon and Tyre)	☎ 07
Mt Lebanon North	☎ 04
Mt Lebanon South (including Beiteddine)	☎ 05
Bekaa Valley (including Zahlé, Chtaura and Baalbek)	☎ 08

There's a government-run telephone office in Beirut (see under Information in that section) where you can make local and international calls.

There are an increasing number of public phones in shops and in the street where local calls can be made for LL500. Otherwise, all over the country there are private telephone offices which charge LL1000 to LL1500 for local calls and US$1 to US$3 per minute for international calls. Hamra Telecom Centre is a central private phone service charging US$1 per minute. At the time of writing it was not possible to make collect calls from Lebanon.

Fax

Faxes can be sent from most mid-range and top end hotels and from many private telephone bureaus and bookshops.

Email & Internet Access

Internet cafes have proliferated in Lebanon in the past couple of years, with cafes in Beirut, Tripoli, Jounieh, Byblos, Sidon and Tyre (see the Information section for each city for details). They generally charge LL5000 or LL6000 per hour for Internet access. The cafes are often packed with young Lebanese playing the latest computer games.

The major Internet service provider in Lebanon is Cyberia (☎ 01-355 156, email info@cyberia.net.lb). A Cyberia starter kit includes software, an email account and 15 free hours access. Intracom (☎ 01-792 340, email info@intracom.net.lb) is another Internet service provider offering a starter kit with 10 free hours for US$20.

BOOKS

People from every side of the political spectrum have written about the civil war. Among the many books is Kamal Salibi's *A House of Many Mansions: The history of Lebanon Reconsidered* which looks at the reasons for the civil war. Meir Zamir's *The Formation of Modern Lebanon* is a detailed study of how modern Lebanon was formed in the wake of the disintegration of the Ottoman empire after WWI. It shows how the creation of Greater Lebanon was bound to lead the country to a civil war. *Pity the Nation: Lebanon at War* by Robert Fisk is a very readable and comprehensive account of the Lebanese war. It chronicles the events of the war since it began in 1975 and explains the different factions and parties involved. Sandra Mackey's *Lebanon: Death of a Nation* is another account of the war and its causes.

There are also quite a few books written on Lebanon's recent history. Focusing on the rebuilding of Beirut is the comprehensive *Projecting Beirut: Episodes in the Construction and Reconstruction of a Modern City* edited by Peter Rowe & Hashim Sarkis. A glossier, more pictorial version of events is *Beirut Reborn: The Reformation and Development of the Central District* by Angus Gavin & Ramez Maluk. Nelda La-Teef's *Women of Lebanon* is an interesting series of interviews with 42 Lebanese women educators, artists, politicians, social workers and home-makers.

Coffee-table books about Lebanon include *Lebanon: Pictures of our Heritage*, a beautiful, three volume series with a book each on public buildings, religious architecture and old homes; and *Eternal Beirut*, which does a nice job of covering many facets of the city.

If you're interested in prewar travel accounts try Colin Thubron's *The Hills of Adonis* or Philip Ward's *Touring Lebanon*. For ancient history *The Phoenicians*, by Donald Harden, is comprehensive and authoritative.

More general Middle East titles, some of which also contain coverage of Lebanon, are listed in the Books section in the Regional Facts for the Visitor chapter at the beginning of this book.

NEWSPAPERS & MAGAZINES

The English-language daily *The Daily Star* provides a good coverage of local events and includes the *International Herald Tribune* as an insert to cover world news. The local French-language *L'Orient Le Jour* newspaper is reasonable, as are the weekly magazines *La Revue du Liban* and *Magazine*.

Bookshops and newsagents stock many foreign publications, including the UK's

LEBANON

The Independent, The Guardian and *The Times*, the French *Le Monde* and *Le Figaro*, as well as German, Italian and Spanish newspapers (they're usually one day late). They also have *Time* and *Newsweek* magazines, *The Economist, L'Express, Le Point* and many more foreign publications.

RADIO & TV

The Lebanese Broadcasting Station has programs in French and English, as do most of the private radio stations. You can pick up the BBC's 24 hour service on 1323 kHz or 720 kHz medium wave.

There are 10 TV stations broadcasting in Arabic, English and French at different times of the day.

PHOTOGRAPHY & VIDEO

Kodak, Agfa, Fuji and other brands are sold everywhere in Lebanon, but good slide film is generally only available in Beirut, the larger towns and some tourist shops (but watch the expiry date). A regular 36 exposure print film costs LL6500 to LL8500 and a slide film LL15,000 (often including developing). Many photo shops have a one hour or same-day developing service (LL13,000 to LL18,000 for a 36 exposure film), and the quality is good. Videotapes are available in all the popular formats.

There's a good range of camera and video equipment and spare parts in Beirut. Check out Kamera on Rue Hamra and Photo Nubar on Rue Neamé Yafet.

LAUNDRY

There are drycleaning services in all the major cities and towns (but no laundrettes) – your hotel can direct you to the nearest one. Drycleaners usually take one day and their prices start at about LL7000 for a simple garment.

TOILETS

There are public toilets at some tourist sites, but otherwise you'll need to use those in hotels and restaurants. The standard is usually good although you sometimes need your own toilet paper.

HEALTH

Medical services in Lebanon are well developed and most doctors have graduated overseas and speak English or French. The best equipped hospitals are usually the private ones, and a medical insurance policy is essential as they are expensive. Pharmacists can prescribe you medicines for minor ailments; most drugs are available over the counter.

The main precaution to take is with food and water. Tap water is *not* drinkable in Lebanon, so either drink bottled spring water, which is widely available (LL750 for 1.5L in grocery stores) or sterilise your water. Always wash fruit and vegetables and avoid eating salads in cheap snack bars. See the Health section in the Regional Facts for the Visitor chapter for more detailed health information.

WOMEN TRAVELLERS

Women should have few hassles travelling in Lebanon. The worst they'll be subjected to is leers or zealous attempts at conversation. Sleeveless tops, shorts and miniskirts are common in Beirut and Jounieh, but outside the main centres long sleeved, loose clothing is preferable.

GAY & LESBIAN TRAVELLERS

There are not a lot of gay hangouts in Lebanon but B018 is one popular gay-friendly nightclub in Beirut and there's also a Cuban bar in Jounieh with a fabulous gay male belly-dancer. See the Beirut and Jounieh Entertainment sections.

TRAVEL WITH CHILDREN

For the kids there's a children's science museum called Planet Discovery which opened in Beirut Central District in 1999. It's temporarily housed on Rue Omar Daouk and will move to a permanent location in Beirut Central District in a couple of years. There are also Luna Park funfairs dotted around the country.

DANGERS & ANNOYANCES

The main danger spot in Lebanon is the south, which can often be subject to Israeli retaliatory shelling or air raids in response to Hezbollah attacks on the Israeli Occupied Zone. This zone is off limit to visitors, but the UNIFIL area which straddles it is accessible to tourists. The UN base in Tyre (Sour) can advise travellers whether it is safe to enter the zone. But outside this area Lebanon is safe to travel in. Since the disarming and disbanding of militias in the early 1990s, it has become possible to go anywhere at night or day without worries about security.

It is always a good idea to be alert to the current situation. Attacks from Israel can happen without warning and at times such as these you would be well advised to stay away from Hezbollah areas (mainly in the south and the Bekaa Valley).

BUSINESS HOURS

Sunday is the end-of-week holiday in Lebanon. Government offices, including post offices, are open from 8 am to 2 pm Monday to Saturday and from 8 to 11 am on Friday. Banks are open from 8.30 am to 12.30 pm Monday to Friday and to noon Saturday.

Shops and businesses open from 9 am to 6 pm Monday to Saturday. Many grocery stores keep later hours and open on Sunday. In summer many shops close around 3 pm.

PUBLIC HOLIDAYS & SPECIAL EVENTS

Most holidays are religious, and with so many different sects in Lebanon there are quite a few events to celebrate:

New Year
   1 January
Mar Maroun (patron saint of the Maronites)
   9 February
Good Friday & Easter Monday
   March-April
Labour Day
   1 May
Assumption
   15 August
All Saints Day
   1 November
Independence
   22 November
Christmas Day
   25 December

Also observed are Muslim holidays of Eid al-Fitr, Eid al-Adha, Prophet's Birthday, Muslim New Year and Ashura. For the more information on these Muslim holidays and dates see Public Holidays & Special Events in the Regional Facts for the Visitor chapter.

COURSES

The American Language Center (☎ 704 717, 343 403) on Rue Hamra in Beirut offers beginner and intermediate courses in Arabic for foreigners. Courses run for 16 weeks and consist of three one-hour classes each week. The 50 hours of tuition in practical Arabic costs US$200. The intermediate course runs for 25 hours and costs US$100. There are also centres in Tripoli and Zahlé.

The AUB (☎ 374 444) has short courses in Arabic, and Roman and Byzantine history. A 12 week course called 'Colloquial Arabic for beginners' has four hours per week of tuition and costs US$375. 'Lebanon in the Roman Period' is a 10 week course studying Roman and Byzantine sites in Lebanon. There is 2½ hours per week of tuition and the fee is US$270.

WORK

You need a work permit to take on any official employment in Lebanon but there are opportunities for foreigners with professional skills. Unless you're being sponsored by a company it's difficult to get a work permit before arriving in Lebanon. Once you're in Lebanon an employer will apply for a work permit on your behalf if they're interested in you. Possible areas of employment are teaching English at language schools such as the American Language Center, sub-editing at *The Daily Star* English-language newspaper, and as a tour guide or in a hotel.

ACCOMMODATION

There's plenty of top end accommodation, but budget and mid-range is a bit more scarce. Lebanon has one camping ground, the Camping Amchit Les Colombes, just outside Byblos (Jbail) on the northern coast. There are cheap places to stay in Beirut, and at least one hotel in Tripoli (Trablous),

Baalbek and Sidon (Saida). Even the cheapest hotels in Lebanon have hot water, though its supply is sometimes limited or costs more.

FOOD

Lebanese cuisine is a real delight, with a variety of foods to suit all tastes. What's more, it's not expensive; even the street food is delicious. Beans, fruits and vegetables are plentiful and mutton is the favourite meat. A typical Lebanese meal consists of a few *mezze* dishes (hors d'oeuvres), a main dish of meat, chicken or fish (usually with rice), a salad and dessert. There are two kinds of bread: the flat, pocket variety found everywhere in the Middle East and the *marqouk*, or mountain bread – a very thin bread baked on a domed dish on a wood fire.

There are sandwich and snack bars all over Beirut and in every town around the country. Restaurants also abound, and cover a variety of cuisines from Middle Eastern to European, Indian and Japanese. There's also plenty of American fastfood and restaurant chains including, as of 1999, the ubiquitous McDonald's. For more information, get the Ministry of Tourism's *Restaurants, Night Clubs and Cafes*, which has a list of most eateries around Lebanon. Available from the Beirut tourist office, it gives the addresses, notes the average price per person and a summary of the cuisine.

Mezze & Snacks

Dishes in this category include *fatayer bi sbanikh* (spinach pies), *humous* (chickpea dip), *baba ghanoug* (eggplant dip), *labneh* (dried yoghurt cheese), *fatayer bi zaatar* or *man'oushi* (thyme pizza), *lahm bi ajin* (meat pizza), stuffed vine leaves, eggplants and peppers cooked in oil and served cold, and *loubieh bi zeit* (string beans cooked with tomatoes, onions and garlic).

Main Dishes

The national dish is *kebbe*, lamb meat mixed with *burghul*, or crushed wheat, which comes in the form of a baked pie or fried balls stuffed with pine nuts. Other main meals include *kharouf mihshi* (lamb stuffed with rice, meat and nuts), *sayadieh* (fish cooked with rice in an onion and tahina sauce) and *ruz wi djaj* (chicken with rice and nuts). There's also all the variety of *kebabs* found in the Middle East.

The two favourite salads are *tabouleh* and *fattoush*. The first consists of parsley, mint, onions and tomatoes mixed with burghul and the second has parsley, lettuce, tomatoes, radishes, onions, cucumbers and toasted bread pieces, and is seasoned with *sumac*, a tangy fruit commonly used to colour and flavour cooking.

Desserts & Sweets

In addition to the syrupy *baklava* varieties, sweets include *mahallabiye* (a milk custard with pine nuts and almonds), *maamoul bi joz* or *tamr* (semolina cakes stuffed with walnuts or dates), and *katayef*, pastries stuffed with cream *(bil qashta)* or walnut *(bi joz)*.

DRINKS
Nonalcoholic Drinks

Like in other Middle Eastern countries, Arabic coffee is popular in Lebanon. It's quite strong and served in small coffee cups. You can have it *sadah* (without sugar), *wassat* (medium sugar) or *hilweh* (sweet). Tea is also available but is not as popular. Western-style coffee is usually called *Nescafé* and comes in small sachets with a pot of hot water and a jug of milk and is usually expensive.

Other popular nonalcoholic drinks include freshly squeezed vegetable and fruit juices, *limonada* (fresh lemon squash), *jellab* (a delicious drink made from raisins and served with pine nuts) and *'ayran* (a yoghurt drink). All kinds of foreign-brand soft drinks are also widely available.

Alcohol

Alcohol is widely available in Lebanon and you'll find everything from local beers and wines to imported whisky and vodka.

The most popular alcoholic drink is *araq*, which is mixed with water and ice and usually accompanies meals. Good local brands include Ksaraq and Le Brun. There are a few wineries in Lebanon, such as Ksara and Kefraya, producing a reasonable variety of red, rosé and white wines. Local beer brands include Laziza and Almaza, which are quite good. There is also Amstel, a Dutch beer brewed locally under licence. For more information on Middle Eastern food and drinks see the Regional Facts for the Visitor chapter.

SPECTATOR SPORTS

There are quite a few events such as motor rallies and football, but you will only get to know about them if you scour the newspapers or ask locals. The Lebanese love football and have a national team and local leagues. There are also international teams for golf, basketball and skiing.

Horse Racing

The *Hippodrome* (☎ 632 520/15) in Beirut holds regular Sunday race meetings, one of the few events which survived throughout the war. The meetings are very popular and are a great way to soak up the local atmosphere. Admission is US$10 to the grandstand and US$3 to the 2nd class stand. The entrance is on Ave Abdallah Yafi, not far from the National Museum.

Skiing

Lebanon's not a country many people associate with skiing, but it's a hugely popular sport and there are some good resorts. The resorts at Faraya and Faqra (45km northwest of Beirut) and The Cedars are the most popular. See Around Beirut and The Cedars sections of this chapter for more information. The Ministry of Tourism publishes a magazine *All Seasons* which in winter details all the ski resorts, facilities and a calendar of competitive events. It's available from the Beirut tourist office.

SHOPPING

Local handicrafts include pottery, blown glass, embroidered materials, caftans, copperware, brass bowls and trays, mother-of-pearl inlaid boxes and backgammon sets, and rugs. You can buy everything in Beirut and the *souqs* (markets) of Tripoli and Sidon are also good places to shop. If you don't have any moral qualms about buying ancient artefacts (it's legal) there's plenty on sale in Byblos, as well as other parts of the country.

Getting There & Away

You can travel to Lebanon by air or overland from Syria or by boat from Cyprus.

AIR
Airports & Airlines

The newly refurbished Beirut international airport, 5km from the city centre, is Lebanon's only airport. Lebanon's carrier, Middle East Airlines (MEA), connects Beirut with most European capitals, other parts of the Middle East and some African capitals. In addition, many European, Middle Eastern and Asian airlines have services to Beirut.

Departure Tax

Airline passengers departing from Beirut international airport must pay a steep US$51.

LAND

The only way into Lebanon by land is through Syria; the border with Israel is closed and will be for the foreseeable future. There is no departure tax when leaving by land. If you're bringing your car into Lebanon, you must have an International Driving Permit and a carnet.

There are daily buses and service taxis leaving Charles Helou bus station in Beirut for Damascus, Aleppo and Lattakia. The same services leave from Tripoli and there is also a service to Homs. See the Tripoli and Beirut Getting There & Away sections for prices and times. It's also possible to take a service taxi direct from Baalbek to Damascus – see the Baalbek section for details.

SEA

It is possible to arrive in Lebanon by sea from Lemesos (Limassol) in Cyprus during

LEBANON

the summer. Louis Tourist Company in Cyprus (☎ 02-678 000) operates a two day cruise which leaves Lemesos at 8 pm on Friday and arrives in Jounieh, just north of Beirut, at 7 am. The return trip includes a cabin bed, food, day excursion to Beirut, Jounieh and Byblos and departure taxes. The cruise operates from the end of May until the end of October and prices start at US$160 per person (US$126 without the day excursion). It's not possible to get a one-way fare, but it's still cheaper to pay the return fare than to fly. At the time of writing, the ferry that once operated between Larnaca and Jounieh was no longer running.

Getting Around

There are no air services or trains operating within Lebanon but there is an ever expanding bus network which is cheap, abundant and covers most city neighbourhoods and major destinations around the country.

BUS

The bus system at first seems completely chaotic and despite there being no timetables it is possible to fathom how it works. A number of private companies offer frequent bus services between Beirut and major towns around Lebanon and the fare is the same whether you're a local or a foreigner. Most towns have an area where buses congregate; in Beirut there are two bus areas, with Charles Helou bus station servicing destinations to the north and the Cola stand servicing destinations to the south.

Charles Helou is systematically divided into three signposted zones: Zone A is for buses to Syria; Zone B is for buses servicing Beirut (where the route starts or finishes at Charles Helou); and Zone C is for express buses to Jounieh, Byblos and Tripoli. Zone A and C have ticket offices where you can buy tickets for your journey.

Buses gather at the Cola bridge for destinations south of Beirut. At the time of writing there were no bus services to Baalbek. The Cola station is not as well organised as

Charles Helou but if someone doesn't find you first (which is what usually happens) ask any driver where the next bus to your destination is leaving from. They usually have the destination displayed on the front window or above it in Arabic only.

There is also a growing number of microbuses covering the same routes which are slightly more expensive than regular buses, but a lot cheaper than service taxis. Microbuses are operated by individuals. The beauty of them is that they are small, comfortable and frequent, but you take your chances regarding the quality of the driver's ability. You pay for your ticket on the microbus, at either the start or end of your journey.

TAXI & SERVICE TAXI

Taxis and service taxis are recognisable by their red number plates and, on some cars, a white sign with 'TAXI' written in red letters. Most of the cars are old Mercedes. Before getting in, always check that the number plate is red as there are many unlicensed drivers operating taxis.

Service taxis usually follow an established route and you can stop them anywhere. To signal the driver to stop just say 'indak' (here). Payment can be made at any point during the trip, though people tend to pay as soon as they get in. To take you anywhere in central Beirut, a service taxi charges LL1000 (LL2000 to outlying districts). You may sometimes have to take more than one service taxi if your destination is not straightforward, ie if it includes more than one of the service taxi's routes. Outside of Beirut, the fares range from LL2000 to LL8000, depending on the destination. Although the fares are not listed anywhere the driver will usually ask for the correct fare. However, always inquire 'servEES?' (service) before getting into the car, especially if there are no other passengers, to avoid being charged a full taxi fare.

The same service taxi can become a taxi if you pay for the fare of the four other seats in the car. This avoids the delay of stopping to let other passengers in or out and the driver will deposit you right outside your destination.

Ordinary taxis are not confined to a set route and take only one fare. You can also order taxis by telephone. They'll take you anywhere in Lebanon and some also have services to Syria and Jordan.

CAR & MOTORCYCLE
Road Rules
Driving is on the right-hand side of the road in Lebanon, but this is where road rules end. Despite the cheap petrol (LL100 per litre), driving is not exactly recommended in Lebanon. Accidents and traffic jams are frequent hazards.

Despite the attempts of traffic police to organise the flow of cars, very few drivers follow road regulations. Some intersections in Beirut do have traffic lights, but they are usually treated as give way signs at best. Sometimes drivers stop at them, but those who do are usually tooted by other drivers to move on.

Driving in the cities is frustrating because of the traffic jams, the double parking and service taxis which stop without warning in the middle of the road to let passengers in or out. On the highways it can be a pretty scary experience as drivers will zigzag among the cars at crazy speeds. In the mountains many roads are narrow with hairpin bends and it's not unusual for drivers to overtake on hidden road bends. In addition, you have to keep an eye out for pedestrians who often walk in the middle of the streets or haphazardly cross highways and roads. That said, local drivers are quite used to driving in these chaotic circumstances.

Rental
There are several car hire companies in Beirut offering competitive rates. Most have small cars starting at US$25 to US$30 per day with unlimited mileage; it's cheaper for longer periods. We recommend that you take out the best insurance policy that you can afford. Many of the firms also offer drivers to go with the cars which costs about US$25 per day.

Rental companies include:

Avis	(☎ 01-861 614)
Budget	(☎ 01-740 740/1)
Prestige	(☎ 01-866 328)

All companies require a refundable deposit, except from credit card holders, and offer free delivery and collection during working hours. The minimum age for hiring a car is 21. Hire cars cannot be taken over the border into Syria.

ORGANISED TOURS
There are a few operators organising tours within Lebanon and to Syria and Jordan. They're a good option as the tours cover most of Lebanon's places of interest and are reasonably priced (most include lunch in the deal). All transport is by air-con coaches. The itineraries vary from company to company but they all cover the main places of interest such as Baalbek, Aanjar, Byblos, Tripoli, The Cedars, Sidon and Tyre. A day trip costs about US$50. The main tour operators are in Beirut:

Nakhal & Cie
    (☎ 01-389 389, fax 389 282, email tours@
    nakhal.com.lb) Ave Sami Solh, Ghorayeb
    Bldg
Tania Travel
    (☎ 01-739 682/3/4, fax 340 473, email tani
    atvl@cyberia.net.lb) Rue Sidani, 1st floor of
    building opposite Cinema Jeanne d'Arc

Beirut

Beirut is the capital of Lebanon and its largest city, with a population of just over a million. It's a city of contrasts, cosmopolitan and glitzy in parts and a bombed-out shell of its former self in others. Expensive new cars vie for the right of way with vendor carts, elegant traditional houses are surrounded by concrete buildings, and the wealthy share the pavement with beggars. Beirut suffered severely from 16 years of war when whole neighbourhoods, including the old city centre, were destroyed. But there's an infectious optimism in the city now and a huge amount of energy going into its speedy and tasteful reconstruction.

Beirut is noisy, crowded and chaotic but it's also sophisticated, vibrant and retains a certain charm, due mainly to the warmth and hospitality of its citizens. Though there's not a lot to see in Beirut itself, it's a good base for travellers, as it's the country's transport hub, with the most distant part of Lebanon no more than three hours drive away. And the nightclub scene is the best in the Middle East.

History
Beryte, as Beirut was originally known, was a modest port during Phoenician times (2nd millennium BC). It became famous in Roman times for its School of Law, one of the first three in the world, which made it a cultural centre until the 6th century AD. Then it went into a long period of decline, and even during Arab times (13th century), when mosques, *hammams* (bathhouses) and souqs were built, it was still relatively obscure. In the 19th century Beirut gained importance as a trading centre and gateway to the Middle East and its port became the largest on the eastern Mediterranean coast. The city soon became a major business, banking and publishing centre and remained so until the civil war undermined its position.

Since the war ended the rehabilitation of the city's infrastructure has begun in earnest and most of it should now be completed. One positive thing which has come out of all the destruction is the uncovering of archaeological sites from Phoenician and classical times which would otherwise never have been found. All efforts are geared towards restoring Beirut as the business and commercial centre of the Middle East.

Orientation
The Hamra district of Beirut is where many visitors stay. It's where you'll find most hotels, the Ministry of Tourism, major banks, many restaurants and cafes, travel agencies, a post office, telephone office and airline offices – all within walking distance of each other. Just north of Hamra is Ras Beirut, home to the American University Beirut

(AUB), and to the south-west is the seaside Raouché area, where there's Beirut's landmark Pigeon Rocks and a host of cafes overlooking the Mediterranean. The Corniche (Ave de Paris and Ave du Général de Gaulle) runs along Beirut's western and northern shores and is a popular spot for walks. Heading east from Hamra is Ain-al Mreisse, where popular American fastfood outlets and Beirut's cheapest hotels are located. Farther east is the newly rebuilt Beirut Central District and continuing east again is Achrafieh, where you'll find some of Beirut's newest restaurants and nightclubs.

When directing you, people refer to landmarks (eg British Bank building) and the names of commercial institutions. You soon get used to this system and getting around Beirut is less difficult than it may at first seem.

Information
Tourist Offices The tourist information office (☎ 340 940/4) is on the ground floor of the office block housing the Ministry of Tourism, on the corner of Rue Banque du Liban and Rue de Rome. The entrance is through a covered arcade that runs underneath the block. It is open from 8 am to 4 pm daily. The staff can supply you with an excellent collection of up-to-date brochures of the main tourist attractions (and some of the minor ones too) but cannot help with a lot of practical information.

Money You won't have difficulty changing money in Beirut as there are banks and moneychangers throughout the city. Banks are open until 12.30 pm (noon on Saturday) while moneychangers stay open until at least 6 pm. There are plenty of banks with ATMs; Banque Audi has branches on Rue Bliss and Rue Hamra and the British Bank on Rue Makdissi has an ATM. Banque du Liban et d'outre Mer has a branch on Rue Bliss where it's possible to get a cash advance on Diner's Club.

The American Express Bank (☎ 341 879/739 830) has a branch on the 1st floor of the Gefinor Centre on Rue Maamari,

BEIRUT

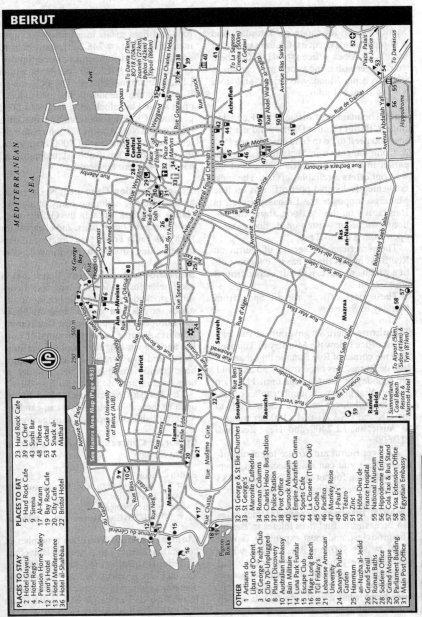

MEDITERRANEAN SEA

Port

To Dawra (7km),
BO18 (10km),
Jounieh (21km),
Byblos (42km) &
Tripoli (85km)

To La Sagesse
Cinema (500m)
& Getawi

Achrafieh

Avenue Charles Helou

Avenue Elias Sarkis

Place Palais
de Justice

To Damascus

Rue Sursock

Rue Gouraud

Rue de Damas

Rue Abdel Wahab al-Inglizi

Avenue Abdallah Yafi

Hippodrome

Rue Weygand

Beirut
Central
District

Rue Monot

Place de
l'Etoile

Place des
Martyrs

Rue Allenby

Avenue du Central Foyad Chehab

Rue Bechara el-Khoury

St George
Bay

Rue Phoenicia

Rue Ahmed Chaouqi

Overpass

Ain al-Mreisse

Riad-es-
Solh

Rue de l'Armée

Avenue de l'Indépendance

Rue Basta

Ras
an-Naba

Boulevard Saeb Salam

Rue Omar ad-Daouq

Rue Clémenceau

Rue Spears

Rue d'Alger

Rue Mar Elias

Mazraa

Sanayeh

Ras Beirut

Avenue de Paris

American University
of Beirut (AUB)

See Hamra Area Map (Page 493)

Rue John Kennedy

Rue de Rome

Rue René
Mowawd

Rue Omar
Daouq

Snoubra

Rue Beni
Maarouf

Boulevard Saeb Salam

Rue al-Rachidine

Rue Bliss

Rue Abdul

Rue Nelf

Manara

Rue Hamra

Rue Emile Edde

Rue Madame Curie

Hamra

Raouché

Rue Verdun

Rue de l'Unesco

Ramlet
al-Baida

To
Summerland,
Coral Beach
Resort (4km) &
Marriott Hotel

To Airport (5km),
Sidon (41km) &
Tyre (81km)

Avenue du Général
de Gaulle

Pigeon
Rocks

PLACES TO STAY
2 Hotel Glayeul
4 Hotel Regis
7 Pension Home Valery
12 Lord's Hotel
13 Hotel Mediterranee
36 Hotel al-Shahbaa

PLACES TO EAT
5 Hard Rock Cafe
9 Sirena
17 Al-Karam
19 Bay Rock Cafe
20 City Cafe
22 Bristol Hotel

23 Hard Rock Cafe
39 Le Chef
43 Sushi Bar
48 Tribeca
53 Coktail
54 Snack al-Mathaf

OTHER
1 Artisans du
Liban et d'Orient
3 St George Yacht Club
6 Club 70-Unplugged
8 Planet Discovery
10 Australian Embassy
11 Bain Militaire
14 Luna Park Funfair
15 Escape Club
16 Plage Long Beach
18 TGI Friday's
21 Lebanese American
University
24 Sanayeh Public
Garden
25 Hammam
an-Nuzha al-Jedid
26 Grand Serail
27 Roman Baths
28 Solidere Office
29 Grand Mosque
30 Parliament Building
31 Main Post Office

32 St George & St Elie Churches
33 St George's
Maronite Cathedral
34 Roman Columns
35 Charles Helou Bus Station
38 Police Station
38 Post Office
40 Sursock Museum
41 Empire Achrafieh Cinema
42 Sports Cafe
44 La Closerie (Time Out)
45 Gotha
46 Pacifico
47 Monkey Rose
49 J-Paul's
50 Téatro
51 Zinc
52 Hôtel-Dieu de
France Hospital
55 National Museum
56 Hippodrome Entrance
55 Cola Taxi & Bus Stand
58 Visa Extension Office
59 Egyptian Embassy

LEBANON

Hamra. It is open from 8.30 am to 12.30 pm, Monday to Friday (noon on Saturday) and will replace lost cheques. On the same floor there's an Amex office (☎ 341 856) where you can get cash using your Amex card from 9 am to 3 pm Monday to Friday and from 8.30 to 1 pm Saturday.

Post The main post office is on Rue Riad Solh in Beirut Central District and it's here that you need to go to send parcels (see Post & Communication in Facts for the Visitor earlier in this chapter). It's a bit out of the way but offers a reliable service. The most conveniently located post office is on Rue Makdissi, opposite the Embassy Hotel, in Hamra. It's on the 1st floor, above the stationer with Star written on its door, and is open from 8 am to 2 pm.

The American University of Beirut on Rue Bliss in Ras Beirut has its own post office which anyone can use. It's open from 8 am to 2 pm.

These post offices are all open from Monday to Saturday.

Telephone There's a government-run telephone office below the Ministry of Tourism, near the corner of Rue Banque du Liban and Rue de Rome. It is open from 7.30 am to 11 pm Monday to Saturday and until 11 am on Friday. You give your number to an operator who will direct you to a booth. Calls to the UK and USA cost LL2100 per minute, to Australia, LL2400 and New Zealand, LL3600.

All over Beirut are private telephone offices where you can make local and international calls, for between US$1 and US$3 per minute, depending on the destination.

Email & Internet Access Internet cafes can be easier to find than felafel in Beirut. The grooviest, and most expensive, is Web Cafe (☎ 348 880) on Rue Khalidi where you can have your Internet with cake and coffee or beer and burgers. Internet access is LL8000 per hour, the food is reasonably priced and it has a cool cafe feel. It's open noon to midnight.

Along Rue Makhoul and also serving food and light meals in a friendly environment is MagNet (☎ 748 223), open from 10 am to 2 am and sometimes closed Sunday. Internet access is LL5000 per hour, with a LL2500 minimum charge. The PC Club on Rue Mahatma Gandhi is full of students, open around the clock and charges LL5000 per hour. Close by and charging the same price is The Net (☎ 740 157), which also offers Internet access for LL4000 after 9 pm. It's open from 9 am to at least midnight, and has ultra-modern keyboards.

Travel Agencies There are travel agencies all over Beirut, including many along Rue Hamra and quite a few in the Gefinor Centre. Among the better ones, and cheapest for flights, is Tania Travel (see Organised Tours in the Getting Around chapter for its details).

Bookshops & Libraries Beirut has a good selection of foreign-language bookshops stocked with academic books, dictionaries, novels and general interest books and European newspapers. On Rue Hamra, Librairie Antoine has a good range of English and French-language books. Four Steps Down and Way In, also on Rue Hamra, have mainly English-language books, as does the Librairie du Liban on Rue Bliss.

The British Council has a small library open to the public where you can catch up with English newspapers and magazines.

Cultural Centres Cultural centres in Beirut include:

British Council
  (☎ 730 459, 739 460) Rue Yamout (off Rue Sadat), Ras Beirut
Institut Culturel Français
  (☎ 387 511/2/3) Cité Bounnour, Rue de Damas

Medical Services There are a number of hospitals in Beirut. The American University of Beirut Hospital (☎ 340 460, 350 000) on Rue du Caire is considered the best and also operates a clinic where you can see a doctor. Hôtel-Dieu de France (☎ 615 300/400) on Rue Hôtel-Dieu is another alternative.

The New Beirut

The rebuilding of Beirut's central district is one of the world's largest and most ambitious urban redevelopment projects. The central district was one of the worst affected areas in the civil war, with most buildings badly shelled or bombed. The project to rebuild the former commercial, financial and administrative centre of Lebanon covers 1.8 million sq metres of land, as well as 60 hectares of reclaimed land, and has attracted tens of millions of dollars in investment.

In 1992 the Lebanese parliament formed the Lebanese Company for the Development and Reconstruction of Beirut Central District, known by its French acronym Solidere. Former prime minister Rafiq Hariri was instrumental in the creation of Solidere and the 10 year government approved master plans and invested about US$120 million of his own money into the redevelopment project. Solidere became an incorporated company in 1994 and now has a share capital of US$1.65 billion.

The rebuilding is a two phase project. Phase One, which at the time of writing was due for completion at the end of 1999, is 40% residential and 30% office buildings. A feature of the central district will be the old souq area, which is set to become a series of shopping and entertainment complexes interspersed with large open squares. The old street grid will be one of the few elements that remains of the former souqs. Phase Two, due to start in 2000, involves a new marina and construction work on reclaimed land which Solidere says will 'evolve into a modern financial, business and luxury residential area, commanding panoramic views on the Mediterranean and surrounding mountains and endowed with a grand public park and cultural and recreational facilities'.

The rebuilding work has unearthed archaeological finds from just about every period of Beirut's history – traces of Canaanite, Phoenician, Persian, Hellenistic, Roman, Byzantine, Umayyad, Abbasid, Crusader, Mamluk, Ottoman and French Mandate have all been revealed. Solidere has been working with archaeologists to preserve some of these ancient finds, including Roman baths and colonnades which have been incorporated as features of the central district.

Most Beirutis are pleased with the redevelopment. In contrast to the unplanned concrete invasions in other parts of Lebanon, the rebuilding has been tastefully and thoughtfully done. In many cases the original facades of buildings have been preserved with the same fine stone masonry and wrought-ironwork. The masterplan has blended new features with the old, including more parkland and plazas as well as a drive-in cinema and museum.

Those unhappy with the development include people who previously owned land in the central district. Although they were compensated for their loss of land with shares in Solidere, many would rather have their land and are still mounting legal challenges.

The reconstructed city is largely complete and awaits people to move in and breathe life into it. There has been concern that some tenants and investors are getting nervous and are backing out of lease arrangements, but even if there is not immediately full occupancy the quality of the rebuilding work and the enthusiasm with which it is generally being received should ensure that Beirut thrives again.

Emergency The following numbers can be useful in case of emergency:

Emergency Police:	☎ 01112
Ambulance:	☎ 372 803/4
Fire Brigade:	☎ 01175
Red Cross:	☎ 739 297

Dangers & Annoyances On the whole Beirut is a safe place to travel around. For pedestrians the traffic poses the biggest hazard. Also beware of masonry falling from damaged buildings and watch for potholes in the road when walking around, especially at night in places where there is little street lighting.

Museums

National Museum This museum on the corner of Rue de Damas and Ave Abdallah Yafi has an impressive collection of archaeological artefacts, statuettes and sarcophagi covering Lebanon's history from prehistoric times to the present. There are fossilised fish dating from 85 million years ago as well as Stone Age weapons and tools. There's a display of Phoenician pottery found at Tyre which date from the 7th century BC and **stelae** (inscribed stone slabs) which are even older. There are statues which have been excavated from Sidon, Tyre, Echmoun and Byblos and also a good collection of mosaics from the Roman and Byzantine periods. The collection of figurines, jewellery, mirrors and vases from Byblos is excellent.

At the time of writing the museum was closed but was due to reopen by the end of 1999. Its opening hours were expected to be from 10 am until 5 pm Wednesday to Sunday with an LL10,000 entry fee.

American University of Beirut Museum The AUB museum (☎ 340 549), just inside the AUB main gate, was founded in 1868 and is one of the oldest in the Middle East. It has a collection of Lebanese and Middle Eastern artefacts dating back to the early Stone Age, a fine collection of Phoenician glass and Arab coins going back to the 5th century BC when coins first appeared. There are also terracotta statuettes, including fertility goddesses, and a large collection of pottery dating back to 3000 BC.

The museum is open from 9 am to 4 pm Monday to Friday. Admission is free.

Sursock Museum Owned by the Sursock family, this all white, Italian influenced mansion is the setting for a museum of contemporary art. The museum (☎ 334 133) on Rue Sursock in Achrafieh has a permanent exhibition but is only open when there are special exhibitions of modern paintings, sculptures and old manuscripts, so phone ahead.

Beirut Central District

In the 1970s the Beirut Central District was exalted as the Paris of the Middle East, in the 80s it was the centre of a war zone, and in the 90s the focus of a massive rebuilding program. The central district is largely rebuilt with loads of new buildings but very few are occupied, and at the time of writing it had a surreal, ghost town feel. Tenants were due to move in by early 2000 when the area was expected to explode into action. Whatever stage it's at when you visit, it's worth spending a couple of hours just wandering around looking at the restored old buildings and the new buildings which are mostly re-creations of those destroyed during the war.

The information office of Solidere (☎ 980 650/60, email solidere@solidere.com.lb), the real estate company which has masterminded the reconstruction of the city, has display models and information boards outlining the redevelopment of the area and information officers on hand to answer questions. The office, in Building 149, Rue Saad Zaghloul, off Rue Foch, is open between 8 am and 6 pm and closed between 1 and 2 pm. It is also often closed for short periods for tours by official visitors so it's worth phoning ahead on the day you plan to visit.

Some of the features include: the **Grand Mosque**, which was badly damaged during the war but is still an impressive building and is being restored; and the **Grand Serail**, a magnificent Ottoman building which has already been restored to its former grandeur. Solidere's excavation and reconstruction work has unearthed some Roman ruins including the **Roman baths** which once served the city's population, and five **Roman columns** which were once part of a grand colonnade.

There are many churches, mosques and other old buildings still under restoration.

Corniche

The Corniche is a favourite promenade spot, especially late in the afternoon and on weekends. You can stop to drink a coffee served from the back of a van or sample the push-cart pedlars' specialities such as hot chestnuts, iced cactus fruit, *kaak* (crisp bread with sesame seeds and thyme), fresh coconut, corn on the cob and green almonds. Or you can stop at one of the open-air cafes for a beer and a *nargila* (water pipe). There is a small funfair called Luna Park on the Corniche which is popular with Lebanese families during summer.

Beaches

Unfortunately, the beaches around Beirut are heavily polluted but there are a few seaside resorts in and around the capital where you can sunbathe or swim in a pool. They're rather on the expensive side, with entry fees ranging from US$6 to US$20. In Ain al-Mreisse there is a women-only swimming resort called **Beach Ajram**, close to Artisans du Liban et d'Orient. It's open from 8 am to 5 pm daily during the summer and admission is LL10,000. **Plage Long Beach** has a huge cafe serving food, coffee and nargila. Don't order the Nescafé here unless you're prepared to pay LL4500. Alternatively you can walk down the cliffs near Pigeon Rocks and sunbathe for free.

Hammam

You can indulge yourself with a full massage, sauna and bath at the Hammam an-Nuzha al-Jedid (☎ 641 298) on Rue Kasti, off Ave du General Fouad Chehab. There's a sign out the front saying Turk Bain. It's open to men and women each day from 7 to 1 am, and costs LL17,000 for the works. Soap and towels are provided.

Bus Ride

One of the most interesting things you can do to get a feel for the city is to just jump on a bus and see where it takes you. It's a cheap way to sightsee at LL500 and a good way to meet some locals. The buses tend to crawl through the traffic so you'll see plenty, in-

cluding the suburbs of Beirut which haven't come under any restoration plan yet.

Places to Stay – Budget

The cheapest accommodation in Beirut is in Ain al-Mreisse and near Charles Helou bus station, however it's not cheap by Middle East standards.

Hotel al-Shahbaa (☎ 564 287, *Rue des Libereteurs, Remeil*) is conveniently placed near the Charles Helou bus station. To get there walk up the steps from the bus station to Avenue Charles Helou and you'll see a sign for the hotel in front of you. It's a friendly place, reasonably clean and beds costs LL5000 in four and five-bed rooms. It has kitchen facilities and the rooms have fans.

Pension Home Valery (☎ 364 906, *Saab Bldg, Rue Phoenicia, Ain al-Mreisse*) is the backpacker favourite with dorm beds for US$5 and basic singles/doubles (some with balcony) with shared bathrooms for US$7/10; showers are an extra LL2500. It's in an unmarked building next to the Wash Me car wash; you can't miss it, as there's a car hanging off the building. Go through the first door on your right after the car wash and walk straight ahead until you reach a lift. There are three hotels in the building, two of them called Pension Home Valery, both with friendly, English-speaking management and charging the same prices. The one on the 3rd floor has better rooms; the 2nd floor version (☎ 362 169) was about to be renovated at the time of writing. The 4th floor hotel, *Pension Mehanna*, is overpriced and not recommended.

Hotel Glayeul (☎ 869 690, *Rue Minet al-Hosn, Ain al-Mreisse*) is in a great position on the waterfront and has rooms with shared bathroom for US$10/20. At the time of writing the rooms and bathroom were rundown but were due to be renovated and the terrace restaurant overlooking the sea was to be reopened.

Hotel Regis (☎ 361 845, *Rue Razi, Ain al-Mreisse*), down a small side street almost opposite the Glayeul, is a step up in quality with 20 standard rooms with bathroom costing US$20/25.

University Hotel (☎ *365 391, Rue Bliss, Ras Beirut*) is the best budget option if you're prepared to pay a little more. Home to many AUB students, it is also open to travellers and charges US$10 in a four-bed dorm; rooms start at US$15/20 and don't have fans but do have private bathrooms and are cheaper for stays of a week or longer. The more expensive rooms (US$20/30) have balconies and great views across the harbour.

San Lorenzo Hotel (☎ *348 604/5, Rue Hamra, Hamra*) is above the Taverne Suisse restaurant. The rooms are clean and have fans and balconies, though the French doors on to the balcony don't seem to lock. Rooms with shared bathroom cost US$17/24; with a private bathroom they cost US$20/30.

Hotel Moonlight (☎ *352 308*) is on a side street between Rue Ibrahim Abdel Ali and Rue Omar ben Abdel-Aziz in Hamra. The rooms are average and cost US$20/25 with bathroom; there's no fan, and hot water in the evenings only.

Places to Stay – Mid-Range

Most of the mid-range hotels are in Hamra and come with bathroom, air-con and TV.

Embassy Hotel (☎ *340 814/5, Rue Makdissi, Hamra*) is a comfortable hotel with a bit of greenery where rooms cost US$35/50 plus 5% tax.

Mace Hotel (☎/fax *344 626/7, 340 720, Rue Jeanne d'Arc, Hamra*) is friendly, pleasant and has some character. Rooms are US$30/40, plus 5% tax, including breakfast.

Cedarland Hotel (☎ *340 233/4, fax 341 759, Rue Omar ben Abdel-Aziz, Hamra*) is new and clean and has a shared kitchen. Rooms cost US$35/40.

West House Residence (☎ *350 450/1, fax 352 450, Rue Sourati, Hamra*) has 24 self-contained studio apartments, each with a double bed or twin beds, a small sitting room and coffee making facilities. The rooms aren't as nice as the other mid-range hotels but it's a good deal at US$32 per room per night and US$200 per week; discounts are available to groups.

Lord's Hotel (☎ *740 383, fax 740 385, Rue Negib Ardati, Manara*) on the Corniche has smallish but pleasant rooms starting at US$40/45 and costing US$50/70 with sea views.

Places to Stay – Top End

All the top end hotels add a 16% service charge and 5% government tax to their prices. Most will also offer discounts of 25 to 50% during winter.

Mayflower Hotel (☎ *340 680, fax 342 038, Rue Neamé Yafet, Hamra*), in the lower range of the top end scale, has a pub downstairs which is a popular watering hole for expats, and a swimming pool upstairs. It's a friendly, pleasant place where rooms cost US$60/70.

Marble Tower Hotel (☎ *346 260, fax 346 262, Rue Makdissi, Hamra*) is a comfortable place with rooms which are a bit overpriced at US$78/90 but you can often negotiate a discount. Breakfast is included in the price.

Hotel Mediterranee (☎ *603 015, fax 603 014, email htlmed@cyberia.net.lb, Avenue du Général de Gaulle, Manara*) has lovely rooms with sea views for US$97/115.

Places to Eat

Beirut is full of eateries catering to all tastes and budgets, and it would be impossible to list them all in this space. Below is a selection in the Hamra, Ras Beirut and Achrafieh areas that should give you an idea of what's on offer and the prices. There are many small shops around this area selling supermarket goods, and a large supermarket, **Consumers Co-op**, downstairs in the building opposite the Marble Tower Hotel on Rue Makdissi.

Street Food Beirut has some of the best street food in the Middle East. Around Hamra and Ras Beirut there are loads of little shops turning out the most amazing food from tiny spaces; what's listed below is a small sampling. The usual system in these places is to order your food, pay at the till and then take your receipt to the food counter.

HAMRA AREA

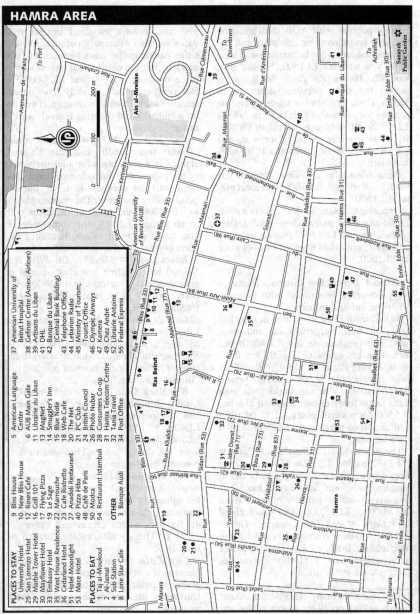

PLACES TO STAY
7   University Hotel
25   San Lorenzo Hotel
29   Marble Tower Hotel
30   Mayflower Hotel
33   Embassy Hotel
35   West House Residence
36   Cedarland Hotel
51   Hotel Moonlight
53   Mace Hotel

PLACES TO EAT
1   Taj al-Moukoul
2   Al-Jamal
4   Sub Station
8   Lone Star Cafe
9   Bliss House
10   New Bliss House
12   Roses Cafe
16   Grill 101
17   Flying Pizza
19   Le Sage
22   Marrouche
23   Cafe Ristretto
27   Anadoli Restaurant
40   Pizza Hiba
48   Café de Paris
50   Modca
54   Restaurant Istambuli

OTHER
3   Banque Audi
5   American Language
      Center
6   AUB Main Gate
11   Librairie du Liban
14   MagNet
15   Smuggler's Inn
18   Blue Note
20   Web Cafe
21   PC Club
24   The Net
26   Photo Nubar
28   Consumers Co-op
31   Hamra Telecom Centre
32   Tania Travel
34   Post Office
37   American University of
      Beirut Hospital
38   Gefinor Centre (Amex; Airlines)
39   Artisans du Liban
41   DHL
42   Banque du Liban
      (Central Bank Building)
43   Telephone Office
44   Lebanon Radio
45   Ministry of Tourism;
      Tourist Office
46   Olympic Airways
47   Kamera
49   Chez André
52   Librairie Antoine
55   Federal Express

To Downtown

To Port

To Achrafieh

To Manara

To American University of Beirut (AUB)

Sanayeh Public Garden

Ain al-Mreisse

Ras Beirut

Hamra

Le Sage (Rue Bliss, Ras Beirut) is extremely popular with AUB students. You can have feta cheese or chocolate and banana melted onto your Lebanese bread base while you wait for LL1500. Farther east, *New Bliss House (Rue Bliss, Ras Beirut)* is one of the most popular takeaways in Beirut. There are always loads of people queuing for *shwarmas* (LL2500) or *kebabs* (LL3500). *Bliss House*, next door on Rue Bliss, has generous serves of icecream and specialises in fresh juices (LL1750/3000 small/large).

Pizza Hiba (Rue de Rome, Hamra) has good, fresh spinach (LL1000) and meat pizzas (LL1500).

Opposite the National Museum is a great *felafel-shwarma place* where fresh felafel sandwiches cost LL1500. Two doors along is *Coktail*, which has huge servings of juice for LL3000.

Fastfood Beirut has fastfood joints of every conceivable variety, with a strong American cultural influence.

Sub Station (Rue Bliss, Ras Beirut) has steak, chicken, burgers, salad and great subs. The vegie delite sub (LL4000) and chocolate brownies (LL2500) are delicious. *Flying Pizza (☎ 353 975, Rue Khalidi, Hamra)* is a reasonably priced pizzeria where you can build your own pizza to eat there or take away. It charges LL5500 for a small pizza, LL11,00 for a medium-sized pizza and LL1250 for each extra topping.

The Ain al-Mreisse *Hard Rock Café (☎ 371 247, fax 369 079, Rue Minet al-Hosn)* is open from noon to midnight daily and to 1 am on Friday and Saturday. It has fabulous views and expensive burgers from LL12,000 to LL15,000. The other *Hard Rock Cafe (☎ 738 444, Concorde Galleria, Rue Verdun, Hamra)* has a bit more atmosphere, loads of Elvis and Beatles memorabilia and a Harley Davidson. There's a DJ every night.

Cafes There are many cafes dotted around the city selling excellent Arabic coffee and sweet pastries and in many establishments you can smoke a nargila. European-style cafes are also extremely popular. In most cafes Arabic coffee costs between LL1000 and LL1500 and pastries and sweets vary in price between LL1000 and LL3000. The European-style cafes usually have an extensive sandwich and salad menu. If you are on a budget avoid ordering Nescafé as it is usually expensive.

Cafe Ristretto (☎ 739 475), on the corner of Mahatma Gandhi and Rue Yamout, Hamra, is a great place for a leisurely read of the papers over breakfast or lunch. The food isn't the cheapest in town, but it's good quality and fresh. The *pain au chocolat* (LL2000) and stack of pancakes with maple syrup (LL5000) are recommended. It also has a range of salads, baguettes and good coffee.

Roses Cafe (☎ 348 153, Rue Bliss, Ras Beirut) has a filling breakfast special of pancakes and juice costing LL4000, with coffee for LL5500. It also specialises in frozen yoghurt.

Café de Paris (Rue Hamra, Hamra), near Librairie Antoine, has a 'watch the world go by' feel to it, as does *Modca (☎ 345 501, Rue Hamra, Hamra)*. Modca offers three cups of coffee for the price of one and traditional Lebanese food.

Bay Rock Cafe (Avenue du Général de Gaulle, Raouché) overlooks Pigeon Rocks and is a popular sunset spot. Crepes are LL4000 to LL6000 and salads are about LL7000. It must have the slowest service in town but this at least allows you time to contemplate the sunset.

Taj al-Moukoul (Ave de Paris, Ras Beirut) is an upmarket looking cafe without the upmarket prices. There's an amazing array of Lebanese sweets to choose from, 48 flavours of ice cream and cakes for LL2500. There's also another branch on Rue Bliss.

City Cafe (☎ 802 288, Rue Sadat, Hamra) is a cosmopolitan, groovy kind of place, popular with Lebanese American University students. It has excellent fresh mint tea.

Tribeca (☎ 339 123, *Rue Abdel Wahab al-Inglis, Yessoueiye*) is the only bagel place in town and has a casual, trendy atmosphere with relaxed background jazz music. Bagels cost about LL8000 and the large cafe lattes are good.

Bristol Hotel (☎ 353 438, *Rue Madame Curie, Snoubra*) has some of the best coffee and cakes in town, but be prepared to pay about LL9000 for morning tea.

Restaurants Beirut has an astounding variety of restaurants. There are many excellent restaurants serving Lebanese food but you'll also find many other international cuisines. Below is a selection with the emphasis on traditional Lebanese food. Most restaurants will add a 9 to 16% service charge to the bill.

Grill 101 (☎ 354 437, *Rue Makhoul, Hamra*) is a groovy kind of place with a good value pasta special. For LL7000 you can choose from a range of pastas and also receive a glass of wine or beer. There's also an à la carte menu with dishes such as calamari and steak ranging from LL12,000 to LL17,000.

Restaurant Istambuli (☎ 352 049, *Rue de Baalbek, Hamra*) serves tasty, traditional Lebanese food, is popular with local families and is excellent value.

Anadoli Restaurant (☎ 340 051, *Rue Makdissi, Hamra*) has interesting decor and good Lebanese food and service. A meal costs about US$10 per person.

Marrouche (☎ 743 185 *Rue Sidani, Hamra*) is a popular local chain with nice, reasonably priced Lebanese food and eclectic decor. The *fuul* (fava bean paste) with garlic (LL2500) is excellent.

Al-Jamal (☎ 364 003, *Ain al-Mreisse*) has good Lebanese food with generous mezzes costing LL2500 to LL4000. It's popular with young people in the evening for eating and nargilas. There are views of the Corniche and the sea from the outdoor balcony tables.

Al-Karam (*Raouché*) is friendly and good value and has a great range of mezzes for LL3000 each.

Lone Star Cafe (☎ 341 605, *Rue Bliss, Ras Beirut*) serves good Mexican food, with generous sized entrees costing LL6000 and main courses costing about LL12,000. This place is also good for a drink (see Entertainment).

Sirena (☎ 804 639, *off Rue Bliss, Ras Beirut*) offers traditional Indian cuisine in a setting that transports you to the sub-continent. The food is very good and costs about US$25 per person.

Sushi Bar (☎ 338 555, *Rue Monot, Achrafieh*) is close to all of Achrafieh's nightclubs and has a great reputation for Japanese food; expect to spend about US$25 per person.

Le Chef (☎ 445 373, *Rue Gouraud, Achrafieh*) is open from 8 am to 6 pm and is always packed at lunchtime; a meal costs about US$5 to US$7 per person.

Entertainment

Beirut is *the* place for nightlife in the Middle East. Thursday, Friday and Saturday are the big nights, but there are bands, music and DJs to be found every night of the week. It's worth ringing ahead and reserving a place at a nightclub, especially on Friday and Saturday night. Some places get so busy they only allow in people on the reservation list, and that doesn't even guarantee you a table; the action doesn't start at most clubs until at least 11 pm. The dress code is smart, but you don't need to go overboard.

There's a sprinkling of bars and clubs around Hamra but most of the popular clubs are in Achrafieh. There are about 10 within walking distance of each other, so it's possible to check out a few in one evening. There are also a few popular clubs on the way to, and in, Jounieh. Unlike the expat bars in Hamra, you won't find the locals just drinking; Beirutis go out to drink and dance or drink and eat or both. Most clubs don't have a cover charge but wine, beer and shots of spirits cost LL10,000 a go.

The 'in' places change quickly and there are new places opening up all the time so

LEBANON

ask around and check the social page of the *Daily Star* for new venues. Beware of the 'super nightclubs' – usually strip joints or brothels rather than superior nightclubs – around Ain al-Mreisse.

Beirut also has a reasonable selection of cinemas showing new release movies.

Bars *Blue Note* (☎ 344 362, *Rue Makhoul, Hamra*) has live jazz music on Friday and Saturday nights with a cover charge of LL6000. A local beer costs LL4500 and imported brands and spirits cost LL6500. There's also a pleasant restaurant offering mezze dishes that start at LL3000 for a humous or eggplant dip and main courses that start at LL8500. It attracts the 25 to 50 year old crowd.

Smuggler's Inn (☎ 354 941, *Rue Makhoul, Hamra*) a few doors down is a popular, laid-back pub popular with 20 to 30 year olds most nights of the week. It has groovy taped music and local beer for LL3000. There's a small menu to order from (the salads are the nicest).

Chez André (☎ 345 662, *Rue Hamra, Hamra*) is one of the nicer bars to survive the war in Lebanon. It's popular with locals over 35 and has an avant-garde kind of feel. Beers are LL2500. It's the third shop on your left-hand side in an arcade off Rue Hamra, and is open daily except Sunday from 8 am until at least 11 pm.

J-Paul's (☎ 204 779, *Rue Abdel Wahab al-Inglizi, Achrafieh*) is a busy, down-to-earth, spacious pub-restaurant with a positive energy. It attracts all ages and if all else fails you can usually get in without a booking.

La Closerie (Time Out) (☎ 331 938, *Rue du Liban, Achrafieh*) is an old house which has been turned into a pub-restaurant. Choose from the three mellow, lounge room-style areas to chill out in. It's one of the few places where it's easy to have a conversation over the music. In summer the pleasant terrace area is also opened up. It's popular with 25 to 40 year olds.

Pacifico (☎ 204 446, *Rue Monot, Achrafieh*) is a down-to-earth bar with good DJ music, popular with 20-somethings. Look hard or you'll miss it.

Téatro (☎ 616 617, *Avenue de L'Independence, Achrafieh*) is an old house turned into a very beautiful pub. The feature chandelier was inspired by the Haunted House at Euro Disney. There are friezes on the wall, reproduction-style paintings, paintings on the table and a theatre-style balustrade. The music level is a bit lower than other places before 11 pm, but cranks up afterwards. It's popular with the 30 to 45 age group.

Zinc (☎ 612 612, *Rue Seifeddine al-Khatib, Achrafieh*) is another old house turned into a music venue. It's decorated tastefully with original art work, mosaic scraps from Beirut Central District, there's an outdoor terrace and an amazing chandelier. It's popular even on Wednesday nights.

Sports Cafe (☎ 335 600, *Avenue du General Fouad Chehab, Achrafieh*) is a Canadian chain pub-restaurant with a multitude of TV sets showing sports events. It attracts a down-to-earth young crowd and is best when there's a big sports event on.

Lone Star Cafe (☎ 341 605, *Rue Bliss, Hamra*) is across the road from the AUB and attracts a young crowd. There's a DJ most nights serving up popular commercial music, while the bar serves some amazing cocktails.

TGI Friday's (☎ 802 587, *Avenue du Général de Gaulle*) is another chain popular with young people. It's a good place to have a drink and watch the sunset over Pigeon Rocks and there's a happy hour most nights.

Clubs *Monkey Rose* (☎ 362 666, *Rue Faculte, Achrafieh*) has great dance music after 11.30 pm and is popular with teenagers and university students.

Club 70-Unplugged (☎ 362 544, *Rue Phoênicia, Ain al-Mreisse*) has live international bands, mostly playing jazz, soul and funk, and doubles as a restaurant. It's got a groovy kind of feel, some nice art work and appeals mostly to the 25 to 45 age bracket. There's a US$10 cover charge.

Gotha (☎ 336 533, Rue Monot, Achrafieh) is French for elite group, and that does tend to be what the clientele think of themselves. There's a live singer and a dance floor, and lots of make-up and expensive cars.

B018 (☎ 03-800 018, next to Forum de Beyrouth, Beirut-Jounieh highway) is the most liberal club in town; gays and lesbians will feel comfortable here. It was the most popular club at the time of writing and has techno-rave music, which turns to Latin-disco after 2 am. It's also got a movable roof to release the cigarette smoke. The nightclub is underground so don't look for a sign. It's about 10km from Beirut Central District; ask a taxi driver for the club or Forum de Beyrouth.

Cinemas There are a few cinemas showing a good selection of foreign films. The most convenient for many travellers will be *Concorde* (☎ 738 440, Rue Verdun), next to the Hard Rock Cafe, with seven screens showing new release movies for LL10,000. It charges LL5000 for matinees and on Monday and Wednesday night. In Achrafieh there's the *Empire Achrafieh* (☎ 328 806, Avenue Du General Fouad Chehab, Achrafieh) and *La Sagesse* (☎ 585 111, Rue Sagesse, Achrafieh).

Shopping

Beirut is full of shops, stalls and markets where you can buy everything from locally woven rugs to electronic calculators and the latest fashion wear, often at good prices.

To buy handicrafts, try Artisans du Liban et d'Orient in Ain al-Mreisse or Artisans du Liban on Rue Clémenceau in Hamra. They both collect the work of artisans from around the country and sell them at reasonable prices to promote the local crafts.

Getting There & Away

Air Beirut international airport is served by the local carrier, Middle East Airlines (MEA), and several Arab, Asian and European airlines.

Several airlines have their offices in the Gefinor Centre in Hamra, including British Airways (☎ 739 813), Cathay Pacific Airways (☎ 361 230), Gulf Air (☎ 361 230), KLM-Royal Dutch Airlines (☎ 510 088) and MEA (☎ 737 000). Elsewhere are the following:

Air Canada
  (☎ 811 690) Rue Verdun
Air France
  (☎ 864 492/3) Rue Bliss
Air India
  (☎ 336 282) Sanayeh
Alitalia
  (☎ 340 280) Rue Hamra
Lufthansa Airlines
  (☎ 349 001) Rue Hamra
Olympic Airways
  (☎ 340 285) Rue Hamra

Bus, Microbus & Service Taxi Buses, microbuses and service taxis to destinations north of Beirut leave from Charles Helou bus station. To the south and south-east they leave from the Cola stand.

Charles Helou Bus Station Ahdab (☎ 587 507) runs new buses to Jounieh (LL1500, 30 minutes), Byblos (Jbail; LL1500, one hour) and Tripoli (LL2000, 90 minutes). Buses leave every five minutes between 6 am and 10 pm. Kotob (☎ 587 506) operates older buses every 15 minutes between 6 am and 6.30 pm to Jounieh, Byblos and Tripoli for a flat fare of LL1000. Microbuses to destinations north leave from Dawra, a suburb of Beirut which was the transport hub before Charles Helou was established. (For more information see the main Getting There & Away and Getting Around sections of this chapter.)

If you're going to Syria you need to go to Zone A of Charles Helou bus station, where you will probably be swamped by people offering you private or service taxis or buses. If you want a bus go straight to the Beirut Pullman Company office (☎ 587 467), which sells tickets for all the private and government buses going to Syria. There are two offices: one sells tickets to all Syrian destinations, the other only sells tickets to Damascus, but the prices are the same. The buses are not super luxurious but they are clean and have allocated (numbered) seats. You can usually get a seat quite easily, but to be sure book the day before. Buses to Damascus (LL7000, four hours) leave every 30 minutes between 5 am and 10 pm; buses to Aleppo (LL10,500, seven hours) leave every 30 minutes between 7 am and midnight; and buses to Lattakia (LL9000, 4½ hours) leave at 10.30 am and 2 pm daily. You must have a Syrian visa or you will not be allowed on the bus.

A service taxi to Jounieh/Byblos/Tripoli will cost LL2000/4000/6000. Service taxis to Damascus cost US$8 while private taxis cost US$40. You usually don't have to wait more than 20 minutes for a service taxi to fill up.

Cola Bus Station The Lebanese Transportation Company (☎ 07-720 566) operates blue and white buses from Cola to Sidon (one hour) and Tyre (two hours) for LL500. Express buses cost LL1250/1500. Microbuses to Sidon/Tyre cost LL1000/2000 and services taxis cost LL2500/5000.

Getting Around
To/From the Airport Beirut international airport is approximately 5km south of Beirut. You can get the bus from the airport but the only hassle is that the airport bus stop is at the roundabout at the airport exit, a 1km walk from the terminal. The red and white Lebanese Commuting Company bus No 1 will take you from the airport roundabout to Rue Sadat in Hamra; bus No 5 will take you to Charles Helou bus station. The blue and white government bus Nos 7 and 10 also stop at the airport roundabout. Bus No 10 goes to Charles Helou bus station and bus No 7 goes to Raouché; from there you can take bus No 9 to Hamra. Fares are LL500. The buses operate between 5.30 am and 6 pm daily and the maximum wait should be 10 minutes.

Taxis from the airport are notoriously expensive, charging US$25 for the trip into town. A cheaper option is to walk 1km to the highway and hail a service taxi into town for LL2000. It's cheaper from Beirut to the airport, as taxis will usually charge LL10,000 for the trip.

During daylight hours microbuses often drop people at the airport so it can be worthwhile waiting at the departures exit for one (LL1000 into town).

Bus Beirut is well covered with a network of buses. The red and white buses are run by the privately owned Lebanese Commuting Company (☎ 744 172) and the large blue and white buses are government owned.

The buses operate on a 'hail and ride' system: just wave at the driver and they'll stop. The only actual bus stops are where the bus starts and finishes.

There are no timetables but buses come usually every five minutes and 10 minutes maximum. At the time of writing Lebanese Commuting Company was planning to hand out bus route maps to all passengers and also to expand its bus routes further. Most of its buses run from 5.30 am to 9.30 pm, though some routes, such as the airport bus, finish at 6 pm.

There are maps of the government-owned bus routes posted up at Charles Helou station; these buses operate between 6 am and 7 pm. The main bus routes are listed. Bus trips cost LL500 (LL1000 for longer journeys).

Lebanese Commuting Company
No 1 Rue Sadat (Hamra), Rue Emile Edde, Hotel Bristol, Rue Verdun, Cola roundabout, airport roundabout, Kafaat

No 2 Rue Sadat (Hamra), Rue Emile Edde, Radio Lebanon, Sassine Square, Dawra, Antelias

No 3 Ain al-Mreisse, Bain Militaire, Raouche, Verdun, Museum, Dawra

No 4 Wardieh, Radio Lebanon, Riad al-Solh Square, Martyrs Square, Fouad Chehab, Yessoueieye, Sfeir

No 5 Charles Helou bus station, Place des Martyrs, Fouad Chehab, Yessoueiye, the airport roundabout, Hay as-Seloum

No 6 Dawra, Antelias, Jounieh, Jbail (Byblos)

No 7 Museum, Beit Meri, Broummana, Baabda

No 12 Wardieh, Radio Lebanon, Cola roundabout, Borj al Brajne

No 13 Charles Helou bus station, Martyrs Square, Riad al Solh Square, Cola roundabout

No 14 Cola roundabout, airport roundabout, Lebanese University, Khalde

No 15 Cola roundabout, airport roundabout, Aquiba

Government Buses

No 1 Bain Militaire, Khalde

No 4 Dawra, Jounieh

No 7 Bain Militaire, airport

No 10 Charles Helou station, airport roundabout

No 11 Charles Helou station, Lebanese University

No 16 Charles Helou station, Cola roundabout

No 17 Museum, Broumanna

No 23 Bain Militaire, Dawra

No 24 Museum, Hamra

Taxi & Service Taxi Private taxi companies usually have meters and can quote you an approximate fare on the phone. If you hail a taxi on the street, chances are it won't have a meter and you have to agree on the fare before getting into the car. Always make sure you do this to avoid any arguments at the end. Within Beirut taxis charge anywhere from LL5000 to LL8000, depending on your destination. Private taxi offices include:

Auto Tour	(☎ 888 222)
Lebanon Taxi	(☎ 353 152/3)
TV Taxi	(☎ 862 489)

Service taxis cover the major routes in Beirut. They can be hailed anywhere around town and will drop you off at any point along their established route. The fare is LL1000 on established routes within the city and LL2000 to outlying suburbs.

Around Beirut

MOUNTAIN RESORTS

There are a few mountain resorts around Beirut which are easy to get to and a welcome change from the heat in summer and the traffic of the city. You may go through some of them while travelling around Lebanon but they also make a nice day trip from Beirut.

Beit Meri & Broummana

Set in pine forests some 800m above and 17km east of Beirut, Beit Meri offers panoramic views over the capital. It dates back to Phoenician times and has Roman and Byzantine ruins, including some fine floor mosaics in a Byzantine church dating from the 5th century. There is also a 17th century Maronite monastery built with the remains of a Roman temple.

About 4km north-east from Beit Meri is Broummana, a bustling town full of hotels, eateries, cafes, shops and nightclubs. Broummana has a lot of charm and is a nice place to wander around, particularly in summer.

Service taxis from the National Museum or Dawra charge LL2000 to Beit Meri or Broummana. You can get off to have a look at Beit Meri and from there either walk to Broummana or take another service taxi (LL1000), or get the No 7 LLC bus or No 17 government bus from near the museum.

Faraya

If you're into skiing, try Faraya, a ski resort 50km north-east of Beirut (about one hour's drive). Faraya resort (☎ 341 034) is equipped with ski lifts and chairs. There are hotels, though they are usually fully booked during the ski season. Weekday/weekend passes cost US$18/28.50 for adults and are slightly cheaper for children.

JOUNIEH

Once a sleepy little village on a magnificent bay, Jounieh, 21km north of Beirut, is a modern resort and high-rise playground full of restaurants, shops and nightclubs. Only the old part of town, centred on Rue Mina which runs along the bay, has retained some of its previous charm. You get glimpses of the water between the beach resorts (entry fees LL8000 to LL10,000) that line Rue Mina.

Jounieh extends from the classy district of Kaslik, full of expensive cars, shops and beautiful people, to Maamaltein, home of the casino. The places to stay and eat mentioned later are midway between the two, close to the British Bank and *baladiyé* (municipality building).

Information

Cafe Net has Internet facilities for US$5 per hour, as well as coffee and cake for sale. To get there head south down Rue Mina, turn left at the roundabout and take your first right (there's a sign to Beirut) and it's about 50m up the hill on your left. The Holiday Suites Hotel also has Internet facilities available to the public for US$6 per hour.

Casino de Liban

This famous casino (☎ 932 933) at the northern end of the bay is a huge complex full of glitter, dancing girls, restaurants and, of course, gambling. The slot machine area is open from noon to 4 am and the gaming rooms are open from 8 pm to 4 am. You're meant to be over 21 and wearing smart casual gear (no jeans and sports shoes) to get in.

Téléphérique

There's a cable car *(téléphérique)* (☎ 914 324) from Jounieh up to the mountain-top Basilica of Our Lady of Lebanon. The views are breathtaking and the return ride costs LL7000/4500 for adults/children. It operates daily except Monday from 10 am (except for Tuesday when it starts at 1 pm) to 7.30 pm (to 11.30 pm between July and October).

Places to Stay & Eat

Hotel St-Joseph (☎ 931 189, Rue Mina), about 100m north of the British Bank, has friendly owners and is really a pension charging US$20 for a basic small room (one or two people) and US$30 for a large room (two or three people), all with shower and toilet. It's a lovely old house with high vaulted ceilings, 12 spacious rooms, and a common lounge, kitchen and terrace.

Holiday Suites Hotel (☎ 933 907, 639 038, email holidaysuites@usa.net, Rue Mina), behind British Bank, is a new hotel with nice rooms overlooking the sea. Pierre, the general manager, is helpful and charges US$55/65/85 for singles/doubles/suites (sleeping three), plus 14% service and 5% tax.

Jus Cocktail (Rue Mina), about 100m south of the British Bank, has a terrace overlooking the sea and excellent fresh fruit juices starting at LL3000 for a (very large) small glass. *J Kabab (Rue Mina)*, 220m south of the British Bank, serves toasted sandwiches, mezzes, salad and grills at reasonable prices.

There are sandwich bars and restaurants on Rue Mina with the standard shwarma, felafel, cheese, meat, chicken etc.

Fahed (one block east of the British Bank and Rue Mina) is a reasonably large supermarket to get supplies from.

Entertainment

There's plenty of nightlife in Jounieh. Beware of the 'super nightclubs' which tend to have tacky dance shows with plenty of female escorts on hand.

Amor Y Libertad (☎ 640 881), below Kaslik Cinema in Kaslik, is an amazing Cuban club-restaurant. If you only go to one nightclub in Lebanon this should be it. It's expensive at US$20 for the cover charge (which entitles you to two drinks) but it's an unforgettable experience. There's a live band playing Latin American and world music, a Blues Brother lookalike singing and dancing on the bar, and a nice crowd, mostly aged between 25 and 50. The highlight though is Musbah, a gay male belly-dancer who is absolutely sensational and has to be seen to be believed. He performs on Thursday, Friday and Saturday at 11.30 pm.

Oliver's (☎ 934 616, Maamaltein) has food, drink and music and is popular with the young local crowd.

Getting There & Away

A combination of two buses will get you to Jounieh for LL1000 (see the Beirut Getting

Around section for details). Service taxis from Hamra to Dawra and then Dawra to Jounieh cost LL2000 each. A private taxi from Jounieh to Hamra costs LL20,000.

JEITTA GROTTO

The stalactites and stalagmites in the caves at Jeitta Grotto (☎ 220 840) are some of the most stunning in the world. The vast honeycomb of galleries and ravines has been known to humans since Paleolithic times but was first surveyed in the 19th century and opened to the public in 1958. This is Lebanon's most touristy site and also the most well looked after. There are walkways through the caves, souvenir shops and restaurants at the entrance to the grotto. Once you're inside a toy train takes you to the caves and a cable car takes you back (a very over the top way of avoiding a five minute walk).

In summer there's a boat ride through the lower caverns (usually closed in winter because of flooding). The upper galleries are open all year. Photography is forbidden. Entrance for adults is LL10,500, children aged four to 14, LL6250 and under four, free. The caves are open from 9 am to 6 pm Tuesday to Saturday and from 8 am to 7 pm Sunday. They're closed Monday, except on public holidays.

You can get a bus or service taxi from Beirut to the turn-off on the right of the Beirut-Jounieh highway to the grotto. There are usually service taxis waiting at the turn-off which should take you to the grotto for LL1000. It's well worthwhile as it's otherwise a 1½ hour walk (mostly uphill). If you're lucky enough to get a service taxi from the grotto to Jounieh it will cost LL2000; otherwise a taxi is LL10,000.

North of Beirut

BYBLOS (JBAIL)

Byblos is one of the world's oldest continually inhabited towns and most of the world's great civilisations were there at one point or another. These days Byblos is a small town where tourism and fishing are the main industries.

History

Excavations have shown that Byblos (biblical name Gebal) was inhabited during the Neolithic period 7000 years ago. In the 3rd millennium BC it became the most important trading port in the area and sent cedar wood and oil to Egypt in exchange for gold, alabaster, papyrus rolls and linen. It continued to be the major Phoenician centre until the 10th century BC and developed an alphabetic phonetic script which was the precursor of modern alphabets.

The Greeks called Gebal Byblos after the Greek word for papyrus, *bublos*, because papyrus was shipped from Egypt to Greece via the Phoenician port. A collection of sheets were called *biblion*, or book, so from the Greek *ta b blia*, or 'the books', the English word 'Bible' was derived.

As of the 1st millennium BC, Byblos suffered successive invasions, from the Persians to Alexander the Great, the Romans, the Byzantines, the Arabs and, finally, the Crusaders, who built a castle and moat using the large stones and granite columns of the Roman temples. Following the Crusaders' departure Byblos was ruled by the Ottomans, who made Beirut their major trading city, and Byblos plunged into obscurity.

Orientation & Information

The town itself stretches from just outside the perimeter of the ruins to the old port which is sheltered by a craggy headland. A hotel and restaurants are clustered around the port. Opposite the entrance to the ruins are more restaurants and sandwich bars and a few souqs full of souvenir shops.

The tourist office (☎ 940 325), about 30m north of the entrance to the archaeological site, is open from 8 am to 4 pm daily (except Sunday in winter) but don't expect much more information than brochures.

For Internet facilities, Bytes Shop (☎ 546 107) is open from noon to 3 am and charges LL6000 per hour. CD Master (☎ 546 238) is open 24 hours and charges LL7500 per hour for use of the Internet.

Byblos Bank on Rue Jbail has an ATM for Visa and MasterCard cash advances. Also on that street, Metropolitan Bank and Banque Libanaise Pour Le Commerce theoretically change travellers cheques but charge a hefty commission (US$1 per cheque with a US$5 minimum and US$4 per cheque respectively) and you must show your purchase receipts (the ones that you're supposed to keep separate from your travellers cheques.)

The post office is just off Rue Jbail. Turn left at the street which has Diab Brothers on the corner and the post office is 20m up the hill on your right. It's on the second floor; there's a small sign at street level.

Ruins

This ancient site is entered through the restored **Crusader castle** which dominates the city's medieval ramparts. The 12th century castle was built from monumental blocks, some of the largest used in any construction in the Middle East. There are some glorious views of Byblos from the castle ramparts which also give you a very clear idea of the layout of the site and a chance to ponder the remains of 17 civilisations.

The earliest remains are **Neolithic huts** from the 5th millennium BC and the crushed limestone floors and low retaining walls can still be seen. The **temple of Baalat Gebal** (the Lady of Byblos) from 2800 BC was the largest and most important temple constructed at Byblos and was rebuilt a number of times in the two millennia that it survived. Ten jars of offerings to the goddess Gebal found during excavations are now in the National Museum. During the Roman period the temple was replaced with a Roman structure and there are the remains of a **Roman colonnade** leading to it. There are also the foundations of a **L-shaped temple** dating from 2700 BC and an **Obelisk temple** from the early 2nd millennium BC where offerings of human figurines encrusted in gold leaf were discovered. There were nine **royal tombs** cut in vertical shafts deep into the rock in the 2nd millennium

BC; some of the sarcophagi found are now housed in the National Museum, including that of King Aharim whose sarcophagus has an early Phoenician alphabet inscription. One-third of the **Roman theatre** has been restored and placed near the cliff edge, giving some great views across the sea. In the centre of the site is a deep depression which was once the **king's well**, a spring that supplied the city with water until the end of the Hellenistic era.

The site is open daily from 8 am to sunset and entrance is LL6000. The gatekeeper can arrange a guide to give a tour of about 45 minutes (US$10); it's worthwhile if you can afford it.

Many remains from the site can be seen in the National Museum in Beirut and in a small collection in the AUB Archaeological Museum. There are also numerous artefacts on sale in the shops of Byblos, more than from most other sites as the director of items decided to sell to a number of collectors antiquities that were not considered unique.

Wax Museum & Church of St John the Baptist

The Wax Museum (☎ 540 463) is on the road to the port. It portrays the history and culture of Lebanon through the ages in a series of rather bizarre and sometimes creepy tableaus. Don't expect the wax works to be anything like the standard of Madame Tussaud's, however the traditional costumes worn by the figures are quite impressive. It's open year-round from 9 am to 6 pm; admission is overpriced at LL5000.

Near the Wax Museum is the Church of St John the Baptist, a Romanesque-style cathedral with three apses, a building the Crusaders began constructing in 1115AD. The church is an interesting mix of Arab and Italian designs and there are some quite well preserved Byzantine mosaics in the areas adjoining the church.

Boat Rides

Down by the port the fishers take visitors on 15 minute rides in their small boats for LL4000 per person from spring until autumn.

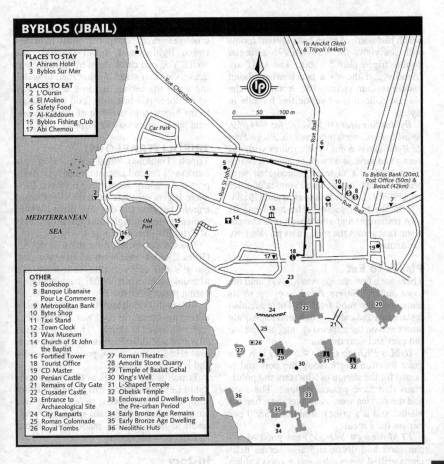

BYBLOS (JBAIL)

PLACES TO STAY
1 Ahiram Hotel
3 Byblos Sur Mer

PLACES TO EAT
2 L'Oursin
4 El Molino
6 Safety Food
7 Al-Kaddoum
15 Byblos Fishing Club
17 Abi Chemou

MEDITERRANEAN

SEA

Old Port

To Amchit (3km)
& Tripoli (44km)

0   50   100 m

To Byblos Bank (20m),
Post Office (50m) &
Beirut (42km)

OTHER
5 Bookshop
8 Banque Libanaise
  Pour Le Commerce
9 Metropolitan Bank
10 Bytes Shop
11 Taxi Stand
12 Town Clock
13 Wax Museum
14 Church of St John
   the Baptist
16 Fortified Tower
18 Tourist Office
19 CD Master
20 Persian Castle
21 Remains of City Gate
22 Crusader Castle
23 Entrance to
   Archaeological Site
24 City Ramparts
25 Roman Colonnade
26 Royal Tombs
27 Roman Theatre
28 Amorite Stone Quarry
29 Temple of Baalat Gebal
30 King's Well
31 L-Shaped Temple
32 Obelisk Temple
33 Enclosure and Dwellings from
   the Pre-urban Period
34 Early Bronze Age Remains
35 Early Bronze Age Dwelling
36 Neolithic Huts

Places to Stay

Camping *Camping Amchit Les Colombes*
(☎ *540 322, 943 782*) in Amchit, 3km north
of Byblos, is a lush camping ground on a
promontory overlooking the sea. With the
capacity for 1500 people, it's fully self-contained and has all necessary amenities, including showers, toilets (with facilities for
handicapped people), kitchen with gas
burners and electrical points for caravans
(220V). A camp site costs US$3 per person
(half price for children) and a tent is

US$1.50. In addition to tent and caravan
sites, there are also fully furnished chalets
(US$25 for two people, US$30 for three or
four people), with their own bathroom and
air-con, and 'tungalows' (a bungalow in the
shape of a tent with two beds and toilet)
which cost US$20 and sleep two people.
Each tungalow comes with a hammock.
The camping ground is set on a wooded
cliff-top with steps down to its own rocky
beach. You can get there by service taxi
from Byblos (LL1000) or Beirut (LL4000).

Hotels *Ahiram Hotel* (☎ 540 440) on the beach just north of town has pleasant rooms with sea views for US$48/68/78 a single/double/triple plus 5% tax. The staff are friendly and there's a beach where hotel residents can swim. The hotel has the biggest collection of antiquities for sale in Byblos.

Byblos Sur Mer (☎ 548 000, fax 944 859, email byblos.mer@inco.com.lb, Plage Port de Byblos) has comfortable rooms with sea views and air-con as well as its own swimming pool. It's tastefully decorated with prints and Byblos artefacts. Singles/doubles are US$60/72 in the low season and US$84/102 in the high season. The hotel has its own restaurant and also operates *L'Oursin* restaurant across the road on its private jetty in summer.

Places to Eat
There are a few cheap takeaways around the town square. *Safety Food* lives up to its name and has good felafels. There are also restaurants and cafes, which tend to be quite smart and on the expensive side, around the old port and near the ruins.

Byblos Fishing Club (☎ 549 213) is in a great location overlooking the port and is famed for the stream of film stars and politicians that have passed through. The food and the service were very average when we visited and it's pricey at about US$30 per person for a meal.

El Molino (☎ 541 555) has good Mexican food and decor and also serves delicious grilled vegetables and a good kahlua chocolate mousse. A meal costs about US$15 per person.

Abi Chemou (☎ 540 484), near the entrance to the ruins, has a cafe downstairs and a restaurant upstairs where a lunch of mezze, a grill, fruit and coffee will set you back about US$15.

Al-Kaddoum (☎ 946 806) has excellent fresh fruit juices and delicious cakes.

Getting There & Away
The service taxi stand is at the town's main square. A service taxi to Beirut or Tripoli costs LL4000. LCC bus No 6 and microbuses travel along the coast road between Byblos and Beirut (LL500, one hour). You can catch them by waiting near the service taxi stand on Rue Jbail or walking up to the service road of the highway where there is a bus stop. You can also go to the highway to hail one of the large private buses on its way to Tripoli.

TRIPOLI (TRABLOUS)
Tripoli (Trablous), 86km north of Beirut, is Lebanon's second largest city and the main port and trading scentre for northern Lebanon. It gets its name from the Greek word *tripolis* because the city had three parts in ancient times, though there are no remains of Tripoli's Phoenician past.

The Crusaders left their mark in the St-Gilles Citadel, which towers over the city, but it's the city's medieval history and Mamluk architecture which make it a fascinating place to visit.

Although Tripoli had its share of fighting during the Lebanese civil war, it was not as badly damaged as Beirut. It has retained the charm of a Middle Eastern city, with its narrow alleys, souqs, slow pace and friendly and hospitable people.

Tripoli is also famous as the sweets capital of Lebanon, so any trip to the city is not complete without a visit to one of its Arabic sweet shops. The main speciality is *halawat al-jibn*, a sweet made from cheese and served with syrup.

History
Like other Phoenician cities along the eastern Mediterranean coast, Tripoli (ancient Arados) had a succession of invaders from the Romans to the Persians and Byzantines. After its occupation by the Arabs in the 7th century AD, it again became an important trading centre. Then in the 12th century it fell to the Crusaders, led by Raymond de St-Gilles, who built the citadel overlooking the city. The Crusaders remained for 180 years, until the city was captured by the Mamluks in 1289. The old city, built around the base of the citadel, dates back to this era.

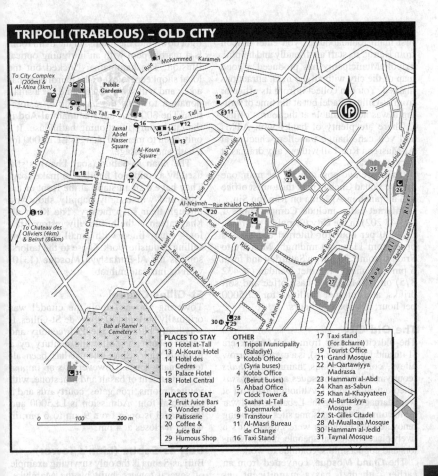

TRIPOLI (TRABLOUS) – OLD CITY

To City Complex
(200m) &
Al-Mina (3km)

Rue Mohammed Karameh

Public
Gardens

Rue Tall

Jamal
Abdel
Nasser
Square

Al-Koura
Square

Rue Fouad Chehab

Rue Cheikh Mohammed al-Jisr

To Chateau des
Oliviers (4km)
& Beirut (86km)

Rue Cheikh Nassif al-Yaziji

Rue Cheikh Nassif al-Yaziji

Rue Cheikh Rachid Mikati

Rue Tall

Al-Nejmeh — Rue Khaled Chebab
Square

Rue Rachid
Rida

Rue Ahmad al-Rifai

Rue Cheikh Nassif al-Yaziji

Bab al-Ramel
Cemetery

Rue Emir Fakhr al-Din

Rue Rachid Karami

Rue Rachid Karami

Abou Ali River

0   100   200 m

PLACES TO STAY	OTHER	
10 Hotel at-Tall	1 Tripoli Municipality	17 Taxi stand
13 Al-Koura Hotel	(Baladiyé)	(For Bcharré)
14 Hotel des	3 Kotob Office	19 Tourist Office
Cedres	(Syria buses)	21 Grand Mosque
15 Palace Hotel	4 Kotob Office	22 Al-Qartawiyya
18 Hotel Central	(Beirut buses)	Madrassa
	5 Ahbad Office	23 Hammam al-Abd
PLACES TO EAT	7 Clock Tower &	24 Khan as-Sabun
2 Fruit Juice Bars	Saahat al-Tall	25 Khan al-Khayyateen
6 Wonder Food	9 Supermarket	26 Al-Burtasiyya
12 Patisserie	8 Transtour	Mosque
20 Coffee &	11 Al-Masri Bureau	27 St-Gilles Citadel
Juice Bar	de Change	28 Al-Muallaqa Mosque
29 Humous Shop	16 Taxi Stand	30 Hammam al-Jedid
		31 Taynal Mosque

Orientation & Information

There are two main parts to Tripoli: Al-Mina (the port area), which juts out into the sea; and the city proper, which includes modern Tripoli and the old medina. The centre is at Saahat at-Tall (pronounced 'at-tahl'), a large square by the clock tower where you will find the service taxi and bus stands, most of the cheap eateries and hotels. (This is where you will be dropped off when you arrive by public transport in Tripoli.)

The old city sprawls east of Saahat at-Tall, while the modern centre is west of the square, along Rue Fouad Chehab. On this street there are banks, moneychangers, travel agencies, bookshops, pharmacies etc.

Between Rue Fouad Chehab and Al-Mina are broad avenues with residential buildings, and a modern shopping complex with Internet cafes, cinemas and restaurants. In Al-Mina, which is also an older part of the city, you'll find more hotels, restaurants and cafes, banks and moneychangers.

The tourist office (☎ 433 590) is on the first main roundabout as you enter Tripoli from Beirut. Its staff are friendly and helpful. Tripoli Municipality has produced a good map of the city with all the main attractions marked. You can collect it from its office or from St-Gilles Citadel but at the time of writing it was not available at the tourist office.

There are plenty of banks with ATMs and you can change travellers cheques at Al-Masri on Rue Tall without any dramas at very good rates.

There are two post offices, the main one on Rue Fouad Chehab near the tourist office and a branch in Al-Mina on Rue Ibn Sin.

Internet cafes include CompuGames 1 (☎ 448 202) in the City Complex, charging LL4000 per hour for Internet access. It's open from 11 am to midnight Monday to Friday, from 2.30 pm on Saturday and from 6 pm on Sunday. Internet Dandan (☎ 432 875) on Al-Mina Ave has coffee and soft drinks, and Internet facilities for LL5000 per hour; it's open 24 hours.

The Old City

The old city, dating from the Mamluk era (14th and 15th centuries), is a maze of narrow alleys, colourful souqs, hammams, *khans* (courtyarded inns), mosques and *madrassas* (theological schools). Although parts of it were damaged during the Lebanese civil war (at the time of writing, some sites were being renovated while others were closed), it's a lively place where craftspeople, including tailors and coppersmiths, continue to work.

The **Grand Mosque**, converted from an earlier cathedral, has a magnificent entrance. The adjoining **Al-Qartawiyya Madrassa** (1316-26), with its facade of alternate black and white facings and honeycomb pattern above the portal is also impressive. The most beautiful mosque is the restored **Taynal Mosque** (1336) with a magnificent inner portal. It's on the outskirts of the old city but well worth the visit.

You have to look up to see the **Al-Muallaqa Mosque** which is suspended over the street. It's very close to the **Hammam al-Jedid**, a palatial ruin of a bathhouse with cupolas studded with glass, casting shafts of light down into the rooms. In the main room is a marble pool with an intriguing optical illusion. The hammam is locked but the local shopkeeper next to the hairdresser has a key and will show you around for a small donation towards the hammam's restoration. The 300 year old **Hammam al-Abd** is the city's only functioning bathhouse. It's only open to men and charges LL15,000 for a bath and massage.

The **Khan as-Sabun** (soap khan) is still used by a couple of families to make soap. They have a small stand at the front of the khan and will usually happily show you through their soap factory. The **Khan al-Khayyateen** is the beautifully restored tailors' souq, lined with small workshops selling exquisite work. Close to the tailors' souq is the **Al-Burtasiyya Mosque** (1310) with its intricate mihrab.

St-Gilles Citadel

Towering above Tripoli the citadel was originally built in 1103-4 by de St-Gilles. It was badly burned in the 13th century and partly rebuilt the following century by a Mamluk emir. Since then it has been altered many times. However, it's an imposing monument of basalt and limestone, with vaulted rooms, iron gates, courtyards and a baptismal font. Admission is LL5000 and the citadel is open from 9 am to 6 pm; in winter it closes at 4 pm.

Burj as-Sebua (Lion's Tower)

Burj as-Sebua is the only surviving example of several towers, built by the Mamluks, along the coast to protect the city. It dates back to the 15th century and is an imposing, impregnable square structure with numerous decorative elements adorning its entrance. It's 2km from the port in the Al-Mina district, about 500m from the old railway terminus. Admission is LL3000 and the tower is open from 9 am to 5 pm daily.

Boat Trips

There are several offshore islands that can be reached from Al-Mina port. The return trip takes two hours, with time for a swim, and costs LL5000 per person, or you can hire a whole boat (10 to 12 people) for LL50,000.

Places to Stay – Budget

Tripoli has the reverse accommodation situation of most Lebanese towns – there is plenty of budget accommodation but not much in the more expensive range.

Hotel des Cedres (no phone, Rue Tall) is very rundown and the shared bathroom is extremely grotty but only costs LL5000 per person in a two to four-bed room.

Palace Hotel (☎ 671 460, Rue Tall), next door, is a stark contrast. It's a beautiful old building with high ceilings and stained-glass windows, though in winter it has a damp feel. It charges US$10 per person in doubles with shared bathroom and US$15/25/30 in singles/doubles/triples with private bathroom.

Hotel at-Tall (☎ 628 407, Rue Tall) is shiny clean with lots of mirrors and neat, clean rooms. Singles/doubles/triples cost LL30,000/40,000/60,000. It's at the other end of Rue Tall from the square.

Al-Koura Hotel (☎ 03-326 803, Rue Izz ad-Dine) is a spotless, homey hotel and is the pick of the bunch. It costs US$15 per person, including breakfast, and some rooms have private bathroom and air-con.

Hotel Central (☎ 631 544, Rue Central) close to the tourist office charges US$10 per person (slippers provided) with shared bathroom. It's on the 6th floor of a dilapidated building but the rooms are fairly clean.

Hotel Hayek (☎ 601 311, Rue Ibn Sina) in Al-Mina is a family-run business and has clean rooms with sea views for US$18/20/30 for singles/doubles/triples with a shared bath. The family also runs Supermarket Hayek on the ground floor. The hotel entrance is from the back; ask at the supermarket if no one is around.

Places to Stay – Mid-Range

Qasr as-Sultan (☎ 601 627, 611 640) is rundown and overpriced at US$36/46 for singles/doubles with bath and breakfast. All rooms come with TV, minibar and air-con. There's a restaurant on the 1st floor. It's right on the Corniche, on the corner of Rue Ibn Sina and Rue al-Meshti.

Places to Stay – Top End

Chateau des Oliviers (☎/fax 629 271) is a private mansion converted into a hotel by the owner Nadia Dibo. It is set a few kilometres south of the city in the Haykalieh region high on a hill. The chateau has a garden, a swimming pool and a small nightclub. It's advisable to book in advance, rooms start at US$100.

Places to Eat

There are lots of cheap places to eat around Saahat at-Tall, where you can get felafel sandwiches for LL500 and shwarmas for LL1000. They are all good value, but at *Wonder Food* you can sit down and eat. There are also some great fresh juice stands, where a medium glass costs LL3000, near the public garden. In the old city, there's a *humous shop* under the bridge near Hammam al-Jedid. It sells some of the best humous around for LL2000 a plate. There's also a cheap *bar* selling coffee (LL500) and fresh juice (LL750) at Al-Nejmeh Square.

Captain's Fish Restaurant in Al-Mina shows you the freezer instead of a menu to choose the fresh fish catch of the day from. Fish dishes are charged by weight and with mezzes will cost about US$10 to US$15.

Paparazzi (☎ 442 455, City Complex, Al-Mina Ave) is a pleasant Italian restaurant where a meal costs about US$15 to US$20 per person.

There's a *patisserie* on Rue Tall, handy to most of the hotels and there's also a well stocked *supermarket*.

Entertainment

Tripoli is not renowned for its nightlife but it does have a good cinema complex showing the latest release English-language movies, with Arabic subtitles. *Ciné Planéte* (☎ 442 471, City Complex, Al Mina Ave) charges LL10,000 per person (half price on Monday).

LEBANON

Getting There & Away

There are two bus companies operating services to Beirut from offices close to Saahat-at Tall. Buses to Beirut leave every 15 minutes until early evening. The new Ahbad buses charge LL2000 and the older Kotob buses (☎ 444 986) charge LL1000. The service-taxi stand is at Saahat at-Tall and service taxis to Beirut cost LL4000.

Tripoli is a good place from which to visit Bcharré, Khalil Gibran's birthplace and the site of his museum, and The Cedars. There are no bus services to Bcharré and The Cedars. Service taxis to Bcharré cost LL3500 (40 minutes) and to The Cedars, LL5500 (50 minutes). The service taxi stand to Bcharré and The Cedars is on Al-Koura Square.

It's possible to get a service taxi or taxi from Tripoli to Baalbek, except during winter when the mountain road is closed. It should cost LL7000 for a service or LL35,000 for a taxi but it can be difficult to get this price.

Syria & Turkey Bus services to Syria are operated by Kotob (☎ 443 986) and Transtour (☎ 03-411 015). Fares are Homs (US$3, two hours), Damascus (US$4, four hours) and Lattakia (US$5, five hours). They also run bus services to all major cities in Turkey for US$30 to US$35 (24 hours). Service taxis to Homs cost LL7000 and to Damascus, LL16,000. They leave when full from Saahat at-Tall.

Getting Around

Service taxis within Tripoli cost LL1000.

BCHARRÉ & THE CEDARS

The trip to Bcharré and The Cedars takes you through some of the most beautiful scenery in Lebanon. The road winds along the mountainous slopes, continuously gaining in altitude and offering spectacular views of gorges. Villages of red-tile roofed houses perch atop hills or cling precariously to the mountain sides. Olive groves and vineyards, lush valleys and mountain peaks rise higher and higher behind every road turn.

Gibran Museum

One of the highlights along this route is the Gibran Museum in the village of Bcharré, the birthplace of the author-artist Gibran Khalil Gibran (1883-1931). Better known as Kahlil Gibran, his most famous work is *The Prophet*. According to his wishes Gibran, who emigrated to the USA in the 19th century, was buried in an old monastery built into the rocky slopes of a hill overlooking Bcharré. The museum, set up in this monastery, houses a large collection of Gibran's paintings, drawings and gouaches, and also some of his manuscripts. His coffin is in the monastery's former chapel, which is cut straight into the rock. In the same room is his bed, a table and chair, other personal objects, as well as a 12th century tapestry of Christ on the cross which Gibran was particularly fond of because it depicted a smiling Christ.

The museum is open from 9 am to 4 pm Tuesday to Sunday and admission is LL3000.

Cedars of Bcharré

From Bcharré the road climbs 6km along a tortuous road until it reaches the last remaining forest of biblical cedars in Lebanon. Known locally as *arz ar-rab* (God's cedars), they are on the slopes of Mt Makmal at an altitude of more than 2000m. It's a small forest, as the cedar tree, which once covered most of Lebanon's high summits, has been overexploited throughout the centuries. The Phoenicians exported cedar to the Egyptians, who considered it the sacred wood of the gods, and to Solomon to build his temple. The site is classified as a national monument as some of these cedars go back more than 1500 years.

Skiing

The Cedars region is a prime ski resort in winter for both downhill and cross-country skiing. There are ski-hire shops and accommodation in the village below the forest; boot and ski hire will cost about US$10 per day. An adult day pass at the Cedars ski resort (☎ 671 073) costs US$25.

Kadisha Grotto

This small grotto extends about 500m into the mountain and has some great limestone formations, it's not as spectacular as Jeitta Grotto but neither is it as touristy. The grotto is a 10 minute walk, providing stunning views of the Katisha Valley, along the mountainside from the signposted path at L'Aiglon hotel. The guide who lives at the grotto sells coffee as well as leading visitors through the cave. Admission is LL2000.

Places to Stay & Eat

St Peter's (☎ 671 490, Main Road, The Cedars) is 500m before you arrive at the Cedar forest, coming from Bcharré. This new hotel charges US$30/40 per person on weekdays/weekends, including breakfast. It's nice, comfortable and offers ski lessons for US$15 per hour on its beginner's slope.

L'Aiglon (☎ 671 529) is in a peaceful setting, but midway between Bcharré and The Cedars it's a bit out of the way if you don't have your own car. It's overpriced at US$50 for standard rooms which sleep one or two with new bathrooms.

Palace Hotel (☎ 671 460) is just below the main road in Bcharré, about 100m west of the huge St Saba church and the village square. It charges US$30/50/60 for standard singles/doubles/triples with new bathrooms.

Hotel Chbat (☎ 06-671 237/230), on Rue Gibran in the upper part of Bcharré, is more expensive at US$65/78/88 for singles/doubles/triples but has terrific views over the gorge.

There are a few restaurants and cafes in Bcharré. *Makhlouf Eli* has good Lebanese food for about US$5 per person and its roof-top terrace has great views. Equally good views but more expensive are *Mississippi* and *River Roc*, just outside Bcharré on the road to Tripoli.

Getting There & Away

From Tripoli service taxis charge LL3500 to Bcharré or LL5000 to The Cedars. Out of the ski season you will probably only get a service taxi as far as Bcharré and then have to take a taxi. Taxi drivers will usually take you to The Cedars, wait 30 minutes and then take you back to Bcharré for LL20,000.

South of Beirut

Travelling south of Beirut is OK all the way to Tyre (Sour), 80km south of the capital, and all over the Chouf Mountains, southeast of Beirut. East and south of Sour the area is under UNIFIL control and is often subject to Israeli shelling, and beyond UNIFIL's area the border strip is under Israeli control and is out of bounds for visitors – Lebanese and foreigners alike.

Cheap accommodation is hard to come by in areas south of Beirut; fortunately most of the places of interest can be visited on day trips from the capital.

SIDON (SAIDA)

Sidon (Saida) is a small port city, set amid citrus orchards and banana groves, 41km south of Beirut. It's a very old settlement, going back 6000 years, and once was a prominent and wealthy Phoenician city. Like other Phoenician capitals, Saida was built on a promontory facing an island to shelter its fleet. It had a succession of invaders, from the Persians to the Assyrians, Alexander the Great, the Romans, the Byzantines, the Arabs, the Crusaders and then the Mamluks. It was destroyed twice by wars between the 7th and 4th centuries BC and by an earthquake in the 6th century AD, so few remains of the ancient city survived. However, it has a particularly good Crusader castle and fine examples of Muslim architecture in its mosques, khans and vaulted souqs. Sidon also has a thriving financial and commercial sector which sits comfortably with its ancient past.

Sidon is famous for orange-blossom water and a sort of crumbly biscuit called *sanioura* which is delicious.

Orientation & Information

The centre of town is around Saahat an-Nejmeh (An-Nejmeh Square), where you'll find cheap eateries, the bus and service taxi stations, the municipality building and the police station. Rue Riad Solh, which runs south off Saahat an-Nejmeh (in reality a huge roundabout), has restaurants, banks, moneychangers, shops, travel agencies etc. The old city, the harbour, the Sea Castle and the one hotel are west of Saahat an-Nejmeh and Rue Riad Solh, while the modern shopping centres and residential buildings are on the eastern side.

Saida Net Centre (☎ 03-464 985), tucked away in the souqs near the Khattakdar Mosque on the way to the Great Mosque, charges LL5000 per hour for Internet access.

The Old City

Old Sidon is behind the buildings fronting the harbour, just across from the wharf. It's a fascinating maze of **vaulted souqs**, tiny alleyways and old buildings dating back to the Middle Ages when most inhabitants lived in the area between the city walls and the harbour.

In the souqs you'll find shops selling everything from spices to fish and vegetables and you'll see craftspeople at work. There's also the **Khan al-Franj** (Inn of the Foreigners), which consists of vaulted galleries surrounding a large rectangular courtyard with a central fountain. It was built with limestone during the reign of Fakhreddine II in the 17th century to accommodate foreign merchants and promote contact with Europe. At the time of writing it was undergoing restoration.

Farther inside the old city is the **Great Mosque**, a beautiful building with vaulted prayer areas surrounding a central courtyard. It replaced a church built by the Crusaders and its outer walls date back to the 13th century. Visitors wishing to enter the mosque must be modestly dressed and women should cover their hair.

Sea Castle

Built by the Crusaders in the early 13th century, the Sea Castle (Qasr al-Bahr) sits on a small island which was formerly the site of a temple to Melkart, the Phoenician Hercules. It is connected to the mainland by an Arab fortified stone bridge (of a later date). It was one of many coastal castles built by the Crusaders for protection and, like many others, was destroyed by the Mamluks to prevent the Crusaders from returning to the region.

However, it's still in a fair state of preservation and consists chiefly of two towers connected by a wall – the west tower is better preserved than the east tower, which has lost its top floor. Roman shaft columns used as transverse trusses support the outside walls, and there are two cisterns in the castle's basement.

It's open all year from 9 am to 6 pm (4 pm in winter) and entrance costs LL2000.

Echmoun

About 5km north-east of Sidon is Echmoun a Phoenician temple site which is well worth a visit. It is Lebanon's only Phoenician site where you can see more than just foundations. There are impressive temple remains and lots of mosaics, though most of them are badly damaged. The temple complex to Echmoun, god of the city of Sidon, was begun in the 7th century BC and other buildings were later added by the Persians, Romans and Byzantines. The temples clearly catered for plenty of worshippers, as the row of ancient shops testifies. The highlight of the site is the throne of Astarte, guarded by winged lions.

From Sidon you can take a taxi to the site for LL5000 or get a service taxi (LL1000) or microbus (LL500) to the turn-off on the highway at the funfair and then walk the 1.5km by orchards to the ruins.

Places to Stay & Eat

Hotel d'Orient (☎ 720 364, Rue Shakrieh) is the only hotel in Sidon. It has prison-cell-like rooms on the 1st floor that sleep four and cost LL8000 per person. On the 2nd floor are rooms with shared bathroom which are basic, but clean and comfortable, and have small balconies overlooking the street which cost LL20,000/30,000 for a single/double. It's above a shop selling toiletries, not far from the Muslim cemetery in the old city. (It's a bit hard to spot so look out for the hotel name on a sign on the balcony.)

There are lots of sandwich stalls and cheap cafes around Saahat an-Nejmeh and the harbour. For a bit of a splurge go to the restaurant of the government-run *Resthouse* on the seafront opposite the Sea Castle. The food is good and it has a variety of dips, grills, fish and alcoholic beverages; it will cost about US$7 for mezze and US$15 for a main course. The restored medieval building is constructed in the traditional Arab style and is worth visiting even if you don't plan to eat there.

Getting There & Away

The bus and service-taxi stands are on Saahat an-Nejmeh. Service taxis charge LL2500 to Beirut or Tyre (Sour), buses cost LL1250 and microbuses cost LL1000.

TYRE (SOUR)

Ancient Tyre was founded by the Phoenicians in the 3rd millennium BC. It originally consisted of a mainland settlement and an island city just off the shore, but these were joined in the 4th century BC by a causeway which converted the island permanently into a peninsula. Its most famous king was Hiram, to whom Solomon appealed for cedars to build the temple of Jerusalem and his palace.

History

For a long time, Tyre had a flourishing maritime trade and, with colonies in Sicily and North Africa, was responsible for Phoenician expansion in the west. It was also famous for its purple dye and glass industries.

The town suffered from successive invasions that left their mark, and excavations have revealed remains of Crusader, Arab,

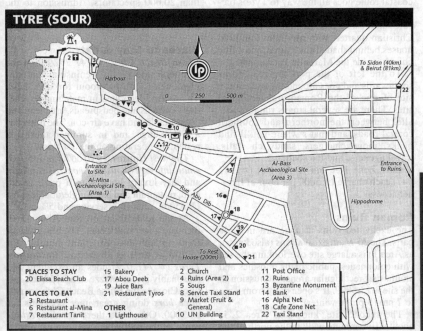

TYRE (SOUR)

To Sidon (40km) & Beirut (81km)

Harbour

0   250   500 m

To Sidon (40km) & Beirut (81km)

Entrance to Site
Al-Mina Archaeological Site (Area 1)

Al-Bass Archaeological Site (Area 3)

Entrance to Ruins

Rue Abu Dib

Hippodrome

To Rest House (200m)

LEBANON

PLACES TO STAY	15 Bakery	2 Church	11 Post Office
20 Elissa Beach Club	17 Abou Deeb	4 Ruins (Area 2)	12 Ruins
	19 Juice Bars	5 Souqs	13 Byzantine Monument
PLACES TO EAT	21 Restaurant Tyros	8 Service Taxi Stand	14 Bank
3 Restaurant		9 Market (Fruit &	16 Alpha Net
6 Restaurant al-Mina	OTHER	General)	18 Cafe Zone Net
7 Restaurant Tanit	1 Lighthouse	10 UN Building	22 Taxi Stand

Byzantine and Graeco-Roman cities. It withstood a 13 year siege by Nebuchadnezzar II, King of Babylon, in the early 6th century BC and in the 4th century BC was besieged for seven months by Alexander the Great, who finally stormed the city. In 68 BC it came under Roman rule and by the 2nd century AD had a large Christian population. The Muslims then ruled it from the 7th to the 12th century, when it became part of the Kingdom of Jerusalem under the Crusaders, to be destroyed by the Muslim Mamluks in 1291.

Tyre has three archaeological sites with Roman ruins; two of them are open to the public.

Orientation & Information

The old part of Tyre is on the peninsula jutting out into the sea and covers a relatively small area. The modern town is on the left-hand side as you arrive from Beirut. The coastal route goes all the way to Tyre's picturesque old port, around which are a few cafes and restaurants. Behind the port is the Christian quarter, with tiny alleys and old houses behind shaded courtyards, and a fine church inside the Maronite Patriarchate.

To the left of the port the road forks southwards and goes around the excavation site of one of the Roman archaeological sites. There are several streets running parallel between the northern and southern coastal roads, and that's where you'll find banks, moneychangers, sandwich stalls, travel agencies and the souq.

Cafe Zone Net and Alpha Net (☎ 347 047) each charge LL5000 per hour of Internet access.

Roman Ruins

The excavated ruins at Tyre are in three parts. The Al-Mina excavations (also known as Area 1) is a large site overlooking the sea with colonnades, public baths, mosaics and an unusual rectangular arena. Admission to the site is LL5000. It's open daily from 8 am to 7 pm (5 pm in winter).

The second site, known as Area 2, is about a five minute walk to the north of the first site. It is fenced off and not open to the public, but you can see the ruins from the road, including the remains of the Crusader Cathedral.

The Al-Bass site (Area 3) has some of Tyre's most impressive archaeological remains. It has a well preserved Roman road leading to the ancient settlement, made of big blocks of paving stones and lined in many parts with marble columns. The road stretches in a straight line for about 1.6km, passing through a monumental archway. It is lined on one side by an aqueduct, and on both sides there are hundreds of ornate stone and marble sarcophagi of the Roman and Byzantine periods which are intricately carved with the names of the occupants or reliefs drawn from the *Iliad*. There's also a U-shaped Roman hippodrome built in the 2nd century AD for chariot racing, one of the largest of the Roman period with a capacity for more than 20,000 spectators. Admission to the Al-Bass site is LL5000 and opening hours are the same as for Al-Mina.

Places to Stay & Eat

Elissa Beach Club (☎ 741 267/8), on the southern side of the peninsula, has single/doubles with bathroom for US$35/50. The rooms, decorated in matching psychedelic curtains and bedspreads, are clean and comfortable and have air-con. The hotel has a TV lounge and in summer there's a restaurant operating on the 1st floor.

The Rest House (☎ 740 667, fax 345 163, email info@resthouse-tyr.com.lb) is a light and airy luxury hotel with a pool, health club, restaurant and bar. Single/doubles cost US$50/60 plus 16% service and 5% tax.

At the roundabout on Rue Abou Deeb there are a few snack bars. The best is *Abou Deeb*, which has excellent felafels for LL500 as well as shwarmas. *Restaurant Tyros* (☎ 741 027) does an excellent and reasonably priced mezze in a laid-back setting. Close to the Elissa Beach Club are two *juice bars* doing great juice cocktails for LL3000. Otherwise there are the *restaurants* on the port where you can eat grilled meat or chicken for about US$5, fish at a much higher price or the standard sandwich fare.

Getting There & Away

The service taxi stand is about 50m before the port on the northern coastal road. Service taxis to Beirut cost LL5000, to Sidon (Saida), LL2500. The Lebanese Transport Company buses do the run to Beirut for LL500 (local bus) or LL1500 (express) and microbuses cost LL2000.

THE CHOUF MOUNTAINS

The Chouf Mountains, just south-east of Beirut, are the southern part of the Mt Lebanon range. Like their northern counterparts, they're spectacularly beautiful with narrow gorges, lush green valleys, fountains and springs, rivers and waterfalls, and cultivated, terraced mountainsides.

Unlike their northern counterparts, however, they're sparsely populated as many inhabitants fled following the Israeli invasion of 1982 and the fighting that broke out in the Chouf in the wake of the Israeli's departure.

At the time of writing, budget accommodation was practically nonexistent in the area. However, all the sites of interest can be visited on day trips from Beirut.

Palace of Beiteddine (Beit ad-Din)

The main attraction of the Chouf Mountains is the Palace of Beiteddine, 45km south-east of Beirut. Sitting majestically atop a terraced hill and surrounded by gardens, the palace was built by Emir Beshir ash-Chehab II in the first half of the 19th century. After WWI the palace was used by the French Mandatory Authorities for local administration. When Lebanon became independent in 1943, the palace became the summer residence of the president. Following the Mountain War in 1983, the palace came under the control of the Druze militias who transformed it into a museum and cultural centre, and renamed it the Palace of the People. In 1999 the Druze handed it back to the government and it will once again be used as the

president's summer residence as well as continuing to be open to visitors.

Although conceived by Italian architects, the palace incorporates all the traditional forms of Lebanese architecture and has an expansive and peaceful feel to it. The gate opens onto a vast, 60m courtyard walled on three sides only; the fourth side has great views out over valleys and hills. A double staircase on the western side leads into the inner court, which consists of a smaller courtyard with a central fountain bordered by buildings on three sides only. Beyond this court is the Dar al-Harim, or women's quarters, with a beautiful hammam. The hammam is often closed, but sometimes staff at the Guidance Office will show you through. All the buildings have arcades along their facades.

The main court houses a couple of museums and a craft shop. The inner court and Dar al-Harim contain vast, vaulted rooms decorated and paved with multicoloured marble or mosaics and richly decorated doorways with exquisite calligraphic inscriptions. The former stables display a collection of Byzantine mosaic floors dating back to the 5th and 6th centuries from Jiyyeh, 30km south of Beirut.

The palace is open daily from 9 am to 6 pm (5 pm in winter) and admission is LL3000. There is no information available at the entrance so it's worth getting the tourist office brochure beforehand. Official guides are available for tours of the palace.

Other Attractions

Farther up the hill and overlooking the village of Beiteddine is the **Mir Amin Palace** (a smaller version of Beiteddine Palace), which belonged to the son of Emir Beshir. It is now a 1st class luxury hotel with 22 rooms, a swimming pool and spectacular views over the hills and valleys. It's worth stopping there at least for a drink.

The picturesque town of **Deir al-Qamar**, 5km from Beiteddine on the way to Beirut, was the seat of Lebanon's emirate during the 17th and 18th centuries. The town square has some fine examples of Arab architecture,

LEBANON

including a mosque built in 1493, a silk khan and a palace.

Places to Stay & Eat

SJS Motel (☎ 05-501 567, *Samqaniye*) has rundown but comfortable rooms with TV, kitchen facilities, lounge and bathroom for US$50. They sleep two to three people. The village of Samqaniye is 4km south-east of Beiteddine.

Mir Amin Palace (☎ /fax 501 315, email *miriamin@bookinn.com, Beiteddine*). This is the place for a splurge. Singles/doubles start at US$103/123 but are heavily discounted in winter.

You'll find *sandwich stalls* (shwarma, chicken, cheese etc) in most of the villages, like those on the town square in Deir al-Qamar, and restaurants (mezzes and grills) in the bigger towns. About 500m from the SJS Motel on the road to Beiteddine is the classic *Restaurant H-Z*. It's decorated with hundreds of bank notes which have been autographed by customers for the owner who has a collection mania. Hanging off the walls of the small restaurant are also ancient ploughs, old weaponry and coffee pots; the menu is as eclectic as the decor. It's open in the evenings only.

Getting There & Away

The easiest way to visit the Chouf Mountains is by car. If there's a few of you travelling, you could hire a taxi from Beirut for the day (US$80); otherwise there are service taxis from the Cola stand to different towns in the Chouf. The fare is from LL2000 to LL4000, depending on where you want to be dropped off. You can get off at the places you want to see along the way and then catch service taxis to your next destination (LL1000), though on certain stretches you may have to wait a while. Alternatively, if you're heading back from Baalbek or Zahlé and don't want to go back to Beirut you can stop at the turn-off at Mdajeid and get a service taxi to Beiteddine (LL3000). You can also get a service taxi from Beiteddine to Sidon for LL2000 or alternatively a service to the Beirut-Sidon

highway (LL1000) and from there get a minibus to Sidon for LL750.

The Bekaa Valley

There are two fascinating sites to visit in the Bekaa Valley, the fertile plain that separates the Mt Lebanon and Anti-Lebanon ranges. One is Baalbek, or ancient Heliopolis, with its Roman ruins of gigantic proportions, and the other is Aanjar, where a whole Muslim Umayyad town was uncovered in the early 1950s.

The Bekaa Valley is reached via the Damascus Highway, which goes through several towns and villages in the Mt Lebanon range. There are also lots of Lebanese and Syrian army checkpoints along this route.

CHTAURA

The first town in the Bekaa Valley is Chtaura, a main stopover halfway between Beirut and Damascus and the transport hub of the different sites around the valley. There's plenty of cheap eateries along the main road going through town and, if you want to stay here *Hotel Khater* (☎ 08-540 133, *Beirut-Damascus Highway*), opposite the police station, has singles/doubles/triples (some with private bath) for US$10 per person. The rooms at the back are quieter and have pleasant views. Service taxis from Beirut to Chtaura charge LL3000 or a microbus will cost about LL2000; they both leave from Cola. Bus Nos 4 and 5 will take you from Chtaura to Zahlé or on to Baalbek for LL500. They leave from the corner where the highway to Damascus intersects with the road to Baalbek.

ZAHLÉ

The other major town in the Bekaa is Zahlé, about 7km north-east of Chtaura. It's a pretty town nestled along the slopes of a narrow valley and is famous for its riverbank cafes and restaurants specialising in mezzes and grills. Most activity centres around Rue Brazil which runs directly off the highway.

Information

The tourist office (☎ 802 566, fax 803 595) is signposted about 1km from the highway turn-off and is on the 3rd floor of the Chamber of Commerce building, just off Rue Brazil. The staff is helpful and the office is open from 8.30 am to 1.30 pm daily except Sunday.

Dataland Internet (☎ 814 825) offers Internet access for LL6000 per hour. It's open from 9 am to midnight daily, and is 1.5km from the highway turn-off on the left side of Rue Brazil, before you reach the Grand Kadri Hotel.

The post office is on Rue Brazil about 750m from the highway turn-off on the right-hand side.

Places to Stay & Eat

Hotel Akl (☎ *820 701, Rue Brazil*) is the pick of the cheaper hotels. It's clean, friendly and very much recommended. It's in a lovely old house and charges LL25,000/30,000 per person without/with bathroom.

Hotel Traboulsi (☎ *820 534, Rue Brazil*) is next door to the Akl and is also a good family-run hotel, where single or double rooms with bathroom cost US$25. Akl and Traboulsi are about 2km from the highway turn-off.

Grand Hotel Kadri (☎ *813 920, fax 803 314, email kadrotel@dm.net.lb, Rue Brazil*) is huge, classy and a lot more expensive. Singles/doubles start at US$130/156 with generous discounts in winter. Facilities include a child care centre, health club, tennis court, night club and four restaurants.

There are plenty of riverside cafes and restaurants to chose from and a typical meal at one of those places would set you back about US$12, but it's well worth the experience; they aren't open during winter. On Rue Brazil, *La Ronda* does good spinach and cheese pastries for LL500 and the place named simply *Restaurant* does a mean felafel for LL1000.

Getting There & Away

To get there, take a service taxi from Chtaura which will drop you in the town centre for LL1000. Bus No 4 or 5 from Chtaura or Baalbek will cost LL500. In Zahlé the bus stops just below the car park which is midway along Rue Brazil.

AROUND ZAHLÉ
Ksara Winery

Lebanon is not traditionally associated with wine making, but it produces some excellent wines. About 5km from Zahlé, the Ksara winery (☎ 813 495) is a worthwhile stop and is well set-up to receive visitors. After a 10 minute video which provides a rose coloured view of the winery's history and production methods you can explore the network of caves (or be shown through if you're part of a tour group) where the barrelled wine is matured before sampling some of Ksara's internationally commended wines. It's open 9 am to 4 pm, closed Sunday. The winery is on the highway almost midway between Chtaura and Zahlé. A service taxi will cost LL1000; ask for Ksara winery, not Ksara village. The No 4 and 5 buses also pass by the entrance.

BAALBEK

The town of Baalbek, 86km north-east of Beirut, was originally named after the Phoenician god Baal. The Greeks later called it Heliopolis, or City of the Sun, and the Romans made it a major worship site for their god Jupiter. The remains of their temples make for one of the Middle East's most spectacular archaeological sites.

Orientation & Information

The town of Baalbek is small with around 12,000 inhabitants. It is easy to tour the whole town on foot and the ruins are close to the centre of town. There are two main roads in Baalbek. Rue Abdel Halim Hajjar is the road you'll arrive at first coming from Beirut. You'll see the Roman ruins on your left-hand side and the Palmyra Hotel is across the road on your right. It's also the street on which you'll find banks, sandwich bars and the Ash-Shams Hotel. It intersects with the other main road, Ras al-Ain Boulevard, where there's the Pension Shuman,

BAALBEK

The acropolis at Baalbek is one of the largest in the world; it is also the most impressive ancient site in Lebanon and arguably the most important Roman ruin in the Middle East. The World Heritage listed site is equally stunning bathed in morning sunlight and floodlit at night and is definitely worth a visit.

The Site

There are only partial remains of the Temple of Jupiter, originally completed around 60 AD, but it gives you a feel for how massive this temple was. You wander through a forecourt and the Great Court, with its sacrificial altar, before reaching the temple itself which is built on a high platform at the top of a monumental staircase. The six remaining, oft-photographed columns which soar 22m are awesome.

Adjacent to the Temple of Jupiter is the Temple of Bacchus which was known in Roman times as the 'little temple'. Built by about 150 AD, it's amazingly well-preserved and gives a whole new meaning to the word little. Its features include the ornately decorated interior, the monumental doorway and the portico around the temple with its richly

Top: Detail from temple ruins (Photo by Gadi Farfour)

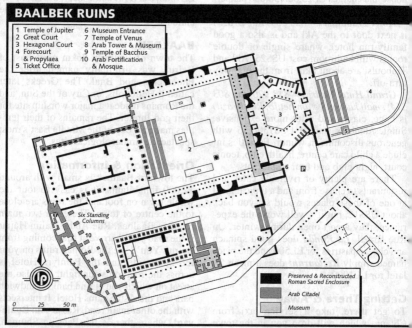

BAALBEK RUINS

1 Temple of Jupiter
2 Great Court
3 Hexagonal Court
4 Forecourt
  & Propylaea
5 Ticket Office
6 Museum Entrance
7 Temple of Venus
8 Arab Tower & Museum
9 Temple of Bacchus
10 Arab Fortification
   & Mosque

Six Standing Columns

Preserved & Reconstructed
Roman Sacred Enclosure

Arab Citadel

Museum

0   25   50 m

decorated walls and ceiling with scenes of the gods at work and play.

At the entrance to the site there is a new museum which has a voluminous amount of information in English, French, German and Arabic about the history of Baalbek. The chronology of the information is a little unclear but it's definitely worth spending an hour or two wandering through. At the corner of the Bacchus temple there is another museum, housed in the 15th century tower added by the Mamluks, which has a good display of sarcophagi.

The best time to visit the Baalbek site is early morning when there are few people around. Allow a few hours to wander through the museum and the ruins and consider taking food and drink to the site with you as there is none available inside. Guides can be organised at the ticket office and cost US$14 for about an hour. It depends how you like to receive your information but a lot of the detail they'll give you is covered in the museum. A ticket to the site costs LL10,000 and it's open daily from 8.30 am until 30 minutes before sunset.

When you leave the site check out the Temple of Venus, near the entrance to the main site. It's closed to visitors but you can wander around the perimeter fence to see this comparatively delicate and exquisite temple which is circular shaped with many fluted columns.

Top Right: Bronze Statue from the Temple of Jupiter

Bottom Left: The Temple of Jupiter's six remaining columns

Bottom Right: Cornice detail from the Temple of Jupiter

GADI FARFOUR

ANDREW HUMPHREYS

more sandwich bars, service taxi office and riverside restaurants.

Bring cash with you. There are no ATMs in Baalbek, the banks don't change travellers cheques and the hotels don't accept credit cards. The BBAC bank will provide a cash advance on Visa and MasterCard for a US$3 minimum fee.

The post and telephone office is about 1km from the ruins, just off Ras al-Ain Boulevard.

Places to Stay & Eat

Ash-Shams Hotel (☎ 373 284, Rue Abdel Halim Hajjar) has four basic but clean rooms (with washbasins) sleeping up to five people. Beds cost US$6 per person and there's a shared toilet and hot-water shower. It's on the 1st floor and the dentist next door can provide keys if there is no one at the hotel.

Pension Shuman (☎ 370 160, Ras al-Ain Boulevard) has the best views and the hardest beds in town. It charges LL10,000 per person and there's a dingy shared bathroom.

Palmyra Hotel (☎ 370 230, Beirut-Baalbek Highway) is opposite the ruins on the right-hand side of the road just before Baalbek and is *the* place to stay. Built in 1874 it remains a beautiful building with an atmosphere of faded grandeur. Set in shady gardens it has singles/doubles/triples with bathroom and balconies overlooking the ruins for US$38/53/65. There are cheaper rooms (which won't be mentioned when you check in, so ask specifically about them) without the view and with a shared bathroom for US$20/25/30. Hot water is only available in the evening. The hotel has a bar and restaurant; the food is reasonably priced but not great quality.

There are lots of cheap eateries on Rue Abdel Halim Hajjar where you can get a plate of ful or humous and sandwiches for LL1500. **Snack Al-Ajami** (Ras al-Ain Boulevard) is a friendly snack bar which does good shwarmas and cheese pizzas.

Getting There & Away

The cheapest way to get between Baalbek and Beirut is by microbus. They leave from Beirut's Cola bus stand and from outside the Palmyra Hotel in Baalbek about every 10 minutes, though the frequency decreases in the afternoon. From Baalbek to Zahlé and Chtaura fares cost LL1000, to Beirut, LL3000; the fares are the same from Beirut.

Alternatively there's a service taxi office on the corner of Rue Abdel Halim Hajjar and Ras al-Ain Boulevard. It charges LL2000 to Zahlé, LL3000 to Chtaura, LL5000 to Beirut and LL8000 to Damascus. In Beirut, service taxis leave from the Cola stand.

If you are travelling to or from Zahlé or Chtaura, bus Nos 4 and 5 leave about every 30 minutes and the fare costs a bargain LL500.

Travel times in a service taxi to Zahlé/Chtaura/Beirut are 30 minutes/40 minutes/two hours; it takes slightly longer in a microbus or bus.

AANJAR

This town is Lebanon's best preserved Islamic archaeological site. It's got loads of historical interest, being the only significant Umayyad site in Lebanon and the only ancient ruin you're likely to see in Lebanon that hasn't been the site for a multiplicity of cities. The Umayyads ruled briefly but energetically from 1660 to 1750 and Aanjar was an important inland commercial centre, located on intersecting trade routes.

The walled and fortified city was built along symmetrical Roman lines; the layout is rectangular – almost square – with two major avenues, each 20m wide, bisecting it. The city walls each have a gate at the midpoint of each side which were protected by towers. In its heyday, the main streets were flanked by palaces, baths, mosques, shops and dwellings. Definitely the most beautiful building at Aanjar is the reconstructed great palace with its graceful arches, though the entire site looks striking against the backdrop of the often snowcapped Anti-Lebanon mountains.

About 600 shops have been uncovered since the site was discovered in the 1940s, and some are occupied by Syrian soldiers; the site is very close to the Syrian border.

The site is open daily from 8 am to sunset and admission is LL6000. It's worth getting the Aanjar brochure, which includes a map and details about the site, from the Zahlé or Beirut tourist offices before you arrive as it's not available at the entrance point.

Getting There & Away

You can catch a service taxi from Chtaura (LL1500, 15km) which will drop you at the turn-off, leaving you with a 2km walk. The No 12 bus also covers this route infrequently for LL500. Walk down the road towards Aanjar and turn left at the road opposite Restaurant Soleil and follow that road around until you reach the entrance to the ruins. Alternatively you may decide to hire a taxi to take you to the site, wait for an hour or so and then return. This will cost about US$10.

Libya

LIBYA

Libya is best known for its radical anti-western political stand, its vast oil reserves and, most of all, for its mercurial leader, Colonel Muammar Gaddafi. In recent times Libya has been subject to United Nations sanctions, imposed due to its perceived role in the 1988 bombing of Pam Am flight No 103, but with the May 1999 lifting of those sanctions the country is attracting tourists keen to see the classical ruins or experience what is probably the best part of the Sahara Desert.

Visitors will find Libya religious without being fanatical, and hospitable without being obsequious. Tourism is bound to make its mark on Libya, but at the moment it is one of the last unspoilt places on the Mediterranean.

Facts about Libya

HISTORY
Libya's history has few parallels with the rest of the Middle East. For most of its history the country has been ruled by a succession of colonising powers. Even during the 17th and 18th centuries when Tripoli was ruled by the local Karamanli dynasty, the country nominally belonged to the Turkish Ottoman sultan. The Sublime Porte had long realised the impracticality of directly ruling all of their foreign possessions, especially the troublesome Barbary ones, and installed puppet rulers who paid a hefty tribute for the privilege. These local rulers became virtually independent over time and often almost forgot the Sultan altogether.

After the Turks regained control of Tripoli in the 19th century they may have remained there if it wasn't for the ambitions of a European power. This last power to seize Libya was to go beyond merely settling for a colony and attempted to add Libya to its own sovereign territory.

In the scramble for African colonies in the late 19th and early 20th centuries, Italy set its sights on Libya. It harboured the dream

Great Socialist Libyan People's Arab Jomhuriyya

Area: 1,759,640 sq km
Population: approx four million
Population Growth Rate: 3.7%
Capital: Tripoli
Head of State: Colonel Muammar Gaddafi
Official Language: Arabic
Currency: Libyan dinar
Exchange Rate: US$1 = LD0.32

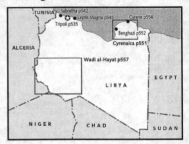

- **Best Nightlife** – watching the Tuareg dancers perform in Ghadhames under the desert stars
- **Best Walk** – through the hidden wadis of the Acacus Mountains to see the cave paintings
- **Best View** – following the Sacred Way through the ancient city of Cyrene and catching the sunset from the Sanctuary of Apollo
- **Best Shopping** – in the covered souqs of the Tripoli medina; get there early to soak up the local atmosphere
- **When in Rome ...** pack up a picnic and head for the beach on Fridays like many Libyan families

of a North African empire and the outbreak of war between Turkey and Italy in 1911 gave the Italians the excuse to invade.

The Italian period was devastating for the Libyan people. Between 1911 and the end of WWII, the indigenous population of about one million was halved by either forced exile or extermination. The Italians viewed Libya as Italy's 'fourth shore' and they embarked upon a complete 'Italianisation' program, sending huge numbers of immigrant farmers (mainly from Sicily) to develop the valuable agricultural land.

Libya suffered the misfortune of being a theatre of war during WWII and the desert campaign left behind huge minefields, many of which still remain today.

In the post-war years, Italy was forced to give up Libya, which was placed under a UN trusteeship until the Allied powers could decide what was to be done with the country. At one stage Libya's three provinces, Tripolitania, Cyrenaica and Fezzan, almost became separate countries but during the final voting session at the UN the motion was defeated by one vote. In December 1951, Libya became a united independent state for the first time in its long history. A monarchy was chosen and King Idris, an ageing Senussi leader from Cyrenaica, took the throne. His appointment as king was not universally popular, especially outside his native province.

The discovery of oil in 1959 meant that cash flowed into the country. From being the Cinderella of Africa, Libya was poised to become wealthy for the first time since the Roman era. However, the oil companies were almost wholly foreign-owned and controlled, and only a small proportion of the oil revenue found its way into the Libyan treasury.

Fired by growing political discontent and the mood of pan-Arabism, which was sweeping the Arab world, a small group of army officers led by the then 27-year-old Captain Gaddafi deposed the king on 1 September 1969 in a virtually bloodless coup. The radical new regime swept away the old establishment at a stroke and drastically changed Libya's former status as a client state of the UK and USA.

Soon after Colonel Gaddafi came to power, the British and Americans were ordered to leave the bases they had occupied since WWII, and the 25,000 descendants of the Italian colonists were also forced to promptly pack their bags and leave. Libya's oil deposits were gradually taken over by a

What to See

Many visitors come to Libya for the well preserved Roman cities of **Leptis Magna** and **Sabratha** with their impressive monuments and mosaics and the beautiful Greek cities of **Cyrene** and **Apollonia** set in the lush and spectacular Jebel Akhdar. As a collection of ruins they are as finer if not finer than any others in the Mediterranean and with few people around to spoil the experience.

The other big attraction in Libya is the vast **Sahara Desert** – not called the greatest desert on earth for nothing. Desert safaris are becoming popular, taking in the unique mud-built desert architecture of **Ghadhames** and the fabulous prehistoric **cave paintings** in the Acacus Mountains in the south. One of the desert's secrets is a series of lakes among the dunes in the **Ramlet Dawada**.

However far off the beaten track you wander be sure to visit **Tripoli** and see Tripoli's castle, former stronghold of Barbary corsairs and the unspoilt medina with its lively souq.

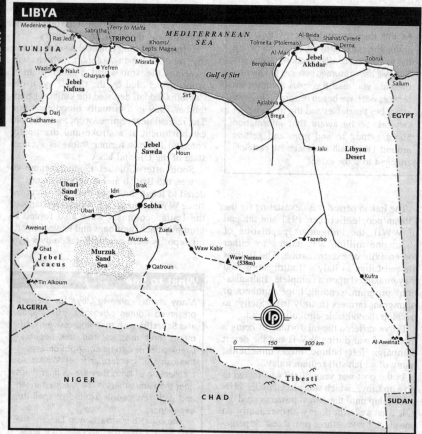

LIBYA

Medenine
Ras Jedir
Sabratha Ferry to Malta
TUNISIA
TRIPOLI
Khoms/ Leptis Magna
Wazin Nalut Yefren
Gharyan
Jebel Nafusa
Misrata
Sirt
MEDITERRANEAN SEA
Tolmeita (Ptolemais) Al-Beida Shahat/Cyrene Derna
Al-Marj
Benghazi
Jebel Akhdar
Tobruk
Sallum
Gulf of Sirt
Ajdabiya
Brega
EGYPT
Darj
Ghadhames
Jebel Sawda
Houn
Jalu
Libyan Desert
Ubari Sand Sea
Idri
Brak
Aweinat
Ubari
Sebha
Ghat
Jebel Acacus
Murzuk
Zuela
Murzuk Sand Sea
Waw Kabir
Tazerbo
Tin Alkoum
Qatroun
Waw Namus (538m)
Kufra
ALGERIA
NIGER
Tibesti
CHAD
SUDAN
Al Aweinat
0   150   300 km

government determined to return control of the country's natural resources to its people. By 1973, all of the foreign oil companies had been forced to accept a minimum 51% Libyan participation.

Throughout the 1970s and 80s, Libya adopted a high international profile based on pan-Arabism, its virulent condemnation of western imperialism, its support of liberation movements around the world and a program of military adventurism in neighbouring African countries.

What angered western countries most was (and continues to be) Colonel Gaddafi's support of real and so-called liberation movements and, particularly, his alleged support of terrorist organisations. These have included various extremist Palestinian groups, the Irish Republican Army, Baader-Meinhof and the Red Army Faction. This support has only served to isolate Libya further from the international community.

The most violent reaction to Libya's international politics, however, came in 1985 from US President Ronald Reagan, who had long harboured a grudge against Colonel Gaddafi for his uncompromisingly anti-US stance. President Reagan ordered the US fleet to assert its rights to sail in international waters in the Gulf of Sirt (claimed by Colonel Gaddafi as Libyan territorial waters). The Libyans saw this as a provocative act, as the fleet was within shelling distance of Libya, and they dispatched fighter planes to confront the warships. During a skirmish several Libyan planes were shot down. This was followed in April 1986 by a US air attack on Libyan mainland targets during which dozens of Libyan citizens were killed, including Colonel Gaddafi's adopted baby daughter.

The most serious crisis to hit Libya during the past decade came following the 1988 bombing and destruction of the US Pan Am airliner over Lockerbie in Scotland. Libya was accused of planting the bomb and two Libyans were named as suspects. Investigators from Scotland and the USA demanded that Libya hand over the two for trial, a request refused by Libya, which denied the charges and argued that the suspects would not receive a fair trial in Britain or the USA. Infuriated by Libya's lack of compliance, the UN security council (under strong pressure from the USA) ordered an embargo on any flights in or out of Libya and also a ban on military sales and related spare parts.

Libya Today

In the winter of 1998, after nearly 10 years of negotiations, a breakthrough came when The Hague offered to hold the trial in Holland. The plan finally had everyone's agreement and in the spring of 1999 the two suspects of the Pan Am disaster were flown to The Hague to be officially charged.

After this breakthrough concessions came quickly with Libya accepting responsibility for the shooting of WPC Yvonne Fletcher and the French airliner which was destroyed over the Sudan. The UN Security Council suspended sanctions in April 1999 and airlines resumed their routes to Libya once again.

At home most Libyans would agree despite everything that Gaddafi has occasionally been a beneficial influence on the country (at least in the early years) and he still enjoys some support from within Libya, especially among the young, who make up most of the population. Libya, however, is a country in rapid transition from a largely nomadic to a modern consumer society and this has resulted in many problems. Not least of these is a high inflation rate and the need to import about 80% of its food. Libya's political future depends on getting back to some sort of normality in its dealing with the outside world and addressing its economic realities.

GEOGRAPHY

Libya is the fourth largest country in Africa with 1,759,640 sq km of mostly desert terrain. It is bordered to the west by Tunisia and Algeria; to the east by Egypt; and to the south by the Sudan, Chad and Niger. Only the narrow coastal strip receives sufficient rainfall for agriculture, and it's here that 90% of the population resides and where the two capitals, Tripoli and Benghazi, are situated. The north-eastern part of the country, the Jebel Akhdar area ('Green Mountains'), is the most verdant region and also one of the most beautiful. The interior of the country is largely uninhabited desert dotted with small oasis communities, the largest being Sebha, capital of the Fezzan. Agriculture in the Fezzan is sustained by subsurface aquifers as the region sometimes does not receive any rainfall for years.

CLIMATE

Due to the lack of natural barriers the Sahara Desert and the Mediterranean Sea both affect the climate. Summer is hot, with temperatures on the coast around 30°C, often with high humidity. In the south, it can reach a sweltering 50°C. In winter, the coast can be cool and rainy, while the desert temperatures can drop below freezing at night. During spring and autumn, the *ghibli*, a hot, dry, sand-laden wind sometimes blows. The ghibli can last from a few hours to several days.

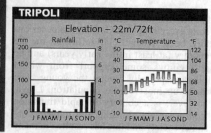

TRIPOLI
Elevation – 22m/72ft

GOVERNMENT & POLITICS

The government of Libya comprises the unique system of People's Committees introduced by Colonel Gaddafi in his *Green Book*. The system swept away all previous administrative structures and replaced them with a pyramidal committee system. The lowest of these are the Basic People's Committees, to which every citizen over the age of 16 belongs. They act as sounding boards and organs of power for local issues and decisions. Once or twice a year a General People's Congress meets; this congress is roughly the equivalent of a parliament, but with General People's Committees to carry out the affairs of state. The system outlaws political parties or activity outside the committees.

Voting for representatives is not carried out by secret ballot and as a result, people tend to vote according to their tribal allegiances, giving rise to some disgruntlement by the weaker factions. The system also stifles independent initiative, so decision-making processes can be rather slow.

Interestingly, under this system there is no formal head of state, though Colonel Gaddafi has adopted the title of Leader of the Revolution. He has held this powerful position for nearly 30 years.

Another curious feature of the system is that Libya technically has two capital cities – Tripoli and Benghazi. This came about because the people of Benghazi (originally a provincial capital) were unhappy about Tripoli being the sole capital.

POPULATION & PEOPLE

Libya has a population of around four million, half of whom are under the age of 15. Most of the population are Arabs, although ethnically there is a mixture of races, including Turks, Berbers and sub-Saharan Africans. In the south, especially around Ghat, there are large Tuareg communities, most of whom now live in towns or settlements rather than pursue a life of desert no-

The Green Book

When Colonel Gaddafi made his historic Zuara Declaration in 1976 he literally dismantled the entire structure of the Libyan state at one stroke. Even his closest revolutionary cronies did not know what was coming. He had withdrawn to the desert for months on end, thinking and secretly writing. The product of this sweated labour was the slender volume of the *Green Book*. Between its covers was the blueprint for Gaddafi's vision of a 'peoples power', a non-state, a Jomhuriyya. Noncapitalist and noncommunist, it was the 'Third Universal Theory' as he modestly called it; the solution to not only Libya's, but to the world's problems.

Briefly, the *Green Book* offers guidance, not only in the economic and political spheres, but also in the areas of sport, men and women, and the home and family. Sayings from the *Green Book* can be seen everywhere in Libya: 'In need freedom is latent'. 'Partners not wage-workers, 'Committees everywhere' and the curious 'Democracy means popular rule not popular expression'.

The *Green Book* has been translated into 84 languages and has spawned thousands of studies, theses and commentaries, enough to fill the library at the Green Book Studies Centre, which exists to dissect the Colonel's slender volume.

madism. Away from the traditionally more cosmopolitan coastal cities tribalism remains strong. It especially affects family relationships, matrimony and social structures.

RELIGION

Libya is virtually 100% Sunni Muslim. The exceptions are foreign workers, who account for the tiny number of Christians and other faiths. There is only one functioning church (in Tripoli) in Libya. The former small Jewish community in Tripoli emigrated en masse to Israel following the revolution.

LANGUAGE

Arabic is the national language of Libya and you are left in no doubt about this fact. All street signs and directions are in Arabic – not even motorway signs are transliterated. Some knowledge of Arabic is therefore extremely helpful. Outside the main cities, where some English or Italian is spoken, few people speak a foreign language. The exception is Ghadhames or Ghat, where some older people speak French. In Jebel Nafusa there are pockets of Berbers who speak Tifinagh, an original Berber language unique to North Africa, as well as Arabic.

Facts for the Visitor

PLANNING

There are two main kinds of trips you can make to Libya: archaeological tours or trips into the desert. You may want to do a combination of both. Winter on the coast can see a surprising amount of rain and cloud in between sunny days. To be sure of good weather, avoid mid-November to March. Travel in the Sahara should be avoided during high summer (June to September) when the temperatures can be extremely high.

The best seasons for travel in Libya are spring and autumn, when the real sting has gone out of the heat in the desert but the weather is still hot and sunny. Spring is particularly recommended for travel in the Jebel Akhdar as the wild flowers are in full bloom among the ruins. The one thing to be aware of in spring and autumn is the occasional blast of the ghibli.

Michelin 953 is the best all-round map for North Africa, while Geoprojects publishes a map of Libya with some city maps included.

VISAS & DOCUMENTS
Passport

Before applying for your Libyan visa, all nationalities must have their passport details translated into Arabic. You can obtain the necessary Arabic stamp from most western embassies or passport offices. Then you will need a translator to write in the details in Arabic. Some Libyan People's Bureaus offer a translation service for a fee, otherwise you will need to get this done privately (or ask an Arabic-speaking friend).

Ensure that your passport has at least two blank pages for the visa and entry/exit stamps. You will not get a visa if your passport has an Israeli stamp in it.

Visas

All nationalities, except those from Arab countries and Malta, require a visa. Some years ago the Libyan government declared that the country was to develop its tourism potential and that all nationalities (except Israeli citizens) were welcome to visit as tourists. In theory, this means that it should be straightforward to obtain a tourist visa, but in practice, this new tourist visa rule is unevenly applied from embassy to embassy. Although there are a few individual exceptions, you must apply for your visa in your home country. For those countries without diplomatic representation (eg the UK, USA, Canada, Australia, New Zealand), you must obtain a visa authorisation from Libya. This can be done through one of the private tourist operators in Libya (see Organised Tours in the Getting Around section). Once authorised, you can get your visa from your local Libyan Interests Section (if you have one) or the UN Libyan mission in the USA. If there is no Libyan representation in your country, as is the case in Australia and New Zealand, you can organise to collect your visa at a nominated Libyan embassy in another specified country. Visas cannot be processed by post.

Visa charges vary from country to country, but the average cost is US$30. Allow at least a couple of weeks for processing. Visas are normally valid for three months from the date of issue for a stay of up to a month. Receiving visas is by no means automatic. Those most likely to be refused include journalists or anyone working in the media. Women travelling alone, especially if unmarried, are also unlikely to be granted visas.

On arrival in Libya, all foreigners must register within seven days at the *jawwazat* (security office). Hotels can do this for you. If you do it yourself, take along someone to translate as the staff only speak Arabic. There is a small fee for the stamp.

Warning It is currently against US law for its citizens to travel to Libya. Those doing so risk a large fine if they are found out by the US authorities.

Visa Extensions Visa extensions are possible, but are not easy to organise. You need to visit the jawwazat (in Tripoli or major towns) and be prepared for a lot of form filling (in Arabic, of course), and you will need two photographs. Tripoli's jawwazat (☎ 021-360 5561, fax 360 5568) is near the junction of sharias An-Nasr and Al-Masirah al-Kubra and is open from 9 am to noon daily except Friday.

Visas for Neighbouring Countries You need a visa to enter the following neighbouring countries of Libya:

Egypt It's possible to get an Egyptian visa at the embassy in Tripoli (see the following Embassies & Consulates in Libya section for the address), but it takes two or three days to come through. The embassy is open from 9 am to 2 pm and you need one passport photo and 20LD.

Tunisia The Tunisian embassy in Libya does not issue visas to nonresidents. Western tourists do not need a visa to visit Tunisia. The only exceptions are Australians and New Zealanders, who should apply at a nominated embassy en route to Libya. Other nationalities should apply in their home country.

Other Documents

It is always useful in Libya to have a supply of passport photos. You will need photos if you want to join a local youth hostel, get a permit to visit the Acacus Mountain area or apply for a visa extension.

If you are planning to drive in Libya, you will need a current international driving licence. If you are bringing your own vehicle, you will need documentary proof that you are the owner. You can buy insurance at the border.

Student cards are not generally recognised in Libya.

EMBASSIES & CONSULATES
Libyan Embassies & Consulates

For the address of the Libyan embassy in Egypt see that country chapter.

Diplomatic representation abroad includes the following:

Belgium
    Embassy:
    (☎ 649 15 03, 649 16 56)
    Ave Victoria 28, 1050 Brussels
Denmark
    Embassy:
    (☎ 26 36 11)
    Rosenvaengets Hovedvej 4, 2100 Ø Copenhagen
France
    Embassy:
    (☎ 01 55 34 070, 01 70 47 160)
    2 Rue Charles Lamoureux, 75116 Paris
Germany
    Embassy:
    (☎ 82 00 90, fax 36 42 60)
    Beethovenalle 12a, 53173 Bonn
Greece
    Embassy:
    (☎ 647 2120, 647 2122)
    Vironoz 13, 152-154 Psychikon, Athens

Italy
  Embassy:
  (☎ 83 09 51)
  Via Nomentana 365, Rome
Malta
  Embassy:
  (☎ 356 34947)
  Dar Tarek, Tower Rd, Sliema
Spain
  Embassy:
  (☎ 548 0500, 548 0458)
  Alphonso Rodriguez Santamaria 6, Madrid
Switzerland
  Embassy:
  (☎ 43 30 76)
  Travelveg 2, Bern
Tunisia
  Embassy:
  (☎ 78 08 66)
  48 Rue du 1er Juin, Tunis
  Consulate:
  (☎ 28 54 02)
  74 Ave Mohammed V, Tunis
UK
  Embassy:
  (☎ 020-7486 8387)
  Libyan Interests Section, Royal Embassy of
  Saudi Arabia, 119 Harley St, London W1
USA
  (☎ 752 5775)
  Libyan Diplomatic Mission (represents Libya
  in the USA and Canada), 309-315 East 48th
  Street, NYC, NY 10017

Embassies & Consulates in Libya

Opening hours are generally from 9 or 9.30
am to anywhere between 11.30 am and 2
pm. All embassies are closed on Fridays
and their own national holidays. All of the
following are in Tripoli:

Belgium
  Embassy:
  (☎ 335 0115/6/7/8)
  1 Sharia Abu Ubeida ibn
  al-Jarrah, PO Box 663
Egypt
  Consulate:
  (☎/fax 333 9876)
  Sharia Omar al-Mukhtar
France
  Embassy:
  (☎ 477 4891/2)
  Sharia Ahmad Lotfi Said, PO Box 312
Germany
  Embassy:
  (☎ 333 0554)
  Sharia Hassan al-Mashay, PO Box 302

Italy
  Embassy:
  (☎ 333 4130/2/3)
  1 Sharia Wahran, PO Box 219
Netherlands
  Embassy:
  (☎ 444 1549, 444 1550)
  20 Sharia Jalal Bayer, PO Box 3801
Spain
  Embassy:
  (☎ 333 5463, 333 6797)
  Sharia al-Jazayir, PO Box 2302
Switzerland
  Embassy:
  (☎ 361 4118/9)
  Sharia al-Wahshi, PO Box 439
Tunisia
  Consulate:
  (☎ 360 7181)
  Sharia Bin 'Ashur
UK
  Embassy:
  (☎ 333 1191)
  British Interests Section, c/o Italian Embassy
USA
  Embassy:
  (☎ 333 7797)
  US Interests Section, c/o Belgian Embassy

CUSTOMS

Clearing customs can be a lengthy process
due to long queues at the border posts, ports
or airports and thorough searches of baggage and vehicles. All pork and alcohol
products are prohibited. Books, magazines
and videos may be confiscated. Although
they are not banned, there have been reports of video cameras and personal computers being confiscated.

Immigration forms are in Arabic and if
you do not read the language you will have
to engage the help of an Arabic-speaking
passer-by.

MONEY
Costs

Libya is by no means cheap. The government has recently closed a loophole
whereby foreigners were paying their hotel
bills with cheap black market dinars. Now
all foreigners have to pay in hard currency
at the expensive official rate. So, unless you
are planning to stay in hostels exclusively,

plan on a budget of at least US$60 per day. The good news is that food and public transport, or shared taxis, are cheap.

Currency

The Libyan Dinar (LD) has a rate fixed by the Bank of Libya that has remained virtually unchanged for years. Dinars are issued in 0.25, 0.50, one, five and 10 notes. Coins, which are rarely used these days, are available in 10, 100 and 250 dirhams. There are 1000 dirhams to a dinar.

Exchange Rates

country	unit		dinars
Australia	A$1	=	LD0.24
Canada	C$1	=	LD0.22
Egypt	E£1	=	LD0.09
euro	€1	=	LD0.43
France	10FF	=	LD0.90
Germany	DM1	=	LD0.20
Japan	¥100	=	LD0.40
New Zealand	NZ$1	=	LD0.20
Tunisia	TD1	=	LD0.32
UK	UK£1	=	LD0.52
USA	US$1	=	LD0.32

Exchanging Money

Undoubtedly, the favoured foreign currency is US dollars, with German marks a close second. Most hard currencies are easily changed in banks or large hotels. The soft currencies of Libya's neighbours are not so popular, so it's best to exchange these before reaching the border.

Changing money at the foreign exchange desks in hotels or banks is no problem – except for the appallingly low rate of exchange they offer. You will be given an official exchange receipt, which you will need to show if you want pay your hotel bill in dinars.

ATMs & Credit Cards Credit cards or any other form of banking cards are of no use in Libya.

Black Market Because of the punitive foreign exchange rate set by the bank, there is a thriving black market in currency ex-

change. Almost all of this illegal money trade is conducted in US dollars in high denomination notes. The difference between the official and black market rate is considerable – about six times the difference. If you choose to change money in this way, be aware that it is *strictly illegal*, with dire punishments if you get caught.

Tipping & Bargaining

Libya does not have a big tipping culture and certainly people never have their hand out expecting one. The exception is in the big hotels, where the staff are mostly from Egypt or Morocco, and where tipping is a different matter entirely. It is useful to have a supply of low denomination US dollars for these occasions.

POST & COMMUNICATIONS
Post

Libya is still sticking to air mail rates even though there is no air mail! Letters to Europe cost 350 dirhams, to the USA and Canada 750 dirhams and to Australia and New Zealand 850 dirhams. Parcel post is not recommended.

Sending Mail

The main towns have a post office where you can buy stamps and send mail. There are mail boxes in the larger hotels. Allow a week to 10 days for mail to arrive from Tripoli, longer if you post from anywhere else.

Receiving Mail

Poste restante services are available for letters, not parcels, in the Tripoli post office. Address mail to: (Your Name), Poste Restante, Main Post Office, Tripoli, Libya. If you know where you will be staying, have your mail sent to your hotel. It is a good idea to let the hotel know you are expecting mail.

Telephone

The country code for Libya is ☎ 218, followed by the area code (minus the zero), then the subscriber number. Area codes for the major cities and regions are:

Benghazi	☎ 061
Derna	☎ 081
Ghadhames	☎ 0484
Gharyan	☎ 041
Ghat	☎ 0724
Khoms	☎ 031
Misrata	☎ 051
Nalut	☎ 0470
Sabratha	☎ 024
Sebha	☎ 071
Sirt	☎ 054
Tripoli	☎ 021
Yefren	☎ 0421

The main post offices also offer public telephone services for local and international calls. The system involves filling in a slip of paper, handing it in at the counter and waiting until you are directed to a booth to make your call; you can omit the 00 for international calls. Pay at the counter when you have completed your call. You may be asked for ID, so take your passport or hotel registration card along.

Fax
The only public access to fax machines is in the larger hotels and using them can be costly. Fax machines are often only available during office hours. Be sure to tell the staff if you are expecting a reply.

BOOKS
Travel
Oasis Kingdom, by Nina Epton. Travels in 1950s Libya.

Around the Shores of the Mediterranean, by Eric Newby. Entertaining account of the writer's visit to Libya before the tourists arrived.

Children of Allah, by Agnes Newton Keith. Across the Libyan desert in the 1960s.

A Cure for Serpents, by Alberto di Pirajno. A doctor's account of his tour round Libya in the 1950s.

History & Politics
The Garamantes of Southern Libya, by Charles Daniels. The only published account of the ancient history of the Garamantian desert empire.

Rome in Africa, by Susan Raven. A detailed and illustrated guide to the Roman empire in Africa, with site maps.

A Traveller's History of North Africa, by Barnaby Rogerson. An authoritative and readable account of the history of the region.

Libya, A Modern History, by John Wright. A detailed and well-written account of the revolution and Gaddafi's rise to power.

More general Middle East titles, some of which also contain coverage of Libya, are listed in the Books section in the Regional Facts for the Visitor chapter at the beginning of this book.

NEWSPAPERS & MAGAZINES
The press in Libya is government controlled and censored. All regular publications are in Arabic. It is virtually impossible to buy imported foreign newspapers or magazines other than titles from the Arab world.

RADIO & TV
There are two government-run local TV stations. Channel One broadcasts an English news summary at 9 pm. Satellite stations are available at the more expensive hotels. They show CNN, BBC World and a number of European stations. The government periodically restricts the hotels from showing satellite broadcasts.

PHOTOGRAPHY & VIDEO
Tripoli and Benghazi have a few camera shops where film, video tape and spare parts (such as special batteries) are available. Prices are high though. For example, a roll of Fuji or Kodak reversal film will cost about 20LD and a lithium battery a whopping 45LD. Processing is possible and results are not bad with colour print film, but E6 processing is not recommended.

HEALTH
Health care is available to foreigners at low cost in either the main hospitals, or in private clinics (in the cities). The standard is reasonably good and even small towns have well-equipped clinics. Pharmacies often sell prescription medicines over the counter, although availability is sometimes limited.

There are relatively few health risks in Libya. There is a tiny risk of malaria in the south-west of the country; it is recommended that you use a good repellent rather than take prophylactics.

LAUNDRY
Getting your washing done is a constant headache as there are no public laundrettes and the hotel laundry services are usually slow and expensive. Most travellers resort to hand washing. A supply of detergent and one of those clever elastic wash lines are a good idea.

TOILETS
Public toilets are nonexistent in Libya. Hotels usually have toilets at lobby level, and these are often your best bet. Restaurants have toilets, which are usually a bit disorderly and dirty. In out-of-the-way places, often the only option is to use the bathrooms at the local mosque. These are always squat-down toilets. Take a supply of toilet paper, as it is nonexistent outside the cities.

WOMEN TRAVELLERS
It is important for women travellers arriving from Tunisia or Egypt to remember that Libya is much more conservative and unused to tourists than either of those two countries. You should therefore dress accordingly. Trousers are perfectly OK, as long as they are loose-fitting. The same applies to T-shirts and other tops, although these should have sleeves to cover the upper arm. It is also a good idea to wear a waistcoat over the top. There is no need to cover your head, except when entering a mosque. Swimsuits (not bikinis) should not be too skimpy and should definitely only be worn on the beach. See Society & Conduct in the Facts about the Region chapter for more details on dress codes.

DANGERS & ANNOYANCES
The deterioration of cars and the subsequent drop in safety is one of the main dangers. It is not unusual to come across cars with only one light or no lights at all, being driven on the highway at night. Also, the lack of internal air transport means that more people are driving long distances and much too fast for safety.

For desert travellers the dangers of land mines from WWII remains. Certain areas of the desert, notably south of Tobruk, still pose a danger to the unwary. The chances of getting blown up by a land mine are very small but real nonetheless. If travelling in areas known to be mined take a local guide and stay on the tracks.

BUSINESS HOURS
Libya has an Islamic working week, with Friday as the day off. Summer business hours are from 7 am to 2 pm, and in the winter 8 am to 1 pm. Government offices are open from 8 am to 2 pm.

PUBLIC HOLIDAYS & SPECIAL EVENTS
Libya observes all the Islamic holidays (see the Facts for the Visitor chapter at the beginning of this book), in addition to several national holidays:

Declaration of the Jamahiriya
  2 March – school holiday and a day of speeches and rallies to celebrate the founding of the Jamahirya.
Evacuation of Foreign Military Bases
  11 June – an excuse for some rousing anti-imperialist speeches and maybe a military parade.
Revolution Day
  1 September – biggest nonreligious holiday on the Libyan calendar. Green Square is often the scene of a big rally with speeches by Colonel Gaddafi. Sometimes it is held in Benghazi for variety. Parades of various kinds can go on for days.
Day of Mourning
  26 October – commemorating the Libyans killed or exiled by the Italians. Everything closes, including the borders, and there are no international telephones, telexes or ferries.

ACCOMMODATION
In Libya most of your budget will probably go on accommodation. As all foreigners have to pay in hard currency at the official rate, it makes even the most modest hotel

room an expensive item. There is a serious shortage of decent budget hotels; most accommodation is in the four star business hotels. There are some fairly cheap and not at all cheerful dives. Few of these cheapies are clean and some are only for the brave. Even the dives will cost about US$25 per night.

The only real budget option in Libya is to use the HI hostels, of which there are several. Some are very good indeed, while others are less so. In some places the hostels listed in the association handbook have been taken over as student accommodation or closed down. The best ones are recommended in the appropriate sections. The head office for Libyan hostels is in Tripoli (☎ 444 5171) on Sharia Amr ibn al-As, and they can answer inquiries about hostels throughout the country.

FOOD & DRINKS

While food in Libya is not wonderful, it is at least tasty and inexpensive. There are reasonably good restaurants in the big hotels (you can pay for meals in dinars), and the better ones can attract a large crowd of nonresident diners. Chefs are often Moroccan, so what is on offer is seldom Libyan cuisine.

In Tripoli and Benghazi, there is also the possibility of finding non-Arabic cuisine. Mostly, the food on offer is standard North African fare, with some Middle Eastern favourites thrown in. Smaller restaurants and snack bars often have the best food; this can include fresh *felafel* (deep-fried chickpeas), Egyptian pizzas, *fuul* (fava bean paste) and *couscous* (steamed semolina served with a meat stew).

Drinks are the most disappointing aspect of dining out, not only because there is no alcohol (Libya is completely dry), but because of the endless number of sweet, gassy drinks that take its place. If you are lucky, you will find a place that sells nonalcoholic beer or an interesting Campari-like drink called Bitter Soda. Otherwise, stick to mineral water – it's really very good.

SHOPPING

The best souq in the country is in Tripoli. One of the best buys is antique silver jewellery. Old rugs and textiles are also a good buy if you can find them.

Apart from the Tripoli souq, Benghazi has a good gold souq and Ghadhames has some interesting leather crafts for sale. Shopping in the regions is rather limited.

Getting There & Away

AIR

For the past 10 years Libya had been subject to sanctions, which affected air travel; there were no flights permitted to enter, leave or even fly over Libyan air space. This meant travellers had to enter the country overland or via the sea.

With the recent suspension of sanctions, however, access to Libya is now becoming a lot easier. Some airlines have already resumed flights to Tripoli, and by the time you read this there will probably be even more flight options available.

Airlines & Routes

As of August 1999, the following airlines were offering a service to Tripoli: British Airways flies from London Gatwick three times a week; Lufthansa from Frankfurt five times a week; Aeroflot from Moscow once a week; Alitalia from Rome twice a week, and from Milan three times a week; Turkish Airlines from İstanbul twice a week; Sudan Airlines from Khartoum on Thursday only; Royal Jordanian from Amman once a week; and Syrian Airlines from Damascus twice a week.

The national carrier, Libyan Airlines, has a depleted fleet due to the UN embargo which forbade the import of aircraft or aircraft parts. At the time of writing it started sporadic flights to Egypt, Malta and Tunisia, but frequency and costs could not be confirmed.

LAND

Almost all travellers to Libya now use the land borders. The two that are open to foreigners are the coastal border post with

Tunisia at Ras Jedir and Sallum at the border with Egypt. International bus services run from Cairo or Alexandria in Egypt, and from Tunis or Sfax in Tunisia. Fares are cheap. One-way tickets to Alexandria cost 42LD, to Cairo 50LD and to Tunis 20LD. Shared taxis also run on these routes as well as from Djerba in Tunisia. In most cases taxis drop you at the border post and you get another one for your onward journey on the other side.

Apart from the two border posts mentioned earlier, no other borders are open to foreigners. Because of the concentration of people crossing at these two points, allow plenty of time to cross. Waits of several hours are not unusual. Also be prepared for a bout of form-filling in Arabic. There have been numerous reports of hassles at the Tunisian border post for those who have just left Libya. These involve delays, excessive passport checks, luggage searches and sometimes the confiscation of guidebooks purchased in Libya.

SEA

There is a daily car ferry to and from Malta to Tripoli operated by the General National Maritime Transport Company (☎ 333 4865), Sharia Magarief, Tripoli. This ferry service is subject to frequent cancellations and delays due to season, weather and general chaos. To book tickets in Malta, ring Sea Malta (☎ 2322 30/9) in Valletta. See the regional Getting There & Away chapter for details.

Getting Around

AIR

Libyan Arab Airlines operates a skeleton air service on some of its domestic routes. There were only two aircraft operating at the time of writing. In theory, there should be one flight a day in each direction between Tripoli and Benghazi, and a couple a week from Benghazi to Sebha. All of these flights are subject to cancellation or delay.

In Tripoli, there is a central Libyan Arab Airlines office in the Al-Kebir Hotel (☎ 333 7500, 335 5686). The head office in Tripoli is on Sharia Haiti (☎ 20333 or 20193). In Benghazi, the main office is on Sharia Gamal Abdel Nasser (☎ 92011/2/3). In Sebha, the airline office (☎ 29120) is on Sharia Mohammed Megharief.

BUS

In the absence of good air connections, the bus services between towns and cities has increased. The downside is that although the services are frequent and cheap, the buses are also very full, and sometimes overbooked. It is strongly recommended that you buy tickets the day before you intend travelling and that you arrive before the departure time (buses have been known to leave ahead of schedule if they are full).

The main bus company for intercity travel is Fast Transport Company, which operates comfortable, air-con vehicles, some of which have video.

The main routes to/from Tripoli are Benghazi, Ghadhames, Gharyan and Jadu, Khoms (for Leptis Magna), Nalut, Ras Jedir (for the Tunisian border), Sebha and Yefren. From Benghazi there are regular buses to Sebha, Sallum (for the Egyptian border), Derna, Al-Beida (for Cyrene) and Tobruk.

SHARED TAXI

An alternative to using buses is to use the shared taxis that operate on many routes, long or short. They are easily identified by their yellow paintwork. All towns have a shared taxi rank of some sort. The fares are similar to buses, or slightly higher, but they offer more flexibility for travel. For long distances though, these taxis can be cramped and hot as the drivers like to pack people in like sardines. If you offer a driver a few more dinars, he will usually make a detour to take you all the way to your destination if it's not too far off his route.

In addition to the routes covered by the buses, shared taxis also serve the smaller towns of the Jebel Nafusa and the Jebel Ahkdar, all the towns on the coast road, plus destinations between Sebha and Ghat, and Sebha and the coast.

CAR & MOTORCYCLE

To enter Libya with a car or motorcycle, you must have proof of ownership and a current international drivers licence. You will have to buy compulsory insurance at the border and will be issued with temporary Libyan plates. There is a deposit of 60LD for these, which is refunded when you leave. The roads in Libya are generally good but those into the desert are subject to *wadi* (water course) flooding occasionally and blockage by sand dunes frequently. For motorcyclists, smaller roads have the added hazard of potholes.

Driving conditions are hazardous as local drivers tend to drive too fast. Beware of cars or other vehicles at night with defective lights (or no lights at all!). Checkpoints are frequent, especially approaching borders, so have your papers and passport handy at all times.

Last but not least is the problem of road signs being only in Arabic script. It is a good idea to familiarise yourself with the written Arabic for your destination. Motorcyclists should contact the Tripoli Motorcycle Federation (☎ 444 1274), PO Box 12794, Tripoli for advice.

Road Rules

Driving is on the right. Speed limits are universally ignored, but they are 80km/h on the highway and 40km/h in town. Priority is from the left on roundabouts; pedestrian crossings exist but few drivers stop unless they have to.

Rental

None of the big name car rental companies operate in Libya; they are all local independent operators. Most have a desk or office in the lobbies of the larger hotels in Tripoli or Benghazi. The average cost for a modest saloon (sedan) is about 50LD per day, with a deposit of 300 to 400LD.

ORGANISED TOURS

There are a number of privately owned travel agents and tour operators in Libya. Some are quite large efficient organisations with their own vehicles whereas some comprise only

one man with a telephone, who will buy in the services you want. The following tour operators are recommended:

Agence Akacus Voyages
   (☎ 2804) Ghat. This French-speaking operation was the pioneer of desert tourism in the deep south and it uses local drivers and guides.
Robban Travel
   (☎ 444 1530, fax 444 8065) 212 Sharia Jamahiriya, PO Box 84272, Tripoli. A small agency that caters for individuals and groups of all sizes. It also offers special caving tours.
Wings Travel & Tours
   (☎ 333 18 55, fax 333 08 81) Sharia Garnata, Tripoli. Runs adventure and special interest tours.
Winzrik Tourism Services Company
   (☎ 361 11 23/4/5, fax 361 11 26) Sharia 7th September, Tripoli. A comprehensive operation in classical and desert tours. It has offices throughout Libya and operates a camp at Lake Gabraoun.

In addition to tours, the agents can arrange visas and book tickets for your onward travel.

Tripoli

Tripoli, known as Tarabulus in Arabic, is the capital of Libya and the country's principal port. It has a population of approximately two million.

Known in the past as 'the white bride of the Mediterranean', Tripoli has lost most of its pristine allure but it still retains a good deal of character. There are many colonial buildings, historic mosques and a lively *medina* (old city). The city is unlike other large cities in North Africa. The Turkish and Italian colonial periods left a distinctive mark on the architecture, and the revolutionary period has ensured that the usual hallmarks of a modern commercial city, such as advertising hoardings, are completely absent.

History

Tripoli was founded by the Phoenicians in about 500 BC, and was one of many settlements established by them along the African coast. After the fall of Carthage in 146 BC,

Tripoli became a Roman protectorate and later a part of the province of Africa Nova. Under the Romans the city grew prosperous and, together with Sabratha and Leptis Magna (the other cities of the 'tripolis'), provided the Roman empire with grain, wild animals and slaves.

When the Vandals overran North Africa in the 5th century, the damage to the city was devastating. Its conquest in 533 by Emperor Justinian's general, Belisarius, and the establishment of Byzantine rule prevented the city from falling into total decay. When the first Arab invasion occurred in the 7th century, a new town was built among the ruins of the old. During the 16th century, the city was occupied in quick succession by the Spanish and the Knights of Malta. The most visible result of their occupation is the extensive work carried out on Tripoli Castle, the Assai al-Hamra, which has been fortified and extended throughout its history.

The most lasting architectural monuments in the old city were built by the Turks, who constructed most of the mosques, *hammams* (Turkish-style bathhouses with sauna and massage) and souqs that are still standing today. Most of today's old town dates from this era.

It was not until the Italians invaded and conquered Libya that the city burst out of the confines of its walls. The area that now comprises central Tripoli used to be farms and gardens. The Italians also built colonnaded streets radiating from the castle. When Libya became independent, many families left the old city to live in the newly vacated Italian apartments and houses. The old city suffered from neglect, a process which is only now beginning to halt.

Orientation

Easily the most dominant feature of Tripoli is the castle, which sits on the northern promontory overlooking what used to be the sea. A recent development has reclaimed about 500m of land and a motorway now runs between the old Corniche (coastal road) and the sea. Next to the castle is Green Square, a vast open area cleared after the revolution as a venue for mass rallies. All the main shopping and business streets sprawl from this square.

The city is divided into western and eastern halves by the castle and the tangle of lanes comprising the medina. In the western half you will find the town's beaches and some seaside hotels, but little else of interest. On the eastern side, there is the old, tree-lined Corniche that leads past a line of Ottoman buildings. This is where most of the business class hotels are located. There are also small green spaces with cafes which are popular with the locals. Farther along to the east, almost opposite Mehari Hotel, is the ferry port. Everything of interest is within walking distance.

Information

Tourist Offices The best source of information is the General Secretariat of Tourism (☎ 360 3405, 360 4006, fax 360 3400, 600291), PO Box 207, Tripoli. It has brochures and maps in several languages and some of the staff speak English. The office is about 2km east from Green Square, along the Corniche. It is a low building overlooking the sea, but there's no sign so you may need to ask directions.

Money The city's main banks are found on or near Green Square, on Sharia 1st September, Sharia al-Magarief and Sharia Omar al-Mukhtar. They are open from 8 am to 2 pm Saturday to Thursday. Outside banking hours, most of the main hotels have an exchange facility and the rates are often the same as the banks.

Post & Communications The main post office is on Midan al-Jazayir, near the former cathedral at the end of Sharia al-Magarief. Apart from the usual services, this post office offers a collectors' counter for special-edition stamps. There is also a smaller post office on the east side of Green Square. Opening hours are from 8 am to 2 pm.

The public telephone office is in a nearby building and is open 24 hours. It is in the large, Art Deco-style complex opposite the

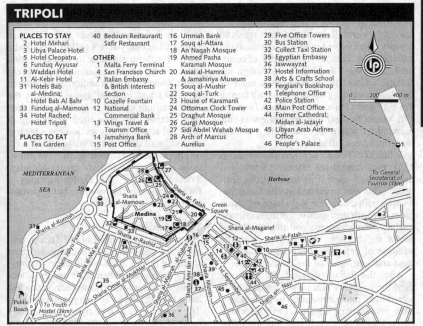

TRIPOLI

PLACES TO STAY
2 Hotel Mehari
3 Libya Palace Hotel
5 Hotel Cleopatra
6 Funduq Ayyusar
9 Waddan Hotel
11 Al-Kebir Hotel
31 Hotels Bab
   al-Medina;
   Hotel Bab Al Bahr
33 Funduq al-Mamoun
34 Hotel Rached;
   Hotel Tripoli

PLACES TO EAT
8 Tea Garden

40 Bedouin Restaurant;
   Safir Restaurant

OTHER
1 Malta Ferry Terminal
4 San Francisco Church
7 Italian Embassy
   & British Interests
   Section
10 Gazelle Fountain
12 National
   Commercial Bank
13 Wings Travel &
   Tourism Office
14 Jamahiriya Bank
15 Post Office

16 Ummah Bank
17 Souq al-Attara
18 An Naqah Mosque
19 Ahmed Pasha
   Karamali Mosque
20 Assai al-Hamra
   & Jamahiriya Museum
21 Souq al-Mushir
22 Souq al-Turk
23 House of Karamanli
24 Ottoman Clock Tower
25 Draghut Mosque
26 Gurgi Mosque
27 Sidi Abdel Wahab Mosque
28 Arch of Marcus
   Aurelius

29 Five Office Towers
30 Bus Station
32 Collect Taxi Station
35 Egyptian Embassy
36 Jawwayzat
37 Hostel Information
38 Arts & Crafts School
39 Fergiani's Bookshop
41 Telephone Office
42 Police Station
43 Main Post Office
44 Former Cathedral;
   Midan al-Jazayir
45 Libyan Arab Airlines
   Office
46 People's Palace

0   200   400 m

MEDITERRANEAN SEA

Harbour

To General
Secretariat of
Tourism (1km)

Sharia al-Mamoun

Medina

Green
Square

Sharia al-Fatah

Sharia al-Magarief

Sharia al-Fatah

Sharia al-Kurnish

Sharia Jabyu Frawa

Sharia al-Ma'ari

Sharia ar-Rashid

Sharia Amri Ibn al-As

Sharia al-Masirah

Sharia 1st September

Sharia Mizran

Sharia an Nasr

Sharia Omar al-Mukhtar

Public
Beach

To Youth
Hostel (3km)

former cathedral. As you enter the courtyard from Midan al-Jazayir, it is on the right. For international calls, you will need to show some ID (your passport or hotel registration card). You can also make calls from the larger hotels but the costs are much higher. Fax facilities are only available at hotels.

Photography & Video There is a good photographic shop on Sharia 1st September, about 200m from Green Square. It sells film and video tapes and can process film.

Travel Agencies There are several good travel agencies in Tripoli. Apart from arranging tours around the country, they can also make reservations for onward travel. The agencies can also handle ticketing and reservations for domestic flights and offer advice. For travel agents details see Organised Tours in the Getting Around section earlier.

Bookshops The only bookshop in Tripoli that sells English and European language books is Fergiani's Bookshop on Sharia 1st September. Fergiani's publishes its own books, mostly faxes of early travels in North Africa, under the DARF imprint. They also have a range of local guidebooks, some English-language fiction, maps and postcards. Unfortunately, their books are extremely expensive.

Medical Services There are several privately run medical clinics in the suburbs of Tripoli as well as a couple of public hospitals. Unless you are fluent in Arabic it is best to ask your hotel to call a recommended doctor who will come to your hotel or arrange for an ambulance to collect you. Medical consultations and facilities are efficient and inexpensive. If the problem is serious, repatriation by air is a possibility.

LIBYA

Tripoli Castle

The Assai al-Hamra, which represented the seat of power in Tripolitania until the 20th century, has evolved over the centuries into a vast citadel containing a labyrinth of courtyards, alleyways and houses. Although the site itself dates from Roman times, much of the castle's existing interior was built during the 17th and 18th centuries. Plans from the 17th century reveal that the castle was surrounded by water. The landside moat has long since been filled in.

When the Turks occupied the castle in 1551, they carried out extensive works and the governors used it as their official residence. This was continued by the Karamanlis, who built the harems and a large reception room in which they received official visitors.

Under the Spaniards and the Knights of Malta, the defences were built up with the addition of defensive towers in the southwest and south-east of the citadel.

After the Italian conquest, the governor used the castle as official offices and parts were turned into a museum. The Italians also cut a road through the citadel to connect the two halves of the city. It is in this space that the Jamahiriya Museum has been built to house the national collection of antiquities. Entry to the castle is through a large gate on the landward side near the Souq al-Mushir. Most of the buildings inside the castle are used by the Department of Antiquities.

Jamahiriya Museum

Entry to this museum is from Green Square through a huge wooden door. The new museum was built in consultation with UNESCO at enormous cost and is extremely well designed. The exhibits are laid out chronologically, starting with prehistory and early Libyan tribal history, and working up through the marble galleries to one devoted to the revolution.

The most impressive parts of the collection are the mosaics, statues and artefacts from classical antiquity. The Roman finds from Leptis Magna are particularly stunning. Overall, this is one of the finest collections of classical art in the Mediterranean.

For those interested in early Islamic architecture, there is a gallery devoted to the various styles and periods of building in Libya. Checking out this gallery can also be useful for those planning to visit the actual sites. There are also various folklore exhibits demonstrating traditional life, both in the cities and in rural areas. Perhaps the most startling exhibit is in the natural history section; for those tired of looking at classical artefacts, this section has a bizarre collection of deformed animals.

The museum is open from 8.30 am to noon and 2 to 5 pm daily except Monday. The entrance fee is 3LD. Photography is forbidden inside the museum but is permitted in the castle grounds.

The Medina

The medina, in the heart of old Tripoli, provides the most visually exciting and best shopping in the city, if not the entire country. The souq has an authentic air and the goods on display cater to local tastes, although a few items of tourist tat have been spotted recently. The good news is that there is absolutely none of the hassle usually associated with a trip to a souq. Shopkeepers are friendly and often curious, but there is no pressure to buy.

The old walled city contains virtually all of Tripoli's historic buildings. Recently, moves have been made to halt the process of dilapidation and undertake sympathetic restoration of the most important buildings. The medina in Tripoli is one of the largest in North Africa and contains a wealth of historic mosques, khans (inns), hammams and houses.

Starting from the castle, the first road into the medina leads past the old Bank of Libya and passes a decorative Ottoman clocktower, built in the 19th century. The road then follows what used to be the coast for a few hundred metres, bringing you to one of the old city gates – a huge decorated door called the Bab Draghut. Behind this is Draghut Mosque, named after a famous corsair admiral. The mosque has an Islamic school and a cemetery where the admiral is buried.

If you continue on the coast road for another 100m, you will come to the Sidi

Abdel Wahab Mosque. Behind the mosque is the only Roman artefact of any significance in Tripoli – the **Arch of Marcus Aurelius**, which, although in some need of restoration, is an impressive decorated triumphal structure.

Immediately behind the arch, and towards the city, is **Gurgi Mosque**, one of the most beautiful in the city. The courtyard has lovely tilework and inlaid marble decorations. The prayer hall alone has 16 domes and the minaret is the tallest in the city. Next door to Gurgi Mosque, on Zenkat Spania, is **Ahmed Pasha's house**, formerly the British consulate. This fine old house has been restored and is to be used as a library and gallery, which will be open to the public.

Another important old building that has been restored is **House of Karamanli**, near an ancient crossroad in the centre of the city called Al-Arba Asaht. The crossroad is marked by four Roman columns set into the corners of the buildings. Note that the name of the old house in Arabic is 'Hosn al-Harem', as you will almost certainly need to ask directions.

Back at the south-eastern end of the medina, near the castle, is **Souq al-Mushir**. The entrance from Green Square is through an archway. Immediately to the left is **Souq al-Attara**, which houses the jewellery shops. If, instead of turning left into Souq al-Attara, you continue straight ahead, you will see on your left the splendid **Ahmed Pasha Karamanli Mosque**, the largest mosque in the old city. Turn left after passing the mosque and follow the road around to the right. You will then enter **Souq al-Turk**, a partly covered market that sells clothes and all manner of general goods. **Mohammed Pasha Mosque** is about 200m along on the right, marked by an elaborately carved door.

The oldest mosque in Tripoli is **An-Naqah Mosque**, which is well worth a look. In all, there are 38 mosques within the walls of the old city. If you only want to see one or two, go for the Ahmed Pasha Karamanli and Gurgi mosques, as their decoration is particularly fine.

Modern City

Outside the medina radiates the modern city, most of which was built during the Turkish and Italian eras. The Italianate colonnaded shopping streets lead off Green Square east and south. At the end of Sharia 1st September is a former **cathedral**. This was built in 1928 by the Italians in a neo-Romanesque style, but since the revolution it has become a mosque. One of the city's small but attractive landmarks is **Gazelle Fountain**, which dates from the 1920s and now sits on a small roundabout surrounded by palm trees. Another 1920s landmark is **People's Palace**, which was previously the royal residence in the days of the monarchy. Some of the best **colonial architecture** in the city from the Turkish period can be found on Sharia Mizran. The old **Arts & Crafts School** has some extremely interesting decorative tilework in the entrance and courtyard.

Places to Stay

Hotels in Tripoli tend to be at one end of the spectrum or the other: either business class establishments or unspeakable dives. What's more, they tend to be heavily booked, especially if there is some kind of gathering (such as 1st September celebrations). Hotels also have a reputation for not always honouring bookings. This often happens when a government department requisitions rooms for a conference at short notice.

Places to Stay – Budget

There are few genuinely cheap places to stay in Tripoli and anything under 20LD is for emergencies or die-hards only. The only really cheap option that doesn't involve sharing your room with the local wildlife is the hostel. The central hostel listed in the HI Handbook is only open for information, the actual hostel is in a suburb of Tripoli.

Youth Hostel (☎ 74755) is in Gagaresh, on the coast about 3km south west from the centre of Tripoli. If you follow the main Gagaresh road south, take the second turn-off on the right after the big post office. This road leads to the sea, and the hostel is a large new building close to a small fishing harbour. It can be difficult to find and is not signposted, so you may have to ask directions. There are frequent shared taxis serving this route. There are no family rooms, only dormitories, but it is clean and modern. There is a large restaurant and meals cost around 5LD. Beds cost 4LD for members and 6LD for nonmembers.

The best of the cheaper hotels on the eastern side of town is *Libya Palace Hotel* (☎ *333 1180/9, Sharia Sidi Issa*) behind the Egyptian Embassy. This large 1960s hotel was formerly in the luxury class but has fallen on hard times. It is a bargain at only 20/25LD for singles/doubles with bathroom. The hotel has two restaurants, where lunch or dinner costs 10LD, and a rooftop coffeehouse with a good view of the city.

If large hotels are not your cup of tea, the small and friendly *Funduq Ayyussar* (☎ *333 0911, 333 7287*) is a good bet. It is tucked away in a nameless back street in Dahra, directly opposite San Francisco Church. Singles/doubles cost 24LD for a room with bath including a simple breakfast. The rooms are by no means luxurious, but they are tolerably clean and the showers are hot. In the same small street there is another hotel a couple of doors on called *Hotel Cleopatra* (☎ *22445*) charging 25LD for singles/doubles.

Closer to the old city there are a few cheap hotels. *Funduq al-Mamoun* (☎ *333 7919, Sharia al-Mamoun*) is good, if simple, and is very close to the shared taxi station. Singles/doubles with bathroom cost 18/22LD and include a light breakfast. There is a small restaurant where meals cost about 10LD. Also recommended is *Hotel Rached* (☎ *4441095, Sharia al-Rached*) which is handy for the main taxi station. Clean singles/doubles cost 10/20LD with a simple dinner available for an extra 10LD. On the same street is *Hotel Tripoli* (☎ *444 1095*) with singles/doubles for 15/25LD with bathroom. Meals are an extra 10LD.

Places to Stay – Mid-Range
Mid-range hotels include *Bab al-Medina Hotel* (☎ *608 051/8, Sharia al-Kurnish*) overlooking the beach. The hotel has a pool

and is comfortable. Rooms cost 30LD with private bathroom and air-con. The hotel has a buffet-style restaurant, where meals cost 12LD and a coffeehouse.

There is also the popular *Waddan Hotel* (☎ *333 0042/6, Sharia al-Fatah*) where singles/doubles cost 35/45LD with bathroom and air-con. This is a popular place with friendly staff and, because it is conveniently situated near the centre, it can be heavily booked. The restaurant serves fixed-price menus for about 15LD for lunch or dinner. The entrance to this place is on the other side of the building – away from the sea.

Places to Stay – Top End
The swankiest place in town is undoubtedly *Hotel Mehari* (☎ *333 4091, 12 Sharia al-Fatah*) with swanky prices to match. Single/double rooms cost 80/95LD and include breakfast. The hotel is large and very comfortable, but is somewhat lacking in the services that would justify its high prices in another part of the world. There are three restaurants, including a sort of nightclub on the roof with live music, and there is also a small pool with a bar. Lunch or dinner will probably set you back about 25LD, which, if you put it on your bill, will be converted to hard currency. It is better to pay cash for meals.

Somewhat cheaper, but still in the luxury class, is *Al-Kebir Hotel* (☎ *444 5945/9, fax 444 5959, Sharia al-Fatah*). It is well situated, being a couple of hundred metres from Green Square, close to the shopping district and within an easy walk of the castle and medina. The hotel has a pool (only filled in high summer), terrace coffeehouse and two restaurants, one buffet-style, the other à la carte. Double rooms cost 65LD with no discount for single occupancy.

Places to Eat
Cafes There are many cafes tucked in among the parks and gardens around Green Square and along Sharia al-Fatah that serve soft drinks and light snacks. There is a simple *tea and coffee place* in the palm grove, just east of Al-Kebir Hotel. The *tea garden*

100m east of Waddan Hotel is also popular in the evenings. In the old city, there are numerous small and cheap *cafes* – one of the most popular is by the clocktower. Apart from drinks, all the cafes offer *narjilehs* (water pipes).

Fastfood Although none of the big international chains exists in Tripoli, there is an increasing appetite for burgers and pizzas and quite a few small places have sprung up recently. These can mostly be found around Green Square and the main shopping streets: sharias 1st September, Omar al-Mukhtar and Magarief. Meals are cheap and are perfect if you are on a strict budget. Another option is felafel. One popular place is on Sharia Magarief, about 100m from Green Square on the right.

Restaurants There is something of a shortage of good, inexpensive restaurants in Tripoli. Apart from ex-pats, a few business people and travellers, there isn't really an 'eating out' culture. The few good cheap restaurants can get extremely full. *Bedouin Restaurant (Sharia al-Baladiyya)* almost directly behind Al-Kebir Hotel is highly recommended. The food is Levantine and lunch or dinner costs about 10 to 12LD, which includes mixed starters, well-cooked grills, delicious stuffed flat bread, salads and pudding. The measure of the quality is that you almost always have to queue for a table; it is, however, worth the wait.

In the same area directly behind Al-Kebir Hotel on Sharia al-Baladiyya, is a Moroccan place, *Safir Restaurant (☎ 47064)* which has good food and a lovely interior of traditional Moroccan tile and stucco. Lunch or dinner costs about 20 to 25LD. This restaurant is often fully booked, being popular with tour groups, so it is best to telephone ahead.

Some of the best bargains are to be found in the hotel restaurants. Particularly popular is Al-Kebir's buffet restaurant on the 1st floor, where a sumptuous spread can be enjoyed for 18LD. It is full every Friday for lunch, so get there early.

All the restaurants in Tripoli seem to close early in the evening, about 10 or 10.30 pm, and if you want a table at the more popular places, it is best to arrive no later than 8.30 pm.

Entertainment
Public entertainment is a bit thin on the ground in Tripoli. Occasionally, there will be some kind of folklore festival or an equestrian event. These are listed in the local press, but if you do not read Arabic, ask around. Hotel reception staff usually know what is going on. If your visit coincides with a national holiday there may well be some parades or other public festivities, which often centre around Green Square.

Spectator Sports
Soccer is a regular favourite with Libyans. There are a large number of teams and there is often a game played in Tripoli (in either the main stadium in the south of the city or in one of the local sports centres). There is also horse racing about 3km west of Green Square, just off Sharia al-Fatah, where there are periodic fixtures.

Getting There & Away
Air Libyan Arab Airlines flies a skeleton service to the main cities in Libya. For details see the Getting Around section earlier.

Libyan Arab Airlines (☎ 333 7500 or 333 5686) has a central booking office in Al-Kebir Hotel on Sharia al-Fatah.

Bus There are frequent cheap bus services to and from Tunisia and Egypt, as well as regional towns around Libya. The buses arrive and leave from the main bus station east of the medina, near the five large towers. The green-and-white buses of Fast Transport Company have a ticket office at the bus station. Fares are cheap. One-way tickets to Benghazi cost 20LD, to Ghadhames 4LD, to Garyan 3LD, to Khoms 3LD and to Sebha 22LD.

Shared Taxis The yellow-and-white shared taxis serve most destinations including those in Tunisia. The main taxi square is on the south-western side of the medina and is packed with taxis. Simply ask which taxi is going to your destination.

Car There are car rental agencies in the lobbies of the main hotels. Tripoli Office Car Rentals has offices in both Al-Kebir (☎ 444 7208, fax 444 5959) and Mehari (☎ 333 4091/6, ext 404) hotels. You will need an international drivers licence and a deposit of about 400LD. Rental charges are between 35 to 60LD per day plus extra kilometres. Unlimited kilometre deals work out at around 250 to 300LD for three days or 600LD for a week.

Getting Around
To/From the Airport There is a shuttle bus service to and from the airport to serve the few flights. The bus leaves from Green Square (double check with the airline office as things change frequently). The fare to the airport is 3LD.

Minibus White minibuses serving the city and the suburbs leave from the taxi square at the south-western end of the medina. Bus stops on the routes are easily recognisable by their concrete shelters. There is a flat fare of 0.25LD. There are no fixed timetables and you will need help in discovering the various routes as they are not signposted (neither at bus shelters or on the buses themselves).

Car & Motorcycle Arriving in Tripoli with your own car presents the problem of where to park safely. Green Square is used as a car park (except during certain public holidays) and is supervised. Otherwise, parking in central Tripoli is a bit of a nightmare.

Taxis Avoid the private black-and-white taxis as they are hideously expensive, even for short rides. For example, a taxi from Al-Kebir Hotel to Waddan Hotel (a two minute journey) costs 12LD – about the cost of a meal in an average restaurant. A ride to the airport would be at least 50LD.

If you do need to use these taxis, they tend to congregate at the entrance to the medina on Green Square, outside Al-Kebir Hotel and in Midan al-Jazayir, next to the large post office. Otherwise, just flag one down.

Tripolitania

Tripolitania covers the entire north-west of the country. The area surrounding Tripoli as far south as the Jebel Nafusa is mostly farm land, with vast groves of fruit and olive trees and date palms. Most of Libya's fresh food comes from this area. Beyond the Jebel Nafusa is the start of the desert, with some spectacular scenery along the way. South-west of the mountains lies the oasis town of Ghadhames, which offers unique attractions that should not be missed.

Sabratha and Leptis Magna, on the coast of Tripolitania, are within easy reach of the capital. As the coast dips towards Sirt the desert meets the coast, forming the desolate natural boundary which, historically, divided the provinces of Tripolitania and Cyrenaica.

SABRATHA
One of the 'must-see' sights in Libya, Sabratha is a well-preserved Roman city, about 67km west of Tripoli. Although the ruins, overall, are less spectacular than those at Leptis Magna, the site is attractively situated overlooking the sea, and there are nearby beaches.

Although it is possible to visit the site as a day trip from Tripoli or as a short stopover on the way to or from Tunisia, it is worthwhile to allow at least a full day to explore the ruins and to view the museum. This will leave you time for a leisurely swim and sunbathe.

History
The city, as seen today, dates from the Roman occupation of Tripolitania and was built during the 1st and 2nd centuries AD. It was destroyed by the Vandals, rebuilt during the Arab occupation and then neglected by the Turks. It was finally exca-

vated during the Italian occupation and partly restored in the 1930s.

Sabratha was first settled by the Phoenicians as a trading post. The exact date of its foundation is largely a question of speculation. The first literary reference to the settlement dates from the late 4th century BC. After the fall of Carthage, the Romans superimposed their ordered town plan over the original, more haphazard, settlement. The transformation took longer than that at Leptis Magna. The early Roman city was concentrated around the forum, where the Liber Pater and Serapis temples were found. It later spread inland on the familiar grid pattern, culminating in the theatre, which is Sabratha's crowning feature.

Sabratha did not enjoy the lavish imperial favour of Leptis and so its decline was not as dramatic. The city did not collapse until the Vandals wrought their usual destruction, although an earthquake in 365 AD had already caused it to decline. When Byzantine armies reclaimed North Africa from the Vandals, Sabratha was in a weak state and new defensive walls were built. A fine church featuring a mosaic floor was also constructed.

After the Arabs arrived in Tripolitania and laid siege to Tripoli, the Sabrathans prepared for their own siege behind their Byzantine walls. Hearing that the Arabs had been repelled, they relaxed their vigilance, even to the point of leaving their gates open. When the Arabs finally took Tripoli, the inevitable happened. Riding through the night they took Sabratha completely by surprise and the city surrendered. Once established, the Arabs moved the market to Tripoli, depriving Sabratha of its means of economic survival. Thereafter, the city declined into obscurity and ruin.

Information

Money There is a bank in Sabratha. It can be found on the right of the road approaching the entrance to the ruins.

Post & Communications The post office is in the same street as the bank. It also has public telephones.

The Ruins

The older sections of the city are in the western area, which correspond roughly to the original Punic city. When the Byzantines rebuilt the city walls they enclosed only this part, leaving the later Roman parts of the city farther to the east exposed and abandoned. The extent of this later, somewhat reduced, city can be seen clearly on the map. The entrance to the site is directly on the city's main *cardo* (Roman thoroughfare), and the museum is just to the south. Straight ahead lies the Byzantine gate to the city.

The site is open from 8 am to sunset daily except Mondays. Entrance fees are 3LD, and you should retain your ticket for entry to two museums. The main museum is well worth seeing. The courtyard has a fine selection of statues. The west wing houses the smaller sculptures of marble and bronze, as well as domestic objects, including a large hoard of coins.

The south wing has the reconstructed setting of the Basilica of Justinian, with its spectacular mosaic floor. The east wing houses the frescoes found on the site as well as an impressive collection of busts, including a monumental one of Jupiter. This is also the home of the famous Neptune mosaic.

In a separate building around the corner is the Phoenician Museum, which houses some painted fragments from the Mausoleum of Bes showing the physically repugnant deity in all his glory, as well as a number of artefacts. The **Mausoleum of Bes** itself is in the residential quarter, found to the left of the Byzantine gate on entering the site. It is mostly a modern reconstruction though it has some rare Aeolic capitals. The mausoleum was originally covered in painted stucco. Passing through the Byzantine gate, the first major building on the left is the South Forum Temple. It is not known to which deity the temple was dedicated, but it is impressive in size and has a large rectangular courtyard.

Farther to the north, the remains of the **forum** visible today date from the 4th century restoration, perhaps carried out to repair earthquake damage. Before the Antonine

SABRATHA

MEDITERRANEAN SEA

To Tripoli
(67km)

Byzantine
Gate

Main Entrance
to Excavations

Entrance
Gate

To Restaurant (1km)

To Hostel
& Town (1km)

0   75   150 m

1 Seaward Baths
2 Basilica of Justinian
3 Curia
4 Temple of Serapis
5 Capitolium
6 Forum
7 Temple of Liber Pater
8 Antonine Temple
9 Basilica of Apuleius
10 South Forum Temple
11 Temple of Hercules
12 Christian Basilica
13 Christian Basilica
14 Baths of Oceanus
15 Temple of Isis
16 Mausoleum of Bes
17 Theatre
18 Peristyle House
19 Museums
20 Site Restaurant

period, the forum was closed to traffic and only accessible via a single entrance. Over time, the shops and offices became more grand and more permanent, and a portico was built with grey columns of Egyptian granite. Surrounding the forum are a number of important buildings. The **Antonine Temple** stands on the other side of the site's main thoroughfare, and the **Temple of Liber Pater**, or Dionysus, is next to it to the north. Also north of the forum is the curia, marked by its restored archway at the entrance. The curia was the meeting place of the city's magistrates and senators.

Opposite the curia is the **Temple of Serapis**. Serapis was a healer and miracle worker and at Sabratha the cult of Serapis, which originally came from Memphis in Egypt, was often associated with that of Isis. The **Capitolium**, or Temple of Jupiter, is the last of the important buildings around

the forum. It is the principal temple of the city. The huge bust of Jupiter that is in the museum was found here.

North-west of the forum area and near the coast is the **Basilica of Justinian**. The magnificent mosaic that is housed in the site museum was discovered here. Seeing the splendour of the mosaic it is easy to imagine the overall grandeur of the church, which has three naves, a raised presbytery, a pulpit and an altar. The pulpit originally formed a part of the cornice on the Capitolium.

There are several baths in Sabratha, the best of which are the **Seaward Baths.** These are famous for their lovely mosaics and for the wonderfully preserved hexagonal latrine, which is paved and lined with fine marble. The baths are a favourite setting for taking pictures. Also worth seeing are the **Baths of Oceanus**, to the north east of the Temple of Hercules. The decoration of hese public baths was extraordinarily lavsh, with marble on every surface.

The lovely **Temple of Isis,** the finest of the emples, sits by the seashore at the eastern end of the city. It has been splendidly restored and is possibly the most complete of ts kind in Africa. The colonnaded courtyard has a row of eight Corinthian columns. Look beyond the temple into the sea and you will see parts of the city lost to the waves.

The most outstanding monument at Sabratha is the theatre. Built in the late 2nd century, it has been beautifully restored, with the imposing three-tiered *scaenae frons* dominating the view. This unusual backdrop is composed of 108 Corinthian columns. The design is reputed to be a replica of the palace built by Septimius Severus in Rome.

The front of the stage is decorated with a series of marble reliefs in recesses showing various mythological and dramatic scenes. Carved dolphins can be found in the semicircular arena below the stage.

Places to Stay

The only place to stay at the moment is the *hostel* situated so close to the ruins that you can see the theatre from its garden. This large, modern establishment is clean, comfortable and has a restaurant. If travelling on the modern highway from Tripoli, turn right after the *baladiyya* (town hall) and the mosque. The hostel is about 1km straight ahead on a bend in the road. Shared rooms cost 4LD and meals (order them in advance) cost 2LD.

Places to Eat

There is a restaurant inside the ruins that has a pleasant outside eating area. It is only open for lunch and you need to place your order when you arrive at the ruins. Expect to pay about 10LD. There is a tourist-style restaurant about 1km west of the site entrance, following the perimeter fence, but it is normally packed with tour groups and the service is slow. You could do worse than take your meals in the garden at the hostel. Even better, take a picnic.

Getting There & Away

Sabratha is on the extremely busy highway between Tripoli and the Tunisian border, and there is no shortage of buses and shared taxis passing through. Buses stop on the main road in the centre of town – 1km walk to the ruins. For a small extra fee, taxis will make the detour from the centre of town to the ruins or the hostel. The fare from Tripoli is 3LD for both bus and taxi.

KHOMS

Khoms is a small coastal town 120km east of Tripoli. It has low-built, modern architecture and little of historical interest for the sightseer, apart from a rather nice old mosque, the Ali Pasha. The real reason for visiting Khoms is its proximity to Leptis Magna, 3km along the road to the east, which is one of the largest and most impressive Roman cities in the Mediterranean. As Khoms is also situated on a particularly fine stretch of sandy beach, it makes a good base to both explore the ruins and swim.

Information

The bank is situated at a turn-off just off the main street, Sharia Khoms, close to the baladiyya, and is open from 8 am to 2 pm. The post office is on the main street and is open from 8 am to 2 pm for counter services. There are also public telephones in the same building.

Places to Stay & Eat

Funduq Kebir al-Khoms (☎ 23333, 26944) is on the main highway, close to the turn-off for Khoms. As well as its 47 rooms, it has a coffee lounge, dining room and laundry facilities. Rooms cost 20LD for a single/double including breakfast. Lunch at the hotel costs between 4 and 10LD and dinner is 15LD.

The best hotel in the area is *Hotel Nagazza* (☎ 26691) 22km west of Khoms and 2km north of the main highway (a signpost in Arabic indicates the turn-off). It is a small hotel set in wooded hills close to the sea. It has six rooms, two suites and 11

LEPTIS MAGNA

Leptis Magna was originally a Phoenician port, settled during the 1st millennium BC. By around the 6th or 7th century BC, it was a permanent colony under the domination of Carthage, but following the third Punic War, when Carthage was razed, Leptis came under Roman rule. During the reign of Trajan (98-117 AD), Leptis Magna and Tripolitania became part of the Roman empire and its inhabitants Roman citizens.

Leptis flourished during the rule of Septimius Severus (193-211 AD), who was born in Leptis, and many of the buildings seen today date from this period. The town fell into decline when the Severan dynasty ended and its occupation by the Vandals in 455 AD signalled the end.

Abandoned finally in the 11th century, it was not until the 20th century that any serious excavations were carried out. Most of the monuments were well preserved under their blanket of sand, and it's the fine condition of the ruins that makes Leptis Magna such an outstanding archaeological site.

The Site

The city has many interesting monuments and you should allow a full day to see everything. Some of the highlights of Leptis Magna include:

- The **Severan Arch** (2nd century) is a particularly fine example of a triumphal arch with rich decorations.
- The **Hadrianic Baths** is the largest outside Rome and features an impressive array of hot and cold rooms and an outdoor swimming pool, all finished in marble and mosaic.

ALL PHOTOS BY PATRICK SYDER

Top: Head of Medusa, Severan Forum

Bottom Left: Detail of the Severus Arch

Bottom Right: Intricately carved Roman Pilasters from the Severan Basilic

- The **Severan Forum** has a distinct similarity to Rome's imperial forum and the scale of the place is similarly immense. Around the ruined portico are giant Medusa and Nereid heads.
- The **Severan Basilica** is just off the forum. This large building has a set of the most fantastically carved columns, solidly worked with acanthus scrolls, animals and figures.

Heading west from the harbour you arrive at the **old forum**. Leading from this are the main temples of the city and public buildings. These temples are in various states of repair, but are nonetheless interesting for their rich diversity.

Leaving the forum area and heading south-west along the *cardo maximus* (major Roman thoroughfare), the **market** is on the right. This is a rectangular open space with two attractive circular pavilions in the centre.

The number one monument at Leptis Magna is the **theatre**. From the upper tiers there is a fabulous view over the city and across to the sea. This showpiece was donated to the city in the year 1 AD by a wealthy citizen, Annobal Rufus, who also built the market.

For details of how to get to Leptis Magna see the Khoms section.

LEPTIS MAGNA

To Beach & Hunting Baths
Late Roman Wall
Western Gate
0   125   250 m
Roman Streets
MEDITERRANEAN SEA
Sand Bar
Byzantine Gate
Wadi Lebda
Old Coast Road
Byzantine Wall
To Circus & Amphitheatre (by beach track 1.5km)
To Zliten (34km)
Entrance
Old Coast Road
To Khoms (3km)
To Circus & Amphitheatre (by road)
To Main Highway (500m)

1 Temple of Liber Pater	13 Severan Forum
2 Temple of Rome & Augustus	14 Severan Basilica
3 Old Forum Church	15 Colonnaded Street
4 Old Forum	16 Temple
5 Curia	17 Doric Temple
6 Lighthouse	18 Church
7 Old Basilica	19 Severan Arch
8 Theatre	20 Palaestra
9 Chalcidicum	21 Nymphaeum
10 Market	22 Hadrianic Baths
11 Arch of Trajan	23 Museum
12 Arch of Tiberius	24 Restaurant

chalets. Single/double rooms with bath cost 25LD and prices include breakfast. Lunch and dinner cost 10LD. There are three good beaches 4km north of the hotel. If you follow the road, you will come to a three-way fork. The road on the left is a bumpy track to a sandy beach; the middle track leads to a rocky beach, good for snorkelling; and the surfaced road on the right leads to a long, sandy beach.

Dining out opportunities in Khoms are limited. Away from the hotels, the only options are the simple hole-in-the-wall restaurants in the centre of town. There are others along Sharia Khoms. These places have a limited but tasty selection of meals, with soup and couscous, for a few dinars. There is also a tourist restaurant attached to the museum at Leptis Magna, where lunches cost about 12LD.

Getting There & Away
There are many shared taxis running between Tripoli and Khoms and the fare is only 3LD. You can find them in the square off Sharia Khoms next to the old barracks. You can walk, but private taxis will take you the 3km, from Khoms to Leptis Magna, for only 4LD. You can arrange for the driver to pick you up again at an agreed time.

MISRATA
Misrata is a fairly large town between Khoms and Sirt whose inhabitants are reputed to be excellent at business dealings. This air of prosperity is due in part to its newish steel mill, which has created something of a boom in the town. The entire area is surrounded by extensive palm and olive groves. Misrata has a totally different atmosphere to other towns in Libya. You will notice the place has a sense of order: the streets are cleaner and the buildings are smarter.

Information
The banks, baladiyya, post office, hotels and shops are all within a 500m radius of Midan an-Nasser, the main square in the centre of town.

Things to See & Do
There is little to interest the tourist, although there is a good beach 5km north of the centre of town. However, Misrata is a good place to stop for the night if you are touring along the coast and want to avoid Sirt. Misrata's main claim to fame is an enormous sand dune just to the west of the town. It is said to be the tallest dune in the world, but nobody has yet measured it for the Guinness Book of Records.

The town also has a thriving carpet industry. You can find the traditional designs of the region, which are mainly in fairly bright colours, in the souqs of the town.

Places to Stay & Eat
A pleasant option is to head for Al-Jazera, the beach resort 5km north of the Midan an-Nasser. Simple beach chalets, costing 5LD per night, are available here throughout the year. You can find a taxi easily around Midan an-Nasser or from the bus station.

The best budget place in the centre of town is *Funduq Misrata Seahi* (☎ 20323, 20037, Sharia Ramadan Asswayhli). This is an old hotel that has been refurbished with traditional furniture, and it has some character. Rooms with TV, air-con and bathroom cost 15LD per person and include breakfast. It has a coffeehouse and restaurant, where meals cost 10 to 15LD.

The best in town is *Koztik Hotel* (☎ 26999, fax 26013) on Sharia Daralry, in the southern part of town. Look for the tall observation tower and the hotel is next door. This place has the works: swimming pool, shops, cinema and two restaurants. Single/double rooms cost 30/45LD. Lunch or dinner here will cost you about 15LD.

Most of the restaurants are on Sharia Ramadan Asswayhli or in the souq area just to the north. They serve the usual Arabic cuisine for less than 10LD. If you crave something different, there is a good pizza and burger place called *Bayt Fitayer* on Sharia Tarabulus, about 800m from Midan an-Nasser. A pizza will set you back 6LD and a burger 8LD. Also worth trying are the two or three nameless fish restaurants on the each, which are open for lunch and dinner. Fish, salad and chips will cost about 12LD.

Getting There & Away
There are daily buses to and from Tripoli and Benghazi, and shared taxis leave throughout the day in both directions.

SIRT
Sitting in the dip of the gulf, Sirt was historically both an important land communication point with the south and an embarkation point for many caravans. Under the Italians it was an administrative centre, and since the revolution, it has increased in importance. The General People's Congress meets in Sirt and the main ministries have offices here. It's a dull, dusty town and the only reason for spending any time here is to rest during the long coastal trip.

Information
The layout of Sirt is simple. There is one main street running through the town and all the services are either on, or close to it. The Wahda Bank is down a turn-off to the left of the Medina Hotel. The post office is in the next road back from the main street, and can't be missed as it has a huge radio tower. Public telephones are in the same building.

Places to Stay & Eat
Medina Hotel (☎ 60160/3) is in the main street (which has no name) and is comfortable and friendly. There is a cafe and restaurant, and all rooms have bathrooms and satellite TV. Singles/doubles cost 30/35LD; lunch or dinner costs 20LD and is not at all bad. The only other restaurant in town is *Naeem Restaurant*, just off the main street at the western end of town. It serves traditional Arabic food, but nothing fancy, for a few dinars.

Getting There & Away
Bus There are two buses a day from Tripoli. These depart at 10 am and 2 pm and costs 7LD. There is also a bus from Khoms to Benghazi that stops at Sirt on the way. The

bus station is just off the main street, almost opposite the Congress Secretariat building.

Taxi There is a taxi station across the road from the bus station where you can easily pick up a shared taxi for most destinations.

GHARYAN
The road south to Gharyan from Tripoli soars steeply up to the jebel, offering fine views across the Jefara Plain. The first sign of the approaching town is the huge amount of pottery being sold by the roadside. Small kilns are often operated out of troglodyte workshops carved into the hillside. The style is quite colourful and funky, but we suspect some of the wares are imported from Tunisia.

Information
Facilities such as the post office, bank, buses and taxis are close to Hotel Rabta, either on Sharia Jamahirya, or just off it. The few small restaurants are also in this area.

Things to See
Of most interest are the Berber **troglodyte houses**. Few of these have been restored and many are sitting next to modern farmhouses owned by families of the former inhabitants, who use the troglodyte structures to house animals. One restored house belongs to Rabta Hotel (although it lies a few kilometres away). Hotel staff will take you there, free of charge if you are a guest, and for a small fee if you are not a guest. However, none of the staff speaks English, which can be a problem. For a small fee, hotel staff will also arrange for you to be taken to springs that are near the town.

Places to Stay & Eat
The good news is that the only hotel in town is a fine establishment. *Hotel Rabta* (☎ 21971/4, Sharia Jamahirya) is modern with clean, comfortable rooms and all the mod cons. The rooms are also a bargain at 20/25LD for singles/doubles with bath and air-con. The *restaurant* serves Libyan and continental meals for 10/15LD. Also

available is a supermarket and a luxury cinema showing imported films at 7.30 and 9.30 pm. Tickets cost 1LD.

Away from the hotel's restaurant, eating out is limited to a few hole-in-the-wall eateries. There is a *restaurant* 100m up the road from the hotel, on the left towards the bus station, which is not bad and is extremely cheap.

Getting There & Away
A bus leaves Tripoli daily at 2 pm for Gharyam. The fare is 3LD. There are also frequent shared taxis coming and going between Tripoli and Gharyan. The bus station is about 500m from Hotel Rabta. Taxis also leave from there.

YEFREN
Yefren is perched on the top of a series of hill crests set in an attractive wooded area. The twisting mountain roads branch out in several directions and there are various monuments and places of interest in the surrounding areas, including several **springs** and a small lake. The deserted, old part of Yefren is 500 years old and sits on the hilltop overlooking the town. The **old grain store** and traditional houses can be explored here.

A **Roman monumental tomb** can be found 18km north of the town at a place called Safit. This monument really stands out from its surroundings and can be seen kilometres away. Other nearby places of interest include **Gasr Bir Niran**, where there are some impressive ruins.

Finding any of these places without help would be difficult, but the good news is that the hostel (see Places to Stay & Eat following) will arrange to take people to the sights around Yefren, either in your car, or one rustled up by the staff (if possible). The manager, Yousef Suleiman Aboud, is helpful and has many photos and loads of information about the various places.

Places to Stay & Eat
The only place to stay in Yefren is the *hostel* (☎ 2585) which is in the centre of town. If approaching from Gharyan, you pass the post office on your right and then come to a

service station on the left. Turn right and you will enter a small square. The hostel is on the right, opposite a park. The atmosphere in this old Italian building is friendly. The coffeehouse has music and, by Libyan standards, is pretty lively. There is a restaurant, which does a full lunch or dinner for 8LD, or members can use the kitchen themselves.

Getting There & Away
If you are travelling from Tripoli there is a direct bus to Yefren at 1 pm daily. The fare is 3LD. There is also a bus that goes from Tripoli via Gharyan at 2 pm daily. The return bus leaves Yefren at 8 am.

NALUT
Nalut is perched high on an escarpment overlooking the plains below. It is the last town on the Jebel Nafusa before the Tunisian border, 30km to the west. Today, Nalut is a small modern town but the real interest for the visitor is a large old town overlooking the new. There is a gigantic *qasr* (fort), which was the grain store rather than a castle, and is probably the best of its type still standing. There are also some old vernacular mosques, which are worth seeing.

The qasr is reckoned to be at least 300 years old and the Alal'a Mosque could be even older. The storage chambers of the qasr were used for oil as well as grain, and each keeper knew exactly how much each family had in storage at any one time, even though there were 400 chambers. There are so few visitors that there are no set opening times. If the door of the qasr is locked, you should inquire at the baladiyya, which is set back from the road near the bus stand.

Places to Stay & Eat
Funduq Nalut (☎ 2204) is, unfortunately, the only hotel in town. It is superbly situated overlooking the ruined old town and was built in 1933 by the Italians. Despite its rather pleasant, solid architecture, the hotel has been allowed to become badly rundown. In fact, it is filthy and bug-infested. If you plan to stay, bring a sleeping bag and some bug spray. There are 18 rooms, each

costing 10LD with a bathroom. Dinner costs 6LD, although we recommend you bring your own picnic.

There are a few simple restaurants around the centre of town and there is a cheap and good place near the roundabout along the Ghadhames road. You can expect to pay about 3LD in these places for lunch or dinner.

Getting There & Away

There are two buses a day, at 7.30 am and 2 pm, from Tripoli to Nalut, and two Ghadhames buses pass through Nalut around lunch time. The fare is 4LD, and the buses stop in the main street, west of the main roundabout. Shared taxis run between Tripoli and Nalut and stop by the roundabout, but they are infrequent.

GHADHAMES

The oasis town of Ghadhames, 650km south-west of Tripoli and 314km from Nalut, is close to the borders with Algeria and Tunisia. If your time in Libya is limited and you want to see one traditional desert place, this is it. Famed for its traditional desert architecture, Ghadhames earned itself the sobriquet 'Pearl of the Desert' in the 1950s, when it was a popular weekend resort for visitors from Tripoli. Since the revolution, a new town has been built around the old, and the inhabitants occupy new houses.

With its thick, mud-brick walls the old town is a quiet and cool retreat from the desert sun. Its dark covered walkways still attract the locals, who congregate in the seating areas built into the narrow streets. The old city is a labyrinth, the dark streets lit only by the occasional overhead skylights and open squares. The town is constructed entirely with mud-bricks that are held together with mud mortar and then whitewashed. The style is eclectic and unique to this part of the Sahara.

The people of Ghadhames are of Arab, African, Berber and Tuareg origin, and the town was formerly on an important trans-Saharan trading route stretching from Tripoli to Lake Chad and beyond. Apart from gold, ivory and wild animals destined

for the Roman arena, slaves formed an important part of the trade in Ghadhames, and many of the people living in Ghadhames today are descendants of former slaves.

With the decline of the trade route and the outlawing of slavery, the town reverted to agriculture to support itself. The date-palm groves still provide a modest living for those who work them, although many locals choose to head for the city and more lucrative jobs.

Information

There is a small bank in the modern town, just north of the main square in an arcade of shops. It is open from 8 am to 2 pm daily except Friday. The tiny post office is also just off the main square. International calls can be made, but with some difficulty, due to the shortage of lines.

Things to See & Do

The town is small enough to be entirely explored on foot. Its main attraction is the architecture of the old town (take a torch with you). Close to 'Ain al-Faras Hotel near the western entrance to the old town, the **House Museum** is an old merchant's house with intact original furnishings and decorations. It serves as a museum of local culture and is well worth seeing, but there are no fixed opening times. Inquire at one of the travel agencies to arrange for it to be unlocked.

The old town is an experience in itself. The square of the Mulberry is the old slave market. Periodically, the local people stage a musical evening, which is open to all, in the old town square near the old **Al-Kebir Mosque**. The minaret of the mosque can be climbed for an excellent view of the old town. The domes seen on the rooftops are family tombs or small prayer rooms.

About 15km outside Ghadhames are (unspectacular) Roman ruins on the hill at **Ras al-Ghoul** (the Haunted Hill), which are worth visiting for the views over the desert. There is also a lake 40km from town that is popular for picnics and swimming. To visit these places, you will need off-the-road transport and a guide.

Places to Stay & Eat

As the town is surrounded by open desert, camping is a possibility. However, bear in mind this is a border area, and that straying across could result in an unpleasant experience with the authorities. Independent tourists are still a rarity, so it would be wise to seek the advice of one of the local tourist agencies if you plan to camp – you may need a permit. Some recommended companies are Ghadhames Travel & Tourism (☎ 2307) or Winzrik Tourism Services (☎ 2533). Winzrik also has camping facilities next to its office on the outskirts of Ghadhames.

There is a fairly clean *hostel* (☎ 858) on the eastern outskirts of town, overlooking the desert and the old cemetery. Most of the 120 beds are in dormitories, but there are a couple of family rooms with private bathrooms for 4LD per night and meals can be arranged.

Hotel al-Waha (☎ 2569/70) is on the outskirts of town and its 20 rooms are fiercely fought over by the tour companies. If you want a room, try and book well in advance through a Libyan travel agent. Singles/doubles cost 25/30LD with bath. Lunch or dinner costs 12LD.

Eating out opportunities are limited. There are a few *cafes* in the new town, around the main square serving snacks and soft drinks, but at night there's nothing at all. Opposite the museum in the old fort is a plain *restaurant*, where you can get a cooked breakfast or a simple hot lunch for a few dinars.

Getting There & Away

Bus There are two buses a day running between Tripoli and Ghadhames. They leave Tripoli at 7 and 10 am and from Ghadhames at 6 and 8 am. The trip takes seven hours and the buses have air-con. They pick up passengers outside the new mosque and you can buy a ticket on the bus for 10LD.

Cyrenaica

The eastern part of Libya is quite different, both geographically and culturally, from the rest of the country. The area's landscape is extremely attractive and, if you have spent any time in the desert, a refreshing change. The Jebel Akhdar (the Green Mountains) lives up to its name and is reminiscent of Crete.

Geography aside, the main reason for visiting the region is to see the wonderful Greek cities of antiquity. Five sites comprise the old 'Pentapolis'. The most glorious of these is Cyrene, followed by Apollonia nearby on the coast. This area also has the best coastline in the country and offers opportunities for divers to explore sunken ruins off the coast. Even for nondivers, the beaches are attractive and often empty.

BENGHAZI

Benghazi, the capital of Cyrenaica, is on the eastern side of the Gulf of Sirt. It is probably most famous for the siege during WWII, when the city constantly changed hands and was under bombardment from both the Allies and the Axis powers. By the time the war

---

Sahara Desert

A great deal of Libya is Sahara Desert and the attraction for travellers is to experience the desert crossing in the footsteps of the early African explorers, although in relative safety and a fraction of the time. Some of the old disused caravan routes are now being rediscovered after years of disuse by travellers and by the Tuareg guides who now take them across the desert in 4WD vehicles.

The Sahara Desert is not very old in geological terms and used to be savannah. The last 'wet phase' ended more than 4000 years ago and many visual records were left of wildlife from that time on the walls of the caves where early humans left their mark. This cave art is a major attraction for those on a desert safari. The most popular desert route today goes from Tripoli to Ghahames and then off the road to Ghat and the Acacus Mountains in the south, taking in the cave paintings and the lakes of the Ramlet Dawada.

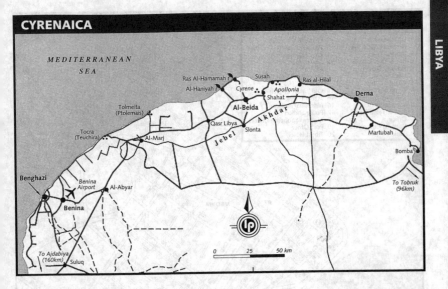

CYRENAICA

MEDITERRANEAN SEA

Ras Al-Hamamah
Al-Haniyah
Susah
Cyrene
Apollonia
Shahat
Ras al-Hilal
Derna
Al-Beida
Tolmeita (Ptolemais)
Qasr Libya
Slonta
Jebel Akhdar
Tocra (Teuchira)
Al-Marj
Martubah
Bomba
Benghazi
Benina Airport
Al-Abyar
Benina
To Tobruk (96km)
To Ajdabiya (160km)
Suluq

0   25   50 km

ended, there was not much left. The British administration did little to restore the city because of the uncertain future of Cyrenaica. After independence, and more particularly after oil was discovered, the development of the city began again. The harbour was enlarged to accommodate more commercial shipping following the revolution.

Orientation

The older part of the city is to the north, near the harbour area. It is in this quarter that most of the shopping and banking facilities can be found. Along the northern shore is a promenade, which at night comes alive with street vendors and families out for a stroll. South of the promenade are the souqs. The farther south you go, the more modern the city becomes. Along the shores of the inner harbour are some of the more expensive hotels and large commercial buildings. The inner harbour is crossed by a bridge that links the older part of the city with the new suburbs to the south.

It is worth walking up to the Central Souq and the Funduq Souq, which sell fruit and vegetables and have a few cafes. The tomb of Omar al-Mukhtar, the famous resistance fighter, is sited in the middle of a roundabout along Sharia al-Magarief.

Information

Money There are plenty of banks in the central area. They are concentrated around Sharia Gamal Abdel Nasser and Sharia Omar al-Mukhtar.

Post & Communications The main post office is on Sharia Omar al-Mukhtar, and there are public telephones in the same building. There is another post office close to Tibesti Hotel on Sharia Gamal Abdel Nasser.

Photography & Video Benghazi Photos in Sharia Gamal Abdel Nasser, near Omar Khayyam Hotel, sells film and has a 24-hour processing service.

Foreign Embassies The Egyptian consulate is on the 1st floor of the Omar Khayyam Hotel and is open daily from 8 to 10 am, except on Friday. An Egyptian visa

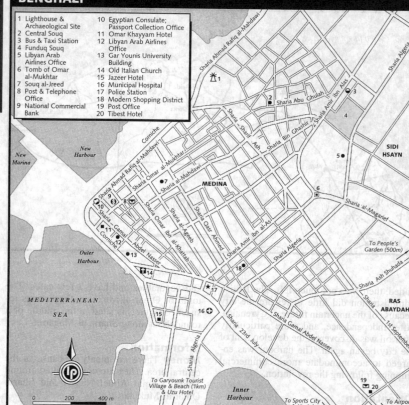

BENGHAZI

1 Lighthouse &
 Archaeological Site
2 Central Souq
3 Bus & Taxi Station
4 Funduq Souq
5 Libyan Arab
 Airlines Office
6 Tomb of Omar
 al-Mukhtar
7 Souq al-Jreed
8 Post & Telephone
 Office
9 National Commercial
 Bank
10 Egyptian Consulate;
 Passport Collection Office
11 Omar Khayyam Hotel
12 Libyan Arab Airlines
 Office
13 Gar Younis University
 Building
14 Old Italian Church
15 Jazeer Hotel
16 Municipal Hospital
17 Police Station
18 Modern Shopping District
19 Post Office
20 Tibest Hotel

costs 20LD and you need a photo. You need
to collect your passport the next day at 2 pm
from the old consulate on the Corniche,
near the old Italian church.

Things to See & Do
Benghazi has little to offer tourists. It is
mainly used as a stopover en route to the
Jebel Akhdar. You can walk around central
Benghazi in a couple of hours. The covered
souqs, including the gold souq, are open
daily but they really come alive on Friday

mornings. The main covered market is
called **Souq al-Jreed,** off Sharia Omar al-
Mukhtar, and it sells all manner of clothes
and household goods. There is a small archaeological excavation from Berenice, the
original Greek settlement, by the lighthouse
at the northern end of the Corniche.

Places to Stay & Eat
There is a *hostel* (☎ 95961) at the Sports
City on the south-eastern side of the inner
harbour. It is popular in summer and can get

full. Accommodation is separate for men and women, but there are a few family rooms. Meals are very cheap at 4LD.

Jazeer Hotel (☎ 96001/7) on the south-western end of the Corniche is the only budget hotel. It is acceptable but everything is grubby, the bathroom ceilings leak and there is seldom hot water. Even so, it is the choice of most budget travellers. Singles/doubles cost 15/20LD, which includes breakfast. A bit more upmarket is the stylish *Omar Khayyam Hotel* (☎ 95101/9, *Sharia Gamal Abdel Nasser*). Singles/doubles with bath cost 25/35LD including breakfast.

Hotels at the top end of the scale are very comfortable and well appointed. They are also expensive. *Uzu Hotel* (☎ 95160/5) on the eastern side of the inner harbour on Sharia Juliana is popular. Singles/doubles cost 45/60LD.

The best hotel in Benghazi is the five star *Tibest Hotel* (☎ 92034) on the eastern side of the inner harbour on Sharia Gamal Abdel Nasser. Singles/doubles cost 45/65LD.

Eating out is a bit limited: it basically boils down to using hotel *dining rooms*; snacking on food from *street stalls* in the Corniche; or perhaps eating from a worker's *hole-in-the-wall* place in the souqs. The latter can be delicious and cheap. Try the *fruit and vegetable souq* on Sharia Amir ibn Alas, near the bus station.

Getting There & Away

Air There is one flight a day to and from Tripoli. The one way/return fare is 28/56LD, although you may have to pay in hard currency. The Libyan Arab Airlines (☎ 92011/3) office is on Sharia Gamal Abdel Nasser.

Bus The main bus station is next to the Funduq souq area. Benghazi is well served by buses, both to and from other Libyan towns and to Cairo, Alexandria and Damascus. There are two buses a day to and from Tripoli, leaving in both directions at 7 and 10 am. The fare is 20LD. It is best to buy tickets the day before you leave as this is a popular route. A bus serving the Jebel

Akhdar area leaves at 7.30 am daily. The are also connections to Sebha on Monday, Wednesday and Saturday. The fare is 20LD.

CYRENE & APOLLONIA

Generally considered the second most important site in Libya after Leptis Magna, Cyrene is a must see. It is the most splendidly preserved of the Greek cities of Cyrenaica, and apart from the wonderful Greek ruins, its location high on a bluff overlooking a plateau across to the sea is quite stunning. Enough of the city has been resurrected to give the visitor an impression of how it originally appeared, but without the over-restored air that detracts from many classical sites. Cyrene still has very few visitors and, correspondingly, few facilities. It is, however, a site that deserves at least an entire day.

History

The city owes its name to the nymph Cyrene, known in Greek as Kurana. It was founded by a group of Greek immigrants who had fled from the island of Thera (Santorini). It is generally agreed that this event occurred in 631 BC, but the historical facts are somewhat shrouded in legend.

King Battus I ruled over the tiny community for the first 40 years and during that time the nucleus of the future great city took shape. Battus was buried in what was to become the agora; and the Temple of Apollo was dedicated close to the spring, which was named after the nymph Cyrene. The city flourished, and was soon attracting many Greek settlers. The dynasty of Battus lasted until 331 BC, encompassing a golden age of considerable power and prosperity for the city. With Barca, Berenice, Tocra and Apollonia, Cyrene was a member of the Pentapolis, a federation of five cities which traded and shared a common coinage.

It was not until 75 BC, following the battle of Actium, that the Pentapolis became part of the Roman empire. The period following the Roman takeover was generally marked by reconstruction and peace. This peace was shattered with devastating effect by the Jewish Revolt in 115 AD. There was

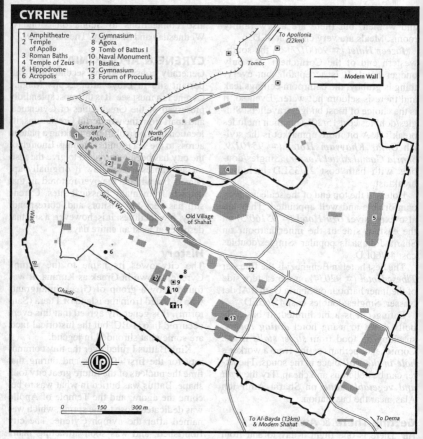

CYRENE

1	Amphitheatre	7	Gymnasium
2	Temple of Apollo	8	Agora
3	Roman Baths	9	Tomb of Battus I
4	Temple of Zeus	10	Naval Monument
5	Hippodrome	11	Basilica
6	Acropolis	12	Gymnasium
		13	Forum of Proculus

a large Jewish community in Cyrenaica at the time and, following the destruction of the Temple in Jerusalem, there was widespread disruption throughout the Middle East.

Cyrene never fully recovered, despite efforts by the emperor Hadrian to reconstruct the buildings and repopulate the city. By the 4th century, it and the other cities of the Pentapolis were virtually deserted. The city lay unexcavated until the Italians began work during the 1920s and 30s.

The Ruins

The site is large and set out on several levels. The best route is to start from the top of the hill, near the modern village of Shahat, and work your way down. Those with limited time can enter by the northern gate to explore the lower ruins and enjoy the spectacular view from the escarpment.

From the southern entrance the first monument is the **agora**. An agora was the principal square of a Greek city, corresponding to the Roman forum. Most of the important civic

civic buildings were around this area and the space would probably also have been used as a market. The remains of many temples can be seen, along with fragments of statues and mosaics. The founder of the colony, Battus I, has the rare honour of being buried not only within the city walls, but in the middle of the principal square. His burial chamber can be reached by descending some steps. In the chamber is an altar, which would have been used for the sacrifice of animals. Also in the agora area is the **Naval Monument**, a stylised ship of war dating from the 3rd century BC.

Following the **Sacred Way** down to the lower levels of the city, you pass caves in which the sacred virgins bathed before entering the sanctuary. On the lower levels of the city is the **Sanctuary of Apollo**. This is part of a cluster of temples and other later buildings, including a **Roman baths**.

Tombs from Cyrene cover a vast area around the site. A concentration of carved rock tombs can be seen going down the hill towards Apollonia. These tombs were later used by nomads for habitation, some of them being quite spacious.

The drive down the hill from Cyrene to Apollonia is stunning, with the road swooping down dramatically from the escarpment to the plain below.

The ancient city of Apollonia was built to provide a port for Cyrene. It is right on the coast in an attractive setting, with the hills as a backdrop. After Cyrene, Apollonia is the most rewarding of the Greek cities to visit. For those with snorkelling or diving equipment, there are underwater ruins just off the ruins as parts of the city have been submerged over the centuries.

If you are approaching from Cyrene you will pass through the small village of Susah, 20km from Shahat. There is a small **museum** in the centre of the old section of Susah. It has a small but interesting collection of Greek funerary statues and some mosaics from Apollonia and nearby Ras al-Hilal. There is also a charming collection of miniature offering figures.

The Cyrene and Apollonia sites are open daily from 8 am to sunset except on Mon-

day. The Apollonia site has several important monuments. At the far eastern end of the site, and also outside the walls, is the **theatre**, carved into the rock abutting the ramparts of the city. Returning along the coast there is an unexcavated **acropolis**.

The main street of the city passes an impressive structure, the **Eastern Church**, which has huge columns of cipolin marble. West of the Eastern Church is the **baths** complex, which has a large courtyard of Corinthian columns. There is also a **Byzantine palace** and **baths**.

Places to Stay

The only place to stay in Shahat is the *hostel (☎ 0853-2102)* which is very close to the ruins. To find it, follow the road to the entrance to the site and you will see two columns straight ahead. Take the turn-off on your left and then turn left again. The hostel is the grey building on the left. It is advisable to phone ahead in summer as it can get full. The nearest hotel is in Al-Beida 12km away. *Funduq Gasr al-Beida (☎ 084-23455/9)* on the main street is another colonial hotel gone to seed. Rooms are 15/20LD, with a disgusting bath thrown in. Meals are OK at 12LD for lunch or dinner. *Hotel Kairo* which is across the street, is the same price. There is not much to choose between them.

Alternatively, you can sleep near the sea. Coming from Cyrene, before you reach Susah, there is a beach resort called *Massif Susah Seahi (☎ 0853-2365)*. It has 80 rooms and 23 chalets, which cost 25LD and 30LD respectively. The *restaurant* serves lunch and dinner for 7LD, and there is a tennis court for guests to use.

Getting There & Away

There are hourly buses between Al-Beida and Shahat, the last leaving Shahat at about 5 pm. Shared taxis also travel this route throughout the day and evening. The fare is 5LD.

From Shahat there are not too many shared taxis running down to Susah, so be prepared to wait. The fare for the 20km ride is 8LD.

The Fezzan

The Fezzan in south-western Libya covers a vast area of uninhabited but varied desert terrain, with a small population concentrated in wadi systems and oases. For lovers of the desert, the Fezzan offers a great experience and some of the best prehistoric rock art to be found in Africa. Presently, the tourism infrastructure is minimal, and there are few hotels and restaurants in the area.

Also bear in mind that guides, 4WD vehicles and accommodation in this remote area do not come cheaply. Even if you bring your own 4WD, there will be occasions when, to get to the most interesting areas, you will be obliged to hire a guide. The Acacus is one example of an area in the Fezzan where the authorities have recently decreed that tourists must be accompanied by a local guide.

SEBHA

Sebha is the capital of the Fezzan and the main transport centre for the region. The town is mostly modern and rather dull, but it is well endowed with services. Sebha has some historical interest because it is where Colonel Gaddafi was educated and where he began his political activities. The only building in town of any historical or architectural interest is the old fort next to the airport. It is not open to the public because it is still used by the military.

Information

There are several banks on Sharia Mohammed Megharief, close to the bus station. These are the only banks in the entire Fezzan with foreign currency exchange facilities. There is a large post office and public telephone office on Sharia Mohammed Megharief, almost opposite the baladiyya. The public telephones are available until 10 pm.

Places to Stay & Eat

Nakhil Hotel (☎ 25049, Sharia Mohammed Megharief) is a small place with only 16 rooms set around a courtyard. It has recently been taken over as a private business

and has a cafe, a fountain in the courtyard and satellite TV. There is also the convenience of a bus stop right outside the hotel. Singles/doubles cost 10/15LD. There is a *restaurant* next door, which has an arrangement with the hotel and serves cheap meals.

Kalha Hotel (☎ 23104, 26650 or 27670, Sharia Gamal Abdel Nasser) is large and comfortable and in the centre of town. It has all the usual facilities of a Libyan hotel this size, including lobby shops, and an empty swimming pool. Singles/doubles cost 25/30LD including breakfast. Lunch and dinner cost 13LD.

Slightly more upmarket is *Al-Fatah Hotel (☎ 23952/5, Sharia Gamal Abdel Nasser)*. Rooms cost 22/27LD and have satellite TV and air-con. There is a rooftop *restaurant* with views over the city. Lunch or dinner costs about 10LD.

The few places to eat in Sebha, apart from the hotels, are mainly along Sharia Mohammed Megharief and cater for local travellers. There are also a few *cafes* near the bus station, but nothing fancy.

Getting There & Away

Air There are a couple of flights a week to Tripoli and Benghazi but they are unreliable. Libyan Arab Airlines (☎ 29120) office is on Sharia Mohammed Megharief, close to the Nakhil Hotel. The one-way fare to Tripoli or Benghazi is 30LD.

Bus Sebha is well served by buses travelling to and from Tripoli. An express air-con bus leaves Tripoli daily at 7 am, returning at 6 am the next day, and the fare is 22LD. There is a daily service along the Wadi al-Hayat to Ubari and Ghat, which leaves early in the morning. The bus station in Sebha is on Sharia Mohammed Megharief.

Taxi There are shared taxis serving the routes around the region. The taxis going to Ubari and Ghat leave from the taxi rank close to the bus station. Those going north and serving the Wadi ash-Shatti are on the next block along, down a turn-off by the Libyan Arab Airlines office.

WADI AL-HAYAT

Wadi al-Hayat is about 400km long, running west from Sebha to Aweinat. A fast road runs through the wadi, which is flanked by a rocky escarpment on the south and by the Ubari Sand Sea on the north. The wadi has various villages, farms and one main town, Ubari, dotted along its length.

Historically, the wadi was important as the capital and seat of power of the Garamantes tribe. Their capital, Garama, near the modern village of Germa, is mostly un-

excavated and the ruins now on view date from a much later occupation. Throughout the region there are distinctive tombs (some dramatically large), water tunnels and other monuments left by the Garamantes, the most notable being the cemetery at Hatya.

RAMLAT DAWADA

This area of the Ubari Sand Sea contains 11 lakes, the origins and extraordinary qualities of which have baffled geographers and explorers alike. To get there, you definitely

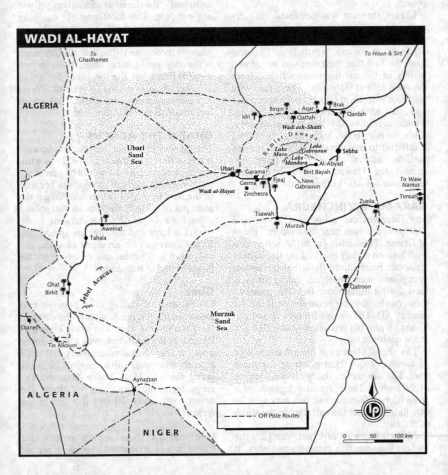

WADI AL-HAYAT

- To Ghadhames
- To Houn & Sirt
- ALGERIA
- Birqin
- Aqar
- Brak
- Idri
- Qattah
- Qardah
- Wadi ash-Shatti
- Ramlat Dawada
- Lake Gabraoun
- Ubari Sand Sea
- Lake Mavo
- Sebha
- Lake Mandara
- Al-Abyad
- Ubari
- Garama
- Bint Bayah
- Germa
- Fjeaj
- New Gabraoun
- To Waw Namus
- Zinchecra
- Wadi al-Hayat
- Tsawah
- Zueila
- Aweinat
- Murzuk
- Timsah
- Tahala
- Ghat
- Birkit
- Jebel Acacus
- Qatroon
- Djanet
- Murzuk Sand Sea
- Tin Alkoum
- Aynazzan
- ALGERIA
- NIGER
- - - - Off Piste Routes
- 0   50   100 km

need a 4WD, and a guide is recommended. Contact Winzrik Travel & Tourism Services (☎ 0728-2726) in New Gabraoun to organise a vehicle and guide.

Lake Mavo is known as the lake that changes colour because the water can be red, sometimes blue or even green. It is thought that the changes are caused by algae in the water. Another permanent lake is **Mandara**, which is picturesque and surrounded by palm trees, although the water level can sometimes drop to that of a muddy pool.

Lake Gabraoun was occupied until recently by the Dawada tribe, whose history also remains the subject of speculation. Their name means 'worm-eater', arising from the fact that their diet was composed mainly of the small creatures fished from the main lake at Gabraoun. These creatures were not worms, of course, but a species of tiny, red shrimp called *Artemia salina*, which thrived in the lake's high salinity. Since the revolution, authorities have found it difficult to maintain any kind of modern facilities at the lake and they have persuaded the Dawada to move to New Gabraoun – a new village on the wadi.

GARAMA & ZINCHECRA
The Garamantian ruins of Garama and Zinchecra are both near the modern village of **Germa**. The earlier capital, Zinchecra, is built high on a bluff overlooking the wadi to the south. Excavations show that the earliest occupation was Neolithic, dating from at least the 1st millennium BC. The promontory continued to be occupied until the 1st century AD. The site is officially open from 8 am to 5 pm, but it is often unattended and is not enclosed.

The site of Garama is behind the village of Germa, about 2km north of the main road. The site was no doubt chosen because of its spring. There are also legends of a large lake at Garama, and this may well be true judging from the salt flats to the south of the city.

About 15km east of Ubari, you pass the ancient Garamantian cemetery at **Hatya**. It

is visible from the highway but you need to look out for it. Heading west, the distinctive mud-brick mausoleums are set about 200m back from the road on the left.

Places to Stay
Fjeaj's *hostel* (☎ 071-28331) is one of the best in Libya, with good rooms. It is popular with desert travellers and can be heavily booked, so it is best to book in advance.

Camping opportunities in and around the wadi are limitless, but you need to be well equipped – the desert is unforgiving if you are careless. The most popular camping places are out in the dunes of the Ramlat Dawada, around one of the lakes (but beware of mosquitos). The lake at Gabraoun is the only one with facilities. You can rent a palm-frond hut for the night for about 20LD. The site is owned by Winzrik Travel & Tourism Services (☎ 0728-2726) which has an office at New Gabraoun.

GHAT & THE ACACUS
The Acacus mountain area (Jebel Acacus) is one of the highlights of Libya. Even without its cave paintings, it would be one of the most stunning parts of the Sahara because of the wild beauty of the terrain. To get the most out of a trip to the Acacus you should allow for a couple of nights camping as the terrain is large and the sites are spread out. Expeditions can be arranged in Ghat, the only town in the area, and a useful base for hiring vehicles and guides.

Ghat
Ghat is a small Tuareg town between two mountain ranges, the Acacus to the east and the Tassili to the west. The town, known as Rhapsa in Roman times, was a key trading post for trans-Saharan caravans and until recently there were still occasional caravans going south to Mali. These days, the Tuaregs have mostly 'come in' from the desert; only about 20 still live out in the Acacus.

Information There are no government tourist offices in Ghat but a couple of private companies have offices in town and are helpful if you want information. Voyages Acacus (☎ 2804) and Winzrik Travel & Tourism Services (☎ 2600) are in the centre of town on the main road.

The small post office is just past the hotel on the main road. You can make telephone calls from there, although connections are often slow.

Things to See There is not a great deal to do in Ghat, apart from exploring the old medina on foot. It has some interesting architecture, including a lovely, old vernacular-style mosque that is still being used today.

Places to Stay & Eat There is only one place to stay in Ghat: *Tassili Hotel* (☎ 2570, 2560). It is set back slightly from the main road, between the school and the post office. Singles/doubles cost 20/25LD and meals about 15LD.

The heady decision about which restaurant to eat in doesn't arise in Ghat because there aren't any. Only the hotel has meals on offer. The alternatives are to bring your own food or buy it locally from shops, which offer a limited choice.

Getting There & Away There are air-con buses running to and from Sebha twice a day, and to and from Ubari daily.

Shared taxis do the run to Ghat from Sebha and leave early. The journey takes six hours.

The Acacus

There are only two ways to see this area: bring your own 4WD and hire a guide in Ghat; or book an all-inclusive excursion from one of the agencies, either locally or in Tripoli. Government rules forbid anyone to travel without a guide into the area. This is for two reasons: firstly, to prevent people from getting lost; and secondly, to prevent the cave paintings from being damaged.

To visit the Acacus you need a permit arranged by the tour agencies in Ghat. You also need two passport photos and 5LD. The agencies usually charge a few dinars for making the applications, but it saves you the hassle of locating the desert patrol office. Allow half a day for the permits to be processed (the next day if you apply in the afternoon).

The usual circuit from Ghat takes you 190km north and comes out near Aweinat. Depending on how much time you have, an interesting route continues through the Acacus via Mathandous and comes out near Germa in the Wadi al-Hayat. There are **rock carvings** throughout the Mathandous area and these are well worth seeing.

There are no roads in the Acacus area and some of the going is pretty rough. It is absolutely essential that you have a good vehicle and carry enough supplies and spares to see you through any delays or breakdowns. Wells are few and far between and it is not a good idea to depend on them for replenishing your water supplies. If you do use them, however, the water is safe to drink.

Oman

In contrast to the vast desert wasteland of Saudi Arabia or the tiny city-states of the Gulf, Oman is a land of dramatic mountains and long, unspoiled coastlines. Its capital, Muscat, does not have the nouveau-riche feel that typifies much of the Gulf.

Tourism is on the increase in Oman and facilities and services for tourists extend to all parts of the country. However, the country has taken a cautious approach to its development, and Oman remains one of the most traditional countries in the Middle East though its traditions are often more outward looking than the country is given credit for.

Facts about Oman

HISTORY

A general history of the Middle East can be found in the Facts about the Region chapter.

At its peak in the 19th century, under Sultan Said bin Sultan (1804-56), Oman controlled Mombasa and Zanzibar and operated trading posts even farther down the African coast. It also controlled portions of what are now India and Pakistan. It was not until 1947 that Oman surrendered its last colonial outpost at Gwadar, in what is now Pakistan.

When Said died the empire was divided between two of his sons. One became the Sultan of Zanzibar, and ruled Said's African colonies, while the other became known as the Sultan of Muscat and Oman – the coast and interior of today's sultanate were then regarded as two separate realms.

The division of the empire cut Muscat off from some of its most lucrative domains, causing the country to stagnate economically during the late 19th century. The British exacerbated this situation by pressing the sultan to end the trade in slaves and arms for which Oman had long been known.

Even though the rest of the empire suffered economically, Zanzibar continued to prosper. The British took advantage of the empire's

The Sultanate of Oman

Area: 309,500 sq km
Population: 2.1 million
Population Growth Rate: 3.7%
Capital: Muscat
Head of State: Sultan Qaboos bin Said
Official Language: Arabic
Currency: Omani riyal (OR)
Exchange Rate: US$1 = OR0.390

- **Best Dining** – for traditional Omani cuisine go to Bin Atique Restaurant in Nizwa
- **Best Walk** – a stroll through Mutrah souq in Muscat
- **Best Activity** – a 4WD safari into one of the country's scenic wadis
- **Best Nightlife** – watching the turtles nesting on the beach at Ras al-Jinz

weakness and in 1891 they made Zanzibar a British protectorate. Administration of the island was taken over by the British consulate and the sultan was stripped of all power, reduced to an honorary figure. The situation continued until the 1950s when an Arab Zanzibarian party was established and assumed the majority at a general election. The British withdrew from the region in 1957.

When Sultan Faisal bin Turki died in 1913, the interior's tribes refused to recognise his son and successor as imam. This led to a split between the coastal areas ruled by the sultan and the interior, which came to be controlled by a separate line of imams.

In 1938 a new sultan, Said bin Taimur, came to power. When he sought to extend his writ into the interior in the early 1950s the British backed him, largely because they believed that there might be oil there. Said did not gain full control of the country until 1959.

Though he ended the long-running revolt in the interior, Said, in many other respects, took Oman backwards. He was opposed to any sort of change and sought to isolate Oman from the modern world. Under his rule, a country that only a century earlier had rivalled the empire-builders of Europe became a medieval anachronism.

In 1958 Said boarded himself up in his palace at Salalah, which he rarely left thereafter. The formation of a nationalist rebel group, the Dhofar Liberation Front (DLF), in 1962 did little to change this. The DLF's battle against the state began in 1965.

The combination of the escalating rebellion and Said's refusal to spend the money he received from oil exports after 1967 soon began to try even London's patience. In July 1970 Said was overthrown by his only son, Qaboos, in a bloodless palace coup.

Sultan Qaboos bin Said promptly repealed his father's oppressive social restrictions and began to modernise Oman's semi-feudal economy. There was a certain urgency in his program to bring the country into the 20th century. In 1970, when development in much of the rest of the Gulf was already well under way, Oman still had only 10km of surfaced road (between Muscat and Mutrah). There were only three primary schools in the country and no secondary schools. There was one hospital, which was run by US missionaries.

Oman's oil revenues were, and still are, small and its resources limited. Qaboos saw the need to move quickly if the oil wealth was to have any real effect on his people's lives. He pushed localisation of the workforce harder than the rulers of the other Gulf countries. Oman needed foreign aid and expertise, but it could hardly afford the luxury of the armies of foreign labourers who had built the infrastructure of places like Kuwait.

What to See

In Muscat be sure to make time for a trip to the **Mutrah souq** – one of the best traditional markets in the region. The **Sultan's Armed Forces Museum** in the capital's Bait al-Falaj district and the **Natural History Museum** in Madinat as-Sultan Qaboos are both 'must-see' sites, as are the capital area's three **forts**.

If you have the time and money the best place to visit is the **Musandam peninsula**, home of some of the most dramatic scenery in the Gulf. Other spots worth visiting outside Muscat include the old fortress and the market in **Nizwa** and the fort at **Jabrin** in the north of the country, **Job's Tomb** just outside of Salalah in the far south, and **Ras al-Jinz**, the easternmost point of the Arabian peninsula.

Despite Qaboos' apparent desire to make a clean break with the past, the Dhofar rebellion continued unabated. It ended only when Oman and South Yemen established diplomatic relations in 1982, and the Aden government cut off its assistance to the rebels.

In foreign affairs Qaboos has carved out a reputation for himself as a maverick. In spite of Oman's past military ties with the shāh, he has managed to maintain friendly relations with post-revolutionary Iran. Oman was also one of only two Arab countries (the other was Sudan) that refused to break diplomatic ties with Egypt after it signed a peace treaty with Israel in 1979. In late 1993 the sultan became the first Gulf leader to welcome a representative of Israel to his country when prime minister Yitzhak Rabin paid a brief visit.

Oman Today

In his latest five year plan, Qaboos has called for greater diversification of the economy in an effort to ensure security and jobs for Omanis. This has become an even more important issue since a drop in oil prices in 1998. Reserves of natural gas are

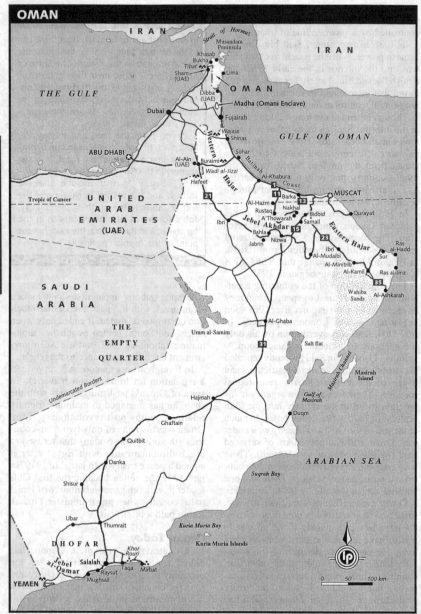

OMAN

being tapped and Oman's mining industry has been given the task of exploiting deposits of gold, copper, silver and coal. A long term goal of the government is to be self-sufficient in food production. Oman has also increased its export market through the manufacture of furniture, textiles, electrical goods and paper and metal products.

Employment of nationals is vital to the achievement of Oman's economic goals. This process is called Omanisation and has resulted in the retrenchment of many expats who are relocating to other Gulf States where there is still a high dependence on foreign labour and professionals. It is far more common to see Omanis in service positions or doing manual jobs than it is to see other Gulf Arabs performing similar jobs.

A further relaxation on issuing tourist visas means tourism is high on the list of growing industries in Oman.

In 1998 Sultan Qaboos was awarded the International Peace Award from the National Council on US-Arab Relations in recognition of his insight, and his role in maintaining peace and stability in the region.

GEOGRAPHY

Oman is 309,500 sq km in area. Its territory includes the Musandam peninsula, which is separated from the rest of the country by the east coast of the UAE.

The northern coastal strip, known as the Batinah coast, is a sand and gravel plain separated from the rest of Arabia by the Hajar Mountains. The highest peak in the country is Jebel Akhdar (Green Mountain) at 2980m. The term Jebel Akhdar, however, generally refers to the entire Hajar range in north-central Oman, rather than to a single peak.

There are also two large areas of salt flats and a sandy desert area, the Wahiba Sands, popular with tourists and expatriates for 4WD trips.

CLIMATE

Oman's varied geography makes for a wide range of climatic conditions. Muscat is hot and humid from mid-March until October, with an average temperature in June of

38°C. It is pleasantly warm from October to March and daytime temperatures from December to February are usually a lovely 25°C. In the Salalah area, humid weather with temperatures approaching 30°C is common, even in December. The Salalah area is drenched by the monsoon rains every year from June to September.

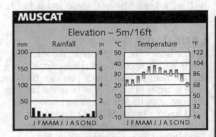

GOVERNMENT & POLITICS

The sultan is the ultimate authority and even relatively minor policy decisions go all the way to his desk before being implemented. In January 1992 an elected *Majlis ash-Shura* (Consultative Council) was convened for the first time, replacing an appointed State Consultative Council that had existed since 1981. Though a far cry from a western parliament, the council is widely seen as a first step towards broader participation in government. It mainly comments on draft laws and such other topics as the sultan chooses to put in front of it.

Sultan Qaboos is not married and has no children. The basic law of the Constitution states that an heir to the throne will be chosen by the royal family within three days of the throne falling vacant.

POPULATION & PEOPLE

Oman's population is estimated to be about two million. While Omanis are Arabs, the country's long trading history has led to a great deal of mingling and intermarriage with other ethnic groups, such as east Africans. There has been an Indian merchant community in Muscat for at least 200 years, and in

OMAN

the north, it is common to find people who are partly of Persian or Baluchi ancestry.

RELIGION

The majority of Omanis (about 75%) follow the Ibadi sect of Islam. However, Oman is very tolerant of other religions and in the capital there are several Christian churches, both Protestant and Roman Catholic, as well as a Lord Shiva Temple and a Lord Krishna Temple.

LANGUAGE

Arabic is the official language, though English is widely spoken in business circles. In the northern coastal areas you can find a large number of expatriates from the Indian subcontinent, traders and sailors who speak Fārsī and/or Urdu. Many Omanis who returned from Africa in the early 1970s speak Swahili and, in some cases, French.

Facts for the Visitor

PLANNING

See the Regional Facts for the Visitor chapter for general information about when to visit this part of the world.

Unusual for the Gulf, southern Oman has a monsoon season, which lasts from June to September, and while you probably do not want to be in Salalah during the rains, it is definitely worth a visit in October when everything in Dhofar is still lush and green.

VISAS & DOCUMENTS
Visas

Everybody except citizens of other Gulf countries needs a visa to enter Oman. To apply you must fill out an application, have at least six months validity on your passport and provide several (probably four) passport-sized photographs. Travellers have on occasion also been asked to produce an onward or return ticket.

If you are not close to an embassy it is possible to obtain a visa through most of Oman's hotels and tour companies. This usually takes about a week. A hotel will usually require a three night minimum stay and will add a visa processing fee to your bill. Costs vary according to your nationality. For example, a standard single-entry tourist visa allowing a stay of three weeks costs OR20 for British passport holders and OR7 for Australians. It is usually tied to the reciprocal arrangement between countries. Multiple-entry visas cost OR40 and are valid for two years.

A standard single-entry tourist visa allows a stay of three weeks, and is valid for entry by land unless it specifically has something to the contrary (like 'By Air Only') written on it. If you get a hotel sponsored visa it is likely to state this, in which case you can only enter the country by air. Multiple-entry visas are available to US and British residents of Gulf Cooperation Council (GCC) countries. They cost OR40 and are valid for two years.

Resident expats in GCC countries can collect visas at land border posts or at the airport on their day of travel. You must have resided in the GCC for at least one year and have six months validity left on your residence visa. These are only available to professional people and their families.

Transit visas are available on arrival at Seeb airport and last for 72 hours. You must have proof of an onward flight.

Visa Extensions In theory, one week extensions are available to everyone. If you want to extend for a longer period you will have to come up with a good reason why you need it. To get an extension go to the Immigration & Passports Directorate in the ministries area in Muscat.

Visas for Neighbouring Countries You need a visa to enter the following neighbouring countries of Oman:

Kuwait If you are a GCC resident you will need a letter of sponsorship from your company, photocopies of the information pages of your passport and an invitation from a company or hotel in Kuwait to apply for a Kuwaiti visa. The fee for a Kuwaiti visa varies — it's free for some nationalities, but

OR7 for US passport holders. The visa takes two days to process.

Tourists on visiting visas cannot get Kuwaiti visas in Oman – applications must be submitted to the Kuwait embassy in your home country.

Qatar GCC residents of certain professions can get a visa for Qatar on arrival in Doha at the airport immigration desk. Others will need to go through a sponsor in Doha. Call airport immigration in Doha (☎ 00974-351550 ext 490) for information on whether you qualify for an automatic visa. The Qatari embassy in Oman does not issue visas to tourists – applications must be submitted to the Qatar embassy in your home country.

Saudi Arabia Visas for Saudi Arabia must be organised through the Saudi embassy in your home country.

United Arab Emirates GCC residents can get a visa for the United Arab Emirates (UAE) if it's organised through a sponsor in the UAE (eg a hotel or tour operator) – see Visas & Documents in the UAE chapter for more details. GCC residents who have been in Oman for a year and have six months validity left on their residence visa can purchase visas for the UAE on arrival at the airport or at major border posts.

However, the UAE embassy in Oman does not issue visas to tourists. This must be organised through the UAE embassy in your home country or through a sponsor (eg a hotel).

Yemen To get a visa for Yemen GCC residents need two photos and a letter of sponsorship from their employer; tourists just need the photos. The visa is processed the same day and costs OR5 for most nationalities but OR23 for British passport holders.

Driving Licence & Permits
Most foreign driving licences are accepted in Oman. If you think that your licence may not be recognised it's best to get an International Driving Permit.

Foreign residents of Oman need a Road Permit to enter or leave the country by land. This regulation does not apply to tourists.

Student Cards
Discounts are given on admission to certain museums and to some beach clubs for people under 18. But a student card is not widely recognised in Oman and you will gain little advantage by having one.

Other Documents
Site Permits When the last edition of this book was written, a permit from the Ministry of Culture & National Heritage in Muscat was needed to visit most archaeological sites, old forts etc. Now the general rule seems to be that only large groups have to call ahead to make arrangements for a visit. Permits are definitely needed, however, for conservation sites such as the green turtle nesting area at Ras al-Jinz. These are available from the Directorate General of Nature Reserves in the Ministry of Regional Municipalities & Environment in Muscat and cost OR1 per person. The ministry is on the sea side of Ministries St in Al-Khuwair. It is the large white building that stands alone.

EMBASSIES & CONSULATES
Omani Embassies & Consulates
Oman does not have embassies in Canada, Australia or New Zealand – for information contact the nearest Omani embassy. For addresses of Omani embassies in neighbouring Middle Eastern countries see the relevant country chapters. Diplomatic representation abroad includes:

France
    Embassy:
    (☎ 01 47 23 01 63, fax 01 47 23 77 10)
    50 Ave de Lena, 75116 Paris
Germany
    Embassy:
    (☎ 228-35 70 31, fax 35 70 40)
    Lindenallee 11, D-53173 Bonn
Netherlands
    Embassy:
    (☎ 70-361 5800, fax 360 7277)
    Koninginnegracht 27, 2514 AB Den Haag

OMAN

OMAN

UK
    Embassy:
    (☎ 020-7225 0001, fax 7589 2505)
    167 Queen's Gate, London, SW7 5HE
USA
    Embassy:
    (☎ 202-387 1980, fax 745 4933)
    2535 Belmont Rd NW, Washington DC 20008

Embassies & Consulates in Oman

Working hours for most embassies/consulates in Oman are generally Saturday to Wednesday from 8 am to 1 or 2 pm.

The UK embassy looks after Irish nationals, and processes visas and handles emergencies for Canadian citizens. Australians should contact the Australian embassy in Riyadh.

Bahrain
    Embassy:
    (☎ 605074, 605133, fax 605072)
    Al-Kharjiyah St, just off Way 3015, Shatti al-Qurm
Egypt
    Embassy:
    (☎ 600411, fax 603626)
    Jameat A'Duwal al-Arabiya St, Al-Khuwair, to the sea side of Sultan Qaboos St, west of the Al-Khuwair roundabout
France
    Embassy:
    (☎ 681800, fax 681843)
    Jameat A'Duwal al-Arabiya St, Al-Khuwair, to the sea side of Sultan Qaboos St, west of the Al-Khuwair roundabout
Germany
    Embassy:
    (☎ 702164, fax 735690)
    Near the Al-Nahdha Hospital on Al-Nahdha St, Ruwi
India
    Embassy:
    (☎ 702957, fax 797547)
    Bank al-Markazi St, Ruwi
Iran
    Embassy:
    (☎ 696944, fax 696888)
    Jameat A'Duwal al-Arabiya St, Al-Khuwair, to the sea side of Sultan Qaboos St, west of the Al-Khuwair roundabout
Kuwait
    Embassy:
    (☎ 699626 or 699627, fax 699628)
    Jameat A'Duwal al-Arabiya St, Al-Khuwair, to the sea side of Sultan Qaboos St, west of the Al-Khuwair roundabout

Netherlands
    Embassy:
    (☎ 603706, 603719, fax 603397)
    Villa 1366, Way 3017, Shatti al-Qurm
New Zealand
    Consulate:
    (☎ 794932, fax 706443)
    Mutrah High St, Mutrah
Qatar
    Embassy:
    (☎ 691152, fax 691156)
    Jameat A'Duwal al-Arabiya St, Al-Khuwair, to the sea side of Sultan Qaboos St, west of the Al-Khuwair roundabout
Saudi Arabia
    Embassy:
    (☎ 601744, fax 603540)
    Jameat A'Duwal al-Arabiya St, Al-Khuwair, to the sea side of Sultan Qaboos St, west of the Al-Khuwair roundabout
UAE
    Embassy:
    (☎ 600302, fax 602584)
    Jameat A'Duwal al-Arabiya St, Al-Khuwair, to the sea side of Sultan Qaboos St, west of the Al-Khuwair roundabout
UK
    Embassy:
    (☎ 693077, fax 693091)
    Jameat A'Duwal al-Arabiya St, Al-Khuwair, to the sea side of Sultan Qaboos St, west of the Al-Khuwair roundabout
USA
    Embassy:
    (☎ 698989, fax 604316)
    Jameat A'Duwal al-Arabiya St, Al-Khuwair, to the sea side of Sultan Qaboos St, west of the Al-Khuwair roundabout
Yemen
    Embassy:
    (☎ 600815, fax 609172)
    Bldg No 2981, Way 2840, Shatti al-Qurm

CUSTOMS

Non-Muslims arriving by air can bring in one bottle of booze. Those arriving by road are not permitted to import alcohol. Customs regulations allow travellers to import a 'reasonable quantity' of cigars, cigarettes and tobacco.

Customs officers are extremely concerned about videotapes and you can expect to have them held at customs for several days.

MONEY
Currency

The Omani riyal (OR) is divided into 1000 baisa (also spelled baiza). Notes come in denominations of 100 and 200 baisa, and 0.5, one, five, 10, 20 and OR50. Coins are five, 10, 25, 50 and 100 baisa, though the 25 and 50 baisa coins are the only ones you are likely to see on a regular basis. A word of warning: the OR5 note and the old OR1 are the same colour and look very similar. It's easy to confuse them. The riyal is a convertible currency and there are no restrictions on its import or export.

The good thing about travelling to Oman from the UAE is that you can use up all your UAE dirhams. They are accepted just about everywhere in the country at an exchange rate of Dh10 to OR1.

Exchange Rates

country	unit		riyal
Australia	A$1	=	OR0.240
Canada	C$1	=	OR0.250
euro	€1	=	OR0.430
France	10FF	=	OR0.650
Germany	DM1	=	OR0.220
Japan	¥100	=	OR0.369
New Zealand	NZ$1	=	OR0.210
UK	UK£1	=	OR0.630
USA	US$1	=	OR0.390

Exchanging Money

Banking hours are Saturday to Wednesday from 8 am to noon, and Thursday from 8 to 11 am. Most banks will change US dollar travellers cheques but they do take a commission. Moneychangers keep similar hours to the banks but are usually also open from around 4 to 7 pm.

Credit Cards & ATMs ATMs are widespread in Oman though few of them appear to be tied into the big international systems. Some British Bank of the Middle East machines accept cards on the Plus system and Cirrus. The National Bank of Oman's ATMs are tied into the Global Access network.

The most popular credit card appears to be Visa, but MasterCard and American Express (Amex) are also accepted at most hotels and restaurants. If you use Amex you may incur a merchant fee of 5%.

Costs

Accommodation is the main barrier to seeing Oman on a budget. Once you get around that problem many other expenses of daily life are quite low. Unless you can find a free bed, plan on spending OR15 per day in Muscat and OR20 to OR25 outside the capital.

Tipping & Bargaining

Tipping is not expected in cheaper places while more expensive restaurants tend to add a service charge to bills (though this often goes to the restaurant, not the waiting staff). If you do decide to leave a tip, 10% should be sufficient.

Hotel, restaurant, bus and microbus prices are fixed. The only things you can expect to haggle over are taxi fares and souvenirs in the souq.

Taxes

A 5% municipality tax and a 4% tourism tax are applied to all hotel and restaurant bills, as is an 8% service charge. If prices are quoted 'net', it means they include all taxes.

POST & COMMUNICATIONS
Post

Sending a postcard to any destination outside the Arab world costs 150 baisa. Postage for letters is 200 baisa for the first 10g and 350 baisa for 10g to 20g. Mailing small packets to countries outside the Arab world costs OR2 to OR4. For parcels of 1kg it costs OR4 to OR6.

Sending Mail

Post offices are open Saturday to Wednesday from 7.30 am until 2 pm, and Thursday until 11 am. If you are staying at a five star hotel you can leave your mail at reception for staff to post for you.

OMAN

OMAN

Receiving Mail

Poste restante service is available at the main post office in Ruwi or the branch post office in Muscat. Have your mail addressed to: Your Name, Poste Restante, Ruwi Central Post Office, Ruwi, Sultanate of Oman; or Muscat Post Office, Muscat, Sultanate of Oman.

Any parcels you receive while in the sultanate will incur a 250 baisa charge for presentation to customs and you may be required to collect them from the post office and have them cleared through customs there.

Telephone & Fax

The country code for Bahrain is ☎ 968, followed by the local six digit number – there are no area or city codes.

There are central public telephone offices, that offer fax services as well, in both Muscat and Salalah and in a few of the smaller cities and towns. With the exception of the call booking office in Muscat however, these offices mainly offer card phones. Phonecards are available from most grocery stores and petrol stations.

The directory assistance number is ☎ 198.

Email & Internet Access

Internet access is available in Oman through the General Telecommunication Organisation (GTO). See Information in the Muscat section for details of Internet cafes. Most five-star hotels in the capital have business centres with Internet access for executive guests.

BOOKS
Lonely Planet

Lonely Planet publishes several detailed guides to various countries in the Middle East. For information on titles, see the Books section in the Regional Facts for the Visitor chapter.

Guidebooks

Oman – a Comprehensive Guide to the Sultanate of Oman is very thorough and includes interesting anecdotal information,
but as it is published under the auspices of the Directorate General of Tourism, it doesn't tend to be very objective. There are a large number of specialist guides to Oman published by companies based in either Muscat or Dubai. All are widely available in larger bookshops or hotels in Muscat for OR5 to OR6.

The *Maverick Guide to Oman* by Peter Ochs is an essential book if you plan to do some off-road exploring. It has detailed and interesting information on off-road sites as well as good instructions on how to get there. *Off-Road in Oman* by Heiner Klein & Rebecca Brickson covers much of the same territory.

Travel

Travels in Oman: On the Track of the Early Explorers by Philip Ward combines a modern travel narrative with the best of the 18th, 19th and early 20th century travellers' accounts of the country. *Sultan in Oman* by James Morris is a travelling journalist's account of a visit to Oman in the 1950s, though you should be aware that it is banned in the country.

Some of the action in Wilfred Thesiger's 1959 classic *Arabian Sands* takes place in and around Salalah, which Thesiger visited at the end of one of his journeys into the Empty Quarter. The final section of the book is an account of a trip around Oman's northern interior.

History

Michael Field's *The Merchants* has a fascinating chapter on the growth of modern Oman built around the story of WJ Towell & Co, one of Oman's biggest family-owned trading companies. *Oman and Its Renaissance* by Sir Donald Hawly covers the first 25 years of Sultan Qaboos' rule, and charts the history of Oman from the end of the Ice Age until the present.

There is also a huge number of coffee table books on Oman that can be found in the bookshops listed in city sections. They cover such topics as Omani architecture, geology, wildlife, crafts and forts.

More general Middle East titles, some of which also contain coverage of Oman, are listed in the Books section in the Regional Facts for the Visitor chapter at the beginning of this book.

NEWSPAPERS & MAGAZINES

The *Times of Oman* and the *Oman Daily Observer* are the local English-language newspapers. Foreign newspapers and magazines, available only in the bookshops in Muscat's five-star hotels and in the suburban shopping centres frequented by the western community, are usually about three days old. Outside of Muscat you can forget about finding foreign papers except, maybe, at the Salalah Holiday Inn and the Salalah Family Bookshop.

Oman Today is a magazine-cum-handbook published every two months and widely available throughout the sultanate for 500 baisa. *Adventure Oman* is a glossy magazine with articles on caving, mountain biking, rock climbing and ecology. It costs OR1.500. Less thorough listings of activities can be found in *What's On*, a monthly publication based in the UAE and available in the sultanate for OR1.200.

RADIO & TV

Omani TV broadcasts a daily newscast in English at 8 pm and shows English-language movies two or three nights a week (usually around 11 pm). Satellite TV is also widely available in the sultanate.

The Sultanate of Oman FM Service is the local English-language radio station. It broadcasts on 90.4 FM (94.3 FM from Salalah) every day from 7 am to 10 pm, with news bulletins at 7.30 am and 2.30 and 6.30 pm. The fare is mostly classical music interspersed with light entertainment.

PHOTOGRAPHY & VIDEO

There is no problem getting film developed in Oman. The labs are reliable and world standard. To have 36 prints developed will cost about OR2.200. All types of films are available in Muscat but you may have difficulty finding particular film out of the capital.

LAUNDRY

There are no laundrettes in Oman. But if you are not a wash-it-in-the-sink sort of person it's fairly easy to get your washing done through hotels or at laundries in the cities. A moderately sized load will cost OR1 or OR2.

TOILETS

Most public toilets in Muscat are western style and are generally clean. You'll find them in shopping centres (though you'll often have to ask a shopkeeper for the key as they are usually just for staff) and in museums. Public toilets in souqs or on the street are usually just for men. Most restaurants and petrol stations outside Muscat will have a toilet out the back but be aware that they are just holes in the ground and are generally in a pretty poor state.

HEALTH

Since his ascension to power Sultan Qaboos has made improving health care and hygiene standards in Oman one of his main priorities. The result today is one of the most squeaky-clean countries you could ever hope to visit. Even the smallest restaurants in the souq are held to quite high standards of cleanliness.

Tap water is drinkable throughout the country and no special vaccinations are necessary, though a gamma globulin (or Havrix) injection as a Hepatitis A preventative is always a good idea. Malaria, virtually endemic only 30 years ago, is no longer a huge problem, but you may want to consider antimalarial medications, particularly if you plan to travel extensively in the south. Western medication and healthcare products are widely available in Muscat but less so out of the capital.

If you are coming from a yellow fever area you will need to have a vaccination at least 10 days before arriving in Oman and be able to produce a certificate on arrival.

DISABLED TRAVELLERS

Although some car parks around the cities have spots for disabled drivers, it seems that services and facilities in Oman end there. If you need any specific information you can contact the Oman Association for the Disabled, PO Box 331, Muscat 113, Sultanate of Oman (☎/fax 597657).

DANGERS & ANNOYANCES

The only danger to speak of is bad drivers. They abound in Oman, so be alert on the roads and don't expect people to drive as considerately as you may be used to.

BUSINESS HOURS

Most businesses are open daily from 8 am to 1 pm and 4 to 7 or 7.30 pm, except Thursday afternoon and Friday. Shops in the Mutrah souq and in some of Muscat's more upmarket shopping malls stay open until 9 or 9.30 pm most nights. Government departments and ministries are open Saturday to Wednesday from 7.30 am to 2.30 pm. Note that during Ramadan government offices are open from 8.30 am to 1.30 pm.

PUBLIC HOLIDAYS & SPECIAL EVENTS

In addition to the main Islamic holidays described in the Regional Facts for the Visitor chapter. Oman observes the following:

New Year's Day
  1 January
Lailat al-Mi'raj
  24 October 2000 (varies each year) – Ascension of the Prophet
National Day
  18 November
Sultan's Birthday
  19 November

ACTIVITIES

The variety of terrain in Oman makes weekend mountain and desert motoring particularly worthwhile. If you are planning to do some wadi bashing on your own, the *Maverick Guide to Oman* and the *APEX Explorer's Guide to Oman* are essential reading. *Desert Driver's Manual* by Jim Stabler is a handy publication with some vital tips on desert driving. But unless you have your own 4WD or can borrow one, taking off on your own can be very expensive due to the exorbitant cost of hiring.

Every tour company in Oman offers 4WD desert safaris and wadi bashing trips, some of them overnight. They usually incorporate a spot of sand-skiing and camel riding as well.

Rock climbing, hiking and caving are increasingly popular activities, especially with the expat community. Sunny Day Tours (☎ 591244, fax 591478) can arrange such activities. As all trips are individually designed there are no fixed prices, but you can roughly estimate a cost of US$100 per day per person.

ACCOMMODATION

The only formal camp site in Oman is at the Ras al-Jinz Turtle Reserve and you need a permit from the Ministry of Regional Muncipalities & Environment to go there (see Ras al-Jinz later in this chapter for details). Camping is mostly a matter of finding a good spot and setting up shop.

In Muscat you can spend anything from OR7 to OR70 on a single hotel room. Most of Oman's provincial towns, however, have only one or two hotels, and they tend to be pretty expensive.

FOOD & DRINKS

Unlike many other countries in the Gulf where the national cuisine is basically Lebanese cuisine, Oman does have some interesting national dishes and flavours. Eating cheaply in Oman almost always means eating Indian. Biryani, shwarma and felafel are available just about everywhere for 200 to 600 baisa. Muscat also has a number of upmarket Indian, Lebanese and Chinese restaurants, and the usual collection of western fastfood establishments. Alcohol is available only in larger hotels and expensive restaurants.

SPECTATOR SPORTS

Camel racing is usually held on Friday mornings at camel tracks around the country. Races are announced in the major Arabic dailies but not necessarily in the English-language newspapers. Alternatively, contact one of the tour companies, which will be able to arrange a camel race outing for you.

Bull fighting, or bull butting as it is more descriptively called, involves a gathering of up to 20 Brahmin bulls paired off to fight each other one pair at a time. The bulls simply butt and push each other with their heads until one of them turns tail and is declared the loser. It doesn't involve any blood or injury. The best place to see bull butting is at Barka, 45km west of Muscat, on Fridays in winter (November to March) from 4 to 6pm.

SHOPPING

Oman is unquestionably the best place on the Arabian peninsula to go souvenir shopping. See the Regional Facts for the Visitor chapter earlier in this book for souvenirs that are common to all Gulf countries.

If you are serious about buying Omani silver and jewellery, you should read *Disappearing Treasures of Oman* by Avelyn Foster.

The country's most distinctive product is the *khanjar*, also spelled *khanja*, the curved dagger worn by Omani men on important occasions, and in rural areas still sometimes worn every day. Khanjars cost anything from OR30 to OR500, depending on the extent and quality of the decoration on the dagger, scabbard and belt. As a rule, however, anything under OR50 tends to be pretty nasty – very shoddy, very battered or both.

Other common items for sale are jewellery, coffee pots, prayer holders, gun powder horns, pottery and woven items such as camel bags, mats and cushion covers.

Getting There & Away

AIR
Airports & Airlines

Seeb airport in Muscat is the only international airport in Oman (see Getting Around in the Muscat section for details on getting

to/from Seeb). Domestic airports are at Sur, 150km east of Muscat, Masirah Island, off the east coast, and Salalah in the south.

The national carrier is Oman Air. It services all the domestic airports, and international destinations include Abu Dhabi, Mumbai (Bombay), Cairo, Colombo, Dhaka, Doha, Dubai, Karachi, Kuwait, Madras and Trivandrum. Gulf Air, of which Oman has a 25% share, is also a national carrier. It services all cities in the Middle East and has flights to most overseas destinations.

Buying Tickets in Oman

There are no bucket shops in Muscat, though you might save 10% or so by shopping around.

Return fares to eastern USA via Dubai generally cost OR350 (US$910) in the low season and up to OR600 (US$1560) in the high season (mid-June to mid-October).

Due to the sheer number of British expats in Oman, air fares are relatively cheap as airlines vie for passengers returning home for the summer or at Christmas time. You should be able to get a return fare to London and other cities in Western Europe for about OR250 (US$650). Low-season (February to August) return fares to Sydney and Melbourne are OR415 (US$1079) return and OR259 (US$673) one way.

Fares to New Delhi cost about OR103 (US$268) one way or OR172 (US$447) return. A return ticket to Cairo is roughly the same.

Sample return fares to some other Gulf cities include: Abu Dhabi OR46 (US$119), Dubai OR44 (US$114), Bahrain OR86 (US$223) and Kuwait OR148 (US$385). Note that to the other Gulf states cheap 'weekend fares' are often available.

Departure Tax

There is an international departure tax of OR3.

LAND

You can travel into Oman by land from Yemen or from the UAE. Oman National Transport Company (ONTC) operates a

OMAN

twice daily Muscat-Dubai and once daily Muscat-Abu Dhabi coach service. There is also a bus service to Muscat from Buraimi, which is just a few minutes from Al-Ain in the UAE. See Muscat Getting There & Away for details.

Yemen

The border between Yemen and Oman in the south is open but there is no public transport between Salalah and San'a or Aden. Getting there involves driving yourself in your own car or hitching a ride. The road from Salalah to the Yemeni border is blacktop but on the other side it gets pretty rough, although work is being done to upgrade it. A 4WD may be your only option at this stage to get to Sana'a. Of course, with the volatile nature of the political scene in Yemen, there are security issues to think about. Hiring an armed guard for the journey is probably a good idea.

SEA

There is a boat service between Bandar Abbas in Iran and Muscat. See the Getting There & Away section of the Iran chapter for details.

Getting Around

AIR

Oman Air is the only domestic airline. Routes, fares and schedules are as follows:

from	to	one way (OR)	return (OR)	times
Muscat	Salalah	27	50	daily, 1½ hours
Muscat	Sur	14	28	three flights per week, 30 mins
Muscat	Khasab	20	40	four flights per week, 1½ hours
Sur	Masirah Island	12	24	three flights per week, 50 mins

Oman Air flights can be booked through just about any travel agent. The central booking number is ☎ 519347.

BUS

Intercity buses are operated by the Oman National Transport Company (ONTC), which has daily services to and from most of the main provincial towns. With the exception of Salalah none of the main intercity routes costs more than OR4 each way. Buses are frequent, cheap and comfortable and are a great way to get around if you are on a budget. Safety standards are high as buses are given a limited life span.

LONG-DISTANCE TAXI & MICROBUS

Oman has an extraordinarily comprehensive system of long-distance taxis and microbuses. Unlike long-distance taxis in other Middle Eastern cities, Oman's service taxis and microbuses do not wait until they are full to leave. Drivers will often depart when they have a few passengers, expecting to pick up and drop off other passengers along the way. This is a very cheap way to get around, provided you are in no particular hurry. You can also, of course, take a taxi or microbus 'engaged' (ie privately) by paying for all of the seats in it.

CAR

Traffic laws are enforced fairly strictly in Oman, especially in Muscat. Seatbelt use is mandatory for passengers in the front seat of cars. The fine for not wearing one is OR10. Right turns are not allowed at red lights. Petrol costs 118 baisa per litre for super and 112 baisa per litre for regular.

Rental

Renting a car in the sultanate is fairly easy but not cheap. Most foreign driver's licences are accepted for people on tourist visas as are International Driving Permits. International rental chains in Oman include Avis, Budget and Thrifty, but there are dozens of small local agencies where rates come down by about OR2 per day. Generally, rates for compact cars start at about OR12 per day plus OR2 to OR3 per day for insurance, with 100 or 150 free kilometres per day. Renting a 4WD will cost you about OR35 per day with 200 free kilometres per day.

ORGANISED TOURS

See Organised Tours in the Getting Around the Region chapter for tours arranged outside Oman.

Tour companies abound in Muscat and Salalah offering camel safaris, 4WD touring, camping, city tours, caving, rock climbing and dhow cruises (aboard a lateen-rigged Arab sailing vessel). Recommended agencies include Bahwan Travel Agencies (☎ 797405), Zubair Travel & Services Bureau (☎ 787563, 708071), Al-Azri Tours (412368), Sunny Day Tours (☎ 591244) and Heide Beale Tours (☎ 799928). *Adventure Oman* and *Oman Today* have complete listings of tour operators.

Muscat

Muscat enchants visitors in a way that no other city in the Gulf can even begin to match. Maybe this is because Muscat does not have that slightly artificial feel that typifies so much of the rest of the region.

Orientation

Muscat, Mutrah and Ruwi are the capital's core districts. Muscat is the old port area. It is the site of the sultan's main palace and a fascinating place to wander around but it has few shops and no hotels. Mutrah, 3km north-west of Muscat, is the main trading port and is the real attraction for tourists. A few kilometres inland from Muscat and Mutrah lies Ruwi, the capital's modern commercial district. Immediately south of Muscat lie the small villages of Sidab and Al-Bustan and, farther south, the huge Al-Bustan Palace Inter-Continental Hotel.

Along the coast to the west of Mutrah and Ruwi are a number of new, mostly residential, districts. The main ones are Qurm, which includes some hotels and five or six big shopping malls; Shatti al-Qurm, where you'll find the Muscat Inter-Continental Hotel and most of the foreign embassies; Madinat as-Sultan Qaboos, an upmarket residential area; and Al-Khuwair, the site of most of Oman's ministries and a couple of museums.

Information

Tourist Offices The official tourism board is under the Directorate General of Tourism (☎ 771 4923). National Travel & Tourism (☎ 568173, fax 566125) is a government-accredited tour operator. It will give you any information you need but you can also pick up brochures and maps from larger hotels and tour operators.

Money Most of the big banks, including the British Bank of the Middle East, can be found in Ruwi. You'll find a plethora of money-changers (plus a few banks) along Souq Ruwi St and on Mutrah Corniche around the entrance to the souq and inside the souq. Amex (☎ 708035) is represented by Zubair Travel & Services Bureau in Ruwi. It is open daily except Friday from 8 am to 1 pm and 4 to 6.30 pm. The office will not cash travellers cheques but they will hold mail. Client's mail should be addressed to: American Express (Client's Mail), PO Box 833, 112 Ruwi, Oman. Thomas Cook (☎ 706798) is represented by Bahwan Travel Agencies in Ruwi.

Post The main post office is at the northern end of Markaz Mutrah al-Tijari St in Ruwi. It is open Saturday to Wednesday from 8 am to 2 pm and 4 to 6 pm. On Thursday, Friday and holidays it keeps a shorter 8 to 11 am schedule. There is a branch post office in Mutrah just west of the Zaharat al-Orchid restaurant on Al-Mina St.

Telephone & Fax The telephone office is on Souq Ruwi St in Ruwi near the intersection with Street 37. You can also send faxes from a desk in the main lobby. The office is open daily from 7.30 am to 10.30 pm.

Email & Internet Access On the Al-Asfoor Plaza ground floor in Qurm commercial

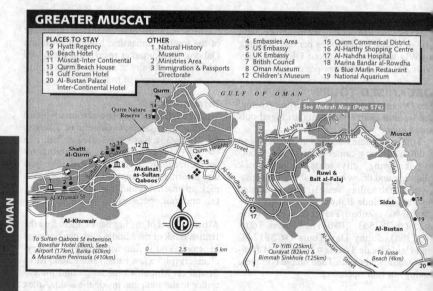

GREATER MUSCAT

PLACES TO STAY	OTHER	4 Embassies Area	15 Qurm Commerical District
9 Hyatt Regency	1 Natural History	5 US Embassy	16 Al-Harthy Shopping Centre
10 Beach Hotel	Museum	6 UK Embassy	17 Al-Nahdha Hospital
11 Muscat-Inter Continental	2 Ministries Area	7 British Council	18 Marina Bandar al-Rowdha
13 Qurm Beach House	3 Immigration & Passports	8 Oman Museum	& Blue Marlin Restaurant
14 Gulf Forum Hotel	Directorate	12 Children's Museum	19 National Aquarium
20 Al-Bustan Palace			
Inter-Continental Hotel			

district, Cyberworld (☎ 566740) charges OR2 per hour or OR1.500 for members for Internet access. It is open Saturday to Wednesday 9 am to 9 pm. The Oman Chamber of Commerce & Industry on the corner of Al-Jaame and Markaz Mutrah al-Tijari Sts in Ruwi has a library on the ground floor that offers public Internet access for OR1.500 per hour. It is open Saturday to Wednesday from 8.30 am to 1.30 pm.

Travel Agencies The capital's greatest concentration of travel agencies can be found in and around Markaz Mutrah al-Tijari St in Ruwi. Two of the larger agencies are Bahwan Travel Agencies (☎ 704455) on Markaz Mutrah al-Tijari St in Ruwi and Mezoon Travel (☎ 796680) on Al-Burj St in Bait Al-Falaj.

Bookshops There aren't many decent English-language bookshops in Muscat. The Family Bookshop has stores in Qurm at the Qurm Commercial Centre, and in Ruwi just across from the White Nile Hotel. Al-Oloum Bookshop in the Al-Harthy Shop-

ping Centre in Qurm stocks many of the same titles. There is a small bookshop on Mutrah Corniche that has a few tourist maps as well as a number of English language coffee table books.

Cultural Centres
British Council
  (☎ 600548) Al-Inshirah St, parallel to Sultan Qaboos St, Al-Khuwair
USA Information Service
  (☎ 698989 ext 201) US embassy, Jameat A'Duwal al-Arabiya St, Al-Khuwair. Open Saturday to Wednesday from 9 am to 4 pm.

Medical Services Should you need hospitalisation it will probably be free, though if things get really serious you are likely to find yourself on the first plane home. The Al-Nahdha Hospital on the outskirts of Ruwi (on the left-hand side as you head from Ruwi towards Al-Khuwair) is the main medical centre in the capital area.

Emergency Phone ☎ 999 to contact the police or the ambulance service, or to report a fire.

Greater Muscat

Jalali, Mirani & Mutrah Forts Mutrah Fort sits on a hill overlooking Mutrah Corniche while Jalali and Mirani forts guard the sea entrance to Muscat. All three forts took on more or less their present form in the 1580s during the Portuguese occupation of Muscat. Of the three, the Portuguese built only Mutrah Fort from scratch, though their alterations to the other two were so extensive that the forts can be said to be of Portuguese rather than Arab construction. All of the forts are still used by the police and/or military and are closed to the public. It's OK to photograph them.

Omani-French Museum The Omani-French Museum, in a restored turn-of-the-century building inside Muscat's walls near the Al-Kabir Gate, is largely an extended celebration of the Sultan's state visit to France in 1989 and former French president François Mitterrand's state visit to Muscat in 1992. There are several galleries detailing relations between the two countries in the 19th and early 20th centuries. The museum is open daily from 8 am to 1.30 pm. Admission is free.

Bait al-Zubair Located on Al-Saidiya St, Bait al-Zubair is a museum and shop, with exhibits of Omani heritage in photographs and documents as well as displays of traditional handicrafts, weapons, furniture and cooking implements. It's open Saturday from 4 to 8 pm; Monday and Wednesday from 4 to 7 pm; and Sunday, Tuesday and Thursday from 9 am to 12.30 pm.

National Aquarium Muscat has by far the best aquarium in the Gulf. It is south of old Muscat between Sidab and Al-Bustan in the Marine Sciences & Fisheries Centre. All of the specimens on display are native to Omani waters and most are accompanied by thorough descriptions in English. Visiting hours are Saturday to Thursday from 7.30 am to 2.30 pm. Admission is free.

Madinat as-Sultan Qaboos

Oman Museum Displays on the ground floor cover the history, geography and geology of Oman from the 3rd millennium BC onwards. There is also a display on shipbuilding. The 1st floor has a small display on Islam, consisting mostly of manuscripts, a fair to middling display of Omani arts and crafts, a display of Omani weapons and an excellent room on architecture in the sultanate with an emphasis on forts.

The museum is open Saturday to Wednesday from 8 am to 2 pm, and Thursday from 9 am to 1 pm. Admission is free. To get there take the exit off Sultan Qaboos St marked for the Muscat Inter-Continental Hotel. If you are coming from Ruwi you will need to cross the bridge to the other side of the road. Turn immediately right onto Al-Inshirah St, walk 850m and take the fifth left, onto Way 1595, then go 400m and turn left onto Way 1526. After another 250m turn right onto Way 1530. From there, go 550m and turn right at the sign for the Oman Museum.

Natural History Museum This is one museum you shouldn't miss. It has displays on Oman's geography, geology, flora and fauna. There are lots of specimens, including stuffed animals and a skeleton of a sperm whale. The museum is on Al-Wazarat St, which runs parallel to Sultan Qaboos St in Al-Khuwair. Look for a small green sign with a drawing of a lynx (the museum's symbol) indicating the exit. The museum is open Saturday to Wednesday from 8 am to 2 pm and Thursday from 9 am to 1 pm. It is also open Sunday and Friday afternoons from 4 to 7 pm.

Mutrah

Mutrah Souq The Mutrah souq is without a doubt the most interesting souq in the Arab Gulf States. As with any good Arab souq the best thing to do here is simply to wander at will. The Mutrah souq is not very big and you are in no danger of getting lost, though there may be moments when it does not look that way.

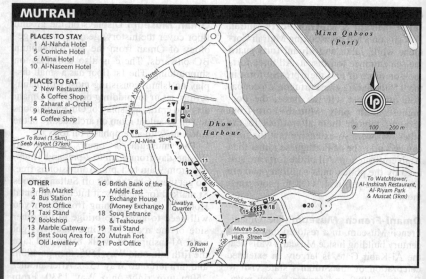

MUTRAH

Mina Qaboos (Port)

PLACES TO STAY
1 Al-Nahda Hotel
5 Corniche Hotel
6 Mina Hotel
10 Al-Naseem Hotel

PLACES TO EAT
2 New Restaurant & Coffee Shop
8 Zaharat al-Orchid
9 Restaurant
14 Coffee Shop

Dhow Harbour

To Ruwi (1.5km), Seeb Airport (37km)
Al-Mina Street

To Watchtower, Al-Inshirah Restaurant, Al-Riyam Park & Muscat (3km)

OTHER
3 Fish Market
4 Bus Station
7 Post Office
11 Taxi Stand
12 Bookshop
13 Marble Gateway
15 Best Souq Area for Old Jewellery

16 British Bank of the Middle East
17 Exchange House (Money Exchange)
18 Souq Entrance & Teahouse
19 Taxi Stand
20 Mutrah Fort
21 Post Office

Liwatiya Quarter

Corniche

Mutrah Souq High Street

To Ruwi (2km)

0   100   200 m

Al-Riyam Park At the eastern end of Mutrah Corniche, opposite the Al-Inshirah Restaurant, is Al-Riyam Park. You can climb up to the large incense burner statue for great views of the area. The park is open Saturday to Wednesday from 4 to 11 pm, and from 9 am to noon on Thursday, Friday and public holidays.

Ruwi

National Museum The National Museum, on A'Noor St near the intersection with Al-Burj St, is definitely worth a look. There are displays of jewellery, traditional costumes and weapons as well as examples of decorated wooden chests and pottery. There is also a large mural showing trade routes throughout Oman's history. The museum is open Saturday to Wednesday from 7.30 am to 2.30 pm. Admission is free but photography is prohibited.

Sultan's Armed Forces Museum This museum, run by the Omani army, is in the Bait al-Falaj Fort, which gives its name to the Bait al-Falaj district. The fort is one of

the oldest buildings in Muscat. It was built in 1845 as a royal summer home, was restored extensively in the early 1900s, and served as the headquarters for the Omani army from WWI until 1978. The museum is quite well presented and the lower floor – which provides an excellent outline of Omani history – is definitely worth a visit. This museum is open Saturday to Thursday from 7.30 am to 2 pm. Admission is 500 baisa for adults, free for anyone under 18. Photography is strictly prohibited.

Beaches & Beach Clubs

There is a nice stretch of public beach with palm trees and *barasti* (palm frond) shelters in Qurm, next to the Gulf Forum Hotel. Jussa, south of Al-Bustan, off the Qantab Rd, there is a popular picnic spot for Omani families, as is Yitti beach, which is about 25km from Ruwi. But the latter two are difficult to reach unless you have your own transport.

Many of the large hotels will let outsiders use their beach facilities for a fee. While a bit expensive, these beaches should definitely be considered by unaccompanied women, who are far less likely to suffer from harassment at one of the hotels than they would be on a public beach. It will cost you anywhere between OR3 and OR6.300 for a day visit.

Organised Tours

Most of Oman's tour operators set their prices by the vehicle, which means up to four people can take the tour for the quoted price. On average a half day city tour costs OR22. A full-day tour to Nizwa, Bahla and Jabrin costs about OR70, and one to Nakhal, Rustaq and Al-Hazm costs OR60. Full-day 4WD excursions to the Wahiba Sands are available for OR120. See Organised Tours in the Getting Around section for some recommended tour operators.

Places to Stay – Budget

Al-Hadow Hotel (☎/fax 799329, Mutrah High St, Ruwi) has Muscat's cheapest beds at OR7/10 for singles/doubles including tax. However, even if you are on a tight budget we don't recommend this place, which appears to be falling apart. The cheap hotels along Mutrah Corniche offer better rooms and the best views and atmosphere in the city for only a bit more money.

Al-Naseem Hotel (☎ 712418, fax 711728) is by far the best hotel on Mutrah Corniche with large, clean, comfortable rooms for OR10.900/15.300 for singles/doubles. Most rooms in other hotels on Mutrah Corniche tend to be cramped and desperately in need of a clean.

Al-Nahda Hotel (☎ 712385, 714196, fax 714994, Mutrah Corniche) near the entrance to Mina Qaboos, is the place to stay on Mutrah Corniche if price remains your main concern. Singles/doubles are OR8.700/12.800 and triples are OR14.600.

Mina Hotel (☎ 711828, fax 714981, Mutrah Corniche) has tiny rooms for OR12.500/15.600. Their card advertises a licensed restaurant but, although still operating, it no longer serves alcohol.

White Nile Hotel (☎ 708989, fax 750778, Al-Iskan St, Ruwi) has small but clean rooms with nice bathrooms for OR13.200/22.

Qurm Beach House (☎ 564070, fax 560761, Way 1622, Qurm) is the only budget hotel out of Mutrah and Ruwi, and is highly recommended. It's in a peaceful location across from the beach, and the rooms, at OR14/18, are clean and appealingly odd.

Places to Stay – Mid-Range

Hotel Mercure al-Falaj (☎ 702311, fax 795853, Al-Mujamma St, Bait Al-Falaj) has rooms for OR42.120/49.120. It has a bar on the top floor that's worth visiting for the great views of Ruwi. There is also a swimming pool and health club.

Ruwi Novotel (☎ 704244, fax 704248, Ruwi St) near the main roundabout is central but noisy. Rooms cost OR39.780/45.630, and as at Hotel Mercure al-Falaj, there is a swimming pool and health club here.

Al-Wafa Hotel Flats (☎ 786522, 786540, fax 786534, Al-Jaame St) near the Ruwi bus station is probably the first hotel you will see if you arrive in Ruwi by bus or microbus. It has one-bedroom and two-bedroom flats for OR20/25. The flats are clean and well maintained and the location is great, even if it is a little noisy.

Beach Hotel (☎ 696601, 696602, fax 696609) in Shatti al-Qurm has rooms for OR40.250/51.175. The hotel looks like a large white villa and you will pass it if you follow the signs for the Muscat Inter-Continental Hotel.

Bowshar Hotel (☎ 501105, fax 501124) is halfway to the airport from Ruwi, close to the ministries and embassies districts. Rooms are very reasonable at OR17.550/23.400 for singles/doubles.

Places to Stay – Top End

Prices quoted here are rack rates and you can almost certainly arrange a discount of some sort.

Sheraton Oman Hotel (☎ 799899, fax 795791, Bait Al-Falaj St, Ruwi) is well located for business travellers. It offers singles/doubles for OR66.700/75.900.

Al-Bustan Palace Inter-Continental Hotel (☎ 799666, fax 799600) is a long way

OMAN

OMAN

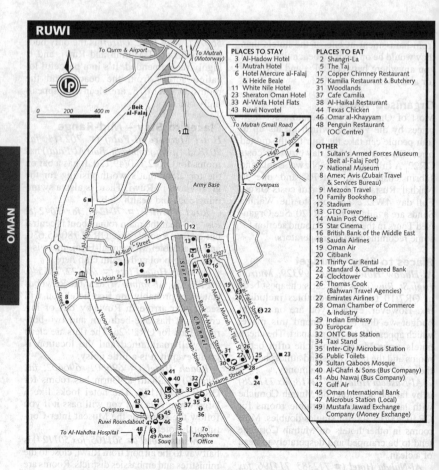

RUWI

To Qurm & Airport
To Mutrah (Motorway)
To Mutrah (Small Road)
To Mutrah

Beit al-Falaj

0   200   400 m

Army Base

Overpass

Al-Mujamma St
Al-Burj Street
Al-Iskan St
Ruwi Street
A Noor Street
Al-Funsan Street
Souq Ruwi St

Way 2307
Bank al-Markazi Street
Markaz Mutrah al-Tijari Street
Al-Jaame Street

Overpass
Ruwi Roundabout
To Al-Nahdha Hospital
Ruwi Souq
To Telephone Office

PLACES TO STAY
3   Al-Hadow Hotel
4   Mutrah Hotel
6   Hotel Mercure al-Falaj & Heide Beale
11 White Nile Hotel
23 Sheraton Oman Hotel
33 Al-Wafa Hotel Flats
43 Ruwi Novotel

PLACES TO EAT
2   Shangri-La
5   The Taj
17 Copper Chimney Restaurant
25 Kamilia Restaurant & Butchery
31 Woodlands
37 Cafe Camilia
38 Al-Haikal Restaurant
44 Texas Chicken
46 Omar al-Khayyam
48 Penguin Restaurant (OC Centre)

OTHER
1   Sultan's Armed Forces Museum (Beit al-Falaj Fort)
7   National Museum
8   Amex; Avis (Zubair Travel & Services Bureau)
9   Mezoon Travel
10 Family Bookshop
12 Stadium
13 GTO Tower
14 Main Post Office
15 Star Cinema
16 British Bank of the Middle East
18 Saudia Airlines
19 Oman Air
20 Citibank
21 Thrifty Car Rental
22 Standard & Chartered Bank
24 Clocktower
26 Thomas Cook (Bahwan Travel Agencies)
27 Emirates Airlines
28 Oman Chamber of Commerce & Industry
29 Indian Embassy
30 Europcar
32 ONTC Bus Station
34 Taxi Stand
35 Inter-City Microbus Station
36 Public Toilets
39 Sultan Qaboos Mosque
40 Al-Ghafri & Sons (Bus Company)
41 Abu Nawaj (Bus Company)
42 Gulf Air
45 Oman International Bank
47 Microbus Station (Local)
49 Mustafa Jawad Exchange Company (Money Exchange)

from anything else in the capital region and is inconvenient if you don't have a car. It is worth the drive, however, just for a look at its massive atrium lobby. Singles/doubles start at a whopping OR132.210/150.930.

Hyatt Regency (☎ 602888, fax 605282) in Shatti al-Qurm rivals the Al-Bustan Palace Inter-Continental Hotel for ostentation. Its atrium is a great place for a coffee and to admire the luxurious decor. Beautifully decorated rooms here cost OR93.600/105.300.

In Shatti al-Qurm, *Muscat Inter-Continental Hotel* (☎ 600500, fax 600012) is another self-contained mini-resort with its own beach, but it's not as grand as the Al-Bustan Palace Inter-Continental Hotel or the Hyatt Regency. Rooms can be had for a mere OR72.540/78.390 (more if you want a sea view).

Gulf Forum Hotel (☎ 560100, fax 560650, Qurm St, Qurm) is in a quiet part of town on a hill overlooking the beach to the west. Rooms cost OR53.820/65.520.

Places to Eat

Street Food Stand-up snacks are available from the kiosk at the bus station on Mutrah Corniche.

Zaharat al-Orchid coffeehouse and restaurant, a short distance inland from the roundabout, has excellent shwarma and also offers cheap sandwiches, burgers and fresh juice. Oddly there are two restaurants with this name a few metres apart. The better of the two is the one farther inland.

The *cafe* next to the Mina Hotel is a popular local gathering spot, particularly on cool evenings when both Omanis and foreigners can be found munching shwarma or felafel and sipping tea.

The *coffeehouse* at the entrance to the Mutrah souq is the one place you must not miss under any circumstances. Sweet tea is 75 baisa a cup, served as you sit on stone benches on either side of the entry archway. No visit to Muscat would be complete without a pit stop here.

Snacks *Al-Badiyeh Restaurant,* near the post office, is your only choice for snacks in Muscat. The menu is mostly medium-priced Indian. Main dishes cost OR1 to OR2.

Cafe Camilia, across Al-Jaame St from the Ruwi bus station, is a good spot for a quick snack, with sandwiches and shwarma for 200 baisa.

Al-Haikal Restaurant, just around the corner from the Ruwi bus station, has delicious spiced fried fillets of king fish with rice, salad and paratha for under OR1.

Texas Chicken at the corner of An-Noor and Al-Jaame Sts in Ruwi has good chicken and burgers, but you should really try its excellent, and cheap, Chinese and Filipino noodle dishes costing OR1.200 each.

Restaurants *Albahr* (which is Arabic for 'the sea') in the Mina Hotel offers a great view of Mutrah and the Indian food is very good. Main dishes cost about OR3 and it is a popular spot for travellers.

Sindebad Restaurant at the Al-Nahda Hotel has curries and biryanis for OR1. The small and private dining area is good for

women travellers who want to enjoy cheap food but don't want the stares as a side dish.

Al-Inshirah, opposite the giant incense burner at the eastern end of Mutrah Corniche, has two restaurants. One is a seafood restaurant specialising in Thai dishes, but it is expensive at OR3 to OR4 a dish. The other restaurant is a US steakhouse that was closed for renovation at the time of writing but, on a previous visit, I had a great burger for OR2.500. It also serves steak and fresh fish. There is a bar and the view of Mutrah at night is superb.

Woodlands is an Indian restaurant off Bank al-Markazi St. It is the place to go if you want to have a drink with dinner and don't want to pay handsomely for the privilege. Most main dishes are fairly spicy and cost OR1.500 to OR2.200.

Copper Chimney Restaurant, just off Markaz Mutrah al-Tijari St in Ruwi, is a good choice if you need an upmarket restaurant for a business meeting. It also serves some of the best Indian food in Muscat and the surroundings are quite dignified. Dinner is fairly expensive at OR5 to OR7, but the food is great.

Shangri-La at the Ruwi end of Mutrah High St, just up from the Al-Hadow hotel, offers what may be the best Chinese food in Oman. Main dishes cost OR3.500 and up, but the portions are very large.

Omar al-Khayyam has good Indian and Chinese food for about OR1.500 for mains. It is in the souq area in the new part of town. Turn left off A'Nahdah St at the taxi stand.

Entertainment

Muscat is rather thin on entertainment although the five-star hotels and some of the smaller ones have bars and nightclubs, usually with live acts. *Oman Today* and the UAE-based *What's On* magazine are your best sources for this information.

Star Cinema (☎ 791641) shows both western and Indian films (though rather more of the latter). Tickets are OR1 and 800 baisa. It is the unmistakable round building with flashing lights near the main post office in Ruwi.

You will have to look hard to find *cof-feehouses* that serve *sheesha* these days (also known as 'hubbly bubbly') as the government periodically bans the practice, saying it pollutes the environment and is detrimental to health.

Shopping

One result of the growth of tourism in Oman has been that the Mutrah souq, while still a great place to wander around and soak in the atmosphere, has become a pretty pricey place to shop for Omani handicrafts. The best place to look for khanjars and silver jewellery is, oddly enough, inside the Sabco Commercial Centre in the Qurm commercial district.

The **Omani Heritage Gallery** in the Al-Shatti Shopping Complex opposite the Muscat Inter-Continental Hotel is a non-profit organisation, set up to encourage traditional handicrafts in rural areas and to put money back into the communities through sales. Prices are high but so is the quality of the work.

Getting There & Away

Air Seeb international airport is 37km from Mutrah. For airport flight information call ☎ 519223 or 519456.

See the Getting Around section earlier in this chapter for details of domestic flights around Oman.

Bus The Ruwi bus station (☎ 708522) is the main depot for buses in the sultanate operated by ONTC. Luggage can be stored in the cargo area (around the side of the ticket office). Timetables in English are posted in the waiting room.

Salalah is the only route on which ONTC has competition. ONTC buses leave daily at 7 am and 7 pm with an extra bus at 6 pm from mid-June to mid-September. The buses leave one hour later during Ramadan. The trip takes 12 hours. The fare is OR8 one way and OR16 return. Booking a day or two early is not necessary but would be a good idea if you really wanted to travel on a particular bus.

Abu Nawaf Road Transport (☎ 785252), just off A'Noor St round the corner from the Ruwi bus station, has buses to Salalah daily at 3.30 pm, arriving at Salalah at 4 am, for OR6 one way and OR11 return. Al-Ghafri & Sons (☎ 707896) has two buses daily at 6.30 am and 4.30 pm for OR7 one way and OR13 return. Bin Qasim Transport (☎ 785059), next door to Al-Ghafri, has a daily bus at 3 pm for OR7 one way and OR13 return.

The only international bus service is to Dubai (twice daily at 7.30 am and 4.30 pm) and Abu Dhabi (once a day at 7 am). Buses leave twice a day, at 7.30 am and 4.30 pm, from the Ruwi bus station. During Ramadan the late bus to Dubai leaves at 5.30 pm. The trips take six hours. The fare is OR9 one way and OR16 return.

If you are coming from or going to the UAE, consider taking the Buraimi bus. The fare is much cheaper at OR3.600 one way and there are three buses a day from both Muscat and Buraimi at 7 am and 1 and 3 pm. The trip takes 4½ hours and goes via Sohar. The Buraimi bus station is on the main street just two minutes drive (or a 10 minute walk) from the centre of Al-Ain.

Taxi & Microbus Muscat has two long-distance taxi stands for both taxis and microbuses. One is in Ruwi across Al-Jaame St from the main bus station while the other is out at the Seeb clock tower (formally the Sahwa Tower) roundabout, beyond the airport. A shared taxi from Ruwi to the clock tower costs 500 baisa. Microbuses charge 300 baisa for the same trip. From Mutrah the taxi/microbus fare is 700/300 baisa.

Some sample taxi/microbus fares are:

to	taxi	microbus
Barka	OR1	300 baisa
Nakhal	OR2	OR1
Nizwa	OR1.500	OR1
Rustaq	OR2	800 baisa
Samail	OR1	500 baisa
Sohar	OR2.500	OR1.700
Sur	OR3.500	OR3

Only taxis make the trip to Buraimi at OR5 per person.

Car There are several rental agencies in the area around the Ruwi roundabout as well as the usual desks in big hotels and at the airport. See the Getting Around section earlier in this chapter for costs.

Getting Around

To/From the Airport Bus Nos 23 and 24 run between the Mutrah bus station and Seeb airport twice an hour from approximately 6.20 am until 9.50 pm daily. On Friday (and on holidays) there is an additional bus at five minutes past the hour, but the buses do not start running until 7.20 am. The trip takes about 50 minutes and the fare is 200 baisa.

Taxis between the airport and the centre cost OR6 (Ruwi and Mutrah) and OR5 (Qurm, Madinat as-Sultan Qaboos and Al-Khuwair). If you share a service taxi you should pay 500 to 700 baisa.

Bus ONTC's system of local buses covers greater Muscat fairly thoroughly. Fares are either 100 or 200 baisa (300 baisa to Sultan Qaboos University), depending on the distance travelled. Destinations are displayed on the front of the buses in Arabic and English. Timetables in English are available at the main bus station on Al-Jaame St in Ruwi (the same place intercity buses leave from). Bus Nos 2, 4, 23, 24, 28, 31 and 32 all run between the Mutrah and Ruwi stations for 200 baisa. Other main routes include: Nos 23 and 24 to Qurm and the Ministries Area in Madinat as-Sultan Qaboos, and No 26 to Qurm and Al-Khuwair.

Microbus In Mutrah, local microbuses cruise the Corniche, particularly the end near the Mina Hotel and the Mutrah bus station, while in Ruwi they park en masse in a lot across Al-Jaame St from the main bus station. Mutrah to Ruwi costs 100 baisa, Mutrah to Muscat 150 baisa; no microbus journey within greater Muscat should cost more than 300 baisa. The only significant exception to this rule is trips to the main microbus station at the Seeb clock tower (beyond the airport). This trip costs 500 baisa.

Taxi Muscat's taxis, like all others in Oman, are orange and white and do not have meters. If you bargain you will inevitably pay two or three times what you ought to. The only way to pay the proper fare is to know it before you get into the cab and not raise the subject of money at all but just hand the driver the proper sum at your destination.

A taxi between Mutrah and Ruwi costs OR1 in either direction if you take it 'engaged', or 200 baisa if shared. Muscat to Mutrah is OR1 engaged and Muscat to Ruwi OR1.500 engaged. There are no shared taxis between Muscat and Ruwi. Mutrah to Qurm is OR3 engaged and 300 baisa shared, and Ruwi to Qurm is OR2 engaged or 300 baisa shared.

If you are taking an engaged taxi to or from a hotel the fare goes way up. From a hotel in Ruwi to a hotel in Mutrah you will be charged OR3, and the trip between a hotel in Ruwi to a hotel in Shatti al-Qurm costs a ridiculous OR4.

Northern Oman

BARKA

Barka, 80km west of Mutrah and Ruwi, makes an excellent day trip outside the capital, or an easy stopover on the way from Muscat to Sohar. The turn-off from the main Muscat-Sohar highway is well signposted, and this is where you will probably be dropped if you take a microbus. From the junction you can pick up another microbus to cover the few extra kilometres to the centre.

The main reason for visiting Barka is to see the **bull butting**, which takes place in winter every second Friday from 4 to 6 pm. There is no blood letting involved in this event, in which two bulls are pitted against each other. It's very much a casual social gathering for the men in the area. To get to the bullring turn left at the T-junction in the centre. After about 2.5km you will see the shallow, concrete structure standing alone on your right.

Barka's **fort** is on your right as you enter town, just before the T-junction. The fort is open daily from 7.30 am to 6 pm but on Friday it closes at 2 pm. Admission is free.

Barka's other point of interest is **Bait Nua'man**, a restored house that gives you an idea of how wealthier residents of Oman's coast lived several generations ago. To reach Bait Nua'man continue along the road that brought you into Barka from the main highway and go 4.8km beyond the fort. This will bring you to a left turn onto a paved road. Take this turn (if you reach a roundabout you've gone too far) and follow the road 1.9km. Bait Nua'man will be on your right.

While you are in Barka you should stop to buy some *halwa*, a gooey Omani sweet, from the little shops at the turn-off from the main highway. It is delicious.

Getting There & Away

There are four buses per day between the Barka turn-off and Muscat's Ruwi bus station (400 baisa, one hour express, 1½ hours regular). Taxis and microbuses can be found both around the T-junction in Barka's centre and at the turn-off from the Muscat-Sohar road. A shared taxi from the Seeb clock tower taxi stand to Barka costs OR1 per person and around OR8 engaged. Microbuses charge 300 baisa per person for the trip from the Seeb clock tower roundabout to Barka.

SOHAR

Sohar, home of the fictional Sinbad the sailor, is one of those places where history casts a shadow over modern reality. A thousand years ago it occupied three times its present area and was the largest town in the country.

The fort and its small museum are quite good but only arguably worth the trip by themselves. If time is not a factor, however, or if you can combine Sohar with the Batinah coast's other sites (Barka, Rustaq, Nakhal etc) it makes a good turn-around point for a two or three day trip out of Muscat and back. If you are passing by anyway (en route from Muscat to Dubai or the Musandam peninsula, for example) it should not be missed.

Orientation & Information

Sohar has two centres – the old centre on the waterfront near the fort, and a more modern business district a couple of kilometres inland. The post office and taxi stand are both in the latter area, around Sohar's souq and the main hospital. To reach the new centre take the 'city centre' exit off the highway from Muscat to Dubai then turn right at the next roundabout onto A'Nahdah St. You should spot the taxis and microbuses in a car park to your left a little way up the road, and the hospital on your right. The post office is 250m past the hospital. To get to the old centre, take the 'city centre' exit off the highway, but keep straight instead of taking A'Nahdah St. You will come to another roundabout after 2.1km. Turn right and you will see the fort and coast road.

Things to See

Sohar's **fort** is a large, whitewashed, slightly irregular rectangle with a single tower rising from its courtyard. It is a dramatic sight after the earth-coloured forts that dominate the rest of Oman. The fort is open Saturday to Wednesday from 7.30 am to 2.30 pm and Thursday and Friday from 8 am to noon and 4 to 6 pm. Admission is free.

There is a small **museum** in the fort's tower. The tower also houses the **tomb** of Sayyed Thuwaini bin Said bin Sultan al-Busaid, the ruler of Oman from 1856 to 1866 and the son of Sultan Said bin Sultan, the 19th century ruler under whom Omani power reached its height.

The **souq** in the new part of town is just behind the taxi and microbus stand. Behind it is the **women's souq** where local women sell perfumes, cheap jewellery, shampoo, henna, cooking spices and oils, and all sorts of incense and incense burners.

Places to Stay & Eat

Al-Wadi Hotel (☎ 840058, fax 841997), just off the main highway about 10km west of Sohar's new centre, is the cheaper of the two hotels in Sohar at OR23.100/31.500 for singles/doubles. To get there from Muscat, turn left off the highway at the second

Sohar roundabout, the one whose centre-piece looks like a mosque dome on stilts.

Sohar Beach Hotel (☎ *841111, fax 843776*) has rooms for OR33.930/40.950. If you can afford the extra money this is one case where the more expensive hotel is definitely better value for money. It is about 6km north of the centre on the coastal road. From the old centre just follow the coast north. From the highway follow the big green signs.

There are a number of good, cheap biryani restaurants within easy walking distance of the fort. ***Ahmed bin Mohammed bin Ali & Partners Restaurant*** on As-Souq St has a few tables outside overlooking the coastal road and the sea when the weather is nice.

Getting There & Away
There are three buses per day between the Sohar hospital and Ruwi bus station. The fare is OR2.200.

The daily express buses between Dubai, Abu Dhabi and Muscat stop in Sohar at the Penguin Restaurant on the main highway, just south-east of the turn-off for the centre. From there you can get a nonstop lift into Muscat for OR5 or to Dubai for OR4. Tickets can be purchased from the driver but you should phone ahead the Ruwi bus station in Muscat (☎ 708522) to make a booking. The Muscat-bound buses come through daily at approximately 10.30 am and 8.30 pm. The Dubai-bound buses arrive at around 9.30 or 10 am and 6.30 or 7 pm.

Microbuses and taxis come and go from a car park across the street from the hospital. A few can also be found at the turn-off on the main highway. Microbuses charge OR1.500 for the trip to the Seeb clock tower roundabout and OR2 to Ruwi. Taxis charge OR2.500 to the clock tower and OR3 to Ruwi. Expect to pay around OR15 if you insist on taking a taxi engaged. There is no direct taxi or microbus service to Rustaq and Nakhal. An engaged taxi will cost OR15.

NAKHAL
Nakhal is a picturesque town dominated by one of Oman's more dramatic forts. The fort in question rises from a hill in Nakhal's small town centre. It is open from 7 am to 5 pm daily. Admission is free.

A few kilometres beyond Nakhal lies the lush **spring** known as A'Thowarah. The spring emerges into a wadi here to form a stream and a small oasis. It is a perfect place for a stroll or a picnic.

There is only one bus per day between Muscat and Nakhal (OR1.500). The bus leaves the Ruwi bus station in Muscat at 6 pm arriving at 7.55 pm. The return trip leaves Nakhal every morning at 8 am, arriving in Ruwi at 10 am. Since there is no place to stay in Nakhal, this could be a bit awkward.

You'll find microbuses and taxis both at the junction with the main road and in the area below the fort. Microbuses charge OR1 for the trip to the Seeb clock tower and 300 baisa to/from the Barka roundabout. Taxis charge about OR2 for the same trip, though most of the cabs in the area appear to specialise in short local runs for a couple of hundred baisa (such as between the main road and the town).

RUSTAQ
Some 175km west of Muscat is Rustaq (Rostaq), a town best known today for its imposing **fort**, though for a time in the Middle Ages it was Oman's capital. The small **souq** near the entrance to the fort has a few antiques and souvenirs but the **new souq** on the main street, about 1.5km from the highway, has left the old one for dead. Here you can buy traditional Omani wooden chests, silver jewellery and khanjars, as well as meat, fish and vegetables.

There is one bus a day to and from Rustaq (OR1.800). Frustratingly, the bus from Muscat leaves Ruwi at 6 pm.

Microbuses can be found a few hundred metres from the fort on the main road to Nakhal and the coast. Microbus fares from Rustaq include: Nakhal, 500 baisa; the junction with the coastal highway, 400 baisa; Sohar OR1; and Muscat-Ruwi, OR1 (800 baisa to the Seeb clock tower). The fare to Muscat in a shared taxi is OR2.

SUR

Sur (pronounced 'soor') is a fairly quiet place but has great beaches and several interesting things to see. It is only 150km down the coast from Muscat as the crow flies, though by road it is a bit over twice that distance. That makes it a bit too far for a day trip but it is still worth a visit.

Orientation & Information

Sur's commercial centre is several kilometres from the government buildings that make up its administrative and historical centre. The commercial centre includes the taxi stand and bus stop, the cheaper of the town's two hotels, and a few restaurants. The post office is on the roundabout between the Sinesla Fortress and the main mosque.

Sinesla Fortress

Sur's main fort, which is on a hill overlooking the town, is relatively simple in construction: a defensive wall that is roughly square in shape, with towers at the four corners. Look carefully and you will notice that the two watchtowers facing the sea are slightly taller than the two that face inland. The fort is open daily from 7.30 am to 6 pm. Admission is free.

Bilad Fort

The more impressive of Sur's two forts is just over 6km from the centre off the road towards Muscat. Follow the green signs. It is open daily from 7.30 am to 6 pm. The fort is approximately 200 years old. Its basic design – lots of open space, little in the way of accommodation – implies that it was a defensive rather than an administrative centre.

Marine Museum

The highlight of this small exhibit is a collection of photographs of Sur in 1905, a striking contrast to the Sur of today. The museum is inside the Al-Arouba Sports Club and is open daily from approximately 8 am to noon and from 4 to 7 pm. Admission is free. The club is across the road from the side of Sinesla through which the fort's compound is entered and about 100m closer

to the centre. Look for a stone wall with sports figures painted on it.

Dhow Building Yard

Sur's dhow yard is one of the town's highlights. At any given time a dozen or more dhows may be under construction here. It is just over 3km east of the centre.

Places to Stay & Eat

There are only three hotels in Sur and all of them are very overpriced.

Sur Hotel (☎ 440090, fax 443798) in the town's centre has noisy rooms for two people at OR17.250 without bath, OR28.250 with bath.

Sur Beach Hotel (☎ 442031, fax 442228) is very expensive at OR39.780/49.140 for singles/doubles. The hotel is 5.3km north of the centre. To get there turn right at the third roundabout after leaving the centre. There are signs for the hotel as you come into Sur from Muscat.

Sur Mercure Hotel (☎ 443777, fax 442626) is the newest hotel and has rooms for OR42.120/50.310. They are definitely better value than those at the Sur Beach Hotel, but the hotel doesn't have the beachfront location. To get there take the same road out of the centre for the Sur Beach Hotel but instead of turning right, continue straight. The hotel is just past the next roundabout.

Arabian Sea Restaurant on the ground floor of the same building as the Sur Hotel (though the entrance faces the other side of the block) is a good enough place to eat. Most main dishes cost OR1 to OR1.500, though you can also get sandwiches for 200 to 500 baisa.

At the **Chinese restaurant** opposite, meals cost roughly the same and Indian meals are served as well.

Getting There & Away

The airport is south of the centre on the Sur-Muscat road. See the Getting Around section earlier for details. Tickets can be purchased, and return flights reconfirmed, through Oman Orient for Travel & Tours (☎ 440279), in the centre.

There are three buses per day between Muscat and Sur (OR3.400, 4¼ hours). Service taxis for Muscat (OR3.500 to the Seeb clock tower roundabout; OR15 engaged) tout for passengers in the car park around the corner from the Sur Hotel. Microbuses make the same trip for OR3.

RAS AL-JINZ

Ras al-Jinz (Ras al-Junayz) is the easternmost point of the Arabian Peninsula. Up to 13,000 turtles come to nest on the beach here annually which is why the area is under government protection.

To get onto the beach or the camp site here you will need a permit (OR1 per person) from the Directorate General of Nature Reserves (☎ 692574, fax 602283) at the Ministry of Regional Municipalities & Environment. The Ministry is on the sea side of Ministries St in Al-Khuwair. It is a large white building with empty blocks either side of it.

From the camp site you will be taken onto the beach at about 10 pm by the park ranger who will show you the turtles.

To get there take the road from Muscat to Sur, then take the turn for Al-Ashkarah at Al-Kamil. There is a signposted turn-off for Ras al-Hadd onto a graded road 40km from Al-Kamil. For the more scenic coast road, continue past this turn-off for another 20km and take the turn for Asylah. Once you get to this sleepy little fishing town the blacktop road ends and a graded road continues north along the coast for 70km to Ras al-Jinz.

If you have a 4WD there is an alternative route via Sur. Take the road to Ayega from Sur. The blacktop road ends shortly after Ayega and a track goes along the coast for about 20km before it heads inland. You will see signs for Ras al-Jinz.

SAMAIL

From the main Muscat-Nizwa road Samail appears to be little more than a bus stop that people usually head straight past. But 10km from the junction with the main road is **Samail Fort**, nestled between a wadi and an oasis of palm trees to one side and a hill of dark, loose stone to the other. Even though you cannot get into the fort, it is worth stopping for a look, and making the climb up to the watchtowers for a view out over the oasis.

To reach the fort turn off the Muscat-Nizwa road (a left turn if you are coming from Muscat) at the big green sign welcoming you to the Samail Wilayat. If you are coming from Nizwa look for a sign saying 'Samail 4km' and pointing right. Follow the road for 10km until you reach a junction with a road going off to the right and a sign saying 'Luzugh 10km', pointing in the direction you are travelling. At this point you should be able to see one of the watchtowers on the hill above you and to the left. About 250m beyond the sign turn left onto a dirt track between two yellowed walls. The fort will be on your left.

The **Masjid Mazin bin Ghadouba Mosque** is Oman's oldest mosque. It has been completely rebuilt and is constructed out of blocks of stone. The wooden window frames and stained glass make it an unusual building. To get there turn right off the main road through Samail at the sign for 'Sefalat Samail'. After 500m there is a T-junction. Turn left and follow the narrow street through town for 1.5km. The mosque will be on your right, opposite a grocery store. If you continue along this road you will come out on the main road at the sign that says 'Luzugh 10km' from where you can get to the fort.

The Samail road junction is a stop on the bus route from Muscat to Nizwa. The fare from either city is 900 baisa. Microbuses charge 500 baisa for the trip from the Seeb clock tower (800 baisa from Ruwi). The shared taxi fare from the clock tower is OR1. From Nizwa to Samail the microbus fare is 700 baisa while taxis charge OR1.500. From the junction to the fort the microbus fare is 200 to 300 baisa each way.

NIZWA

Only 45 years ago Wilfred Thesiger was forced to keep well clear of Nizwa. As the seat of the imams who then ruled much of the country's interior it had a reputation for ferocious conservatism. Today, visitors need have no such worries – Nizwa has rapidly emerged as one of Oman's major tourist centres. It is probably the country's most popular destination after Muscat.

Orientation & Information

Nizwa's main landmark is the large, blue-domed mosque that is on your left if you enter the town from the direction of Muscat.

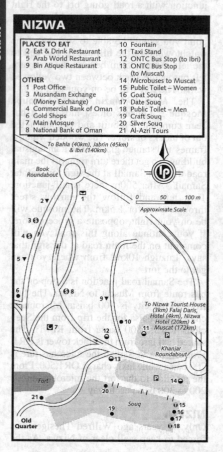

NIZWA

PLACES TO EAT
2 Eat & Drink Restaurant
5 Arab World Restaurant
9 Bin Atique Restaurant

OTHER
1 Post Office
3 Musandam Exchange (Money Exchange)
4 Commercial Bank of Oman
6 Gold Shops
7 Main Mosque
8 National Bank of Oman
10 Fountain
11 Taxi Stand
12 ONTC Bus Stop (to Ibri)
13 ONTC Bus Stop (to Muscat)
14 Microbuses to Muscat
15 Public Toilet – Women
16 Goat Souq
17 Date Souq
18 Public Toilet – Men
19 Craft Souq
20 Silver Souq
21 Al-Azri Tours

To Bahla (40km), Jabrin (45km) & Ibri (140km)

Book Roundabout

0   50   100 m
Approximate Scale

To Nizwa Tourist House (3km) Falaj Daris, Hotel (4km), Nizwa Hotel (20km) & Muscat (172km)

Khanjar Roundabout

Fort

Old Quarter

Souq

The souq is the citadel-like area on the left before you get to the mosque. Past the mosque the main street swings around to the right into the town's business area. The taxi stand and bus stop are both in the car park on either side of the road running past the souq. The post office is in the souq. You can change money at any of the several banks on the main street.

Nizwa Fort

The fort was built in the mid-17th century by Sultan bin Saif, the first imam of the Al-Ya'ribi dynasty. For the next 300 years it was the primary seat of the imamate, serving as a combination palace, seat of government and prison. It is open daily from 7.30 am to 4 pm (until 5 pm from June to September). Admission is free.

Nizwa Souq

Despite having been moved into more 'modern' quarters a few years ago the souq retains much of its colour and vitality. The bad news is that the souq's popularity with package tours has made it one of the worst places in the sultanate to shop for souvenirs. The best thing to do is to avoid the silver souq altogether and spend your time wandering among the merchants buying and selling fish, meat, fruits and vegetables, household goods, dates and goats.

Places to Stay & Eat

Nizwa Tourist House (☎/fax 412402) is the cheapest place to stay in Nizwa. Rooms here are large and comfortable, even if a little sparse, and are the best value in town at OR14. You'll find it on the main highway, 3km from the khanjar roundabout towards Muscat.

Nizwa's other two hotels will both put a dent in your budget.

Falaj Daris Hotel (☎ 410500, fax 410430) is better value for money than the Nizwa Hotel with singles/doubles for OR21.800/ 29.500. The hotel is 1km past the Nizwa Tourist House towards Muscat. It's on the left if you are coming from the capital.

Nizwa Hotel (☎ 431616, fax 431619) is about 20km from the centre of Nizwa out towards Muscat. Rooms cost OR37.950/43.700.

Bin Atique Restaurant is the place to go for traditional Omani food in a traditional setting. It is on a sidestreet that runs past the fountain opposite the souq. Look for the sign. Meals are around 750 baisa to OR1.

Eat & Drink Restaurant tells it like it is and serves Indian and Chinese meals for 600 baisa to OR1. It's on the main street, just past the Musandam Exchange.

Getting There & Away

ONTC operates six buses per day between Nizwa and Muscat (OR1.600, 2½ hours express, three hours regular). There are also regular buses from Nizwa to Ibri. You can catch the southbound bus from Muscat to Salalah at the roundabout on the edge of Nizwa where the highway from Muscat to Ibri meets the road coming up from Salalah. The buses come through Nizwa every day at approximately 9 am and 9 pm. The fare from Nizwa to Salalah is OR7.200 one way. You might want to telephone the Ruwi bus station in Muscat (☎ 708522) to reserve a seat in advance.

Taxi/microbus fares from Nizwa to the Seeb clock tower roundabout outside Muscat are OR1.500/1 (to Ruwi add 500 baisa). Microbuses go to Samail for 700 baisa while service taxis charge OR1.500 for the same trip. Ibri is OR2 by taxi or OR1.500 by microbus.

BAHLA

Bahla, 40km west of Nizwa, is famous as the **pottery** capital of Oman. Most pottery bought in Muscat or other towns in northern Oman will have come from here. The town's **souq** is about 1km along the road that comes off to the right (if you are coming from Nizwa) just past the fort. As far as aesthetics go, it's the nicest souq in Oman. Bahla's huge **fort**, listed by UNESCO as a World Heritage Site, was undergoing extensive restoration at the time of writing. When work on it is complete the site, which lies smack on the main road from Nizwa to Jabrin and Ibri, should be a major tourist attraction.

Between the bus stop and the fort you can see a **well**, which is still in use, and behind the fort you will find a portion of Bahla's **city wall**. West of the centre, there are more **fortifications** guarding the approach to the town.

The only hotel in the area is the circular *Bahla Motel (☎ 420211, fax 420212)*, 5.4km east of the centre on the road coming from Nizwa. It has large rooms at OR15/20 for singles/doubles.

Buses for Bahla leave Muscat (OR2, three hours express, 3½ hours regular) three times a day. From Nizwa the trip takes about 45 minutes and costs 300 baisa. Microbuses charge 500 baisa from Nizwa and taxis are OR10 engaged.

JABRIN

Jabrin (Jibreen) is one of Oman's most dramatic forts. It is large and imposing and its location commands the entire plain and surrounding hilltops. Jabrin is worth visiting if only for the restoration job, which is one of the best in Oman. It is a much more impressive place than Nizwa's fort and its restored state gives you some sense of what it looked like in its prime.

To reach the fort from Nizwa follow the Ibri road for 45km then turn at a sign for Jabrin. After another 4km the pavement ends at a small roundabout. Turn right, go 500m, and you will reach the fort. The fort is open from 8 am to 4 pm daily. Admission is free.

Buses from Muscat to Ibri and vice versa stop at the road junction for Jabrin. The trip from Muscat takes four hours by express bus or five hours on a regular bus, and costs OR2.200.

BURAIMI

The long-disputed Buraimi oasis straddles the border between Oman and Abu Dhabi in the UAE. Both the Omani and the Emirati sides of the oasis are covered in this book's UAE chapter. This is because the Omani portion of the oasis is effectively in a customs union with Abu Dhabi.

OMAN

Approaching the oasis from the Omani side requires that you pass through outgoing Omani customs. Once through this checkpoint (53km from the border) you can pass freely between the Omani town of Buraimi and the city of Al-Ain in the UAE. You can also continue up the road to anywhere else in the UAE. Approaching the oasis from the UAE side does not involve a customs check or require any documentation beyond that ordinarily required to enter the UAE.

There are three buses per day between Buraimi and Muscat (OR3.600, 4½ hours). Taxis will make the trip for OR5.

Southern Oman

SALALAH

Oman's second city, the capital of the province of Dhofar and the birthplace of Sultan Qaboos, Salalah is a striking change from Muscat. It catches the Indian summer monsoon (called the *khareef*) and, as a result, it is cool, wet and green from mid-June to mid-September just as the rest of Arabia is going through the worst of the summer heat.

Orientation & Information

Salalah's centre is the intersection of A'Nahdah and A'Salam Sts. Both the ONTC bus station and the Redan Hotel are a 10 to 15 minute walk from this intersection and the gold souq is right around the corner. Most of the city's businesses are either along, or just off, one of these streets.

Money There are several banks and a few exchange houses around the intersection of A'Nahdah and A'Salam Sts. The British Bank of the Middle East's branch on A'Salam St has an ATM linked into the Global Access cash machine network. Amex is represented by Zubair Travel (☎ 235581, 235582) which can be found in the lobby of the Holiday Inn. It cannot cash cheques for clients but it will hold mail. Mail should be addressed to: American Express (Client's Mail), c/o Zubair Travel & Services Bureau – Salalah Branch Office, PO Box 809, Postal

Code 211, Oman. The office is open Saturday to Thursday from 8 am to 1 pm and from 4 to 6.30 pm.

Post & Communications The main post office is on A'Nahdah St, next to the telephone company's administrative centre, though you have to exit A'Nahdah St and enter the building from the back. It is open Saturday to Wednesday from 7.30 am to 1.30 pm and Thursday from 9 to 11 am.

Wilfred Thesiger

The last of the region's great explorers, Sir Wilfred Thesiger, made countless journeys through Arabia, Northern Africa, Iraq, Afghanistan, Kurdistan and Pakistan in the 1940s and 50s. He estimates that he has walked more than 100,000 miles.

The most amazing journey of all, though, was his epic 1000km crossing of the Empty Quarter, or Rub al-Khali, one of the harshest, driest and hottest spots on the planet. This lonely sea of dunes stretches from southern UAE to eastern Saudi Arabia and across to Oman. Thesiger was accompanied by four Bedouin from the Beit Kathir tribe of southern Oman.

In his book, *Arabian Sands*, Thesiger wrote of this legendary crossing of the Empty Quarter. He talks of the hardship and danger and the complete solitude that the desert imposes on any living creature that dares to be there. He had to rely heavily on the companionship of the Bait Kathir, so that the stark emptiness of the desert would not destroy him.

Even though others have made this crossing since, vehicles have been used and the hardship, therefore, hasn't been as extreme. It wasn't until early 1999 that three Canadian explorers successfully retraced Thesiger's steps and completed the crossing by camel from Salalah in southern Oman to Abu Dhabi. They, too, were accompanied by the Beit Kathir and they too felt the loneliness that was felt by Thesiger.

SALALAH

PLACES TO STAY
4 Salalah Tourist Hotel
9 Al-Zahra al-Omania Centre
   (Haffa House, Gulf Air
   & Oman Air)
10 Dhofar Hotel
11 Al-Hanaa Hotel
13 Redan Hotel
16 Bin Hangosh Residences
17 Al-Arooqah Residences

PLACES TO EAT
7 Al-Fareed Tourist
   Restaurant
18 Omar al-Khayyam
   Restaurant
20 Chopsticks
25 Southern Desert Trading
   Enterprises Coffee Shop
26 Pizza Hut
27 Penguin Restaurant

OTHER
1 Cultural Centre
2 Dhofar Governor's Office
3 Main Post Office
5 ONTC Bus Station
6 New Souq
8 Gulf Transport Company
12 Al-Miyasa Rent-a-Car
14 Laundry
15 British Bank of the Middle East
19 Malatan On-Land Transport
21 Oman United Agencies
   Travel Centre

22 Family Bookshop
23 Police & Fire Stations
24 Al-Fawaz Travel &
   Tourism
28 Gold Souq
29 Oman United Exchange
   Company
30 Bank of Muscat
31 Telephone Office
32 Petrol Station
33 Sultan's Palace
34 Cinema
35 Al-Husn Souq

To Hamdan Plaza Hotel (1km),
Job's Tomb (30km) & Mughsail (45km)

A' Robat Street

To Airport (1km)

Clock
Tower
Roundabout

A' Robat Street

23rd July Street

A' Nahdah

A' Salam Street

Al-Montazah Street

Al-Noor Street

Al-Hafah Street

0   250   500 m

To Salalah Holiday Inn (5.5km),
Taqa (36km), Khor Rouri (43km)
& Mirbat (70km)

Sultan Qaboos Street

A' Sharooq Street

To Al-Balid (3.5km)

A'Bahri Street

ARABIAN SEA

OMAN

The telephone office is at the intersection of A'Nahdah and Al-Montazah Sts. It's open from 7.30 am to 11.30 pm daily. Fax and telex facilities are also available but these close down around 9 pm.

Museum

Salalah's museum is in the Cultural Centre on Ar-Robat St (access is from the back, via A'Nahdah St). There is no English lettering on the building, but it is the huge white place, the second building west of the in-

tersection of Ar-Robat and A'Nahdah Sts. The museum is open Saturday to Wednesday from 8 am to 2 pm. Admission is free. Make sure you stop in the lobby to look at the exhibit of Wilfred Thesiger's photographs of Salalah and other parts of Arabia in the 1940s and 50s.

Al-Husn Souq

This is the place to buy your genuine Dhofari frankincense. Your sense of smell will be blitzed after you've smelt all the incenses and been daubed with a dozen or so perfumes. There are also a number of silver shops selling khanjars, swords and jewellery. There are lots of Omani halwa shops on the corner of Al-Hafah and Sultan Qaboos Sts. This is really good stuff and you are likely to become addicted.

Al-Balid

The ruins of Al-Balid, site of the ancient city of Zafar, lie about 4.5km east of the centre on the coast road, just west of the Holiday Inn. Zafar's heyday was in the 11th and 12th centuries AD when it was an active trading port. Coins from as far away as China have been found at the site. There is a fence around the site and you need a permit to enter. Alternatively, you can go with a tour guide.

Organised Tours

Zubair Travel & Services Bureau (☎ 235581, 235582), in the lobby of the Holiday Inn, has a three hour city tour for OR23. It also offers a half-day tour to Job's Tomb and Mughsail blowholes for OR36. For the same price a tour goes east to Taqa and Mirbat. Al-Fawaz Travel & Tourism (☎ 294324, fax 294265) on A'Nahdah St is a little bit more expensive at OR40 for the same half-day tours. It also has a tour to the Lost City of Ubar, 175km from Salalah, then to the edge of the great Empty Quarter and back via Wadi Hanoon for OR120 with lunch. Prices are per vehicle (ie up to four people).

Places to Stay

Al-Hanaa Hotel (☎ 298305, fax 291894, 23 July St) near the corner of Al-Matar St is very good value for money with bright, clean rooms for OR10/15 for singles/doubles. These prices include tax and breakfast.

Salalah Tourist Hotel (☎ 295332, fax 295626), opposite the ONTC bus station just north of 23 July St, is equally good value for money with large, comfortable rooms and friendly staff for OR10/15, also including tax and breakfast.

Al-Arooqah Residences (☎ 294538) on A'Salam St has the cheapest rooms in town

with one bed for OR8, two beds for OR12, three beds for OR15 and four beds for OR18. Most rooms have private baths. The hotel is on an upper floor of the building beside which the Al-Ghafri buses stop.

Redan Hotel (☎ 292266, fax 292255, A'Salam St) in the centre has singles/doubles for OR14/17. The location is good and the rooms are large and clean.

Dhofar Hotel (☎ 290484, 292300, fax 294358, Al-Matar St) is more upmarket, with rooms for OR18.720/23.400.

Haffa House (☎ 295444, fax 294873), in the Al-Zahra al-Omania Centre at the clock tower roundabout on the corner of Al-Matar and Ar-Robat Sts, charges OR19.800/22. The rooms are large and comfortable and there is a pool and restaurant.

Hamdan Plaza Hotel (☎ 211025, fax 211187), on the main road leading west out of the city, is a huge five star place with very large rooms for OR32.200/40.250.

Salalah Holiday Inn (☎ 235333, fax 235137), on the coast, about 5.5km east of the centre, charges OR38.610/48.555. It has a pool, private beach, health club, two bars and an expensive seafood restaurant.

Al-Mughsail Beach Tourist Resthouse (☎ 290641, 298805), 45km west of Salalah, offers cabins on the beach for OR20.

Places to Eat

There are plenty of small restaurants in the centre along A'Salam St offering Indian food.

Omar al-Khayyam on 23 July St has good Chinese and Indian food. Entrees are about OR1 and mains OR1.500 to OR2. This is a popular place and is usually pretty full in the evenings.

Al-Fareed Tourist Restaurant, across the road from Omar al-Khayyam on 23 July St, has similar meals for roughly the same price. They also have buffet dinners most evenings with a mixture of Lebanese and Indian food.

Lou Lou'A restaurant in the Hamdan Plaza Hotel offers basic western meals. The view over Salalah is great but the food is a little expensive.

Shopping

Among Dhofar's most distinctive souvenirs are the small, bead-covered plastic bottles used by women to carry kohl for decorating their eyes. They can be purchased in the new souq for OR3 to OR5, depending on size. Other locally made crafts available in the new souq include pottery incense burners. These cost OR1.500 to OR10, depending on size. A small bag of frankincense will cost you about OR1.

If you are looking for khanjars, the best place to go is A'Sharooq St behind the Al-Husn souq. The large khanjars here are beautifully crafted but they are expensive at OR100 to OR250. They are not antiques but they are some of the most beautifully made khanjars in Oman.

Getting There & Away

Air Salalah's small airport is served only by Oman Air (☎ 295747). Its office is on the 1st floor of the Al-Zahra al-Omania Centre by the clock tower roundabout. There are two flights per day to Muscat. The fare is OR27 one way and OR50 return.

Bus Buses leave the ONTC bus station in the new souq for Muscat every day at 7 am and 7 pm, with an extra bus at 6 pm from mid-June to mid-September (OR8 one way, OR16 return, 12 hours). Departures are one hour later during Ramadan. You can store luggage in the ONTC ticket office at the new souq.

Al-Ghafri & Sons (☎ 293574) also runs buses to Muscat every day at 7 am and 4.45 pm. Departures are from the office, which is actually called Malatan On-Land Transport, just off A'Salam St. At OR8 one way and OR14 return, the fare is a bit cheaper than ONTC's, but the buses are older and clunkier.

Taxi & Microbus Salalah's taxis and microbuses hang out in front of the British Bank of the Middle East on A'Salam St. Taxis will generally only make intercity trips on an engaged basis, which is invariably expensive (OR10 to Taqa, for example). Microbus fares from Salalah include: Mirbat, 500 Baisa; Mughsail, OR1; and Muscat, OR8.

Getting Around

Generally a microbus ride inside the city costs around 200 baisa and a taxi ride about 500 baisa. To farther destinations like the Holiday Inn, OR1.500 should be sufficient. From the airport there seems to be a fixed price of OR2.500 to anywhere in the city.

If you want to rent a car in Salalah check out Al-Miyasa Rent-a-Car (☎ 296521) on A'Salam St next door to the Redan Hotel. It offers small cars for OR14, including insurance and 200 free kilometres per day. Budget (☎ 235160) has a desk at the Holiday Inn and there is an Avis desk at Zubair Travel (☎ 235581).

AROUND SALALAH

There are very good **beaches** all along the road to Mughsail once you're about 5km out of Salalah. Overnight camping on the beach is not allowed.

Mughsail

Mughsail (Mugsail) is 45km west of Salalah. It offers beautiful unspoiled beaches as well as some spectacular scenery, including several groves of **frankincense trees**, on the drive out. Here you will also be able to see blowholes that spray sea froth high into the air. Drive past the Al-Mughsail Beach Tourist Resthouse to a path leading around a bluff. You should be able to see the **blowholes** at the end of the path.

If you continue beyond Mughsail on the road towards the Yemeni border the landscape becomes even more spectacular.

Microbuses charge OR1 in either direction for the trip between Salalah and Mughsail.

Job's Tomb

In religious terms the mortuary known as Job's Tomb (and referred to in Arabic simply as 'Nabi Ayyub' – Prophet Job) is probably the most important site in Dhofar. Regardless of your religious convictions the tomb – situated on an isolated hilltop overlooking Salalah – is a must-see both for the beautiful drive up to its mountain site and for the excellent view over Salalah that the car park affords on a clear day.

OMAN

The tomb is just over 30km from Salalah's centre. To reach it take the main west-bound road from the centre towards Mughsail and turn right at the sign for Ittin when you are on the outskirts of Salalah, just after passing the Hamdan Plaza Hotel. From the turn-off follow this road for 22km and then turn left off the main road at a sign that says 'An-Nabi Ayyub 1½ km'. After 1.4km you will come to a fork in the road. Keeping right takes you to the restaurant, while going left takes you to the car park outside the tomb enclosure. There is no public transport to or from the tomb.

Khor Rouri

Centuries ago Khor Rouri was an important port holding down the southern end of the frankincense route. Today, little remains of the city except the ruins of a palace-cum-fort sitting atop a mound of rather nondescript-looking rubble. The calm here is almost unearthly, but it is strangely easy amid that calm to imagine a time 18 or 20 centuries ago when this quiet bay was one of the most important ports on earth.

The site is completely fenced in and trespassing is not allowed. It is possible to visit the site with a guide only, which means taking a tour with one of the companies in Salalah. Even if you don't take a tour it's worth going out of your way to visit the dramatic setting.

To get there take the road from Salalah towards Mirbat and turn at the Khor Rouri sign, about 7km beyond Taqa's centre. The site is 2.5km off the main road along a bumpy dirt track. The microbus fare from Salalah should be 300 to 400 baisa.

Mirbat

The town of Mirbat (Mirbaat), just over 70km east of Salalah, is about as far east of Salalah as you can go without a 4WD. The town's small **fort** has a lonely, end-of-the-road feel about it as it overlooks both the town and the coastline trailing off back towards Salalah.

Mirbat's other noteworthy site is the **Bin Ali Tomb**, a small and quite photogenic

mosque built in a style typical of Yemen's Hadhramawt region. The tomb is 1km off the main road. It is the larger of the two white tombs in the cemetery – the one closer to the parking area.

Musandam Peninsula

Separated from the rest of Oman by the east coast of the UAE, and guarding the southern side of the strategically important Strait of Hormuz, the Musandam peninsula is a land of stark beauty. It is the least developed part of the Gulf's least developed country; an area of fjords, small villages and dramatic, mountain-hugging roads.

Apart from the spectacular coast road from Tibat, there are no paved roads around Musandam except in the town centres of Khasab, Bukha and the Omani portion of Dibba which is on the east coast. Public transport exists more in theory than in practice and some of the region's settlements are accessible only by boat. It is also very expensive, even by Omani standards.

The good news is that the widely held belief that you cannot move about outside of Khasab without a 4WD is not true. This section lists most of the places in the Musandam you can visit using a regular car.

KHASAB

The Musandam peninsula's capital is small but far from sleepy. Its port bursts with activity, much of it involving the smuggling of US cigarettes to Iran, and its souq is filled with both visitors from other parts of the Musandam and an ever-increasing number of tourists.

Orientation & Information

For such a small place Khasab is surprisingly spread out. The town's commercial centre is the port and the small souq a few kilometres or so south-east of it. Another 1.5km to the east is the town's new souq. This consists of a few restaurants and gro-

MUSANDAM PENINSULA

Strait of Hormuz

Musandam Island

0   10   20 km

Khor Ash Shamm

Kumzar

ARABIAN GULF

Al-Harf
Hanah
Qulda
Tawi
Khasab
Telegraph Island

Bukha

Tibat (Oman)

Sham

Khor Habalayn

Khor Najd

OMAN

Sayh

1488m

▲1924m

Lima

Rawdah Bowl
Rawdah Checkpoint

GULF OF OMAN

Ras al-Khaimah

To Dubai (90km)

1527m

Dibba Bayah (Oman)

Road Passable with 4WD Vehicle Only

UNITED ARAB EMIRATES

Dibba Muhallab (UAE)

Dibba Hisn (UAE)

To Masafi

To Fujairah (60km)

OMAN

cery stores, the post office, a couple of banks and the Oman Air office. The Khasab Hotel and the airport lie a short distance to the south of the new souq.

Khasab Fort

There is nothing especially remarkable about Khasab Fort. What sets this fort apart is the setting. The fort dominates the bit of coast that provides access to Khasab's older sections. Its opening hours are a bit erratic. Government office hours (from 7.30 am to 2.30 pm Saturday to Wednesday) are your best bet. Admission is free.

Activities

Diving Diving around the Musandam peninsula is reputed to be some of the best in the world, though conditions in the water are suitable only for experienced divers with a minium of a PADI Open Water Cer-

tificate and 50 logged dives. The only way to arrange a trip is with Scuba International in Dubai (☎ 00968-4-420 553) or Khasab Travel & Tours (☎ 830464).

There is a small **beach** suitable for swimming just outside Khasab. Follow the road from the port towards Bukha. The beach is at a lay-by on the right exactly 1km after the point where the pavement ends.

Organised Tours

Khasab Travel & Tours (☎ 830464) in the old souq offers full-day and half-day boat trips around Musandam's fjords. These trips are for groups really and are very expensive at OR30. A trip to Kumzar will cost you up to OR60 but you should be able to get one of the fishermen to take you there and back for around OR30.

There is also a kayaking trip in the fjords that can be combined with a two night camping trip and hiking for a whopping OR200 (minimum four people). You can also design your own tours if you are prepared to pay OR80 per day for a 4WD and driver.

Places to Stay & Eat

The only hotel in Musandam is *Khasab Hotel* (☎ *830267, fax 830989*) 1km south of the new souq roundabout. At OR20.475/33.930 for singles/doubles, including the tax and service charge, it is rather overpriced. Because the hotel is small, calling ahead for reservations is a very good idea.

Khasab Travel & Tours has two three-bedroom villas for OR40 per night. This is much better value if you are a group, and you can do your own cooking. It is about 200m from Khasab Hotel.

Bukha Restaurant in the old souq has biryanis that are more subtly spiced than those usually found in Muscat. These cost 600 baisa per serving. Roast chicken and kebabs are available in the evening and the place is popular with the Iranian cigarette smugglers – always a good sign.

Getting There & Away

Air Oman Air's office (☎ 830543) is on the new souq's main roundabout, between the

OMAN

Khasab Hotel and the port area. It has flights to Muscat four days a week. Fares are OR20 one way and OR40 return, a price you will find hard to beat by going overland unless you have your own car.

Long-Distance Taxi The 10-passenger 4WD pick-up trucks that serve as the Musandam's long-distance taxis gather in Khasab's old souq, near the port. It's most likely, however, that you will have to take a taxi 'engaged'. The standard engaged rates are: Bukha, OR5; Tibat or Khor Najd, OR10; Dibba, OR25; and Muscat, OR70.

Though it is only about 70km from Ras al-Khaimah to Khasab there are no service taxis making the run on a regular basis. The Khasab pick-up drivers charge OR15 for the trip to Ras al-Khaimah (about two hours if there are no problems at the border). From Ras al-Khaimah service-taxi drivers demand Dh200 for the trip to Khasab, though for Dh40 they will take you to the Sham border post, from where you can try to hitch a ride into Khasab. To leave the UAE by road you will also have to pay a Dh20 road tax.

Car Rental There is no car rental company in the Musandam peninsula. However, we were told at the Khasab Hotel that it could arrange rental with one of the locals for OR30 per day, though you should be able to haggle this outrageous fee down to OR25 or less, depending on demand.

Getting Around

To/From the Airport Khasab may have the only airport in the world that is completely devoid of taxis. Khasab Hotel staff will meet your flight if you have a reservation there and can also give you a lift to the airport when it is time to leave. Either of these services costs OR3. If someone offers you a lift into town but expects to be paid for the service do not agree to pay more than OR2, as the distance is only a few kilometres.

Taxi There are orange and white taxis that will take you around town for 200 or 300 baisa but these are usually permanently booked up by locals. The only other form of public transport is open 4WD pick-up trucks with benches in the back. Should one of these vehicles actually be moving, the driver will charge a couple of hundred baisa for a lift within the town.

TAWI

About 10km from Khasab port lies the village of Tawi, site of a handful of prehistoric **rock carvings**. To reach the carvings turn off the Khasab-Bukha road and onto a dirt track at Quida. Coming from Khasab the track is just beyond the sign with the village's name on it but before you pass any of Quida's houses. Follow this track up the Wadi Quida for 2.3km. The carvings will be to your left on two rocks at a point where the track bends sharply to the right just before a large white house. Across the track from the carvings is an ancient **well** that is still used by Tawi's residents.

BUKHA

Bukha has two forts. The more interesting of the two is **Bukha Fort**, on the coast. If you are coming from Khasab the fort is the first thing you will arrive at. The other fort, which is in ruins, is on a hill a short distance inland and north of Bukha Fort.

On the other side of Bukha on the way to Tibat there is a great camping spot on the beach with shelters and drinking water.

KHOR NAJD

Khor Najd (Khor an-Najd) is the only one of the Musandam's fjords that can be reached from Khasab in an ordinary car, though it needs to be a car in fairly decent repair considering how steep (both climbing and descending) the last portion of the drive is. It is 24.5km by road from Khasab's centre, about a 30 minute drive. The small beach is better suited to camping than swimming, and is a popular weekend spot with both Omani and Emirati families, particularly since it has a concrete ramp for launching boats. There are a few shelters and drinking water available.

To reach Khor Najd go south from the new souq roundabout. After a few kilometres you'll come to a T-junction with a sign pointing right to the airport and left to Dibba; turn left here. After 8.5km you will see a green sign pointing to, among other places, 'Khor an-Najd 10km'. Turn left, follow this road for another 5.6km and then turn left again. After another 1.5km you will come to a three-way fork in the road; take the road that winds up the mountain. After 2.3km you will reach the outlook, and your first view of Khor Najd. Another (even steeper) 2.8km descent brings you to the water's edge.

KUMZAR

Set on an isolated cove at the northern edge of the Musandam peninsula, Kumzar is accessible only by boat. The village's residents do not speak Arabic. Their language, known as Kumzari, is a mish-mash of Fārsī, Hindi, English, Portuguese and Arabic.

The village's only 'sight' is a **well** 500m or so up the wadi that serves as Kumzar's main 'street'. The well, which is now brackish, was Kumzar's sole source of water until the government built a small desalination plant next to the harbour in the 1970s. The old **stone houses** are also interesting to look at, quite unlike anything you will see in the rest of Oman. The main attraction of a visit to Kumzar is really the spectacular scenery on the way there.

Water taxis travel between Khasab and Kumzar most days, charging OR3 per person. This can be a pretty harrowing trip. Most of the speedboats used as water taxis have no seats and maybe 15cm clearance between deck and gunwale. Alternatively, you could hire an entire boat. With a little tenacity you should be able to get someone to take you over to Kumzar, wait around there for two or three hours and then bring you back for OR40. If you can split this cost among several people you will have a faster and, probably, safer trip, not to mention a more comfortable ride and and best of all, a guaranteed lift back.

Qatar

The strangely shaped peninsula of Qatar has been largely forgotten in recent history, and continues to be ignored by most travellers. Qatar only started issuing visas to tourists in 1989, and while it does little to attract visitors, and it's a far cry from the tourist centres of the United Arab Emirates, there's enough to see and do to justify a stopover for a few days.

Facts about Qatar

HISTORY

A general history of the Middle East is given in the Facts about the Region chapter.

For most of its recent history, Qatar has been dominated by the Al-Thani family who arrived in the mid-18th century, when Qatar was already well established as a pearling centre, and became the peninsula's rulers about 100 years later. Historically, Doha (now the capital) was never a particularly important trading port, and throughout the 19th and early 20th centuries Qatar remained very poor, even by pre-oil Gulf standards.

In 1915 the Emir of Qatar expelled the Turkish garrison then based in Doha. With Britain and Turkey on opposite sides in WWI, and the British controlling the rest of the Gulf, a switch in alliances seemed wise. After expelling the Turks, Qatar's emir signed an exclusive agreement with the British, under which Britain guaranteed Qatar's protection in exchange for a promise that the ruler wouldn't deal with other foreign powers without British permission.

Even before the collapse of the pearl market around 1930, life in Qatar was rough. With poverty, hunger, malnutrition and disease all widespread, the emir welcomed the oil prospectors who first arrived in the early 1930s. A concession was granted in 1935 and the prospectors struck oil in 1939. Because of WWII, however, production did not begin for another 10 years.

The State of Qatar

Area: 11,437 sq km
Population: approx 640,000
Population Growth Rate: 3.4%
Capital: Doha
Head of State: The Emir, Sheikh Hamad bin Khalifa al-Thani
Official Language: Arabic
Currency: Qatari riyal (Qr)
Exchange Rate: US$1 = Qr3.65

- **Best Dining** – the best place for a meal or a drink is anywhere overlooking the bay, such as the Al-Bandar group of restaurants at the end of the jetty
- **Best Walk** – Al-Corniche is about 7km long, and offers plenty of shade and superb views; it is particularly pleasant in the late afternoon and evening
- **Best View** – most visitors can't afford to stay at the Doha Sheraton Hotel but the views of the bay from the restaurants upstairs, and from the opulent foyer, are wonderful
- **Best Activity** – if you have access to a 4WD, or can go on an organised tour, the 'inland sea' and sand dunes at Khor al-Adaid are truly spectacular
- **When in Rome ...** find out when the camel races are being held at Ash-Shahhainiya, and career alongside the track in a car while the races are in progress

QATAR

Ras Abu Amran
Ar-Ruweis
Abu Dhalouf
Al-Khuwair
Al-Ghariya
Al-Arish
Madinat al-Shamal
Al-Zubara
Fuwairit
Hawar Islands (Ownership Disputed)
Al-Ghuwairiyah
Al-Khor Gardens
Al-Dakhira
Al-Jumailiyah
Al-Khor
THE GULF
Umm Salal Ali
Umm Salal Mohammed
Dukhan
Ash-Shahhainiya
Al-Rayyan
DOHA
Umm Bab
Al-Wukair
Al-Wakrah
Mukeinis
Al-Kharrarah
Mesaieed
Sealine Beach Resort
Salwa
Khor al-Adaid
0   15   30 km
SAUDI ARABIA
Undemarcated Border
Dukhan Heights

What to See

Doha is a bit short on attractions. The highlight is undoubtedly the comprehensive **Qatar National Museum**, but the **Ethnographic Museum** and **Doha Fort** are also worth a look. In the evening, take a long walk along **Al-Corniche** and enjoy a **boat ride** around the bay. A trip to **Palm Tree Island** is also a pleasant diversion.

Outside the capital, the **camel races** at Ash-Shahhainiya are spectacular and the **fort museum** at Al-Zubara is interesting if only for the bleak, desert landscape. There are also several **museums** and decent **beaches** in southern and northern Qatar. The highlight is undoubtedly the 'inland sea' and sand dunes at **Khor al-Adaid**, but this is only accessible by 4WD.

GEOGRAPHY

The Qatar Peninsula is 11,437 sq km, about 160km long and 55 to 80km wide. The desert tends to be flat (the highest elevation is only about 98m above sea level) and gravelly, and there is very little natural vegetation.

CLIMATE

Summer (May to September) temperatures generally average 35°C, but it's not uncommon to get up to 50°C. The 90% humidity also means that summers can be very uncomfortable. The winter months are

When the British announced they would withdraw by the end of 1971, Qatar entered talks with Bahrain and the Trucial States (now the United Arab Emirates) with the intention of forming a confederation. When Bahrain pulled out of the talks, Qatar followed suit and declared independence on 1 September 1971. Six months later Sheikh Khalifa bin Hamad al-Thani, a cousin of the emir, and for many years Qatar's ruler in all but title, took power in a coup.

Qatar Today

In June 1995, Sheikh Khalifa was unexpectedly replaced as emir by his son Hamad. In many ways, Qatar remains a sleepy backwater, but it is becoming more liberal compared to other Gulf states: the press has relative freedom, and women were allowed to vote in municipal elections in early 1999.

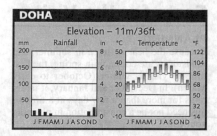

DOHA

Elevation – 11m/36ft

Rainfall
mm   in
200   8
150   6
100   4
50   2
0   0
J F M A M J J A S O N D

Temperature
°C   °F
50   122
40   104
30   86
20   68
10   50
0   32
-10   14
J F M A M J J A S O N D

QATAR

much milder with pleasant, cool evenings. Sandstorms are common throughout the year, especially in the spring. Although it doesn't rain much, there are a few weeks of wet weather in December and January.

GOVERNMENT & POLITICS

Qatar is ruled by an emir: Sheikh Hamad bin Khalifa al-Thani, who is also minister of defence and commander-in-chief of the armed forces. His third son, Sheikh Jasim bin Hamad al-Thani, is the official heir apparent; and the prime minister and minister of the interior is Sheikh Abdullah bin Khalifa al-Thani.

POPULATION & PEOPLE

Qatar is one of the smallest countries in the Arab world by population: about 640,000. Of these, only 25% are indigenous Qataris. Most are of Najdi (central Arabian) ancestry, though there are also people of Persian descent. The foreign population is a mix of people from South-East Asia, the Indian subcontinent and the Arab world; Britons make up the largest contingent of western expatriates.

RELIGION

Most Qataris adhere to the austere Wahhabi sect of Islam, which is less severe than the Saudi variety.

LANGUAGE

The national language is Arabic. English is also widely spoken, and is a lingua franca among the foreign population, but is not widely understood by less educated Qataris.

Facts for the Visitor

PLANNING

Because the heat is fierce in summer, and sandstorms are common in spring, the best time to visit is winter (October to early March). In December and January, it rarely rains for more than a few days at a time so this need not be a consideration in planning your trip.

VISAS & DOCUMENTS
Visas

Residents of, and expatriates living in, other countries of the Gulf Cooperation Council (GCC) can enter Qatar without a sponsor or visa, but it's still prudent to check this before coming.

UK citizens can get a visa at a Qatari embassy/consulate without a sponsor. US citizens can obtain a visa at an embassy/consulate but need a confirmed hotel reservation (but no sponsor). Almost all other nationalities need a sponsor from within Qatar – and for most, this means arranging a hotel to sponsor you.

At the time of writing, the Qatari authorities planned to increase visa fees considerably: tourist visas (normally valid for a maximum of 14 days) will cost Qr200; multi-entry tourist and business visas of less than six months, Qr300; and multi-entry tourist and business visas for six to 12 months, Qr500.

At the Embassy If you can get a visa at a Qatari embassy/consulate, you must fill out three forms and provide three passport-sized photos. Anyone requesting a business visa may be asked to supply a letter from the company they will be visiting. Visas will normally take one week to process.

Via a Hotel Most tourists will need to be sponsored by a hotel. Only mid-range and top end hotels can do this – for a variable fee (Qr50 to Qr100). The following hotels (listed under Places to Stay in the Doha section later) can arrange visa sponsorship: Ramada Hotel, Doha Sheraton, New Capital Hotel, Doha Palace Hotel and Oasis Hotel.

Contact the hotel (preferably by fax or email), book a room and request sponsorship. Send them your passport details, reason for visit (business, tourism etc), arrival and departure dates and flight numbers. The hotel sort of 'controls' your visa and stay, so it's almost impossible to change hotels after you arrive.

The hotel must send you a letter or fax (email probably won't be accepted by the immigration authorities) acknowledging your reservation, and quoting a visa number. Give this letter/fax to the immigration counter at Doha international airport, and (hopefully) you'll obtain an unimpressive (extendable) visa for the length of your stay (maximum of 14 days). The visa fee, and fee for arranging the sponsorship, will probably be added to your hotel bill. Allow at *least* six (Qatari) working days (nothing will get done on Thursday afternoon and Friday).

Visa Extensions Tourist visas can be extended for an additional 14 days and business visas for seven days. The charges for overstaying are very high: between Qr200 and Qr500 *per day* for any type of visa. If you were originally sponsored by a hotel, the hotel must arrange your extension which costs Qr300 plus hotel fees. If you obtained your visa through an embassy/consulate, go to the Department for Passports, Nationality & Residence in Doha (☎ 882 882).

Visas for Neighbouring Countries You need a visa to enter the following neighbouring countries of Qatar:

Kuwait Only residents of Qatar can get a visa for Kuwait.

Oman A visa for Oman requires three photos, costs about Qr10 and takes two to four days to process.

Saudi Arabia Only residents of Qatar can get a visa for Saudi Arabia.

United Arab Emirates Again, only residents of Qatar can obtain a visa for the UAE.

Yemen A visa for Yemen requires two photos, costs about US$50 and takes less than one week to process. A letter from a travel agency helps but is not mandatory.

Exit Visa The situation was unclear at the time of writing, but the Qatari authorities will soon charge visitors Qr200 for an 'exit visa' – probably in lieu of a departure tax.

Other Documents
No other special permits are required. Student cards are worthless. Refer to Car & Motorcycle in the Getting Around section later for information about driving permits and licences in Qatar.

EMBASSIES & CONSULATES
Qatari Embassies & Consulates
For addresses of Qatari embassies in neighbouring Middle Eastern countries see the relevant country chapters.

France
    Embassy:
    (☎ 01 45 51 90 71)
    57 Quai D'Orsay, 75007, Paris
Germany
    Embassy:
    (☎ 228-957 520)
    Brunnen alle 6, 53177 Bonn
UK
    Embassy:
    (☎ 020-7370 6871, visa info ☎ 0891-633 233)
    1 South Audley St, London, W1Y 5DQ
USA
    Embassy:
    (☎ 202-274 1600, fax 237 0061)
    4200 Wisconsin Ave, NW, Suite 200, Washington DC 20016
    Consulate:
    (☎ 212-486 9355)
    747 3rd Ave, 22nd floor, New York, NY 10017

Embassies & Consulates in Qatar
Most embassies are located in the 'Diplomatic Area', past the Doha Sheraton Hotel and few have specific addresses. All are open from about 8 am to 3 pm from Saturday to Wednesday. There is no Bahrain embassy.

France
    Embassy:
    (☎ 832 283, fax 832 254)
    Diplomatic Area
Germany
    Embassy:
    (☎ 876 959, fax 876 949)
    Al-Jezira al-Arabiyya St
Kuwait
    Embassy:
    (☎ 832 111, fax 832 042)
    Diplomatic Area

QATAR

Oman
  Embassy:
  (☎ 670 744, fax 670 747)
  41 Ibn al-Qassem St, Villa 7, Hilal district
Saudi Arabia
  Embassy:
  (☎ 832 722, fax 832 720)
  Diplomatic Area
United Arab Emirates
  Embassy:
  (☎ 885 111, fax 882 837)
  Off Al-Khor St, Khalifa Town district
UK
  Embassy:
  (☎ 421 991, fax 438 692)
  Al-Istiqlal St, Rumailiah district
USA
  Embassy:
  (☎ 864 701, fax 861 669)
  149 Ahmed bin Ali St
Yemen
  Embassy:
  (☎ 432 555, fax 429 400)
  Near the As-Saad roundabout, Al-Jezira district

CUSTOMS

Customs procedures can be tiresome at the Doha international airport but foreigners are often waved through. Books, photographs and videos may be confiscated for further scrutiny but they will be returned. Duty-free allowances are: 800 cigarettes, 100 cigars or 500g of tobacco, and 250ml of perfume.

MONEY
Costs

Food is reasonably inexpensive but cheap beds are almost impossible to find because most visitors must be sponsored by a mid-range or top end hotel – many budget places won't accept foreigners anyway. To stay in the cheapest hotel that will sponsor visas, eat in the cheapest restaurants and walk everywhere will cost about Qr150/100 per person per day if travelling as a single/double.

Currency

The Qatari riyal (Qr) is divided into 100 dirhams. Notes come in one, five, 10, 50, 100 and Qr500 denominations. Dirham coins no longer exist, though some prices are still quoted in dirhams. If you're charged, for ex-

ample, Qr1.25 for a (soft) drink, the amount will be rounded down to Qr1; something costing Qr1.5 is rounded up to Qr2.

The Qatari riyal is fully convertible so there's no black market and exchange controls. Many shops also accept Saudi riyals at par for small transactions.

Exchange Rates

The Qatari riyal is fixed against the US dollar. Exchange rates for the major currencies are:

country	unit		riyals
Australia	A$1	=	Qr2.32
Canada	C$1	=	Qr2.42
euro	€1	=	Qr3.79
France	10FF	=	Qr6.10
Germany	DM1	=	Qr2.09
Japan	¥100	=	Qr2.99
New Zealand	NZ$1	=	Qr1.99
UK	UK£1	=	Qr5.86
USA	US$1	=	Qr3.65

Exchanging Money

Moneychangers will offer about Qr3.64 for US$1; banks about Qr3.63 for US$1. The difference is not worth worrying about unless you're changing a huge amount. The top end hotels offer about US$1 for Qr3.50. Currencies from Bahrain, Saudi Arabia and the United Arab Emirates are easy to buy and sell at banks and moneychangers.

Credit Cards & ATMs

All major credit cards are accepted in large shops, and many can be used in ATMs. The Commercial Bank of Qatar accepts American Express (Amex), Diner's Club, Visa, MasterCard and Cirrus; and the British Bank of the Middle East, and the Qatar National Bank, take Visa, MasterCard and Cirrus.

Tipping & Bargaining

A service charge is usually added to restaurant (and top end hotel) bills, but this rarely goes to staff. Local custom does not require that you leave a tip though it would certainly be appreciated – 10% is fine.

QATAR

POST & COMMUNICATIONS

Postal Rates

Postal rates are standard for most western countries: postcards cost Qr1, and letters weighing 10g cost Qr2 and a further Qr2 for every subsequent 10g. The first 1kg for parcels costs Qr73 to USA/Canada and UK/Europe, and Qr88 to Australia/New Zealand. Every subsequent kilogram costs Qr57 to USA/Canada, Qr27 to UK/Europe and Qr50 to Australia/New Zealand.

Sending Mail

There is a main post office in northern Doha, and a more convenient one in central Doha – refer to that section for details. Major international express mail and package services are available.

Receiving Mail

Poste restante is not available and Amex does not keep mail for clients. Your hotel will probably hold mail for a short time prior to your arrival.

Telephone

The country code for Qatar is ☎ 973, followed by the local number – there are no area or city codes.

All communications services are provided by the Qatar Public Telecommunication Corporation (Q-Tel), and the telephone system is excellent. Local calls cost about 50 dirhams, but to make a local or international call from a payphone you must buy a phonecard (Qr30, Qr50 and Qr100), available in many shops around Doha.

Operator-assisted calls from the Main Telecommunications Centre (MTC) in Doha are more expensive than dialling directly from a payphone using a phonecard. The cost of a direct-dial call to the USA/Canada and UK/Europe is about Qr7 per minute, and to Australia/New Zealand it costs about Qr9. Rates are cheaper from 8 pm to 7 am and all day Friday and on holidays.

Email & Internet Access

There are email facilities at most top end hotels, and an Internet cafe in the capital – refer to the Doha section later for details. The only Internet Service Provider is Internet Qatar, part of Q-Tel.

BOOKS

One of the few books which focuses entirely on Qatar is Helga Graham's *Arabian Time Machine*. Subtitled 'Self-Portrait of an Oil State', the book is a collection of interviews with Qataris about their lives and traditions before and after the oil boom.

Anyone intending to stay in Qatar for a while, should pick up one of the following practical books (available at major bookshops in Doha). The 2nd edition of *Qatar: A MEED Practical Guide* (Qr45) unashamedly toes the government line in its coverage of politics, religion and history, but is always useful. *Welcome to Qatar* (Qr35) by the American Women's Association of Qatar is more practical but caters more to US residents.

More general Middle East titles, some of which also contain coverage of Bahrain or Qatar, are listed in the Books section in the Regional Facts for the Visitor chapter at the beginning of this book.

NEWSPAPERS & MAGAZINES

Two decent English-language newspapers are published daily (except Friday). *Gulf Times* is bright and colourful; and *The Peninsula* is informative. International newspapers and magazines, mostly from the UK, are available one or two days after publication at major bookshops in Doha.

RADIO & TV

QBS (Qatar Broadcasting Service) offers radio programs in English on 97.5FM and 102.6FM, and has a French-language service on 100.8FM. The BBC and Armed Forces Radio are also available on local FM frequencies.

Channel 37 on QTV (Qatar Television) broadcasts programs in English every day from late afternoon. With a good antenna, English-language stations from Abu Dhabi, Dubai (UAE), Saudi Arabia and Bahrain can be picked up. Most hotels, except for the smallest ones, offer satellite TV.

QATAR

PHOTOGRAPHY & VIDEO

Shops offering print film and developing, and video cassettes, are plentiful in Doha. A roll of 24/36 print film costs about Qr6/8, and about Qr31/43 to develop (including a free film). Slide film is hard to find and very difficult to get developed so bring your own. Many photographic shops also arrange passport photos.

LAUNDRY

There are no laundrettes, but most hotels offer a laundry service for guests. There are several cheap laundries, which charge about Qr2 to Qr3 for a shirt, and Qr4 to Qr5 for trousers or a skirt – refer to the Doha section later for details.

HEALTH

Vaccination certificates are not required, unless you're arriving from an area where cholera, yellow fever or some similar disease is endemic. The only disease which local authorities consider a 'health risk' in Qatar is rabies. Refer to the Health section in the Regional Facts for the Visitor chapter at the beginning of this book for a general overview about health issues in the region.

The standard of health and health care in Qatar is very high, and hospital care is free for residents *and* tourists. A list of up-to-date contact details for hospitals and pharmacists are printed in the two daily English-language newspapers. Refer to the Doha section later for more details.

BUSINESS HOURS

Qataris love their 'siesta', and Doha almost resembles a ghost town in the early afternoon, especially in the summer. Shops and offices are open from around 8 am to noon and from 4 to 7 pm in winter and about 5 to 8 pm in summer. The modern, western-style shopping centres stay open all day from about 9 am to 9 pm.

PUBLIC HOLIDAYS & SPECIAL EVENTS

In addition to the main Islamic holidays in the Public Holidays & Special Events sec-

tion in the Regional Facts for the Visitor chapter, Qatar observes Qatar National Day on 3 September.

ACCOMMODATION

The few designated camp sites around the countryside are not available to tourists, and camping in the desert is not a lot of fun because of fierce sandstorms, lack of water and the bumpy ground.

There are no really cheap hotels nor youth hostels, and most budget places won't accept foreigners. Most visitors end up in pricey mid-range and top end hotels because it's the only way to get a visa (see Visa & Documents earlier in this section). If you're not tied to any hotel, prices for most rooms are negotiable and weekend (Thursday/Friday) specials are commonly offered.

FOOD & DRINKS

Refer to the special section on Middle Eastern cuisine in the Facts about the Region chapter at the beginning of this book for more information.

Qatar does not have an indigenous cuisine that's worth mentioning, and restaurant that serve decent Arabic food are surprisingly scarce. Apart from the restaurants at the big hotels (which offer predictable and expensive western fare), Doha is filled with well known fastfood joints with set-price meals (about Qr15); and Indian/Pakistani eateries, which offer cheap but tasty curry and *biryani* dishes for about Qr10. The cheapest places are the 'cafeterias', which serve sandwiches and burgers, and the 'juice stalls', with their *felafel*-style snacks.

The average Qatari restaurant offers little more than fruit juice and soft drinks (sodas). All of the larger hotels have a bar and a restaurant which serves liquor. Any sign in the hotel lobby which advertises 'entertainment' in the 'lounge' is an advertisement for the bar. They're open to guests and 'members'. If you're desperate for a drink but are not a hotel guest, ask the hotel about entrance regulations.

SPECTATOR SPORTS

Qatar hosts many international sports events, such as the Qatar Masters golf tournament; the Qatar Open tennis tournament; and the Qatar International squash championship. In 1998, Qatar hosted an international grand prix athletics meeting, the first in the GCC to allow foreign and local women to participate.

SHOPPING

There is little in the way of Arabian souvenirs in Doha, and much of the Arabian stuff (eg incense burners) is actually made in Pakistan or Syria. Refer to the Doha section later for information about souqs, markets and shopping centres.

Getting There & Away

AIR
Airports & Airlines

Qatar is one of the four part-owners of Gulf Air, which has one or more flights a week from Doha to the hubs of Frankfurt, London and Paris; several each day to major cities on the subcontinent and all around the Middle East; and weekly services elsewhere around the world, via Bahrain and Abu Dhabi. Qatar's own national carrier, Qatar Airways, also has services from Doha to London and Munich, and to most cities in the Middle East. The country's only airport, Doha international, is only 2.5km from central Doha.

Departure Tax

The departure tax for Qatar, currently Qr20, is payable at the airport. Since November 1999, visitors have been slugged Qr200 for an 'exit visa' which may be in lieu of a departure tax.

LAND

There are no international bus or taxi services to Saudi Arabia or the United Arab Emirates (UAE). Residents of Qatar, Saudi Arabia and UAE can drive across the Qatar-Saudi border, but foreigners are normally not allowed to because sponsored visas must be collected at Doha international airport.

SEA

No passenger ferry nor boats currently service Qatar.

Getting Around

BUS

The local bus service is no use to visitors. Infrequent, unreliable and uncomfortable buses link Doha with major cities, such as Dukhan, Ar-Ruweis and Mesaieed, but the service is so irregular that locals don't even know if/when the buses are running.

LONG DISTANCE TAXI

For short trips taxis are useful, but to visit most sights around the countryside you're better off hiring a car. Taxi drivers will use the meter, but need a little encouragement. The flagfall is Qr2 during the day (Qr3 at night), and then 100 dirhams per 100m. You can negotiate a set fare for a longer trip, but it will still probably be cheaper using the meter. Some private cars offer cheaper rates than taxis, but they're illegal, and an unmetered fare in a private car will still probably cost foreigners more than a metered fare in an official taxi.

CAR & MOTORCYCLE

If you're driving around Doha, you'll discover that roundabouts are common, disorientating and large. Finding the right way out of Doha can also be difficult: if you're heading south towards Al-Wakrah or Mesaieed, take the airport road (Al-Matar Rd); the main road to all points north is 22nd February Rd (north from Ar-Rayyan Rd); and to the west, continue along Ar-Rayyan Rd.

Driving in Qatar is on the right-hand side. There are two grades of petrol: regular costs 65 dirhams per litre; super costs 70 dirhams. Numerous reputable service stations are located around Doha, and along the highways.

Rental

Foreigners can rent a car (there is nowhere to rent a motorcycle) with their normal driving licences from home – but *only* within seven days of arriving in Qatar. After that, a temporary licence must be obtained. This is issued by the Traffic Licence Office, costs Qr50 and lasts three months – the larger rental companies can arrange this. The minimum rental period for all agencies is 24 hours and drivers must be at least 21 years old.

Rental costs (which include unlimited kilometres but not petrol) do vary, so shop around. Expect to pay about Qr110/700 per day/week for the smallest sedan. Most rental companies have a compulsory Collision Damage Waiver of Qr20 to Qr40 per day, which is a good idea anyway to avoid an excess of Qr1500 to Qr2500 in case of accidents. A few companies also add a compulsory Personal Accident Insurance Fee.

There are some less reputable agencies around Doha but it's better to use a well-known company. The following companies have booths at the airport, and some have offices in top end hotels: Avis (☎ 447 766, fax 441 626, email avis@qatar.net.qa), also at the Gulf Sheraton and Ramada hotels; Budget (☎ 419 500, fax 419 077); Europcar (☎ 411 982), also at Hotel Sofitel; and Hertz (☎ 622 891, fax 621 291).

ORGANISED TOURS

Qatar Holidays, which has offices at the Gulf Sheraton (☎ 495 585) and Doha Sheraton (☎ 854 829) hotels, organises tours around Doha and trips to the desert, camel farms and oil fields around Dukhan. German-speaking guides can be arranged. Prices range from Qr75/200 for half/full-day tours to Qr450 for overnight 'desert safaris'.

Doha

Around the Gulf, Doha (where 80% of Qatar's population lives) has earned the unenviable reputation of being the dullest place on earth. You will be hard-pressed to find anyone who'll claim the place is exciting, but there is nothing *wrong* with Doha; the bay is pleasant, there are some interesting sights around town and it's the obvious base for day trips around the country.

INFORMATION
Money

Moneychangers are dotted around central Doha; there's a small collection just south of the Doha Fort. Amex is represented by Darwish Travel & Tourism (☎ 422 411) on western Ar-Rayyan Rd. There are ATMs at the Commercial Bank of Qatar, the Doha Club, the airport, The Centre and The Mall shopping complexes, the Gulf Sheraton and Doha Sheraton hotels, the British Bank of the Middle East and the Qatar National Bank. See under Money in the Facts for the Visitor section earlier in this chapter for more details.

Post

The General Post Office is in northern Doha, but there is a more convenient one on Abdullah bin Jasim St. It's open from 7 am to 1 pm and 4 to 7 pm from Saturday to Thursday and from 8 to 10 am on Friday.

Telephone

The Main Telecommunications Centre is open 24 hours a day and also offers fax, telex and telegram services. Refer to Post & Communications in the Facts for the Visitor section earlier in this chapter for more information.

Email & Internet Access

At the business centres of the Gulf Sheraton, Doha Sheraton and Ramada hotels (see Places to Stay later), Internet access costs about Qr60 per hour. Internet Cafe (☎ 350 711, email sales@ig.com) in the Gulf Commercial Center, Gulf St, charges a more reasonable Qr15 per hour.

Bookshops

The Centre and The Mall shopping complexes have decent bookshops. The Journal Bookshop in the Gulf Sheraton Hotel is pretty good, but the best is in the Doha Sheraton Hotel.

CENTRAL DOHA

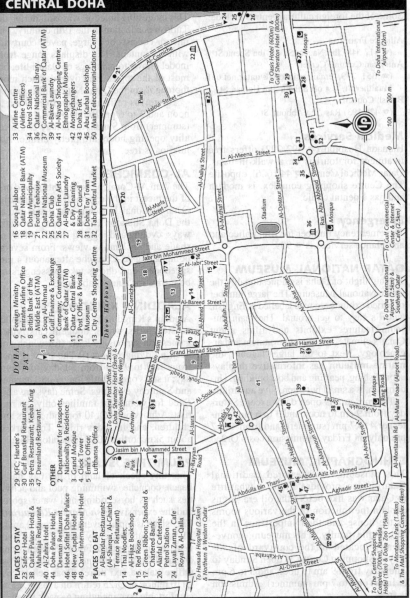

PLACES TO STAY
23 Safeer Hotel
38 Qatar Palace Hotel &
   Maharaja Restaurant
40 Al-Zahra Hotel
44 Doha Palace Hotel;
   Desman Restaurant
46 Hotel Sofitel Doha Palace
48 New Qatal Hotel
49 Qatar International Hotel

PLACES TO EAT
1 Al-Bandar Restaurants
   (Al-Sharqui, Al-Gharbi &
   Terrace Restaurant)
14 Thai Noodles;
   Red Rose
15 Al-Hilaz Bookshop
17 Green Ribbon; Standard &
   Chartered Cafeteria;
   Petrol Station
20 Alantal Cafeteria;
24 Layali Zaman, Cafe
   Royal & Al-Qalla

OTHER
2 Department for Passports,
   Nationality & Residence
3 Grand Mosque
4 Clock Tower
5 Emir's Office;
   Lufthansa Office

29 KFC; Hardee's
30 Gulf Broasted Restaurant
35 Petra Restaurant; Kebab King
47 Dreamland Restaurant

6 Foreign Ministry
7 Emirates Airline Office
8 British Bank of the
   Middle East (ATM)
9 Souq Al-Ahmad
10 Gulf Finance & Exchange
   Company; Commercial
   Bank of Qatar (ATM)
11 Qatar Central Bank
12 Post Office & Postal
   Museum
13 City Centre Shopping Centre

16 Souq al-Jabor
18 Qatar National Bank (ATM)
19 Doha Municipality
21 Forda Teahouse
22 Qatar National Museum
25 Qatari Fine Arts Society
27 Al-Rayes Laundry
   & Dry Cleaning
28 British Council
31 Doha Toy Town
32 Tabri Central Market

33 Airline Centre
   (Airline Offices)
34 Petrol Station
36 Qatar National Library
37 Commercial Bank of Qatar (ATM)
39 Al-Baker Laundry
41 Al-Nayad Shopping Centre;
   Ethnographic Museum
42 Moneychangers
43 Doha Fort
45 Abu Karbal Bookshop
50 Main Telecommunications Centre

QATAR

Cultural Centres

Some of the foreign cultural centres include:

Alliance Française
(☎ 417 548) Ibn Naeem St, off Ibn Seena St
American Cultural Center
(☎ 351 279, email usisdoha@qatar.net.qa)
Muaither St, just off Suhaim bin Hamad St
British Council
(☎ 426 193) Ras Abu Abboud St

Medical Services

Hamada Hospital (☎ 392 222) offers free treatment for tourists on a walk-in basis. Qatar Medical Centre (☎ 440 606), opposite The Centre shopping complex, is modern and has a dental clinic.

Emergency

The emergency number for fire, police and ambulance services is ☎ 999.

QATAR NATIONAL MUSEUM

The highlight of Doha is unquestionably the Qatar National Museum. The large number of varied exhibits are well labelled in English, and it's easy to get around. The main museum features exhibits and films about Qatar's climate, history, environment and archaeology. Next to the large 'lagoon', the **marine museum** has informative displays about fishing, pearling and boat building. Underneath, is a small but impressive **aquarium**.

The museum is open daily except Saturday from 9 am to noon and 3 to 6 pm (winter) or 4 to 7 pm (summer); and from 4 to 7 pm only on Friday. Admission costs Qr2.

ETHNOGRAPHIC MUSEUM

This museum, in a restored traditional Qatari house, provides a look at what life in Qatar was like before the oil era. Signs explain the function of the various rooms in the house and their importance in the life of the family. The museum, conveniently located in the courtyard of Al-Nayad Shopping Centre, is open Sunday to Thursday from 9 am to noon and 3 to 6 pm (winter) or 4 to 7 pm (summer). Admission is free.

DOHA FORT

This interesting little fort was built during the Turkish occupation in the 19th century. The interior consists of a large, paved courtyard with a fountain. The displays range from model dhows to paintings of Qatari life, but most of the topics are covered much more thoroughly in the Qatar National Museum.

The fort is officially open from 9 am to noon and 3 to 6 pm (winter) and 4 to 7 pm (summer) from Sunday to Friday but in reality opening hours are pretty erratic. Admission is free.

AL-CORNICHE

The 7km Al-Corniche is delightful, and one of the nicest in the region. It starts opposite Qatar National Museum and peters out at the Doha Sheraton Hotel. There are walkways, cycling and jogging tracks, plenty of shade and enchanting views. From several points along Al-Corniche after about 4 pm, speedboats and dhows take passengers on boat trips for a negotiable fare.

ALADDIN'S KINGDOM

Aladdin's Kingdom (☎ 831 001) has a roller coaster, ferris wheel, dodgem cars, video games and serious go-karts (for which you need a driving licence!). The park is open from 3.30 to 9 pm from Sunday to Thursday; it stays open a little longer on Thursday and Saturday evenings. Some days are allocated for women or families only, so ring first. Admission is Qr40 for both adults and children, and includes rides. The park is about 5km north of Doha Sheraton Hotel.

PALM TREE ISLAND

This tiny speck of land in the bay has a beach, corniche, swimming pool and activities such as horse riding and water sports, and the expensive *Fish Market Restaurant*. The island is 'open' every day from 9 am to 11 pm. Boats currently leave from a spot next to an American Fried Chicken stand along Al-Corniche and near the General Post Office (take a taxi there). Boat tickets cost Qr10 return; or Qr25 return on a faster, more comfortable boat including a snack lunch.

PLACES TO STAY

See under Visa & Documents in the Facts for the Visitor section earlier for a list of hotels that sponsor visas. No budget hotels in Doha will accept foreigners or sponsor visas.

PLACES TO STAY – MID-RANGE

All of the rooms at these hotels have aircon, a TV (normally satellite), fridge and private bathroom (with hot water).

New Capital Hotel (☎ 445 445, fax 442 233, Al-Musheireb St) is the cheapest place in town for anyone who craves a swimming pool and needs a sponsor. Singles/doubles are good value for Qr125/150 but look a little dated. The hotel is clean, comfortable and central.

Safeer Hotel (☎ 353 999, fax 353 888, Al-Mathaf St) is close to Qatar National Museum. It has large, well-furnished rooms for Qr130/180 and is very good value.

Qatar International Hotel (☎ 361 222, fax 442 413, Al-Musheireb St) is reasonable, but the rooms for Qr120/150 are musty.

Qatar Palace Hotel (☎ 421 515, fax 321 515, Al-Asmakh St) has large, well-furnished and quiet rooms in a central location for Qr176/220.

Doha Palace Hotel (☎ 4360 101, fax 423 955, email dpalace@qatar.net.qa, Al-Musheireb St) is probably the best in this range. It has helpful staff and plenty of comfortable rooms for Qr150/180 in a noisy but convenient location.

PLACES TO STAY – TOP END

Doha Sheraton Hotel (☎ 854 444, fax 832 323) is incredibly opulent but inconvenient. Single/doubles cost a whopping Qr1170/1287, but the management will negotiate a little. It's still worth a visit for the location and views.

Oasis Hotel (☎ 24 424, fax 327 096, Ras Abu Abboud St) is large, has nicer views and is better value than the nearby Gulf Sheraton (on the same street). The rooms in the Oasis could do with some renovation but they're well-furnished and cost Qr350/470.

Ramada Hotel (☎ 417 417, fax 410 941) at the intersection of Salwa and C Ring roads is an unmistakable orange building. It's luxurious, close to The Centre shopping complex and costs Qr643/761.

PLACES TO EAT
Snacks

There are several western fastfood outlets at the intersection of C Ring and Salwa roads; and in The Centre and The Mall shopping complexes. The cheapest places for a snack are the cafeterias, such as *Alanfal Cafeteria*, along Al-Corniche. One of the best *bakeries* is in The Centre shopping complex.

Street Food

In the older part of the city, just south of the Postal Museum, there are a few cheap Indian/Pakistani places. *Thai Noodles* is small, popular and serves interesting Middle Eastern versions of Thai cuisine.

Restaurants

Desman Restaurant (Abdul Aziz bin Ahmed and Al-Musheireb Sts) offers good, cheap Chinese and Indian food.

Red Rose (☎ 413 807, Al-Jabr St) is a pleasant surprise. The cool, if a little dark, restaurant upstairs has a wide range of Chinese, Indian, Filipino and western food. Soup costs Qr7, and Chinese dishes about Qr10.

Petra Restaurant (☎ 412 720, Ras Abu Abboud St) sells excellent felafel sandwiches (Qr3) and very tasty roast chicken. *Kebab King* (☎ 444 215) next door is clean and good value. *Gulf Broasted Restaurant* serves tasty burgers (Qr6 to Qr8), and chicken meals (from Qr12).

Caravan Restaurant (☎ 412 277) on the corner of Salwa and C Ring roads has great buffets (about Qr40). *Green Ribbon* (Abdullah bin Jasim St) is of a similar standard for a la carte, but is not open for lunch.

Layali Zaman (☎ 351 413) is the extraordinary place at the southern end of Al-Corniche. The restaurant is expensive, but the adjoining *Cafe Royal* is a pleasant place to enjoy (cold or hot) drinks, snacks and views.

Al-Bandar is an atmospheric collection of restaurants at the end of the jetty. It includes the outdoor and cheaper *Terrace*

Restaurant, where burgers cost Qr12, pizzas Qr18 and seafood a lot more.

ENTERTAINMENT

Check the 'Events' sections in the two English-language daily newspapers to find out what's going on.

Cinema

Two cinema complexes show modern, western films: Gulf Cinema on C Ring Rd, and one in The Mall shopping complex. Tickets cost about Qr15.

Theatre

Qatar National Theatre (☎ 831 250) along Al-Corniche in northern Doha, sometimes features Arabic plays. Doha Players stage impressive shows at its small theatre on Ar-Rayyan al-Jedid Rd. British Council also sometimes sponsors shows from the UK.

Bars & Nightclubs

Hotel bars are normally only open to guests and 'members' (who pay 'membership' of about Qr100 per year). One of the few nightclubs that serves alcohol and is open to the general public is *Al-Qalla*, in the Layali Zaman building along Al-Corniche.

Arabic Teahouses

Forda Teahouse along Al-Corniche, has views, simple meals and hot and cold drinks in a reasonably authentic atmosphere.

SHOPPING

The 'souqs' are disappointing: they're just a small, western-style, air-con and undercover collection of shops. The two main shopping complexes are The Centre on Al-Musheireb St and The Mall on D Ring Rd. The Central Market on Salwa Rd (about 4km south-west of The Centre) has a range of fresh fruit, vegetables, meat and fish.

GETTING THERE & AWAY

Doha international airport (☎ 622 999 for inquiries) has offices for Gulf Air (☎ 455 444) and Qatar Airways (☎ 621 681). Many airlines have offices in the Airline Centre

on Ras Abu Abboud St, and As-Saad Plaza, on C Ring Rd south of the city centre.

GETTING AROUND
To/From the Airport

If you have arranged your visa with a top end hotel, it should provide free transport to and from the airport. A taxi between the airport and central Doha costs about Qr10; up to Qr20 if you don't persuade the driver to use the meter.

Taxi

There are lots of taxis in the city, but don't forget to gently persuade the driver to use the meter.

Around Qatar

ASH-SHAHHAINIYA

Ash-Shahhainiya is a good place to see camels roaming around the desert, and to see **camel races** in the purpose-built stadium. If you have a car – a 4WD is not necessary – it's more fun to drive along the 18km race-track during the race. Check the two English-language daily newspapers for race times.

The village and stadium are well sign posted from the main Doha to Dukhan road.

AL-WAKRAH

Al-Wakrah and the village of Al-Wukair have several interesting **mosques** and **traditional houses**. Al-Wakrah also has a small **museum**, which keeps unpredictable hours: officially 8 am to noon and 3 to 6 pm from Sunday to Friday. Behind the museum are the **ruins** of what is thought to be a palace.

There are some good **beaches** south of Al-Wakrah, and along the coast between Al-Wakrah and Mesaieed, plenty of flamingos come to roost during winter.

Al-Wakrah is easy to reach by car from Doha; follow Al-Matar Rd past the airport.

MESAIEED

Mesaieed (formerly known as Umm Said) is an industrialised region but it does boast some of the best beaches in Qatar.

Sealine Beach Resort (☎ 772 722, fax 772 733) is wonderfully located on a pleasant beach and near some awesome sand dunes and it's a great base from which to explore Khor al-Adaid (see the following section). Ring for current rates, and ask about any special offers.

Mesaieed is easy to reach by car from Doha; follow the road past the airport and through Al-Wakrah.

KHOR AL-ADAID

Understandably touted as the major attraction in Qatar this 'inland sea' is actually a huge lake jutting into the desert and surrounded by awesome sand dunes. The best time to go is in the late afternoon but to really appreciate the changing landscapes between day and night camp overnight or go on an organised tour (see the Getting Around section earlier in this chapter).

However, this region is *only* accessible by 4WD, and independent travellers should accompany someone who knows the area, and can really drive a 4WD. From Doha, head towards Salwa for about 60km, and look for the turn-offs to Khor al-Adaid. You can also do a day trip from Sealine Beach Resort in Mesaieed (see the previous section).

UMM SALAL MOHAMMED

This small town has a **fort** but it's normally only open when someone is around to unlock the door (mornings are your best bet). Near the fort is a small **mosque** with an old minaret that has been restored to its original state. Umm Salal Mohammed is the first town north of Doha. To the fort, drive through, and then past, the town for about 1.5km, and look for the signs. If in doubt, ask for directions.

UMM SALAL ALI

This field of very old **grave mounds** probably dates from the 3rd millennium BC and is worth visiting if you haven't seen the more impressive collections in Bahrain. A small mound field lies just north of the town and more mounds are scattered among the buildings in the town centre. Umm Salal Ali is easy to reach from along the main road north from Doha.

AL-KHOR

Al-Khor is a pleasant town with a nice Corniche. The small **museum** has some archaeological and cultural artefacts from the region, but is often closed. A number of old **watchtowers** are scattered around the town; several have been restored to their original form. From the old mosque, the **view** of the ocean is splendid.

Ain Helaitan Restaurant & Coffeeshop and *Pearl of Asea*, both along the Corniche, serve decent food.

Al-Khor is easy to reach from Doha. Along the road into Al-Khor, follow the signs to the Corniche. The road then passes the museum and mosque, about 700m farther along the coast.

AL-KHOR GARDENS

The new Al-Khor Gardens are a pleasant respite from the unending desert landscape. It has plenty of greenery, several places to eat and a children's playground. The main turn-off to the gardens is about 2km north of the turn-off to Al-Khor along the main highway from Doha. Admission is free.

AL-ZUBARA

Al-Zubara occupies an important place in Qatari history, and was a large commercial region in the 18th century. All that remains is a fort, which has been restored and converted to the **Al-Zubara Regional Museum**. It has some mildly interesting exhibits of archaeology and pottery, and some bleak **views** from the towers.

Admission is free, but the caretaker offers a small pamphlet, with limited information in English, and expects a 'donation' (Qr1 to Qr2 is enough). The museum is open from 9 am to noon and 3 to 6 pm (winter) and 4 to 7 pm (summer) daily except Saturday.

The fort is at the intersection of a road from Doha and Ar-Ruweis. From Doha, follow the signs; from Ar-Ruweis, follow the road to Abu Dhalouf, and keep going.

Saudi Arabia

Arabia has intrigued travellers for centuries. Vast and mostly arid, it is the cradle of the Islamic religion, the Arab race and the Arabic language – a language considered holy by Muslims. Today's Saudi Arabia retains that mystique, in part because it is so incredibly difficult to visit. Yet, contrary to popular belief, the kingdom has an abundance of attractions. Even more intriguingly, Saudi Arabia offers the traveller the rare opportunity of exploring a country where tradition and modernity are still working out how to accommodate one another.

Facts about Saudi Arabia

HISTORY

A general history of the Middle East can be found in the Facts about the Region chapter.

Until the 18th century the history of what is now Saudi Arabia is largely the history of the coastal regions. In the Gulf this history goes as far back as any yet recorded. Parts of what is now eastern Saudi Arabia were first settled in the 4th or 5th millennium BC by migrants from what is now southern Iraq. The best known of the western Arabian kingdoms was that of the Nabataeans. At one point their empire, which thrived in the 1st century BC, stretched as far north as Damascus.

In the early 18th century the Al-Saud, the royal family of modern Saudi Arabia, were the ruling sheikhs of the oasis village of Dir'aiyah, near modern Riyadh. What is now called the First Saudi empire grew from an alliance, cemented circa 1744, between Mohammed bin Saud, the ruler of Dir'aiyah, and Mohammed bin Abdul Wahhab (born 1703), a preacher who espoused a simple, unadorned and strict form of Islam. The result of this was Wahhabism, the back-to-basics religious movement which remains the official form of Islam in Saudi Arabia today.

The Kingdom of Saudi Arabia

Area: 1,960,600 sq km
Population: 20.8 million
Population Growth Rate: 3.4%
Capital: Riyadh
Head of State: King Fahd ibn Abdul Aziz al-Saud
Official Language: Arabic
Currency: Saudi Riyal (SR)
Exchange Rate: US$1 = SR3.75

- **Best Dining** – if you're going cheap Alkhobar, in the Eastern Province, is the place to be for both quality and selection. Asian food is especially good and plentiful. If money is no object when dining out, head for Jeddah.

- **Best Shopping** – Najran, in the south-west corner of the country is the best place to shop for Bedouin jewellery.

- **Best Walk** – Jeddah's Old City; there is no better place in the kingdom to wander for a few hours.

- **When in Rome ...** try to visit the huge camel market outside Riyadh or the more remote weekly Bedouin market at Nairiyah. A morning in either place will tell you a lot more about traditional Saudi life than a month in a Saudi city.

Mohammed bin Abdul Wahhab's religious fervour and Mohammed bin Saud's military skill proved to be a potent combination which outlived its two founders. After conquering and converting to Wahhabi doctrine most of the tribes of Najd (north-central Arabia), the Saudi-led forces swept out across the peninsula. By 1806 they controlled most of the territory of today's kingdom of Saudi Arabia as well as a large section of what is now southern Iraq.

None of this went down well in Constantinople as western Arabia was, at least in theory, part of the Ottoman empire. An expedition to retake Arabia was launched in 1812. The Saudis were driven back to Dir'aiyah, which fell in 1818.

The Al-Saud family's revival began in 1902 when Abdul Aziz bin Abdul Rahman al-Saud (often called Ibn Saud in the west) recaptured Riyadh from the Al-Saud family's traditional rivals, the Al-Rashids, beginning a string of conquests that built the modern kingdom of Saudi Arabia.

In 1933 Abdul Aziz granted an oil concession to Standard Oil of California (Socal, the precursor of today's Chevron). Oil was found in commercial quantities in 1938 and by 1950 the kingdom's royalties were running at about US$1 million per week. By 1960, 81% of the Saudi government's revenues came from oil.

Under King Faisal Saudi Arabia was a central player in the 1973-74 Arab oil embargo. In its wake the price of oil increased fourfold and Faisal, who controlled 30% of OPEC's overall production, became a force to be reckoned with on the world stage. Between 1973 and 1978 the country's annual oil revenues went from US$4.35 billion to US$36 billion. A building boom began: money poured into utility and infrastructure projects and construction of a petrochemical industry commenced.

Faisal, however, did not live to see it. In 1975 he was assassinated by a nephew, who was said to have been deranged. He was succeeded by his half-brother, Khaled, with another half-brother, Fahd, as crown prince.

It is difficult today to appreciate the extent to which Saudi Arabia was modernised during King Khaled's reign (1975-82). Most accounts of Riyadh and Jeddah in the late 70s describe the cities in terms of huge construction sites. The physical growth of these cities was staggering. For example, in the early 70s Riyadh's old airport, which today appears to be fairly close to the centre, was well outside the city.

In the late 70s everyone seemed to be making easy money. Some Saudis, however, were troubled by the outside influences flooding into the kingdom. This tension in Saudi society became clear in November 1979 when some 300 radicals seized control of the Grand Mosque in Mecca. It took government troops 10 days to retake the mosque, an operation in which over 250 people died.

What to See

Saudi Arabia's best known sites are the Muslim Holy Cities of **Mecca** and **Medina**. These, however, are strictly closed to all non-Muslims. The country's most famous archaeological site is **Madain Salah**, the remote area of Nabataean ruins in the country's north-west.

If you are not Muslim, and do not have the time to travel to Madain Salah, make Jeddah's **old city** your top priority. There are several fine examples of houses built of coral from the Red Sea, and a vibrant souq that blends the ancient and the modern.

The south-west offers two attractions worth going out of your way for: the mountain city of **Abha** is the gateway to the often-dramatic **Asir National Park**. Further south, **Najran**, near the Yemeni border, is one of the kingdom's undiscovered gems.

The Friday camel market at **Nairiyah** is a long but worthwhile side trip – at least four hours each way (by car) from either Riyadh or Dhahran.

SAUDI ARABIA

King Khaled died in June 1982 and his half-brother, Fahd, became the fourth of Abdul Aziz's sons to rule Saudi Arabia. Fahd was well prepared for the job. Khaled's health had long been poor and for much of his reign Fahd, then crown prince, had been king in all but name.

Saudi Arabia Today

As the 1990s drew to a close Saudi Arabia's politics were dominated by two things: King Fahd's increasingly fragile health and the long term security of the Al-Saud monarchy.

Meanwhile, internal challenges to the Saudi monarchy are increasing. In late 1995 a bomb went off outside a Riyadh office used by the US military, and in mid-1996 a huge truck bomb exploded near a housing complex in the Eastern Province used by both US and Saudi troops. These incidents highlight the continuing controversy surrounding the western military presence in the kingdom.

Saudi Arabia's challenge is not unique in the Gulf, but because of the country's size it may be the most difficult to face. The days of easy oil money are now a fond memory. The country's population is growing rapidly (the average Saudi woman bears 6.38 children), and two generations of generous public assistance have not inculcated the country's youth with a strong work ethic. Government payrolls are swelled by employees who often have little to do, while private businesses (both local and foreign) often find it cheaper to hire their staff from overseas.

The late 1990s saw the first, tentative opening of the country to a select number of high-end tour groups. But lingering problems with internal dissidents have led the government to approach change even more cautiously than in the past. Many of the government's harshest critics believe it is too liberal and want to see the country purged of all western influences.

GEOGRAPHY

Saudi Arabia is about 1.96 million sq km in area, most of it desert. Western Saudi Arabia is dominated by a mountain chain running the entire length of the country and

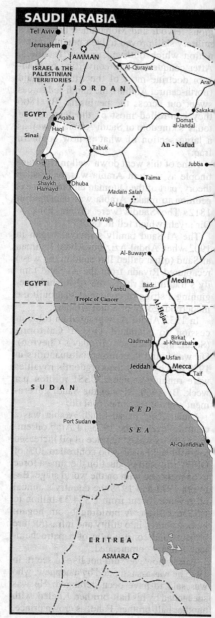

SAUDI ARABIA

Tel Aviv
Jerusalem
AMMAN
ISRAEL & THE PALESTINIAN TERRITORIES
Al-Qurayat
Arar
JORDAN
EGYPT
Aqaba
Haql
Sinai
Sakaka
Domat al-Jandal
An - Nafud
Tabuk
Jubba
Ash Shaykh Hamayd
Dhuba
Taima
Madain Salah
Al-Ula
Al-Wajh
Al-Buwayr
Medina
EGYPT
Yanbu
Badr
Tropic of Cancer
Al-Hejaz
Qadimah
Birkat al-Khurabah
Usfan
Jeddah
Mecca
Taif
SUDAN
RED
Port Sudan
SEA
Al-Qunfidhah
ERITREA
ASMARA

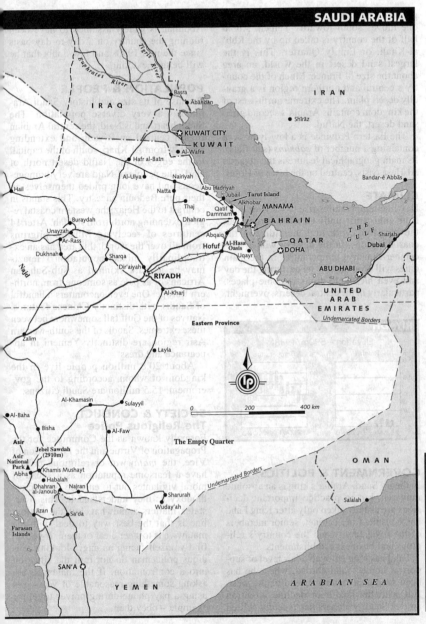

SAUDI ARABIA

IRAQ

IRAN

Euphrates River

Tigris River

Basra

Ābādān

Shīrāz

KUWAIT CITY

KUWAIT

Al-Wafra

Hafr al-Batn

Al-Ulya

Nairiyah

Abu Hadriyah

Bandar-é Abbās

Hail

Natta

Thaj

Tarut Island

Jubail

Alkhobar

MANAMA

Qatif

Dammam

BAHRAIN

Buraydah

Dhahran

Unayzah

Abqaiq

THE GULF

Sharjah

Ar-Rass

Hofuf

Al-Hasa Oasis

QATAR

Dubai

Dukhnah

Sharqa

Uqayr

DOHA

Dir'aiyah

RIYADH

ABU DHABI

Al-Kharj

UNITED ARAB EMIRATES

Najd

Undemarcated Borders

Zalim

Eastern Province

Layla

Al-Khamasin

Sulayyil

Al-Baha

Bisha

Al-Faw

The Empty Quarter

OMAN

Asir

Jebel Sawdah
(2910m)

Asir National Park

Khamis Mushayt

Abha

Habalah

Undemarcated Borders

Dhahran al-Janoub

Najran

Salalah

Jizan

Sharurah

Farasan Islands

Sa'da

Wuday'ah

SAN'A

YEMEN

ARABIAN SEA

0   200   400 km

SAUDI ARABIA

generally becoming higher and broader as one moves south towards Yemen. About half of the country is taken up by the Rub' al-Khali, or Empty Quarter. This is the largest sand desert in the world, an area about the size of France. Much of the country's central and northern region is a gravelly desert plain. The extreme north-west of the kingdom contains Arabia's second great sand desert, the Nafud.

The Eastern Province is a low-lying area containing a number of *sabkhas* (salt flats). Its main geographical feature is the gigantic Al-Hasa oasis, centred on the town of Hofuf.

CLIMATE
Daytime temperatures rise to 45°C or more from mid-April until October throughout the kingdom, with high humidity in the coastal regions. In the dead of winter (December-January) temperatures in the main cities will drop into the teens during the day and even hit single digits in some places, particularly in the central deserts, overnight.

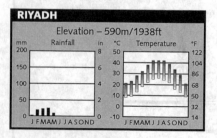

RIYADH
Elevation – 590m/1938ft

GOVERNMENT & POLITICS
In theory Saudi Arabia's king is an absolute monarch, but in practice important decisions are usually taken only after King Fahd has consulted the cabinet, senior members of the royal family and the country's religious and business establishments.

Fahd has long enjoyed a fair level of support at home – and abroad, where he has been seen as a staunch friend of the west. But with his health in decline attention among Saudi-watchers has recently shifted

to his half-brother, Crown Prince Abdullah. Abdullah is widely assumed to have been running the country on a day-to-day basis since the mid-1990s and few doubt that he will be the next king.

POPULATION & PEOPLE
Because of its size and history Saudi Arabia has a very diverse population. The Saudi heartland is Najd, the central Arabian region centred on Riyadh and extending roughly from Al-Kharj, south of the capital, to the edges of the Nafud desert north of Hail. The people of Najd are very homogeneous and have long prided themselves on their pure Bedouin ancestry. This stands in contrast to the Hejaz, the western coastal region extending north from Jeddah. After 14 centuries of receiving Muslim pilgrims from all over the world, this area has an extraordinarily mixed population. Hejazis may be as dark skinned as sub-Saharan Africans or as pale as someone from northern Europe. One even encounters a handful of Saudis with distinctly Chinese features. Natives of the Gulf fall somewhere between these extremes. Saudis of the south-western Asir region are distinctly Yemeni in appearance and dress.

About 20.8 million people live in the kingdom of whom, according to the government, 15.5 million are Saudi citizens.

SOCIETY & CONDUCT
The Religious Police
Formally known as the Committee for the Propagation of Virtue and the Prevention of Vice, the *matawwa*, or religious police, have a fearsome reputation as a squad of moral vigilantes out to enforce Islamic orthodoxy as they understand it. This overstates matters somewhat, but the bottom line is that the best way to deal with the matawwa is to steer clear of them. If you do find yourself facing an angry-looking religious policeman do not turn the situation into a confrontation. If the matawwa are asking something reasonable of you – not using a pay phone during prayer time, for example – obey them.

RELIGION

Most Saudis are Sunni Muslims who follow the Wahhabi sect of Islam. The country's Shi'ite minority constitutes between five and 10% of the population. Most of the Shi'ite live in the Eastern Province, where they may account for as much as a third of the population. There are also small Shi'ite communities in the Asir region, near the Yemeni border.

LANGUAGE

Arabic is the official language of Saudi Arabia. English is the universal language of commerce in the kingdom and you should have no trouble getting by with it in all of the main cities and towns.

Facts for the Visitor

PLANNING

The best time to visit is between November and February when the climate is mild. The Asir mountains are at their best a bit earlier and a bit later than the rest of the country – during the winter they are often locked in fog.

The best maps of Saudi Arabia are those drawn by Zaki Mohammed Ali Farsi, commonly known as the Farsi Maps. They are available at most bookshops and hotels in the kingdom for about SR20 each.

VISAS & DOCUMENTS
Visas

Saudi Arabia has a well-deserved reputation as one of the hardest places in the world to visit. Tourist visas are not issued. Your options consist of visitor's or transit visas and, for Muslims, *haj* and *umrah* visas.

To obtain a visitor visa (ie a business visa) you must have a Saudi sponsor. This can be a company or individual. The sponsor obtains permission for you to enter the country, is issued a visa number and passes this number on to you. You then go to the Saudi embassy or consulate and get the visa. If you do not have a visa number do not bother going to the embassy. No number, no visa. If you show up with the number in the morning, you can usually pick up your visa the same afternoon. Visitor visas can be picked up at any Saudi diplomatic mission, though the pick-up site has to be specified when the visa application is filed by the sponsor in the kingdom.

The 24 and 48-hour transit visas are for people passing through Saudi airports. These are issued by Saudi embassies after you have shown them your airline tickets and convinced the embassy that when purchasing these tickets you had absolutely no choice other than an overnight transit in Saudi Arabia.

People driving between Jordan and either Kuwait or Yemen are usually issued three-day transit visas. People driving between Jordan and Bahrain or the United Arab Emirates (UAE) often get seven-day transit visas. As a general rule these are only issued in the countries that actually border Saudi Arabia. You have to go to the embassy with your carnet and proof that you already have a visa for the country at the other end of the road. In theory it is possible to hitch a ride on any of these routes, though in practice you probably will not get a transit visa unless you are already attached to a vehicle. Check your visa carefully as it may contain restrictions concerning the route you are allowed to take through the kingdom.

From the first of Ramadan each year Saudi embassies in Muslim countries issue only haj visas until the haj is over about three months later. There's no longer a ban on issuing visas to people whose passport contains an Israeli stamp, but this could cause you problems with some border guards who may not be aware of the new regulations.

A final note: all official business in Saudi Arabia is conducted according to the Muslim Hejira calendar. Any Gregorian date you see on a document is there solely for the foreign community's convenience. A visa valid for a one month stay is valid for a Hejira month, not a Gregorian month. If you stay for a month according to the western calendar you will have overstayed your visa by a day or two – and you will be in trouble.

Travel Letters

Foreigners living in the kingdom need permission from a sponsor to travel outside the city they reside in. In practice this is only enforced between provinces. Foreigners on a visitor visa can travel with only a passport.

Site Permits

To visit virtually any fort, ruin or archaeological site in the kingdom you must first obtain a permit. Permits for all sites are issued by the Department of Antiquities office at the Riyadh Museum. Permits for the Eastern Province outside Al-Hasa oasis can be obtained at the Regional Museum of Archaeology & Ethnography in Dammam.

In Riyadh you have to file the application one morning and return a day or two later to collect the permit. In Dammam they can often issue permits the same day provided you arrive before 10 am. Resident foreigners will have to bring their *iqama*, or residence permit, and, if the site involves a trip to a province other than the one where they live, a travel letter. People in the country on a visitor visa require only a passport.

Once you get to the place you plan to visit you may have to take the permit to the local branch of the antiquities office.

EMBASSIES & CONSULATES
Saudi Embassies & Consulates

For Saudi embassies and consulates in the Middle East, see individual country chapters.

Australia
  (☎ 06-286 2099)
  12 Culgoa Circuit, O'Malley, Canberra 2606 ACT
UK
  (☎ 020-7235 0303)
  30 Belgrave Square SWIX
USA
  (☎ 202-342 3800)
  601 New Hampshire Ave NW, Washington DC, 20037

Embassies & Consulates in Saudi Arabia

All of the following embassies are in Riyadh's Diplomatic Quarter. The best idea

if you need to visit one of these places is to call the embassy and ask for directions, for which it helps to be good with national flags.

Australia	(☎ 488 7788)
Bahrain	(☎ 488 0044)
Canada	(☎ 488 2288)
France	(☎ 488 1255)
Germany	(☎ 488 0700)
Ireland	(☎ 488 2300)
Kuwait	(☎ 488 3500)
New Zealand	(☎ 488 7988)
Qatar	(☎ 482 5544)
UAE	(☎ 482 6803)
UK	(☎ 488 0077)
USA	(☎ 488 3800)

The Omani embassy (☎ 482 3120) is located in the Al-Ra'id District, behind the petrol station opposite the main gate of King Saud University

There are also a few consulates in Jeddah. The UK consulate (☎ 654 1811) is off Al-Andalus St, one block east of the Sheraton Al-Bilad Hotel, in the Al-Shate'e district. The British also handle diplomatic matters for citizens of Canada, Australia and New Zealand in Jeddah. The US consulate (☎ 667 0080) is on Falasteen St.

CUSTOMS

The import of anything containing alcohol or pork is strictly forbidden. Customs officers also pay close attention to any books, magazines or photographs you are carrying. Videotapes are often held at the airport for a day or two for screening by censors. Anything deemed pornographic (which, in Saudi Arabia, could include vacation photos of your family and friends at the beach) or politically sensitive may be confiscated.

MONEY
Costs

While Saudi Arabia isn't cheap, it is possible to travel there relatively cheaply if you put your mind to it. Filling your stomach for SR15 (US$4) or less is never a problem. Beds generally bottom out at SR8 (US$2.50) in youth hostels, SR55 to SR90 (US$15 to

US$24) in hotels. It is possible to cross the peninsula for less than SR200 (US$53). Travelling around the kingdom can be done on about SR50 (US$13) a day, though SR100 (US$26) is a more realistic low-budget estimate (SR200 if you don't stay in the youth hostels).

Currency

The Saudi riyal (SR) is divided into 100 halalas. It is a hard currency and there are no restrictions on its import or export. Notes come in one, five, 10, 50, 100 and SR500 denominations. Coins come in five, 10, 25 and 50 halala and SR1 denominations.

Exchange Rates

The riyal is pegged to the US dollar, so while the US$/SR rate rarely moves by more than a halala or so either side of SR3.75, the rates against other western currencies change constantly.

Australia	A$1	=	SR2.46
Canada	C$1	=	SR2.54
euro	€1	=	SR3.88
France	10FF	=	SR5.90
Germany	DM1	=	SR1.98
Japan	¥100	=	SR3.51
New Zealand	NZ$1	=	SR2.00
UK	UK£1	=	SR6.05
USA	US$1	=	SR3.75

Exchanging Money

Moneychangers are among some of the kingdom's larger banking operations and can usually offer slightly better rates than the banks.

Changing travellers cheques can be a pain in the neck. Many banks and money changers either will not take them, will only change brands they sell or will only cash them for account holders. You should always carry your original purchase receipt with you as the few places that will change travellers cheques won't consider touching them without it.

ATMs linked to the major international cash-machine networks are easy to find in all of the main cities.

Tipping & Bargaining

Tips are not generally expected in restaurants. However, the service charge added to your bill is not an automatic tip but goes straight into the till. Most waiters are paid very little and a few extra riyals would certainly be appreciated.

In Saudi Arabia the price of almost anything is negotiable up to a point. Outside of a Bedouin market, however, bargaining frequently means asking for a discount and being offered it. After that initial offer the price may not go much lower.

POST & COMMUNICATIONS
Post

Airmail letter postage to addresses outside the Arab world is SR1.50 for the first 10g and SR1 for each additional 10g. Postcard postage is SR1.

Sending Mail

The queues in Saudi post offices tend to be rather long, especially at the end of the month when many foreign workers are sending their salaries home to their families.

Receiving Mail

There are no poste restante facilities and American Express (Amex) does not hold mail. The best approach is to find a sympathetic friend who will let you get mail through his or her company, or to make do without.

Telephone

Saudi Arabia has an excellent telecommunications system. Almost every town has a telephone office through which international calls can be made.

The country code for calls to Saudi Arabia is ☎ 966 plus the area code for the individual city. Telephone codes for some of the main cities are:

Abha	☎ 07
Dammam	☎ 03
Hail	☎ 06
Hofuf	☎ 03
Jeddah	☎ 02
Najran	☎ 07

Riyadh	☎ 01
Sakaka	☎ 04
Taif	☎ 02

Fax

In addition to the telephone centres, you can send faxes from the business centres in most big hotels and from some of the larger copy shops. The latter offer a much better deal.

BOOKS

Richard Burton's *Personal Narrative of a Pilgrimage to Al-Madinah & Meccah*, originally published in 1855, is one of the few accounts of the Holy Cities written by a non-Muslim. A more recent Arabian travel classic is Wilfred Thesiger's 1959 memoir *Arabian Sands* in which he recounts his two journeys across the Empty Quarter in the late 1940s. You might also want to look for *At the Drop of a Veil* by Marianne Alireza, a Californian who married into the Jeddah-based merchant family in the 1940s. The best work on modern Saudi Arabia is Robert Lacey's *The Kingdom* though it only carries the country's history up through the mid-1980s.

NEWSPAPERS & MAGAZINES

The *Arab News* and *Saudi Gazette* are the country's main English-language newspapers. Major foreign newspapers and magazines are widely available in the kingdom's main cities. Periodicals usually appear two or three days after publication, by which time they have received a very thorough going-over by Saudi censors.

RADIO & TV

Channel 2 of Saudi Arabian TV broadcasts exclusively in English, except for a French-language newscast every night at 8 pm. The programs are a mixture of old and heavily edited American shows and locally made documentaries and talk shows. In the Eastern Province you can also receive Channel 3 – the Aramco television station. It tends to be a more up-to-date version of Channel 2.

Many hotels, even small ones, also have satellite television.

PHOTOGRAPHY & VIDEO

Film is easy to find in main cities, but check that it has not passed its expiry date. There are numerous shops specialising in one- or two-hour photo processing, but most of them handle only colour prints. Slides or B&W film tend to take a lot longer and the results are often less than satisfactory.

HEALTH

The standard of health care in Saudi Arabia is very high and almost any ailment can be treated inside the country. Many diseases which were once endemic, such as malaria, are now virtually unknown. Though a cholera shot and a gamma globulin booster might not be a bad idea if you are planning to spend a lot of time far off the beaten track, there are no special precautions which need to be taken before visiting Saudi Arabia.

The quality of drinking water varies greatly; on the whole you should probably stick to bottled water.

WOMEN TRAVELLERS

Men and women are strictly segregated in Saudi society and, as time goes by, things seem to be getting more, not less, strict. Restaurants which do not have a family section often will not serve women and there has been a trend in recent years to bar women entirely from some smaller shops and fast-food outlets. Women are not allowed to drive and unaccompanied women may not travel by intercity bus or train.

An unaccompanied woman cannot check into a hotel without a letter from her sponsor, and it would probably also be a good idea for the sponsor to contact the hotel in advance. Saudi Arabia's youth hostels are entirely off-limits to women.

Strictly speaking, it is not necessary for a foreign woman to wear the *abeyya* (a long, black cloak-like garment) and a floor-length skirt but, in practice, it's usually a good idea. In the main cities there is no need for foreign women to cover their heads. In more remote or conservative areas (Hail, Najran, Sakaka, Tabuk) it is advisable for foreign women to cover their heads. Women who are, or appear to be, of Arab descent are likely to be held to far tighter standards of dress than western or Asian women, especially outside the main cities.

DANGERS & ANNOYANCES
Saudi Arabia is a very safe country and street crime is almost unknown. Petty theft, particularly things being stolen out of cars, is sometimes a problem in the cities.

The main thing that you will have to worry about is the rather frightening way that people drive. As a rule the driving gets crazier as one moves farther west.

BUSINESS HOURS
Banks and shops are open from 8 or 8.30 am until 1 or 1.30 pm Saturday to Wednesday. Many shops, and some banks, reopen in the afternoon from about 4 to 7 pm. Big shopping centres, particularly in Riyadh, Jeddah and Alkhobar, may stay open until 10 pm. Few businesses are open on Thursday afternoons and almost everything is shut up tightly on Friday.

At prayer time *everything* closes; even Saudia airlines stops answering its telephone numbers for reservations. The length of the prayer break can be anything from 20 minutes to an hour. If you are already inside a restaurant and eating, the staff may let you hang around and finish your meal, or they may throw you out.

PUBLIC HOLIDAYS & SPECIAL EVENTS
Wahhabism is so strict on matters of observance that no holidays other than Eid al-Fitr and Eid al-Adha are observed in the kingdom. Saudi National Day is 23 September though it is not widely observed.

The kingdom's only cultural and folkloric festival, the Jinadriyah National Festival, takes place every February at a special site about 45km north-east of central Riyadh.

ACCOMMODATION
Saudi Arabia's youth hostels (*beit ash-shabab* in Arabic) are excellent and, at SR8

per night, very cheap. The down side is that they are open only to men. Saudi Arabia is a Hostelling International (HI) member and hostel cards are always required.

Saudi law requires the presentation of proper documents to check in at any hotel or hostel. For visitors this means a passport. Expatriates will require their iqama and a travel letter from their sponsor. Small hotels and youth hostels often will ask you to go out and make a photocopy of these documents if you did not arrive with xeroxes in hand. Women travelling alone need a letter from their sponsor to check into any hotel.

FOOD
Grilled chicken, *fuul* and *shwarma* are the most common cheap dishes. For more up-market dining, every large city has a selection of moderately priced Asian restaurants. Filipino and Thai food are the cheapest and Chinese food tends to be the most expensive. This is because there are many more low-paid Filipino and Thai workers than Chinese in the kingdom.

DRINKS
Saudi Arabia is 'dry' so beverages consist of soft drinks, mineral water and fruit juice. 'Saudi Champagne', which you will sometimes see on menus and which can generally be ordered by name, is a mixture of apple juice and Perrier.

SHOPPING
Among the best buys is silver Bedouin jewellery. The *souqs* of Khamis Mushayt and Najran have the best selection, and a few shops in Riyadh and Jeddah also carry a good range.

If you have a lot of space in your luggage, woven Bedouin bags make great souvenirs. Prices, after bargaining, range from SR50 to SR1000, depending on the size and the quality of the work. The best place to look for weavings is the Hofuf souq or the weekly camel market in Nairiyah.

Most of the other souvenirs you will see in shops – incense burners, for example – come from somewhere else, usually Pakistan.

Getting There & Away

AIR

Saudia (Saudi Arabian Airlines) flies to dozens of cities in Europe, the USA and Asia and to just about every place worth mentioning in the Middle East. Riyadh, Jeddah and Dhahran airports are also served by most of the major European carriers, a few Asian airlines and the major carriers from the subcontinent (Air India, PIA etc). There are also a handful of international flights to and from Medina (Medina airport is open to non-Muslims).

The cheapest way into Saudi Arabia is often via Egypt or Jordan. It's generally best to arrive with an onward or return ticket because one-way travel out of Saudi Arabia is often more expensive than purchasing a round-trip ticket to the same destination.

There is an airport fee of SR50 per person for international flights. The fee does not apply to domestic air travellers.

LAND

There are regular daily buses from Dammam/Alkhobar to Bahrain. It is also easy to get a bus from any of the major cities to Egypt, Jordan, Syria or Turkey. On all routes (except Turkey) SAPTCO, the Saudi Arabian bus company, competes with foreign companies. Generally SAPTCO has the best fares and the best-maintained buses.

SEA

The car ferry connecting Jeddah with Suez is the main sea route in and out of the country. There are also regular passenger services from Jeddah to Safaga (Egypt), Port Sudan and to Musawwa (Eritrea). See the Jeddah section for details and fares.

Getting Around

AIR

All domestic air services in the kingdom are operated by Saudia, which is quite reliable.

The most frequent and efficient service is on the Jeddah-Riyadh-Dhahran corridor. Considering the distances involved, Saudia's domestic services, though no great bargain, are reasonably priced. See the individual city listings for information on direct air connections to and from each city. You can also stop by any Saudia office for an up-to-date timetable.

BUS

Getting around by bus is probably your best bet if you are not pressed for time and do not have a car. Bus fares are one-half to two-thirds of the equivalent airfare. Buses are operated by SAPTCO, which has comfortable, air-con buses that usually run on time. You can buy bus tickets only on the day of departure or one day in advance. When purchasing tickets you will also have to show identification and, for residents, a travel letter.

TRAIN

Saudi Arabia has the only stretch of train track in the entire Arabian peninsula – one line from Riyadh to Dammam, via Hofuf and Abqaiq. Trains leave three times a day in each direction every day except Thursday, when there is only one train. See the relevant city entries for fares.

TAXI

Service taxis usually cluster around the bus station in each city and cover most of the destinations the buses go to at the same prices. They leave when full, which could mean anything from five to 11 passengers, depending on the size of the vehicle.

CAR

Driving in Saudi Arabia is on the right. Petrol is cheap but, contrary to what you may hear, it is not virtually free. Saudi Arabia is a very car-oriented society, and getting petrol is never a problem. If the road is sealed, there will be a petrol station sooner or later. That said, it is obviously important to watch your fuel gauge on any serious cross-desert drive.

Rental

If you are in the country on a visitors visa you can rent a car on a driving licence from most western countries. Rental rates are government controlled with insurance and the collision-damage waiver mandatory. Rates start at SR110 for a Toyota Corolla or similar. That includes insurance and 100 free kilometres per day. Additional kilometres are 40 halalas each. A discount of 20, 25 or 30% on this price is almost always available for the asking.

HITCHING

Hitching is common in the kingdom among less well-off Saudis and Indians, Pakistanis, Filipinos etc. It is rare enough among westerners that anyone trying it would be likely to attract the unwelcome attention of the first policeman who happened by. In the Hejaz and Asir regions, hitchers are usually expected to pay the equivalent of the bus fare along the same route.

Riyadh

While Riyadh, and the nearby oasis town of Dir'aiyah, are the ancestral home of the Al-Saud family, it is only in the last generation that Riyadh has become the kingdom's centre of government. Though technically Saudi Arabia's capital since the nation's establishment in 1932, it was eclipsed by Jeddah until quite recently; the ministries, embassies and just about everything else were headquartered in Jeddah well into the 1970s.

Orientation

The first thing you should do is learn the names of the main districts. Al-Bathaa is the central, older portion of town; immediately adjacent are Masmak, Al-Murabba and Al-Wazarat. North of these areas lie Olaya and Suleimaniyya, the main residential and business areas for the capital's business community.

To the extent that Riyadh has any centre at all it is Al-Bathaa, more or less the area around Al-Bathaa St and Al-Malek Faisal St, which is also called Al-Wazir St, between Al-Washem and Tariq ibn Ziyad Sts. The bus station, GPO and everything else a traveller needs, however, are around Al-Bathaa, and it's the cheapest part of town.

Informal names are commonly used for some of Riyadh's main streets. These include (formal name first):

Al-Malek Abdul Aziz St:	Old Airport Rd
Al-Malek Faisal St:	Al-Wazir St
Al-Amir Soltan ibn Abdul Aziz St:	Tallateen St
Salah ad-Din al-Ayyubi St:	Sitteen St
Al-Imam Faisal ibn Torki ibn Abdulla St:	Al-Khazan St
Al-Ihsa St:	Pepsi Cola St

Information

Money Riyadh has no shortage of banks. A good place to start looking is along Olaya St between the Al-Khozama Hotel and Makkah Rd. They all change money, as do the various moneychangers in Olaya and Al-Bathaa.

Amex is represented by Ace Travel (☎ 464 8813) on Makkah Rd near the junction with Al-Ma'ther St. It's open from 9 am to 1.30 pm and from 4.30 to 8 pm Saturday to Thursday, closed Friday. Cheques are cashed for card holders through a nearby bank. The Amex clients' mail service is not available.

Post The GPO, on Al-Malek Abdul Aziz St, near the intersection with Al-Bathaa St, is open from 7.50 am to 2.50 pm and from 4 to 10.30 pm Saturday to Wednesday, closed Friday.

Telephone There are several sets of international call cabins around the city. The most central ones are by the Al-Foutah Garden at the intersection of Al-Dhahirah and Al-Imam Faisal ibn Torki ibn Abdulla Sts. There are also call cabins on Jareer St, near the intersection with Salah ad-Din al-Ayyubi St.

Bookshops The best selection of English, French and German books is at the Jarir Bookstore. They have two branches in Riyadh. One is on Olaya St just south of the

RIYADH

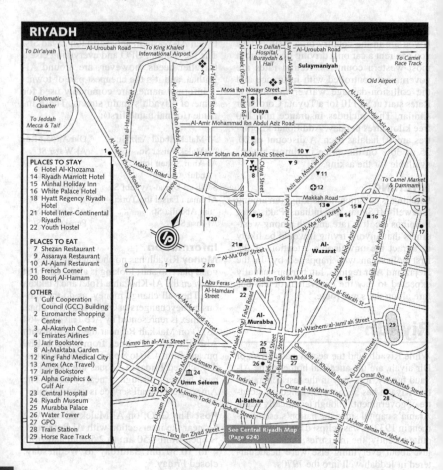

PLACES TO STAY
6 Hotel Al-Khozama
14 Riyadh Marriott Hotel
16 Minhal Holiday Inn
16 White Palace Hotel
18 Hyatt Regency Riyadh Hotel
21 Hotel Inter-Continental Riyadh
22 Youth Hostel

PLACES TO EAT
7 Shezan Restaurant
9 Assaraya Restaurant
10 Al-Ajami Restaurant
19 French Corner
20 Bourj Al-Hamam

OTHER
1 Gulf Cooperation Council (GCC) Building
2 Euromarche Shopping Centre
3 Al-Akariyah Centre
4 Emirates Airlines
5 Jarir Bookstore
8 Al-Maktaba Garden
12 King Fahd Medical City
13 Amex (Ace Travel)
17 Jarir Bookstore
19 Alpha Graphics & Gulf Air
23 Central Hospital
24 Riyadh Museum
25 Murabba Palace
26 Water Tower
27 GPO
28 Train Station
29 Horse Race Track

intersection with Mosa ibn Nosayr St, the other is on Al-Ihsa St in Al-Malaz District.

Medical Services Though Riyadh has an abundance of hospitals many of the best known ones are either reserved for the royal family, the military or some other class of VIP, or they are highly specialised. The Dallah Hospital (☎ 454 5277) at the intersection of King Fahd Rd and Al-Imam Saud ibn Abdul Aziz ibn Mohammad Rd takes emergency cases on a walk-in basis.

Things to See

Riyadh Museum Start your tour of Riyadh at the museum in the Department of Antiquities office on Al-Imam Abdul Aziz ibn Mohammed St in the Umm Seleem district, near the Central Hospital. It's open from 8 am to 2 pm Saturday to Wednesday and admission is free.

The displays in the main hall are well laid out with signs in both English and Arabic. These cover the history and archaeology of the kingdom from the Stone Age to early Islam. The galleries are particularly thorough on geography and archaeology. The last room of the exhibit has an interesting display on Islamic architecture. There is also a separate Ethnographic Hall.

Masmak Fortress This was the citadel in the heart of Old Riyadh that Abdul Aziz took in January 1902 to regain control of the city. During the raid one of the future king's companions heaved a spear at the door with such force that the head is still lodged in the doorway (look just to the right of the centre panel of the small door set into the main door). The fortress is built of dried mud. It is now used as a museum honouring Abdul Aziz. Masmak is open from 8 am to noon and from 4 to 8 pm Saturday to Wednesday. Sunday and Tuesday are for families only. Admission is free and permits are not required.

Murabba Palace This combination fortress and palace was built by King Abdul Aziz in 1946. It's open from 8 am to 2 pm Saturday to Wednesday.

King Faisal Centre for Research & Islamic Studies The King Faisal Centre has a gallery of manuscripts and Islamic art in its complex behind the Hotel Al-Khozama in Olaya. The Centre usually has an exhibit focusing on some aspect of Islamic art or culture, though not always. Admission is free.

King Saud University Museum King Saud University, on the western edge of Riyadh near the Diplomatic Quarter, has a small museum displaying finds from the university's archaeological digs at Al-Faw and Rabdhah. The museum is open from Saturday to Wednesday mornings, but to visit it you must first make an appointment through the university's public relations office (☎ 467 8135).

Camel Market Around 30km from the centre on the outskirts of the city is one of the largest camel markets in the Middle East. Trading is heaviest in the late afternoon. To reach the market take the Dammam Rd to the Thumamah exit – the last one before the road heads off east across the desert.

Al-Thumairi Gate On Al-Malek Faisal St, near the Middle East Hotel, this is an impressive restoration of one of the nine gates which used to lead into the city before the wall was torn down in 1950. Across the street, opposite the hotel, is the New al-Thumairi Gate, a more modern structure vaguely resembling a triumphal arch.

Places to Stay

Youth Hostel (☎ 405 5552) is on Shabab al-Ghansani St, a sidestreet between Al-Malek Fahd Rd and the junction of Al-Amir Sa'ad ibn Abdul Aziz and Abu Feras al-Hamdani Sts in the Al-Namodhajiyah District. Beds are SR8. The hostel is not on any bus route nor is it within walking distance of the bus station.

The cheap hotels are all clustered in the vicinity of the bus station. The prices quoted here include the service charges, where applicable. In most cases it should be possible to bargain SR10 to SR15 off the quoted price, particularly if you are staying for more than a few days.

Middle East Hotel (☎ 411 1994) on Al-Malek Faisal St is a bit out of the way but certainly the cheapest place in town after the youth hostel. Singles/doubles cost SR45/75 (none with private bath). The rooms are very small and a bit cramped and the toilet is nothing to write home about. Still, the price is hard to beat.

Cairo Hotel (☎ 401 4045) on Abu Ayyub al-Ansari St, just off Al-Bathaa St, is drab but clean though some of the rooms are windowless. The central location makes up for some of this. Rooms are SR65/100 with bath.

West of Al-Bathaa St there are several good-value hotels along Al-Imam Faisal ibn Torki ibn Abdulla St (Al-Khazan St).

Al-Rawdah Hotel (☎ 412 2278) has rooms for SR66/99 with bath. Across the street *Al-Medina Hotel* (☎ 403 2255) charges SR55/83 though none of their singles have attached baths.

SAUDI ARABIA

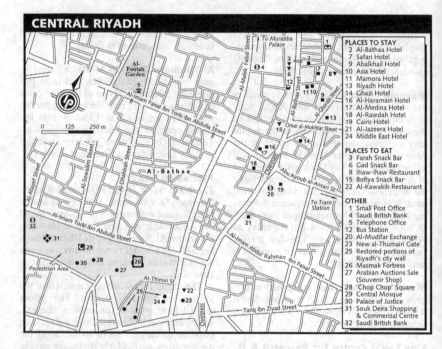

CENTRAL RIYADH

PLACES TO STAY
2 Al-Bathaa Hotel
7 Safari Hotel
9 Abalkhail Hotel
10 Asia Hotel
11 Mamora Hotel
13 Riyadh Hotel
14 Ghazi Hotel
16 Al-Haramain Hotel
17 Al-Medina Hotel
18 Al-Rawdah Hotel
19 Cairo Hotel
21 Al-Jazeera Hotel
24 Middle East Hotel

PLACES TO EAT
3 Farah Snack Bar
6 Gad Snack Bar
8 Ihaw-Ihaw Restaurant
15 Bofiya Snack Bar
22 Al-Kawakib Restaurant

OTHER
1 Small Post Office
4 Saudi British Bank
5 Telephone Office
12 Bus Station
20 Al-Mudifar Exchange
23 New al-Thumairi Gate
25 Restored portions of
   Riyadh's city wall
26 Masmak Fortress
27 Arabian Auctions Sale
   (Souvenir Shop)
28 'Chop Chop' Square
29 Central Mosque
30 Palace of Justice
31 Souk Deira Shopping
   & Commercial Centre
32 Saudi British Bank

Hotel Alrajehi (☎ 412 3557), up an alley behind the Al-Rawdah Hotel, is a bit more upmarket at SR80/120 for rooms with bath, including breakfast. This is a particularly good value.

Al-Haramain Hotel (☎ 404 3085), on Al-Bathaa St, has clean rooms with TV for SR77/116 with bath, SR66/99 without.

Mamora Hotel (☎ 401 2111), on Al-Bathaa St (the entrance is on a small side-street around the corner), is a good option if you're looking for something a bit more upmarket in the Al-Bathaa area. Rooms are an excellent value at SR80/120 for singles/doubles. Another good mid-range option is *Safari Hotel* (☎ 405 5533) parallel to Al-Bathaa St. Singles/doubles are SR100/140 though you might be able to talk them down a bit. The Safari would be a good choice for a married couple or a family with children.

Places to Eat

The area around the bus station is packed with small coffee shops, shwarma stands and restaurants. A meal, usually consisting of a half chicken and a huge pile of rice, costs between SR7 and SR10. Near the Middle East Hotel and the Thumairi Gate you will find *Al-Kawakib*, a particularly good place for roasted chicken and rice. Half a chicken with a big plate of rice costs SR8. Back on Al-Bathaa St try *Bofiya Snack Bar* for good, quick snacks (shwarma, juice etc). The sign is in Arabic but look for the orange and yellow stripes. Another good place for shwarma, pastries and something that resembles pizza is *Farah*, on Al-Bathaa St just across from the Al-Bathaa Hotel. Look for a sign in Arabic with red and white lettering and a picture of a hamburger.

Gad is a similar place nearby; there's also a larger and swisher version of it in

Olaya just off Al-Amir Soltan ibn Abdul Aziz St, near the King Faisal Centre.

There are several dozen places selling cheap Filipino food on the streets behind the Al-Bathaa Hotel. Try *Ihaw-Ihaw* a couple of short blocks in along the street separating the Al-Bathaa and Safari hotels. Their 'budget lunch' consisting of rice, one selection from their cafeteria line and a drink is a bargain at SR7.

Al-Amir Soltan ibn Abdul Aziz St (Tallateen St) in Olaya is a good place to look for affordable food of all types. Good, cheap Lebanese food can be had at *Al-Ajami Restaurant*, a cafeteria style eatery just over 1km east of the intersection with Olaya St. Mezze cost SR5 to SR10 apiece and kibbeh can be ordered by the piece at SR2 each.

A notch up the scale is *Assaraya*, a popular Turkish restaurant on Al-Amir Soltan ibn Abdul Aziz St. Excellent kebabs cost SR12 to SR15. It's highly recommended.

French Corner on Al-Amir Abdul-Aziz ibn Mosa'ad ibn Jalawi St is the Riyadh branch of a popular kingdom-wide chain. They have good coffee, a wide selection of pastries for SR5 to SR7 and full, but generally unimpressive, meals for SR20 to SR40.

Shopping

Spices, and occasionally woven-items, can be found if you wander deep into the Souq al-Bathaa. The best place in Riyadh to buy Yemeni silver and other Arabian souvenirs is Arabian Auctions Sale, near the Masmak Fortress. A number of smaller shops dealing in (mostly imported) souvenirs are located in and around Thumeiri St, near the fortress.

Getting There & Away

Air King Khaled international airport is a long way from the city – nearly 40km from Al-Bathaa. Saudia's main reservations office is at the intersection of Al-Amir Torki ibn Abdul-Aziz (Al-Thani) St and Olaya St far to the north of the centre.

Riyadh is Saudia's base of operations and there are frequent flights to just about everywhere in the kingdom. Sample one-way economy-class fares include: Jeddah SR270, Dhahran and Hofuf SR140, Gassim (Buraydah) SR130, Hail SR190, Taif and Medina SR240, Abha and Najran SR270, Tabuk SR380.

Bus The bus station just off Al-Bathaa St is SAPTCO's intercity depot. You'll need identification to buy a ticket and the queues tend to be long. Unaccompanied women are not allowed to travel by bus.

There are 11 buses every day to Jeddah (SR130, 13 hours) via Taif (SR100, 10 hours). These buses go around Mecca and are OK for non-Muslims. If you are a non-Muslim bound for Jeddah it would be prudent to double-check that the routing has not changed.

Other routes include: 11 daily to Dammam (SR60, 4½ hours); three daily to Hofuf (SR45, four hours) with an extra bus on Thursday. To Buraydah (SR60, 4½ hours) there are nine buses every day. There are three buses per day to Hail (SR100, eight hours), ten daily to Abha (SR125, 13 hours), two daily to Jizan (SR160, 18 hours), three daily to Najran (SR115, 12 hours), two daily to Tabuk (SR200, 17 hours), and two daily to Sakaka (SR175, 14 hours).

For Muslims only, buses leave for Mecca (SR115, 10 hours) five times per day and for Medina (SR140, 12 hours) three times daily.

International service is available to Egypt, Syria, Jordan and Turkey. SAPTCO and a number of foreign companies serve all of these routes. The foreign companies all have offices around the bus station, can usually undercut SAPTCO's price, and might throw in a few meals as well. The Amman and Cairo routes are particularly competitive. On the other hand, SAPTCO's buses are often newer and may be more comfortable. Expect to pay around SR350 to SR400 to Cairo, SR200 to Damascus or Amman and SR260 to İstanbul. SAPTCO will also sell you a through ticket to Bahrain (SR100) or Abu Dhabi (SR195), but these routes require a change of bus in Dammam if you're going to Bahrain and in Hofuf if you are headed to the UAE.

Train The train station (☎ 473 1855) is on Al-Amir Abdul Aziz ibn Abdullah ibn Torki St, 2.5km east of the bus station. Trains leave for Dammam via Hofuf and Abqaiq three times daily, except Thursday when there is only one train. Fares in 1st/2nd class are SR60/40 to Dammam, SR52/34 to Abqaiq and SR45/30 to Hofuf.

Car Rental Prices are fixed by the government. Expect to pay SR110 per day, including insurance, for the smallest cars available (usually Toyota Corollas) from all the companies. With whatever discount they are offering at the time that should drop the net price to SR90 to SR100. Most big hotels also have a car hire desk and you can find a number of car hire offices along Olaya St near the Al-Khozama Hotel.

Service Taxi These leave from the SAPTCO station, though, in general buses are a better bet than service taxis. Expect to pay SR150 to Jeddah, SR60 to Buraydah, SR70 to Dammam, SR55 to Hofuf and SR120 to Hail. All service taxis leave when they are full. Most carry either five or seven passengers.

Getting Around

To/From the Airport There is no bus service to King Khaled international airport. The buses and minibuses marked 'Airport' go to the old airport via Al-Malek Abdul Aziz St. Your only option is a taxi, which could cost anything from SR30 to SR70, depending on where in the city you start. From the airport the white limos have a set tariff of SR50 or SR60 to most districts in the city though a few of the areas closer to the airport are only SR45.

Bus SAPTCO buses and privately run minibuses cover most of the city. Fares on either are SR2. Routes are posted on the front of the bus (the signs on the minibuses are in Arabic only).

Taxi There are two kinds of taxis: white-and-orange and yellow cabs. In both cases a flag-drop is SR3 after which the meter ticks over in 50 halala increments at SR1 per kilometre. The drivers in the white cabs are more likely to speak English.

AROUND RIYADH
Dir'aiyah

Riyadh's most interesting site is outside the city. On the capital's northern outskirts, about 30km from Al-Bathaa, lie the ruins of Dir'aiyah, the first capital of the Al-Saud clan and the kingdom's most popular and easily accessible archaeological site (no permits required). The site is open from 7 am to 6 pm Saturday to Thursday and from 1 to 6 pm on Friday. Admission is free.

To reach Dir'aiyah from Riyadh, leave the city centre following the signs for the airport. Once you're on the expressway to the airport look for signs for Dir'aiyah. Once you exit the expressway you should see the ruins in the distance to your left. Follow the road until you reach a T-junction. Turn left, and left again when you reach a roundabout. Go straight, and look for the small white signs indicating a right turn to reach the ruins.

If you can find it, *Dir'aiyah*, by Stevie Wilberding & Isabel K Cutler, contains some excellent photographs, a good historical essay on the city and three 30 to 60-minute walking tours of the site. It used to be widely available but has become difficult to find in Riyadh's bookshops.

Najd (Central Region)

HAIL

Hail (pronounced Hay-El), 640km northwest of Riyadh, was formerly the seat of the Al-Rashid family, the Al-Saud clan's most formidable rivals. It is now the centre of the kingdom's vast agricultural program, and most of Saudi Arabia's wheat crop comes from the surrounding area.

Hail's main street runs north-south and centres on Commercial District Square by the Saudi Hollandi Bank building. Old Hail is roughly east of this street and the newer areas are west of it, except for the Al-Qashalah Fortress. The bus station is at the Al-Qashalah Fortress, three blocks south of Commercial District Square.

Things to See

Before doing any sightseeing your permit has to be validated at the Antiquities Section of the Ministry of Education office in town (ask for *maktab al-athaar*). The office is on the 1st floor and is open from about 8 am to 1 pm Saturday to Wednesday. These are also more or less the hours during which you can visit the sites.

The **Al-Qashalah Fortress**, next to the bus station, was built in the 1930s and was used mostly as a barracks for Abdul Aziz's troops in Hail. The small square building in the courtyard contains a display of artefacts from Hail and the surrounding desert region. **'Airif Fort**, on a hill just outside the centre is much older. It was built about 200 years ago as a combination observation post and stronghold. Also in the centre, on Barazan Square, you can see two restored **towers**, all that remains of another of Hail's palaces.

Places to Stay & Eat

Youth Hostel (☎ 533 1485) is at the stadium, a 20 to 30-minute walk south of the bus station along Hail's main street. Beds are SR8. Alternately, walk into town from the bus station and catch a minibus from the parking lot in front of the Saudi Hollandi Bank building. The fare is SR2.

Hail Hotel (☎ 532 0180, fax 532 7104, *King Khaled St*) has singles/doubles with bath for SR132/170. To reach the hotel walk west from Commercial District Square and turn left at the first set of traffic lights. The hotel will be on your right.

Lahore Restaurant, across from the Hail Hotel, is a decent and clean place with the usual selection of chicken dishes and curries. Another good bet is *Wajabat Srea'a* a small Indian place across from the Al-Bank al-Saudi al-Fransi office, offering cheap samosas (50 halalas apiece) and other quick eats. For shwarma and fresh juice try *Fast*

Food on the Main Rd across from the southern edge of the park.

Getting There & Away

Hail's small airport is south-west of the centre. There are two or three flights a day to/from Riyadh (SR190 one way, economy class), daily service to Jeddah (SR240) and one or two flights a week to Dhahran (SR310).

SAPTCO runs three buses a day to Riyadh (SR100, eight hours) via Buraydah (SR40, four hours). There are daily buses to Medina and Tabuk.

Jeddah

Once a modest port living mostly off the pilgrim trade, Jeddah (Jiddah, Jidda) has evolved into one of the Arab world's most important commercial centres. Within its walls Jeddah occupied about one sq km of land. Today it is approximately one thousand times that size.

Orientation

Everything centres on Al-Balad: the strip of buildings on the coast between the old foreign ministry building and the bus station, and on the old city which lies directly inland from them. Al-Madinah al-Munawwarah Rd (Medina Rd, for short) is the principal street running north from the centre, flanked to the east by Al-Amir Fahd St and to the west by Al-Andalus St.

As in Riyadh, there are a number of streets with commonly used, but unofficial, names. The most important one to know is Al-Amir Fahd St, which is commonly called Sitteen St or King Fahd St. Al-Dahab St is sometimes referred to as King Faisal St. The names of several main streets are commonly anglicised. These include Filasteen St (Palestine St) and Al-Malek Abdel Aziz St (King Abdel Aziz St).

Information

Money There is an Al-Rajhi Banking & Investment Company branch on Al-Malek

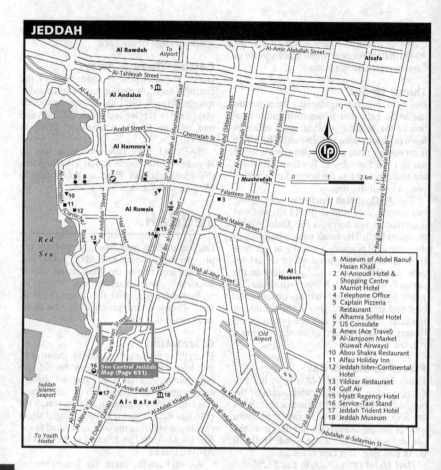

JEDDAH

Al Rawdah
To Airport
Al-Amir Abdallah Street
Alsafa
Al-Tahleyah Street
Al Andalus
1
Arafat Street
Ghernatah St
Al Hammra'a
2
Mushrefah
Falasteen Street
9 8
7
6
5
3
10
11
Al Ruwais
12
13
14 15
Bani Malek Street
Red Sea
Wali al-Ahd Street
Al Naseem
Old Airport
See Central Jeddah Map (Page 631)
16
Jeddah Islamic Seaport
Al-Amir Fahd Street
17
18
Al-Balad
Ba Kahshab Street
Makkah al-Mukarramah Rd
To Youth Hostel
Abdallah al-Sulayman St
Al-Madinah al-Munawwarah Road
Al-Amir Fahd (Sitteen Street)
Al-Makarounah Street
Majed Street
Al-Amir Street
Khaled ibn al-Walid Street
Ring Road Expressway (Al-Haramain Road)
Al-Andalus Street
Al-Kournaish Road
Hail Street
Corniche
Ba'ashan Street
Al-Falah Street
Al-Minia Street
Al-Dahab (Zahab) St
Al-Malek Khaled Street
Al-Al-Murtadi St

0   1   2 km

1 Museum of Abdel Raouf Hasan Khalil
2 Al-Amoudi Hotel & Shopping Centre
3 Marriot Hotel
4 Telephone Office
5 Captain Pizzeria Restaurant
6 Alhamra Sofitel Hotel
7 US Consulate
8 Amex (Ace Travel)
9 Al-Jamjoom Market (Kuwait Airways)
10 Abou Shakra Restaurant
11 Alfau Holiday Inn
12 Jeddah Inter-Continental Hotel
13 Yildizar Restaurant
14 Gulf Air
15 Hyatt Regency Hotel
16 Service-Taxi Stand
17 Jeddah Trident Hotel
18 Jeddah Museum

Abdel Aziz St opposite the Shaheen Hotel, and a Saudi British Bank branch in the shopping arcade at the Red Sea Palace Hotel. There are a large number of money-changers along Al-Qabel St in Al-Balad between Al-Malek Abdel Aziz St and the tunnel that goes underneath Al-Dahab St.

Amex is represented by Ace Travel (☎ 665 1254), on Filasteen St near the intersection with Al-Hamra St. They can replace lost and stolen cards and cash personal cheques for Amex clients but will not hold mail. The of-

fice is open from 9 am to 1.30 pm and 4.30 to 8 pm Saturday to Wednesday. They are open on Thursday only during the morning hours, closed Friday.

Post The GPO is the large red-and-white building opposite the bus station, between Ba'ashan and Al-Bareed Sts. The entrance is on the Al-Bareed St side of the building. The GPO is open from 7.30 am to 9.30 pm Saturday to Wednesday. On Thursday only the Mumtaz Post (express mail) windows are open from 7.30 am to 2 pm. The post office is closed on Friday.

Telephone The telephone office is on Abu Bakr al-Siddiq St in the Al-Sharafiyya district, south of the Filasteen St intersection.

Things to See & Do

Jeddah Museum Jeddah's Regional Museum of Archaeology and Ethnography is in an awkward location near the Al-Khozam Palace and the Islamic Development Bank. The displays are quite similar to those at the Riyadh Museum. The museum is open from 8 am to noon Saturday to Wednesday, admission is free.

Walking Tour & Old City Walls Many of Jeddah's sites lie along the course of the old city walls, which were torn down in the late 1940s. The walls ran along Al-Malek Abdel Aziz St, Makkah al-Mukarramah Rd and Ba'najah St. A circuit of these streets should take under an hour on foot.

Along the route are the three reconstructed city gates – all that remains of the wall. Near the North City Gate are several good examples of traditional Jeddah architecture in various states of preservation. Many of the older houses within the old city walls are constructed not of stone but of coral quarried from reefs in the Red Sea.

The Shorbatly House Just east of the North City Gate, this house is one of the best known examples of the city's traditional architecture. In the immediate area around it you will see several other old houses, also in various states of repair.

Municipality Museum The museum is in the restored traditional house opposite the National Commercial Bank's headquarters building. It is open from 7.30 am to 1.30 pm Saturday to Wednesday. Admission is free, but you must first make an appointment with the curator (☎ 642 4922).

The house, which is approximately 200 years old, is the only surviving building of the WWI-era British Legation in Jeddah. TE Lawrence stayed at the Legation when he visited in 1917. Like many Jeddah buildings of that era it is built of coral quarried from the Red Sea. A photographic display at the far end of the entrance hall includes aerial photographs of Jeddah in 1948, 1964 and 1988, dramatically illustrating the city's growth.

The Naseef House Along the old city's main thoroughfare, Souq al-Alawi, stands one of the city's most famous houses. The Naseefs are one of Jeddah's old-line merchant clans. The larger of the two trees to the left of the house's front door was, as recently as the 1920s, the only tree in all of Jeddah and thus an indicator of the family's wealth and importance.

Al-Shafee Mosque The Al-Shafee mosque, near the centre of Al-Balad, is one of the oldest in the city. The easiest way to reach it is to enter the souq near Bab Makkah.

The Museum of Abdul Raouf Hassan Khalil This private museum really has to be seen to be believed. It contains over 10,000 items crammed into four 'houses' that look like the sort of mock-Arab buildings you might expect to see at Disney World. The museum is open from 9 am to noon and from 5 to 9 pm Saturday to Thursday, closed Friday. Admission is SR20.

Though signs in various parts of Jeddah point to the museum, actually finding it can be a bit tricky. Take either Al-Madinah al-Munawwarah Rd or Al-Andalus St to Tahleyah St. Turn off Tahleyah St on to Ibrahim al-Jufali St (if you are starting from Al-Madinah al-Munawwarah Rd this will require a U-turn). Go 500m and turn right onto Al-Madani St. Take the first left, and then turn right onto Al-Mathaf St. The museum will be on the right after about 150m.

Organised Tours Red Sea Palace Hotel (☎ 642 8555) offers a 1½ hour city tour at 10 am every Friday for SR25. You do not have to be staying in the hotel to take the tour. Telephone the concierge for reservations or further information.

SAUDI ARABIA

Places to Stay

Youth Hostel (☎ 688 6692) is at the stadium, 12km east of the city centre on the Mecca Expressway. Beds are SR8 per night. The hostel is behind the green buildings of the Sporting City. There is no access by bus. The easiest way to reach it by car is to take exit No 8 from the expressway, *not* the stadium exit which is farther on.

Shaheen Hotel (☎ 642 6582, fax 644 6302), in an alley between Al-Malek Abdel Aziz St and the Corniche Commercial Centre, has long been one of Jeddah's best budget buys. Singles/doubles are SR60/80.

Ba'najah St is a good place for moderately priced beds. **Hotel Makkah** (☎ 647 7439) would probably be a good choice for a couple or a family with children. Rooms with bath cost SR66/100.

Al-Almen Hotel (☎ 648 3953, fax 648 2621), a few doors away, near the intersection with Al-Dahab St also has good rooms, though some of the air-conditioners are old and rather loud. Singles/doubles cost SR88/132 with bath and SR77/115 without.

Tysir Hotel (☎ 647 7777) has rooms with bath for SR100 single or double.

A bit more upmarket are **Al-Marwa Hotel** (☎ 643 2650, fax 644 4273) at SR94/140 and **Atlas Hotel** (☎ 643 8520, fax 644 8454) at SR90/135, opposite each other on Al-Dahab street.

Places to Eat

There are a lot of cheap places in the centre, one, however, stands out from the rest: **Al-Falah**, a cafeteria near the Saudia office on Al-Malek Abdel Aziz St. They offer Arab staples like humous (SR5) and a wide range of Chinese and Filipino dishes at SR10 to SR15 as well as burgers and pizza. The clientele is as varied as Jeddah's population and the food is always good.

Texas, on Al-Malek Abdel Aziz St, around the corner from the Shaheen Hotel, is another good bet. They have both shwarma and the traditional burgers, fries and fried chicken fast-food menu. There are a couple of cheap Filipino places on the ground floor of the Corniche Commercial Centre.

Lebanese Nights Restaurant is well outside the centre at the intersection of Al-Amir Abdullah and Al-Amir Sultan Sts in North Jeddah but is still a good bet for moderately priced Lebanese food.

One expensive place bears mention. **Al-Alawi Traditional Restaurant**, just off Souq al-Alawi St in the old city. The 'traditional' food is Moroccan, not Saudi, but it's a great place with a nice garden. Main dishes are SR30 to SR45 but you can pay much less by sticking to the appetisers. Try the *harira* (a thick beef and vegetable soup) for SR8.

Entertainment

Ak Wan Restaurant-Coffeeshop, a short distance south of the entrance to the Souq al-Alawi, is one of central Jeddah's better traditional coffeehouses. Also worth trying are **Harat ash-Sham Coffeehouse**, near the footbridge that crosses over Al-Dahab St, and the **Al-Fishawi Coffeehouse**, near the intersection of Al-Dahab St and Maydan al-Bayal.

Shopping

The old city's gold souq is particularly good. The Al-Alawi Traditional Restaurant has a small pottery workshop on the premises. Across a small plaza from the Al-Alawi is a good 'oriental' gift shop called Old Jeddah Arts and Crafts. You can also find a few stalls selling silver jewellery and other souvenirs along Al-Qabel St.

Getting There & Away

Air The King Abdul Aziz International airport is about 25km north of the city on Al-Madinah al-Munawwarah Rd. Saudia flights, both domestic and international, leave from the south terminal. Foreign airlines use the north terminal.

Jeddah is Saudia's second hub, after Riyadh, and you can fly directly from here to pretty much anywhere in the kingdom. There are usually about 10 flights per day to Riyadh (SR270 one way, economy class) and four or five to Dhahran (SR380).

Bus The SAPTCO bus station (☎ 648 1131) is on Ba'ashan St. Thanks to a change in

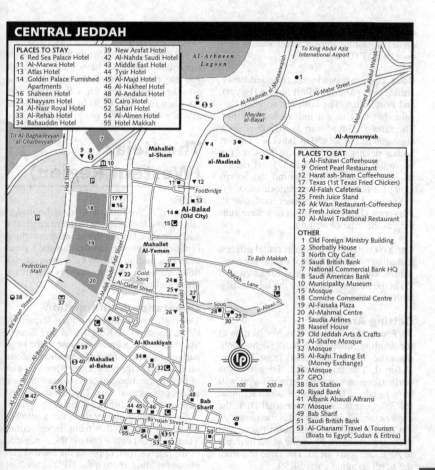

CENTRAL JEDDAH

PLACES TO STAY
6 Red Sea Palace Hotel
11 Al-Marwa Hotel
13 Atlas Hotel
14 Golden Palace Furnished Apartments
16 Shaheen Hotel
23 Khayyam Hotel
24 Al-Nasr Royal Hotel
33 Al-Rehab Hotel
34 Bahauddin Hotel
39 New Arafat Hotel
42 Al-Nahda Saudi Hotel
43 Middle East Hotel
44 Tysir Hotel
45 Al-Majd Hotel
46 Al-Nakheel Hotel
48 Al-Andalus Hotel
50 Cairo Hotel
52 Sahari Hotel
54 Al-Almen Hotel
55 Hotel Makkah

PLACES TO EAT
4 Al-Fishawi Coffeehouse
9 Orient Pearl Restaurant
12 Harat ash-Sham Coffeehouse
17 Texas (1st Texas Fried Chicken)
22 Al-Falah Cafeteria
25 Fresh Juice Stand
26 Ak Wan Restaurant-Coffeeshop
27 Fresh Juice Stand
30 Al-Alawi Traditional Restaurant

OTHER
1 Old Foreign Ministry Building
2 Shorbatly House
3 North City Gate
5 Saudi British Bank
7 National Commercial Bank HQ
8 Saudi American Bank
10 Municipality Museum
15 Mosque
18 Corniche Commercial Centre
19 Al-Faisalia Plaza
20 Al-Mahmal Centre
21 Saudia Airlines
28 Naseef House
29 Old Jeddah Arts & Crafts
31 Al-Shafee Mosque
32 Mosque
35 Al-Rajhi Trading Est (Money Exchange)
36 Mosque
37 GPO
38 Bus Station
40 Riyad Bank
41 Albank Alsaudi Alfransi
47 Mosque
49 Bab Sharif
51 Saudi British Bank
53 Al-Ghanami Travel & Tourism (Boats to Egypt, Sudan & Eritrea)

---

routings, eastbound intercity buses no longer go through Mecca and, therefore, are all open to non-Muslims. Non-Muslim passengers, though, would be well advised to double-check this – it changed once so, presumably, it could change back.

There are 10 buses every day to Riyadh (SR130, 12 hours) via Taif (SR30, 2¾ hours). To Dammam (SR190, 17 hours) there are two direct buses per day, at 4.30 and 9 pm. There are also daily buses to Abha (SR90, nine hours) and Khamis Mushayt (SR90, 9½

hours), Al-Baha (SR60, seven hours), Bisha (SR100, 8½ hours), Jizan (SR100, 12 hours), Najran (SR120, 8½ hours), Yanbu (SR60, 4½ hours) and Tabuk (SR130, 13 hours).

For Muslims only, buses go to Mecca (SR15, 1¼ hours) 16 times a day, and to Medina (SR50, five hours) 21 times per day.

SAPTCO's international services depart from the same terminal as their domestic ones. There are daily buses to Cairo, Amman and Damascus. Buses to İstanbul leave several times per week. International services are also offered by several Turkish bus companies operating from a small station next door to SAPTCO.

Boat You can travel by sea from Jeddah Islamic Port to Suez and Port Safaga (Egypt), and Port Sudan. The fares are no great bargain, but they're not unreasonable either. The fares to Egypt start at SR205 in deck class and run to SR450 in 1st class. To Port Sudan tickets cost SR320 to SR420. Try Al-Aquel Travel (☎ 647 5337), off Ba'najah and Al-Dahab Sts, behind the Sahari Hotel for tickets and more information.

Service is also sometimes available to Mussawa (Eritrea), though none were running at the time of writing.

Car You will find a lot of car rental offices, including outlets of most of the bigger companies, along Al-Madinah al-Munawwarah Rd in the 3km or so north of the intersection with Filasteen St.

Getting Around
To/From the Airport Bus No 20 runs to the south terminal (all Saudia flights, both domestic and international) from Maydan al-Bayal. The fare is SR3. To get to the north (foreign carriers) terminal you will have to take a taxi from the south terminal (SR35). A taxi to either terminal from the centre costs SR30 to SR50 on the meter.

Coming into the centre from the airport there are set tariffs. From the south terminal to Al-Balad costs SR40. The same trip from the north terminal costs SR50.

Bus & Taxi It's best to stick to the orange and white SAPTCO buses for getting around town. Bus trips anywhere in the city are SR2, the sole exception being the airport which costs SR3. Thrifty Tickets (three trips for SR5) can be purchased at the SAPTCO intercity terminal.

Some good routes to know include: No 7 which largely follows the circuit of the old city walls; the airport bus (No 20) which heads up Al-Madinah al-Munawwarah Rd from Maydan al-Bayal and vice versa; and

No 11, a section of which goes back and forth along both Filasteen St and Al-Matar St.

The cabs, which are white with an orange stripe down the side, have meters, though you may have to remind the driver to turn it on. They charge SR3 for a flag-drop. The fare then increases in 50 halala increments at a rate of about SR1 per kilometre.

The Hejaz (Western Region)

TAIF
Taif (Tai'if, Al-Taif), nestled in the mountains above Mecca, is the summer capital of Saudi Arabia. During the summer months it is noticeably cooler than Jeddah and a great deal less humid. The town's main attractions are its weather, its scenery and its relaxed atmosphere.

Orientation & Information
Taif centres on a nameless square formed by the intersection of King Faisal and Shubra Sts. It looks like a square because of the large parking lot across from the Saudi telephone office. Most of the budget hotels are a bit east of this intersection and cheap restaurants are all over the central area. The bus station and airport are some distance north of the centre.

For changing money there are a number of banks around the main intersection. There is a post office just off the south side of the intersection, opposite the Saudi Telephone building, though the GPO is north of town, near the bus station.

Things to See
Abdallah bin Abbas Mosque Taif's central mosque is a good example of simple, refined Islamic architecture. The mosque is named for a cousin of the Prophet who was also the grandfather of the founder of the Abbasid dynasty. Abdullah bin Abbas died in Taif circa 687 AD at the age of 70.

Tailor's Souq One of the few surviving bits of traditional Taif can be found just off the main square at the intersection of Shubra and King Faisal Sts around the corner from the post office. Next to a Turkish restaurant and several small grocery stores is an archway of sand-coloured stone. The short alleyway behind this arch, part of the tailor's souq, is a quick trip into old Taif. At one time much of the city (and many other Middle Eastern cities) consisted of small, alley-like streets of this kind making up the various souqs.

Shubra Palace This beautifully restored house on the edge of the centre doubles as the city's museum. It is open from 7.30 am to 2.30 pm Saturday to Wednesday. Admission is free. The palace itself was built around the turn of the century. The materials used included marble imported from Italy and timber from Turkey. King Abdul Aziz used to stay here when he visited Taif in his later years and it was also used as a residence by King Faisal.

Two other old houses that have also been maintained (sort of) are **Beit Kaki** and **Beit Khatib**, once the summer residences of two of Mecca's leading merchant families.

Places to Stay
Taif is crowded on summer weekends (ie from Wednesday afternoon until Friday afternoon). From May to September reservations are strongly recommended.

Mohammed (570-632 AD)

Mohammed was born in Mecca, a prosperous centre of trade and pilgrimage, into a less well-off branch of the Quraysh, the ruling tribe. His father had died before he was born and his mother died when he was seven, so he was raised by his grandfather and uncle. As a young man he worked as a shepherd and as a merchant's agent. He married at age 25 and had four daughters and two sons. Both of the boys died in infancy. After the death of his first wife he took further wives – perhaps as many as nine.

Mohammed received his first revelation at the age of 40 while meditating in a cave. He began preaching in public three years later in 613, but his verbal assaults on the pagan pilgrim trade – on which Mecca prospered – so angered the local establishment that he was forced to flee to Medina (then called Yathrib).

Over the next eight years Mohammed's following increased dramatically and the Medina-based Muslims fought a series of battles with the Meccan pagans, who eventually surrendered in 630. Mohammed continued to reside in Medina but in 632 he travelled back to Mecca on a pilgrimage, thus establishing the ritual of *haj* that all Muslims follow to this day. He died later that year.

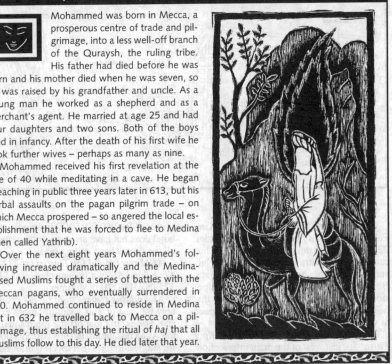

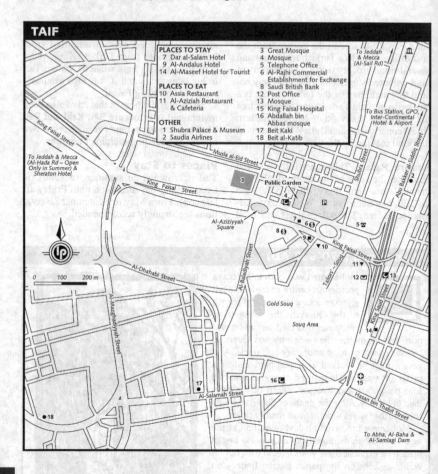

TAIF

PLACES TO STAY
7 Dar al-Salam Hotel
9 Al-Andalus Hotel
14 Al-Maseef Hotel for Tourist

PLACES TO EAT
10 Assia Restaurant
11 Al-Aziziah Restaurant
& Cafeteria

OTHER
1 Shubra Palace & Museum
2 Saudia Airlines
3 Great Mosque
4 Mosque
5 Telephone Office
6 Al-Rajhi Commercial
Establishment for Exchange
8 Saudi British Bank
12 Post Office
13 Mosque
15 King Faisal Hospital
16 Abdallah bin
Abbas mosque
17 Beit Kaki
18 Beit al-Katib

King Faisal Street

To Jeddah & Mecca
(Al-Hada Rd – Open
Only in Summer) &
Sheraton Hotel

Musla al-Eid Street

King Faisal Street

Public Garden

Al-Aziziyyah Square

Al-Dhahabi Street

Al-Baladiyah Street

Al-Muzghadiyah Street

Gold Souq

Souq Area

Talbot – Souq

King Faisal Street

To Jeddah
& Mecca
(Al-Sail Rd)

To Bus Station, GPO,
Inter-Continental
Hotel & Airport

Shubra Street

Abu Bakker al-Siddiq Street

King Saud Street

Al-Salamah Street

Hasan bin Thabit Street

To Abha, Al-Baha &
Al-Samlagi Dam

0   100   200 m

Youth Hostel (☎ 725 3400) is at the King Fahd Sporting City in the Hawiyah district, 22.5km north of the centre. The No 10 bus runs from the centre to the hostel via the bus station and stops about 100m from the gate. Beds are SR8. The hostel is infinitely superior to any of the hotels listed under this heading and is far more likely to have space at weekends.

Dar al-Salam Hotel (☎ 736 0124, *King Faisal St*), just west of the main intersection, is the only real cheapie in town. Singles/dou-

bles are SR40/60 (SR50/70 in summer). The hotel does not have air-conditioning, though all the rooms have ceiling fans.

Al-Maseef Hotel for Tourist (☎ 732 478, *King Saud St*) is a decent choice at SR80/125 (SR100/170 in summer).

Al-Andalus Hotel (☎ 732 8491) is probably the best of Taif's slightly more expensive places. It's just off the main square by the Assia restaurant. Rooms cost SR100/150 for singles/doubles (SR150/180 in summer). The rooms are large and very clean.

SAUDI ARABIA

Places to Eat

Al-Aziziah Restaurant Cafeteria, on King Faisal St near the intersection with Abu Bakker al-Siddiq St, is one of the best of Taif's many small Turkish restaurants. Grilled chicken or a kebab with rice, bread and salad costs around SR12.

Assia Restaurant is a friendly place on King Faisal St similar, though not quite as good. The prices are about the same as those at the Al-Aziziah.

Port Said Coffeehouse is the place to go for traditional coffeehouse pursuits (backgammon, TV etc). It is above the Al-Rajhi Commercial Establishment for Exchange office on the main square and is entered through a small door on the north side of the building, next to a stationery shop.

Getting There & Away

The airport is 25km north of the town. Daily flights operate to Riyadh and Dhahran. Direct flights are also available to Jeddah, Abha, Medina, Tabuk and Sharurah.

The bus station (☎ 736 9924) is on Al-Matar Rd, 2.5km north of the main intersection. There are numerous buses every day to both Riyadh (SR100, nine hours) and Jeddah (SR90, 2¾ hours). Jeddah buses are generally going around Mecca and, therefore, are open to non-Muslims, but it is always a good idea to double-check before purchasing a ticket. Regular services also operate to Abha and Al-Baha.

MADAIN SALAH

The spectacular rock tombs at Madain Salah, some 300km north of Medina, are Saudi Arabia's most famous archaeological site. The tombs were mostly carved between 100 BC and 100 AD when Madain Salah was ruled by the Nabataeans, in whose empire it was second in importance only to Petra in present-day Jordan. In later centuries the pilgrim road from Damascus to Medina passed near the site and it was by following this that Charles Doughty, in the 1880s, became the first westerner to see the tombs.

The Saudi Arabian Department of Antiquities publishes a useful guide to Madain Salah. It costs SR15 and can be purchased at the Riyadh Museum or from any number of Saudi men cruising the site in pick-up trucks, though they charge SR20 to SR30 per copy.

There are no hotels or restaurants available at Madain Salah, though accommodation and food can both be found 22km away at Al-Ula.

Things to See & Do

Madain Salah's tombs are less spectacular than those at Petra but they're better preserved. You do not need a 4WD to get around the site, though it might make life easier. You should, however, have a vehicle of some sort – the distances are large.

Be sure to see **Qasr Farid**, the largest tomb at Madain Salah. It is carved from a single large outcrop of rock standing alone in the desert. **Qasr al-Bint**, which translates as 'The Girl's Palace', is another important site. If you step back and look up near the northern end of its west face you'll see a tomb that was abandoned in the early stages of construction and would, if completed, have been the largest in Madain Salah.

The Diwan, or 'meeting room', is carved into a hillside a few hundred metres northeast of Qasr al-Bint. The name owes more to modern Arab culture than to the Nabataeans, who probably used the area as a cult site. As you pass through this mini-Siq note the small altars carved into the cliff face and the channels which brought water down into several small basins. After passing through the mini-Siq go straight for 150 to 200m and then climb up and to the right for a good view over the site.

On the northern edge of the site is an abandoned station from the **Hejaz Railway**, of *Lawrence of Arabia* fame (though Lawrence never operated this far south). The complex of 16 buildings includes a large workshop building where a restored WWI-era engine is on display.

Organised Tours

Organised tours to Madain Salah are run by the *Medina Sheraton* (☎ 04-846 0777, fax 846 0385) and Golden Eagle Services of

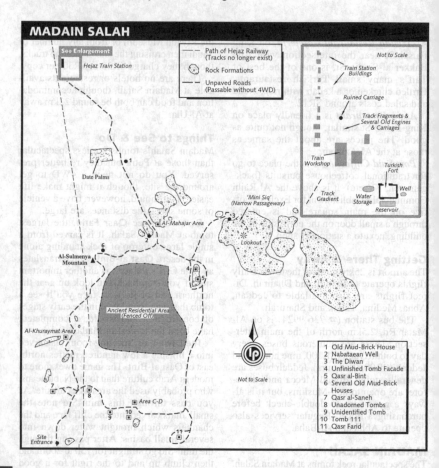

MADAIN SALAH

See Enlargement

Hejaz Train Station

——— Path of Hejaz Railway (Tracks no longer exist)

🪨 Rock Formations

- - - - Unpaved Roads (Passable without 4WD)

Date Palms

Al-Mahajar Area

Al-Sulmenya Mountain

Al-Khuraymat Area

Ancient Residential Area (Fenced Off)

'Mini Siq' (Narrow Passageway)

Lookout

Not to Scale

Train Station Buildings

Ruined Carriage

Track Fragments & Several Old Engines & Carriages

Train Workshop

Turkish Fort

Track Gradient

Water Storage

Well

Reservoir

Site Entrance

Area C-D

Not to Scale

1 Old Mud-Brick House
2 Nabataean Well
3 The Diwan
4 Unfinished Tomb Facade
5 Qasr al-Bint
6 Several Old Mud-Brick Houses
7 Qasr al-Saneh
8 Unadorned Tombs
9 Unidentified Tomb
10 Tomb 111
11 Qasr Farid

Riyadh (☎ fax 01-491 9567). The Medina Sheraton does the site as a day trip for SR925 per person. Golden Eagle offers camping trips where you sleep in tents at the site for SR950 per person (SR500 for children under 12). Both tours are geared towards groups but allow single people to join groups that are already going. In either case you should book three to four weeks in advance so that the necessary permits can be arranged. Note that Medina airport and the Medina Sheraton are both open to non-Mus-

lims, as is Medina's *Youth Hostel* (☎ 04-847 4092, fax 847 4344).

Getting There & Away

Madain Salah is some 330km north of Medina, off the main road from Medina to Al-Ula. To reach the site from Medina take the north-bound Tabuk/Hail exit when you are about 20km south of Al-Ula. Follow this road 25km to another junction. Exit, turn right and after a short distance you will see a sign saying 'Madain Salah 18km'. About

1km from this sign you will see a paved road running off into the desert to your left. Turn here. Note that in the direction you are travelling this road is not signposted. After another 6km turn right at a sign marked 'Antiquities'. Another 1.7km brings you to the site gate.

Asir (The South-West)

The dramatic mountains of the Asir range are on the edge of the same geological fault line that emerges farther to the south-west as Africa's Great Rift Valley. The mountain chain includes Jebel Sawdah, the 2910m peak near Abha which is the highest point in Saudi Arabia. Asir was an independent kingdom until it was conquered by Abdul Aziz in 1922. It has long had close ties with Yemen. The region's architecture has a distinctly Yemeni look about it. The most distinctive feature of the houses are the shingles sticking out from their sides. These are designed to deflect rain away from the mud walls of the house.

Another common sight are hamadryas baboons which can often be seen along the main roads throughout Asir. Allow yourself time to stop and explore this fascinating place.

AL-BAHA

Al-Baha, 220km south of Taif and 240km north of Abha, is the secondary tourist hub of the Asir region. The area's attraction has mainly been that it is a lot less developed than Abha. The **Raghdan and Shaba Forests** are nice spots with some good views, but the scenery is better farther south.

ABHA

If Saudi Arabia ever opens up to tourism, Abha, the capital of the south-western province of Asir, is likely to be one of the main attractions. The relatively cool weather, forested hills and striking mountain scenery have made it a very popular

weekend resort. Like Taif, it is crowded on summer weekends and reservations are strongly recommended.

You'll need to have a car in Abha as taxis are hard to find and local buses do not serve the main areas of the Asir National Park.

Orientation

The main streets are King Khaled and King Abdul Aziz Sts; the area stretching from their intersection to the governate office is Abha's nominal centre. (King Khaled St is called Al-Bahar St between King Abdul Aziz and King Faisal Sts). These names come from the Farsi maps. On the ground you will find few, if any, street signs.

You'll find several banks in the area around the main intersection. The post office and telephone office are side by side on King Abdul Aziz St, near the intersection with Prince Abdullah St.

Things to See

Shada Palace Abha's only in-town site is the Shada Palace. It was built in 1927 as an office/residence for King Abdul Aziz's governors in the region. The palace is the large, traditional tower immediately behind the police station on King Faisal St, across from the bus station. It is open from 9 am to 1 pm and from 4.30 to 7.30 pm Saturday to Thursday. Admission is free; children under 12 are not allowed inside.

Asir National Park Visitors Centre The Asir National Park Visitors Centre sits imposingly on the southern edge of the Ring Rd. It is not a tourist office but rather an introduction to the Asir National Park. It is open only to families and only in the summer, when its hours are from 4 to 8 pm daily. If you want to see it in the winter, or you are male and have no women and/or children along, you must first obtain a permit from the park headquarters on the Qara'a road, 1.8km from the junction with the Ring Rd.

Asir National Park The park covers some 450,000 hectares of land from the Red Sea

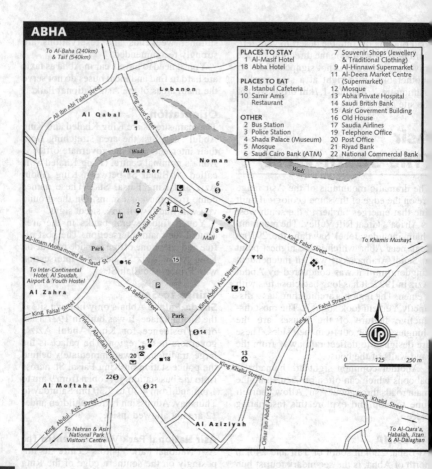

ABHA

To Al-Baha (240km)
& Taif (540km)

PLACES TO STAY
1   Al-Masif Hotel
18 Abha Hotel

PLACES TO EAT
8   Istanbul Cafeteria
10 Samir Amis
    Restaurant

OTHER
2   Bus Station
3   Police Station
4   Shada Palace (Museum)
5   Mosque
6   Saudi Cairo Bank (ATM)

7   Souvenir Shops (Jewellery
    & Traditional Clothing)
9   Al-Hinnawi Supermarket
11 Al-Deera Market Centre
    (Supermarket)
12 Mosque
13 Abha Private Hospital
14 Saudi British Bank
15 Asir Goverment Building
16 Old House
17 Saudia Airlines
19 Telephone Office
20 Post Office
21 Riyad Bank
22 National Commercial Bank

Lebanon

Al Qabal

Al Ibn Abi Taleb Street

King Saud Street

Wadi

Manazer

Noman

Wadi

To Inter-Continental
Hotel, Al Soudah,
Airport & Youth Hostel

Park

King Faisal Street

Al-Imam Mohammed Ibn Saud St.

Mall

King Fahd Street

To Khamis Mushayt

Al Zahra

Al-Bahar Street

King Abdul Aziz Street

Fahd Street

King Faisal Street

Prince Abdullah Street

Park

King Khalid Street

King

Omar Ibn Abdul Aziz St.

King Khalid Street

Al Moftaha

Al Aziziyah

To Nahran & Asir
National Park
Visitors' Centre

King Abdul Aziz Street

To Al-Qara'a,
Habalah, Jizan
& Al-Dalaghan

0   125   250 m

---

coast to the desert areas east of the mountains. The two main mountain areas are **Al-Soudah**, a few kilometres beyond the Inter-Continental Hotel, and the remote **Al-Sahab** area. Al-Soudah, which is near the summit of Jebel Sawdah (2910m), is the most spectacular part of the park.

The main park areas to the south-east of Abha are **Al-Dalaghan** (Dalgan), 26km from Abha, and, farther down the same road, **Al-Qara'a** (Qara), for which the road is named. Both areas consist of a large area

of rounded boulders and small evergreen trees. Wild baboons can often be seen in both areas.

Places to Stay

Abha's *Youth Hostel* (☎ 227 0503) is at the Sporting City, 20km west of Abha and 8km off the Abha-Khamis road. Beds are SR8 but there is no bus service.

Every place except the youth hostel has higher rates in the summer (May to September). Don't arrive in Abha on a Wednesday or Thursday during summer without a reservation.

Shamasan Hotel (☎ 225 1808), just outside the centre, is probably the best value for money in Abha after the hostel. They charge SR100/150 for singles/doubles (SR150/180 in summer).

The only hotel in the centre is **Abha Hotel** (☎ 224 8775, King Abdul Aziz St), where rooms cost SR100/150 (SR120/220 in summer).

Up in the mountains **Inter-Continental Hotel** (☎ 224 7777) has fairly standard five-star rates, but it's worth dropping by to marvel at its sheer scale. The hotel is said to have been originally designed as a palace for a Saudi prince.

Places to Eat

There are a few restaurants scattered around the centre but, on the whole, the pickings are rather thin.

Samir Amis Restaurant on King Abdul Aziz St has good kebabs and grilled chicken.

Istanbul Cafeteria (a sign over the doorway says 'Turkey Cafeteria'), near the Al-Hinnawi supermarket, is a good place for a quick snack. Grilled chicken, egg, beef or liver sandwiches cost SR2. Several other small places are in the area immediately around the Samir Amis.

Getting There & Away

The airport is 25km from town. To get there, take the Abha-Khamis Rd to the turn-off just beyond the turn for the Sporting City. There are several flights each day to Jeddah and Riyadh and one per day to Dhahran.

The SAPTCO station is in the big parking lot on King Faisal St, a couple of blocks north of the intersection of King Khaled and King Abdul Aziz Sts. Buses to Jeddah (8½ hours) leave nearly hourly during the day. There are also several buses per day to Taif and Jizan. For buses to Riyadh you must go to Khamis.

Local buses run between the Abha and Khamis bus stations every 30 minutes from 6.30 am to 10.30 pm. The trip takes about 35 minutes and the fare is SR2.

KHAMIS MUSHAYT

Khamis Mushayt (Khamis, for short) is 26km east of Abha. Khamis is usually spoken of as Abha's twin city, though it is a bit difficult to see what the two places have in common. It is as flat and dull as Abha is hilly and interesting.

Khamis' main attraction is its small, modern souq (just off the main square), which is a good place to shop for silver jewellery.

HABALAH

The deserted village of Habalah (Habella), about 60km from the centre of Abha, is one of the most dramatic sites in the Asir National Park. It appears to hang from a 300m-high cliff face above terraced fields and a broad valley. A cable car takes visitors down to the remains of the village but it only runs when eight people can be scared up to make the trip. Assuming enough people are present, the cable car operates daily from 8.30 am to 7.30 pm. The trip down offers some of the most dramatic views in the country and is well worth the long drive from Abha.

To reach Habalah take the Qara'a road from Abha past Al-Dalaghan. Three kilometres beyond the Al-Dalaghan turn, the road ends in a T-junction. Turn left and follow the road to the village of Wadiain where you will see a sign pointing towards 'Al-Habla Park'. Follow the sign and keep left at the white sign with a picture of a cable car.

NAJRAN

Najran (Nejran) is one of the most fascinating and least visited places in Saudi Arabia; Yemen's cultural influence is stronger here than anywhere else. This is obvious in both the local architecture and the attitude of the people towards outsiders. Najranis are extremely outgoing and deeply conservative at the same time.

Orientation & Information

Najran is easy to find your way around. Driving in from Abha, you hit a T-junction; this is the only road leading to Najran and everyone calls it the Main Rd. Turning left at the junction takes you to the Holiday Inn, Najran airport and the Empty Quarter (in that order). Turning right leads you into Faisaliah, a modern business district just before Najran.

Most of the shops and businesses, the youth hostel, the other two hotels, Saudia, the telephone office, two post offices (the main one in Faisaliah and a smaller one near the turn for the Najran Fort) and the bus station are all along, or a short distance off, the Main Rd in Faisaliah. Except for the bus station all of them are on the right-hand side of the road if you are coming from Abha or the airport. Continuing on Main Rd you reach Najran's centre, where the fort and the souq are located.

Things to See

Parts of **Najran Fort (Qasr al-Imara)** are said to date from pre-Islamic times, but the present fort was begun in 1942 as a royal residence. The fort is more or less in the centre of town, across from the fruit and vegetable market. It is open from 8 am to 5 or 6 pm daily (depending on the time of the sunset prayer). Admission is free and you don't need a permit to get in.

Some 5km west of Najran's centre, **Al-Aan Palace** (also known as the Saadan Palace) is a five storey tower dominating the oasis from an outcrop of rock. The building is a private residence and is not open to the public. The best way to see it is to backtrack towards Faisaliah along the Main Rd and turn (left if coming from Najran, right if coming from Faisaliah) at the sign for Maratah. Follow the road for 7km from this point and turn off in front of the large house with a white and yellow wall around it directly beneath the palace.

Najran's **museum** is open from 8.30 am to 2 pm Saturday to Wednesday. It is several kilometres off the Main Rd, next to the Al-Ukhdood archaeological site. To reach the museum, turn off the Main Rd at the sign for 'Okhdood'. After 3km you will reach a T-junction. Turn right. The museum will be on your left after 2km.

Places to Stay

Najran's **Youth Hostel** (☎ 522 5019) is about 9km from the fort. As you pass through Faisaliah watch out for the Najran Municipality on your right. Past this the Main Rd swings around to the left while a smaller street continues on straight. Keep going straight on the smaller road. Take the first right (immediately beyond the first petrol station) and then take the second right. The hostel will be on your right after less than 200m. It's across the street from a school.

Aside from the youth hostel there are two cheap/mid-range hotels in Najran, both just off the Main Rd, approximately 10km from the fort and 3km from the junction with the Abha road.

Okhdood Hotel (☎ 522 2614) has rooms for SR132/170, but will discount these by about 15% when things are slow.

Najran Hotel (☎ 522 1750), about 1km closer to the centre, is slightly better value at SR88/150.

Places to Eat

In Faisaliah there are a number of good places in the general vicinity of the youth hostel.

Cafeteria al-Beek has good shwarma served, unusually, in submarine sandwich rolls. The sign is only in Arabic but it is on the south side of the road about 500m back towards Abha from the turn for the youth hostel.

Al-Ramal ash-Shaabi, around the corner from the youth hostel, is one of the Najran area's best bets. The kebabs and grilled chicken dishes are excellent, as is the rice. At breakfast they do great *hadas* (a spicy bean dish eaten with pita bread), served sizzling in front of you for SR4. The restaurant's sign is only in Arabic. Look for the models of two Yemeni-style houses framing the entrance.

Getting There & Away

The Saudia office is on the Main Rd about 1km towards the centre from the turn for the youth hostel. There are daily flights to Riyadh and Jeddah. The bus station is on the Main Rd, 1.7km from the turn for Abha. There is direct service to Riyadh and Jeddah via Abha and Khamis Mushayt. There is also one bus each day to Sharurah.

SHARURAH

The town of Sharurah lies deep in the Empty Quarter, about 340km east of Najran. The desert scenery on the road to Sharurah is spectacular and includes a drive of about 60km through what can only be described as a canyon of sand dunes rising to heights of 100m or more on each side of the road.

There is nothing to see in Sharurah itself. If you need to eat try *Naseef al-Qamar*, an Egyptian-run restaurant on the main street.

The North-West

TABUK

Tabuk (Tabouk), the largest city in northwestern Saudi Arabia, is largely a military town, so be careful where you point your camera. It also has a conservative reputation – another reason to tread carefully.

Most of Tabuk's essential services are on or near Prince Fahd bin Sultan St. The local antiquities office is in the education ministry building 400m west of the Al-Balawi Hotel. Moving from the hotel towards the centre you will see two white buildings opposite each other on either side of the street. Coming from the hotel the education building is the one on the right. The antiquities office is on the 2nd floor.

The main attractions are **Tabuk Fort**, a 17th century Ottoman structure, once a stop on the pilgrim's road from Damascus to Mecca, and the reconstructed **Hejaz Train Station** a few blocks away.

DOMAT AL-JANDAL

Domat al-Jandal is one of the kingdom's little known gems. This modest town boasts two of the country's most interesting antiquities – the ruined **Qasr Marid** and the still-in-use **Mosque of Omar**, both of which are a short walk from the **Jof Regional Museum**.

The museum is open from 8 am to 1 pm Saturday to Wednesday. Admission is free.

By far the best way to get to this remote corner of the kingdom is to fly. The regional airport appears in Saudia's domestic timetables as 'Jouf'.

The museum is 1.2km off the main road from Tabuk to Sakaka. Coming from Sakaka turn right off the main road just past the second Domat al-Jandal petrol station and 350m beyond the police station. Follow this road for 1.2km. The museum will be on the right.

Qasr Marid is immediately adjacent to the museum. Its foundations date to Nabataean times, and Roman-era records mention Marid by name. The fortress was repaired in the 19th century and again served as the regional seat of government in the early years of the 20th century. The Mosque of Omar, on the far side of Marid from the museum, is one of the oldest in the kingdom.

Outside the centre a small portion of Domat al-Jandal's once-formidable **city wall** has been restored and can be viewed without a permit. The wall is 3.6km from the museum. Ask at the museum for directions.

Places to Stay & Eat

Actually, there isn't anywhere to stay in Domat al-Jandal. You'll have to stay 50km down the road in the regional capital, Sakaka.

Sakaka's *Youth Hostel* (☎ 624 1883, fax 624 8341) is 1.5km west of the town's main intersection on the big street that goes out of the intersection immediately to the west of the mosque. Beds are SR8 per night. Look for a green sign with white lettering in Arabic and a small blue-and-white IYHF logo in the upper left hand corner.

Al-Yarmook Hotel (☎ 624 9333), on the road running north and east out of the main intersection, is your best low-budget bet in Sakaka. The rooms cost SR70/100, all with bath.

Al-Buraq Restaurant-3 near the youth hostel, is an excellent cheap eatery. The surroundings are good and the kebabs are especially well-seasoned. Lunches and dinners cost SR7 to SR15, depending on the size of your appetite.

The Eastern Province

DAMMAM

The provincial capital, Dammam, is the longest settled and largest town of the Dhahran-Dammam-Alkhobar group. It is a bit run-down compared to Alkhobar but a lot cheaper.

Orientation & Information

Downtown Dammam is roughly the area bounded by King Abdul Aziz St to the north, King Khaled St to the south, 9th St to the east and 18th St to the west. The centre is the area around the intersection of 11th St, which appears on some maps and street signs as Dhahran St, and King Saud St. There are banks and moneychangers at the intersection of 11th and King Saud Sts. The main post office is at the corner of 9th and Al-Amir Mansour Sts.

The Regional Museum of Archaeology & Ethnography

The museum (☎ 826 6056) is at the railroad crossing on 1st St near the Dammam Tower and across the street from the Al-Waha mall. It's on the 4th floor and is open from 7.30 am to 2.30 pm Saturday to Wednesday. Many of the explanatory texts are in Arabic only, though most of the items in the display cases are labelled in English, too.

The museum is also the place to pick up permits for visiting the Eastern Province's main archaeological sites. The only exceptions are the sites in the Hofuf area, for which permits must be obtained in Riyadh.

Places to Stay

Youth Hostel (☎ 857 5358) is at the Sports Centre on the Dammam-Alkhobar expressway. Beds are SR8 per night. Take bus No 1 from either city and get off midway between the two at the buildings in front of the stadium (not the green buildings nearby, and not at the big stadium on the edge of Dammam).

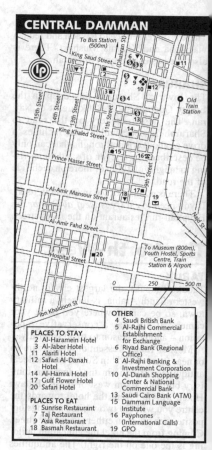

CENTRAL DAMMAM

To Bus Station (500m)
King Saud Street—(Dhahran St)
15th Street
14th Street
13th Street
11th Street
King Khaled Street
Prince Nasser Street
Al-Amir Mansour Street
Al-Amir Fahd Street
Hospital Street
9th Street
Najd St
Old Train Station
Ibn Khaldoon St

To Museum (800m), Youth Hostel, Sports Centre, Train Station & Airport

0   250   500 m

PLACES TO STAY
2 Al-Haramein Hotel
3 Al-Jaber Hotel
11 Alarifi Hotel
12 Safari Al-Danah Hotel
14 Al-Hamra Hotel
17 Gulf Flower Hotel
20 Safari Hotel

PLACES TO EAT
1 Sunrise Restaurant
7 Taj Restaurant
9 Asia Restaurant
18 Basmah Restaurant

OTHER
4 Saudi British Bank
5 Al-Rajhi Commercial Establishment for Exchange
6 Riyad Bank (Regional Office)
8 Al-Rajhi Banking & Investment Corporation
10 Al-Danah Shopping Center & National Commercial Bank
13 Saudi Cairo Bank (ATM)
15 Dammam Language Institute
16 Payphones (International Calls)
19 GPO

Al-Haramein Hotel (☎ 832 5426), just off King Saud St, west of the intersection with 11th St, has singles/doubles for SR88/115, all with private bath, mini-fridge and TV.

Gulf Flower Hotel (☎ 826 2170), on 9th St across from the main post office, has rooms at SR99/132, all with bath, TV and telephone. It's OK, but old and a bit creaky.

Dammam Hotel (☎ 832 9000), a set of prefabricated buildings behind the five star Dammam Oberoi Hotel, is a good medium-priced option, though it is a bit out of the entre. Rooms are SR165/224, including the 10% service charge. This place is much nicer inside than it looks from the street.

Places to Eat

Asia Restaurant, on King Saud St, is a good place for a quick, cheap meal. You can get two main dishes, rice, soup, dessert and a soda or mineral water for only SR10. Even by the standards of the Eastern Province's many cheap Filipino eateries this deal is hard to beat.

Basmah Restaurant on Al-Amir Mansour St, a couple of blocks from the GPO, has good shwarma and *fatar* (seasoned bread). The service is pretty bad but the food and prices make up for it.

Over in nearby Alkhobar, however, is where you will find the Eastern Province's best cheap food.

Getting There & Away

Air Dhahran International Airport (DHA) is between Alkhobar and Dhahran, near the University of Petroleum & Minerals and the US consulate general. A new airport (King Fahd international) is under construction in the desert, 60km north of the present airport. This project has been under way for years so it is difficult to say when it may open.

There are about eight or 10 flights per day to Riyadh and four or five to Jeddah. There are also daily flights to Abha and Taif and regular service to Medina and a host of smaller cities.

Bus Dammam's SAPTCO bus station is a few blocks north of the centre on 11th St between King Abdul Aziz St and the Corniche. The services to Qatif, Safwa and Tarut Island are classified as local and leave from the same part of the station as the routes to Alkhobar and the airport. The fare for any of these trips is SR2. Intercity buses depart regularly for Hofuf and Riyadh.

The Saudi-Bahraini Transport Company's buses to Bahrain (SR40/70 one way/return, three hours) leave five times a day.

Train The train station is south-east of the city centre, near the Dammam-Alkhobar Expressway and a housing development. Trains leave three times daily except Thursday for Riyadh (SR60/40 1st/2nd class, approximately four hours) via Abqaiq (SR10/6, 45 minutes) and Hofuf (SR20/15, 1½ hours). On Thursday there is only one train.

ALKHOBAR

Alkhobar (Al-Khubar, Khobar) is the newest – and most upmarket – of the three cities that make up the Dhahran area. For the budget traveller its main attraction is as a place to eat. The area bounded by Dhahran St, 4th St, the Gulf and Prince Bandar St is filled with good, cheap restaurants.

Phuket Restaurant, on King Faisal St one block north of Dhahran St, has good Thai meals for SR20 to SR25. Across the street and a few doors down is *Aristocrat Restaurant* with friendly staff and particularly good SR10 set meals.

Turkey Cock on 28th St, across from the Pepsi Cola bottling plant, has excellent set meals for SR15.

DHAHRAN

Aside from the airport, Dhahran consists of the Aramco compound, which is a small city in itself, the US consulate, and the University of Petroleum & Minerals. Admission to any of these requires identification showing that you live, work, study or have business there.

The **Aramco Exhibit** is open to the public and is the kingdom's best museum bar none. Open from 8 am to 6.30 pm Saturday to Wednesday, from 9 am to noon and from 3 to 6.30 pm Thursday and from 3 to 6.30 pm Friday. Thursday and Friday are for families only; admission is free. For the layperson, the centre is a comprehensive guide to the oil industry with a minimum of pro-Big Oil preaching and an emphasis on explaining the technical side of the industry. It's also fun, especially for kids, with lots of buttons to push, user-participation displays and quizzes.

TARUT ISLAND

For centuries the small island of Tarut has been one of the most important ports and military strongholds on the Arabian side of the Gulf. **Tarut Fort** is one of Saudi Arabia's most photographed ruins. What you see today was built by the Portuguese in the 16th century on top of a site that has been used since the 3rd millennium BC. Tarut's other site is **Qasr Darin** – so exposed and so thoroughly ruined that you do not need a permit to see it. It was built in 1875 to guard the sea approaches to the island.

Tarut is connected to the mainland by a causeway. Once you're on the island turn right at an intersection-cum-roundabout. Follow a narrow road through Tarut town for about 1km and you will see Tarut Fort on the right. To reach Qasr Darin continue on the same road for 2km until it swings around to the right. At that point just keep hugging the coastline for another 6km and you'll see the ruins on the right, near the pier.

NAIRIYAH

One of the Eastern Province's most interesting day trips is the Bedouin Market which takes place every Friday morning in the village of Nairiyah, about 250km north of Dammam. To reach Nairiyah from Dammam take the Jubail Expressway to the Abu Hadriyah turn-off and follow the signs to Nairiyah. Once in the town head for the large mosque with a low green dome, and follow the crowd. Get an early start as the market usually ends by 10 am.

HOFUF

The Al-Hasa oasis, centred on the town of Hofuf, is the largest in Arabia and one of the largest in the world. The oasis seems to go on and on and, if you have time and a car, exploring the small villages scattered through this large, lush area can be a pleasant way to spend an afternoon or two.

Orientation & Information

King Abdul Aziz St is the main commercial street and intersects with Al-Khudod St to form a central square containing the bus station, bounded by a mosque and the large, white Riyad Bank building. Both of the centre's hotels are an easy walk from this intersection.

There are several banks and moneychangers around this main area. The telephone office is north of the centre at the intersection of the Dammam Rd (officially Prince Abdullah Ben Jalawi St) and Hajer Palace Rd. It is open from 7.30 am to midnight daily.

Things to See

The **Hofuf Museum** is especially good on Eastern Province archaeology and, with everything labelled in English, is a much better introduction to the region than the Dammam museum where many of the explanatory texts appear only in Arabic. The museum is open from 8 am to 2 pm Saturday to Wednesday. Admission is free. It is about 5km from the main intersection, but getting there can be a bit tricky. From the main intersection head west on Al-Khudod St and turn left at the first traffic signal past Qasr Ibrahim. Follow this road for 1.2km and turn left at the third set of traffic lights (Al-Safir supermarket will be across the intersection from you). Go about 100m and turn right at the next traffic signal. Follow this road for 1.8km and turn left at the second traffic signal. Go left again after 700m (at the first traffic signal). The museum will be on your left after a farther 600m.

In the centre is Hofuf's best known site, the Ottoman fortress of **Qasr Ibrahim**. You'll need a site permit to visit the interior. Once inside, take a look at the jail, next to the mosque, and the underground cells inside it. The Turkish bath near the north-west corner of the compound was used during Abdul Aziz's time to store dates, the smell of which still lingers inside. The stairs along the eastern wall lead to what were the commanding officer's quarters.

Hofuf's real treat is the **souq**. It's just off King Abdul Aziz St, about 300m south of the main intersection. Several shops also have good collections of Bedouin weaving and a few have old silver jewellery. You

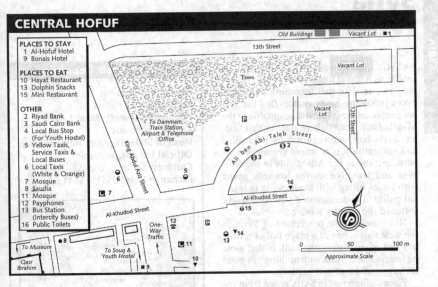

CENTRAL HOFUF

PLACES TO STAY
1 Al-Hofuf Hotel
9 Bonais Hotel

PLACES TO EAT
10 Hayat Restaurant
13 Dolphin Snacks
15 Mini Restaurant

OTHER
2 Riyad Bank
3 Saudi Cairo Bank
4 Local Bus Stop
  (For Youth Hostel)
5 Yellow Taxis,
  Service Taxis &
  Local Buses
6 Local Taxis
  (White & Orange)
7 Mosque
8 Saudia
11 Mosque
12 Payphones
13 Bus Station
  (Intercity Buses)
16 Public Toilets

Old Buildings ▨▨ Vacant Lot ■1
13th Street
Vacant Lot
Trees
Vacant Lot
12th Street
To Dammam,
Train Station,
Airport & Telephone
Office
Ali ben Abi Taleb Street
King Abdul Aziz Street
16
Al-Khudod Street
Al-Khudod Street
One-Way Traffic
To Museum
Qasr Ibrahim
To Souq &
Youth Hostel
0   50   100 m
Approximate Scale

will also find a few shops selling woven materials near Qasr Ibrahim.

Places to Stay

Youth Hostel (☎ 580 0028) is at the stadium. Beds are SR8. To reach the hostel take Bus No 2 to the large T-junction by the prison. There is a stadium behind it but that's not the one. Turn right at the junction and follow the road for 500m until it forks. Keep left at the fork and follow the road for another 2.5km. A cab from the bus station costs SR12 to SR15.

Bonais Hotel (☎ 582 7700, King Abdul Aziz St) is your best bet in town. Singles/doubles cost SR110/165.

Al-Hofuf Hotel (☎ 587 7082, 13th Street) has some affordable 'two star' rooms at SR132/198. They also have a 'four star' section where the rooms are triple that price.

Places to Eat

Hofuf is a bit short on restaurants but there is a very good small place across the main

intersection from the bus station. A meal of chicken, rice and salad costs SR12. It's called *Al-Haramein Restaurant* but the sign is written only in Arabic. Keep an eye out for a small black sign with yellow and white lettering.

Sargam Restaurant, just west of the bus station, serves up good, cheap Indian food; chicken or mutton curry with rice costs only SR7.

Getting There & Away

The bus station (☎ 587 3687) is at the intersection of King Abdul Aziz and Al-Khudod Sts. There are buses to Dammam throughout the day as well as regular service to Riyadh. Service taxis congregate in the parking lot across the street from the bus station.

The train station (☎ 582 0571 for information) is a long way from the town centre. To reach it, head north on the Dammam Rd and turn west onto Hajer Palace Rd at the telephone office.

SAUDI ARABIA

Syria

As Syria slowly comes in from the cold, its profile as a travel destination is also beginning to rise. Not that travelling there was ever a problem – many visitors find the Syrian people among the most hospitable in the Middle East, or anywhere else for that matter. Syria has long been run by a hardline and not entirely benevolent regime but its participation on the Allied side in the Gulf War and tentative moves towards peace with Israel, along with a relaxation in internal political and economic strictures, have softened the country's image.

Nevertheless, the perception of Syria in the west still is one of a place full of terrorists and other nasties; the truth is that most travellers leave Syria with nothing but good feelings – it's that sort of place.

Places of interest in Syria range from romantic Crusader castles perched on mountain ranges overlooking the coast to Roman ruins beside desert oases. Damascus, the capital, is claimed by many to be the oldest continuously inhabited city in the world.

Facts about Syria

HISTORY

Historically Syria included Jordan, Israel, Lebanon and modern Syria. Due to its strategic position, its coastal towns were important Phoenician trading posts and later the area became an equally pivotal part of the Roman, Persian, Egyptian and Babylonian empires – and for that matter many others in the empire-building business. For more details on these eras see the History section in the Facts about the Region chapter.

Syria finally ended up as part of Ottoman Turkey and (along with Lebanon) was dished out to France when the Turkish empire broke up after WWI. This caused considerable local resentment, as the region had been briefly independent from the end of WWI until Paris took over in 1920.

The Syrian Arab Republic

Area: 185,180 sq km
Population: 17 million
Population Growth Rate: 3.4%
Capital: Damascus
Head of State: President Hafez al-Assad
Official Language: Arabic
Currency: Syrian pound (S£)
Exchange Rate: US$1 = S£41.85

- **Best Dining** – Aleppo and Damascus have some fantastic restaurants in beautifully restored 17th century town houses
- **Best Walk** – either through the Old City of Damascus or through the souqs of Aleppo
- **Best View** – standing on top of the world on the Jebel Ansariyya looking out over the Al-Ghab plain
- **Best Activity** – making like Indiana Jones and exploring the overgrown Dead Cities south of Aleppo
- **When in Rome ...** occupying a table at some alfresco restaurant and passing the evening dabbing at mezze and slowly emptying a bottle of araq

The French never had much luck with their Syria-Lebanon mandate and during WWII agreed to Syrian and Lebanese independence. The French proved reluctant to make good on the proposal and it was only in 1946 that they finally withdrew.

A period of political instability followed and by 1954, after several military coups, the Ba'athists in the army rose virtually unopposed to power. A brief flirtation with the Pan-Arabist idea of a United Arab Republic (with Egypt) in 1958 proved unpopular and coups in 1960, 1961 and 1963 saw the leadership change hands yet again. By 1966 the Ba'ath party was back in power, but it was severely weakened by loss in two conflicts – the Six Day War with Israel in 1967 and the Black September hostilities in Jordan in 1970. At this point, defence minister Hafez al-Assad seized power.

Assad has maintained control longer than any other post-independence Syrian government with a mixture of ruthless suppression and guile. In 1998, he was elected to a fifth seven year term with a predictable 99.9% of the vote.

Syria Today

The lack of an obvious successor to Assad remains a glaring problem, but fears of growing instability were lulled in the early 1990s by Assad's astute exploitation of the Gulf War and improvements in the economy.

Assad is dragging behind in the peace process with Israel. Neither side is apparently willing to make sufficient concessions to the other on the subjects of security, Israeli withdrawal from the Golan Heights and terrorist attacks on Israel emanating from Lebanon. With the recent change of government in Israel peace is at least back on the agenda but nobody is holding their breath.

GEOGRAPHY

Syria is a bit over half the size of Italy. It is bordered in the south-west by Lebanon, in the south by Jordan, in the east by Iraq and in the north by Turkey. The country has four geographical regions: a fertile 180km-long coastal strip between Lebanon and Turkey; the Jebel Ansariyya (also known as Jebel an-Nusariyya) mountain range, with

What to See

Damascus is a thoroughly charming capital with an old city that can keep you enraptured for days, although you should drag yourself away for at least a day trip down to **Bosra** for the Roman theatre. Syria's premier, must-see attractions are the ruins of the desert city of **Palmyra** and the Crusader castle **Krak des Chevaliers**, the latter of which is best visited from **Hama**, a small town with good food and accommodation. From a Hama base it's certainly also worth visiting the Roman site of **Apamea**.

Aleppo is Syria's second great city, an historical commercial centre with a fabulous souq. It also makes a good base from which to explore the surrounding countryside and its littering of Byzantine sites, the best of which is undoubtedly **Qala'at Samaan**.

an average height of 1000m, an impenetrable ridge running north-south inland from the coast with the Jebel Lubnan ash-Sharqiyya (Anti-Lebanon Range) forming a 2000m high border between Lebanon and Syria; the cultivated steppes that form an arc on the inland side of the mountain range and include the main centres of Damascus, Homs, Hama, Aleppo and Qamishle; and the stony Syrian desert of the south-east.

CLIMATE

Syria has a Mediterranean climate with hot, dry summers and mild, wet winters close to the coast. Inland it gets progressively drier and more inhospitable. On the coast average daily temperatures range from 29°C in summer to 10°C in winter and the annual rainfall is about 760mm. Temperatures on the cultivated steppe area average around 35°C in summer and 12°C in winter. Rainfall varies from about 250 to 500mm. In the desert the temperatures are high and rainfall is low. In summer the days average 40°C and highs of 46°C are not uncommon.

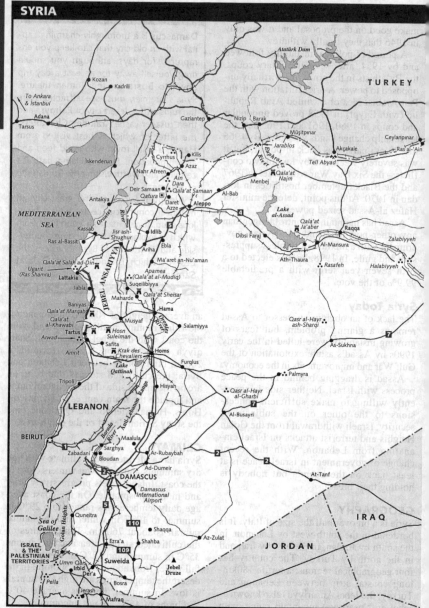

Facts about Syria 649

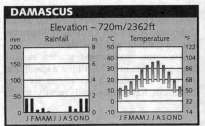

DAMASCUS

Elevation – 720m/2362ft

Rainfall | Temperature

J F M A M J J A S O N D

GOVERNMENT & POLITICS

The president, as leader of the Arab Ba'ath Socialist Party, has the power to appoint ministers, declare war, issue laws and appoint civil servants and military personnel. At the time of the promulgation of the constitution, which guarantees freedom of religious thought and expression, there was outrage that Islam was not declared the state religion. Bowing (but not all the way) to the pressure, President Assad and his government amended it to say that the head of state must be Muslim.

The country is divided into 14 governorates, or *muhafazat,* which in turn are subdivided into smaller units of local government.

POPULATION & PEOPLE

Syria has a population of 17 million, and its annual growth rate of 3.4% (one of the highest in the world) is way out of proportion with its economic growth.

About 90% of the population are Arabs, which includes some minorities such as the Bedouin (about 100,000). The remainder is made up of smaller groupings of Kurds (about one million), Armenians, Circassians and Turks.

RELIGION

Islam is practised by about 86% of the population – 20% of this is made up of minorities such as the Shi'ite, Druze and Alawite, while the remainder are Sunni Muslims.

Christians account for most of the rest and belong to various churches including the Greek Orthodox, Greek Catholic, Syrian Orthodox, Armenian Orthodox, Maronite, Roman Catholic and Protestant.

Since the government started issuing them passports in 1992, all but a handful of the several thousand Jews who lived in Damascus have emigrated, mostly to the USA.

LANGUAGE

Arabic is the mother tongue of the majority. Kurdish is spoken in the north, especially towards the east, Armenian in Aleppo and other major cities, and Turkish in some villages east of the Euphrates.

Aramaic, the language of the Bible, is still spoken in two or three villages.

English is widely understood and increasingly popular as a second language, while French, although waning, is still quite common among older people.

For helpful hints on Arabic see the Language chapter later.

Facts for the Visitor

PLANNING

Spring is the best time to visit as temperatures are mild and the winter rains have cleared the haze that obscures views for much of the year. Autumn is the next choice.

If you go in summer, don't be caught without a hat, sunscreen and water bottle, especially if visiting Palmyra or the northeast. Winter can be downright unpleasant on the coast and in the mountains.

The best Syria map is one produced by Freytag & Berndt, distinguished by a red cover. It covers the country at a scale of 1:800,000 and on the reverse carries very good city plans of Damascus and Aleppo. It's widely available in Syria where it's published under licence by the Avicenne bookshop and costs S£250 (roughly US$5). There's also another, mediocre sheet map put out by GEOprojects, based in Beirut, on a scale of 1:1,000,000, also with city plans. The tourist offices throughout Syria have free handout city and regional maps but they are generally way out of date and of very little use.

VISAS & DOCUMENTS
Visas

All foreigners entering Syria should obtain a visa in advance. The most sure way to get your visa is to apply for it in your home country well before you intend travelling. Avoid applying in a country that is not your own or that you don't hold residency for as the Syrians don't like this. At best they will ask you for a letter of recommendation from your own embassy (which is often an expensive proposition); at worst, they'll turn you down flat. In fact, US citizens must get their visas at home as US embassies abroad have a policy of not issuing letters of recommendation. The only place you can get around this is at the Syrian embassy in Cairo which, at the time of writing, didn't ask for a letter. If your home country doesn't have a Syrian embassy or consulate, then there's no problem with you applying anywhere else.

The Syrian embassy in Amman issues visas only to nationals and residents of Jordan and to nationals of countries that have no Syrian representation. So, if you are from a country like the UK, the USA or France that has a Syrian embassy then you cannot get a Syrian visa in Jordan. Of course, as there will always be, there is the odd traveller who has proved the exception – but you cannot count on it. In Turkey, you can get Syrian visas in both Ankara and İstanbul without too much of a problem.

There are two types of visa issued: single entry and multiple entry, but both are valid only for 15 days inside Syria and must be used within three months of the date of issue (six months for multiple-entry visas). Don't be misled by the line on the visa stating a validity of three months – this simply means the visa is valid *for presentation* for three months.

The cost of visas varies according to nationality and on where you get them. There seems to be little rhyme or reason in deciding which nationalities pay what, except in the case of UK passport-holders, who always pay a lot.

If there is any evidence of a visit to Israel in your passport, your application will be refused.

Visas at the Border The official line is that if there is no Syrian representation in your country, you are entitled to be issued a visa on arrival at the border, airport or port. That said, there's no Syrian embassy or consulate in the Netherlands yet we've had letters from Dutch people who were turned back at the Turkish-Syrian border. Our advice has got to be that you most definitely should secure your visa in advance certainly to be on the safe side.

Visa Extensions If your stay in Syria is going to be more than 15 days you have to get a visa extension while in the country. This is done at an immigration office, which you'll find in all main cities. The length of the extension appears to depend on a combination of what you're willing to ask for and the mood of the official you deal with. They are usually only granted on the 14th or 15th day of your stay, so if you apply earlier expect to be knocked back. The specifics vary from place to place but there are always several forms to complete and you need from three to five passport photos. The cost is never more than US$1.

Re-Entry Visas If you don't have a multiple-entry visa and want to leave Syria and re-enter (for example, to visit Lebanon) it is possible to arrange this by visiting the immigration office in central Damascus.

Visas for Neighbouring Countries You need a visa to enter the following neighbouring countries of Syria:

Egypt Applications for visas can be made from 9 to 11 am Saturday to Thursday. Collect your passport and visa the same day at 2 pm. It costs US$34 for US citizens, US$61 for UK citizens and US$54 for most other nationalities.

Jordan Visa applications can be made from 9 to 11 am Saturday to Thursday. Get your passport and visa the same day at 1 pm. For UK citizens it's US$21, free for Australians, Canadians pay US$31 and US citizens pay US$26. You can get a Jordanian visa at the border, but it's cheaper to get it in advance.

Iraq & Lebanon The Iraqi embassy is closed and there is no Lebanese representation in Damascus. Get Lebanese visas at the border.

Other Documents
Student cards get massive discounts off site admissions. If you don't have one you can probably pick one up in Palmyra.

EMBASSIES & CONSULATES
Syrian Embassies & Consulates
Following are addresses of Syrian embassies and consulates in cities around the world:

Australia
    Consulate:
    (☎ 03-9347 8445, fax 9347 8447)
    57 Cardigan St, Carlton, Victoria 3053
    Consulate:
    (☎ 02-9597 7714, fax 9597 2226)
    10 Belmore St, Arncliffe, NSW 2205
France
    Embassy:
    (☎ 01 45 51 82 35)
    20 rue Vaneau, 75007 Paris
Germany
    Embassy:
    (☎ 030-220 20 46)
    Otto Grotewohl Str 3, Berlin
    Consulate:
    (☎ 228-81 99 20, fax 81 92 99)
    Andreas Hermes Str 5, D-53175 Bonn
    Consulate:
    (☎ 40-30 90 54 14, fax 30 90 52 33)
    Brooktor 11, 20457 Hamburg
UK
    Embassy:
    (☎ 020-7245 9012, fax 7235 4621, visa line 0891-600 171)
    8 Belgrave Square, London SW1 8PH
USA
    Embassy:
    (☎ 202-232 6313)
    2215 Wyoming Ave NW, Washington DC 20008
    Consulate:
    (☎ 212-661 1313)
    820 Second Ave, New York NY 10017

Embassies & Consulates in Syria

Most embassies and consulates are open from around 8 am to 2 pm and are closed Friday, Saturday and any public holidays.

Australia
(☎ 613 2626, fax 613 2478)
128A Sharia al-Farabi, Al-Mezzeh, about 6km west of the city centre
Belgium
(☎ 333 2821, fax 333 0426)
Sharia al-Jala'a
Canada
(☎ 611 6692, fax 611 4000)
Block 12, Al-Mezzeh, about 4km west of the city centre
Egypt
(☎ 333 3561, fax 333 7961)
Sharia al-Jala'a
France
(☎ 332 7992)
Sharia Ata Ayyubi, Salihiyya
Germany
(☎ 332 3800/1, fax 332 3812)
53 Sharia Ibrahim Hanano
Iran
(☎ 222 6459, fax 222 0997)
Autostrad Al-Mezzeh, about 4km west of the city centre
Jordan
(☎ 333 4642, fax 333 6741)
Sharia al-Jala'a
Netherlands
(☎ 333 6871, fax 333 9369)
Sharia al-Jala'a
Saudi Arabia
(☎ 333 4914)
Sharia al-Jala'a, Abu Roumana
Turkey
(☎ 333 1411)
58 Sharia Ziad bin Abi Soufian
UK
(☎ 371 2561, fax 373 1600)
11 Sharia Mohammed Kurd Ali, Malki
USA
(☎ 333 2315, fax 224 7938)
2 Sharia al-Mansour, Abu Roumana

MONEY
Costs

It is possible to get by on US$15 a day or maybe less if you are willing to stick to the cheapest hotels (you can get a bed for as little as S£150, or US$3), make felafel, shwarma and juice the mainstay of your diet, and carry a student card to offset the site admission costs. If you stay in a modest hotel room with fan and private bathroom, eat in regular restaurants, with the odd splurge, and aim to see a couple of sites each day, you'll spend around US$20 to US$30 a day.

To give an indication of daily costs, a felafel costs about S£15 to S£25 (around US$0.30 to US$0.50) and shwarma S£25 to S£35 (US$0.50 to US$0.70), while a meal in an average restaurant costs around S£150 (US$3). If you go a little upmarket you can usually eat very well for E£250 (US$5) per person. A beer costs S£35 (US$0.70) in a liquor shop and about S£50 to S£65 (US$1 to US$1.30) in a restaurant or bar.

Getting around the country is cheap: the four hour bus ride between Damascus and Aleppo costs only S£150 (US$3) on a luxury air-con bus, while if you want to slum it on an old battered bus you can do it as cheaply as S£60 (US$1.20).

Many museums, castles and other sites cost S£300, which at the official exchange rate is over US$7. While such a fee is justified at sites such as Krak des Chevaliers, there will be times when you have to ask yourself if a sight is worth paying such money. We've tried to give an indication of whether a site is worth its entry fee. A way around this is to own a student card.

Currency

The currency is the Syrian pound (S£), known locally as the *lira*. There are 100 piastres (*qirsh*) to a pound but the smallest coin you'll find now is one pound. Notes are five, 10, 25, 50, 100 and S£500.

Exchange Rates

Australia	A$1	=	S£27.09
Canada	C$1	=	S£28.23
euro	€1	=	S£44.09
France	10FF	=	S£67.20
Germany	DM1	=	S£22.54
Japan	¥100	=	S£37.02
New Zealand	NZ$1	=	S£22.13
UK	UK£1	=	S£67.17
USA	US$1	=	S£41.85

Black market rates (see the following section) are usually about 15% higher depending on what part of the country you are in and how good your bargaining skills are.

Exchanging Money
Cash & Travellers Cheques There's at least one branch of the Commercial Bank of Syria (CBS) in every major town and most of them will change cash *and* travellers cheques in most major currencies, although each branch has its own quirks – some charge commission, some don't: some require the bank manager's signature to authorise transactions, some just hand over the cash without any form filling whatsoever. There are also a small number of officially sanctioned private exchange offices. These change cash and sometimes travellers cheques at official bank rates but generally don't charge any commission. The other advantage is that whereas banks usually close for the day at 12.30 or 2 pm, the exchange offices are often open until 7 pm.

Credit Cards & ATMs Major credit cards such as American Express (Amex), Visa, MasterCard and Diners Club are increasingly being accepted by bigger hotels and stores for purchases. They are also handy for buying air tickets (as the only alternative is cash) and with some car rental companies (it will save you having to leave a large cash deposit).

Cash advances are officially not possible as the CBS has no links with any credit card companies, however, a few individual entrepreneurs carry out transactions via Jordanian or Lebanese banks. The rate they offer may not be too great and you may also have to pay a commission.

There are no ATMs at all in Syria.

Black Market At the time of writing, the best rate you could hope for was S£50 to the US dollar. Outside Damascus you are looking at more like S£48. Treat the black market like any other transaction and bargain. It's not hard to find people to change money but be discreet as this is an illegal activity.

Tipping & Bargaining
Tipping is expected in the better restaurants and occasionally waiters deduct it themselves when giving you your change. Whatever you buy, remember that bargaining is an integral part of the process and listed prices are always inflated to allow for it. If you are shopping in the souqs, bargain – even a minimum amount of effort will almost always result in outrageous asking prices being halved.

POST & COMMUNICATIONS
Post
The Syrian postal service is slow but effective enough. Letters mailed from the main cities take about a week to Europe and anything up to a month to Australia or the USA. Mailing letters to the UK and Europe costs S£17, while to the USA and Australia it's S£18; stamps for postcards to the UK and Europe cost S£10, while to Australia and the USA it's S£13. In addition to post offices, you can also buy *tawaabi* (stamps) from most tobacconists.

The poste restante counter at the main post office in Damascus is more or less reliable. You must take your passport as identification and be prepared to pay an S£8 pick-up fee.

Telephone
The country code for Syria is ☎ 963 followed by the national area code minus the initial zero then the subscriber's number. Some national area codes for places mentioned throughout this chapter are listed as follows:

Aleppo	☎ 021
Bosra	☎ 015
Damascus	☎ 011
Deir ez-Zur	☎ 051
Der'a	☎ 015
Hama	☎ 033
Hassake	☎ 052
Homs	☎ 031
Lattakia	☎ 041
Palmyra	☎ 031
Qamishle	☎ 053

Quneitra	☎ 014
Raqqa	☎ 022
Suweida	☎ 016
Tartus	☎ 043

Booking an international call through the operator at the phone office is the traditional way of doing things and away from the big cities it's often the only option. There is a three minute minimum charge and you can wait up to two hours for a connection to be made. Bring your passport along, as the operator will want to see it. Most main phone offices are open from early morning until late at night and occasionally around the clock.

Thankfully, card phones are becoming more prevalent – they're all over central Damascus and are starting to appear at telephone offices in smaller towns like Palmyra and Hama. The phonecards come in denominations of S£200 and S£500 and are sold either at the post office or, in the case of Damascus, also from outlets close by the card phones. With a card phone you dial direct and there is no minimum call period. The international access code is ☎ 00.

Normal rate phone calls with card phones or through the operator cost S£100 per minute to most destinations in Europe, S£115 per minute to Australia and S£125 to the USA. There is a cheap rate, but the hours differ wildly from one country to the next. For Australia, cheap rate calls cost S£58 per minute from 2 to 7 pm. The cheap rate to the USA is S£63 and calls can be made from 3 to 8 am. Cheap calls to Europe cost S£50 per minute and can be made from 1 to 7 am.

Local calls have to be made with normal coin-operated telephones – if you can find one in working order. You can identify working local call booths by the queues that form around them. They accept S£10 coins. It's actually much easier to make such calls from your hotel and as long as it's only a local call most hotels don't charge.

Fax & Telex
It is possible to send telexes, telegrams and faxes from telephone offices or sometimes from main post offices but they are very expensive. For faxes normal phone call rates are charged, and what you pay depends on how long it takes for the fax to go through. For instance, to fax the UK from the main telephone office in Damascus costs S£180 for the first minute and S£90 for any further minutes. As there's a two minute minimum charge that means that at the least your fax will cost S£270. To Australia it's S£220 for the first minute and S£110 per minute beyond that.

Email & Internet Access
The Syrian government forbids Internet service providers (ISPs) in Syria, effectively banning email and access to the Web. To our knowledge the only publicly accessible online terminal in Syria is at the Al-Assad National Library out in the west of Damascus on Saahat Umawiyeen. There's just the one terminal and users, we are told, are nervously scrutinised by a permanent 'cyber guardian'.

If you are lugging around your own laptop then you can get connected in some of the better hotels by using an RJ-11 standard telephone connector but this, apparently, is not entirely legal, so be discreet.

BOOKS
In English there are two fine architectural guides to Syria; the better of them is *Monuments of Syria: An Historical Guide* by Ross Burns, which is a wonderfully comprehensive and opinionated gazetteer of Syria's castles, Islamic monuments and archaeological sites. It's widely available in Syria in a cheap locally published edition, but it's a bit big for your backpack. The other is Warwick Ball's *Syria: A Historical and Architectural Guide*.

Cleopatra's Wedding Present by Robert Tewdwr Moss is a very individual take on Syria. His experiences (such as an affair with a Palestinian commando) are unlikely to be shared by many but they do make for entertaining reading.

Lonely Planet's *The Gates of Damascus* by Lieve Joris also goes far deeper than just a traveller's tale. Through her friendship with a local woman and her family, Joris paints a grim and claustrophobic picture a million miles from the Syria most visitors will encounter – which is perhaps all the more reason for reading the book.

Of the various coffee-table titles available in the hotel bookshops of Damacus, Michael Jenner's *Syria in View* contains some excellent photography.

NEWSPAPERS & MAGAZINES

The English-language daily newspaper the *Syria Times* is published under direct government control and is predictably big on anti-Zionist, pro-Arab rhetoric and short on news. Foreign newspapers and magazines are irregularly available in Damascus, Aleppo and Homs. Any articles on Syria or Lebanon are so lovingly torn out you'd hardly notice there was anything missing.

RADIO & TV

The Syrian Broadcasting Service seems to have dropped much of its foreign language broadcasting. For news of the world, you can tune into retransmitted British Broadcasting Corporation (BBC) and Voice of America (VOA) broadcasts. Try 9.41 MHz, 9.51 MHz, 21.7 MHz and 15.31 MHz for the BBC and 11.84 MHz for VOA. If you have a short-wave set you'll have no trouble.

Syrian TV reaches a large audience and programs range from news and sport to American soaps. There is news in English on Syria 2 at around 10 pm. A few hotels, even at the budget end, have satellite TV.

PHOTOGRAPHY

In Damascus and Aleppo there's a good choice of film available including Ektachrome, Elite, Kodak Gold and K-Max film, sold at specialist photo shops which seem to take pretty good care of their stock. Film generally costs as much as, if not more than, it does in the west.

The Thousand and One Nights

After the *Bible*, *The Thousand and One Nights* (in Arabic *Alf Layla wa Layla*) must be one of the most familiar, while at the same time, largely unread, books in the English language. It owes its existence in the popular consciousness almost entirely to the Disneyfied tales of *Aladdin*, *Sinbad* and *Ali Baba & the 40 Thieves* that appear in children's books, cartoon films and Christmas pantomimes.

That the actual text itself is largely ignored is unsurprising considering that in its most famous English-language edition (translated by the Victorian adventurer Sir Richard Burton), it runs to 16 volumes. In fact, an old Middle Eastern superstition has it that nobody can read the entire text of *The Nights* without dying.

But what constitutes the entire text is a matter of academic debate. *The Thousand and One Nights* is a portmanteau title for a mixed bag of colourful and fantastic tales, and the many historical manuscripts that carry the famed title collectively contain many thousands of stories, sharing a core of exactly 271 common tales. They all, however, employ the same framing device – that of a succession of stories related nightly by the wily Sheherezade to save her neck from the misogynistic King Shahriyar.

Sheherezade and her tales have their origins in pre-Islamic Persia, but over the ages (and in endless retellings and rewritings) they were adapted, expanded and updated, drawing on sources as far flung as Greece and India. As they're known to us now, the stories are mainly set in the semi-fabled Baghdad of Haroun ar-Rashid (reigned 786-809 AD), and in Mamluk-era Cairo and Damascus. Regarding the last two cities in particular, *The Nights* provides a wealth a rich period detail, from shopping lists and prices of slaves, through to vivid descriptions of types and practices of assorted conjurers, harlots, thieves and mystics. *The Thousand and One Nights* is revered as much by medieval scholars as it is by Walt's animators.

Colour print processing costs vary depending where you go but in Damascus we paid S£25 for processing plus S£10 per print and the quality was fine.

LAUNDRY

Syria's laundries are not always particularly easy to find, so if you want to use one ask your hotel where the nearest is. Be aware, though, that the going rate is a pricey S£25 to S£35 *an item*. We're not talking about one hour laundrettes either – expect anything from 24 hours to a three or four day turnaround time.

TOILETS

Toilets are generally the hole-in-the-floor variety. Toilet paper is not always available so it's a good idea to carry tissues with you.

HEALTH

No inoculations are required in order to enter Syria unless you are coming from a disease-affected area, but it is a good idea to have preventative shots for hepatitis A, polio, tetanus and typhoid before you go. If you plan on spending a great amount of time along the Euphrates River in the north of Syria, your doctor may also recommend that you take anti-malarial tablets such as chloroquine.

The occasional outbreak of cholera still occurs in Syria, but as the vaccine is not all that effective, your best bet is to keep your eyes open. An encouraging sign is a notable absence of salad, especially parsley, being served in restaurants. (Cholera can be transmitted via the water that salad greens are washed in.)

In the major towns the tap water is safe to drink but if your stomach is a bit delicate or you find yourself in out-of-the-way places, bottled water is widely available. As ice cream in Syria rarely contains dairy products, it's also OK unless you are having problems coping with the water.

Medical services in Syria are well developed in the larger towns and cities and many of the doctors have been trained overseas and speak English. Your embassy will usually be able to recommend a reliable doctor or hospital if the need arises.

For more general health information see the Health section in the Regional Facts for the Visitor chapter at the beginning of this book.

BUSINESS HOURS

Government offices, such as immigration and tourism, are generally open from 8 am to 2 pm daily except Friday and holidays. Other offices and shops keep similar hours and often open again from 4 to 6 or 7 pm. Most restaurants and a few small traders stay open on Friday.

Banks generally follow the government office hours but there are quite a few exceptions to the rule. Some branches keep their doors open for only three hours from 9 am, while some exchange booths are open as late as 7 pm.

Museums and sites tend to be closed on Tuesday.

PUBLIC HOLIDAYS & SPECIAL EVENTS

Most holidays are religious (Islamic and Christian) or celebrations of important dates in the formation of the modern Syrian state. Most Christian holidays fall according to the Julian calendar, which can be as much as a month behind the western (Gregorian) calendar.

For Islamic holidays see the table of holidays in the Regional Facts for the Visitor chapter. Other holidays, not all of which imply any disturbance in day-to-day affairs, are:

New Year's Day
  1 January – official national holiday but many businesses stay open.
Christmas
  7 January – Orthodox Christmas is a fairly low-key affair and only Orthodox businesses are closed for the day.
Commemoration of the Revolution
  8 March – celebrates the coming to power of the Arab Ba'ath Socialist Party.
Commemoration of the Evacuation
  17 April – celebrating the end of French occupation in Syria.

Easter
    Different dates each year. The most important
    date on the Christian calendar.
May Day
    1 May – official national holiday.

Martyrs' Day
    6 May – celebrates all political martyrs who
    died for Syria.

COURSES
If you develop an interest in the Arabic language, there are several options in Damascus. The Arabic Teaching Institute for Foreigners (☎ 222 1538), PO Box 9340, Jadet ash-Shafei No 3, Mezzeh-Villat Sharqiyya, runs two courses, a short one in summer (June to September) and another in winter (October to May). The Goethe Institut and the Centre Culturel Français also run courses in colloquial Arabic.

ACCOMMODATION
Rooms in most of the cheap hotels are let on a shared basis and will have two to four beds. If you want the room to yourself you'll often have to pay for all the beds. For solo male travellers these shared rooms are quite OK and your gear is generally safe. Solo females will usually have to take a room for themselves.

Most hotels will want to keep your passport in the 'safe' overnight. This is generally to ensure payment – tell them you need it to change money at the bank. If you want to hang on to it, the hotel may insist on advance payment for the room.

Hotels officially rated two-star and up generally require payment in US dollars. The more expensive hotels sometimes accept credit cards and with some it is possible to change travellers cheques for the appropriate amounts.

FOOD
Food in Syria can be excellent. While the street food staples of felafel and shwarma are nothing too exciting, there are some excellent restaurants around. If you've already spent time in other Middle Eastern countries, particularly Lebanon, then much of the menu

will be familiar fare but there are also a few local specialities to look out for. *Maqlubbeh* is steamed rice topped with grilled slices of eggplant or meat, grilled tomato and pine nuts. A good dish that, ordered in sufficient quantity, could easily make a very satisfying main course is *mar-ya*, not unlike Turkish *lahmacun*. It is a thin pastry base with a minced meat and spice topping, folded over and cut into sandwich-like squares.

A dessert native to the town of Hama, and well worth seeking out, is *halawat al-jibna* – a soft doughy pastry filled with cream cheese and topped with syrup and ice cream.

Getting There & Away

AIR
Syria's two international airports are at Damascus and Aleppo. Both, but especially Damascus, have regular connections to Europe, other cities in the Middle East, Africa and Asia.

As it's not a popular destination you won't find much discounting on fares to Syria. Nevertheless, prices do vary from one agency to the other, so take the time to call around. At the time of writing the best deals were with either Air France or Turkish Airlines.

If you're planning to tour either Jordan or Turkey as well as Syria, you should consider flying to Amman or Istanbul, as a greater range of airlines serve those cities with a wider spread of fares. Another option worth looking into is taking a charter plane to Adana in southern Turkey and a local bus from there.

People flying out of Syria must pay S£300 airport departure tax.

LAND
Turkey
There are at least four border posts between Syria and Turkey. The busiest and most convenient links Antakya in Turkey with

Aleppo via the Bab al-Hawa border station. This is the route all cross-border buses take and traffic can get fairly congested here with waits of up to a couple of hours.

From Syria, there are direct buses to İstanbul and several other Turkish destinations from Damascus and Aleppo – for details of fares see the Getting There & Away sections for those cities. You can also make your way by microbus from Lattakia, north to an alternative border post near the village of Kassab and on via Yayladağ. There has traditionally been a train that travels once a week between Aleppo and İstanbul's Haydarpaşa station but at the time of writing this service was suspended. It was supposed to resume sometime in 1999 but we haven't been able to confirm whether it has yet.

Jordan
The main border crossing between Syria and Jordan is at Der'a/Ramtha. You can cross by direct bus, service taxi or by using a combination of local transport and walking – for details of the latter see the Der'a section later in this chapter.

From Damascus there is one air-con Karnak bus and one JETT bus daily to Amman. You need to book in advance as demand for seats is high. For details of departure times and prices see the Getting There & Away part of the Damascus section.

As this book was going to print we learnt that a new three-times weekly express train service had begun between Damascus and Amman but no further details were available. It's not known whether this service supplements or replaces the old 'Hejaz' service that operates one a week on this route. See the Damascus Getting There & Away section for further details.

Lebanon
There are plenty of buses from Damascus to Beirut, although to travel direct to Baalbek the only option is a service taxi. You can also travel into Lebanon, to Beirut via Tripoli, from Homs and Lattakia by bus or service taxi; see the relevant city entries later in this chapter.

Saudi Arabia & Kuwait
It is possible to go direct from Syria to Saudi Arabia by bus, passing through Jordan in transit. There are also irregular services all the way across to Kuwait. For details see Getting There & Away in Damascus.

Bringing Your Own Vehicle
It's no problem bringing your own vehicle to Syria, although you should get a *carnet de passage en douane* and your own insurance. The UK Automobile Association requires a financial guarantee for the carnet, which effectively acts as an import duty waiver, as it could be liable for customs and other taxes if the vehicle's exit is not registered within a year. The kind of deposit it requires can be well in excess of US$1000. It is essential to ensure that the carnet is filled out properly at each border crossing or you could be up for a lot of money. The carnet may also need to have listed any more expensive spares that you're planning to carry with you, such as a gearbox.

All this said, drivers have brought their vehicles into Syria without a carnet. In such a case, you have to buy what amounts to a temporary customs waiver on arrival. In Syria it appears this costs about US$50, plus possible bribes to grumpy customs officials. Third-party insurance also has to be bought at the border at the rate of US$36 a month. This supposedly also covers you for Lebanon, but double check. The real value of these compulsory insurance deals is questionable, and it is worth making sure your own insurance company will cover you for Syria.

Obviously, you will need the vehicle's registration and ownership papers, but you do not strictly speaking need an International Driving Permit – your national licence is generally sufficient.

Getting Around

AIR
Syrianair operates a reasonable internal air service and flights are cheap by international standards. Bear in mind that, given

the time taken to get to and from airports, check in and so on, you're unlikely to save much time over the bus; the Damascus-Qamishle run is the only exception to this.

Sample one-way fares from Damascus are as follows: Aleppo S£600; Deir ez-Zur S£600; Qamishle S£900; and Damascus to Lattakia S£500. Return fares are exactly double.

BUS
Syria has a well-developed road network and public transport is frequent and cheap. Distances are short and so journeys rarely take more than four hours. Carry your passport at all times as you may need it for ID checks; you definitely will need it to buy tickets.

Bus/Minibus
The bottom category of buses connect all major towns, and minibuses serve the smaller places. They have no schedule, are often luridly decorated (especially on the inside) and leave when full, so on the less popular routes you may have to wait for an hour or so until one fills up. Note that locals generally call the old minibuses *meecros*. For the sake of clarity, we have distinguished them from the modern vans that are now taking over the roads (see Microbus).

These buses are far less comfortable than the more modern alternatives but as the distances are short it's no real hardship, and it is one of the best ways to meet local people. Conversations on buses can lead to an invitation to someone's house or village.

Journey times are generally longer than with the other buses, as they set people down and pick them up at any point along the route. This has earned them the nickname of 'stop-stops' among some of the locals.

Microbus
The term microbus is blurred, but in general refers to the increasingly popular modern (mostly Japanese) vans on Syrian roads. These are used principally on short hops between cities (such as Homs to Hama) and on many routes to small towns and villages. They are replacing the clat-

tering old minibuses with which they compete, and are more expensive. They too leave when full but because they are smaller and there is no standing room, departures are considerably more frequent.

Karnak & Pullman Buses
The orange-and-white buses of the state-run Karnak company were once the deluxe carriers of the Syrian highways. The company and its buses have barely changed and with so many rival companies employing newer vehicles, Karnak looks a pretty poor cousin. Its buses are perfectly acceptable and connect most major centres, but its network is shrinking. Tickets cost roughly double those on the old buses.

At the end of the 1980s, private companies emerged with buses of the same vintage as Karnak, and in some cases superior. As a rule, they were (and remain) cheaper than Karnak by a few pounds and went by the general name of Pullman. The denomination seems to have fallen into disuse, but for the purposes of this guide is as good as any to distinguish them from the most recent crop of modern buses now roaming Syria's roads. Quality of these buses can vary greatly, and the real distinction is between these and the antique buses in circulation mentioned above. As with Karnak, you must always buy a ticket, with seat assigned, prior to boarding.

Luxury Bus
For want of a better word, we are calling the latest crop of buses 'luxury'. These new companies arrived on the scene in the early 1990s, and in general fares are at least 50% higher than with Karnak. A rigid no-smoking rule is imposed on most, and in the course of the journey a steward will distribute sweets and the occasional cup of water.

Tickets must be bought in advance and buses leave strictly according to a timetable. In some towns all these companies share a bus station, but in others it is a matter of tracking down each company's office. Among the better companies are Qadmous, Al-Ahliah and Al-Ryan.

TRAIN

Syria has a fleet of fairly modern trains made in Russia. They are inexpensive and punctual but the main disadvantage is that the stations are usually several kilometres from the town centres and services only ever seem to pass through in the dead of night.

First class is air-con with aircraft-type seats; 2nd class is the same without air-con.

The main line connects Damascus, Aleppo, Deir ez-Zur, Hassake and Qamishle. A secondary line runs from Aleppo to Lattakia, along the coast to Tartus and again inland to Homs and Damascus. For further details see the relevant Getting There & Away sections.

SERVICE TAXI

The service taxis (shared taxis) only operate on the major routes and can cost three times the microbus fare – sometimes more. Unless you're in a tearing hurry, there's really no need to use them.

CAR

Traffic runs on the right-hand side of the road in Syria. The speed limit in built-up areas is 60km/h, 70km/h on the open road and 110km/h on major highways. The roads are generally quite reasonable in Syria, but when heading off into the backblocks you will find that most signposting is in Arabic only. Night driving can be dangerous and is best avoided.

Rental

Europcar has been joined by Budget and Avis, as well as a gaggle of sometimes dodgy local companies. With the latter, keep your eye on insurance arrangements, which seem quite lackadaisical. Budget's cheapest standard rate is US$45 a day for a Ford Fiesta or something similar, including all insurance and unlimited mileage. Rental for a week comes out at US$259. The local companies can be cheaper, but it's best to look around.

BICYCLE

There is no real problem with riding a bike through Syria, although the summer heat is not ideal for it, particularly in desert areas. Decent spare parts are hard to come by.

HITCHING

Hitching is easy as few people have private cars and it is an accepted means of getting around. Some payment is often expected, as drivers will take passengers to subsidise their own trip. As always, women should think twice before hitching alone. It's been done without incident, but it is risky.

Hostage to Hospitality

The number one rule of travel in Syria is be flexible. It's not that the transport system is bad – on the contrary, all manner of four-wheeled vehicles go wherever you need to go, frequently, and for very little money. But you share your journey with local Syrians and that adds an element of unpredictability. As a foreigner – a guest – you can expect to receive frequent invitations to talk, share in food, and often to come back home or accompany your fellow passenger to wherever it is they're going. Depending on how open you are to this proffered hospitality, you can find yourself alighting from the bus several stops earlier than anticipated in the company of a new companion heading off to go for tea, meet the family, look at some photos, watch some TV ... We've had letters from readers who've spent days with such spontaneous hosts.

All of this is wonderful as long as you're not in any kind of hurry. Anybody with rigid schedules and a strict quota of four sites a day should probably stick to luxury buses, but for anyone with a more relaxed attitude to sightseeing, then taking the locals up on their offers of tea and such is a fine way to experience the country through its people rather than just its old stones.

Damascus

Damascus (Ash-Sham or Dimashq in Arabic) is the capital of Syria and, with an estimated population of six million, its largest city. It owes its existence to the Barada River, which rises high in the Jebel Lubnan ash-Sharqiyya (Anti-Lebanon Range). The waters give life to the Ghouta oasis, making settlement possible in an otherwise uninhabitable area.

Damascus is claimed to be the oldest continuously inhabited city in the world – there was an urban settlement here as long ago as 5000 BC. Later it was a Persian capital, fell to Alexander the Great, became a Greek centre and then a major Roman city. In 635 AD, with Byzantine power on the decline, Damascus fell to the Muslims and rose to primacy in the rapidly expanding Muslim Arab empire. In 1200 it was sacked by the Mongols and then endured centuries of slow decline under the Mamluks and the Ottomans before eventually passing to the French mandate and finally independence.

It is a fascinating city of contrasts, retaining much of the mystery of the oriental bazaars and the gracious, somewhat decayed charm of some of the Islamic world's greatest monuments. Exuding just a hint of its more remote past too, Damascus is well worth spending a few days exploring. Many travellers find themselves caught up in its spell and stay much longer.

ORIENTATION

The city centre is compact and finding your way around on foot is no problem. The heart of the city is Martyrs' Square, and many of the cheap hotels and restaurants are close by. Locals know it as Al-Merjeh.

The main street, Sharia Said al-Jabri, begins at the Hejaz train station and runs north-east, changes its name a couple of times and finishes at the Central Bank building. The entire street is about 1km long and on it you'll find the central post office, tourist office, various airline offices and many mid-range restaurants and hotels.

The Barada River is unfortunately not much more than a smelly drain flowing through the city. On its banks to the west of Martyrs' Square is the Takiyya as-Suleimaniyya mosque and the National Museum.

INFORMATION
Immigration Office
For visa extensions, the central immigration office is on Sharia Filasteen, one block west of the Baramke bus station. Go to the 2nd floor to begin filling in the three forms, for which you'll need three photos (a couple of photographers with ancient cameras across the road can do some awful photos for you). You can get extensions of up to one month. It costs S£25 and takes a working day to process – pick up your passport at 1 pm the following day.

There is another immigration office on Sharia al-Furat, just west of Martyrs' Square, which deals with re-entry visas.

Tourist Office
The main office (☎ 222 2388) is on Sharia 29 Mai, just up from Saahat Yousef al-Azmeh in the centre of town. There's a second, smaller place (☎ 221 0122) in the Ministry of Tourism building by the Takiyya as-Suleimaniyya, near the National Museum.

Money
There are several branches of the Commercial Bank of Syria as well as exchange booths where you can change money fairly easily. The booth on Martyrs' Square is open from 9 am to 6 pm Saturday to Thursday and from 10 am to 2 pm Friday and will change cash and travellers cheques.

The local Amex agent (☎ 221 7813, fax 222 3707) is on the 1st floor above the Sudan Airways office on Sharia Balkis, which is a small street running between sharias al-Mutanabi and Fardous. It can't cash cheques, it can only replace stolen ones. Thomas Cook is represented by Nahas Travel (☎ 223 2000, fax 223 6002) on Sharia Fardous. Again, it can't cash travellers cheques, only arrange for replacements for any stolen. Nahas can

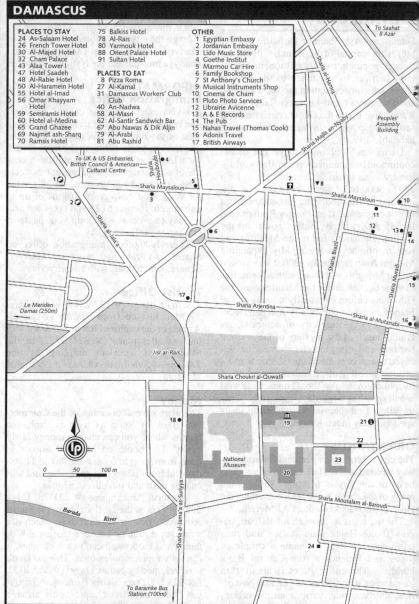

DAMASCUS

PLACES TO STAY
24 As-Salaam Hotel
26 French Tower Hotel
30 Al-Majed Hotel
32 Cham Palace
43 Alaa Tower I
47 Hotel Saadeh
48 Al-Rabie Hotel
50 Al-Haramein Hotel
55 Hotel al-Imad
56 Omar Khayyam
   Hotel
59 Semiramis Hotel
60 Hotel al-Medina
64 Grand Ghazee
69 Najmet ash-Sharq
70 Ramsis Hotel

75 Balkiss Hotel
78 Al-Rais
80 Yarmouk Hotel
88 Orient Palace Hotel
91 Sultan Hotel

PLACES TO EAT
8 Pizza Roma
27 Al-Kamal
31 Damascus Workers' Club
   Club
40 An-Nadwa
58 Al-Masri
62 Al-Santir Sandwich Bar
67 Abu Nawas & Dik Aljin
79 Al-Arabi
81 Abu Rashid

OTHER
1 Egyptian Embassy
2 Jordanian Embassy
3 Lido Music Store
4 Goethe Institut
5 Marmou Car Hire
6 Family Bookshop
7 St Anthony's Church
9 Musical Instruments Shop
10 Cinema de Cham
11 Pluto Photo Services
12 Librairie Avicenne
13 A & E Records
14 The Pub
15 Nahas Travel (Thomas Cook)
16 Adonis Travel
17 British Airways

To Saahat
8 Azar

Peoples'
Assembly
Building

Sharia al-Hamra
Sharia Majlis an-Nyaby
Sharia Maysaloun
Sharia Maysaloun

To UK & US Embassies,
British Council & American
Cultural Centre

Sharia Hboubi(?)
Sharia Maysaloun

Sharia al-Jala'a

Sharia Brazil
Sharia Muradi

Le Meriden
Damas (250m)

Sharia Arjentina
Sharia al-Mutanabi

Jisr ar-Rais

Sharia Choukri al-Quwatli

National
Museum

Sharia al-Jama'a as-Sunnya

Sharia Mousalam al-Baroudi

Barada   River

0   50   100 m

To Baramke Bus
Station (100m)

DAMASCUS

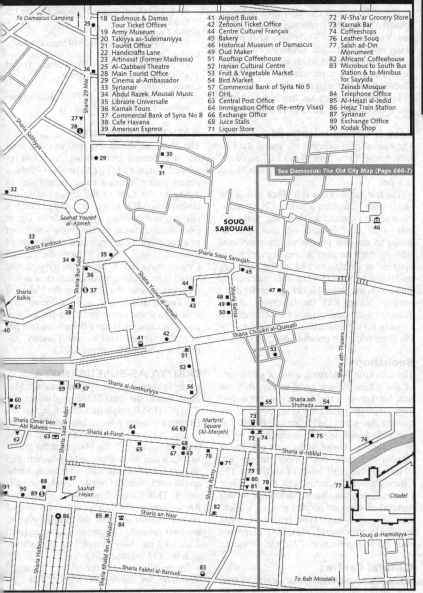

18 Qadmous & Damas
   Tour Ticket Offices
19 Army Museum
20 Takiyya as-Suleimaniyya
21 Tourist Office
22 Handicrafts Lane
23 Artinasat (Former Madrassa)
25 Al-Qabbani Theatre
28 Main Tourist Office
29 Cinema al-Ambassador
33 Syrianair
34 Abdul Razek Mousali Music
35 Librairie Universale
36 Karnak Tours
37 Commercial Bank of Syria No 8
38 Cafe Havana
39 American Express

41 Airport Buses
42 Zeitouni Ticket Office
44 Centre Culturel Français
45 Bakery
46 Historical Museum of Damascus
49 Oud Maker
51 Rooftop Coffeehouse
52 Iranian Cultural Centre
53 Fruit & Vegetable Market
54 Bird Market
57 Commercial Bank of Syria No 5
61 DHL
63 Central Post Office
64 Immigration Office (Re-entry Visas)
66 Exchange Office
68 Juice Stalls
71 Liquor Store

72 Al-Sha'ar Grocery Store
73 Karnak Bar
74 Coffeeshops
76 Leather Souq
77 Salah ad-Din
   Monument
82 Africans' Coffeehouse
83 Microbus to South Bus
   Station & to Minibus
   for Sayyida
   Zeinab Mosque
84 Telephone Office
85 Al-Hejazi al-Jedid
86 Hejaz Train Station
87 Syrianair
89 Exchange Office
90 Kodak Shop

See Damascus: The Old City Map (Page 666-7)

SOUQ
SAROUJAH

arrange to have money wired to you in a matter of hours and can also give you cash against a Visa card (it represents MasterCard and Visa in Syria). Travellers also report being able to get cash advances on a Visa card at a shop on the south side of Martyrs' Square that has a prominent Visa/Diners Club/MasterCard sign outside.

To change money on the black market just walk down the Souq al-Hamidiyya.

Post & Communications

The central post office is on Sharia Said al-Jabri and is open from 8 am to 7 pm daily except Friday and holidays, when it closes at 1 pm.

The telephone office is a block east of the Hejaz train station on Sharia an-Nasr and is open around the clock. However, you can't make operator calls and will instead be directed to the card phones on the street outside. As there are card phones at every major junction in Damascus and as the cards are sold throughout the city at places indicated by stickers on the phone kiosks, you really don't need to bother with the telephone office. Telegrams can be sent from this office during vaguely set daytime hours, as can faxes. For the latter you must present your passport.

Bookshops

The Librairie Avicenne, a block south-east of the Cham Palace hotel is possibly the best bookshop in the country as far as foreign-language publications are concerned – though that's not saying much. It also has a selection of days-old international press. The Librairie Universalle, just off Sharia Yousef al-Azmeh, has a more current crop of novels plus shelf-loads of art books. The Cham Palace, Sheraton and Le Meridien Damas hotels also have bookshops with a handful of standard airport novels, a selection of coffee-table type books on Syria and the Islamic world, plus *Time* magazine and maybe *International Herald Tribune*.

Cultural Centres

Bring your passport as many cultural centres require ID before they'll let you enter.

American Cultural Center
　(☎ 333 8443) off Sharia Mansour near the US embassy
British Council
　(☎ 333 8436, fax 332 1467) 10 Sharia al-Jala'a
Centre Culturel Français
　(☎ 224 6181, fax 231 6194) off Sharia Yousef al-Azmeh in central Damascus
Goethe Institut
　(☎ 333 6673, fax 332 0849) 4 Sharia Houboubi, off Sharia Maysaloun

NATIONAL MUSEUM

The National Museum is well worth at least one visit. Behind the imposing facade (the relocated entrance of Qasr al-Heir al-Gharbi, a desert palace/military camp near Palmyra dating to the time of the Umayyad caliph Hisham in 688) is a fantastic array of exhibits ranging from written cylinders from Ugarit (Ras Shamra) using the first known alphabet to a complete room decorated in the style of the 18th century Azem Palace (see the Old City section). Highlights are the hypogaeum, which is an amazing reconstruction of an underground burial chamber from the Valley of the Tombs at Palmyra, and the fresco-covered synagogue recovered from Dura Europos. The museum is open from 9 am to 6 pm (4 pm in winter) daily except Tuesday; admission is S£300 (students S£25).

TAKIYYA AS-SULEIMANIYYA

Lying immediately east of the National Museum and to the west of the post office, the Takiyya (1554) was built to the design of the Ottoman empire's most brilliant architect, Sinan, builder of İstanbul's Blue Mosque and Süleymaniye. It has two parts: the graceful black and white mosque to the south, and an arcaded courtyard with additional rooms on the north side that would have housed pilgrims. This former hostel area is now the **Army Museum** with a mixed collection of military hardware from the Bronze Age to the near present. The museum is open from 8 am to 2 pm daily except Tuesday; admission is S£15 (students S£5).

Immediately east of the takiyya is a small *madrassa*, or theological school, that now serves as the **Artisanat**, an appealing handicraft market where the former students' cells are now workshops and sales spaces.

OLD CITY

Most of the sights of Damascus are in the old city, which is surrounded by what was initially a **Roman wall**. The wall itself has been flattened and rebuilt several times over the past 2000 years. The best preserved section is between Bab as-Salaama (the Gate of Safety) and Bab Touma (Thomas Gate – named after a son-in-law of Emperor Heraclius) in the north-east corner.

Next to the citadel is the entrance to one of the main covered markets, the **Souq al-Hamidiyya**. This cobbled souq with its bustling crowds, hawkers and tenacious merchants is worlds away from the traffic jams and chaos of the streets outside. Most of the shops sell handicrafts.

At the far end of the market the vaulted roof gives way to two enormous Corinthian columns supporting a decorated lintel – the remains of the western gate of the old Roman **Temple of Jupiter** dating from the 3rd century AD.

Salah ad-Din (1138-93)

In contrast to the dishonourable reputation of the Crusaders, Salah ad-Din (Saladin) tends to be portrayed as a true knight in the romanticised European tradition of chivalry. He was born in Tikrit in modern Iraq to Kurdish parents. At the age of 14 he joined other members of his family in the service of Nur ad-Din (Nureddin) of the ruling Zangi dynasty. By the time Nur ad-Din died in 1174, Salah ad-Din had risen to the rank of general and had already taken over de facto control of Egypt. He quickly took control of Syria and in the next 10 years extended his control into parts of Mesopotamia, careful not to infringe too closely on the territory of the now largely powerless Abbasid caliphate in Baghdad. In 1187 Salah ad-Din crushed the Crusaders in the Battle of Hittin and stormed Jerusalem. By the end of 1189, he had swept the Franks out of Lattakia and Jabla to the north and castles such as Kerak and Shobak (both in Jordan) inland. The blitzkrieg provoked Western Europe into action, precipitating the Third Crusade and bringing Salah ad-Din up against Richard III 'the Lionheart' of England. After countless clashes and sieges the two rival warriors signed a peace in November 1192, giving the Crusaders the coast and the interior to the Muslims. Salah ad-Din died three months later in Damascus.

SYRIA

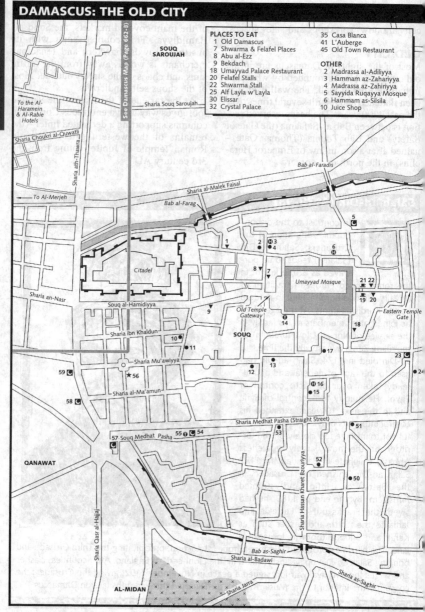

DAMASCUS: THE OLD CITY

SOUQ
SAROUJAH

To the Al-
Haramein
& Al-Rabie
Hotels

See Damascus Map (Page 662-3)

Sharia Choukri al-Quwatli

Sharia ath-Thawra

Sharia Souq Saroujah

To Al-Merjeh

Sharia al-Malek Faisal

Bab al-Faradis

Bab al-Farag

Bab al-Farag

Citadel

Sharia an-Nasr

Souq al-Hamidiyya

Old Temple
Gateway

Umayyad Mosque

Eastern Temple
Gate

Sharia ibn Khaldun

SOUQ

Sharia Mu'awiyya

Sharia al-Ma'amun

Sharia Medhat Pasha (Straight Street)

QANAWAT

Souq Medhat Pasha

Sharia Hassan Kharet Bzouriyya

Sharia Qasr al-Hajaj

Bab as-Saghir

Sharia al-Badawi

Sharia as-Saghir

AL-MIDAN

Sharia Jarra

PLACES TO EAT
1 Old Damascus
7 Shwarma & Felafel Places
8 Abu al-Ezz
9 Bekdach
18 Umayyad Palace Restaurant
20 Felafel Stalls
22 Shwarma Stall
25 Alf Layla w'Layla
30 Elissar
32 Crystal Palace

35 Casa Blanca
41 L'Auberge
45 Old Town Restaurant

OTHER
2 Madrassa al-Adiliyya
3 Hammam az-Zahariyya
4 Madrassa az-Zahiriyya
5 Sayyida Ruqayya Mosque
6 Hammam as-Silsila
10 Juice Shop

DAMASCUS: THE OLD CITY

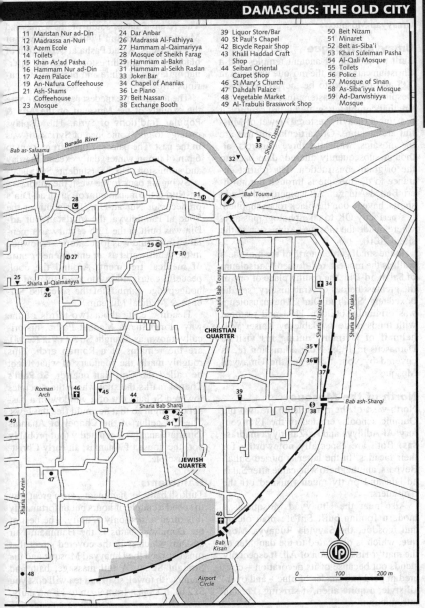

Opposite the end of the market is the Umayyad Mosque.

Umayyad Mosque

Built on the site of ancient temples and a Christian cathedral, the mosque was built in 705 and designed to be the greatest ever. Despite several disasters, including a huge fire that completely gutted it last century, it remains a (heavily restored) jewel of Muslim architecture. Of particular interest are the mosaics, while the three minarets, although subsequently altered, date back to the original construction. The tourist entrance to the mosque is through the northern Bab al-Amarah. All women, and men in shorts, have to don the black robes supplied. It's perfectly OK to take photographs anywhere inside the mosque. Admission to the site is S£10.

In the small garden north of the mosque's walls is the modest, red-domed Mausoleum of Salah ad-Din, the resting place of one of the greatest heroes of Arab history (see the boxed text 'Salah ad-Din'). The mausoleum was originally built in 1193 and restored with funds made available by Kaiser Wilhelm II of Germany during his visit to Damascus in 1898. Your admission fee is covered by your ticket for the Umayyad Mosque.

North of the Mosque

North-west of the mausoleum are two old Quranic schools, erected in the 13th century: Al-Adiliyya and Az-Zahiriyya madrassas. Both are especially noteworthy for their facades. In the latter is buried Sultan Beybars, another hero who came after Salah ad-Din and pretty much finished off the Crusaders.

Also near the Umayyad Mosque is a modern Iranian-built Shi'ite mausoleum and mosque, the Sayyida Ruqayya Mosque, which is dedicated to the daughter of the martyr Hussein, son of Ali. It especially stands out because of its decoration – covered in gold and shades of blue – and overall style, a quite alien, if striking, Persian introduction.

South of the Mosque

The Azem Palace, south of the Umayyad Mosque, was built in 1749 by the governor of Damascus, As'ad Pasha al-Azem, out of black basalt and limestone, and the alternating layers of white and black give a curious effect.

The rooms of the modest palace also house the exhibits of the Museum of the Arts & Popular Traditions of Syria. The displays manage to give some idea of Syria as it was in the past. The palace is open from 9 am to 6 pm (4 pm in winter) daily except Tuesday and admission is S£300 (students S£25).

Swinging back to the west, the Madrassa an-Nuri is the mausoleum of Salah ad-Din's predecessor Nur ad-Din. Just south of the Souq al-Hamidiyya, the Maristan Nur ad-Din was built in the 12th century as a mental hospital and was for centuries renowned in the Arab world as an enlightened centre of medical treatment. Around the cool, peaceful courtyard inside are displayed the hodgepodge exhibits of the so-called Science & Medical Museum.

Heading east, about two-thirds of the way along Sharia Medhat Pasha, historically known as Straight Street (Via Recta), are the remains of a Roman arch. This roughly marks the boundary of what might be called the Christian quarter. St Paul's Chapel marks the spot where the disciples lowered St Paul out of a window in a basket one night so that he could flee the Jews. The old cellar of the Chapel of Ananias (Sharia Hanania) is reputedly (but probably not) the house of Ananias, an early Christian disciple.

Hammams

Turkish baths, or hammams, are a great way to spend a couple of hours but unfortunately it is often a men-only activity. The best of the Damascus baths is the Hammam Nur ad-Din, which is in the covered street that runs between the Umayyad Mosque and the Straight Street. A full massage, bath and sauna with towel, soap and tea will cost you S£240. It's open from 9 am to 11 pm daily.

continued on page 675

MOSQUES

Embodying the Islamic faith, and representing its most predominant architectural feature is the mosque, or *masjid* or *jamaa*. The building was developed in the very early days of the religion and takes its form from the simple, private houses where the first believers gathered to worship.

The house belonging to the Prophet Mohammed is said to have provided the prototype for the mosque. It had an enclosed oblong courtyard with huts (housing Mohammed's wives) along one wall and a rough portico providing shade. This plan developed with the courtyard becoming the *sahn*, the portico the arcaded *riwaqs* and the houses the *haram* or prayer hall.

Top: Geometric Patterns often cover doors and ceilings. (Photo by Davor Pavichich)

Right: The Umayyad Mosque, Damascus, with arcaded riwaq and minaret from where the muezzin traditionally made the call to prayer.

ANDREW HUMPHREYS

Typically divided into a series of aisles, the centre aisle in the prayer hall is wider than the rest and leads to a vaulted niche in the wall called the *mihrab*; this indicates the direction of Mecca, which Muslims must face when they pray.

Before entering the prayer hall and participating in communal worship, Muslims must perform a ritual washing of the hands, forearms and face. For this purpose mosques have traditionally had a large ablutions fountain at the centre of the courtyard, often carved from marble and worn by centuries of use. These days, modern mosques just have rows of taps.

The mosque also serves as some kind of community centre, and often you will find groups of small children or even adults receiving lessons (usually in the Quran), people in quiet prayer and others simply enjoying a peaceful nap – mosques provide wonderfully tranquil havens from the hustle and bustle of the streets outside.

Visiting Mosques

With the exception of Saudi Arabia and Yemen, non-Muslims are generally quite welcome to visit mosques at any time other than during Friday prayers. You must dress modestly. For men that means no shorts; for women that means no shorts, tight pants, shirts that aren't done up, or anything else that might be considered immodest. Some of the more frequently visited mosques provide wrap-around cloaks for anyone that is improperly dressed. Shoes have to be removed or, again, some mosques will provide slip-on shoe covers for a small fee.

In Yemen some historical mosques that are not in active ritual use can be entered but you must remember never do so without asking permission first.

Top: The mihrab indicates the direction of Mecca.

Bottom: The minbar is platform on which the imam stands to deliver his sermon.

DAMIEN SIMONIS

Stylistic Developments

The earliest of the grand mosques inherited much from Byzantine models (the Dome of the Rock is a basilica) but with the spread of the Muslim domain various styles soon developed, each influenced by local artistic traditions. The Umayyads of Damascus, for example, favoured square minarets; the Abbasids of Iraq built spiral minarets echoing the ziggurats of the Babylonians; the Fatimid dynasty of North Africa made much use of decorative stucco work.

The vocabulary of mosque building quickly became very sophisticated and expressive, reaching its apotheosis under the Mamluks (1250 to 1517). A military dynasty of former slaves ruling out of Egypt, the Mamluks were great patrons of the arts and built many mosques, *madrassas* (theological schools), *khanqahs* (monasteries) and mausoleum complexes. Their buildings are characterised by the banding of different coloured stone (a technique known as

Top: Every mosque has some form of ablutions fountain for ritual washing before prayer.

Right: Carved dome from the Northern Cemetery, Egypt

ablaq) and by the elaborate carvings and patterning around windows and in the recessed portals. The best examples of their patronage are found in Cairo but impressive Mamluk monuments also remain in Damascus and Jerusalem.

The Mamluks were eventually defeated by the Ottoman Turks who followed up their military gains with an equally expansive campaign of construction. Designed on the basic principle of a dome on a square, and instantly recognisable by their slim pencil-shaped minarets, Ottoman mosques can be found throughout Egypt, Israel, the Palestinian Territories, Lebanon, Syria and Iraq. The most impressive monuments of this era, however, were built at the heart of the empire – the Süleymaniye Mosque in İstanbul and the Selimiye Mosque at Edirne, both the work of the Turkish master architect Sinan.

Of all the non-Gulf regions of the Middle East, Persia was the one area that did not fall to the Turks. The Persian Safavid dynasty proved strong enough to hold the Ottomans at bay and thus Iran, and neighbouring Afghanistan, have a very different architectural tradition to anywhere else in the Middle East. Persian architecture has its roots not in Byzantium/Constantinople but in the eastern lands occupied by the Mongols who swept down from Central Asia. Their grand buildings are much simpler in form but made startling by the sumptuous use of cobalt blue and turquoise tiling which often covers every available surface.

Left: Lavishly decorated late Mamluk minaret from the Mosque of Amir Qurqumas (1506) with its characteristic three tiers.

Middle: Early Mamluk minaret from the Mosque of Beybars al-Jashankir (1307) with square base and pepper pot cap.

Right: Ottoman pencil-minaret from the Mosque of Süleyman Pasha (1528) at the Citadel.

BRADLEY MAYHEW

KRISTEN HELLSTROM

Top: The entrance to the 17th century Sheikh Lotfollāh Mosque, Meidūn-é Emām Khomeinī, Esfahān, Iran

Middle: Dazzlingly white and visible throughout the surrounding countryside, the Ahmad ibn Alwan Mosque, Yifrus, Yemen, is over 500 years old.

Bottom: The spectacular Sultan Ahmet Camii (Blue Mosque) in İstanbul is notable for its six slender minarets and its luminous blue impression.

DIANA MAYFIELD

CHRIS MELLOR

PATRICK SYDER

ANDREW HUMPHREYS

Top Left: The Emām Mosque in Esfahān, one of the most stunning pieces of architecture in Iran, changes colour according to the light conditions.

Top Right: Although the Mamluk dynasty ended almost 500 years ago, their decorative mosque building style of patterned domes and three-tiered cylindrical minarets has come back into vogue in the 20th century, as at the Mosque of Abu Abbas al-Mursi (1943) in Alexandria, Egypt.

Bottom: The architectural style of the Dome of the Rock in Jerusalem, one of the earliest mosques ever built, was never subsequently imitated and it remains unique in the Islamic world.

Mosques Not to be Missed

Dome of the Rock (688), Jerusalem – One of the earliest mosques ever built and with its octagonal plan and mosaic-encrusted exterior, one of the most unique of all Islamic structures. (See page 343)

Umayyad Mosque (705), Damascus – An adaptation of a Christian cathedral (itself built on the site of a Roman temple), this mosque is notable for its age, size and the stunning golden mosaics that cover the courtyard walls. (See page 668)

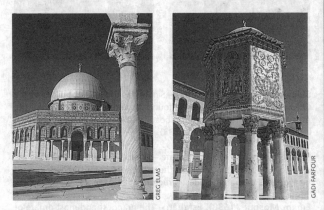

Left: Dome of the Rock

Right: The Umayyad Mosque

Mosque of ibn Tulun (879), Cairo – Claimed to be the first building to use the pointed arch that has since come to typify Islamic architecture, it also has a wonderful spiral minaret based on Iraqi models. (See page 161)

Azīm-é Gōhar Shād Mosque (1418), Mashhad – This is the jewel at the heart of this pilgrimage city's holy shrine complex, built by the wife of the son of the Central Asian warlord Timur (Tamerlane); it shows a clear kinship with the mosques of Samarkand and Bukhara. (See page 267)

Left: Mosque of ibn Tulun

Right: Azīm-é Gōhar Shād Mosque

MOSQUES

EDDIE GERALD

TOM BROSNAHAN

Left: Süleymaniye

Right: Selimiye Mosque

Süleymaniye (1557), İstanbul – Sinan was the master builder of the Ottoman empire and his work is found throughout the region, but the grandest of his mosques are the beautiful Blue Mosque and the even larger Süleymaniye. (See page 733)

Selimiye Mosque (1574), Edirne – Sinan's showpiece mosques are in İstanbul but his masterpiece, the most harmonious and elegant of his works, is this more modest structure. (See page 742)

Emām Mosque (1638), Esfahān – The grandest and most ornate of the garish Persian mosques, with almost every surface covered by shimmering turquoise tiles and the whole thing topped by a great 54m-high dome. (See page 258)

JOHN BORTHWICK

Left: Emām Mosque

continued from page 668
PLACES TO STAY
Camping
Damascus Camping, also known as *Harasta Camping* (☎ 445 5870), 4km out of town on the road to Homs, charges S£250 per person a day. The location is inconvenient but it is popular with some of the overland truck tours that make their way through here.

Hotels
Damascus has a big selection of cheap hotels grouped around Martyrs' Square. However, many double as brothels and will turn away foreigners who genuinely want a bed only, or will invite them in for a bed with extras.

The true travellers' ghetto is in Saroujah district in Sharia Bahsa, off Sharia Choukri al-Quwatli. *Al-Haramein Hotel* (☎ 231 9489, fax 231 4299, Sharia Bahsa) is an enchanting old house converted into a hotel. Rooms are basic with no private bathrooms and there are only two terrible toilets, but there are hot showers in the basement and the central courtyard is beautiful. Beds in share rooms cost S£150, while singles/doubles/triples go for S£200/325/425. You can also sleep on the roof for S£100. This place is *the* travellers' favourite in Damascus, so book in advance to secure a room.

Al-Rabie Hotel (☎ 231 8374, fax 231 1875, Sharia Bahsa) is another old house with a courtyard that's even more attractive than at Al-Haramein, however the rooms are not as good. Singles/doubles are S£200/350.

There's little to choose between the rest of the cheapies but *Najmet ash-Sharq* (☎ 222 9139, Martyr's Square), on the south-west corner of the square above the juice stalls, is relatively clean and a bit less seedy than most of the other places around here. Singles/doubles with fan and bathroom are S£300/500.

Al-Rais (☎ 221 4252), one block east and south of Al-Merjeh, is recommended. It has basic rooms that contain nothing more than a bed but it comes with fresh sheets and the bathrooms are scrubbed regularly. A double with ensuite goes for S£400.

If you can't get into the Al-Haramein or Al-Rabie then our advice would be to push the budget a little and consider staying at one of the following, listed cheapest first.

Yarmouk Hotel (☎ 221 3283) is one of the better options among the proliferation of two-star joints in the sidestreets off Al-Merjeh. While the rooms are basic, they are clean and most have balconies with partial views of the square. Singles/doubles are US$17/23.

Sultan Hotel (☎ 222 5768, fax 224 0372, Sharia Mousalam al-Baroudi), just west of the Hejaz train station, is quite easily the best of the cheaper mid-range hotels. It's a well run place with a desk staff that speaks English, plus there's a small library, a notice board and a decent reception/breakfast area with satellite TV. Some of the rooms are a bit shabby and only have a fan but others are air-con and fine. Rates are US$18/24, or US$24/30 with breakfast.

As-Salaam Hotel (☎ 221 9764, fax 231 7457), south off Sharia Mousalam al-Baroudi, is a close second best to the Sultan. It has two floors of spotlessly clean air-con rooms all with newly fitted bathrooms. Singles/doubles are US$17/24.

French Tower Hotel (☎ 231 4000, fax 231 4002, Sharia 29 Mai) has clean, bright air-con rooms with ensuites. There's also a nice breakfast terrace with views of northern Damascus and Jebel Qassioun. The rooms are a bargain at S£1200/1500.

Al-Majed Hotel (☎ 232 3300, fax 232 3304) just off Sharia 29 Mai, behind the Cinema al-Ambassador, represents even more of a bargain; it's new and modern and has spacious air-con rooms with fridge, satellite TV and spotless new bathrooms. At the time of writing it was charging S£1500 a double.

PLACES TO EAT
Budget Dining
The sidestreets off Martyrs' Square are crowded with cheap eateries, mostly offering shwarma and felafel, while some of the pastry shops also do some good savouries – we particularly recommend *Abu Rashid*, which is at the top of the steps down the alley at the south-east corner of the square.

Al-Masri (*Sharia Said al-Jabri*) is an excellent cheap lunch place heavily patronised by local office workers. The name means 'the Egyptian' and much of the menu is the kind of home-cooked fare you'd find in the backstreet eateries of Cairo, including no-frills dishes like *shakshouka* (fried egg and mince meat; S£65), *fuul* (mashed beans) and a variety of *fatahs* (bread soaked in humous and oil, topped with chickpeas and meat; S£80). It's filling stuff.

An-Nadwa Restaurant (*Sharia al-Mutanabi*), off main Sharia Bur Said, is more like a work canteen than a restaurant, with a basic menu and average but cheap food. Kebabs are S£60 to S£80 and *mezze* (hors d'oeuvres) are under S£20. Beer is also served and it's about the cheapest in town at S£36 (but send the 'complimentary' nuts back as they'll appear on the bill and cost more than the drink).

Since most people like to spend the bulk of their time in Damascus in the old city, it's a logical place to look for a bite to eat too. The best bet is the small alley east of the Umayyad Mosque; just past the two coffee-houses are a couple of very good shwarma places and a stall that does probably the best value felafel in town – a truly fat felafel with salad will cost you S£25. There's another collection of felafel and shwarma hole-in-the-wall eateries in the covered market lane that runs north off Souq al-Hamidiyya just before you reach the mosque.

Restaurants

The cheaper restaurants are in the Martyrs' Square area.

Al-Arabi, off the south-west corner of the square, is the name of two adjacent cheap restaurants, both run by the same management and sharing the same extensive menu with an unusually wide range of meat and vegetable dishes. The food is hit and miss and there are no prices given, but for a main dish plus a couple of mezze you can expect to pay S£200. The staff is known to be extremely rude but if you can get a table out on the pavement it's worth putting up with them.

Abu Nawas and *Dik Aljin,* on the south-west corner of Martyrs' Square, are two ad-

jacent new eateries, both very clean and efficiently run, and with similarly short menus of mezze, kebabs and chicken. A main meal with a couple of mezze and a cold Barada beer will come to S£200.

Damascus Workers' Club, off Sharia 29 Mai behind the Cinema al-Ambassador, is a garden restaurant in the sprawling courtyard of an old house, complete with fountain and plenty of greenery. A lot of people come here just to drink but the food is extremely good – it's standard fare like mezze, kebabs and *shish tawouk* (grilled, skewered chicken) but all very well done and reasonably priced (two mezze, two kebabs and two beers came to S£385). It's open from 5 pm to midnight.

Al-Kamal (*Sharia 29 Mai*), beside the tourist office, has a menu that features many home-style dishes like mixed vegetable stews but the best are on the changing daily menu – try the *kabsa*, which is exotically spiced rice with chicken or lamb. Main dishes are around S£90, while mezze are S£15 to S£30.

Crystal Palace (☎ 542 0052, Sharia Qasr al-Ballur), just outside the Old City walls near Bab Touma, is a good, moderately priced open-air restaurant. It's a garden-type affair, separated from the main road by vine-covered trellises and is fairly small and intimate with friendly staff. The menu's composed of mezze (around S£30 each) and grilled meats (S£100), and the food, while not exceptional, is good. Beer is available, though raki is definitely the drink of choice with most of the patrons.

Elissar (☎ 542 4300, Bab Touma) offers perhaps the best dining in Damascus. It's an enormous old house with tables filling the courtyard and two upper levels of terraces. While the menu of typical Syrian cuisine offers few surprises, the food is as good as it gets. Of course, it doesn't come cheap: entrées are in the region of S£60, while main dishes clock in at around S£250. Our bill for two was S£800 (which included two local beers and a huge platter of complimentary fruit) but we considered it money well spent. Reservations are recommended.

ENTERTAINMENT

The finest place to relax in Damascus is at either of the two coffeehouses nestled in the shadow of the Umayyad Mosque's eastern wall. Bar-wise, about the most convenient and a popular haunt with locals and backpackers alike is the *Karnak* above the Hotel Siyaha on Martyrs' Square – just head up the stairs in the street entrance off the square. You can eat here, but really it's more a serious drinking place with patrons knocking back the beers (S£50) or araq until 2 am. You wouldn't bring your mother here. On the other hand, she'd probably love *Damascus Workers' Club* – see Places to Eat. Though people do eat here, plenty take a table and order a beer (S£55). It's open to midnight.

Most of the cinemas around show pretty appalling fare. The exception is the *Cinema de Cham* at the Cham Palace hotel on Sharia Maysaloun. This place regularly screens almost-current Hollywood releases in its two wide-screen auditoriums. Tickets cost S£150. The only way to find out what's showing is to drop by.

GETTING THERE & AWAY
Air

There are several Syrianair offices scattered about the city centre (for example, in Sharia Fardous and on Sharia Said al-Jabri across from the post office); central sales and reservations numbers include ☎ 223 2154, ☎ 223 2159 and ☎ 222 9000. The telephone numbers for Damascus airport are ☎ 543 0201/9.

From Damascus Syrianair flies once or twice daily to Aleppo (S£600 one way, one hour), three times a week to Deir ez-Zur (S£600 one way, one hour), three times a week to Qamishle (S£900 one way, 80 minutes), and once a week to Lattakia (S£500 one way, 45 minutes).

Most of the other airline offices are grouped across from the Cham Palace Hotel on Sharia Maysaloun or one block south on Sharia Fardous.

Bus

There are two main bus stations in Damascus: Harasta, which has luxury bus services to the north, and Baramke, which deals with services to the south, plus international services to Jordan, Lebanon, Egypt and the Gulf. In addition there are several minibus and microbus stations serving regional destinations.

The Harasta station is about 6km northwest of the city centre. All the big private bus companies have their offices here, as well as Karnak. Prices are much of a muchness and average one-way fares include Aleppo (S£150, five hours), Deir ez-Zur (S£175, six hours), Hama (S£85, 2½ hours), Homs (S£70, two hours), Lattakia (S£150, 4½ hours), Palmyra (S£130, four hours) and Tartus (S£110, 3½ hours). To get up to Harasta you can take a microbus from Martyrs' Square (ask for 'karajat Harasta') for S£5 or a taxi will cost S£30 on the meter.

Cheaper, old buses go from the Baramke station, which is about a 15 to 20 minute walk west of Martyrs' Square. This is also where you catch the buses for Beirut (4½ hours, S£175), departing every hour from 7.30 am to 4.30 pm, and to Amman, with services at 7 am and 3 pm for a fare of US$6 or JD5 (no Syrian pounds accepted). All these services go from outside the Karnak office, which is in the south-west corner of the station (the furthest away from you if you approach from Hejaz train station).

Buses to İstanbul (S£1500, 30 hours) and other Turkish destinations such as Antakya (S£350) and Ankara (S£1200) all go from Harasta. There are frequent departures during the day – just show up and book a ticket on the next bus out. Note, if you are on a tight budget then it's cheaper to get local transport to Aleppo and on to the border and then get Turkish buses once you're across.

The Aman bus company has a daily service to Riyadh (S£1500) at 11 am, one to Jeddah (S£1000) on Tuesday, Thursday and Saturday, and buses to Kuwait (S£2500) on Saturday, Wednesday and Thursday. These buses go from the Baramke terminal and tickets should be bought in advance.

Minibus & Microbus

From Baramke station microbuses depart for destinations south-east and north-east of

Damascus including Khan Arnabeh (for Quneitra). From a large minibus station in the district of Bab Mousala (known as 'karajat Bab Mousala', or also 'karajat Der'a'), about 2km south of the Old City, services depart for south of Damascus including Suweida and Der'a (for Bosra and the Jordanian border). The easiest way to get to the depot is by taxi, which should cost about S£25 from Martyrs' Square.

Train

Most trains leave from the Khaddam train station, about 5km south-west of the centre (a shuttle bus connects with the Hejaz station in the centre). Trains are infrequent and slower than the buses; they run daily to Homs, Hama, Aleppo, Raqqa, Deir ez-Zur, Hassake, Qamishle, Tartus and Lattakia. The trip to Qamishle can take 16 hours or more.

The only trains leaving from the Hejaz train station are the 7 am Friday service south to Der'a (S£26, three hours) and the weekly service to Amman (stopping at Der'a). The latter departs at 7 am Monday morning and costs S£157 (one class for all). If you are catching this train, double-check the departure day – traditionally it departs Sunday but at the time of research had been switched.

Service Taxi

There is a service-taxi station which is part of the Baramke terminal. Taxis leave throughout the day and night for Amman (five hours, S£385 or JD5.500) and Beirut (three hours, S£191 or S£291 depending on where in Beirut).

GETTING AROUND
To/From the Airport

The airport is 35km south-east of Damascus. Local buses leave every 30 minutes from next to the Choukri al-Quwatli flyover from 5.30 am to 11 pm. The trip costs S£10 and takes about 45 minutes.

Bus & Taxi

Damascus is well served with a local bus and microbus network, but as the centre is so compact you'll rarely have to use them.

All the taxis are yellow and there are hundreds of them. A ride across town should never cost more than S£25.

South of Damascus

Much of the area from Damascus south to the Jordanian border, about 100km away, is intensively farmed, fertile agricultural land. Around the border and to the south-east, the good soil gives way to an unyielding black basalt plain, and the region is known as the Hauran. The capital of the Hauran is Suweida, 75km south of Damascus. It's a dull place but it does possess a good museum with some stunning mosaics which alone almost make the trip worthwhile. You get here by microbus from Damascus' Baramke terminal (S£22, 1¾ hours).

To the west of Suweida the land rises to the Golan Heights, occupied by Israel since 1967 and the principal bone of contention in the on-again off-again Israeli-Syrian peace talks.

DER'A

There's not a lot of interest in this southern town, 100km from Damascus, although most travellers have to pass through to get to the ruins at Bosra or to the border with Jordan. We do not recommend staying here overnight but if you have to then there are a clutch of grotty hotels on the main drag, Sharia Ibrahim Hanano. Of these *Orient Palace Hotel* (☎ *238 304*), aka the Al-Chark, is easily the best.

Getting There & Away

The bus station lies about 3km east of the centre of town. Buses and minibuses to and from Damascus (Bab Mousala station) cost S£25 and take about two hours, while microbuses cost S£50 and take 1½ hours.

The diesel train for Amman from Damascus passes through Der'a at about noon on Sunday and costs S£150. The same train passes back through on its way to Damascus (S£25) on Monday at 10.30 am but it would be worth checking the departure days as these recently changed. There is an additional service between Der'a and Damascus on Friday.

Jordan Service taxis shuttle between the bus stations in Der'a and Ramtha (on the Jordanian side), and cost S£150 or JD2 per person. Alternatively, you can hitch a ride or walk.

BOSRA

The town of Bosra is 40km east of Der'a. Once important for its location at the crossroads of major trade and, under the Muslims, pilgrimage routes, it is now little more than a backwater. But what a weird and wonderful backwater it is. Apart from having possibly the best preserved Roman theatre in existence, the rest of the town is built in, around and over old sections of Roman buildings, and made almost entirely out of black basalt blocks.

Bosra can be seen as an easy day trip from Damascus.

Things to See

The **citadel** is a curious construction as it is largely a fortified **Roman theatre**. The two structures are in fact one – the fort was built around the theatre to make it an impregnable stronghold. The first walls were built during the Umayyad and Abbasid periods, with further additions being made in the 11th century by the Fatimids.

The big surprise on entering the citadel is the magnificent 15,000 seat theatre – a rarity among Roman theatres in that it is completely freestanding rather than built into the side of a hill.

Other sites in town include various **monumental gates**, **Corinthian columns**, **Roman baths**, a **monastery**, and the **Mosque of Omar**, dating to at least the 12th century.

Places to Stay & Eat

Bosra has the most unusual accommodation in all Syria – a *hostel* in one of the towers inside the citadel. It's extremely basic, just a room with some beds in it, and you'd be wise to bring a sleeping bag or at least your own sheets, but it's a unique experience and you're free to wander the fortress and citadel

all night. There's a shower and toilet available and the cost is S£300 per person.

Bosra's only other accommodation option is the expensive yet unappealing *Bosra Cham Palace* (☎ 790 881, fax 790 996), where singles/doubles cost US$100/120.

Getting There & Away

There are direct Bosra buses (S£50, two hours) from Damascus' Baramke station run by the Jameel bus company but departures are infrequent – one every two to 2½ hours or so. It's probably more convenient to go via Der'a. You do have to change minibus but it's a case of stepping off one and straight on to another. The whole trip, Damascus-Der'a-Bosra, takes 1½ to 2½ hours and costs S£34 by minibus or S£65 by smaller, faster microbus.

Mediterranean Coast

The 180km long Syrian coastline is dominated by the rugged mountain range that runs along its entire length. The extremely fertile and heavily cultivated coastal strip is narrow in the north and widens towards the south.

The beaches along the coast are certainly nothing to rave about as the water is murky and the sand is littered with garbage but they are popular with Syrians on holiday.

LATTAKIA

Lattakia is not a typical Syrian town. A busy port since Roman times, the place is less inward-looking than the rest of the country. With wide, tree-lined boulevards and sidewalk cafes it feels almost European. Its comparative liberalism aside, the city itself has no real attractions but it makes a comfortable base for visits to the ruins of the ancient city of Ugarit and the Crusader castle of Qala'at Salah ad-Din.

Information

The tourist centre (☎ 416 926) is in the foyer of a severe municipal building at the fork at the end of Sharia 14 Ramadan. It is

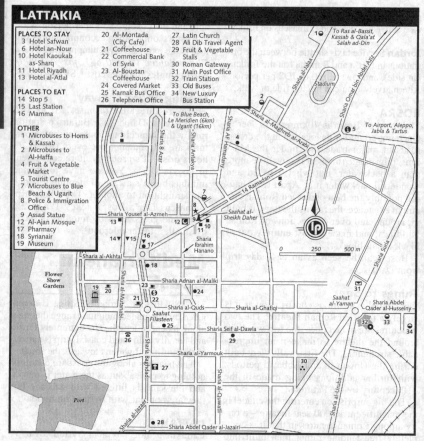

LATTAKIA

PLACES TO STAY
3 Hotel Safwan
6 Hotel an-Nour
10 Hotel Kaoukab as-Sharq
11 Hotel Riyadh
13 Hotel al-Atlal

PLACES TO EAT
14 Stop 5
15 Last Station
16 Mamma

OTHER
1 Microbuses to Homs & Kassab
2 Microbuses to Al-Haffa
4 Fruit & Vegetable Market
5 Tourist Centre
7 Microbuses to Blue Beach & Ugarit
8 Police & Immigration Office
9 Assad Statue
12 Al-Ajan Mosque
17 Pharmacy
18 Syrianair
19 Museum

20 Al-Montada (City Cafe)
21 Coffeehouse
22 Commercial Bank of Syria
23 Al-Boustan Coffeehouse
24 Covered Market
25 Karnak Bus Office
26 Telephone Office

27 Latin Church
28 Ali Dib Travel Agent
29 Fruit & Vegetable Stalls
30 Roman Gateway
31 Main Post Office
32 Train Station
33 Old Buses
34 New Luxury Bus Station

open from 8 am to 8 pm daily except Friday. For visa extensions, the immigration office is on the 3rd floor of the police building opposite the Al-Ajan Mosque on Saahat al-Sheikh Daher. The office is open from 8 am to 2 pm daily except Friday. Extensions are issued on the spot.

The Commercial Bank of Syria is on Sharia Baghdad and is open from 8.30 am to 1.30 pm and 5 to 8 pm daily except Friday. You can change cash and travellers cheques and no commission is charged on either.

Things to See

There's a small **museum** down near the waterfront housed in what was once an old *khan* (merchants' inn). It contains little and is certainly not worth the S£300 admission.

Places to Stay

Hotel Kaoukab as-Sharq (☎ 478 452, Saahat al-Sheikh Daher) by the Assad statue is slightly better than most of the other cheapies in this area in that it does at least provide clean sheets. Singles/doubles are S£175/275, while rooms with a shower and toilet cost S£325/425.

Hotel al-Atlal (☎ *476 121, Sharia Yousef al-Azmeh*), 400m west of Saahat al-Sheikh Daher, is a quiet, family-run establishment with freshly laundered sheets on the beds and a pleasant common area with a fridge stocked with soft drinks. It charges S£250 per person and hot water is available at all times in the common showers.

Hotel Safwan (☎ *478 602, Sharia Mousa bin Nosier*), just a little north of the centre off the Corniche, is possibly Lattakia's best budget deal. It's fairly new and clean and all rooms have their own ensuites with hot water on tap. It's S£250 per person in doubles, or there are three and five-person suites with kitchenettes for S£700/1500.

Moving up into the dollar-price bracket, the **Hotel Riyadh** (☎ *479 778, Sharia 14 Ramadan*) is a comfortable place with fairly modern air-con rooms high enough up to neutralise much of the street noise and with hot water and balconies. Singles/doubles cost US$24/28.

Hotel an-Nour (☎ *423 980, fax 468 340, Sharia 14 Ramadan*) is similar in standard to the Riyadh but given a choice between the two we go for this one because of its comfortable lounge area and breakfast room. Singles/doubles cost US$23/28, breakfast included.

Places to Eat

As with accommodation, the cheapest source of dining is around the Saahat al-Sheikh Daher area. A quick hunt will turn up the old faithfuls – felafel, chicken, kebabs and shwarma. For something a bit different you could try **Mamma** (*Sharia 8 Azar*), a takeaway style place that does reasonable pizzas (S£80 to S£120) as well as things like spaghetti bolognaise (S£65), burgers (S£80) and escalope (S£150).

There are a few restaurants along Sharia Baghdad and a couple of seafood places along the Corniche but in recent times so many new places have opened on or just off Sharia al-Mutanabi that it's acquired the nickname the 'American Quarter'. **Stop 5**

(☎ *477 919, Sharia al-Mutanabi*) more resembles a bar than a restaurant with shelves of spirits, posters advertising happy hours, and a TV locked in to MTV. The food is surprisingly affordable and very good.

Last Station (☎ *468 871*) is a little more formal than Stop 5, opposite, and caters for a more mature crowd. Its a definite restaurant as opposed to a bar/restaurant (though it does serve beer) but with a menu that is a mix of international and Middle Eastern standards – the latter mainly variations on the kebab theme and the two we tried were excellent and very good value at around S£120.

Getting There & Away

Air There's a flight once a week to Damascus from Lattakia's airport, about 25km south of the town.

Bus The new main bus station from where all the big luxury buses depart is on Sharia Abdel Qader al-Husseiny about 200m east of the train station. All the numerous private companies have their offices here and between them they operate frequent services to Damascus (S£150, four hours), Aleppo (S£100, 3½ hours) and to Tartus (S£35, under an hour). In addition buses go from here to Antakya, İskenderun, Ankara and İstanbul in Turkey, and to Amman, Beirut and Cairo.

Karnak buses also depart from this station but the booking office (☎ *233 541*) is on Sharia Seif al-Dawla, just off Sharia Baghdad. Prices are slightly cheaper than the luxury buses but you need to book one day in advance.

There's a second bus station between the luxury station and the train station from where real old, clapped out vehicles totter forth for Damascus (S£55) and Aleppo (S£40) – cheap yes, but recommended, no.

Microbus The main congregation of microbuses is 1.5km north of the town centre near the stadium. From a great big lot up there a confusion of services (just walk around and listen for your destination being shouted) depart frequently for Baniyas (S£10, 45 minutes), Tartus (S£35, one hour),

Homs (S£60, two hours) and Kassab (S£20, 1½ hours) for the Turkish border.

Microbuses for Al-Haffa (for Qala'at Salah ad-Din) and Jabla depart from a lot near the junction of sharias Al-Maghreb al-Arabi and Al-Jalaa, off to your left just before you get to the stadium

Microbuses for Ugarit (Ras Shamra) and Blue Beach (Shaati al-Azraq) go from a back alley down the side of the big white school on Saahat al-Sheikh Daher.

Train The train station is about 1.5km east of the city centre on Saahat al-Yaman. There are three daily departures for Aleppo (S£67/40,1st/2nd class). The trip normally takes 3½ hours on the 6.45 am and 3.30 pm trains, and 2½ hours on the 9 pm express. The route is said to be beautiful and it may be worth passing on the greater convenience and comfort of the bus just once.

Service Taxi Service taxis to Beirut and Tripoli in Lebanon leave from a rank on Sharia 14 Ramadan outside the Hotel Kaoukab al-Sharq. They depart when full (and they fill up faster in the mornings) and the one-way fare to Beirut is US$10 per person.

AROUND LATTAKIA
Ugarit
Ugarit (Ras Shamra) was once the most important city on the Mediterranean coast. From about the 16th to the 13th century BC, it was a centre for trade with Egypt, Cyprus, Mesopotamia and the rest of Syria. Writing on tablets found here is widely accepted as being the earliest known alphabet. The tablets are on display in the museums in Lattakia, Aleppo and Damascus, as well as the Louvre in Paris. Today, the masonry left behind shows you the layout of the streets and gives you some vague idea of where the most important buildings were.

The site is open daily from 9 am to 6 pm (4 pm in winter) and entry costs S£200.

Getting There & Away Microbuses make the trip to Ugarit regularly from Lattakia.

Qala'at Salah ad-Din
Although much less celebrated than Krak des Chevaliers, TE Lawrence was moved to write of Qala'at Salah ad-Din, 'It was I think the most sensational thing in castle building I have seen'. This sensational aspect is largely down to the site – the castle is perched on top of a heavily wooded ridge with near precipitous sides dropping away to surrounding ravines.

The castle is 24km east of Lattakia and is a very easy half-day trip. It's open from 9 am to 6 pm (4 pm in winter) daily except Tuesday and admission costs S£300 (students S£30).

Getting There & Away Take a microbus from Lattakia to Al-Haffa (S£10, 30 minutes) from where you have to haggle with a taxi; the local price is S£20 per person but you'll have to be a pretty stiff bargainer to get that.

Qala'at Marqab
This citadel was originally a Muslim stronghold, possibly founded in 1062. After falling into Crusader hands in the early 12th century, the fortifications were expanded. The main defensive building, the dungeon, is on the southern side, as the gentler slopes made that aspect the castle's most vulnerable. After several attempts, Salah ad-Din gave up trying to take Marqab. It eventually fell to the Mamluks in 1285.

The walls and towers are the most impressive element of what is left today, and the interior of the citadel is rapidly being overrun with vegetation. It is open from 9 am to 6 pm (4 pm in winter) daily except Tuesday and entry is S£300 or (students S£30).

Getting There & Away To get there, take a microbus (S£5) from Baniyas on the coast for Zaoube – it goes right past.

TARTUS
Tartus, Syria's second port, is an easy-going town with what could be a reasonable beach if it weren't so utterly covered in garbage. The compact remnants of the old city (known to the Crusaders as Tortosa) are a fascinating

warren of old and new, as is the once fortified island Arwad. Again, however, stench and rubbish seem to be a big theme here.

Things to See

Don't be put off by the rather austere exterior of the 12th century **cathedral**, the interior is all graceful curves and arches and houses a good little museum. From the outside it looks more like a fortress, and that is no coincidence as its construction was conceived with its own defence in mind.

If you head down to the waterfront, pretty well directly in front of the cathedral, you will see remains of the **medieval town walls** and **ramparts**. The area of the **old city** is small and crowded and still buzzing with activity.

Arwad, a few kilometres south-west of Tartus, could be a real gem if only it weren't so filthy – as it is, it's thoroughly depressing.

Places to Stay & Eat

There are several cheapies (around S£150 a bed) clustered around the junction of sharias Ath-Thawra and Al-Wahda but these are very, very dire – bedding down on one of the mattresses in these places could be the start of a long-lasting relationship with a dermatologist. Instead, the best bet is the *Daniel Hotel* (*☎ 312 757, fax 316 555, Sharia al-Wahda*). Rooms are large and beds are big with clean sheets. The ensuites are aged but the creaky plumbing delivers constant hot water. Singles/doubles cost S£250/500.

Hotel Raffoul (*☎ 220 616 or 220 097, Saahat Manchieh*), across from the cathedral, is a converted apartment with 10 rooms. Two of the rooms have ensuites, the rest share facilities. It's quiet and very well looked after. Rates are S£200 per person. If the hotel is locked up (and it usually is) you need to go to the grocers on the corner which is owned by the same guy who is behind the hotel.

Hotel Shahine (*☎ 222 005, fax 315 002, Sharia Ahmed al-Azawi*) is a modern, eight storey place one block back from the sea – rooms on the 3rd floor and above have good sea views. Singles/doubles with air-con, en-

suite and fridge are very decent and clean and cost US$32/34 plus taxes.

The usual cheap restaurants and snack places (for felafel, shwarma, grilled chicken) are clustered around the clock tower and Sharia al-Wahda and south down Ath-Thawra. There's also a cluster of cheap eats places along Sharia Ahmed al-Azawi, which is the place to hang out for the local youth. *Al-Ayounak*, a snack bar at the sea front end of this street, is run by a friendly guy who lived for 17 years in Sydney.

Al-Nabil, one block back from the small marina, specialises in heavily spiced and salted baked fish but also does more regular dishes like chicken and kebabs for around S£100. Local beer (S£50) is available too.

Pizza Hut, just off Sharia Beirut, east of Ath-Thawra, may have the name, logo and shiny red plastic furniture, but the pizzas are thoroughly Syrian. They make a welcome change from shwarma, kebabs and the like. Prices range from S£115 to S£180 and there's beer too.

Getting There & Away

The luxury bus company Qadmous has a station just off the big roundabout north of the park. It has frequent services to Damascus (S£110, four hours), Aleppo (S£115, four hours), Lattakia (S£35, one hour) and Homs (S£40, one hour). The Karnak office is out east of town just off Sharia 6 Tichreen, the main highway, by the train station; it has just one bus a day to Damascus (S£100) and one to Homs (S£40), as well as a daily service to Beirut (S£150) via Tripoli (S£100) departing at 7.15 am.

Microbuses also depart from Sharia 6 Tichreen. The trip to Lattakia by microbus costs S£35 and takes just over an hour; Baniyas is S£11 and 30 minutes away. There are also plenty of buses heading for Homs (S£23, 1½ hours) and Damascus (S£53, four hours). You can also get a microbus to Safita (S£8, 45 minutes) from here.

KRAK DES CHEVALIERS

For a description of the castle see the special section ' Krak des Chavaliers.

KRAK DES CHEVALIERS

Author Paul Theroux described the Krak des Chevaliers as the epitome of the dream castle of childhood fantasies; of jousts and armour and pennants. TE Lawrence simply called it 'the finest castle in the world'. Take their word for it, the remarkably well-preserved Krak des Chevaliers (in Arabic Qala'at al-Hosn) is one of Syria's prime attractions. Impervious to the onslaught of time, it cannot have looked a great deal different 800 years ago, and such is its size and state of completeness that you could easily spend several hours here absorbed in exploring.

The first fortress known to have existed on this site was built by the Emir of Homs in 1031 but it was the Crusader knights around the middle of the 12th century who largely built and expanded the Krak into the form in which it exists today. Despite repeated attacks and sieges the castle held firm. In fact, it was never truly breached. Instead, the Crusaders just gave it up. By 1271, when the great Muslim warlord Beybars marched on the castle, the knights at the Krak were a last outpost. Jerusalem had been lost and the Christians were on the retreat. Numbers in the castle, which was built to hold a garrison of

Top: The south-west tower and square tower in the foreground with the Warden's Tower rising up behind. (Photo by Andrew Humphreys)

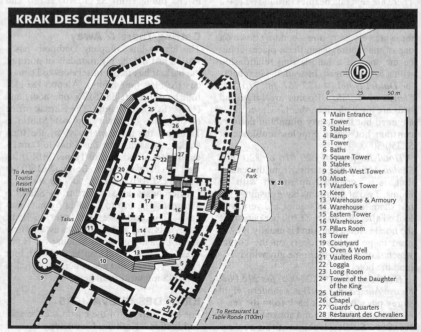

KRAK DES CHEVALIERS

1 Main Entrance
2 Tower
3 Stables
4 Ramp
5 Tower
6 Baths
7 Square Tower
8 Stables
9 South-West Tower
10 Moat
11 Warden's Tower
12 Keep
13 Warehouse & Armoury
14 Warehouse
15 Eastern Tower
16 Warehouse
17 Pillars Room
18 Tower
19 Courtyard
20 Oven & Well
21 Vaulted Room
22 Loggia
23 Long Room
24 Tower of the Daughter of the King
25 Latrines
26 Chapel
27 Guards' Quarters
28 Restaurant des Chevaliers

To Amar Tourist Resort (4km)
Talus
Car Park
To Restaurant La Table Ronde (100m)

2000, were depleted to around 200. Surrounded by the armies of Islam and with no hope of reprieve, the Krak must have seemed more like a prison than a stronghold. Even though they had supplies to last for five years, after a month under siege the Crusaders agreed to depart the castle in return for safe conduct.

The Castle

The castle comprises two distinct parts: the outside wall with its 13 towers and main entrance; and the inside wall and central construction, which are built on a rocky platform. A moat dug out of the rock separates the two walls.

A suggested route for exploration is to walk from the main entrance up the sloping ramp and out to the moat. Visit the **baths**, which you can get down to by a couple of dogleg staircases over in the corner off to your left, then on to the **great hall**, from where you can gain access to the three towers that punctuate the southern wall.

Continue around and enter the inner fortress through the tower at the top of the access ramp into an open courtyard. The **loggia**, with its Gothic facade, on the western side of the yard, is the most impressive structure in the Krak. Opposite is a **chapel** that was converted to a mosque after the Muslim conquest and the **minbar** (pulpit) still remains. The staircase that obstructs the main door is a later addition and leads to the upper floors of the fortress. You can make your way over to the round tower in the south-west corner which is known as the **Warden's Tower** – on a clear day there are some magnificent views from the roof.

Krak des Chevaliers is open from 9 am to 7 pm (5 pm in winter) daily (except public holidays), and entry costs S£300 (students S£30).

Right: Described by any as 'the finest castle in the world', Krak des Chevaliers is one of Syria's prime attractions.

ANDREW HUMPHREYS

Places to Stay & Eat

Restaurant La Table Ronde (☎ 031-734 280), about 200m south of the main entrance, has basic rooms with three beds for S£500. You can also camp. It's probably the best choice of places to eat too. The Krak is an easy day trip from Tartus, Homs or even Hama. The latter offers the best accommodation possibilities.

Getting There & Away

Krak des Chevaliers lies some 10km north of the Homs to Tartus motorway. From Homs there are several microbuses to the village of Hosn (S£20) before noon. They will drop you right at the castle. The other alternative, and the only choice from Tartus, is to catch one of the buses which shuttle between the two cities and alight at the turn-off. From there you will have to hitch or flag down a passing local microbus.

Orontes Valley

The Orontes River (Nahr al-Assi in Arabic) has its headwaters in the mountains of Lebanon near Baalbek. The river flows through the industrial city of Homs before reaching Hama, where the only obstruction to the flow is the ancient *norias*, or water wheels. The Orontes once used to flow north-west from Hama and seep away in the swamps of Al-Ghab but those swamps have long been drained to form one of the most fertile plains in Syria.

HOMS

There's little of interest in Homs but it is one of those crossroads most travellers have to pass through at some stage. Roads head north to Hama, east to Palmyra and the Euphrates, south to Damascus and west to Tartus and the coast. You will find a small information booth beside the footpath along Sharia al-Quwatli, the town's main east-west street. For visa renewals, go to the 3rd floor of a multistorey administration building at the end of a tiny side lane north of Al-Quwatli.

The only building of great note is the **Khaled ibn al-Walid Mosque** on the Hama road about 600m north of the town centre. It holds the tomb of the commander of the Muslim armies who brought Islam to Syria in 636 AD.

Places to Stay & Eat

The cheap hotels are on or around Sharia al-Quwatli between the tourist office and the souq. *An-Nasr al-Jedid Hotel (☎ 227 423, Sharia al-Quwatli)*, entered from a side-street just off Sharia al-Quwatli, is about the best of the lot. It's a bit grubby and basic but the sheets are clean and one of the showers along the corridor can be cranked up to give out some hot water (S£50 per shower). Singles/doubles cost S£200/300.

Grand Basman Hotel (☎ 225 009) has rooms with bath and fan for US$15/22. The entrance is in the middle of a small shopping arcade. It's not bad, but as is so often the case with the lower end hotels charging US dollars, it's well overpriced and tends to be a haunt for some dubious passing trade.

The cheap restaurants are all in a group one block south of Sharia al-Quwatli and have the same old stuff – kebabs, chicken, felafel, humous and salad. One of the better is the *Al-Shalaal as-Sihai Restaurant*, which is a really busy place with a take-away section downstairs and seating upstairs. It has a menu in English and does shwarma, hamburgers and juices.

Getting There & Away

There are two bus stations: the Karnak station which is about 1.5km north of the city centre up the Hama road and a new luxury bus station, which is almost 1km farther on. At the latter are all the usual bus companies and between them they have buses for Damascus (S£70, two hours), Aleppo (S£75 to S£85, 2½ hours), Tartus (S£40, one hour) and Palmyra (S£70, two hours). The quickest way to Hama is to jump in a microbus (S£17, 40 minutes) – they leave every 10 minutes or so. Battered old minibuses go from the Karnak station to all over for fares that are considerably cheaper than the bigger buses, but they're generally cramped and uncomfortable with nowhere to put baggage. The fare to Aleppo on one of these is S£30, Tartus is S£17, Palmyra S£22 and Hama S£10. For the Krak des Chevaliers you need to catch a Tartus bus or minibus and ask to be let off on the highway at the castle junction – tell the driver you want 'Qala'at Hosn'. All the service taxis gather around the corner of the Al-Khayyam Hotel on Sharia al-Quwatli and run to Damascus, Aleppo, and Beirut and Tripoli (Lebanon).

HAMA

This is one of the most attractive towns in Syria with the Orontes River flowing through the town centre, its banks lined with trees and gardens. There's not an awful lot to see, but the town's peaceful atmosphere makes it a pleasant place. In fact, Hama is far preferable to Homs as a base for excursions to Krak des Chevaliers and other sights in the area.

Information

For visa extensions the immigration office is hidden away up three flights of stairs in a building opposite the footbridge in the centre of town (there's a small sign reading 'passports' in English). The local tourist office (☎ 511 033) is in a small building in the gardens in the centre of town just north of the river though apart from the usual free hand-out map, the staff here don't have an awful lot to tell you and certainly they aren't as well tuned in to travellers' needs as the staff at the Cairo and Riad hotels.

The Commercial Bank of Syria on Sharia al-Quwatli, just east of the clock tower and next door to the post office, is open from 8.30 am to 12.30 pm daily except Friday. It accepts cash and travellers cheques (no commission) at the exchange counter on the first floor.

Things to See

Hama's main attraction is its **norias** – wooden water wheels up to 20m in diameter – built centuries ago to provide water for the town and to irrigate the surrounding

fields by a series of mini aqueducts. Because both the wheels and the blocks on which they are mounted are wooden, the friction when they turn produces a mournful groaning. The norias right in the centre of town are surrounded by a popular park where people gather to relax. The most impressive wheels, however, are about 1km east, upstream from the centre. The four norias here, known as the Four Norias of Bechriyyat, are in two pairs on a weir straddling the river. About 1km west of the centre is the largest of the norias, known as the Al-Mohammediyya. The town's **museum** is housed in the old Azem Palace, the residence of the governor, As'ad Pasha al-Azem, who ruled the town from 1700 to 1742. The palace is reminiscent of the more grandiose building of the same name in Damascus which is hardly surprising as the latter was built by the same man upon his transfer to Damascus.

Places to Stay

Cairo Hotel (☎ *222 280, fax 511 715, Sharia al-Quwatli*) and neighbouring *Riad Hotel* (☎ *239 512, fax 517 776, Sharia al-Quwatli*), near the clock tower in the centre of town, are the two best budget hotels in all Syria. Rooms are spotlessly clean with fridge (stocked with soft drinks) and the ensuites and shower units are new and have constant hot water. Of the two, the Riad is marginally cheaper: a bed in a shared room will cost S£150, while ensuite doubles go for S£400. You can also sleep on the roof for S£100. Both hotels run a variety of day trips.

Costing a little more, *Noria Hotel* (☎ *512 414, fax 511 715, Sharia al-Quwatli*) is an extremely comfortable place with good service, a smart reception, central air-con and excellent food. Singles/doubles are US$18/28 and there are also triples and suites available.

Hama Tower Hotel (☎ *226 864, fax 521 523*) is one block north of Sharia al-Quwatli and occupies the top floors of a tower block overlooking the river. The views are great but the hotel is badly maintained. We were asked US$31 for a double with ensuite but rates seemed negotiable.

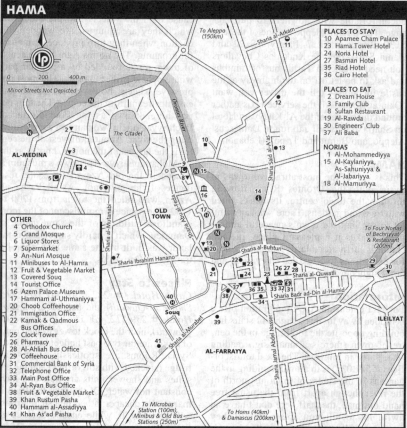

HAMA

0   200   400 m

Minor Streets Not Depicted

To Aleppo
(150km)

Sharia al-Arkam

The Citadel

AL-MEDINA

Orontes River

OLD
TOWN

Sharia Jalal al-Feda

Sharia al-Mutanabi

Sharia Said al-A'as

Sharia Ibrahim Hanano

Sharia al-Buhturi

To Four Norias
of Bechriyyat
& Restaurant
(200m)

Souq

Sharia al-Quwatli

Sharia Badr ad-Din al-Hamid

ILEILYAT

Sharia al-Murabet

Sharia Jamal Abdel Nasser

AL-FARRAYYA

To Microbus
Station (100m),
Minibus & Old Bus
Stations (250m)

To Homs (40km)
& Damascus (200km)

PLACES TO STAY
10 Apamee Cham Palace
23 Hama Tower Hotel
24 Noria Hotel
27 Basman Hotel
35 Riad Hotel
36 Cairo Hotel

PLACES TO EAT
2 Dream House
3 Family Club
8 Sultan Restaurant
19 Al-Rawda
30 Engineers' Club
37 Ali Baba

NORIAS
1 Al-Mohammediyya
15 Al-Kaylaniyya,
   As-Sahuniyya &
   Al-Jabariyya
18 Al-Mamuriyya

OTHER
4 Orthodox Church
5 Grand Mosque
6 Liquor Stores
7 Supermarket
9 An-Nuri Mosque
11 Minibuses to Al-Hamra
12 Fruit & Vegetable Market
13 Covered Souq
14 Tourist Office
16 Azem Palace Museum
17 Hammam al-Uthmaniyya
20 Choob Coffeehouse
21 Immigration Office
22 Karnak & Qadmous
   Bus Offices
25 Clock Tower
26 Pharmacy
28 Al-Ahliah Bus Office
29 Coffeehouse
31 Commercial Bank of Syria
32 Telephone Office
33 Main Post Office
34 Al-Ryan Bus Office
38 Fruit & Vegetable Market
39 Khan Rustum Pasha
40 Hammam al-Assadiyya
41 Khan As'ad Pasha

Places to Eat

In the couple of blocks along Sharia al-Quwatli west of the Cairo Hotel and in the sidestreets running north to the river are all the usual cheap kebab and chicken restaurants. *Ali Baba* on Sharia al-Quwatli (sign in Arabic only but look for the painted Ali Baba figure) is said to do some of the best felafel in all Syria; it also has basics like fuul and humous.

Dream House (☎ *411 687*) is a fairly newish place in the Al-Medina quarter, a block north of the Orthodox church. It's a bit large and soulless but it is very clean and smart and the food is good. The menu starts with pizzas and filling burgers with fries and salad (S£100 to S£130) and ranges up to steaks, fillets and oriental grills (S£120 to S£170). It's open 10 to 1 am, and is a good lunch option.

Sultan Restaurant benefits from a wonderful setting in part of a Mamluk-era complex. The main dining room is bare stone with wooden ceilings and a central fountain but, best of all, right outside is one of the great old norias providing a groaning aural backdrop to your meal. The menu is limited to mezze and several varieties of kebab (S£70 to S£80), which are merely okay.

Four Norias is just over 500m east of the centre on the banks of the river beside, what else, four norias. It's a large open-air place popular with groups and families which gets pretty lively on summer evenings. Food is the standard mezze and kebabs but it's good.

Getting There & Away

Hama has no modern bus station. Instead, there are several bus company offices in the town centre and the services pull up outside – see the map for locations. Fares include to Damascus (S£90), Aleppo (S£65), Homs (S£20), Tartus (S£70) and Lattakia (S£100). The minibus and old bus stations are on the southern edge of town about 1.5km from the centre; you walk down Sharia al-Murabet to where it joins with the main Damascus road and then bear left. The main microbus station is a 10 minute walk from the centre of town at the south-west end of Sharia al-Murabet in a triangular lot at the junction with the main Damascus road. They run to Homs (S£17), Suqeilibiyya (S£20) and Salamiyya (S£13).

APAMEA

If it weren't for the unsurpassable magnificence of Palmyra, Apamea (Afamia in Arabic) would be considered a wonder and one of the unmissable highlights of Syria. As it is, Apamea is like a condensed version of the pink sandstone desert city, but executed in grey granite and transposed to a high, wild grassy moor overlooking the Al-Ghab plain. The city was founded in the 2nd century BC by Seleucus I, one of Alexander the Great's generals. It prospered through into the Byzantine period but then the city was sacked by the Persians in 540 AD and again in 612. Barely a quarter of a century later Syria was seized by the Muslims and Apamea fell into decline. The city was all but flattened in a devastating earthquake in

1157. Beside the site is the village of Qala'at al-Mudiq, sheltered in a Medieval castle, while down below, beside the main road is a small **mosaic museum**. The site of Apamea has no set opening hours as it's unfenced and there's nothing to stop anyone wandering across it at any time, however there is an admission fee of S£300 (S£25 for students). Officials patrol the site checking tickets. It's is open from 8 am to 2.30 pm daily except Tuesday and entry is S£150 (students S£15).

Getting There & Away

Minibuses (S£10) and microbuses (S£20) regularly run the 45km from Hama to Suqeilibiyya, and from there microbuses go on to Qala'at al-Mudiq (S£10). The whole trip usually takes about an hour.

Aleppo

Called Haleb by the locals, Aleppo, with a population of about three million, is Syria's second-largest city. Since Roman times it has been an important trading centre between the countries of Asia and the Mediterranean, and the long presence of a strong corps of merchants from Europe goes some way to account for the vaguely European feel of its tree-lined streets, parks and upmarket restaurants.

There is a large Christian population comprised mainly of Armenian refugees from Turkey, and if you walk around certain quarters of the city, you'll see as many signs in the condensed-looking script of Armenian as you'll see in the familiar 'shorthand' with which many people equate Arabic. An influx of traders from the ex-Soviet Union has also left its mark – Russian seems like the third language.

With its fascinating covered souqs, the citadel, museum and *caravanserais* (merchants' inns), it is a great place to spend a few days. There are also interesting sights in the vicinity such as the Church of St Simeon (Qala'at Samaan), which was the largest Christian building in the Middle East when built in the 4th century.

SYRIA

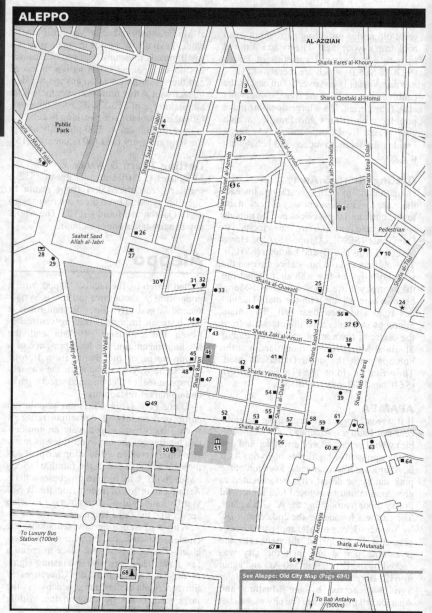

ALEPPO

AL-AZIZIAH

Sharia Fares al-Khoury

Sharia Qostaki al-Homsi

Public Park

Sharia al-Malek Faisal

Sharia Saad Allah al-Jabri

Sharia al-Aryubi

Sharia Jbrail Dalal

Sharia ash-Shohada

3

4

7

6

5

8

Pedestrian

Saahat Saad Allah al-Jabri

26

27

28

29

9

10

Sharia al-Tilal

30

31 32

33

Sharia al-Quwatli

25

24

34

35

36

37

Sharia al-Walid

44

43

Sharia Zaki al-Arsuzi

Sharia Rashid

38

40

Sharia Baron

45

46

42

41

Sharia Bab al-Faraj

Sharia al-Jalaa

48

47

Sharia Yarmouk

54

39

Sharia al-Dala

49

52

53 55

57

58 59

61

62

Sharia al-Maari

56

60

63

50

51

64

To Luxury Bus Station (100m)

67

66

Sharia Bab Antakya

Sharia al-Mutanabi

68

See Aleppo: Old City Map (Page 694)

To Bab Antakya //(500m)

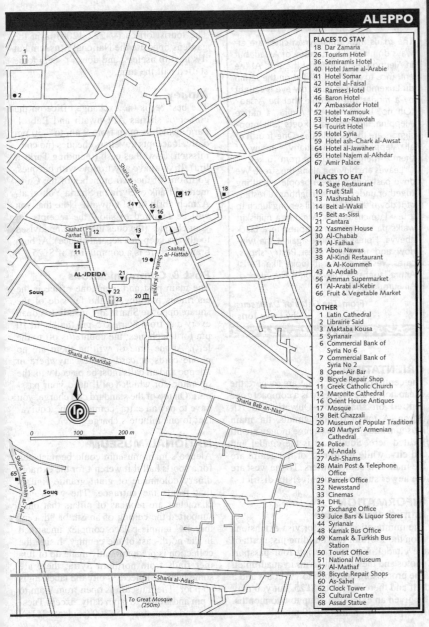

ALEPPO

PLACES TO STAY
18 Dar Zamaria
26 Tourism Hotel
36 Semiramis Hotel
40 Hotel Jamie al-Arabie
41 Hotel Somar
42 Hotel al-Faisal
45 Ramses Hotel
46 Baron Hotel
47 Ambassador Hotel
52 Hotel Yarmouk
53 Hotel ar-Rawdah
54 Tourist Hotel
55 Hotel Syria
59 Hotel ash-Chark al-Awsat
64 Hotel al-Jawaher
65 Hotel Najem al-Akhdar
67 Amir Palace

PLACES TO EAT
4 Sage Restaurant
10 Fruit Stall
13 Mashrabiah
14 Beit al-Wakil
15 Beit as-Sissi
21 Cantara
22 Yasmeen House
30 Al-Chabab
31 Al-Faihaa
35 Abou Nawas
38 Al-Kindi Restaurant
   & Al-Koummeh
43 Al-Andalib
56 Amman Supermarket
61 Al-Arabi al-Kebir
66 Fruit & Vegetable Market

OTHER
1 Latin Cathedral
2 Librairie Said
3 Maktaba Kousa
5 Syrianair
6 Commercial Bank of
   Syria No 6
7 Commercial Bank of
   Syria No 2
8 Open-Air Bar
9 Bicycle Repair Shop
11 Greek Catholic Church
12 Maronite Cathedral
16 Orient House Antiques
17 Mosque
19 Beit Ghazzali
20 Museum of Popular Tradition
23 40 Martyrs' Armenian
   Cathedral
24 Police
25 Al-Andals
27 Ash-Shams
28 Main Post & Telephone
   Office
29 Parcels Office
32 Newsstand
33 Cinemas
34 DHL
37 Exchange Office
39 Juice Bars & Liquor Stores
44 Syrianair
48 Karnak Bus Office
49 Karnak & Turkish Bus
   Station
50 Tourist Office
51 National Museum
57 Al-Mathaf
58 Bicycle Repair Shops
60 As-Sahel
62 Clock Tower
63 Cultural Centre
68 Assad Statue

AL-JDEIDA

Souq

Saahat
Farhat

Saahat
al-Hattab

Sharia as-Sissi

Sharia al-Kayyali

Sharia al-Khandak

Sharia Bab an-Nasr

Sharia Hammam at-Tal

Souq

Sharia al-Adasi

To Great Mosque
(250m)

0   100   200 m

LP

Aleppo

The roads into other Syrian cities are always dominated by a statue of Assad, but in Aleppo I see nothing of the sort. At the entrance to a park modelled on the Jardin du Luxembourg in Paris, my eye is caught by a modest bust. Could that be Assad? 'Oh no, that's a poet,' Amira, a native Aleppine, informs me. Poets and monsignors are the local heroes. One-fourth of all Aleppines are Christians – many of them Armenians who fled from Turkey.

Leaves are blowing along the street. We drive past a cafe where people are sitting together under subdued lighting; a restaurant down the block is still serving lunch to a few late customers. A girl in a miniskirt walks past a woman wrapped in a black abeyya. I press my nose against the window and feast my eyes. Pastry shops, cafes, restaurants – it looks like Paris! Amira laughs. 'I knew you'd like Aleppo. All Europeans do.'

**From *The Gates of Damascus*
by Lieve Joris**

ORIENTATION

The centre of town and the area where the cheap hotels are clustered is a compact zone centred on sharias Al-Quwatli and Al-Baron. A lot of the restaurants, the main museum and places to change money are all located here. South-east is the citadel and old city, while north-east of the centre are the main Christian quarters. To the west are the newer suburbs and university district.

INFORMATION
Immigration Office

The immigration office for visa extensions is on the 1st floor of a building just north of the citadel. You must bring four passport photos and then fill out forms in quadruplet. The processing takes one to 1½ hours and a half and there's a fee of S£25, but you may be given an extension of up to two months. It's open from 8 am to 1.30 pm.

Tourist Office

The tourist office (☎ 222 1200) is in the gardens opposite the National Museum but it's next to useless, and doesn't seem to be staffed half the time.

Money

The best bet is the exchange office on the corner of sharias Al-Quwatli and Bab al-Faraj, which is open from 9 am to 7.30 pm daily. It accepts travellers cheques (no commission) as well as cash (including Turkish lira). If you have any trouble with cheques, go to one of the two branches of the Commercial Bank of Syria on Sharia Yousef al-Azmeh north of Al-Quwatli. Note that you will be required to show the receipts for your cheques (the ones that you are advised to always keep in a separate place). At both branches there is a commission of S£25.

Post & Communications

The main post and telephone office is the enormous building on the far side of the square opposite Sharia al-Quwatli. It's open every day from 8 am to 5 pm (and until 10 pm for telephones; the counter is off to the left). At the time of writing there are no phone cards or card phones anywhere in Aleppo and all calls must be placed with the operator, for which you'll need your passport. On top of the standard call charge, you have to pay an extra 'commission', equivalent to one minute's charge.

NATIONAL MUSEUM

Aleppo's main museum could be mistaken for a sports hall if it weren't for the extraordinary colonnade of giant granite figures that fronts the entrance. The wide-eyed characters are replicas of pillars that once supported the ceiling of an 8th or 9th century BC temple-palace complex unearthed in the north-east of the country. Inside the collection is predominantly made up of further finds from northern Syria; there are some beautiful pieces – pity the labelling is so poor. The museum is open from 9 am to 1 pm and from 4 to 6 pm daily, except Tuesday and admission is S£300 (students S£15).

THE OLD CITY

The fabulous covered souqs of the Old City are Aleppo's main attraction. This partially covered network of bustling passageways extends over several hectares, and once under the vaulted stone ceiling, you're swallowed up into another world. Parts of these markets date to the 13th century but the bulk of the area is an Ottoman-era creation. In among the souqs are numerous khans (see the boxed text 'The Medieval Mall'), the most impressive of which is the **Khan al-Jumruk**, opposite the Great Mosque. Completed in 1574, at one time it housed the consulates and trade missions of the English, Dutch and French, as well as 344 shops. Its days as a European enclave are now long gone but the khan is still in use, serving now as a cloth market.

The souq is at its most labyrinth immediately south and east of the Great Mosque. This is the area where you'll find gold and silver and carpets and kilims, and the area in which you'll be most implored to come, sit, and take tea or coffee.

It's worth visiting the souq at least a couple of times, including on a Friday, when all the shops are closed and the lanes are silent and empty. Relieved of the need to keep flattening yourself against the wall to let the little over-laden Suzuki vans squeeze by, you are free to appreciate architectural details that at other times get lost in the crush.

It's also worth seeking out the wonderful **Bimaristan Arghan** (it has railings out front with a little nameplate affixed), which is south of the souq. A former mental asylum, it's a lovely little building with a tree shaded courtyard off which is a series of tight, claustrophobic passages leading to tiny cells where the insane were confined.

Citadel

The citadel dominates the city at the eastern end of the souqs. Its moat is spanned by a bridge on the southern side, and this leads to the 12th century fortified gate. Once inside, the fort is largely in ruins, although the

The Medieval Mall

Motel, warehouse and shopping centre rolled into one, the *khan* provided for the needs of the merchant caravans rolling into Syria from India, China, Central Asia and Europe. They were basic rectangular or square buildings whose outwardly blank walls had one main entrance that could be closed and locked at night. That entrance – wide and tall enough to admit heavily laden camels and horses – led through to a central courtyard, usually open to the sky and surrounded on four sides by two storeys of small rooms. On the ground floor these would serve as storage bays, stabling, shops and maybe even a coffeehouse, while the upper floor provided accommodation for the merchants.

Khan building reached its apogee in Cairo during the reign of the Mamluks who, in partnership with Venice, enjoyed a virtual monopoly on east-west trade. Some of the splendid khans they built (called *wikalas* or *caravanserais* in Egypt) were up to four or five storeys high. Most of Syria's khans date from the later, Ottoman period, when the importance of Cairo as a trading centre was in decline and the Syrian cities were more favoured. There are plenty of them – virtually every second building in the old souq areas of Damascus and Aleppo is a khan. Less ostentatious than their Cairene counterparts, Damascene khans are nevertheless unique in that many of them were roofed over by domes. Many of these domes have long-since collapsed but you can still see where they used to be.

Although they no longer provide for travelling caravans, most of Syria's remaining khans are still busy centres of commerce, continuing to provide warehousing and sales space for modern-day merchants. No Big Macs or hot tubs, though.

SYRIA

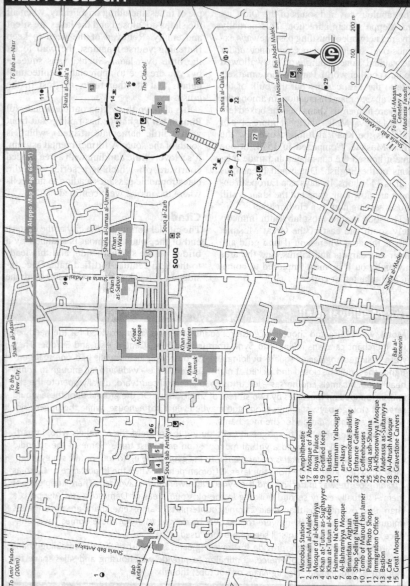

ALEPPO: OLD CITY

To Bab an-Nasr

Sharia al-Qala'a

The Citadel

Sharia al-Qala'a

Sharia Mouisalam Ibn Abdel Malek

To Bab al-Maqam,
Cemetery &
Madrassa Faradis

Sharia Bab al-Maqam

See Aleppo Map (Page 690-1)

0   100   200 m

Sharia al-Jamaa al-Umawi

Khan
al-Wazir

Souq al-Zarb

SOUQ

Sharia al-Adasi

Khan
as-Sabun

Sharia al-Mader

To the
New City

Great
Mosque

Khan an-
Nahaseen

Khan
al-Jumruk

Bab al-
Qinnesrin

To Amir Palace
(200m)

Sharia Bab Antakya

Souq Bab Antakya

Sharia Bab Antakya

Bab
Antakya

1	Microbus Station
2	Hammam al-Maleki
3	Mosque of al-Kamiliyya
4	Khan at-Tutun as-Sughayyer
5	Khan at-Tutun al-Kebir
6	Hammam Na'eem
7	Al-Bahramiyya Mosque
8	Bimaristan Arghan
9	Shop selling Nateh
10	Tomb of Mouruf Ibn Jamer
11	Passport Photo Shops
12	Immigration Office
13	Bastion
14	Cafe
15	Great Mosque
16	Amphitheatre
17	Mosque of Abraham
18	Royal Palace
19	Fortified Keep
20	Bastion
21	Hammam Yalbougha an-Nasry
22	Governorate Building
23	Entrance Gateway
24	Souvenir Shops
25	Souq ash-Shouna
26	Al-Khosrowiyya Mosque
27	Madrassa as-Sultaniyya
28	Al-Atrush Mosque
29	Gravestone Carvers

throne room above the entrance has been lavishly restored. Two buildings that survived pillage and earthquake are a small 12th century mosque attributed to Nur ad-Din (known as the Great Mosque) and the 13th century great mosque. But the best thing is the views from the walls, which are terrific. The Citadel is open from 9 am to 6 pm daily except Tuesday and admission is S£300 (students S£30).

Great Mosque

On the northern edge of the souqs is the Great Mosque (Jamaa al-Kebir), the younger sibling (by 10 years) of the great Umayyad Mosque in Damascus. Its most impressive feature is its freestanding minaret dating to 1090. Inside the mosque is a fine, carved wooden *minbar* (pulpit) and behind the railing to the left of it is supposed to be the head of Zacharias, the father of John the Baptist, after whom the mosque is named. There's no admission fee but you have to remove your footwear, which will then be watched over by a custodian who customarily receives S£25.

CHRISTIAN QUARTER

A beautifully maintained warren of long, narrow stone-flagged alleyways, occasionally arched, and with walls like canyons, the Christian quarter of Al-Jdeida is the most charming part of Aleppo. It's currently undergoing something of a rebirth with age-old townhouses being converted into gorgeous hotels, restaurants and bars. There are also several churches worth visiting, including the 15th century **40 Martyrs' Armenian Cathedral** where mass is still performed on a Sunday, and there's the **Museum of Popular Tradition** (labelled Le Musee des Traditions) occupying a beautiful 18th century residence. Entrance to the latter is S£150 (students S£10) and it's open from 8.30 am to 2 pm daily except Tuesday.

HAMMAMS

Just to the south-east of the Citadel, the **Hammam Yalbougha an-Nasry** is one of Syria's finest working bathhouses. Origi-

nally constructed in 1491 it was most recently restored in 1985. Prices are clearly listed: entry is S£150, or it's S£365 for the whole package including massage, rubdown, soap, towels and tea. Women are admitted from 10 am to 5 pm on Monday, Wednesday (winter only), Thursday and Saturday, the rest of the time it's men only (Sunday, Tuesday, Friday and from 5 pm to 2 am all other days).

PLACES TO STAY

The bulk of the budget hotels are in the block bounded by sharias Al-Maari, Al-Baron, Al-Quwatli and Bab al-Faraj.

Hotel al-Jawaher (☎ 223 9554, fax 239 554) behind the cultural centre, just off Bab al-Faraj, is highly recommended. Rooms are modern and clean, and there's a very comfortable common area with satellite TV. Singles/doubles/triples cost S£350/650/950. This place is always busy so you need to book in advance.

Hotel Najem al-Akhdar (☎ 223 9157, Sharia Hammam al-Tal), also known as the Green Star, is buried off a busy market street south-east of the clock tower. It's a bit scruffy but still one of the better options in that it's frequented almost exclusively by travellers rather than Russian traders. Doubles with shower and toilet go for S£500.

Hotel ar-Rawdah (☎ 223 3896, Sharia al-Maari), one block east of the junction with Sharia al-Baron, has small doubles with an extremely cramped shower for S£500, or you can get a bed in a shared room for S£200.

Hotel Syria (☎ 221 9760, Sharia al-Dala) is passable: sheets are at least changed regularly, the rooms have functioning ceiling fans and the bathrooms have hot water. Singles/doubles with bathroom are S£250/400 or S£200/350 without.

Hotel Yarmouk (☎ 221 7510, Sharia al-Maari) is a last resort sort of place. It's dingy and can be noisy but despite that, it somehow continues to be popular with travellers. It charges S£250 per person, and doubles have private shower and toilet.

Tourist Hotel (☎ 221 6583, Sharia al-Dala) remains Aleppo's best budget option

– it's immaculately clean and there's always hot water – although management can be rude and intrusive. Rooms cost S£350 per person and booking in advance is essential.

At the famed **Baron Hotel** (☎ *221 0880, fax 221 8164, Sharia al-Baron*), where previous guests have included Lawrence of Arabia and Agatha Christie, you have to be prepared for a bit of a trade-off: for its character and air of Gothic romance, you have to let go any attachments to more physical luxuries – the beds are old and squeaky, the air-con clatters like it was powered by diesel, the decor is spartan and the plumbing is antediluvian. Singles/doubles with breakfast in the grand dining hall cost US$30/40.

PLACES TO EAT

In the block bounded by sharias Al-Maari, Bab al-Faraj, Quwatli and Al-Baron are the cheapies offering the usual stuff – the price is more variable than the food so check before you sit down. A row of excellent juice stands lines up at the Bab al-Faraj end of Sharia Yarmouk.

Across from the juice stands are the kebab restaurants **Al-Kindi Restaurant** and **Al-Koummeh**. They are none too hot on hygiene but offer reasonable food at budget prices.

Al-Chabab is a good alfresco restaurant with a fountain in a sidestreet off Sharia al-Baron, just up from the Syrianair office, while the nearby **Al-Faihaa** is a clean and immensely popular felafel place (takeaway only).

Abou Nawas on Sharia Rashid has a menu that stretches way beyond the basics to include the kind of dishes that are usually only ever served up at home – to help you select, you'll be invited into the kitchen to see what's cooking. A two course meal for two will come in at about S£250 to S£300.

Al-Andalib on Sharia al-Baron is a rooftop restaurant one block north of the Baron Hotel. The atmosphere is boisterous and the place is packed most evenings with locals. It's a set menu – a platter of kebab, huge amounts of salads, humous, baba ghanoug and fries – for an all-in price of S£200.

Ebla and **Al-Challal** (☎ *224 3344*) are two of a bunch of pleasant places on Sharia Georges and Mathilde Salem in upmarket Al-Aziziah. Al-Challal is more chic and modern with lots of large glass windows. Its menu combines mezze and Middle Eastern grills (around the S£120 mark) with international dishes like escalope, steak diane (S£220) and a very decent spaghetti bolognese (S£120). Cold beer is served at both restaurants.

Beit al-Wakil (☎ *221 7169*) and **Beit as-Sissi** (☎ *221 9411*) in the Al-Jdeida quarter both have courtyard dining areas complete with jasmine and lemon trees and gently splashing fountains. Both specialise in local variations on Levantine cuisine and the dishes change according to the season. Expect to pay S£600 to S£700 for a full meal for two, wine not included.

GETTING THERE & AWAY

Air

Aleppo has an international airport with some connections to Turkey, Europe and other cities in the Middle East. Internally, there is a daily flight to Damascus for S£600.

Bus

The main station, as far as most travellers are concerned, is the one for luxury, long-distance buses, located on Sharia Ibrahim Hanano about 800m west of the National Museum. From here a variety of companies run buses to Damascus (S£150, five hours), Deir ez-Zur (S£125, five hours), Hama (S£65, 2½ hours), Homs (S£100, 3½ hours), Lattakia (S£100, 3½ hours), among others. In addition there are seven daily buses from here to Beirut (S£300, six hours).

The other important station – actually little more than a parking lot – is north of the tourist office and behind the Karnak office on Sharia al-Baron. This is shared between state-owned Karnak buses and several private companies running services to Turkey and a handful of other international destinations. Karnak is maybe 10% cheaper than the luxury buses but services are far fewer. There are at least five buses a day to İstanbul (approx S£950, 22 hours) and more to Antakya (S£200 to S£250).

Cheaper old buses, as well as minibuses and microbuses, go from a collection of stations south of the Amir Palace hotel.

Train

The train station, about 15 minutes walk from the central hotel area, is north of the big public park. Local trains run daily to Damascus, Lattakia, Deir ez-Zur and Qamishle in the north-east.

At the time of writing weekly services to İstanbul had been suspended but in theory it departs every Tuesday at midnight and takes 36 hours. There is no sleeper carriage and the fare should be around the S£500 mark.

AROUND ALEPPO
Qala'at Samaan

This is the Basilica of St Simeon, also known as St Simon of Stylites, who was one of Syria's most unusual early Christians. In 423, he sat on top of a 3m pillar and went on to spend the next 36 years atop this and other taller pillars. After his death in 459, an enormous church was built around the most famous pillar. The church today is remarkably well preserved, with the arches of the octagonal yard still complete, along with much of the four basilicas. Admission is S£300 (students S£30).

Getting There & Away Microbuses from Aleppo leave every hour or so from the main microbus station for the one hour trip (S£10) to the village of Daret' Azze. It is about a farther 8km from Daret' Azze to Qala'at Samaan and it's a matter of negotiating with a local for transport or hitching.

The Desert

The Damascus to Aleppo highway marks roughly the division between the cultivable land to the west and the barren desert that stretches east to the Euphrates.

The wide fringe of the desert gets sufficient rain to support enough vegetation to graze sheep and goats. The desert fringe-dwellers build beehive-shaped houses as protection against the extreme heat. You can see them on the road from Homs to Palmyra, in the area south of Lake al-Assad and around Aleppo.

Dotting this desert are the oases – the main one is Palmyra – that once served as way-stations for the caravans on their way between the Mediterranean and Mesopotamia.

PALMYRA

Known to the locals as Tadmor (its ancient Semitic name), Palmyra is Syria's prime attraction and one of the world's great historical sites. If you're only going to see one thing in Syria, make it Palmyra. Although mass tourism is making itself felt and the place's popularity is growing, there's still a good chance you'll be able to enjoy it with relatively few other people about.

The oasis is really in the middle of nowhere – 150km from the Orontes River to the west and 200km from the Euphrates to the east.

The ruins of the 2nd century AD city have been extensively excavated and restored and cover some 50 hectares. The new town is rapidly growing around it, spreading out with particular speed towards the west, and counts 40,000 inhabitants.

History

Palmyra was at one time a Greek outpost of considerable importance. It was an Assyrian caravan town for over 1000 years but only enjoyed its later Greek period of glory for two centuries. It was annexed by Rome in 217 AD and became a centre of unsurpassed wealth.

The city's most famous character was Zenobia, the half-Greek, half-Arab ruler of Palmyra from 267 AD, after the death in suspicious circumstances of her husband Odenathus. Claiming descent from Cleopatra, she was a woman of exceptional ability and ambition. She even set her sights on Rome, although her troops were soundly beaten by the forces of Aurelian in 271, and the city was put to the torch by him two years later.

PALMYRA

Bel was the most important of the gods in the Palmyrene pantheon and the **Temple of Bel** is the most complete structure and single most impressive part of the ruins. Once inside, you'll see that the complex consists of two parts, a huge walled courtyard and at its centre, the temple proper, or *cella*, which dates from 32 AD.

Formerly connected to the temple by a colonnade – of which only some column stubs remain – the **monumental arch**, now serves as the entrance to the site proper. The arch is interesting in that it is actually two arches joined like a hinge to pivot the main street through a 30° turn. This slight direction switch, and a second one just a little farther west, are in themselves evidence of the city's unique development – a crooked street like this would be quite unimaginable in any standard Roman city.

South of the main **colonnaded street** (impressively restored in the section immediately east of the arch) is the city's theatre, which until the 1950s was buried by sand. Since its discovery it has been extensively restored but large sections now look just a bit too shiny and new.

About one-third of the way along the colonnaded street is the reconstructed **tetrapylon**, a monumental structure that served to mark a

Top: The only remaining part of the portico that once ran all the way round the *cella* in the Temple of Bel. (Photo by TM Flower)

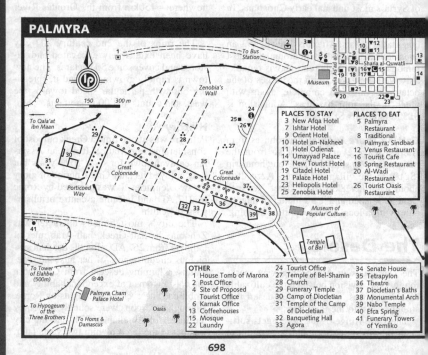

PALMYRA

To Bus Station
To Qala'at ibn Maan
Zenobia's Wall
Museum
Sharia As'ad al-Amin
Sharia al-Quwatli
0   150   300 m
Great Colonnade
Great Colonnade
Porticoed Way
Museum of Popular Culture
Temple of Bel
To Tower of Elahbel (500m)
Palmyra Cham Palace Hotel
To Hypogeum of the Three Brothers
To Homs & Damascus
Oasis

PLACES TO STAY
3 New Afqa Hotel
7 Ishtar Hotel
9 Orient Hotel
10 Hotel an-Nakheel
11 Hotel Odienat
14 Umayyad Palace
17 New Tourist Hotel
19 Citadel Hotel
21 Palace Hotel
23 Heliopolis Hotel
25 Zenobia Hotel

PLACES TO EAT
5 Palmyra Restaurant
8 Traditional Palmyra; Sindbad
12 Venus Restaurant
16 Tourist Cafe
18 Spring Restaurant
20 Al-Wadi Restaurant
26 Tourist Oasis Restaurant

OTHER
1 House Tomb of Marona
2 Post Office
4 Site of Proposed Tourist Office
6 Karnak Office
13 Coffeehouses
15 Mosque
22 Laundry
24 Tourist Office
27 Temple of Bel-Shamin
28 Church
29 Funerary Temple
30 Camp of Diocletian
31 Temple of the Camp of Diocletian
32 Banqueting Hall
33 Agora
34 Senate House
35 Tetrapylon
36 Theatre
37 Diocletian's Baths
38 Monumental Arch
39 Nabo Temple
40 Efca Spring
41 Funerary Towers of Yemliko

junction of thoroughfares. From here the main street continues north-west, and another smaller pillared street leads south-west to the **agora**, or forum, and north-east to the **Temple of Bel-Shamin**, a small shrine dedicated to the god of storms and fertilising rains.

Beyond the tetrapylon the main street continues for another 500m. This stretch has seen much less excavation and reconstruction and the way is littered with tumbled columns and assorted blocks of masonry. The road ends in the impressive, portico of a **funerary temple**, dating from the 3rd century. The area around here is

ANDREW HUMPHREYS

also littered with broken and tumbled masonry, in places just heaped up into small hillocks of fragments of statuary and decorated friezes and panels – it gives you a chance to look at the intricacy of the carving at close quarters.

South of the funerary temple along the porticoed way is **Diocletian's camp**, erected after the destruction of the city by Aurelian, possibly on the site of what had been the palace of Zenobia, although excavations so far have been unable to prove this. The camp lay near what was the Damascus Gate, which gave on to a 2nd century colonnaded street that supposedly linked Emesa (Homs) and the Euphrates.

Over to the south at the foot of some low hills are a series of tall, free-standing square-based towers; these are funerary towers. The towers contain coffins – or rather, did contain coffins – in niches like pigeon holes that rise for up to five levels.

Although there is no admission fee to the site, you pay S£300 to enter the Temple of Bel, S£150 to get into the Arab castle up on the hill overlooking the site (a good place to be at sundown) and S£200 to have the funerary towers unlocked for investigation (payable at the museum, where you also have to arrange transport).

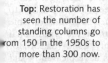

Top: Restoration has seen the number of standing columns go from 150 in the 1950s to more than 300 now.

Bottom: Most of the time you have the ruins to yourself, especially if you choose to get up early in the morning.

JEAN-BERNARD CARILLET

SYRIA

This was the beginning of the end for Palmyra. It fell to the Muslims in 634 and was finally and completely destroyed by an earthquake in 1089.

Information

The tourist office is about halfway between the town and the site proper. There is no bank or exchange office in Palmyra, although the black market thrives and you can change at the Palmyra Cham Palace Hotel.

Museum

With no labelling to speak of and poor presentation it's debatable whether Palmyra's modest museum is worth a visit or not. But there is a good large-scale model of the Temple of Bel that gives an excellent idea of how the complex would have looked in its original uneroded state, as well as a couple of very dynamic mosaics that were found in what are presumed to be nobles' houses, located just east of the Temple of Bel. There are also countless busts and carved portraits that formed part of the panels used to seal the tombs in Palmyra's many funerary towers.

The museum is on the edge of the new town and open from 8 am to 1 pm and 4 to 6 pm (2 to 4 pm in winter) daily except Tuesday. The entrance fee is S£300 (students S£25).

Places to Stay

New Tourist Hotel (☎ 791 0333, Sharia al-Quwatli) was at one time about the only hotel in town. It's failed to keep up with the times and is looking a bit grotty and battered. A bed in a share room is S£150, while singles/doubles with ensuites are S£200/ 325, or S£175/275 without.

New Afqa Hotel (☎ 791 0386) is maybe the best backpackers' option in town. Rooms are spartan but clean, and charged at S£250 per person with ensuites or S£600 for a triple with shared facilities. You can also sleep on the roof for S£100.

Umayyad Palace (☎/fax 910 755, Saahat al-Jamarek) had only been open a few months when we visited and many rooms

were still under construction. It looked to have great potential with a lovely courtyard area, and we stayed in a fine ensuite double for a 'discount price' of S£400, however, there have been complaints about sleazy behaviour by staff here, so female travellers beware.

Citadel Hotel (☎ 791 0537, Sharia As'ad al-Amir), which faces the side of the museum, is a fairly nondescript place with a few simple rooms with shared facilities charged at S£200 per bed, or a couple of ensuite doubles that are seriously overpriced at S£700.

Palace Hotel (☎ 791 3941, fax 911 707) is not bad at all, quiet and well-looked after, and some of the rooms have good views of the ruins. The place is used a lot by French groups. Ensuite singles/doubles are listed at US$17/24 but, again, we were offered a generous discount.

Ishtar Hotel (☎ 791 3073, fax 913 260, Sharia al-Quwatli) is about the first place you come to, on the left, as you enter the town. It's new and modern and the rooms, if a little on the small side, are immaculately kept with clean sheets and towels. Ensuite air-con singles/doubles are US$17/24. It also has cheaper, basement doubles with shared facilities for S£500.

You can camp at *Hotel Zenobia* out by the ruins but it's expensive at S£200. The hotel itself has rooms for US$55/66/76 in high season.

Places to Eat

Most travellers seem to end up at one of the trio of restaurants on the main drag, Sharia al-Quwatli: *Traditional Palmyra*, *Sindbad Restaurant* next door, or *Spring Restaurant* across the street. There's little to choose between them. The food is variable although the *mansaf* at the Traditional Palmyra is reasonably good (S£250 for two). All three places have pleasantly laid back atmospheres and greatly benefit from the fact that there's little to do at night in Palmyra except take a streetside table and linger over a meal and several teas (none of the three serves beer).

Venus Restaurant on Sharia an-Nasr, just north of the main drag, is a relatively new place that's trying hard (very friendly, enthusiastic staff) but serves very bland fare. It is, however, cheap and it does serve beer.

Palmyra Restaurant on the main square, opposite the museum, does fairly awful food but the garden setting with fountains and plenty of leafy shade is extremely pleasant. Beer is served (S£75).

Tourist Oasis Restaurant is something similar – an open-air place with seating among the date palms – and while we did not get a chance to eat there, a couple of travellers' reports have been favourable.

Getting There & Away

The government-run Karnak bus company has its office on the main square opposite the museum. From here there are three buses a day on Tuesday, Friday and Sunday direct to Damascus (S£125, three hours), while on other days there's just one Damascus service, which goes via Homs (S£65, two hours to Homs). In the other direction there are five buses a day to Deir ez-Zur (S£75, three hours) and one to Qamishle (S£160, six hours), which goes via Hassake (S£135, five hours).

Otherwise, you can try to jump on any of the buses regularly passing through en route between Damascus and Deir ez-Zur (and beyond). For Deir ez-Zur, the best bet is to wait at one of the restaurants on the Deir ez-Zur highway (head north about 1.5km up Sharia As'ad al-Amir, the highway forms a T-junction about 200m past the last tree).

If you're in a hurry, there is also a bus station north of the centre with frequent departures to Damascus, Deir ez-Zur and Homs but the vehicles are old and many are minibuses rather than proper big air-con buses. The fares are about a half to two-thirds those of Karnak. To get to the station, walk west out of town past the Assad Gardens and north to a T-junction; at this junction, bear right, then take the first left. In all it's about a 1km walk from the museum.

The Euphrates River

The Euphrates River (Al-Furat in Arabic) starts out high in the mountains of eastern Anatolia in Turkey and winds through north-eastern Syria into Iraq, finally emptying into the Shatt al-Arab waterway and the Persian Gulf – a total distance of over 2400km.

One of the few tributaries of the Euphrates, the Kabur, flows down through north-eastern Syria to join it below Deir ez-Zur. These two rivers make it possible to irrigate and work the land, and wheat and cotton grown here are an important source of income for the country.

RAQQA

From 796 to 808 AD, the city of Raqqa (then Ar-Rafika) reached its apex as the Abbasid caliph, Haroun ar-Rashid, made it his summer residence.

Practically nothing of the city's old glory has been preserved, but the partly restored **Baghdad Gate**, about a 10 minute walk to the east of the clock tower, is a central landmark when you arrive in the city. The old Abbasid city **wall**, restored at some points to a height of 5m, runs north from the gate past the **Qasr al-Binaat** (Daughters' Palace), which served as a residence under the Ayyubids.

A small **museum**, located roughly halfway between the Baghdad Gate and the clock tower, has some interesting artefacts from excavation sites in the area. It is open daily except Tuesday from 9 am to 6 pm (4 pm in winter), and entry costs S£150.

There are a few hotels around the clock tower, all of them amazingly expensive. The best of a bad lot is *Ammar Hotel* (☎ 222 2612, Sharia al-Quneitra), just north of the clock tower, which has very basic, grotty rooms with shared shower and toilet facilities at S£400 for a double. Food-wise, the *Aladdin* just across from the museum is about the best there is.

Getting There & Away

There's a new bus station about 300m south of the clock tower. Several companies have their offices here and between them there are regular services to Aleppo (S£85, 2½ hours), Damascus (S£225, seven hours) and Deir ez-Zur (S£60, two hours).

RASAFA

This startling walled city lies in the middle of nowhere, and seems to rise up out of the featureless desert as you approach it. Fortified by the Romans, the Byzantine emperor Justinian gave it much of its present look, a religious basilica complex devoted to St Sergius and a military outpost. The Umayyads later built a palace here which was subsequently destroyed by the Abbasids.

Getting There & Away

Catch a microbus from Raqqa to Al-Mansura (S£15, 20 minutes) – that's the easy bit. Now it's just a matter of waiting at the signposted turn-off for a pick-up to take you the 35km to the ruins for about S£20 – or hitching.

DEIR EZ-ZUR

This is a pleasant town on the Euphrates and a crossroads for travellers visiting the northeast of Syria. It has prospered recently with oil discoveries in the surrounding areas.

There's not much to see, apart from a reasonable new **museum** about a kilometre west of the centre, but a stroll along the riverbank is a popular activity. On the other side of the suspension bridge is a small recreation ground where you can swim with the locals, though this is probably not advisable for women travellers.

Places to Stay & Eat

There are several cheap dumps around the main square but these are all to be avoided. About the only budget place we could recommend (and it's a hesitant recommendation at that) is *Al-Jamia al-Arabiyya* (☎ 222 1371) on Sharia Khaled ibn al-Walid east of the square; it has clean sheets, hot showers and a friendly manager and charges S£200 per person.

Otherwise *Hotel Raghdan* (☎ 222 2053, fax 222 1169) on Sharia Abu Bakr as-Siddiq overlooking the canal has grotty air-con

singles/doubles for US$17/23 with bathroom, or US$14/20 without.

Hotel Mari (☎ 222 4340, fax 221 657) is even worse value than the Raghdan; rooms are very badly looked after but are charged at US$24/33, and we found the staff thoroughly unpleasant.

Restaurant as-Said on the south side of the main square is a very basic kebab and grilled chicken place but one which stands out from the competition by virtue of having some notion of hygiene. *Al-Aseel* is a small place on Sharia Abu Bakr as-Siddiq beside the canal, about 750m west of the centre. It has outside seating in the summer and an indoor restaurant for the colder months but most importantly, according to one long time expat resident, it does the best kebabs in Syria.

There are also a couple of restaurants on the south bank of the Euphrates – *Tourist Blue Beach* just to the north of the suspension bridge and *Al-Jisr al-Kebir* (Big Canal) just to the south. Both are little more than open-air terraces but with excellent riverside settings that go some way to compensating for indifferent, overpriced food.

Getting There & Away

The airport is about 7km east of town and the weekly flight between Deir ez-Zur and Damascus costs S£600.

The new luxury bus station is about 2km south of town, at the end of Sharia 8 Azar. Several companies have their offices here and between them they offer regular services to Damascus (S£175, seven hours) via Palmyra (S£100, three hours) and to Aleppo (S£135, five hours) via Raqqa (S£60, two hours). There's little need to book in advance – just show up and get a ticket for whichever bus is going out next. Services to Hassake (S£75, two hours) and Qamishle (S£110, three hours) are less frequent – in fact, to the latter there's only one service a day, operated by Qadmous and departing at 3.30 pm.

The minibus station is on Sharia 8 Azar about 1km south of the main square. From here there's an hourly minibus to Raqqa (S£60, two hours) and plenty to Hassake in the north-east (S£75) and on to Qamishle on the Turkish border (S£125). There are also frequent departures to Abu Kamal (often pronounced 'bukaMEL') by minibus (S£30) and by microbus (S£50).

The train station is across the river to the north of town, about 3km from the centre. The train to Aleppo leaves at 1.30 am daily (S£90/60 in 1st/2nd class, S£225 for a sleeper), while the Damascus service departs at 8.30 pm (S£155/105 in 1st/2nd class, S£430 for a sleeper). Several trains run to Hassake and on to Qamishle (S£60/40, three hours), although, all but the 12.30 pm service are in the early hours of the morning.

SOUTH OF DEIR EZ-ZUR

The route south-east of Deir ez-Zur follows the Euphrates down to the closed Iraqi border. It is dotted with sites of archaeological and historical interest.

Dura Europos

For the uninitiated, the extensive, largely Hellenistic/Roman fortress city of Dura Europos is by far the most intriguing site to visit on the road from Deir ez-Zur to Abu Kamal. The riverside walls overlook the left bank of the Euphrates, 90m below. It is renowned for its apparent religious tolerance, seemingly confirmed by the presence of a church, synagogue and other Greek, Roman and Mesopotamian temples side by side.

Mari

The ruins of Mari (Tell Hariri), an important Mesopotamian city dating back some 5000 years, are about 10km north of Abu Kamal. Although fascinating for their age, the mud-brick ruins do not grab the imagination as much as you might hope.

The **Royal Palace of Zimri-Lim** was enormous, measuring 200m by 120m with over 300 rooms. The palace is the main point of interest; it is now sheltered from the elements by a modern protective roof.

Getting There & Away
Local microbuses run alongside the river from Deir ez-Zur to Abu Kamal (three hours, S£50).

The North-East

Bordered by Turkey and Iraq, there are no major monuments or sights in the north-eastern corner of the country, but this does not mean it is empty of attractions. Perhaps the greatest is the chance to meet the Kurds, a people without a country, who have yet to give up their struggle. Only about one million of a total of around 20 million Kurds live in Syria.

The numerous *tells* (artificial hills) dotted around the place are a sign that the area has been inhabited since the 3rd millennium BC.

HASSAKE

The capital of the governorate of the same name, Hassake doesn't offer the visitor an awful lot to do, but it's not a bad base from which to explore the area, unless you're planning on entering Turkey here, in which case you may as well push on to Qamishle.

Hassake is serviced by a variety of buses and microbuses, and there are trains to Qamishle, Damascus, Deir ez-Zur and Aleppo.

QAMISHLE

Situated right at a crossing point on the Turkish border in the north-east, Qamishle is full of Kurds and Turks and the cheaper hotels will sometimes quote prices in Turkish lira rather than Syrian pounds.

There is nothing to see in Qamishle, but the mix of people makes the place interesting. Because of its proximity to the border, you can expect passport checks at the hotels (even during the night), and when getting on or off buses or trains.

Places to Stay & Eat

Among the cheapest and worst is *Umayyad Hotel,* in a sidestreet across from *Hotel Semiramis*. A bed here costs S£100. Just around the corner is *Chahba Hotel*, which is nothing to write home about and asks S£100 a bed (women must take a double). The upstairs terrace is OK.

Mamar, a block south, is better value, although a tad more expensive. Singles/doubles cost S£300/400. The rooms with balconies are quite good and they have hot water.

Opposite the Chahba is a pleasant *restaurant* with an outdoor section. A good meal of kebabs and the usual side orders will cost about S£200.

Getting There & Away

The Turkish border is only about 1km from the centre of Qamishle.

There are three flights a week to Damascus (S£900).

Several private companies operate buses to Damascus (10 hours, S£340) and Aleppo (five hours, S£175). More rickety buses do the trips for half the price.

There are three daily trains that go as far as Aleppo, and one or two of them go all the way to Damascus (S£740 for a sleeper; S£198/132 in 1st/2nd class).

The Dead Sea at sunset, Israel

Boat at sunset, Egypt

Pamukkale at sunset, Turkey

View over Shihara, Yemen

Wadi Rum desert, Jordan

ANDREW HUMPHREYS

Palmyra, Syria

RUSSELL MOUNTFORD

GREG ELMS

Luxor, Egypt

The Dome of the Rock, Jerusalem, Israel

JON DAVISON

Celsus Library, Ephesus, Turkey

PATRICK SYDER

Leptis Magna, Libya

Turkey

Turkey is the bridge between Europe and the Middle East, both physically and culturally. The Ottoman sultans ruled the entire Middle East for centuries, and traces of Turkish influence remain in all of the countries once controlled from İstanbul.

Turkey was the first formerly Ottoman Muslim land to establish a republic and to achieve democracy, as well as the first to look westward, to Europe and North America, for cultural models. The tourism boom of the 1990s brought even more European influence, from rock music to topless beaches. It may be one of the least exotic countries you encounter in this region, but it's no imitation Europe. With more ancient cities than any other country in the region, 4000km of warm-water coastline, varied countryside and excellent food, Turkey has lots to offer. The Turks are mostly very friendly, especially when you escape the coastal resorts.

Facts about Turkey

HISTORY
A general history of the Middle East can be found in the Facts about the Region chapter. Following Turkey's defeat in WWI, Mustafa Kemal Atatürk, the father of modern Turkey, made his name by repelling the Anzacs (the Australian and New Zealand forces) in their heroic but futile attempt to capture Gallipoli and then by out-manoeuvring the last weak Ottoman rulers and the Allied forces in the War of Independence. Victory for the Turks came in 1923 at Smyrna (İzmir) where the invading Greeks were pushed out of Anatolia for good. The treaties of WWI, which left the Turks with almost no country, were renegotiated and a new Turkish republic, reduced to Anatolia and part of Thrace, was born.

Atatürk embarked on a rapid modernisation program, including establishing a secular democracy, the introduction of Latin script and European dress, and the theoretical

Turkish Republic (Türkiye Cumhuriyeti)

Area: 788,695 sq km
Population: 61 million
Population Growth Rate: 2.1%
Captial: Ankara
Head of State: President Süleyman Demirel
Official Language: Turkish
Currency: Turkish lira (TL)
Exchange Rate: Subject to 55% inflation

- **Best Dining** – İstanbul offers far and away the widest choice of food
- **Best Nightlife** – soaking up the atmosphere of the Chimaera at Olimpos beneath a full moon
- **Best Walk** – through the Ilhara Gorge in Kapadokya
- **Best View** – the Bosphorus from the ruined castle at Anadolu Hisarı
- **Best Activity** – visiting a hamam (see 'The Hamam Experience' boxed text)
- **When in Rome ...** watching camels spit and snarl at each other during a camel-wrestling bout at Selçuk

adoption of equal rights for women. The capital was also moved from İstanbul to Ankara. But such sweeping changes did not come easily and some of the battles (eg over women's head covering) are still being fought today.

Since Atatürk's death, Turkey has experienced three military coups and considerable political turbulence. During the 1980s and 90s it has also been wracked by the conflict with the PKK (Kurdistan Workers Party), led by Abdullah ('Apo') Ocalan, which has been agitating for the creation of a Kurdish state in Turkey's south-east corner. This conflict has led to an estimated 30,000 deaths and huge population shifts inside the country, and has wreaked havoc on the economy. In 1999 Ocalan was brought to trial in Turkey for treason and separatist activity and sentenced to death, a sentence which, at the time of writing, was yet to be carried out.

Turkey Today

Modern Turkey is suffering from an identity crisis. Despite the fact that it entered a customs-union agreement with the European Union (EU) in 1995, hopes that it would move rapidly to full membership of the EU look forlorn at present, and have been made worse by the passing of the

death sentence on Ocalan. The festering dispute with Greece, symbolised by the seemingly insoluble problem of Cyprus, is no nearer to being resolved, and the secular society established by Atatürk is coming under strain as a result of resurgent Islamic fundamentalism.

Some commentators foresee a brighter future, especially for the south-east, if the struggle with the PKK can be resolved. The collapse of the Soviet Union has brought unparalleled opportunities for trade with Eastern Europe and the Turkish republics of former Soviet Central Asia; but, in 1999, the Turkish economy was in dire straits, not least because of the collapse of tourism in the face of threats from the PKK. That a newly elected coalition government made up of representatives of the right-wing MHP (National Unity Party), the right-of-centre ANAP (Motherland Party) and the left-wing DSP (Democratic Socialist Party) will prove strong enough to resolve any of these problems must be doubtful.

TURKEY

What to See

Set on the Bosphorus, **İstanbul** is one of the world's great romantic cities and could keep you entertained for days on end. Heading down the Aegean from İstanbul, top places to stay include **Çanakkale** for the battlefields of Gallipoli and the ruins of Troy; and **Selçuk**, for excursions to the ruins at Ephesus, Priene, Miletus and Didyma. Along the Mediterranean coast, particularly inviting smallish resorts include **Dalyan**, **Kaş** and **Olimpos**, all good bases for exploring the Graeco-Roman and Lycian archaeological sites along the coast. The beach at **Patara** is one of the best in Turkey.

Inland, Turkey's premier attraction is the spectacular landscape of **Kapadokya (Cappadocia)** where the village of Göreme is a particularly popular place to stay. From there you can easily travel west to **Konya** to see the beautiful tomb of the Mevlâna; east to **Nemrut Dağı** to see the giant Commagenian heads; and south to the exotic bazaars of **Sanlıurfa**.

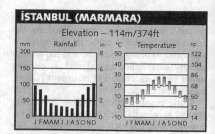

GEOGRAPHY

Turkey is divided into Asian and European parts by the Dardanelles, the Sea of Marmara and the Bosphorus strait. Eastern Thrace (European Turkey) comprises only 3% of the total 788,695 sq km land area. The remaining 97% is Anatolia, a vast plateau rising eastward towards the Caucasus Mountains. Turkey's coastline is over 6000km long, much of it colonised for holidaymaking.

CLIMATE

The Aegean and Mediterranean coasts have mild, rainy winters and hot, dry summers. In İstanbul, summer temperatures average around 28°C to 30°C; the winters are chilly but usually above freezing, with rain and perhaps a dusting of snow. The Anatolian plateau is cooler in summer and freezing in winter. The Black Sea coast is mild and wet in summer, chilly and wet in winter.

Mountainous eastern Turkey is very cold and snowy in winter, and only pleasantly warm in high summer. The south-east is dry and mild in winter and baking hot in summer, with temperatures above 45°C not unusual.

ECOLOGY & ENVIRONMENT

The embryonic environmental movement in Turkey is making slow progress, exemplified by the fact that the government is considering building a new nuclear power plant on the Mediterranean coast at Akkuyu Bay, in a known earthquake region. Greenpeace Mediterranean (☎ 236 4238, fax 236 4215, PO Box MBE 109, Dolapdere Caddesi 283, Pamgaltı, İstanbul) has the details.

For information on the few remaining nesting sites of the loggerhead turtle in Turkey (at Dalyan, Olimpos etc), contact The Society for the Protection of Sea Turtles (☎ 242-825 7260) in Çiralı. The Society for the Protection of Nature (☎ 212-281 0321, fax 279 5544, Doğal Hayat 1/2 Koruma Derneği, PK 18 Bebek, 80810 İstanbul) has information on many other environmental issues.

See also the Ecology & Environment section in the Facts about the Region chapter at the beginning of this book.

GOVERNMENT & POLITICS

In theory Turkey is a multiparty democracy on the Western European model, although in practice it has proved more of a semi-democracy with the military wielding considerable power behind the scenes. During the 1990s no one political party has been able to win absolute control of parliament in elections based on proportional representa-

Atatürk (1881-1938)

It won't take you long to discover the national hero, Mustafa Kemal Atatürk. Though he died on 10 November 1938, his picture is everywhere in Turkey, a bust or statue (preferably equestrian) is in every park, quotations from his speeches and writings are on every public building. He is almost synonymous with the Turkish Republic.

A man of great intelligence and even greater energy, Atatürk was possessed by the idea of giving his fellow Turks a new lease of life. In contrast to many leaders, he had the ability to realise his obsession almost single-handedly. His achievement in turning a moribund empire into a forward-looking nation state was taken as model by 1950s Egyptian president Abdel Nasser and the Shāhs of Iran.

tion. This has resulted in a series of weak coalition governments with increasing representation from parties of the extremes. In 1995, for the first time since the creation of the Turkish republic, an overtly religious party leader became prime minister although he was speedily sidelined. In the 1999 elections the right-wing MHP took a share of power for the first time, a shock result which probably reflects increasing Turkish nationalism as a reaction to Kurdish nationalism.

The current prime minister of Turkey is the veteran left-winger Bulent Ecevit, while the president is the equally long-serving Süleyman Demirel. Turkey has had 57 governments since the creation of the republic in 1923. Three parties with little in common are now sharing power; it remains to be seen how long the present one can last.

POPULATION & PEOPLE

Turkey's nearly 61 million people are predominantly Sunni Muslim Turks, with a significant minority (perhaps 12 million) of mainly Muslim Kurds and small groups of

Laz, Hemsin, Arabs, Jews, Greeks and Armenians. Most of the Laz and Hemsin people still live along the north-eastern corner of the Black Sea. South-east Turkey is pretty solidly Kurdish, although the problems of the last 15 years have led many to head west in search of a better life.

Turkey's five biggest cities are İstanbul (12 million people), Ankara (3 million), İzmir (2 million), Adana (1.6 million) and Bursa (1 million).

SOCIETY & CONDUCT

Ottoman Turkey was ruled by Sharia'a (Islamic religious law) but republican Turkey has largely adapted to a modern westernised lifestyle. Liberal western attitudes born of Atatürk's reforms are strongest in the urban centres of the west and along the coasts, and among the middle and upper classes. You will feel quite comfortable among these Turks, who look to western culture as the ideal, and accept the validity of other religious beliefs.

The working and farming classes, especially in the east, are more conservative, traditional and religious. There's a small but growing segment of 'born again' Muslims, fervent and strict in their religion but otherwise modern.

RELIGION

Turkey is 99% Muslim, predominantly Sunni, with Shi'ites and Alawites in the east and south-east.

The small Jewish community is descended from those who fled the Spanish Inquisition in 1492 and found tolerance in the Ottoman empire. The Ecumenical Orthodox Patriarch is based in İstanbul, but the Orthodox minority dwindled after the Cyprus crisis of the 1970s. In general, religious minorities live freely although there is increasing intolerance of difference in the east.

LANGUAGE

Ottoman Turkish was written in Arabic script, but Atatürk switched to Latin script in 1928. In big cities and tourist areas, many locals know at least some English, French and/or German. In the south-east, Kurdish or Arabic is often the first language.

Facts for the Visitor

PLANNING

Spring (late April/May) and autumn (late September/October) are the best times to visit. The weather is fine and usually not too rainy, and the crowds have yet to appear. In the high season (July to mid-September) the weather can be very hot, and major tourist destinations are crowded and overpriced. Though winter is generally rainy and cold, with high air pollution, accommodation prices are low, and there are no crowds. Try to avoid travelling during Kurban Bayramı, Turkey's most popular public holiday, when half the country is on the move.

The free map of Turkey provided by the tourist offices is excellent and shows the site of most attractions. The Bartholomew Euromap of Turkey, in two sheets at 1:800,000, is also excellent. Many locally produced maps are sketchy and inaccurate.

It's worth packing mosquito repellent (from April to September); sunblock cream; a universal sink plug; a towel; and reading matter. Women should bring their favoured sanitary protection.

VISAS & DOCUMENTS
Visas

Nationals of the following countries (partial list) can enter Turkey for up to three months with just a valid passport; no visa is required: Belgium, Canada, Denmark, Finland, France, Germany, Holland, Japan, New Zealand, Norway, Sweden and Switzerland. Nationals of Australia, Austria, Greece, Ireland, Israel, Italy, Portugal, Spain, the UK and the USA must buy a sticker visa on arrival at the airport or overland border rather than at an embassy in advance; make sure to join the queue to buy your visa before the one for immigration. How much you pay depends on your nationality and changes fairly frequently; at the time of writing British citizens paid UK£10 (bank note only), Australians US$20 and citizens of the USA a hefty US$45. No photographs are required.

The standard visa is valid for three months and, depending on your nationality, usually allows for multiple entries. In theory a visa can be renewed once after three months, but the bureaucracy and costs involved mean that it's much easier to leave the country (usually to one of the Greek islands) and then come back in again.

Visas for Neighbouring Countries You need a visa to enter the following neighbouring countries of Turkey:

Armenia Armenia has no embassy or consulate in Turkey; would-be visitors to Armenia should try the consulate of the Russian Federation (☎ 292 5101, İstiklal Caddesi 443, İstanbul) for information.

Georgia Georgia has a consulate in Trabzon where visas are issued on the spot. They cost US$20 for 15 days. See the Trabzon section for further details.

Iran The embassy in Ankara and consulate in İstanbul will readily issue a transit visa good for five days but you need to show a visa for an onward country. Applications for tourist visas, valid for 20 days or more, are sent to Tehrān for approval, which can take 10 or more days. You also have to pay US$50 on application, which is not returned if your application is knocked back. In Doğubeyazıt there are men who say they can sort out a visa in a day, but it's a long way to go on the off chance.

Iraq Foreign Office advice is don't even consider it. We can't imagine any circumstances under which you could get an Iraqi visa as a tourist in Turkey.

Syria The embassy in Ankara and consulate in İstanbul will both issue visas but a letter of recommendation from your embassy is necessary (for UK citizens this costs an unbelievable UK£35). Costs for the visa itself varies by nationality – for Aussies it's free but UK and US citizens pay US$55. Drop your passport off between 9.30 am and 11 am and collect it the next day between 2 and 2.30 pm.

Other Documents

Holders of International Student Identity Cards (ISICs) are granted discounts of 25% to 33% on some museum admission fees. They also get discounts of 10% on Turkish State Railways and Turkish Maritime Lines.

An international driving permit may be handy if your driving licence is from a country likely to seem obscure to a Turkish police officer.

EMBASSIES & CONSULATES
Turkish Embassies & Consulates

For addresses of Turkish embassies in neighbouring Middle Eastern countries see the relevant country chapters.

Australia
  Embassy:
  (☎ 02-6295 0227, fax 6239 6592)
  60 Mugga Way, Red Hill ACT 2603

Canada
  Embassy:
  (☎ 613-789 4044, fax 781 3442)
  197 Wurtemburg St, Ottawa, Ontario KIN 8L9
France
  Embassy:
  (☎ 01 45 24 52 24, fax 01 45 20 41 91)
  16 Ave de Lamballe, 75016 Paris
Germany
  Embassy:
  (☎ 49-228 9538, fax 228 3488)
  Utestr 47, 53179 Bonn 2
Ireland
  Embassy:
  (☎ 1-668 5240, fax 668 5014)
  11 Clyde Rd, Ballsbridge, Dublin 4
Netherlands
  Embassy:
  (☎ 70-360 4912, fax 361 7969)
  Prinsessgracht 28, 2514 AP, The Hague
New Zealand
  Embassy:
  (☎ 4-472 1290, fax 472 1277)
  15-17 Murphy St, Level 8, Wellington
UK
  Embassy:
  (☎ 020-7393 0202, fax 7393 0066)
  43 Belgrave Square, London SW1X 8PA
USA
  Embassy:
  (☎ 202-659 8200, fax 659 0744)
  1714 Massachusetts Ave, NW Washington, DC 20036

Embassies & Consulates in Turkey

Embassies are in Ankara but many nations also have consulates in İstanbul and some also in İzmir. In general embassies and consulates are open from 9.30 am to 3.30 pm Monday to Friday, although there's usually an hour off for lunch. The embassies and consulates of some Islamic countries (particularly Iran) close on Friday but may be open on Sunday.

Australia (Avustralya)
  Embassy:
  (☎ 436 1240, fax 445 0284)
  Nene Hatun Caddesi 83, Gaziosmanpaşa, Ankara
  Consulate:
  (☎ 257 7050, fax 257 7054)
  Tepecik Yolu 58, 80630 Etiler, İstanbul

Bulgaria (Bulgaristan)
Embassy:
(☎ 426 7456, fax 427 3178)
Atatürk Bulvarı 124, Kavaklıdere, Ankara
Consulate:
(☎ 269 0478, 269 2216)
Zincirlikuyu Caddesi 44, Ulus, Levent,
İstanbul
Canada (Kanada)
Embassy:
(☎ 436 1275, fax 446 4437)
Nene Hatun Caddesi 75, Gaziosmanpaşa,
Ankara
Consulate:
(☎ 272 5174)
Büyükdere Caddesi 107/3, Bengün Han, 3rd
floor, Gayrettepe, İstanbul
France (Fransa)
Embassy:
(☎ 468 1154, fax 467 1489)
Paris Caddesi 70, Kavaklıdere, Ankara
Consulate:
(☎ 243 1852, fax 249 9168)
İstiklal Caddesi 8, Taksim, İstanbul
Germany (Almanya)
Embassy:
(☎ 426 5451/65, fax 426 6959)
Atatürk Bulvarı 114, Kavaklıdere, Ankara
Consulate:
(☎ 251 5404, fax 249 9920)
İnönü Caddesi, Selim Hatun Camii Sokak 46,
Ayazpaşa, Taksim, İstanbul
Consulate:
(☎ 421 6995, fax 463 4023)
Atatürk Caddesi 260, Alsancak, İzmir
Greece (Yunanistan)
Embassy:
(☎ 436 8861, fax 446 3191)
Ziya-ur-Rahman Caddesi (Karagöz Caddesi)
9-11, Gaziosmanpaşa, Ankara
Consulate:
(☎ 245 0596, fax 252 1365)
Turnacıbaşı Sokak 32, Ağahamam, Beyoğlu,
İstanbul
Iran (İran)
Embassy:
(☎ 429 4320, fax 468 2823)
Tahran Caddesi 10, Kavaklıdere, Ankara
Consulate:
(☎ 513 8230)
Ankara Caddesi 1/2, Cağaloğlu, İstanbul
Iraq (Irak)
Embassy:
(☎ 468 7421, fax 468 4832)
Turan Emeksiz Sokak 11, Gaziosmanpaşa,
Ankara

Consulate:
(☎ 230 2930/3, fax 234 5726)
Halide Edip Adıvar Mahallesi, İpekböceği
Sokak 1, İstanbul
Ireland (İrlanda)
Honorary Consulate:
(☎ 246 6025, fax 248 0744)
Cumhuriyet Caddesi 26/A, Pegasus Evi, Har-
biye, İstanbul
Israel (İsrail)
Embassy:
(☎ 446 3605, fax 426 1533)
Mahatma Gandhi Caddesi 85, 06700 Gazios-
manpaşa, Ankara
Consulate:
(☎ 225 1040, fax 225 1048)
Valikonağı Caddesi 73/4, Nişantaşi, İstanbul
Netherlands (Holanda)
Embassy:
(☎ 446 0470, fax 446 3358)
Uğur Mumcu Caddesi 16, Gaziosmanpaşa,
Ankara
Consulate:
(☎ 251 5030, fax 251 9289)
İstiklal Caddesi 393, Tünel, Beyoğlu
New Zealand (Yeni Zelanda)
Embassy:
(☎ 446 0768, 446 0732, fax 445 0557)
Kızkulesi Sokak 42/1, Gaziosmanpaşa, Ankara
Pakistan
Embassy:
(☎ 427 1410)
İran Caddesi 36, Kavaklıdere, Ankara
Consulate:
(☎ 233 5800, fax 233 5802)
Abide-i Hurriyet Caddesi, Gecit Sokak 11, Kat
6, Hacionbasılar İshanı, Şişli, İstanbul
Syria (Suriye)
Embassy:
(☎ 438 8704, fax 439 4588)
Abdullah Cevdet Sokak 7, Çankaya, Ankara
Consulate:
(☎ 232 6721)
Maçka Caddesi 59, İstanbul
UK (İngiltere, Birleşik Krallığı)
Embassy:
(☎ 468 6230, fax 468 3214)
Şehit Ersan Caddesi 46/A, Çankaya, Ankara
Consulate:
(☎ 293 7545, fax 245 4989)
Meşrutiyet Caddesi 34, Tepebaşı, Beyoğlu,
İstanbul
Consulate:
(☎ 463 5151, fax 421 2914)
Mahmut Esat Bozkurt Caddesi, 1442 Sokak
No 49, İzmir

USA (Amerika Birleşik Devletleri, Amerika)
  Embassy:
  (☎ 468 6110, fax 467 0019)
  Atatürk Bulvarı 110, Kavaklıdere, Ankara
  Consulate:
  (☎ 251 3602, fax 267 0057)
  Meşrutiyet Caddesi 104-108, Tepebaşı,
  Beyoğlu, İstanbul
  Consulate:
  (☎ 21 3643)
  Turkish-American Association (Turk-
  Amerikan Derneği) Büyük Efes Oteli Arkası,
  İzmir

CUSTOMS

You may import, duty free, two cartons of
cigarettes (400), 50 cigars or 200g of smoking tobacco, and 5L of liquor. Duty-free
items are on sale in both arrival and departure areas of Turkey's international airports.

Although Turkey is full of antiquities, it
is strictly illegal to buy, sell or export them.
Penalties are severe – if caught, you may go
to jail. Customs officers spot-check the luggage of departing passengers.

MONEY
Costs

Turkey is still relatively cheap although
prices in İstanbul and along the coast are
rising rapidly. You can travel on as little as
US$15 to US$20 per person per day using
buses, staying in pensions and eating one
restaurant meal daily. For US$20 to US$35
per day you can travel more comfortably by
bus and train, stay in one and two-star hotels with private baths, and eat most meals
in average restaurants. For US$30 to US$70
per person per day you can move up to three
and four-star hotels, take the occasional
flight and dine in restaurants all the time.
Costs are lowest in small eastern towns off
the tourist track, but Kapadokya (Cappadocia) still manages to offer bargain prices.

Currency

The Turkish lira (TL) comes in coins of 5000,
10,000, 25,000, 50,000 and 100,000 liras, and
notes (bills) of 50,000, 100,000, 250,000,
500,000, one million and five million liras,
with higher denominations issued regularly
as inflation (around 55% per annum) de-

values the currency. Prices in this chapter are
quoted in more stable US dollars.

Exchange Rates

The Turkish lira is subject to rapid devalu-
ation caused by inflation. Check exchange
rates shortly before your visit to Turkey and
be prepared for them to change.

country	unit		Turkish lira
Australia	A$1	=	TL288,838
Canada	C$1	=	TL300,550
euro	€1	=	TL474,663
France	10FF	=	TL723,610
Germany	DM1	=	TL242,691
Japan	¥100	=	TL408,724
New Zealand	NZ$1	=	TL232,181
UK	UK£1	=	TL718,668
USA	US$1	=	TL447,880

It's easy to buy Iranian rials at a good rate
in Doğubeyazıt and Syrian pounds in Antakya. Changing these currencies back
again is unlikely to be a profitable business.

Exchanging Money

Exchanging major currencies is fast and easy
in most banks, exchange offices, post offices
(PTTs), shops, hotels etc. Cashing even
major travellers cheques is less easy and the
exchange rate is usually slightly lower. Many
places charge a *komisyon* (commission).

Although Turkey has no black market, you
can often spend US dollars or Deutschmarks
in place of liras.

Credit Cards & ATMs The most useful
credit cards in Turkey are Visa and Master-
Card/Access, which are quite widely ac-
cepted by hotels, restaurants, carpet shops
etc but not by pensions and local eateries.
American Express (Amex) is rarely useful.
You can also get cash advances on Visa and
MasterCard.

ATMs dispense cash in Turkish lira but are
quick and easy to use and spreading around
the country like wildfire. They accept Visa,
MasterCard, Cirrus, Maestro and Eurocard.
You can get by in Turkey just using your
home banking card, provided you remember

to draw out money in the towns to tide you through the villages.

International Transfers Western Union operates in Turkey through Interbank; for info ☎ 212 6666 in İstanbul.

Tipping & Bargaining
Turkey is more European in its approach to tipping than other parts of the Middle East; you won't be pestered by demands for bak-sheesh here. Waiters, hairdressers and bath attendants appreciate around 10% of the bill; a hotel porter US$0.50 to US$1; and a cinema usher a few coins or a small lira note. You might round up your taxi fare slightly but there's no need to tip *dolmuş* (minibus) drivers.

Taxes & Refunds
Value-added tax of 15 to 20% is included in the price of most items and services: look for signs saying KDV *dahil* (VAT in-cluded). A few hotels and shops give dis-counts if you agree not to request an official receipt; this way, they don't have to pay the tax and you save.

If you buy an expensive item (eg carpet, leather jacket) for export, ask the shopkeeper for a KDV *iade özel fatura* (special VAT re-fund receipt). Get it stamped as you clear cus-toms, then get your refund at a bank branch in the airport departure lounge (usually not open); or you can mail the receipt and be sent a cheque (be patient and ever-hopeful).

POST & COMMUNICATIONS
Turkish post offices are called PTTs – look for the black-on-yellow signs.

Postal Rates
Postcards to Europe cost US$0.50; to Aus-tralia, New Zealand and the USA US$0.60. Letters to Europe cost US$0.60; to Aus-tralia, New Zealand and the USA will cost you US$0.85.

Sending Mail
It's best to post letters in the post office slots rather than in a letter box. The *yurtdışı*

slot is for mail to foreign countries, *yurtiçi* is for mail to other Turkish cities and *şehir içi* is for mail within the city.

The PTT operates an express mail courier-type service called *acele posta servisi* (APS), which competes with inter-national express carriers like Federal Ex-press. If you must have something reach its destination fast, ask for this. Don't confuse this courier service with the traditional, slower *ekspres* (special delivery) service.

To mail packages out of the country, you must have your package opened for customs inspection, and you may have to endure a bit of frustrating red tape. Have paper, box, string, tape and marker pens with you.

To be sure that a parcel will get to its des-tination intact, send it by APS, an interna-tional courier service (DHL, Fedex, UPS) or at least *kayıtlı* (registered mail).

Receiving Mail
Most main post offices have a poste restante section. If you need to receive mail, you can use the poste restante service, where letters are sent to a post office for you to collect. Letters should be addressed in this form:

(Name)
Poste Restante
General Post Office
City
Country

To collect your mail, go to the main post of-fice in the town and show your passport. Let-ters sometimes take several weeks to arrive (packets even longer), so have them sent to a place where you're going to be for a while or will be passing through several times. There are too few Amex offices for it to make much sense to have your mail sent there.

Telephone
Phoning home from Turkey can be very ex-pensive; it costs around UK£1 to phone Britain for one minute, US$3 to phone the USA and even more to call Australia. Cheaper rates are only available from mid-night to 7 am and on Sunday. Hotels often levy exorbitant surcharges, even on local

phone calls. Wherever possible, it's probably wise to make collect (reverse charge) calls, although note that this facility is not currently available to New Zealand.

The country code for Turkey is 90, followed by the area code (minus the zero), then the subscriber number. Area codes for some cities, towns and regions are:

Adıyaman	☎ 416
Alanya	☎ 242
Amasya	☎ 358
Ankara	☎ 312
Antakya	☎ 326
Antalya	☎ 242
Avanos	☎ 384
Ayvalık	☎ 266
Behramkale (Assos)	☎ 286
Bergama	☎ 232
Bodrum	☎ 252
Bursa	☎ 224
Çanakkale	☎ 286
Demre (Myra)	☎ 242
Diyarbakır	☎ 412
Doğubeyazıt	☎ 472
Edirne	☎ 284
Erzurum	☎ 442
Fethiye	☎ 252
Gelibolu (Gallipoli)	☎ 286
Göreme	☎ 384
Güzelyurt	☎ 382
Ihlara	☎ 382
İstanbul	☎ 212 (European side)
İstanbul	☎ 216 (Asian side)
(Assume ☎ 212 unless stated otherwise)	
İzmir	☎ 232
Kahta	☎ 416
Kalkan	☎ 242
Kars	☎ 474
Kaş	☎ 322
Kayseri	☎ 352
Konya	☎ 332
Kuşadası	☎ 256
Marmaris	☎ 252
Malatya	☎ 422
Olimpos	☎ 242
Ölüdeniz	☎ 252
Ordu	☎ 452
Pamukkale	☎ 258
Patara	☎ 242
Safranbolu	☎ 372
Samsun	☎ 362
Şanlıurfa	☎ 414
Selçuk	☎ 232
Side	☎ 242
Sivas	☎ 346
Trabzon	☎ 462
Ürgüp	☎ 384
Van	☎ 432

Turkey's public telephones, now operated by Türk Telekom, take *jeton* (tokens) or, increasingly, *telekart* (telephone cards), both sold at telephone centres and some shops.

Fax

It's easiest to send and receive faxes at your hotel for a fee (ask in advance). Türk Telekom centres have faxes, but require more paperwork.

Email & Internet Access

Turkey has taken to the Internet like a duck to water. There are Internet cafes in most big towns, and lots of hotels, pensions, tour operators, even carpet shops are hooked up. Fees are usually around US$2 for 30 minutes. See the individual city sections for addresses and further details.

CompuServe has nodes (9600 bps) in Ankara (modem 468 8042) and İstanbul (modem 234 5168). America Online's İstanbul node is 234 5158 (28,800 bps). You may have to pay additional charges; consult your online service for more information.

Many phones use US-style RJ11 modular plugs (common in expensive hotels). In cheaper hotels you must buy a three-prong *telefon fişi* (Turkish phone plug) and make an adapter.

BOOKS

For a short cut to understanding Turkey, read the definitive *Atatürk: The Rebirth of a Nation* by Lord Kinross. A gripping account of the decline of the Ottoman empire from its peak under Süleyman the Magnificent is *Lords of the Golden Horn* by Noel Barber. Readable accounts of modern Turkey include Jeremy Seal's entertaining *A Fez of the Heart* and Tim Kelsey's more sober *Dervish*.

More general Middle East titles, some of which also contain coverage of Turkey, are listed in the Books section in the Regional Facts for the Visitor chapter at the beginning of this book.

NEWSPAPERS & MAGAZINES

The local English-language paper, the *Turkish Daily News* is especially worth reading on Sundays for its supplement, *Turkish Probe*. In major tourist areas you'll find many day-old European and US newspapers and magazines. Although there's little overt censorship in Turkey and you can read criticism of the government both in Turkish newspapers and in widely available foreign publications, certain subjects (criticism of Atatürk, any suggestion that the Kurds have a right to a separate identity, however moderately phrased) are likely to lead to headaches for journalists and editors – some of whom have disappeared or been killed.

A free magazine produced by Fez Travel and worth keeping an eye out for is *Fark Etmez*, available all over Turkey, particularly in western Turkey; it's a good resource for travellers.

RADIO & TV

Broadcasting is by the government-funded Turkish Radio & Television (TRT) and independent stations. TRT has news broadcasts in English each morning and evening on radio, and late each evening on TV.

PHOTOGRAPHY & VIDEO

Film costs about US$5, plus developing, for 24 Kodacolor exposures. Kodachrome is scarce, pricey and can't be developed in Turkey, though the simpler E-6 process films such as Ektachrome and Fujichrome are readily available and speedily processed in city photo shops – watch the prices in popular tourist resorts.

Most big towns have camera shops that can take passport photos on the spot for about the same price as you'd pay at home.

You must usually pay to use still cameras in most museums. To use a flash or tripod, you must normally obtain written permission from the staff (not easy). Video fees are usually even higher.

LAUNDRY

Laundrettes are beginning to appear in the larger cities, but most *çamaşır* (laundry) is done in hotels. *Kuru temizleme* (dry cleaners) are readily found in the cities; ask at your hotel.

TOILETS

All mosques have toilets, though most are pretty smelly. Major tourist sites have better ones. Almost all public toilets require payment of a small fee (around US$0.25).

Though most hotels and many public toilets have the familiar raised bowl commode, you'll also see traditional flat toilets – holes in the floor with footrests on either side. The custom is to wash with water (from a jug or little pipe attached to the toilet) using the left hand. Doesn't appeal? Then always carry toilet paper with you.

HEALTH

In general, Turkey is a pretty healthy country to travel in, although many people will experience the odd day of stomach upset. It's wise to stick with bottled water and to take all the usual precautions over food hygiene, especially in July and August. There's a small but growing risk of contracting malaria in south-eastern Turkey, where the lakes created by the GAP project have made it easier for mosquitoes to breed.

An *eczane* (pharmacy) can advise on minor problems and dispense many drugs for which you would need a prescription at home. Emergency medical and dental treatment is available at simple *sağlık ocağı* (dispensaries), *klinik* (clinics) and *hastane* (government hospitals). Look for signs with a red crescent or big 'H'. Payment is required, but is usually low.

The standard of hygiene and care in Turkey's state hospitals is not high; make sure you have insurance that will cover treatment in a private hospital.

For more detailed information, see Health in the Regional Facts for the Visitor chapter.

GAY & LESBIAN TRAVELLERS

Though not uncommon in a culture that traditionally separates men and women in society, overt homosexuality is not socially or legally acceptable in Turkey. It's not strictly illegal, but laws prohibiting 'lewd behaviour' are often used to suppress it. Even so, it exists openly at a small number of gay bars and clubs in major cities and resorts. Be discreet.

For more information, surf to www.qrd .org/qrd/www/world/europe/turkey.

DANGERS & ANNOYANCES

Although Turkey is one of the safest countries in the region, you must still take precautions. Wear a money belt under your clothing. Be wary of pickpockets and purse-snatchers in buses, markets and other crowded places.

In İstanbul, single men are sometimes lured to a bar or nightclub (often one of those along İstiklal Caddesi) by new Turkish 'friends'. The man is then made to pay an outrageous bar bill whether he drank or not.

There have been isolated incidents of rape and even murder at resorts, crimes that were virtually unheard of before the tourism boom.

Drugging is becoming quite a problem. Sometimes it happens on bus journeys – the person in the seat next to you buys you a drink, slips a drug into it and, as you sleep, makes off with your luggage. However, it can also happen in hostels and pensions so be a tad wary of who you befriend.

More commonly, the hard-sell tactics of carpet-sellers can drive you to distraction; be warned that 'free' lifts and suspiciously cheap accommodation often come attached to near compulsory visits to carpet showrooms.

If you're travelling to the south-east, be sure to read the warning at the start of the section.

PUBLIC HOLIDAYS & SPECIAL EVENTS

In addition to the main Islamic holidays described in Public Holidays & Special Events in the Regional Facts for the Visitor section, Turkey observes:

New Year's Day
  1 January
Kurban Bayramı
  February/March
National Sovereignty Day
  23 April

Youth & Sports Day
  19 May
International İstanbul Music Festival
  June/July
Victory Day
  30 August
Republic Day
  29 October
Atatürk's Death
  10 November
Mevlâna Festival
  10-17 December

LANGUAGE COURSES

The author of this chapter spent a month studying Turkish for four hours a day, five days a week at Tömer in İstanbul (☎ 252 5154, İnönü Caddesi, Prof Dr Tarık Zafer Tunaya Sokak 18, Taksim) for US$250. Morning, afternoon and evening classes are available at a variety of different levels. There are other branches at İzmir and Antalya. Another possibility is International House (☎ 282 9064, fax 282 3218), Nispetiye Caddesi, Güvercin Durağı, Erdölen İşhani 38, Kat 1, Levent, İstanbul.

Turkish Daily News carries ads for private tutors, as does *İstanbullshit*, a freebie available at the Orient hostel in İstanbul.

ACCOMMODATION

You'll find camping facilities dotted about Turkey. Some hotels and pensions let you camp in their grounds and use their facilities for a small fee (US$2 to US$4). Well-equipped European-style camp sites are available in a few resorts.

Until recently Turkey had no real system of hostels. Several places are now affiliated to the IYHA. Some are real hostels with dorms, others little different from the cheapest pensions. The terms *yurt* (hostel or lodge) and *öğrenci yurdu* (student hostel) usually apply to extremely basic dormitory lodging meant for low-budget Turkish students from the provinces. They're not normally affiliated with the International Youth Hostel Federation, nor are they often located near the major sights, though they may open their doors to foreign students in summer. Tourist offices have details.

The Hamam Experience

The history of steam baths goes back millennia and many of Turkey's natural spas were enjoyed by the ancient Greeks and Romans. Turks built beautiful, elaborate baths (hamams) to serve their communities, partly because Islam demands high standards of personal hygiene, and partly because bathing is such a pleasure. Most Turkish towns still have hamams of varying degrees of fanciness, although they are becoming scarcer in the west as homes acquire plumbed-in bathrooms. The custom of going to the hamam continues because the public facilities are so much grander than anything available at home, and because, for Turks, it is still a social occasion.

What happens in a hamam? Well, you will be shown to a *camekan* (cubicle) where you undress, store your clothes, lock up your valuables and wrap the *peştamal* (the cloth that's provided) around you. A *tellak* (attendant) will lead you through to the hot room where you sit and sweat for a while. Then you have to make a choice. It's cheapest to wash yourself with the *sabon* (soap), *şampuan* (shampoo) and *havlu* (towel) you brought with you. The hot room will be ringed with individual basins that you fill from the taps above before sluicing the water over yourself with a plastic scoop. You should try not to get soap into the water in the basin, and avoid splashing your neighbours, especially on a Friday when someone who has completed their ritual wash would have to start all over again if soaked by an infidel. But it's far more enjoyable to let an attendant wash you. In the hot room you'll be doused with warm water and then scrubbed with a *kese* (coarse cloth mitten), loosening dirt you never suspected you had. Afterwards you'll be lathered with a sudsy swab, rinsed off and shampooed.

When all this is done you'll be offered the chance of a massage, an experience worth having at least once during your trip. Some massages are carried out on the floor or a table but often you'll be spread out on the great marble bench beneath the dome. The massage over, you'll be led back to the cold room, there to be swathed in towels and taken to your cubicle for tea or coffee.

Traditional hamams have separate sections for men or women or admit the sexes at separate times. Opening hours for women are almost invariably more restricted than those for men.

You'll also find hamams throughout Syria – although note: in Arabic the word is pronounced 'ham-mam' with a distinctly double-sounded consonant; the short 'hamam' means 'pigeon'.

Turkey's cheapest hotels are rated by the local municipality and are mostly used by working-class Turkish men travelling on business. They usually cost from US$4 per bed in a small town up to US$20 or US$30 for a double room in a large city. Virtually all hotels above this basic standard are rated by the Ministry of Tourism. One-star hotels are just a step above the cheap places rated by the municipalities. At the top, the five-star places are the big international chains – the Hiltons, Hyatts, Ramadas and Sheratons.

Not surprisingly, the most difficult place to find a really good cheap room is İstanbul. In most other cities good, inexpensive beds can be found fairly easily. The cheapest places are not always suitable for lone women, who will attract less unwanted attention by asking for *aile* (family) accommodation.

In smaller tourist towns like Fethiye and Selçuk, touts for hotels and pensions may accost you as you step from your bus. Many are legitimate agents – or even pension owners – looking for customers, but the obnoxious ones are usually freelancers who extort commissions from pension owners for bringing you to them.

FOOD

Turkish food has often been called the French cuisine of the east, with good reason. You'll find the *kebapçı*, a cheap eatery specialising in roast lamb, everywhere; *şiş kebap* (shish kebap), lamb grilled on a skewer, is a Turkish invention. Try the ubiquitous *döner kebap* – lamb packed onto a vertical revolving spit and sliced off when done.

The best cheap and tasty meal is *pide*, Turkish pizza. Fish, though excellent, is often expensive – be sure to ask the price before you order. A proper meal consists of a long procession of dishes. First come the *mezze* (hors d'oeuvres), such as:

beyaz peynir – white sheep's milk cheese
börek – flaky pastry stuffed with white cheese and parsley
(kuru) fasulye – (dried) beans
kabak dolması – stuffed squash/marrow
patlıcan salatası – puréed aubergine salad
patlıcan tava – fried aubergine
pilaki – beans vinaigrette
yaprak dolması – stuffed vine leaves

Dolma is made of all sorts of vegetables (aubergine, peppers, cabbage or vine leaves) served cold and stuffed with rice, currants and pine nuts, or hot with lamb. The eggplant (aubergine) is Turkey's number one vegetable. It can be stuffed as a dolma *(patlıcan dolması)*, served puréed with lamb *(hünkar beğendi)*, stuffed with minced meat *(karnıyarık)* or appear with exotic names like *imam bayıldı* – 'the imam fainted' – which means stuffed with ground lamb, tomatoes, onions and garlic.

For dessert, try *fırın sütlaç* (baked rice pudding), *kazandibi* (caramelised pudding), *aşure* (pudding made from up to 40 different ingredients), *baklava* (flaky pastry stuffed with walnuts or pistachios, soaked in honey), or *kadayıf* (shredded wheat with nuts in honey). The famously chewy sweet called *lokum*, or Turkish delight, has been made here since the 18th century. There's not a bus station in the country that doesn't sell it. Whether you'll like it or not is another matter.

DRINKS

Good bottled water is sold everywhere. Beers, such as Tuborg or Efes Pilsen, the sturdy Turkish pilsener, supplement the familiar Turkish soft drinks. There's also good Turkish wine – red or white – or fierce aniseed *rakı*, which is like Greek *ouzo* or Arab *araq* (the Turks usually cut it by half with water).

Kahve (Turkish coffee) is legendary. Order it *sade* (no sugar), *az şekerli* (slightly sweet), *orta* (medium-sweet) or *çok şekerli* (very sweet); *süt* (milk) is not always available. *Çay* (Turkish tea), grown on the eastern Black Sea coast, is served in tiny glasses, with sugar. A milder alternative is the wholly chemical *elma çay* (apple tea).

SPECTATOR SPORTS

Turks are fanatical football fans and barely a day goes by without some match on TV. If you want to soak up the atmosphere of the real thing, try and get a ticket for one of the three İstanbul biggies – Galatasaray, Fenerbahçe or Beşiktaş.

More unusual sports include oil wrestling and camel wrestling. The main oil wrestling bouts take place at Edirne in June, with camel wrestling at Selçuk in January, but it's worth keeping an eye out for details of smaller, more local events too.

SHOPPING

As well as the legendary Turkish carpets, you may also want to buy clothes, jewellery, onyx or carved meerschaum as souvenirs. The widest choice is available in İstanbul but many people find the hard-sell tactics of the carpet salespeople off-putting. Bargaining is absolutely essential. You may prefer to postpone your purchases until you reach the more easygoing atmosphere of Kapadokya (Cappadocia).

Carpets & Kilims

Turkey is famous for its beautiful carpets and kilims and wherever you go you'll be spoilt for choice as to what to buy. Traditionally, village women wove carpets for their own family's use, or for their dowry. Knowing they would be judged on their efforts, the women took great care over their handiwork, hand-spinning and dyeing the wool, and choosing what they judged to be the most interesting and beautiful patterns. These days many carpets are made not according to local traditions but according to the dictates of the market. For example, weavers in eastern Turkey might make carpets in popular styles native to western Turkey.

A good carpet shop will have a range of pieces made in a variety of techniques. Besides the traditional pile carpets, they may offer double-sided flat woven kilims. Older, larger kilims may actually be two narrower pieces of similar but not always identical designs stitched together. As this is now rarely done, any such piece is likely to be fairly old. Other flat-weave techniques include *sumak*, a style originally from Azerbaijan in which coloured threads are wrapped round the warp. In Turkey the sumak technique was only used for saddlebags, so big sumak pieces must be from elsewhere in the Turkic world. *Cicims* are kilims with small, lively patterns interwoven into the design.

When deciding what to buy, there's no substitute for shopping around. Not only can you compare prices but you will end up with a good idea of what you really like which should, ultimately, be the main consideration. However, some general guidelines might help you make up your mind.

A good-quality, long-lasting carpet should be 100% wool, fine and shiny with signs of the natural oil still present. More expensive carpets may be of a silk and wool blend. Cheaper ones may be made of mercerised cotton. You can tell by inspecting the fringes or by turning the piece over and checking for the fine, frizzy fibres common to wool but not to cotton. There's nothing wrong with buying a cotton carpet if you like it – if the dyes and design are ugly, even a 100% wool carpet can be a bad buy – but you shouldn't be persuaded to pay for wool.

In general, the tighter the weave and the smaller the knots, the better the quality of the carpet, but bear in mind that the oldest carpets sometimes had quite thick knots, so consider the number of knots alongside the colours and quality of the knots.

Compare the colours on the back and the front. Spread the nap with your fingers and look at the bottom of the pile. Slight colour variations could occur in older carpets, but richer, deeper colour in the pile is often an indication that the surface has faded in the sun. Natural dyes don't fade as readily as chemical dyes. There's nothing wrong with chemical dyes but natural dyes tend to fetch higher prices.

New carpets can be made to look old, and damaged or worn carpets can be rewoven (good work, but expensive), patched or even painted. There's nothing wrong with a dealer offering repaired carpets provided they point out what has been done.

Be realistic about your budget. These days real bargains are hard to come by unless you can afford the sort of outsize carpets that are priced down because few people have homes big enough to contain them! Bear in mind, too, that if you do your shopping on a tour or when accompanied by a guide, the price will be hiked to cover their commission.

It may be wise to go for something small but of high quality rather than for a room-sized cheapie. Another way to make the money stretch is to go for one of the smaller items made from carpet materials: old camel bags and hanging baby's cradles opened out to make rugs; decorative grain bags; cushion covers; even the bags that once held rock salt for animal feed.

Getting There & Away

AIR

Airports & Airlines

Turkey's most important airport as far as foreign travellers are concerned is İstanbul; the cheapest fares are almost always to İstanbul, and to reach other Turkish airports, even Ankara, you usually have to transit İstanbul. In the last few years Turkey has built an increasing number of new airports around the country, all of them accessible on domestic flights from İstanbul, some also accessible from Ankara.

Turkish Airlines has direct flights from İstanbul to two dozen European cities and New York, as well as the Middle East, North Africa, Bangkok, Karachi, Singapore and Tokyo.

European airlines like Aeroflot, Air France, Alitalia, Austrian Airlines, British Airways, Finnair, KLM, Lufthansa, SAS and Swissair fly to İstanbul; British Airways, Lufthansa and the independent airline İstanbul Airlines have flights to Ankara, Antalya, İzmir or Dalaman as well. One-way full-fare tickets from London to İstanbul can cost as much as US$425; it's usually advisable to buy an excursion ticket (from US$300) even if you don't plan to use the return portion.

European airlines also fly one-stop services from many North American cities to İstanbul; Lufthansa has perhaps the most cities and the best connections. In summer Turkish Airlines flies daily nonstop from New York (Newark) to İstanbul and three times a week from Chicago. Delta flies from various US cities to various European cities and has direct flight from New York to İstanbul via Frankfurt. Round-trip fares range from US$500 to US$900.

There are direct flights from Australia to İstanbul offered by Malaysian Airlines (via Kuala Lumpur and Dubai) and Singapore Airlines (via Singapore and Dhahran) with round-trip fares for about A$1800. Cheaper are Middle Eastern Airlines, Gulf Air and EgyptAir, with round-trip fares for about A$1600. There are also connecting flights via Athens, London, Rome, Amsterdam or Singapore on Thai International, British Airways, Olympic, Alitalia, KLM, Turkish Airlines and Qantas.

All these airlines have regular 'specials' (usually during the European low season of mid-January to the end of February and the start of October to mid-November) with most offering fares for A$1400 or less. Usually these must be booked and paid for in advance.

Eastern Mediterranean nonstop Turkish Airlines flights occur daily from İstanbul to Athens (1½ hours), Cairo (2½ hours) and Tel Aviv (two hours), five a week to Amman (2¼ hours), five to Baku (2½ hours), two to Beirut (one hour), two to Damascus (2½ hours), three to Dubai (6¼ hours), four to Jeddah (5½ hours), two to Riyadh (5¾ hours), two to Kuwait (4¼ hours), three to Tehrān (4½ hours) and four to Tunis (two hours).

Daily nonstop flights on Turkish Airlines, Cyprus Turkish Airlines and İstanbul Airlines connect İstanbul, Ankara and Nicosia (Turkish: Lefkoşa). There are also nonstop flights between Nicosia and Adana, Antalya and İzmir several times a week.

New Turkish airlines have started to compete with Turkish Airlines and İstanbul Airlines. These include Onur Air (☎ 256 8500) in İstanbul.

Buying Tickets in Turkey

Travel agencies in İstanbul, especially along Divan Yolu in Sultanahmet, specialise in selling cheap tickets to anywhere in the world. Some agencies in popular resort areas may have links that enable them to sell these same tickets but in general you'll need to head for the big city to shop around for bargains. Single tickets start at US$120 to Frankfurt, US$260 to New York and US$160 to London.

Departure Tax

A departure tax of about US$12 is usually included in the cost of your ticket if you buy it in Turkey.

LAND

There are plenty of ways to get into and out of Turkey by rail or bus across the borders of seven countries. You'll need a transit visa for any country except Greece. There are consulates in İstanbul (and a few in İzmir) as well as embassies in Ankara.

Turkey's relationship with most of its neighbours tends to be tense, which can affect the availability of visas and when/where you can cross overland. Always check with the relevant embassy for the most up-to-date information before leaving home.

Europe

At the time of writing there were no direct trains between western Europe and Turkey. Instead there were daily direct train services between Budapest and İstanbul (Balkan Express, 31 hours) and Bucharest and İstanbul (Bucharest-İstanbul Express, 17 hours).

Despite the romantic appeal of train journeys, getting to Turkey overland is usually cheaper and faster by bus. Several Turkish bus lines, including Ulusoy, Varan and Bosfor, offer reliable, comfortable services between İstanbul and major European cities like Frankfurt, Munich and Vienna. One-way tickets range from US$85 to US$140, not much of a saving on the cheapest air tickets.

Greece

Most people come to Greece by boat from the Eastern Aegean islands (see Sea later in this section for more details). If you're planning on travelling from the mainland, note that the daily Thessaloniki-İstanbul passenger train takes 16 to 18 hours to cover the 850km. The bus covers the distance in greater comfort in about half the time.

Syria

Daily buses connect Antakya, on Turkey's eastern Mediterranean coast, with the Syrian cities of Aleppo (Halab, US$12, four hours) and Damascus (US$20, eight hours), and Amman in Jordan (US$28, 10 hours).

For more information on getting to Syria, including taking local buses to the border, see the Antakya section later in this chapter.

You can also buy tickets direct from İstanbul to Aleppo (approximately 24 hours) or Damascus (30 hours). The ticket costs in the vicinity of US$24 to US$30, depending on which company you travel with. Buses leave daily, usually with five or six departures between about 11 am and the early evening.

Some readers have written to suggest there's less delay involved in crossing the border by train. Trains run from Gaziantep, Kahramanmaraş and Osmaniye in Turkey to Aleppo in Syria.

Georgia

The border crossing at Sarp on the Black Sea coast is open and daily buses run to Batumi and Tbilisi (Turkish: Tflis) from Trabzon. Obtain a Georgian visa in advance at the Georgian consulate in Trabzon; for more details see the Trabzon section later in this chapter.

Armenia

The train line from Ankara to Erzurum runs as far as Kars but at the time of writing the Turkish-Armenian border was closed to foreign travellers. The situation was expected to change so it's worth rechecking.

Iran

For details on the border crossing from Turkey, see the Doğubeyazıt section later in this chapter.

SEA

Turkish Maritime Lines (TML) runs car ferries from Antalya, Marmaris and İzmir to Venice weekly from May to mid-October. Fares start at US$215 one way with reclining seat; mid-price cabins are priced from US$390 per person. In summer TML also offers ferry services four times a week from Brindisi; fares are often undercut by Med Link Lines. Poseidon Lines also runs summer ferries from Bari (Italy) to İzmir. For more details, see the regional Getting There & Away chapter.

Private ferries link Turkey's Aegean coast and the Greek islands, which are in turn linked by air or boat to Athens. Services are usually daily in summer, several times a week in spring and autumn and perhaps just once a week in winter. In summer expect boats connecting Lesbos-Ayvalık, Lesbos-Dikili, Chios-Çeşme, Samos-Kuşadası, Kos-Bodrum, Rhodes-Marmaris, Rhodes-Bodrum, Rhodes-Fethiye and Kastellorizo-Kaş. The cheapest and most frequent ferries are Samos-Kuşadası and Rhodes-Marmaris. The most expensive and certainly a hassle is Lesbos-Ayvalık. For more details see the Ayvalık, İzmir, Kuşadası, Bodrum and Marmaris sections later in this chapter.

There are daily boats and hydrofoils to Turkish Cyprus from Taşucu (near Silifke) – see the regional Getting There & Away chapter.

Getting Around

AIR

Turkish Airlines (Türk Hava Yolları, THY) links all the country's major cities, servicing routes such as the busy İstanbul-Ankara corridor (US$90, 50 minutes). Domestic flights fill up rapidly; book in advance. İstanbul Airlines competes with Turkish Airlines on a few routes, offering lower fares, but less frequent flights. Smoking is prohibited on domestic flights.

Following are the addresses/phone numbers of some useful Turkish Airlines' offices:

Ankara
(☎ 428 0200) Atatürk Bulvarı 154
Antalya
(☎ 243 4383) Özel Idare İşhanı, Altı Cumhuriyet Caddesi
Bodrum
(☎ 313 3172) Neyzen Tevfik Caddesi 208
Erzurum
(☎ 218 1904) 50 Yıl Caddesi, SSK Rant Tesisleri No 24
İstanbul
(☎ 663 6363) Cumhuriyet Caddesi 199, Kat 3, Elmadağ
İzmir
(☎ 445 5365) Gaziosmanpaşa Bulvarı 1/F, Büyük Efes Oteli Altı
Trabzon
(☎ 321 1680) Kemerkaya Mah Meydan Park Karşışı 37/A

from	to	hours	frequency of service	one way ($US)
İstanbul	Ankara	1	hourly	65
İstanbul	Antalya	1¼	seven flights a day	75
İstanbul	Bodrum	1¼	one flight a day	67
İstanbul	Erzurum via Ankara		three flights a day	74
İstanbul	İzmir	1	10 flights a day	65
İstanbul	Trabzon	1¾	three flights a day	67

BUS

Buses go everywhere in Turkey frequently and cheaply (around US$2.25 to US$2.75 per 100km). Kamil Koç, Metro, Ulusoy and Varan are premium lines, more comfortable (hostess service, soft drinks) and with better safety records than most, an important consideration since traffic accidents claim hundreds of lives each year.

The *otogar* (bus terminal) is often on the outskirts, but the bigger bus companies usually have free *servis* minibuses between the city centre and the otogar. The larger otogars usually have an *emanet* (left-luggage room) with a small charge. Don't leave valuables in unlocked luggage. If there's no emanet, leave luggage at your bus line's ticket office.

Tickets for long-distance services should be reserved in advance. On local routes you pay the conductor.

All Turkish bus services are officially smoke-free, however you may want to avoid the front seats near the driver and conductor, the only people still allowed to puff away freely.

TRAIN

Turkish State Railways (TCDD) has a hard time competing with the long-distance buses for speed and comfort. Only on the special express trains such as the *Fatih* and *Başkent* can you get somewhere faster than by bus.

Ekspres and *mototren* services are sometimes one class only. If they have 2nd class it costs 30% less. Student and return fares are discounted too. These trains are a little slower than and comparable in price with buses, and they are sometimes more pleasant because you can get up and move around. On *yolcu* and *posta* trains you could grow old and die before reaching your destination. Trains east of Ankara are not as punctual or comfortable as those to the west.

Sleeping-car trains linking İstanbul, İzmir and Ankara are good value; the cheaper *örtülü kuşetli* carriages have four simple beds per compartment.

CAR & MOTORCYCLE

Türkiye Turing ve Otomobil Kurumu (TTOK), the Turkish Touring & Automobile Association (☎ 282 8140, fax 282 8042, Oto Sanayi Sitesi Yanı, Seyrantepe, 4 Levent, İstanbul), can help with questions and problems.

Carnets are not required for stays of less than three months, but details of your car are stamped in your passport to ensure it leaves the country with you.

Mechanical services are easy to find, reasonably competent and cheap. The most easily serviced models are Fiat, Renault and Mercedes, with Volkswagens and Toyotas starting to show up in large numbers as well. In the west petrol stations have been sprouting like cabbages recently and the new places usually come equipped with flashy *dinlenme tesisleri* (rest facilities). Farther east you shouldn't expect such splendour. There are also some roads with fewer petrol stations than you might hope to find – the road from Eğirdir to Konya is one example.

In the major cities plan to park your car and use public transport – traffic is terrible and parking impossible.

Rental

All the main car rental companies are represented in İstanbul, Ankara and İzmir, but car hire in Turkey is pricey and driving a hazardous pastime.

Avis
(☎ 246 5256) Hilton Girişi, Arcade, Taksim, İstanbul
Europcar
(☎ 254 7799) Topçu Caddesi No 1, Talimhane, İstanbul
Hertz
(☎ 233 7101) Cumhuriyet Caddesi No 295, Harbiye, İstanbul

BOAT

Every Monday from June to early October a Turkish Maritime Lines car ferry departs from İstanbul, heading for Trabzon and ports along the way. It departs from Trabzon on Wednesday for İstanbul, arriving on Friday. Fares from İstanbul to Trabzon (per person, no meals) range from US$35 for a reclining seat to US$160 for a bed in the best cabin. A car costs US$56.

A similar car-ferry service departs from İstanbul on Friday (all year) and arrives the next morning in İzmir. It departs on Sunday afternoon for the return trip to İstanbul. Fares are US$16 (reclining seat) to US$100 (luxury cabin bed), plus US$60 for a car.

Fast ferries from İstanbul to Bandırma (US$3) also connect with a daily train service to İzmir (the *Marmara Express*). Heading to İzmir the train leaves Bandırma daily at 3 pm; returning to İstanbul it leaves Bandırma daily at 2.12 pm.

ORGANISED TOURS

Most independent travellers find tours in Turkey expensive. Almost all tours park you in a carpet shop for an hour (the guide gets a kickback). In general, it's faster and cheaper to make your own travel arrangements. Be particularly careful if booking a tour out of İstanbul; some of these are ludicrously expensive compared with doing it yourself.

Visitors who want to see the battlefield sites at Gelibolu (Gallipoli) in a hurry may need to take a tour; see the Çanakkale section later in this chapter for details.

If you're on a whistlestop tour of Kapadokya (Cappadocia) you may also need to take a tour to see all the sights quickly; see the Göreme section later in this chapter for details of some good local operators. Kirkit

Voyage (☎ 511 3259, Atatürk Caddesi 50, Avanos) also offers a wide range of environmentally sensitive walking and riding tours.

The Fez Bus (☎ 516 9024, fax 517 1626, Aybıyık Caddesi, Sultanahmet, İstanbul) is a hop-on, hop-off bus service linking the main tourist resorts of the Aegean and the Mediterranean with İstanbul and Kapadokya. A two-month pass costs around US$150.

İstanbul

İstanbul, formerly Constantinople, is a treasure trove of places and things to see. After a day of wandering around mosques, ruins and tangled streets where empires have risen and fallen, you'll realise what is meant by the word 'Byzantine'. Nor should it be forgotten that it was here, 5½ centuries ago, that the final fragment of the Roman empire crumbled, and that through Europe's Dark Ages this city carried European civilisation on from its Greek and Roman origins.

History

Late in the 2nd century AD, Rome conquered the small city-state of Byzantium. In 330 AD Emperor Constantine moved his capital there from Rome and renamed the city Constantinople.

The city walls kept out barbarians for centuries as the western part of the Roman empire collapsed before invasions of Goths, Vandals and Huns. When Constantinople fell for the first time it was to the misguided Fourth Crusade. Bent on pillage, the Crusaders abandoned their dreams of Jerusalem in 1204 and then ravaged Constantinople's churches, shipping out the art and melting down the silver and gold. When the Byzantines regained the city in 1261 it was only a shadow of its former glory.

The Ottoman Turks attacked in 1314, but withdrew. Finally, in 1453, after a long and bitter siege, the walls were breached just north of Topkapı Gate on the western side of the city. Mehmet II, the Conqueror, marched to Aya Sofya (Hagia Sofia) and

İstanbul Highlights

- **Best Dining** – eating fish alfresco in Kumkapı; but be careful to ask the price of everything you order and to check the bill afterwards
- **Best Nightlife** – duck down the side streets off İstiklal Caddesi in Taksim for small live-music bars where you can listen to folk songs updated for a modern clientele while tucking into pistachios and a beer
- **Best Walk** – up Divan Yolu from the square between Aya Sofya and the Blue Mosque; the trams keep the traffic at bay, and you can stop to drink tea and smoke a water-pipe in several converted graveyards on the way
- **Best View** – the Blue Mosque floodlit on a winter night from the Rami restaurant
- **Best Activity** – listening to a summer concert inside the atmospheric Yerebatan Sarnıcı

converted the church to a mosque. The Byzantine empire had ended.

As capital of the Ottoman empire the city entered a new golden age. During the glittering reign of Süleyman the Magnificent (1520-66), the city was graced with many beautiful new buildings. Even during the empire's long and celebrated decline, the capital retained much of its charm. Occupied by Allied forces after WWI, it came to be thought of as the decadent capital of the sultans, just as Atatürk's armies were shaping a new republican state.

When the Turkish Republic was proclaimed in 1923, Ankara became the capital. But İstanbul (its new name), the much beloved metropolis, remains the centre for business, finance, journalism and the arts.

Orientation

The Bosphorus strait, between the Black and Marmara seas, divides Europe from Asia. On its western shore, European İstanbul is further divided by the Golden Horn

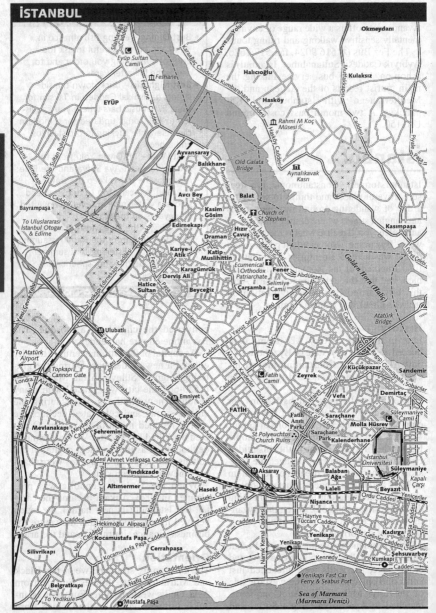

İSTANBUL

TURKEY

Okmeydanı

Silahtarağa Caddesi

Karaağaç Caddesi

Çevre Yolu

Eyüp Sultan Camii

Feshane

Feshane Caddesi

Halıcıoğlu

Kumbarahane Caddesi

Kulaksız

EYÜP

Hasköy

Hasköy Caddesi

Rahmi M Koç Müsesi

Piyale Paşa

Ayvansaray

Balıkhane

Old Galata Bridge

Demirhisar Caddesi

Aynalıkavak Kasrı

Avcı Bey

Balat

Bayrampaşa

Kasım Gösim

Edirnekapı

Draman

Hızır Çavuş

Balat İskelesi Caddesi

Mürsel Paşa Caddesi

Church of St Stephen

Kasımpaşa

To Uluslararası İstanbul Otogar & Edirne

Topkapı Edirnekapı Caddesi

Savaklar Caddesi

Fevzi Paşa Caddesi

Kariye-i Atik

Katip Muslihittin

Karagümrük

Derviş Ali

Our Ecumenical Orthodox Patriarchate

Fener

Abdülezel Paşa Caddesi

Golden Horn (Haliç)

Hatice Sultan

Beycegiz

Çarşamba

Selimiye Camii

Atatürk Bridge

Ulubatlı

Adnan Menderes Caddesi

Yavuz Selim Caddesi

Haliç Caddesi

Ragıp Gümüşpala Caddesi

To Atatürk Airport

Topkapı Cannon Gate

Tatlıpınar Caddesi

Guraba Caddesi

Akşemsettin Caddesi

Macar Kardeşler Caddesi

Küçükpazar

Sarıdemir

Londra Asfaltı

Turgut Özal Caddesi

Hastanesi

Fatih Camii

Zeyrek

İtfaiye Caddesi

Vefa

Demirtaç

Mevlanakapı Yolu

Çapa

Emniyet

FATİH

Aqueduct of Valens

Süleymaniye Camii

Mevlanakapı

Seyit Ömer

Şehremini

Turgut Özal Caddesi

Oğuzhan Caddesi

Bulvarı

Fatih Anıtı Park

Saraçhane

St Polyeuchtos Church Ruins

Saraçhane Park

Molla Hüsrev

Kalenderhane

İstanbul Üniversitesi

Süleymaniye

Fındıkzade

Kızılelma Caddesi

Aksaray

Balaban Ağa

Kapalı Çarşı

Altımermer

Haseki

Aksaray

Laleli

Beyazıt

Yeniçeriler Caddesi

Haseki Caddesi

Nişanca

Ordu Caddesi

Hekimoğlu Alipaşa

Cerrahpaşa Caddesi

Hayriye Tüccarı Caddesi

Çifte Gelinler Caddesi

Kadırga

Gedikpaşa Caddesi

Silivrikapı

Kocamustafa Paşa

Cerrahpaşa

Kocamustafa Paşa Caddesi

Küçük Langa Caddesi

Namık Kemal Caddesi

Yenikapı

Şehsuvarbey

Kumkapı

Caddesi

Belgratkapı

A Nafiz Gürman Caddesi

Sahil Yolu

Yenikapı Fast Car Ferry & Seabus Port

To Yedikule

Mustafa Paşa

Kennedy

Sea of Marmara (Marmara Denizi)

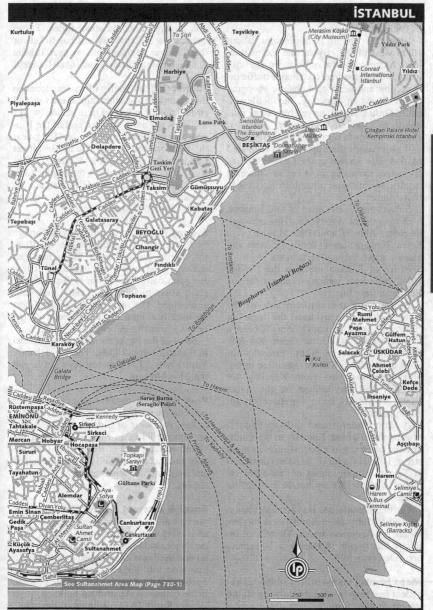

İSTANBUL

Kurtuluş
Teşvikiye
Merasim Köşkü (City Museum)
Yıldız Park

To Şişli

Abdi İpekçi Caddesi

Harbiye
Conrad International Istanbul
Yıldız

Piyalepaşa

Dolapdere Caddesi
Kadırgalar Geçidi
Kurtuluş Caddesi

Elmadağ
Luna Park
Swissôtel Istanbul The Bosphorus
Beşiktaş
Deniz Müzesi
Çırağan Caddesi
Çırağan Palace Hotel Kempinski İstanbul

Yenişehir Dere Caddesi
Dolapdere

BEŞİKTAŞ
Dolmabahçe Sarayı

Taksim Gezi Yeri
Taskim

Tarlabaşı
Taksim
Gümüşsuyu

Tepebaşı
Galatasaray
BEYOĞLU
Kabataş

Cihangir

Tünel
Fındıklı

İstiklal Caddesi
Meşrutiyet Caddesi

Tophane

To Bostancı

To Bosphorus

Bosphorus (İstanbul Boğazı)

Karaköy
Kemeraltı Caddesi
Necatibey Caddesi
Kemankeş Caddesi

To Üsküdar

Rumi Mehmet Paşa Ayazma
Gülfem Hatun

Salacak
ÜSKÜDAR

Galata Bridge

Ahmet Çelebi

Kefçe Dede

Kız Kulesi

İhsaniye

Reşadiye Caddesi
Rüstempaşa
EMİNÖNÜ
Tahtakale

Saray Burnu (Seraglio Point)

Kennedy
Şirkeci
Sirkeci

Mercan
Hobyar
Hocapaşa

Sururi

Topkapı Sarayı

Aşçıbaşı

Tayahatun

Gülhane Parkı

To Haydarpaşa & Kadıköy

Alemdar
Aya Sofya

Emin Sinan
Çemberlitaş
Divan Yolu

Gedik Paşa

Cankurtaran
Cankurtaran

Harem
Harem Bus Terminal
Selimiye Camii

Küçük Ayasofya

Sultan Ahmet Camii

Sultanahmet

At Meydanı

Selimiye Kışlası (Barracks)

See Sultanahmet Area Map (Page 730-1)

0   250   500 m

TURKEY

(Haliç) into Old İstanbul in the south and Beyoğlu in the north.

İstanbul's otogar is at Esenler, about 10km west of the city on the metro tram line. Aksaray, halfway between the city walls and Sultanahmet, is a major traffic intersection and heart of a chaotic shopping district. East of Aksaray, the boulevard called Ordu Caddesi, served by a tram, runs uphill to İstanbul University, where it changes names to become Yeniçeriler Caddesi as it passes the Kapalı Çarşı (Covered Market, also known as the Grand Bazaar). It changes names again to Divan Yolu as it heads downhill past other historic sites to Sultanahmet.

Sultanahmet is the heart of Old İstanbul, with the ancient Atmeydanı (Hippodrome), the Sultan Ahmet Camii (Blue Mosque), Aya Sofya, Topkapı Sarayı (Topkapı Palace), and many cheap hotels and restaurants.

North of Sultanahmet, on the Golden Horn, is Sirkeci station, terminus for the European train line.

Beyoğlu, on the northern side of the Golden Horn, is considered the 'new' or 'European' city, although there's been a city here since Byzantine times. Karaköy (formerly Galata) is where cruise ships dock at the Yolcu Salonu (maritime terminal). Ferries depart from Karaköy for Kadıköy and Haydarpaşa on the Asian shore; hydrofoils leave for more distant Asian points.

A short underground railway (Tünel) runs up the hill from Karaköy to the southern end of Beyoğlu's pedestrianised main street, İstiklal Caddesi. At its northern end is Taksim Square, heart of 'modern' İstanbul with its luxury hotels and airline offices.

On the Asian side, Haydarpaşa station (served by ferry from Karaköy) is the terminus for Anatolian trains. There's an intercity bus station at Harem, a 10 minute taxi ride north.

Maps İstanbul tourist offices supply an excellent free map of the city showing all the important attractions.

Information

Ask at Sirkeci station about trains. Travel agencies in Sultanahmet sell bus tickets or there are bus company offices near Taksim Square on Mete Caddesi and İnönü Caddesi.

Tourist Offices Tourist offices are found in the Atatürk airport international arrivals hall (☎ 663 6363); in Sirkeci train station (☎ 511 5888); at the north-western end of the Hippodrome in Sultanahmet (☎ 518 1802); near the UK consulate in Beyoğlu at Meşrutiyet Caddesi 57, Tepebaşı (☎ 243 2928); in Taksim Square (☎ 245 6876) on İstiklal Caddesi; and in the İstanbul Hilton arcade on Cumhuriyet Caddesi (☎ 233 0592), two long blocks north of Taksim Square.

Money Divan Yolu is lined with foreign exchange offices and travel agencies offering speedy, hassle-free exchange facilities at fairly good rates. Most exchange offices are open daily from 9 am to 9 pm. Other good areas to look are Sirkeci and Taksim/İstiklal. The rates offered at the airport are usually at least as good as those offered in town, sometimes better.

Most of the banks along İstiklal Caddesi in Taksim have ATMs. There's a handy Yapı Kredi ATM between Aya Sofya and the Blue Mosque.

Post For poste restante go to the *merkez postane* (main PTT) on Şehinşah Pehlevi Sokak, just west of Sirkeci station. There are branch PTTs in Sultanahmet and the Grand Bazaar, and in Beyoğlu at Galatasaray and Taksim, as well as in the domestic and international departure areas at Atatürk airport.

Email & Internet Access You can check your email at several backpackers' hostels and cafes in Cankurtaran, south of Sultanahmet, including the Orient Youth Hostel and the Mavi Guesthouse (see Places to Stay); and at Yağmur Cybercafe (☎ 292 3020), near the American consulate general, in the Çitlembik Apartımanı building, Şeyh Bender Sokak 18, Asmalımescit, Beyoğlu.

Travel Agencies Divan Yolu in Sultanahmet is lined with travel agencies, all of them selling cheap air and bus tickets; some can also arrange train tickets and minibus transport to the airport. Shop around for the best deals. One respected agent is Marco Polo, Divan Yolu 54/11 (☎ 519 2804).

Another established and reputable travel agency/tour operator with English-speaking staff is Orion-Tour (☎ 248 8437, fax 241 2808), Halaskargazi Caddesi 284/3, Marmara Apartımanı, Şişli, about 2km north of Taksim. Orion sells tickets to anywhere, and tours to anywhere in Turkey.

Bookshops In general books in English are extremely expensive; you'd do well to bring anything you need with you from home. Failing that, your best bet is to head for the Tünel end of İstiklal Caddesi where there are several bookshops selling English titles. Best is probably Homer (☎ 249 5902, Yeni Carşı Caddesi), along the road beside the Galatasary Lisesi, which doesn't at present add a mark-up to the original cover prices. Other possibilities include Robinson Crusoe (☎ 293 6968, İstiklal Caddesi 389); Dünya Aktüel (☎ 249 1006, İstiklal Caddesi 469); and Pandora (☎ 245 1667, Büyükparmakkapı Sokak 3), off İstiklal Caddesi.

Cultural Centres
American Library
  (☎ 251 2675) Meşrutiyet Caddesi 108, Tepebaşı. Open noon to 4 pm Monday to Friday.
British Council
  (☎ 252 7474 ext 115) Örs Turistik İş Merkezı, İstiklal Caddesi 151-253, Beyoğlu. The library is open from 10.30 am to at least 5.30 pm Tuesday to Friday and from 9.30 am to 2.30 pm Saturday.
French Cultural Centre
  (☎ 249 0776) İstiklak Caddesi 8, Beyoğlu

Laundry Try the Hobby Laundry, Caferiye Sokak 6/1, Sultanahmet, in the Yücelt Interyouth Hostel, or Active Laundry, Dr Emin Paşa Sokak 14, off Divan Yolu beneath the shabby Arsenal Youth Hostel.

Medical Services For hospitals, the Amerikan (☎ 231 4050), at Güzelbahçe

Sokak, Nişantaşı (2km north-west of Taksim Square), and the International (☎ 663 3000), Çınar Oteli Yanı, İstanbul Caddesi 82, in Yeşilköy near the airport, do good work.

Emergency Try the tourist police (☎ 527 4503), Yerebatan Caddesi 6, Sultanahmet, across the street from Yerebatan Sarnıcı (Sunken Palace Cistern). The İstanbul Blue Line (☎ 638 2626), staffed by multilingual counsellors, can help with anything from emotional to financial queries.

The ordinary police (☎ 155 in an emergency) are less experienced in dealing with foreigners.

Old İstanbul

Sultanahmet is the first place to go, with all the major sights arranged around the Hippodrome. There is a sound and light show on summer evenings; a notice in front of the Blue Mosque says which nights are in which language.

Aya Sofya (Church of Holy Wisdom)

Also known as Hagia Sofia or Sancta Sophia, Aya Sofya was begun under Emperor Justinian in 532 AD and was intended to be the grandest church in the world. For 1000 years it was certainly Christendom's largest church. Despite scaffolding that seems to have become a permanent feature, the interior reveals the building's magnificence; stunning even today, it must have been overwhelming centuries ago when it was covered in gilded mosaics.

Climb up to the gallery to see the splendid surviving mosaics (the gallery closes from 11.30 am to 1 pm). After the Turkish conquest and the subsequent conversion of Aya Sofya to a mosque, the mosaics were covered over, as Islam prohibits images. They were not revealed until the 1930s when Atatürk declared Aya Sofya a museum. The minarets were added during the centuries when Aya Sofya was a mosque. The church is open from 9 am to 4 pm daily except Monday, later in summer; admission is US$5.

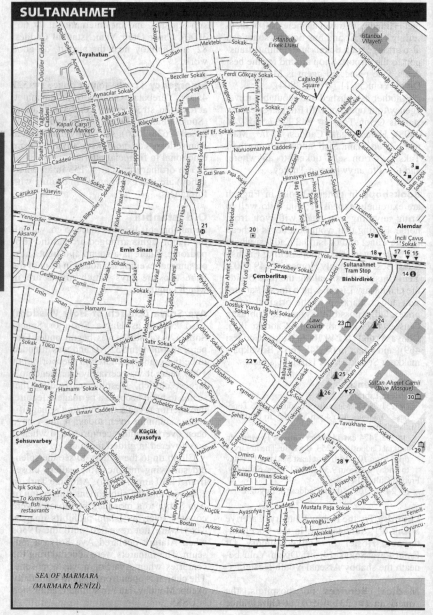

SULTANAHMET

SEA OF MARMARA
(MARMARA DENİZİ)

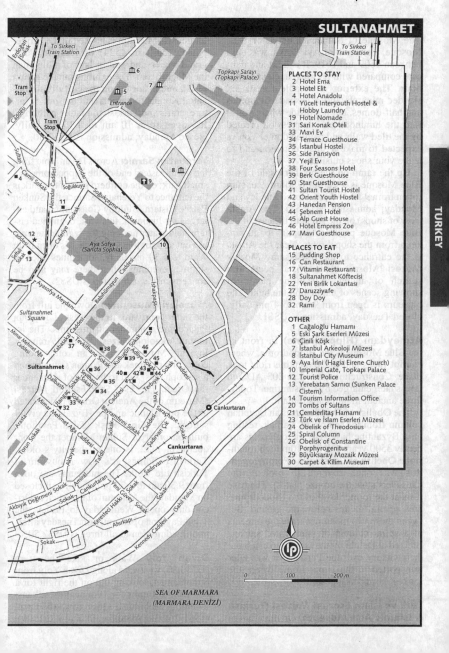

SULTANAHMET

PLACES TO STAY
2 Hotel Ema
3 Hotel Elit
4 Hotel Anadolu
11 Yücelt Interyouth Hostel &
   Hobby Laundry
19 Hotel Nomade
31 Sari Konak Oteli
33 Mavi Ev
34 Terrace Guesthouse
35 İstanbul Hostel
36 Side Pansiyon
37 Yeşil Ev
38 Four Seasons Hotel
39 Berk Guesthouse
40 Star Guesthouse
41 Sultan Tourist Hostel
42 Orient Youth Hostel
43 Hanedan Pension
44 Şebnem Hotel
45 Alp Guest House
46 Hotel Empress Zoe
47 Mavi Guesthouse

PLACES TO EAT
15 Pudding Shop
16 Can Restaurant
17 Vitamin Restaurant
18 Sultanahmet Köftecisi
21 Yeni Birlik Lokantası
27 Daruzziyafe
28 Doy Doy
32 Rami

OTHER
1 Cağaloğlu Hamamı
5 Eski Şark Eserleri Müzesi
6 Çinili Köşk
7 İstanbul Arkeoloji Müzesi
8 İstanbul City Museum
9 Aya İrini (Hagia Eirene Church)
10 Imperial Gate, Topkapı Palace
12 Tourist Police
13 Yerebatan Sarnıcı (Sunken Palace
   Cistern)
14 Tourism Information Office
20 Tombs of Sultans
22 Çemberlitaş Hamamı
23 Türk ve İslam Eserleri Müzesi
24 Obelisk of Theodosius
25 Spiral Column
26 Obelisk of Constantine
   Porphyrogenitus
29 Büyüksaray Mozaik Müzesi
30 Carpet & Kilim Museum

TURKEY

Sultan Ahmet Camii (Blue Mosque)

The Mosque of Sultan Ahmet I, or Blue Mosque, just south of Aya Sofya, was built between 1609 and 1619. It is light and delicate compared with its squat ancient neighbour. The exterior is notable for its six slender minarets and a cascade of domes and half-domes, but it's inside where you'll find the luminous blue impression created by the tiled walls and painted dome. You're expected to make a small donation and to leave your shoes outside.

Up the ramp on the northern side of the Blue Mosque is a **Carpet & Kilim Museum** (open from 9 am to 4 pm, closed Sunday and Monday; admission is US$1). The **Arasta** (row of shops) on the street to the east of the Blue Mosque provides support for its upkeep from the shops' rents. Near the Arasta is the entrance to the **Büyüksaray Mozaik Müzesi** (Mosaic Museum), a spectacular stretch of ancient Byzantine pavement showing scenes of nature and the hunt. The museum is open from 9 am to 4 pm daily, closed Tuesday; admission is US$1.

Atmeydanı (Hippodrome)

In front of the Blue Mosque is the Hippodrome, where chariot races and the Byzantine riots took place. Construction started in 203 AD and it was later enlarged by Constantine. Today, three ancient monuments remain.

The **Obelisk of Theodosius** is an Egyptian column from the temple of Karnak, resting on a Byzantine base. The hieroglyphics are nearly 3500 years old. The 10m high roughstone **Obelisk of Constantine Porphyrogenitus** was once covered in bronze (the Crusaders stole the bronze plates). The base rests at the former level of the Hippodrome, now several metres below the ground. Between these two monuments are the remains of a **spiral column** of intertwined snakes. Erected at Delphi by the Greeks to celebrate their victory over the Persians, it was later transported to the Hippodrome where the snakes' heads disappeared.

Türk ve İslam Eserleri Müzesi (Turkish & Islamic Arts Museum)

On the western side of the Hippodrome, the Turkish & Islamic Arts Museum is housed in the former palace (built in 1524) of İbrahim Paşa, grand vizier and son-in-law of Süleyman the Magnificent. The exhibits run the gamut of Islamic history, from beautifully illuminated Korans to carpets and mosque furniture, crafts and Turkish miniature paintings. It's open from 10 am to 4.30 pm daily, closed Monday; admission is US$2.50.

Yerebatan Sarnıcı Across Divan Yolu from the north-eastern end of the Hippodrome is a small park; on the northern side of the park is the entrance to Yerebatan Sarnıcı, the Sunken Palace Cistern. Built by Constantine and enlarged by Justinian, this vast, columned cistern held water not only for regular summer use but also for times of siege. It's open from 9 am to 5.30 pm daily, sometimes later on summer evenings when there may also be concerts; admission is US$2.

Müzeleri (Museums) Down the hill from the outer courtyard, to the west of Topkapı Palace, are a number of museums. The **İstanbul Arkeoloji Müzesi** (İstanbul Archaeological Museum) has an outstanding collection of Greek and Roman statuary, and a sarcophagus, said to be that of Alexander the Great. The **Eski Şark Eserleri Müzesi** (Museum of the Ancient Orient) is dedicated to the pre-Islamic and pre-Byzantine civilisations. The **Çinili Köşk** (Tiled Pavilion), built on order of Sultan Mehmet the Conqueror in 1472, is one of the city's oldest Turkish buildings. It's now a museum of Turkish tile work. The museums are open from 9.30 am to 4.30 pm (they're all closed on Monday; the Museum of the Ancient Orient only opens Wednesday to Friday; the Tiled Pavilion opens only on Tuesday afternoon); admission to all three is US$2.50.

Divan Yolu Walk or take the tram (US$0.30) westward along Divan Yolu from Sultanahmet, looking out on the right for a complex of **tombs** for 19th century sultans, including Mahmut II (1808-39), Abdülaziz (1861-76) and Abdülhamid II (1876-1909).

A bit farther along, on the right, is the **Çemberlitaş** (Banded Stone), a monumental column erected by Constantine the Great sometime during the 4th century. Within a century it had to be strengthened with iron bands. During a storm in 1105 Constantine's statue toppled off the top, killing several people sheltering below. In 1779 the column was badly damaged by a fire, and was further strengthened with the iron hoops you see today. Nearby is the popular **Çemberlitaş Hamamı**.

Kapalı Çarşı (Covered Market) The Kapalı Çarşı (Covered Market, also known as the Grand Bazaar) is a labyrinthine medieval shopping mall. It's fun to wander among the 65 streets and 4400 shops, and a great place to get lost – which you certainly will.

The bazaar is divided into areas: carpets, jewellery, clothing, silverware and so on. West of the bazaar proper, across Çadırcılar Caddesi, beside the Beyazıt Camii, is the **Sahaflar Çarşısı** (Old Book Market), with many stalls selling secondhand books, mostly in Turkish. The bazaar is open from 8.30 am to 6.30 pm Monday to Saturday.

Beyazıt & Süleymaniye Beyazıt takes its name from the graceful **Beyazıt Camii**, built in 1506 on the orders of Sultan Beyazıt II, son of Mehmet the Conqueror. In Byzantine times this plaza was the **Forum of Theodosius**, laid out in 393 AD. The great gateway on the north side of the square is that of **İstanbul University**. The gateway, enclosure and buildings behind it date mostly from Ottoman times, when this was the Ministry of War.

Behind the university to the north-west rises İstanbul's grandest mosque complex, the **Süleymaniye**. Construction was completed in 1557 on orders of Süleyman the Magnificent; he and his foreign-born wife Roxelana (Hürrem Sultan) are buried in a **mausoleum** behind the mosque to the south-east. Süleyman's great architect, Sinan, is entombed near the sultan. The buildings surrounding the mosque were originally a hospital, *medrese* (seminary), soup kitchen, baths and hospice.

Theodosian Walls Stretching for 7km from the Golden Horn to the Sea of Marmara, the Theodosian city walls date back to about 420 AD. Many parts have been restored during the past decade.

At **Yedikule**, close to the Sea of Marmara, you can visit a Byzantine-Turkish fortress where obstreperous diplomats and inconvenient princes were imprisoned. It's open from 9.30 am to 5 pm daily; admission is US$1.

Near **Edirnekapı** (Adrianople Gate) is the marvellous **Kariye Müzesi** (Chora Church), a Byzantine building with the best 14th century mosaics east of Ravenna. Built in the 11th century, it was restored and converted to a mosque, and is now a museum. It's open from 9 am to 4 pm (closed Wednesday); admission is US$3. To get there, take an Edirnekapı bus along Fevzi Paşa Caddesi.

Turkish Baths İstanbul's most interesting historical baths are now very touristy and not always good value for money. The **Cağaloğlu Hamamı**, at Yerebatan Caddesi 34, a short stroll north-west of Sultanahmet, has separate entrances for men and women (around the corner). The baths are open from 7 am to 10 pm daily for men and from 8 am to 8 pm for women. Prices here would be outrageous anywhere else in Turkey: about US$20 for an assisted bath with massage, supposedly inclusive of tips.

Eminönü

At the southern end of Galata Köprüsü (Galata Bridge) looms the large **Yeni Cami** (New Mosque), built between 1597 and 1663. Beside it is the **Mısır Çarşısı** (Egyptian Bazaar), full of spice and food vendors. To the west, in the fragrant market streets, is the **Rüstem Paşa Camii**, a small, richly tiled mosque designed by the great Ottoman architect Sinan.

Beyoğlu

Cross the new Galata Bridge (1992), and head uphill towards the Galata Tower.

TOPKAPI SARAYI

Near Aya Sofya stands the sprawling, world-famous Topkapı Sarayı. Mehmet the Conqueror built the first palace shortly after the Conquest in 1453, and lived here until his death in 1481. Many sultans followed him until the 19th century when Mahmut II (1808-39) was succeeded by sultans who preferred living in European-style palaces like the Dolmabahçe.

The Site

You enter the palace through the Ortakapı (Middle Gate), which leads to the Second Court, which was used for the business of running the empire. It was constructed by Süleyman the Magnificent in 1524.

The second courtyard has a beautiful, park-like setting. Unlike European-style palaces, Topkapı is not one large building with outlying gardens. Instead it's a series of pavilions, kitchens, barracks, audience chambers and kiosks built around a central enclosure.

On the left side of the Second Court is the ornate **Imperial Council Chamber**, beneath the Adalet Kulesi tower. The imperial council met here to discuss matters of state while the sultan eavesdropped through a grille high on the wall.

Beside the Kubbealtı (Imperial Council Chamber) is the entrance to the 300-odd sumptuously decorated rooms that make up the **harem**. The harem is usually imagined as a place where the sultan could engage in debauchery. In fact, these were the imperial family quarters, and every detail of harem life was governed by tradition, obligation and ceremony.

Many of the rooms were constructed during the reign of Süleyman the Magnificent (1520-66), but others were added or reconstructed over the years. In 1665 a fire destroyed much of the complex, which was rebuilt by Mehmet IV and later sultans.

Top: No expense was spared in decorating th Sultan's palace, as this detail of the ceiling demonstrates. (Photo b Geoff Stringer)

Bottom: The harem wa actually the private quarters of the sultan and his family.

DAVOR PAVICHICH

The main gate into the Third Court leads into what was the sultan's private domain. Just inside is the audience chamber, constructed in the 16th century but refurnished in the 18th century. Important officials and foreign ambassadors came here to conduct the business of state.

In the Third Court are the sultan's ceremonial robes and the fabulous **treasury**, containing an incredible wealth of gold and gems. The **sacred safe keeping rooms** holds a solid-gold casket containing the Prophet Mohammed's cloak and other Islamic relics.

The Fourth Court contains four pleasure domes set amid gardens. The **Mecit Kiosk** was designed according to 19th century European models.

Up the stairs at the end of the tulip garden are two particularly enchanting kiosks. Sultan Murat IV (1623-40) built the **Erivan Kiosk** in 1635, and the **Baghdad Kiosk** in 1638. Just off the terrace overlooking the Bosphorus is the Circumcision Room.

Topkapı is open from 9.30 am to 5 pm daily, closed Tuesday. Admission is US$6. You pay an extra US$2.50 to visit the harem, which is open from 10 am to noon and 1 to 4 pm. In summer be at the door when it opens and head straight for the harem; individual travellers can't always get in as tour groups book all the slots in advance. Allow at least half a day to see everything.

Top: The exquisite detail of Topkapı Sarayı's ceiling can hold a visitor's attention for hours.

Bottom: The Hünkar Sofası (Emperor's Chamber) is decorated with Delft tiles.

TOPKAPI SARAYI (TOPKAPI PALACE)

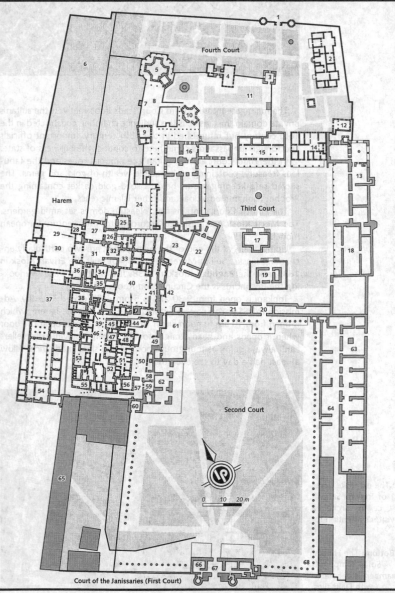

Fourth Court

Third Court

Second Court

Harem

Court of the Janissaries (First Court)

0   10   20 m

TOPKAPI SARAYI (TOPKAPI PALACE)

SECOND COURT
61 Inner Treasury (Enderun Hazinesi; Arms & Armour)
62 Divan Salonu
63 Restored Confectionery (Helvahane)
64 Palace Kitchens (Porcelain & Glass Exhibits)
65 Imperial Stables (Has Ahırları)
66 Bookshop
67 Middle Gate (Ortakapı; Bab-üs Selâm)
68 Imperial Carriages

THIRD COURT
13 Imperial Treasury (Hazine)
14 Museum Directorate
15 Treasury Barracks (Hazine Koğuşu; Calligraphy, Illumination & Miniatures)
16 Sacred Safe Keeping Rooms (Mukaddes Emanetler Dairesi; Prophet's Relics)
17 Library of Ahmet III
18 Dormitory of the Expeditionary Force (Seferli Koğuşu); Imperial Robes
19 Audience Chamber (Arz Odası)
20 Gate of Felicity (Bab-üs Saade)
21 White Eunuchs Quarters (Akağalar)
22 Mosque/Library (Ağalar Camii)

FOURTH COURT
1 Gate of the Privy Gardens (Has Bahçe Kapısı)
2 Mecit Kiosk (Mecidiye Köşkü); Konyalı Restaurant
3 Doctor's Room (Hekimbaşı Odası)
4 Mustafa Paşa (Sofa) Köşkü
5 Baghdad Kiosk (Bağdat Köşkü)
6 Lower Gardens of the Imperial Terrace; Fig Garden; Elephant Garden (Sofa-i Hümayun Alt Bahçeleri; İncir Bahçesi; Fil Bahçesi)
7 Canopy for Breaking the Fast (İftariye Kameriyesi ve Mehtaplık)
8 Marble Terrace & Pool (Mermer Teras ve Havuz)
9 Circumcision Room (Sünnet Odası)

10 Erivan Kiosk (Revan Köşkü)
11 Tulip Garden
12 Sofa or Terrace Mosque (Sofa Camii)

HAREM
23 Harem Mosque
24 Favourites Courtyard & Apartments (Gözdeler Mabeyn Taşlığı ve Daireleri)
25 Double Kiosk with Stained Glass
26 Beautifully Tiled Antechamber
27 Privy Chamber of Murat III
28 Library of Ahmet I; Dining Room of Ahmet III (Fruit Paintings)
29 Ahmet III Dining Room
30 Terrace of Osman III
31 Emperor's Chamber (Hünker Sofası)
32 Room with Hearth (Ocaklı Oda); Room with Fountain (Çeşmeli Oda)
33 Consultation Place of the Genies
34 Valide Sultan's Hamam
35 Sultan's Hamam
36 Chamber of Abdül Hamit I
37 Harem Garden
38 Valide Sultan's Quarters (Valide Sultan Taşlığı)
39 Sultan Ahmet Köşkü

40 Courtyard of the Valide Sultan
41 Golden Road (Altınyol)
42 Birdcage Gate (Kuşhane Kapısı)
43 Main Gate (Cümle Kapısı) with Gilded Mirrors & Sentry Post; Second Guard Room
44 Chief Black Eunuch's Room (Kızlarağası)
45 Concubines' Corridor (Cariyeler Koridoru)
46 Concubines' & Consorts' Courtyard (Cariye & Kadinefendi Taşlığı)
47 Harem Kitchen
48 Imperial Princes' School
49 Harem Chamberlain's Room
50 Black Eunuchs' Courtyard (Ağalar Taşlığı)
51 Black Eunuchs' Dormitories (Ağalar Koğuş)
52 Women's Hamam
53 Women's Dormitory
54 Harem Hospital
55 Laundry Room
56 Black Eunuchs' Mosque
57 Guard Room/Hall with Şadırvan
58 Harem Eunuchs' Mosque
59 Tower of Justice (Adalet Kulesi)
60 Carriage Gate & Dome with Cupboards (Dolaplı Kubbe)

Decorative water fountain

Imperial tuğra, Middle Gate

Galata Tower In its present form the tower dates from 1216, when Galata was a Genoese trading colony. Later it served as a prison, an observatory, then a fire lookout before it caught fire itself in 1835. In 1967 it was completely restored as a supper club. The observation deck, an excellent place for views and photos, is open from 9 am to 9 pm daily for US$1.75 (US$1 on Monday). Find the sign announcing that during the 17th century an intrepid local 'birdman' launched himself from the top and made the first intercontinental flight across to Asian İstanbul.

İstiklal Caddesi & Taksim At the top of the hill is İstiklal Caddesi, once called the Grand Rue de Péra, now a pedestrian way served by a restored tram (US$0.50, always overcrowded). The famed Pera Palas Oteli (rooms for US$180 a double) is off to the west; huge consulates – embassies in Ottoman times – line the avenue. At Galatasaray is the colourful **Balık Pazar** (Fish Market) and **Çiçek Pasajı** (Flower Passage), an assortment of fish-and-beer restaurants.

Taksim Square, with its huge hotels, park and Atatürk Cultural Centre, is the hub of modern İstanbul.

The Bosphorus

North from İstanbul towards the Black Sea are some beautiful old Ottoman buildings, including the imposing but overpriced **Dolmabahçe Palace** and several big mosques; **Rumeli Hisar**, the huge castle built by Mehmet the Conqueror on the European side to complete his stranglehold on Constantinople; and many small and surprisingly peaceful villages that are now the city's suburbs. Towns on the Asian side in particular have charm, open space and good food.

Any bus heading out of Karaköy along the Bosphorus shore road will take you to Dolmabahçe. Get off at the Kabataş stop. Just north is the Dolmabahçe mosque, and beyond it, the palace. To get to Rumeli Hisar, take any bus or dolmuş going north along the European shore of the Bosphorus to Bebek, Emirgan, Yeniköy or Sarıyer. A ferry ride up the Bosphorus is *de rigueur* for all İstanbul tourists. See also Organised Tours later in this section.

The Princes' Isles

Once the site of monasteries and a haven for pirates, this string of nine spotless little *adalar* (islands) is a popular weekend and summer getaway for İstanbul's middle class. With good beaches, open woodland and transport by horse-drawn carriages, the isles make a pleasant escape from the noise and hustle of İstanbul. Ferries (US$3.50) and *deniz otobüsü* (hydrofoils, US$5) depart the dock at Kabataş, just south of Dolmabahçe.

Organised Tours

A cruise along the Bosphorus is likely to be a highlight of your trip. Organised excursion ferries depart from Eminönü daily at 10.35 am and 12.35 and 2.10 pm each weekday, and stop at Beşiktaş on the European shore, Kanlıca on the Asian shore, Yeniköy, Sarıyer and Rumeli Kavağı on the European shore; and Anadolu Kavağı on the Asian shore (1¾ hours). Extra trips are added on Sunday and holidays, with boats departing from Eminönü at 10 and 11 am, noon, 1.30 and 3 pm.

The weekday round-trip fare is US$5, half price on Saturday and Sunday. Hold on to your ticket; you need to show it to reboard the boat for the return trip. The standard 1¾ hour tourist cruise from Eminönü to Sarıyer on a normal ferry costs US$4 one way (half price on Sunday). Or, you can take the shorter 'poor-person's sunset cruise' across the Bosphorus and back by boarding any boat for Üsküdar.

Special Events

The annual İstanbul International Music Festival from early June to early July attracts top name artists from around the world.

Places to Stay

Hostels and camp sites aside, İstanbul's accommodation is quite pricey nowadays. The best area to stay is Cankurtaran, immediately south-east of Sultanahmet, where the quiet streets play host to a range of cheap and moderate hotels, mostly with stunning views from their roof terraces.

For four and five-star hotels, head across the Bosphorus to Taksim.

Places to Stay – Budget

Camping Camping is not particularly convenient and costs about as much as staying in a cheap hotel (around US$10 for a tent and two people). *Londra Kamping* (☎ 560 4200) is a truck stop with a large camping area behind it on the south side of the Londra Asfaltı between the Topkapı district and the airport (coming east from the airport, follow the *servis yolu* signs). *Ataköy Tatil Köyü* (☎ 559 6000), on the shore south-east of the airport, and *Florya Turistik Tesisleri* (☎ 574 0000) are holiday beach-hotel-bungalow complexes with camping facilities. To get to them, take the *banliyö* (suburban) train from Sirkeci train station.

Hostels Most İstanbul hostels charge US$7/8 for a bed in summer, less in winter. In high summer even the hostels fill up (with the inevitable problems of noise and overstretched facilities), and roof space becomes available for less than US$5. These days most of the hostels boast a few private rooms, Internet access and extras like cafes or games rooms.

A little way from the other hostels, the 320-bed *Yücelt Interyouth Hostel* (☎ 513 6150, Caferiye Sokak 6/1, Sultanahmet) has lots of facilities including a mini-gym and laundry. Some rooms look onto Aya Sofya, right beside it.

Heading into Cankurtaran, the *İstanbul Hostel* (☎ 516 9380, Kutlugün Sokak) is new and immaculate, and shows movies in its basement bar. Farther along is the small and welcoming *Mavi Guesthouse* (☎ 516 5878, Kutlugün Sokak 3) – not to be confused with the expensive Mavi Ev nearby – which charges US$7/8 a single/double for a bed in a four-bed dorm, including breakfast. The cosy ground-floor lounge is a plus.

One block over is Akbıyık Caddesi, with lots of places to stay and eat. The popular

Orient Youth Hostel (☎ 518 0789, Akbıyık Caddesi 13) has a top-floor cafe with marvellous Bosphorus views and a basement bar that features belly-dancers and water-pipes. The smaller *Sultan Tourist Hostel* (☎ 516 9260, Terbıyık Sokak 3), just around the corner, also boasts Marmara views from its cafe.

Hotels Yerebatan Caddesi runs north-west from Aya Sofya. A block past the Sunken Palace Cistern, turn right on Salkım Söğüt Sokak to find a couple of budget-priced places. *Hotel Ema* (☎ 511 7166) and *Hotel Elit* (☎ 526 2549) are both on the left, *Hotel Anadolu* (☎ 512 1035), down the street on the right. The Anadolu and Elit are cheapest and quietest at US$10 and US$15 per person for rooms with sink; hot showers are free.

Places to Stay – Mid-Range

Many Cankurtaran pensions are gradually turning themselves into classy small hotels.

Heading down from Aya Sofya you'll come to Utangaç Sokak on the right where the friendly *Side Pansiyon* (☎ 517 6590) has singles/doubles from US$20/35; the adjoining hotel has the same owners and excellent-value rooms for US$40/50/60 a single/double/triple.

Turn right opposite Four Seasons Hotel then left into Kutlugün Sokak for the cosy *Berk Guest House* (☎ 516 9671), where comfortable doubles with bath cost from US$50. From the roof terrace you can look into the grounds of the Four Seasons. *Terrace Guesthouse* (☎ 638 9733, Kutlugün Sokak 39) has only a few rooms, but they're cheerful enough for US$40 to US$45 a double.

Opposite the Orient Youth Hostel, *Star Guest House* (☎ 638 2302, Akbıyık Caddesi 18) has doubles with shower from US$25. Walk down Adliye Sokak for *Alp Guesthouse* (☎ 517 9570) at No 4, where pleasingly decorated singles/doubles with bath cost US$35/50. *Hanedan Pension* (☎ 516 4869) opposite has similarly priced rooms and a small roof-top cafe. A few doors away is the new *Şebnem Hotel* (☎ 517 6623), where comfortable, colour-coordinated singles/doubles cost from US$35/50.

Hotel Empress Zoe (☎ 518 2504, Akbıyık Caddesi, Adliye Sokak 10) is built around a Byzantine cistern next to an old Ottoman hamam. Rooms are tiny but stylish for US$50/70. The rooftop bar-lounge-terrace affords good views of the sea and the Blue Mosque.

The immaculate *Sarı Konak Oteli (☎ 638 6358, Mimar Mehmet-Ağa Caddesi 42)* has very comfortable rooms for US$60/80, together with a mosaic-floored breakfast room and a rooftop dining room with sweeping views of the Bosphorus.

Hotel Nomade (☎ 511 1296, Divan Yolu, Ticarethane Sokak 15), just off busy Divan Yolu, charges US$45/60 with private shower and breakfast. There are more good views from the roof terrace.

Places to Stay – Top End

Cankurtaran also harbours some wonderful hotels in restored Ottoman mansions or buildings designed to imitate them. Classiest is probably *Yeşil Ev (☎ 517 6785, Kabasakal Caddesi 5)*, a 22-room Ottoman house furnished with period pieces and antiques. Behind it is a nice shaded garden-terrace restaurant. Singles/doubles will set you back US$115/150.

Mavi Ev (☎ 638 9010, Dalhbastı Sokak 14) offers comfortable rooms and excellent morning views of the Blue Mosque from its rooftop restaurant for US$110/130 a single/double.

Of course *the* place to stay must be the gorgeous *Four Seasons Hotel (☎ 638 8200, Tevkifhane Sokak 1)*, an ex-prison turned luxury hotel. Even at US$240/270 a single/double it's often full.

Places to Eat

Nowadays, the *Pudding Shop*, officially known as the *Lale Restaurant* and once a legend among travellers, is just one of a string of medium-priced *lokantalar* (restaurants) along Divan Yolu opposite the Hippodrome – typical meals cost US$4 to US$6. Try *Can Restaurant*, or *Vitamin Restaurant*, a brightly lit, hyperactive place. *Sultanahmet Köftecisi* serves delicious grilled meatballs with salad, bread and a drink for US$4 or less.

At the far (south-western) end of the Hippodrome, walk up Üçler Sokak one short block to the *Yeni Birlik Lokantası*, at No 46, a large fast food restaurant favoured by lawyers from the nearby law courts. Meals cost US$2.50 to US$4.

The favourite is *Doy Doy* ('Fill up! Fill up'); at the south-eastern end of the Hippodrome, walk downhill to Şifa Hamamı Sokak 13. This is a simple, cheap restaurant busy with locals and backpackers. *Kuru fasulye* (broad beans in tomato sauce), *pilav* (rice), bread and a soft drink costs about US$2.

Vegetarians should head for Taksim and the streets off İstiklal Caddesi. A great newcomer is *Nuh'un Ambarı (☎ 528 2030, Yeni Çarşı Caddesi 54)*, near the Galatasaray Lisesi, a conservation centre with a cafe where you can also buy things like organic wine.

For that special occasion *Rami (☎ 517 6593, Utangaç Sokak 6)*, in a restored house behind the Blue Mosque, serves interesting Ottoman specialities like grilled lamb and aubergine purée; a meal is likely to cost about US$20 to US$30 per person. The rooftop terrace has fine views of the Blue Mosque.

Daruzziyafe (☎ 518 1351, Atmeydanı 27), on the Hippodrome to the right of the Blue Mosque, also serves good Ottoman cuisine. A full lunch might cost US$10 to US$15.

The neighbourhood called Kumkapı, following the shoreline 800m south of Beyazıt along Tiyatro Caddesi, boasts dozens of good seafood *restaurants*. In fair weather the whole place is one big party. A meal of fish and rakı is likely to cost US$12 to US$20. For a cheaper lunch, buy a fish sandwich from one of the boats near the Galata Bridge for just US$1.

Getting There & Away

Air İstanbul is Turkey's airline hub. Most foreign airlines have their offices near Taksim, or north of it, along Cumhuriyet Caddesi. Most domestic flights with Turkish Airlines cost under US$100. For reservations, call ☎ 663 6363 (fax 240 2984).

İstanbul Airlines (☎ 231 7526, fax 246 4967, Cumhuriyet Caddesi 289) flies to Adana, Ankara, Antalya, Dalaman, İzmir and Trabzon, as well as many European cities. Most domestic flights cost US$55 to US$70.

Bus The Uluslararası (international) İstanbul Otogarı (☎ 658 0036, fax 658 2858) at Esenler has 168 ticket offices and buses leaving for all parts of Turkey and beyond. To get to it from Sultanahmet take the metro from Aksaray and get out at the otogar.

Buses depart for Ankara (US$15 to $US24, six hours) roughly every 15 minutes, day and night; buses for most other cities depart at least every hour. Heading east to Anatolia, you might want to board at the smaller otogar at Harem (☎ 216-333 3763), north of Haydarpaşa on the Asian shore, although choice is more limited.

For information on getting buses from İstanbul to Syria see the Getting There & Away section earlier in this chapter.

Train Sirkeci is the station for trains to Edirne, Greece and Europe. Haydarpaşa, on the Asian shore, is the terminus for trains to Anatolia. Ask at Sirkeci station (☎ 527 0051) or Haydarpaşa station (☎ 216-336 0475) for rail information. From Sirkeci there are three express trains a day to Edirne (US$3, 6½ hours), but the bus is faster (US$6, three hours). The nightly *Balkan Expresi* goes to Budapest via Skopje, the *Bükreş Ekspresi* to Bucharest.

From Haydarpaşa there are seven express trains a day to Ankara (US$6.50 to US$58, seven to 10 hours); one has only sleeping cars.

Boat For information on car ferries to İzmir and along the Black Sea coast to Trabzon, see the introductory Getting Around section in this chapter. Buy tickets at the Turkish Maritime Lines (Denizyolları) office (☎ 249 9222 for reservations, ☎ 244 0207 for information), Rıhtım Caddesi, Karaköy, just east of the Karaköy ferry dock.

Yenikapı, south of Aksaray Square, is the dock for intracity catamarans and for *hızlı*

A Wave of Destruction

As this book went to print, a massive earthquake hit north-western Turkey with devastating consequences. The death toll was yet to be confirmed but was expect to exceed 20,000, with thousands more injured or made homeless. Although more than 1000 people died in İstanbul, the Sultanahmet area, most popular with visitors, was little affected.

Although Bursa and Eskişehir were hit by the quake the older districts survived intact. Many smaller settlements around the Sea of Marmara were virtually destroyed. In particular, Yalova, the terminus for the high-speed catamarans from İstanbul and popular for its thermal springs, was almost obliterated.

---

feribot (fast car ferries) on routes across the Sea of Marmara. Heading for Bursa, take a Yalova ferry or catamaran, which will get you to Yalova in less than an hour for US$35 (car and driver). The voyage to Bandırma takes less than two hours and costs US$70 (car and driver) or US$12 (pedestrian/passenger).

Ferries for the Princes' Isles depart from Eminönü (see the Princes' Isles section earlier).

Getting Around
The Airport The fastest way to get into town from the airport is by taxi (US$10 to US$20, 20 to 30 minutes); the fare depends on what part of the city you're headed for and whether it's *gündüz* (night) or *gece* (day).

A cheaper but slower alternative is the Havaş airport bus (US$3.50, 35 to 60 minutes), which departs from the international terminal, stops at the domestic terminal, then goes to Taksim Square. Buses leave every 30 minutes from 5.30 to 10 am, every hour from 10 am to 2 pm, every 30 minutes from 2 to 8 pm, and every hour from 9 to 11 pm (no buses between 11 pm and 5.30 am).

TURKEY

It's even cheaper if you find two or three other thrifty travellers and share a taxi (US$5 total; make sure the driver runs the meter) from the airport to the Yeşilköy *banliyö tren istasyonu*, the suburban train station in the neighbouring town of Yeşilköy. From here, battered trains (US$0.50) run every 30 minutes or less to Sirkeci station. Get off at Yenikapı for Aksaray and Laleli, at Cankurtaran for Sultanahmet, or at Eminönü (end of the line) for Beyoğlu.

Many of the Divan Yolu travel agencies and Sultanahmet hostels book minibus transport from the hotels to the airport for about US$5.

Bus City buses are crowded but useful. Destinations and intermediate stops are indicated at the front and side of the bus. You must have a ticket (US$0.30) before boarding; some long routes require two tickets. Stock up on tickets in advance from the white booths near major stops or nearby shops.

Ferries The cheapest and nicest way to travel any considerable distance in İstanbul is by ferry, although the old ferries have been replaced on many routes by fast, modern catamarans called *deniz otobüsü* (seabus), which cost several times as much.

The main ferry docks are at the mouth of the Golden Horn (Eminönü, Sirkeci and Karaköy) and at Kabataş, 3km north-east of the Galata Bridge, just south of Dolmabahçe Palace. Short ferry rides cost US$0.60, most longer ones US$1.20.

Train To get to Sirkeci train station, take the *tramvay* (tram) from Aksaray or Sultanahmet, or any bus for Eminönü. Haydarpaşa train station is connected by ferry to Karaköy (US$0.60, at least every 30 minutes).

Banliyö trenler (US$0.40) run every 20 minutes from Sirkeci along the southern walls of Old İstanbul and westward along the Marmara shore. There's a handy station in Cankurtaran.

Tram The useful *hızlı* (fast) tramvay has two lines. The first runs between Eminönü

and Aksaray via Divan Yolu and Sultanahmet; the second runs west from Aksaray via Adnan Menderes Bulvarı through the city walls to the otogar. Another restored tram trundles along İstiklal Caddesi to Taksim. All tram tickets cost US$0.30.

Underground The Tünel (İstanbul's underground train) mounts the hill from Karaköy to Tünel Square and İstiklal Caddesi (US$0.40, every 10 or 15 minutes). The underground line from Taksim north to 4 Levent should also be operational by the time you read this.

Taxi İstanbul has 60,000 yellow taxis, with meters, though not every driver wants to run them. From Sultanahmet to Taksim costs around US$5; to the otogar around US$10.

Around İstanbul

EDİRNE

European Turkey is known as Trakya (Thrace). If you pass through, stop in Edirne, a pleasant town with several fine old mosques. Have a look at the **Üçşerefeli Cami**, the **Eski Cami**, and especially the **Selimiye Camii**, the finest work of Süleyman the Magnificent's master architect, Sinan. The impressive **Beyazıt II Camii** complex is on the outskirts. There are several good, cheap hotels a few blocks from the tourist office (☎/fax 225 1518, Hürriyet Meydanı 17) in the town centre. Buses run every 20 minutes to İstanbul (US$6, three hours); and five times a day south to Çanakkale (US$7, four hours).

BURSA

Sprawling at the base of Uludağ, Turkey's biggest winter sports centre, Bursa was the Ottoman capital prior to İstanbul's conquest. It retains several fine mosques and pretty neighbourhoods from early Ottoman times, but its big attraction, now and historically, is its thermal springs. Besides healthy hot water, Bursa produces lots of succulent fruit and most of the cars made in Turkey. It's also famous for its savoury kebaps.

Orientation & Information

The city centre, with its banks and shops, is along Atatürk Caddesi between the Ulu Cami (Grand Mosque) to the west and the main square, Cumhuriyet Alanı, commonly called Heykel (*heykel* means 'statue'), to the east. The PTT is on the southern side of Atatürk Caddesi opposite the Ulu Cami. Some cheap hotels are 1.5km down the mountain slope from the city centre. Çekirge, with its hot springs, is about 6km west of Heykel.

The Bursa Şehirlerarası Otobüs terminalı is 10km north of the centre on the Yalova road. Special 'Terminal' buses (grey with a blue stripe) shuttle between the bus station and the city centre. The *doğ garaj* (eastern garage) and *batı garaj* (western garage) – separate minibus terminals east and west of the city centre – serve regional routes.

You can get maps and brochures at the tourist office (☎ 251 1834) in the Orhangazi Altgeçidi subway, Ulu Cami Parkı, opposite the Koza Han (Silk Market).

Things to See & Do

The largest of Bursa's mosques is the 20-domed **Ulu Cami** (Grand Mosque), built in 1399, on Atatürk Caddesi in the city centre. About 1km east of Heykel in a pedestrian zone are the early Ottoman **Yeşil Cami** (Green Mosque, built in 1424), its beautifully tiled **Yeşil Türbe** (Green Tomb, open from 8.30 am to noon and 1 to 5.30 pm daily; admission is free), and the **Turkish & Islamic Arts Museum**, open from 8.30 am to noon and 1 to 5 pm daily, closed Monday. Admission is US$1.25.

A few hundred metres farther east is the **Emir Sultan Mosque** (1805). To get there, take a dolmuş or bus No 18 ('Emir Sultan') east from Heykel.

Uphill and west of the Grand Mosque, on the way to Çekirge, are the 14th century **Tombs of Osman & Orhan**, the first Ottoman sultans. A kilometre beyond is the **Muradiye Mosque Complex**, with its decorated tombs, dating from the 15th and 16th centuries.

Bursa's **covered market** is behind the Koza Park (Fountain Plaza), by the Ulu Cami. You can also take a stroll in the vast

Kültür Park west of the centre on the way to Çekirge. **Mineral baths** can be found in the suburb of Çekirge.

It's worth going up **Uludağ**. From Heykel take bus No 3 or a dolmuş east to the *teleferik* (cable car) which you can catch up the mountain (US$5, half price Wednesday). Alternatively take a dolmuş (US$6) from the otogar for the 22km to the top.

Places to Stay

Bursa hotels tend to be rather pricey. That said, the Tahtakale/İnebey district just south of the Ulu Cami is an interesting area with many narrow streets and historic houses. Some of these are being restored, and will probably become expensive shops and 'boutique' hotels. The cheapest rooms here are at *Otel Güneş* (☎ 222 1404, İnebey Cad-desi 75), where you can stay in a waterless single/double for US$8/12.

Though somewhat overpriced, the nearby *Otel Çamlıbel* (☎ 221 2565, İnebey Caddesi 71) is a renovated hotel with a quiet location and constant hot water. Rates are US$20/30 with private shower; breakfast costs extra. Better is the *Hotel Çeşmeli* (☎ 224 1511, Gümüşçeken Caddesi 6), a few steps north of Atatürk Caddesi. It's friendly, fairly quiet and very clean. Rooms cost US$28/42 with shower and breakfast.

Hotel İpekçi (☎ 221 1935, Çancılar Cad-desi 38), about four blocks north of Heykel near the Karakedi Camii, has quiet rooms for US$12/20 with shower (less with just a sink).

Most Çekirge hotels have their own facil-ities for taking the waters. You may find that the bathtub or shower at your hotel runs only mineral water, or there may be private or public bathing rooms in the hotel basement.

Çekirge's main street is I Murat Caddesi (Birinci Murat Caddesi). To get there, take a bus or dolmuş from Heykel or along Atatürk Caddesi to 'Çekirge' or 'SSK Hastanesi'. Good bets here include *Öz Yeşil Yayla Oteli* (☎ 236 8026, Çekirge Caddesi, Selvi Sokak 6), between the Boyugüzel and Yıldız II ho-tels at the upper end of the village, which charges US$22 a double for rooms with sink but free use of the mineral baths.

Next door, **Boyugüzel Termal Otel** (☎ 233 3850, fax 233 9999) on Selvi Sokak, charges US$22 for a double with sink and toilet; 30 minutes in the mineral bath downstairs is thrown in.

Opposite the Osman and Orhan tombs, **Safran Oteli & Restaurant** (☎ 224 7216, Kale Sokak) is a restored Ottoman house in a historic neighbourhood. Singles/doubles with private bathroom and TV cost US$55/80, breakfast included.

For real luxury try the three-star **Termal Hotel Gönlü Ferah** (☎ 233 9210, fax 233 9218, I Murat Caddesi 24), in the very centre of the village. Some of the 62 rooms have fine views over the valley. Rates are US$70/90 with breakfast.

Places to Eat

Bursa is renowned for İskender kebap (döner kebap topped with savoury tomato sauce and browned butter). Competition for patrons is fierce among kebapçıs. **Kebapçı İskender** (Ünlü Caddesi 7), just east of Heykel, dates back to 1867 and has a posh atmospheric dining room but low prices – about US$6 with a soft drink. *Adanur Hacıbey*, opposite, costs the same but is less fancy.

Çiçek Izgara (Belediye Caddesi 15), just north of the half-timbered *Belediye* (city hall) in the flower market, is bright and modern, good for women unaccompanied by men, and open from 11 am to 3.30 pm and 5.30 to 9 pm daily.

For cheaper eats, head for the small eateries in the Tahtakale Çarşısı (the market across Atatürk Caddesi from the Ulu Cami). For a jolly evening of seafood and drinks, explore Sakarya Caddesi, off Altıparmak Caddesi.

Getting There & Away

The fastest way to İstanbul is a bus to Yalova, then a catamaran or fast car ferry to İstanbul's Yenikapı docks. Get a bus that departs at least 1½ hours before the scheduled boat departure.

Buses going all the way to İstanbul are designated either karayolu ile (by road), or feribot ile (by car ferry). Karayolu ile buses take four hours and drag you all around the Bay of İzmit. Those designated feribot ile take you to Topçular, east of Yalova, and drive aboard the car ferry to Eskihisar, a much quicker and more pleasant way to go. You must also determine whether your chosen bus terminates its journey at İstanbul's Harem bus station on the Asian shore, or at the Esenler otogar; some buses stop at both.

Getting Around

To/From the Otogar Take the special 'Terminal' bus (grey with a blue stripe; US$0.75) to travel the 10km between the otogar and the city centre. A taxi costs US$6.

Bursa's city buses (BOİ; US$0.40) have destinations and stops marked on the front and kerb side. A major set of stops is by Koza Parkı on Atatürk Caddesi. Catch a bus from *peron* (stop) No 1 for Emir Sultan and Teleferuç (Uludağ cable car); from peron No 2 for Muradiye; from peron No 4 for Altıparmak and the Kültür Parkı; and from the BOİ Ekspres peron for the Osman gazi and Orhan Gazi tombs and Muradiye.

The Aegean Coast

Olive groves and history distinguish this gorgeous coast. Gelibolu (Gallipoli), Troy and Pergamum are just some of the famous places to be visited.

ÇANAKKALE

Çanakkale is a hub for transport to Troy and across the Dardanelles to Gelibolu (Gallipoli). It was here that Leander swam what was then called the Hellespont to his lover Hero, and here too Lord Byron did his Romantic bit and duplicated the feat. The defence of the straits during WWI led to a Turkish victory over Anzac (Australian and New Zealand) forces on 18 March 1916, now a big local holiday.

Orientation & Information

The helpful tourist office (☎ 217 1187), all the cheap hotels and a range of good cafes are within a block or two of the ferry pier, near the town's landmark clock tower.

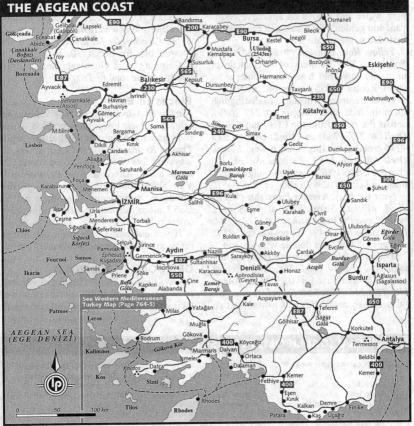

THE AEGEAN COAST

Things to See

The **Ottoman castle** built by Sultan Mehmet the Conqueror in 1452 is now the **Army & Navy Museum**. Just over 2km south of the ferry pier, the **Archaeological Museum** (closed Monday) holds artefacts found at Troy and Assos.

Places to Stay

Except on Anzac Day, Çanakkale has hotels in all prices. Many are less well kept, less well run and less friendly than in other Turkish towns.

Anzac House (☎ 217 1392, *Cumhuriyet Bulvarı*) provides clean, simple budget accommodation with a choice of dorm beds for US$4, singles for US$6 and doubles for US$10. Some of the doubles are claustrophobic, windowless boxes.

Hotel Efes (☎ 217 3256, *Aralık Sokak 5*), behind the clock tower, is bright and cheerful charging US$6/8 for singles/doubles without running water, a little more with shower.

The quaint old *Hotel Kervansaray* (☎ 217 8192, *Fetvane Sokak 13*) is a good choice.

Very basic rooms cost US$6/8 without running water and there's an attractive courtyard and garden. Make sure that breakfast is included in the price.

Yellow Rose Pension (☎ 217 3343, Yeni Sokak 5) is 50m south-east of the clock tower in an attractive old house on a quiet sidestreet. Rooms (US$5 per person) are basic.

Other cheapies, with little to distinguish them, include *Hotel Akgün (☎ 217 3049)*, across the street from the Efes; and *Erdem Oteli (☎ 217 4986)* and *Ümüt Otel (☎ 213 4246)*, nearer to the clock tower. *Konak Oteli (☎ 217 1150, Fetvane Sokak 14)* charges US$6/10 for waterless singles/doubles; and US$8/12 with shower.

Near the bars, *Avrupa Pansiyon (☎ 217 4084, Matbaa Sokak 8)* is also US$8/12 with shower. *Otel Fatih 2 (☎ 217 7884, İnönü Caddesi 149)*, opposite the PTT, charges US$12 for a double with shower.

You can't miss the two star *Otel Anafartalar (☎ 217 4454, İskele Meydanı)* offering bath and breakfast for US$31/42. *Anzac Hotel (☎ 217 7777, Saat Kulesi Meydanı 8)*, more or less facing the clock tower, is a two star place with rooms for US$30/40 without breakfast (US$5). A good choice because it's clean and new is *Hotel Temizay (☎ 212 8760, Cumhuriyet Meydanı 15)*, with singles/doubles for US$20/30.

Camping is at Güzelyalı Beach, 15km south, off the road to Troy.

Places to Eat

Gaziantep Aile Kebap ve Pide Salonu, behind the clock tower, serves good, cheap pide and more substantial kebaps, while *Trakya Restaurant*, on the main square, always has lots of food ready and waiting 24 hours a day. *Aussie & Kiwi Restaurant* in Yalı Sokak does its best to oblige Antipodeans, serving up Vegemite toast for US$2 alongside cheap kebaps and *köfte* (meat balls).

If you eat at the waterfront fish restaurants, ask for *all* prices in advance.

GELİBOLU (GALLİPOLİ)

Always the first line of defence of İstanbul, in WWI the Dardanelles defences proved their worth. Atop the narrow, hilly peninsula,

GELİBOLU (GALLİPOLİ) PENINSULA

1 Büyük Kemikli Picnic Area	19 The Nek	37 Beach (Hell Spit) Cemetery
2 Hill 10	20 Lala Baba Cemetery	38 Mehmetçiğe Saygı Anıtı
3 Lala Baba	21 Embarkation Pier Cemetery	(Memorial to Mehmetçik)
4 Green Hill	22 New Zealand No 2 Outpost	39 Kabatepe Information Centre
5 Hill 60 New Zealand Memorial	Cemetery	& Museum
6 'B' Beach	23 No 2 Outpost Cemetery	40 Gelibolu Tarihi Milli Park
7 7th Field Ambulance Cemetery	24 57th Regiment (57 Alay)	(Gallipoli National Historic
8 Kocaçimentepe	Cemetery	Park), Ziyaretçi Merkezi
9 Hill Q	25 Bomba Sırt (Bomb Ridge)	(Park Visitors' centre)
10 Chunuk Bair New Zealand	26 Quinn's Post	& Picnic Area
Memorial	27 Yüzbaşı Metrmet Şehitliği	41 Twelve Tree Copse Cemetery
11 The Farm	28 Courtney Steele's Post	& NZ Memorial
12 Conkbayırı Mehmetçik	29 Canterbury Cemetery	42 Redoubt Cemetery
Memorials	30 Anzac Memorial & Arıburnu	43 Pink Farm Cemetery
13 Place where Atatürk Spent the	31 Anzac Cove	44 Kerevizdere Picnic Area
Night of 9-10 August 1915	32 Kırmızı Sırt (125. Alay	45 Skew Bridge Cemetery
14 Talat Göktepe Monument	Cephesi)	46 Lancashire Landing Cemetery
15 Kemalyeri (Scrubby Knoll,	33 Johnston's Jolly	47 Cape Helles British Memorial
Turkish HQ)	34 Lone Pine (Kanlı Sırt) Cemetery	48 İlk Şehitler & Yahya Çavuş
16 Düztepe (10 Alay Cephesi)	35 Shrapnel Valley (Korkudere) &	Memorials
17 Mehmet Çavuş Cemetery	Plugge's Plateau Cemeteries	49 'V' Beach Cemetery
18 Baby 700 Cemetery &	36 Kanlı Sırt Kitabesi (Bloody	50 French Memorial & Museum
Mesudiye Topu	Ridge Inscription)	51 Çanakkale Şehitleri Abidesi

GELİBOLU (GALLİPOLİ) PENINSULA

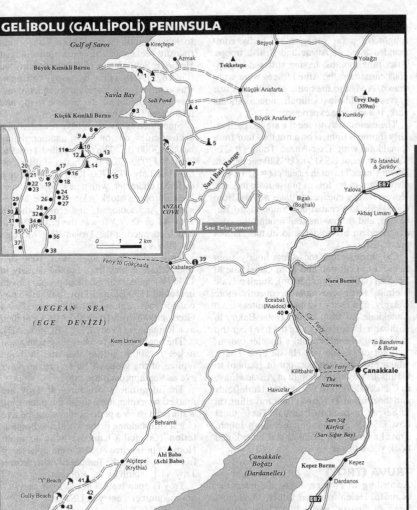

Mustafa Kemal (Atatürk) and his troops fought off a far superior but badly commanded force of Anzac and British troops. After nine months, having suffered horrendous casualties, the Allied forces were withdrawn. A visit to the battle grounds and war graves of Gelibolu (Gallipoli), now a national park, is a moving experience.

The easiest way to see the sights, particularly if time is tight, is on a minibus tour from Çanakkale with Troy-Anzac Tours (☎ 217 5849) for about US$15 to US$20 per person. Down Under Travel in Eceabat (☎ 814 2431) also comes in for lots of praise from readers. However, it's cheaper to take a ferry from Çanakkale to Eceabat and a dolmuş to Kabatepe, and follow the trail around the sites described in a booklet sold at the visitors centre there.

Car ferries cross the straits hourly from Lapseki to Gallipoli and from Çanakkale to Eceabat (US$0.50 per person). Small private 'dolmuş' ferries cross more frequently, more cheaply, and faster (15 to 20 minutes) from Çanakkale (in front of the Hotel Bakır) to Kilitbahir. Buses also make the five hour trip to Gallipoli from İstanbul's Esenler otogar.

A lot of people use Hassle-Free Tours, which provides transport out of İstanbul to Gallipoli, staying one night at Anzac House in Çanakkale before visiting the battlefields and the ruins at Troy and either travelling on to Selçuk or back to İstanbul. These tours cost US$49 per person, including lunch. Travel agencies in İstanbul and Selçuk can book you a ticket.

TRUVA (TROY)

According to Homer, Paris abducted the beautiful Helen from her father, Menelaus, King of Sparta, and whisked her off to Troy, thus precipitating the Trojan War. When 10 years of carnage couldn't end the war, Odysseus came up with the idea of the wooden horse filled with soldiers, against which Cassandra warned the Trojans in vain. It was left outside the west gate for the Trojans to wheel inside the walls.

The approach to modern Troy is across low, rolling grain fields, dotted with villages. This is the ancient Troad, all but lost to legend until German-born Californian treasure-seeker and amateur archaeologist Heinrich Schliemann (1822-90) excavated it in 1871. At that time the poetry of Homer was assumed to be based on legend, not history. Schliemann got permission to dig and uncovered four ancient towns.

Since then excavations have revealed nine ancient cities, one on top of another, dating back to 3000 BC. The cities called Troy I to Troy V (3000-1700 BC) had a similar culture, but Troy VI (1700-1250 BC) took on a different character, with a new population of Indo-European stock related to the Mycenaeans. Archaeologists argue over whether Troy VI or Troy VII was the city of Priam which engaged in the Trojan War. Most go for Troy VI.

Troy VII lasted from 1250 to 1050 BC. The Achaeans may have burned the city in 1240 BC; an invading Balkan people moved in around 1190 BC and Troy sank into a torpor for four centuries. It was revived as a Greek city (Troy VIII, 700-85 BC) and then as a Roman one (Troy IX, 85 BC-500 AD).

The booth where you buy your admission ticket is 500m before the site. A huge replica of the **wooden horse** catches your eye as you approach the ruins.

The identifiable structures at Troy are marked by explanatory signs: the interesting **walls** from various periods, including the five oldest still standing in the world; the **Bouleuterion** (Council Chamber) built at about Homer's time (circa 800 BC); the stone **ramp** from Troy II; and the **Temple of Athena** from Troy VIII, rebuilt by the Romans.

Troy is open from 8 am to 5 pm daily (7 pm in summer); entry is US$2.

Places to Stay

Tevfikiye, the farming village 1km before the site, has a few small *pensions* charging US$8 to US$12 a double. The restaurants near the ruins are inevitably pricey.

Getting There & Away

In summer frequent dolmuşes run the 32km from Çanakkale (US$1.50). Walk inland from the ferry pier to Atatürk Caddesi, and turn right towards Troy; dolmuşes wait by the bridge.

BEHRAMKALE (ASSOS)

Once known as Assos, Behramkale, 19km south-west of Ayvalık, has a hilltop **Temple of Athena** looking across the water to Lesbos in Greece. Considered one of the most beautiful cities of its time, attracting even Aristotle, it's still beautiful – particularly the little *iskele* (port) 2km beyond the village.

On the heights, *Halıcı Han* and other pensions can put you up for US$12 a double and the *Kale Restaurant* will feed you. The lovely port hotels charge US$40/60 a single/double with half board in summer. These places fill up quickly so phone ahead: *Behram* (☎ 721 7016), *Kervansaray* (☎ 721 7093), *Assos Şen* (☎ 721 7076) and *Yıldız* (☎ 721 7025). *Dost* provides camping at the port for US$5.50. Visit in the low season if possible.

AYVALIK

Once inhabited by Ottoman Greeks, this small, pleasant fishing port and beach resort is the departure point for ferries to Lesbos.

The otogar is 1.5km north of the town centre, the tourist office (☎/fax 312 2122) 1km south, opposite the marina. Offshore is **Alibey Island**, with open-air restaurants, linked by ferries and a causeway to the mainland (take the red 'Ayvalık Belediyesi' bus north).

Places to Stay & Eat

The most interesting place to stay is *Taksiyarhis Pansiyon* (☎ 312 1494, İsmetpaşa Mahallesi, Mareşal Çakmak Caddesi 71), a renovated Ottoman house, five minutes walk east of the PTT behind the former Taxiarkhis church. At just US$5 per person plus US$2 for breakfast, it's often full in summer, so reserve in advance if possible.

The faded *Turistik Çiçek Pansiyon* (☎ 312 1201) is about 200m south of the main square, just off the main road. Very basic rooms with showers cost US$4 per person without breakfast. *Biret Pansiyon* (☎ 312

2175), at the other end of Mektep Aralığı, and *Melisa Pansiyon* (☎ 312 6584) around the corner take the overflow.

The best camping is on Alibey Adası but at the southern end of Çamlık, on the way to Sarımsaklı Plaj, there's a national forest camping ground (*Orman Kampı*) and several private camping grounds.

Off İnönü Caddesi are several good, cheap restaurants such as *Ayvalık* and *Anadolu Döner ve Pide Salonu*. *Öz Canlı Balık Restaurant* on the waterfront is priceyer but good for seafood. Alibey Adası is wall-to-wall fish restaurants.

Getting There & Away

Boats operate to Lesbos, Greece, every other day from late May to September but the price is an outrageous US$50 one way or US$65 for a same-day round trip.

BERGAMA

From the 3rd century BC to the 1st century AD, Bergama (formerly Pergamum) was a powerful and cultured kingdom. A line of rulers beginning with a general under Alexander the Great ruled over this small but wealthy kingdom, whose **asclepion** (medical school, 3.5km from the city centre, admission US$2.50) grew famous and whose library rivalled that of Alexandria in Egypt. The star attractions here are the city's ruins, especially the **acropolis** (a hilltop site 6km from the city centre, entry US$2.50), and an excellent **Archaeology & Ethnography Museum** (closed at the time of writing but check in case it's reopened).

The tourist office (☎ 633 1862) is at İzmir Caddesi 57, midway between the otogar and the market. Taxis wait here, and charge US$5 to the acropolis, US$10 total if they wait and bring you back down. If you're a walker, follow the path down through the ruins instead. A taxi tour of the acropolis, the asclepion and the museum costs US$20.

Places to Stay & Eat

The spotless, family-run *Böblingen Pension* (☎ 633 2153, Asklepion Caddesi 2) is at the start of the road to the asclepion, with doubles for US$12. Near the *çarşı hamamı* (Turkish bath, for men only) on the main street, **Pergamon Pension** (☎ 632 3492, *Bankalar Caddesi 3*) has rooms of all sizes for US$8 to US$12 but check the location of the bathroom before reserving.

With touching honesty **Pension Athena** (☎ 633 3420, *İmam Çıkmazı 5*) admits 'we are not the best but trying to get there'. Rooms with/without shower cost US$7/5; breakfast is another US$2. To find it, follow the signs from the Meydan Restaurant. Cross the nearby bridge and turn left to find **Nike Pension** (☎ 633 3901, *Tabak Köprü Çıkmazı 2*), which has bigger rooms in a 300-year-old Ottoman-Greek house. Rooms cost US$8 including breakfast.

For luxury, **Hotel Berksoy** (☎ 633 2595), east of the town, charges US$55 a double amid well-kept gardens with a pool.

Hotel Berksoy and, just west of it, **Karavan Camping** have sites for tents, caravans and camper vans. Sometimes cheaper places pop up for a brief life nearer to the coastal highway.

About 150m south-west of the old Red Basilica on the main street is the **Meydan Restaurant** charging about US$5 or US$6 for a three course meal on vine-shaded terraces. The simpler **Sarmaşık Lokantası** has no outdoor seating, but is cheaper. Heading south-west towards the museum and pensions, **Şen Kardeşler** and **Çiçeksever Kebap Salonu** are good, cheap eating alternatives.

Getting There & Away

Buses shuttle between Bergama and İzmir every half-hour in summer (US$4, 1½ hours). Four buses a day connect Bergama's otogar and Ayvalık (US$2); or you can hitch out to the highway and catch a bus.

İZMİR

Turkey's third-largest city, İzmir (once Smyrna) was the birthplace of Homer in about 700 BC. Today it's a transport hub, but otherwise a good place to skip if you can. It's spread out and baffling to find your way around, and its hotels are overpriced.

Work on building a new metro will also be causing disruption during the lifetime of this book.

Orientation

Central İzmir is a web of *meydanlar* (plazas) linked by streets that aren't at right angles to each other. Instead of names the back streets have numbers. You'll go mad without a map – the tourist office supplies a good one.

Budget hotel areas are near the Basmane train station. To the south-west, Anafartalar Caddesi twists and turns through the labyrinthine bazaar to the waterfront at Konak, the commercial and government centre. Atatürk Caddesi, also called Birinci Kordon, runs north-east from Konak along the waterfront 1.4km past Cumhuriyet Meydanı and its equestrian statue of Atatürk, the main PTT, luxury hotels and tourist and airline offices.

At Atatürk Caddesi's northern end is the harbour, Alsancak (Yeni) Limanı, and the smaller, mostly suburban Alsancak train station. İzmir's outdated otogar is 2km east of Alsancak train station.

Information

The tourist office (☎ 484 2147, fax 489 9278) is next to the Turkish Airlines office in the Büyük Efes Oteli at Gaziosmanpaşa Bulvarı 1/C, Cumhuriyet Meydanı, with another at Adnan Menderes airport. There's a good city information desk at the otogar.

Things to See

If you stay in İzmir, enjoy the 2nd century Roman **agora**, the hilltop **Kadifekale** fortress, the **Archaeology & Ethnography museums** (closed Monday) and the **bazaar**.

Places to Stay

For the cheapest places to stay, walk out of the front of Basmane train station, turn left, cross the large street and walk up shady Anafartalar Caddesi. Take the first small street on your right, which is 1296 Sokak, lined with small hotels. The cheapest charge about US$8 for a waterless double

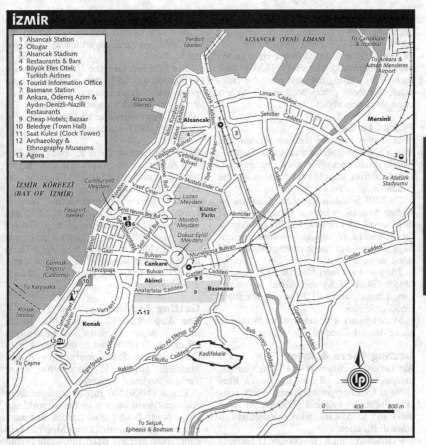

İZMİR

1 Alsancak Station
2 Otogar
3 Alsancak Stadium
4 Restaurants & Bars
5 Büyük Efes Oteli;
   Turkish Airlines
6 Tourist Information Office
7 Basmane Station
8 Ankara, Ödemiş Azim &
   Aydın-Denizli-Nazilli
   Restaurants
9 Cheap Hotels; Bazaar
10 Belediye (Town Hall)
11 Saat Kulesi (Clock Tower)
12 Archaeology &
   Ethnography Museums
13 Agora

room but prices rise to US$15 for a room with private shower. The hotels seem to improve in quality and fall in price the farther you walk. Look at several rooms before making your choice.

Anafartalar Caddesi winds into the bazaar. Near the Hatuniye Camii is *Otel Saray* (☎ 483 6946, Anafartalar Caddesi 635), which has been popular with backpackers for years. Get a room on the upper floor (it's quieter there) for US$14 a double with sink. Up 945 Sokak is the cleaner, more comfort-

able *Otel Hikmet* (☎ 484 2672) at No 26, for about the same money.

For other hotels, walk straight down Fevzipaşa Bulvarı from Basmane station and turn right (north). In 1368 Sokak and its westward continuation, 1369 Sokak, are half a dozen good, clean, quiet and cheap hotels such as *Divan*, *Akgün*, *Ova* and *Çiçek Palas*, with doubles for US$12 with sink, US$18 with shower.

Hotel Baylan (☎ 483 1426, 1299 Sokak No 8) has good two-star singles/doubles for

US$55/70 with breakfast, subject to negotiation. Another good choice is the new *Otel Antik Han* (*☎ 489 2750, Anafartalar Caddesi 600*), in a restored house right in the bazaar. Singles/doubles cost US$20/30 with baths, TVs, ceiling fans and plenty of character, but these prices are unlikely to last once word gets about.

Places to Eat

Immediately opposite Basmane station, the *Ankara, Ödemiş Azim* and *Aydın-Denizli-Nazilli* restaurants offer quick, cheap meals. Little eateries are also scattered along the budget-hotel streets.

On 1296 Sokak is the cheap *Güneydoğu Kebap Salonu*, where a kebap plate and drink cost US$4 or less. But the restaurants on 1368 and 1369 sokaks, just across Fevzipaşa Bulvarı, are much more pleasant and some serve alcohol.

The excellent *Dört Mevsim Et Lokantası* (*1369 Sokak 51/A*) specialises in meats, serves drinks, and will fill you up for about US$5 or US$6.

More upmarket restaurants are by the sea along Atatürk Caddesi.

Getting There & Away

Air Turkish Airlines (*☎ 484 1220*, Gaziosmanpaşa Bulvarı 1/F), in the Büyük Efes Oteli at Cumhuriyet Meydanı, offers nonstop flights to İstanbul (US$85, 50 minutes) and to Ankara, with connections to other destinations.

İstanbul Airlines (*☎ 489 0541*, Gaziosmanpaşa Bulvarı 2/E) has some flights to İstanbul, and numerous flights between İzmir and Europe.

Bus Many bus companies have ticket offices situated around Dokuz Eylül Meydanı, just north of Basmane, and west along Gazi Bulvarı. They may also provide a *şehiriçi servis* (free minibus shuttle service) to the İzmir otogar, which is 3km east of the city centre.

Train An evening train (US$7, 14 hours) hauls sleeping and dining cars from Bas-

mane station to Ankara. The evening *İzmir Express* service to Ankara (15 hours) has 1st/2nd class carriages which will cost you US$6/5.

For İstanbul, take the *Marmara Express* to Bandırma (US$3), then a fast ferry. Four pokey but cheap trains a day go from Basmane to Selçuk/Ephesus (US$1.50, 2½ hours); three continue to Denizli (for Pamukkale; US$3, six hours).

Boat The Getting There & Away and Getting Around sections earlier in this chapter have information on ferries to İstanbul, the Greek Islands and Venice.

Chios ferries go from Çeşme, west of İzmir, every day in summer (US$30 one way, US$40 same-day return trip). To get there you will need to catch a bus from Dokuz Eylül Meydanı to the Çeşme Garaj at Üçkuylar in western İzmir. From there, buses travel to Çeşme about every 20 minutes (US$2).

Getting Around

The Airport A Havaş bus (US$2.50, 30 minutes) departs from the Turkish Airlines office which is located at the Büyük Efes Oteli for the 25km journey to Adnan Menderes airport 1½ hours before every Turkish Airlines' departure.

Trains (US$0.50) run every hour from Alsancak train station to the airport, and some south-bound trains from Basmane also stop at the airport. From Montrö Meydanı, 700m north of Basmane, south-bound 'Adnan Menderes Belediyesi' buses travel to the airport during the day for US$1. A taxi will cost you anywhere from US$18 to US$35.

Local Transport City buses and dolmuşes connect the bus and train stations for US$0.70; signs say 'Basmane' or 'Yeni Garaj'.

The No 50 city bus (US$0.40, make sure to buy your ticket before boarding) links the Yeni Garaj and Konak; Çankaya Meydanı is the closest stop to Basmane. A taxi costs about US$3.

SELÇUK & EPHESUS

Selçuk is an easy 1¼ hour (80km) bus trip south of İzmir. Almost everybody comes here to visit the splendid Roman ruins of Ephesus (Efes). In its Ionian heyday only Athens was more magnificent, and in Roman times this was Asia's capital.

Orientation & Information

Although touristy, Selçuk is modest compared with coastal playpens like Kuşadası and most backpackers prefer it. On the eastern side of the highway (Atatürk Caddesi) are the otogar, restaurants, some hotels and the train station; on the western side behind the museum are the pensions. There's a tourist office (☎/fax 892 1328) and town map in the park on the western side of the main street, across from the bus station.

Ephesus is a 3km, 35 minute walk west from Selçuk's bus station along a shady road (turn left – south – at the Tusan Motel). Alternatively, there are frequent minibuses from the bus station to the motel, leaving you just a 1km walk.

Things to See

The site seems to be permanently swamped with coach groups and is open from 8.30 am to 5.30 pm daily (7 pm in summer). Entry fees are US$6, plus US$1.25 to park a car. In high summer it gets extremely hot here. You would be better off to start exploring early in the morning, then retire to a shady restaurant for lunch at the peak of the heat. Unfortunately this is what the coach parties also do; lunch time is when you're most likely to avoid the tour groups. If your interest in ruins is slight, half a day may suffice, but real ruins buffs will want to continue their explorations well into the afternoon.

TURKEY

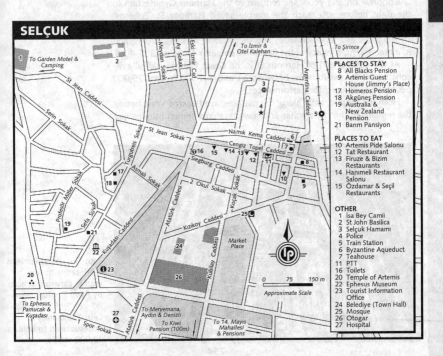

SELÇUK

To İzmir & Otel Kalehan
To Şirince
To Garden Motel & Camping
Meydan Sokak
Ay Sokak
Eski İzmir Cad
Argentina Caddesi
St Jean Caddesi
Sefin Sokak
Turgutreis Sokak
St Jean Sokak
Asmalı Sokak
Namık Kemal Caddesi
Cengiz Topel Caddesi
Siegburg Caddesi
2 Okul Sokak
Atatürk Caddesi
Koçak Sokak
Profesör Müller Sokak
Sefa Sokak
Kuşadası Caddesi
Kızıkoy Caddesi
Kubilay Caddesi
Market Place
To Ephesus, Pamucak & Kuşadası
Atatürk Caddesi
1 Spor Sokak
To Meryemana, Aydın & Denizli
To Kiwi Pension (100m)
To 14. Mayıs Mahallesi & Pensions

0   75   150 m
Approximate Scale

PLACES TO STAY
8 All Blacks Pension
9 Artemis Guest House (Jimmy's Place)
17 Homeros Pension
18 Akgüneş Pension
19 Australia & New Zealand Pension
21 Barım Pansiyon

PLACES TO EAT
10 Artemis Pide Salonu
12 Tat Restaurant
13 Firuze & Bizim Restaurants
14 Hanımeli Restaurant Salonu
15 Özdamar & Seçil Restaurants

OTHER
1 İsa Bey Camii
2 St John Basilica
3 Selçuk Hamamı
4 Police
5 Train Station
6 Byzantine Aqueduct
7 Teahouse
11 PTT
16 Toilets
20 Temple of Artemis
22 Ephesus Museum
23 Tourist Information Office
24 Belediye (Town Hall)
25 Mosque
26 Otogar
27 Hospital

EPHESUS (EFES)

Ephesus is the best-preserved classical city on the eastern Mediterranean, and among the best places in the world to get a feel for what life was like in Roman times.

Ancient Ephesus was a great trading and religious city, a centre for the cult of Cybele, the Anatolian fertility goddess. In time, Cybele became Artemis, the virgin goddess of the hunt and the moon, and a fabulous temple was built in her honour. When the Romans took over and made this the province of Asia, Artemis became Diana and Ephesus became the Roman provincial capital.

As a busy Roman town, Ephesus quickly acquired a sizeable Christian congregation. St Paul later wrote the most profound of his epistles to the Ephesians.

The Site

As you walk into the site you pass the **Gymnasium of Vedius** (2nd century AD) on your left. The road descends to the car park. To the right are the ruins of the Church of the Virgin Mary, site of the third Ecumenical Council (431 AD) which condemned the Nestorian heresy.

Continue on and you'll see remains of the **Harbour Gymnasium** to the right before you reach the marble-paved **Harbour St**. Ephesus' grandest street had water and sewer lines beneath the marble flags, 50 streetlights along its colonnades and shops along its sides. It was, and is, a grand sight, a legacy of the Byzantine emperor Arcadius (395-408).

At the eastern end of Harbour St is the **Great Theatre**, skilfully reconstructed by the Romans between 41 and 117 AD to seat 25,000 people. It's still used for performances.

From the theatre, walk along the marble-paved **Sacred Way**, noting the remains of the city's water and sewer systems beneath the paving

Top: The site at Ephesus is littered with fine marble carvings. (Photo by Peter Ptschelinzew)

Left: The Library at Ephesus used to hold 12,000 scrolls.

T M FLOWER

JON DAVISON

stones and the ruts made by wheeled vehicles. The large open space to the right of the street was the agora or marketplace, heart of Ephesus' business life. On the left towards the end of the street is an elaborate building which some archaeologists call a brothel.

In 114 AD, Consul Tiberius Julius Aquila erected a huge **library** in memory of his father Tiberius Julius Celsus. The fine building you see now used to hold 12,000 scrolls in niches around its walls. Architectural trickery was used to make it look bigger than it really was.

On the left is the **Gate of Augustus**, leading into the agora where food and handicrafts were sold.

As you head up Curetes Way, a passage on the left leads to the men's toilets. The famous figure of Priapus (now in Selçuk's Ephesus Museum) with the penis of most men's dreams was found nearby. You can't miss the impressive Corinthian-style **Temple of Hadrian** on the left. Dedicated to Hadrian, Artemis and the people of Ephesus in 118 AD, it was greatly reconstructed in the 5th century. Curetes Way ends at the two-storey **Gate of Hercules**, constructed in the 4th century AD.

Top: The ruins are extensive enough to suggest what life in a Roman city would have been like.

Right: The impressive Corinthian-style Temple of Hadrian was built in 118 AD but greatly restored in the 5th century.

PETER PTSCHELINZEW

EPHESUS

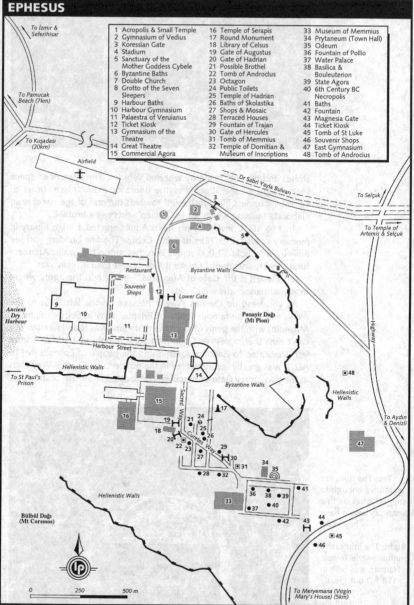

1 Acropolis & Small Temple	16 Temple of Serapis	33 Museum of Memmius
2 Gymnasium of Vedius	17 Round Monument	34 Prytaneum (Town Hall)
3 Koressian Gate	18 Library of Celsus	35 Odeum
4 Stadium	19 Gate of Augustus	36 Fountain of Pollio
5 Sanctuary of the	20 Gate of Hadrian	37 Water Palace
Mother Goddess Cybele	21 Possible Brothel	38 Basilica &
6 Byzantine Baths	22 Tomb of Androclus	Bouleuterion
7 Double Church	23 Octagon	39 State Agora
8 Grotto of the Seven	24 Public Toilets	40 6th Century BC
Sleepers	25 Temple of Hadrian	Necropolis
9 Harbour Baths	26 Baths of Skolastika	41 Baths
10 Harbour Gymnasium	27 Shops & Mosaic	42 Fountain
11 Palaestra of Veruianus	28 Terraced Houses	43 Magnesia Gate
12 Ticket Kiosk	29 Fountain of Trajan	44 Ticket Kiosk
13 Gymnasium of the	30 Gate of Hercules	45 Tomb of St Luke
Theatre	31 Tomb of Memmius	46 Souvenir Shops
14 Great Theatre	32 Temple of Domitian &	47 East Gymnasium
15 Commercial Agora	Museum of Inscriptions	48 Tomb of Androcius

The excellent **Ephesus Museum** in Selçuk (open from 8.30 am to noon and 1 to 5 pm; admission US$3.50) has a striking collection of artefacts. Don't miss the exquisite figure of the Boy on the Dolphin in the first room, the marble statues of Cybele/Artemis with rows of egg-like breasts representing fertility, and several effigies of Priapus, the phallic god. The foundations of the **Temple of Artemis**, between Ephesus and Selçuk, are all that remain of one of the Seven Wonders of the Ancient World – see the 'Temple of Artemis at Ephesus' boxed text on the following page.

Places to Stay

Selçuk has almost 100 small pensions so finding a room shouldn't be too difficult, except at the busiest times. Rooms in these modest, friendly places cost from $US6 to

---

The Temple of Artemis at Ephesus

'Whoever looks will be convinced that a change of place has occurred; that the heavenly world of immortality has been placed on the earth'; so wrote Philo, the Byzantine historian who listed the temple of Artemis among his Wonders of the World. It was larger than the Parthenon at Athens (which was never considered a Wonder), with 127 columns, all of which had figures carved around the base.

Gothic fleets sacked and plundered Ephesus and fired the temple in 262 AD. Although it was rebuilt in the 5th century AD, the cult of Artemis was subsumed by Christianity and the temple partially dismantled for building materials. By the 10th century the site had been buried by silt from the nearby River Cayster and it disappeared completely until rediscovered in 1869 by an English archaeologist, John Turtle Wood.

All that's left today is a single re-erected column in a rectangular pit, which is the result of Wood's diggings. It's difficult to make out the outline of the temple. In the town of Selçuk you can find fragments of the temple embedded in a Byzantine aqueduct, a slab from the altar forming part of the walls of a mosque, and other remnants incorporated into the ancient church up on the hill of Ayasuluk.

TURKEY

US$8 a single, US$8 to US$12 a double without bath; or from US$8 to US$10 a single, US$12 to US$15 a double with private shower. In some cases it's possible to sleep on the roof or camp in the garden for US$2 to US$3 per person.

Garden Motel & Camping (☎ 892 1163) is west of Ayasoluk, the hill bearing the citadel and Basilica of St John; walk past the basilica, down the hill, then turn right at the İsa Bey Camii. Quiet tent and caravan sites amid fruit orchards cost US$7. There are also some pension rooms with a few dorm beds for US$3 per person.

There are many pensions up the hill behind the Ephesus Museum. Good choices are *Barım Pansiyon* (☎ 892 6923, *Turgutreis Sokak 34*), the first street back from the museum, and *Australia & New Zealand Pension* (☎ 892 1050, *Profesör Mitler Sokak 17*), the second street back. Also worth seeking out are *Homeros Pension* (☎ 892 3995, *Asmalı Sokak 17*); and *Akgüneş Pension* (☎ 892 3869, *Turgutreis Sokak 14*), with private showers.

The most promising newcomer to the Selçuk pension scene is the five storey *All Blacks* (☎ 892 3657, *1011 Sokak 1*), overlooking an aqueduct with storks' nests and close to the train station. Another newcomer receiving good reports is *Artemis Guest House* (☎ 892 6191, *1012 Sokak 2*), also known as Jimmy's Place.

South of the centre are quiet neighbourhoods of modern apartment blocks. Some of them have been converted into small pensions. *Kiwi Pension* (☎ 891 4892, *Kubilay Caddesi 8*) has been recommended by readers.

For luxury, the best place is the atmospheric 50 room *Otel Kalehan* (☎ 892 6154), on the main road just north of the Shell station. Single/double/triples with showers, minifridges and air-con cost US$30/50/60. There's a pool as well.

Cengiz Topel Caddesi, a pedestrian street between the Cybele fountain at the highway and the town square by the train station, has several decent hotels with private bath for US$25 a double.

Places to Eat

Cengiz Topel Caddesi has many outdoor restaurants and cafes; *Özdamar Restaurant* and *Seçil*, facing the fountain, are perennially popular. The nearby *Hanımeli Restaurant* advertises vegetarian food. For cheap pide, try *Artemis Pide Salonu*, a half-block south of the tea garden at the eastern end of Cengiz Topel, where Turkish-style pizza goes for US$1.50 to US$2.50.

On the next block, *Firuze* and *Bizim* are a bit simpler, and may have slightly lower prices. Particularly popular is the *Tat* where a full meal with wine will cost around US$7.

Getting There & Away

Selçuk's otogar is across from the Tourism Information Office. Most services are local. Long-distance services usually start somewhere else (İzmir, Kuşadası, Bodrum) and pick up passengers on the way through.

Minibuses leave frequently for Kuşadası (US$0.90, 30 minutes) and the beach at Pamucak (US$0.75, 10 minutes), passing the Ephesus turn-off (US$0.50, five minutes). Taxis to Ephesus charge at least US$4; ask for the *güney kapısı* (southern gate) so you can walk downhill.

KUŞADASI

This cruise-ship port is a cheerfully shameless tourist trap. The main reason to visit is to catch a boat to the Greek island of Samos, although there are several attractions nearby and a raging nightlife.

Information

The tourist office (☎ 614 1103, fax 614 6295) is right beside the pier. The otogar is 1.5km south-east of the centre on the highway. Three lines sail to Samos (Sisam) daily in summer for US$30 (one way), US$35 (same-day round trip), or US$55 (open round trip); all have ticket offices near the tourist office.

Things to See

There's a 16th century **castle** (once used by pirates, now a nightclub) on an island in the harbour, and an old **caravanserai** (merchants' inn, now a hotel) in the old town. Kuşadası is a good base for visits to the ancient cities of **Priene**, **Miletus** and **Didyma** to the south (take a US$20 tour from the otogar). There are also good beaches and Dilek National Park at **Güzelçamlı**, 25 minutes to the south by dolmuş.

Places to Stay

The *Önder* and *Yat Mocamp* camp sites, north of town on the waterfront near the marina, charge US$8 for two people in a tent.

Most cheaper pensions have pleasant rooms, sometimes with sinks, sometimes with private bath. Expect to pay between US$16 and US$24 a double in the high season. There are several clusters of places to stay near the centre. To find them, when coming from the harbour walk up Barbaros Hayrettin Caddesi, turn right towards the Akdeniz Apart-otel, and take Yıldırım Caddesi, the road to the left of the Akdeniz, or Aslanlar Caddesi, the road to the right. These take you into the neighbourhood called Camiatik Mahallesi, which has lots of pensions and inexpensive hotels.

Walk up steep Yıldırım Caddesi to the *Düsseldorf Pansiyon* (☎ 613 1272), an excellent choice with spotless rooms for US$6 per person, plus another US$2 for breakfast arrayed in front of a secluded garden. Readers have also recommended *Cennet Pension* (☎ 614 4893), farther up the street, where bathless rooms cost US$5 per person.

Su Pansiyon (☎ 614 1453, *Aslanlar Caddesi 13*) is an old reliable option; *Pension Golden Bed* (☎ 614 8708), just off Aslanlar Caddesi (follow the signs), is quiet and family run, with a cafe terrace. Nicer than these is the 14 room *Park Pension* (☎ 614 3917, *Aslanlar Caddesi 17*), with simple rooms in a restored house set around a shady courtyard with orange trees.

Newly restored *Hotel Stella* (☎ 614 1632) costs more (US$55 a double) but boasts stunning harbour views.

To stay in the historic *Hotel Kervansaray* (☎ 614 4115) near the harbour costs US$50/80 for singles/doubles with breakfast; you're better off just enjoying a drink in the courtyard bar. Costing less (US$22/ 36) and providing more comfort, stay at a hotel (*Köken*, *Çidem* or *Akman*) on İstiklal Sokak, 1km north-east of the centre.

Places to Eat

Good seafood places along the waterfront close to the wharf charge US$15 to US$25 for a fish dinner, depending on the fish and the season. Cheaper meals (US$4.50 to US$6) are served on Sağlık Caddesi between Kahramanlar Caddesi and İnönü Bulvarı. Try the *Konyalı* at No 40.

The Kaleiçi district shelters several charming cafe-bars, a million miles better in atmosphere than the crass offerings of Barlar Sokak (Bar Lane).

Getting There & Away

Kuşadası's otogar is situated at the southern end of Kahramanlar Caddesi on the bypass highway. Direct buses depart for several far-flung parts of the country, or you can transfer at İzmir (US$2.50, every 30 minutes). There are frequent direct buses to Bodrum (US$6) and Denizli (for Pamukkale; US$7) in summer.

For Selçuk (US$1, 30 minutes) you need not bother going to the otogar; instead, pick up a minibus on Adnan Menderes Bulvarı.

PAMUKKALE

Three hours east of Selçuk, Pamukkale is renowned for the brilliant white ledges, or travertines, with pools that flow down over the plateau edge. Sadly, in recent years the water supply has started to dry up and you can no longer swim in the pools. Behind this natural wonder are the extensive ruins of the Roman city of **Hierapolis**, an ancient spa. There are tourist offices on the ridge at Pamukkale (☎ 272 1077, fax 272 2077), and in Denizli train station (☎ 261 3393), although neither is very helpful.

Things to See & Do

You pay admission (US$3) to the ridge as you climb the hill. Soak your bones in one of the many hotel **thermal baths**; one reader likened it to 'swimming in warm Perrier'. The most famous (and most expensive, at US$4 for two hours), complete with sunken Roman columns, is at Pamukkale Motel at the top of the ridge. Some pensions in town, at the bottom of the ridge, have baths too.

If time allows, on your way back to Selçuk or Kuşadası take a detour to **Aphrodisias** (Geyre), south of Nazilli near Karacasu, a beautiful ruined city thought by many to rival Ephesus.

Places to Stay

The bargain pensions and hotels (over 60 of them) are below the travertines in Pamukkale village – the farther from the highway, the cheaper they are. For cheerful service and decent rooms, good bargains are *Kervansaray Pension* (☎ 272 2209), where rooms cost US$12/18, and the nearby *Aspawa* (☎ 272 2094). Readers have also recommended *Weisse Burg Pension* (☎ 272 2064), where rooms cost US$12, breakfast US$2 and dinner US$5.

The inviting *Koray Motel* (☎ 272 2300), a few streets south, has a restaurant, bar and pool; doubles cost US$18, including breakfast.

Places to Eat

Taking meals in your pension or hotel is usually best here. Of the restaurants in the town, the *Gürsoy*, opposite the Yörük Motel in the village centre, has the nicest terrace, but the *Han*, around the corner facing the square, offers best value for money. Meals at either cost US$4 to US$6.

Getting There & Away

In summer, Pamukkale has a surprising number of direct buses to and from other cities. At other times of year it's best to assume you'll have to change in Denizli.

Municipal buses and dolmuşes make the half-hour trip between Denizli and Pamukkale every 30 minutes or so, more frequently on Saturday and Sunday, for US$1; the last bus runs at 10 pm in summer, probably around sunset in other seasons.

BODRUM

Bodrum (formerly Halicarnassus) is the site of the Mausoleum, the monumental tomb of King Mausolus, which is another of the Seven Wonders of the Ancient World.

Orientation & Information

The otogar is 500m inland along Cevat Şakir Caddesi from the Adliye (Yeni) Camii, a small mosque at the centre of the town. The PTT and several banks are on Cevat Şakir. The tourist office (☎ 316 1091, fax 316 7694) is beside the Castle of St Peter.

Things to See

There is now little left of the **mausoleum** (admission US$1.75; closed Monday). Placed between Bodrum's perfect twin bays is the Gothic **Castle of St Peter**, built in 1402 and rebuilt in 1522 by the Crusaders, using stones from the tomb. It's now the **Museum of Underwater Archaeology** and contains finds from the oldest Mediterranean shipwreck ever discovered. The museum is open from 8 am to noon and from 1 to 5 pm (closed Monday); admission is US$3.50, and another US$1 each to visit the ancient wreck and a model of a Carian princess' tomb.

West past the marina and over the hill, **Gümbet** has a nicer beach than Bodrum proper but is solid package-holiday territory. **Gümüşlük**, to the far west of the Bodrum peninsula, is the least spoilt of the many smaller villages nearby. Dolmuşes run there every hour (US$1).

Places to Stay

Some of the smaller villages on the peninsula such as Bitez Yalısı and Ortakent Yalısı have camp sites. There are more on the peninsula's northern shore.

The narrow streets north of Bodrum's western harbour have pleasant family-run pensions, which tend to be quieter than those on the eastern bay because they're farther from the Halikarnas Disco, famed as one of the loudest nightclubs around the Med. Pensions charge from US$18 to US$25 a double for rooms in high summer. Some rooms have

TURKEY

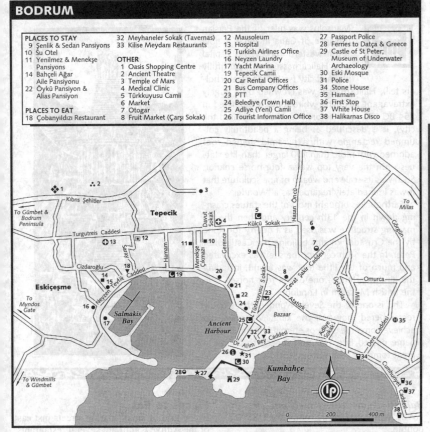

BODRUM

PLACES TO STAY
9 Şenlik & Sedan Pansiyons
10 Su Otel
11 Yenilmez & Menekşe
    Pansiyons
14 Bahçeli Ağar
    Aile Pansiyonu
22 Öykü Pansiyon &
    Alias Pansiyon

PLACES TO EAT
18 Çobanyıldızı Restaurant
32 Meyhaneler Sokak (Tavernas)
33 Kilise Meydanı Restaurants

OTHER
1 Oasis Shopping Centre
2 Ancient Theatre
3 Temple of Mars
4 Medical Clinic
5 Türkkuyusu Camii
6 Market
7 Otogar
8 Fruit Market (Çarşı Sokak)
12 Mausoleum
13 Hospital
15 Turkish Airlines Office
16 Neyzen Laundry
17 Yacht Marina
19 Tepecik Camii
20 Car Rental Offices
21 Bus Company Offices
23 PTT
24 Belediye (Town Hall)
25 Adliye (Yeni) Camii
26 Tourist Information Office
27 Passport Police
28 Ferries to Datça & Greece
29 Castle of St Peter;
    Museum of Underwater
    Archaeology
30 Eski Mosque
31 Police
34 Stone House
35 Hamam
36 First Stop
37 White House
38 Halikarnas Disco

private facilities, some include breakfast in the price. Off season, prices drop, and the breakfast, which costs extra in season, may be included in the price.

Türkkuyusu Sokak starts just north of the Adliye Camii and goes north past several good, cheap, convenient pensions, mostly with shady courtyards. Try *Şenlik Pansiyon* (☎ *316 6382*), at No 115, right on the street and charging US$12 a double. Behind it is the family-run *Sedan* (☎ *316 0355, Türkkuyusu Sokak 121*), where newer doubles with shower go for US$24; older doubles without water are US$16.

Two nearly identical quiet, modern places renting double rooms with showers for US$20 are on Menekşe Çıkmazı, a narrow alley which begins between Neyzen Tevfik 84 and 86: *Yenilmez* (☎ *316 2520*) at No 30, and *Menekşe* (☎ *316 5890*) at No 34. During the quieter months breakfast is included.

Set back from the seafront at the end of a passage beside the Turkish Airlines office is

The Mausoleum of Halicarnassus

Mausolus was ruler of the Persian province of Caria in what is now south-western Turkey; his capital was Halicarnassus. A beautifully planned city (so the classical scholars tell), Halicarnassus was crowned by a hugely extravagant gleaming white tomb. Completed in 354 BC (20 years before Alexander captured the city), it is described as being a beautifully columned rectangle with a pyramid-shaped roof adorned with more than 100 larger-than-life statues – on the very top was a four-horse chariot. Such was its scale and wealth of fine sculpture that it was immediately regarded as a 'Wonder'.

Earthquakes brought most of the statues crashing down in the 13th century and then the remaining structure was used as a quarry for stone by the Crusader knights building the Castle of St Peter. In the 19th century the site was excavated and much of the little that was found, including the hind quarters of one of the four horses, is in the British Museum in London.

This is one of the Seven Wonders that's rarely remembered; however the king, Mausolus, did achieve some measure of eternal fame in that his name passed into common speech to denote a great tomb, or 'mausoleum'.

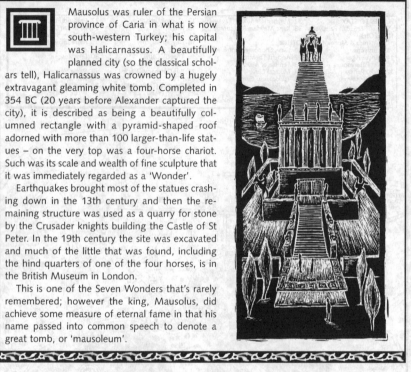

Bahçeli Ağar Aile Pansiyonu (☎ 316 1648), with quiet, basic rooms for US$20 a double.

Right on the seafront, the small *Öykü Pansiyon* (☎ 316 4604, Neyzen Tevfik Caddesi 200) has slightly cramped rooms but lovely views from its rooftop terrace. Beds cost US$10 including breakfast. *Alias Pansiyon* (☎ 316 3146) nearby has small, rather crowded cabins set around a pool. In high season expect to pay US$20 per person.

Best of all is *Su Otel* (☎ 316 6906, Turgutreis Caddesi, 1201 Sokak) – follow the signs – with a charming flower-filled courtyard, a swimming pool and rooms decorated with local crafts; singles/doubles with bath cost US$30/55 in summer.

Places to Eat

In the grid of small market streets just east of the Adliye Camii are several restaurants. *Babadan* and *Ziya'nin Yeri* are patronised by locals as well as foreigners and serve plates of döner for about US$3, beer for US$1.50. For very cheap eats, buy a *dönerli sandviç* (sandwich with roast lamb) for less than US$2 at a streetside *büfe* (buffet).

For cheaper fare, continue eastward to a little plaza filled with open-air restaurants serving pide and kebap. *Nazilli* is the favourite here, but *Karadeniz* is almost as good. A pide topped with meat or cheese costs only US$3 or so.

In warm weather, check out Meyhaneler Sokak (Taverna St), off İskele Caddesi. Wall-

In warm weather, check out Meyhaneler Sokak (Taverna St), off İskele Caddesi. Wall-to-wall *tavernas* serve food and drink to happy crowds nightly for US$12 to US$18.

Of all the upmarket places, *Çobanyıldız* (☎ 316 7060) on the western bay is the best, with meals for around US$15 per person. Alternatively, head for the fish restaurants lining the eastern side of the harbour – but be sure to check all the prices before ordering.

Getting There & Away

The new Bodrum international airport (☎ 523 0129) is actually nearer to Milas. Havaş buses meet arrivals and charge US$4 to take you to Bodrum. The taxi fare is US$30 (or US$14 to Milas).

Bodrum offers fast and frequent bus services to Antalya (US$12, 11 hours), Fethiye (US$6, 4½ hours), İstanbul (US$24, 14 hours), İzmir (US$10, four hours), Kuşadası and Selçuk (US$5, three hours), Marmaris (US$8, three hours) and Pamukkale (US$6, five hours).

Hydrofoils and boats go to Kos (İstanköy) frequently in summer for US$20 one way, US$25 return. In summer there are also boats to Datça, Didyma, Knidos, Marmaris and Rhodes (Rhodos); check with the ferry offices near the castle.

TURKEY

The Colossus of Rhodes

No trace has ever been discovered of the Colossus of Rhodes, which is perhaps why it remains one of the Seven Wonders most shrouded in myth. Medieval etchings portray the giant statue standing with its legs bridging the harbour entrance, tall enough for ships to pass under, but such an engineering feat would have been impossible at that time. In fact, earlier Classical accounts make no mention of the Colossus spanning the harbour entrance. What they do say is that the giant figure stood 110 feet tall (by way of comparison, the Statue of Liberty is about 150 feet high) and, according to Roman encyclopedist Pliny, it was built between 292 and 280 BC, collapsing 56 years later in an earthquake.

Most likely the Colossus was situated on the tip of the mole dividing the island's two harbours where the small, round fortress of St Nicholas stands today. The statue was dedicated to the sun god Helios but what it really looked like nobody can say, as no contemporary images or accurate descriptions exist. One theory, though, is that the Colossus was cast in the likeness of Alexander the Great, who had died half a century before.

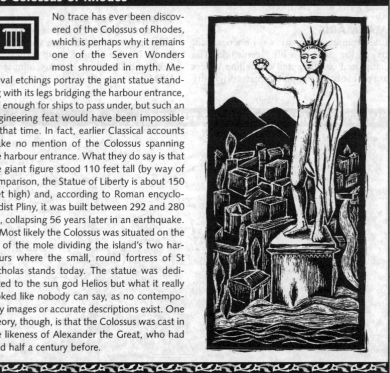

The Mediterranean Coast

Turkey's Mediterranean coastline winds eastward for more than 1200km from Marmaris to Antakya on the Syrian border. East of Marmaris the 'Turquoise Coast' is perfect for boat excursions, with many secluded coves and quiet bays all the way to Fethiye. The rugged peninsula east of Fethiye to Antalya – immortalised by Homer as 'Lycia' – and the Taurus Mountains east of Antalya are wild and beautiful. Farther east you pass through fewer seaside resorts and more workaday cities. The entire coast is liberally sprinkled with impressive ruins, studded with beautiful beaches and washed by pellucid water ideal for sports.

MARMARİS
Like Bodrum, Marmaris sits on a beautiful bay at the edge of a hilly peninsula. The sculptured coastline and crystalline waters are probably the reason Marmaris originally became Turkey's premier yachting port although these days careless overdevelopment has robbed it of most of its charm. The Greek island of Rhodes (Rodos) is a short trip south.

Orientation & Information
İskele Meydanı (main square) and the tourist office (☎ 412 1035) are by the ferry pier north-east of the castle and near the waterfront. The centre is mostly a pedestrian precinct, and new development stretches many kilometres to the south-east.

The new otogar is north of town, off the road to Bodrum. Hacı Mustafa Sokak, also known as Bar St, runs inland from the bazaar; action here keeps going until the early hours of the morning.

The PTT is on Fevzipaşa Caddesi.

Things to See & Do
The small **castle** has a few unexciting exhibition rooms but offers fine views of Marmaris. It's open from 8 am to noon and 1 to 5.30 pm daily except Monday; admission is US$1.

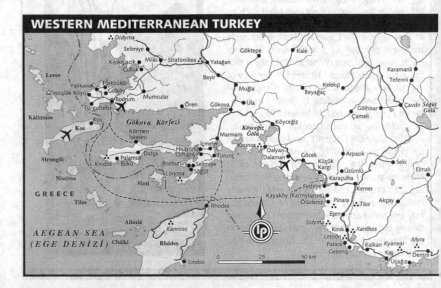

WESTERN MEDITERRANEAN TURKEY

Numerous boats along the waterfront offer day tours of the harbour, its beaches and islands. Summer departures are usually at 9 am. Before deciding on your boat, talk to the captain about where the excursion goes, what it costs, whether lunch is included and, if so, what's on the menu. A day's outing usually costs around US$16 to US$20 per person, much less in off season, when boats also leave later in the day.

The most popular daily excursions are to **Dalyan** and **Kaunos** or to the bays around Marmaris but you can also take longer, more serious boat trips to Datça and Knidos.

Datça, two hours out on the Reşadiye peninsula, has now been 'discovered' but is still a great place to visit; less developed is **Bozburun**, not as far west. At the tip of the peninsula are the ruins of the ancient port of **Knidos**, accessible by road or excursion boat.

Places to Stay

Although Marmaris has several hundred hotels and pensions, the cheaper places are being squeezed out by the relentless rise in the number of hotels serving package holi-

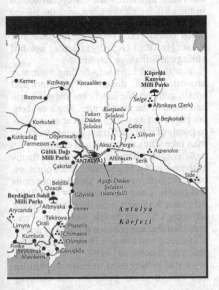

daymakers. The cheapies that remain may be fairly central but often they're noisy. There are several moderately priced hotels a short walk from İskele Meydanı. Most of the really expensive hotels are well around the bay from the town, some as far out as İçmeler.

Ask at the tourist office about the few remaining *ev pansiyonları* (home pensions), renting double rooms for US$8 to US$12. Otherwise, for the cheapest accommodation, go to the district called Kemeraltı Mahallesi. Walk along the waterfront to Abdi İpekçi Park. Turn inland just past the park and left at the first street, then right and past Ayçe Otel. Cross a footbridge for *Maltepe Pension* (☎ 412 1629), with beds for US$10 per person in a room with private shower. The bigger *Özcan Pension* (☎ 412 7761, Çam Sokak 3) next door charges similar prices.

Marmaris has two Interyouth hostels, neither of which require hostel cards. Walk inland from the Maltepe, cross the road and look for *Interyouth Hostel (1)* (☎ 412 6432, İyiliktaş Mevkii 14), offering beds in dormitory rooms for US$6, a roof-terrace bar, laundry, restaurant, baggage storage room and free hot showers. There are also bathless 'pension' rooms for US$13 a double. The other *Interyouth Hostel (2)* (☎ 412 3687, Tepe Mahallesi, 42 Sokak 45) is deep in the bazaar right at the town centre. Prices and services are similar.

Pension Yılmaz (☎ 412 3754, 107 Sokak) is inland from the park just east of the Turkish Airlines office (124 Sokak goes alongside the park). This close to the centre and charging just US$15 a double, it's a real find.

For lodgings and camping on the beach, take a 'Siteler-Turban' minibus along the waterfront road to the last stop at *Turban Marmaris Tatil Köyü* holiday village, 4km south-west of the main square. Besides *Berk Camping*, with tent sites for US$6 and cabins for US$18, there are several small pension-like hotels renting double rooms for around US$25: *Birol, Yüzbaşı, Sembol, Villa Erel* and *Tümer*.

Hotel Begonya (☎ 412 4095, Hacı Mustafa Sokak 71) is a delightful place, with a courtyard filled with plants, but there are

TURKEY

heaps of bars along this street – good news if you're in for a big night. If sleep's more important, look elsewhere.

Places to Eat

There are concentrations of restaurants all along the harbour, along Kordon Caddesi and out along the shore to Uzunyalı, with more places to eat in the bazaar and along Hacı Mustafa Sokak.

For the cheapest fare, explore the bazaar and the streets beyond it looking for 'un-touristy' local Turkish places selling pide, ke-baps and fast food. Head for the PTT on 51 Sokak in the bazaar. Just inland from it are several good, cheap restaurants including *Sofra*, *Marmaris Restaurant* and *Liman Restaurant* off 51 Sokak at 40 Sokak 32. Any of these places will serve you lunch or dinner for US$4 to US$7. Farther inland, *Yıldız Restaurant* is less crowded and cheaper.

Walk inland from the Atatürk statue along Ulusal Egemenlik Bulvarı and turn right opposite the big Tansaş shopping cen-tre to find *Kırçiçeği Pide Pizza Çorba Kebap ve Tandır Salonu*. It's always crowded with locals; a bowl of soup and a baked pide need cost no more than US$3.

The *waterfront restaurants* south and east of the tourist office have pleasant out-door dining areas but prices are higher than those inland and the extra pays for the set-ting rather than the quality of the food. As-sume you'll spend between US$10 and US$20 per person for a full meal with wine.

If the crowds prove unpleasant, follow the signs up to *Kartal Restaurant & Ter-race Bar* (☎ 412 3308, Eski Cami Sokak). You'll pass a number of small restaurants with fine views of the town, quiet dining rooms and terraces and moderate prices. A three course meal with drinks will cost US$12 to US$18.

Getting There & Away

The nearest airports to Marmaris are at Bo-drum and Dalaman.

Marmaris otogar, north of town off the Bodrum road, has frequent direct buses and minibuses to all places in the region, includ-ing Antalya (US$11, seven hours), Bodrum (US$7, three hours), Dalyan (via Ortaca; US$4, two hours), Datça (US$3.50, 1½ hours), and Fethiye (US$5, three hours). Bozburun minibuses run at least once a day (US$3, 1½ hours). Car ferries run to Rhodes daily in summer (less frequently in the off season) for US$45 one way or US$75 return (plus US$13 port tax at Rhodes and US$10 to re-enter Turkey).

MARMARİS TO FETHİYE

East of Marmaris is Dalaman, which has an international airport. A few scheduled flights supplement the holiday charters. Although there are hotels and pensions in all prices, you'd do better to head straight out; buses run to all points along the coast and beyond.

The most obvious destination is Dalyan. Set in lush river-delta farming country, nearby Dalyan has it all: fertile soil, a placid river meandering by, excellent fishing and, to the south at İztuzu, beautiful **beaches** that are the natural nesting ground of the *car-retta carretta*, or sea turtle.

As if that were not enough, Dalyan also has ruins: dramatic rock-cut **Lycian tombs** in the cliff facing the town, and the ruined city of **Kaunos** within easy boat-excursion reach downriver. Upriver on the shores of Köyceğiz Gölü (Köyceğiz Lake) are **hot springs** at Sultaniye Kaplıcaları.

You'll need little help finding your way around Dalyan; dozens of pensions and small, comfortable hotels are ranged north and south of the town centre. The local boat cooperative fixes rates for river excursions to points of interest. To get there from Dala-man take a bus to Ortaca and change.

Köyceğiz, 75km east of Marmaris, stands at the edge of a placid lake. It's a pleasant, peaceful farming town with a few pensions and hotels; *Tango Pansiyon* (☎ 262 2501, Ali Ihsan Kalmaz Caddesi) is a new place charging US$24 a double with shower and breakfast that has come in for a lot of praise.

Heading east towards Fethiye from Dala-man you'll come to Göcek, a small fishing town still getting used to tourism. With an odd mix of cheap pensions and camping grounds for backpackers, and white-table-cloth restaurants for sailing enthusiasts, Göcek is pleasant and laid-back, even though it lacks good beaches.

FETHİYE & ÖLÜDENİZ
Fethiye has superb beaches and cheap lodgings, crowded in summer but well worth a visit. This is the site of ancient Telmessos, with giant Lycian stone sarcophagi from about 400 BC littered about and the rock-cut Tomb of Amyntas looming from a cliff above the town.

Orientation & Information
Fethiye's otogar is 2km east of the centre. As you come into town you pass near the government buildings, the PTT and the museum, skirt the market district on the left, then curve round the bay past the tourist office (☎/fax 614 1527) next to the Dedeoğlu Otel, and then by the yacht marina on the western side of the town.

Things to See & Do
The Tomb of Amyntas is open from 8 am to 7 pm; admission is US$1. Dolmuşes run to the nearby Ottoman Greek 'ghost town' of Kayaköy. The beach at Calış, 5km northeast of the centre, is many kilometres long, and backed by hotels and pensions.

To the south, 17km over the mountains, is the gorgeous lagoon of Ölüdeniz ('Dead Sea'), too beautiful for its own good and now one of the most famous beach spots on the Mediterranean. Inland from the beach are moderately priced bungalows and camping areas, as well as some hotels.

If you stay in Fethiye, be sure to take the '12 Island Tour' boat excursion. With its swimming, cruising and sightseeing, it may be your most pleasant day in Fethiye. Prices start at around US$8 per person. Don't miss the Turkish bath in the bazaar either. It's open from 7 am to midnight and the full treatment costs about US$10.

Places to Stay
There's a cluster of pensions near the stadium just west of the otogar. To find it, walk straight down the road heading north from the minibus station. Typically, *Göreme Pansiyon* (☎ 614 6944, Dolgu Sahası, Stadyum Yanı 25) has spotless singles/doubles for US$10/16.

In the town centre *Ülgen Pansiyon* (☎ 614 3491) up a flight of steps off Çarşı Caddesi, has a warren of assorted, ramshackle rooms. Plumbing arrangements and the number of beds differ from room to room, but the standard rate is US$5 per person, with breakfast costing US$2 extra.

Other pensions are uphill from the yacht marina along Fevzi Çakmak Caddesi. *Yıldırım* (☎ 614 3913), *Pınara* (☎ 614 2151), *Derelioğlu* (☎ 614 5983) and *İrem* (☎ 614 3985) all charge around US$16/30 for singles/doubles.

İdeal Pension (☎ 614 1981, Zafer Caddesi 1) has superb views from its terrace but is a bit more expensive. Even farther uphill, *İnci Pansiyon* (☎ 614 3325) has marvellous views and is blissfully quiet, with similar prices. On the left, follow signs to *Pension Savaşçı* (☎ 614 6681), which charges US$15/24 for rooms with spectacular harbour views.

Places to Eat
On Çarşı Caddesi a block off Atatürk Caddesi, *Özlem Pide ve Kebap Salonu* will serve you köfte, salad, and soda for less than US$4. A bit farther south on Çarşı Caddesi are *Pizza Pepino* and *Pizza Villa*; Pepino serves tasty pizzas under a shady vine for reasonable prices; a good vegetarian pizza costs US$6.

Directly across Çarşı Caddesi from the Özlem on Tütün Sokak is *Sedir Lokantası & Kebap House*, a local favourite serving pizzas for US$2 to US$3.50 and meat for US$4 to US$5. In Eski Cami Geçidi Likya Sokak look out for the very popular *Meğri* with a wide range of piping hot meals. There's another branch in the bazaar.

The market district is packed with open-air restaurants, where you should watch out for bill fiddling. *Güneş Restaurant* has indoor dining rooms as well as open-air cafe dining in fine weather. There's a good range of meat and fish dishes and cold starters here and prices aren't bad either (chicken kebap for US$5), but service can be slow.

Getting There & Away

If you're going nonstop to Antalya, note that the *yayla* (inland) route is far shorter and cheaper (US$6) than the *sahil* (coastal) route (US$8).

Buses from the otogar also serve Kalkan (US$3.25) and Kaş (US$3.50). Minibuses depart from their own terminal, 1km west of the otogar towards the centre, on short hops to other points along the coast, like Patara (US$3.25), Kınık (for Xanthos; US$2.25) and Ölüdeniz (US$1).

In high summer a hydrofoil service operates between Rhodes (Greece) and Fethiye on Tuesday and Thursday. A one-way ticket costs US$50, a same-day round trip US$75 and an open return US$95.

RUINS NEAR FETHİYE

Lycia was heavily populated in ancient times, as shown by the large number of wonderful old cities, reached by minibus from Fethiye. **Tlos** is far up into the mountains near Kemer on the yayla route to Antalya. **Pınara**, 46km east of Fethiye then 6km south, right off the road, is also a mountainous site.

Letoön, 63km east of Fethiye, a few kilometres off the highway in a fertile valley filled with tomato greenhouses, has excellent mosaics, a good theatre and a pool sacred as the place of worship of the goddess Leto.

Xanthos, a few kilometres south-east of Letoön above the village of Kınık, is among the most impressive sites along this part of the coast, with its Roman theatre and Lycian pillar tombs. At **Patara**, 7km farther south (turn at Ovaköy), the attraction is not so much the ruins as the incredible 20km beach. Lodgings in Patara village, 2.5km inland from the beach, range from camping to cheap pensions and hotels to the three-star *Otel Beyhan Patara* (☎ 844 5098).

KALKAN

Kalkan, everybody's idea of what a small Turkish fishing village should be, is 11km east of the Patara turn-off. It tumbles down a steep hillside to a yacht marina (in ancient times, the port).

Kalkan's old stone and wood houses have been restored as lodgings – some expensive, some moderate, some still fairly cheap. The streets above the marina are lined with atmospheric open-air restaurants. There are no good beaches, but excursion boat tours (or minibuses) can take you to Patara Beach and secluded coves along the coast. More information on things to do is available from www.kalkan.org.tr.

Places to Stay

If you decide to stay, look for cheap pensions (US$12/18 a single/double) at the top of the town.

On the main shopping street *Özalp Pansiyon* (☎ 844 3486) is good, as is the simple *Çelik Pansiyon* (☎ 844 212, *Yalıboyu 9*). *Holiday Pension* and, up the hill across from it, *Gül Pansiyon*, are both more basic and slightly cheaper.

Near the harbour, *Akın Pansiyon* (☎ 844 3025) has some waterless rooms for US$17 a double; rooms lower down with private showers cost US$22, breakfast included. *Akgül* (☎ 844 3270) around the corner is similar. *Çetin Pansiyon* (☎ 844 3094) is quieter, at US$16 a double.

Pricier but very atmospheric is *Balıkçı Han* (☎ 844 3075), designed to look like an older building, with stone fireplaces and red-tiled floors. Rooms with private shower cost US$34 a double, breakfast included.

On the road winding down past the mosque to the harbour is nicely decorated *Daphne Pansiyon* (☎ 844 3547, *Hasan Altan Caddesi*), where you pay US$16/30 for singles/doubles including breakfast on a pleasant roof terrace.

Almost hidden beneath its veil of bougainvillea is *Patara Pansiyon* (☎ 844 3076), a lovely stone house with views. Rooms cost US$16/24 with breakfast.

KAŞ

Called Antiphellus in ancient times, Kaş has a picturesque quayside square, friendly people and a big **market** on Sunday. It's a fine, laid-back place to spend some time. The tourist office (☎ 836 1238, fax 836 1368) is on the square.

Things to See & Do

Apart from enjoying the town's ambience and a few small pebble beaches, you can walk west a few hundred metres to the well-preserved **theatre**. Lycian stone **sarcophagi** are dotted about the streets, and tombs are cut into the cliffs above the town.

A popular boat excursion is to **Kekova** and **Üçağız**, about two hours away, where there are several interesting ruins. The cost is from US$10 to US$14 per person.

You can also visit **Meis Adası** (Kastellorizo), the Greek island just off the coast. The fare is likely to be about US$26.

Other excursions go to the **Mavi Mağara** (Blue Cave), Patara and Kalkan. There are also overland excursions to the 18km **Saklıkent Gorge** and villages farther inland.

Places to Stay

Kaş has everything from camp sites to cheap pensions and three-star hotels. *Kaş Camping* (☎ 836 1050), in an olive grove 1km west of town past the theatre, also has simple bungalows.

At the otogar you'll be accosted by pension-pushers. Yenicami Caddesi (or Recep Bilgin Caddesi), just south of the otogar, has lots of places, including *Orion Hotel* (☎ 836 1286), with tidy rooms and sea views for US$13/22 for singles/doubles, breakfast included. Farther along the street, or just off it, are *Anıl Motel* (☎ 836 1791), *Hilal* (☎ 836 1207) and the *Melisa* (☎ 836 1068). At the southern end of the street by the mosque is *Ay Pansiyon* (☎ 836 1562), where the front rooms have sea views.

Turn right at Ay Pansiyon and follow the signs to the quieter *Kale Pansiyon* (☎ 836 1094), right by the theatre ruins. Up the hill behind it is the slightly pricier *Korsan Karakedi Motel* (☎ 836 1887) with a lovely roof bar. Rooms cost US$15/23.

On the other (eastern) side of town many more pensions offer similar but noisier ac-

commodation. Try *Koşk* (☎ 836 1017), behind the Sun Cafe and with fine sea views.

For more comforts and services, head east for *Hotel Kayahan* (☎ 836 1313) above Küçük Çakıl Plaji, where rooms with wonderful sea views cost US$28/34; or the three star *Hotel Club Phellos* (☎ 836 1953), the fanciest place in town, with a swimming pool and comfortable rooms for US$40/60, including breakfast.

Places to Eat

On the main square, *Noel Baba* is a favourite cafe-restaurant for breakfast and light meals from US$1.50 to US$4. *Corner Cafe*, at the PTT end of İbrahim Serin Caddesi, serves juices or a vegetable omelette for US$1, yoghurt with fruit and honey for US$1.75. *Cafe Merhaba* across the street is good for cakes and western newspapers.

Eriş, behind the tourist office, is a favourite, as much for its setting as its food; expect to pay US$6 to US$12. *Mercan Restaurant* is the town's best place to dine because of its longstanding service, waterfront location and seafood. A fish dinner with mezes and wine can cost from US$12 to US$18 per person.

South of the mosque, the tiny *Asma Cafe* receives the local seal of approval for its salad lunches and pleasant ambience. Beyond it (head out towards the quay and turn right) is a row of restaurants that are great for breakfast or a sunset drink. *Elit Bar*, at the western end, has a concrete sun deck and unobstructed view of Kastellorizo.

KAŞ TO ANTALYA

Hugging the coast and backed by pine-clad mountains, the main road goes east from Kaş, then north to Antalya, passing the ruins of a dozen ancient cities.

Demre (Kale)

Demre (ancient Myra, also known as Kale), set in a rich alluvial plain covered in greenhouses, is interesting because of its generous 4th century bishop who, according to legend, gave anonymous gifts to dowryless girls, thus enabling them to marry. He was later canonised as St Nicholas, the original Father Christmas or Santa Claus (Noel Baba in Turkish). For US$4 you can visit the restored 12th century **Church of St Nicholas** built to hold his tomb. About 2km inland from the church at Demre is a rock face honeycombed with ancient **tombs**, right next to a large **Roman theatre**. Both are open from 8 am to 5.30 pm daily; admission is US$2.75.

Most people don't stay overnight here, but if you do *Hotel Şahin (☎ 871 5686, Müze Caddesi)* is on the way to the Church of St Nicholas. Singles/doubles with private bath and breakfast cost US$14/20.

East of the main square on PTT Caddesi, *Hotel Simge (☎ 871 4511)* is probably OK for US$10/16 a single/double. Farther along the street, the two star *Grand Hotel Kekova (☎ 871 3462)* is Demre's quietest and best value for money, charging US$14/25.

About 300m south of the Myra ruins, *Kent Aile Pansiyon (☎ 871 2042)* has pleasant gardens and low prices (US$6/10).

Şehir and *Çınar* restaurants near the main square provide basic sustenance. In the high season, better fare is offered 5km west at **Çayağzı**, the ancient Andriake, Demre's harbour, where the beach, the views and the food are fine.

Olimpos

After climbing into the mountains, you reach a turn-off marked for Olimpos. From here it's just over 8km down a winding unpaved road to the village, and a farther 3.5km along an ever-worsening road to the site of ancient Olimpos. A wild, abandoned place, the Olimpos ruins peek out from forest copses, rock outcrops and river banks – perfect for the rough camper. There are a few small restaurants and the beach is magnificent, although pebbly.

Along the road leading to the Olimpos ruins are several restaurants that allow camping as well. *Kadir's (☎ 892 1250)* offers treehouses amid rustic ramshackle charm but with Internet connections too. Kadir charges US$7 per person for a bed in a treehouse (communal showers and toilets)

or US$10 for a more conventional room, breakfast and dinner included. Nearby *Olimpos, Olimpos Şerif, Türkmen, Çamlık, Orange* are similar places.

Çavuşköy/Adrasan, on the next cove to the east, has another half a dozen simple hotels and pensions.

Chimaera

According to legend, the Chimaera (Yanartaş), a natural eternal flame, was the hot breath of a subterranean monster. Easily sighted by mariners in ancient times, it is today a mere glimmer of its former flamy self but no less inspiring for all that.

Turn off the highway less than 1km east of the eastern Olimpos turn-off; the road is marked for Çıralı, 7km towards the sea. The standard price for a pension double room with private bath and breakfast here is US$24. The best places are down by the beach. Walking along the beach towards the Olimpos ruins you'll come to the delightful *Olympos Lodge (☎ 825 7171)*, set among citrus orchards and well-tended gardens near the beach. Everything is well maintained, and the price, at US$63/85 for singles/doubles, justifies a splurge.

To get to the Chimaera, follow the signs for 3km east down a neighbouring valley. A half-hour climb along a good path leads to the flames.

Phaselis

About 2km from the highway, Phaselis is a collection of ruins framing three small, perfect bays, a good place for a swim. The ruins are open from 7.30 am to 7 pm daily; admission is US$2.75.

Kemer

Built to the specifications of resort planners and architects, Kemer was custom-made for the package holiday traveller. Its white buildings and straight streets seem sterile, but there's a nice little beach by the marina and, above it, a **Yörük Park** (Nomad Park), with exhibits showing aspects of traditional life from the region. The place to stay here is *King's Garden Pension (☎ 814 1039)*, on the northern side of town, 400m north-east of the minibus station. Simple rooms cost US$40 for two with all meals, or you can camp.

ANTALYA

The main town of the coast, Antalya has one of the most attractive harbour settings in the Mediterranean. It's fun to kick around in Kaleiçi, the old restored Ottoman town by the Roman harbour – now the yacht marina. The bazaar is interesting and the archaeological museum outstanding. The beaches are out of town, to the west (Konyaaltı Plajı, a pebble beach) and the east (Lara Plajı, a sand beach).

Orientation & Information

The main otogar is 4km north of the centre on the D 650 highway to Burdur. The city centre is at Kalekapısı, a major intersection right next to Cumhuriyet Meydanı, with its dramatic equestrian statue of Atatürk. Kaleiçi, the old town, is south of Kalekapısı down the hill.

The *doğu garaj* (eastern otogar) is 600m east (left) of Kalekapısı along Ali Çetinkaya Caddesi. Atatürk Caddesi, 100m east of Kalekapısı, goes south past Hadriaynüs Kapısı (Hadrian's Gate).

The tourist office (☎/fax 241 1747) can be found at Cumhuriyet Caddesi 91. It's 600m west of Kalekapısı on the right-hand side in the Özel İdare Çarşısı building, after the police headquarters but before the pedestrian bridge over the roadway – look for 'Antalya Devlet Tiyatrosu' emblazoned on it. The Turkish Airlines office (☎ 243 4383) is situated in the same building. The PTT is around the corner on Güllük (Burdur) Caddesi.

Things to See

Behind the clock tower is Antalya's symbol, the Yivli Minare (Grooved Minaret), which rises above an old mosque turned art gallery.

From Kalekapısı, head east 100m along Ali Çetinkaya Caddesi to Atatürk Caddesi, then south to the Hadriaynüs Kapısı (Had-

rian's Gate), a monumental gate built for the Roman emperor's visit in 130 AD. A bit farther along is Karaali Park, perched on cliffs above the sea.

In Kaleiçi, the Kesik Minare (truncated minaret) marks a ruined Roman temple.

Cumhuriyet Caddesi leads west to the excellent Antalya Museum, 2km from Kalekapısı. It's open from 9 am to 6 pm Tuesday to Sunday, and the admission fee is US$3.50. Past the Sheraton and Falez hotels along Cumhuriyet Caddesi is Konyaaltı Beach.

Places to Stay

Parlar Mocamp, 14km north on the Burdur highway (D 650), has unshaded tent and campervan sites. *Camping Bambus*, on the road to Lara Plajı, has modern facilities on the beach.

Kaleiçi is full of pensions, most of them clearly signed. *Erkal Pansiyon* (☎ 241 0757, Kandiller Geçidi 5) rents fine double rooms with fan or air-con for US$14 to US$22.

Excellent value for money and a safe haven for women travellers is *Senem Family Pension* (☎ 247 1752, Kılınçaslan Mahallesi, Zeytin Geçidi Sokak 9), near the Hıdırlık Kulesi. Clean, simple rooms cost US$15 to US$18. The neighbouring *Keskin Pansiyon* (☎ 241 2865) is two converted houses with equally low rates but much lower standards.

The unrestored *Adler Pension* (☎ 241 7818, Civelek Sokak 16) is among the cheapest pensions in the neighbourhood at US$9/15 for singles/doubles with shared baths. *Erken Pansiyon* (☎ 247 6092, Hıdırlık Sokak 5) is a well-preserved Ottoman house charging US$18 a double.

Hadriyanüs Pansiyon (☎ 244 0030, Kılınçarslan Mahallesi, Zeytin Çıkmazı 4/A-B) is a series of old, mostly unrestored buildings around a refreshingly large walled garden. The owners are friendly and charge US$14/20.

For a bit more money Kaleiçi has many other beautiful pensions and hotels, including the prettily decorated *Atelya Pension*

(☎ 241 6416, Civelek Sokak 21), where doubles cost US$30 including breakfast.

Pricier but worth it is the spotless *Hotel Frankfurt* (☎/fax 247 6224, Hıdırlık Sokak 17), excellent value at US$25/35 in high summer.

Places to Eat

Many pensions serve good meals at decent prices. Otherwise Eski Sebzeciler İçi Sokak, a short street just south-west of the junction of Cumhuriyet and Atatürk caddesis, is filled with **open-air restaurants** where a kebap, salad and drink can cost as little as US$5. The speciality is Antalya's own *tandır kebap* (mutton cooked in an earthenware pot).

For grills, you can't beat *Parlak Restaurant*, a block up Kazım Özalp/Şarampol Caddesi on the left. Skewered chicken and lamb kebaps sizzle as patrons drink rakı and beer. A full meal of meze, grills and drinks costs from US$8 to US$16 a person.

For unobstructed sunset views of the bay and Beydağları mountains *Mermerli Restaurant* perched above the eastern end of the harbour, can't be beaten. The bonus is lower prices than at most harbour restaurants: full meals for US$8 to US$12.

Getting There & Away

Turkish Airlines has daily nonstop flights from Antalya to Ankara and İstanbul, and weekly nonstop flights to Amman, Lefkoşa (Nicosia), London, Tel Aviv and Zürich. İstanbul Airlines also has frequent flights to İstanbul. The airport is 10km east of the city centre; the airport bus costs US$2, a taxi about US$10, or take any eastbound minibus and walk the final 2km.

Beach buses leave from the Doğu Garaj on Ali Çetinkaya Caddesi – the Konyaaltı minibus goes west, the Lara minibus east. You can get to the local ruins from here too: take an 'Aksu' dolmuş for Perge, and 'Manavgat' for Side.

From the otogar, buses go to Alanya (US$4, two hours), Göreme (US$12, 10 hours), Konya (US$12, six hours), Olimpos (US$2.50, 1½ hours), Side (US$2, 1½ hours) and other towns.

AROUND ANTALYA

This stretch of coast has plenty more spectacular Greek and Roman ruins. **Perge**, east of Antalya just north of Aksu, boasts a 12,000 seat stadium and a theatre for 15,000. **Aspendos**, 47km east of Antalya, has Turkey's best preserved ancient ruins, dating from the 2nd century AD; it is still used for performances during the Antalya Festival in September. **Termessos**, high in the mountains off the Korkuteli road, to the west of Antalya, has a spectacular setting but demands some vigorous walking and climbing to see it all.

SİDE

Once an idyllic seaside village, Side ('SEE-deh') has been overrun by tourists, and by carpet and leather shops. It is now a tawdry, overcrowded caricature of its former self unless you visit out of season. Impressive ancient structures include a **Roman bath** (now a small museum, open from 8 am to noon and 1 to 5 pm daily; admission is US$2.50), the old **city walls**, a huge **amphitheatre** (closed for restoration at the time of writing) and seaside marble **temples** to Apollo and Athena. Its excellent beaches are packed in summer.

The village is 3km south of the highway at Manavgat; minibuses (US$0.30) run between the two. To and from Antalya and Alanya you'll find more connections at Manavgat.

The tourist office (☎ 753 1265, fax 753 2657) is on the road into town, an inconvenient 1.5km from the centre.

The village itself is packed with pensions and hotels, all of which fill up in summer. Inland, *Pettino's Pension* (☎ 753 3608) offers rooms in a cheerfully decorated house for US$10 per person. More pensions can be found just off Liman Caddesi on the right-hand side as you walk towards the waterfront. Promising is *Yaşa Motel* (☎ 753 4024, Turgut Reis Caddesi), where beds can cost as little as US$6 each.

Continue down Turgut Reis Caddesi for *Hanımeli Pansiyon* (☎/fax 753 1789), a beautifully restored stone house, reasonably priced at US$24 a double.

ALANYA

Dominated by the ruins of a magnificent Seljuk fortress perched high on a promontory, Alanya is second only to Antalya as a Turkish Mediterranean resort. Once a pretty, easy-going place, it has grown in recent years into a bustling, noisy city where it's hard to find a reasonably priced bed, especially in summer, even though the good beaches to the east and west are lined with hotels.

The bus station is 3km west of the centre; to get to town take a dolmuş or a municipal bus (marked 'ALSO') and get off at the roundabout by the little mosque. Downhill towards the big mosque is the old waterfront area with trendy shops and good food; uphill (south) above the harbour are the few remaining cheap hotels. The tourist office (☎/fax 513 1240) is on the western side of the promontory.

Things to See & Do

If you stop here, visit the Seljuk Kızıl Kule (Red Tower, built in 1226), down by the harbour. It's open from 8 am to noon and 1.30 to 5.30 pm daily except Monday; admission is US$2.50. Also worth seeing is the kale (fortress, also built in 1226) atop the promontory. It's open from 8 am to 7 pm daily; admission is US$2.50. Hire a boat (US$5.50 to US$8) for an excursion to caves beneath the promontory.

Places to Stay

Camping is available at the Forestry Department site of İncekum, 19km west of town. Sadly, cheap accommodation has virtually disappeared as pensions give way to self-catering flats for package holidaymakers.

There are a couple of places left on noise-ridden İskele Caddesi, above the harbour. The first is *Baba Hotel* (☎ 513 1032, İskele Caddesi 6), where mundane singles/doubles cost US$6/12 without shower. *Alanya Palas* (☎ 513 1016) next door is similar.

More expensive but infinitely preferable is *Hotel Temiz* (☎ 513 1016, İskele Caddesi 12), a few steps farther along towards the Red Tower. Comfortable singles/doubles with showers cost US$12/18.

A little farther along and upstairs on the right is *Yili Hotel* (☎ 513 1017), offering the most basic of waterless rooms for US$6 per person.

At the southern end of Bostancı Caddesi near the big mosque, the Kuyularönü Camii, is *Çınar Otel* (☎ 512 0063), where faded rooms are US$8/11 with shower.

Places to Eat

The best cheap food area is between the first two waterfront streets, near the Kuyularönü Camii, where the alleys are filled with tables and chairs. Most places here will serve you a big döner kebap, salad and beer for US$4. *Yönet* and *Mahperi* along the waterfront promenade are worth visiting for evening meals (around US$8 to US$12). Along Kültür Caddesi *Ottoman House Restaurant* serves dishes like swordfish for US$6 in the gardens of an old wooden house.

THE EASTERN COAST

East of Alanya the coast sheds some of its touristic freight. About 7km east of **Anamur** there is a wonderful castle, built by the emirs of Karaman in 1230, right on the beach, with pensions and camping grounds nearby. The ghostly ruins of Byzantine **Anamurium** are 8.5km west of the town.

Silifke has a Crusader castle and a ruined Roman temple, but is mostly a transport point. At **Taşucu**, 11km south-west of Silifke, boats and hydrofoils depart daily for Girne (Kyrenia) in Turkish Cyprus (see the Getting There & Away chapter for details). **Kızkalesi** (Maiden's Castle) is a growing holiday resort with a striking Crusader castle offshore. **Mersin** is a modern city of no great interest. **Tarsus**, just east of Mersin, was the birthplace of St Paul and the place where Antony first ran into Cleopatra.

Hectic, overcrowded **Adana** is the country's fourth largest city, an important agricultural centre and a bus interchange for eastern Turkey; don't stop unless you have to.

HATAY

South-east of Adana, a tongue of Turkish territory – the Hatay – licks at the mountains of north-western Syria. You'll pass several impressive castles on the way to İskenderun (formerly Alexandretta), where Alexander the Great defeated the Persians and Jonah is thought to have been coughed up by the whale. It's still an important port city although you're unlikely to want to linger.

ANTAKYA

The biblical Antioch, where St Peter did a spell of converting, was said to be the most depraved city in the Roman empire. You can see his church, the **Senpiyer Kilisesi**, 3km outside the town. There are magnificent Roman mosaics in the **Antakya Museum** (open 8 am to noon and 1.30 to 5 pm, closed Monday; admission is US$2).

The tourist office (☎ 216 0610) is 1km north of the museum. Cheap hotels are south of the otogar. *Jasmin Hotel* (☎ 212 7171, İstiklal Caddesi 14) has basic doubles with shared baths for US$6. *Hotel Güney* (☎ 214 9713, İstiklal Sokak 28), one narrow street east of İstiklal Caddesi, charges US$10 for a double without shower, US$12 with. *Divan Oteli* (☎ 215 1518, İstiklal Caddesi 62) costs about the same.

Hotel Orontes (☎ 214 5931, İstiklal Caddesi 58) charges US$26/36 for air-con singles/doubles, some with river views. Newest in town is *Onur Hotel* (☎ 326-216 2210, İstiklal Caddesi, İstiklal Sokak 14), on the edge of the bazaar but quiet at night. Comfortable singles/doubles cost US$30/44.

Getting There & Away

For information about getting buses from Antakya through to Aleppo and Damascus, see the Getting There & Away section earlier in this chapter. Syrian visas are not normally issued at the border, but this depends partly upon your nationality and partly upon current regulations.

Local Buses If you are really determined to save money you could take a local bus from Antakya to Reyhanli from where you can catch a dolmuş to the border; after crossing on foot (a long and sweaty couple of kilometres in summer) you can try to pick up a

lift on the Syrian side. This can greatly lengthen an already tiresomely slow procedure and the savings in cost are minimal.

From Antakya you also have the alternative of catching a dolmuş south to Yeydağ (these go from beside the Etibank, opposite the entrance to the otogar), from where you pick up a taxi or hitch a few kilometres farther to the border. Once across (and crossing takes all of 15 minutes here), you're just 2km from the Syrian mountain village of Kassab from where regular microbuses make the 45 minute run to Lattakia (S£25). To get to Kassab, from the border walk about 10 minutes to where you join the main road at a point where it curves sharply to your right and then flag down any north bound microbus. (Southbound microbuses will be heading to Lattakia coming from Kassab, but as microbuses only tend to depart when they have a full complement of passengers, they'll most likely already be full and won't pick you up here.)

Central Anatolia

Realising that the Anatolian plateau was Turkey's heartland, Atatürk moved the capital to Ankara. Try not to think of this area as a great central nothingness; cruise across the undulating steppe to Kapadokya (Cappadocia) and you'll be amazed by a region that looks as if it belongs in another world.

ANKARA

Capital of Turkey since 1923, Ankara's site was a Hittite settlement nearly 4000 years ago. The Museum of Anatolian Civilisations aside, it's not of special interest to visitors, but because of its central location there's a good chance you'll at least pass through.

Orientation

Ankara's *hisar* (citadel) crowns a hill 1km east of Ulus Meydanı (Ulus Square), centre of Old Ankara, and near most of the cheap hotels. 'New Ankara' (Yenişehir) is 3.5km to the south, centred on Kızılay Meydanı (Kızılay Square).

ANKARA

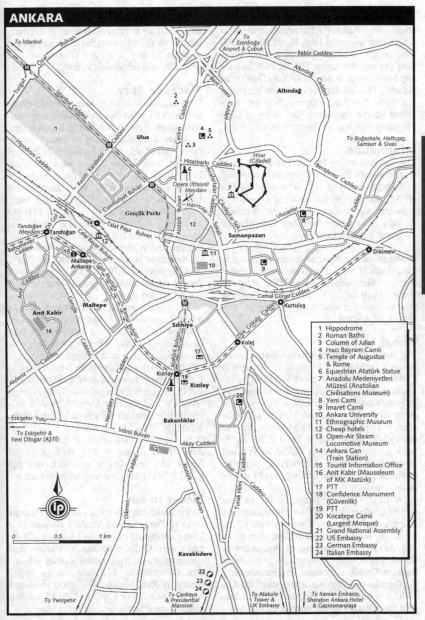

To İstanbul

Oral Bulvarı
Turgut
İstanbul Caddesi

To Esenboğa
Airport & Çubuk

Babür Caddesi

Bent Deresi Caddesi

Albındağ Caddesi

Altındağ

Hipodrom Caddesi

Kazım Karabekir Cad

Ulus

Çankırı Caddesi

To Boğazkale, Hattuşaş,
Samsun & Sivas

Hisarparkı Caddesi

Hisar
(Citadel)

Bentderesi Caddesi

Cumhuriyet Bulvarı

Opera (İtfaiye)
Meydanı

Atatürk Bulvarı

Talat Paşa Bulvarı

Hacırıcılar

Gençlik Parkı

Çankıraları Caddesi

Peliene Caddesi

Tandoğan
Meydanı

Tandoğan

Celal Bayar Bulvarı

Ceyhun Atıf Kansu Sokak

Ulucanlar

Samanpazarı

Dikimevi

Bahçelievler
Caddesi

Maltepe
Ankaray

Anıt Caddesi

Gençlik Cad

Maltepe

Kemal Bulvarı

Mustafa Kemal Bulvarı

Cemal Gürsel Caddesi

Kurtuluş

Anıt Kabir

Akdeniz

Anıt Caddesi

Sıhhiye

Ziya Gökalp Caddesi

Eskişehir Yolu

To Eskişehir &
Yeni Otogar (AŞTİ)

Necatibey Cad

Atatürk Bulvarı

Kolej

Kızılay

Kızılay

İnönü Bulvarı

Bakanlıklar

Akay Caddesi

Dikmen Caddesi

Esat Caddesi

Tunalı Hilmi Caddesi

Atatürk Bulvarı

Kavaklıdere

To Yenişehir

To Çankaya
& Presidential
Mansion

To Atakule
Tower &
UK Embassy

To Iranian Embassy,
Sheraton Ankara Hotel
& Gaziosmanpaşa

0   0.5   1 km

1	Hippodrome
2	Roman Baths
3	Column of Julian
4	Hacı Bayram Camii
5	Temple of Augustus & Rome
6	Equestrian Atatürk Statue
7	Anadolu Medeniyetleri Müzesi (Anatolian Civilisations Museum)
8	Yeni Cami
9	İmaret Camii
10	Ankara University
11	Ethnographic Museum
12	Cheap hotels
13	Open-Air Steam Locomotive Museum
14	Ankara Garı (Train Station)
15	Tourist Information Office
16	Anıt Kabir (Mausoleum of MK Atatürk)
17	PTT
18	Confidence Monument (Güvenlik)
19	PTT
20	Kocatepe Camii (Largest Mosque)
21	Grand National Assembly
22	US Embassy
23	German Embassy
24	Italian Embassy

TURKEY

Atatürk Bulvarı is the city's main north-south axis. Ankara's mammoth otogar is 6.5km south-west of Ulus Meydanı, the historic centre, and 6km west of Kızılay Meydanı, the modern centre. The Turkish Airlines city bus terminal is next to Ankara Garı (train station), 1.4km south-west of Ulus Meydanı.

Opera Meydanı (Opera Square, also called İtfaiye Meydanı), just south of Ulus Meydanı, has lots of cheap hotels.

Information
The tourism office (☎/fax 231 5572) is at Gazi Mustafa Kemal Bulvarı 121, opposite Maltepe Ankaray station. The main PTT is on Atatürk Bulvarı just south of Ulus Meydanı, although there's a handy branch beside Ankara Garı where you can also change cash and travellers cheques.

Embassies The diplomatic area is Çankaya, 5km south of Kızılay, and the adjoining districts of Gaziosmanpaşa and Kavaklıdere. See the Facts for the Visitor section earlier in this chapter for addresses of foreign embassies in Ankara.

Things to See
The **Anadolu Medeniyetleri Müzesi** (Anatolian Civilisations Museum), Hisarparkı Caddesi, is Ankara's most worthwhile attraction. With the world's richest collection of Hittite artefacts, it's an essential supplement to visiting central Turkey's Hittite sites. It's uphill from Ulus Meydanı, next to the citadel, and is open from 8.30 am to 5.15 pm; admission is US$2.50 (closed Monday in winter). Afterwards, continue up the hill and wander among the old streets of the citadel.

North of Ulus Meydanı, on the eastern side of Çankırı Caddesi (the continuation of Atatürk Bulvarı), are some **Roman ruins**, including the **Column of Julian**, erected in 363 AD and the **Temple of Augustus & Rome**. Right next to the temple is the **Hacı Bayram Camii**, a mosque commemorating the founder of a dervish order established in 1400. On the western side of Çankırı Caddesi are remains of the **Roman Baths**.

The **Anıtkabir** (Mausoleum of Atatürk), 2km west of Kızılay Meydanı, is a monumental tomb and memorial to the founder of modern Turkey. It's open from 9 am to 5 pm daily and admission is free.

Places to Stay
Ulus has numerous budget and mid-range hotels. Yenişehir has good mid-range hotels. The top end hotels are in Kavaklıdere.

Along the eastern side of Opera (or İtfaiye) Meydanı, on the corner of Sanayi Caddesi and Tavus Sokak near the Gazi Lisesi high school, try *Otel Devran* (☎ *311 0485, Tavus Sokak 8)*, with doubles for US$15 with shower, US$18 with bath. *Sipahi* (☎ *324 0235, Kosova Sokak 1)* is old and dingy but serviceable at a pinch, and cheap at US$10 for a double with shower, or even less without. Perhaps the best value on the street is at *Otel Fuar* (☎ *312 3288, Kosova Sokak 11)*, where US$9 gets you a decent double room with sink, and showers (US$3) down the hall.

For more comfort, *Otel Mithat* (☎ *311 5410, Tavus Sokak 2)* has shower-equipped doubles for US$17. It's a better choice than the adjoining *Otel Akman* (☎ *324 4140, Tavus Sokak 6)*, which charges more.

North of Ulus and one street west of Çankırı Caddesi, the three-star *Hotel Oğultürk* (☎ *309 2900, Rüzgarlı Eşdost Sokak 6)* has rooms with TV and minibar for US$26/40 a single/double, breakfast included. The nearby *Yıldız* (☎ *312 7581)* is similar.

In 'new' Ankara south of Kızılay Meydanı, *Hotel Ergen* (☎ *417 5906, Karanfil Sokak 48)*, near Olgunlar Sokak, charges US$25/35 for singles/doubles with bath.

Places to Eat
At the south-eastern corner of Ulus, *Akman Boza ve Pasta Salonu (Atatürk Bulvarı 3)* is in the courtyard of a huge block of offices and shops. Order a sandwich or snack and consume it at terrace tables around a fountain. Overlooking this place, on the upper storey, is *Kebabistan*, with good food and low prices – about US$3 to US$5 for a full meal of roast lamb, less for just pide.

Çankırı Caddesi north of Ulus Meydanı also has numerous restaurants. *Çiçek Lokantası* serves drinks with meals (US$6 to US$10).

For a memorable meal at very reasonable cost (US$6 to US$12 per person), try *Zenger Paşa Konağı* (☎ 311 7070, *Doyran Sokak 13*), an old house in the hisar with wonderful crafts and ethnographic displays, as well as good Ottoman-style food. *Kınacılar Evi* (☎ 312 1010, *Kalekapısı Sokak 28*), straight uphill from the hisar entrance, has airy rooms and some traditional dishes such as *mantı* (Turkish ravioli).

Getting There & Away

Air Turkish Airlines (☎ 419 2800), at Atatürk Bulvarı 167/A, Bakanlıklar, has daily nonstop flights to most Turkish cities. Most international routes require a connection in İstanbul. İstanbul Airlines (☎ 432 2234), Atatürk Bulvarı 64/1, Kızılay, serves several Turkish cities, but more foreign ones.

Bus Ankara's huge otogar (AŞTİ) is the vehicular heart of the nation, with coaches to all places day and night. For İstanbul (US$10 to US$18, six hours) they depart at least every 15 minutes. Other sample fares are Antalya (US$15, eight hours), Bodrum (US$20, 13 hours), Erzurum (US$18, 12 hours), İzmir (US$14.50 to US$20, eight hours) and Göreme/Kapadokya (Cappadocia, US$10, 4½ hours).

Train For details of trains to İstanbul and İzmir see Getting There & Away in those sections.

Trains heading east of Ankara are not as comfortable or punctual as those travelling westward. The *Doğu Express*, hauling carriages and sleeping cars, departs each evening for Erzincan, Erzurum (US$15, or US$32 for a bed, 25 hours) and Kars. On alternate mornings the *Güney Express* departs for Diyarbakır (US$15, 26½ hours), and the *Vangölü Express* departs for Elaziğ.

For full train information phone Ankara Garı (☎ 311 0600).

Getting Around

The Airport Ankara's Esenboğa airport is 33km north of the city centre. Havaş buses (US$3.50, 40 minutes in light traffic) depart the Turkish Airlines city terminal at the train station 1½ hours before domestic and two hours before international Turkish Airlines flights. A taxi costs about US$25. Cheaper shared taxis run from the train station to the airport as well.

Local Transport Many city buses run the length of Atatürk Bulvarı. Buy a *bilet* (ticket) for US$0.50) from kiosks by bus stops, or from a shop saying 'EGO Bilet(i)'. City bus No 198 runs to the otogar from the train station and Ulus; bus 623 goes via Kızılay to Gaziler.

Taxis are multitudinous, metered and often suicidal. A taxi between the otogar and the train station costs about US$2.75; to Ulus or Kızılay it's about US$3.25.

The Ankaray underground train runs between AŞTİ otogar in the west through Kızılay to Dikimevi in the east. A five-ride pass (US$2) is the cheapest ticket.

The first line of Ankara's metro system runs from Kızılay north-west via Sıhhiye, Maltepe and Ulus to Batıkent, connecting with the Ankaray line at Kızılay.

BOĞAZKALE

The Hittites ruled central Anatolia from about 2000 to 1180 BC. Boğazkale (called Hattuşaş in Hittite), 29km off the Ankara-Samsun road (to the south), was the ancient capital of the Hittites until it was destroyed by the Phrygians. There is little left today apart from the walls and foundations of the buildings. But what walls! Though they are crumbling, they stretch for over 10km and have five entrances, including the **Royal Gate**, the **Lion Gate** (flanked by stone lions) and the underground tunnel, **Yer Kapı**. The massive foundations are also imposing, although visited only by the occasional curious sheep. Largest is the site of the **Great Temple of the Storm God**, which has no fewer than 70 storerooms. The natural rock temple of **Yazılıkaya**, 2km from the main

TURKEY

site, has bas-reliefs of Hittite deities carved into the rock face.

The village of Boğazkale has a small **museum**. Several small hotels with camping facilities are open in summer. Take a bus to Sungurlu, then a minibus to Boğazkale.

Alacahöyük, 36km north-east of Boğazkale near the main Ankara-Samsun road, is a pre-Hittite site, probably 6000 years old. The remains, however, including the Sphinx Gate, are Hittite. There's another small museum here.

KONYA

Known as Iconium in Roman times, Konya, due south of Ankara, is a conservative place but a showcase for some striking Seljuk architecture. It was the capital of the Seljuk Turks, and it was here, in the 13th century, that the poet Mevlana Rumi inspired the founding of the whirling dervishes, one of Islam's important mystical orders. You can see them whirling here during the **Mevlana Festival** every December.

Orientation & Information

The centre of town stretches from Alaettin Tepesi, the hill topped by the Alaettin Mosque (1221), along Alaettin Caddesi and Mevlana Caddesi to the tomb of Mevlana, now called the Mevlana Müzesi. The otogar is 3.5km north of the centre. Minibuses will ferry you to the town centre (US$0.30).

The tourist office (☎ 351 1074) is at Mevlana Caddesi 21, across the square from the Mevlana Müzesi.

Things to See

Mevlana's **tomb** (US$1) is topped by a brilliant green-tiled tower. It's a powerful place to visit, very popular with pilgrims, and you should be especially careful about dressing modestly when you go in.

Outstanding Seljuk buildings around the Alaettin Tepesi are the **Büyük Karatay Müzesi**, once a Muslim theological seminary, now a ceramics museum; and the **İnce Minare Medresesi** (Seminary of the Slender Minaret), now the Museum of Wood & Stone Carving.

Places to Stay & Eat

First choice is **Hotel Ulusan** (☎ 351 5004, Kurşuncular Sokak 2), immediately behind the PTT. Singles/doubles here are simple but clean and, with sink, cost US$9/12. Other reasonable places near the Mevlana Müzesi are **Mavi Köşk** (☎ 350 1904) and **Derviş** (☎ 351 1688) hotels, side by side in Bostan Çelebi Sokak, which both charge US$14.50/18.

Just doors away from them is **Öztemel Lokantası**, where you can sample Konya's own fırın kebap (oven-roasted mutton) with a drink for US$4.

KAPADOKYA (CAPPADOCİA)

Cappadocia, the region between Ankara and Malatya, between the Black Sea and the Taurus Mountains, is famous for the fantastic natural **rock formations** of its valleys. Over the centuries people have carved houses, churches, fortresses, even complete underground cities where early Christians sought refuge, into the soft, eerily eroded volcanic stone. Attractions include the Göreme and nearby Zelve valleys; the rugged Ihlara Valley (south of Aksaray) dotted with ancient churches; Soğanlı with its scores of stone-cut chapels; and the huge underground cities at **Kaymaklı** and **Derinkuyu** (open from 8 am to 5 pm, 6.30 pm in summer; admission US$3).

Nevşehir is a loud, unattractive town but a vital transport base for the region; catch buses here for Derinkuyu and Kaymaklı, or to **Niğde**, much farther south, but with more rock-carved monasteries and churches, Hittite traces and interesting mosques.

Information

Ürgüp, Avanos and Uçhisar all have a good selection of hotels and pensions, but Göreme village is most attractive to low-budget travellers. You can camp almost everywhere, most conveniently in the gardens of pensions.

In summer buses departing twice an hour link Nevşehir, Uçhisar and Avanos, stopping in Göreme. Dolmuşes depart year round twice an hour linking Göreme with Nevşehir.

KAPADOKYA (CAPPADOCIA)

Good tours of the region are offered by Ötüken Voyage (☎ 271 2757), Neşe Tour (☎ 271 2525) and Zemi Tour (☎ 271 2576) in Göreme, by Kirkit Voyage (☎ 511 3259) in Avanos and by Argeus (☎ 341 4688) in Ürgüp. The most useful tourist offices are in Nevşehir (☎ 213 3659) and Ürgüp (☎ 341 4059).

Göreme & Zelve Valleys

The Göreme Valley is one of Turkey's most amazing sights. Over the centuries a thick layer of volcanic tufa has been eroded into fantastic, eerie shapes, dubbed fairy chimneys by the locals. Early Christians carved chambers, vaults and labyrinths into them for use as churches, stables and homes.

Painted **frescoes** can be seen in the rock-hewn monastery, nunnery and several dozen cave churches of the **Göreme Open-Air Museum**. Some date from the 8th century, though the best are from the 10th to 13th centuries. Unlit for many centuries, they've hardly faded at all, though vandals have left an indelible mark. The museum is open from 8 am to 5.30 pm daily (4.30 pm in winter); entry is US$6 with an extra US$6 to see the newly restored Karanlık Kilise (Dark Church).

The nearby **Zelve Valley** (same opening times), just off the road to Avanos, is less visited. On the way you can stop to see some of the finest fairy chimneys at **Paşabağ**.

About 3km in the opposite direction is **Uçhisar**, a picturesque town built around, and into, a prominent peak. A room-to-room scramble through its rock citadel leads to fine views from the summit (US$1).

Places to Stay At the lower end of the Göreme Valley, Göreme Köyü (Göreme Village) has lots of good-value pensions, some carved into the rocks. You can camp in the gardens of many pensions, or at the *Dilek* or *Berlin* camp sites, side by side amid wonderful rock formations on the road leading to the open-air museum.

Göreme's abundance of pensions charge US$3.50 per bed in a dorm, US$5 in a waterless private room, or US$7 per bed with private facilities. One of the most popular is *Köse* (☎ 271 2294), near the PTT, with a good restaurant and book exchange. Other favourites are the *Kelebek* (☎ 271 2531), with spectacular views, *Paradise* (☎ 271 2248), *Ufuk (Horizon)* (☎ 271 2157), *Gümüş* (☎ 271 2438), *Flintstones* (☎ 271 2555), *Walnut House* (☎ 271 2564), *L'Elysee Pension* (☎ 271 2244), *Tuna* (☎ 271 2236) and *Peri* (☎ 271 2136). *Cave Hotel Melek* (☎ 271 2463) has rock-cut waterless double rooms for US$10, or US$16 with private bath, breakfast included.

Ottoman House (☎ 271 2616) boasts that it offers luxury at affordable prices: US$15 a head. The new *Göreme House* (☎ 271 2060) is similar.

Places to Eat Restaurants offering standard fare at slightly above average prices cluster around the otogar; best is the *Orient* facing the popular *Cafedoki@*. For a splurge, head uphill to *Konak Türk Evi*, where a 19th century paşa's house is now a beautiful restaurant. Expect to pay around US$8 to US$15 to dine in frescoed splendour.

Avanos

Set on the northern bank of the wide Kızılırmak (Red River), Avanos is known for its pottery. Best value among the pensions is *Kirkit Pansiyon* (☎ 511 3148), where beds cost US$8 in waterless doubles, US$10 with shower, breakfast included; from the northern end of the bridge, walk east and bear left at the first alley.

Immediately facing the northern end of the bridge is *Ilhan's Guesthouse* (☎ 511 4828, Orta Mahalle Zafer Sokak 1), with similar prices. Another low-price favourite is *Panorama Pension* (☎ 511 1654), a five minute walk uphill through the backstreets of the old town, with impressive views from the terrace. B&B costs from US$6 to US$11, depending upon whether the room has a private shower.

Moving up the price and comfort scale, *Sofa Motel* (☎ 511 5186), across the northern end of the bridge, has tastefully decorated rooms in a group of old houses for US$20/35 for singles/doubles with private bath.

Ürgüp

Despite being a bigger town, Ürgüp still has plenty of appeal, with its old sandstone buildings, cobbled streets and a stone hill shot through with rooms and passages. Cappadocia's best wineries are on the outskirts. The helpful tourist office (☎/fax 341 4059) is in the park, downhill on Kayseri Caddesi.

Places to Stay & Eat *Hotel Elvan* (☎ 341 4191, Dutlu Cami Mahallesi, Barbaros Hayrettin Sokak 11) has rooms arranged around a small courtyard for US$20 to US$25 a double. South of the market *Hotel Kilim* (☎ 341 4481, Dumlupınar Caddesi 47) offers clean singles/doubles for US$10/16.

Güllüce Sokak, the street south of Kayseri Caddesi, has many similarly priced cheapies. From the centre, you come to *Sarıhan Pansiyon* (☎ 341 8813) and *Merkez Pan-*

siyon (☎ *341 2746*), as well as *Otel Snowball* (☎ *341 2356, Elgin Sokak 2*).

Göreme Turist Pansiyon (☎ *341 4022*) just off Kayseri Caddesi also offers simple rooms for US$10/16 a single/double, but the owner is often ready to agree a lower rate.

The prettiest place to stay is the immaculately kept *Esbelli Evi* (☎ *341 3395, fax 341 8848*) behind Turban Hotel, at US$55/75, excellent breakfast included; reserve in advance.

The town's most prominent eatery is *Şömine Restaurant*. Right on the main square, its high terrace provides outdoor tables to supplement those inside. Ürgüp-style kebaps baked on tiles are a speciality; full meals cost from US$8 to US$14. Otherwise, there's the usual range of cheap kebap places around the otogar.

Ihlara Gorge & Güzelyurt

Ilhara is Cappadocia with a physical challenge – a once-remote, beautiful canyon full of churches dating back to Byzantine times. Most people visit as part of a whistlestop tour of the region but there's nothing to stop you staying and walking the entire 16km length of the gorge.

The village of Ihlara Köyü is 85km south-west of Nevşehir and 40km southeast of Aksaray. *Anatolia Pansiyon* (☎ *453 7440*), on the road running along the top of the gorge between Ihlara village and the official entrance, has doubles with shower for US$18, or camping for US$3. On the road towards Aksaray *Akar Pansiyon* (☎ *453 7018*) charges marginally less. There are more pensions and a camp site in the gorge itself at the village of Belisırma.

About 14km from Ihlara, on the road east to Derinkuyu, is the village of Güzelyurt, a quiet Cappadocian farming village of stone houses, the perfect antidote to the Göreme hustle. Beautiful *Otel Karballa* (☎ *451 2103*) offers B&B for US$14 per person or half-board for US$20; you eat your meals in what was once a monastic refectory.

Buses run to Ihlara several times a day from Aksaray otogar (US$0.75). Several dolmuşes a day also connect Aksaray with Güzelyurt.

Kayseri

Sitting in the shadow of snowy Mt Erciyes, Kayseri (Caesarea in Roman times) was the provincial capital of Cappadocia. A religiously conservative but fast modernising town, it's full of mosques, tombs and old seminaries.

Near the tourist office (☎ 222 3903, fax 222 0879) is the beautiful **Hunat Hatun mosque**, **tomb** and **seminary** (now the Ethnographic Museum). Opposite, behind the massive 6th century city walls, is the **Ulu Cami** (Great Mosque), begun by the Seljuks in 1136. Also inside the walls is the ancient and smelly **Vezirhanı**, once a caravanserai, now a market for sheepskins. Farther out are the **Gıyasiye ve Şifaiye Medreseleri** (Twin Seminaries) in Mimar Sinan Park, a Seljuk hospital now housing a medical museum. Don't miss the **Güpgüpoğlu Konağı**, a beautifully decorated 18th century stone mansion.

Places to Stay & Eat Cheapest is *Hunat Oteli* (☎ *232 4319, Zengin Sokak 5*), behind the Hunat Mosque, with waterless rooms priced at US$7 a person. Better is the *Hotel Sur* (☎ *222 4367, Talas Caddesi 12*), not far from the tourist office, with good double rooms for US$26/32 a single/double with shower. *Hotel Çamlıca* (☎ *231 4344, Bankalar Caddesi, Gürcü Sokak 14*), is in the bazaar, with serviceable rooms for US$14 a double with sink, US$16 with shower.

For comfort, you can't go past two good hotels near Düvenönü Square charging US$30 to US$35 for a double with breakfast: *Hotel Çapari* (☎ *222 5278*) and *Hotel Konfor* (☎ *320 0184*).

It's almost worth coming to Kayseri just to eat at the *Beyaz Saray* (*Millet Caddesi 8*). The İskender kebap is in the award-winning category, beautifully presented and absolutely delicious for just US$3.50.

Safranbolu

A charming town between İstanbul and Ankara, Safranbolu is well worth visiting for its wonderful old half-timbered houses. If you can afford to splash out for accommodation, this is the place to do it. *Ev Pansiyonculuğu Geliştirme Merkezi (Home Pension Development Centre)* (☎ 712 7236, Yemeniciler Arastası 2), next to the tourist office, makes reservations for overnight stays in restored houses for US$19 to US$26 a single, US$29 to US$38 a double, breakfast included. Or you can book into the beautiful *Havuzlu Asmazlar Konağı* (☎ 725 2883, fax 712 3824) at US$30/40 for singles/doubles with bath.

Can't afford it? Then the Ottoman-style *Çarşı Pansiyon* (☎ 725 1079), not far from the Cinci Hanı, charges only US$10/15, breakfast included.

The tourist office (☎/fax 712 3863) is next to the Köprülü Mehmet Paşa Camii mosque in the Çarşı district.

Amasya

A mountain town set dramatically on river banks hemmed in by sheer cliffs, Amasya has rock-cut tombs of the Pontic kings dating from before Christ, a lofty citadel, fine old houses and several imposing Seljuk buildings. The tourist office (☎ 218 7428, Mustafa Kemal Bulvarı 27) is on the river bank in the centre.

Things to See Look for the **Gök Medrese Camii** (1276), the **Burmalı Minare Camii** (Spiral Minaret, 1242), the Mongol-built **Bimarhane Medresesi** (1308), the octagonal **Büyük Ağa Medresesi** (1488) and the Ottoman **Sultan Beyazit II Camii** (1486). The **museum** is good, with the bonus of some gruesome mummies.

Places to Stay The best place to stay is the beautifully restored *İlk Pansiyon* (☎ 218 1689, Hitit Sokak 1), charging US$12 to US$25 a single, US$16 to US$35 a double. Also good is *Yuvam Pension* (☎ 218 1324, Atatürk Caddesi 24/5). The quiet *Zümrüt Pansiyon* (☎ 218 2675, Hatuniye Mahallesi, Hazeranlar Sokak 28) has rooms without toilet or sink for US$7 per person and garners lots of praise from readers.

Sivas

Sivas used to be an important crossroads on the caravan route to Persia and Baghdad, and has many marvellous Seljuk buildings to prove it. In 1919, Atatürk convened the second congress of the War of Independence here.

The tourist office (☎ 221 3535) is in the Vilayet building on the main square. The buildings to see are in the adjoining park: the **Çifte Minare Medrese** (Twin Minaret Seminary), **Şifaiye** and **Bürüciye** seminaries, the **Ulu Cami** and the **Gök Medrese** (Blue Seminary).

Places to Stay & Eat

The better cheap hotels are 700m southeast of Konak Meydanı, at the junction of Atatürk Caddesi and Kurşunlu Sokak. Best of the newer places is *Hotel Yavuz* (☎ 225 0204, Atatürk Caddesi 86), south-east of the intersection with Kurşunlu Caddesi. Singles/doubles cost only US$8/12 with shower; a double with bathtub costs US$19.

Otel Çakır (☎ 222 4526) charges US$12/16 for clean singles/doubles with bath, including breakfast. The nearby *Otel Fatih* (☎ 233 4313, Kurşunlu Caddesi 15) charges a bit more. Around the corner at Atatürk Caddesi 176, *Otel Ergin* (☎ 221 2301) offers beds from US$4. Single women would probably be better off at the Çakır or Fatih.

Top places are *Otel Sultan* (☎ 221 2986, Eski Belediye Sokak 18), at US$20/28, and the slightly pricier, noisier *Otel Köşk* (☎ 221 1150, Atatürk Caddesi 11).

For cheap meals look behind the PTT on 1 Sokak, just off the main square.

Black Sea Coast

This region is dramatically different from the rest of Turkey – steep and craggy, damp and lush, isolated by the Pontic Mountains along most of its length. It's the country's dairyland, and its hazelnuts make Turkey the world's biggest exporter of these nuts. The tea you drink in İstanbul probably comes from east of Trabzon; the cigarette smoke you endure probably comes from tobacco grown west of Samsun.

Legend has it that the coast was first settled by a tribe of Amazons. Its kingdoms have tended to be independent-minded; Trabzon was the last Byzantine bastion against the Ottomans. Overseas tourism hasn't penetrated very far, though you'll find plenty of cheap hotels and camping. Samsun and Trabzon aside, less English is spoken here than is usual in Turkey.

Partly because of heavy industry around Zonguldak, the coast west from Sinop to the Bosphorus is almost unknown to tourists, though the fishing port of **Amasra**, with its Roman and Byzantine ruins and numerous small, cheap hotels, is worth a look. **Sinop**, three hours north-west of Samsun, is a fishing and boat-building town that was the birthplace of Diogenes, the Cynic philosopher. Thanks to the development of Samsun's harbour, Sinop is a fine little backwater. There are beaches on both sides of the peninsula, as well as a few historic buildings and numerous good, cheap hotels.

SAMSUN

Under the Seljuks, Samsun was a major trading port and had its own Genoese colony. When the Ottomans looked set to capture it in the 15th century, the Genoese fled after burning the city to the ground. Consequently, there's little of interest here now, although it's a good starting point for coastal travel and a port of call for the ferry from İstanbul. Atatürk landed here on 19 May 1919 to begin the Turkish War of Independence.

The otogar is 3km east of town. The town centre is the traffic roundabout near the Atatürk statue. Inland to the north-east, next to the Archaeological Museum, is the tourist office (☎ 431 1228).

SAMSUN TO TRABZON

There are excellent cold-water beaches around the cheerful resort town of **Ünye**, on a wide bay 85km east of Samsun. Beaches are the only reason to stop in the glum town of **Ordu**, 80km east of Ünye. A tourist office (☎/fax 223 1608) is half a block east of the central Atatürk statue and mosque.

Europe's first cherry trees came from **Giresun** courtesy of Lucullus, the Roman general and famous epicure, and the town is still surrounded by cherry orchards.

The dramatic remains of a large Byzantine fortress stand on a headland beside the friendly village of **Akçakale**, about 22km west of Trabzon.

TRABZON

Trabzon is by far the most interesting place on the Turkish Black Sea coast, with mild weather, lots of Byzantine architecture, a bazaar full of honest merchants, beaches and the amazing Sumela Monastery. Known as Trebizond in Byzantine times, this was the last town to fall to the Ottoman Turks, and an earlier holdout against the Seljuks and Mongols as well.

Orientation & Information

Modern Trabzon is centred on Atatürk Alanı (Atatürk Square), on a steep hill above the harbour. The tourist office (☎/fax 321 4659) is off the southern side of the square, near Hotel Nur. The Georgian Consulate (☎ 326 2226, fax 326 2296) is off the northern side of the square at Gazipaşa Caddesi 20 (Georgian visas cost US$20 for 15 days, US$25 for 30 days).

On the coastal highway at the foot of the hill are two minibus yards: north of the bazaar for points west, and on the eastern side near the ferry pier for points east. A third yard, north of Atatürk Alanı, has buses to Rize. To reach Atatürk Alanı from any of them, just take the steepest climb up. About 3km to the east is the otogar for long-distance buses.

Things to See

A 20 minute walk west of Atatürk Alanı are the dark walls of the Byzantine city. The **old town**, with its timber houses and stone bridges, still looks medieval.

Trabzon has many **Byzantine churches**, the oldest being the 7th century Küçük Ayvası Kilisesi (St Anne Church), and the best

TRABZON

PLACES TO STAY	OTHER	9 Fatih Sultan Hamamı	19 Buses to Ordu
25 Hotel Nur	1 Atapark	10 Tabakhane Camii	20 Buses to Rize
26 Hotel Benli	2 Gülbahar Hatun	11 Küçük Ayvasil Kilisesi	21 Georgian Consulate
28 Otel Horon	Camii & Tomb	(St Anne Church)	23 Police Station
29 Santa Maria	3 Zağanos Paşa Köprüsü	12 Sekiz Direkli Hamamı	24 Tourist Information
Katolik Kilisesi	4 Fatih Parkı	13 Çarşı Camii	Office
30 Hotel Gözde	5 Ortahisar Fatih	14 PTT	27 Tourist Police
31 Hotel Anıl	Büyük Camii	15 Türkiye İş Bankası	32 Kale Park
	6 Russian Consulate	16 Kostaki Konağı	33 Buses to Rize
PLACES TO EAT	7 Kültür Merkezi	17 Banks with ATMs	34 Turkish Maritime Lines
22 Cheap	8 Yeni Cuma Camii	18 Turkish Airlines	Terminal
restaurants	(St Eugenius Church)	(THY) Office	35 Otogar

preserved the 13th century Aya Sofya, now a museum (take a minibus from Atatürk Alanı; admission is US$1). Among its more beautiful **Ottoman mosques** are the Gülbahar Hatun Camii (1514) west of the city walls and the Çarşı (or Osmanpaşa) Camii in the bazaar. For a look at a beautiful 19th century villa, visit the **Atatürk Köşkü** high above the town.

Many travellers come to Trabzon just to visit the nearby 14th century **Sumela Monastery**, built into a cliff face like a swallow's nest. Inhabited right up to this century, it boasts fine murals (much damaged by vandals) and amazing views. Ulusoy buses (US$6) depart for Sumela from a small terminal on Taksim Caddesi, across the street and uphill a few steps from Atatürk Alanı. Entry to Sumela National Park costs US$2 (half price with a student card) per person. It's open from 9 am to 6 pm in summer.

Places to Stay

Sadly, petty traders and prostitutes from the former Soviet states often fill the cheapest hotels, so you may have trouble finding somewhere affordable and tolerable. The cheapest rooms are east of Atatürk Alanı on Güzelhisar Caddesi and surrounding streets. *Hotel Anıl* (☎ 326 7282, *Güzelhisar Caddesi 10*) has a flashy lobby and fairly clean singles/doubles with shower for US$12/18.

Hotel Gözde (☎ 321 9579, *Salih Yazıcı Sokak 7*), just off Güzelhisar Caddesi, has a dingy lobby but better rooms for US$12 a double, with shower.

Hotel Benli (☎ 321 1022, *Cami Çıkmazı 5*) is uphill behind the Belediye. Small, old and drab, it has clean rooms for US$5/10 with sink, US$2 more with shower. Facing it is the newly renovated *Hotel Nur* (☎ 323 0445, *Cami Sokak 4*), a good bet for single women.

Travellers are also welcome at the hostel of the *Sankta Maria Katolik Kilisesi (☎ 321 2192, Sümer Sokak 26)*, a few blocks downhill (north) from Atatürk Alanı. Leave a realistic donation for use of spotless simple rooms and hot showers.

For more comfort, try the two star *Otel Horon (☎ 322 6455, fax 321 6628, Sıra Mağazalar Caddesi 125)*, off Güzelhisar, with modern rooms for US$30/40.

Places to Eat

Lots of cheap food is available right around Atatürk Alanı. Try *Derya* and *Volkan 2* near the cheap hotels for sulu *yemek* (fast food). *Murat Balık Salonu* on the northern side of the square fries up mackerel (US$3) and *hemsin*, a Black Sea delicacy when in season. *Güloğlu Baklava ve Kebap Salonu* serves a wide range of meals in cheerful surroundings.

Getting There & Away

Air Turkish Airlines (☎ 321 1680), at the south-western corner of Atatürk Alanı, has daily nonstop flights to Ankara and İstanbul. You'll need to take a dolmuş from Atatürk Alanı to get to the airport.

Bus West-bound dolmuşes go as far as Ordu, from the minibus yard on the highway below the bazaar. Dolmuşes going east as far as Rize, and minibuses to Maçka and Sumela, go from the yard east of Atatürk Alanı near the ferry terminal. Rize city buses leave from the foot of Gazipaşa Caddesi, north below Atatürk Alanı. From the otogar, minibuses go to Rize, Hopa and Artvin every 30 minutes. A dozen buses a day go to Erzurum, a beautiful ride via Gümüşhane. There are dolmuş taxis operating between the otogar and Atatürk Alanı (US$0.50).

Boat See the Getting Around section at the beginning of this chapter for details on car ferries to İstanbul and the Getting There & Away chapter at the beginning of this book for details on the Karden Lines service to Sochi in Russia.

KAÇKAR MOUNTAINS

The eastern end of the coastal mountain range is dominated by 3937m Kaçkar Dağı, inland from Rize. The surrounding area offers excellent opportunities for camping, wilderness treks, and even white-water boating on the Çoruh River. The many small villages offer cheap accommodation.

At Uzungöl, 50km east of Trabzon and 50km inland, is an **alpine lake**, with camping, bungalows and a few small hotels. Ayder, 40km east of Rize and 40km inland, has **hot springs**, and is a good base for day hikes and trekking towards Kaçkar Dağı. For more information, ask at the tourist office in Trabzon.

Eastern Turkey

The harshest, hardest part of the country, Turkey's eastern region nonetheless rewards visitors with dramatic landscapes – like majestic views of 5165m Mt Ararat (legendary resting place of Noah's Ark) – and some unusual historical relics. In the winter, bitterly cold weather blows in direct from the Russian steppes, so unless you're well equipped and something of a masochist, avoid travelling here from October through to April.

For full coverage of this region see Lonely Planet's *Turkey*.

ERZURUM

Eastern Turkey's main transport hub and military centre for hundreds of years, Erzurum is famous for its harsh climate but has some striking Seljuk buildings that justify a stay of a day or so.

Orientation & Information

The tourist office (☎ 218 5697, fax 218 5443) is inconveniently far out on Cemal Gürsel Caddesi, the main street, west of the Atatürk statue. The otogar is also inconveniently located 3km from the centre on the airport road. Luckily the centre itself is compact, with all the main sites within walking distance of each other.

Erzurum's Iranian consulate (☎ 218 3876), off Aliravi Caddesi, across from the

ERZURUM

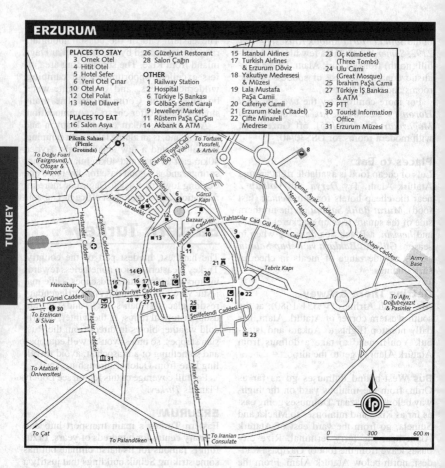

PLACES TO STAY	26 Güzelyurt Restoran	15 İstanbul Airlines	23 Üç Kümbetler
3 Örnek Otel	28 Salon Çağın	17 Turkish Airlines	(Three Tombs)
4 Hitit Otel		& Erzurum Döviz	24 Ulu Cami
5 Hotel Sefer	OTHER	18 Yakutiye Medresesi	(Great Mosque)
6 Yeni Otel Çınar	1 Railway Station	& Müzesi	25 İbrahim Paşa Camii
10 Otel An	2 Hospital	19 Lala Mustafa	27 Türkiye İş Bankası
12 Otel Polat	6 Türkiye İş Bankası	Paşa Camii	& ATM
13 Hotel Dilaver	8 Gölbaşı Semt Garajı	20 Caferiye Camii	29 PTT
	9 Jewellery Market	21 Erzurum Kale (Citadel)	30 Tourist Information
PLACES TO EAT	11 Rüstem Paşa Çarşısı	22 Çifte Minareli	Office
16 Salon Asya	14 Akbank & ATM	Medrese	31 Erzurum Müzesi

Eğitim Fakültesi (Education Faculty), is open every day except Friday from 8 am to 1 pm and 2 to 4 pm. You are supposed to be able to get a visa here in one day if you apply from Monday to Thursday. However, it may be safer to apply at the Iranian embassy in your home country.

Things to See

The well-preserved walls of a 5th century **Erzurum Kale (Citadel)** loom over a maze of narrow streets. From here you get a good

view of the town's layout and the bleak surrounding plains.

The beautifully symmetrical **Çifte Minareli Medrese** (1253) is a famous example of Seljuk architecture. Its classic carved portal is flanked by twin minarets, which also frame a conical dome behind.

The oldest mosque is the **Ulu Cami** (1179), next door to the Çifte Minareli. Farther west along Cumhuriyet Caddesi is an open square with an Ottoman mosque and, at the western corner, another seminary, the

Warning

When this guidebook went to press, the Kurdish insurgency continued in portions of eastern Turkey. It's still possible to travel to most towns in the region, and as the insurgency dies down (as seems to be happening), more of the region will become safe for travel. The last kidnappings of foreigners occurred in 1994, although it's hard to know whether that's because of better security or because there are fewer travellers about to kidnap. For now, travellers to the east should scrupulously observe the following rules:

Contact your embassy or consulate in advance, ask about current conditions, tell them your plans and ask their advice. The British Foreign and Commonwealth Office has a hotline for travellers giving their most up-to-date advice. You can access it on ☎ 020-7238 4503 or on www.fco.gov.uk/travel/countryadvice.asp. Travel only during daylight, only on major highways (or preferably by air) and restrict your stops to major cities, towns and sites. Transport stops early in the day in the south-eastern corner bordered by Doğubeyazıt, Elazığ and Diyarbakır.

Frequent military checkpoints are a fact of life east of Malatya. In most cases the soldiers pay little attention to foreigners, although they'll probably want to see your passport and visa.

Yakutiye Medresesi, built by the local Mongol emir in 1310, and now a museum of Turkish arts.

Places to Stay

Erzurum has lots of cheapies, although some are pretty dismal. Kazım Karabekir Caddesi has lots of bargain-priced accommodation, including *Hitit Otel* (☎ 218 1204), at No 26, charging US$8/11 a single/double with sink, US$9/12 with shower, and very close by the similarly priced *Örnek Otel* (☎ 218 1203).

Otel Arı (☎ 218 3141, Ayazpaşa Caddesi 8), next to the Ayazpaşa mosque, charges only US$7/10 for a single/double with sink. Nearby is the well-regarded, friendly *Yeni Otel Çınar* (☎ 233 9892, Ayazpaşa Caddesi 18), which is more comfortable for US$8 a double with sink, US$10 with shower. To find it, look for the Gürpınar Sineması (cinema) in the bazaar. The street opposite leads to the Çınar.

A step up in quality, *Otel Polat* (☎ 218 1623, Kazım Karabekir Caddesi 4) posts rates of US$20/30, but may drop them if it's quiet. *Hotel Sefer* (☎ 218 6714, İstasyon Caddesi), near Aşağı Mumcu Meydanı, is another good choice, charging US$15/20, breakfast included, for rooms with private bath.

The best rooms in town are at the three star *Hotel Dilaver* (☎ 235 0068, Aşağı Mumcu Caddesi Petit Meydani), with TV and air-con for US$60/85.

Places to Eat

There are several reasonable choices along Cumhuriyet Caddesi near the Yakutiye Medresesi. *Güzelyurt Restorant*, though Erzurum's fanciest, is cheap and good: have the *mantarlı güveç* (lamb and mushroom casserole), with drinks, for less than US$10. *Salon Çağın* and *Salon Asya*, a block away, are even cheaper, and still quite good.

Getting There & Away

Air Turkish Airlines (☎ 218 1904), at 100 Yıl Caddesi at the north-western end of Kazım Karabekir Caddesi, has at least one daily nonstop flight (US$85) to Ankara, with connections to İstanbul and İzmir. A taxi to the airport costs about US$6.

Bus The otogar, 3km from the centre along the airport road, handles most of Erzurum's intercity traffic. City bus No 2 passes the otogar and will take you into town for US$0.30; a taxi costs about US$2.50. Bus company offices are uphill from the train station at Gürcü Kapı.

For Iran, take a bus to Doğubeyazıt and then catch a minibus to the Iranian frontier.

TURKEY

Train Erzurum Garı is at the northern end of İstasyon Caddesi, within walking distance of most of the hotels. City buses depart from the station forecourt every 30 minutes and circulate through the city.

Erzurum has good rail connections with İstanbul and Ankara via Kayseri, Sivas, Divriği and Erzincan. *Yeni Doğu Ekspresi* travels between Erzurum and Ankara in 21 hours; the *Doğu Ekspresi* takes about 25 hours. Neither runs every day, though.

KARS

About 260km north-east of Erzurum this much-fought-over frontier town has a suitably massive fortress. Nearby are the ruins of ancient Ani on the border with Armenia.

The **museum** (closed Monday), northeast of the train station on Cumhuriyet Caddesi, has exhibits dating from the Bronze Age. The tourist office (☎ 223 2300, fax 223 8452, Gazi Ahmet Muhtar Paşa Caddesi 135) is at the corner of Faik Bey Caddesi; come here for permits for Ani.

Rock bottom places to stay include *Otel Kervansaray* (☎ 223 1990, Faik Bey Caddesi 124), which charges only US$6/13 for singles/doubles; the neighbouring *Otel Nur Saray* (☎ 223 1364) is similar.

Up a notch, *Hotel Temel* (☎ 223 1376, Kazım Paşa Caddesi 4/A) is good value for US$12/20. *Hotel Güngören* (☎ 212 0298, Halit Paşa Caddesi, Millet Sokak 4) offers more comfort for US$15/25 with bath.

For real comfort, go to the three star *Hotel Karabağ* (☎ 212 3480, Faik Bey Caddesi No 84), with good rooms for US$40/60.

Several shops near the Temel and Güngören hotels sell Kars honey and the local *kaşar peynir* (mild yellow cheese) – perfect for a picnic. *Cafe Kristal* (Atatürk Caddesi) is the most cheerful place to eat.

ANİ

Ani, 45km east of Kars, was completely deserted in 1239 after a Mongol invasion, but before that it had been an important city and a capital of both the Urartian and Armenian kingdoms. Fronted by a hefty wall, the ruins lie in fields overlooking the Arpaçay River, which forms the border with Armenia. A ghost city, it's extremely dramatic and there are several notable churches, including a cathedral built between the years 989 and 1010.

In a piece of nonsense left over from Cold War days, to visit Ani you must first apply for written permission at Kars tourist office, then have your application approved at the Emniyet Müdürlüğü (Security Headquarters) and finally buy a ticket (US$2) at Kars museum. Only then can you flag a taxi to the ruins (around US$30, fair enough for a group but a lot if you're on your own). Ani is open from 8.30 am to 5 pm. Allow at least 2½ hours at the site.

AĞRI DAĞI (MT ARARAT)

When the 40 days and 40 nights finally ended, Noah and his flock are said to have landed on Mt Ararat – a nice theory, but difficult to test since climbing is no longer allowed for security reasons.

Even so, the snowcapped dormant volcano makes an impressive view rising sheer from a level plain alongside the main road between Erzurum and the Iranian border.

DOĞUBEYAZIT

Known jocularly as 'dog biscuit', this drab town is the last Turkish outpost on the road to Iran. It's dramatically sited at the far side of a sweeping grass plain that runs to the foot of Mt Ararat. Everything is within a handy five minute walk of the centre.

Apart from spectacular views of Mt Ararat, there's an interesting **palace-fort**, the İshak Paşa Sarayı (open from 8 am to 5 pm daily; entry US$2), 5km east of town. Perched romantically among rocky crags, it overlooks the town and the plains. The occasional dolmuş passes nearby, but unless you want to walk, you'll probably have to negotiate for a taxi (US$5).

Take excursions to the **meteor crater, Diyadin hot springs** and another supposed resting-place of **Noah's Ark**.

If you decide to stay, *Murat Camping*, on the road to the İshak Paşa Sarayı, has tent spaces for US$1. *Hotel Erzurum* (☎ 312

5080, Belediye Caddesi), with spartan waterless rooms for US$8 a double, is typical of the many cheap and cheerful hotels.

A good choice is the friendly *Ararat Hotel* (☎ *312 4988)*, facing the otogar and beside the busy bazaar, with comfortable doubles, some with fine views, for US$15. *Hotel İsfahan* (☎ *215 5139, Emniyet Caddesi 26)* has comfy singles/doubles for US$20/35.

Getting There & Away
Minibuses to the Gürbülak border for Iran cost US$1; assume the crossing will take at least 20 minutes even if your visa is in order. The border usually closes from 11 pm to 6 am. A shared taxi on to Maku will cost around US$0.35.

SOUTH-EASTERN TURKEY
Turkey's south-eastern corner, along the border with Syria and Iraq, is the region once known as Upper Mesopotamia, drained by the historic Tigris (Dicle) and Euphrates (Fırat) rivers. The cities of Şanlıurfa, Mardin and Diyarbakır were all centres for the Hurri-Mitanni civilisation of 4000 years ago. More recently they have been some of the places most adversely affected by the dispute between the PKK and the Turkish government.

Nemrut Dağı
North of Şanlıurfa, south of Malatya, pretty much in the middle of nowhere, is Nemrut Dağı (Mt Nimrod), on whose summit is a 2000 year old **memorial sanctuary** for an obscure Commagene king, with the heads of enormous statues of gods and kings toppled by earthquakes scattered on the ground.

You can trek to Nemrut Dağı from the north via Malatya, a farming city that specialises in apricots, or from the south via the grim oil-prospecting towns of **Adıyaman** and **Kahta**. Daily minibus tours (US$30; April to mid-October) leave from Malatya tourist office (☎ 323 3025, fax 324 2514); these include a sunset visit, a night at a hotel near the summit and a dawn visit. From Kahta the bonus is stops at other ancient sites along the way: Karakuş, a Roman

bridge, Yeni Kale and splendid Arsameia. These days many people prefer to take a three day tour from Göreme in Kapadokya (Cappadocia), which, for US$150 per person, takes in other sites in the east too.

Places to Stay
Malatya *Otel Tahran* (☎ *324 3615, PTT Caddesi)* offers basic singles/doubles with sinks for US$5/6. The nearby *Merkez* and *Özen* are similar. A better choice would be the welcoming *Otel Kantar* (☎ *321 1510, Atatürk Caddesi 81)*, where a clean if simple double room costs US$6 with sink or US$10 with a shower. Best in town is *Malatya Büyük Otel* (☎ *321 1400)*, with singles/doubles for US$15/19.

Adıyaman Adıyaman's hotels are expensive and usually full of oil prospectors but in the shopping streets off Atatürk Bulvarı, south of the Vilayet, are two good bets for backpackers, both in Harıkçı Caddesi. *Otel Yolaç* (☎ *216 1301)* has fairly basic rooms with showers but shared toilets for US$9 per person without breakfast. *Ünal* (☎ *216 1508)* is similar. *Beyaz Saray Pansiyon* (☎ *216 2100, Atatürk Bulvarı 136)*, on the highway in the eastern part of town, has singles/doubles with shower for US$6/10. The three star *Hotel Antiochos* (☎ *216 3377, Atatürk Bulvarı 141)* has good rooms for US$21/30 with breakfast and swimming pool.

Kahta Cheaper rooms are in Kahta, 35km to the east, in *Anatolia Pension* (☎ *725 1774)*, at US$3 per person; and *Hotel Kommagene* (☎ *725 1092)*, at the start of the Nemrut road, with singles/doubles for US$7/10. *Zeus Camping* charges US$3 a tent. Kahta's helpful tourist office (☎ 725 5007) is on the main road near the Hotel Kommagene.

Şanlıurfa
Once known as Edessa and commonly called Urfa, this hot, dusty but delightful city boasts that it harbours the **cave** where the patriarch Abraham was born. Pilgrims come, pay their respects, then feed fat carp in a shady pool

nearby. You can visit the fine old bazaar, some graceful mosques, a good museum, the citadel and the sacred pool. A day trip 50km to the south brings you to **Harran**, one of the oldest continuously occupied settlements, with distinctive beehive houses.

Places to Stay Urfa has accommodation to suit all tastes and budgets. Most hotels are near the Belediye. A backpackers enclave is growing up in Köprübaşı Caddesi behind the Özel Sanmed Hastanesi. The popular *Hotel İpek Palas* (☎ 215 1546) has singles/doubles for US$12/17 with private showers. A few doors along the very basic *Otel Günbay* (☎ 313 9797) charges about the same. At *Otel Uğur* (☎ 313 1340), up a perilous flight of steps at the end of Köprübaşı Caddesi, dorm beds in the most basic rooms cost just US$3.

Heading towards the bazaar you'll find *Park Otel* (☎ 216 0500, Göl Caddesi 4). Waterless rooms here are clean but as basic as they come for US$4 per person.

Urfa's best place to stay only has six rooms and tends to be booked up. *Şanlıurfa Valiliği Konuk Evi* (☎ 215 9377, Yeni Nahalesi) is a delightful 19th century stone building. The prices, at US$21/30 for singles/doubles, are surprisingly reasonable.

The other long-time favourite is the three star *Hotel Harran* (☎ 313 2860, Köprübaşı Caddesi), directly opposite the Belediye. Rates are US$20/38 for singles/doubles, or US$50 for a double with bathtub. The swimming pool is a big plus in summer.

Diyarbakır

The great basalt walls of Diyarbakır surround a city of medieval mosques, narrow streets and Kurdish separatist feelings. At the centre of the Kurdish insurgency, Diyarbakır can have the feel of an armed camp.

The tourist office (☎ 221 2173, fax 224 1189) is inside the Dağ Kapısı, by a busy road junction. If you walk along the tops of the walls, do it in a group as robbery and mischief are real problems.

Take a dolmuş from the otogar to Dağ Kapısı (3.5km) to find cheap hotels such as *Hotel Kenan* (☎ 221 6614, İzzetpaşa Caddesi 24), with shower-equipped singles/doubles for US$5/8. Also good is *Hotel Güler* (☎/fax 224 0294, Kıbrıs Caddesi, Yoğurtçu Sokak 7), offering a quiet location, clean, comfortable rooms and lots of hot water for US$18/21 a single/double.

Van

On the south-eastern shore of the vast salt lake of the same name, Van has a 3000 year old **citadel** at the Rock of Van, and an interesting **museum**. The 10th century church on **Akdamar Island** in the lake is a fascinating piece of Armenian architecture in a beautiful setting, with frescoes and reliefs depicting biblical scenes. Ferries make the trip from near Gevaş but you need a group of people to pay the US$18 to US$20 cost of the boat; dolmuşes to the harbour run from Beş Yol in Van (US$1). The tourist office (☎ 216 2018) is at Cumhuriyet Caddesi No 127.

Places to Stay Van is well supplied with cheap hotels although several were undergoing renovation at the time of writing which looked likely to push them up a price category. Those in the bazaar to the west of Cumhuriyet Caddesi tend to be cheapest, those to the east slightly more expensive, but also cleaner and more comfortable.

Several hotels in the bazaar area charge US$4.50 per person in rooms with sink and/ or private shower. Among the better ones are *Otel İpek* (☎ 216 3033, Cumhuriyet Caddesi, Sokak No 3) and the more basic *Aslan Oteli* (☎ 216 2469).

Hotel Bayram (☎ 216 1136, Cumhuriyet Caddesi 1/A) is a good choice, with clean, modern singles/doubles with shower and sink for US$9/15. Better is *Büyük Asur Oteli* (☎ 216 8792, Cumhuriyet Caddesi, Turizm Sokak 5), charging US$18/25 for singles/doubles with shower and plenty of hot water.

Büyük Urartu (☎ 212 0660) is the high-status place in town but it's overpriced at US$65/78.

The United Arab Emirates

Travel agencies in Europe push the United Arab Emirates (UAE) as a land of contrasts: mountains, beaches, deserts and oases, camel racing, Bedouin markets and the legendary duty-free shopping of Dubai. Brochures trumpet the 'Arabian Experience' and are clearly aimed at upmarket tourists in search of an exotic but comfortable destination. But the UAE is also one of the best places in the Gulf for the independent traveller.

A union of seven sovereign sheikhdoms, the UAE was formed in 1971 when the British withdrew from the Gulf. Despite the small size of the emirates, each has its own, distinct features. The capital, Abu Dhabi, is one of the most modern cities on earth, while Dubai is unquestionably the most vibrant city in the Gulf.

Facts about the UAE

HISTORY

Like much of the rest of the Gulf, what is now the UAE has been settled for many centuries. The earliest significant settlements are from the Bronze Age. In the 3rd millennium BC a culture known as Umm an-Nar (after the island where it was discovered) arose near modern Abu Dhabi. Umm an-Nar's influence extended well into the interior and down the coast of what is now Oman. There were also settlements at Badiyah (near Fujairah) and at Rams (near Ras al-Khaimah) during the second half of the 3rd millennium BC.

The Greeks were the next major cultural influence in the area. Ruins showing strong Hellenistic features have been found at Meleiha, about 50km from Sharjah, and at Ad-Dour in the emirate of Umm al-Qaiwain.

During the Middle Ages much of the area was part of the Kingdom of Hormuz, which

The United Arab Emirates

Area: 83,600 sq km
Population: 2.4 million
Population Growth Rate: 3.5%
Capital: Abu Dhabi
Head of State: The President, Sheikh Zayed bin Sultan al-Nahyan
Official Language: Arabic
Currency: UAE dirham (Dh)
Exchange Rate: US$1 = Dh3.673

- **Best Dining** – treat yourself to an omelette sandwich for Dh2.50 at Mina restaurant in Abu Dhabi
- **Best Activity** – an overnight camel safari and barbecue in the desert
- **Best View** – go to the top floor of the Jumeira Beach Hotel for the best view of Dubai
- **Best Walk** – a stroll around the Heritage and Arts areas in Sharjah
- **When in Rome ...** relax with a sheesha and a chat after dinner at any one of the many coffeehouses

controlled the entrance to, and most of the trade in, the Gulf. The Portuguese first arrived in 1498 and by 1515 they had occupied Julfar (near Ras al-Khaimah) and built a customs house through which they taxed the Gulf's flourishing trade with India and the Far East. The Portuguese stayed on in the town until 1633.

The rise of British naval power in the Gulf in the mid-18th century coincided with the rise of two important tribal confederations along the coast of the lower Gulf. These were the Qawasim and the Bani Yas, the ancestors of the rulers of four of the seven emirates that today make up the UAE.

The Qawasim, whose descendants now rule Sharjah and Ras al-Khaimah, were a seafaring clan based in Ras al-Khaimah. Their influence extended, at times, to the Persian side of the Gulf. This brought them into conflict with the British, who dubbed the area the Pirate Coast and launched raids against the Qawasim in 1805, 1809 and 1811. In 1820 a British fleet systematically destroyed or captured every Qawasim ship it could find, imposed a General Treaty of Peace on nine Arab sheikhdoms in the area and installed a garrison in the region. As life there quietened down Europeans took to calling the area the Trucial Coast, a name it retained until 1971.

Throughout this period the main power among the Bedouin tribes of the interior was the Bani Yas tribal confederation, made up of the ancestors of the ruling families of modern Abu Dhabi and Dubai. The Bani Yas were originally based in Liwa, an oasis on the edge of the Empty Quarter desert, but moved to Abu Dhabi in 1793. They engaged in the traditional Bedouin activities of camel herding, small-scale agriculture, tribal raiding and extracting protection money from caravans passing through their territory. The Bani Yas divided into two main branches in the early 19th century when Dubai split from Abu Dhabi.

So long as their rivals were kept out of the region and the lines of communication to India remained secure, the British, who formally established a protectorate over the Trucial Coast in 1892, did not really care what happened in the Gulf. The area became a backwater. Throughout the late 19th and early 20th centuries the sheikhdoms were all tiny enclaves of fishers, pearl divers and Bedouin.

What to See

Dubai is the most vibrant city in the Gulf, and should be a stop on any traveller's itinerary. The museum and Deira souqs are worth a look, but the city's real attraction is its atmosphere.

The **Buraimi oasis** is an easy trip from Dubai. There are a number of historical and archaeological sites in the area, and the contrast between the Emirati and Omani sides of the oasis is greater than you might think.

If you have more time, consider a trip from **Fujairah** to **Dibba** on the east coast where there is some of the best scenery in the country and some great beaches.

It was the prospect of oil that changed the way the British ran their affairs on the Trucial Coast. After the collapse of the world pearl market in the early 20th century, the entire coast was plunged into abject poverty. In 1939, Sheikh Shakhbut, the ruler of Abu Dhabi, granted the first of several oil concessions on his territory. It was not until 1958, however, that oil was found in the emirate. Exports began in 1962 and, with a population at the time of only 15,000, Abu Dhabi was obviously on its way to becoming very rich.

Throughout this period Dubai was cementing its reputation as the region's busiest trading centre. In 1939 Sheikh Rashid bin Said al-Maktoum quickly moved to bolster the emirate's position as the lower Gulf's main entrepôt. Dubai was already becoming a relatively wealthy trading centre when, in 1966, it was found to have oil of its own.

Britain's 1968 announcement that it would leave the Gulf in 1971 came as a shock to most of the ruling sheikhs. Britain's original plan was to form a single state consisting of Bahrain, Qatar and the Trucial Coast. Plans for such a grouping were announced in February 1968 but collapsed almost immediately. Negotiations over the next three years

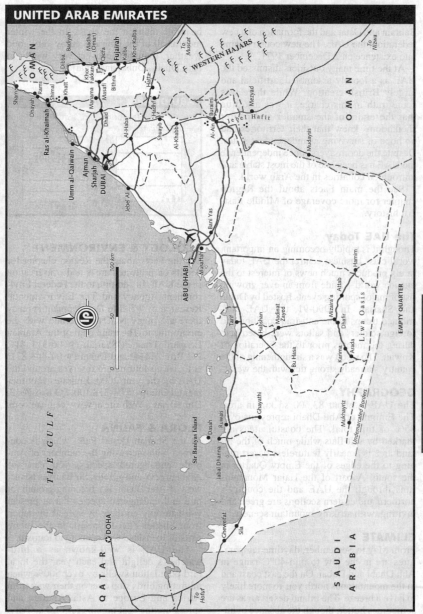

eventually resulted in independence for Bahrain and Qatar and the formation of a new federation: the UAE. The new country came into existence on 2 December 1971.

At the time many outsiders dismissed the UAE as a loosely assembled, artificial and largely British creation. While there was some truth in this charge, it was also true that the emirs of the smaller and poorer sheikhdoms knew that their territories had no hope of surviving as independent states. Despite the doomsayers, since independence the UAE has been one of the most stable and untroubled countries in the Arab world.

See the main Facts about the Region chapter for more coverage of Middle Eastern history.

The UAE Today

Though it is rapidly becoming an important, world-class business centre, the UAE today rarely produces much news of interest to the outside world – aside from an ever-growing list of major sporting events hosted by Dubai and Sharjah. In 1990-91, the UAE contributed troops to the anti-Iraq coalition and foreign soldiers and sailors were based here during the months prior to the liberation of Kuwait. The result was a strengthening of the country's already strong ties with the west.

GEOGRAPHY

The UAE is about 83,600 sq km in area. The Emirate of Abu Dhabi represents over 85% of this total. The coastal areas are marked by salt flats while much of the inland area is a nearly featureless desert running to the edges of the Empty Quarter in the south. A part of the Hajar Mountains runs through the UAE and the country's northern and eastern sections are green and inviting, with striking mountain scenery.

CLIMATE

From May to September, daytime temperatures are in the low to mid-40°C range in Abu Dhabi and Dubai. On the east coast and in the mountainous north you're more likely to have a breeze. The inland desert areas are sometimes hotter, though the absence of hu-

midity makes the heat here much more bearable than on the coast. In the winter months all of the emirates enjoy very good weather, though it can get very windy in Abu Dhabi, Dubai and Sharjah.

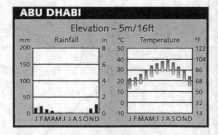

ECOLOGY & ENVIRONMENT

See the Facts about the Region chapter for details on protected areas and conservation in the UAE. In addition to the Federal Environment Agency and The Environmental Research & Wildlife Development Agency there are many NGOs concerned with the environment. The main goal of the Arabian Leopard Trust in Sharjah (☎ 06-311 411, PO Box 24444) and Dubai (☎ 04-444 871) is to set up four nature reserves around the UAE by the year 2000. Emirates Environmental Group (☎ 04-318 100, PO Box 7013, Dubai) has a Web site at www.eeg.uae.com.

FLORA & FAUNA

At the Sharjah Desert Park, which is concerned with increasing the numbers of Arabia's endangered species, you can see Arabian oryx and gazelle. Sir Baniyas Island, west of Abu Dhabi, is a breeding ground for rare and endangered species but at present you can only go there by special invitation from Sheikh Zayed himself. In the future parts of the island will open up to tourism.

The UAE is well-known as a birdwatcher's delight and each year the local bird population swells by over 500% when migrating birds stop over on their way from Africa and Europe to Asia. Autumn and spring are the best months for bird activity.

In Dubai, thousands of flamingos inhabit an area of swampy land along Oud Metha Rd that has been set aside as a waterbird and wildlife sanctuary. In the parks, golf courses and wadis you will see parakeets, shrikes, doves, Indian rollers and little green bee-eaters. On the coasts you'll see Socotra cormorants and swift terns. The mangrove swamp of Khor Kalba on the east coast is the only home in the world to the Khor Kalba white collared kingfisher, and the mangroves at Umm al-Qaiwain are home to abundant bird species.

Birdwatchers can arrange tours through Colin Richardson of the Emirates Bird Records Committee (☎ 04-472 277).

GOVERNMENT & POLITICS

Though there is a federal government over which one of the emirs presides, each of the rulers is completely sovereign within his own emirate.

In 1991, Sheikh Zayed bin Sultan al-Nayan of Abu Dhabi was elected to his fifth term as president, a position he seems likely to hold for life. Sheikh Maktoum, the ruler of Dubai, is the country's vice president and prime minister.

The degree of power which the seven emirs should cede to the federal government has been one of the country's hottest topics of debate since independence in 1971. The forum where these and other issues are discussed is the Supreme Council, the highest body in the country, which comprises the seven emirs. There is also a cabinet in which the posts are distributed among the emirates. Most of the federal government's money comes from Abu Dhabi and Dubai so they get to hold most of the important Cabinet posts.

The cabinet and Supreme Council are advised, but cannot be overruled, by the Federation Council of Ministers. This is a 40 member consultative body whose members are appointed by the respective emirs. All the council's members come from leading merchant families.

The UAE does not align itself with any other country but it is committed to Arab unity in the region.

POPULATION & PEOPLE

There's an estimated 2.4 million people living in the UAE, of whom about 27% (650,000) are UAE citizens (or 'nationals' as they are usually referred to). The expat community makes up the rest of the population, the majority of whom are from India, Pakistan and other Arab countries. The Emiratis themselves come from a number of different backgrounds. All of the northern emirates

The Easy Life

The European and US presence in the Middle East, which began with the 19th century 'discovery' and plunder of the orient continues today in the form of a huge western expatriate workforce. From Tehrān to Tripoli, every major Middle Eastern city has its community of westerners, some just there on a short-term work contract, others who've entered into a longer term relationship with their host country and may well never leave. Just look at the benefits. For the 45,000 or so western expats living in the UAE, life is a fantasy world of no taxes, often no rent and a free air fare home once or twice a year. A typical expat existence is one of disposable income, continuously sunny weather, weekend camping and 4WD trips, beach resorts, pubs and restaurants. It's a life few could ever expect to maintain back in their own country.

But money is not the only driving force. There is also the opportunity to explore the Arab culture and enjoy its hospitality and warmth. The crime rate is low and the streets are safe and many people choose to bring up children here too. Ask any western expat when they're going home for good and the common answer is 'Oh, in another 12 months or so' but be sure, you can come back in another couple of years and find that same person, still frequenting the same places, and you can ask your question again and you'll hear the same procrastinations. The expat lifestyle can be very seductive indeed.

have substantial communities of people of Persian, Indian or Baluchi ancestry.

RELIGION

Most Emiratis are Sunni Muslims subscribing to the Maliki or Hanbali schools of Islamic law. Many of the latter are Wahhabis, though UAE Wahhabis are not nearly as strict and puritanical as the Saudi Wahhabis. There are also smaller communities of Ibadi and Shi'ite Muslims. Other religions are tolerated and there are a number of Christian churches throughout the country.

LANGUAGE

Arabic is the official language of the UAE but English is very widely understood. In Dubai and Abu Dhabi, you could also get by using the Persian language, Farsi. Urdu can be useful because of the large number of Pakistani expatriates.

Facts for the Visitor

PLANNING
When to Go

For information about when to visit this part of the world see the Regional Facts for the Visitor chapter. A trip to the UAE in high summer (July/August) is simply a bad idea – however, if you enjoy temperatures of 48°C you will be treated to heavily discounted hotel rates. Many hotels also offer up to 50% off their normal rates during Ramadan.

VISAS & DOCUMENTS
Visas

Citizens of other Gulf Cooperation Council (GCC) countries and British nationals with the right of abode in the UK do not need visas to enter the UAE. Everyone else has to arrange a transit visa (two weeks, Dh120) or visit visa (two months, Dh110) through a sponsor. This can be a hotel, a company or a resident of the UAE. Most hotels will charge you about Dh180, and in some cases Dh300 or more, for arranging one. Emirates Airlines and Gulf Air can arrange visas for a total cost of Dh150.

If you are arranging a visa through a hotel you will usually be required to stay there for up to three nights. Once you have the visa, however, you are free to move to a cheaper hotel. Processing the visa can take anywhere from two days to three weeks. While there are a lot of cheap hotels that claim to sponsor visas, many of them provide rather questionable service.

Multi-entry visas are available for British, US, Canadian and German passport holders. These cost Dh400 on average and are valid for two years.

The immigration authorities say they will issue an on-the-spot three week visa to westerners of certain professions (management-type jobs usually) holding a GCC residence permit who turn up at airports and at land border posts.

Officially, if your passport shows any evidence of travel to Israel you will be denied entry to the UAE, but we have heard from travellers who have visited Israel and have had no problem entering the UAE.

Visas for Neighbouring Countries You need a visa to enter the following neighbouring countries of the UAE:

Kuwait GCC residents need a sponsorship letter from their employer, photocopies of the information pages of their passport plus an invitation from a company or hotel in Kuwait. The fee varies; it's free for some nationalities, Dh70 for US passport holders. The visa takes two days to process.

Tourists on visit visas cannot get Kuwaiti visas in the UAE – it has to be done from the Kuwait embassy in their home country.

Oman GCC residents need a sponsorship letter from their company plus photocopies of the information pages of their passport. The fee varies, eg Dh70 for Australians, US citizens and New Zealanders; Dh200 for Brits. The visa takes two days to process. It's the same deal for tourists but they don't have to have a sponsorship letter (obviously).

GCC residents who have been in the country for at least one year and have six months validity left on their residence visa can purchase visas at major border posts or at the airport on arrival. Have two photos and a copy of your passport ready.

Qatar GCC residents with certain professions can get a visa on arrival in Doha at airport immigration; phone them (☎ 00974-351550 ext 490) for information on whether or not you qualify for an automatic visa. Others will need to go through a sponsor in Doha. The Qatari embassy in the UAE does not issue visas to tourists; this must be done from your home country.

Saudi Arabia You must organise a visa through the Saudi embassy at home.

Yemen GCC residents need a sponsorship letter from their employer; tourists need a letter of recommendation from their embassy. The visa costs Dh50 for most nationalities but it costs Dh230 for British passport holders, and it's processed on the same day.

Other Documents

International Student Cards are generally not recognised in the UAE and having one will not get you discounts at hotels or sites. Most foreign driving licences are accepted for car rental.

EMBASSIES
UAE Embassies

For addresses of UAE embassies in neighbouring Middle Eastern countries see the relevant country chapters.

Australia
    Embassy:
    (☎ 2-6286 8802, fax 6286 8804)
    36 Culgoa Circuit, O'Malley ACT 2606
France
    Embassy:
    (☎ 01 45 53 94 04, fax 01 47 55 61 04)
    3, rue de Lota, 75116 Paris
Germany
    Embassy:
    (☎ 228-267 070, fax 267 0714)
    Erste Fahrgasse, D-54113, Bonn

UK
    Embassy:
    (☎ 020-7581 1281/4113, fax 7581 9616)
    30 Princes Gate, London SW1
USA
    Embassy:
    (☎ 202-338 6500, fax 337 7029)
    3000 K St, NW, Suite 600, Washington DC 20007

Embassies in the UAE

Core opening hours are 9 am to noon Saturday to Wednesday, although many embassies either open an hour earlier or close an hour later than this. The following are all in Abu Dhabi.

Australia
    Embassy (temporary):
    (☎ 789 946, fax 779 909)
    Gulf Business Centre, corner of Salam and Hamdan Sts, Abu Dhabi; 8 am to 5 pm Saturday to Wednesday; for more information call the Australian consulate in Dubai (☎ 313 444, fax 314 812)
Bahrain
    Embassy:
    (☎ 312 200, fax 311 202)
    Al-Najda St, behind Abu Dhabi Islamic Bank
Canada
    Embassy:
    (☎ 456 969, fax 458 787)
    Al-Nahayan St, near the Batin Palace
France
    Embassy:
    (☎ 435 100, fax 434 158)
    Al-Nahayan St, near the Batin Palace
Germany
    Embassy:
    (☎ 435 630, fax 455 712)
    Al-Nahayan St, near the Batin Palace
Iran
    Embassy:
    (☎ 447618, fax 448 714)
    Diplomatic Area, Airport Rd, behind Pepsi factory, about 10km south of the centre
Ireland
    Citizens of Ireland are represented through the embassy in Riyadh
Kuwait
    Embassy:
    (☎ 446 888, fax 444 990)
    Diplomatic Area, Airport Rd, behind the Pepsi factory, about 10km south of the centre
Netherlands
    Embassy:
    (☎ 321 920, fax 313 158)
    Al-Masaood Tower (look for the Standard & Chartered Bank at street level of the same

building), 6th floor, Shaikh Hamdan bin Mohammed St

Oman
Embassy:
(☎ 463 333, fax 464 633)
Airport Rd, next to the Immigration Department, about 8km south of the centre

Qatar
Embassy:
(☎ 493 300, fax 493 311)
Diplomatic Area, Airport Rd, behind Pepsi
factory, about 10km south of the centre

Saudi Arabia
Embassy:
(☎ 445 700, fax 446 747)
Diplomatic Area, Airport Rd, behind Pepsi
factory, about 10km south of the centre

UK
Embassy:
(☎ 326 600, fax 342 676)
Khalid bin al-Walid St, slightly south of the
Corniche

USA
Embassy:
(☎ 436 691, fax 435 441)
Sudan St, between Al-Karamah St and the in-
tersection where King Khalid bin Abdul Aziz
St becomes Al-Nahayan St

Yemen
Embassy:
(☎ 448 457, fax 447 978)
Diplomatic Area, Airport Rd, behind Pepsi
factor, about 10km south of the centre

CUSTOMS

The duty-free allowances for tobacco are
huge: 2000 cigarettes, 400 cigars or 2kg of
loose tobacco (this is *not* a country cracking
down on smoking). Non-Muslims are allowed to import 2L of wine and 2L of spirits, unless they are arriving in Sharjah,
where alcohol is prohibited. You are not allowed to bring in alcohol if you enter the
country by land. If you bring videos into the
country, or even if they are sent to you by
mail, they are likely to be confiscated for
about a month while they are inspected.

MONEY
Costs

The UAE is not a low-budget country like
Egypt or Iran but it is possible to keep costs
under control. Decent hotels can be found for
Dh100 to Dh150 in Dubai but they tend to be
more expensive elsewhere. Eating for Dh10
to Dh15 is rarely a problem though if you include alcohol the bill will be a lot higher.
Getting around is cheap in shared long-distance taxis and minibuses and admission to
most museums etc is free. Plan on spending
Dh150/200 per day for budget/mid-range
travel. In Dubai, Fujairah and Sharjah, which
have good youth hostels, you might be able
to keep your budget down to half that.

Currency

The UAE dirham (Dh) is divided into 100
fils. Notes come in denominations of five,
10, 20, 50, 100, 200, 500 and Dh1000.
Coins are Dh1, 50 fils, 25 fils, 10 fils and 5
fils. The government recently issued new
coins that are smaller than the old ones.
Both types remain legal tender.

Exchange Rates

The dirham is fully convertible and is pegged
to the US dollars. Exchange rates are:

country	unit		dirham
Australia	A$1	=	Dh2.368
Canada	C$1	=	Dh2.464
euro	€1	=	Dh3.892
France	10FF	=	Dh5.930
Germany	DM1	=	Dh1.990
Japan	¥100	=	Dh3.352
New Zealand	NZ$1	=	Dh1.904
UK	UK£1	=	Dh5.894
USA	US$1	=	Dh3.673

Exchanging Money

Moneychangers sometimes have better
rates than banks, and some do not even
charge a commission (others charge quite
big ones). The problem with moneychangers is that some of them either will not take
travellers cheques or will take only one
type. Currencies of neighbouring countries
are all easily changed with the exception of
the Yemeni riyal, which was out of circulation at the time of writing.

Credit Cards & ATMs

ATMs at branches of the British Bank of
the Middle East are linked to the Global
Access system. ATMs at Emirates Bank In-

ternational and Abu Dhabi Commercial Bank are also on Global Access, as well as Cirrus, Plus and, sometimes, Switch. All major credit cards are accepted, though you may be hit with a 5% merchant fee if you use Amex.

Tipping & Bargaining

Tips are not generally expected in the UAE as there is a service charge added to your bill (this goes to the restaurant, not the waiter, however). If you want to leave a tip, 10% should be sufficient.

Bargaining in souqs in the country can be exhausting. Be prepared to spend some time at it and you'll find that prices may come down by as much as 50%. Even in shopping centres you can ask for a discount or for their 'best price'. The more touristy souqs in the cities will not usually offer this much of a discount.

Taxes & Refunds

In Dubai most hotel and restaurant bills will have 10% tacked on for a service charge and another 10% for a municipality tax. In Abu Dhabi hotels and restaurants have a 16% service charge added to their bills and in Sharjah it's 15%. If a price is quoted 'net', this means that it includes all taxes and service charges.

POST & COMMUNICATIONS

Post

Letters up to 20g cost Dh3 to Europe; Dh3.50 to the USA, Australia and Asia and Dh2.50 to the Indian subcontinent. Postcard rates are Dh2 to Europe, the USA, Australia and Asia and Dh1 to Arab countries. Sending a 1kg package to Australia, the USA and Asia costs Dh130; to Europe and South Africa it costs Dh85 and to the Indian subcontinent Dh68.

Sending Mail

Mail generally takes about a week to Europe or the USA and eight to 10 days to Australia. Mumtaz Speed Post or Express Mail Services are available from main post offices in each emirate but they are very expensive and you might save money by using a courier.

Receiving Mail

Poste restante facilities are not available in the UAE. The American Express (Amex) offices in Abu Dhabi and Dubai will hold mail for clients (see city entries for addresses). If you are checking into a five star hotel the reception desk will usually hold letters and small packages for two or three days prior to your arrival. Be sure to mark the envelope 'Guest in Hotel' and 'Hold for Arrival'.

Telephone

The country code for the UAE is ☎ 971, followed by the area code (minus the zero), then the subscriber number. Area codes for the major cities and regions are:

Abu Dhabi	☎ 02
Ajman	☎ 06
Al-Ain	☎ 03
Dubai	☎ 04
Fujairah	☎ 09
Liwa oasis	☎ 088
Ras al-Khaimah	☎ 07
Sharjah	☎ 06
Umm al-Qaiwain	☎ 06

The UAE has a splendid telecommunications system and you can connect up with just about anywhere in the world from even the remotest areas. The state telecom monopoly is ETISALAT, recognisable in each city by the giant golf ball on top of its office buildings. Coin phones have almost completely been taken over by card phones. Phonecards are available from street vendors around ETISALAT offices and from grocery stores.

Fax

You can send faxes from ETISALAT offices. They may ask for your local address and contact number before they'll send it. The service is fairly good but it is expensive at Dh10 per page to most international destinations.

Email & Internet Access

Internet connection is available though ETISALAT. Internet cafes are in most cities (see city entries for details). Five-star hotels offer Internet access to their guests though sometimes this is only available to guests staying in executive suites.

BOOKS

The *Abu Dhabi Explorer* and *Dubai Explorer* include information on just about everything there is to see and do – particularly useful for expats. For those who have 4WDs, *Off Road in the Emirates I* and *II* by Dariush Zandi is a must if you want to go exploring, although directions to places can be vague and confusing.

Father of Dubai: Sheikh Rashid bin Said Al Maktoum by Graeme Wilson is a tribute to the acknowledged founder of modern Dubai. For an intimate view of life on the Trucial Coast before oil was discovered, read Wilfred Thesiger's classic *Arabian Sands*, originally published in 1959.

For an Emirati view of local history and Britain's role in the Gulf see *The Myth of Arab Piracy in the Gulf* by Sultan Muhammad al-Qasimi, the Emir of Sharjah. *Mother Without a Mask* by Patricia Holton is an easy to read account of a British woman's involvement with a family from Al-Ain.

More general Middle East titles, some of which also contain coverage of the UAE, are listed in the Books section in the Regional Facts for the Visitor chapter at the beginning of this book.

NEWSPAPERS & MAGAZINES

Gulf News and *Khaleej Times*, both based in Dubai, are the UAE's two English-language newspapers. Both cost Dh2 and carry pretty much the same international news, though *Gulf News* is widely regarded as the better of the two.

What's On (Dh12) is a monthly magazine catering mostly to the expatriate community. It's a pretty good source of information about what's new at hotels, bars, clubs and discos.

RADIO & TV

Abu Dhabi and Dubai each have an English-language TV channel, though outside the two main cities reception is decidedly mixed. In various parts of the country you can also pick up English-language signals from Qatar and Oman. Most hotels, even small ones, offer satellite TV.

Abu Dhabi and Dubai also have English-language FM radio stations. Dubai FM is at FM 92 and Channel 4 FM is at 104.8. Abu Dhabi's Capital Radio is at FM 100.5.

PHOTOGRAPHY & VIDEO

Getting colour prints developed is never a problem – 20-minute services are advertised by photo developers on nearly every street in the country. A 36 exposure roll of film will cost you about Dh38 for developing. You'll also get another film and a photo album thrown in. The best place to get slides and B&W film developed is at Prolab in Dubai (☎ 669 766).

LAUNDRY

There are few laundrettes in the UAE's cities but small laundries abound and are very cheap. An average load might cost you Dh10. Dry cleaning services are also offered in most cities.

TOILETS

The best advice is to go when you can, because there is not an abundance of public toilets in the UAE. Most public toilets in shopping centres, museums or hotels are western style. The only toilets you're likely to find out of the cities are holes in the ground out the back of restaurants or petrol stations.

HEALTH

The standard of health care is quite high throughout the UAE. Should you get sick consult either the hotel doctor, if you are in a big hotel, or your embassy or consulate. If this is not possible, you can go to any hospital. Western medicines are widely available in larger cities.

Tap water in Abu Dhabi and Dubai is safe to drink, but often tastes bad and is heavily chlorinated. Stick to bottled water. See the Health section in the Facts about the Region chapter for more health information.

DISABLED TRAVELLERS

Contact North Tours (☎ 04-737 474) in Dubai; it can arrange all kinds of tours specifically designed for disabled travellers and book hotels with facilities for disabled guests. It will also sponsor visas.

DANGERS & ANNOYANCES

The main danger is bad driving. Many drivers in the UAE don't seem to have a concept of other cars and courtesy on the road simply does not exist. People will cut in front of you, turn without indicating, and race each other on freeways. They have a tendency to zoom into roundabouts at frightening speeds, and try to exit them from inside lanes. Pedestrian crossings are no guarantee that drivers will stop or even slow down. Watch out!

BUSINESS HOURS

Government offices open at 7 or 7.30 am and finish at 1 or 1.30 pm from Saturday to Wednesday. Banks, private companies and smaller shops open Saturday to Wednesday from 8 am to 1 or 1.30 pm and in the afternoon from 4 to 7 or 8 pm. Shopping centres and souqs open every day to about 10 pm.

There are local variations: in Ras al-Khaimah, for example, all shops are required to close for about 30 minutes at prayer time.

PUBLIC HOLIDAYS

Apart from the Islamic holidays described in the Regional Facts for the Visitor chapter, the UAE observes:

New Year's Day
  1 January
Lailat al-Mi'raj
  24 October 2000 (varies each year) – Ascension of the Prophet
National Day
  2 December

Each emirate may also observe its own holidays (eg in Abu Dhabi 6 August is a holiday marking the accession of Sheikh Zayed).

ACCOMMODATION

There are no camp sites adjacent to the UAE's cities but camping in the desert is quite common. There are youth hostels in Dubai, Sharjah and Fujairah (see these sections for details). HI cards are required at all three hostels. Most of the country's cheap hotels are in and around the Dubai souq. These bottom out at around Dh70/90 for a single/double but we can't recommend these places to single women travellers. The cheapest places providing reliable visa-sponsorship service cost around Dh250/350.

FOOD & DRINKS

Eating cheap in the UAE means eating either in small Indian/Pakistani restaurants or having street food, such as shwarma. Inexpensive Lebanese, Chinese and Filipino food is also available, as is the usual American fastfood. See the Middle Eastern cuisine section in the Facts about the Region chapter for a general discussion of Middle Eastern delicacies.

Alcohol can only be sold in restaurants and bars in hotels. The prices are pretty outrageous – expect to pay around Dh18 for a pint of beer. Alcohol is not available in Sharjah.

SPECTATOR SPORT

The most popular spectator sport in the UAE is camel racing (although after 10 minutes a single race can get exceedingly boring to watch). Early Friday mornings are the best time to see races or training.

The Dubai Desert Classic is one of the richest PGA golf tournaments and is held at Dubai Creek Golf & Yacht Club each February. The Dubai Tennis Open, also held in February, is a part of the ATP world series tour. The Dubai World Cup is well known as the world's richest horse race with prize money of US$5 million. It is held at Nad al-Sheba racecourse, 5km south-east of Dubai.

SHOPPING

Dubai has a well established reputation as a shoppers' paradise, mostly due to its duty-free status. There are a few shops in Al-Ain, Abu Dhabi and Dubai dealing in Bedouin souvenirs, most of which come from Oman. If you have a lot of money to spend try the gold souq in Dubai or the carpet merchants in

Sharjah's new souq. Dubai is also the cheapest place outside of Iran to buy Iranian caviar.

Getting There & Away

AIR
Airports & Airlines
Dubai and Abu Dhabi are the country's main international airports, though an increasing number of carriers serve Sharjah as well. There are also small international airports at Ras al-Khaimah, Fujairah and Al-Ain.

Emirates Airlines and Gulf Air are the main airlines operating in the UAE. There are daily services from Abu Dhabi and Dubai to major European and Middle Eastern cities. Strictly speaking there are high and low seasons but special fares are offered at any time of the year so shop around. There are no bucket shops in the UAE.

Buying Tickets in the UAE
The only airline flying nonstop from Dubai to New York is Malaysian Airlines; the fare of Dh3700 is about the best you can get. Return air fares to Europe range from Dh3000 to Dh3500. You can get to Athens for Dh1300 one way. During summer and Christmas, when many expats return home, airlines often have special fares to London, sometimes as low as Dh2000 return.

Sample return air fares to other destinations in the Middle East are Amman Dh2000 (US$543), Beirut Dh1810 (US$492), Cairo Dh1800 (US$490), Doha Dh360 (US$98), Muscat Dh500 (US$136) and Tehrān Dh1240 (US$337).

LAND
There is a daily bus service between Dubai and Muscat, and Abu Dhabi and Muscat via Al-Ain, though the lack of a UAE border post at Dibba, Buraimi or Hatta can present some visa problems for travellers. Essentially, you can leave the UAE this way with no problems, but if you want to enter at these points you will not receive an entry stamp and therefore will be considered to be in transit and have 48 hours to leave – whether by air, sea or road. After that you will incur a fine of Dh100 per day when you do try to leave. Having a valid UAE visa in your passport makes no difference.

To enter through Sila, the checkpoint near the Saudi-UAE border, or Sham, on the UAE-Oman border north of Ras al-Khaimah, you will get a border stamp and can remain in the country for as long as your visa allows.

There are dozens of bus companies with services to Syria via Saudi Arabia and Jordan. A ticket costs around Dh500 return, including the cost of the Saudi transit visa. The trip takes 35 hours and buses leave three times a week. You'll find these companies around the bus stations in major cities.

SEA
There are passenger services between Sharjah and the port of Bandar Abbas in Iran. The trip takes 12 hours and costs Dh160 one way. For more details contact Oasis Freight Co (☎ 06-596 325) in Sharjah. Make sure that the hotel organising your visa deposits it at Sharjah port for you to pick up.

There is a passenger and car ferry between Jebel Ali and Umm Qasr Port in Iraq, departing once a week on Saturday. Bookings are handled by Al Majid Travel Agency (☎ 04-211 176). One-way/return fares will cost Dh830/1280 in economy and Dh1065/1640 in 1st class, including meals and port taxes. GCC residents can get a visa on arrival in Iraq for US$100 but they must submit to a blood test. The trip takes 1½ days.

DEPARTURE TAX
There is no airport departure tax. If you leave by boat or road, there's a Dh20 tax, though at some crossing points there are no border posts to collect it.

Getting Around

AIR
At the time of writing there were no air services between the emirates although there

were plans for a charter service between Dubai and Al-Ain.

MINIBUS
Dubai transport has had a minibus service to all the emirates since mid-1998 but at the time of writing there was still no return service. Yes, that's right. The buses go back to Dubai empty.

LONG-DISTANCE TAXI
Shared taxis can be a bit cramped but they are cheap and a great way to meet people. The main problem is often that, aside from the busy Abu Dhabi-Dubai route, they do not fill up very quickly. You can also take them engaged if you are willing to pay for all of the seats.

CAR
Major roads around the UAE are good. Rental for small cars starts at about Dh120 per day with another Dh20 to Dh30 for insurance, but you may be able to negotiate this down to a net rate of around Dh100 per day, with insurance, at the smaller agencies. The first 100 or 150km per day are usually free. If you rent a car for more than three days you will usually be given unlimited kilometres.

ORGANISED TOURS
There are several companies in Dubai, Abu Dhabi, Sharjah and Ras al-Khaimah offering tours of the various emirates. They also run desert safaris, dhow cruises, camel rides and camping trips. For a list of tour companies in Dubai and Abu Dhabi see the *Explorer* guides or the Tourist Guide section at the front of the telephone book.

Most operators are based in Dubai but have branches in other emirates. Some of the main ones are Arabian Adventures (☎ 04-343 9966), Orient Tours (☎ 04-828 238), Alpha Tours (☎ 04-223 229), Gulf Ventures (☎ 04-305 102) and Oasis Tours (☎ 04-626 556). Bear in mind that, with what you spend on a day's tour with one of these companies, you could hire a car for up to three days and take yourself to lots more places in your own time.

Abu Dhabi

Everything in the UAE's capital is modern, sleek and shiny. Abu Dhabi is often accused of being a rather soulless place, but that's probably going a bit too far: it may not be the most exciting place around but it does have its attractions.

Orientation
The city of Abu Dhabi sits at the head of a T-shaped island. The airport is about 30km from the centre. The main business district is the area bounded by Shaikh Khalifa bin Zayed and Istiglal Sts to the north, Zayed the Second St to the south, Khalid bin al-Walid St to the west, and As Salam St to the east. Some of the streets have names that are in more common use than their official ones. These include (formal name first):

Shaikh Rashid bin Saeed al-Maktoum St – Airport Rd or Old Airport Rd
Zayed the Second St – often called Electra St
Shaikh Hamdan bin Mohammed St – referred to as Hamdan
Al-Falah St – often called Passport St

Information
Money In the centre, and especially along Hamdan and Shaikh Khalifa bin Zayed Sts, it often seems like every third building is a bank. If you're looking for a moneychanger instead of a bank, try Leewa St, around the corner from Hamdan.

Amex (☎ 213 045) is represented by Al-Masaood Travel & Services on Al-Nasr St near the intersection with Khalid bin al-Walid St. All the usual Amex services are provided, including cheque cashing and holding mail. Mail should be addressed c/o American Express, PO Box 806, Abu Dhabi, UAE, and should be clearly marked 'Client's Mail'. The office is open from 8.30 am to 1 pm and 4 to 6.30 pm Sunday to Thursday.

Post The main post office is on East Rd between Al-Falah and Zayed the Second Sts.

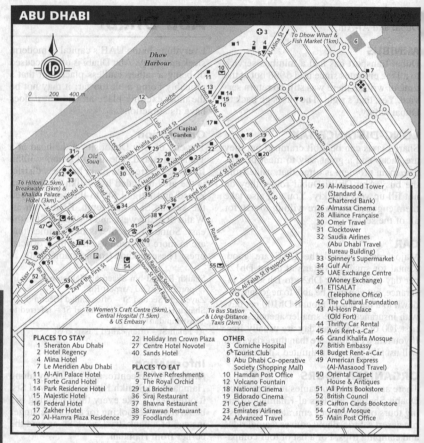

ABU DHABI

Dhow Harbour

0   200   400 m

PLACES TO STAY
1 Sheraton Abu Dhabi
2 Hotel Regency
4 Mina Hotel
7 Le Meridien Abu Dhabi
11 Al-Ain Palace Hotel
13 Forte Grand Hotel
14 Park Residence Hotel
15 Majestic Hotel
16 Federal Hotel
17 Zakher Hotel
20 Al-Hamra Plaza Residence

22 Holiday Inn Crown Plaza
27 Centre Hotel Novotel
40 Sands Hotel

PLACES TO EAT
5 Revive Refreshments
9 The Royal Orchid
29 La Brioche
36 Siraj Restaurant
37 Bhavna Restaurant
38 Sarawan Restaurant
39 Foodlands

OTHER
3 Corniche Hospital
6 Tourist Club
8 Abu Dhabi Co-operative
   Society (Shopping Mall)
10 Hamdan Post Office
12 Volcano Fountain
18 National Cinema
19 Eldorado Cinema
21 Cyber Cafe
23 Emirates Airlines
24 Advanced Travel

25 Al-Masaood Tower
   (Standard &
   Chartered Bank)
26 Almassa Cinema
28 Alliance Française
30 Omeir Travel
31 Clocktower
32 Saudia Airlines
   (Abu Dhabi Travel
   Bureau Building)
33 Spinney's Supermarket
34 Gulf Air
35 UAE Exchange Centre
   (Money Exchange)
41 ETISALAT
   (Telephone Office)
42 The Cultural Foundation
43 Al-Hosn Palace
   (Old Fort)
44 Thrifty Car Rental
45 Avis Rent-a-Car
46 Grand Khalifa Mosque
47 British Embassy
48 Budget Rent-a-Car
49 American Express
   (Al-Masaood Travel)
50 Oriental Carpet
   House & Antiques
51 All Prints Bookstore
52 British Council
53 Carlton Cards Bookstore
54 Grand Mosque
55 Main Post Office

It is open from 8 am to 8 pm Saturday to Wednesday, from 8 am to 6 pm Thursday and from 8 to 11 am Friday.

Telephone & Fax The ETISALAT office, on the corner of Zayed the Second St and Airport Rd, is open 24 hours a day. Fax, telex and telegram services are also available.

Internet Access The Cyber Cafe is above Choitram's on the corner of Zayed the Second and Bani Yas Sts. There is a separate computer room for women. Havana Cafe also has Internet access and is on the corner of Hamdan and As-Salam Sts. Rates at both places are Dh20 per hour.

Bookshops All Prints Bookstore on Al-Nasr St has an excellent selection of English-language books. Carlton Cards also has a good selection of English-language books but it doesn't sell maps. It has two stores, one on Zayed the First St, west of Khalid bin al-Walid St, and another at the

Hamdan Centre on East Rd, near the corner of Hamdan.

Cultural Centres The UAE is not brimming with cultural organisations but the constant increase in the number of expat residents means that more centres are opening their doors.

Alliance Française
(☎ 260 404) is behind the north side of Shaikh Hamdan bin Mohammed St between Leewa and Lulu Sts. The office is behind the Lulu Centre, above the Jameela supermarket.
British Council
(☎ 659 300) is on Al-Nasr St (Fifth St), off Tariq ibn Ziyad St. It's open from 9 am to 1 pm and 4.30 to 7 pm Monday to Wednesday.
US Information Service (USIS) cultural centre
(☎ 436 567) is at the US embassy on Sudan St.

Medical Services Abu Dhabi's central hospital (☎ 214 666 for the general switchboard or ☎ 344 663 for the emergency unit) is on Al-Manhal St. The emergency entrance is on the corner of Al-Manhal and Karamah Sts. The Corniche Hospital (☎ 724 900 for the general switchboard or ☎ 202 4221 for emergency) is next to the Sheraton at the eastern end of the Corniche.

Emergency For the police dial ☎ 999; ambulance ☎ 998; fire ☎ 997.

The Cultural Foundation

This large, faceless building on Zayed the First St is more interesting inside than its outward appearance would indicate, and is worth a visit. It houses the National Archives, the National Library and the Institution of Culture and Art. There are often interesting exhibits on local history and Islamic art as well as modern art exhibits and musical concerts. The foundation is open from 7.30 am to 1.30 pm and 4 to 10 pm Saturday to Wednesday, from 7.30 am to noon and 4 to 9 pm Thursday and is closed Friday. Admission is free.

Al-Hosn Palace

Al-Hosn Palace, commonly known as the Old Fort or the White Fort, is one of the few

buildings in Abu Dhabi that's more than 30 years old. It was built in the late 19th century and is the oldest building in Abu Dhabi. Its interior has been completely modernised and is now used by the Cultural Foundation as a documents and research centre. The fort is on the corner of Khalid bin al-Walid and Hamdan Sts. It's open from 7.30 am to 1.30 pm Saturday to Wednesday and from 7.30 am to noon Thursday. Admission is free.

The Old Souq

If you're looking for a break from the world of banks and boutiques that is modern Abu Dhabi take a walk through what remains of the old souq in the small area east of Al-Ittihad Square and north of Shaikh Khalifa bin Zayed St.

Women's Craft Centre

This is a government-run operation where traditional weavings and other crafts are displayed and sold. The centre is open from 9 am to noon Saturday to Wednesday and from 9 to 11 am Thursday and is closed Friday. Admission is Dh2.

To reach the centre simply take Airport Rd south from the centre and exit at the small black and white sign pointing right (it is easy to overshoot the turn-off so watch the road closely). It is in a compound marked 'Handicraft Industrial Centre'.

Dhow Wharf & Fish Market

At the eastern end of the Corniche, near the port, lies Abu Dhabi's fish market and small dhow wharf. It is rather disappointing compared with Dubai's waterfront but it does offer good local colour and an excellent view back towards the city.

Places to Stay

There are really no cheap hotels in Abu Dhabi. That's the bad news. The good news is that a youth hostel will open some time in the future. The rates quoted here are the hotels' rack rates (standard high-season rates). It's usually possible to negotiate some sort of discount. Service charges have been included in the prices.

Places to Stay – Budget

Zakher Hotel (☎ *275 300, fax 272 270, Umm al-Nar St*) is the only place in Abu Dhabi where you can get a room for under Dh200 per night. Singles/doubles start at Dh150/200, including the service charge.

Federal Hotel (☎ *789 000, fax 794 728, Shaikh Khalifa bin Zayed St*) is in a good central location but the rooms (Dh200/225) are not as good as those in the hotels nearby with similar rates.

Park Residence (☎ *742 000, fax 785 656*) is next to Federal Hotel. It has comfortable rooms for Dh200/225.

Majestic Hotel (☎ *710 000, fax 741 221*) is next to Federal Hotel near the corner of Shaikh Khalifa bin Zayed St and Umm al-Nar St. Single rooms cost Dh300 and have two beds and, for some reason, are more expensive than the double rooms (two beds pushed together) which cost Dh250.

Hotel Regency (☎ *765 000, fax 777 446*) is an excellent hotel with five-star amenities. It is behind Mina Hotel on the corner of Al-Mina and As-Salam Sts. Singles/doubles cost Dh250/350 and all rooms have kitchenettes. Guests here have the advantage of being able to use the beach and health club at the Sheraton hotel across the road.

Places to Stay – Mid-Range

At *Al-Hamra Plaza Residence* (☎ *725 000, fax 766 228, Zayed the Second St*), a little farther away from the Corniche near Bani Yas St, rooms cost Dh350/450.

Sands Hotel (☎ *335 335, fax 335 766*) is farther west along Zayed the Second St and has rooms for Dh402.50/437.

Centre Hotel Novotel (☎ *333 555, fax 343 633, Hamdan*) is right in the heart of the commercial and shopping district and has rooms for Dh400/500.

Al-Ain Palace Hotel (☎ *794 777, fax 795 713*), near the eastern end of the Corniche, has rooms for Dh460/575.

Places to Stay – Top End

The following hotels all have private beach clubs and health facilities as well as numerous restaurants and bars.

Abu Dhabi Hilton (☎ *681 1900, fax 669 696, Corniche*) offers singles/doubles for Dh975/1090.

Le Meridien Abu Dhabi (☎ *776 666, fax 729 315, Zayed the Second St*) is a luxurious hotel with the best health club and restaurant complex in town. Singles/doubles are Dh840/920.

Forte Grand Hotel (☎ *742 020, fax 742 552, Umm al-Nar St*) has large rooms starting at Dh750/850.

Radisson SAS (☎ *666 220, fax 666 291, Zayed the First St*) is designed for long-term guests and offers large suites for Dh1276 as well as standard singles/doubles for Dh638. All rooms have cooking facilities, and the rooftop pool has some great views of Abu Dhabi from 18 floors up. The hotel doesn't have its own beach club but guests can use the Khalidia Palace Hotel beach club.

Places to Eat

Street food If you don't want to spend much on filling your stomach try the little *shwarma shops* that can be found all over the centre. Another choice for cheap snacks are the *Indian-run restaurants* where you can tuck into omelette sandwiches, burgers, chicken sandwiches and Indian snacks such as *kima* (tasty mince meat served with salad and flaky bread) and biryanis for Dh2.50 to Dh7. You can buy tea and (Nescafe) coffee for 50 fils a cup.

Snacks *Revive Refreshments* on Al-Mina St near the Mina Hotel has the best omelette sandwiches in the country. It's the one with the red bench seats inside. Keep in mind that when you ask for a sandwich you will get either arabic bread or Indian *puri* (fried) bread. If you want to be sure you get the less greasy arabic bread, ask for it.

Bhavna Restaurant on Zayed the Second St has vegetarian Indian food. Samosas are Dh2.50 each and the *masala dosa* (curried vegetables in a pancake-like shell) is quite good for Dh3. It also carries a selection of Indian sweets.

La Brioche on Shaikh Khalifa bin Zayed St, between Lulu and Leewa Sts, offers good coffee, pastries and baguette sandwiches and is worth the extra dirham or two.

Restaurants If you're looking for a particular type of restaurant, pick up a copy of *What's On* to get a complete listing of restaurants by cuisine.

Foodlands is a popular Chinese/Indian restaurant on Zayed the Second St. The food is varied (you may find beef stroganoff on the menu along with carrot halva) and the servings are generous. Main dishes cost Dh10 to Dh25.

Bukhara is in the Hotel Regency. It bills itself as a Central Asian restaurant which, in practice, means that the menu features both Indian and Persian dishes with the emphasis on subtle combinations of spices rather than sheer heat. Main dishes cost Dh15 to Dh30.

As-Sofon and *Al-Sufina* are both Arabic-style fish restaurants on the Breakwater. They are worth visiting at night for the spectacular views of Abu Dhabi. To get to the Breakwater turn to the right at the Hilton roundabout at the western end of the Corniche.

Pizzeria Italiana in the Federal Hotel has pizzas and pastas for Dh12 to Dh18. The food is good and makes a welcome change from biryanis and shwarma, and you can enjoy a glass of house wine with your meal.

Self-Catering For fresh fruit and vegetables try the markets out by the port area. For Arabic breads and sweets there are a number of 'modern' bakeries around town. For European breads head straight to La Brioche, where a wide selection of white and brown loaves are baked daily, on Shaikh Khalifa bin Zayed St. Western-style bread from the supermarkets is usually sweetened and stale.

Entertainment
Abu Dhabi is probably not as boring as its reputation, but it does lack Dubai's energy and nightclub scene.

The Tavern, a British-style pub at the Sheraton Hotel, is a good place for a drink. *Eldorado Cinema* on Zayed the Second St and *Almassa Cinema* on Shaikh Hamdan bin Mohammed St show western films.

The best coffeehouse in the country has to be *Breakwater Local Cafe*. It's hardly an intimate place but it has a lovely setting overlooking the water and the city. A late night visit here is a must. To get to the Breakwater turn to the right at the Hilton roundabout at the western end of the Corniche.

Shopping
Al-Nasr St has a number of shops with a good selection of carpets and Arabian souvenirs, though most of these are actually made elsewhere, generally in Egypt, Syria, Iran, India or Pakistan. The large complex behind the Abu Dhabi Co-op near the Meridien Hotel has similar items for sale. Locally made crafts are available at the Women's Craft Centre south of the city centre (see Women's Craft Centre earlier this chapter).

Getting There & Away
Air Abu Dhabi international airport is on the mainland, about 30km from the centre or town. Call ☎ 757 611 for airport information. Gulf Air (☎ 332 600) is on the corner of Airport Rd and Hamdan St. Emirates Airlines (☎ 315 888) is on Hamdan, between East Rd and Bani Yas St.

Bus The main bus terminal is on East Rd, south of the centre. Intercity service is only available within the Abu Dhabi emirate. Buses run to Al-Ain every 30 minutes from 6 am to 10 pm every day. Buses for Madinat Zayed leave every hour, finishing at 8 pm. Both trips take 2½ hours and cost Dh10. Change at Madinat Zayed for Liwa.

Minibus These are found with the long-distance taxis next to the main bus station on East Rd. They take 14 passengers and charge Dh20 per person to Dubai and Dh25 to Sharjah. If there are enough passengers, and depending on the mood of the driver, you may be able to catch a minibus farther north to Umm al-Qaiwain and Ajman. Minibuses also go to the same places within Abu Dhabi emirate as the large coaches for the same price, but only if they have a full load.

Long-Distance Taxi These leave from the same place as minibuses. To catch an engaged taxi to Dubai, Sharjah or Al-Ain costs Dh150. Don't pay more than this. A shared taxi with five to seven people costs Dh30 per person. If you have luggage you will have to pay Dh30 for that too.

Car Rental There are a number of car hire companies on Al-Nasr St near the corner of Khalid bin al-Walid St. You will also find agencies in the lobbies of most four and five-star hotels.

Getting Around
To/From the Airport Bus No 901 runs from the main bus station to the airport around the clock, departing every 20 minutes (every 30 minutes between midnight and 6 am). The fare is Dh3. Airport limos and Al-Ghazal taxis charge Dh65 from the airport to the city. A regular taxi to or from the city centre costs around Dh40.

Bus You will notice large municipal buses throughout Abu Dhabi. These are cheap – fares are only Dh2 or Dh3 depending on the distance travelled – but they are nearly useless for the traveller because they follow no fixed routes. All of the buses originate at the main bus station on East Rd. From there they go down one of the three main roads and end up in various industrial zones and labourers' camps on the mainland, where they turn around and head back into the souq.

AL-AIN & BURAIMI
The Buraimi oasis straddles the border between Abu Dhabi and Oman. In the days before the oil boom, the oasis was a five day overland journey by camel from Abu Dhabi. Today, the trip takes about two hours on a tree-lined freeway. Once in the oasis, you can cross freely between the UAE and Oman – people driving up from Muscat pass through customs 50km before reaching the Omani town of Buraimi.

One of Al-Ain's main attractions come summer is the dry air – a welcome change from the humidity of the coast. The cool

and quiet date palms are nice to wander through at any time of the year.

Orientation
The Al-Ain/Buraimi area can be very confusing. All of the streets in Al-Ain look pretty much the same. The main streets in Al-Ain are Khalifa ibn Zayed St (known as Khalifa St) and Zayed ibn Sultan St (known as Main St). The main north-south cross streets are Abu Bakr al-Siddiq St, which extends into Buraimi, and Al-Ain St. The two landmarks you need to know for navigational purposes are the clock tower and coffeepot roundabouts.

Distances in both Al-Ain and Buraimi are large. You could walk from the bus or taxi station in Al-Ain to Buraimi's cheap hotels, but with any luggage it would be a hell of a hike, especially when it's hot.

Information
There is no tourist office in either city but it's fairly easy to find most of the things worth seeing in Al-Ain by following the big purple tourist signs. There is an Internet cafe (☎ 628 686) at the Al-Ain International Centre on Al-Qattara St. It costs Dh15 per hour.

Money There are banks in Al-Ain near the clock tower roundabout. The area around the Grand Mosque has several moneychangers. In Oman you'll see several banks on the main road. UAE currency is accepted in Buraimi at a standard rate of OR1 for Dh10 but you'll find that Omani currency is not as widely accepted in Al-Ain.

Post & Communications Al-Ain's main post and telephone office are at the clock tower roundabout. The post office is open from 8 am to 1 pm and 4 to 7 pm Saturday to Wednesday, from 8 am to 4.30 pm Thursday and from 8 to 11 am Friday. The ETISALAT office is open from 7 am to 3 pm Saturday to Wednesday, and from 8 am to 1 pm on Thursday. Buraimi's post office, across from the Yameen Restaurant, is open from 8 am to 2 pm Saturday to Wednesday, and from 8 to 11 am Thursday. It's closed Friday.

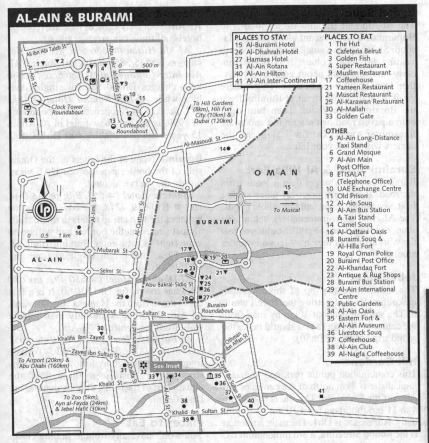

AL-AIN & BURAIMI

PLACES TO STAY
15 Al-Buraimi Hotel
26 Al-Dhahrah Hotel
27 Hamasa Hotel
31 Al-Ain Rotana
40 Al-Ain Hilton
41 Al-Ain Inter-Continental

PLACES TO EAT
1 The Hut
2 Cafeteria Beirut
3 Golden Fish
4 Super Restaurant
9 Muslim Restaurant
17 Coffeehouse
21 Yameen Restaurant
24 Muscat Restaurant
25 Al-Karawan Restaurant
30 Al-Mallah
33 Golden Gate

OTHER
5 Al-Ain Long-Distance
  Taxi Stand
6 Grand Mosque
7 Al-Ain Main
  Post Office
8 ETISALAT
  (Telephone Office)
10 UAE Exchange Centre
11 Old Prison
12 Al-Ain Souq
13 Al-Ain Bus Station
  & Taxi Stand
14 Camel Souq
16 Al-Qattara Oasis
18 Buraimi Souq &
  Al-Hilla Fort
19 Royal Oman Police
20 Buraimi Post Office
22 Al-Khandaq Fort
23 Antique & Rug Shops
28 Buraimi Bus Station
29 Al-Ain International
  Centre
32 Public Gardens
34 Al-Ain Oasis
35 Eastern Fort &
  Al-Ain Museum
36 Livestock Souq
37 Coffeehouse
38 Al-Ain Club
39 Al-Nagfa Coffeehouse

UNITED ARAB EMIRATES

Eastern Fort & the Al-Ain Museum

The museum and fort are in the same compound, south-east of the overpass near the coffeepot roundabout. As you enter the museum, look at the Bedouin *majlis* (reception area) and see the display of photographs of Al-Ain in the 1960s. The fort was the birthplace of Abu Dhabi's current ruler, Sheikh Zayed. The museum is open from 8 am to 1 pm and 3.30 to 5.30 pm (4.30 to 6.30 pm from May to October) Sunday to Wednesday.

On Thursday it's open from 8 am to noon and Friday from 9 to 11.30 am. It's closed all day Saturday. Admission is 50 fils.

Livestock Souq

You can see the entrance to this souq from the museum/fort car park. The souq, which sells everything from Brahmin cows to Persian cats, attracts people from all over the southern UAE and northern Oman. The best time to be there is early in the morning (before 9 am) when the trading is at its heaviest.

Camel Souq

The Al-Ain and Buraimi camel souq is in Buraimi on a large vacant block off Al-Masoudi St. It's quite a small market but worth visiting for local colour. It is open from early morning until about noon every day, then from about 4 pm til dusk. To get there go 4km up the main street of Buraimi from the Buraimi roundabout. Then turn right onto a paved road just after a red and white transmitter tower. Go for 1.5km and the camels will be on your left.

Buraimi Souq & Al-Hilla Fort

Buraimi's souq is bigger than it looks from the road. It's a very practical place selling fruit, vegetables, meat and household goods. The Al-Hilla Fort, immediately behind the souq, is not open to the public but if you ask the workers nicely they may let you wander around.

Jebel Hafit

The views from the top of this mountain make the effort of getting there well worth it. The summit is about 30km by road from the centre of Al-Ain (a taxi should make the round trip for about Dh50).

Hili Gardens

This combination public park and archaeological site is 8km north of the centre of Al-Ain, off the Dubai Rd. The site is open from 4 to 11 pm (holidays from 10 am to 10 pm) daily. Admission is Dh1. The main attraction is the **Round Structure**, a 3rd millennium BC tomb, possibly connected with the Umm an-Nar culture. The park can be reached by bus Nos 80, 100 and 203. The fare is Dh1.

Zoo

Al-Ain's zoo, one of the better ones in the Gulf, is about 5km south of town. It is open from 7 am to 5.30 pm daily and is closed Saturday. Admission is Dh2. It has indigenous species including Arabian oryx and gazelle, saluki dogs and bustards. It also has kangaroos, pygmy hippos, vultures etc. The zoo can be reached via bus No 110 to Ayn al-Fayda or bus No 60 to Zakhe.

Places to Stay

Al-Ain Your only choices here are five-star hotels; all three can arrange visas.

Al-Ain Hilton (☎ *686 666, fax 686 888*) charges Dh535/585 for singles/doubles. *Al-Ain Inter-Continental* (☎ *686 686, fax 686 766*) charges Dh464/580 for singles/doubles while *Al-Ain Rotana Hotel* (☎ *515 111, fax 515 444*), opened at the beginning of 1999, is the only new hotel in Al-Ain in 15 years. Singles/doubles cost Dh550/600.

Buraimi None of the hotels on the Omani side of the border can sponsor UAE visas, nor do they serve alcohol.

Hamasa Hotel (☎ *651 200; in the UAE call ☎ 050-619 4248, fax 651 210*) is the better of the two cheap hotels in town. It sits almost smack on the border, and will be on your right as you enter Buraimi from Al-Ain. Clean and bright singles/doubles are Dh150/200.

Al-Dhahrah Hotel (☎ *650 492, fax 650 881*) has rooms for Dh130/160. It is a few doors down from the Hamasa Hotel towards Al-Ain. Both hotels are only a 10 minute walk from the centre of Al-Ain.

Al-Buraimi Hotel (☎ *652 010, fax 652 011; in the UAE call ☎ 050-474 954*) can be found easily enough by following the signs strategically positioned throughout the Omani part of the oasis. Singles/doubles are Dh420/500.

Places to Eat

You won't have any trouble finding cheap eats in the centre of Al-Ain.

Muslim Restaurant just north of the overpass on Abu Bakr al-Siddiq is definitely recommended. Offering the usual fare of rice with mutton, chicken or fish for Dh7, it also makes very good *hadas* (a spicy lentil paste) for Dh3 and bakes its own bread.

Golden Gate Restaurant is more upmarket and serves very good Chinese and Filipino food. Main dishes cost Dh15 to Dh25.

The Hut is a western-style coffee shop on Khalifa ibn Zayed St. It offers good coffee as well as a wide selection of cakes, pastries and sandwiches. Costing Dh6 for a cappuccino the prices are a bit high, but the comfortable surroundings make up for it.

Super Restaurant is a very popular Indian restaurant. It has a large menu and meals are around Dh10 to Dh12.

Buraimi has a number of eating places but you'll probably find your options limited to biryani dishes and shwarma.

Getting There & Away

Air Al-Ain's airport is approximately 20km from the centre. Gulf Air offers direct services from Al-Ain to Bahrain, Doha and Muscat. EgyptAir, Royal Jordanian and PIA service the airport. For airport information call ☎ 855 555 ext 2211.

Bus Buses run from Al-Ain to Abu Dhabi (Dh10, 2½ hours) every 30 minutes from 6 am to 9.30 pm. The bus station is behind the Al-Ain Co-op, near the Livestock Souq. Oman's bus company, ONTC, has three buses a day to and from the Ruwi station in Muscat (five hours; OR3.600) via Sohar. They leave from the bus station on the main street in Buraimi, just over the Al-Ain border.

Long-Distance Taxi Al-Ain's taxi station is in the big car park lot behind the Grand Mosque. There is another at the bus station near the livestock souq. It costs Dh30 to Dubai and Dh20 to Abu Dhabi.

Getting Around

Bus No 500 is an express service that runs every 30 minutes between Al-Ain's bus station and the airport. The fare is Dh3 and the trip takes about 40 minutes. A taxi to or from Al-Ain should cost about Dh25. All of Al-Ain's buses run roughly on the 30 minutes from 6 am to midnight. Most fares are Dh1. There are no local buses in Buraimi.

If you're going by taxi it's better to use the Al-Ain ones, which have meters. Al-Ain's taxis are gold and white, Buraimi's are orange and white.

LIWA

Liwa oasis is a popular weekend getaway spot for Emiratis and expatriates. Lying on the edge of the Empty Quarter, its main attractions are its dunes. The long stretches of green agricultural plots stretching from the roadside to the base of these mountains of sand make the place quite a sight. The extension of the paved roads deep into the desert has made it possible to see some of Liwa's desert scenery without a 4WD. Liwa is actually a collection of small villages spread out over a 150km arc of land.

The bus from Abu Dhabi (Dh15, 3½ hours) takes you as far as **Mizaira'a** roundabout. Notice Sheikh Zayed's huge palace on the right at the first roundabout you come to in Mizaira'a. There's not much else to see except a couple of three-towered forts: one is off the Arada road and the other is in the village of Attab.

Two local routes serve the oasis communities. The more interesting route goes east to the village of **Hamim** (Dh3), where the paved road ends and the bus turns around. The other route, 40km west to **Karima** (Dh2), is flatter and more open. Liwa's *Resthouse* (☎ 088-22075, fax 29311) is about 7km west of the bus station along the Arada road. Rooms cost Dh165 for a single or double, including breakfast. Book ahead if you plan a weekend visit. A taxi to Liwa from Abu Dhabi costs Dh160.

Dubai

In all the Middle East, there is no place quite like Dubai. It's a bastion of anything-goes capitalism – sort of an Arab version of Hong Kong. You won't find a more easy-going place anywhere in the Gulf – or a place with better nightlife.

Orientation

Dubai is really two towns: Deira to the east, and Dubai to the west. They are separated by the *al-khor* (creek), an inlet of the Gulf. The Dubai side is sometimes referred to as Bur Dubai. Deira, however, is the city centre.

Activity in Deira focuses on Beniyas Rd (which runs along the Creek), Beniyas Square (which used to be called Nasr Square

DUBAI

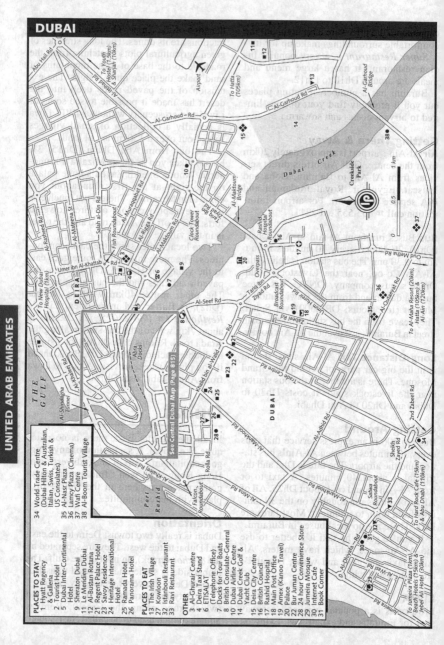

See Central Dubai Map (Page 815)

PLACES TO STAY
1 Hyatt Regency & Galleria
2 Tourist Hotel
5 Dubai Inter-Continental Hotel
9 Sheraton Dubai
11 Le Meridien Dubai
12 Al-Bustan Rotana
21 Regent Palace Hotel
23 Savoy Residence
24 Heritage International Hotel
25 Ramada Hotel
26 Panorama Hotel

PLACES TO EAT
13 The Irish Village
27 Kowloon
32 Istanbouli Restaurant
33 Ravi Restaurant

OTHER
3 Al-Ghurair Centre
4 Deira Taxi Stand
6 ETISALAT (Telephone Office)
7 Docks for Tour Boats
8 British Consulate-General
10 Dubai Airline Centre
14 Dubai Creek Golf & Yacht Club
15 Deira City Centre
16 British Council
17 Rashid Hospital
18 Main Post Office
19 Amex (Kanoo Travel)
20 Palace
22 Bur Juman Centre
28 24 hour Convenience Store
29 Jumeira Mosque
30 Internet Cafe
31 Book Corner

34 World Trade Centre (Dubai Hilton & Australian, Italian, Swiss, Turkish & US Consulates)
35 Al-Nasr Plaza
36 Lamcy Plaza (Cinema)
37 Wafi Centre
38 Al-Boom Tourist Village

and is still generally known by that name) and the areas along Al-Maktoum Rd, Al-Maktoum Hospital Rd, and Naif Rd.

Information

Tourist Office The Department of Tourism & Commerce Marketing has a Welcome Bureau you can call on ☎ 245 252 or 244 098. There are also three visitor's centres: one at the airport arrivals area, another in Beniyas Square in Deira and one on the road to Dubai from Abu Dhabi, about 40km from Dubai.

Money In central Deira, especially along Beniyas Rd and on Beniyas Square, every other building seems to contain a bank or a moneychanger. In Bur Dubai there are lots of moneychangers (though most of them only take cash) around the *abra* (water taxi) dock.

Amex (☎ 365 000 ext 222) is represented by Kanoo Travel. The office is on the 1st floor of the Hermitage building, next to the main post office on Za'abeel Rd. It's open from 8.30 am to 1 pm and 3 to 6.30 pm daily except Friday. It doesn't cash travellers cheques but will hold mail for clients. Address mail to: c/o American Express, Client's Mail, PO Box 290, Dubai, UAE.

Post The main post office is on the Dubai side, on Za'abeel Rd. It's open from 8 am to 11.30 pm Saturday to Wednesday, from 8 am to 10 pm Thursday, and from 8 am to noon Friday. There is also a small post office on the Deira side of the Creek, on Al-Sabkha Rd near the intersection with Beniyas Rd.

Telephone & Fax The ETISALAT office on the corner of Beniyas and Omar ibn al-Khattab roads is open 24 hours a day.

Email & Internet Access The Internet Cafe (☎ 453 390) on Al-Dhiyafa Rd in Jumeira charges Dh15 per hour and is open from 10 am to 3 am Saturday to Thursday and from 2 pm to 3 pm Friday.

Bookshops Dubai's best bookshop, Magrudy Books, is on Jumeira Rd, just over 5km west of the large roundabout by the

Dubai bus station. In the centre, try Book Corner at Deira City Centre or on Al-Dhiyafa Rd in Jumeira. Most of the larger hotels have small selections in their bookshops. The House of Prose is an excellent secondhand bookshop in the Jumeira Plaza on Jumeira Rd.

Medical Services Dubai's Rashid Hospital (☎ 371 111 or 371 323 for emergency) is on the Dubai side of the Creek, just east of the Al-Maktoum Bridge. The New Dubai Hospital (☎ 229 171 or 215 636 for emergency) is off Al-Khaleej Rd in Deira.

The Creek

The obvious place to start your tour of Dubai is at the waterfront. Abras make the crossing all day for 50 fils per person. The best idea is to hire one for an hour or so. For around Dh30 (for the whole boat, not per person) the captain should take you most of the way to Al-Maktoum Bridge and back. Also take some time to walk along the cargo docks on the Deira side of the Creek. Dhows bound for every port from Kuwait to Bombay to Aden dock here to load and unload all sorts of interesting cargo.

Dubai Museum

Dubai's museum occupies the Al-Fahidi Fort on the Dubai side of the Creek, just south-east of the Ruler's Office. Al-Fahidi Fort was built in the early 19th century and is thought to be the oldest building in Dubai. The museum has recently been remodelled and expanded and is definitely worth visiting. It's open from 7.30 am to 2 pm and 3 to 9 pm Saturday to Thursday and from 3 to 9 pm Friday. Admission is Dh7 (Dh3 for children up to age eight).

The Bastakia Quarter

This area on the waterfront, between the Dubai souq and the Ruler's Office, has some old windtower houses that were once the homes of wealthy Dubai merchants. Built at the turn of the century, they have been declared a conservation area and restoration work is being carried out on a few of them.

Sheikh Said al-Maktoum House

The house of Sheikh Said, the grandfather of Dubai's present ruler, has been restored as a museum of pre-oil times. The 30 room house was built in the late 19th century and served as a residence for the Al-Maktoum family. It lies next to the Heritage and Diving villages on Al-Shindagha Rd in Dubai. It's open from 7.30 am to 9.30 pm Saturday to Thursday and from 3 to 9.30 pm Friday. Admission is Dh2.

Heritage & Diving Villages

These villages on Al-Shindagha Rd were under construction at the time of writing. The Diving Village will show displays of pearl diving, once the livelihood of the city. The Heritage Village will re-create traditional Bedouin and village life. At the time of writing, a small souq selling traditional handicrafts, Bedouin jewellery, pottery and paintings was open. There is a restaurant and coffeehouse overlooking the Creek and

city. The villages are open from 7.30 am to 9 pm daily but close between 2 and 3 pm.

Souqs

The **Deira souq**, or spice souq as it is also known, offers a taste of traditional Dubai and is a wonderful place to take in the aroma of spices, nuts and dried fruits. The **Deira covered souq**, off Al-Sabkha Rd, sells just about anything.

Deira's **Gold souq**, on and around Sikkat al-Khail St, is probably the largest such market in Arabia and is a 'must-see'.

Places to Stay – Budget

Dubai's *youth hostel* (☎ 625 578, Qusais Rd) is on the eastern outskirts of the city, between the Al-Ahli Club and the Jamiat al-Islah relief agency. Beds are Dh35 per night in two and three-bed dorms. Women as well as men can be accommodated. Bus Nos 13 and 19 go to the hostel.

Dubai's cheap hotels are concentrated around the Deira souqs. Few of Dubai's cheapest hotels still arrange visas, which is probably just as well considering the chequered record some of these places had in terms of getting the paperwork done properly and on time. Some hotels advertise themselves as a 'family hotel'. This means that they will not accept single men but will usually accept single women. Beware of the ultra cheap hotels though: apart from probably being turned away you'll find that they are more brothel than hotel.

Tourist Hotel (☎ 229 388, fax 248 992) next to the Deira taxi stand is very good value, although it's a bit of a walk from the souqs. The staff are friendly and helpful and rooms are the standard of a mid-range hotel and cost Dh150/180.

Al-Karnak Hotel (☎ 268 799, fax 452 793, Naif Rd) is probably the best value hotel in Deira with large, clean rooms at Dh120 for singles and doubles.

Al-Noor Hotel (☎ 255 455, fax 291 682) off Sikkat al-Khail St is your next best bet in Deira. The hotel had almost finished refurbishment at the time of writing and everything was new and clean. Rooms are large

The Other Expats

For the 1.5 million or so Asian expats living in the UAE, life is very different to that of a western expat. Most Pakistanis, Indians, Sri Lankans, Bangladeshis and even some Chinese and Filipinos are employed as labourers. Working on building sites without proper safety precautions or digging roads in 45°C heat is hardly the easy life, but it is preferable to financial struggles back home. Even though salaries are often one-fifth that of a western expat, they're likely to be making three or four times as much as they could at home. One man is able to support an extended family back in India on his pay packet alone. Living here is not really a means to an end for many Asian expats – it is simply a better existence. What this means is that many men stay here not just for a few years but for 20 years or more, without seeing their families except for a trip home for one month every two years.

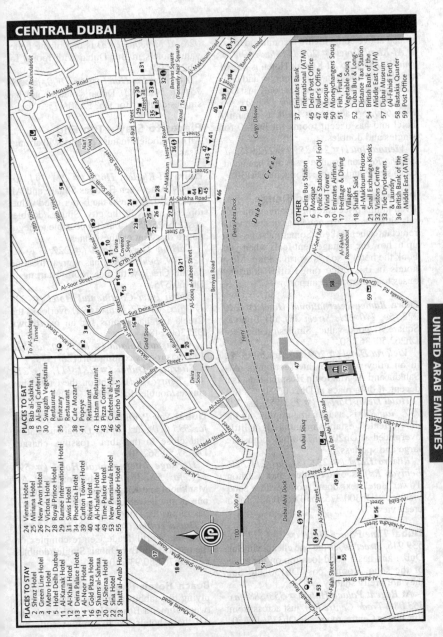

CENTRAL DUBAI

PLACES TO STAY
2 Shiraz Hotel
3 Green Line Hotel
4 Metro Hotel
5 Royal Prince Hotel
11 Hotel Delhi Darbar
12 Al-Khail Hotel
13 Ramee International Hotel
14 Swiss Hotel
16 Deira Palace Hotel
19 Al-Noor Hotel
22 Gold Plaza Hotel
23 Shams al-Sahraa
  Sina Hotel
  Shatt al-Arab Hotel

24 Vienna Hotel
25 Miriana Hotel
26 New Avon Hotel
27 Victoria Hotel
28 Carlton Tower Hotel
31 Phoenicia Hotel
34 Deira Palace Hotel
39 Riviera Hotel
40 Al-Khaleej Hotel
44 Al-Sheraa Hotel
49 Time Palace Hotel
53 New Peninsula Hotel
55 Ambassador Hotel

PLACES TO EAT
8 Bab al-Sabkha
15 Al-Burj Cafeteria
30 Swagath Vegetarian
  Restaurant
35 Entezary
  Restaurant
38 Cafe Mozart
41 Popeye
  Restaurant
42 Hatam Restaurant
43 Pizza Corner
46 Cafeteria al-Abra
56 Pancho Villa's

OTHER
1 Deira Bus Station
6 Mosque
7 Police Station (Old Fort)
9 Wind Tower
10 Emirates Airlines
17 Heritage & Diving
  Villages
18 Shaikh Said
  al-Maktoum House
21 Small Exchange Kiosks
32 Visitors Centre
33 Tide Drycleaners
36 British Bank of the
  Middle East (ATM)

37 Emirates Bank
  International (ATM)
45 Deira Post Office
47 Ruler's Office
48 Mosque
50 Moneychangers Souq
51 Fish, Fruit &
  Vegetable Souq
52 Dubai Bus & Long-
  Distance Taxi Station
54 British Bank of the
  Middle East (ATM)
57 Dubai Museum
  (Al-Fahidi Fort)
58 Bastakia Quarter
59 Post Office

UNITED ARAB EMIRATES

and cost Dh120/165. All three hotels mentioned above come highly recommended.

Al-Khail Hotel (☎ 269 171, fax 269 226, *Naif Rd*), next to Al Karnak Hotel, is one of the cheaper hotels in Deira (singles and doubles cost Dh100) but rooms are only just OK.

Deira Palace Hotel (☎ 290 120, fax 255 889, 67th St) advertises itself as a family hotel and has decent rooms for Dh150 for singles and doubles.

Vienna Hotel (☎ 218 855, fax 212 928, *Al-Sabkha Rd*) can arrange visas and has good, clean single and double rooms for Dh130.

Places to Stay – Mid-Range
Even in this price category many of the hotels either won't arrange visas or seem very reluctant when asked. Sometimes it's just up to how the management feels when you book the hotel – so it's worth asking. Most hotels in this price range offer courtesy buses to and from the airport.

Deira *Ramee International Hotel* (☎ 240 222, fax 240 221, *Street 38*), off Beniyas Square, is good value. Singles/doubles are Dh262.50/ 367.50.

Victoria Hotel (☎ 269 626, fax 269 575), in an alley near the intersection of Al-Sabkha and Al-Maktoum Hospital Rds, is a decent, if dull, place at Dh200/250.

Hotel Delhi Darbar (☎ 733 555, fax 733 737, *Naif Rd*) is, as its name implies, an Indian-oriented establishment. It is a little overpriced at Dh201/287.50 but rooms are large and spotless.

Riviera Hotel (☎ 222 131, fax 211 820, *Beniyas Rd*) is better value than Carlton Tower Hotel next door; rooms with a souq view cost Dh300/375; or Dh350/425 for a creek view.

Dubai *Time Palace Hotel* (☎ 532 111, fax 539 948, *Street 34*) is the one cheapie in Bur Dubai and has a good location on the edge of the souq. Rooms cost Dh150/240 but they are pretty shabby.

At *Regent Palace Hotel* (☎ 353 888, fax 353 080, *Trade Centre Rd*), just across from Bur Juman Centre, rooms are Dh375/ 437.50.

Panorama Hotel (☎ 518 518, fax 518 028, *Al-Mankhool Rd*) is one of the better value hotels in Bur Dubai with rooms for Dh220/275.

Ambassador Hotel (☎ 531 000, fax 534 751, *Al-Falah Rd*), Dubai's oldest hotel, has singles/doubles for Dh312.50/475.

Places to Stay – Top End
All of the hotels in this category will arrange visas.

Deira *Al-Khaleej Hotel* (☎ 211 144, fax 237 140), between Beniyas Square and Al-Sabkha Rd, is one of the better good value, top end hotels in the city. Singles/doubles cost Dh625/750 – but it's possible to negotiate a discount on these rates.

Carlton Tower Hotel (☎ 227 111, fax 228 249, *Beniyas Rd*) has a great location on the Creek with nice rooms starting at Dh460/575.

Dubai Inter-Continental Hotel (☎ 227 171, fax 284 777, *Beniyas Rd*) overlooks the Creek and has rooms for an overblown Dh1360/1486.

Al Bustan Rotana (☎ 820 000, fax 828 100) has rooms costing Dh1125/1375.

Sheraton Dubai (☎ 281 111, fax 213 468, *Beniyas Rd*), right on the Creek, has singles/doubles for Dh930/1030.

Dubai *New Penninsula Hotel* (☎ 533 000, fax 535 010), next to the Dubai bus station and close to the abra crossing, charges Dh437.50/562.50.

Heritage International Hotel (☎ 590 111, fax 590 181), on the corner of Al-Mankhool and Khalid bin al-Walid Rds, is one of the newer hotels in Bur Dubai and has rooms for Dh660/780.

Dubai Hilton (☎ 314 000, fax 313 383) is in the World Trade Centre complex on the outskirts of Bur Dubai. Singles/doubles cost Dh787.50/937.50.

Beach Hotels Five-star hotels are multiplying like rabbits along the waterfront between Jumeira Beach Hotel and Jebel Ali. All these hotels are like mini-resorts but they are a long way from the centre – about 20 minutes in a taxi.

Jumeira Beach Hotel (☎ 480 000, fax 482 273) is easily recognised by the spectacular Arabian Tower rising up out of the water; it's become a landmark of the city. Rooms are very expensive at Dh1375/1500. This is the only hotel we have come across in Dubai that does not reduce its rates in summer. You should visit the hotel for a view of Dubai from one of the top floors.

Oasis Beach Hotel (☎ 846 222, fax 846 200), with its 'Gilligan's Island' feel, has rooms for Dh687.50/812.50. It seems to be *the* place for German package tourists.

Le Meridien Beach Hotel (☎ 845 555, fax 845 264) is a little more upmarket and costs Dh1062.50/1187.50.

Places to Eat

Street food *Cafeteria al-Abra*, next to the abra dock in Deira, is good for a quick and cheap meal while watching the activity on the Creek. It has shwarma and samosas along with fruit juice, soda, and coconut juice served fresh in the shell.

Popeye Restaurant, a bit farther up the road, has shwarma, burgers and other snacks. It has a pretty good offer of two shwarma and one drink for Dh5.

Snacks *Pizza Corner*, on Beniyas Rd not far from the abra dock, is a good medium-priced place with pizzas and burgers. Sandwiches go for Dh9 to Dh16.

Cafe Mozart serves excellent coffee and re-creates the atmosphere of a Viennese cafe, right down to the change purse carried by the waitress. The pastries and croissants cost about Dh4 each and are good.

Restaurants On Beniyas Square *Entezary Restaurant* offers a dinner of kebab, rice, soup, salad, humous, bread and tea for only Dh15.

Hatam Restaurant, on Beniyas Rd, is one place we can highly recommend. It serves excellent Persian food at very reasonable prices. A traditional *chelo kebab* (sultan kebab on the menu) costs Dh17, including soup and salad. Most other meals are under Dh20.

Ravi is a Pakistani restaurant just off Al-Dhiyafa Rd in Satwa and comes highly recommended by readers. A meal consisting of a curry or biryani with bread, salad and a drink comes to about Dh15.

The Irish Village behind the Aviation Club on Al-Garhoud Rd, opposite Dubai Creek Golf & Yacht Club, is a real slice of Britain and is popular with western expats. You can get a stew, bangers and mash, baked potatoes, fish and chips etc for Dh20 to Dh30.

The Blue Elephant at the Al-Bustan Rotana Hotel serves some of the best Thai food in the world. The restaurant is decked out like a Thai village, complete with a pond, and the service is impeccable. Mains will set you back about Dh40 to Dh50.

Pancho Villa's, a Tex-Mex restaurant in the Astoria Hotel on the edge of the Dubai souq, is one of the Gulf's best known restaurants (its bumper stickers can be seen far and wide). Appetisers and main dishes cost Dh20 to Dh50. The restaurant is a bit cheaper at lunch, when a variety of specials is available.

There is a *dinner cruise* along the Creek every night from 8.30 to 10.30 pm. It leaves from Al-Boom Tourist Village near Al-Gharoud Bridge and costs Dh110. Call ☎ 341 444 to make a booking.

Self-Catering Those on a self-catering budget will find a number of small *grocery stores* in the area between Al-Sabkha Rd and Beniyas Square. Reasonably fresh fruit can be purchased at stalls around the bus stop on Al-Sabkha Rd. There is a 24 hour *convenience store* on Rolla Rd in Bur Dubai.

Entertainment

Check *What's On* to see what's happening each month around town. *Pancho Villa's* at the Astoria Hotel has long been one of Dubai's most popular nightspots. *Hard Rock Cafe* next to the Dubai Park Hotel off Shaikh Zayed Rd down near Jebel Ali had just opened a new club at the time of writing. We've always liked Duke's Bar on the top floor at *Al-Khaleej Hotel*, between Beniyas

Square and Al-Sabkha Rd. The view over the Creek at sunset really is worth a beer or two. Another good place for a drink is *The Old Vic* at Ramada Hotel on Al-Mankhool Rd.

You can catch relatively recent western flicks at *Galleria*, the shopping complex attached to Hyatt Regency Hotel or at the cinema in *Lamcy Plaza*.

Shopping

If you're looking for cheap electronics try the area at the Al-Sabkha Rd end of Beniyas Square. The gold souq has to be seen to be believed: even veterans of Middle-Eastern gold markets are likely to be blown away be the sheer scale of it. Persian carpets are said to be cheaper at the souq in Sharjah. Carpet shoppers in Dubai should try the Deira and Al-Mansour Towers on Beniyas Square, both of which have lots of small carpet boutiques.

If you're looking for Middle Eastern souvenirs, including Bedouin jewellery, there are a couple of small shops along Beniyas Rd near the abra dock that are worth browsing around. For similar merchandise try the shops in the Heritage Village on Al-Shindagha Rd.

Getting There & Away

Air You can fly to almost anywhere from Dubai international airport (DXB). The Emirate's long-standing reputation as the travel hub of the Gulf was built on a combination of easy landing rights for transiting aircraft and a very big and cheap duty-free shop at the airport. For general airport information call ☎ 245 777 or ☎ 245 555.

Dubai is the base for Emirates Airlines. Its main booking office (☎ 295 3333) is at the Airline Centre on Al-Maktoum Rd, Deira. There is another office on Naif Rd next to the Al-Karnak Hotel.

Bus Intercity buses operate within the Dubai emirate only. To go to another emirate, you have to take a Dubai Transport minibus. There are six buses daily to Hatta (Dh7, 80 minutes). The Hatta buses leave from the Deira bus station, near the gold souq, and also stop at the Dubai bus and long-distance taxi station. There are also

two buses per day to Muscat, Oman. These depart at 7.30 am and 5.30 pm from the car park of the Dubai Airline Centre on Al-Maktoum Rd, Deira. The trip takes five to six hours and costs Dh75 one way, Dh140 return (Dh48/96 for children). For information, call ☎ 203 3799. Tickets are available at the Airline Centre or from the bus driver.

Long-Distance Taxis You can only take these to other emirates 'engaged'. You'll need to haggle over a price but it should be roughly five times as much as the individual minibus fares in the following section.

Minibuses Dubai Transport has replaced the private long-distance taxis, once the only means of transport between the emirates, with minibuses. The minibuses carry 14 passengers and run every 15 or 20 minutes depending on when they fill up. They are very clean and efficient and fixed prices save you the hassle of bargaining for a seat.

Minibuses leave Deira from the bus and taxi station near the intersection of Omar ibn al-Khattab and Al-Rigga Rds. Prices per person are: Sharjah Dh5, Ajman Dh7, Umm al-Qaiwain Dh10, Ras al-Khaimah Dh20 and Fujairah Dh25. To get to Khor Fakkan and Dibba you will need to get a long-distance taxi in Fujairah.

Minibuses for Abu Dhabi and Al-Ain leave from the Dubai bus station on Al-Ghubaiba Rd, on the Dubai side of the Creek. It's Dh30 to Abu Dhabi or Al-Ain.

Car For rentals of more than a few days, Cars Rent-a-Car (☎ 692 694) can usually undercut the bigger agencies. It has an office in Bur Dubai at the Bur Juman Centre. It also has offices in a number of other cities around the UAE. We've also had good experience with Hanco Emirates Rent-a-Car (☎ 699 544) on Al-Ittihad Rd just outside the centre.

Of the big agencies try Europcar (☎ 520 033), Hertz (☎ 824 422) or Budget (☎ 823 030).

Getting Around

To/From the Airport From the Deira bus station, bus Nos 4 and 11 go to the airport about every 30 minutes for Dh1. Only the beige coloured taxis are allowed to pick up passengers at the airport. These charge Dh30 to any point in the city centre. A ride from the Deira souq area to the airport in a metered cab costs Dh10 to Dh12.

Bus Local buses operate out of stations in both Deira and Bur Dubai. The Deira bus station is off Al-Khor St, near the intersection with Al-Soor St. The Bur Dubai bus station is on Al-Ghubaiba Rd. Numbers and routes are posted on the buses in English as well as Arabic. Timetables and route maps are available from Dira and Bur Dubai bus stations for free. Fares are Dh1 to Dh3.50. The best way to get to where you're going is just to say where you want to go and someone will point you to the right bus. Tell the bus driver where you're going and he'll tell you when to get off.

Taxi The starting fare in Dubai Transport's beige coloured taxis is Dh3. Most of Dubai's orange and white taxis have no meters. Negotiate the fare in advance. Expect to pay Dh4 or Dh5 for trips around the centre that do not involve crossing the Creek. For trips across the Creek pay Dh7. Drivers will expect a 50% premium after midnight.

You can also call Dubai Transport (☎ 313 131) to send a taxi to pick you up.

Abra Abras leave constantly from early morning until about midnight. On the Deira side of the Creek the dock is at the intersection of Al-Sabkha and Beniyas roads. On the Dubai side the dock is near the entrance to the souq. The fare is 50 fils, which is collected once you are out on the water.

The Northern Emirates

SHARJAH
The third largest of the seven emirates, Sharjah is a place that too many visitors to the UAE either miss entirely or pass through

too quickly. It pushes itself as the cultural capital of the UAE and, with the proliferation of new museums, galleries and theatres in the last couple of years, it's easy to see why. Sharjah has some of the most interesting architecture in the country. Its new souq offers shopping to rival that of Dubai and its recently restored old souq offers a window on an older way of life that has now all but disappeared.

Orientation
Sharjah's business district is the area between the Corniche and Al-Zahra Rd, from the Central Market to Shaikh Mohammed bin Saqr al-Qasimi Rd (or Mohammed Saqr St). This is not a huge area and it's pretty easy to get around. It is a dreadful place for driving, however, because the streets are so crowded.

Information
On Burj Ave (also called Bank St), nearly every building contains a bank. Moneychangers can be found on the small streets immediately to the east and west of it. The main post office is on Government House Square. It's open from 8 am to 8 pm Saturday to Wednesday and from 8 am to 6 pm Thursday. The ETISALAT office is on Al-Safat Square (formerly Kuwait Square). It's open 24 hours a day.

Al-Hisn Fort
This fort, originally built in 1822, has been fully restored and houses a fascinating collection of photographs and documents, mainly from the 1930s. As you enter the fort there is a room on your left showing footage of the first Imperial Airways flights from London, which landed here on their way to India. The difference between Sharjah then and now is really incredible. The fort sits in the middle of Burj Ave and is open from 8 am to 1 pm and 5 to 8 pm. On Friday it is open from 4.30 to 8.30 pm and it is closed on Monday. Admission is free.

The Heritage Area
All the buildings in this block, just inland from the Corniche Rd between Burj Ave and

Al-Ayubi Rd, have been faithfully constructed following traditional designs. Coming from Burj Ave the first place you will come across is **Literature Square**. It was under construction at the time of writing but when completed it will house a library and be a meeting place for writers. Across from here is **Bait Shaikh Sultan bin Saqr al-Qasimi**, a house set around a courtyard, displaying traditional costumes, jewellery, ceramics, cooking utensils and furniture. The **Heritage Museum** displays much the same thing. Next door is the **Islamic Museum** which definitely should not be missed. Everything inside is to do with Islam or comes from somewhere in the Islamic world.

All of the museums are open from 8 am to 1 pm and from 5 to 8 pm. Wednesdays are for ladies only at most places and they are all closed on Monday. Admission is free but it seems you are obliged to sign each and every visitor's book.

The Arts Area

Tucked away on the other side of Burj Ave from the Heritage area is the arts area. There is a large **Art Museum** exhibiting modern art from local as well as foreign artists and some 19th century European paintings. It's open from 9 am to 1 pm and from 5 to 8 pm daily except Friday.

The **Bait Obeid al-Shamsi** next to it is a restored house that is now used as artists' studios. It is a lovely building featuring intricate plasterwork and pillars on the upper level. The **Arts Cafe**, on the main square serves traditional snacks such as hot milk with ginger (delicious) for about Dh1.

Souqs

Al-Arsah souq, just in from the Corniche on the southern side of Burj Ave, was restored by the government after large sections of it fell to pieces during the 1970s and 80s. The *arish* (palm frond) roof and wooden pillars give it a traditional feel and it's a lovely place to wander around and buy Arabic and Bedouin souvenirs.

The **central market** (also called the new souq, the blue souq or the Sharjah souq) has the best selection of oriental carpets in the country. From certain angles it looks like a set of monster-size oil barrels that have tipped over and had windtowers glued to their sides. The **animal souq** is just off Al-Mina St and, like the Al-Ain livestock souq, has all kinds of animals for sale, including falcons. The **plant souq** runs along the Corniche near the taxi stand. Farther south along the same road is the **fish souq**.

Sharjah Archaeological Museum

This museum is on Shaikh Rashid bin Saqr al-Qasimi Rd, just off Cultural Square. It's open from 8.30 am to 12.30 pm and 5 to 8 pm daily. On Friday it is open only in the afternoon. Admission is free. All exhibits are labelled in English, French and Arabic.

Sharjah Science Museum & Planetarium

This museum is a really fun place. The displays are all interactive and you can easily spend more than a couple of hours trying everything out. Especially spooky is the shadow tunnel. The museum is next to the Archaeological Museum on Shaikh Rashid bin Saqr al-Qasimi Rd, just off Cultural Square. It is open from 3.30 to 8.30 pm daily and is closed on Sunday.

Places to Stay – Budget

Sharjah's *youth hostel* (☎ 225 070, *Al-Zahra Rd*) is about 1.5km north-east of Al-Zahra Square, next to the Children's Hospital. Beds cost Dh30 per night and HI cards are required. The hostel is generally only open for men.

Khaleej Tourist Hotel (☎ 597 888, fax 598 999, King Faisal Rd) charges Dh90/120 for its rooms. It is simple but clean and has unbelievably small bathrooms (some with Turkish toilets).

Sharjah Plaza Hotel (☎ 377 555, fax 373 311, Al-Qasimia Rd), Government House Square, is basic and rooms are small but clean. Singles/doubles are Dh120/150 but are negotiable. The hotel can sponsor visas.

Federal Hotel (☎ 724 106, fax 724 394, King Faisal Rd) doesn't look much from the

SHARJAH

THE GULF

Port Khalid

Khalid Lagoon (Sharjah Creek)

To Ajman (3km) &
Ras al-Khaimah (75km)

To Ajman (3km)

Shaikh Mohammed

Ibn Saqr al-Qasimi Road
(Mohammed Saqr Street)

Al-Khalij
Al-Arabi Road

To Archaeological &
Science Museums (2km)

Corniche

Al-Arouba Road

Al-Zahra Road

Al-Zahra Square

Al-Ghazal Road

Rolla Square

Al-Safat Square

Shaikh Zayed Road

Al-Mina Street
(Harbour Road)

Al-Qasimia Rd

Al-Soor Road

Government
House Square

Al-Kuwait Road

To Airport (15km),
Natural History Museum (35km),
Sharjah Desert Park (40km)
& Fujairah (100km)

Al-Ittihad
Square

King Faisal Road

Corniche Road

Al-Estiqlal Road

Al-Zahra Road

Al-Wahda Rd

To Dubai (10km)

0   250   500 m

OTHER
3 Taxi Stand for
   Umm al-Qaiwain &
   Ras al-Khaimah
4 Al-Hamra Cinema
5 Arts Area
6 Al-Arsah Souq
7 Public Coffeehouse
8 Heritage Area
9 Al-Hisn Fort
13 ETISALAT
   (Telephone Office)
14 Amiri Diwan
   (Ruler's Office)
15 Main Post Office
16 SNTTA
25 Watchtower
26 Animal Souq
27 Plant Souq
28 Souq
29 Fruit & Vegetable Souq
30 Taxi Stand for Dubai,
   Abu Dhabi & Al-Ain
31 Fish Souq
32 King Faisal Mosque
33 Central Market
34 Amusement Park

PLACES TO STAY
1 Holiday Inn Resort
2 Youth Hostel
11 Al-Rolla International
   Hotel
12 Sharjah Plaza Hotel
18 Golden Beach Motel
19 Howard Johnson
   Beach Hotel
20 Summer Land Motel
21 Lou' Lou'a
   Beach Resort
22 Beach Hotel
23 Sharjah Grand Hotel
24 Sharjah Carlton Hotel
36 Federal Hotel
37 Marbella Resort
   Sharjah
38 Hotel Holiday
   International
39 Khaleej Tourist Hotel

PLACES TO EAT
10 Thriveni & Satkar
   Restaurants
17 Kowloon
35 Sharjah Dhow
   Restaurant

outside but rooms are large, clean and comfortable. Singles/doubles cost Dh176/200.

Places to Stay – Mid-Range

Al-Rolla International Hotel (☎ *512 000, fax 512 111*), on the southern edge of Rolla Square, has rooms for Dh295/375 but you should be able to negotiate a substantial discount on this. The hotel sponsors visas.

The following hotels are all on Shaikh Sultan al-Awal Rd, south-west of the centre on the other side of Khor Khalid.

Golden Beach Motel (☎ *281 331, fax 281 151*) is one place we can highly recommend. It has large rooms with kitchens and cooking facilities (but no utensils) and balconies overlooking the beach. The 70s decor suits this place down to the ground and rooms cost Dh200.

Beach Hotel (☎ *281 311, fax 285 422*) charges Dh200/250 for B&B and is just as good as the top end hotels along this road.

Summer Land Motel (☎ *281 321, fax 280 745*) has rooms with sitting area for

Dh200. Guests here can use the Beach Hotel's private beach. It caters to a largely Russian clientele.

Places to Stay – Top End

Unless otherwise noted, all of the following hotels can arrange visas.

Holiday Inn Resort (☎ 371 111, fax 524 090), at the Corniche end of Shaikh Mohammed bin Saqr al-Qasimi Rd, is Sharjah's top hotel. Rooms are Dh690/805 but if you are in Sharjah on a weekend this rate drops to Dh300 for a double, including tax and two breakfasts. This is incredibly good value for the standard of hotel but you'll need to book ahead.

Marbella Resort Sharjah (☎ 741 111, fax 726 050, Corniche) has nicely decorated Spanish-style villas set among trees and gardens. Junior suites (bedroom, bathroom and lounge) are Dh517.50 and master suites (bedroom, bathroom, lounge, dining area and kitchenette) are Dh805. Book ahead if you want to stay here.

The following top end places are outside the city centre along Shaikh Sultan al-Awal Rd.

Sharjah Grand Hotel (☎ 285 557, fax 282 861) charges Dh460/575. Many of its customers are Germans on package tours.

Sharjah Carlton Hotel (☎ 283 711, fax 284 962) asks Dh345/460, more if you want a sea view from your room. It will only sponsor visas for US citizens and western Europeans.

Places to Eat

The Public Coffeehouse in the Al-Arsah souq is one place that you really must visit while in Sharjah. For Dh10 you not only get a fairly large biryani but also salad and a bowl of fresh dates for dessert. The restaurant is a traditional coffeehouse, with seating on high benches. Backgammon sets are available and sweet tea is served out of a huge urn.

Thriveni Restaurant and the slightly fancier *Satkar Restaurant* are on Rolla Square. The surroundings are pleasant and you get a nice view out onto the square. Meals are around Dh5.

Sharjah Dhow Restaurant is next to the Marbella Resort on Corniche Khalid. Prices are quite reasonable although the menu is pretty uninspired.

Kowloon a Chinese restaurant on Al-Mina St has the best Chinese food we have tried in the UAE. Soups cost Dh10 to Dh12 and most main dishes are in the Dh20 to Dh30 range.

Getting There & Away

Sharjah international airport is 15km from the centre. The phone number for airport information is ☎ 581 111.

There is no bus service to, from or through Sharjah but the city does have two long-distance taxi stations. Taxis for Umm al-Qaiwain (Dh28 engaged, Dh7 shared) and Ras al-Khaimah (Dh50 engaged, Dh15 shared) leave from Al-Arouba Rd across from the Al-Hamra cinema. Taxis for Dubai (Dh30 engaged, Dh5 shared), Abu Dhabi and Al-Ain (Dh175 engaged, Dh30 shared) depart from a stand next to the fruit and vegetable souq.

Getting Around

Since Sharjah has no bus system, getting around without your own car means either taking taxis or walking. The taxis have no meters and trips around the centre should cost Dh5 to Dh10 (agree on the fare before you get in). When the heat is not too debilitating Sharjah's centre can be covered on foot quite easily.

AROUND SHARJAH
Sharjah Natural History Museum

The Sharjah Natural History Museum is quite extraordinary – possibly the slickest, most modern museum in the entire Gulf. Unfortunately for the casual visitor, it also happens to be out in the desert, 35km east of Sharjah's centre on the road to Fujairah. At least the exit is well marked. Many of the museum's exhibits are aimed at children – most can be touched and there are a large number of interactive displays – but adults will probably find it fascinating as well.

A desert park and breeding centre are adjacent to the museum complex. This area is gradually being developed into a small safari park featuring endangered species native to Arabia.

The museum is open from 9 am to 7 pm (2 to 8 pm on Friday and public holidays). It is closed on Sunday. Admission is Dh5. Photography is not allowed inside and cameras will be kept at the entrance for you.

AJMAN

The smallest of the seven emirates, Ajman occupies a small stretch of coast between Sharjah and Umm al-Qaiwain and also has

two inland enclaves. The public beach stretches from Sharjah to the Ajman Beach Hotel. It is wide and clean and one of the best spots on the gulf to swim.

Things to See

The **Ajman Museum** occupies the old police fort on the central square. The fort was built in the late 18th century and served as the ruler's palace and office until 1970. From 1970 to 1978, it was Ajman's main police station. The museum is open from 9 am to 1 pm

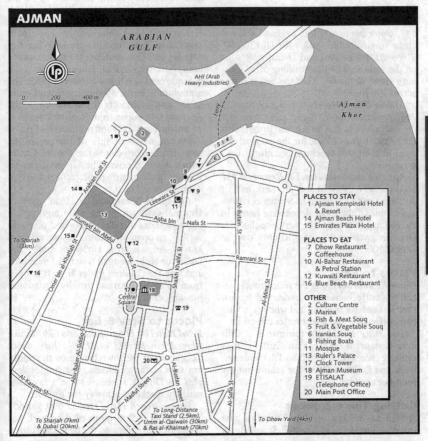

AJMAN

ARABIAN GULF

AHI (Arab Heavy Industries)

Ferry

Ajman Khor

0   200   400 m

To Sharjah (3km)

Arabian Gulf St
Humaid bin Abdul
Omer bin al-Khattab St
Leewara St
Aqba bin
Nafa St
Al-Butain St
Ramrani St
Al-Mina St
Aziz St
Shaikh Khalifa St
Abu-Baker Al-Siddiq St
Al-Karama St
Marfut Street
Al-Bustan Street
Al-Safia St

Central Square

To Long-Distance Taxi Stand (2.5km), Umm al-Qaiwain (30km) & Ras al-Khaimah (70km)

To Sharjah (7km) & Dubai (20km)

To Dhow Yard (4km)

PLACES TO STAY
1 Ajman Kempinski Hotel & Resort
14 Ajman Beach Hotel
15 Emirates Plaza Hotel

PLACES TO EAT
7 Dhow Restaurant
9 Coffeehouse
10 Al-Bahar Restaurant & Petrol Station
12 Kuwaiti Restaurant
16 Blue Beach Restaurant

OTHER
2 Culture Centre
3 Marina
4 Fish & Meat Souq
5 Fruit & Vegetable Souq
6 Iranian Souq
8 Fishing Boats
11 Mosque
13 Ruler's Palace
17 Clock Tower
18 Ajman Museum
19 ETISALAT (Telephone Office)
20 Main Post Office

UNITED ARAB EMIRATES

except Thursday, when it closes at noon; it reopens in the afternoon from 4 to 7 pm (5 to 8 pm from May to August). It is closed on Friday morning and all day Saturday. Admission is Dh4. Photography is not permitted.

Fruit and vegetables and meat and fish are sold in two purpose-built souqs along the coast, off Leewara St. Also here is the **Iranian souq**, a fascinating place to wander around. You are unlikely to find much in the way of souvenirs (unless your idea of a souvenir is a plastic washing bucket), though you can sometimes find interesting pottery.

Places to Stay

Emirates Plaza Hotel (☎ 445 777, fax 446 642, Omer bin al-Khattab St) has basic but clean single/double rooms for Dh130/150. The staff are helpful and friendly. Rooms on the right side of the building offer stunning views of the Gulf and the beach is just across the road.

Ajman Beach Hotel (☎ 423 333, fax 423 363, Arabian Gulf St) was, until recently, the only place to stay in Ajman. Rooms cost Dh200/250. Don't look for the pool advertised in the hotel brochure because it isn't there.

Ajman Kempinski Hotel & Resort (☎ 451 555, fax 451 222), at the northern end of Arabian Gulf St, opened in September 1998 and is one of the most impressive hotels in the country. It seems to be very popular with German package tourists. Rooms start at Dh862.50/977.50.

Places to Eat

Dhow Restaurant along the waterfront is actually a coffeehouse in a traditional *barasti* shelter. Look for the blue and white sign with two coffee pots and a rosewater urn on it.

The Blue Beach Restaurant is a Chinese restaurant on Arabian Gulf St. It is rather expensive at Dh10 to Dh15 for entrees and Dh20 to Dh30 for mains but the food is excellent.

Getting There & Away

Ajman has no bus service. There's a taxi stand on Omar ibn al-Khattab St just down

from the Emirates Plaza Hotel. If you want to go farther north along the coast, you'll have to go to the taxi stand at the main roundabout on the highway just out of town.

UMM AL-QAIWAIN

With a population of around 35,000, Umm al-Qaiwain (Umm al-Quwain, Umm al-Qawain) is the least populous of the seven emirates. It lies on a narrow peninsula of sand jutting north from the main road linking Dubai and Sharjah with Ras al-Khaimah. The old town and the emirate's small business district are at the northern tip of the peninsula, particularly along King Faisal Rd.

The small **fort** at the intersection of Al-Hason and Al-Lubna roads was under restoration at the time of writing. When finished it will be a museum for the emirate's many archaeological finds. There is a **mosque** next to it that was built in 1962. The **aquarium** is in the Marine Research Centre at the end of Moalla Rd at the tip of the peninsula. It's open from 8 am to 1 pm (8 to 11 am on Thursday) and is closed on Friday.

On the northern side of the peninsula, just off the Corniche is the **Tourist Centre** which offers a private beach, boat and jet ski hire, a swimming pool, jacuzzi and bar. Admission is Dh20.

Aquapark Dreamland is 10km north of Umm al-Qaiwain on the main highway. It has a plethora of rides, slides and pools, as well as an open-air theatre, restaurants and kiosks. Admission is Dh30 for adults and Dh20 for children aged five to 12 year olds and free for children under five. It is open from 10 am to 7 pm and usually closes later in summer.

Places to Stay & Eat

Pearl Hotel (☎ 666 678, fax 666 679, Shaikh Ahmed bin Rashid al-Moalla Rd), about 5km south of the town centre on the northern side of the peninsula, has singles/doubles for Dh250. It seems to be a favourite naughty weekend getaway for Emiratis.

Palma Beach Hotel (☎ 667 090, fax 667 388), about 2.5km north of the Pearl, has prefabricated cabins on the beach starting at

Dh220. Newer, motel-style rooms off the beach start at Dh260.

Umm al-Quwain Beach Hotel (*☎ 666 647, fax 667 273, Moalla Rd*) is another 1km back towards the centre on the southern side of the peninsula. It's a slightly musty place with one-bedroom aluminium cabins on the beach for Dh400. Behind these there are roomier brick bungalows starting at Dh700. This hotel is very popular with groups of young Emiratis. The turn off for the hotel is about 50m past KFC on the left as you enter Umm al-Qaiwain.

All the ***hotel restaurants*** serve up similar Western and Arabic meals (Dh20 to Dh30) and snacks (Dh10 to Dh12). The centre of town also has a collection of ***Indian restaurants*** around the top of King Faisal Rd.

Getting There & Away
Without your own car the only way in or out of Umm al-Qaiwain is by taxi. The taxi stand is at the top of King Faisal Rd, across from the Al-Salamia restaurant.

AROUND UMM AL-QAIWAIN
Ad-Dour
Inhabited from 200BC until sometime in the 4th century AD, this **Hellenistic site** is easily accessible because it is literally by the roadside. The many artefacts found here will be on display at the Umm al-Qaiwain museum when it is opened.

To get there, drive 10km north along the main highway from the Umm al-Qaiwain roundabout. Turn right at the sand track about 200m before the Emirates petrol station and double back parallel to the road for about 50m until you come to some stone foundations, believed to be a **ruler's house** because of its large size overlooking the sea.

From here continue through the gate and along the track for about 500m until you come to two trees standing very close to each other. All around this area are the remains of **tombs**. Head along the track veering off to the left and after 100m you'll come to the remains of a 4th century **fort**. The fort is surrounded by the remains of the village's houses.

Back at the two trees continue straight along the track for about 300m and you will come to the remains of a 1st century AD **temple**, on your left. The stone walls are covered in gypsum plasterwork, once decorated with grapevine reliefs. The large stone block in the middle of the temple is believed to be a basin used for sacrificial purposes.

RAS AL-KHAIMAH
Ras al-Khaimah is one of the nicer spots in the UAE, although the town itself is a bit of a dump. It is the northernmost, and most fertile, of the emirates, bordered by sea, mountains and desert. It's a favourite weekend getaway for people from Dubai and is also increasingly popular with package tourists from northern Europe.

Orientation & Information
Ras al-Khaimah is really two cities: Ras al-Khaimah proper, which is the old town on a sandy peninsula along the Gulf coast; and Al-Nakheel, the newer business district on the other side of Ras al-Khaimah's creek.

You can change money at any of the banks along As-Sabah St in Ras al-Khaimah or Oman St in Al-Nakheel. The main post office is a red brick building on King Faisal St, about 4km north of the Bin Majid Beach Hotel. The ETISALAT office is on Al-Juwais Rd in Al-Nakheel.

Things to See
Ras al-Khaimah's **museum** is in the old fort on Al-Hosen Rd, next to the police headquarters. The fort was built in the mid-18th century. Until the early 1960s it was the residence of the ruling Al-Qasimi sheikhs. The courtyard of the fort is paved with stones from the fossil-bearing strata of Wadi Haqil in the emirate. It's open from 8 am to noon and 4 to 7 pm daily except Tuesday. Admission is Dh2.

Ras al-Khaimah's **old town** is a nice place for a wander. The **souq area**, south of the museum, has a number of small tailors' shops but the main attraction is the unspoiled atmosphere.

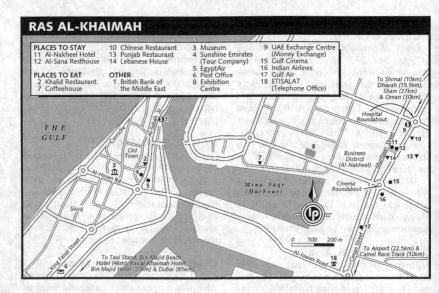

RAS AL-KHAIMAH

PLACES TO STAY
11 Al-Nakheel Hotel
12 Al-Sana Resthouse

PLACES TO EAT
2 Khalid Restaurant
7 Coffeehouse

10 Chinese Restaurant
13 Punjab Restaurant
14 Lebanese House

OTHER
1 British Bank of
   the Middle East

3 Museum
4 Sunshine Emirates
   (Tour Company)
5 EgyptAir
6 Post Office
8 Exhibition
   Centre

9 UAE Exchange Centre
   (Money Exchange)
15 Gulf Cinema
16 Indian Airlines
17 Gulf Air
18 ETISALAT
   (Telephone Office)

Places to Stay & Eat

The two top end hotels and the As-Sana Resthouse can arrange visas for tourists, though it would be a good idea to give them two weeks or more warning if you need one.

As-Sana Resthouse (☎ 229 004, fax 223 722, Oman St), at Dh70/120 including breakfast, is the cheapest place in town to stay.

Al-Nakheel Hotel (☎ 222 822, fax 222 922, Muntaser St), in Al-Nakheel, has the cheapest bar in town and rooms cost Dh140/190.

Bin Majid Beach Hotel (☎ 352 233, fax 353 225, King Faisal St) is the favoured haunt of Russian tour groups. Rooms are Dh250/350 including breakfast and the beach here is lovely.

Ras al-Khaimah Hotel (☎ 362 999, fax 362 990, Khuzam Rd) has rooms for Dh330/440 but is overpriced compared with the Bin Majid.

Punjab is a Pakistani and northern Indian restaurant in the souq area of Al-Nakheel. A chicken curry costs Dh6, dahl costs Dh3 and all meals include bread and salad.

As-Sana Restaurant, next to the As-Sana Resthouse, is highly recommended. It has western, Chinese, Indian and Filipino food. Meals should not run to more than Dh15 to Dh20.

You should definitely drop in at the barasti *coffeehouse* near Mina Saqr, overlooking the Creek. Very sweet tea costs 50 fils a cup (Dh1 with milk) and you can also get snacks. Until recently sheesha was served here but the municipality has banned it, saying that it's bad for health and disrupts family life.

Getting There & Away

Ras al-Khaimah's small airport is 22.5km south of Al-Nakheel. Gulf Air flies twice a week to Muscat then on to Karachi, and once a week to Doha and Bahrain. Indian Airlines flies once a week to Calicut and EgyptAir has a weekly flight to Cairo. For airport information call ☎ 448 111.

The taxi station is on King Faisal St, just south of the Bin Majid Beach Hotel. Taxis to Dubai and Sharjah charge Dh15 per person or Dh70 engaged.

AROUND RAS AL-KHAIMAH

Shimal

The village of Shimal, 5km north of Ras al-Khaimah, is the site of some of the most important archaeological finds in the UAE. The area has been inhabited since the late 3rd millennium BC. The main attraction is the **Queen of Sheba's Palace**, a set of ruined buildings and fortifications spread over two small plateaus overlooking the village.

To reach the site travel north for about 4km from the Hospital roundabout in Al-Nakheel and turn right onto a paved road where there are a number of signs. One has a red arrow, another has red Arabic script on a white background and another has the falcon crest on it. Follow this road for 1.5km until you reach a roundabout. Turn right and follow the road for another 2.3km through a village until you come to the People Heritage Revival Association, a new building made to look like a fort. Turn left. After about 400m the sealed road ends. Continue on a dirt track through the village. You will pass a small green and white mosque on the left. Keep going straight, heading for the base of the hills and get onto the paved road to your left. Continue along this road for about 1km until you see a track leading to a large green water tank. At this point you will see a gap in the fence on your right. Walk through the gap in the fence and follow a faint track to the base of the closest hill. At the top of this hill (which will be on your right) you should see the remains of a stone wall. The 15 minute climb is a little strenuous due to the loose rocks underfoot.

HATTA

An enclave of Dubai nestled in the Hajar Mountains, Hatta is a popular weekend getaway spot. It is 105km from Dubai by road, about 20km of which runs through Omani territory. There is no customs check as you cross this portion of the road but remember that if you are driving a rental car your insurance does not cover accidents in Oman.

There's a **rug souq** about 12km west of Hatta on the main highway, where you can pick up some great bargains. Hatta's main attractions are its relatively cool, dry climate (compared with that of the coast) and the mountain scenery. It is also a good jumping-off point for off-road trips through the mountains. At the time of writing the government was building a **Heritage Village**, a re-creation of a traditional mountain village from the pre-oil era.

The only place to stay in Hatta is *Hatta Fort Hotel* (☎ 085-232 11, fax 235 61) where singles/doubles cost Dh440 on weekdays, Dh495 on weekends.

There are six buses per day from Dubai to Hatta (Dh7, 80 minutes) and vice versa. In Hatta, the buses depart from the red bus shelter near the Hatta Palace Grocery.

The East Coast

FUJAIRAH

Fujairah is not cheap but it is attractive and a good base for exploring the east coast.

Orientation & Information

The main business area is Hamad bin Abdullah Rd, between the Fujairah Trade Centre and the coast. Along this stretch of road you'll find the ETISALAT office, several banks and, at the intersection with the coast road, the central souq. The main post office is on Al-Sharqi Rd, just off Hamad bin Abdullah Rd.

The coastal road changes its name three times, which can be confusing. Passing through the city from south to north it is called Regalath Rd, Gurfah Rd and Al-Faseel Rd, in that order.

Things to See

At the time of writing the **museum** had been closed for six months. It will eventually re-open in a restored building in the old town area. The **old town** is best described as spooky. **Ain al-Madab Garden** on the edge of town is a pretty sorry sight. However, the swimming pools here are clean, cool and segregated. It is open from 10 am to 10 pm and the pools are open 10 am to 7 pm. Admission

FUJAIRAH

PLACES TO STAY
1 Fujairah Beach Motel
3 Youth Hostel
7 Fujairah Hilton
17 Ritz Plaza Hotel

PLACES TO EAT
6 Diner's Inn
8 Al-Meshwar Restaurant
9 National Restaurant
12 New Palace Restaurant
    & Cafeteria
22 Taj Mahal Restaurant

OTHER
2 Sports Club
4 Sheikh's Palace
5 Fujairah Fort
   & Old Town

10 Ghorfah Post
    Office
11 Central Souq
13 British Bank of
    the Middle East
14 National Bank of
    Abu Dhabi
15 Indian Airlines
16 Car Rental
    Companies
18 Main Post Office
19 Exhibition Centre
20 Fujairah Trade Centre
    (Gulf Air)
21 ETISALAT (Telephone
    Office)
23 Cinema
24 Central Hospital
25 Airport Terminus

To Khor Fakkan (20km)
& Dibba (45km)

GULF
OF
OMAN

To Ain al-Madab
Gardens &
Heritage Village
(2km)

To Taxi Stand, Al-Hayl
Caste (13km), Masafi
(35km), Sharjah (100km)
& Dubai (110km)

To Kalba (12km)
& Oman (15km)

Date Gardens

0   250   500 m

to the park is Dh2; Dh5 if you want to swim.
There is a small **heritage village** across from
the garden that is open from 9 am to 6 pm
every day.

Places to Stay & Eat

Fujairah's *youth hostel* (☎ 222 347) is just
off Al-Faseel Rd near the sports club. Beds
are Dh15. The hostel will only accommodate women if it is empty enough to segre-
gate them from the men. Considering how
small the hostel is, that means a single

woman stands a fairly high chance of being
turned away.

Fujairah Beach Motel (☎ 228 111, fax
228 054) is 3km north of the centre on the
coast road and has rooms for Dh262.50. It
is frequented mainly by Russians.

Fujairah Hilton (☎ 222 411, fax 226
541, Al-Faseel Rd) is closer to the centre.
Rooms cost Dh598/666.

Ritz Plaza Hotel (☎ 222 202, fax 222
203, Hamad bin Adbullah Rd) has comfortable, small rooms at Dh460/575.

UNITED ARAB EMIRATES

There are a number of cheap restaurants on the Corniche road near the Hilton.

Taj Mahal serves excellent Indian and Chinese food at Dh10 to Dh12 for mains. We can highly recommend it. It is at the back of the building directly opposite ETI-SALAT on Hamad bin Abdullah Rd.

Al-Meshwar, on King Faisal Rd, is a medium-priced Lebanese restaurant with mezze from Dh7 to Dh12 and main dishes from Dh12 to Dh25.

On the way to Kalba there are two traditional barasti *coffeehouses*. One is between the coast road and the inland road, 2.3km from the coffee pot roundabout in Fujairah. The other is called Gorfa Nights Public Cafe and is on the right just before the big roundabout that leads into Kalba.

Getting There & Away

Fujairah international airport is served by Gulf Air (one flight a week to Bahrain and Doha and two to Muscat) and Indian Airlines (one flight a week to Calicut). For airport information call ☎ 226 222.

The taxi station is on the edge of town on the road to Sharjah and Dubai. The fare to Dubai or Sharjah is Dh25 per person or Dh175 shared. Shared taxis to Dibba are Dh20, Dhaid Dh10 and Masafi and Khor Fakkan Dh5.

AROUND FUJAIRAH

The largely residential town of **Kalba**, just south of Fujairah, is part of the Sharjah emirate. It is also the site of the oldest mangrove forest in Arabia. This conservation reserve has abundant bird life and is the only home in the world to the Khor Kalba white collared kingfisher. It's possible to hire canoes and paddle up the inlets into the mangroves. Make a deal with the fishermen on the beach.

Breeze Motel (☎ 778 877, fax 776 769) is the only place to stay. Run-down cabins are Dh250/300 but those rates can drop by up to Dh100 if things are slow.

KHOR FAKKAN

One of Sharjah's enclaves and the largest town on the east coast after Fujairah, Khor Fakkan must be the most beautiful spot in the UAE. It's also a trendy weekend resort, but while the port has proved to be a roaring success, the development of tourism has been somewhat held back by Sharjah's ban on alcohol.

The sweeping Corniche is bounded by the **port** and **fish market** at the southern end and the luxury Oceanic Hotel to the north, with a nice beach in between. The fort that once dominated the coast is long gone.

If you have your own transport it's worth a drive to **Rifaisa dam** in the mountains above the town which resembles a Swiss mountain lake without the greenery. To get there turn inland from the main street at the Select N Save store, just near the mosque. The road swings round to the right and over a bridge. Turn left immediately after the bridge onto a dirt road. Follow this road for 4.7km to the dam.

Places to Stay & Eat

Oceanic Hotel (☎ 09-385 111, fax 387 716), at the northern end of the Corniche, is expensive with singles/doubles for Dh460/575. The hotel is unashamedly 70s. It can arrange visas with five days notice.

Al-Khaleej Hotel (☎ 09-387 336) is one of the first buildings you will see on the right upon entering Khor Fakkan from Fujairah. It only has doubles for Dh150 with bath which is far too much for the sparsely furnished and dirty rooms.

Lebanon Restaurant, on the Corniche, has mezze for Dh5 to Dh15 and main dishes for around Dh20. Avoid the appealing looking *Irani Pars* restaurant at the roundabout on the Corniche near the souq. It is overpriced at Dh20 to Dh25 for mains and the food is average at best. The restaurant on the top floor of the *Oceanic* is expensive but try to drop in for a cup of coffee and a chance to admire the view over the bay.

BADIYAH

Badiyah, 8km north of Khor Fakkan but in the Fujairah emirate, is one of the oldest towns in the Gulf. Archaeological digs have shown that the site of the town has been settled more or less continuously since the 3rd millennium BC. Today, it is known mainly for its **mosque**, a small whitewashed structure of stone, mud brick and gypsum built around 640 AD. It is the oldest mosque in the UAE, and is still in use. It is built into a low hillside along the main road just north of the village. On the hillside above and behind it are several ruined **watchtowers**. You may be asked for baksheesh by the Sri Lankan minders here.

There is no place to stay in Badiyah but 6km to the north, near the village of Al-Aqqa, there's *Sandy Beach Motel* (☎ 09-445 555, fax 445 200). Hotel rooms are Dh267.50 and one-bedroom chalets cost Dh399. There is a diving centre here where you can organise dives or just hire snorkelling gear to explore the coral reef just 100m from the beach. The stretch of beach next to the hotel is a popular *camping* spot.

DIBBA

Dibba lives in Islamic history as the site of one of the great battles of the Ridda Wars,

the reconquest of Arabia by Muslim armies in the generation after the death of the Prophet. The victory at Dibba in 633, a year after the Prophet's death, traditionally marks the end of the Muslim reconquest of Arabia. The graveyard on the vast flat area before the mountains plunge directly into the sea is the only evidence of these past battles. Thousands of headstones protrude from the flat ground. It really is quite an amazing sight.

These days, Dibba is a quiet set of seaside villages. In fact, there are three Dibbas, each belonging to a different ruler: Dibba Muhallab (Fujairah), Dibba Hosn (Sharjah) and Dibba Bayah (Oman). As in Al-Ain, you can walk or drive freely across the Omani border or you may want to explore some of the Omani villages at the southern edge of the spectacular Musandam peninsula.

Dibba is a really nice spot. There is nothing much to see, and there are no hotels. Nevertheless, the quiet pace of life here makes it worth the trip.

Yemen

Over 3000 years of recorded history have left Yemen with a unique cultural heritage, evident in the architecture of the towns and villages of the country. Today Yemen is furiously modernising a society that only opened up to the rest of the world a generation ago. It is the privilege of today's traveller to witness the endurance of the world of *The Thousand and One Nights* in the grip of an abrupt change.

After an era of isolation, which for some parts of the country had lasted decades, for other parts a thousand years, Yemen is more accessible today than it has ever been. Tourists have been cautiously welcomed since the late 1970s, but a lack of resources and recurrent political crises have hampered the development of a tourist infrastructure: there are no holiday resorts in Yemen, western-style hotels are rare and many of the country's attractions are inaccessible. However, many visitors have found their trip far too short, dictating a return.

Facts about Yemen

HISTORY
The Frankincense Trade
The earliest known civilisations in southern Arabia existed more than 1000 years before Christ. The ancient kingdoms based their existence on agriculture and trade. The most important products of the region were myrrh and frankincense, the resins of the *Commiphora* and *Boswellia* tree genera, which grow only on the coasts of the Gulf of Aden. These aromatics, highly valued for the pleasant odours they released when burned as incense, had great ritual value in many different cultures – from the Egyptian to the Greek and Roman.

These commodities were carried by sea or land. Around the 11th century BC, overland travel through Arabia vastly improved with the introduction of camels, as they could

---

The Republic of Yemen

Area: 532,000 sq km
Population: 15.8 million (1994 census)
Population Growth Rate: 3.7%
Capital: San'a
Head of State: President Ali Abdullah Salih
Official Language: Arabic
Currency: Yemeni riyal (YR)
Exchange Rate: US$1 = YR155

- **Best Dining** – black-fried whole fish on a *khubz* bed in a street restaurant in any of the coastal towns
- **Best Walk** – stroll around old Sa'da on top of the town wall
- **Best View** – from Jebel Kawkaban; walking the footpath up from Shibam makes the view unforgettable
- **Best Activity** – early morning walk from one mountain village to another, anywhere in the highlands
- **When in Rome ...** attend a *qat* party with somebody who can interpret the chat to you

walk much longer distances without requiring as much rest or water as donkeys. This meant that routes could be plotted through dry lands, with only a few stops needed for food, water and lodgings along the way.

From the important frankincense production area of Qana (today's Bir Ali), on the coast of the Arabian Sea, it became possible to reach Ghaza (Egypt) in a matter of two months. In addition to fragrances, the convoys carried gold and other precious items that came to Qana by sea from India.

Saba & its Rivals

In southern Arabia, several mighty kingdoms along the trade route rose and fell within a period of 1500 years. The most important of these was Saba, which existed for at least 14 centuries from about 1000 BC.

The capital of Saba was located in Ma'rib, strategically positioned by the natural land routes from Qana and through the Hadramawt valley. The agricultural wealth of Saba was based on the famous dam in Ma'rib, which was built in the 8th century BC and stood for over 1000 years.

However, Saba had powerful rivals along the trade route: Najran (today in southern Saudi Arabia), Ma'in, Awsan, Qa'taban and Hadramawt (all in present-day Yemen). Between the 6th century BC and 2nd century AD, these states alternately fell under Sabaean rule and freed themselves from it.

In the 1st century AD, Greeks and Romans discovered how to utilise monsoon winds on their voyages to India, transferring their cargo from camels to ships. New rivals off the land-based routes emerged, who were able to control the ports of Aden and Al-Muza near the Bab al-Mandab Strait: the Himyarites, with their capital Dhafar (now a small village in the Ibb governorate), and the Ethiopians on the opposite shores of the strait. For five centuries control of the region alternated between Ethiopians, Sabaeans and Himyarites.

With the rise of Christianity on the shores of the Mediterranean, the use of 'pagan' ritual fragrances was abandoned. The total conversion of the Roman Empire in 395 AD put an end to the demand for frankincense, and the Sabaean kingdom faced a decline. Maintenance of the great Ma'rib dam was neglected and in 570 AD the dam broke. The inhabitants abandoned Ma'rib, wandering the Arabian peninsula to settle in new locations.

In the same year, the Ethiopians were finally defeated by the Himyarites who had allied themselves with the Persians. By 575 AD the Persians managed to subdue the region, along with the rest of the peninsula.

Medieval Islamic Yemen

In 628 Badhan, the Persian governor of Yemen, converted to Islam and the general population soon followed. By the early 630s the first Yemeni mosques were built in San'a, Al-Janad and near Wadi Zabid. The first two still stand today.

After the Prophet's death in 632, the capital of the newly founded Islamic empire was quickly moved away from the Arabian peninsula: first to Damascus in 661, by the Umayyad caliphs, and to Baghdad in 750 by

---

What to See

Reasons to visit Yemen include the country's long history, the extraordinary architecture that is in perfect harmony with the mountainous landscape and the unique culture developed during centuries of isolation and preserved to this day.

Time has not treated southern Arabia gently. Still, the sites of the once-mighty towns of **Qana**, **Shabwa**, **Timna'**, **Ma'rib** and **Baraqish** along the ancient incense route offer plenty to experience, even if the ruins are modest when compared to those in Egypt or Turkey.

Yemeni culture is overwhelmingly present in the capital, **San'a**, simultaneously a bustling modern city and a huge open-air museum. Mountain regions such as those around **Manakha** and **Al-Mahwit** offer good opportunities for trekking, while the towns of **Ibb** and **Ta'izz** are not to be missed. **Wadi Hadramawt** offers a totally different setting with equally fascinating towns and buildings. **Aden**, the country's most cosmopolitan city, will remind you of the colonial past.

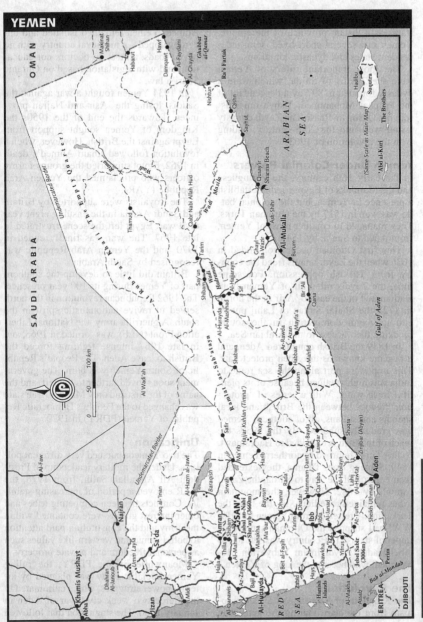

YEMEN

OMAN

Makinat
Shihan
Habarut
Hawf
Damqawt
Al-Faydami
Ghabbat
al-Qamar
Al-Chayda
Nishtun
Ra's Fartak

ARABIAN
SEA

Sayhut
Sharma Beach
Qusay'ir
Qabr Nabi Allah Hud
Ash-Shihr
Al-Mukalla
Ghayl
Ba Wazir
Burum

SAUDI ARABIA

Al-Faw

Thamud

Wadi Masila

Wadi Hadramaut

Tarim
Say'un
Shibam
Al-Hajarayn
Al-Mashhad
Sif
Bir 'Ali
Qana

Al-Hurayda

Shabwa

Mayfa'a
Habban
Al-Mahfid
Yashbum

Ar-Rawda
'Azan

Ataq

Al-Wadi'ah

Ramlat as-Sab'atayn

Al-Rub' al-Khali (The Empty Quarter)

Undemarcated Border

100 km
50
0

Najran

Al-Hazm al-Jawf
Baraqish
Ma'rib
Harib
Bayhan
Nuqub
Al-Bayda
Lawdar
Zinjibar (Abyan)
Shuqra

Hammam Damt
Rada'a

Dza'taba
Al-Hablayn

Aden

Khamis Mushayt

Abha

Dhahran
Al-Janoub

Sa'da
Suq al-Inan

Umm Layla

Shihara

Midi

Al-Qanawis

Hajja
Thilla
Shiban
Amran
Al-Mahwit
Jabal an-Nabi
Shu'ayb (3660m)

SAN'A'

Manakha
Ma'bar
Dhamar
Bayt al-Faqih

Beit al-Faqih
Yarim

Dhafar
Ibb
Jibla
At-Turba
Sheikh Uthman

Lahj
(Al-Hawta)

Az-Zaydiya
Bajil

Al-Hudayda

Zabid
Hays
Al-Khawkha
Jebel Sabir (3006m)

Hamish
Islands

Ta'izz

Yifrus

Al-Makha

Assab

Perim

Bab al-Mandab

Jizan

RED SEA

DJIBOUTI

ERITREA

Gulf of Aden

(Same Scale as Main Map)
Hadibu
Suqutra
The Brothers
'Abd al-Kuri

YEMEN

the Abbasid caliphs. With its diminishing status as a distant province of the empire, Yemen saw several short-lived, semi-independent states and dynastic kingdoms.

The most important rulers of Yemen were the Zaydis of Sa'da, which were a dynasty founded in 897 by a descendant of the Prophet Mohammed, Yahya bin Hussein bin Qasim ar-Rassi. The Zaydi dynasty lasted well into the 20th century, ending with the revolution of 1962.

Yemen Under Colonial Powers

In the early 16th century, the Portuguese and the Mamluks of Egypt tried to establish a presence in Yemen, but the colonial battle was won in 1517 by the Ottoman Turks. They managed to conquer most of Yemen, from Aden to San'a, by 1548.

This first Ottoman occupation ended in 1636 when the Zaydi imams freed the country from Turkish oppression. For some time, the Zaydis ruled all of Yemen from Hadramawt in the east to 'Asir in the north. In 1728 the Shafai Sultan of Lahij put an end to Zaydi domination in the south, blocking their access to the Arabian Sea.

In 1839 the British conquered Aden, and it became known as the Aden protectorate. This important port along the sea route to India was highly valued because of its plentiful fresh water. With a series of 'protection' treaties between the British and local sheikhs and sultans, all of southern Yemen was gradually subdued. By the 1950s the reach of the British extended to Hadramawt.

The Turks returned to northern Yemen in 1849. Starting from Tihama, they extended their control all the way to Sa'da, the Zaydi capital, by 1882. However, the mountain tribes remained rebellious. By the time the Turks finally retreated from Yemen in 1919, WWI had stripped the Ottoman state of its imperial status. The country was left to the rebel leader, Zaydi Imam Yahya ibn Mohammed, who became the king of Yemen.

The Revolutions

The Kingdom of Yemen was an anachronism from the start. During the autocratic reigns of Imam Yahya and his son, Imam Ahmed, Yemen remained isolated and underdeveloped – a medieval country with no paved roads, almost no doctors nor education, and with legislation based on Quranic Shari'a law.

In 1934 Yemen fought a war against the Saudis, losing the 'Asir and Najran provinces. Towards the end of the 1950s the Kingdom of Yemen sought support from Egypt against the British. However, when a revolution followed Imam Ahmed's death in 1962, Egypt supported the group of army officers who proclaimed the Yemen Arab Republic (YAR).

The Royalists were supported by Britain and Saudi Arabia in the ensuing eight year civil war. Egypt left the scene frustrated in late 1967. The war was finally ended in 1970, and the Yemen Arab Republic was recognised by Saudi Arabia.

Britain did little to develop the southern part of Yemen during its 100 year presence. The 1962 Republican revolution in the north served to revive nationalistic spirit in the south. A guerrilla army, the National Liberation Front (NLF), was formed in 1963, and in late 1967 intense fighting forced the British to leave Aden. The People's Republic of South Yemen was born. The government soon moved farther to the left, and the name of the first and only Marxist Arab state was changed to the People's Democratic Republic of Yemen (PDRY) in 1970.

Unification

The two Yemens pursued very different politics. Under the military leadership of President Ali Abdullah Salih, from 1978, the YAR enjoyed a period of increasing stability. Conflicts between competing tribes and other interest groups were contained within the army and the constitution paid attention to both Islamic and western-like values such as personal freedom and private property.

Meanwhile, in the PDRY, the ruling Yemen Socialist Party was plagued by internal power struggles, which culminated in the fierce two week civil war of Aden in January 1986. The stagnation that followed developed into virtual bankruptcy when the Soviet Union collapsed and the flow of both ideological and financial aid ceased.

The 1970s had marked an era of mutual suspicion between the two Yemens. The short border wars of 1972, 1978 and 1979 were futile for both parties. Instead, the quest for the unification of Yemen remained strong. The mid-1980s discovery of oil fields in the desert area on both sides of the undemarcated border accelerated the progress towards unity. The economic cul-de-sac of the PDRY was solved by the declaration of the unified Republic of Yemen on 22 May 1990.

The unification was sealed in a referendum held in May 1991, and reconfirmed in a two month civil war in 1994. The war was prompted by a secession attempt led by ex-PDRY politicians in the South, who were frustrated by their isolation from the power plays of San'a.

Yemen Today

Since 1994, Yemen has slowly crawled towards greater stability, with occasional setbacks. Politically, all parties now stand behind the unity of the country, with President Salih as the grand unifying figure. Religious extremists tried to extend their power shortly after the War of Unity in 1994, but their profile is markedly low now. The widely publicised kidnapping incident of December 1998, which left four western tourists dead, was apparently masterminded from abroad (several of the perpetrators were British and Algerian citizens). In general, security is getting better even if the thorny issue of unruly tribes in the Ma'rib and Al-Jawf governorates remains unsolved.

The main problem is dissatisfaction with the slow pace of economic development. The government has followed IMF and World Bank guidelines and gradually lowered subsidies on foodstuffs and fuel, prompting sporadic riots and unrest in the cities. The riyal, which had gained unforeseen stability in 1998, was sent into a new nose dive in 1999 after the decline of tourism and yet another round of lifted subsidies.

GEOGRAPHY

Yemen is 532,000 sq km in area, with two thirds of it uninhabited. Saudi Arabia and Oman are its neighbours. The Hanish Islands in the Red Sea, and Suqutra in the Arabian Sea also belong to Yemen.

The topography is the most varied of any country in the Arabian peninsula. Adjacent to the Tihama, a 20 to 50km-wide coastal strip, the western mountains rise to well over 3000m. Between the western and the lesser eastern mountains, fertile high plateaux lie at over 2000m. The capital San'a sits at the centre of the San'a basin at an altitude of 2250m.

Several parts of the highlands are volcanically active with hot springs and occasional earthquakes. The eastern mountains slowly descend to about 1000m at the Omani border. From the north, the great sands of the vast Arabian desert, Ar-Ruba' al-Khali (The Empty Quarter), extend to the southernmost tip of Yemen.

CLIMATE

Yemen is the most arable spot on the Arabian peninsula. Twice-yearly monsoon winds often bring ample rains from the south and south-west. However, the rains are irregular; in different years they may come in different months and, some years, a monsoon may deliver no rain.

The coastal region is arid as rainfall is scant, with most of the rain falling between late July and September. The western mountains receive most of the rainfall; in the governorate of Ibb, daily rains bring a monthly rainfall of almost 500mm in August, while

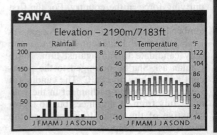

SAN'A

Elevation – 2190m/7183ft

Rainfall / Temperature charts

YEMEN

San'a may get a fourth of that. During the winter and mid-summer no rainfall at all occurs except infrequently in Ibb. Towards the east, the rainfall gradually diminishes. In Ruba' al-Khali no rain ever falls.

Temperatures vary considerably according to location and calendar. The Tihama and the southern coast are hot throughout the year, with very humid air. The highlands are mild and San'a's maximum daily temperatures range from 25°C to 30°C throughout the year. Minimum nightly temperatures are around 0°C in January (the dry season) and 10°C in July (between the rainy seasons).

GOVERNMENT & POLITICS

Yemen is the only parliamentary democracy in the Arabian peninsula, and in the two elections held to date (1993, 1997) almost 40 parties competed for the 301 parliamentary seats. The People's General Congress (PGC) of the North holds 187 seats, while the biggest religious party, Islah, is a distant second with 54 seats. The rest of the seats are splintered between small parties and independents. The present government is formed almost exclusively by the PGC with Abdul Karim al-Iryani as prime minister.

The Yemen Socialist Party of the South (YSP) lost its influence in the War of Unity and boycotted the last elections.

After the War of Unity in 1994, President Ali Abdullah Salih stood out as the undisputed leader of Yemen. In power since 1978, the president of the former YAR has survived a rumoured 100 assassination attempts and is now widely respected as *the* unifying force in the country. For the first free presidential elections, set for 23 September 1999, no serious rivals emerged. As Islah supported President Salih, too, the only candidate to run against him, Najib Qahtan ash-Sha'bi, belonged to the president's own party, the PGC. The candidates were elected by the parliament in the vote of 22 July from 31 nominees but no representative of the opposition achieved the necessary 10% support.

POPULATION & PEOPLE

Yemen is the most populous country in the Arabian Peninsula. The most recent census in December 1994 counted the population at

The Tribal Spirit

Unlike other countries of the peninsula, Yemen is still very much a tribal society. These tribes form even bigger units that could be called tribal federations. Two powerful federations remain in the northern part of Yemen today: the Hashids and Bakils of the mountains. The Zaraniqs of Tihama no longer have a strong role. In the south and in the east, the Communist PDRY pursued a strongly anti-tribalist policy, but even there tribes have enjoyed a sort of revival since unification. Tribal units have a strong influence in Yemen, to the extent that no cabinet can be formed without balancing tribal representation.

The tribal ties are at their strongest in the mountainous areas, where the mobility of the population is at its lowest. Unlike the nomadic Bedouin, the Yemeni farmer families have stayed in their villages for centuries, marrying their sons and daughters only to members of respectable families from the same region and, of course, from the same tribe.

The famous Yemeni historian, Hassan ibn Ahmed al-Hamdani, recorded the tribal structure of northern Yemen in astonishing detail in his ten-volume tome *Al-Iklil*, written around 930-40 AD. A town or village he describes as Bakil or Hashid has stayed the same ever since. As every tribe, and every Yemeni, trace their origins all the way to Qahtan, son of the Prophet Hud, who in turn was a great-grandson of Noah's son Shem, genealogy is an integral part of the Yemeni mind set. In tribal areas one can meet old men who know by heart their ancestors of five or six generations, and who can accurately describe the relations between themselves and every inhabitant of their own and the neighbouring villages.

YEMEN

15.8 million, with more than 80% from the former YAR. With an annual growth rate at 3.7% the figure is predicted to reach 20 million in the year 2001. Ethnically, Yemenis can be divided into three main groups. Mountain dwellers represent the purest Yemeni blood, the people of Tihama have mixed with their African neighbours while on the southern coast and in Wadi Hadramawt, Indian and south-east Asian influences are evident.

RELIGION

The state religion of Yemen is Islam. Most people in the Tihama and the southern and eastern parts of the country belong to a Sunni sect called the Shafa'i. The northernmost governorates are inhabited mainly by Zaydis, a Shi'ite minority sect, who make up a third to a half of the Yemeni population. Members of another Shi'ite sect, the Ismailis, constitute a very small percentage of the population. The sects use each others' mosques freely.

A small but important Jewish minority existed throughout the first 14 Islamic centuries. After the creation of the state of Israel, about 50,000 Jews left Yemen; a few hundred remain in the country.

LANGUAGE

Arabic is the official language of Yemen and the only language of most of the inhabitants. Having some Arabic at your command makes all the difference. English is widely taught in the schools, with pretty poor results. It is easier to get by with English in Aden and other southern governorates due to the region's colonial past. Tour guides may speak various European languages. For more details about the Arabic language, see the Language chapter.

Facts for the Visitor

PLANNING
When to Go

Climatic conditions vary greatly between regions. If you plan to visit the Tihama region or Aden and Hadramawt, avoid the unbearably hot summer. In contrast, nights in the highlands can get quite cold in winter. From late November to early January San'a may have nightly frosts and, in the mountains, it is chilly. The dry season of late October to early February causes most of the country to become parched and dusty.

The rainy seasons – the lighter one in March-April and the heavier one in August-September – offer pleasant temperatures, but heavy downpours and fogs make the mountains less pleasant. The moderate periods just after the rainy seasons, April-May and September-October, might be your best bet.

VISAS & DOCUMENTS
Visas

Everybody, except citizens from the Gulf Cooperation Council countries, needs a visa to enter Yemen. Any Yemeni consulate will issue you with an entry visa. Citizens of the European Union countries, except the UK, can get their visa at San'a airport on arrival but the procedure is lengthy and not recommended.

Entry fees are generally about US$35. At most embassies the rates are US$5 to US$10 higher for applicants who are not citizens of the country the embassy is located in.

The period covered by an entry visa varies from one to three months. The maximum duration of stay is usually one month for tourist visas.

Depending on the embassy, you will need one or two photographs for your visa application. If you're travelling on business, you will need a reference in Yemen – usually a letter from the Yemeni company or organisation with which you are dealing.

As a rule, it takes 48 hours (two working days) for any embassy to process a visa application, but sometimes you may get a visa the next day. On the other hand, should any problem occur (eg you sent insufficient funds when applying by mail) they'll be in no hurry to try fixing that (they might wait for you to contact them instead of informing you of the problem). It is not possible to get a visa on a land border post, sea port (except possibly transit visas in Aden in the near future) nor at any other airport but San'a.

YEMEN

Visa Extensions You can get one-month visa extensions from the immigration office of the Ministry of Interior for YR1500. There are immigration offices in San'a, Ta'izz, Al-Hudayda and Aden. You'll need a medical certificate to show you are not HIV positive.

Visas for Neighbouring Countries You need a visa to enter the following neighbouring countries of Yemen:

Oman To get a visa for Oman in San'a you need two photographs; the fee is US$21, and you should allow two to four days.

Saudi Arabia You can get a transit visa for Saudi Arabia if you are travelling with a vehicle of your own. You will need documents showing the ownership of the car plus one photograph; the fee is SR50, and because you need to apply for the visa in person you should budget up to one week for the process.

UAE The UAE embassy in San'a is not in the business of granting visitor visas as you need a sponsor in the country and the visas are arranged for you to pick up at the airport.

Other Documents
Visitors flying directly from Western Europe need no health cards, but if you are coming from a place where cholera or yellow fever is rampant you'll need an international vaccination certificate.

Cars are usually rented with drivers, but for self-drive an international drivers' permit is recognised if properly stamped by Yemeni police.

EMBASSIES & CONSULATES
Yemeni Embassies & Consulates
For addresses of Yemeni embassies in neighbouring Middle Eastern countries see the relevant country chapters.

Canada
    Embassy:
    (☎ 613-729 6627, fax 232 8276)
    Suite 1100, 350 Sparks St, Ottawa, Ontario, K1R 570

France
    Embassy:
    (☎ 01 47 23 61 76, fax 01 47 23 69 41)
    25, rue Georges Bizet, 75016 Paris
Germany
    Embassy:
    (☎ 49-228 220451, fax 228 229364)
    Adenauerallee 77, 5300 Bonn
Netherlands
    Embassy:
    (☎ 703-653936, fax 563312)
    Noordeinde 41, 2414 GC The Hague
UK
    Embassy:
    (☎ 020-7584 6607, fax 7589 3350)
    57 Cromwell Rd, London SW7 2Ed
USA
    Embassy:
    (☎ 202-337 8117, fax 337 2017)
    Suite 705, 2600 Virginia Avenue, N.W. Washington, D.C. 20037
    Consulate:
    (☎ 212-355 1730, fax 750 9613)
    Room 435, 866 UN Plaza, New York, NY 10017

Embassies & Consulates in Yemen
All of the following embassies are based in San'a. Opening times vary but are generally from 8 am to 1 pm.

Australia
    Australian travellers in Yemen are asked to register their presence with the Australian embassy in Riyadh, Saudi Arabia (☎ 1-488 7788, fax 488 7973).
Canada
    Consulate:
    (☎ 208814, fax 209523)
    Mogadishu St, South of Hadda Rd
France
    Embassy:
    (☎ 268882, fax 269160)
    St 21, near Khartum St, PO Box 1286
Germany
    Embassy:
    (☎ 413174, fax 413179)
    Hadda Area
Netherlands
    Embassy:
    (☎ 264078, fax 415646)
    Hadda St (after Ring Rd)
Oman
    Embassy:
    (☎ 208875, fax 204586)
    Villa 7, St 5, off Baghdad St

Saudi Arabia
    Embassy:
    (☎ 240429, 240430, fax 240859)
    Bldg 1, Al-Quds St, Southern Ring Rd
UAE
    Embassy:
    (☎ 248777, fax 248779)
    South Ring Rd
UK
    Embassy:
    (☎ 264081, fax 263059)
    129 Hadda St (Al-Hasan al-Hamadani St), PO
    Box 1287
USA
    Embassy:
    (☎ 238842, fax 251563)
    Sa'wan St, Dhahr Himyar Zone, Sheraton
    Hotel District

MONEY
Costs
If you conform to the traditional Yemeni lifestyle, you can travel very cheaply here, but if you demand steak grilled medium, beer and private guided tours, you will find that it was only the flight ticket that was cheap. If you try something in-between, you will find Yemen is still reasonable.

Basic food is cheap. For example, a glass of tea or a loaf of bread costs YR10 to YR20 and you can have a simple but nourishing dinner in a street-level restaurant for YR100 to YR400. A live chicken sells for YR150 to YR200 in the market while the bill for a grilled one in a restaurant is YR400 to YR600.

As for hotels, you'll find everything from absolutely basic inns at YR300 to YR500 per bed to western-style five-star deluxe hotels charging US$210 a night. Doubles in clean and perfectly adequate mid-range tourist hotels cost YR2000 to YR3500.

Transport, your third main expense, is not expensive either. San'a to Al-Hudayda takes four hours and costs YR500, while Aden to Al-Mukalla takes 12 hours and costs YR900. A seat in a service taxi may cost 20 to 50% more for the same distance. At the high end of the scale, a private 4WD with a driver costs YR9000 to YR20,000 per day, depending on distance covered and the roughness of the road.

Currency
The Yemeni riyal is denoted in this book by the abbreviation YR. There is both a coin and a banknote worth five and 10 riyals and banknotes of 20, 50, 100, 200, 500 and 1000 riyals. The notes are bilingual; values are printed in Arabic on one side, English on the other, and can be recognised by their colours. Coin values are shown only in Arabic.

Exchange Rates
Exchange rates at the time of research were:

country	unit		Yemeni riyals
Australia	A$1	=	YR103
Canada	C$1	=	YR107
euro	€1	=	YR169
France	10FF	=	YR250
Germany	DM1	=	YR86
Japan	¥100	=	YR145
New Zealand	NZ$1	=	YR83
UK	UK£1	=	YR256
USA	US$1	=	YR159

Exchanging Money
It is best to bring US dollars in cash; major European currencies are also accepted, as are Saudi and Omani riyals. US$100 bills will get you better rates than smaller denominations. Travellers cheques are a nuisance as they are only accepted by a few banks (such as Indo-Suez) and moneychangers in San'a and possibly Aden and Al-Hudayda. It is far too time-consuming to hunt for a place willing to exchange your particular brand, and it's not worth paying for the extra protection travellers cheques provide as theft is so uncommon in Yemen.

You can change money at the exchange counter at San'a airport, in commercial banks or at moneychangers' offices in larger cities – the rates are usually quite similar. In smaller towns you won't be able to exchange money at all.

There is no real black market.

Credit Cards & ATMs
Credit cards (Amex, Visa) are only accepted by the biggest hotels, tour operators and airline offices. ATM's are nonexistent.

YEMEN

Tipping & Bargaining

Tipping is unknown in Yemen as service is included in restaurant and hotel prices.

Time-consuming bargaining was never the rule in Yemen but tourists have recently introduced the habit in the more popular silver souqs and hotels. Compare the prices and use your better judgement.

POST & COMMUNICATIONS
Post

Postal services in Yemen are relatively developed and you can send your postcards, parcels and express mail from San'a and Aden with fair confidence that they will reach, say, Europe in a week or two. Post offices can also be found in towns everywhere in the country. Print the country of destination in Arabic after the address to make sure the handlers route your mail first to San'a or Aden, the hubs of international traffic.

Receiving mail is only possible at San'a poste restante or big hotels belonging to international chains.

The rates are reasonable; for example, a postcard to Europe costs YR50.

Telephone & Fax

The phone services in Yemen are generally quite good. In the bigger towns you can find International Telephone Centre offices with phone booths for domestic and international calls. The phones have small LCD displays showing the riyal charge of your call as it progresses. Domestic rates are very reasonable, while international rates comply with the international price level anywhere.

The international dialling code for Yemen is ☎ 967. When calling in Yemen, dial ☎ 0 before the area code, ☎ 00 for international calls. For inquiries, dial ☎ 118. Area codes for the governorates are:

San'a	☎ 1
Aden, Abyan, Lahij	☎ 2
Al-Hudayda	☎ 3
Ta'izz, Ibb	☎ 4
Shabwa, Hadramawt, Al-Mahra	☎ 5
Dhamar, Al-Bayda, Al-Jawf	☎ 6
Ma'rib	☎ 630
Al-Mahwit, Hajja, Sa'da	☎ 7

Most hotels have fax facilities that guests can usually use for a fee.

Email & Internet Access

At the time of writing, Internet use in Yemen was in its infancy, and no Internet cafes or similar public services were available. Some pioneering hotels offer computers for their customers to use; hefty fees reflect the high charges of TeleYemen, the only Internet service provider at the moment.

BOOKS

Highly recommended are *Yemen: Travels in a Dictionary Land* by Tim Mackintosh-Smith and *Impressions of Yemen* by Pascal & Maria Maréchaux. Check the bookshop of the Taj Sheba hotel in San'a for its random selection.

More general Middle Eastern titles, some of which also contain coverage of Yemen, are listed in the Books section in the Regional Facts for the Visitor chapter at the beginning of this book.

NEWSPAPERS & MAGAZINES

The most interesting newspaper for the English-reading visitor is the political weekly *Yemen Times*, which is proof of the freedom of Yemeni press. *Time* and *Newsweek* are also available in some centrally located newsstands in the bigger cities and at a couple of luxury hotels in San'a.

RADIO & TV

Two radio stations, one transmitting from San'a the other from Aden, broadcast mainly in Arabic. All TV programs are in Arabic, except for the 9 and 11 pm news, which are broadcast in English. Dish antennas for receiving satellite broadcasts became legal in 1991 and are popular even in the remotest of villages.

PHOTOGRAPHY & VIDEO

Photographers will find film available in the bigger cities, though not in the smaller towns. For processing, fully automated development labs only take a couple of hours and cost about YR750 for 36 colour prints.

You can have passport photos taken in San'a and Aden.

LAUNDRY

Outside the most expensive hotels, laundry services for tourists are a new idea in Yemen. The dry-cleaning outlets around San'a and other cities are mainly geared to handle the jackets of Yemeni men – your shirts and underwear will not be accepted.

TOILETS

As a rule, the restaurants in smaller towns do not have toilets, and public toilets are rare. If you ask for one, you are usually shown to a nearby cheap hotel or to a service station. Women travellers seeking relief in a strange town should ask a pre-teen boy, who will take you to the male-only *lukanda* you could not otherwise enter.

HEALTH

Health care standards are dismally low in Yemen. Western medical aid is mainly available in the hospitals of San'a and Aden. The pharmacies of bigger towns are relatively well-stocked. For detailed health information, see the Health section in the Regional Facts for the Visitor chapter.

DANGERS & ANNOYANCES

In the latter half of the 1990s many travellers and expats have found themselves kidnapped by local groups trying to blackmail the government for various ends. This has grown into a major problem in certain Bedouin governorates (especially Ma'rib, Al-Jawf and northern Shabwa). Usually the incidents last a few days only and very few travellers have been physically harmed to date. The glaring exception is the December 1998 catastrophe where four tourists got killed in a shoot-out between government troops and UK-based Jihad terrorists.

Inquire about the current situation at the General Tourism Authority in San'a.

In some northern mountain towns and cities (like Sa'da), children throwing small rocks at tourists and cyclists have become a nuisance.

BUSINESS HOURS

Government offices and banks are open from 8 or 9 am to about noon or 1 pm and are closed in the afternoon. On Friday and other public holidays, offices stay closed. Most shops and restaurants are open during mornings and evenings and close their doors for a few hours at qat time in the early afternoon.

PUBLIC HOLIDAYS

In addition to those in the Muslim calendar (see the boxed text 'Islamic Holidays' in the Regional Facts for the Visitor chapter for dates), the following secular holidays are observed:

Labour Day
 1 May
Day of National Unity
 22 May
Victory Day
 7 July
Revolution Day (of the YAR)
 26 September
National Day (of the YAR)
 14 October
Independence Day (of the PDRY)
 30 November

LANGUAGE COURSES

The Yemen Language Center (☎ 205125, email language@y.net.ye, PO Box 16961, San'a) offers Arabic courses for foreigners. See their web site at *ylcint.com* for registration forms, schedules and fees. Other options include the Yemen International Language Institute (☎ 206917, email arwauniversity@y.net.ye, Hadda St, San'a) and the Center for Arabia Language and Eastern Studies (☎ 286776, fax 281700, email cales@y.net.ye, Old San'a).

ACCOMMODATION

The cheapest form of Yemeni accommodation is the *lukanda*, a place often open to the street and with a large *mada'a* (waterpipe) dormitory and loud TV. Sometimes rooms are also available, with filthy mattresses on the floor and blankets (no sheets). Prices vary from YR300 to YR400 per person.

YEMEN

Not much cleaner is the *funduq* (traditional hotel) with one sheet on the bed, changed weekly. It may offer doubles, but rooms usually contain four or more beds. Pricing is per bed, typically from YR300 to YR500. Common bathrooms in the corridor usually have cold tap water only.

A cleaner variation is the palace hotel, found in tourist-populated towns and villages. A palace hotel is an old-style Yemeni tower house converted into a hotel serving western tourists only, charging negotiable prices from YR1000 to YR1500 per mattress with sheets and blankets on the floor.

In western-style tourist hotels, beds have two sheets and prices are based on room capacity, with doubles at YR800 to YR2000. Bathrooms are usually private with hot showers. In the Tihama and the southern governorates, it is worth paying extra for air-conditioning.

The top end category ranges from excellent tourist hotels charging YR2000 to YR5000 per double to a few members of western and Indian hotel chains, charging in dollars only, from US$60 to US$210 a night for fabulous service.

FOOD & DRINKS

Yemeni restaurants are eateries rather than places of social interaction. Lunch is the main meal of the day. A knife and fork are not used; fingers of the right hand and a piece of bread usually do the job.

Bread comes in 30 varieties and is baked once or twice daily. Common are *khubz tawwa* (ordinary bread fried at home), *ruti* (bought from shops) and *lahuh* (a festive pancake-type bread made of sorghum).

The national dish is a thick, fiery stew called *salta*. It contains lamb or chicken with lentils, beans, chickpeas, coriander, spices and any other kitchen leftovers and is served on a bed of rice. Yemenis also like their *shurba* – a cross between a soup and a stew. Varieties include *shurba bilsan* (a lentil soup) and *shurba wasabi* (a lamb soup). Fenugreek (the much celebrated *hilba* soup) is something you can't help but encounter.

Chewing Qat

Yemenis are set apart from other Arabs by their passionate love of qat, the national narcotic. The fresh leaves of *Catha edulis*, a small, evergreen tree or bush that prospers only at relatively high altitudes (1500m to 2500m), are a mild stimulant when chewed. The leaves are not swallowed, instead the chewed paste is pushed against the cheek, which bulges as the slimy lump grows – no wonder old Yemenis' cheeks appear so wrinkled when empty!

Qat is above all a social drug, chewed at qat parties that take place in the afternoons in the *mafraj* of Yemeni houses. Every male Yemeni has to attend a chew at least once a week lest he be regarded as a loner, a voluntary social outcast. Each one offers his house in turn, and qat parties serve to enforce the social fabric of the local community. When asked if you, the foreigner, have chewed qat, a negative answer reveals you are either new or want to retain your foreigner's status, while a positive answer shows you have some Yemeni friends, which will win you respect.

Although most talk in qat chews is just everyday chatter, decision-making also requires qat; nobody has a say in Yemeni politics if he's not invited to President Salih's qat parties.

Qat is not cheap. A *rubta*, or small bundle of six or 10 qat branches containing enough leaves for a typical three to four-hour chewing session, may cost anything from YR200 to YR2000 (a quarter to double an unskilled labourer's daily wage) depending on supply and demand, the season and the quality of the qat. The ability to pay for your qat is an important means of showing affluence.

A typical Yemeni dessert is *bint as-sahn*, an egg-rich, sweet bread that you dip into a mixture of clarified butter and honey.

Bottled mineral water and soft drinks are readily available around the country, even in the tiniest villages. *Never* drink water from the standard plastic jars in restaurants.

Qahwa, or coffee, often flavoured with ginger and other spices, is not as common as *shai*. It is often made not from the beans themselves but from their shells (called *qirsh*). As for alcohol, the Quranic ban is enforced in most of the country except Aden.

SHOPPING

In the silver markets of the souqs of San'a, Sa'da and Ta'izz, old and old-looking jewellery is sold. Traditionally, all Yemeni silverware was crafted by the Jews of Yemen. A common component in the jewellery is the Maria Theresa thaler, a sizeable silver coin originally minted in Austria. It was introduced to Yemen by the Ottoman Turks and served as the currency to the end of the imamate.

An object that is indisputably typical of countries in southern Arabia is the sharply curved tribesman's ceremonial dagger, known as a *jambiya*. It is worn by men on a special belt at the waist. The elite, such as a *qadi* or a *sayyid*, wear more slenderly curved *dhumas*. Prices range from a few hundred riyals for a simple jambiya to tens of thousands for more ornate dhumas with silver and gold decorations.

The most highly valued daggers have handles made from African rhinoceros horn. In fact, Yemen is the chief consumer of this rare material, jeopardising the survival of the entire species.

Getting There & Away

AIR

The San'a airport is used for most of the international flights. Aden airport is only used by Ethiopian and Tanzanian airlines.

The national carrier of Yemen, Yemenia Airways, offers flights from San'a to: Frankfurt, London, Paris and Rome in Europe; Abu Dhabi, Amman, Bahrain, Beirut, Cairo, Damascus, Doha, Dubai, Jeddah, Riyadh, and Sharjah in the Middle East; Karachi and Mumbai in Asia; and Addis Ababa, Asmara, Djibouti, Khartoum and Nairobi in Africa.

San'a and Aden abound with airline agencies, but don't count on finding any bargains. The one-way economy fare to Paris or Frankfurt, for example, is YR231,010.

Presently, no charter packages are offered to Yemen, and bargains are few.

Departure Tax

An airport tax of US$10 is also payable in Yemeni currency.

LAND

To Saudi Arabia, only the Tihama road from Bajil to Jizan is open for non-Muslims travelling on a transit visa with a car of their own. Yemeni customs and immigration formalities are handled in Haradh. The paperwork is horribly time-consuming – expect to spend a full day at the border.

You must have proof of ownership of your vehicle and hefty insurance is essential. Should you be involved in an accident in which a Saudi or Yemeni citizen dies, you will be held liable for considerable compensation of up to tens of thousands of dollars to the victim's family. Make sure you check the procedures with your insurance company beforehand.

The border between Oman and Yemen was opened in late 1992. The coastal road from Salalah is closed for foreigners, but the desert road via Makinat Shihan is open for anybody. Both roads require 4WD's on the Yemeni side of the border. There is no public cross-border traffic, but it is possible to hitch-hike. If you come with your own car, you have to arrange for a local driver and a guard to cross Yemen's easternmost governorates, Al-Mahra and Hadramawt. Hiring a guard is a requirement imposed by the local police administration for security reasons.

YEMEN

Getting Around

AIR

Yemenia (☎ 201822, fax 201821) in San'a, connects all major towns and cities in the country, and has offices in all towns served. The most useful routes include:

from	to	flight time	one way (YR)	flights per week
San'a	Say'un	1h	15,600	6
San'a	Aden	½h	9750	7
San'a	Al-Mukalla	1h	13,650	7
Aden	Say'un	1h	15,600	4
Aden	Al-Mukalla	1h	13,650	4

BUS

Buses travel major asphalt roads only. Usually they leave terminal towns between 6 and 9 am, with afternoon buses leaving between 1 and 3 pm on shorter and more frequented lines. On some long-haul lines such as Aden to Al-Mukalla (nine hours) there may only be a 6 am bus. Buy tickets beforehand from offices at every bus terminal or at major stops along the way. Ticket offices are only open an hour or so before departures.

City Bus

The bigger cities have plenty of minibuses, *dhabar*, that drive along defined routes and pick up passengers from the streets. Prices are around YR10 to YR25 per person. There are no route maps nor schedules.

LONG-DISTANCE TAXI

Service taxis run between all towns in Yemen and are the preferred form of transport. A rule of thumb is that the fares are about 15 to 50% higher than the corresponding bus fare. It is possible to hire the complete taxi by paying for all the seats; ask for *inqis* (private taxi).

CAR RENTAL

Cars are usually hired complete with driver from local tour organisers. A 4WD vehicle with a driver will cost you at least the equivalent of US$65 (YR9000) a day.

Renting cars without drivers is discouraged. It might be cheaper but don't think about renting a 4WD vehicle unless you know how to handle it across the very rough terrain. Poor maps and missing road signs mean you need local experience. Moreover, while driving along Yemeni roads you are subject to Islamic and tribal law.

ORGANISED TOURS

Universal Travel Company (☎ 272861, fax 272384), Bawniya St, PO Box 10473 San'a, and Yemen Arab Tourism Agency (☎ 224 236), PO Box 1153 San'a, are two of the many tour agencies in San'a. There are plenty of others in Old San'a and around Ali Abdul Mogni St, Az-Zubayri St.

HITCHING

It is relatively easy to get a ride in Yemen, except on the asphalt roads served by buses and taxis. However, in remote areas where tourists are rare, people may wish to avoid contact with strangers. After the ride, always offer some money, equivalent to what you would pay for a seat in a service taxi.

For more information see Hitching in the Getting Around chapter.

San'a

According to Yemeni folklore, San'a is one of the first sites of human settlement, and was founded by Noah's son, Shem. The first written history claims the city wall was built in the late 2nd century AD. The name San'a literally means a fortified city.

Later, San'a served as the capital of the Himyarites during the reigns of several kings. Following the arrival of Islam in Yemen in 628 AD, all non-Muslim palaces were destroyed and mosques were built in their place.

During subsequent centuries, San'a often served as a capital but new sultans on various occasions seized power and moved the throne elsewhere. The city was destroyed by Abbasid troops in 803 AD, by the Zaydis in 901 AD and internal dynastic battles in 1187 AD. During the two Turkish Ot-

Yemeni Architecture

Yemeni architecture is unique. Houses are built from local materials: mud, brick and reed are used for structures on the plains and along the wadis, and stone is used in mountain areas. The building styles and facade decorations vary from region to region. Human settlements always display a fantastic harmony with the natural surroundings.

In the Tihama, houses are low; the only structures of considerable height are the minarets of mosques. The most common type of house in the countryside is the African-style reed hut – a round or rectangular one room house with a sharply pointed roof. In the larger villages and towns, one or two storey houses are built of brick. Decorations on the outer walls include patterns of protruding unfinished bricks or elaborate plastered ornaments.

In the highlands, the most commonly seen dwellings are multistorey tower houses. These buildings are made of stone, brick or mud, depending on locally available material, and embody the architectural style so reminiscent of Yemen. Each house is home to one extended family.

The biggest tower houses have five or six floors, each serving a different function. The ground floor is typically for house animals and bulk storage. The rooms on the 1st floor often serve as storage spaces for agricultural products and household items. The 2nd floor may include the *diwan*, or reception room for guests.

The next two or three floors are generally used as bedrooms for the several generations of families occupying the house. The kitchen is on one of these storeys, often equipped with a well that goes straight through the lower storeys into the ground.

On the top floor is the large *mafraj*, or 'room with a good view', where the owner's guests gather to chew qat in the afternoons. The *manzar*, a separate attic on the roof, serves the same purpose.

In the wadis of the southern governorates, mud-plastered mud brick architecture dominates. In Al-Mukalla and the Hadramawt valley, the decoration of many houses shows Indian and Javanese influences. Sa'da, in the north, has some fine examples of *zabur* architecture. Walls are built by laying clay courses on top of each other, letting one layer dry before the next one is laid.

---

toman occupations, San'a was again conquered, first in 1636, then again in 1872. In 1918 the city became the capital of the independent Kingdom of Yemen. However, in 1948, Imam Ahmed moved the capital to Ta'izz.

After the 1962 revolution, San'a regained its capital status. In 1990, when the two Yemens united, San'a became the capital of the new Republic of Yemen.

In 1962 the city wall was completely intact, embracing a city of 34,000 inhabitants in the midst of green fields. After the revolution San'a experienced a period of unprecedented growth, doubling in size every four years. By the mid-1980s the city had spread in all directions, swallowing the nearby villages. Today the population is about one million.

Orientation

San'a is best defined in terms of its main squares and old gates. Maydan at-Tahrir (Liberation Square), or simply Tahrir, at the point joining the separate parts of the old city, is the post-revolutionary centre of the city. It is connected to the other squares by intracity buses.

Bab al-Yaman, the Gate of Yemen, south of the old city's eastern part, gathers the greatest crowds of people. Less important squares include Bab ash-Sha'ub, by the north gate, and Midan al-Qa', by the west gate.

continued on page 850

YEMEN

OLD SAN'A

The most imposing sight in San'a is the old city. Many houses are more than 400 years old and all are built in the same unique style of 1000 years ago. The old walled city originally comprised separate western and eastern parts, connected at the present-day Ali Abdul Mogni St around the Mutwakil Mosque. The eastern part is one of the largest completely preserved medinas in the Arab world.

Old San'a is highly regarded for its cultural heritage, and in 1984, UNESCO launched an international campaign hoping to raise US$223.5 million to safeguard the city. The success of this campaign has since spawned several bilateral daughter campaigns on a national level.

The best remaining examples of San'a's city wall are by the western side of the Sa'ila and by Az-Zubayri St, between the Sa'ila and Bab al-Yaman. The wall was originally built of mud only; the stony lower part was built in 1990 as an act of restoration, preserving the structure but altering its spirit. On the northern side of the medina, near Bab ash-Sha'ub, restored stretches of the wall still stand. San'a tower houses represent a mix of Yemeni styles and materials. The lower floors are built of dark basalt stone and the upper storeys of brick. Facades are ornamented with elaborate friezes, and plastering with white gypsum is used imaginatively. The *takhrim* windows, with their complex fretwork of superimposed round and angular shapes, are made of alabaster panes or coloured glass. The paving of streets in old San'a was begun in the late 1980s with Italian aid. Before the introduction of motorised vehicles, which threatened to pulverise the streets, paving was

Top: Window in Old San'a (Photo by Bethun Carmichael)

Bottom: Material vendo in Old San'a

unnecessary. People, goats, camels and donkeys trampled the soil down, so dust was no problem; neither was mud, with only 30 or so rainy days per year. Paving was recently extended to Sa'ila, the seasonal river flowing through the city, used as a motor track.

BETHUNE CARMICHAEL

The overall structure of the city steers you along the main streets. If you enter the smaller alleys, you may soon find they are dead ends. Before you reach that point, some friendly souls may approach to ask you where you want to go; boundaries between public streets and private courts are vague here but the privacy of homes is inviolable.

Hammams, or bathhouses, abound in the city, many dating from the Turkish era. It is possible for a visitor to have an inexpensive bath in one of them, preferably with a local guide.

Private gardens hide behind mud walls. There are hectares of them, with entries only from the backyards of the houses or mosques. Travellers can best enjoy these improbable oases from the *manzars* of palace hotels or by looking over walls. The city used to be self-sufficient in vegetables and fruit; the gardens are actively cultivated to this day.

On the south-eastern tip of the walled city, the old citadel stands on an elevation, surrounded by massive walls. It is used by the military forces and cannot be entered.

JULIET COOMBE

Top Right: The tower houses of San'a use natural, dressed stone in their lower floors and fired brick in their upper storeys.

Right: Striking window design on one of the buildings of Old San'a

OLD SAN'A

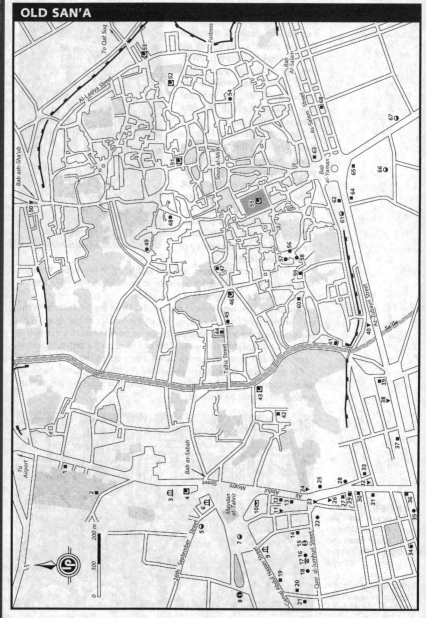

PLACES TO STAY
1 Sam City Hotel
2 Hilltown Hotel
12 Al-Anwar Hotel
13 Al-Makha Hotel
14 International Hotel
19 Manakha Hotel
20 Al-Mukalla Hotel
21 Queen Arwa Tourism Hotel
27 Gulf of Oman Tourist Hotel
29 Say'un Hotel
30 Shabwa Hotel Tourism
31 Taj Sheba Hotel
33 Alshamiri Plaza Hotel
34 Al-Ikhwa Hotel
36 Asia Hotel
37 Middle East Tourist Hotel
39 Sinbad Tourism Hotel
42 Sultan Palace Tourist Hotel
44 Golden Daar Tourist Hotel
47 Taj Talha Hotel
57 Old San'a Palace Hotel
60 Al-Qasmy Hotel
62 Adwa al-Yaman Hotel
63 Tourist Hotel
64 Aden Tourist Hotel

65 Himyar Land Hotel
68 Reidan Palace Hotel

PLACES TO EAT
11 Al Dobaey Fish Restaurant
23 Teahouse
24 Palestine Restaurant
26 Shazarwan Restaurant
32 Teahouse of 26th September
38 Al-Afrah Restaurant
40 Teahouse
50 Teahouse

OTHER
3 National Museum
4 Al-Mutwakil Mosque
5 Shared taxis to Matbah
6 Museum for Arts & Crafts
7 Buses to Bab al-Yaman,
   Bab ash Sha'ub & Qa'al-Yahud
8 General Tourist Corporation
9 Military Museum
10 Post Office
15 Credit Agricole Indosuez
16 Bookshop
17 International Telephone Centre

18 Bookshop
22 Stadium
25 Sinama Bilqis
28 Yemenia
35 Moka Tours
41 Voyages Au Yemen
43 Qubbat al-Mahdi Mosque
45 Al Mokalla Tours
46 Qubbat Talha Mosque
48 Centre for Arabia Language
   and Eastern Studies
49 Handcraft Centre
   (Women Branch)
51 Al-'Aqil Mosque
52 Salah ad-Din Mosque
53 Qubbat al-Bakiriya Mosque
54 Former Site of Qalis
55 Great Mosque
56 Soqatra Tours
58 Magellan Tours
59 Caravan Tours
61 Bus Office, Buses to Al-Hudayda,
   Ta'izz, Ibb & Al Mahwit
66 City Bus & Taxi Station
67 Taxis to Ta'izz, Al-Hudayda
   & Aden

View of Old San'a from the gate of Old San'a Palace

JULIET COOMBE

continued from page 845

Information

Tourist Offices The office of the General Tourist Corporation is at the western end of Maydan at-Tahrir. It is open from 9 am to 1 pm. Its Handicraft Exhibition (souvenir shop) is good for maps, postcards and posters.

The headquarters of the General Tourism Authority are in Hasaba, in the northern part of San'a. Go there to inquire about the current security situation and travel restrictions. A taxi will take you there for YR200.

Visa Extensions Visa extensions can be obtained at the Immigration Office. It is on the eastern side of Ta'izz Rd, next to Yemen Commercial Bank. A minibus takes you there in 10 minutes from Bab al-Yaman for YR20 per person.

Money There are banks in the vicinity of Maydan at-Tahrir that exchange both cash and travellers cheques. Moneychangers offices abound on Ali Abdul Mogni St, Qasr al-Jumhuri St and Gamal Abdul Nasser St.

Post The main post office is at the southeastern corner of Maydan at-Tahrir.

Telephone For calls inside Yemen, the phone booths in the main post office may be used. For overseas calls, there are several International Telecommunication Centres in San'a. A central one is at Qasr al-Jumhuri St, three blocks from Ali Abdul Mogni St.

Travel Agencies Flight bookings can be made at any travel agency on Ali Abdul Mogni St between Maydan at-Tahrir and Az-Zubayri St, or along Az-Zubayri St between the Sa'ila and Hadda St.

Bookshops For English books, the souvenir shops in the Taj Sheba and Sheraton hotels are worth checking, although their selections are limited. Otherwise, try the bookshops on Qasr al-Jumhuri St.

Medical Services The hospital of choice among expatriates in San'a is the Kuwait Hospital (☎ 283282) on Kuwait St, near the junction of the Wadi Dhahr Rd.

Souq al-Milh

The central market area begins at Bab al-Yaman and extends past the Great Mosque, 500m north of Bab al Yaman. Bab al-Yaman was built in the 1870s by the Turkish occupiers.

The souq is open daily but is best visited in the morning, when activity peaks, or between 6 and 7 pm. The area is called Souq al-Milh (Salt Market), but it consists of about 40 smaller souqs, each specialising in things like vegetables, spices, qat, corn, raisins, pottery, clothes, woodworks or copper.

Near Bab al-Yaman, modern consumer items are sold. Moving farther into the souq, better defined sub-souqs emerge, many of them selling traditional products. In the Jambiya Souq you can watch the complicated manufacture of ceremonial weapons. The prosperity of the silver market is largely based on tourists paying high prices.

Traditionally, within each souq there was a *samsara*, a building that served as both storehouse for wares and an inn for those bringing the wares for sale. Fifteen of them can still be found next to the corresponding souqs; many have been restored in the 1990s. **Samsarat an-Nahas** and **Samsarat al-Mansura** today house handicraft and modern art centres.

Mosques

For Muslim visitors, the place to visit in San'a is, of course, the **Great Mosque**, or Al-Jami' al-Kebir, on the westernmost side of Souq al-Milh. Entrance is not granted to non-Muslims. The mosque was built around 630 AD, when the Prophet Mohammed was still alive. Most of the present structures, including the minarets, date from the 12th century.

Salah ad-Din Mosque, in the eastern part of the city, is built in authentic Yemeni style, while the **Qubbat Talha**, in the western part of the medina, shows Turkish influence in its cupolas.

The beautiful, brightly lit minaret of the small **Al-'Aqil Mosque** can be seen at night, overlooking Souq al-Milh. The relatively recent Turkish-style **Al-Mutwakil Mosque** is on Ali Abdul Mogni St, near the northernmost corner of Maydan at-Tahrir next to the Museum of Arts & Crafts. It was built by Imam Yahya in the early 20th century.

The **Qubbat al-Bakiriya**, in the eastern part of the old city by Al-Laqiya St, was built in the early 17th century and restored in the late 19th century – both times by the Turks.

Museums

The **National Museum** is on Ali Abdul Mogni St, about 100m north of Maydan at-Tahrir, after Al-Mutwakil Mosque. It is housed in Dar as-Sa'd (House of Good Luck), a former royal palace built in the 1930s. The museum occupies five floors, with rooms dedicated to ancient kingdoms such as Saba, Ma'rib, Ma'in and Himyar, Yemen's Islamic past and an ethnographic section of 20th century Yemeni folk culture. It's open from 9 am to noon and 3 to 5 pm daily, except Friday (mornings only).

The **Museum for Arts & Crafts**, in Dar ash-Shukr (House of Thanks), another imamic palace near Tahrir, specialises in traditional everyday artefacts of Yemen.

The **Military Museum**, by the south-western corner of Tahrir, is easy to spot; the building is exuberantly decorated with military hardware. This surprisingly good museum tells the story of Yemen from the very relevant military point of view. It is open from 9 am to noon and 4 to 8 pm daily except Friday and the last Thursday of each month.

Places to Stay – Mid-Range

Ali Abdul Mogni St and Gamal Abdul Nasser St have plenty of old hotels where prices stay around YR1000 for a double, often with shared bathrooms. Several are now newly renovated and clean, with private bathrooms. In *Say'un Hotel (☎ 272318, fax 279357)* and *Gulf of Oman Tourist Hotel (☎ 278817)* doubles/triples are YR1800/2200. All these are on Ali Abdul Mogni St, near Shazarwan Restaurant.

Asia Hotel (☎ 272312, fax 272324) near Taj Sheba Hotel is a better alternative with fridge and air-con in the rooms, charging YR2500/3100/5500 for spacious singles/doubles/suites.

Sinbad Tourism Hotel (☎ 272539, fax 272728) on Az-Zubayri St, before Sa'ila, is in the same category, charging YR2500/3500 for smallish singles/doubles.

In Old San'a, several traditional tower houses have been turned into 'palace hotels' with doubles for YR2000 to YR2500, more in the high season. The central *Al-Qasmy Hotel (☎ 273816, fax 271997)* west of Souq al-Milh, *Taj Talha Hotel (☎ 287130, fax 287212)* north of it, and *Sultan Palace Tourist Hotel (☎ 276175, fax 273766)* to the west of Sa'ila are among the best. *Al-Hamd Palace Hotel (☎ 283119, fax 283117)*, the oldest and most luxurious of them all, is in the western centre of San'a, and charges YR4100/5700 for singles/doubles.

Places to Stay – Top End

Hilltown Hotel (☎ 278426, fax 278427), about 200m from the National Museum, charges US$45/61 for singles/doubles. *Al-shamiri Plaza Hotel (☎ 274346, fax 272604, Ali Abdul Mogni St)* has singles/doubles/triples at US$30/50/65. The gorgeous *Taj Sheba (☎ 272372, fax 274129)* offers singles/doubles at US$160/175. *San'a Sheraton (☎ 237500, fax 251521)*, is similarly priced but farther away from the centre, on Ring Rd in the eastern suburbs. *Hadda Hotel (☎ 415215, fax 463094)*, on southern Hadda St, offers singles/doubles/suites for YR13,000/15,000/25,000 plus 12% tax.

Places to Eat

Small restaurants abound all around San'a, but the best selection can be found near Bab al-Yaman and Maydan at-Tahrir.

Shazarwan Restaurant is by the Gulf of Oman Tourist Hotel, opposite the cinema on Ali Abdul Mogni St. It is clean and busy; the grilled chicken is some of the best you will find in Yemen. A good, cheap place is *Al-Afrah Restaurant* on Az-Zubayri St between Ali Abdul Mogni St and the Sa'ila.

YEMEN

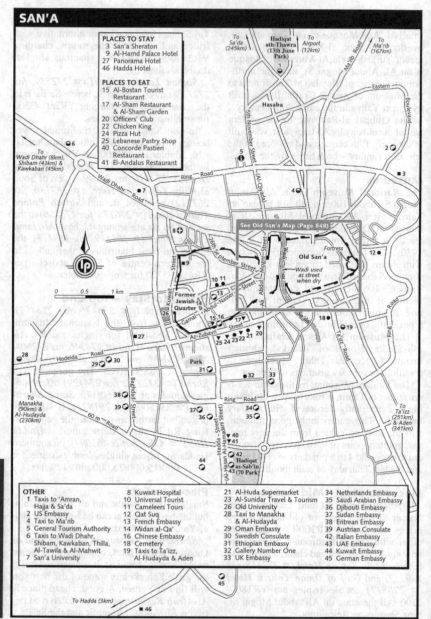

SAN'A

PLACES TO STAY
3   San'a Sheraton
9   Al-Hamd Palace Hotel
27 Panorama Hotel
46 Hadda Hotel

PLACES TO EAT
15 Al-Bostan Tourist Restaurant
17 Al-Sham Restaurant & Al-Sham Garden
20 Officers' Club
22 Chicken King
24 Pizza Hut
25 Lebanese Pastry Shop
40 Concorde Pastieri Restaurant
41 El-Andalus Restaurant

To Sa'da (245km)
Hadiqat ath-Thawra (13th June Park)
To Airport (12km)
To Ma'rib (167km)

Hasaba

To Wadi Dhahr (8km), Shibam (43km) & Kawkaban (45km)

Wadi Dhahr — Road

Ring — Road

See Old San'a Map (Page 848)

Old San'a

Fortress

Wadi used as street when dry

26th September Street

Kuwait Street

Former Jewish Quarter

Gamal — Abdul-Nasser — Street

Az-Zubayn

Ali Abdul Mogni — Street

Hodeida — Road

Park

To Manakha (90km) & Al-Hudayda (230km)

60 m — Road

Baghdad — Street

Ring — Road

Ta'izz — Road

To Ta'izz (251km) & Aden (341km)

Hadda — Street (Al-Hasan Al-Hamdani Street)

Hadiqat as-Sab'in (70 Park)

To Hadda (3km)

0   0.5   1 km

OTHER
1   Taxis to 'Amran, Hajja & Sa'da
2   US Embassy
4   Taxi to Ma'rib
5   General Tourism Authority
6   Taxis to Wadi Dhahr, Shibam, Kawkaban, Thilla, Al-Tawila & Al-Mahwit
7   San'a University
8   Kuwait Hospital
10 Universal Tourist
11 Cameleers Tours
12 Qat Suq
13 French Embassy
14 Midan al-Qa'
16 Chinese Embassy
18 Cemetery
19 Taxis to Ta'izz, Al-Hudayda & Aden
21 Al-Huda Supermarket
23 Al-Sunidar Travel & Tourism
26 Old University
28 Taxi to Manakha & Al-Hudayda
29 Oman Embassy
30 Swedish Consulate
31 Ethiopian Embassy
32 Gallery Number One
33 UK Embassy
34 Netherlands Embassy
35 Saudi Arabian Embassy
36 Djibouti Embassy
37 Sudan Embassy
38 Eritrean Embassy
39 Austrian Consulate
42 Italian Embassy
43 UAE Embassy
44 Kuwait Embassy
45 German Embassy

YEMEN

In the small street near Ali Abdul Mogni St, between the post office and Qasr al-Jumhuri St, try the black-fried fish of *Al Dobaey Fish Restaurant*, served on a huge khubz bed. The Lebanese *Al-Sham Garden*, just behind the Arab Bank at Az-Zubayri St and Sayf Ben Thi Yazin St junction, has a big family section complete with children's playgrounds, billiard and board games for the young. Run by the same family is the tiny *Al-Sham Restaurant*, connected to the Al-Sham Garden by an underground corridor.

The south-western part of the city has several good restaurants aimed at expatriates and tourists alike. *El Andalus Restaurant* and *Concorde Pastieri Restaurant* are farther south on Hadda St, while *Al-Bostan Tourist Restaurant* near its junction, on the other side of the Az-Zubayri St, is a park restaurant with children's playground, caged birds and rabbits.

Getting There & Away
There is a bus station and few taxi stations in San'a, each serving a different destination.

Buses to Ta'izz, Aden and Al-Hudayda leave from Az-Zubayri St, south-west of Bab al-Yaman. Taxis leave from the huge taxi station on Ta'izz Rd, just south of Az-Zubayri St, behind the house blocks.

Brown-striped taxis going to Hajja, Sa'da and 'Amran leave from Hasaba, at the junction of the Sa'da road and the road to the airport.

Yellow-striped taxis to Ma'rib operate from the square in Al-Jomhuriyya St, 500m north of Bab ash-Sha'ub, where the city bus leaves you.

Getting Around
The Airport Only private taxis serve the airport; the official fare is YR800, but YR1000 is commonly demanded. About 100m from the airport building you can find shared taxis for YR50 per seat, but the drivers are sometimes reluctant to serve foreign tourists.

Bus San'a's most important sub centres, Bab al-Yaman, Bab ash-Sha'ub and Midan al-Qa', are linked to Maydan at-Tahrir by city buses. They leave when full and cost YR10 per person. The route between Tahrir and Bab al-Yaman is served most frequently.

Black-striped minibuses shuttle along main streets such as Az-Zubayri St, Ali Abdul Mogni St (the airport road), Hadda St (Al-Hasan al-Hamadani St) and parts of Ring Rd. The usual fare is YR10 per person, YR15 to YR25 for longer hauls.

Taxi Black-striped shared taxis often operate on the same principle as minibuses, driving back and forth along a certain street. The charges vary from YR20 to YR30 per person. Check the price before entering.

Within the urban area you'll need private taxis if you are uncertain about how to get to your destination. Even then, be prepared to encounter a driver no wiser than yourself.

Around San'a

To the north-west of San'a there are several places of interest, suitable for half or full-day excursions. Wadi Dhahr, Shibam and Thilla are served by black-striped taxis stationed in Matbah, north-west of San'a. The fare per seat is YR80 to YR150.

WADI DHAHR
Only about 15km north-west of San'a lies Wadi Dhahr, a fertile valley of small villages and clay-walled orchards. Just before the road descends into the *wadi* (river), the **White Butterfly Garden** is an open space with good views. Families come here for picnics and wedding parties dance here on Friday mornings.

The taxi will probably take you to the front of **Dar al-Hajar** (Rock Palace). The five storey palace was built in the 1930s by Imam Yahya as a summer residence. It was built over the ruins of a prehistoric building on top of the most extraordinary rock formation. The well, penetrating the rocks by the house, is said to be original.

The palace is government property and has remained empty from the time of the revolution. It was renovated in a project started in 1990 with Dutch aid. The building can be visited for a fee of YR100 from 8 am to 1 pm and from 2 to 6 pm.

To the north of Dar al-Hajar you'll find the beautiful village of **Qaryat al-Qabil** with its small Friday market. It is shadowed by an impressive precipice formed over millions of years by fast-flowing waters. Spot the caves in the cliff; the region was already inhabited in Himyarite times. Ancient rock carvings of animals and hunters can be found 2km north of the village. Ask the children for directions.

SHIBAM & KAWKABAN

Not to be confused with the Shibam of Hadramawt, Shibam is a smaller town with quite a past. It stands on the edge of the San'a basin, by a mountain rising steeply from 2500m to 2850m and is the eastern-most town of the Al-Mahwit governorate.

During the 1st century AD, it was the capital of one of the small and short-lived independent states then common in the highlands. Both Sabaean and Himyarite inscriptions can be found on stones in the city gate of Shibam, in the mosque and in other older constructions.

From 845 to 1004 AD, Shibam became the capital again, when the Bani Ya'fur dynasty ruled here. They built the Shibam mosque on the site of a Himyarite temple.

Kawkaban, on top of the 350m cliff shadowing Shibam, originally served as the town's fortification. Water cisterns carved out of the rock collected water during the rainy seasons and grain silos were filled during the years of peace. During crises, the inhabitants were evacuated to the fortress, and survived a siege of almost any length.

The steep path winding its way from Shibam was easily defended; many an attacker found their sophisticated guns useless against Yemenis throwing rocks down the cliffs. A walk from Shibam to Kawkaban takes one hour. The paved footpath starts from behind the big mosque.

From Kawkaban, another ancient town with a mountain fortress can be seen in the distance; **Thilla**, only 9km from Shibam, is also well worth a visit.

Places to Stay

If you plan to extend your visit to Thilla or Al-Mahwit, you can stay overnight in Shibam in *Hotel Al-Shamsi Shibam* (☎ 450465). It has sheets on its mattresses and is in a clean and quiet house some 10 minutes' walk from the noisy town. Facing the mountain at the central square, take the street to your right and walk until you exit the tightly-built area; ask for directions. The staff charge YR700 per person for a room and a further YR200 with breakfast.

Hotel Jebel Kawkaban (☎ 450170) and *Kawkaban Hotel* (☎ 450154), in Kawkaban, offer charming no-sheet accommodation in old-style tower houses. The latter is cleaner and offers better value with hot showers and a reasonable restaurant. An outrageous scenery tax brings the cost of staying overnight to around YR2000 per person for full board, but you may try to bargain.

AL-MAHWIT GOVERNORATE

This small governorate is to the west of the San'a governorate. It is an impressive mountain district, full of small villages and hamlets and very suitable for trekking. From Shibam you can catch a service taxi to At-Tawila (29km; YR100) or to the governorate's capital, Al-Mahwit (80km; YR200), where *Hotel Mahweet* (☎ 404767, fax 404591) near the market has doubles at US$35.

MANAKHA

The western Haraz Mountains benefit from ample monsoon rains and are intensely cultivated. In the centre of the region stands the proud mountain village of Manakha (altitude 2200m). Its location was of strategic importance during the Ottoman occupation of Yemen; from here the Turks were able to protect the supply lines between San'a and Al-Hudayda, in the Tihama.

Manakha is an excellent base for trekking. In the Haraz region, old fortified villages and hamlets are scattered on hilltops and between the terraces that extend across the steepest slopes. The place of pilgrimage for members of the Ismaili sect, **Al-Khutayb**, lies only about 5km downhill, south-east from Manakha. Another fine village, the tightly built **Al-Hajjara**, 5km west of Manakha, has developed into a popular trekking centre for tourists.

Places to Stay

All the hotels in the region offer similar services for around YR1500 per person. This normally means a mattress in a dormitory (four persons minimum), shared showers with hot water, breakfast and dinner plus a 'party' (a folklore music and dance performance held nightly in each hotel's *mafraj* or 'room with a view'). Bargaining is possible if occupancy is low: vegetarians can bring the price down to YR1000.

Just before the entrance of Manakha, you'll find *Tawfiq Tourist Hotel*, while on the main street is *Manakha Tourist Hotel*. In Al-Hajjara, *Al-Hajjarah Tourist Hotel* and *Shibam Haraz Hotel (☎ 460270)* are your choices. The three latter hotels are all run by the same family.

Getting There & Away

Buses and taxis to Al-Hudayda leave from Bab al-Yaman in San'a; buy a ticket to the village of Al-Maghraba (82km from San'a by the old Al-Hudayda road), a small roadside market. The fare to Al-Maghraba is YR300 by bus or taxi.

From Al-Maghraba, a 6km road takes you up to Manakha. Local taxis charge YR30 for the ride but walking the distance could be a substitute for more extensive trekking elsewhere in the region.

Hajja

The town of Hajja (also spelt Haddzhah or Haggah) is a modern provincial capital standing on top of a mountain. The town once served briefly as the capital of the Zaydi state but other than the citadel on top of Hajja's highest peak, built by the Turks, there is little to see.

It is the journey along the Hajja road that makes a trip to Hajja worthwhile. The 65km stretch between 'Amran and Hajja offers spectacular views of terraced mountain slopes. The Chinese-built road first climbs to an altitude of 2800m then, after crossing the highest pass, descends steeply and serpentines all the way down to Wadi Sharas, a mere 1000m above sea level. Hajja itself stands at 1700m.

Places to Stay

Funduq Ghamdan Hajja (☎ 220420, fax 220423) is your only decent alternative. It stands on top of the hill to the west of central Hajja, a 10 minute walk from the central cross-roads (take the road left from San'a St). It offers singles/doubles for YR3150/3575.

Getting There & Away

Taxis from San'a to Hajja leave from Hasaba, and cost YR300. The 115km ride takes 2½ to three hours.

SHIHARA

Shihara (also spelt Shaharah) in the northern Hajja governorate is one of the most famous mountain fortress villages in Yemen. Situated on top of the 2600m high Shihara mountain, the almost inaccessible village of Shihara was never conquered by the Ottoman occupiers. Only during the 1960s civil war, when Shihara served as the headquarters of the Royalists, was it defeated for the first time, a victim of the Republican air force.

Shihara has 23 water cisterns. The two parts of the village, located on neighbouring mountain peaks, are connected over a 300m deep gorge by a stone bridge built in the early 17th century.

Places to Stay

The price of an overnight stay in a no-sheet dormitory at one of the two old-style funduqs varies greatly, from YR1000 to YR2000 per person, with breakfast and dinner.

Getting There & Away

Unfortunately, it is very expensive to get to Shihara as you can only visit using a tour operator from San'a, who will provide you with a car and driver for US$65 to US$85 a day. Due to bad road conditions near Shihara, you'll need two days for the visit.

At Al-Qabai, a village at the foot of Jebel Shihara, the locals won't allow the San'a tour operators to drive you to the top of the mountain. Instead, you have to hire a local car and pay another YR6000! Walking up the 1400m ascent offers extraordinary views and takes five to seven hours.

Sa'da

The northernmost provincial capital of Yemen, Sa'da (also spelt Saadah) was inhabited long ago in the days of frankincense trade but the recorded history of Sa'da begins in 901 AD. An outsider, Yahya bin Hussein bin Qasim ar-Rassi from Basra (Iraq), had been called to Sa'da in 892 to mediate between the warring Hashid and Bakil tribes. He was a follower of Zaydism, which is a Shi'ite sect. He proclaimed himself the imam and made Sa'da his capital.

The Zaydi state is led by the imam, chosen from the *sada*, or those descended directly from Ali and Fatima, the son-in-law and daughter of the Prophet. The Zaydi dynasty lasted for more than 1000 years, with Sa'da remaining the spiritual, if not always the governmental, capital of the country. It was the holy city of the imamate until the 1962 revolution, and it still has an influence in Yemeni politics.

Orientation & Information
You will be dropped off in front of Bab al-Yaman, Sa'da's southern gate. The hotels, restaurants, bus office, taxi station, police and hospital are on San'a St, within a few kilometres of the city wall.

Things to See
The holiest place of the Zaydis is the **Great Mosque of Sa'da**, built in the 12th century. Imam Yahya, who introduced Zaydism to Yemen, is buried here with 11 later imams, under 12 cupolas. Entry into this mosque is

not allowed to non-Muslims. The fortification on the central hill is used by the government and cannot be entered either.

Most rewarding is a walk around Sa'da on top of the town wall, which is still largely intact and partly renovated. Of special interest is **Bab Najran**, the northern gate, surrounded by imaginatively twisted walls. The houses of Sa'da are an excellent example of zabur architecture, with walls that are built of layers of clay.

In town, the Sunday market is best. This is the place to buy Yemeni silver jewellery as there is a local Jewish community that has retained its silversmith traditions.

Just outside the town, to the west, is a huge Zaydi graveyard. Among the many elaborately carved stone plates and tombstones there are a few small domes, marking the graves of distinguished Zaydis.

Places to Stay
Apart from the rock-bottom holes in the vicinity of Bab al-Yaman, Sa'da has some nice hotels on San'a St, about 2km from the old town. *Bilqis Throne Hotel* (☎ 512973) is a clean one-sheet inn, offering triples with private bathroom and hot water at YR1200. Farthest from town, the two-sheet *Taj Bilqis Hotel* (☎ 512459, fax 512203) is the cleanest of the town's hotels; it has singles/doubles for YR1035/1265.

Rahban Hotel (☎/fax 7512856) is in a modern but dilapidated house, which is curved like a *dhuma* (nobleman's dagger), and is just outside the old town. Frequented by tour operators, this hotel is perfect for women travelling without a male companion. Spacious doubles with private bathrooms go for YR1400/1900 without/with breakfast.

Places to Eat
Sanabel Restaurant, on the main street in front of Bab al-Yaman, has an excellent tourist menu, a cross-breed of Yemeni and western cuisine; its *shish kebab* comes with khubz, rice, fries and tea at YR300. *Rahban Restaurant* has menus printed in German. Farther along San'a St, *Kanaru Restaurant* is a popular, if not fancy, place for lunch.

Getting There & Away

From San'a, Sa'da can be reached by taxi. From Hasaba, brown-striped taxis will take you to Sa'da for YR500 a seat. The 231km trip takes about four hours.

Al-Hudayda

The coastal plain of the Red Sea, the Tihama, is economically the most important part of Yemen with approximately one-third of the country's population and almost half the country's agricultural output produced here. For the visitor, it's of limited interest due to the monotonous landscape, the lack of spectacular architecture and the extremely hot and humid climate that is exacerbated by sandy winds.

Al-Hudayda (also spelt Hodeida) is the largest city of the Tihama. It is a young city, plagued by recurrent wars in the 19th and 20th centuries. Only after the Saudi-Yemeni war in 1934 was Al-Hudayda allowed to develop without disturbance. The real boom for the port city began after the revolution, and especially after the 1960s civil war, in the explosive years of foreign (import) trade. Today, Al-Hudayda is Yemen's fourth largest city.

Orientation & Information

Although Al-Hudayda is a fairly large city it is quite easy to find your way around it. The main street, San'a St, enters the city from the east as a continuation of the San'a and Ta'izz roads. San'a St ends at the modern park of Hadiqat ash-Sha'b (People's Garden), which has a huge fountain.

Everything of interest in Al-Hudayda lies within about 2km of the People's Garden, between San'a St and the coastline – bus stations, taxis, accommodation, the 'old' city, shops, markets, pharmacies, banks and the fishing port.

Things to See & Do

The oldest part of Al-Hudayda is formed by the **Turkish quarters** near the old market area, which is as lively as any Yemeni

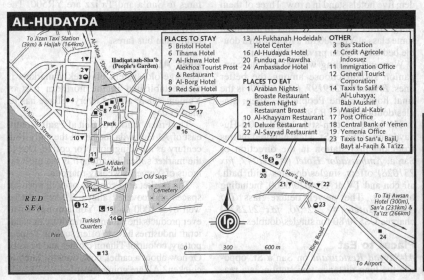

AL-HUDAYDA

To Jizan Taxi Station (3km) & Hajjah (164km)

Hadiqat ash-Sha'b (People's Garden)

Al-Kornish Street

Al-Mina Street

Park

Park

Midan at-Tahrir

Old Suqs

Cemetery

Turkish Quarters

Pier

RED SEA

San'a Street

Ring Road

To Taj Awsan Hotel (300m), San'a (231km) & Ta'izz (266km)

To Airport

PLACES TO STAY
5 Bristol Hotel
6 Tihama Hotel
7 Al-Ikhwa Hotel Alekhoa Tourist Prost & Restaurant
8 Al-Borg Hotel
9 Red Sea Hotel
13 Al-Fukhanah Hodeidah Hotel Center
16 Al-Hudayda Hotel
20 Funduq ar-Rawdha
24 Ambassador Hotel

PLACES TO EAT
1 Arabian Nights Broaste Restaurant
2 Eastern Nights Restaurant Broast
10 Al-Khayyam Restaurant
21 Deluxe Restaurant
22 Al-Sayyad Restaurant

OTHER
3 Bus Station
4 Credit Agricole Indosuez
11 Immigration Office
12 General Tourist Corporation
14 Taxis to Salif & Al-Luhayya; Bab Mushrif
15 Masjid al-Kabir
17 Post Office
18 Central Bank of Yemen
19 Yemenia Office
23 Taxis to San'a, Bajil, Bayt al-Faqih & Ta'izz

0   300   600 m

YEMEN

market but with the extra flavour of sailors from various countries.

The typical old Red Sea house found in Al-Hudayda is three or four storeys high with wooden balconies or window covers and plaster-decorated walls. One of the best examples, with a rare dome on its roof, faces the Red Sea by Al-Kurnish St.

The shoreline is under intense development with new hotels and cafeterias being built. In the mornings the fishing port in the south abounds with fishers returning from the sea carrying numerous different species of fish and shellfish. Many fishers still use traditional wooden vessels.

Places to Stay

If you arrive by taxi from San'a or Ta'izz and walk a few blocks west along San'a St, you'll find *Funduq ar-Rawdha*, a modest hotel where an air-con double with private bathroom costs YR1500. A better place of this type is 500m farther along, on the same side of the street – *Al-Hudayda Hotel* (☎ 239100, fax 212577). A triple with common bathroom costs YR1600.

On the southern side of the People's Garden, five hotels stand in a row. Three of them are similar to those just mentioned, while *Al-Borg Hotel* (☎ 239279) tries to maintain some class at YR2000 for a room with a double bed and a clean private bathroom.

Women travelling without a male companion should choose among the better ones. *Bristol* (☎ 239197, fax 239760) is the final hotel on the People's Garden; singles/doubles cost YR3980/5255.

The most western-style hotels in Al-Hudayda are on San'a St, a few hundred metres from the taxi station in the direction of San'a. *Ambassador Hotel* (☎ 231247, fax 231028) offers singles/doubles with bath, air-con and TV at YR4020/6200, including breakfast. The newer deluxe-class *Taj Awsan Hotel* (☎ 212570, fax 212577) charges US$70/80 for singles/doubles.

Places to Eat

Al-Sayyad Restaurant on San'a St, opposite the long-distance taxi station, is a reasonably priced, simple place. Fried fish big enough for two, with rice, tea and Shamlan is YR350 only. *Al-Khayyam Restaurant*, *Arabian Nights Broaste Restaurant* and *Eastern Nights Restaurant Broast* on the street running from the People's Garden to Tahrir Square, are popular among the expatriate community of Al-Hudayda. The menus of these restaurants have long lists of dishes, and the prices vary from YR150 for eggs, salads or kebab to YR550 for shrimps. Of the hotel restaurants, the ground floor of the Al-Ikhwa Hotel houses *Alekhoa Tourist Prost & Restaurant*, a much better place than the hotel itself, and slightly cheaper than the previous ones.

Getting There & Away

Buses from San'a to Al-Hudayda leave from Bab al-Yaman. There are two asphalt roads; the northern one passes through the western mountains near Manakha. Most buses and taxis nowadays choose the less scenic southern route via Ma'bar and the monotonous Wadi Siham.

The bus station of Al-Hudayda is on the western side of the People's Garden. The fares to San'a and Ta'izz are YR500. The station for taxis serving San'a and Ta'izz is on San'a St. Taxi fares are YR40 to YR100 more than bus fares.

BEIT AL-FAQIH

The age-old system of weekly markets is well-established in the northern part of Yemen, where almost every village has its market day.

The Friday market of Beit al-Faqih (southeast of Al-Hudayda) began in the early 18th century as a trading point for coffee. Due to the market's ideal location, it is the most famous of Yemen's weekly markets.

The market area consists of both open-air spaces and covered alleys. There must be well over 1000 traders. You can buy whatever products the Tihami agriculture or handicraft industries have to offer, such as Yemeni pottery, colourful Tihami clothes and baskets. Or how about a camel, cow, donkey, lamb or chicken? All are going cheap!

Orientation & Information
If you arrive by taxi, the driver will probably take you straight to the 'supermarket'. If you come by bus, you will be left at the crossroads, about 1km out of town, from where you can walk or take a motorbike taxi.

Places to Stay & Eat
Staying overnight in Beit al-Faqih is not recommended but Friday lunch here is not a bad idea. Choose anything that has been boiled; full meals are served indoors. There is an alley full of eateries. If it's not a market day, you might want to resort to biscuits.

In the extremely hot and moist atmosphere of Tihama any food that is not thoroughly heated is suspect, especially in rural places such as Beit al-Faqih.

Getting There & Away
Buses (YR60) depart from Al-Hudayda at 7 am and taxis (YR100) leave at any time. The 55km trip along an asphalt road takes only an hour. Coming from Ta'izz is less practical because the trading activities peak between 7 and 10 am, and you may be late for the market. By Friday afternoon most of the vendors have packed and gone, and the town is almost as quiet as it is during the rest of the week.

By taxi from Beit al-Faqih, YR100 should take you to Zabid, and YR350 to Ta'izz.

ZABID
About 37km south of Beit al-Faqih lies Zabid, a town with a remarkable past. Zabid was founded in 820 AD by Mohammed ibn Abdullah ibn Ziyad who also laid the foundations for the 200 year Ziyadid dynasty. He brought a prominent Mufti (Islamic religious expert), At-Taghlabi, from Baghdad, who founded an Islamic university, an ever-growing compound of Quran schools and mosques. Zabid became a famed centre of learning, attracting scholars from abroad.

Besides Islamic law, other disciplines were studied in the university: grammar, poetry, history and mathematics. The word 'algebra' has been attributed to a Zabidi scholar, Ahmed Abu Musa al-Jaladi, who called his mathematical system *al-jabr*.

The Zabid University outlived the Ziyadid dynasty, reaching its peak during the Rasulid era (1229-1454), when approximately 5000 students occupied the 200 or more schools and mosques of Zabid. During the Tahirid rule (1454-1526) the Zabid University started its gradual decline, which continued for centuries.

In 1994 UNESCO included Zabid on its World Heritage list.

Orientation
From the junction on the Al-Hudayda to Ta'izz road, an alley leads through the eastern gate to the souq area of Zabid. To your left there is a large square just before the town itself, with a citadel and other imposing buildings behind it.

Once in the town, closely built winding alleys and blocks provide no visual axes or hills. The city appears reserved, because the modest street facades of the houses conceal the splendour of their interiors. If you manage to get a glimpse of the inner courtyards of these houses, the dazzling white, richly ornamented walls will reveal the aesthetic preferences of the Zabid elite.

Things to See
During the golden days of the Zabid University there were 236 mosques. Over the centuries two out of three mosques have vanished but Zabid, with its 86 mosques, is still extraordinary.

The cupolas of many of these remarkable mosques, including the vast **Al-Asha'ir Mosque**, or the **Great Mosque**, don't reach great heights but extend over a wide area. The **Iskandar Mosque** with its 60m high minaret stands just outside the old city, inside the citadel walls. The **Mustafa Pasha Mosque** is another mosque of Turkish origin, standing with a dozen cupolas on the eastern side of the Ta'izz to Al-Hudayda highway.

The **Nasr Palace** by the citadel was built in the late 19th century and today serves as a government building. Inside the citadel, the tiny **Zabid Granary Museum** houses some archaeological finds and an ethnographical collection.

YEMEN

Places to Stay

Just before the main square, *Shibam Tourist Rest House* has a large, open multipurpose hall with souvenir stalls, tables (for having refreshments and meals) and beds with a fan. You can stay overnight and have dinner and breakfast here for YR500.

AL-MAKHA

This coffee-trading and manufacturing port in the southernmost part of Tihama gave mocha coffee its name but is today a small village with few (if any) attractions. As one disappointed visitor put it, Al-Makha is 'for name-addicted romantics only'.

By the time Europeans appeared in the 16th century, Al-Makha was already a prospering city. Coffee, grown in the Yemeni mountains and the latest craze in Europe, was Yemen's most important product. Trade had started in the late 15th century, greatly expanded under the first Ottoman rule, and flourished during the first half of the Zaydi rule, and Al-Makha was the main export port.

In 1618 the English and Dutch built Al-Makha's first coffee factories. They were soon followed by other Europeans, even Americans. By the 1630s coffeehouses were being opened in Venice, Amsterdam and elsewhere, and the demand for coffee rose to such heights that Yemen was no longer able to meet it on its own. Prices soared and the prosperous coffee merchants of Al-Makha built gorgeous villas in the city.

Yemen's monopoly on the coffee beans was broken by the early 18th century, when coffee plants were smuggled out of the country, and new plantations were established in Ceylon. The decline of Al-Makha had begun. The final blow came in 1839, when the British captured Aden and started to develop it as the main port of southern Arabia, robbing Al-Makha of the remaining trade.

Things to See

The **Ash-Shadhli Mosque**, with its beautiful Zabid-influenced architecture, is about 500 years old. Some of the ruins of the coffee merchants' villas still stand, but most have already become sand-covered rubble.

Places to Stay

The clean *Hotel Al-Rasheed* (☎ 046-2357), in a modern house just outside the town, has doubles with private bathrooms and air-con for YR1400. There is a busy restaurant on the ground floor.

Getting There & Away

A seat in a taxi from Ta'izz should not cost more than YR250 for the 105km ride.

Ta'izz

Ta'izz is dramatically located at an altitude of 1400m in the northern foothills of the majestic Jebel Sabir. In 1175 AD the Ayyubid ruler Turan Shah decided to live in Ta'izz because of its pleasant climate. During the Rasulid era (1229-1454), Ta'izz prospered as Yemen's capital. The period of Rasulid rule was followed by the 'dark centuries' when the city was controlled by various foreign conquerors and local rulers.

In 1948 Imam Ahmed made Ta'izz his residence and the new capital of Yemen. Much of the current prosperity of Ta'izz derives from the period between 1948 and 1962.

Orientation & Information

Two main streets wind their way through the city in an east-west direction. Gamal Abdul Nasser St serves as the main thoroughfare and buses leave at either end of the street. The southern 26th September St passes by the walls of the old town. At one point, near the Haud al-Ashraf part of town, the streets run very close to each other. There are plenty of hotels and restaurants in this area.

Things to See

The liveliest part of the old town is definitely the market area by the northern wall. The market is small: just a couple of parallel alleys joining the wall's two main gates, Bab Musa (the Gate of Sheikh Musa) and Bab al-Kabir (the Great Gate).

The twin minarets of the **Al-Ashrafiya Mosque** overlook the old town. The mosque was built in the 13th and 14th centuries.

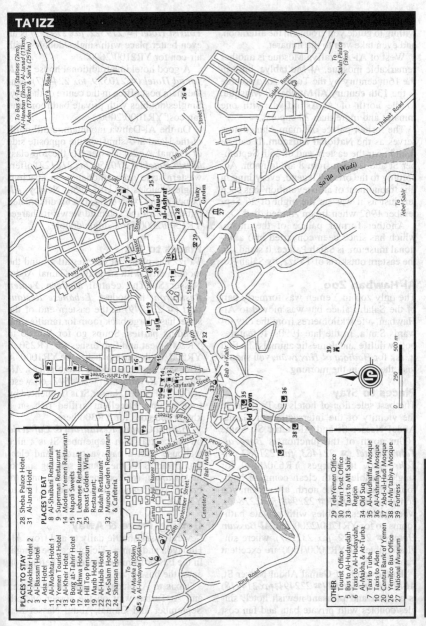

TA'IZZ

To Bus & Taxi Stations (2km),
Al-Hawban (3km), Al-Janad (11km),
Aden (178km/km) & San'a (251km)

San'a Road

To Salah Palace
(3km)

Salah Road

Thabat Road

13th June Street

San'a Street

Sa'ila (Wadi)

Unity
Garden

To
Jebel Sabir

Haud
al-Ashraf

Asayfarah Street

Jamal Abdul Nasser Street

26th September Street

Bab al-Kabir

Al-Tahrir Street

As-Sayfarah Street

Old Town

Bab Musa

Masallah Street

Jamal Abdul Nasser Street

Wadi Street

Cemetery

Bab Musa

Ring Road

26th September Street

To
Al-Mukha (105km)

To
Al-Hudayda (266km)

0   250   500 m

PLACES TO STAY
1   Al-Mokhtar Hotel 2
2   Al-Bassam Hotel
3   Asia Hotel
11 Al-Mokhtar Hotel 1
12 Yemen Tourist Hotel
13 Al-Kheir Hotel
16 Borg at-Tahrir Hotel
17 Al-Ikhwa Hotel
18 Hill Top Pensoun
19 Marib Hotel
22 Al-Habib Hotel
23 As-Salam Hotel
24 Shamsan Hotel

28 Sheba Palace Hotel
31 Al-Janad Hotel

PLACES TO EAT
8   Al-Shaibani Restaurant
9   Superman Restaurant
14 Modern Yemen Restaurant
15 Napoli Sweets
21 Lebanese Restaurant
25 Broast Golden Wing
    Restaurant;
    Radah Restaurant
32 Muroui Garden Restaurant
    & Cafeteria

OTHER
4   Tourist Office
5   Bus to Al-Hudaydah
6   Taxis to Al-Hudaydah,
    Al-Makha & At-Turba
7   Taxi to Turba
10 Taxis to Aden
20 Central Bank of Yemen
26 Yemitco Bus Office
27 National Museum

29 TeleYemen Office
30 Main Post Office
33 Taxis to Mt Sabir
    Region
34 Old Suq
35 Al-Mudhaffar Mosque
36 Al-Ashrafiya Mosque
37 'Abd-al-Hadi Mosque
38 Al-Mu'tabiya Mosque
39 Fortress

YEMEN

Children from the Quran school may be willing to guide you around in the afternoon, and even take you to the minaret.

West of Al-Ashrafiya Mosque is another remarkable mosque, **Al-Mu'tabiya**, built in the 16th century by the Turks. Also notable is the 13th century **Al-Mudhaffar Mosque**, to the north of Al-Ashrafiya, with one minaret and more than 20 cupolas.

The former palace of Imam Ahmed now serves as the **National Museum**. It can be found near the eastern end of 26th September St and is open from 8 am to noon. According to the official legend, everything in this 'monument of anti-revolution' has been left just as it was on the night of 26 September 1962 when Imam Ahmed died.

Another former palace of the imam, which has since been converted into a national museum, is **Salah Palace**. It stands on the eastern outskirts of Ta'izz, by Salah Rd.

Al-Hawban Zoo
The only zoo in Yemen was formerly part of the Salah Palace but was moved to Al-Hawban, a few kilometres from the city towards San'a, in the late 1990s. It features both wildlife and domestic animals. To find it, ask for *Hadīqat al-Hayawān*; you should visit the zoo in the morning.

Places to Stay
The best selection of hotels in Ta'izz is in the vicinity of the intersection of Gamal Abdul Nasser St and Al-Tahrir St. Some 100m north of the junction is *Borg at-Tahrir Hotel* (☎ 221483, fax 221482, Al-Tahrir St). It charges YR650/1100 for singles/doubles with clean common bathrooms. Farther to the north, after 500m you come to *Asia Hotel* (☎ 222948, fax 227846), where singles/doubles with private bathrooms go for YR1700/2200, and *Al-Bassam Hotel* (☎ 211412, fax 232287), where singles/doubles at YR1000/1500 are excellent value.

To the south of Gamal Abdul Nasser St, *Al-Mokhtar Hotel 1* (☎ 222491, fax 214718) is a clean and pleasant newish hotel; singles/doubles with private bath and fan cost YR1650/1850. The neighbouring *Yemen Tourist Hotel* (☎ 219522, fax 219525) is an even better place with singles/doubles with air-con for YR2100/2600.

A good hotel in a traditional house is *Al-Janad Hotel* (☎ 210529, fax 224497), near the main post office in the centre of the city. Singles/doubles with private bathroom and fan cost YR1000/2000.

On the Al-Dabwa mountain, a hill north of the Haud al-Ashraf, on the opposite side of Gamal Abdul Nasser St, the top-class *Marib Hotel* (☎ 210350, fax 212122) offers western-style accommodation in spacious singles/doubles for US$30/50. Nearby, *Al-Ikhwa Hotel* (☎ 210364) is a bit dilapidated but cheap for the splendid views; it charges YR1500/2000 for a single/double.

Places to Eat
Ta'izz has plenty of eateries all around the modern city, with several on Gamal Abdul Nasser St. The central *Modern Yemen Restaurant* is modest. *Lebanese Restaurant* (☎ 231749) at the eastern end of the street has a large back room for families and wedding parties. Soups go for YR100 to YR200, meat and fish dishes for YR250 to YR500, while shrimp dishes are YR1000. A 10% service fee is added to the prices. *Al-Shaibani Restaurant* (☎ 234647) on western Gamal Abdul Nasser St is frequented by tour groups. Excellent grilled fish on a khubz bed goes for YR300 here.

Muroui Garden Restaurant & Cafeteria on the central 26th September St is a nice teahouse with a papaya garden and electronic games for the young, serving snacks of *shwarma*, (grilled meat served on pitta bread) bread and chicken for YR130 to YR150.

Getting There & Away
Several buses shuttle daily to and from Al-Hudayda and San'a. Tickets can be bought in the bus or from the bus office before you enter the bus.

Taxis to Al-Hudayda (and to Al-Makha and At-Turba) wait on the corner of 26th September and Gamal Abdul Nasser Sts, while the main taxi station for San'a and Aden is on San'a Rd, east of the centre.

Getting Around

Black-striped minibuses shuttle along Gamal Abdul Nasser St, 26th September St and other long streets. The fare is YR15 to YR20 per person.

AROUND TA'IZZ

You can make a couple of short excursions in the area around Ta'izz. **Jebel Sabir**, the 3006m high mountain to the south of Ta'izz, is well worth the ascent. Depending on the weather, the views can be extraordinary or, especially in the afternoon, completely obscured by clouds or rain. The 1½ hour climb along the really bumpy road from Bab al-Kabir can be made in a 4WD taxi. A seat costs about YR200.

Hujjariya (also spelt Huggariyah) is the countryside south-west from Ta'izz. Taxis to the main town, **At-Turba**, notable for its location on a steep cliff by Wadi al-Maqatira, leave from the western taxi station in Ta'izz. A seat for the 1½ hour trip should not cost more than YR200. After about a third of the ride there is the 500 year old white mosque of **Yifrus** on your right-hand side. It was built by the last Tahirid ruler Amir bin Abd al-Wahab.

Another fine mosque, originally built before the Prophet's death in 632 AD, can be found in **Al-Janad** (also spelt Al-Ganad), 6km to the north of Ta'izz and another 5km east from the San'a highway, and served by no regular taxis.

IBB

Ibb was originally built on a hilltop (1850m). The old town of stone tower houses is well worth visiting. Ibb is also a good stopping place between San'a and Ta'izz for a side trip to Jibla.

Orientation & Information

The San'a to Ta'izz highway no longer passes through the centre of Ibb. If you arrive by bus, you will be dropped off at the junction of the Al-'Udayn Rd; look for a black striped taxi to take you east to the town centre, which is just below the old town.

Places to Stay

Arhab Hotel Garden, or **Alrehab** (☎ 403 955) is at the junction of the Old San'a Rd and the new Al-'Udayn St. A double with private, hot showers costs YR1000. On the Main St, less than 500m towards Ta'izz, the pleasant **Al-Aqsa Tourist Hotel** (☎ 403432) offers singles/doubles/triples for YR800/1000/1200, mostly with private bathrooms. **Bilquis Throne Tourist Hotel** (☎ 512973), can be found after another 500m, on the old Ta'izz road. Clean doubles with private bathrooms and hot water go for YR1200.

On Al-'Udayn St, about 1.5 km from the central junction, **Nashwan Tourist Hotel** (☎ 408182) offers doubles at YR1000; common bathrooms have hot water.

Places to Eat

Mataam az-Zahban, close to the central taxi station, is a good place to eat, with a family room upstairs. Or try **Kentaky Alekil** on your way up to the old town.

Getting There & Away

The bus fare from San'a (193km) is YR400 and from Ta'izz (65km) it's YR160. For a seat in a shared taxi, add YR50 from San'a and YR20 from Ta'izz.

JIBLA

A small town with a big history, Jibla is only 8km south of Ibb, 3km from the Ta'izz road. It is another former Yemeni capital from the time of the Sulayhids, which was a dynasty founded by Ali as-Sulayhi in 1064. After the death of his son, his daughter-in-law, Arwa bint Ahmed, became the queen. She moved the capital to Jibla and ruled for almost 70 years until her death in 1138. Jibla still bears signs of prosperity from her time.

Things to See

Jibla is attractively located on a basalt hill between two wadis that join immediately under the town. Once in town after crossing the bridge, take the first street to the left, just after the small funduq and before the **Qubbat Beit az-Zum**. You will see the souqs and, eventually, the **Mosque of Queen Arwa**. It is big with two minarets and can occasionally be visited. Queen Arwa is buried in the mosque.

As you enter the town you can choose to continue straight through, past the beautiful small mosque, Qubbat Beit az-Zum, to your left. This road leads to the upper slopes of the hill. From here an aqueduct, built in the days of Queen Arwa, still brings water from the mountains past the graveyard to the town.

Aden

The natural deep-water port of Aden is built on a site of past volcanic activity. It served as the port for the ancient kingdom of Awsan between the 5th and 7th centuries BC. A long sequence of different rulers included Saba and other ancient kingdoms, local sheikhs and sultans in the early Islamic era, and finally distant colonists from Egypt and Europe. All were attracted by the port's convenient location on the major sea route between India and Europe.

The British ruled their South Arabian Protectorate from Aden, and the city served as the capital of the PDRY after their exit in 1967. However, the development of the city was stalled under the rule of the communists. When the two Yemens united, Aden became a free trade zone. The city suffered badly in the War of Unity, but has since been declared the winter capital of Yemen. With the opening of the free port in 1999 the city is finally showing signs of recovery.

Orientation & Information

Hot and steamy Aden actually consists of several towns: the classical port city of Aden; the industrial Little Aden with its huge oil refinery; and the new government centre, Medinat ash-Sha'b. North of the old city are the suburbs of Khormaksar and Sheikh Othman. Between these two is Aden's international airport.

The old city is scattered around the almost 600m high volcano that forms Cape Aden. The oldest part is the Crater (or Critir). To

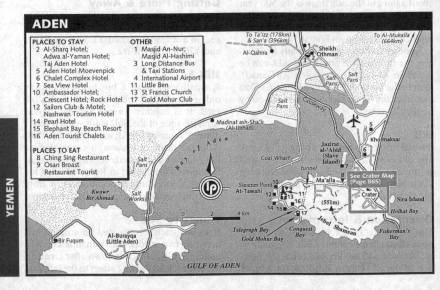

ADEN

PLACES TO STAY
2 Al-Sharq Hotel;
   Adwa al-Yaman Hotel;
   Taj Aden Hotel
5 Aden Hotel Moevenpick
6 Chalet Complex Hotel
7 Sea View Hotel
10 Ambassador Hotel;
   Crescent Hotel; Rock Hotel
12 Sailors Club & Motel;
   Nashwan Tourism Hotel
14 Pearl Hotel
15 Elephant Bay Beach Resort
16 Aden Tourist Chalets

PLACES TO EAT
8 Ching Sing Restaurant
9 Osan Broast
   Restaurant Tourist

OTHER
1 Masjid An-Nur;
   Masjid Al-Hashimi
3 Long Distance Bus
   & Taxi Stations
4 International Airport
11 Little Ben
13 St Francis Church
17 Gold Mohur Club

To Ta'izz (178km) & San'a (396km)
To Al-Mukalla (664km)

Sheikh Othman
Al-Qahira
Salt Pans
Salt Pans
Salt Pans
Causeway
Madinat ash-Sha'b (Al-Itihad)
Jazirat al-'Abid (Slave Island)
Khormaksar
Coal Wharf
tunnel
Bay of Aden
See Crater Map (Page 865)
Ma'alla
Crater
Sira Island
Steamer Point
At-Tawahi
Salt Pans
(551m)
Holkat Bay
Kwawr Bir Ahmad
Salt Works
Jebel Shamsan
Fisherman's Bay
Bir Fuqum
Al-Burayqa (Little Aden)
Telegraph Bay
Gold Mohur Bay
Conquest Bay
0   2   4 km

GULF OF ADEN

YEMEN

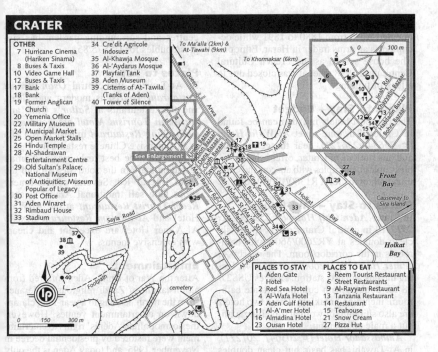

CRATER

OTHER
7 Hurricane Cinema
  (Hariken Sinama)
8 Buses & Taxis
10 Video Game Hall
12 Buses & Taxis
17 Bank
18 Bank
19 Former Anglican
   Church
20 Yemenia Office
22 Military Museum
24 Municipal Market
25 Open Market Stalls
26 Hindu Temple
28 Al-Shadrawan
   Entertainment Centre
29 Old Sultan's Palace;
   National Museum
   of Antiquities; Museum
   Popular of Legacy
30 Post Office
31 Aden Minaret
32 Rimbaud House
33 Stadium

34 Cre'dit Agricole
   Indosuez
35 Al-Khawja Mosque
36 Al-'Aydarus Mosque
37 Playfair Tank
38 Aden Museum
39 Cisterns of At-Tawila
   (Tanks of Aden)
40 Tower of Silence

To Ma'alla (2km) &
At-Tawahi (9km)

To Khormaksar (6km)

See Enlargement

Front
Bay

Causeway to
Sira Island

Holkat
Bay

PLACES TO STAY
1 Aden Gate
  Hotel
2 Red Sea Hotel
4 Al-Wafa Hotel
5 Aden Gulf Hotel
11 Al-A'mer Hotel
16 Almadina Hotel
23 Ousan Hotel

PLACES TO EAT
3 Reem Tourist Restaurant
6 Street Restaurants
9 Al-Rayyam Restaurant
13 Tanzania Restaurant
14 Restaurant
15 Teahouse
21 Snow Cream
27 Pizza Hut

the west of Crater is the modern centre of
Ma'alla. Around the western tip (Steamer
Point) of the cape is At-Tawahi, and to the
south the beaches of Gold Mohur Bay.

Banks in Aden are open from 7.30 am to
12.30 pm. Moneychangers operate on Main
Bazaar Rd in central Crater. The Yemenia
office is on Queen Arwa Rd in Crater.

Things to See
The so-called **Tanks of Aden** (Cisterns of
At-Tawila) high above Crater on the slopes
of Jebel Shamsan are among the oldest
sights in Aden. The 18 cisterns, probably
built by the Himyarites in the 1st century
AD, can store a total of 45 million litres of
water. The present appearance of the tanks
is the result of renovations carried out by
the British in the mid-19th century.

The **Aden Museum**, in a garden just by
the tanks, is only open on request. The Mili-

tary Museum, the pride of the former
PDRY, on Sayla Rd in central Crater, has
been closed since the War of Unity in 1994
but is bound to reopen.

The **National Museum of Antiquities**,
with numerous treasures from excavations at
Awsan kingdom towns, such as Qa'taban,
Shabwa and Hadramawt, and the **Museum
Popular of Legacy** (sic), with a fine ethnographic exhibition, are both housed in the old
sultan's palace in northern Crater. The museums are open from 8 am to 1 pm daily.

The **Al-'Aydarus Mosque** (also spelt Al-
Aidrus), on Aidrus St, is one of the oldest
mosques in Aden. It was first built in the
14th century, then rebuilt in 1859. The blaz-
ingly white **Aden Minaret** in central Crater,
not far from the main post office, belonged
to an 8th century mosque.

The **Rimbaud House** near the main post
office was renovated in 1991 as homage to

YEMEN

the French poet Arthur Rimbaud. He frequented Aden from 1880 to 1891 while occupied as an arms trader in Harar, Ethiopia. The house served as the French Cultural Centre until 1998 when it was closed due to a lack of funding.

Places to Stay – Budget
The cheapest hotels in Aden can be found in Crater. The one-sheet *Al-Wafa Hotel* (☎ 256340/256121), near the central taxi and bus stations of Crater, offers clean doubles/triples/quadruples with air-con and common bathrooms for YR1300/1700/1900.

Places to Stay – Mid-Range
In Crater, *Aden Gulf Hotel* (☎ 253900, fax 251710) in central Crater offers spotlessly clean doubles at YR2600/3600 with bathrooms in the corridor/room. The nearby *Al A'mer Hotel* (☎ 252600, fax 256304), facing the bus and taxi station, charges US$27/ 38 for doubles with common/private bathroom, including breakfast. These two hotels are also suitable for women travelling without a male companion.

Ambassador Hotel (☎ 203641, 201271), in At-Tawahi, has basic but clean doubles with private baths for YR3000. *Nashwan Tourism Motel* (☎ 202908), in the westernmost part of the cape, has spacious singles/doubles for YR3000/5000 in nice chalets and a restaurant/discotheque in a separate building. Farther to the south, *Pearl Hotel* (☎ 202267, fax 204853, Funduq Al-Lu'lu'a) offers peaceful doubles for YR4000. That's good value, as every three or four rooms have a common kitchen, lobby and balcony with a sea view.

Places to Stay – Top End
Aden Hotel Moevenpick (☎ 232911, fax 232947) in Khormaksar, near the airport, is a luxury hotel where doubles cost US$210. In At-Tawahi, *Crescent Hotel* (☎ 203471, fax 204597) is a recently renovated, historical hotel with a British atmosphere. It charges US$50/60 for spacious singles/doubles with breakfast included. *Elephant Bay Beach Resort* (☎ 202055, fax 201082) in

Gold Mohur Bay, with fitness and business centres and surrounding garden, has singles/doubles for US$75/85.

Places to Eat
In At-Tawahi, the central *Osan Broast Restaurant Tourist* is modern and clean, and the restaurants at *Sailor's Club* and *Nashwan Tourism Motel* are good also. *Ching Sing Restaurant* in eastern Ma'alla is an expensive Chinese restaurant.

In Crater, the best teahouses and small restaurants are in the souq area around the Main Bazaar Rd. Several confectionery shops here sell traditional Arabic sweets. *Reem Tourist Restaurant* at the Al-Wafa Hotel and *Al-Rayyam Restaurant* next to Al-A'mer Hotel are excellent and cheap, with extensive menus.

Entertainment
After the War of Unity, Aden suffered from an onslaught of Zaydi religious intolerance from the north, leading to a year-long clampdown on entertainment venues. However, the cosmopolitan Adenis' rights to entertainment were restored by presidential decree in November 1995, and today Aden is the only place in Yemen with nightlife to speak of.

Gold Mohur Club with its fine beach, once reserved for diplomats, is now open to the public. The entrance fee is YR100; for banquet nights, up to YR1500 is charged. In Crater, next to Yemen's first Pizza Hut outlet, the incredible *Al-Shadrawan* entertainment centre has a nightly disco, expensive restaurants and banquets.

Getting There & Away
Aden's main bus station is in Sheikh Othman. Buses leave at 6 am and 1 pm for San'a (YR700 per person) and 'Ataq (YR450), 6.30 am for Al-Mukalla (YR900), and at 6.30 and 11 am for Ta'izz (YR400).

Buses are often full but you can always use service taxis. The station is a couple of blocks from the bus station in Sheikh Othman. Shared taxi fares are at least 20% higher than bus fares. Taxis to Al-Mukalla also leave from the city bus station in Crater.

It is advisable to show up no later than 7 am to be sure of getting a seat for the long hauls.

Getting Around

Small buses and shared taxis shuttle between the stations in the city's sub centres. Seats cost YR20 to YR25 regardless of distance. The private cabs should take you between any two points on the cape of Aden for YR200 and to Sheikh Othman for YR400.

Ma'rib

Ma'rib, the capital of the ancient kingdom of Saba, is the most remarkable archaeological site in Yemen. In the 8th century BC, a 680m long dam was built here between two mountains to catch the waters of Wadi Adhana. Over the centuries the dam was gradually enlarged and strengthened until its height finally reached 16m.

For more than 1000 years the dam provided irrigation to 96 sq km of fields, sus-taining a population of 30,000 to 50,000 people. Peaceful periods alternated with wars, but in the 2nd century AD the traditional dynasty of Saba came to an end and was replaced by various rulers from the highlands.

The dam was neglected and damaged several times by flooding during the following centuries. In 570 it was irrevocably washed away, and most of the inhabitants of Ma'rib fled to various parts of the Arabian peninsula. Ma'rib was reduced to a village with only a few families, remaining basically the same for 1400 years.

In the 1970s, pump irrigation revived agriculture in the region, and in the early 1980s, Hunt Oil Corporation found oil east of Ma'rib. Yemen's first oil well went into production in 1986, and the new town of Ma'rib and a new dam were built. Today, Ma'rib is a bustling place.

The unruly tribes of Ma'rib every so often campaign against the government and at the time of research, due to kidnapping fears, travellers were barred from visiting

---

Who was the Queen of Sheba?

The legend of the meeting of King Solomon (965 BC to 925 BC) and the Queen of Sheba, or Saba, appears in three holy books: the Jewish and Christian Old Testament (1 Kings 10:1-13); the Ethiopian Orthodox Kebra Nagast; and the Muslim Quran (sura of Ants, 20-44). A wealth of ancient Jewish and Islamic scriptures and folklore expand on the theme.

Today the story is well known throughout the western world. The image of a powerful woman ruling a remote but influential corner of the world has caught the imagination of countless poets, tale-tellers, painters, sculptors, cartoonists and movie directors.

However, nowhere is her legend as alive and well as on both sides of the southern Red Sea. There are many Islamicised versions of the story, with the main plot being her conversion to the faith of Solomon's God, ultimately leading to Islam. Arabian tradition also tells us that Menelik, the son of King Solomon and Queen Bilqis, became the ruler of Aksum, in today's Ethiopia. The intriguing love story between the king and the queen is not mentioned at all in the Quran and only vaguely hinted at in the Bible, but the Ethiopian Kebra Nagast is explicit about it. Indeed, Menelik's ancestry was then claimed by all Ethiopian leaders up to Haile Selassie (ruled 1930-74), who traced his lineal descent from her through 237 generations.

How did the same queen live and rule both sides of the Red Sea? The legends obviously contradict each other. Actually, no hard archaeological proof exists that Saba was indeed ruled by a queen at the time of King Solomon, although Sabaean queens are mentioned in scriptures from later times. While scholars keep debating the unresolved issue, no Yemeni would ever doubt the reality of the legend, and many Yemeni girls are still named Bilqis after her.

Ma'rib independently – instead you must be part of a group tour.

Orientation & Information

The 'New Ma'rib' is a collection of shops and petrol stations just past the rancid Ma'rib airport. You can stop here to eat and to buy bottles of fresh water to endure the heat of the afternoon.

The old village of Ma'rib is visible in the distance. Just before the village a new road branches to the right, leading to the dam sites a little way upstream. Seeing all the archaeological sites, widely scattered around the wadi, involves a 30km round trip along asphalt roads that wind through the sand.

Things to See

On a tiny hill by the wadi bank stands Old Ma'rib. Of the almost demolished village, some impressive small-windowed mud buildings remain, their stone basements often sporting stones with ancient Sabaean inscriptions.

On the other side of the wadi, just a couple of kilometres south-west of Old Ma'rib, you will find the remnants of remarkable Sabaean temples. They are marked by a sign reading 'Balqis Palace'. A few hundred metres to the west stand the five and a half remaining pillars of the Temple of the Moon (called 'Arsh Bilqis, or the Throne of Bilqis by the locals, after the Yemeni name for the legendary queen of Saba).

Continuing farther in the direction of Safir and turning right at the sign reading 'Sun Temple' you will find the Mahram Bilqis, or 'Temple of Bilqis'. Archaeological studies from 1950 to 1952 indicate that the temple was built around 400 BC. Today the desert has reclaimed much of the temple, leaving only pillars rising from the sands.

Turning back and branching left before Old Ma'rib, you will come to the ancient Great Dam of Ma'rib. Only the ruins of the sluice gates remain on each bank. Continuing just a couple of kilometres upstream, you will come to the 40m high and 760m long New Dam of Ma'rib, built in the 1980s as a US$75 million gift from Sheikh Zayed bin Sultan al-

Nahyan, the ruler of Abu Dhabi. His ancestors lived in Wadi Nahayan, near Ma'rib, and migrated to the shores of the Persian Gulf after the great disaster of 570 AD.

Places to Stay & Eat

The '1st class' Hotel al-Jannattyn (☎ 2309, fax 2116) is just outside the new town, on your right if you are heading for Old Ma'rib. It charges YR2100/2900 for singles/doubles with air-con. A gorgeous holiday resort hotel is Bilqish Mareb Hotel (☎ 2372, fax 2378), offering singles/doubles for US$68/81, with breakfast.

Apart from hotel restaurants, El-Hahna Tourist Restaurant, with fine paintings on the walls of the dining hall, is popular among oil workers and tourists alike.

Getting There & Away

For security reasons, tourists are currently only allowed to visit Ma'rib on a group tour.

Shabwa & Hadramawt

The sparsely populated governorates of Shabwa and Hadramawt form the bigger part of eastern Yemen.

SHABWA

Ancient Shabwa, capital of the Hadramawt kingdom for maybe 1000 years before its fall around 220 AD, is today a less-visited archaeological site in the middle of the desert. The modest ruins of Timna', the capital of the state of Qa'taban, lie near the town of Bayhan. It is thought to have been originally founded by the Sabaeans around 400 BC.

To visit Shabwa or Bayhan you might want to hire a car and driver since public transport is scarce. Sometimes unrest in these Bedouin regions prevents visits; disputes over grazing lands or age-old tribal vendettas may explode into small-scale wars, and the police won't let travellers past check points whenever this is the case.

Shabwa can most conveniently be visited on a desert trip from Ma'rib to Wadi Hadramawt. There is also a dirt road from 'Ataq, 45km from **Habban**, which is a wadi settlement of striking appearance, about 340km east of Aden on the Al-Mukalla road. **Bayhan** is located about 180km to the west of 'Ataq and 150km south-east of Ma'rib by a good asphalt road.

The southern end of the frankincense route was in ancient Qana, on the coast of the Arabian Sea. The place is marked by today's fishing village of **Bir Ali** on the Aden to Al-Mukalla road.

AL-MUKALLA

Al-Mukalla in southern Hadramawt is a prosperous sea port and fishing centre. Founded as a fishing village in 1135 AD, today it has more than 100,000 inhabitants.

The beautiful but shrinking old town with white buildings represents a fascinating mix of Yemeni, Arabic and Indian elements. The notable **Ar-Rawdha Mosque** and the **Mosque of Omar** on Main al-Mukalla St are worth a look. The **Al-Mukalla Museum** by the bay is housed in the former palace of the Qu'ayti sultans. Just out of the town is **Hosn al-Ghuwayzi**, a photogenic and tiny fortress, which is poised on an imposing cliff.

Places to Stay – Mid-Range

In the western part of the town, the *Star Hotel* (☎ 304122, fax 303925, Funduq an-Nujum) charges YR1800 for a clean and spacious double with air-con and private bathroom. *Al-Riyan Hotel* (☎/fax 353038) offers the cheapest sea views: doubles go for YR1700/1200 with/without air-con, triples with air-con are YR2000.

Al-Maseela Hotel (☎ 303811, fax 354798), in the northern part of the town is well suited for women travellers also. Prices for singles/doubles with air-con are YR2500/3000, including breakfast.

Funduq al-Mukalla (☎ 303547, fax 303349) is attractively situated by the seashore in the old town, next to the Ar-Rawdha Mosque. Prices range from YR1600 for a double with fan to YR2400

for a triple with air-con, all with common bathrooms.

Places to Stay – Top End

Hadhramaut Hotel (☎ 302060, fax 303134) is *the* western-style hotel in Al-Mukalla, 2km to the east of the city with a magnificent view of the sea. Singles/doubles cost US$85/104. The hotel sports a bar, tennis court, swimming pool and a diving school.

Places to Eat

Instead of the hotel restaurants, try the numerous small fish or chicken *restaurants* in the old town. Tuna, pilchard and lobster are common here but the real winner is dried shark, simply called *lakhum* (meat) – it's subject to availability.

Mukalla Club Cafeteria in the huge two storey building east of the Al-Mukalla Hotel is a nice teahouse with views over the town and the sea.

Getting There & Away

Buses and taxis to Aden leave from the bank of the wadi that divides Al-Mukalla in two. Buses leave daily at 6.30 am – arrive at the station 30 minutes before the bus leaves. A bus ticket to Aden costs YR900, a seat in a taxi YR1200.

The taxi station serving the eastern and northern directions is in the northern suburb of Hai Uktubr. The trip to Say'un costs YR600 and takes six hours, with traffic starting only in the morning.

The desert airport of Riyan is 26km north-east of Al-Mukalla. A seat in a shared taxi costs YR120. The Yemenia office is in the western part of the town facing the wadi.

WADI HADRAMAWT

Wadi Hadramawt, the biggest wadi in the Arabian peninsula, runs for 160km, west to east, amid the most arid stone desert, about 160km from the coast. The main valley is about 300m deep, with the wadi bottom at an altitude of 700m.

Wadi Hadramawt with its numerous tributaries is very fertile, making it possible for

WADI HADRAMAWT & WADI DAW'AN

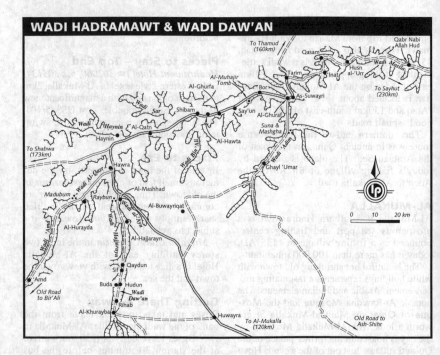

a population of 200,000 to live on agriculture and goat-herding.

Archaeological sites show that the region has been settled throughout human history. Before the 3rd century AD the area was ruled from Shabwa, at the far western end of the wadi.

In 951 Sayyid Ahmed ibn Isa al-Muhajir, a descendant of the Prophet Mohammed, settled in Hajrayn, in the eastern part of the wadi, establishing Shafaism in the region. The tomb of Al-Muhajir near Say'un is still an important place of pilgrimage.

In 1488 the Kathirids of Hamdanis, a San'a tribe, conquered Hadramawt and eventually settled in the eastern part of the wadi, with Tarim and then Say'un as their capital.

In the 16th century the western part of the wadi fell under the rule of the Qu'aytis, a Yafi'i tribe originally brought to the region by the Kathirids as paid soldiers. The

Qu'ayti sultanate made the town of Al-Qatn the capital. The disputes and wars between Qu'aytis and Kathirids continued throughout the centuries, resulting in the division of the wadi between Shibam and Say'un in the mid-19th century.

Colonial Britain slowly extended its rule to the hinterlands, mediating between the sultanates of Al-Qatn and Say'un by the 1940s. However, the 1967 revolution brought about a final resolution to the dispute; the sultans fled to Saudi Arabia and old ruling institutions were replaced by communist ones.

Since unification, tribalism has been undergoing a revival and a few sultans have returned.

Orientation & Information

Say'un, midway along the wadi, has an airport, other central traffic facilities and several hotels.

The asphalt road from Al-Mukalla descends to the wadi at the town of Haura, passing the towns of Al-Qatn and Shibam before reaching Say'un. The road then continues to Tarim and beyond. Numerous tributaries are also worth exploring, most notably Wadi Daw'an with its spectacularly painted houses.

Getting There & Away
The traditional land route from San'a through Aden and Al-Mukalla takes three full days in a taxi or bus. You can skip Aden and ride from San'a to Al-Mukalla via Al-Bayda. From Al-Mukalla a bus ticket costs YR600, a seat in a taxi YR800. A spectacular alternative is to hire a Bedouin taxi over the desert from Ma'rib to Say'un. The Bedouin request US$300 per car for the eight hour ride. When security allows, San'ani tour operators do the trip for US$100 as part of a larger tour.

Getting Around
Taxis shuttle along the asphalt road that links the towns of the wadi. Seats cost YR100 from Say'un to Shibam and YR120 from Say'un to Tarim.

SHIBAM
Shibam is the 'Manhattan of the desert', a tight collection of about 500 tower houses, five to seven storeys high, crammed into an area of perhaps only half a sq km.

It is a very old city, having served as the capital of the Hadramawt area several times since the 3rd to the 16th century. Today it has a population of 7000. Most of the present houses date from the 16th century; many were rebuilt about 100 years ago.

The buildings are made exclusively of mud brick. This applies not only to houses but also to mosques, tombs, wells and walls. In the 1980s Shibam, like San'a, was included in a UNESCO program to safeguard human cultural heritage.

Things to See
The citadel by the main square dates from the 13th century AD. It is not to be confused with the neighbouring Sultan's Palace, which was not built until the 1920s.

The biggest of the mosques is the **Friday Mosque**, built in 904 AD by Caliph Haroun ar-Rashid on the site of an earlier mosque. Since then it has been rebuilt several times, most recently in the 1960s. The first mosque you see as you enter the city through the main gate is the **Ma'ruf Mosque**, which is also over a thousand years old, but was rebuilt in the 1940s.

In the western palm grove stands the splendid white **Mosque of Sheikh Ma'ruf**, which is over 400 years old.

SAY'UN
Say'un, 'the town of a million palm trees', with its 30,000 people, is the largest town in the Hadramawt valley.

Things to See
The **Sultan's Palace** in Say'un, next to the souqs and close to the bus and taxi stations, is perhaps the most pompous of all South Yemeni palaces: a multistorey white-plaster colossus with light-blue window decorations. The palace was converted into a museum after the 1967 revolution. It is open daily from 8 am to noon, with a permanent archaeological show and sections dedicated to folklore themes and recent history. The turquoise **Tomb of Habshi** is the next most eye-catching structure in the centre of Say'un. It dates from the 1910s. The nearby **Mosque of al-Haddad** is much older, dating from the 16th century.

Places to Stay – Mid-Range
Trade & Housing Tower Hotel (☎/fax 403575) has a swimming pool and doubles costing YR1000/1500 without/with air-con. The hotel is on the main road, which is an easy walk from Say'un centre towards Tarim. *Rayboon Tourist Hotel* (☎ 405393, fax 402686) is right in the central souq area. The clean and amiable place has spacious doubles/triples with air-con and private bath at YR1500/2000.

Towards Tarim, 1.5km from the town centre, the pleasant *Samara Hotel* (☎ 403997, 405416, fax 405414), offers singles/doubles/triples with air-con, private bathrooms and a wealth of satellite TV channels for YR1200/ 1500/2000. *Al-Sallam Hotel* (☎ 403208, 403641, fax 403181) opposite the junction, has singles/doubles with air-con and private bathrooms for YR1831/2441, including breakfast. The hotel complex also has a swimming pool and a souvenir shop.

Places to Stay – Top End

The huge *Seiyun Hotel* (☎ 404254), about 3km east from the centre of Say'un, high on the mountain, offers doubles for YR2430 with breakfast, suites for YR3660.

About 3km in the direction of Shibam you'll find *BMC Hotel* (☎ 402524, fax 402935). It has singles, doubles and triples; low season it costs only YR2500 regardless of the head count. Another road side attraction, about 4km towards Tarim from Say'un, is the business class *Samah Seiyun* (☎/fax 403623), which has singles/doubles for US$45/55, with half-board.

Places to Eat

All the hotels mentioned earlier have restaurants. Among the many eateries in the town, *Restaurant Capital Modern* in the northern part of the centre is a nice, walled outdoor place. Here you can have tasty shwarma and rice for YR300.

The best coffee in town can be had at *Ryboon Cafe* in the middle of the new souq. You can choose either *qirsh* or coffee, Yemeni-style or western.

TARIM

Tarim, with its 15,000 inhabitants, is about 35km to the east of Say'un. It is overshadowed by vast rock cliffs on one side and surrounded by palm groves on the other.

From the 17th to the 19th centuries the numerous mosques of Tarim were as important in spreading the Shafai teachings in and from Hadramawt as those of Zabid were in the Tihama.

Things to See

Tarim is a beautiful town marked by the high minarets of its many mosques. The most famous, the **Al-Muhdar Mosque**, with its 50m high square minaret, is the symbol of the town.

The **Al-Afqah Library** was founded in 1972 to preserve the spiritual heritage of the region's Islamic teachers. About 14,000 volumes, including 3000 antique manuscripts, were gathered from all over Wadi Hadramawt. The books are locked behind glass doors.

The finest palace in Tarim with its 19th century Javanese Baroque style is the **Al-Kaf Palace**, also known as the **Ishsha Palace**, built by Sayyid Omar bin Sheikh al-Kaf, near the Al-Muhdar Mosque.

The graveyards of Tarim, to the south of the town centre, are worth a glimpse through the gates. The uniformly designed sandstone monuments with their deft calligraphy represent a style unique in Yemen.

Language

ARABIC

Arabic is the official language of all Middle Eastern countries except Afghanistan, Iran, Israel and Turkey. While English (and to a lesser extent, French – mainly in Lebanon and Syria) is widely spoken in the region, any effort to communicate with the locals in their own language will be well rewarded. No matter how far off the mark your pronunciation or grammar might be, you'll often get the response (usually with a big smile), 'Ah, you speak Arabic very well!'.

Learning the basics for day-to-day travelling doesn't take long at all, but to master the complexities of Arabic would take years of constant study. For a more comprehensive guide to the language, get a copy of Lonely Planet's *Egyptian phrasebook*.

Transliteration

It's worth noting here that transliterating from Arabic script into English is at best an approximate science. The presence of sounds unknown in European languages, and the fact that the script is 'incomplete' (most vowels are not written), combine to make it nearly impossible to settle on one method of transliteration. A wide variety of spellings is therefore possible for words when they appear in roman script – and that goes for place and people's names as well.

The Transliteration Dilemma

TE Lawrence, when asked by his publishers to clarify 'inconsistencies in the spelling of proper names' in *Seven Pillars of Wisdom* – his account of the Arab Revolt in WWI – wrote back:

'Arabic names won't go into English. There are some "scientific systems" of transliteration, helpful to people who know enough Arabic not to need helping, but a washout for the world. I spell my names anyhow, to show what rot the systems are.'

The matter is further complicated by the wide variety of dialects and the imaginative ideas Arabs themselves often have on appropriate spelling in, say, English: words spelt one way in a Gulf country may look very different in Syria, heavily influenced by French (not even the most venerable of western Arabists have been able to come up with an ideal solution).

Pronunciation

Pronunciation of Arabic can be tongue-tying for someone unfamiliar with the intonation and combination of sounds.

Much of the vocabulary that follows would be universally understood throughout the Arab world, although some of it, especially where more than one option is given, reflects the region's dialects. Arabic pronunciation is not easy, and to reflect sounds unknown in English, certain combinations of letters are used in transliteration. Pronounce the transliterated words slowly and clearly.

Vowels

Technically, there are three long and three short vowels in Arabic. The reality is a little different, with local dialect and varying consonant combinations affecting their pronunciation. This is the case throughout the Arabic-speaking world. More like five short and three long vowels can be identified:

a	as in 'had'
e	as in 'bet'
i	as in 'hit'
o	as in 'hot'
u	as in 'push'

A macron over a vowel indicates that the vowel has a long sound:

ā	as in 'father' or as a long pronunciation of the 'a' in 'had'
ī	as the 'ea' in 'eagle'
ū	as the 'oo' in 'food'

The Arabic Alphabet

Final	Medial	Initial	Alone	Transliteration	Pronunciation
‍ا			‍ا	ā	as the 'a' in 'father'
‍ب	‍ب‍	ب‍	ب	b	as in 'bet'
‍ت	‍ت‍	ت‍	ت	t	as in 'ten'
‍ث	‍ث‍	ث‍	ث	th	as in 'thin'
‍ج	‍ج‍	ج‍	ج	j	as in jam; in some countries as 'g' in 'go'
‍ح	‍ح‍	ح‍	ح	H	a strongly whispered 'h', almost like a sigh of relief
‍خ	‍خ‍	خ‍	خ	kh	as the 'ch' in Scottish loch
‍د	‍د		د	d	as in 'dim'
‍ذ	‍ذ		ذ	dh	as the 'th' in 'this'
‍ر	‍ر		ر	r	a rolled 'r', as in the Spanish word caro
‍ز	‍ز		ز	z	as in 'zip'
‍س	‍س‍	س‍	س	s	as in 'so', never as in 'wisdom'
‍ش	‍ش‍	ش‍	ش	sh	as in 'ship'
‍ص	‍ص‍	ص‍	ص	ṣ	emphatic 's'
‍ض	‍ض‍	ض‍	ض	ḍ	emphatic 'd'
‍ط	‍ط‍	ط‍	ط	ṭ	emphatic 't'
‍ظ	‍ظ‍	ظ‍	ظ	ẓ	emphatic 'z'
‍ع	‍ع‍	ع‍	ع	'	the Arabic letter 'ayn; pronounce as a glottal stop – like the closing of the throat before saying 'Oh oh!' (see Other Sounds on p.875)
‍غ	‍غ‍	غ‍	غ	gh	a guttural sound like Parisian 'r'
‍ف	‍ف‍	ف‍	ف	f	as in 'far'
‍ق	‍ق‍	ق‍	ق	q	a strongly guttural 'k' sound; in Egyptian Arabic often pronounced as a glottal stop
‍ك	‍ك‍	ك‍	ك	k	as in 'king'
‍ل	‍ل‍	ل‍	ل	l	as in 'lamb'
‍م	‍م‍	م‍	م	m	as in 'me'
‍ن	‍ن‍	ن‍	ن	n	as in 'name'
‍ه	‍ه‍	ه‍	ه	h	as in 'ham'
‍و			و	w	as in 'wet'; or
				ū	long, as the 'oo' on 'food'; or
				aw	as the 'ow' in 'how'
‍ي	‍ي‍	ي‍	ي	y	as in 'yes'; or
				ī	as the 'e' in 'ear', only softer; or
				ay	as the 'y' in 'by' or as the 'ay' in 'way'

Vowels Not all Arabic vowel sounds are represented in the alphabet. See Pronunciation on the previous page.

Emphatic Consonants To simplify the transliteration system used in this book, the emphatic consonants have not been included.

Names

While we have tried to standardise all spellings in this book there are some instances in which flexibility seemed to be more appropriate than consistency. For example, while we use the more accepted 'beit' (house) and 'sheikh' throughout the book, in the Oman and The United Arab Emirates chapters we decided to go with 'bait' and 'shaikh' as these are the spellings any visitor to those countries will find on local maps and road signs.

Differences in spelling also arise through the same word appearing modified in the different languages of the region – 'square' in Arabic is traditionally transliterated as 'midan', but in Turkish it's written 'maydan' and in Persian 'meidun' (or 'meidun-é; 'the square of'). Here lies great potential for confusion, as in the case of 'hamam' which is Turkish for the famed 'bathhouse', but Arabic for 'pigeon'; if you're looking for a good steam-cleaning in Arabic you ask for 'hammam', with two distinctly sounded syllables.

We have also been forced to modify some spellings because of regional differences in Arabic pronunciation. The most obvious example of this is the hard Egyptian sounding of the letter *jīm*, like the 'g' in 'gate', whereas elsewhere in the Arab world it's a softer 'j' as in 'jam' – hence we have used both 'gadid' and 'jadid' (new), and 'gebel' and 'jebel' (mountain).

Consonants

Pronunciation for all Arabic consonants is covered in the alphabet table on the preceding page. Note that when double consonants occur in transliterations, both are pronounced. For example, *el-hammām* (toilet), is pronounced 'el-ham-mam'.

Other sounds

Arabic has two sounds that are very tricky for non-Arabs to produce, the 'ayn and the glottal stop. The letter 'ayn represents a sound with no English equivalent that comes even close. It is similar to the glottal stop (which is not actually represented in the alphabet) but the muscles at the back of the throat are gagged more forcefully – it has been described as the sound of someone being strangled. In many transliteration systems 'ayn is represented by an opening quotation mark, and the glottal stop by a closing quotation mark. To make the transliterations in this language guide (and throughout the rest of the book) easier to use, we have not distinguished between the glottal stop and the 'ayn, using the closing quotation mark to represent both sounds. You should find that Arabic speakers will still understand you.

Greetings & Civilities

Arabs place great importance on civility, and it's rare to see any interaction between people that doesn't begin with profuse greetings, enquiries into the other's health and other niceties.

Arabic greetings are more formal than greetings in English, and there is a reciprocal response to each. These sometimes vary slightly, depending on whether you're addressing a man or a woman. A simple encounter can become a drawn-out affair, with neither side wanting to be the one to put a halt to the stream of greetings and well-wishing. As an *ajnabı* (foreigner), you're not expected to know all the ins and outs, but if you come up with the right expression at the appropriate moment, they'll love it.

The most common greeting is *salām 'alaykum* ('peace be upon you'), to which the correct reply is *wa alaykum as-salām* ('and upon you be peace'). If you get invited to a birthday celebration or are around for any of the big holidays, the common greeting is *kul sana wa intum bi-khēr* ('I wish you well for the coming year').

After having a bath or a haircut, you will often hear people say to you *na'iman*, which roughly means 'heavenly' and boils down to an observation along the lines of 'nice and clean now, huh'.

Arrival in one piece is always something to be grateful for. Passengers will often be greeted with *al-hamdu lillah 'al as-salāma*, meaning 'Thank God for your safe arrival'.

Hi.	*marhaba*
Hello. (literally 'welcome')	*ahlan wa sahlan/ahlan*
Hello. (response)	*ahlan bīk* or *ya hala*
Goodbye.	*ma'a salāma/ Allah ma'ak*
Good morning.	*sabah al-khayr*
Good morning. (response)	*sabah an-nūr*
Good evening.	*masā al-khayr*
Good evening. (response)	*masā an-nūr*
Good night.	*tisbah 'ala khayr*
Good night. (response)	*wa inta min ahlu*
Please. (request)	*min fadlak* (m)/ *min fadlik* (f)
Please. (polite, eg in restaurants)	*law samaht* (m)/ *law samahtı* (f)
Please. (come in/ go ahead)	*tafadal* (m)/*tafadalı*(f)/ *tafadalu* (pl)
Thank you.	*shukran*
Thanks a lot.	*shukran jazīlan*
You're welcome.	*'afwan* or *ahlan*
How are you?	*kayf hālak?* (m)/ *kayf hālik?* (f)
Fine. (literally 'thanks be to God')	*al-hamdu lillah*
Pleased to meet you. (departing)	*fursa sa'ida*
Pardon/Excuse me.	*'afwan*
Sorry!	*'assif!*
Congratulations!	*mabrūk!*

Basics

What's your name?	*shu-ismak?* (m)/ *shu-ismik?* (f)
My name is ...	*ismı...*
Where are you from?	*min wayn inta?*
Do you speak ...?	*btah-ki ...?/ hal tatakallam ...?*
I speak ...	*ana bah-ki .../ ana atakallam ...*

English	*inglīzi*
French	*faransi*
German	*almāni*
I understand.	*ana af-ham*
I don't understand.	*ma bif-ham/la af-ham*
What does this mean?	*yānī ay?*
I want an interpreter.	*urīd mutarjem*
I (don't) like ...	*ana (ma) bahib/ ana (la) uhib ...*
Yes.	*aywa/na'am*
No.	*la*
No problem.	*mish mushkila*
Never mind.	*ma'alesh*
I'm sick.	*ana marīd* (m)/ *ana marīda* (f)

Questions like 'Is the bus coming?' or 'Will the bank be open later?' generally elicit the inevitable response *in sha' Allah* (God willing) an expression you'll hear over and over again. Another less common one is *ma sha' Allah* (God's will be done) sometimes a useful answer to probing questions about why you're not married yet!

Getting Around

How many kilometres?	*kam kilometre?*
airport	*al-matār*
bus station	*mahattat al-bās*
train station	*mahattat al-qitār*
car	*as-sayāra*
1st class	*daraja awla*
2nd class	*daraja thani*
here/there	*hena/henak*
left	*yasār*
right	*shimal/yamīn*
straight ahead	*'ala tūl*

Around Town

Where is (the) ...?	*wayn ...?*
bank	*al-masraf/al-bank*
hotel	*al-funduq*
market	*as-sūq*
Mohammed St	*sharia Mohammed*
mosque	*al-jāmi'/al-masjid*
museum	*al-mat'haf*

passport & immi- gration office	maktab al-jawāzāt wa al-hijra
pharmacy	as-saydaliyya
police	ash-shurta
post office	maktab al-barīd
restaurant	al-mat'am
tourist office	maktab as-siyāHa

Accommodation

Do you have ...?	fi'andakum ...?
a room	ghurfa
a single room	ghurfa mufrada
a double room	ghurfa bı sarīrayn
a shower	dūsh
hot water	mayy harr
a toilet	twalet/mirhad/ hammām
soap	sābūn
air-con	kondishon/takyīf
electricity	kahraba

Shopping

How much?	qaddaysh/bikam
How many?	kam wahid?
How much money?	kam fulūs?
money	fulūs/masāri
big	kabīr
small	saghīr
bad	mish kwayyis/ mu kwayyis
good	kwayyis
cheap/expensive	rakhīs/ghali
cheaper	arkhas
closed	maghlūq/musakkar
open	maftūh

Time

What is the time?	adaysh as-sā'a?
It's 5 o'clock.	as-sa'a khamsa
When?	mata/emta?
yesterday	imbārih/'ams
today	al-yōm
tomorrow	bukra/ghadan
minute	daqiqa
hour	sa'a
day	yom
week	usbu'
month	shaher
year	sana

Numbers

Arabic numerals are simple to learn and, unlike the written language, run from left to right. Pay attention to the order of the words in numbers from 21 to 99.

0	٠	sifr
1	١	wāhid
2	٢	itnīn
3	٣	talāta
4	٤	arba'a
5	٥	khamsa
6	٦	sitta
7	٧	sab'a
8	٨	tamanya
9	٩	tis'a
10	١٠	'ashra
11	١١	hida'shar
12	١٢	itna'shar
13	١٣	talat-ashar
14	١٤	arba'at-ashar
15	١٥	khamas-ta'shar
16	١٦	sitta'shar
17	١٧	sabata'shar
18	١٨	tamanta'shar
19	١٩	tisata'shar
20	٢٠	'ishrīn
21	٢١	wāhid wa 'ishrīn
30	٣٠	talatīn
40	٤٠	arba'īn
50	٥٠	khamsīn
60	٦٠	sittīn
70	٧٠	sab'īn
80	٨٠	tamanīn
90	٩٠	tis'īn
100	١٠٠	miyya
101	١٠١	miyya wa wāhid
1000	١٠٠٠	alf

Days & Months

Monday	al-itnīn yom
Tuesday	at-talāta yom
Wednesday	al-arbi'ā yom
Thursday	al-khamīs yom
Friday	al-jum'a yom
Saturday	as-sabt yom
Sunday	al-ahad yom

The Islamic year has 12 lunar months and is 11 days shorter than the western year (the

Gregorian calendar), so important Muslim dates will fall 11 days earlier each (western) year.

There are two Gregorian calendars in use in the Arab world. In Egypt and the Gulf States, the months have virtually the same names as in English (January is *yanāyir*, October *octobir* and so on), but in Lebanon, Jordan and Syria, the names are quite different. Talking about, say, June as 'month six' is the easiest solution, but for the sake of completeness, the months from January are:

January	*kānūn ath-thāni*
February	*shubāt*
March	*āzār*
April	*nisān*
May	*ayyār*
June	*huzayran*
July	*tammūz*
August	*'āb*
September	*aylūl*
October	*tishrīn al-awal*
November	*tishrīn ath-thani*
December	*kanūn al-awal*

The Hejira months, too, have their own names:

1st	*Moharram*
2nd	*Safar*
3rd	*Rabī' al-Awwal*
4th	*Rabī' ath-Thāni*
5th	*Jumada al-Awwall*
6th	*Jumada al-Akhīra*
7th	*Rajab*
8th	*Sha'bān*
9th	*Ramadān*
10th	*Shawwāl*
11th	*Zūl-qe'da*
12th	*Zūl-hijja*

FĀRSĪ

Fārsī (Persian) is the national language of Iran. Although the vast majority of Iranians can speak it, it's the first language for only about 60% of the population. The most predominant minority languages are Āzarī, Kurdish, Arabic, Baluchi and Lorī.

Pronunciation

A macron above a vowel indicates that its sound is lengthened.

ā	between 'a' in 'father' and the 'a' in 'what'
ī	as the 'i' in 'machine'
ō	as the 'o' in 'bone'
ū	as the 'u' in 'ruse'
a	as in 'map'
e	as in 'beg'
é	as in French *café*
o	between the 'o' in 'god' and the 'o' in 'good'
eι	as in 'rein'

The letters **b**, **d**, **f**, **j**, **k**, **l**, **m**, **n**, **p**, **s**, **sh**, **t**, **v** and **z** are pronounced as in English.

ch	as in 'chip'
g	as in 'go'
y	as in 'yak'
zh	as in 'Zhivago'
r	slightly trilled as in Italian *caro*
h	always pronounced; like **r**, it doesn't lengthen the preceding vowel
kh	as the 'ch' in Scottish *loch*
gh	a soft guttural sound like the noise made when gargling
'	a weak glottal stop, like the double 't' in the Cockney pronunciation of 'bottle'

Double consonants are always pronounced as two distinct sounds. Stress generally falls on the last syllable of a word (but **é** is never stressed).

Greetings & Civilities

Hello.	*salām*
Peace be upon you.	*salām aleikom*
Goodbye.	*khodāfez*
	khodā hāfez (more polite)
Good morning.	*sobh bekheir*
Good night/	*shab bekheir*
Good evening.	
Please. (request, literally 'kindly')	*lotfan*

Please. (offering something) — *befarmed/befarmā'īd*

Thank you. — *mersī/tashakkor/ motashakkeram*

Don't mention it. — *ghābel nabūd*

Excuse me/ I'm sorry. — *bebakhshīd*

Yes. — *balé*

No. — *nakheir/ na* (less formal)

OK. — *dorost*

Small Talk

Where are you from? — *shomā ahl-é kojā hastīd?*

Do you speak ...? — *shomā ... baladīd?*
  English — *engelīsī*
  French — *ferānsé*
  German — *ālmānī*

I'm sorry, I don't speak Persian. — *bebakhshīd, fārsī balad nīstam*

Getting Around

Where is the ... (to Tabrīz)? — *... (betabrīz) kojāst?*
  bus — *otōbūs*
  train — *ghetār*
  boat — *ghāyegh*
  ship/ferry — *kashtī*
  taxi (any kind) — *tāksī*
  car (or taxi) — *māshīn*
  minibus — *mīnībūs*

airport — *forūdgāh*
jetty/dock/harbour — *eskelé*
bus/train station — *termīnāl/īstgāh*
ticket — *belīt*
ticket office — *daftar-é belīt forūshī*
open/closed — *bāz/ta'tīl*

left — *dast-é chap*
right — *dast-é rāst*
far (from) — *dūr (az ...)*
near (to ...) — *nazdīk (-é ...)*
straight ahead — *mostaghīm*

Around Town

Excuse me, where is the ...? — *bebakhshīd, ... kojāst?*
  town centre — *markaz-é shahr*

embassy — *safārat*
consulate — *konsūlgarī*
post office — *postkhūné*
mosque — *masjed*
church — *kelīsā*
restaurant — *restōrān/chelō kabābī/sālon-é ghezā*
toilet — *dast shū'ī*
street/avenue — *kheyābūn*

Shopping

How many? — *chand tā?*
How much is it? — *chand é?*
cheap/expensive — *arzūn/gerūn*

Accommodation

hotel — *hotel/mehmūnkhūné*
cheap hotel/ guesthouse — *mosāferkhūné*

Do you have a ... for tonight? — *emshab ... dārīd?*
  room — *otāgh*
  single room — *otāgh-é ye nafarī*
  double room — *otāgh-é do nafarī*
  cheaper room — *otāgh-é arzūntar*
  better room — *otāgh-é behtar*

How much is the room per night? — *otāgh shabī chand é?*

Time & Dates

When? — *kei?*
At what time? — *chī vaght?*
(at) ... o'clock — *sā'at-é ...*
today — *emrūz*
tonight — *emshab*
tomorrow — *fardā*
(in the) morning — *sobh*
(at) night, evening — *shab*

Saturday (1st day of Muslim week) — *shambé*
Sunday — *yekshambé*
Monday — *doshambé*
Tuesday — *seshambé*
Wednesday — *chahārshambé*
Thursday — *panjshambé*
Friday — *jom'é*

Numbers

1	yek
2	do
3	sé
4	chahār
5	panj
6	shesh
7	haft
8	hasht
9	noh
10	dah
11	yāzdah
12	davāzdah

HEBREW

Written from right to left, Hebrew has a basic 22-character alphabet – but from there it starts to get very complicated. Like English, not all these characters have fixed phonetic values and their sound can vary from word to word. You just have to know that, for instance, Yair is pronounced 'Ya-ear' and doesn't rhyme with 'hare' or 'fire'.

As with Arabic, transliteration of Hebrew script into English is at best an approximate science. The presence of sounds not found in English, and the fact that the script is 'incomplete' (most vowels are not written) combine to make it nearly impossible to settle on one consistent method of transliteration. A wide variety of spellings is therefore possible for words when they appear in roman script, and that goes for place names and people's names as well.

For a more comprehensive guide to Hebrew than can be given in this chapter, get a copy of Lonely Planet's new *Hebrew phrasebook*.

Basics

Hello.	sha-LOM
Goodbye.	sha-LOM
Good morning.	BO-ker tov
Good evening.	erev tov
Goodnight.	lie-la tov
See you later.	le-HIT-rah-OTT
Thank you.	to-DAH
Please.	be-va-ka-SHA
You're welcome.	al low da-VAAR
Yes.	ken
No.	loh
Excuse me.	slee-KHA

Wait.	REG-gah
What?	mah?
When?	mah-tye?
Where is ...?	AYE-fo ...?
I don't speak Hebrew.	AH-NEElo m'dah-BEHR ee-VREET
Do you speak English?	ah-TAH m'dah-BEHR ang-LEET?

Getting Around

Which bus goes to ...?	AYE-zeh auto-boos no-SE-ah le ...?
Stop here.	ah-TSOR kahn
airport	sde t'oo-FAH
bus	auto-boos
near	ka-ROV
railway	rah-KEH-vet
station	ta-cha-na

Food & Accommodation

food	OKHEL
water	my-im
restaurant	MISS-ah-DAH
breakfast	ah-roo-CHAT BO-ker
lunch	ah-roo-KHAT-tsa-ha-RYE-im
dinner	ah-roo-KHAT erev
menu	taf-REET
egg	bay-TSA
vegetables	YEH-rah-KOHT
bread	LEKH-hem
butter	khem-AH
cheese	g'VEE-nah
milk	kha-LAV
ice cream	glee-DAH
fruit	pay-ROT
wine	yain
bill	KHESH-bon
hotel	ma-LON
room	khe-der
toilet	she-ru-TEEM

Around Town

How much is it?	KA-mah zeh ule?
money	KES-sef
bank	bank
post office	dūgh-ar
letter	mich-tav
stamps	boolim
envelopes	ma-ata-FOT

postcard	gloo-yah
telegram	miv-rack
air mail	dügh-ar ah-veer
pharmacy	bait mer-kah-KHAT
shop	kha-NOOT
expensive	ya-KAR
cheap	zol
right (correct)	na-CHON

Time & Days

What is the time?	MA ha-sha-AH?
seven o'clock	ha-sha-AHSHEV-vah
minute	da-KAH
hour	sha-AH
day	yom
week	sha-voo-ah
month	KHO-desh
year	sha-NAH

Monday	shey-NEE
Tuesday	shlee-SHEE
Wednesday	reh-vee-EE
Thursday	cha-mee SHEE
Friday	shee-SHEE
Saturday	sha-BAT
Sunday	ree-SHON

Numbers

1	eh-HAD
2	SHTA-yim
3	sha-LOSH
4	AR-bah
5	cha-MAYSH
6	shaysh
7	SHEV-vah
8	sh-MO-neh
9	TAY-shah
10	ESS-er
11	eh-HAD-ess-RAY
12	shtaym-ess-RAY
20	ess-REEM
21	ess-REEM v'ah-KHAD
30	shlo-SHEEM
31	shlo-SHEEM v'ah-KHAD
50	cha-MEESHLEEM
100	MAY-ah
200	mah-tah-YEEM
300	shlosh may-OAT
500	cha-MAYSH may-OAT
1000	alef
3000	shlosh-ET alef-EEM
5000	cha-maysh-ET alef-EEM

TURKISH

Ottoman Turkish was written in Arabic script, but it was phased out when Atatürk decreed the introduction of Latin script in 1928. In big cities and tourist areas, many locals know at least some English and/or German. In the south-eastern towns, Arabic or Kurdish is the first language.

For a more in depth look at the language, including a comprehensive list of useful words and phrases, get a copy of Lonely Planet's new edition *Turkish phrasebook*.

Pronunciation

The letters of the new Turkish alphabet have a consistent pronunciation; they're reasonably easy to master, once you've learned a few basic rules. All letters except ğ (which is silent) are pronounced, and there are no diphthongs.

Vowels

A, a	as in 'shah'
E, e	as in 'fell'
İ, i	as 'ee'
I, ı	as 'uh'
O, o	as in 'hot'
U, u	as the 'oo' in 'moo'
Ö, ö	as the 'ur' in 'fur'
Ü, ü	as the 'ew' in 'few'

Note that ö and ü are pronounced with pursed lips.

Consonants

Most consonants are pronounced as in English, but there are a few exceptions:

Ç ç	as the 'ch' in 'church'
C c	as English 'j'
Ğ ğ	not pronounced – it draws out the preceding vowel
G g	as in 'go'
H h	as in 'half'
J j	as the 's' in 'measure'
S s	as in 'stress'
Ş ş	as the 'sh' in 'shoe'
V v	as the 'w' in 'weather'

Basics

Hello.	*Merhaba.*
Goodbye/	*Allaha ısmarladık/*
Bon Voyage.	*Güle güle.*
Yes.	*Evet.*
No.	*Hayır.*
Please.	*Lütfen.*
Thank you	*Teşekkür ederim.*
That's fine/	*Bir şey değil.*
You're welcome.	
Excuse me.	*Affedersiniz.*
Sorry. (Excuse me/	*Pardon.*
Forgive me.)	
How much is it?	*Ne kadar?*

Language Difficulties

Do you speak	*Ingilizce biliyor*
English?	*musunuz?*
Does anyone speak	*Kimse Ingilizce biliyor*
English?	*mu?*
I don't understand.	*Anlamiyorum.*
Just a minute.	*Bir dakika.*
Please write that	*Lütfen yazın.*
down.	

Getting Around

Where is the bus/	*Otobüs/tramvay*
tram stop?	*durağınerede?*
I want to go to	*(İsmir)'e gitmek*
(İzmir).	*istiyorum.*
Can you show me	*Haritada gösterebilir*
on the map?	*misiniz?*
Go straight ahead.	*Doğru gidin.*
Turn left.	*Sola dönün.*
Turn right.	*Sağa dönün.*
far/near	*uzak/yakın*

When does the ...	*... ne zaman kalkar/*
leave/arrive?	*gelir?*
ferry/boat	*feribot/vapur*
city bus	*şehir otobüsü*
intercity bus	*otobüs*
train	*tren*
tram	*tramvay*

next	*gelecek*
first	*birinci/ilk*
last	*son*

I'd like a ... ticket.	*... bileti istiyorum.*
one-way	*gidiş*
return	*gidiş-dönüş*
1st class	*birincısınıf*
2nd class	*ikincısınıf*

Accommodation

Where is a cheap hotel?	*Ucuz bir otel nerede?*
What is the address?	*Adres ne?*
Please write down the address.	*Adresıyazar mısınız?*
Do you have any rooms available?	*Boş oda var mı?*

I'd like ...	*... istiyorum.*
a single room	*tek kişilik oda*
a double room	*Ikıkişilik oda*
a room with a bathroom	*banyolu oda*
to share a dorm	*yatakhanede bir yatak*
a bed	*bir yatak*

How much is it per night?	*Bir gecelik nekadar?*

Signs

Camping Ground	*Kamping*
Entrance	*Giriş*
Exit	*Çıkış*
Full	*Dolu*
Guesthouse	*Pansiyon*
Hotel	*Otel(i)*
Information	*Danışma*
Open	*Açık*
Closed	*Kapalı*
Police	*Polis/emniyet*
Police Station	*Polis Karakolu/*
	Emniyet Müdürlüğü
Prohibited	*Yasak(tır)*
Rooms Available	*Boş oda var*
Toilet	*Tuvalet*
Train Station	*Gar/İstasyon*
Student Hostel	*Öğrencıyurdu*

May I see it?	*Görebilir miyim?*
Where is the bathroom?	*Banyo nerede?*

Around Town

I'm looking for the/a ...	*... arıyorum*
bank	*bir banka*
city centre	*şehir merkezi*
... embassy	*... büyükelçiliğini*
hotel	*otelimi*
market	*çarşıyı*
police	*polis*
post office	*postane*
public toilet	*tuvalet*
telephone centre	*telefon merkezi*
tourist office	*turizm danışma bürosu*
beach	*plaj*
bridge	*köprü*
castle	*kale/hisar*
church	*kilise*
hospital	*hastane*
island	*ada*
lake	*göl*
mosque	*cami(i)*
old city	*tarihişehir merkezi*
palace	*saray*
ruins	*harabeler/kalıntılar*
sea	*deniz*
square	*meydan*
tower	*kule*

Food

breakfast	*kahvaltı*
lunch	*öğleyemeği*
dinner	*akşamyemeği*
I'd like the set lunch, please.	*Fiks menü istiyorum, lütfen.*
Is service included in the bill?	*Servis ücretıdahil mi?*
I don't eat meat.	*Hiç et yemiyorum.*

Health

I'm diabetic/ epileptic/ asthmatic.	*Şeker hastasıyım/ saralıyım/ astımlıyım.*
I'm allergic to antibiotics/ pennicillin.	*Antibiyotiklere/ penisiline/ alerjim var.*

antiseptic	*antiseptik*
aspirin	*aspirin*
condom	*prezervatif*
contraceptive	*gebeliğıönleyici*
diarrhoea	*ishal/diyare*
medicine	*ilaç*
nausea	*bulantı*
sunblock cream	*güneş blok kremi*
tampon	*tampon*

Time

What time is it?	*Sāt kaç?*
today	*bugün*
tomorrow	*yarın*
in the morning	*sabahleyin*
in the afternoon	*öğleden sonra*
in the evening	*akşamda*

Days of the Week

Monday	*Pazartesi*
Tuesday	*Salı*
Wednesday	*Çarşamba*
Thursday	*Perşembe*
Friday	*Cuma*
Saturday	*Cumartesi*
Sunday	*Pazar*

Months

January	*Ocak*
February	*Şubat*
March	*Mart*
April	*Nisan*
May	*Mayıs*
June	*Haziran*
July	*Temmuz*
August	*Ağustos*
September	*Eylül*
October	*Ekim*
November	*Kasım*
December	*Aralık*

Numbers

0	*sıfır*	18	*on sekiz*
1	*bir*	19	*on dokuz*
2	*iki*	20	*yirmi*
3	*üç*	21	*yirmibir*
4	*dört*	22	*yirmiiki*
5	*beş*	30	*otuz*
6	*altı*	40	*kırk*
7	*yedi*	50	*elli*
8	*sekiz*	60	*altmış*
9	*dokuz*	70	*yetmiş*
10	*on*	80	*seksen*
11	*on bir*	90	*doksan*
12	*on iki*	100	*yüz*
13	*on üç*	200	*ikiyüz*
14	*on dört*	1000	*bin*
15	*on beş*	2000	*ikibin*
16	*on altı*		
17	*on yedi*	one million	*bir milyon*

Glossary

Here, with definitions, are some unfamiliar words and abbreviations you might meet in the text or on the road in the Middle East:

Abbasids – Baghdad-based successor dynasty to the *Umayyads*. Ruled from 750 until the sack of Baghdad by the Monguls in 1258.
abd – servant, slave
abeyya – woman's full-length black robe
abra – small motorboat
abu – father; saint
acropolis – high city; hilltop citadel and temples of a classic Hellenic city
agal – (also *'iqal*) headropes used to hold a *kaffiyeh* or *gutra* in place
agora – open space for commerce and politics in a classic Hellenic city
ahwa – see *qahwa*
aile salonu – family room for use of couples, families and single women in a Turkish restaurant
ain – (also *ein*, *ayn*) spring, well
Al-Ahram – the pyramids
arg (Persian) – citadel
Ayyubids – Egyptian-based dynasty founded by *Saladin* (1169-1250)

bab – gate
bait – see *beit*
barasti – traditional method of building palm-leaf houses and the name of the house itself
barjeel – wind towers
bazbort – (also *basbut*, *pispot*) passport
beit – house
biblion (Greek) – book
bijous (Egyptian) – service taxi
Book of the Dead – ancient Egyptian theological compositions, or hymns, that were the subject of most of the colourful paintings and reliefs on tomb walls. Extracts from these so-called books were believed to assist the deceased person safely into the afterlife via the Kingdom of the Dead. The texts were sometimes also painted on a roll of papyrus and buried with the dead.
bublos (Greek) – papyrus
burj – tower (*burg* in Egypt)

caliph – Islamic ruler
cami(i) (Turkish) – mosque
Canopic jars – pottery jars which held the embalmed internal organs and viscera (liver, stomach, lungs, intestines) of the mummified pharaoh. They were placed in the burial chamber near the sarcophagus.
caravanserai – see *khan*
çarşı (Turkish) – market, bazaar
cartouche – oblong figure enclosing the hieroglyphs of royal or divine names
chador – one-piece head-to-toe black covering garment, as worn by many Iranian women

Decapolis – a league of 10 cities, including Damascus, in the north-east of ancient Palestine
deir – monastery, convent
dervish – Muslim mystic; see also *Sufi*
dhabar (Yemeni) – minibus
dhuma (Yemeni) – nobleman's curved dagger
Diaspora – Jewish dispersion or exile from the Land of Israel; the exiled Jewish community worldwide
dishdasha – name of man's shirt-dress worn in Kuwait and the UAE
diwan – reception room
doner kebab – see *shwarma*

Eid al-Adha – Feast of Sacrifice marking the pilgrimage to Mecca
Eid al-Fitr – Festival of Breaking the Fast; celebrated at the end of *Ramadan*
ein – see *ain*
emām (Persian) – see *imam*
emir – Islamic ruler, military commander or governor; literally, prince
Eretz Y'Israel – the Land of Israel, commonly used today by Israel's right wing to

refer to their preferred borders for the modern Jewish State, which includes the Gaza Strip, the West Bank and sometimes Jordan and/or the Sinai, too

falaj – irrigation channel
Fatimids – a Shi'ite dynasty (908-1171) from North Africa, later based in Cairo, claiming descent from Mohammad's daughter Fatima; founders of Al-Azhar, the oldest university in the world
felafel – deep-fried balls of chickpea paste with spices served in a piece of flat bread with tomatoes or pickled vegetables
fellaheen – the peasant farmers or agricultural workers who make up the majority of Egypt's population; fellaheen means 'ploughman' or 'tiller of the soil'
funduq – hotel
fuul – paste made from fava beans

galabeyya – full-length robe worn by men
GCC – Gulf Cooperation Council; members are Saudi Arabia, Kuwait, Bahrain, Qatar, Oman and the UAE
gebel (Egyptian) – see *jebel*
gutra – white headcloth worn by men in Saudi Arabia and the Gulf States

haj – annual Muslim pilgrimage to Mecca
Hamas – militant Islamic organisation which aims to create an Islamic state in the pre-1948 territory of Palestine; acronym (in Arabic) for Islamic Resistance Movement
hammam – (also *hamam*) Turkish steam bath
hared or **hasid** – (pl *haredim* or *hasidim*) member of an ultraorthodox Jewish sect
hejab – woman's headscarf, worn for modesty (*hegab* in Egyptian)
hejira – migration; also name of Islamic calendar
hisar – fortress, citadel; same as *kale*
hypostyle hall – hall in which the roof is supported by columns

imam – prayer leader, Muslim cleric
Intifada – the Palestinian uprising against Israeli authorities in the Occupied Territories and Jerusalem (literally 'shaking off')
'iqal – see *agal*

iskele(si) (Turkish) – landing-place, wharf, quay
iwan – vaulted hall, opening into a central court in the madrassa of a mosque

jambiya – tribesman's ceremonial dagger
jebel – (also *gebel*) hill, mountain
jihad – literally: striving in the way of the faith; holy war

ka – spirit, or 'double', of a living person which gained its own identity with the death of that person. The survival of the ka, however, required the continued existence of the body, hence mummification.
kale(si) (Turkish) – fortress, citadel; same as *hisar*
khan – (also *caravanserai* or *wikala*) a travellers' inn usually constructed on main trade routes, with accommodation on the 1st floor and stables and storage on the ground floor around a central courtyard
khanjar – (also *khanja*) Omani curved dagger
khedive – Egyptian viceroy under Ottoman suzerainty (1867-1914)
kibbutz – (pl *kibbutzim*) communal settlement; originally farms, but now involved in additional industries
kibbutznik – member of a *kibbutz*
kiosk – open-sided pavilion
knanqah – *Sufi* monastery
Knesset – Israeli parliament
Koran – see *Quran*
kosher – food prepared according to Jewish dietary law
köy(ü) (Turkish) – village
kufeyya – headscarf
kufic – a type of highly stylised old Arabic script

Likud – major Israeli right-wing political party
liman(ı) (Turkish) – harbour

madrassa – Muslim theological seminary; also modern Arabic word for school
mafraj – room with a view; top room of a tower house
mahalle(si) (Turkish) – neighbourhood, district of a city

majlis – formal meeting room; also parliament

Mamluk – slave-soldier dynasty that ruled out of Egypt from 1250-1517

manzar – attic; room on top of a tower house

mashrabeyya – ornate carved wooden panel or screen; a feature of Islamic architecture

mastaba – Arabic word for 'bench'; a mud-brick structure above tombs from which the pyramids were developed

medina – old walled centre of any Islamic city

medrese(si) (Turkish) – see *madrassa*

menorah – seven pronged candelabra; an ancient Jewish symbol associated with the Hanukkah Festival

meydan(ı) (Turkish) – see *midan*

midan – town or city square

mihrab – niche in a mosque indicating the direction of Mecca

minbar – pulpit used for sermons in a mosque

Misr – another name for Egypt and Cairo; also written as Masr

moshav – cooperative settlement, with a mix of private and collective housing and industry

moulid – festival celebrating the birthday of a local saint or holy person

muezzin – cantor who sings the call to prayer

nargila – water pipe used to smoke tobacco

Nilometer – pit descending into the Nile and containing a central column marked with graduations. The marks were used to measure and record the level of the river, especially during the inundation.

obelisk – monolithic stone pillar, with square sides tapering to a pyramidal top; used as a monument in ancient Egypt.

Omayyad – see *Umayyad*

OPEC – Organisation of Petroleum Exporting Countries

otogar – bus station

pansiyon – pension, B&B, guesthouse

PLO – Palestine Liberation Organization

PTT – Posta, Telefon, Telǧraf: post, telephone and telegraph office

pylon – monumental gateway at the entrance to a temple

Qaaba – (also *Kabaa*) the rectangular structure at the centre of the Grand Mosque in Mecca (containing the Black Stone) around which haj pilgrims circumambulate

qahwa – (also *ahwa*) coffee

qasr – castle

qat – mildly narcotic leaves commonly chewed in Yemen

Quran – the holy book of Islam; also spelt Koran

rakats – cycles of prayer during which the Qur'an is read and bows ad prostrations are performed in different series

Ramadan – the Muslim month of fasting

ras – cape or headland; also head

sabil – public drinking fountain

Saladin – (in Arabic *Salah ad-Din*) Kurdish warlord who retook Jerusalem from the Crusaders; founder of the *Ayyubid* dynasty

Şehir (Turkish) – city; municipal

serdab – hidden cellar in a tomb, or a stone room in front of some pyramids, containing a coffin with a life-size, lifelike, painted statue of the dead king. Serdabs were designed so that the pharaoh's *ka* could communicate with the outside world.

settler – a term used to describe those Israelis who have created new communities on territory captured from the Arabs during the 1967 War

Shabbat – the Jewish sabbath and shutdown, observed from sundown Friday to sundown Saturday

shari'a – Islamic law

shai – tea

sheesha – see *nargila*

sheikh – (also *shaikh*) a venerated religious scholar

sherut – shared taxi (fixed route)

shwarma – grilled meat sliced from a spit and served in a pitta bread with salad; also known as doner kebab

souq – market

stele – (pl *stelae*) stone or wooden commemorative slab or column decorated with inscriptions or figures

Sufi – follower of any of the Islamic mystical orders which emphasise dancing, chanting and trances in order to attain unity with God

sultan – the absolute ruler of a Muslim state

ta'amiya – see *felafel*

takiyya – Ottoman name for a *khanqah*

TC – Türkiye Cumhuriyeti (Turkish Republic) which designates an official office or organisation

tell – an ancient mound created by centuries of urban rebuilding

thobe – term used in Saudi Arabia, Bahrain and Qatar for man's shirt-dress; similar to a *dishdasha*, but more tightly cut

THY – Türk Hava Yolları: Turkish Airlines

Torah – the five books of Moses (the first five Old Testament books); also called the Pentatuch

Umayyads – (also *Omayyad*) first great dynasty of Arab Muslim rulers, based in Damascus (661-750)

wadi – dried up river bed; seasonal river

wikala – see *khan*

zawiya – a small school dedicated to the teaching of a particular *sheikh*

Acknowledgments

THANKS
Thanks to the many travellers who took the time and trouble to write to us about their experiences in the Middle East. They include:

A Goodwin, Alan & Brenda Stockwell, Alistair Reid, Allen Sanderson, Amanda Martin, Andrea King, Andrew Thorburn, Andy Johnson, Anita Hayhoe, Anne Bruford, Barbara Ledbetter, Benjamin Richards, Bill Stoughton, Brad Myer, Brett King, Carolyn List, Chris Ganahl, Chris Tremann, Chris Ziersch, Danielle Seminiuk, Dave Poirier, David Martin, David Siddhartha Patel, Deian Krailah, Didomizio Joel, Doris Smith, Douglas B Piil, Douglas Poole, Dyan Eastman, Ed Bobeff, Eleonora Humphreys, Elizabeth Barnett, Ellis Ryan, Emiliano Lo Manto, Emma Cain, Emma Whitewood, Esther Shannon, Fahmi Jabari, Farid Sabounchi, Fiona Clarkson, Frank Ellsworth, Fred Spengler, Gabriel Kuhn, Gill Lobel, Gordon Bailey, Graham Egerton, Gregg Butensky, Harry Pol, Heidi Klaschka, Helen Black, Hoe Habboushe, Ilse Stevenson, JC Gwilliam, J Heine, J Tucker, James Wood, Jamie Maler, Jan Mansfield, Jane Roberts, Jane Stewart, Jason Kane, Jason Mathwin, Jason Williams, Jedidiah J Palosaari, Jeff Bell, Jeff Blundell, Jennifer Perrin, Jeremy Gray, Joanne Nathan, Jocelyn Biathelot, John Lea, Johnny Groethe, Jolm Ball, KJ Aitken-Meehan, Kannan Amaresh, Karen L Rae, Kathryn Beer, Kathryn Harkin, Keith A Law, Kevin Wall, Kip Ault, Krawinkler Karl Heinz, Krista Bernard, Laura M Bertolotto, Lisa Berry, Lucinda Coates, Luke Haas, M Idress, M Ishaq, Maddalena Antonina Monachesi, Maike Juta, Maitreyee Mishra, Malcolm James, Marcel Wissink, Mark Hayman, Mark Hunt, Mark Nicholls, Mark Tinker, Martin Sher, Mathew McGillan, Michael Carroll, Michael Donovan, Michael van Os de Man, Michelle Cook, Miniam Tobolowsky, Neil Donnelly, Nick Elzinga, Olly Francis, P Abraham, Papantom, Patrick & Beryl Chambers, Patrick Barclay, Patrick Weinrauch, Paul Zoglin, Peg Schlekat, Pertti Malo, Peter Buechel, Przemyslaw Pochec, RG Wells, RN McLean, Rachel Grant, Rebekah Nathan, Renato Soares Figueiredo, Richard Groom, Richard Hamel, Richard Hill, Rob Hart, Robert A Estes, Robert Dale Hajek, S Bregman, Scott Morrison, Sean Flannery, Shane Delphine, Sharon Peake, Sharon Yopp-Schaefer, Simon Kutcher, Sonja Bregman, Sophie Collins, Stephen Bateson, Steve Hewitt, Sue Bellamy, Sven Barter, Thomas Nolte, Tim Dymond, Tina Calov, Tom Tolk, Trevor Williams, Trine Viken Sumstad, Vicki Schnaedelbach, Vincent Gray, W Berryman, Wallace & Shirley Herridge, Wendy McCarty, Wolf Gotthilf, Zavodnik Ales, Zdenek Kvinta.

LONELY PLANET

Phrasebooks

Lonely Planet phrasebooks are packed with essential words and phrases to help travellers communicate with the locals. With colour tabs for quick reference, an extensive vocabulary and use of script, these handy pocket-sized language guides cover day-to-day travel situations.

- handy pocket-sized books
- easy to understand Pronunciation chapter
- clear & comprehensive Grammar chapter
- romanisation alongside script to allow ease of pronunciation
- script throughout so users can point to phrases for every situation
- full of cultural information and tips for the traveller

'...vital for a real DIY spirit and attitude in language learning'
– *Backpacker*

'the phrasebooks have good cultural backgrounders and offer solid advice for challenging situations in remote locations'
– *San Francisco Examiner*

Arabic (Egyptian) • Arabic (Moroccan) • Australian *(Australian English, Aboriginal and Torres Strait languages)* • Baltic States *(Estonian, Latvian, Lithuanian)* • Bengali • Brazilian • British • Burmese • Cantonese • Central Asia • Central Europe *(Czech, French, German, Hungarian, Italian, Slovak)* • Eastern Europe *(Bulgarian, Czech, Hungarian, Polish, Romanian, Slovak)* • Ethiopian (Amharic) • Fijian • French • German • Greek • Hebrew phrasebook • Hill Tribes • Hindi/Urdu • Indonesian • Italian • Japanese • Korean • Lao • Latin American Spanish • Malay • Mandarin • Mediterranean Europe *(Albanian, Croatian, Greek, Italian, Macedonian, Maltese, Serbian, Slovene)* • Mongolian • Nepali • Pidgin • Pilipino (Tagalog) • Quechua • Russian • Scandinavian Europe *(Danish, Finnish, Icelandic, Norwegian, Swedish)* • South-East Asia *(Burmese, Indonesian, Khmer, Lao, Malay, Tagalog Pilipino, Thai, Vietnamese)* • South Pacific Languages • Spanish (Castilian) *(also includes Catalan, Galician and Basque)* • Sri Lanka • Swahili • Thai • Tibetan • Turkish • Ukrainian • USA *(US English, Vernacular, Native American languages, Hawaiian)* • Vietnamese • Western Europe *(Basque, Catalan, Dutch, French, German, Greek, Irish)*

Lonely Planet Journeys

J ourneys is a unique collection of travel writing – published by the company that understands travel better than anyone else. It is a series for anyone who has ever experienced – or dreamed of – the magical moment when they encountered a strange culture or saw a place for the first time. They are tales to read while you're planning a trip, while you're on the road or while you're in an armchair in front of a fire.

These outstanding titles explore our planet through the eyes of a diverse group of international writers. JOURNEYS books catch the spirit of a place, illuminate a culture, recount a crazy adventure or introduce a fascinating way of life. They always entertain, and always enrich the experience of travel.

MALI BLUES
Traveling to an African Beat
Lieve Joris (translated by Sam Garrett)

Drought, rebel uprisings, ethnic conflict: these are the predominant images of West Africa. But as Lieve Joris travels in Senegal, Mauritania and Mali, she meets survivors, fascinating individuals charting new ways of living between tradition and modernity. With her remarkable gift for drawing out people's stories, Joris brilliantly captures the rhythms of a world that refuses to give in.

THE GATES OF DAMASCUS
Lieve Joris (translated by Sam Garrett)

This best-selling book is a beautifully drawn portrait of day-to-day life in modern Syria. Through her intimate contact with local people, Lieve Joris draws us into the fascinating world that lies behind the gates of Damascus. Hala's husband is a political prisoner, jailed for his opposition to the Assad regime; through the author's friendship with Hala we see how Syrian politics impacts on the lives of ordinary people.

THE OLIVE GROVE
Travels in Greece
Katherine Kizilos

Katherine Kizilos travels to fabled islands, troubled border zones and her family's village deep in the mountains. She vividly evokes breathtaking landscapes, generous people and passionate politics, capturing the complexities of a country she loves.

'beautifully captures the real tensions of Greece' – *Sunday Times*

KINGDOM OF THE FILM STARS
Journey into Jordan
Annie Caulfield

Kingdom of the Film Stars is a travel book and a love story. With honesty and humour, Annie Caulfield writes of travelling in Jordan and falling in love with a Bedouin with film-star looks.

She offers fascinating insights into the country – from the tent life of traditional women to the hustle of downtown Amman – and unpicks tight-woven western myths about the Arab world.

LONELY PLANET

Guides by Region

Lonely Planet is known worldwide for publishing practical, reliable and no-nonsense travel information in our guides and on our Web site. The Lonely Planet list covers just about every accessible part of the world. Currently there are thirteen series: travel guides, shoestring guides, walking guides, city guides, phrasebooks, audio packs, city maps, travel atlases, diving and snorkeling guides, restaurant guides, first-time travel guides, healthy travel and travel literature.

AFRICA Africa – the South • Africa on a shoestring • Arabic (Egyptian) phrasebook • Arabic (Moroccan) phrasebook • Cairo • Cape Town • Cape Town city map• Central Africa • East Africa • Egypt • Egypt travel atlas • Ethiopian (Amharic) phrasebook • The Gambia & Senegal • Healthy Travel Africa • Kenya • Kenya travel atlas • Malawi, Mozambique & Zambia • Morocco • North Africa • South Africa, Lesotho & Swaziland • South Africa, Lesotho & Swaziland travel atlas • Swahili phrasebook • Tanzania, Zanzibar & Pemba • Trekking in East Africa • Tunisia • West Africa • Zimbabwe, Botswana & Namibia • Zimbabwe, Botswana & Namibia travel atlas
Travel Literature: The Rainbird: A Central African Journey • Songs to an African Sunset: A Zimbabwean Story • Mali Blues: Traveling to an African Beat

AUSTRALIA & THE PACIFIC Auckland • Australia • Australian phrasebook • Bushwalking in Australia • Bushwalking in Papua New Guinea • Fiji • Fijian phrasebook • Islands of Australia's Great Barrier Reef • Melbourne • Melbourne city map • Micronesia • New Caledonia • New South Wales & the ACT • New Zealand • Northern Territory • Outback Australia • Out To Eat – Melbourne • Papua New Guinea • Papua New Guinea (Pidgin) phrasebook • Queensland • Rarotonga & the Cook Islands • Samoa • Solomon Islands • South Australia • South Pacific Languages phrasebook • Sydney • Sydney city map • Tahiti & French Polynesia • Tasmania • Tonga • Tramping in New Zealand • Vanuatu • Victoria • Western Australia
Travel Literature: Islands in the Clouds • Kiwi Tracks • Sean & David's Long Drive

CENTRAL AMERICA & THE CARIBBEAN Bahamas and Turks & Caicos • Bermuda • Central America on a shoestring • Costa Rica • Cuba • Dominican Republic & Haiti • Eastern Caribbean • Guatemala, Belize & Yucatán: La Ruta Maya • Jamaica • Mexico • Mexico City • Panama • Puerto Rico
Travel Literature: Green Dreams: Travels in Central America

EUROPE Amsterdam • Amsterdam city map • Andalucía • Austria • Baltic States phrasebook • Barcelona • Berlin • Berlin city map • Britain • British phrasebook • Brussels, Bruges & Antwerp • Budapest city map • Canary Islands • Central Europe • Central Europe phrasebook • Corsica • Croatia • Czech & Slovak Republics • Denmark • Dublin • Eastern Europe • Eastern Europe phrasebook • Edinburgh • Estonia, Latvia & Lithuania • Europe • Finland • France • French phrasebook • Germany • German phrasebook • Greece • Greek phrasebook • Hungary • Iceland, Greenland & the Faroe Islands • Ireland • Italian phrasebook • Italy • Lisbon • London • London city map • Mediterranean Europe • Mediterranean Europe phrasebook • Norway • Paris • Paris city map • Poland • Portugal • Portugal travel atlas • Prague • Prague city map • Provence & the Côte d'Azur • Romania & Moldova • Rome • Russia, Ukraine & Belarus • Russian phrasebook • Scandinavian & Baltic Europe • Scandinavian Europe phrasebook • Scotland • Slovenia • Spain • Spanish phrasebook • St Petersburg • Switzerland • Trekking in Spain • Ukrainian phrasebook • Vienna • Walking in Britain • Walking in Ireland • Walking in Italy • Walking in Switzerland • Western Europe • Western Europe phrasebook
Travel Literature: The Olive Grove: Travels in Greece

INDIAN SUBCONTINENT Bangladesh • Bengali phrasebook • Bhutan • Delhi • Goa • Hindi/Urdu phrasebook • India • India & Bangladesh travel atlas • Indian Himalaya • Karakoram Highway • Kerala • Mumbai • Nepal • Nepali phrasebook • Pakistan • Rajasthan • Read This First: Asia & India • South India • Sri Lanka • Sri Lanka phrasebook • Trekking in the Indian Himalaya • Trekking in the Karakoram & Hindukush • Trekking in the Nepal Himalaya
Travel Literature: In Rajasthan • Shopping for Buddhas

LONELY PLANET

Mail Order

Lonely Planet products are distributed worldwide. They are also available by mail order from Lonely Planet, so if you have difficulty finding a title please write to us. North and South American residents should write to 150 Linden St, Oakland, CA 94607, USA; European and African residents should write to 10a Spring Place, London NW5 3BH, UK; and residents of other countries to PO Box 617, Hawthorn, Victoria 3122, Australia.

ISLANDS OF THE INDIAN OCEAN Madagascar & Comoros • Maldives • Mauritius, Réunion & Seychelles

MIDDLE EAST & CENTRAL ASIA Arab Gulf States • Central Asia • Central Asia phrasebook • Hebrew phrasebook • Iran • Israel & the Palestinian Territories • Israel & the Palestinian Territories travel atlas • Istanbul • Istanbul to Cairo • Jerusalem • Jordan & Syria • Jordan, Syria & Lebanon travel atlas • Lebanon • Middle East on a shoestring • Syria • Turkey • Turkish phrasebook • Turkey travel atlas • Yemen
Travel Literature: The Gates of Damascus • Kingdom of the Film Stars: Journey into Jordan

NORTH AMERICA Alaska • Backpacking in Alaska • Baja California • California & Nevada • Canada • Chicago • Chicago city map • Deep South • Florida • Hawaii • Honolulu • Las Vegas • Los Angeles • Miami • New England • New Orleans • New York City • New York city map • New York, New Jersey & Pennsylvania • Pacific Northwest USA • Puerto Rico • Rocky Mountain States • San Francisco • San Francisco city map • Seattle • Southwest USA • Texas • USA • USA phrasebook • Vancouver • Washington, DC & the Capital Region • Washington DC city map
Travel Literature: Drive Thru America

NORTH-EAST ASIA Beijing • Cantonese phrasebook • China • Hong Kong • Hong Kong city map • Hong Kong, Macau & Guangzhou • Japan • Japanese phrasebook • Japanese audio pack • Korea • Korean phrasebook • Kyoto • Mandarin phrasebook • Mongolia • Mongolian phrasebook • North-East Asia on a shoestring • Seoul • South-West China • Taiwan • Tibet • Tibetan phrasebook • Tokyo
Travel Literature: Lost Japan

SOUTH AMERICA Argentina, Uruguay & Paraguay • Bolivia • Brazil • Brazilian phrasebook • Buenos Aires • Chile & Easter Island • Chile & Easter Island travel atlas • Colombia • Ecuador & the Galapagos Islands • Latin American Spanish phrasebook • Peru • Quechua phrasebook • Rio de Janeiro • Rio de Janeiro city map • South America on a shoestring • Trekking in the Patagonian Andes • Venezuela
Travel Literature: Full Circle: A South American Journey

SOUTH-EAST ASIA Bali & Lombok • Bangkok • Bangkok city map • Burmese phrasebook • Cambodia • Hanoi • Healthy Travel Asia & India • Hill Tribes phrasebook • Ho Chi Minh City • Indonesia • Indonesia's Eastern Islands • Indonesian phrasebook • Indonesian audio pack • Jakarta • Java • Laos • Lao phrasebook • Laos travel atlas • Malay phrasebook • Malaysia, Singapore & Brunei • Myanmar (Burma) • Philippines • Pilipino (Tagalog) phrasebook • Singapore • South-East Asia on a shoestring • South-East Asia phrasebook • Thailand • Thailand's Islands & Beaches • Thailand travel atlas • Thai phrasebook • Thai audio pack • Vietnam • Vietnamese phrasebook • Vietnam travel atlas

ALSO AVAILABLE: Antarctica • The Arctic • Brief Encounters: Stories of Love, Sex & Travel • Chasing Rickshaws • Lonely Planet Unpacked • Not the Only Planet: Travel Stories from Science Fiction • Sacred India • Travel with Children • Traveller's Tales

FREE Lonely Planet Newsletters

We love hearing from you and think you'd like to hear from us.

Planet Talk

Our FREE quarterly printed newsletter is full of tips from travellers and anecdotes from Lonely Planet guidebook authors. Every issue is packed with up-to-date travel news and advice, and includes:

- a postcard from Lonely Planet co-founder Tony Wheeler
- a swag of mail from travellers
- a look at life on the road through the eyes of a Lonely Planet author
- topical health advice
- prizes for the best travel yarn
- news about forthcoming Lonely Planet events
- a complete list of Lonely Planet books and other titles

To join our mailing list, residents of the UK, Europe and Africa can email us at go@lonelyplanet.co.uk; residents of North and South America can email us at info@lonelyplanet.com; the rest of the world can email us at talk2us@lonelyplanet.com.au, or contact any Lonely Planet office.

Comet

Our FREE monthly email newsletter brings you all the latest travel news, features, interviews, competitions, destination ideas, travellers' tips & tales, Q&As, raging debates and related links. Find out what's new on the Lonely Planet Web site and which books are about to hit the shelves.

Subscribe from your desktop: www.lonelyplanet.com/comet

Lonely Planet Travel Atlases

Lonely Planet has long been famous for the number and quality of its guidebook maps. Now we've gone one step further and produced a handy companion series: Lonely Planet travel atlases – maps of a country produced in book form.

Unlike other maps, which look good but lead travellers astray, our travel atlases have been researched on the road by Lonely Planet's experienced team of writers. All details are carefully checked to ensure the atlas corresponds with the equivalent Lonely Planet guidebook.

- full-colour throughout
- maps researched and checked by Lonely Planet authors
- place names correspond with Lonely Planet guidebooks
- no confusing spelling differences
- legend and travelling information in English, French, German, Japanese and Spanish
- size: 230 x 160 mm

Available now: Chile & Easter Island • Egypt • India & Bangladesh • Israel & the Palestinian Territories • Jordan, Syria & Lebanon • Kenya • Laos • Portugal • South Africa, Lesotho & Swaziland • Thailand • Turkey • Vietnam • Zimbabwe, Botswana & Namibia

Lonely Planet TV Series & Videos

Lonely Planet travel guides have been brought to life on television screens around the world. Like our guides, the programs are based on the joy of independent travel, and look honestly at some of the most exciting, picturesque and frustrating places in the world. Each show is presented by one of three travellers from Australia, England or the USA and combines an innovative mixture of video, Super-8 film, atmospheric soundscapes and original music.

Videos of each episode – containing additional footage not shown on television – are available from good book and video shops, but the availability of individual videos varies with regional screening schedules.

Video destinations include: Alaska • American Rockies • Argentina • Australia – The South-East • Baja California & the Copper Canyon • Brazil • Central Asia • Chile & Easter Island • Corsica, Sicily & Sardinia – The Mediterranean Islands • East Africa (Tanzania & Zanzibar) • Cuba • Ecuador & the Galapagos Islands • Ethiopia • Greenland & Iceland • Hungary & Romania • Indonesia • Israel & the Sinai Desert • Jamaica • Japan • La Ruta Maya • The Middle East (Syria, Jordan & Lebanon • Morocco • New York • Northern Spain • North India • Outback Australia • Pacific Islands (Fiji, Solomon Islands & Vanuatu) • Pakistan • Peru • The Philippines • South Africa & Lesotho • South India • South West China • South West USA • Trekking in Uganda • Turkey • Vietnam • West Africa • Zimbabwe, Botswana & Namibia

The Lonely Planet TV series is produced by: Pilot Productions
The Old Studio
18 Middle Row
London W10 5AT, UK

Lonely Planet On-line

W hether you've just begun planning your next trip, or you're chasing down specific info on currency regulations or visa requirements, check out Lonely Planet On-line for up-to-the minute travel information.

As well as mini guides to more than 250 destinations, you'll find maps, photos, travel news, health and visa updates, travel advisories, and discussion of the ecological and political issues you need to be aware of as you travel. You'll also find timely upgrades to popular guidebooks which you can print out and stick in the back of your book.

There's also an on-line travellers' forum where you can share your experience of life on the road, meet travel companions and ask other travellers for their recommendations and advice.

And of course we have a complete and up-to-date list of all Lonely Planet travel products including travel guides, diving and snorkeling guides, phrasebooks, atlases, travel literature and videos, and a simple on-line ordering facility if you can't find the book you want elsewhere.

Lonely Planet Diving & Snorkeling Guides

B eautifully illustrated with full-colour photos throughout, Lonely Planet's Pisces Books explore the world's best diving and snorkeling areas and prepare divers for what to expect when they get there, both topside and underwater.

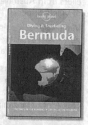

Dive sites are described in detail with specifics on depths, visibility, level of difficulty, special conditions, underwater photography tips and common and unusual marine life present. You'll also find practical logistical information and coverage on topside activities and attractions, sections on diving health and safety, plus listings for diving services, live-aboards, dive resorts and tourist offices.

Index

Abbreviations

Text

Boxed Text & Special Sections

MAP LEGEND

BOUNDARIES

- International
- State
- Disputed

HYDROGRAPHY

- Coastline
- River, Creek
- Lake
- Intermittent Lake
- Salt Lake
- Canal
- Spring, Rapids
- Waterfalls
- Swamp

- **⊙ CAPITAL** .... National Capital
- **◉ CAPITAL** .... State Capital
- **● CITY** .... City
- **● Town** .... Town
- **● Village** .... Village
- ○ .... Point of Interest
- ■ .... Place to Stay
- ▲ .... Camping Ground
- ▼ .... Place to Eat
- ▯ .... Pub or Bar
- ✈ .... Airport
- .... Ancient or City Wall
- .... Castle or Fort/Ruins
- .... Bank
- .... Beach
- .... Border Crossing

ROUTES & TRANSPORT

- Freeway
- Highway
- Major Road
- Minor Road
- Unsealed Road
- City Freeway
- City Highway
- City Road
- City Street, Lane

- Pedestrian Mall
- Tunnel
- Train Route & Station
- Metro & Station
- Tramway
- Cable Car or Chairlift
- Walking Track
- Walking Tour
- Ferry Route

AREA FEATURES

- Building
- Park, Gardens
- Cemetery
- Market
- Beach, Desert
- Urban Area

MAP SYMBOLS

- Coffeehouse
- Canoe/Ski
- Cave
- Church
- Cliff or Escarpment
- Dive Site
- Embassy/Consulate
- Hammam
- Hospital
- Islamic Monument
- Kibbutz
- Lighthouse/Lookout
- Monument
- Mosque
- Mountain or Hill
- Museum

- National Park
- Norias
- One Way Street
- Parking/Petrol
- Pass
- Police Station
- Post Office
- Shopping Centre
- Stately Home
- Synagogue
- Telephone/Toilets
- Temple/Classical
- Tomb
- Tourist Information
- Transport
- Zoo/Bird Sanctuary

Note: not all symbols displayed above appear in this book

LONELY PLANET OFFICES

Australia
PO Box 617, Hawthorn, Victoria 3122
☎ 03 9819 1877 fax 03 9819 6459
email: talk2us@lonelyplanet.com.au

USA
150 Linden St, Oakland, CA 94607
☎ 510 893 8555 TOLL FREE: 800 275 8555
fax 510 893 8572
email: info@lonelyplanet.com

UK
10a Spring Place, London NW5 3BH
☎ 020 7428 4800 fax 020 7428 4828
email: go@lonelyplanet.co.uk

France
1 rue du Dahomey, 75011 Paris
☎ 01 55 25 33 00 fax 01 55 25 33 01
email: bip@lonelyplanet.fr
www.lonelyplanet.fr

World Wide Web: www.lonelyplanet.com *or* AOL keyword: lp
Lonely Planet Images: lpi@lonelyplanet.com.au